AUSTRALIA AND PAPUA NEW GUINEA: THE TRANSITION TO SELF-GOVERNMENT 1970–1972

The mission of the Historical Research Section is to publish an accurate, comprehensive and impartial record of Australia's foreign and trade policy. Volumes in the series *Documents on Australian Foreign Policy* are produced and financed by the Department of Foreign Affairs and Trade. The editors of these volumes, whether officers of the Department, consultants employed by the Department, or scholars working on commissioned projects, operate under the guidance of the Historical Research Section with full editorial independence. An Editorial Advisory Board advises the Minister for Foreign Affairs with respect to the *Documents on Australian Foreign Policy* series. The Board's role is to uphold the editorial independence of the volumes' editors, ensure the scholarly standards and integrity of the series and assist the Historical Research Section in gaining access to relevant documents. A Committee of Final Review consisting of the Minister for Foreign Affairs and delegates of the Prime Minister and Leader of the Opposition examines each volume. Its approval signifies that material has been selected and edited according to appropriate non-partisan practice.

**DOCUMENTS ON
AUSTRALIAN FOREIGN
POLICY**

*Australia and
Papua New Guinea:
The Transition to
Self-Government
1970–1972*

BRUCE HUNT and STEPHEN HENNINGHAM
Editors

AUSTRALIAN DEPARTMENT OF FOREIGN
AFFAIRS AND TRADE

UNSW PRESS

A catalogue record for this
book is available from the
National Library of Australia

ISBN   9781742237176 (hardback)
         9781742249681 (ePDF)

Printer Everbest

UNSW
SYDNEY

Foreword by Minister for Foreign Affairs and Minister for Women

It gives me great pleasure to be associated with the publication of the latest volume in the Documents on Australian Foreign Policy (DAFP) series. This volume is on Australia's relations with Papua New Guinea from January 1970 to December 1972. Dealing with a formative period of our shared history—and one little known to most Australians—the volume highlights Australia's links to Papua New Guinea and its people, as well as some of the constraints on those connections. It underlines the importance of close, constructive personal relationships, exemplified by the rapport that developed between Andrew Peacock, in his role as Minister for External Territories, and Michael (later Sir Michael) Somare, who became Chief Minister of Papua New Guinea from early 1972.

Australia's relationship to the people of Papua New Guinea and their Government remains a highest order priority. We have deep and abiding political, economic, development, defence, church, community and cultural connections. Australia's High Commission in Port Moresby is one of our largest, with this mission's work supported by a Consulate-General in Lae. Understanding Papua New Guinea is a priority for Australia's political leaders and officials just as it should be for business leaders and ordinary citizens.

From the late 1940s, successive Australian Governments took forward reforms that led first to Papua New Guinea's self-government and then to its independence. Paul (later Sir Paul) Hasluck, Minister for Territories from 1951 to 1963, guided these reforms, with bipartisan support from Arthur Calwell, Leader of the Opposition and Australian Labor Party. Hasluck—who later served as Minister for Defence, Minister for External Affairs and Governor-General—favoured gradual reforms in order to lay sound foundations. One of his key legacies was the House of Assembly of Papua and New Guinea, opened in mid-1964 following territory-wide democratic elections. From early 1970 the pace of change quickened, as Prime Minister John Gorton pushed ahead with the reforms which led to self-government.

The present volume provides insights into the complexities of preparing for self-government. In addition to increasing the authority and powers of Papua New Guinea's elected representatives, the Australian Government accelerated the localisation of public sector positions; encouraged unity; provided increased financial support; considered the roles of Papua New Guinea's defence and police forces; worked to ensure that Papua New Guinea maintained good relations with Indonesia; and gave initial consideration to bilateral relations after independence.

This is the second of three volumes on Australia's involvement with Papua New Guinea. The first covered the 1966 to 1969 period. A third volume—on the 1973 to 1975 period— is scheduled to be released in 2022. This volume is a welcome addition to the Australian Government's DAFP series. DAFP's instigator was Sir Paul Hasluck, who among his other attainments was a distinguished historian of Australian public policy. The first DAFP volume appeared in 1975, the year of Papua New Guinea's independence; it is fitting that forty-five years later, this volume is concerned with a key phase of Australia's relations with its steadfast friend and closest neighbour.

Senator the Hon Marise Payne
Minister for Foreign Affairs and Minister for Women

Foreword by General Editor

This latest volume in the series *Documents on Australian Foreign Policy*, on Australia's relations with Papua New Guinea during its transition to self-government from 1970 to 1972, is the second of three dedicated volumes on the subject. The first, *Australia and Papua New Guinea, 1966–1969*, compiled and edited by Dr Stuart Doran, was published in 2006 and should be read in conjunction with this volume. A third, taking the story up to Papua New Guinea's independence in September 1975, is scheduled for publication in 2022. When completed, the three volumes will comprise more than 1,200 of the most important documents charting the relationship at this critical juncture.

Work on these two volumes was initially taken forward by Dr Bruce Hunt, a former officer of the Department of Foreign Affairs and Trade (DFAT), a subject specialist and a Visiting Fellow in the History Department in the College of Arts and Humanities at the Australian National University. While working on both volumes, Bruce also published a sweeping survey, based on his doctoral thesis, entitled *Australia's Northern Shield? Papua New Guinea and the Defence of Australia since 1880* (Monash University Publishing, 2017). This important study, which drew on a number of the documents contained in this collection, also made extensive use of the Cabinet notebooks—one of the first publications to tap into this rich resource, which only recently became available to researchers.

In March 2018—just a day after submitting a draft manuscript of the two volumes to the Department's Historical Research Section—Dr Hunt died suddenly, in a cruel blow to his family and friends. His passing thus left unfinished the two planned volumes on Australia and Papua New Guinea from 1970 to 1975. Bruce had devoted an enormous amount of energy, commitment and enthusiasm to producing the drafts of both volumes, but substantial work was still required. It was incumbent on the Department of Foreign Affairs and Trade to bring these two volumes to publication, both because of the intrinsic importance of the subject and to honour Bruce's contribution. The Office of the Pacific provided some financial assistance which allowed the project to move forward.

Subsequently, Dr Stephen Henningham—another long-term DFAT officer and Pacific specialist—agreed to take both volumes through to publication. His contribution has involved adding several dozen documents to those already selected; rewriting the introduction, drawing in part on Dr Hunt's initial working draft; preparing the editorial notes; adding substantially to the discursive footnotes which provide the reader with essential context; and revising the biographical notes.

Dedicated to the memory of Bruce Hunt, this volume provides a wealth of insights into the Commonwealth Government's relations with Papua New Guinea—Australia's closest neighbour—during its transition to self-government.

Contents

Documents on Australian Foreign Policy

General Editor

Matthew Jordan

Editorial Advisory Board

Chair

Peter Varghese, AO

Members

Joan Beaumont, AM

James Curran

Joy Damousi

Alan Oxley

Shirley Scott

Christina Twomey

Representing the Prime Minister

Roderick Brazier

Representing the Leader of the Opposition

Senator the Hon. Penny Wong

The Department of Foreign Affairs and Trade, the Department of Defence and the National Archives of Australia are entitled to be represented for the purposes of consultation.

Abbreviations

ABC	Australian Broadcasting Commission
ADB	Asian Development Bank
AEC	Administrator's Executive Council
AGD	Attorney-General's Department
ALP	Australian Labor Party
AMM	Assistant Ministerial Member
ANZUS	Australia, New Zealand and United States security treaty
ASCAP	Asian and Pacific Council
ASEAN	Association of Southeast Asian Nations
ASIO	Australian Security Intelligence Organisation
ASOPA	Australian School of Pacific Administration
BCPL	Bougainville Copper Proprietary Limited [also referred to as BCL: Bougainville Copper Limited]
BSIP	British Solomon Islands Protectorate
CCS	Chairman of the Chiefs of Staff
CNGT	Commonwealth New Guinea Timber
CPC	Constitutional Planning Committee
CPD	*Commonwealth Parliamentary Debates*
CRA	Conzinc Riotinto of Australia
CSIRO	Commonwealth Scientific and Industrial Research Organisation
DAC	District Advisory Council
DC	District Commissioner
DCA	Department of Civil Aviation
DDA	Department of District Administration
DEA	Department of External Affairs
DET (DOET)	Department of External Territories
DFA	Department of Foreign Affairs
ECAFE	Economic Commission for Asia and the Far East
EEC	European Economic Community
FAO	Foreign Affairs Officer
GATT	General Agreement on Tariffs and Trade

HANKAM	*Pertahanan dan Keamanan* [Indonesian Ministry of Defence and Security]
HR	House of Representatives [Australian Parliament]
IBRD	International Bank for Reconstruction and Development
IDCC	Inter-Departmental Co-ordinating Committee
IOT	Institute of Technology
JPC	Joint Planning Committee
LGC	Local Government Council
MA	Mataungan Association
MHA	Member of the House of Assembly [Papua New Guinea]
MM	Ministerial Member
MRC	Multi-Racial Council
NAA	National Archives of Australia
NCG	National Coalition Government
NLA	National Library of Australia
NZ	New Zealand
OTC	Overseas Telecommunications Commission
Pangu Pati	Papua and New Guinea Union Party
PIR	Pacific Islands Regiment
PM&C	Department of Prime Minister and Cabinet
PMD	Prime Minister's Department
PNG	Papua and New Guinea/Papua New Guinea
PNG DCC	Papua New Guinea Defence Co-ordinating Committee
PNGIC	Papua New Guinea Intelligence Committee
PPP	People's Progress Party
PRC	People's Republic of China
PSA	Public Service Association
PSB	Public Service Board
QANTAS	Queensland and Northern Territory Aerial Services Limited [Australia's national carrier, at that time Commonwealth owned]
RAAF	Royal Australian Air Force
RAN	Royal Australian Navy
RPNGC	Royal Papua New Guinea Constabulary

SITREP	Situation Report
TAA	Trans Australia Airlines
TIC	Territory Intelligence Committee
TPNG	Territory of Papua New Guinea
UK	United Kingdom
UN	United Nations
UNCDT	United Nations Conference on Trade and Development
UNDP	United Nations Development Programme
UNGA	United Nations General Assembly
UNIDO	United Nations Industrial Development Organization
UNNY	Australian Mission to the United Nations, New York
UP	United Party
UPNG	University of Papua [and] New Guinea
US	United States [of America]

Introduction

Introduction

The destiny of Papua and New Guinea is to become a self-governing country developed for independence if and when it is clearly demonstrated by the majority … that this is what they wish.[1]
Richard (Lord) Casey, Governor-General of Australia, March 1968

[The] Government view is that ineffective government would result from haste, but if people want Australia out it would get out.[2]
George Warwick Smith, Secretary, Department of External Territories, August 1969

If we believe that we have a good Administrator and good ministerial members, then now is the time to decentralise a great deal of decision-making.[3]
John Gorton, Prime Minister of Australia, February 1970

It is Australia's objective to disengage from Papua and New Guinea in a way which promotes a peaceful, economically and politically viable state well-disposed to Australia and receptive to Australian influence.[4]
Cabinet Submission, June 1970

Sir, my Government is grateful for what Australia has done....We are prepared to do much more to help ourselves, however, we need special help to get over the last few hurdles. With that help our future is assured and Australia has discharged its trust.[5]
Michael Somare, Chief Minister of Papua New Guinea, July 1972

This is a matter where I can repeat what I said in the Parliament—what Mr Somare himself believes—that the term as the Minister for External Territories of Mr Andrew Peacock made the development of, or the progress towards independence in Papua New Guinea, very much easier than any of us could have expected.[6]
Gough Whitlam, Prime Minister of Australia, December 1972

---

1   Stuart Doran (ed.), *Documents on Australian Foreign Policy: Australia and Papua New Guinea, 1966–1969* (hereafter Doran, *Australia/PNG 1966–69*), Department of Foreign Affairs and Trade, Canberra, 2006, Document 199, para. 5.

2   Ibid., Document 304.

3   Document 15.

4   Document 47, para. 41.

5   Document 337.

6   Document 412.

At the end of the 1960s Australia maintained firm control over the territory of Papua and New Guinea (PNG). All the important decisions, and many lesser ones, were made in Canberra. The chief decision-maker was Charles Edward (Ceb) Barnes, the Minister for External Territories. Barnes, who had succeeded Paul (later Sir Paul) Hasluck in 1963, wanted to delay further steps towards self-government until the mid-1970s, thought independence was two or three decades away, and favoured independence with some form of very close association.[7] Barnes relied heavily on George Warwick Smith, Secretary of the Department of Territories (DET), a fellow Queenslander who shared his conservative instincts but not his courteous style.[8]

Early in 1970, however, Prime Minister John Gorton quickened the pace of change and indicated its expected destination was full independence. By December 1972, when the Australian Labor Party (ALP) won office in Australia, the Liberal/Country Party Coalition Government had made great progress towards implementing self-government, with independence in prospect within the next few years.

Taken together, the 413 documents in this volume illuminate the context, conception and development of Australian policies towards Papua (and) New Guinea from January 1970 to early December 1972, and provide insights into the complex process of transferring power. After a survey of the nature and evolution of Australia's relations with Papua New Guinea during the 1960s and the political and social context in which the Territory's transition to self-government occurred, this Introduction reviews the main themes of the volume.

Australia and Papua and New Guinea in the 1960s

From around 1960 the context within which the Australian Government shaped its approach on Papua and New Guinea became more complex and difficult. As newly-independent countries joined the United Nations the pressure for decolonisation increased.[9] In February 1960 British Prime Minister Harold Macmillan declared: 'We have seen the awakening of national consciousness in peoples who have for centuries lived in dependence upon some other power … The wind of change is blowing … this growth of national consciousness is a political fact. We must all accept it as a fact, and our national policies must take account of it.'[10] This 'wind of change' speech signalled that Britain would not seek to delay the transition of its African or other colonies to independence. Other Western powers were also increasing their pace of 'colonial devolution' in sub-Saharan Africa, while in April 1960 the Dutch announced a ten-year plan to bring West New Guinea to self-government.[11]

Prime Minister Robert Menzies, earlier a supporter of Western colonial rule,[12] accepted the new realities. In May 1960 he acknowledged at a meeting of Commonwealth prime ministers

---

7   Doran, *Australia/PNG 1966-69*, pp. xxiii–xxviii and Documents 25 (paras 50–62), 143, 254, fn. 2, & 257.

8   Ibid., pp. xxii-xxiii; and Donald Denoon, *Trial Separation: Australia and the Decolonisation of Papua New Guinea*, Australian National University, Pandanus Books, Canberra, 2005, pp. 40–42.

9   Matthew Jordan, 'Decolonisation', in James Cotton and David Lee (eds), *Australia and the United Nations*, Department of Foreign Affairs and Trade, Canberra, 2012, pp. 115, 119–20; and Paul Hasluck, *A Time for Building. Australian Administration in Papua and New Guinea, 1951–1963*, Melbourne University Press, Carlton, 1976, p. x.

10 Harold Macmillan, Address to South African Parliament, 3 February 1960, available at https://web-archives.univ-pau.fr/english/TD2doc1.pdf (consulted 23 May 2019).

11 David Goldsworthy, *Losing the Blanket. Australia and the End of Britain's Empire*, Melbourne University Press, Carlton South, 2002, p. 44.

12 Peter Edwards has noted that in the late 1940s 'Menzies had famously described support for independence movements against European colonial powers as "the very ecstasy of suicide"'. See Peter Edwards, *Arthur Tange: Last of the Mandarins*, Allen & Unwin, Crows Nest, 2006, p. 52.

in London that independence was arriving or would soon arrive in many countries. Back in Australia in June he told the press that:

> Whereas at one time many of us might have thought that it was better to go slowly in granting independence so that all the conditions existed for a wise exercise of self-government, I think the prevailing school of thought today is that if in doubt you should go sooner, not later. I belong to that school of thought myself now, though I didn't once.[13]

Asked if that applied to 'New Guinea' he said: 'I would apply that to any country'.[14] In December 1960 the UN General Assembly overwhelmingly passed a Soviet-initiated Declaration which called for immediate steps 'in Trust and Non-Self-Governing territories which have not yet attained independence, to transfer all powers to the peoples of these territories, without any conditions or reservations.'[15]

During the 1960s, nonetheless, successive Coalition governments were willing to discount UN views,[16] though they did accept that some reforms were needed in Papua and New Guinea.[17] In his June 1960 comments to the press Menzies mainly had in mind developments in Africa and Asia.[18] In Papua and New Guinea, where nationalist sentiments were generally lacking, the pace of change towards self-government increased only slightly.

Barnes saw himself as working within the gradualist and paternalist tradition established by his predecessor, Paul Hasluck. In June 1960 Hasluck said that whereas 'political advancement' followed on from 'social and economic advancement', political change was 'not necessarily followed by social and economic improvement'. Accordingly, Australian policy had concentrated 'on major efforts to establish law and order, health, hygiene, education, a better food supply and means of earning a living among people who are still largely primitive.' Australia wanted, Hasluck said, 'political advancement to go hand in hand with these measures and not in isolation from them.'[19]

In March 1966 the Australian Cabinet decided against adopting 'a particular posture towards the long term political future of the Territory', wishing to retain as 'much flexibility as possible'. It had excluded statehood within the Commonwealth as an option while noting— but not endorsing—a proposal from Barnes that the Territory's future should involve very close association with Australia.[20] In subsequent public comments Barnes gave no indication that change would be other than slow and gradual.

In the late 1960s, differences of view emerged between David (later Sir David) Hay and Barnes and Warwick Smith. Hay—a former senior diplomat with a distinguished war record—had been appointed as Administrator of Papua and New Guinea in January 1967. A year later Hay—in a letter to Barnes to which Barnes made no substantive response—

---

13 Goldsworthy, *Losing the Blanket*, pp. 45–46 and Ian Downs, *The Australian Trusteeship: Papua New Guinea, 1945–75*, Australian Government Publishing Service, Canberra, 1980, p. 215.

14 Goldsworthy, *Losing the Blanket*, p. 46. Menzies commented in this memoirs: 'in other words, "much too soon" would provoke disaster; "a little too soon" would be preferable to "a little too late".' See Robert Menzies, *The Measure of the Years*, Cassell Australia Ltd, North Melbourne, 1970, p. 221.

15 Cited in Jordan, 'Decolonisation', p. 120.

16 For Barnes's views on UN pressure, see Document 248. See also Doran, *Australia/PNG 1966–69*, Document 143.

17 Goldsworthy, *Losing the Blanket*, p. 46; Jordan, 'Decolonisation', pp. 123–24.

18 See Paul Hasluck, *A Time for Building*, pp. 254–57.

19 Stuart Doran, *Full Circle: Australia and Papua New Guinea, 1883–1970*, Department of Foreign Affairs and Trade, Canberra, 2007, p. 5.

20 Doran, *Australia/PNG 1966–69*, Documents 25 & 34.

implicitly questioned the value of maintaining Australia's presence. In his view this presence was primarily shaped by Australia's interpretation of its obligations to the United Nations and by 'sentiment, derived from war-time association and personal contacts, from interest in the work of the missions and from a certain pride in doing a job which needs to be done'.[21] Most UN members supported immediate independence but Hay thought an immediate hand-over 'would probably lead to a chaotic situation'. Australia was engaged in the long-term task of seeking to set up 'a manageable (not even a viable) economy'. Defence interests were not a 'primary reason' for a continued presence; though useful, existing facilities were not of 'overwhelming importance'. There was 'no economic advantage to be derived by the government sufficient to outweigh the heavy expenditure of manpower and monetary resources on our administration'. Private individuals and companies had economic interests, of course, but these were of marginal importance to the Australian economy. Maintaining a presence did not benefit Australia's relations with the wider world: Australia got 'no thanks internationally except from our closest allies'.[22]

In January 1968, John Grey Gorton unexpectedly became the Prime Minister, following the disappearance in December 1967 while swimming of Harold Holt, and by March there were already intimations of a new approach. The Australian Governor-General, Lord Casey, in his speech opening the Parliament, announced the transfer of the domestic Australian responsibilities of the Department of Territories to the Department of the Interior, with Papua and New Guinea and the smaller external territories now coming under a new Department of External Territories. He said this change recognised 'that the present problems and future destiny of the Northern Territory differ from those of Papua and New Guinea'. He said PNG's 'destiny … is to become a self-governing country developed for independence if and when it is clearly demonstrated by the majority of the indigenous population that this is what they wish'. He also referred to the possibility of a future 'special relationship' between Australia and a self-governing Papua and New Guinea while discouraging the idea that it might become Australia's 'seventh state'.[23]

The reformed House of Assembly, which began its four-year term in June 1968, was more widely representative than its predecessor, but the extent of real change was limited. Among its 84 elected members 17 were expatriates, of whom 11 had won one of the 15 regional electorates where expatriates had an advantage because an educational qualification was required.[24] The other six expatriates had each won one of the 69 local electorates, known as 'open' electorates because no educational qualification applied. Although a minority, and although their views varied, the elected expatriate members had great influence. In addition the Assembly included 10 Administration-appointed 'official members' whose role was to explain and support official policy. From mid-1968 some Assembly members served in a quasi-ministerial role as 'ministerial members' in the Administrator's Executive Council (AEC). In shaping the working arrangements for these reforms Barnes and Warwick Smith had sought to

---

21 Ibid., Document 155.

22 Ibid.

23 Ibid., p. 451 and Document 199, para. 5. See also Downs, *Australian Trusteeship*, p. 288.

24 Registered voters had the right to vote twice, once in their open electorate and once in their regional electorate. The educational qualification to stand for a regional electorate was the Territory Intermediate Certificate or the equivalent thereof. Most adult expatriates—but only a very small minority of their indigenous counterparts—were thus qualified. The regional electorates broadly aligned with the Territory's administrative districts. See Documents 155 (para. 22) & 162. See also R. S. Parker and Edward P. Wolfers, 'The Context of Political Change', in A. L. Epstein, R. S. Parker & Marie Reay (eds), *The Politics of Dependence: Papua New Guinea 1968*, Australian National University Press, Canberra, 1971, pp. 20–22, 36–38.

slow the pace of political and constitutional change. Overall, the new arrangements increased the scope for elected members to influence the governance of the territory only moderately.[25]

Hay thought that Barnes and Warwick Smith were too cautious and too controlling. In part he was motivated by the calculation that it would be in Australia's interests for a territorial government with greater powers to take greater responsibility for harsh measures to curb dissidence in Bougainville and the Gazelle Peninsula, thus reducing potential criticism of the Commonwealth Government. In 1968 and 1969 he recommended the delegation of more authority to his administration, improved consultation in the Territory, and the extension of more authority to the ministerial members of the Administrator's Executive Council.[26] Barnes and Warwick Smith showed little sympathy.[27] It appears their response was shaped in part by Warwick Smith's suspicion that Hay mainly wanted to arrogate more power to himself and his officials.[28]

Another, more radical, advocate for change was Gough Whitlam, leader of the Australian Labor Party and the Opposition from February 1967. Whitlam had been closely following PNG developments since entering parliament in 1952. During a visit to Papua and New Guinea in 1965 he declared that 'the rest of the world will think it anomalous' if the Territory 'was not independent by 1970'.[29] In May 1968 Whitlam told Parliament that the Government's approach carried 'gradualism to the point of imperceptibility' and contended that 'The Administration is paternalistic, insensitive to the feelings and attitudes of the indigenous people, complacent and self-satisfied'.[30] By the late 1960s opinion in the media, among academics and among members of the interested public was shifting in the same direction.

Barnes, however, did not see any reason to alter his approach. In September 1967 he said that he 'felt that time was on our side with [Papua] New Guinea'.[31] In April 1969 he told the press: 'I believe we have made a tremendous step forward in the last constitutional changes—why not let it settle down for a term of two [of the House or Assembly] until they really know where they are heading, really know what they want'.[32] Doran has remarked that around this time, 'the prospect of revolutionary change in government policy was contemplated by no-one'.[33]

At the end of the 1960s members of the expatriate (almost all Australian) population numbered about 50,000 while the indigenous population numbered an estimated 2.4 million.[34] Australian men held the higher-ranking and most of the middle-ranking positions in the public service,

---

25 Doran, *Australia/PNG 1966–69*, pp. xxxi–xxxii, li–liv; Downs, *Australian Trusteeship*, pp. 379–80; Denoon, *Trial Separation*, pp. 55–59; and Doran, *Full Circle*, pp. 14–15.

26 Doran, *Australia/PNG 1966–69*, pp. xxxi–xxxiii, xxxix–xliii, l–liv and Documents 144, 155, 229, 259 & 316.

27 Ibid., Document 316.

28 Ibid., pp. xli–xliii.

29 Gough Whitlam, *The Whitlam Government, 1972–1975*, Penguin Books, Melbourne, 1985, p. 84.

30 Doran, *Australia/PNG 1966–69*, p. 492.

31 Ibid., Document 143.

32 Ibid., Document 254, fn. 2.

33 Doran, *Full Circle*, p. 16. On political circumstances in 1969, Donald Denoon has commented: 'A generation later, it is hard to image a time when decolonisation seemed neither inevitable nor perhaps achievable'. Denoon, *Trial Separation*, p. 85.

    Mr Jeremy Hearder has recalled that when—as a young External Affairs officer—he made an extensive visit to Papua and New Guinea in 1966, senior officials told him without exception that they did not expect independence until the end of the century. Discussion, Henningham and Hearder, 1 April 2019.

34 Commonwealth Bureau of Census and Statistics, *Official Year Book of the Commonwealth of Australia, 1971*, Government Printer, Canberra, 1971, p. 990.

known as the 'Administration', as well as most of the professional and the technical positions. Australian women, most of them married to other expatriates, held administrative, teaching and support positions.[35] Australian men dominated the business sector, although indigenous participation was significant in coffee production. Older indigenous men exercised power within their kinship groups. Several thousand indigenous men exercised some measure of wider authority, as members of the House of Assembly, as middle rank public servants, as members of local government councils, as pastors and catechists, and as middle rank officers in the police and defence forces. A few hundred indigenous women, most of them educated by the Christian missions, worked as teachers or nurses or in secretarial and administrative support roles.[36] Marriages between members of the expatriate and indigenous populations were rare. Although in decline, racial prejudice and condescension were far from uncommon among expatriates.[37]

The large majority of the very numerous indigenous communities in the territory were accepting of, or at least acquiescent in, Australian rule, in part because this rule impinged only lightly on most of them and brought benefits in terms of public order, health and education services and economic development. Australia's authority had been challenged in the late 1960s, however, by strong protests in Bougainville and in the Gazelle Peninsula.[38] Local communities in Bougainville opposed the massive Conzinc Riotinto of Australia Limited (CRA) copper mining project, and many Bougainvilleans favoured secession.[39] By the beginning of 1970 the dissent in Bougainville had been contained, at least for the moment, and the Administration was mainly concerned with the challenge from the Mataungan[40] Association (MA) on the Gazelle Peninsula. Members of the Tolai community formed the MA in May–June 1969 and started campaigning, at times violently, against the formation of a multi-racial town council and the introduction of new local taxes.[41] Numbering around 70,000, the Tolai comprised a large majority of the population of the area. The MA wanted the continuation of a mono-racial (that is, a Tolai-only) council because it feared a multi-racial council would threaten Tolai identity and interests. The MA successfully encouraged many Tolai not to pay taxes to the new council, and campaigned for extensive control over local affairs. It also sought to foster locally-based economic development which did not involve expatriate capital or expertise.

---

35   Document 389; and Downs, *Australian Trusteeship*, p. 317.

36   See Anne Dickson-Waiko, 'Women, Nation and Decolonisation in Papua New Guinea, *Journal of Pacific History*, 48(2), 2013, pp. 177–93.

37   See Documents 201 (para. 3) & 252.

38   These protests can be seen as part of a broader phenomenon of 'micro-nationalism' based on strong regional and local identities. See R. J. May, 'Micronationalism in Papua New Guinea', in R. J. May (ed.), *State and Society in Papua New Guinea. The First Twenty-Five Years*, Crawford House Publishing, Adelaide, 2001, pp. 48–106.

39   Don Woolford, *Papua New Guinea: Initiation and Independence*, University of Queensland Press, Brisbane, 1976, pp. 28–42.

40   According to Tristan Moss, Mataungan can be translated as 'alert' or 'watchful'. Tristan Moss, *Guarding the Periphery: The Australian Army in Papua New Guinea, 1951–1975*, Cambridge University Press, Cambridge, 2017, p. 162. See also Downs, *Australian Trusteeship*, p. 339.

41   For background on the Association and on official responses to it, see Doran, *Australia/PNG 1966–69*, pp. xxxvi, xlvii–l, and pp. 909–12 and 954–58; Denoon, *Trial Separation*, pp. 62–64; Downs, *Australian Trusteeship*, pp. 169–74, 330–40, 424–39; Scarlett Epstein, 'The Mataungan Affair: The First Radical Mass Political Movement', *New Guinea*, December 1969–January 1970; and Woolford, *Papua New Guinea*, pp. 43–67.

Any broad sense of national identity was lacking; for almost all the members of the indigenous population identities and loyalties were strongly local and primarily kinship-based.[42] The first significant sign of an embryonic nationalist consciousness had come in January 1967, when a small group of Papua New Guineans, supported by sympathetic Australians, called for extensive reforms.[43] In mid-1967 members of this 'Group of 13' became founding members of the Pangu Pati (Papua and New Guinea Union Party). Pangu said it wanted a modest amount of 'home rule' and 'years of experience' of self-government under Australian guidance, leading eventually to independence.[44] Pangu failed to impress Barnes who in June 1967 said: 'The amount of publicity being given it [Pangu] is out of all proportion to how it is regarded by the people of [Papua] New Guinea … My impressions are that the people … do not want independence. They want self-government, but this does not mean that they want independence.'[45] Pangu's support at this time was indeed modest; it won around 10 per cent of the votes in the 1968 elections, gaining 13 of the 84 elected-member seats in the House of Assembly.[46]

A wind of change was beginning to blow, however, though it was emerging more from the changing views of Australian political leaders and their advisers—influenced by UN attitudes, and by the challenges posed by local protests—than from nationalist pressures.

Political and Constitutional Developments

From 28 December 1969 to 12 January 1970 Whitlam disturbed PNG's holiday season torpor with a barnstorming tour which included Port Moresby, Daru, Lae, Goroka, Mt Hagen, Madang, Wewak, Rabaul, Kavieng, Manus and Bougainville. The visit attracted great attention. *The Age* described the visit as a 'catalyst' in the debate over Papua New Guinea's future.[47] The small minority of younger, educated Papua New Guineans mostly responded favourably, albeit cautiously, to Whitlam's views, but many other people had strong reservations. At one meeting a local councillor was applauded after he angrily told Whitlam that only the indigenous people of the Territory should 'decide when they should receive self-government and later independence'. People in the highlands region feared self-government would result in their domination 'by the more sophisticated coastal people'.[48] Many were concerned lest Australian aid cease with self-government and independence.

---

42   According to one study, at the time of the 1968 elections an 'indigenous political elite was barely beginning to emerge'. See Epstein, Parker and Reay (eds), *Politics of Dependence*, p. 3.

  In mid-2019, the distinguished journalist Sean Dorney commented: 'Papua New Guinea is still struggling with governance, it's true. This is due to how rapidly it has moved from more than 1000 tiny, subsistence nation-states to a single country. Its eight to nine million people speak 860 distinct languages'. See Sean Dorney, 'The Papua New Guinea Awakening: Inside the forgotten colony', *Australian Foreign Affairs*, 6 (2019), pp. 71–87.

43   Doran, *Australia/PNG 1966–69*, Document 97 & Document 58 (note 3). See also Parker and Wolfers, 'The Context of Political Change', pp. 32–33.

44   Doran, *Australia/PNG 1966–69*, p. xxxiv and Documents 120 & 122, fn. 2; and Downs, *Australian Trusteeship*, pp. 385–88.

45   Downs, *Australian Trusteeship*, p. 389.

46   Ibid., pp. 391–93.

47   *The Age*, 14 January 1970. For assessments of the visit see Denoon, *Trial Separation*, pp. 78–80; Doran, *Full Circle*, pp. 25–35; Ian Downs, *Australian Trusteeship*, pp. 466–69; James Griffin, 'Papua New Guinea', in W. J. Hudson (ed.), *Australia in World Affairs, 1971–75*, George Allen & Unwin, Sydney, 1980, p. 348; and Woolford, *Papua New Guinea*, pp. 68–71.

48   Doran, *Full Circle*, pp. 26–27.

The views Whitlam expressed met with strong responses from Gorton and Barnes to which in turn Whitlam responded.[49] In public, the Government was combative, but behind the scenes there was movement. In early 1970, after failing in earlier efforts to encourage Barnes to take a different approach, Hay had raised his concerns with Gorton. While on leave in Australia in December 1969/January 1970 he spoke to Sir James Darling, his and Gorton's former headmaster. Darling passed on Hay's views to Gorton and encouraged a meeting between the two men. Gorton's principal private secretary, Ainsley Gotto, and the Minister for Social Security, William Charles Wentworth, helped shape Gorton's views. Unbeknown to Barnes and Warwick Smith, on 22 January Gorton and Hay discussed Australia's policies.[50] Hay then wrote to Gorton with a suggested draft reply to a letter Barnes had sent Gorton on 19 January.[51]

Drawing heavily on Hay's draft letter Gorton wrote to Barnes on 2 February 1970 to say that the Government's stance needed to encourage 'the early achievement of internal self-government'. Gorton wanted to grant ministerial members of the PNG House of Assembly full authority in defined fields. He did not want, as Barnes had suggested, to wait until after the next House of Assembly elections in early 1972 to test public opinion on self-government. He concluded: 'now is the time to decentralise a great deal of decision-making, now is the time to allow some mistakes to be made if that should happen'.[52] Barnes responded urging caution. He referred to the substantial 'requirements by way of social, political and economic development' required for a transition to self-government, questioned whether a 'reasonably broad majority' of the people of the Territory would find self-government acceptable and warned against alarming expatriates and discouraging investors.[53] Gorton was not swayed by Barnes's views.

Gorton's inclination to a fresh approach appears to have been strengthened by the protests in Bougainville and on the Gazelle Peninsula in 1969 and by the interest of the ALP opposition and the Australian media and educated public in those protests.[54] Early in 1970 he was presumably motivated in part by a wish to blunt opposition and media criticisms and to strengthen his authority. His government had won the October 1969 elections only very narrowly and he had strong critics within his own party.[55] Even without such pressures, however, Gorton was inclined to question established policies and had sought to re-evaluate Australia's international role.[56] Downs has recalled that 'two well-qualified observers' had separately confirmed to him 'Gorton's personal determination [in the late 1960s] to accelerate home rule as a prelude to an independent national status' for the Territory.[57] In mid-1969 Gorton said the people of Papua and New Guinea could 'become self-governing and independent as soon as a method is devised.'[58] Andrew Peacock has recalled that Gorton was not comfortable with Australia's

---

49   Documents 1–6 & 8–10.

50   Doran, *Full Circle*, pp. 32–35.

51   Letter, Hay to Gorton, undated (c. late January 1970), NAA: M3787, 14.

52   Document 15.

53   Document 20.

54   See Doran, *Full Circle*, pp. 17–21.

55   Ian Hancock, *John Gorton. He Did It His Way*, Hodder, Sydney, pp. 252–54; Alan Trengrove, *John Grey Gorton, An Informal Biography*, Cassell Australia, Melbourne, 1969, pp. 201, 212–13, 234–40; and Peter Howson (ed. Don Aitkin), *The Howson Diaries: The Life of Politics*, Viking Press, Ringwood, Vic., 1984, pp. 14–15, 481–82, 543–44, 586–89 & 591–94.

56   Trengrove, *Gorton*, pp. 201–3; Hancock, *Gorton*, pp. 156–7, 180, 200; and *Howson Diaries*, p. 181.

57   The two observers were Tony Voutas, a former patrol officer, a member of the House of Assembly from 1968 to 1972 and a founding member of the Pangu Pati; and Peter Hastings, a prominent journalist and leader writer. Downs, *Australian Trusteeship*, pp. 469–70.

58   Ibid.

colonial history and administrative role in the Territory.[59] Behind the scenes, contingency planning on a transition to self-government and to independence in the longer term had begun in the first half of 1969.[60]

The first public sign of a new approach came on 3 March 1970. In his speech opening the new parliament Casey's successor as Governor-General, Sir Paul Hasluck, referred to the transfer of 'enlarged and additional' powers.[61] A few weeks later Hay told Gorton that news of forthcoming changes had been 'received enthusiastically' in Port Moresby by advocates of reform.[62] Hay had reservations about the extent of the reforms proposed, and stressed the need to consult opinion in the House of Assembly.[63] His concerns, however, were largely ignored. On 23 June ministers endorsed Submissions 327 and 328 on PNG's future.[64] In response to 327 they accepted the need to give 'a great deal more bite' to 'the existing policy of increasing the extent to which native people participate in political, social and economic affairs'.[65] They noted that international experience suggested the period between self-government and independence tended to be brief.[66] In response to 328 they agreed to transfer powers in defined fields to ministerial members and assistant ministerial members, so that henceforth they would have full authority rather than sharing it with their departmental heads. The Administrator was to act on the advice provided.[67]

Gorton accompanied his reforms by personally ensuring changes in senior staff. Hay took over as Secretary of External Territories in early July, with Warwick Smith transferred to the Department of the Interior. Les (later Sir Les) Johnson succeeded Hay.[68] Formerly the Assistant Administrator, Johnson managed sensitive political issues deftly and he and his wife Dulcie had built up rapport with PNG's emerging leaders. Downs has recalled that Hay and Johnson:

> had developed a personal understanding while working together in the Territory. They both believed that self-government had to be encouraged. These two appointments meant that for the first time in the post-war period there was total absence of friction and complete co-operation between the Department in Canberra and the Administration.[69]

59 Telephone conversation, Peacock and Hunt, 8 September 2017.

60 Doran, *Australia/PNG 1966–69*, Document 293.

61 Document 25.

62 Letter, Hay to Gorton, 11 May 1970, NAA: M3787, 14.

63 Document 42. See also Documents 44–45.

64 Documents 53 & 54. For the submissions see Documents 47 & 48. See also Document 52 for the view expressed by Hay that: 'the Commonwealth should lean towards rather than against the early achievement of internal self-government'.

65 Documents 47 & 53. The paper attached to Submission 327 said 'the Commonwealth's purpose is to advance the native people and not to preserve the positions of Australians in the Territory'. In the past policies of this kind had perhaps been 'applied somewhat hesitantly because of resistance by those Australians—both in private enterprise and in the public service—who exercise the authority which would be transferred to native hands' (Document 47, para. 38).

66 Document 47, para. 15.

67 Documents 48 & 54.

68 In part because of frustration with Warwick Smith's discourteous micro-management, Johnson had resigned in April 1970 as Assistant Administrator and had accepted the position of Principal of the Tasmania College of Advanced Education. He was back in Australia when Gorton rang him one evening and persuaded him to return to the Territory. Hancock, *John Gorton*, p. 289, and information kindly provided by Mrs Fay Redgrave, daughter of Les Johnson, in a discussion with Bruce Hunt in Sydney on 1 December 2017. For further details on these changes see also Downs, *Australian Trusteeship*, pp. 399–401, 471–72; and Denoon, *Trial Separation*, p. 81.

69 See Downs, *Australian Trusteeship*, p. 401.

In taking forward reform Hay and Johnson were supported by several talented and committed officials in Canberra and Port Moresby.

Gorton visited from 5 to 11 July 1970 to publicise the new approach.[70] Prime ministerial visits were rare: Sir Robert Menzies had made the first in 1957 and the second in 1963.[71] Gorton's itinerary followed that of Whitlam but took a third of the time.[72] On 6 July he told the Administrator's Executive Council that the Territory was on 'the road to self-government. You have started on it'. He announced the transfer of authority over several areas. The appointed official members of the Council would still provide advice but henceforth would not vote on expenditure proposals.[73]

Gorton stressed that change was on its way. In Goroka he 'assured highlanders that Australia would not force Papua and New Guinea into self-government against the people's wishes'. He added, however, that the Territory was 'on the road to self-government and there was no turning back'.[74] In Lae, according to Don Woolford, 'Gorton heard from that forgotten minority, the Chinese. They feared that their position after independence would be untenable … Gorton offered them little comfort'.[75] In Rabaul Gorton faced angry MA supporters.[76] Meanwhile some House of Assembly members were concerned they had not been properly consulted. The House later declared that 'any future transfers of power or constitutional changes … will be unacceptable' unless a majority of members had agreed to them.[77]

Like 1970, 1971 began with a visit by Whitlam, who again spoke in strong terms.[78] Barnes responded that Whitlam 'had shown contempt for the standing of the … House of Assembly in trying to impose his own arbitrary timetable for self-government and independence'.[79] Whitlam made less impact in January 1971 than a year earlier because of the progress with reforms.[80] Barnes wrote to Gorton on 11 February 1971 noting Johnson's advice that an 'obvious foreshortening in the independence time-scale' had occurred. Barnes thought public debate had gone ahead without consideration of: the likely cohesiveness and effectiveness of leadership in the new House of Assembly which would be elected in early 1972; the risk that 'indigenization, now being accelerated, could be chaotic if the key expatriates leave'; challenges to national unity; weaknesses in law and order capacity; the limited capacity to raise internal revenue; and the 'inadequate constitutional and legal foundations for self-government'. He thought it would be 'a folly to conduct a debate about the date of self-government or independence without reference to such factors' and said every year counted in terms of preparations for self-government.[81] Unconvinced, Gorton responded that Australia should 'move with any

---

70 Document 49, fn. 1. He was accompanied by his wife Bettina and by Barnes and Hay.

71 Bruce Hunt, *Australia's Northern Shield? Papua New Guinea and the Defence of Australia Since 1880*, Monash University Publishing, Clayton, 2017, pp. 93, 174

72 Downs, *Australian Trusteeship*, p. 472.

73 Document 64. See also Downs, *Australian Trusteeship*, pp. 472–74.

74 Document 67.

75 Woolford, *Papua New Guinea*, p. 78. See also Document 104, para. 43.

76 Ibid, pp. 78–80.

77 See Downs, *Australian Trusteeship*, pp. 395, 398.

78 Document 127 & 128.

79 Document 129.

80 Downs, *Australian Trusteeship*, pp. 468, 516; Graham Freudenberg, *A Certain Grandeur. Gough Whitlam's Life in Politics*, Revised Edition, Penguin, Camberwell, Vic., 2007, pp. 204–05; Whitlam, *Whitlam Government*, pp. 90–91.

81 Document 137.

fore-shortening of the independence timetable', and that it was important to avoid any impression of an attempt 'to delay the achievement of internal self-government'.[82]

In 1970 and early 1971, with Australian officials providing support and exerting influence, the House of Assembly's Select Committee on Constitutional Development undertook extensive consultations.[83] Presenting its final report in early March 1971 the Committee recommended the preparation 'for internal self-government during the life of the next House of Assembly'. It also made proposals on the legislature (an expanded single chamber), the government (a central government), the ministry (to be chosen solely from the legislature), and on a national crest and flag.[84] The House agreed on 11 March to almost all the recommendations and, at a later meeting, dropped the 'and' from the Territory's name, which thus became 'Papua New Guinea'.[85]

The deliberations of the House of Assembly broadly coincided with the replacement of Gorton by William McMahon, until then the Minister for Foreign Affairs. Prime Minister McMahon and his ministers maintained the broad policy directions Gorton had set. One concern appears to have been that of maintaining the political initiative against the challenge posed by the ALP.[86] Some coalition ministers and parliamentarians took an active interest in the Territory, but most went with the flow.[87] Ministers accepted the burden of spending on Papua New Guinea but hoped it would eventually decline.[88] Disengaging had become easier because Papua New Guinea's perceived defence significance had waned because of improved relations with Indonesia since Soeharto had replaced Sukarno and because of the measure of reassurance provided by Australia's alliance relationship with the United States. Moreover, because of the emergence of separatist pressures and other unrest in Papua New Guinea from the late 1960s onwards, Australian policy-makers were becoming concerned about the risk of Australia becoming embroiled in responding to internal unrest following the transition to self-government and independence.[89]

Despite his reservations Barnes loyally implemented the new approach. In early April 1971 he sought Cabinet agreement to the Select Committee recommendations. He noted the Committee had found that PNG majority opinion 'favoured internal self-government no sooner than the life of the 1976–80 House of Assembly'. Because the rate of political development was quickening, however, it had recommended preparations for internal self-government in the life of the 1972–76 House, should this be required. Barnes also rehearsed his concerns about 'limiting factors'.[90] On 20 April Cabinet agreed to Barnes's recommendations and proposed that Barnes follow up 'as he considered appropriate' on the possibility of establishing a bicameral system.[91] Barnes had earlier advocated for an upper house but did not take the idea

---

82   Document 140.

83   Downs, *Australian Trusteeship*, pp. 397–401; Woolford, *Papua New Guinea*, pp. 90–103.

84   Document 142.

85   Documents 155, 159–160 & 163–64.

86   See Howson, *Howson Diaries*, pp. 606, 608.

87   One coalition member who took a close interest was Peter Howson. See ibid, pp. 515, 544, 549, 611 617, 619, 629, 634 & 743–44.

88   For Gorton's earlier views, see Documents 64 & 65.

89   Document 141 and Hunt, *Australia's Northern Shield?*, pp. xxiv, 219–26.

90   Document 155, paras 8, 9 & 12.

91   Documents 159.

any further, presumably because it conflicted with the Select Committee's views and with Gorton's broad intention to have a strong central PNG government.[92]

After a PNG tour from late January to early March 1971 a UN Trusteeship Council Mission concluded that: 'Recent advancements involving substantial transfer of authority to local ministerial members seem to be working well.'[93] In early May the Department of Foreign Affairs (DFA) advised its overseas posts that circumstances had 'changed markedly over the last few months'. Australia had 'tended to take a somewhat defensive approach' in the past but 'a more positive attitude' could now be taken, with an emphasis on Papua New Guinea 'as a country rapidly approaching self-government and one which will soon take its place in the world.'[94]

Estimates of the likely pace of change varied. At a meeting in November 1971 with defence representatives Hay said his department was planning for self-government in 1975 and thought a date for independence in 1977 or 1978 'seemed a reasonable guess'. The participants agreed, at least with respect to defence planning, that they should plan on self-government in 1975 with independence in 1976 or 1977.[95] Foreign Affairs officials thought change would come more swiftly. In June 1971 they were already 'working on the premise' that self-government would be attained following the 1972 House of Assembly elections, with independence coming 'fairly soon thereafter'.[96] In April 1972, DFA Secretary Sir Keith Waller said that DET's indicative target date for full self-government of September 1975 was 'almost certainly unreal'.[97]

Successive external/foreign affairs ministers (McMahon, Bury and Bowen) and their officials thought that because DFA would assume responsibility for relations with Papua New Guinea after independence it should be fully involved in policy discussions and decisions from early on, in order to help shape the transition process in a way beneficial to Australian interests.[98] For this reason, and because they believed change would be faster than DET envisaged, they wanted formal arrangements for whole-of-government coordination. At first this proposal was resisted. On 7 July 1970 Waller wrote to John Bunting, the Secretary of the Cabinet Office, advising that his minister wished to propose that an inter-departmental committee be set up.[99] Bunting responded a month later that: 'the Prime Minister has marked the papers to the effect that he sees no need for an inter-departmental committee.'[100] DFA revived the proposal in October 1971 but was again rebuffed.[101] Hay's view was that DET should manage the transition to self-government and that there would be no need for substantial DFA involvement until a later stage.[102] Eventually, however, formal coordination arrangements were put in place, with a

---

92   See Downs, *Australian Trusteeship*, p. 399. For the views of Barnes and Warwick Smith on the addition of an upper house to the House of Assembly, see Documents 11 & 13 and Doran, *Australia/PNG 1966–69*, pp. lii–liii and Documents 184, 254, 256, 258, 270, 304 & 316.

93   Document 169.

94   Document 163.

95   Document 233

96   Document 187, para. 4.

97   Document 283.

98   Documents 107, 151, 153, 187 & 200.

99   Document 66.

100 Letter, Bunting to Hay, NAA: A452, 1970/3046.

101 Documents 225, 242 & 251.

102 Documents 239 & 242.

cabinet standing committee and an inter-departmental committee set up in April/May, 1972.[103]

In November 1971 Barnes gained parliamentary agreement to amendments to the *Papua and New Guinea Act*. These changes included creating the role of AEC Deputy Chairman, a position later known as Chief Minister, enlarging the House of Assembly, confirming the name 'Papua New Guinea', replacing the terms ministerial member and assistant ministerial member with 'minister' and 'assistant minister', and adding three ministers.[104]

Australian officials were determined to maintain the pace of change. Following a visit to Papua and New Guinea in late 1971 France's Ambassador to Australia, Gabriel Van Laethem, warned of the risk of a PNG 'panic' involving the departure of skilled expatriates, capital flight and a cessation of investment, and offered France's support to help seek reduced pressure for change from the United Nations.[105] Waller acknowledged the reasons for this 'general feeling of unease' but argued: 'The longer we delay independence the harder it may become to grant it, not least because of the separatist tendencies already apparent'.[106] Pressure for change no longer came mainly from the United Nations. Rather, 'it [was] the people of the Territory who will decide the pace of progress towards self-government'.[107] Hay responded that despite the 'obvious risks' he did not 'see any reason to be diverted from existing policy'.[108] He said Barnes broadly concurred with the Ambassador's views but did not agree that UN pressure 'has in recent years weighed heavily with the Government or political leaders in Papua New Guinea'.[109] Hay met Van Laethem on 21 December and politely declined his offer of French assistance.[110]

On 2 February 1972 Andrew Peacock, Minister for the Army since 1969, succeeded Barnes. Hay advised his new minister of the 'importance of building up a relationship of confidence'. Peacock annotated Hay's submission: 'Most important: establishment of relations of mutual confidence between our governments'.[111] Peacock also took other advice: that of Sir Robert Menzies who referred to his view that when pressure for change had emerged in a colony it was better to transfer power sooner rather than later.[112] The advice from Hay and Menzies chimed well with Peacock's liberal and moderate instincts. When appointed he at once flew to Papua New Guinea. He visited four more times in his first five weeks as minister and made several more visits in the course of the year.[113] Johnson has recalled that Peacock 'was forthcoming, eminently approachable and eager'.[114]

---

103 Documents 284 & 296, para. 2(g). The Cabinet committee comprised the Prime Minister, the Deputy Prime Minister, the Treasurer, the Attorney-General, the Minister for External Territories and the ministers for Foreign Affairs, Trade and Industry, and Defence.

104 See Document 234.

105 Document 244.

106 Document 246.

107 Ibid.

108 Document 248.

109 Ibid.

110 Ibid., fn. 4.

111 Document 260, including fn.1.

112 Peacock's recollection as conveyed to Hunt by telephone on 8 September 2017.

113 Downs, *Australian Trusteeship*, p. 481; Griffin, 'Papua New Guinea', p. 352; and Denoon, *Trial Separation*, p. 101.

114 Les Johnson, *Colonial Sunset: Australia and Papua New Guinea 1970–1974*, University of Queensland Press, St Lucia, 1983, p. 96.

The elections to the expanded House of Assembly took place in February–March 1972. Nine of the 100 elected members were expatriates compared with 17 of 84 in the 1968 House. There were four appointed official members, down from ten previously.[115] Elected as MHA for Central regional, Josephine Abaijah became the first woman to serve in the House. After a visit shortly before a government was formed DFA officer Lew Border predicted that: 'The mood of the House will be rather different from that of the old one. It was relatively easy for the Administration to get its proposals through ... The new Ministry is likely to be much more independent ... The impression I gained was of a rising nationalism and increasing resentment of white domination.'[116]

Peacock made it clear in March 1972 that he favoured a prompt transition to self-government. He hoped a Papua New Guinean would serve as Speaker. Papua New Guineans should predominate 'overwhelmingly' in the ministry and occupy 'key portfolios'. The Deputy Chairman (later to be known as the Chief Minister) should choose his cabinet and 'be seen to be, in practice, the leader of the Government'. He wanted future negotiations to be with local leaders and not expatriates. He wished to start discussions with PNG leaders in mid-year and to prepare a program for movement to self-government.[117]

With around 40 seats the conservative highlands-based United Party (UP) emerged as the strongest single grouping in the new House. Johnson had thought it likely conservative members would have a commanding position, delaying movement towards self-government.[118] The UP was united only in name, however; it lacked cohesion and effective leadership.[119] Instead, Pangu Pati leader Michael Somare and his colleagues adroitly put together a National Coalition Government (NCG). After initial caution because of the difficulty in managing his diverse coalition he and his supporters pushed for rapid progress. Over the following four years he showed great skill in holding the NCG together.[120]

Hasluck said at the opening of the new House on 20 April that it was government policy: 'to encourage the movement towards self-government but not to impose self-government upon Papua New Guinea. To this end my Government looks to this House to represent the wishes of the majority of the people and to take the initiative on the pace and nature of constitutional development.'[121] In early May Johnson reported that 'opinion is likely to move more strongly in the direction of self-government and any attempts by the Commonwealth to influence legislation which it might not favour will be resented and possibly diminish Australian influence in the longer term'.[122] In mid-May Cabinet endorsed a submission by Peacock on the 'Programme of Movement towards Internal Self-Government', noting his advice that 'planning for the establishment of internal self-government should proceed on the basis that it might be expected to come into effect in 1974'.[123] The Government did not however refer to this timeframe in public statements, presumably to avoid alarming conservative PNG opinion

---

115 Downs, *Australian Trusteeship*, p. 487

116 Document 277, paras 5 & 6.

117 Document 263.

118 Documents 217 & 275. See also Document 233, para. 3.

119 See Documents 310 & 376.

120 Document 310; Downs, *Australian Trusteeship*, pp. 489–90; Denoon, *Trial Separation*, pp. 101–3; and Griffin, 'Papua New Guinea', pp. 353–54. A Special Branch report of around January 1967 had noted with respect to Somare that: 'By virtue of his education and proven ability to speak and organise he could become a formidable force in local affairs'. Doran, *Australia/PNG 1966–69*, Document 91, fn. 7.

121 Document 281.

122 Document 289.

123 Document 296. For the submission, see Document 278.

and to maintain business and investor confidence. Cabinet agreed that party leaders outside of Somare's coalition should be consulted 'so that Australia's position is as far as possible accepted by all sections of political opinion in the Territory'.[124]

In early June 1972 DFA officer Colin McDonald reported that the emergence of the National Coalition Government and the increased pressure for change had caught many Administration officials by surprise.[125] On 23 June Somare set up a cross-party group—the Constitutional Planning Committee (CPC)—to recommend on 'a constitution for full internal self-government in a united Papua New Guinea with a view to eventual independence'.[126] A few days later he said: 'self-government should not occur before December 1, 1973, but that it should come as soon as possible after that'.[127] At talks in Port Moresby in July–August Peacock made clear his commitment to the further transfer of powers and to a provisional timetable. He sought agreement on the administrative and legislative steps required and accepted Somare's target date for self-government.[128]

In August Peacock gained support in Parliament for an amendment to the *Papua New Guinea Act* to abolish the limit on the number of ministers he could appoint at the Chief Minister's request.[129] Presumably the purpose was to give Somare greater flexibility to shore up his unwieldy coalition.[130] Reporting to Cabinet on 30 August, Peacock noted the command shown by Somare at the Port Moresby talks and Somare's wish to have authority in all areas transferred as soon as practicable. He said Somare and his colleagues were not distinguishing between self-government powers and those more appropriate to a state of independence. Papua New Guinea could thus find itself virtually independent at the time when internal self-government was attained. This could lead to political problems for Somare, especially in the conservative highlands region. Peacock did not argue, however, for a slowing of the pace of change.[131] Cabinet endorsed his approach. It also—while recognising the likelihood of a shortened interval between self-government and independence—expressed a preference for the transition to independence to take place in the term of the next House of Assembly, that is, in the four years from April 1976.[132]

The CPC presented its first report in October 1972. DFA officer Ross Burns expressed concern about apparent ambitions 'to turn the CPC into a constitution-making body with a status verging on that of a constituent assembly', involving the risk of delaying progress with constitutional negotiations.[133] In late November 1972 Johnson reviewed the state of play. He said the ministers in the National Coalition Government generally arrived at AEC meetings 'poorly informed'. Reflecting their suspicions of 'a colonial and largely white senior public service' they at times had been 'reluctant to accept departmental advice', relying instead on private advisers who he thought lacked knowledge and experience. He concluded that: 'it would be idle to pretend that at present the Government is working smoothly and efficiently, but the fact remains that it is working, it is making its own decisions and it is surviving.'[134]

---

124 Document 296.

125 Document 310.

126 Document 317.

127 Document 318.

128 Document 336. See also Documents 345–347 & 351.

129 Documents 295, 338 & 341 and *CPD*, HR, vol. 79, 16 August 1972, pp. 240–41.

130 See Downs, *The Australian Trusteeship*, p. 490.

131 Document 361. On the highlands region, see Document 376.

132 Document 370.

133 Document 388.

134 Document 406. See also Document 397.

On 2 December the ALP won office in Australia. In offering his congratulations Somare said Whitlam could 'justifiably claim some of the credit for the recent changes of Australian policy towards Papua New Guinea'. He also regretted the loss of a 'dynamic and proven' minister in Andrew Peacock.[135] For his part Whitlam declared: 'It is altogether probable that Papua New Guinea will be fully independent and, one trusts, admitted to both the United Nations and the Commonwealth of Nations ... no more than two years from now'. He said Peacock had made PNG's 'progress towards independence ... very much easier than any of us could have expected'.[136] Whitlam's enthusiasm for independence in less than two years contrasted with the preference of McMahon's government for independence in the 1976 to 1980 period.[137] Somare responded cautiously. He said at a press conference that Whitlam had made his statement on the timing for independence 'during a period of excitement after becoming the new Prime Minister ... He did not think that Mr Whitlam would thrust independence on PNG without consultations with its leaders'.[138]

Economic Support

In 1968 Barnes had said it was not Australia's 'policy that self-government must wait on complete economic self-sufficiency'. For the foreseeable future the Territory would require 'continued outside aid'. Barnes also thought, however, that 'without substantial economic self-reliance, self-government or independence would be a mockery'.[139] A year later, he declared that: 'I am not prepared to see a drift into a situation in which the Commonwealth provides two-thirds of funds for the government of the Territory and does not control expenditure'.[140]

Nonetheless, the political and constitutional changes implemented from early 1970 obliged Barnes to accept a gradual drift into that situation. In financial year 1969–70 Australia's total government expenditure in the Territory amounted to over $204 million. Revenue raised within the Territory comprised around $72 million of this total. Australia's direct grant of $97.2 million had increased by over 10 per cent on the 1968–69 grant. In addition to the funds administered by DET, other Australian departments and agencies expended around $30 million during the financial year.[141] Downs has noted: 'Vast expenditures by these [other] instrumentalities in diverse forms of assistance and in their regular functions were not a charge against the Territory's funds nor taken into account when determining the annual grant-in-aid'.[142] Overall, Australia provided nearly 60 per cent of total public expenditure in 1969–70, with this pattern broadly continuing over the 1970–72 period.[143] The notion of linking

---

135 Document 410.

136 Document 412.

137 Document 370.

138 Document 413.

139 Barnes, as quoted by Ballard in Doran, *Australia/PNG 1966–69*, Document 284.

140 Ibid., Document 299.

141 Downs, *Australian Trusteeship*, p. 397. See also Doran, *Australia/PNG 1966–69*, Document 292.

142 Downs, *Australian Trusteeship*, p. xiv.

143 Documents 33 & 35; Doran, *Australia/PNG 1966–69*, Document 328; and ibid., p. 397.

   Document 97 in the present volume refers to grants totalling $100 million for financial year of 1970/71. The figure quoted in this document presumably refers only to the direct grant. Document 110 refers to spending by other Commonwealth departments and instrumentalities 'of an economic nature' of an estimated $14.5 million in 1970/71. This figure did not include spending on defence and other matters because this expenditure was not 'of an economic nature'. In 1969/70 defence expenditure in the Territory amounted to over $10.2 million, 'excluding a relevant portion of major supporting defence overheads borne by Australia' (Document 100, Para. 33).

movement towards self-government with increased economic self-reliance was abandoned.[144]

The Commonwealth Government continued, however, to call for greater economic self-reliance. Speaking to the AEC on 6 July 1970 Gorton said the House of Assembly should take greater responsibility for levying revenue. Under new arrangements the purposes of the funds Australia provided would be clearer. Direct funding would supplement local revenues to cover administrative and operational costs, with additional funding provided for development spending.[145] In a meeting on the same day with the Speaker of the House, John Guise, Gorton said that 'with power comes ... financial responsibility', and warned that in the in future 'the Australian taxpayer would query the continuance of large amounts of money to the Territory'.[146]

While Cabinet subsequently confirmed the direct grant for 1970–71 and agreed to allow the Administration 'some flexibility' to borrow funds, Barnes remained concerned about the absence of self-reliance. He told Gorton in February 1971 that internal revenues would provide only 29.8 per cent of the budget in 1970–71, if account were taken both of the direct grant and of separate Commonwealth spending. A large part of Papua New Guinea's internal revenues, moreover, comprised tax payments by expatriate individuals and companies, and there was a risk the expatriate presence would decline sharply after independence. Meanwhile measures 'to broaden the indigenous economic base' would 'take some years to show effective results'.[147]

Barnes told Parliament in mid-September 1971 that Australian 'aid of an economic nature' would amount to nearly $131 million in the 1971–72 financial year, and that over the eight years to 1970–71 total economic aid had amounted to $716 million. He noted that 'if self-government and independence were to mean anything at all to the people of Papua New Guinea they must not be too dependent economically on Australia and other countries'. He highlighted some progress towards greater self-reliance: in 1971–72 internal revenue would provide 'about 36 per cent of total Administration expenditure in Papua New Guinea compared with about 25 per cent in 1963/64'.[148]

Soon after succeeding Barnes Peacock said revenue-raising was a 'vital prerequisite' to self-government.[149] Prospects for a substantial increase in local revenue-raising remained poor, however. In mid-February 1972, Hay advised Peacock that the economy still relied heavily on expatriates, including for tax revenues, and was also 'heavily dependent on an increasing annual Australian grant'.[150] In a speech on 8 June Peacock said Australia had: 'made it clear

---

144 Donald Denoon seems to suggest that it was Peacock who 'cut the link between economic development and constitutional change'. Denoon, *Trial Separation*, p. 101. But this link had already been abandoned when Gorton insisted on moving ahead with reforms, despite the reservations of Barnes (Documents 20 & 137).

In a July 1969 television interview Gorton had referred to 'the great drain [from the Australian budget] for New Guinea development, with the suggestion that this economic dependence would complicate a transition to self-government and independence, but in early 1970 he decided to push ahead with reforms anyway.

For Gorton's comments in July 1969, see Downs, *Australian Trusteeship*, p. 469.

145 Document 64. On efforts to improve the management of spending see also Documents 31, 32, 48, & 132, item (f).

146 Document 65.

147 Document 137.

148 Document 214.

149 Document 261.

150 Document 260.

that it looks to Papua New Guinea to progressively increase its financial self-reliance by raising the level of its domestic revenue'. Despite Australia's best efforts, however, Papua New Guinea was 'likely to be heavily dependent on foreign aid after independence.'[151]

In June 1972 Peacock recommended to Cabinet that support for Papua New Guinea for 1972–73 should amount to $132.5 million, up from $120 million the previous financial year.[152] Treasury had strong reservations. The Treasurer expressed 'the strongest doubts whether such a large increase is in the longer-term best interests of the Territory' and said he did 'not believe it can be justified'.[153] It appears DFA was also inclined to have reservations.[154] Cabinet appears to have taken account of these concerns; the allocation was reduced to $127.8 million.[155]

In late 1972 Somare and other PNG leaders expressed interest in a renegotiation of the Bougainville Copper Agreement. If successful, a renegotiation had the potential to increase PNG's economic self-reliance. DET officials opposed the idea, however, arguing that the 'Agreement represented the best deal that could be negotiated at the time', and warning that Papua New Guinea might take steps that caused 'a drying-up of investment'. Moreover 'an unfavourable reaction ... in Australia might make it difficult for the Government to maintain its present generous attitude to aid to Papua New Guinea'. Peacock responded: 'This is an implied threat and should not be put to PNG at this stage'.[156] Later on, in negotiations that concluded in October 1974, and with PNG's bargaining position greatly boosted by the high mineral prices at that time, the Somare Government attained a more favourable deal.[157] But as Denoon has argued, there was a 'fatal' continuity with the original negotiation in that in the renegotiation 'no-one represented either Bougainville or the landowners'.[158]

The Transfer of Powers and Responsibilities

As noted earlier, Gorton had announced the transfer of several domestic portfolios during his July 1970 visit.[159] From then onwards DET officials took these and other transfers forward. The task was substantial: the department had limited resources and as Warwick Smith had noted in late 1968, 'in the Territory we are obviously concerned with the whole field of government'.[160]

At first Hay had believed that separate banking and currency arrangements were 'a long way off'.[161] An interdepartmental committee was nonetheless set up in September 1971 to take forward the transfer of banking.[162] Several of those involved were reportedly 'men of essentially conservative disposition with little direct experience of Papua New Guinea', while the senior

---

151 Document 309.

152 Document 315.

153 Document 329. See also Denoon, *Trial Separation*, p. 128.

154 See Joseph's views in Document 232.

155 Document 333.

156 Document 384. See also Document 390.

157 Denoon, *Trial Separation*, pp. 133–36. See also Woolford, *Papua New Guinea*, pp. 204–5; and Donald Denoon, *Getting Under the Skin: The Bougainville Copper Agreement and the Creation of the Panguna Mine*, Melbourne University Press, Carlton South, 2000.

158 Denoon, *Trial Separation*, p. 135.

159 Document 64. See also Document 40.

160 Doran, *Australia/PNG 1966–69*, pp. 451–52.

161 Document 43, para. 2(f).

162 Document 218.

Treasury representative was said to be 'a person with no evident empathy for developments in Papua New Guinea'.[163] These attitudes probably contributed to slow progress, but—building in part on earlier Reserve Bank preparatory work[164]—progress was nonetheless made. In July 1972 Cabinet approved a joint Treasury/DET submission on the transfer of responsibility for banking.[165] A complication over the Commonwealth Banking Corporation's interests then slowed progress. In November 1972, however, DET sought and gained Peacock's approval to obtain the views of the PNG Government on the committee's final report before the end of the year, in support of the objective of setting up a new PNG banking system in advance of self-government.[166]

Officials proceeded cautiously with respect to PNG's currency arrangements lest they unsettle business and investor confidence.[167] The Treasury's position evolved as political circumstances changed. In May 1972 Treasury Secretary Frederick Wheeler advised Hay that the Treasurer's attitude had been that this 'complex question … should not be dealt with in a precipitate fashion'. But now it could be considered more closely for various reasons, including the emergence of 'an indigenous leadership group' with whom 'more permanent solutions' could be discussed.[168] Hay responded by noting the need to proceed 'without delay'.[169] Consideration was given to Papua New Guinea continuing to use Australian currency after independence, but this idea was not taken forward.[170] In October 1972 the Treasury advised DET on the need for 'a separate PNG monetary area with its own identifiable currency'. The Treasury wanted to avoid any problems arising from the continued use of Australian currency.[171] Arrangements were finalised in the years that followed, with a new PNG currency inaugurated in April 1975.[172]

A PNG minister began exercising authority on immigration from late 1970 but ultimate responsibility remained with the Minister for Territories. A DET paper advised in July 1972 'that migration policy should be transferred to local control immediately'.[173] In August 1972 Somare told the House of Assembly agreement had been reached on the formal transfer of various powers, including over immigration. His government and its predecessor 'had been exercising these powers without reference to the Commonwealth for some time.' The step now to be taken would formalise these arrangements in constitutional terms.[174]

Consideration was given to establishing a PNG citizenship.[175] In June 1970 Hay thought legislation on citizenship was 'an essential' with respect to an early transition to

---

163 This was the view of Dr Ronald May, who served as a senior economist in the PNG branch of the Reserve Bank in the late 1960s and early 1970s. See R. J. May, 'Nugget, Pike, et al.: The Role of the Reserve Bank of Australia in Papua New Guinea's Decolonization', in R. J. May, *State and Society in Papua New Guinea: The First Twenty-Five Years*, ANU Press, Canberra, 2004, pp. 359–61.

164 Ibid, pp. 358–60, 364.

165 Documents 323, fn. 5.

166 Document 404. See also May, 'The Role of the Reserve Bank', pp. 363–64.

167 Documents 220, 224 & 237; and May, 'The Role of the Reserve Bank', pp. 370–78.

168 Document 298.

169 Document 302.

170 Document 321. See also Document 323.

171 Document 387. See also Document 326.

172 May, 'The Role of the Reserve Bank', pp. 377–78.

173 Document 324. See also Document 135.

174 Document 362. See also Documents 316, 348 (para. 10) & 355.

175 Documents 118, 149, 152, 176 & 181.

self-government.[176] Officials envisaged that expatriates would be eligible for PNG citizenship, with eligibility to be considered with respect to a commitment to Papua New Guinea and long-term residence of 'at least seven and perhaps ten years' and with those expatriates who became PNG citizens retaining their Australian citizenship at least until independence.[177] In January 1972 Barnes advised McMahon that the House had debated a statement on citizenship the previous September, but the debate had been adjourned and was unlikely to resume until after the forthcoming elections to a new House. Most members had been 'opposed to any arrangement under which Australians could obtain the benefits of domestic citizenship without committing themselves in any definite way to Papua New Guinea or foregoing any benefits of Australian citizenship'. Barnes told McMahon he had accepted the advice that 'the Government should not attempt to set the pace in this field but should leave it to the House of Assembly.'[178] No progress was made on this issue in the remainder of 1972.[179]

DET coordinated transfers from other civilian departments, agencies and instrumentalities.[180] In July and August 1969 DET and Administration officials had given initial thought to what would be involved.[181] Cabinet decided on a review in June 1970.[182] In February 1971 the committee working on this task agreed that 'so far as it is a function of self-government, every case is appropriate for transfer in the long run'. It decided that immediate staff localisation was not essential because the PNG Government could assume responsibility while Australia continued to provide staff. The functions of some bodies—for example QANTAS and the Overseas Telecommunications Commission (OTC)—would probably not be transferred until independence, but steps could be taken now to ensure there would be people in the Territory familiar with their operations. Should there be any choice over timing, 'it should be sooner rather than later'.[183] Barnes gained Cabinet agreement in late 1971 to the transfer of the work of number of bodies 'outside the aegis of the Administration' subject to consultations with the AEC on timing.[184]

Steps were taken to transfer defence powers.[185] The Army Secretary visited Port Moresby in September 1971 to take forward the setting up of a 'local department staff for immediate Army functions and as the nucleus of an eventual Territory Defence Forces Department'.[186] Defence

---

176 Document 43, item (h).

177 Document 182. See also Documents 186 & 199.

178 Document 254.

179 See Documents 256, 257 & 260, item (b) (vii). In September 1972 DFA advised its posts that PNG and Australian officials would undertake 'an early examination' of 'the establishment of an "international citizenship"' for Papua New Guinea (Document 364). It seems however that no examination of this kind took place in the remaining months of 1972.

180 These bodies included: the Australian Broadcasting Commission, the Australian School of Pacific Administration, the Auditor-General's Office, the Bureau of Agricultural Economics, the Department of Civil Aviation, the Commonwealth Banking Corporation, the Council for Scientific and Industrial Research, the Bureau of Meteorology, the Division of National Mapping, the Bureau of Mineral Resources, the Postmaster General's Department, the Department of Public Health, the Department of Shipping and Transport, the Department of Trade and Industry, the Overseas Telecommunications Commission, and the Department of Works and Housing.

181 Doran, *Australia/PNG 1966–69*, Documents 293 (Attachment) & 304.

182 Documents 47 (para. 9) & 53. See also Documents 64, 94 & 110.

183 Document 138. See also Document 143.

184 Document 250, fn. 7.

185 At this time Australia's defence, army, navy, and air departments exercised these powers. In 1973 these bodies were reorganised into the Department of Defence.

186 Documents 221 & 236.

Minister David Fairbairn referred in November 1971 to the preparation of 'studies of future …
defence and security requirements and of appropriate means of transferring responsibilities'.[187]
In June 1972 Somare said that he envisaged the transfer of internal security 'at self-government
and not at independence'. This was accepted on a revocable basis.[188] The Commonwealth
agreed to appoint defence and police spokesmen within the Somare Government, in order to
inform and engage local leaders.[189] By late 1972 progress had been made but there was further
work to be done.[190]

The Department of External Affairs (later Foreign Affairs) had been preparing for the transfer
of foreign affairs powers since the late 1960s.[191] From 1970 it took forward the training of
young PNG officials in foreign affairs, including by deploying some of them to Australia's
overseas missions, and deployed a foreign affairs adviser and accompanying staff to Port
Moresby.[192] It also proposed political education to 'create an awareness of the facts of
international life in the community'.[193] This commitment to foreign affairs training was not
necessarily shared elsewhere. When Gorton was asked in February 1970 about training for
diplomats he responded that this idea didn't 'fill him with much excitement'. He said he
would rather see Australian funds 'spent on another school or hospital'.[194] In March 1971 DFA
expressed concern that there was only 'a very limited amount of time available either to create
the machinery for PNG to conduct its own foreign affairs or to achieve the atmosphere that
we would like to exist at independence'.[195] In November 1972 it reaffirmed these concerns.[196]

Trade and economic powers were also transferred. In late 1971 Australia arranged for
continued access to UK markets for PNG's agricultural produce after the United Kingdom
joined the European Economic Community.[197] In October 1972 Australian and PNG ministers
issued a joint communiqué on the interim delegation of fisheries licensing powers and the
preparation of separate PNG fisheries legislation.[198] During a visit in October/November 1972
Australian trade officials handed over 'a large amount of briefing material' and confirmed their
department 'would be happy to assist in any way possible, for example training local officers
in Canberra or sending … officers to Papua New Guinea to train and advise'.[199]

Localisation

From 1970 to 1972 the localisation of employment, a process begun in the 1960s,[200] was taken
forward. Somare and his supporters strongly favoured localisation. By June 1969 the number of
indigenous officers in mid-ranking positions had begun to increase but skilled expatriates were

---

187 Document 240. Fairbairn listed 17 studies. See also Document 241.

188 Document 322. See also Documents 334 & 367.

189 Document 347. See also, among others, Documents 355 (para. 9) and 359.

190 See Documents 401 (paras 20–24) & 409 (paras 5–60).

191 Doran, *Australia/PNG 1966–69*, Documents 322, 326 & 355.

192 Documents 151, 153, 161, 170, 187, 200, 201, 277 (paras 44–47), 335, 366, 368, 381 & 391–92.

193 Document 187.

194 Document 19.

195 Document 151, para. 11.

196 Document 402.

197 Document 253. See also Doran, *Australia/PNG 1966–69*, p. 396 and Document 146.

198 Document 378. On trade and broader economic issues, see also Documents 180 & 214.

199 Document 398. See also Documents 374 & 375.

200 Doran, *Australia/PNG 1966–69*, Documents 80, 208 (para. 9), 210 (para. 7), 225, 259 & 326.

still very much required.[201] In February 1970 Cabinet approved 'a practical training scheme to give suitable Papuans and New Guineans opportunities for on-the-job training in Australia'.[202] In April 1970 the chairman of the PNG Public Service Board responded to criticism about slow progress by highlighting recent achievements.[203] Two months later, however, Hay referred to the need for a stable and experienced 'judiciary and public service' and suggested that 'Widespread localisation [was] not likely before [the] early to mid–1980s'.[204] Robert (Bob) Furlonger, the Director of the Joint Intelligence Organisation (JIO), reported in August that localisation had 'not progressed much'.[205] In July 1971 Johnson underlined the importance of substantial progress by 1975.[206] Around this time a senior DFA official commented: 'In some fields, e.g. health and education, localisation has progressed quite well. However, where it counts most, localisation has progressed least, namely, in the formation of a solid cadre of middle and senior level administrators'.[207]

In December 1971 expatriates comprised only around a third of the 25,000-strong public sector but held most of the senior and mid-ranking positions.[208] Hay commented in February 1972 that: 'The administrative framework ... still depends on expatriates (though much less so than five years ago)'.[209] In mid-July 1972 DET official Tim Besley suggested that:

> We perhaps need to promote the notion of *selective localisation* to dispose of any view that we should be working towards total localisation within the next few years or even within the next decade—unless of course the country is prepared to pay the price of a less efficient Public Service and a slowing down in the rate of development and growth of services.[210]

Somare took a different view: in late July 1972 he complained about slow progress and the cost of expatriate wages.[211] In September 1972 Johnson reported that Somare and his ministers wanted 'to begin to run down the total number of expatriates'. He thought about 300 to 400 positions would be immediately considered, involving both officers 'who are useless and can be dispensed with ... and those who are politically unacceptable ... some of whom would leave quite substantial gaps'.[212] In late 1972 Somare said that the number of expatriate public servants would be reduced by 1975 from around 7,000 to around 3,500.[213] Johnson reported there was 'little difference between any political group' on localisation. Opposition members, however, were concerned 'that the baby might be thrown out with the bath water'.[214]

The localisation of the middle and senior ranks of the locally-recruited but Australian-led defence and police forces was taken forward.[215] From the mid–1960s progress had been made

---

201 Ibid., Document 284, Annex.

202 Documents 21 and 22.

203 Document 37.

204 Document 43, para. 2(c).

205 Document 104, para. 43(c).

206 Document 193. See also Document 132, item (t).

207 Document 201.

208 See Documents 266 & 268.

209 Document 260, item (f), (iii).

210 Document 327.

211 Document 340.

212 Document 371.

213 Document 389.

214 Document 406.

215 The official title of the police force was 'The Royal Papua New Guinea Constabulary'.

in training and developing indigenous non–commissioned and commissioned defence force officers.[216] In September 1970 the main component of the PNG defence force, the Pacific Islands Regiment (PIR),[217] had a ceiling strength of 3,209, including 650 Australians. Planners envisaged that by 1974/75 the regiment would increase slightly to 3,460 personnel, but with the Australian component declining to 375, with increased mid-range and senior localisation.[218] Not much had been done, however, to localise PNG's mainly civilian defence administration.[219] The localisation of senior police positions was meanwhile proceeding slowly and localisation had 'hardly begun' in the police administration.[220]

Efforts to Retain Key Expatriate Staff

In concert with localisation key expatriate staff were encouraged to stay on. In early May 1970 Barnes restated assurances and said additional measures were being considered. His focus was on 'key administrative, professional or technical people'.[221] In July 1970 Gorton announced plans for a new Australia-based service, comprising around a thousand selected individuals.[222] In the event, however, the Commonwealth did not set up a service of this kind. In the remainder of 1970 and during 1971 little progress was made.[223] In December 1971 Johnson advised that probably 'the gravest problem' for the year ahead was the 'perceptible weakening' of the public service because it was hard to retain key expatriates while young educated Papua New Guineans to take up positions were in scarce supply.[224] Hay reported in February 1972 that many expatriates were 'not in the mood to stay on'.[225] In May 1972 Cabinet was unable to agree on a proposal from Peacock for the establishment of 'a separate Commonwealth service to which overseas officers would be appointed for the purpose of secondment to the Papua New Guinea government', and instead decided on an independent enquiry.[226] In August 1972 Peacock announced that the enquiry would be undertaken by a leading business figure, A. M. Simpson.[227] In October, the Cabinet considered Simpson's report and agreed in principle to arrangements whereby Australian officers could be deemed to be Commonwealth employees when responsibility for the public service was transferred.[228] Despite these efforts, it was clear by late 1972 that it would remain difficult to encourage key expatriate officers to stay on.

---

216 See Document 277, paras 24 & 42. See also Doran, *Australia/PNG 1966-69*, Documents 216 & 262 (para. 20) and Moss, *Guarding the Periphery*, pp. 175–77.

217 The PIR had a distinctive Territory identity, but for most practical purposes operated as part of the Australian Army.

218 Document 100, fn. 14.

219 Document 221.

220 Document 222, section 1.

221 Document 38. See also Document 36.

222 Document 64. See also Document 48, para. 22.

223 See Documents 179, 204 & 205.

224 Document 252.

225 Document 260, item (f), (iii). See also Document 217, para. 29.

226 Document 279, fn. 6. The Commonwealth also encouraged Australian departments and agencies to second key staff to Papua and New Guinea, in an apparent effort to compensate in part for expatriate departures. See Office of the Public Service Board, Circular No. 1972/9, undated (c. May or June 1972), NAA: A1838, 3080/10/1 PART 2.

227 Document 344.

228 Documents 394 & 395.

Challenges to Unity

Over the period challenges to territorial unity continued.[229] On 5 June 1970 Hay commented that given the absence of:

> any strong feeling of unity, some means would have to be found to create a degree of mutual confidence between [the] main groupings. As an interim measure, safeguards might be provided through agreed proportional representation of [the] main groupings in Territory Cabinet with understanding that before independence there would be [a] full enquiry as to whether the various parts want to remain together.[230]

A report included with a cabinet submission in June 1970 noted that 'Highlanders, Sepiks and the people of Buin in Bougainville have said that if early self-government occurred they would secede from the self-governing country and perhaps seek to retain association with Australia'. It observed: 'What unity there is has been imposed by the Administration'. Withdrawing 'outside authority could lead to pressures for Australian intervention to maintain law and order or to prevent secession'.[231]

During his July 1970 visit Gorton warned the AEC of the 'dangers of fragmentation' because different regions enjoyed different levels of economic progress and made clear Australia's preference for an 'advance as a unit towards nationhood'.[232] In Rabaul he underlined the negative economic consequences for the Tolai people if their area became a separate self-governing entity.[233] In Bougainville he argued that the future would be better for the local people if they remained 'part of a much bigger unit'.[234] In a television interview he highlighted the challenge of maintaining unity.[235] In stressing the material benefits of unity Gorton overlooked the strong local identities underlying separatist sentiments, notably in Bougainville and among the Tolai on the Gazelle Peninsula.

The ALP supported this commitment: in a 1972 essay Whitlam declared: 'To its credit, the Australian government has always made it clear that it accepts its responsibility to hand over independence to a single government of Papua New Guinea'. Despite the evidence of strong indigenous agency he claimed: 'In the background of every separatist movement—usually not too far in the background—are expatriates'.[236]

Uncertainty was created by the distinction between New Guinea as a UN trust territory and Papua as a 'possession of the Crown'.[237] Individuals born to indigenous parents in New Guinea were Australian Protected Persons but not citizens. Individuals born to indigenous parents

---

229 For background on challenges to unity in the late 1960s, see Doran, *Australia/PNG 1966–69*, Documents 242, 250, 256, 268 & 273.

230 Document 43.

231 Document 47, Attachment, paras 32, 43 & 44. See also Document 104, paras 16–17 & 27–36.

232 Document 64.

233 Document 68.

234 Document 69. See also Document 30 and see Downs, *Australian Trusteeship*, p. 478.

235 Document 85.

236 Gough Whitlam, 'Australia and Her Region', in John McLaren (ed.), *Towards a New Australia*, Cheshire Publishing, Melbourne, 1972, pp. 15–16.

237 In 1920 the League of Nations granted Australia a mandate over New Guinea; earlier, in 1914, Australia had seized it from the German Empire.

In 1907 Britain had transferred ownership of British New Guinea to Australia; it was renamed Papua. Australia at first ruled the two entities separately but began administering them as a single unit in the final years of the Second World War, with this combined administration formally established in 1949. In 1946, under the auspices of the United Nations, New Guinea had become a UN Trust Territory under Australian administration.

in Papua were Australian citizens by birth. Under Section 3 of the Migration Act, however, Papuans did not have an automatic right to migrate to the Commonwealth, defined as mainland Australia and Tasmania.[238] In September 1970 senior officials commented that establishing a form of domestic citizenship: 'could be valuable as a means of playing down the separateness of Papuans.'[239] But as noted earlier arrangements for citizenship were not resolved.

Throughout 1971 ministers and senior officials feared that the Papuans would demand a separate referendum.[240] On 20 May Johnson released a statement reaffirming the Government's commitment to 'advance Papua New Guinea to internal self-government and independence as a united country.'[241] The Opposition took the same stance. During his January 1971 visit Whitlam had declared: 'This so-called Australian citizenship is nominal only. Papuans are not Australian citizens in any meaningful sense … It is a fraud on the Papuan people to tell them that they are Australian citizens.'[242]

The Department of Prime Minister and Cabinet (PM&C) had reservations. A senior PM&C official advised McMahon in May 1971 that 'separatism is a recurring feature' and that 'if the Australian Government stands flat-footed behind unity' it could 'find itself opposed to steadily rising internal pressures'.[243] The official recalled Gorton had left some wriggle room during his visit the previous July. Gorton had described the emergence of a Papua independent of New Guinea as 'a very retrograde step', which Australia would discourage, but added that 'if and when self-government comes and ultimately independence should come then that would be a matter for decision by those who were then fully responsible for the running of this Territory'.[244] PM&C did not press the point, however, and official statements continued to encourage unity.

In June 1971 the House of Assembly called for a visit by an Australian parliamentary committee 'to determine the wishes of the Papuan people and to learn of their concerns at first hand'.[245] The Government declined to send a delegation but agreed to accept a Papuan delegation visit. In advance of the visit, which took place in late October, DET investigated the legal basis of any possible request for a plebiscite.[246] Officials noted 'the situation was somewhat unique in that usually most "colonies" were seeking a break away from their dominant country, whereas here it was a case of the nationals having, perhaps, an interest in continuing in association with Australia'. With respect to international law and the UN stance, moreover, it might 'be difficult for Australia to justify not holding one [a plebiscite] if the Papuans requested one'.[247]

Despite these concerns the delegation's visit went smoothly. The delegation complained that Papua had not been fully consulted on PNG's future and that Papuans were disadvantaged 'in the allocation of resources'. It also, however, went on record 'in favour of national unity'. In response, Barnes pledged measures to support Papua's economic development.[248] Johnson

---

238 Documents 125, 126, 176, 181, 206, 217, 223 & 226. See also Goldsworthy, *Losing the Blanket*, p. 55.
239 Document 118, para. 5.
240 Documents 171, 188, 223, 226, 228 & 229.
241 Document 173.
242 Whitlam, *Whitlam Government,* p. 91. See also Document 128.
243 Document 174. See also Documents 172 and 211.
244 Document 174.
245 Document 198, paras 13 & 14. The original motion called for a UN visit, but was amended to refer to an Australian parliamentary visit.
246 Documents 223, 226, 228 & 229.
247 Document 223.
248 Document 230.

later suggested that although the separate administration of Papua before the war had led to 'some sense of Papuan unity, the clamour of the Papuans was largely generated by hopes of ... economic advantage'.[249]

Johnson thought Bougainville separatism posed a more serious challenge. He said in September 1971 that the people of Bougainville 'feel different, have money and see no advantage in staying with Papua New Guinea.' Ultimately the question might be 'how much force would be used to hold Bougainville in Papua New Guinea?' Although 'a question for a future independent government it would raise an issue for Australia as to whether or not it could stand aside in such circumstances'.[250]

During 1972 the Papua and Bougainville issues generally remained quiet, but unrest continued on the Gazelle Peninsula. In July 1972 Somare admitted that he 'saw no immediate solution'. The Tolai 'had told him plainly that they did not want to have anything to do with the central government'. Somare and his ministers wanted 'some authority to act on this matter of handing over power to a regional government without having to refer it to Canberra'.[251] Johnson responded that handing over power to the Mataungan Association 'would pre-empt the whole basis of the work of the Constitutional Committee'. If the Tolais were given the degree of autonomy apparently being considered, 'then the Hulis and the Engas and other tribal groups might demand the same'.[252]

Separatist sentiments in Bougainville had implications for territorial-level politics. Johnson commented in late 1972 that Somare's appointment of 'two Bougainvilleans to Cabinet rank and a third to head up the Constitutional Committee' amounted to 'an attempt to hold Bougainville by committing its parliamentary representatives to the Government of a united Papua New Guinea'.[253]

Smaller-scale separatist movements also posed challenges. Following a late 1972 visit DFA officer Mick Shann reported that 'all sorts of ideas [were] floating around' on local autonomy. He predicted 'real problems' in 'developing a viable constitution which takes care of the inhibitions about central authority of the many localised power bases, bases which are far smaller than areas like Bougainville, the Highlands or the Gazelle'.[254]

Public Order

Over the 1970 to 1972 period senior figures gave substantial attention to challenges to public order, and especially to the Mataungan Association's campaign. In June 1970 the Administration advised: 'If [a] confrontation [is] inevitable it [is] preferable [the] Administration choose [the] time and place by bringing it on'.[255] In advance of Gorton's July visit to the Territory officials recommended the dropping of the Gazelle segment from the itinerary. When told it would be

---

249 Document 252.

250 Document 217, paras 18 and 19. See also Document 252, in which Johnson described secessionism in
    Bougainville as 'a grave problem for the future'.

251 Document 339.

252 Ibid.

253 Document 406.

254 Minute, Shann to Waller, 15 December 1972, NAA: A1838, 3080/16/2, PART 2.

255 Document 55.

going ahead they proposed various precautionary measures to which, however, Gorton did not assent.[256]

In January 1970 Whitlam had been greeted in Rabaul with cheering and singing but in the following July Gorton faced rowdy and hostile crowds. The presence of 800 police helped maintain the peace but the mood was very tense.[257] Barnes advised Defence Minister Malcolm Fraser on 14 July 1970 that: 'The situation … continues to deteriorate. Although the visit of the Prime Minister went off with very little incident that was largely due to the fact that the Administration had not taken up the challenges of the Mataungan Association and breaches of the law during the weeks prior to the Prime Minister's visit.'[258]

Barnes sought Fraser's agreement to an immediate recommendation seeking in principle approval of a call-out of the Pacific Islands Regiment to support the police. He said 'the larger the force [that] can be seen to exist in the area concerned the less resistance we can expect'.[259] The call-out question had been considered in the late 1960s,[260] was again considered early in 1970, and received very close attention in the course of July.[261] Gorton and Barnes strongly urged a call out, but Fraser and External Affairs Minister McMahon and their officials had strong reservations, including over the negative impact on international and domestic Australian opinion of any use of military force against civilians.[262] On 16 July Fraser complained to the Governor-General about Gorton's failure to consult Cabinet on this and other matters.[263] After further high level exchanges, culminating in an emergency Cabinet meeting on the Sunday morning of 18 July, the Executive Council approved a call-out on the afternoon of 18 July.[264] But despite all the excitement the implementation of a call-out was not needed.[265]

A fresh approach by Les Johnson, who took up the position of Administrator on 23 July, initially had a calming effect. On 27 July Johnson announced a reduction of the police presence along with other measures, including a readiness to support 'viable propositions' for economic development (Document 98). On 29 July he announced that renowned anthropologist Professor Richard F. Salisbury of McGill University would visit the area and prepare a report.[266]

After a visit in late July/early August JIO Director Bob Furlonger concluded that poor intelligence arrangements had 'probably contributed to the over-reaction … on the basis of

---

256 Document 62. See also Downs, *Australian Trusteeship*, p. 475. On 2 July senior DET officer John Greenwell reported that he had been 'called over to see Miss Gotto to be given an "ever so elegant" blast through her from the Prime Minister' about a DET proposal that a Pacific Islands Regiment honour guard be deployed at Rabaul for the forthcoming visit, to be on hand to protect Gorton should unrest get out hand. Defence Minister Fraser had reportedly visited Gorton the previous night, 'very agitated' about the idea. Greenwell noted that 'The Prime Minister was most annoyed that we should have made this request without his concurrence' and had told Fraser 'he wanted no such Guard'. Minute, Greenwell to Secretary, 2 July 1970, NAA: A452, 1970/2973.

257 Downs, *Australian Trusteeship*, pp. 476–77.

258 Document 73.

259 Ibid.

260 Doran, *Australia/PNG 1966–69*, pp. xlviii–xlix and Documents 311, 313 & 341 (fn. 6).

261 Documents 27 & 47 (Attachment, para. 24(b)), 71–76, 79–84, 86–93, and 95–96. See also Moss, *Guarding the Periphery*, pp. 162–65.

262 Documents 74, fn. 2, 75 & 84.

263 Document 92.

264 Ibid. See generally, Documents 86–89.

265 Documents 93 & 95–96.

266 Documents 98 & 99. In the event, however, Salisbury's report failed to provide a satisfactory way forward (Document 217).

reports later found to be false'.[267] In his assessment: 'The problem for the Government [was] that recognition of Tolai political demands would encourage separatism; a government back down now would affect its credit elsewhere in the Territory; and acceptance of the Tolai attitude towards land ownership would throw all alienated land in dispute.'[268]

Tensions continued, with occasional violence. In early July 1971 police used tear gas and riot guns in a clash.[269] On 19 August 1971 dissidents murdered Jack Emanuel, the East New Britain District Commissioner. Johnson reported that some MA members had been threatening to kill Emanuel and other officials, and that 'it can be assumed that if the MA was not directly involved it must bear at least an indirect responsibility for creating an atmosphere encouraging violence.'[270] Officials feared the death heralded further serious violence. Although this did not eventuate, tensions continued into 1972. In late 1971 Johnson described the role of the Administration as that 'of sitting on the lid'.[271]

Defence remained cautious about support to the police, including for occasions not involving a formal call-out. In July 1971 Defence Secretary Sir Arthur Tange underlined that any such use required his minister's approval.[272] Johnson followed up later in 1971 seeking support from the defence forces in circumstances when a call-out was not needed. He wanted this support 'without too much red tape—in short, [to] have some delegated authority to act'.[273] In early 1972, the Defence Committee offered provisional views on this and related questions and noted that they would be further examined.[274]

During the 1970–72 period the overall law and order situation became worse. In mid–1971 Border referred to a perception that 'The main reason for this deterioration ... is that officials including police are not allowed now to be tough enough—they cannot quieten things down by "breaking a few heads" as they did in the old days'.[275] Barnes said in August 1971 that he wanted the AEC and the House of Assembly to take greater responsibility for law and order. He favoured 'the problem ... being seen as a Territory one which required measures which were not necessarily of the same kind as would be suitable in ... [Australian] circumstances ... where the tradition of respect for law has ... a longer history'.[276] Barnes does not appear to have considered the risk that harsh measures would worsen rather than reduce local discontents. In September 1971 Johnson reportedly said the internal security situation could become critical 'at any time'.[277] In late December he reported that there had been 'growing disregard for the established law and for those administering it, which has resulted in a substantial increase in violent crime'. Referring to PNG's fragile 'new society', he said 'any serious failure to maintain firmly a coherent body of law would result in either the fragmentation of that society or the alienation of most of its members'.[278]

---

267 Document 104, para. 46(f).

268 Ibid., para. 30.

269 Documents 190–192.

270 Documents 207 & 208.

271 Document 217.

272 Document 194.

273 Document 215. See also Document 219.

274 Document 266.

275 Document 201, para. 6.

276 Document 210.

277 Document 215.

278 Document 252.

The Police and Defence Forces

Over the 1970–72 period ministers and senior officials concerned themselves with the capacities and roles of the police and defence forces. In March 1970 Police Commissioner Ray Whitrod urged that the police force be increased by at least 1,000, in part on the assumption that the armed forces would only be used as a last resort.[279] After visiting Papua New Guinea in July 1971 a senior DFA officer reported that Johnson thought 'the police were badly officered and not a very effective force'.[280] In October 1971 Johnson advised Hay that efforts to strengthen the 'administrative structure' of the police force by recruitment and secondment had not 'achieved much success'.[281] Police Commissioner Norm Nicholls had told him that police headquarters lacked 'sufficient and skilled staff' and that the force was 'virtually administratively bankrupt'.[282] Early in 1972 Brigadier Jim Norrie, the incoming Commander of the PNG Defence Force, said 'it was vital to have an efficient, well-trained, well-equipped and widely-respected police force. The present force was none of these.'[283] Progress in strengthening the police force was slow but some modest efforts were made. From early 1972 five Australian police officers were deployed to take up specialist roles. In July 1972 Peacock announced that 31 further Australian police would be seconded later in the year. They would help address the force's shortage of commissioned officers and 'would have special responsibility for training'.[284]

In a substantial outcome of a process initiated by the Cabinet in late 1968[285] the Defence Department's Joint Planning Committee presented a substantial 'Review of Defence Forces in Papua/New Guinea' on 30 July 1970.[286] This review projected forward on the basis of existing arrangements, assumed continued very close Australian involvement, made optimistic assumptions about the availability of Australian funding, and had not drawn on any consultations with PNG political leaders.[287] Tange expressed dissatisfaction several months later with the kind of thinking embodied in the July 1970 document. He demanded advice on what 'PNG will need forces to *do*, what will be the main tasks and what capabilities will they need for *PNG purposes* … Our present forces there are to protect Australia. The task is to describe what forces *PNG will need* for its purposes after independence'.[288]

Civilian officials thought the Pacific Islands Regiment should make a greater contribution to supporting the police in maintaining internal security. In March 1970 Hay complained that it was 'absurd that an armed force of 3,000 men, highly trained, well-disciplined and well-led, is being maintained in the Territory and is not available for use for law and order purposes.'[289] In mid–1971, Johnson reportedly said that he thought 'the PIR … should be used as an internal security force'.[290] Later that year Johnson noted he had often raised 'the need to supplement

---

279 Document 24.

280 Document 201. See also Document 217, para. 22.

281 Document 222.

282 Attachment to Document 222.

283 Document 264, para. 4.

284 Document 332. See also Document 259.

285 Doran, *Australia/PNG 1966–69*, Documents 216 & 222.

286 Document 100.

287 See Documents 116 & 117. See also Document 150.

288 Document 158. Italics in original. See also Documents 167, 197 & 277 (paras 29–31).

289 Document 27.

290 Document 201, para. 6.

the Police effort with the almost totally unused capacity of the Army'.[291] Some observers proposed merging the two forces. Brigadier Norrie did not agree: in early 1972 he said he believed two forces were needed, in part because of 'the danger of dictatorship if all armed forces were put under the control of one Minister'.[292] He also, however, underlined the need to make procedures 'relevant to PNG'.[293] After an April 1972 visit, Border concluded:

> the role of the PIR after independence would be given a different emphasis. There was a general consensus that the PIR would have to justify its cost, and that the politicians would not accept arguments based on external threats as justification. Some people thought it could be reorganised as a para-military police force (mostly civilians) while others thought it ought to maintain its military identity (mostly servicemen).[294]

Fairbairn called in mid-1972 for 'the further development of the defence force towards post-independence needs'.[295] DET received Peacock's in-principle endorsement in mid-November 1972, and apparently also that of Fairbairn, of the proposed functions and roles for the PNG security forces after independence. It was envisaged that two separate forces be maintained, although with 'increased involvement' of the defence force to support the police 'in internal security roles'.[296]

Relations with Indonesia

Papua New Guinea's relations with Indonesia received close attention. There was considerable sympathy in the Territory with protest against Indonesian control of the western half of the island of New Guinea and with dissidents who sought refuge across the border.[297] The border region remained generally quiet over the 1970 to 1972 period but there was concern that disturbances there could damage Indonesia/PNG relations, with implications for Australia.[298] In March 1971, a DFA paper commented that, with respect to helping Papua New Guinea develop its international relationships: 'our primary effort should be directed at Indonesia. Possible problems and pinpricks should be removed before independence and it would be essential to associate Territory leaders and the embryo PNG Foreign Ministry in the international discussion about these problems.'[299] Australian ministers and officials, in consultation with PNG political leaders, worked with Indonesian counterparts to resolve issues and foster constructive relations.[300] DFA officials thought their DET counterparts were giving insufficient priority to the effective management of border crossers and of related issues.[301]

---

291 Document 252. See also Document 334, para. 9.

292 Document 264.

293 Ibid. See also Document 277, para. 25.

294 Document 277, para. 26.

295 Document 311. See also Document 312.

296 Documents 369, 396 & 403.

297 Documents 334 & 385. For the background in the late 1960s, see Doran, *Australia/PNG 1966–69*, Documents 246 (para. 20), 265, 305 & 308. See also Downs, *Australian Trusteeship*, pp. 230–32; and June Verrier, 'The Origins of the Border Problem and the Border Story to 1969', in R. J. May (ed.), *Between Two Nations. The Indonesian–Papua New Guinea Border and West Papua Nationalism*, Robert Brown and Associates, Bathurst, 1986, pp. 18–48.

298 Documents 104 (para. 41), 141, 151 (para. 6), 277, 296 (para. 2(e)) & 380.

299 Document 151, para 6.

300 Documents 187 (para. 20), 301, 308, 343 & 360. See also Peacock's July 1972 comment that Indonesia would occupy a 'special place' in PNG's foreign relations (Document 320) and Somare's August 1972 comments on border crosser issues (Document 353).

301 See Document 277, 325, 330, & 385.

International Borders

Australian officials sought to ensure disputes did not arise over the delineation and management of the boundaries between Papua New Guinea and Indonesia.[302] Between 1971 and 1973 Australia and Indonesia, in consultation with the National Coalition Government, settled the land border and maritime boundaries. Agreement was reached on administrative arrangements to manage land border issues in 1974.[303] The demarcation of the Torres Strait border was also at issue.[304] In the late 1960s Ebia Olewale and other PNG leaders had called for the redrawing of the border considerably further south.[305] Some DFA officials favoured this idea, as did Whitlam.[306] Peacock sought to resolve this matter, but without success.[307] It was resolved after independence, in a manner compatible with the interests and preferences of the people of the Torres Strait Islands.[308] During the period no significant issues arose with respect to PNG's boundaries with the US Trust Territory of the Pacific Islands to the north and the British Solomon Islands Protectorate to the east.

Future Relations with Papua New Guinea

As the pace of change quickened ministers and their officials considered what they wanted in terms of Australia's relations with an independent Papua New Guinea, to the place Papua New Guinea would take in the world, and to how best to advance Australian interests after independence. Australian policies would need to take account of PNG views, but PNG thinking on these issues was at an early stage. Johnson reported in November 1972 that the Somare Government had not as yet discussed foreign policy issues in depth. It 'recognised that the major influences on Papua New Guinea will be Indonesia, Australia and Japan and Ministers appear to be groping towards a policy that will balance out the power and influence of these countries on Papua New Guinea'. He noted that there was: 'in some quarters, a tendency to overreact against a long period of Australian paternalism but it seems that Australian ties will remain firm and enduring'.[309]

In May 1972 Cabinet asked for a study of national interests with respect to Papua New Guinea and on relations after independence.[310] The initial outcome was a DET paper of 6 November which suggested that in the immediate post-independence period, given PNG's proximity and

---

302 Documents 296 (para. 2(e)), 360 & 380.

303 Document 360. See also Department of Foreign Affairs, 'Papua New Guinea and International Relations', *Current Notes on International Affairs*, vol. 43, 1972, pp. 492–97; and J. R. V. Prescott, 'Problems of International Boundaries with Particular Reference to the Boundary between Indonesia and Papua New Guinea', in May (ed.), *Between Two Nations*, pp. 3, 5, 12.

304 Document 277, para. 23.

305 Niwia Ebia (Ebia) Olewale, a leading member of the Pangu Pati, served as the MHA for South Fly from 1968–1972 and was re-elected in 1972. For his views, see Doran, *Australia/PNG 1966–69*, Document 321, para. 14. See also Denoon, *Trial Separation*, pp. 164–6.

306 For the views of two External Affairs officers—C. R. (Robin) Ashwin and Colin McDonald—in the late 1960s, see Doran, *Australia/PNG 1966–69*, Documents 217 & 257. For Whitlam's views, see his *Whitlam Government*, pp. 93–4; and Downs, *Australian Trusteeship*, p. 496.

307 Documents 270 & 274. See also Documents 296 (para. 2(f)), 297 & 413.

308 See Donald Denoon, *The Hundred Fathers of the Torres Strait Treaty*, National Archives of Australia and the Department of Foreign Affairs and Trade, Canberra, 2009. See also Denoon, *Trial Separation*, p. 166.

309 Document 406.

310 Document 296. See also Documents 283 & 349.

'the close involvement of the Australian Government, Australian enterprises and Australian citizens', a 'special relationship' should be continued, with options kept open for extending a relationship of that kind beyond that period.[311]

The paper's conclusions were consistent with established DET views on Australia's relations with Papua and New Guinea. In the late 1960s, as noted earlier, Barnes had thought PNG's independence should involve very close association with Australia. In late February 1970 Warwick Smith suggested that 'unique action' could be required to address the 'unique problems' arising from Australia's close links with Papua and New Guinea, with the implication that continued very close links should be maintained both during the transition to self-government and afterwards.[312] In early June 1970 Hay said that the 'Main implication of early self-government would be that Australia would have to be prepared to underpin [the] Papua and New Guinea Government more or less indefinitely,' with the position 'more akin to that of French territories in West Africa than to that of British territories'.[313] He presumably had in mind France's tradition of strong engagement in its colonial possessions and their post-independence successors, as compared with the more 'hands off' and *laissez faire* British approach.

After taking over from Barnes, and despite some initial caution,[314] Peacock worked hard for a prompt and smooth transition to self-government and independence. Yet while supporting a swifter pace of change than Barnes had been comfortable with, Peacock was also sympathetic to a special relationship. In an April 1972 discussion he 'seemed very much in favour of a special relationship and of the need to settle this as a policy base at the earliest practicable time'. This would involve continued 'special treatment' of Papua New Guinea as an aid recipient'.[315] He referred to the 'special relationship' theme in public speeches in June and July 1972.[316]

He did not envisage, however, a relationship of this kind precluding Papua New Guinea from diversifying its international links. In June 1972 he said:

> While Australia will remain important to Papua New Guinea, we should not seek to build an exclusive relationship ... Looked at from Papua New Guinea's point of view, Indonesia, Singapore, Malaysia, the Philippines and Japan, as well as the island nations of the Pacific, will have important places ... Other Governments will be seeking to assist Papua New Guinea. We will do well to recognise this. Not to do so might adversely affect both our and Papua New Guinea's relations with third countries.[317]

Other departments and agencies did not share the sympathy of Barnes and Peacock and their officials for a special relationship. At a meeting in late November 1972 the DET representative confirmed that his department 'was very much in favour of a special relations concept as it saw this as important to PNG achieving a status of independence as a viable state. It might not do this without considerable support'. His Treasury counterpart, in contrast, did not support DET's view on 'the extent of support necessary' and thought Papua New Guinea needed 'to face up to the realities of independence'. The Trade and Industry representative supported the 'special relations concept' but said 'this was not necessarily a firm departmental view'.

---

311 Document 399, para. 67.

312 Document 23.

313 Document 43.

314 Document 261.

315 Document 285.

316 Documents 309 & 320.

317 Document 309.

The DFA and Defence representatives did not comment directly on the concept, although the Defence official noted that the future defence relationship was being considered.[318]

Successive Foreign Affairs ministers and their officials did not favour the concept of special relations.[319] Their emphasis was on encouraging strong and constructive relations and preparing Papua New Guinea to conduct itself as effectively as possible as an independent state. They expected, nonetheless, that for reasons of proximity and history the future relationship would be close and friendly.[320]

Senior DFA officials focused on the prospects for future bilateral relations. Before a visit in late November 1972 Shann declared: 'I am not interested in aid, economic development, mines, or any infrastructure works. I *am* interested in the ethos of our relationship with a new country … I want to know what they think they may be, what they think of us, the Indons, the Japs, the UN and so on'.[321] DFA also prepared for a future Australian official presence. It deployed staff to Papua New Guinea; took steps to set up an Australian Commission office during the self-government period that would become a High Commission after independence; arranged for the construction of an office building for the future High Commission; and considered setting up consulates in Lae and elsewhere.[322] In late 1972 Australian trade officials gave initial attention to Australia's future trade relationship with an independent Papua New Guinea.[323]

Over the 1970 to 1972 period the Defence Department and its associated service departments considered Papua New Guinea's likely future strategic circumstances and Australia's post-independence role.[324] In March 1971 a senior Defence official confirmed that Australia 'unreservedly accepted' its obligation to provide for Papua New Guinea's defence until independence. It was not clear, however, how long Australia would retain defence responsibilities; PNG leaders appeared to have given this question little thought. They seemed to hope that 'Australia would continue to make some provision for defence or at least pay for it'.[325] The official also said that after independence 'the main threat … would come from a possible breakdown in law and order from secessionist movements. Trouble might also arise from an immoderate reaction by a Papua/New Guinea government to incidents on the West Irian border.'[326] In June 1972, Fairbairn said it was 'extremely important to us that PNG, our nearest neighbour, should be friendly and should not be taken over by an enemy'. An independent Papua New Guinea would control its defence force, but Australia would be ready

---

318 Document 407.

319 See Documents 232 & 277 (para. 38). See also Document 349.

320 Document 151, paras 7 & 11.

321 Notation by Shann on a minute from Waller, 9 November 1972, NAA: A1838, 3080/10/4/7 PART 1. Italics in original.

322 Document 200.

323 Documents 374, 375 & 398. After independence the two countries formalised 'long-standing preferential access arrangements for PNG goods into Australia'. See Richard H. Snape, Lisa Gropp and Tas Luttrell (eds), *Australian Trade History, 1965–1997. A Documentary History*, Allen & Unwin, St Leonards, 1998, pp. 470, 544–45. See also Doran, *Australia/PNG 1966–69*, Documents 249 & 251.

324 This work was completed in November 1973. See Hunt, *Australia's Northern Shield?*, pp. 245–52.

325 Document 141. In July 1971 Hay noted that 'Defence thinking' was that the Commonwealth needed 'to form some broad judgement at this stage as to the financial commitment [for PNG defence spending] which the Commonwealth is prepared to make (Document 197)'. In July 1972 Somare raised the idea of Australia continuing to fund the PNG defence force (Document 340). See also Documents 112, 116, & 277 (paras 29 & 30).

326 Document 141.

to provide 'Australian senior officers and Australian technicians'.[327] In late November 1972 Defence officials envisaged that forthcoming discussions with PNG ministers 'would help in ensuring that Australia's own Defence interests are adequately protected in further decisions by the Papua New Guinea Government'.[328]

Conclusion

From 1970 to 1972 the Australian Government had ensured that substantial steps were taken in Papua New Guinea towards self-government and eventual independence. At the start of 1970 Canberra took all the important decisions, but from the latter half of 1970 PNG ministers began to exercise considerable authority. The Australian Government initiated the reform process but PNG leaders soon demonstrated their readiness to take reforms forward. Following the election of the Whitlam Government in early December 1972 the pace of change was set to accelerate further.

Editorial Practice

As is the practice for all volumes in the series *Documents on Australian Foreign Policy* the editors of this volume have operated with full editorial independence and selected documents according to traditional scholarly principles unencumbered by political interference. The views expressed in the introduction and editorial notes are entirely those of the authors and should not be regarded as representative of the Australian Government's views. The documents have been examined by a Committee of Final Review comprising the Minister for Foreign Affairs and representatives of the Prime Minister and Leader of the Opposition. The Committee's approval signifies its satisfaction that the material has been selected and edited according to appropriate standards of non-partisan practice, and that the volume is a representative selection of documents. The Committee of Final Review has approved publication of this volume.

A diligent effort has been made to ensure that the texts of the documents provided are faithfully reproduced. Extracts of some documents are included rather than the full text. The words *matter omitted* indicate the omission of one or more paragraphs for reasons of relevance, comparative importance or length. In some cases a footnote summarises or indicates the nature of the matter omitted.

Editorial insertions in square brackets are used to indicate changes other than minor corrections to spelling or punctuation. Care has been taken to ensure the additions do not alter sense; annotations are used where precise meaning is in doubt. Layout and presentation have been standardised for print but as far as possible the paragraphing and headings follow the original text.

A Note on Terminology

Australia assumed responsibility for British New Guinea in 1906, renaming it Papua, and seized German New Guinea in 1914. In 1920 the League of Nations granted Australia a mandate over this area, now known as New Guinea. In December 1946 the mandate was converted to a UN trusteeship. Australia began jointly administering Papua and New Guinea towards the end of the Second World War, with this arrangement formalised in 1949 by the *Papua New Guinea Act*.

Until 1971 many people used the term 'New Guinea' to refer to the Territory as a whole, and the term 'New Guineans' to refer to its inhabitants as a whole. In a more restricted context, these

---

327 Document 313.

328 Document 409. See also Document 401; and Hunt, *Australia's Northern Shield?*, pp. 222–26.

terms were used to refer to New Guinea proper and its population as distinct from Papua and its population. Following a House of Assembly decision in April 1971, 'Papua New Guinea' became the official name for the Territory, and 'Papua New Guinean' became the term for its indigenous inhabitants. In this volume the term 'Papua and New Guinea' is generally used in reference to circumstances and events before April 1971, with the term 'Papua New Guinea' used after that. In some instances the acronym 'PNG' is used in place of the noun 'Papua New Guinea' or the adjective 'Papua New Guinean'.

The Department of External Affairs (DEA) was renamed the Department of Foreign Affairs (DFA) on 6 November 1970. The former term is generally used when referring to this department and its officials until then, with the latter term used after that.

From 1970 to 1972 Australia's national government was officially known as the Commonwealth Government, and this term is generally used. (In 1973, the Whitlam Government passed legislation establishing the 'Australian Government' as the official title of the national government.) At times 'Australia' and 'Australian' are used as shorthand references to the Commonwealth Government and its views and policies.

The distinction between 'open' and 'regional' electorates of the House of Assembly has been noted earlier. Members of the House (MHAs) are described in this volume by reference to the name of their electorate, whether open or regional, but with the term 'open' omitted with respect to members representing the open electorates—for example, 'John Guise, MHA for Alotau' and 'Michael Somare, MHA for East Sepik regional'.

Acknowledgements by Bruce Hunt

This volume was prepared through a collaboration between the Historical Research Section, Department of Foreign Affairs and Trade, and the Australian National University's School of History. Professor Frank Bongiorno oversaw the School's involvement in the project.

The guidance provided by Dr David Lee and Dr Matthew Jordan from the Historical Research Section in DFAT was of immeasurable value. The helpful responses to request for assistance by Gina Dow from the Section were also greatly appreciated. It would be difficult to over-estimate the importance of the assistance provided by the staff at the National Archives of Australia. Andrew Cairns, who served as point of contact on this project, showed great and inexhaustible professionalism and dedication as he responded to each request for assistance. The support and encouragement given by Colin Milner, who is editing a volume of documents on Nauru, was most helpful.

Special mention should be made of the invaluable assistance and advice provided by Alan Kerr and John Greenwell, both former senior officers of the Department of External Territories and both actively involved in the development and execution of Australia's policy in bringing Papua New Guinea to independence. Mr Kerr also provided a number of photographs of events and personalities. The contribution of Christine Goode who served in the Australian Office in Port Moresby was invaluable. The assistance offered by Tim Besley, former First Assistant Secretary in the Department of External Territories, and the detailed comments, insights and information provided by Pat Galvin, who served with External Territories in both Canberra and Port Moresby, were greatly appreciated.

Bill Standish, who has dedicated his academic career to researching Papua New Guinea, must also be recognised for his support and advice, as must Dr Ron May, David Hegarty and Anthony Regan from the ANU. Mr Hegarty's willingness to make available various photographs and images from his personal collection of material on PNG now held by the Menzies Library at the ANU was greatly appreciated. Christine Bryan from the Menzies Library provided expert help in identifying photographs and images. Deveni Temu, also from the Menzies Library, was generous in his advice and comments on the best approaches to researching Papua New Guinea. The guidance and technical assistance offered by Geoff Hunt from the ANU proved vital in enabling the author to manage the large volume of documents from which this collection was selected and often saved the project and author from failure. I owe a particular debt of gratitude to Fay Redgrave, daughter of Les Johnson, for her advice as well as her willingness to make available a number of photographs from her family collection.

The comments and opinions provided by Andrew Peacock, Minister for External Territories from February to December 1972, in telephone conversations were particularly valuable and contributed significantly to a greater understanding of the development of Australia's policy towards Papua New Guinea during the period of the Gorton and McMahon Governments.

In addition I wish to extend my sincere thanks to Sue and my family and friends for their interest, patience and support.

Acknowledgements by Stephen Henningham

I would like to express my warm thanks for the advice, support and *camaraderie* offered by friends and colleagues in the Historical Research Section at the Department of Foreign Affairs. Matthew Jordan provided astute guidance and ensured the volume met his rigorous standards; Jeremy Hearder provided helpful background information on attitudes and individuals; and Gina Dow compiled the list of documents and showed initiative in searching for the map and the photographs.

Our thanks for their helpful and courteous assistance go to Kay Dancey and Jenny Sheehan of the Cartographic Unit at the Australian National University with respect to the map.

We are grateful to several people for their prompt, courteous and efficient assistance with the photographs—Helen Tsogas, Deanna Cronk and Brenton McGeachie of the Digitisation and Document Delivery Team at the National Library of Australia; Andrew Cairns and colleagues at the National Archives of Australia; Dianne McInnes, author of the two-volume *Papua New Guinea's Pictorial History*; and Keitha Brown of the Pictorial Press.

I wish to acknowledge Michael Harrington, who prepared the indexes with his characteristic thoroughness and sharp eye for detail, and Peter Fuller, who completed a final proofread, in a tight time frame, with great care, and offered helpful suggestions.

I am also very appreciative of the assistance and collegiality provided by our colleagues in the Department's Archival Examination and Access Section.

My understanding of Australia's official relations with Papua New Guinea in the early 1970s has been enriched over the years by reading the publications of—and in some cases through the great privilege of personal interaction with—several people, including Donald Denoon, Stuart Doran, Sean Dorney, the late Ian Downs, the late James (Jim) Griffin, David Hegarty, Ronald (Ron) May, the late Hank Nelson, the late Bill Standish, Edward P. (Ted) Wolfers and Don Woolford.

Last—though certainly not least—I warmly thank my family for their generous good humour and support: Catherine, Elizabeth, Patrick and David.

BRUCE HUNT   **STEPHEN HENNINGHAM**

Documents

Part 1

Documents,
January–December 1970

5

'What unity there is has been imposed by the Administration': Key Developments in 1970

From early 1970 Prime Minister John Gorton quickened the pace of change in the Territory of Papua and New Guinea (PNG), in some measure in response to a visit there in January by Australian Labor Party (ALP) leader Gough Whitlam.[1] Gorton took this initiative despite the reservations of his Minister for External Territories, Charles Barnes (Documents 11, 15 & 20).

The new approach was set out in early March in the speech to open Parliament by Sir Paul Hasluck, the Governor-General. Hasluck said the Government would 'take steps to advance Papua and New Guinea further along the road to self-government and eventual independence'. In a riposte to United Nations and ALP calls for a timetable for independence, he added: 'My Government does not believe that an arbitrary date for independence ... should be set by it, even against the wishes of the people of the Territory, and it will not do so.' He nevertheless announced that the Government would transfer 'enlarged and additional' powers (Document 25).

Efforts continued to take forward the 'localisation' of positions in the Territory's public service, a process begun in the 1960s. Expatriates comprised only around a third of the 25,000-strong public sector but held most of the senior and mid-ranking positions (Documents 267 & 268).

In April the Chairman of the PNG Public Service Board responded to criticism about slow progress by referring to recent achievements (Document 37). In June, David Hay, the Administrator of the Territory, suggested that 'Widespread localisation [was] not likely until before [the] early to mid-1980s' (Document 43).

In June the Cabinet agreed to transfer responsibility for several areas of government to the Administrator's Executive Council (AEC), an embryo cabinet formed from Papua New Guinea's House of Assembly, and increased the authority of the AEC's ministerial members (Documents 47, 48, 53 & 54). Gorton visited Papua and New Guinea in early July and made it clear that the Territory 'was on the road to self-government and there was no turning back' (Document 67). His whirlwind visit was mostly favourably received. In Rabaul on the Gazelle Peninsula, however, he faced angry protests from supporters of the Mataungan Association (MA), a body representing members of the Tolai community at odds with the Administration over land and other issues.

Gorton's visit also included Bougainville where he told his audience that their future would be better if they remained 'part of a much bigger unit' (Document 69).[2] There had been strong protests in Bougainville challenging Australia's authority in the late 1960s. Local communities had opposed land acquisition for the Conzinc Riotinto of Australia Limited (CRA) copper

---

1   Whitlam's visit ran from 28 December 1969 to 12 January 1970 and included Port Moresby, Daru, Lae, Goroka, Mt Hagen, Madang, Wewak, Rabaul, Kavieng, Manus and Bougainville. Travelling in an RAAF plane, Whitlam was accompanied by leading ALP colleagues Kim Beazley (senior) and Bill Hayden, along with three ALP parliamentary staffers, four journalists, and his son, Antony. Gough Whitlam, *The Whitlam Government, 1972–1975*, Penguin Books, Melbourne, 1985, pp. 86–7; Ian Downs, *The Australian Trusteeship: Papua New Guinea, 1945–75*, Australian Government Publishing Service, Canberra, 1980, pp. 462–66.

Downs has suggested the size of the group and its form of travel—in contrast with the more modest scale of ministerial visits to the Territory, and their use of commercial air services—gave a misleading impression of Whitlam's standing and role to many of the people he encountered. *Australian Trusteeship*, p. 463.

2   See also Document 30; and Downs, *Australian Trusteeship*, p. 478.

mining project, and many Bougainvilleans favoured secession.[3] *From late 1969, however, dissent in Bougainville had quietened, and Australia's main concern from 1970 to 1972 was with the MA campaign in the Gazelle Peninsula.*

Separatist sentiments were present in several parts of Papua and New Guinea. In June a report included with a Cabinet submission had noted that 'Highlanders, Sepiks and the people of Buin in Bougainville have said that if early self-government occurred they would secede from the self-governing country and perhaps seek to retain association with Australia. Papuans stress their present Australian citizenship.' The paper also observed: 'What unity there is has been imposed by the Administration'. Withdrawing 'outside authority could lead to pressures for Australian intervention to maintain law and order or to prevent secession (Document 47)'.[4] *In the latter half of July the challenge to public order from the Mataungan Association led to Cabinet deciding—despite the reservations of some ministers—to authorise the calling out of troops in aid of the civil power, should the police not be able to maintain control (Documents 86–92).*

At the end of July a substantial 'Review of Defence Forces in Papua/New Guinea' was presented to the Defence Committee, an inter-departmental committee of senior officials (Document 100). This review led to several further studies concerning, among other subjects, PNG's defence needs, the roles of the defence and police forces, the question of defence force support to the police to maintain internal security, and Australia's longer-term defence interests in and in relation to Papua (and) New Guinea.

In the course of the year the House of Assembly's Select Committee on Constitutional Development, which had been set up in June 1969, took forward extensive consultations in Papua and New Guinea, supplemented by study tours to East and West Africa, India, Ceylon, the United States Trust Territory of the Pacific, American and Western Samoa, Tonga, Fiji and the Solomon Islands.[5]

---

3   Don Woolford, *Papua New Guinea: Initiation and Independence*, University of Queensland Press, Brisbane, 1976, pp. 28–42.

4   See also Document 104, paras 16–17 & 27–36.

5   Woolford, *Papua New Guinea*, pp. 90–103.

1   ADDRESS BY WHITLAM

Rabaul, 7 January 1970

[*matter omitted*]

The Labor Party believes that New Guineans can now govern themselves, and it wants to help New Guineans with money and advice so they can govern themselves. What we will do straight after we become the Government, is to make a New Guinean the Administrator of Papua New Guinea. A New Guinean, maybe from Papua, maybe from the mainland of New Guinea, maybe from the Islands, but a New Guinean will become the Administrator of New Guinea.[1] And we will make some New Guineans District Commissioners. There mightn't be enough New Guineans who can do the job of all the District Commissioners. But there are some already and we will make them District Commissioners. Then in the House of Assembly we will take [away] the official members. There will only be elected members in the House of Assembly. And the laws which the House of Assembly makes will become the laws straight away. They won't have to wait until the Australian Government approves them and the Australian Government will no longer disallow laws made by the elected members of the House of Assembly.

Now I want you particularly to believe and be convinced that when you have your own House of Assembly and your own Administrator and some of your own District Commissioners, Australia will still give money to New Guinea and Australia will still lend or keep experts here if you want them. Don't believe any expatriates, Europeans or Australians or Chinese who tell you that when you have self-Government [sic] Australia will get out [and] leave you in the lurch. That is not true.

When New Guinea has self-Government New Guinea will still be able to ask Australia to pay for any professors or teachers or doctors or agricultural experts or engineers or airline people, radio people if you want them still. And when New Guinea has self-Government Australia will still protect New Guinea and Australia will still speak to other countries on behalf of New Guinea. In, what your next House of Assembly, your third House of Assembly discusses with Australia and agrees with Australia that you can protect yourself and speak to other countries on your own behalf then you will have independence.

When you are independent you will have your fourth House of Assembly and you will be able to be, have New Guinea as a member of the United Nations and if you want, New Guinea can become a member of the Commonwealth of Nations like Australia, and Britain and Canada and India and the African countries. And New Guinea, if she wants to, can become a member of Regional Associations with other countries in the Pacific and Indian Ocean.

And when you are independent in your fourth House of Assembly, Australia will make a treaty with New Guinea if New Guinea wants to have a treaty, for financial and technical assistance, for money and experts from Australia. I now want to ask you to help us in the Labor Party in Australia to persuade Australians that you are now ready to govern yourselves.

If there are riots in Rabaul, if the Tolai[2] bash each other or if there are, if there is violence in the Gazelle or in Rabaul, many Australians will say New Guineans are not yet ready to

---

1   In his use of the term 'New Guineans', Whitlam was referring to the people of the whole Territory of Papua and New Guinea, and not just to people from the entity of (Australian) New Guinea. Similarly, he refers in this and other documents to 'New Guinea' with the intention of referring to the entire Territory.

2   The term 'Tolai' does not vary between the singular and the plural form. The large (by PNG standards) and self-confident Tolai community numbered around 70,000 and comprised the large majority of the population of the Gazelle Peninsula.

govern themselves. When people bash each other or use violence, when other people in New Guinea get frightened and they don't understand or support what you want and Australians get frightened and they don't understand or support what you want. But when there are hundreds of men and women who come together to discuss matters as you have this afternoon or thousands who went into Matupit oval yesterday afternoon, then Australians know that New Guineans are thoughtful, disciplined, patriotic people. And when New Guineans get together and speak like that then Australians listen and they're impressed and other New Guineans in other parts, the other Islands or in Papua or in the mainland of New Guinea, they listen and are impressed.

Now you are able to make out a new powerful, impressive case for what you want. You have some very impressive spokesmen. If there hadn't been violence then three of your best spokesmen would not be in the calaboose now they would still be working with you and for you.

Therefore, I ask you always to behave in a wise, quiet way. Have big meetings like this. See that your spokesman tell expatriates what they want. I will tell Australians what I have learnt here and some of the people who have taught us must have been Tolai and people working in Rabaul and in the Gazelle Peninsula.

And if the Australian people make the Labor Party, my party, the Government at the next elections then I know that the Australian people will want to see that New Guineans are able to make laws and carry out Administration well. Australia will be a good neighbor to New Guinea and New Guinea will be a good neighbour to Australia.

Mr President, I thank you very much for having told me of your problems. I thank the Warbete[3] society very much for having organized this very great meeting and I thank you for having interpreted us to each other.

[NAA: A452, 1970/0637]

---

3   The Warbete society comprised the population of several villages which had refused to have local councils or pay council taxes. Its approach aligned with that of the Mataungan Association (MA). See Ian Downs, *The Australian Trusteeship: Papua New Guinea, 1945–75*, Australian Government Publishing Service for the Department of Home Affairs, Canberra, 1980, pp. 137, 431.

The MA's formation was announced in June 1969 shortly after the elections for the first multi-racial council (MRC) of the Gazelle Peninsula. Fearing the MRC would threaten Tolai interests, the MA opposed its creation. The MA wanted the continuation of a mono-racial (that is, a Tolai-only) council. The MA successfully encouraged many Tolais not to pay taxes to the new council, and aspired to extensive local autonomy verging on independence. See ibid., pp. 424–7. See also Documents 2–4, 6 & 8.

2   PRESS RELEASE

Port Moresby, 8 January 1970

Gazelle Peninsula Developments

The attached statement on developments in the Gazelle Peninsula has been considered and approved by the Administrator's Executive Council and has also been circulated to Members of the House of Assembly.

Attachment

Administration Statement on the Recent Gazelle Peninsula Developments

[*matter omitted*]

The Mataungan Approach

1.   The stand taken initially by the Mataungan Association[1] was that it was totally opposed to the Council in its reconstituted—so called 'Multi-racial'—form and it sought the revocation of the establishing proclamation and reversion to the earlier Council. The principal ground for this stand was that the Multi-racial Council was liable to domination by non-indigenous members, and the only way to avoid such domination was to exclude all non-indigenous persons from the Council. The merits of this proposition were canvassed in the earlier House of Assembly debate. The Mataungan Association refused to accept the normal electoral machinery as a means of testing relevant opinion on this issue, and claimed to have the support of a larger majority of the Tolai people. The Association advocated a referendum as a means of testing opinion, but only upon its own terms with the leaders of the opposing groups standing out in the open, with their respective supporters lining up with them. It rejected the ideal of a secret ballot.

2.   More recently the Association has modified its stand to the extent that it no longer calls for the restoration of the pre-reconstitution status quo of the Council. In place of this it seeks legal recognition under the Local Government Ordinance as a co-terminous Council with the Gazelle Peninsula Council, but with each Council retaining its own adherents. However, the Association has not come up with a detailed and practical plan by which its proposition could be satisfactorily implemented.

3.   The Administration is mindful that the amendments which will be needed to the Local Government Ordinance to give effect to the Mataungan proposals would require approval of the House of Assembly. However, the present system of local government seems well suited to the Territory as a whole and no proposals have been made by elected members for variation of the basic concepts of the present legislation.

Events of the 7th December

4.   The events of Sunday, 7th December, have already received wide publicity. On that day a number of Councillors and Council supporters were the victims of attacks by members and supporters of the Mataungan Association. The attacks occurred at several different places throughout the Gazelle Peninsula, and a large number of persons, perhaps 150, took part in them.

---

1   For further details on the MA and the official Australian attitude to it see (among others) Documents 1, 3–4, 6 & 8.

5.   Another incident occurred at Malaguna when a party including His Honour the Administrator[2] was jostled and abused by a large group of men, and one officer was struck heavily from behind and then again in the face.

6.   Because Court proceedings in respect of particular assaults are still taking place, or are to be commenced, it would not be proper to use this opportunity to comment on the attacks.

7.   Directly following the attacks, the Secretary of the Department of the Administrator, Mr Ellis, with a number of his senior officers, flew to Rabaul. The Administrator cancelled a proposed visit to Kieta, to remain in Rabaul until 10th December and thus be on hand to direct action aimed at restoring order and public confidence and at bringing those responsible for the attacks to justice. Police reinforcements were flown in and order was restored without further incident. Police action subsequent to the attacks has resulted in 33 arrests being made of persons involved in the attacks against whom hearings of a total of 73 charges leading to 40 convictions have so far commenced. Several of the persons involved in the attacks, including the President, Secretary and Treasurer of the Mataungan Association, are currently serving gaol sentences.

8.   On 17th December the Administrator's Executive Council met the Minister. Administration action in containing the violence which has erupted in the Gazelle was discussed and both the Minister and the Council endorsed the steps which had been taken and deplored the incidents which led to them.

Administration Attitude to Amending Constitution of Gazelle Peninsula Council

9.   During the House debate on this matter it was stated that the Administration does not have a closed mind on the subject of a referendum being held to determine the majority view on the form the council should take. The Administration does not preclude the possibility that the Council might be reconstituted so as to reduce the size of individual electorates and increase the number of representatives to make increased Tolai representation possible. The Council with the assistance of the Administration, is working towards the election of Ward Committees. The Administration is prepared to consider the holding of general Council Elections before the end of 1970. Nothing that has happened since the last session of the House has affected these views. The Administration is still prepared to consider all these things, subject to Council concurrence. The Council had demonstrated a willingness to enter bona fide negotiations on these and associated matters with the Mataungan Association. The Council has further demonstrated a willingness to submit to new elections if this will help resolve the dispute in the area. To date the Mataungan Association has not demonstrated any inclination to meet the Council half way. Their attitude has been uncompromising opposition to any form of multi-racial Council. The Administration will continue its efforts to negotiate with the Council and the Mataungan Association in any moves taken to heal the divisions, which are currently damaging the Tolai people so deeply, and will continue to make initiatives directed at these ends.

[*matter omitted*]

Conclusion

This statement has sought to relate comprehensively the recent events in the Gazelle Peninsula, and to outline the Administration's reactions to those events, and as well to outline Administration action directed at longer term solutions to the problems which exist.

---

2   David Hay.

The Administration believes that solutions to the differences which have developed can be found, given goodwill and a desire to reach agreement on all sides. The Administration will not, however, tolerate any breaches of the law, and any group or individual seeking to attain objectives by the use of force will be dealt with according to the law. The Administration will continue to take all possible action to reduce the causes for tension in the Gazelle Peninsula and calls upon all groups to cooperate in restoring a peaceful situation wherein they can continue to contribute to the Territory's social, economic and political growth.

[NAA: A1838, 936/4/16 PART 3]

3   STATEMENT TO THE PRESS BY GORTON

Canberra, 9 January 1970

Prime Minister's Telegrams to New Guinea in reply to complaints of damage caused by Mr Whitlam

Following are texts of telegrams received yesterday by the Prime Minister from the Planters' Association of New Guinea and Bali Plantations Ltd.:

Planters' Association of New Guinea

'This Association is shocked that the leader of the Opposition party publicly supports convicted law breakers who are against the basic tenets of self-government that is the organisation, election and working of local government councils. Further that in visiting another country the Leader of the Opposition and his associates have shown grave discourtesy in criticising this country's government and leaders with little basic knowledge of the people's culture, upbringing and beliefs. Mr Whitlam's visit has caused grave disquiet [and] lack of confidence in the future by all residents including the majority of Papuans and New Guineans and it is the considered opinion of this Association that every effort be made by you to visit this territory as early as possible to counteract the damage which has been done. Would appreciate acknowledgement.'

Bali Plantations Ltd

'This Company deplores the Labor Party promotion activities of Leader of the Opposition in the Gazelle Peninsula as a further aggravation to recent troubles here which must result in a complete negation of costly official action in restoring law and order. This has resulted in an increased lack of confidence in investment by both indigenous and overseas investors. We respectfully request that the Prime Minister visit this district immediately to refute the promises made by Mr Whitlam who is regarded by the Tolais as the leading Government official to visit Rabaul for many years particularly whilst he appears to sympathise with the rebellious attitude of the minority repeat minority of the indigenous population.'

Today the Prime Minister, Mr John Gorton, sent the following reply to each of the above:

'Your telegram received. I believe Mr Whitlam's statements are calculated to worsen the divisions amongst the Tolai people in the Gazelle Peninsula and to encourage extremists.

'The Government believes the legally elected Multi-Racial Council, which includes 34 natives and 4 non-natives, is acceptable to the majority of the Tolai people and is in the best interests of good government in the Gazelle Peninsula. The government was prepared to test this belief by a referendum held by secret ballot. The Mataungan Association refused to agree to such a secret ballot referendum being held and said it would not, in any case, abide by the result of such a ballot. The Mataungan Association have withheld taxes, refused to join in discussion of this question, and have resorted to violence.

'Mr Whitlam's support of this attitude and action is emphatically repudiated by the Government and we wish this to be known to all in the Gazelle Peninsula. The Government's attitude has been expressed by the Administrator's Executive Council. We will not tolerate breaches of the law, will invoke the law against the use of force, and call upon all groups to cooperate in restoring a peaceful situation.

'I regret that I am unable at present to accept your suggestion that I visit the area, but I hope this expression of the Government's intentions will help to repair the damage caused by Mr Whitlam.'

This afternoon, the following telegram was received from the Gazelle Peninsula Council:

'Gazelle Peninsula Council East New Britain deeply concerned and distressed by ill-considered and ill-informed statements made by Whitlam Leader of the Opposition. His support of the Mataungan Association [and] his admiration for its leaders and its aims considered seriously detrimental to the peace, order and good government of the Gazelle Peninsula and Territory. Whitlam's confident statement that he will be prime minister by 1972 or earlier and will grant immediate home rule accepted by many Tolais as fact. Implication that Mataungan Association will achieve all its objectives which include destruction of Multi-Racial Council [and] return of alienated land must be refuted at all costs. Failure of Whitlam to support duly elected Multi-Racial Council particular in Council tax issue will have adverse effect throughout Territory. Mataungan members had every opportunity contest June elections but declined to do so. Whitlam's statements will destroy effective government in this area unless refuted. Further bloodshed and violence likely if no positive action taken. Council considers the Australian Government must restore the confidence of all people in the Territory and in particular of Gazelle area by clear restatement of your Government's policy and plans for our future political, social and economic development.'

[*matter omitted*]¹

[NAA: A452, 1970/0637]

---

1   The omitted material comprised the text of the telegram which Gorton sent to the Gazelle Peninsula Council. The text was almost identical to that of the telegram sent to the other organisations, the only difference being that the words 'I regret that I am unable at present to accept your suggestion that I visit the area' were not included.

4   TELEX TO CANBERRA

Port Moresby, 11 January 1970

2543. UNCLASSIFIED

Statement by Mr E. G. Whitlam, QC, MP

Mr Gorton's first statement[1] ever on New Guinea affairs strengthens elements whose chief fear is any discussion or investigation which would expose to the people of Australia the injustices and indignities being perpetrated in their name. While Workers' Associations' claims have been ignored for months, Mr Gorton promptly acknowledges and agrees with associations of those who pay their workers $5 a month.

The difference between Mr Gorton's action and mine is this: he has supported and encouraged those who, some through incompetence and some through malevolence, have created a perilous situation in the Gazelle. I have spoken directly to the people to deplore violence, to encourage peaceful and orderly processes and to reassure them that the people of Australia will listen and will care. There is no surer path to violence than by allowing these people to believe that no one will listen. It is not by speaking the truth, but by suppressing the truth that the real damage is being done.

There is a deep-seated fear among these people. Hate, the companion of fear, cannot be far behind. Emotions like this will not be suppressed by mechanical appeals to law and order. Unless people have faith in the law, or believe that unjust laws can be changed by orderly processes, there can be neither law nor order.

Mr Gorton joins his correspondents in describing the Mataungan Association as extremists. I know of no way of drawing up such an indictment against 11,600 people, one–sixth of the whole Tolai people.

The 11,000 people to whom I spoke at Rabaul have not been charged with any offence. They live in the closest family and clan relationships with all other Tolais. Their leaders include close relatives by marriage of a Ministerial Member of the House of Assembly. Many of their leaders are good Catholics. They have the support of the whole the Rabaul native Ex-Servicemen's Association the very group of men who are most proud of their service and loyalty to Australia. In an act of remarkable self-discipline, the people have paid their taxes into a fund now totalling $30,000 pending a settlement of the dispute.

The Tolai fear of the Multi-Racial Council is not in fact a radical emphasis on race but a conservative fear of losing land. This fear was aggravated by Government action in attempting to force the people of Bougainville to sell their land. Tear gas and batons were used in that attempt.

At the Mataungan meeting at Rabaul we were greeted by the Mataungan Choir, an ecumenical combination of Catholics and Methodists singing the National Anthem and subsequently singing hymns of praise to our Lord. I commended their patriotic fervour and religious fervour. I urged the people to adhere to orderly expressions of their views. I deliberately avoided any expression of opinion whatsoever on the issues of the Multi-Racial Council, taxes or gaolings. Perhaps by doing so I disappointed a deeply troubled and bewildered people.

The people find the attitude of the Administration incomprehensible and so would most Australians. They are confused by ambiguous and precipitate action on the part of the authorities. They are motivated perhaps more than any other people to assert the manhood

---

1   Document 3.

of the people of New Guinea in the face of a policy of glaring race discrimination in law, economic opportunity and wages.

Among the most tragic victims of the Australian Government's insensitivity are the native members of the Multi-Racial Council. Because of their own dignity and integrity, they are being forced into the intolerable choice between their loyalty to the Administration and their loyalty to their own people.

Mr Gorton has created further confusion amongst the people and the Councillors by now stating that the Australian Government was prepared to hold a referendum on the Multi-Racial Council. He blames the Mataungan Association for rejecting it. Yet on the very day Mr Gorton made his statement Mr Oscar Tammur, the Mataungan Patron, was voting in the House of Assembly for a referendum. Every Administration representative voted against it.

In June 1967 Mr Thomas Tobunbun, the distinguished Tolai leader who is opposed to the Mataungan Association on this issue, proposed such a referendum. He was officially informed it was impossible because it would cost $2,000. The subsequent police actions which stem from the official rejection of that referendum have cost more than $1,500,000.

Before any violence occurred, my colleague, Mr Beazley, wrote to Mr Melchior Tomut, the Secretary of the Mataungan Association, urging a referendum and urging against any violence. Copies of his letter were sent to the Administration and Mr Barnes, both of whom replied to him. Mr Barnes' reply did not indicate any support for a referendum.

If Mr Gorton is concerned for the rule of law he might well look at the unprincipled exclusion from hearing Mataungan cases of one of Rabaul's Magistrates, apparently as punishment for having technically acquitted three Mataungan leaders at a previous trial.

Mr Gorton and his colleagues, a section of expatriate Australians and a section of the Administration are knowingly or unknowingly combining to create in New Guinea the classic pattern of disruptive colonialism which ultimately destroys both the ruled and the rulers. I will not be silenced or intimidated on these matters. I am not prepared to allow Australia's name to be besmirched, dishonoured and disgraced, even under the cloak of technical legality.

[NAA: A452, 1970/0637]

5   PRESS RELEASE

Canberra, 12 January 1970

Mr Whitlam's Apologia
Statement by the Prime Minister, Mr John Gorton[1]

Mr Whitlam is clearly trying to extricate himself from the result of those indiscretions which have led to native leaders in New Guinea to tell him to pack up and go home and cease fomenting trouble.

The facts are that Mr Whitlam made a flying visit to a troubled area—the Gazelle Peninsula. Once there he engaged in ill-considered demagogy and increased the chances of trouble and violence in that area. He deepened and worsened the divisions among the Tolai people[2]—divisions which the Government has been seeking to heal. He spoke to one section of the Tolai people and left the impression, in an unsophisticated area, that he and the people of Australia supported not only the aims but the methods—including violence—to which that section has resorted.

He refrained from calming the fears felt by some of the Tolai that their land may be endangered by the multi-racial Council. Yet he must know this fear to be baseless.

He must have known that the Administrator and Government officials were subjected to violence when they went to the area to 'listen' and to discuss this problem. Yet he publicly admires the 'fervour' of those who used that violence.

Either through foolishness or by design he has made a difficult situation worse. He has refused to support what he calls 'technical legality' and has instead tacitly encouraged clearly illegal action. If this results in greater violence and Australia's name is thereby damaged he will to a very large degree be responsible—if responsible is a word which can properly be used in relation to his actions in this matter.

The Government will seek to remove the fears felt by a section of the Tolais, to relieve the difficulties in the region, and to repair the damage done by this visit. But this will now be more difficult.

[NAA: A452, 1970/0637]

---

1   This was a response to Whitlam's statement of 11 January (Document 4).

2   The large, self-confident Tolai community numbered around 70,000 and comprised a large majority of the population of the Gazelle Peninsula.

6   TELEX TO CANBERRA

Port Moresby, 12 January 1970

2481. U<small>NCLASSIFIED</small>

Statement by the Leader of the Opposition, Mr E. G. Whitlam
Labor's Plan for New Guinea

In the past fortnight Mr Beazley,[1] Mr Hayden[2] and I have talked to some thousands of New Guineans and talked with hundreds of elected persons, administrators, teachers and students who will soon be assuming even more responsibility for their country's affairs. New Guinea is already rich in leadership. The time when that leadership will assume its full and proper responsibilities cannot and must not be long delayed.

1.   We quickly found that our most urgent and difficult task was to reassure the people and their leaders, and even expatriates, about Australia's relationship with New Guinea after self-government and after independence. We have been appalled to discover how widespread and deeply rooted is the impression that either independence or even self-government mean the end of Australian concern and Australian help for this country. I make no comment about the origins of this falsehood. Any Australian who propagates it does a grave disservice to the people of Australia and the people of New Guinea.

The plain fact is that for the rest of this century Australian governments will be formed by either the Labor Party or the Liberal Party. All members of the Australian parliament have supported the quadrupling of Australian aid in the past decade. While the consensus which existed on New Guinea during Sir Paul Hasluck's administration has broken down under Mr Barnes, there is no divergence between the parties on this crucial point. It is Labor policy and it is Liberal policy that aid in finance and advice will continue. It is our firm belief that it will increase. It is certain that for the rest of this century at least Australia will be a donor nation to developing nations. New Guinea will long be a principal recipient.

To emphasise the solemnity and sincerity of this undertaking, we have suggested that Australian assistance should be made part of treaty arrangements between the constitutional government of an independent New Guinea and the government of Australia.

2.   Our second task has been to clear away fundamental misunderstanding about the reality of Australia's present relationship to New Guinea. Australia would not have been permitted to remain in New Guinea as trustee had she not promised to prepare New Guinea for independence. The government of 112 nations have just called on Australia to transfer full executive and legislative powers to elected New Guineans. The fact of independence is just not negotiable. There is not nearly as much negotiability about the postponement of independence as some New Guineans and many Australians seem to assume. Australians who think that the United Nations need not be taken seriously may be more respectful of the United States. Anybody who doubts the seriousness of America's purposes on this matter is fooling himself.

---

1   Kim E. Beazley (Snr), Labor MP for Fremantle, was Spokesman on New Guinea Affairs for the Opposition.

2   Bill Hayden, Labor MP for Oxley, 1961–88.

The Australian Parliament has responsibilities beyond New Guinea. Its primary responsibility is to the people of Australia. It has the responsibility of protecting the reputation and the relations of the nation with all countries. These are the responsibilities of the elected persons of the Australian Parliament and the elected government, and of no others, elected or non-elected. The Australian Parliament cannot escape or share this responsibility.

Therefore it is either misleading or meaningless to assert that the decision for independence is one for the people of New Guinea alone. The form of independence is certainly for them to decide for themselves. The fact of independence has already been decided.

Steps After the Next Election

3.   These two tasks of reassurance and clarification were responsibilities we accepted for the Australian people as a whole. We accepted a third task on behalf of our own party, the Australian Labor Party.

An Australian election must be held by the end of 1972 at the latest. It may be earlier. It is our belief that a Labor Government will emerge from those elections. We therefore felt it obligatory to indicate how a Labor Government would discharge its responsivities to the people of Australia and its obligations to the people of New Guinea, including those Australians whose families and fortunes are at stake in New Guinea.

New Guineans will have home rule as soon as a Labor Government can make the necessary arrangements with the House of Assembly which will also be elected in 1972.

This means that laws made by the Assembly will no longer be subject to veto by the Australian Government; that all matters affecting the welfare of the New Guinean people except defence and foreign affairs will be subject to laws made by the Assembly alone; and that those laws will be administered by a public service responsible only to the House of Assembly.

Australians who remain in the service of the New Guinea government will equally be responsible to the House of Assembly, but the Australian Government will accept responsibility for their salaries and the welfare of their families.

The House of Assembly will decide the form of the constitution New Guinea is to have after independence.

It is certain that the assumption of an increasing measure of responsibility will accelerate the desire and ability to accept total responsibility. In this sense it is true that the people of New Guinea will decide their own time-table for independence.

Elements in the Administration, and in the expatriate community, are anxious to postpone every delegation of power to the Papua–New Guinea people into an indefinite future. Most disturbing is the open hostility in the Administration to those who have, if perhaps in gravely mistaken ways, attempted to assert their rights. The manner in which the Department of External Territories endeavoured to enforce the sale of Bougainville land disqualifies those responsible for the policy from any claim to have the well-being of the people at heart. Batons and tear gas have no place in land sales. This incredible exercise in the techniques of violent expropriation has shaken confidence. It threatens to create deep and enduring hatred against Australia and Australians. It is a factor underlying the Mataungan misunderstandings.

Immediate Steps

4.   Fourthly, we have seen there is a need for a far more systematic preparation of the country for self-government. Urgent needs in the Territory which should be the subject of immediate attention are:

A reasonable minimum wage;

An arbitration system for plantation workers and all labourers;

An end to the shame whereby Australia's name is associated with plantation wages of $5 a month or less—the worst wages in the Pacific and probably the worst in the world.

In New Guinea every industrial dispute is automatically a dispute between an Australian or an Australian company on one hand and New Guineans on the other. The Territory has moved to the position where the Workers' Associations should be treated seriously. We heard from workers' leaders, engaged in struggles to lift wages as low as $6 a week, that claims to private employers for wage increases simply went unacknowledged. Even worse, the Administration itself for months on end ignored wage claims from officially recognised workers' associations. It needs to be quite clear that salary and wage discrimination is the basis of every other form of discrimination.

There has been a clear deterioration in race relations, reflected in the movement of battalions of police to Bougainville and Rabaul. There are more police in Rabaul than in any Australian city except Sydney and Melbourne. Australians in Papua-New Guinea are not in their own country. The whole direction of administration needs re-orientation. The basis of Australian policy should be discrimination in favor of the people whose country this is. Only discrimination in favor of the underprivileged can reduce inequality.

The Department of External Territories, which rules, should become a Department of Pacific Relations, which advises. Australian officers should not be masters but envoys, not rulers but helpers. The best of them are. There is cause for pride in much done in health, education, communications, agriculture, and public works, and in the defence services. There is no cause whatever for pride in labour relations. This is the Achilles heel of the whole Australian position in New Guinea. It is full of danger for the near and distant future.

Nor can we have any pride in the fact that in the five largest towns there is no local government, and no businesses, factories or even taxis owned by locals. In New Guinea commercial enterprise has become synonymous with expatriate enterprise.

We have tried to impart a feeling not only of urgency but of self-confidence in the ability of New Guineans to make their own decisions. There are New Guineans who are well equipped to fill the highest political and administrative positions in their country. Indeed, no Australian could claim the contrary without reflecting on Australia's record of administration at its crucial point.

The House of Assembly and its members should now be taken seriously as the representatives of their people and treated by all Australians with proper respect and seriousness.

The only thing in which New Guinea is really unique among the countries of the world is that alone among significant populations its people make no final decisions on any matter affecting their welfare.

It is not unique in its economy, in the difference of economic standards between sections of the country, its educational or social standards, its need for economic aid from abroad, its need for advisers, the diversity of its local customs, or even the multiplicity of its languages.

All these matters present complex and difficult problems for any future government of New Guinea.

None of these problems require colonial rule for their solution or easing. In fact, many of them will worsen if foreign techniques, methods, laws and customs continue to exclude local customs, knowledge and experience.

An outside administration cannot teach or impose unity. It can by errors unite a people against it. This is the very situation which Australians at home will not permit, and Australians in New Guinea must most avoid.

[NAA: A452, 1970/0240]

7   MINUTE FROM BALLARD TO KERR

Canberra, 13 January 1970

I met Hay in Melbourne today (13 January 1970) and he expressed some concern about the tenor of the press exchanges which had been continuing between the Prime Minister and the Leader of the Opposition.

[*matter omitted*]

Hay's principal concern about the statement was [that there] was a good deal of substance in some parts of Whitlam's criticism. I understand this relates particularly in his mind to the need to give more authority to Ministerial Members (or the AEC?).[1]

[*matter omitted*]

He did not think it was wise to let ourselves get into a situation in which anything Whitlam said would be automatically rubbished by the Government. He was afraid that the exchange which had already taken place would stratify opinion in connection with the Mataungan Association so that any further attempt (he thought one should be made) to reconcile the parties would be much more difficult if not impossible. He wanted to make the point that the sort of damage that he was afraid had been done so far as the Mataungan Association was concerned would not be followed through to other broad general areas of Government policy in Papua and New Guinea.

[NAA: A452, 1970/0637]

---

1   Administrator's Executive Council.

8   PRESS RELEASE

Canberra, 13 January 1970

Mr Whitlam's Support of Mataungan Association
Statement by the Prime Minister, Mr Gorton

Mr Whitlam has reached new heights of arrogance.

He went to speak to the Mataungan Association—a section of the Tolai people who had used violence, who were refusing to pay taxes, who were refusing to abide by a legally elected council. He told them—according to newsmen whom he admits 'faithfully reported' him—that he admired this Association, its expression, and its spokesmen and was impressed by the patriotic fervor with which they expressed their feelings.

If he does not feel that this supported and encouraged that organisation he must be the only one who doesn't. Certainly the responsible leading natives of New Guinea,[1] who told him to go home and stop fermenting [sic][2] trouble, don't agree with him. I fear he has increased the risk of violence in the area.

If any apology is required it should come from Mr Whitlam to the Australian people for stating he had undertaken this journey on their behalf, and suggesting he was their spokesman, when the Australian people had so recently refused him the right either to govern them or to speak for them.

[NAA: A1838, 936/4/1, PART 3]

---

1   In this reference to 'New Guinea' Gorton was presumably referring to the Territory of Papua and New Guinea as a whole.

2   Presumably the intended word here was 'fomenting'.

9   PRESS RELEASE

Port Moresby, 15 January 1970[1]

Minister Refutes Opposition Leader's Statements on Papua and New Guinea

The Minister for External Territories, Mr Barnes, said yesterday that the claims made on Tuesday by the Leader of the Opposition[2] on wages paid to native people in the Territory were completely misleading.

[*matter omitted*]

Other statements by Mr Whitlam reported in the Press on 13th January were also incorrect.

Mr Barnes said that contrary to Mr Whitlam's statement that an arbitration system should be established now for plantation workers and labourers, legal provision had existed for settlement of disputes of this kind since 1963.

In answer to Mr Whitlam's claims that a Workers Association should be taken seriously and that the Administration had for months on end ignored wage claims from officially recognised Workers' Associations, Mr Barnes said that the development of Workers' Associations in the Territory is encouraged by the Government and that during the past year Workers' Associations had negotiated 18 new awards, 10 of which had already been registered, six are awaiting registration and the remaining two are awaiting formal ratification.

There was no record of the Administration having ignored a wage claim formally presented by an officially recognised Workers' Association.

Mr Barnes said that because of the rapid changes taking place in economic and social development in the territory the government had been closely examining the question of wages in the Territory and he had foreshadowed last week the appointment of an expert and an independent Board of Enquiry on rural wages.

Referring to Mr Whitlam's comment that 'there are New Guineans that are well equipped to fill the highest political and administrative positions in their country', Mr Barnes said that this is well recognised by the Australian Government since New Guineans are already acting as heads of Public Service departments and as members of the Public Service Board. The Speaker of the House of Assembly is a Papuan and all except one of the ministerial members and assistant ministerial members are Papuans and New Guineans.

Mr Barnes said Mr Whitlam had said that the governments of 112 nations had just called on Australia to transfer full executive and legislative powers to elected New Guineans. He omitted altogether to quote that part of the resolution which stresses that this should be 'In accordance with the freely expressed wishes of the people'.

The Government's policy was in accordance with the resolution in that it was acting and would continue to act in accordance with the freely expressed wishes of the people. He and other Ministers would be meeting the Select Committee on Constitutional Development of the House of Assembly in Canberra shortly.

Mr Barnes said that he noted that Mr Whitlam had said that the Tolai fear of the multi-racial council is a conservative fear of losing land. Mr Whitlam appeared to be unaware of the fact

---

1   This press release was issued by the Department of Information and Extension Services in the PNG Administration. It comprises a press statement released in Canberra the previous day, 14 January 1970.

2   Document 5.

that some 16,000 acres of land is being made available to help overcome land shortage in the Gazelle Peninsula and the action that is being taken in this connection has been known in the area since last September.

Mr Barnes said that the reckless and irresponsible statements by Mr Whitlam had confused and angered Territory people.

[NAA: A452, 1970/0637]

10   LETTER FROM BARNES TO HAGON[1]

Canberra, 19 January 1970

Thank you for your letter[2] dealing with repercussions from Mr Whitlam's visit and possible means of combating the adverse reactions therefrom within the Territory and Australia.

I think that you will agree that Mr Whitlam's image in Australia consequent upon his visit to the Territory has received the worst setback since he has been Opposition Leader. There would be resistance by the Press to any further criticism of him as you will notice *The Australian* and *The Sydney Morning Herald* are already operating a salvage exercise. They have watered down statements that I and others have made.

I know that sections of his party are very critical of him.

You are best able to judge what the position is in the Territory and I believe that people like yourself would achieve much by explaining to local people [the] consequences of actions by Whitlam should he ever become Prime Minister.

Mr Whitlam has stated that financial assistance from Australia to the Territory would continue after 'Home Rule' but he has never stated how much.

My Department has spent tens of thousands of dollars on publicity through booklets, films, press feature articles etc., but we seem unable to get the truth of the situation across.

It requires only a Maori Kiki or Kaputin in a few days featured as spokesmen for their people in press and radio to achieve far more than we are able to do.

This year I intend to bring articulate local people to Australia to speak on behalf of the great majority of the people. I hope only that they get the same publicity.

[NAA: A452, 1970/0637]

---

1   Mr H. R. (Dick) Hagon, Gumanch Plantations Pty Limited, Mt Hagen.

2   Not published. Hagon had written to Barnes on 19 January 1970.

11   LETTER FROM BARNES TO GORTON

Canberra, 19 January 1970

The House of Assembly of Papua and New Guinea has established a second Select Committee on Constitutional Development.[1]

This is setting about its task in much the same way as the earlier Committee which commenced its substantive work with a general discussion with me. The last Committee then canvassed the views of the Territory people and put forward certain specific propositions they wished to discuss with the Government. Following consideration by Cabinet a group of Ministers then met the Select Committee who gave definite answers on behalf of the Government.

The Committee will meet me during the first week of February in Canberra for general discussions. The Committee have said that they would also wish to discuss various aspects of the work of the Select Committee with you, the Deputy Prime Minister,[2] the Attorney-General,[3] the Minister for External Affairs,[4] as well as Mr Whitlam, Senator Gair[5] and a number of others—mainly academics—who are not members of Parliament. I do not myself feel that the Committee should have discussions with other Ministers before it has formulated specific propositions and the policy on these has been determined by Cabinet. If, however, this is convenient to you I would propose that the Committee call on you in Sydney on Thursday, 5th February after the discussions with me.

In addition I would propose to invite any Ministers in Canberra at the time to a reception to meet the members of the Committee informally. I would also propose that senior officers of the Departments of External Territories, Prime Minister's, Treasury, Attorney-General's and External Affairs should take part in discussions with the Committee.

In my own discussions with the Committee I would stress that the Government will be guided by the wishes of the people themselves. The major step the Territory has to take is when it moves to responsible self government and not when it moves from self government to independence and I would run through with the Committee the pre-requisites for self government (in the sense of local Ministers accepting full responsibility to the House of Assembly for their actions). In this context I would point out that the rising expectations of Territory people for a better life cannot be met principally by overseas aid but that the Territory must rely first on developing its own resources. I would seek the Committee's views on a suggestion that the decision on whether the Territory should become self governing might be the subject of a test of Territory opinion possibly by Territory elections in 1972 being fought on this issue.

---

1   The First House of Assembly, which ran from 1964 to 1968, had appointed the first Select Committee in May 1965. The Committee, in close consultation with Barnes and his officials, had proposed reforms which were largely taken account of in a Cabinet submission of 27 January 1966. This submission recommended, subject to confirmation from the Committee's further enquiries '… that there is a strong and widespread popular support for early constitutional changes in Papua and New Guinea', the progressive devolution of authority to Port Moresby and that elected members of the House of Assembly, within defined limits, 'carry some responsibilities of a ministerial character'. Cabinet agreed to this approach in Cabinet Decision 23 of 15 February 1966. See Stuart Doran, (ed.), *Documents on Australian Foreign Policy: Australia and Papua New Guinea, 1966–1969*, Department of Foreign Affairs and Trade, Canberra, 2006, Documents 5 & 13.

     The Second House of Assembly, which ran from 1968 to 1972, appointed the second Select Committee in mid-1969. Its terms of reference included preparing proposals on future constitutional development in the Territory. See ibid., Documents 261 (fn. 2), 289 & 318.

2   Jack McEwen.

3   Tom Hughes.

4   Billy McMahon.

5   A Queensland senator and a former Queensland premier, Senator Vincent Gair was the Leader of the Democratic Labor Party.

I would then lead the discussions to the present Ministerial Member system stressing that this is capable of expansion to confer authority on Ministerial Members to the full extent approved by Cabinet in Decision 23 of 1966. I would say that the Government considers it desirable to increase the number and role of the Ministerial Members so that they are covering substantially the whole range of Administration business by the next Territory elections.

There has been some indication of a wish to change the name of the Territory and I would indicate that the Government would be willing to vary the Papua and New Guinea Act immediately to change this if the people wish such a change. I also have it in mind to discuss with the Committee the possibility of a Second Chamber having regard particularly to the inclination of the present House to pass legislation without adequate consideration and to the desirability of removing the present regional electorates from the Lower House.

[NAA: A1209, 1968/9698 PART 3]

12   MINUTE FROM BALLARD TO WARWICK SMITH

Canberra, 27 January 1970

Discussion with Hay—Constitutional Development

During discussions Besley and I had with Hay he said that he agreed broadly with all the background papers that had been prepared for [the] Select Committee. He was, however, concerned that there was no proposal for further devolution of authority to Ministerial Members, and referred to his letter proposing devolution to the AEC.[1]

[*matter omitted*]

Hay said that he would see no objection to
-   placing the Ministerial Members above the Departmental Heads.
-   Ministerial Members covering the whole say of Administration business.
-   removal of officials from the House of Assembly or providing for them to be called to answer questions concerning their own Departments (in this context he cited a New Caledonia precedent).
-   removal of all officials other than himself (and possibly the person who would act as his deputy during his absence) from the AEC.
-   limiting the appointments of deputies under Section 17 to occasions when he was absent and a Deputy Administrator actually did his job (he said that action was going ahead to delegate statutory authorities to Ministerial Members (MMs) under Section 17 now).

Hay would like to see amendments to the Act (unspecified) and the arrangements under Section 25 taken now as a Government initiative and suggested that this should not be left until just before the next election. The Select Committee would have plenty of other things to discuss but an initiative on these lines would show the young people that we were not always saying 'no'.

[*matter omitted*]

[NAA: A452, 1970/460]

---

1   This is probably a reference to Hay's letter to Barnes of 20 October 1969 in which he argued for greater devolution to the House of Assembly and to the Administrator's Executive Council. See Stuart Doran, (ed.), *Documents on Australian Foreign Policy: Australia and Papua New Guinea, 1966–1969*, Department of Foreign Affairs and Trade, Canberra, 2006, Documents 259 & 325.

13   NOTES FOR MINISTER[1]

Canberra, 29 January 1970

Constitutional development is a continuing process.

Last Select Committee said:

'It is realised that at this stage of the Territory's development, conditions could alter considerably over a four year period. Therefore the framework of any proposals adopted now should make allowance for changing circumstances. The capability of a Minister could develop to the extent that he is able to assume sole ministerial responsibility for the Department. Also, the needs of, or situation within, a department could warrant an increase in the Minister's authority. Accordingly, the powers and duties of Ministers should be reviewed by the House after a minimum period of two years.'

Government has had under review desirability of changes in June.

Present arrangements not training [of] political leaders. Second reading speech in the House of Representatives on 2 May 1968:

'The Government does not, however, believe that political development to the point of self-government or independence or other status which the Territory may ultimately assume can have substance if it is not accompanied by progress towards self-reliance in economic matters—in other words political development cannot be divorced from economic development. At the same time it has to be recognised that the road to economic development is a long hard road.'

[*matter omitted*]

Present situation: Minister responsible to Parliament; Administrator responsible to Minister; Ministerial Members *represent* Administration in the House of Assembly but *responsible* to Administrator.

In discussions with officials the Select Committee might examine to see whether the Ministerial Member system or full self-government reflects true situation in the social and economic fields and the people's wishes.

Select Committee may have views on whether wishes of the people on self-government might be sought at next Territory general election.

Difficult step is from present system to responsible government, not from self-government to independence because responsibility shifts—including responsibility for raising money.

Government feels that now is the time for additional authority for elected members within the Ministerial Member system.

Legislation could be introduced to the autumn session to enable this to come into force in June.

Would appreciate the views of the Committee on the following proposed changes:
-    removing the office of Assistant Ministerial Member and increasing the number of Ministerial Members to, say, 12 or 13 (excluding Treasury, Law but not DDA[2] or Lands)
-    reducing the number of official members of the House of Assembly to, say, five and withdrawing their right to vote.

---

1   These notes were prepared for Barnes for the discussions with the Select Committee to be held in February 1970.

2   Department of District Administration.

–   reducing the number of officials on the AEC to the Administrator and one other (his Deputy).

Government also feels that House of Assembly has reached a stage where all members should be elected on same basis from open electorates.

There may be a need for a second chamber to take the place of present regional electorates.

Select Committee should consider desirability of a second chamber generally. Ask what Committee has done on name, flag, and anthem.

Government could amend Commonwealth legislation to enable change of name to take place.

[NAA: A452, 1970/460]

John Gorton meeting members of the House of Assembly's Select Committee on Constitutional Development in Canberra in February 1970. From left: Walter Lussick, Les Johnson, Donatus Mola, Ebia Olewale, Matthias Toliman, Gorton, Paulus Arek (Chair of the Committee), Matiabe Yuwi, Tom Leahy, Michael Somare, Oala Oala Rarua, Sinake Giregire, John Middleton, Tei Abal and Geoff Littler.

[PHOTO COURTESY OF FAY REDGRAVE]

Gough Whitlam, Australian Labor Party and Opposition Leader, with members of the Select Committee.

[PHOTO COURTESY OF DIANNE McINNES]

Top: John Grey Gorton, Australian Prime Minister, 1968–71; and Charles Barnes, Minister for Territories, 1963–68 and External Territories, 1968–72.

Bottom: George Warwick Smith, Secretary of the Department of Territories, 1964–68 and of External Territories, 1968–70; and David Hay, Administrator of the Territory, 1967–70 and Secretary of the Department of External Territories, 1970–73.

[NAA]

Gough Whitlam, Australian Labor Party and Opposition Leader from 1967, and Prime Minister from December 1972.

[NAA]

Ainsley Gotto, Principal Private Secretary to Prime Minister John Gorton, 1968–71.

[GOTTO PAPERS]

Papua and New Guinea's second House of Assembly, which ran from 1968 to 1972. Expatriate members wielded substantial influence in the 1964 and 1968 Houses of Assembly, but their presence and influence faded in the 1972 House.

[PHOTO COURTESY OF DIANNE McINNES]

Les Johnson succeeded David Hay as PNG Administrator in mid-July 1970. Here Johnson is pictured with the Administrator's Executive Council (AEC), an embryo cabinet.

Front row from left: Toua Kapena, Tom Leahy, Johnson, Tore Lokoloko and Tei Abal.
Second row from left: Tom Ellis, Harry Ritchie, Roi Ashton and Angmai Bilas.
Back row from the left: Tony Newman, Matthias Toliman and AEC Executive Officer Paul Ryan. Sinake Giregire is absent.

[PHOTO COURTESY OF DIANNE McINNES]

THE WEEK WHICH LAY AHEAD

Port Moresby,
5th, 6th, 7th July.

Goroka, 7th July.

Mount Hagen, 7th, 8th July.

Mendi, 8th July.

Wewak, 8th July.

Madang, 8th July.

Lae, 9th July.

Rabaul, 9th, 10th July.

Kieta, 10th July.

Buka, 10th July.

Port Moresby, 10th, 11th July.

> *"There is very much to do in the future of this country and I express a strong hope that that will be done by a partnership of the coastal people, of the Highlanders, of the people from the islands and from Australians, and that working in harmony to build and achieve we will be able to give this country the economic base which must be there for full political stability. I hope that we can avoid any division which would hamper the task which together can be so well done."*
>
> John Gorton, Lae, 9th July.

The Route and Centres Visited

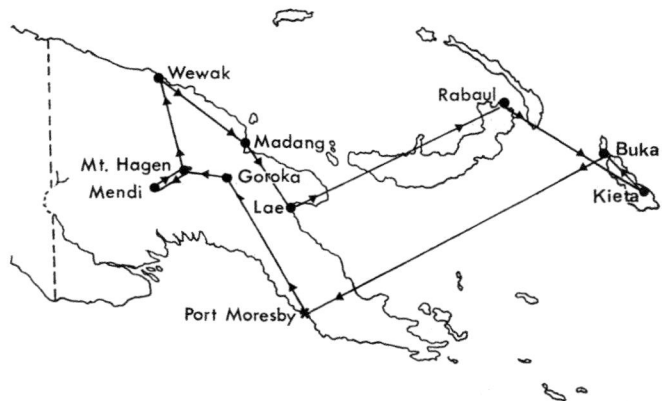

Gorton's itinerary in July 1970. The image is from a PNG Administration brochure on Gorton's visit.

[NLA]

*House of Assembly Speaker John Guise greets Gorton and Barnes
on their arrival at the House in July 1970.*

[DFAT]

Gorton speaks in Port Moresby during his July 1970 visit.

[PNG NATIONAL ARCHIVES & PUBLIC RECORDS SERVICE]

Top: Mataungan Association supporters assembled for Gorton's visit to Rabaul in July 1970.
Bottom: John Kaputin addresses the crowd in Rabaul, flanked by Barnes and Gorton.
[PNG NATIONAL ARCHIVES & PUBLIC RECORDS SERVICE]

Gorton speaks in Buka, Bougainville, during his July 1970 visit.
He encouraged the people of Bougainville to consider the advantages
of remaining part of a united Papua and New Guinea.

[DFAT]

14   LETTER FROM HAY TO BARNES[1]

Port Moresby, 1 February 1970

CONFIDENTIAL

In this letter, following my custom of the last two years,[2] I submit to you some general observations on the main trends in Territory affairs in 1969 and some suggestions which I hope the government will take into account in determining its policies for 1970.

In outline, the year 1969 was one of real achievements, both political and economic, which have been satisfactory to the great majority of Territory people. The CRA[3] decision to proceed with the mining of copper in Bougainville was the outstanding event because it has opened up for the first time the prospect of the territory's dependence on outside aid levelling off and beginning to decline. Of a lesser order of magnitude but perhaps more important from the point of view of confidence in the Administration by rural people and their elected members, has been the successful launching of the Rural Development Programme of $1,000,000 allocated to Districts for self-help projects which have in the main been initiated by Councils and to which they have contributed substantial local government resources by their own efforts.

But the real economic achievements have been overshadowed by four events—the strong attack mounted by a number of critics of the government's development programmes; the adverse publicity on the use of police at Rorovana in Bougainville;[4] the activities of the Mataungan Association[5] in the Gazelle Peninsula; and finally the visit of Mr Whitlam to the Territory. These events have to be assessed against a background which includes a growing divergence between the traditional leaders and the increasing number of younger, educated and articulate Papuans and New Guineans. This divergence is marked, on the part of the traditional leaders, by a strong inclination towards repressive action, and on the part of the younger group by a mistrust amounting to contempt. As a result, there is now a degree of uncertainty and tension in the Territory which is in very marked contrast to the calm which prevailed a year ago.

I have previously drawn to your attention to the political and social stresses involved in a forced development programme, and the likelihood that human frustrations and ambitions would affect the chances of orderly progress in the government's policy of balanced economic, social and political development, with the pace of movement towards self-government regulated by the necessarily slow progress in economic development. I have stressed that slow and orderly progress in economic development depended on the full involvement of Papuans and New Guineans, through accepted leaders, in the government's policies and their execution. A strenuous effort has been made to this end through the Ministerial Members, the Administrator's Executive Council and the House of Assembly. There has been a greater degree of consultation on policy matters than ever before. But the Administration, either alone or with the willing support of the Ministerial Members, has not been able to inspire

---

1   Hay forwarded a copy of this letter to Prime Minister Gorton. They had met on 22 January and Hay had agreed to forward a copy of the letter to him. The relevant documents are held on NAA: M3787, 14.

2   For Hay's two previous end-of-year round up letters see Stuart Doran, (ed.), *Documents on Australian Foreign Policy: Australia and Papua New Guinea, 1966–1969*, Australian Department of Foreign Affairs and Trade, Canberra, 2006, Documents 155 & 259.

3   Conzinc Riotinto Australia.

4   See Doran, *Australia and Papua New Guinea, 1966–1969*, xlv–xlvii.

5   For further details on the MA and the official Australian attitude to it see (among others) Documents 1–4, 6 & 8.

the national effort that is necessary. And the Administration's capacity to enforce unpopular policies in the face of determined local resistance has to be assessed against the damage to its general standing which, because it is essentially an external authority, it is likely to suffer.

I am convinced that only an early transfer of some real power, on a selective basis, to the Territory can secure the sense of involvement and responsibility needed to cause leaders here to espouse and work for the kinds of policies which will set the Territory economically on its own feet, and offer the prospect of something like national support for such policies, including the support of younger Papuans and New Guineans on whom the Territory's development must increasingly depend.

This entails risks, notably the risk that important but unpopular policies will be eroded or materially changed because the political leaders who espouse them will feel their own electoral position jeopardised. The present holders of Ministerial office have no party, and no electoral organisation, to fall back on. They may prefer that it be the Administration which takes responsibility for unpopular decisions such as those on taxation, and use the authority which it has as a government to put them into effect. Another risk is that of alienating the goodwill of the great majority of the population, the rural element, which may interpret any early transfer of power as 'self-government' and take fright because they think self-government signals the end of Australian aid or because they think that the exercise of authority by the Administration, whatever its shortcomings, is preferable to its exercise by native Papuans and New Guineans not of their own tribe.

In my opinion, these risks must be accepted. They are preferable to the risks to the whole Australian position in the Territory which are incurred, and which will increasingly be incurred, when unpopular policies are imposed, however right and generous they are, in the face of active opposition. It is true that the Administration, in accordance with the government's basic policy, has been meticulous in securing the support of the Administrator's Executive Council and the House of Assembly for all important decisions and executive actions. There has been a sharing of the decision making process. But essentially the policies have been Australian ones and it is precisely this feature which I believe we should now set about changing.

The risks can be overstated. There is no need to suppose that existing economic policies will be abandoned. The size of the grant and the degree of dependence in other respects will contribute to this. The goodwill of the conservative rural element can be retained if it is made clear that selective transfer of power will not mean the end of Australian aid or of a strong and just exercise of authority. And not even the most radical voices in the Territory are at present raised in favour of early independence.

A readiness to transfer power is not to be seen as an isolated policy change. It is better seen as a new element in an existing disposition on the part of the government to encourage the taking of responsibility in the Territory. That disposition has already been demonstrated in late 1969 by positive steps in localisation of senior positions in the public service. But the attack has been on a narrow front. It needs to be on a wide front, with greater emphasis on localisation in economic affairs. The idea also needs to be spread that major policies relevant to a self-governing country should receive early consideration by the Territory's House of Assembly. The views of the House should be actively sought on such matters as citizenship, immigration, foreign investment and banking legislation. Clearly the formulation of policies on such basic matters will take many months. But the idea of internal self-government being within sight and not many miles away could have a significant effect on the morale and attitude of the more articulate elements whose support is vital to development. A positive and flexible attitude on the part of the Administration over a much wider front than in the past could generate a sense of urgency and enthusiasm on the part of educated younger Papuans and New Guineans without raising panic among their elders.

I do not recommend an immediate formal move towards internal self-government. That is something which needs careful and no doubt lengthy consideration by the Territory Select Committee on Constitutional Development and, in due course, the House of Assembly, as well as by the government. What I have in mind is a marked change within the context of existing policy as stated by the Governor-General to the House of Assembly in June 1968:

'The destiny of Papua and New Guinea is to become a self-governing country developed for independence if and when it is clearly demonstrated by the majority of the indigenous population that this is what they wish. The Australian Government's basic policy for Papua and New Guinea is therefore to develop it for self-determination.'

The change would be seen as an encouragement of early internal self-government rather than discouragement, exemplified by a de facto transfer of power in selected fields, accompanied by a readiness to encourage the determination of policy issues such as those mentioned above by elected representatives in the Territory.

We need to consider realistically how and to whom selected powers should be transferred. In the immediate future, and short of legislation, the options seem to be confined to delegation by the Commonwealth of certain powers it legally holds, both legislative and executive, and/or the establishment of a convention that it will not exercise those particular powers. So far as legislation is concerned, the House of Assembly already has the power to 'make ordinances for the peace, order and good government of the Territory'. This power is subject to the requirement, inter alia, that the Administrator 'reserve for the Governor-General's pleasure' ordinances relating to a list of subjects such as the armed forces, the Public Service, land. What I have in mind here is the establishment of a convention that the Governor-General does not exercise the right of withholding assent except in relation to ordinances on reserved subjects, and that the Administrator does not indefinitely withhold assent to ordinances which the Act does not require to be reserved for the Governor-General's pleasure. Another convention which could be quickly established is that official members of the House of Assembly confine their activity to explaining government views and refrain from voting.

So far as the executive government of the Territory is concerned, the procedure would be for the Minister either to refrain from directing the Administrator in the selected fields in which authority is transferred, or formally to delegate that authority. He would also need to direct the Administrator, subject to such safeguards as may be thought fit, to seek and accept the advice of the Administrator's Executive Council on all matters within the selected fields. Consequential changes in the 'Arrangements' made under Section 25 of the Papua and New Guinea Act would also be required, e.g. to raise the status of Ministerial Members above that of Departmental Heads.

The transfer of powers in selected fields by the means described above would be meaningless unless it embraced the financial authority necessary to put decisions into effect. Safeguards would need to be included in order to ensure that mutually agreed policies, e.g. those incorporated in the development programme, were not jeopardised. Possibly a review would need to be made of the way in which the Commonwealth's annual grant is calculated and contributed.

It will, of course, be evident, that these suggestions (which follow closely those of my letter to you of 28th February 1969—LH.2722)[6] go further than those in the departmental briefs prepared for the preliminary visit to Australia in early February of the Select Committee on Constitutional Development. Those briefs include a number of references to changes in the 'Arrangements' which would be most welcome. But none of these amount to a transfer to the Territory of definite power.

---

6   Doran, *Australia and Papua New Guinea, 1966–1969*, Document 259.

The mechanics of handing over selected powers on a de facto basis are simple enough. It would be normal to suppose that the powers be handed over to the present Ministerial Members (although their number may need to be enlarged). This in itself may not attract national support on the scale we need. The preponderance of uneducated men among the Ministerial Members is not attractive to the younger, educated group. I therefore believe that an attempt should be made to induce the Pangu Pati to nominate one or more Ministerial Members and form what would in effect be a national government.

The justification for the early transfer of some powers on the above-mentioned lines is that it offers the prospects (a) of involving elected Members of the House effectively in the difficult and perhaps unpopular decisions which need to be made, and (b) of inspiring a sense of urgency and national effort , particularly from younger, educated Papuans and New Guineans, sufficient to win acceptance of the strains of development and to counter the natural disruptive forces at work as well as the new anti-white radicalism which may well soon spread beyond the Gazelle. The action proposed is a mild form of shock treatment. As earlier stated, it is seen as a new element in an existing disposition to encourage the taking of responsibility in the Territory. Together with other new elements already referred to, it amounts to a change of attitude or posture. Public acceptance of such a change would, so far as the Territory is concerned, be reinforced by a clear definition of the reason for Australia's presence in the Territory. I dealt with this at some length in my annual letter dated 31st January 1968,[7] in which I stated my understanding that the Australian presence and policy of economic aid stemmed from its obligations under the UN Charter and from 'sentiment derived from war-time association and personal contacts, from interest in the work of the missions and firm and certain pride in doing a job which needs to be done.' I assumed then, and still do, that our defence interests are not a primary reason for our continuing to administer the Territory, and that these interests could equally well be served by the continuance of close and friendly relations with the Territory's government and people. I said that I saw no economic advantage in our continuing in the Territory, beyond the economic interests of some thousands of Australians. Because these interests have not been stated publicly for some time, I see, from the Territory angle, advantage in a clear statement of them at an early date, provided (which I believe to be still the case) that the government intends to fulfil its obligations in relation to economic aid and does not regard them as discharged upon the Territory's achievement of self-government (which again I take to be the case).

I have pressed in this letter for an early change of posture. I have done so in the knowledge that it may cause concern to a number of strong supporters of the Administration in Papua and in the rural areas of New Guinea, particularly the Highlands. This possibility needs to be borne in mind and steps taken to guard against it. The main fears of the rural people are that upon self-government, which they equate with independence, Australian aid will cease and they will be left to the mercy of other tribes or regional groups who are either more numerous (as the Papuans say of the Highlanders) or more educated (as the Highlanders say of the coastal Papuans and New Guineans). I hope the government will be disposed to allay the first fear by clear statements that the immediate actions proposed do not amount to internal self-government, which in any event is quite different from independence, and involves neither the discharge of Australia's obligations nor the end of its policy of aid to the Territory. The continued Australian presence after self-government will allay, but not dispose of, the second fear. That can only be done by evidence, not yet in sight, that the Territory can maintain largely from its own personnel a strong, just and well-managed government.

---

7   Ibid., Document 155.

The change of posture proposed in this letter also has to be considered from the point of view of its effect on the attitudes and morale of Australians in the Territory, in the business sector and in the public service. I doubt whether the expatriate businessman with a real stake in the Territory in primary or secondary industry is much worried by talk of self-government in itself. He is much more concerned at the type of people likely to be in power, their policies and their ability to hold the country together and keep law and order. Increasingly he appears ready to adjust to what he regards as inevitable. The conjunction of the Whitlam visit and the resignation of two senior officers, following on law and order difficulties in Bougainville and New Britain and an increase in crimes such as assault and cases of molestation in urban areas, have adversely affected morale in the expatriate section of the public service. I have previously expressed to you the opinion, which I still hold, that excessive direction of Administration activity by departmental officers under the guise that the Minister has to be responsible to the Australian Parliament for every detail which happens in the Territory, has had a frustrating effect. Divided control has made it difficult to achieve a united and willing effort by senior officers here. These difficulties should be relieved by the course of action proposed in this letter, but I think we must anticipate an even greater difficulty than before in holding good staff.

This factor leads me to emphasise, as a priority target for 1970 and the years immediately ahead, the building up of an effective administrative machine and police force. I am not sanguine on either count. The pace of localisation and the propensity of good expatriate officers to resign are already having an adverse effect on the efficiency of the public service and its capacity to carry out a complex task such as the five year development programme. Because so much has had to be referred to Canberra the Territory is short of the built-in checking and probing processes that are common in the Commonwealth Treasury, and priority needs to be given to this.

The force required to maintain the authority of the government depends heavily on the district administration system and the police. The former, though suffering from inexperienced officers, is in relatively good shape. The latter is not developing at a rate or with the quality needed to cope with the future. In the 1969 emergencies, the police did very well and both morale and discipline were exemplary. Time is badly needed to build up the field force and train officers and men in more complex and sophisticated aspects of police work. As already recognised, this is one of the main tasks for 1970. In the meantime, enforcement of law and order cannot be taken for granted and the possibility of an urgent requirement to use the PIR[8] cannot be excluded. It is to my mind essential that the PIR continue to have aid to the civil power as one of its openly declared aims, and that it be trained for this task.

I emphasise once again the urgent need for more attention to public relations. This applies both to the Territory and to Australia. Regrettably there was no effective public relations planning for the Rorovana affair in early August.[9] I doubt whether either the Administration or the Department is much better placed now for effective presentation of what is being done. I have for three years sought a suitable person as an adviser for the Administration. It is only now that an attractive salary is available, but no appointment is in sight. In Australia I see great advantage in you yourself and senior officers of both the Department and the Administration holding briefing sessions for editorial staff, and getting to know specialist writers and encouraging them to acquaint themselves with the real facts. In the Territory we need in particular a more effective liaison with the *Post-Courier*.[10] This paper has been strongly anti-Administration

---

8   The Pacific Islands Regiment (PIR) was PNG's locally-recruited but Australian-led defence force.

9   See Doran, *Australia and Papua New Guinea, 1966–1969*, xlv–xlvii.

10   The *Papua New Guinea Post–Courier* was established on 30 June 1969. Its Australian parent company was The Herald and Weekly Times Ltd.

in tone and policy over the past year. Because it is widely and uncritically read by educated Papuans and New Guineans, it has strong influence in an important area.

The year 1969 imposed a number of strains on the Administration and its senior officers. I express to you our warm appreciation of the strong support which we have received from you personally and your departmental officers in times of crisis. In turn, I assure you of our strong support of yourself and the government in the year ahead.

I am sending a copy of this letter to the Secretary, Department of External Territories.

[NAA: M3787, 14]

15   LETTER FROM GORTON TO BARNES[1]

Canberra, 2 February 1970

Thank you for your letter of 19 January[2] about the visit to Australia of the Select Committee on Constitutional Development. As you know, I shall be happy to see the Committee in Sydney on Friday 6 February at 9:30 am.

I take it to be your intention that the meetings between the Committee and yourself be regarded as preliminary, and that definitive expression of government views be left to a later time, when the Committee will have consulted Territory opinion and formulated its own views.

While I believe this to be a sensible approach in relation to constitutional issues of a long-term nature, such as the relationship between the Executive and the Legislature or your own suggestion for a Second Chamber, I do not think the Government should await the Select Committee's recommendations before addressing itself to the questions of how quickly and by what means the Territory should move towards internal self-government.

I think it most important that from the outset, including the preliminary discussions with the Committee, the Government's stance be one which encourages rather than discourages the early achievement of internal self-government. Your statement that 'The major step the Territory has to take is when it moves to responsible self-government and not when it moves from self-government to independence' seems to carry the connotation that self-government is to be obtained by one step. While this is true as regards the final, concluding step, I think that intermediate steps should be taken and that now is the time to take them.

The concept of waiting until 1972 and then testing Territory opinion is not one which appeals to me unless significant steps are taken before 1972 so that, if the territory then wants self-government, it is the more equipped to exercise it.

The implications of the early achievement of internal self-government will, of course, need to be gone into fully and placed before the Cabinet. In advance of this, I shall want to indicate publicly the stance described above and to reinforce it with evidence that in practice, a good deal more power will be given to Ministerial Members in the near future.

If we believe that we have a good Administrator and good Ministerial Members, then now is the time to decentralise a great deal of decision making, now is the time to allow some mistakes to be made if that should happen, now is the time to move closer to the position which an efficient Head Office of an international company would take in allowing its offices in other countries autonomy—subject to periodic reports on progress and the reserve power to interfere if those reports were not satisfactory.

You say in your letter that the present Ministerial Member system is capable of expansion 'to confer authority on Ministerial Members to the full extent approved by Cabinet in Decision 23 of 1966'. If that decision, based on the constitutional position that formal authority over the whole range of government activity in the Territory rests with Australia, is narrowly interpreted as I think it is at present, then the authority conferred in Ministerial Members will not be definitive. Would you therefore look into the possibility that in advance of any changes

---

1   This letter was largely based on a draft prepared by David Hay and passed to Gorton, attached to a personal note from Hay, and dated 24 January 1970. The draft was apparently prepared following a private meeting between Hay and Gorton on 22 January. Paragraphs two, three, the first half of paragraph 4, paragraph 6 and parts of paragraph 8 of Gorton's letter to Barnes drew almost word for word on Hay's draft. The text of Hay's draft and his accompanying letter to Gorton are held on NAA, M3787, 14.

2   Document 11.

in the Papua and New Guinea Act, the Government, by convention or by delegation, can enable Ministerial Members to exercise full authority in defined fields, either individually or collectively (through advice to the Administrator in the Administrator's Executive Council). The exercise of power in this practical way would have to carry with it the responsibility for the financial consequences of decisions. Safeguards would have to be built into any arrangements to ensure, for example, that agreed policies incorporated in the five year development programme are not affected without the government's agreement.

I think, too, that it is important to make the point in the preliminary discussions that the achievement of internal self-government will not alter Australia's intention to assist the political, economic and social advancement of the Territory. The transfer to the Territory of many of the powers now held and experienced by Australia need not lead to fears on the part of Papuans and New Guineans that Australian aid will run down—though we will need to retain a general—not detailed—oversight of aid we may provide.

I have no other comment at this stage on the contents of your letter beyond stressing the point that you yourself make in other words—that the kind of constitutional arrangements under which the Territory will eventually govern itself should be decided by its own elected representatives.

[NAA: A452, 1970/1327]

16   STATEMENT BY BARNES

Canberra, 4 February 1970

Talks with Select Committee on Constitutional Development

The Minister for External Territories, Mr Barnes, said today that valuable and constructive discussions had been held with the Select Committee on Constitutional Development from the House of Assembly.

The Chairman of the Select Committee, Mr Arek, had indicated that the Committee would visit selected overseas countries and would then travel the territory extensively. Discussions with the Minister were seen as a preliminary to assessing the wishes of Territory people.

The Committee's report would then be presented to the House of Assembly and if accepted by the House, the Committee's proposals would be passed to the Government.

Mr Barnes said he had made it clear that the Australian Government would readily make changes if the people of the Territory wanted them. All the Government's policies were directed towards the economic, social and political advancement of the indigenous people of the Territory to build with them a self reliant nation.

During their visit to Canberra the Committee had discussions with the Solicitor-General,[1] Senator Greenwood and members of the diplomatic and academic communities. They would meet the Prime Minister and the Leader of the Opposition in Sydney and a group of Members would meet Senator Gair[2] in Brisbane.

Mr Barnes said that constitutional development was a continuing process and changes to ensure that effect is given to what the people want are continuously under review by the Government.

[NAA: A452, 1970/460]

---

1   Robert James (Bob) Ellicott, QC.

2   Senator Vincent Gair, a senator for Queensland and a former Queensland premier, was the Leader of the Democratic Labor Party.

17   STATEMENT BY SELECT COMMITTEE

Canberra, 5 February 1970

Talks in Canberra

On behalf of the Select Committee on Constitutional Development of the Papua and New Guinea House of Assembly the Chairman, Mr Paulus Arek, said that the Committee felt very satisfied with the discussions in Canberra with the Minister for External Territories and officers of his Department and with other Commonwealth officers and private citizens.

The talks were intended to be exploratory only and there was a free exchange of views and a good deal of common ground.

Among matters which were discussed were whether the possible future constitutional development of Papua and New Guinea should be aligned with the Westminster system or with the American presidential system or whether variants of those systems appropriate to local conditions would be more suitable.

The development of the present Ministerial Member system was also dealt with at some length.

The nature of possible future financial relationships between Papua and New Guinea and the Australian Government is naturally of paramount importance and occupied a good deal of discussion time.

[NAA: A452, 1970/460]

18   DISCUSSION BETWEEN BARNES AND THE PNG SELECT COMMITTEE[1]

Canberra, 5 February 1970

Committee were looking for ideas from the Government and came forward with few of their own.

Minister made it clear that Government wanted faster rather than slower political progress and looked to the Committee to assess views of Territory people on what they wanted.

- Self government (in the sense of Ministers being responsible to the House of Assembly) not excluded;
- Sought views on a number of amendments to the Papua and New Guinea Act (increase number of Ministerial Members to cover all Departments except Treasury, Law and Administrator; abolish position of Assistant Ministerial Member; reduce number of official members in House of Assembly and Administrator's Executive Council and withdraw their vote);
- Changes in present arrangements to give more authority to present Ministerial Members (without amending the Act) would in any case be made by the Minister as it is the present policy to progressively increase the powers of Ministerial Members.

Committee proposed a change in the designation of 'Ministerial Member' to 'Minister' at the present state.

Minister opposes this on the ground that the term 'Minister' should be used only when the Ministers themselves were fully responsible for their position to the House of Assembly.

On financial matters the Committee asked for a Budget to give them control over local revenue and part of the Australian grant.

- Minister said that a split budget would not work while Territory revenue was so small a proportion (40% of total Budget);
- The large Australian grant was given in accordance with a resolution of the House of Assembly under the five year development programme and position should be reviewed when this comes to an end in 1972/73;
- The Government has responsibility to the electorate for how Australian funds are spent; no donor country gives aid without regard to how it is spent;
- Within the agreed Budget Ministerial Members in charge of certain Government Departments could be wholly responsible subject only to Administrator's Executive Council;
- Improved methods of consultation between Administrator's Executive Council and Minister on unitary budget;
- The Minister undertook to examine an allocation of funds for rural development to be allocated by Administrator's Executive Council in consultation with present Budget Committee of House of Assembly.

Some discussion on possibility for second chamber.

---

1   The Select Committee members in attendance were Paulus Arek (Chair), Thomas Leahy, John Maxwell Middleton, Oala Oala Rarua, Tei Abal, Michael Somare, Matthias Toliman, Ebia Olewale, Peter Johnson (MHA for Angoram), Walter Lussick (MHA for Manus and New Ireland regional), Matiabe Yuwi (MHA for Tari) and Donatus Mola (MHA for North Bougainville).

Committee will raise with the Prime Minister their concern:

- That Commonwealth authorities not within the Administration (Army, Civil Aviation) were not the concern of the House of Assembly and were isolated from political progress; there should be designated spokesmen for Army and Civil Aviation in House of Assembly;
- At the loss of experienced overseas officers; they want an arm of the Commonwealth services which will give career security and encourage the more experienced people to stay on;
- About electoral difficulties of Ministerial Members who have to spend long periods away from their electorates. Minister considers that something might be done in the way of electoral Secretary.

[NAA: A452, 1970/460]

19   NOTES ON MEETING BETWEEN GORTON AND PNG SELECT COMMITTEE[1]

Sydney, 6 February 1970

CONFIDENTIAL

(These notes are designed particularly to record what the Prime Minister said and do not necessarily include fully all that was said to him.)

Arek: Opened by asking the Prime Minister his comments on change of designation of 'Ministerial Member' to 'Minister' and removal of Assistant Ministerial Members.

Prime Minister: 'I would not have any worries about the name of the Minister but that cannot be all that is wanted. What is wanted is for people to have powers of decision. Merely to call someone Minister would not mean that they have the same powers as a Minister here.'

Leahy: 'We want to create an image in the Territory and the term 'Minister' will do this.'

Prime Minister: 'If this is really a public relations exercise I would have no objection but Territory Ministers would not be responsible to the House of Assembly in the same way as down here. After all they call people Ministers in the United States and they are not responsible to the Congress. I will take that up with the Minister and the Government.'

Lussick: Asked about more powers for the AEC.

Prime Minister: Made two points:

(1)   'I do not see how there can be full control of the budget or partial control of the budget. A large portion comes from Australia and there must be some Australian control.

(2)   'With regard to spending within the Departments I would like to see more capacity for a Ministerial Member to make decisions of detailed spending on the amounts in the Departments.

'I have talked to the Minister about both these points. Side by side with this there would need to be someone representing the Australian Government to come along every three months or so to see how things are going on. This would be just like a company from the United States operating in Australia.'

Leahy: Said that for their part they would not see any objection to having a permanent Australian representative for this purpose.

Prime Minister: Replied 'If someone was there all the time it would need to be clear that he was only there to be consulted and not to control.'

Middleton: Asked whether this would mean that some functions of the budget could become subject to local control.

Prime Minister: 'Functions would need to be spelled out but there are and should be functions which would become subject to local control. Taking the example of high schools, Australia would need to agree on the standards, e.g. space per pupil. That having been done the letting of contracts, the selection of the site and actual building would be the Territory's responsibility. We won't want to wait for the conclusion of the enquiries by the Select Committee to say this sort of thing. We need to do something on these lines quickly.'

Lussick: 'It is important to let the local people make their own mistakes.'

---

1   For the Select Committee members in attendance, see Document 18, fn. 1.

Prime Minister: 'Yes. That is why we need three-monthly examinations to pick these up. We have said and we mean what we say that self-government is going to come and this cannot happen except by the local leaders learning by doing.'

Leahy: Said that the people were worried about the loss of senior public servants. He mentioned Johnson.[2] He said that this was much more serious than the Bougainville or the Gazelle situation. There would be anarchy if everyone went. Contract officers do not replace men with years of experience.

Oala: Asked whether the Government would consider some sort of guarantee so that [the] Commonwealth took over Australian officers.

Lussick: Said that at present the worst loss was in administrative field. He referred to discussions that the Select Committee had had with diplomats who had all stressed the need for uncorrupted and dedicated public service. He said (wrongly) that this was because under the British arrangements they had had security to return to the British Home Service.

Tei Abel: 'I am very worried about this matter. I am pleased that you have said we can have more power but how can we do this if we have no good public servants. They must have security. If an officer is a Class 8 in Papua and New Guinea he should be given the opportunity of being a Class 8 in Australia. Contract officers cannot do what we need.'

Prime Minister: 'But I do not know enough about this. I know the Minister is giving some thought to this but I am not aware of the position in any depth. Therefore I cannot be as firm on this matter as I am firm in my own mind on other matters. What is the position about replacement of expatriates by Papuans and New Guineans?'

[Peter] Johnson: 'There is as yet a very limited number of Papuans and New Guineans with sufficient experience to take over senior jobs. There are only a handful of graduates and it would be in 1973 or 1974 before we had enough and they would all be very young.'

Prime Minister: Said that he did not think it was necessary for positions all to be filled by University graduates.

Somare: Said that the gap was at the intermediate level and it was at this level that local people get to be given the opportunity to get experience.

Leahy: Said that there were dangers of putting people in positions of acting Director when they were very young men. He agreed with Somare that they should be put in the middle bracket.

Prime Minister: 'I am sure that is right.'

Somare: Asked whether the new Commonwealth scheme for transferability of superannuation would apply to Papua and New Guinea.

Prime Minister: Explained the scheme and said that it was not yet law and that he would find out whether the scheme would apply to pensionable officers in Papua and New Guinea.

---

2   This was presumably a reference to the impending departure of Les Johnson. In early 1970, in part because of frustration with the micro-management of George Warwick Smith, Johnson had announced his resignation as Assistant Administrator after having accepted the position of Principal of the Tasmania College of Advanced Education. Later in the year Johnson was persuaded to return to the Territory to replace Hay as Administrator, with Hay then replacing Warwick Smith as Territories Secretary. See Ian Hancock, *John Gorton: He Did It His Way*, Hodder, Griffin Press, Adelaide, 2002, p. 289; Ian Downs, *The Australian Trusteeship: Papua New Guinea, 1945–75*, Australian Government Publishing Service, Canberra, 1980, pp. 399–401, 471–2; and Donald Denoon, *Trial Separation. Australia and the Decolonisation of Papua New Guinea*, Australian National University, Pandanus Books, Canberra, 2005, p. 81. In a discussion with Bruce Hunt on 1 December 2017, Ms Fay Redgrave, the daughter of Les Johnson, recalled that Gorton had telephoned Johnson at home in Australia in early 1970 to persuade him to return to the Territory as Administrator.

(It would not and it is not thought that this would make much difference since secondment of Commonwealth and State officers is already possible to the Territory under existing legislation with retention of their existing rights).

[Peter] Johnson: Said that the implementation of this scheme might encourage more public servants to move out.

Prime Minister: Asked whether the position might be held when the Ministers get more power because that would give the public servants more power to advise the people on the spot.

Leahy: Said that there is a real fear that something could go wrong in the Territory.

Middleton: Said that as well as security the Public Service wanted continuity.

Lussick: Said that they are losing promotional and current progress. Could there be a separate Commonwealth Service for them which could gradually be absorbed?

Somare: 'Have asked whether the base payment for overseas officers could be paid from the Territory and differential allowances paid direct from the Australian budget.' This was supported by *Oala* as a way of removing discrimination.

Prime Minister: 'I see little difficulty in this and I understand the human difficulties that may arise from differential rates of pay. We have the same problems too with US companies.'

Arek: Asked what would happen when political parties came and there was a political party which was able to command a majority in the House. What would then happen to the Administrator's Office?

Prime Minister: 'I do not know. It would be worked out and discussed and agreed when the time arises. There will still need to be an Administrator of some kind with some powers. It is most unlikely that Australia will pay a lump sum and let the Territory leaders spend it. We will want to allocate the purposes and be able to ensure that the money is spent for the purposes for which it is voted here and there must be someone to supervise the expenditure.'

Abel: Asked the Prime Minister how he felt about a Minister who could not read or write.

Prime Minister: 'It must be clear that they must be supported by expatriates of [the] Public Service who will have to do the reading and writing.'

Toliman: Asked whether the Prime Minister agreed that Ministerial Members should work side by side with Department officers.

Prime Minister: Said that there should be someone beside him but that the man beside him must not make the final decision.

Olewale: Said that there were cases where experienced Public Servants were reluctant to pass their experience to local officers. If overseas officers were sure they would get jobs in Australia when they were no longer needed in the Territory this attitude might change.

Yuwi: 'Many people do not understand the work of Ministerial Members. I think that if we make further changes now such as giving further powers to Ministerial Members people will not understand it. We should give them a little more extra power but not too much. It would be alright to change the name of the country but we could fall down with rapid change.'

Prime Minister: 'We have been talking about the transference of more power to Ministerial Members. This must begin now. I am not talking about particular duties. I am not talking about self government in 1972 and independence by 1976. But the first step should be taken along the road. You will have to work out the details of this with the Minister.'

Lussick: Said that political education was vital.

Toliman: Said that political pressure is growing every year and we have to strike a balance and the only way of doing this is to give a little responsibility.

Mola: Spoke of the dangers of secession in the New Guinea Islands—Bougainville in particular.

Prime Minister: Said that he could see that the real danger for the future was fragmentation.

Oala: Said that Ministers in Australia were backed by the party machine and decisions such as raising tax did not effect them as members in their own electorate in the same way as independent Ministers in the Territory.

Prime Minister: Agreed that it would be appropriate to look to providing secretarial assistance in the electorate as well as additional assistance in departments.

Abel: Agreed with this approach. The danger is that the Ministerial Members will lose their seats and all that they have learned will be lost.

Prime Minister: Said that it could be that the Westminster System would not be the best for the Territory and you might not want Ministers in the House, but this decision is a very long way ahead.

Arek: Asked whether the Prime Minister thought that training should begin for Territory diplomats.

Prime Minister: Replied that this did not fill him with much excitement. The money for this might be spent on something which might be urgently required. He would sooner see the Australian part of the grant was spent on another school or hospital. The Prime Minister went on to say that what we are talking about is future and quick steps towards transfer of authority to the Administrator in the Administrator's Executive Council and to Ministerial Members leading to a lessening of need to refer matters to Canberra for decision.

Somare: 'We want it guaranteed in the long run that after self government there will be close association with Australia—especially in finance and external affairs.'

Prime Minister: Said that he expected that there would be a continuing need to provide the aid and assistance which Australia now provides but aid must continue to be controlled in bulk by the people who provide it. There is going to be aid but it will in the broad continue to be controlled. As for external affairs and defence I would think they would still be functions of Australia when Papua and New Guinea gets self-government-but this would have to be discussed at the time.

Arek: Asked what the Prime Minister thought the Select Committee would say to the Press.

Prime Minister: Said that he thought that at the present time the less said the better. Perhaps they might say something on the lines of 'We met the Prime Minister to discuss the next step on the road to self-government. We mentioned the need for continued financial aid and the Prime Minister said that this would continue but would have to continue to be controlled in bulk by the Australian Government.'

[NAA: A452, 1970/4962]

20   LETTER FROM BARNES TO GORTON

Canberra, 12 February 1970

In your letter of 2nd February[1] you wrote about Papua and New Guinea's progress towards self-government.

In replying I should say first that the reference in my letter of the 19th January[2] to a possible test of Territory opinion in 1972 about self-government was connected with my belief—at least in relation to the present prevailing opinion in the Territory—that the result of such a test would be a heavy vote against early self-government, and that this would counter some of the criticism of the 'gradual' approach. In the event, so far as last week's talks were concerned, the Territory Select Committee did not want to talk about independence, self-government or target dates, and the matter did not arise.

I agree that self-government is not to be obtained by one step—that the actual formal move to self-government should be the culmination of a series of intermediate steps, and that such intermediate steps should be taken now and in the future.

A step-by-step approach was the sense of the policy laid down by Cabinet in March 1966—'by progressively giving the Territory more financial autonomy as its capacity to contribute to its own revenues increases; ... and to enlarge progressively the measure of self-government'.[3]

In accordance with this policy, in 1968 I introduced in the political field the Ministerial Member system—which is of course a purely transitional arrangement—and in 1969, in the administrative area, I increased the financial delegations to Ministerial Members, the Administrator's Executive Council, and officials. I propose shortly to increase the authority of the present Ministerial Members (by making them responsible for their Departments instead of as at present sharing the responsibility with their Departmental Heads), to increase the authority of the Administrator's Executive Council, and subject to the views of the Council to introduce new procedures which will give elected members a greater participation in the framing of the Territory Budget for the coming financial year and in future years.

These will be definite, though not major, changes. They will not require any amendment to the Papua and New Guinea Act (which was drafted to allow successive increases in authority to be conferred on Ministerial Members by the Minister), and they will be taken within weeks, so that there will be no question of awaiting any Select Committee report.

These changes will be within the present system under which formal authority rests with Australia, but I have also put in hand the examination you suggested of the possibility of enabling Ministerial Members to exercise full authority in defined fields. There may be some problems here—for example, how far definitive authority can be conferred on Ministerial Members without their being finally responsible in a collective sense for decisions on revenue-raising as well as for decisions on spending, and there may be some problems of demarcation. Nevertheless, I expect that conventions or rules of practice could be established which would substantially achieve the objective in specified fields of government without amendment of the Act.

---

1   Document 15

2   Document 11.

3   See Stuart Doran, (ed.), *Documents on Australian Foreign Policy: Australia and Papua New Guinea, 1966–1969*, Australian Department of Foreign Affairs and Trade, Canberra, 2006, Documents 25 & 34 (para. 6).

I shall be glad to prepare for Cabinet the study you propose of the implications of the early achievement of internal self-government, and I have in mind that in due course I will send you the draft submission before I circulate it.

In this connection the steps you have suggested—or others—may be taken short of self-government, but in my view the requirements by way of political, social and economic development for the achievement of responsible self-government on a reasonably effective basis are substantially greater than those for the subsequent move from self-government to independence (whether with or without treaty relationships). Moreover, in this area there can be no back-tracking.

On Australia's attitude to aid to the Territory in the future, we have agreed that it will continue at a substantial level, that prompt steps will be taken towards making Australian supervision general rather than detailed in character and that effective over-sight of aid expenditure will still, of course, need to be maintained after self-government.

As I have said, we have been working on the step-by-step basis, but your letter indicates a definite change of pace—that we should speed up intermediate measures and load as much responsibility as we can upon the Territory itself (i.e. on to Territory politicians), and that we should encourage the idea of early self-government; but I take it that it is not our aim to push the people of the Territory into actual self-government ahead of the time when that status is acceptable to a reasonably broad majority of them. On this basis I quite agree with the line of approach you have set out, provided our public statements of position leave no room or excuses for alarm among expatriates already in the Territory about a precipitate withdrawal by Australia, or for discouragement to prospective investors, and provided we take definite action to shore up the expatriate Public Service of the Territory.

This last part goes back to your proposition that we can decentralise decision-making now if we believe we have a good Administrator and good Ministerial Members. The present Ministerial Members are as good as we are likely to get. You have met some of them. I believe they need strong support at the official level, and this will not be forthcoming from native public service resources for some considerable time. The Administrator too must depend heavily on the men available to him. Keeping good people, or replacing those who leave, is becoming increasingly difficult. A significant change of pace in the devolving of authority to the Territory may affect morale, and cause more resignations, and will increase the pressure and strain on the expatriates in key positions. We will run a serious risk of the machinery of government there not functioning adequately, and indeed of its disintegrating, unless definite action is taken. I have already mentioned this to you and I understand members of the Select Committee spoke about it last week to you as well as to me.

One aspect of the need is that in passing greater authority to the Territory there is a risk as I said to you that the real authority will stay in the hands of expatriate officials and will be exercised by them instead of by elected Ministerial office-holders. I think a Service of the kind I have spoken to you about will make it easier to avoid this because by giving in selected cases a measure of career security with the Commonwealth independent of developments in the Territory it will tend to reduce any interest (conscious or unconscious) some expatriate officials may have in perpetuating their own jobs.

Another aspect is that with greater local responsibility we may find an increasing need to supply small 'task forces' of experts to do a particular job thus relieving the Territory Public Service at points of special pressure. The kind of new Service I contemplate would be well adapted because of its flexibility to providing this kind of help to the Territory as well perhaps as to giving effect to the 'reserve power to interfere' to which you refer.

In my view effective 'shoring-up' action is necessary to accompany the change of pace, and subject to your agreement I will ask the Department of External Territories to talk to Treasury,

Prime Minister's Department, Public Service Board and External Affairs and as a matter of some urgency to prepare a proposal for Cabinet along the lines I have mentioned to you.

[NAA: A1209, 1968/9698]

21   CABINET SUBMISSION 124[1]

Canberra, 16 February 1970

CONFIDENTIAL

Papua New Guinea—Practical Training in Australia of Papuans and New Guineans

This submission seeks approval for a scheme to give Papuans and New Guineans practical on-the-job training and experience in Australia.

2.   Although a wide range of educational and training institutions has been developed within the Territory there is a lack of practical training opportunities for local people in numbers of fields. For some years small numbers of Papuans and New Guineans have been coming to Australia on an ad hoc basis for on-the-job training and experience. Greater numbers of mature people with basic educational and vocational skills are becoming available who would benefit greatly from such training. It is proposed to step up the tempo of this training and accelerate localisation both in the Territory Public Service and in private enterprise by establishing a scheme of practical training in Australia for Papuans and New Guineans.

Objects of Scheme

3.   The objects of the scheme would be twofold: firstly, to provide Papuans and New Guineans with a range of training and experience which would enable them to upgrade the level of their skills and to advance more rapidly to positions of greater complexity and responsibility; secondly, to assist in strengthening links between Papua and New Guinea and Australia. It is in Australia's interest to remain in the context of reference for Papua and New Guinean leaders when they seek assistance in the future; the habit of looking to Australia should be established now in as many fields as possible or else Papuans and New Guineans may later prefer to go elsewhere. Further, by working and living with Australians, Papuans and New Guineans will broaden their outlook, will gain greater knowledge and understanding of Australia and Australians and the experience will greatly increase their confidence, poise and initiative. The opportunity of coming to Australia is prized and will give potential indigenous leaders prestige assisting them in their own society. Conversely, Australians would benefit by gaining greater understanding of Papuans and New Guineans.

Types of Training

4.   Training in Australia would only be given in fields where it was not available in the Territory. The essential characteristic of the type of training envisaged is practical experience in a working situation, accepting actual responsibility, taking practical decisions and generally 'learning by doing'. The scope of activity would range from the skilled trade and technical levels to professional and senior administrative levels. For example there is an immediate need for training of such categories as auto-electricians, refrigerator mechanics, radiographers

---

1   Submitted by Barnes.

and manual arts instructors and middle-ranking businessmen and public servants. It is not proposed that base level training would be given in Australia. The period of training envisaged is from 3–12 months with an average period of perhaps 6 months but this would be subject to the lessons of experience in operation of the scheme.

[*matter omitted*]

10. Australia has a special and close relationship with Papua and New Guinea which it wishes to endure even after self-determination; a scheme run specifically for the people of the Territory will emphasise and support this special relationship. To a considerable extent the type of person coming for training would be different from that for sponsored Asian and African students. So far as cooperation from Australian commerce and industry (and for that matter the State Government) is concerned, there is considered to be a wide measure of interested goodwill towards assisting Papuans and New Guineans, especially in down-to-earth practical learning. Additionally, however, the quite considerable number of firms with direct or indirect interests in the Territory may be expected to exert themselves more actively in providing opportunities for Papuans and New Guineans than for 'learners' from foreign countries. It is considered therefore that the Papua and New Guinea practical training scheme should be established as a new and separate scheme although, as proposed above, a liaison committee would ensure coordination with existing training schemes.

[*matter omitted*]

Recommendation

17. I recommend that subject to the views of the Administrator's Executive Council in the Territory:

(1) a practical training scheme be established to give suitable Papuans and New Guineans opportunities for on-the-job training in Australia where such training opportunities are not available in the Territory (paragraphs 2 and 4);

(2) the scheme be administered by the Department of External Territories (paragraph 7) and the costs of operation be carried by the Commonwealth on that Department's appropriation;

(3) a Papua and New Guinea Centre be established for the purposes of the scheme in close cooperation with a voluntary agency.

[NAA: A5869, VOLUME 6]

22   CABINET DECISION 166

Canberra, 25 February 1970

Submission No. 124: Papua and New Guinea—
Practical Training in Australia of Papuans and New Guineans

The Cabinet approved the principal recommendation that, subject to the views of the Administrator's Executive Council, there be established a practical training scheme to give suitable Papuans and New Guineans opportunities for on-the-job training in Australia where such training opportunities are not available in the Territory.

[*matter omitted*][1]

3.   Under the basic framework as the Cabinet saw it, the Department of External Territories should have responsibility for selecting the trainees and for specifying the types of training to be provided. However, the Cabinet took the view that the Department's responsibility should not go beyond this to the arrangements for the placement of trainees and their actual training, since it was generally felt that there should be reliance on the machinery for this purpose which already exists within the responsibility of the Departments concerned with international training programmes. At the same time, it was conceded that the Department of External Territories should be allowed a right of close touch with the progress of trainees.

4.   The Cabinet asked that the Departments of External Territories, External Affairs, Labour & National Service, Education & Science and the Treasury should, against this background, evolve detailed procedures for the administration of the scheme and report further to Cabinet on them. The Departments were asked to report also on the welfare aspect of administration. The Cabinet did not define any position at this stage on the issue of where departmental responsibility for welfare should lie.

[NAA: A5869, VOLUME 6]

---

1   The omitted material concerned administrative arrangements for the training scheme, with departments instructed to look into them further. Cabinet noted the 'proposal for a Papua and New Guinea Centre' but did not give it 'any particular consideration'. In the event, it appears that the proposed Centre was never established.

23   MINUTE FROM WARWICK SMITH TO KERR

Canberra, 27 February 1970

Among the 'implications' [of self-government] would you please ensure we list a readiness on the part of departments and the Government to change the status quo even in ways which are novel or unfamiliar to take account of the particular problems of Papua and New Guinea on the basis that it is *sui generis* and collating the assorted information to demonstrate this last point, e.g. in no other country outside Australia do you find a War Service Land Settlement Scheme for Australians, in no other country do we provide 6,000 Public Servants, in no other country have we sold to Australians properties expropriated from an enemy country, in no other country does there exist already an Australian citizenship as in Papua and so on and so on and try to get from Cabinet a direction to departments to regard Papua and New Guinea as presenting unique problems which may need to be solved by unique action.[1]

[NAA: A452, 1970/1327]

---

1   For background on DET Secretary Warwick Smith's views about the unique character of Australia's relations with Papua and New Guinea see Stuart Doran, (ed.), *Documents on Australian Foreign Policy: Australia and Papua New Guinea, 1966–1969*, Department of Foreign Affairs and Trade, Canberra, 2006, p. 452.

24   LETTER FROM WHITROD[1] TO WARWICK SMITH

Konedobu,[2] 2 March 1970

Royal Papua and New Guinea Constabulary—Establishment

I have made an examination of the manpower requirement of the Constabulary to maintain public order in the Territory if:

(i)   The existing situation in Rabaul continues for some time;

(ii) A similar situation elsewhere occurs, contemporaneously;

(iii) Severe restrictions are placed on the use of normal riot control techniques, i.e., no tearsmoke, no firearms;

(iv) Intervention by the Armed Services is confined strictly to a 'Last Resort' situation.

2.   As you know the Extended Training Programme, which is now in its initial stages, is not designed to increase the numbers beyond the current establishment. The present establishment was determined some years ago and apparently it made only limited provision for the control of internal disturbances e.g., one mobile unit of 30 men at Koki[3] and one unit at Bomana.[4]

3.   The continued deployment of 500 police on the Gazelle is severely taxing our manpower resources and our accommodation difficulties are great. Nevertheless it is the presence of these police with an available speedy 'back-up' of another 500 men which is a prime factor in peaceably maintaining order.

4.   Recent events in Northern Ireland and in England support the proposition that in the current political climate police must forego their customary advantages of being better equipped and instead rely almost solely on brute physical strength to control mass political or industrial disturbances.

5.   You are aware of our current endeavour to obtain additional police from any over-manned stations and detachments, and by seeking the return of police from prison and fire service duties. However, our total gain from these sources is likely to total less than 200 men, that is the extent of the present deficiency between strength and establishment totals.

6.   During the past week I had an opportunity to discuss briefly with Brigadier [John Gilbert] McKinna, Commissioner of Police, South Australia, the possibility of increasing the Royal Papua and New Guinea Constabulary establishment to meet current and future demands on it.

7.   If the Constabulary is to operate in the conditions set out, my assessment is that it will require a minimum of 1,000 additional police, perhaps 1,500 would not be too many—as quickly as possible.

8.   If approval is given to increase the strength by 1,000 men, finance, recruitment, training, equipping and the provision of offices will present problems. The best solution seems to be to endeavor to double the present recruitment intake of 28 to 56 constables monthly, to double the Cadet Officer intake, and to attempt an early repeat of the Assistant Inspector recruitment programme.

---

1   R. W. Whitrod, PNG Commissioner of Police, 1969–70.

2   Konedobu, a suburb in Port Moresby, was the location of the offices of the Administration and the Administrator's residence.

3   A suburb of Port Moresby.

4   A village near Port Moresby.

9.   The greatest difficulty is likely to be the provision of accommodation. As you know we are already occupying quite inadequate premises at Tomaringa[5] and are likely to do so for a further 18–20 months. When our new buildings are available, we can house 280 men under better conditions. This arrangement will mean a continuous police strength on the Gazelle Peninsula of 500 men.

10.   Another of the problems experienced in the last ten months has been the necessity for and the unavailability of, air transport. Lae is the best Territorial centre for obtaining air charters and is reasonably central for rapid deployment of reserve police to any district. As the Extended Training Programme already provides for strategic reserves of police at Mt. Hagen, Port Moresby, Wewak, and Rabaul, Lae appears as a suitable base.

11.   Because of the scarcity of instructors and suitable Officers, it has not been possible to restrict the selection for the Extended Training Programme to single officers or unmarried NCOs. Accommodation for the extra 1,000 men cannot therefore be confined to single men's barracks and married housing will have to be made available.

12.   The only accommodation of this nature in the Morobe District seems to be Igam Barracks[6]. I understand Police were offered some temporary accommodation there on an earlier occasion and on our not taking it up, it has become occupied by junior staff from a nearby educational institute.

13.   In discussion with the Administrator he stated that he would be sending you his own memorandum on this subject. He expressed concern that the police strength would be increased by 1,000 members while the Pacific Islands Regiment exists comparatively unused. I have, however, pointed out that there are serious constitutional dangers in seeking to use soldiers as police even when they are sworn in as 'specials'. I am also certain that the soldiers would have to remain under the command of their own officers so that it would be to all intents and purposes an Army, not a Police operation. To substitute as police they would necessarily have to be responsible to a civil police officer. This arrangement would not be acceptable to the Army Command.

[NAA: A452, 1970/3761]

---

5   A police barracks in East New Britain.

6   Igam Barracks is located in Lae.

25   SPEECH BY GOVERNOR-GENERAL[1]

Canberra, 3 March 1970

[*matter omitted*]

My Government will take steps to advance Papua and New Guinea further along the road to self-government and eventual independence.

My Government does not believe that an arbitrary date for independence of Papua and New Guinea should be set by it, even against the wishes of the people of the Territory, and it will not do so.

But my Government does believe in constant advancement towards self-government. Consideration of major changes in constitutional arrangements for self-government should await presentation to the Territory House of Assembly of the Report of the Select Committee on Constitutional Development, which is at present inquiring into this matter.

My Government will, however, take early steps to introduce new arrangements within the scope of the present Papua and New Guinea Act.

This will result in Ministerial Members accepting full day-to-day responsibility for their Departments instead of sharing that responsibility as at present with a Departmental Head. The Ministerial Member will be responsible to the Administrator's Executive Council.

The scope of the responsibilities of the Administrator's Executive Council will be enlarged and additional powers will be transferred to that Council, and to Ministerial Members who form a majority of that Council.[2]

The procedures by which the Territory Budget is framed will be changed so that elected Members will have a greater voice in the actual drafting of the Budget.

The Territory of Papua and New Guinea is developing economically and will in the future develop faster.

But the level of local savings in Papua and New Guinea is low and finance for major development projects comes predominantly from outside the Territory.

Because of this the Administration has in the past acquired—for future disposal to the people of the Territory—substantial equity holdings in certain enterprises, notably the Bougainville Copper Project and the New Britain Oil Palm Project.

My Government now proposes to ask the Territory House of Assembly for legislation to establish a statutory corporation to acquire equity in major investment projects in the Territory.

This new institution would have a close link with the Papua and New Guinea Development Bank and its principal functions would be to take up shares in appropriate enterprises and hold them for future disposal to the people of the Territory, to underwrite local share issues, and to establish unit trusts or investment companies.

My Government will, this month, introduce a new scheme for practical, down to earth training of Papuans and New Guineans in Australia, in areas of training not available in the Territory.[3]

---

1   Paul Hasluck, who delivered the speech when opening the Parliament. Before becoming Governor-General in April 1969, Hasluck was Minister for Territories (1951–63), Minister for Defence (1963–64), and Minister for External Affairs (1964–69).

2   From the late 1960s 'ministerial members' and 'assistant ministerial members' drawn from the House of Assembly had shared some authority with heads of department in the PNG Administration.

   For a list of the areas involved see Ian Downs, *The Australian Trusteeship: Papua New Guinea, 1945–75*, Australian Government Publishing Service, Canberra, 1980, p. 418.

3   See Documents 21 & 22.

In doing this my Government will seek the cooperation of private organisations, so that the scheme may be a human and economic success and, through the training provided, help Papuans and New Guineans to accept greater responsibilities in both private and government activity in their own country.

[*CPD*, HR, vol. 66, 3 March 1970, pp. 6–7]

26   STATEMENT BY BARNES[1]

Canberra, 4 March 1970

Papua and New Guinea House of Assembly

In harmony with the Government's approach indicated in the Governor-General's Speech[2] the Government intends to introduce some immediate changes within the provisions of the present Papua and New Guinea Act which will give Ministerial Members drawn from the Papua and New Guinea House of Assembly increased powers both individually in relation to the functions of their departments and collectively as members of the Administrator's Executive Council. During the parliamentary recess there were Ministerial discussions in Canberra with the Territory Select Committee on Constitutional Development, which were helpful to both sides.

Following the recommendations of the Select Committee on Constitutional Development set up by the first House of Assembly the Papua and New Guinea Act was amended in May 1968 to provide for further constitutional development in Papua and New Guinea. The main changes made at that time provided for increased participation by elected members in the executive government of the Territory through a system of Ministerial offices and the replacement of the former Administrator's Council by the Administrator's Executive Council. It was emphasized that these arrangements were essentially transitional in character. It was stated that under section 25 the role and functions of Ministerial Members and Assistant Ministerial Members could be adapted in the light of experience.

The Act sets out that the functions of Ministerial office holders are generally to assist in the administration of the Government of the Territory to the extent and in the manner provided by arrangements approved by the Minister for External Territories under section 25. In 1968 in accordance with the amendments to the Act 7 Ministerial Members and 8 Assistant Ministerial Members were appointed from elected members of the House of Assembly.

These office holders were selected from elected members of the House jointly by the Ministerial Nomination Committee of the House and the Administrator before being nominated to the Minister for appointment. There are Ministerial Members for Agriculture, Stock and Fisheries, Education, Labour, Posts and Telegraphs, Public Health, Public Works, and Trade and Industry. At present Ministerial Members share responsibility with the departmental heads for overall departmental activities and for the framing of policy proposals including proposals for expenditure.

The Government considers that the time has now come to invite Ministerial Members to assume more responsibility in the administration of the government of the Territory. New arrangements have therefore been approved for Ministerial Members under section 25 of the

1   Barnes made the statement to the House of Representatives.
2   Document 25.

Act. I table the approved arrangements.[3] These include also the arrangements applying in respect of Assistant Ministerial Members. Subject to the overall responsibly of the Minister for External Territories, acting through the Administrator, these approved arrangements provide that a Ministerial Member will be fully responsible to the Administrator's Executive Council for the day-to-day running of the department instead of, as at present, acting jointly with the departmental head and sharing the responsibility with him.[4]

As set out in the approved arrangements a Ministerial Member will within the framework of broader Government policy make decisions regarding policy and administration in day to day activities related to the matters for which he is responsible. He will formulate plans and proposals for departmental expenditure including draft departmental estimates. It is the Government's intention that these changes should come into effect in practice at once and without waiting for amendments to Territory Ordinances which will be necessary. The Government looks to officials who may now hold statutory powers by delegation or otherwise to exercise these with the concurrence of the Ministerial Member in the spirit of these arrangements.

Some changes are also being made in relation to the Administrator's Executive Council. Again these changes are within the framework of the existing Papua and New Guinea Act. The Council has been exercising increasing authority over the past 2 years and its scope is now being further enlarged. Under the present arrangements the council advises the Administrator, who is broadly free to accept or disregard the advice. However, the Government has been consulting the Council on a widening range of issues and has increasingly accepted the Council's views. In future the Council's authority will be enhanced in 3 ways: Firstly, it will be consulted on all significant policy issues; secondly, it will advise on the more important departmental questions referred to it by a Ministerial Member; thirdly, it will have a greater voice in the procedures for the framing of the Territory budget, as explained later. May I interpose that I propose to delegate powers which will be advised at a later date.

Apart from these specific matters the Government has been giving and will continue to give increasing weight to the views and advice of the Administrator's Executive Council. The increase in the power and influence of the Council is qualitative in character. It is not to be measured in terms of specific powers, individual acts of administration or areas of policy or increased financial delegations, but it will be apparent by the degree to which the Administrator's Executive Council in future influences the Government's attitude on important issues. An example of this kind of increasing influence is the recent reference to the Council by the Minister of the question whether the Papuan Medical College should become part of the University of Papua and New Guinea. This is a matter related to the responsibilities of the Ministerial Member for Health. The Council concluded that it was highly desirable for the Medical College to become part of the University provided arrangements could be made for Government controls to be maintained over costs and the broad direction of the medical course. Such a formula would meet the difficulties previously seen by the Government and the Government has said it accepts the Council's conclusion so that if the University agrees to the Council's recommendations they will be put into effect.

Having regard to the changes I have mentioned, regulations will be made under the Act to govern some procedural matters including the recording of Council decisions and their transmission to the Commonwealth Government. There will also be changes in the procedures by which the Territory budget is framed so that elected members of the House of Assembly

3   Not published.

4   See Documents 15 & 25.

will have a greater say in the budget. The Administrator's Executive Council will be invited to establish immediately an Estimates Sub-committee. Officials of the Territory Treasury will keep the Sub-committee closely in touch with plans and progress in respect of the forthcoming financial year's estimates. The Sub-committee will be invited to discuss the draft estimates with the Minister for External Territories before these are finalized. After those discussions no important alterations will be made in the draft estimates without the knowledge of the Estimates Sub-committee and without their having a full opportunity to comment. Throughout the period during which the budget is being framed it is expected that the Estimates Sub-committee of the Council will keep in touch with the existing Budget Committee of the House of Assembly, a body made up wholly of elected members, with a view to informing themselves of any points which members of the House may wish to have considered in the draft estimates for the following year.

Self-government will not be forced on the people against their wishes. Nevertheless the Government considers steps should be taken now so that the elected representatives of the people take on additional responsibilities in the government of the Territory. The Government is satisfied that the changes now proposed accord with the climate of opinion of the House of Assembly and of the Territory generally. The changes I have outlined reflect the Government's approach of progressively transferring responsibility to elected members of the Territory House of Assembly. The new arrangements are a definite and material step along the road to self government.

Further constitutional changes to be put into effect later this year are now under examination. None of the changes I have outlined requires amendment to the Papua and New Guinea Act. Important or major changes in the constitutional arrangements for Papua and New Guinea of the sort that might be expected to require substantial amendment to the Act should in the Government's view await consideration by the Territory House of Assembly of the report of the Select Committee on Constitutional Development so that such substantial amendment of the Act would be decided upon in the light of the views of the Territory people.

[*matter omitted*]

[*CPD*, HR, vol. 66, 4 March 1970, pp. 47–49]

27   LETTER FROM HAY TO WARWICK SMITH

Port Moresby, 16 March 1970

CONFIDENTIAL

The Commissioner of Police has shown me a note on which he is basing a submission to you advising that if certain assumptions which you have suggested to him are accepted, he will require an additional 1,000 police in order to guarantee the maintenance of law and order.[1]

I am not aware that one of the assumptions, namely that which places 'severe restrictions on the use of normal riot control techniques' is a matter of government policy. I would like to be advised whether it is. In the meantime, I am assuming that it is not.

The arguments which the Police Commissioner makes in his note for an additional 1,000 men over a three year period are persuasive. However, the consequences in terms of finance, accommodation and sufficiency of officers are such that they ought to be analysed and assessed

---

1   Document 24.

in detail before a decision is taken. To have a large but discontented or ill-disciplined or ill-led police force is worse than having a small, efficient and well-disciplined force. Furthermore, the diversion of resources to recruit, train, house and maintain an additional 1,000 police must have implications for the Development Programme.

The first purpose of this letter, therefore, is to suggest that the full financial, administrative and economic implications of recruiting an additional 1,000 police be examined by experts in the immediate future.

The second purpose of this letter is to request a re-examination of the possible use of the Army in some way or another. It is, from a total government point of view, absurd that an armed force of 3,000 men, highly-trained, well-disciplined and well-led, is being maintained in the Territory and is not available for use for law and order purposes. If there are reasons of Government policy which prevent the Army being used in an aid-to-the-civil-power role, then those reasons ought to be re-examined. If the reasons still hold good, then we ought to examine whether, in the light of the extra effort required to produce an enlarged police force, the Government can afford to maintain an Army of the present size. If the answer is still affirmative, then we ought to proceed to examine ways of using trained soldiers in a police role which would avoid objections raised under present policies. The Police Commissioner has suggested, for instance, that Rifle Companies of the PIR[2] might take over the normal patrol duties which police constables perform on behalf of DDA[3] in a number of outlying districts. This would permit a considerable reduction in police constables posted to rural patrol posts. These constables could be withdrawn to a central point for training and be held there as additional strength for emergency purposes.

Another alternative which I believe should be looked into is for the nomination of one or more rifle companies in each battalion of the PIR to be trained for special police duties and to be made actual reserve constables. In these circumstances, these companies could be used in a police role rather than an Army role, with police weapons rather than army weapons, and under Army officers who are also reserve policemen. This would require special training but the Army would have facilities for this in cooperation with the police.

Either of these alternatives would involve a much more rational use of government manpower and resources. I strongly recommend that the Minister consider such alternatives with a view to asking the government to reconsider.

I have discussed this letter with the Police Commissioner. I should be glad if you would place it before the Minister.

[NAA: A452, 1970/3761]

2   Pacific Islands Regiment.
3   Department of District Administration.

28   LETTER FROM BARNES TO HAY

Canberra, 19 March 1970

You will recall that you, the Secretary, the Public Service Commissioner and I discussed the need for a separate Department of Local Government on 15th October, 1968. The record of that meeting reads:

> 'It is expected that within the next few years there would be a separate Department of Local Government: an announcement may be made soon to this effect, but no establishment action would be taken for some time.'

No such announcement was then made, nor did official members adopt this line when subsequently a separate Department was pressed in the House of Assembly.

I understand, however, that it was in the context of moves in the House of Assembly that the matter was again discussed between you and the Secretary in November 1969. At that stage the Secretary said that a separate office of local government in the Department of the Administrator would be supported by the Department, but I have seen no recommendation to implement this.

The Government's policy in relation to increased powers of Ministerial Members now, however, introduces an important new consideration. The Government's policy expressly stated by both the Prime Minister and myself in the dispute over the Gazelle Local Government Council is that it seeks a form of local government which the people in the Council area want. In my opinion it now becomes essential for a switch round to be made of the functions of Ministerial Members so that one takes full responsibility for local government. It would be inconsistent with the Government's approach of conferring authority in local matters on the elected representatives of Territory people for this matter to remain under the control of an official Departmental Head.

For this reason I have concluded that the time has now come to separate the local government function from the Department of the Administrator and to establish a quite separate Department. I am asking the Secretary of the Department of External Territories to inform the Chairman of the Public Service Board of my views and to instruct him to discuss with you the early implementation of my decision.

While policy cannot be determined by the Opposition the comments made in debates in Parliament do indicate the need to separate the local government advisers from the representatives of the Administration in the field. Whether or not Council advisers do in fact intervene in Council matters in the way that has been alleged by the Opposition it is necessary to ensure that the Administration organisation does not of itself lend support to these allegations as I think it does at present.

It is likely to be necessary for me to mention this decision in the course of the debates in Parliament but I should be happy to let you make the announcement locally in the Territory if you think this would be helpful.

[NAA: A452, 1970/1867]

29   LETTER FROM BARNES TO HAY

Canberra, 20 March 1970

The changes in the form of administration announced in the Governor-General's Speech and by me in a statement in Parliament[1] are of course the precursor of other changes designed to increase the authority of elected members of the House of Assembly.

Perhaps no aspect of these changes is more important than their explanation to, and implementation by, senior expatriate officials. As you know I was most concerned by the misunderstanding of the Government's intention which was shown when official members of the House of Assembly were issued with motor vehicles carrying MM number plates.[2] No similar misunderstanding can now be allowed to occur.

I must therefore ask you to make it clear that the changes which have been announced and changes which may be anticipated in the future are in no sense designed to transfer increased authority to expatriate officials in Port Moresby. Under the new arrangements the Government would expect to be able to adopt the views of the elected members in areas which are now the responsibility of Ministerial Members on the basis that the decision has been taken by the elected member concerned. It is of course to be hoped that the elected member would act in accordance with the advice of his departmental head; and to this extent the actual influence of the departmental head is increased. No such change, however, applies to departmental heads of Departments which have no Ministerial Members who remain responsible to the Government through you in the same way as before.

I should be glad if you would ensure that the substance of this letter is passed to all departmental heads and District Commissioners.

[NAA: A452, 1970/1867]

1   Documents 25 & 26 (respectively).

2   'MM' referred to 'Ministerial Member'. For details on the role of ministerial members, see Document 25, fn. 2. In addition to its 84 elected members, the 1968 House of Assembly included ten appointed 'official members' whose role it was to explain and support government policy. It appears that at an earlier stage they had been wrongly provided with vehicles carrying MM number plates.

30   PRESS RELEASE

Canberra, 25 March 1970

Bougainville Situation

The Minister for External Territories, Mr Barnes, today completed a five-day visit to Bougainville.

Mr Barnes said today that his main impression of his visit had been the industry and prosperity now evident on the Island.

He had visited Rorovana village, the centre of a land dispute last year, and learned from the people that they were now happy both with their compensation and with their relations with the mining company; some of their menfolk were working for Bougainville Copper Pty Ltd.

All over the Island people were beginning to appreciate benefits to the whole community through new roads, schools, hospitals and business opportunity.

Bougainville Copper Pty Ltd had achieved a high degree of social integration at Panguna and was employing international experts to give advice on a number of matters including safety requirements and future agricultural development.

The Company had offered 7,000 shares in the operation as part of compensation to local landholders and more shares could be offered.

Mr Barnes said that during his visit he had discussed the problems of the people extensively at meetings with Local Government Councillors, members of cooperatives, landowners, missionaries, school children and local Administration staff.

There was concern in the Kieta area[1] and to a lesser extent in the southern part of the Island about possible domination of Bougainville by the rest of Papua and New Guinea after independence.

In the other parts of the Island, notably in the Buka area, people had expressed their opposition to an unofficial referendum which was being conducted to seek the views of the people of the Island on the possibility of secession.

Mr Barnes said that when discussing the possibility of secession he had stressed the advantages of national unity to the people of Bougainville as well as to the people of the Territory as a whole.

Mr Barnes said that the Roman Catholic Bishop of Bougainville, Bishop L. Lemay, had told him that mission teachers in Bougainville were concerned about the unified education system proposed in the House of Assembly.

This seemed to have resulted from a misunderstanding of the new arrangements which he understood were acceptable to missions elsewhere.

The unified system would provide greater Government support for mission schools electing to join the system. At the same time the identity of mission schools and their right to religious teaching would be safeguarded.

Mr Barnes said he had asked the Administration of Papua and New Guinea to send officials from Port Moresby to explain the proposed system to mission teachers and the people of Bougainville.

[NAA: A452, 1970/1335]

---

1   Kieta is located on the south-east coast of Bougainville.

31   LETTER FROM WHITELAW TO GUTMAN

Canberra, 2 April 1970

CONFIDENTIAL

Assistance to Papua and New Guinea

For a variety of reasons we feel that the time may have arrived when it would be desirable to move away from the present practice of making a global cash grant to the Territory each year to help the Administration to finance its annual budget.

2.   What we have in mind is that, beginning next financial year, if possible, we might break-down the total financial assistance we provide to the Territory each year into a number of different categories or separate items.

3.   At this stage we have no firm views as to what these categories or items might be but our preliminary thinking runs along the following lines:

(a) A base grant, fixed in money terms for a number of years ahead, towards the annual Territory budget.

(b) A general subvention, which would vary over time as circumstances change, to cover the *difference* between the total emoluments (e.g. salary plus all relevant allowances) paid to expatriates and indigenes employed by the Administration.

(c) Additional capital for the Papua and New Guinea Development Bank.

(d) Initial capital for the proposed equity investment corporation (we might need to come to some arrangement with the Administration regarding the provision of additional capital for this institution in later years).

(e) Contribution towards agreed *infrastructure projects* in the Territory public works programme in certain specific fields such as education, transportation, power and telecommunications, but *not* housing.

(f) Matching Assistance (for transfer by the Administration on some pre-determined basis) to local government councils for agreed capital works and development projects at the district level.

4.   I would emphasise that the above are tentative suggestions only and that we are not wedded to them in any way, especially (f). In this regard, there may also be something to be said for the idea that any assistance which we provide to Papua and New Guinea in future for institutions or projects of a self-financing nature under categories (c), (d) and (e) should take the form of a loan rather than a grant. This possibility might also be explored.

5.   It may be that your own Department and/or the Administration itself could suggest some other categories of expenditure which might prove suitable for the Commonwealth Government to finance on some agreed basis with the Administration in future.

6.   The actual amounts to be provided for each category could, of course, only be determined when we come to look at the overall picture for next year at Budget time.

7.   In this regard we need to bear in mind that we shall be called upon to make separate provision in 1970–71 for further payments against the repayable advance to the Administration for construction of the Arawa township.[1] In all probability, we shall also have to provide for

---

1   The Administration had undertaken to build a township at Arawa in south-eastern Bougainville to support the Bougainville mining project.

an advance of $12.5 million to the Administration to enable it to meet the second instalment of its equity subscription to the Bougainville copper project.

8.   I should be grateful for your comments on the basic idea outlined in this memorandum and, assuming you do not disagree, would welcome any suggestions you may care to offer as to how it might best be implemented, having regard to the need to ensure that any changes we might wish to introduce next year do not mislead people in Australia and in the Territory as to our future intentions regarding aid to Papua and New Guinea and arouse suspicions which lead to political difficulties.

[NAA: A452, 1970/1645]

32   MINUTE FROM GUTMAN TO BESLEY

Canberra, 3 April 1970

CONFIDENTIAL

The attached classified letter[1] was delivered to me but its subject seems to fall principally within the province of the Finance Branch. No doubt Economic Division will have an opportunity to comment on a draft reply to Treasury. Meanwhile by way of a first up reaction to the Treasury proposal you may find the following comments helpful:

(a) The proposal appears to be much along the lines of our own thinking here. Its principal merit is that it puts the grant on a functional or project basis in the broad sense of the term.

(b) This has the advantage that the grant determined on that basis becomes more useful as an instrument of achieving definite objectives of (Australian) government policy in the Territory irrespective of the extent of Australian administrative control over Territory government.

(c) These arrangements would give incentive towards relating Territory budgets clearly to the achievement of stated objectives and to the carrying out of specific projects. This would make for clearer definition of policy issues as well as stimulate the development of better budgetary procedures in the direction of performance budgeting and project budgeting.

(d) I would like to think further about the specific categories of grants set out by Treasury. I specifically have some doubts about (c) and (f) and think the whole question of categories needs to be reviewed closely in the context of our long term policies in the Territory. (I will ask Economic Policy and Research Branch to provide some comments on this aspect.) I think there should be some machinery in the grant mechanism which provides strong incentive towards early and substantial increases in Territory revenue through the adoption of additional revenue measures. I am not sure that straight matching grants are the best way of achieving it. They certainly have the obvious drawback that aid increases with the availability of local revenue whereas from another point of view one would argue that aid should decrease as local revenues go up. This matter certainly needs further consideration.[2]

[NAA: A452, 1970/1645]

---

1   Document 31.

2   Besley noted 'yes' against all four of the points made by Gutman.

33   CABINET SUBMISSION 213[1]

Canberra, 3 April 1970

CONFIDENTIAL

Papua and New Guinea Administration—Revised Estimates 1969/70

The purpose of this Submission is to seek Cabinet endorsement of the arrangements which have been agreed between the Treasurer[2] and myself:

(a) To provide a supplementary grant of $1 million to the Administration as additional capital for the Papua and New Guinea Development Bank;

(b) To create a 'Papua and New Guinea Trust Account' for budget equalization purposes; and

(c) To pay $3 million into this Trust Account this year to cover an estimated deficiency of roughly that amount in the Territory's budget for 1969–70.

Papua and New Guinea Development Bank

2.   Decision No. 1159(M) of 24 July 1969 concerning the grant to Papua and New Guinea in 1969–70 stated that:

'The Ministry agreed that it would be desirable to restate publicly, as was done last year and the year before, that if the Papua and New Guinea Development Bank needed more funds in 1969–70, the Government would consider assisting the Administration to make an additional contribution towards the Bank's capital.'[3]

3.   In its second year of operation (1968–69), the Bank approved loans amounting to $5.5 million and this rate of new approvals has continued in the current financial year. On the basis of the above indication that additional capital would be forthcoming, if required, the Bank has entered into lending commitments which it is estimated will involve it in payments totalling roughly $6 million in 1969–70. Many of the advances in respect of which payments will be required this year were in fact approved before 30 June 1969. To meet these commitments, the Bank estimates that it will require an additional $1.5 million this year.

4.   Bearing in mind the other demands which Papua and New Guinea is making upon the Budget at the present time, the Treasurer and I have agreed that the Bank should seek to develop other sources of financing for its lending activities in future, as is provided for in its Charter (*viz.* borrowings, both internally and overseas, and the acceptance of deposits) instead of continuing to rely solely on periodic infusions of interest-free capital from the Commonwealth Government via the Administration's budget.

5.   Accordingly, it is proposed to supplement the Bank's capital by only $1 million at the present time. The Bank will be expected to borrow such additional funds as it may require to tide it over this year, if need be obtaining funds on a temporary basis from the Reserve Bank until regular borrowing arrangements can be instituted for the future. We have reason to believe that the Reserve Bank will agree to help out in this way.

6.   Ministers may be interested to know that the Bank is doing everything it can to promote loans to indigenes. Lending to expatriate borrowers absorbs much the greater part of total Bank

---

1   Submitted by Barnes.

2   Leslie Harry Ernest (Les) Bury, Treasurer, 1969–71.

3   See Decision 1159(M), 'Grant for Papua and New Guinea Administration in 1969/1970', 24 July 1969, NAA: A5868, 655.

loans and this is helping to sustain the recent fairly rapid rate of development of the Territory economy. Loans to indigenes are however growing at a more rapid rate both in numbers and by amount. Apart from loans to indigenes for land settlement purposes, which currently amount to more than $1m., loans to indigenes for sundry other purposes have increased from 125 for a total of $123,000 in 1967/68 to 299 for a total of $411,000 in the six months ended 31st December, 1969. This trend is expected to continue in future.

Territory Budget Position 1969–70

7. The Administration's revised estimates for this year disclose the possibility that total expenditure will exceed total receipts by up to $3 million, assuming that the aforementioned grant of $1 million additional capital for the Papua and New Guinea Development Bank is provided by the Commonwealth Government. Details are set out in Appendix A.

8. Revenues are expected to exceed the Budget estimate by $4.1 million but this will be largely offset by a likely shortfall of $3.5 million in loan raisings.

9. Some of the additional expenditures in prospect, which total $7.9 million in all, will be financed by drawing $2 million of the repayable advance which the Commonwealth Government recently approved for the construction of the Arawa township (Cabinet Decision No. 126 of 11 February 1970)[4] and by increased drawings of $700,000 against existing IDA[5] credits. The additional capital of $1 million to be provided to the Development Bank is, of course, to be financed separately.

10. Other unavoidable expenditures for which additional finance will be required this year amount to a net $4.2 million and include:

	$ million
(a) Costs involved in applying recent Australian arbitration awards and other salary increases to overseas officers	2.6
(b) Emergency expenditures in connection with the influenza epidemic and the Rabaul, Kieta and border situations.	.8
(c) Restoration of Port Moresby store damaged by fire.	.5
(d) Purchase of additional land on Bougainville Island (apart from $1.4 million provided for this purpose in the Budget estimates).	.6

11. The Administrator's Executive Council, with whom this matter was discussed, did not deem it desirable to introduce any new taxation measures during the course of this financial year to meet these increased expenditures, although they have accepted the need for some steps of this kind to be taken when the Territory budget for 1970–71 is drawn up.

Creation of Trust Account

12. Not surprisingly, the Administration experiences some difficulty in accurately estimating receipts and expenditures for the year ahead in such a rapidly changing environment as now exists in the Territory.

13. The Treasurer and I both feel that it would be desirable if some permanent machinery were to be established which would enable the Administration to cope with these uncertainties

---

4   The PNG public service had three divisions. The 'First Division', which numbered around 20, consisted of the most senior officers. The 'Second Division' comprised senior and mid-range officers, while the 'Third Division' comprised officers engaged in support and menial tasks. See Document 39.

5   International Development Association.

and enable it to finance marginal deficits which arise from time to time and also give the Administration some incentive to achieve surpluses in years when for one reason or another these become possible.

14.   We have therefore agreed to the establishment of a 'Papua and New Guinea Trust Account' within the Commonwealth Public Account to be used solely for budget equalization purposes. This Trust Account would be nominally under the control of the Minister for External Territories.

15.   Provided the Treasurer and I are satisfied that the Administration cannot reasonably avoid a deficit in the Territory budget in any year, it would be permitted to finance that deficit by drawing on the balance in the Papua and New Guinea Trust Account *on the understanding that, in formulating its budget for the ensuing year, the Administration would restore the balance in the Trust Account* (at least to its initial level on establishment).

16.   On the other hand, should the Administration achieve a surplus in any year, over and above any amount which it may have been required to pay into the Trust Account to restore its balance, that surplus could also be credited to the Trust Account and be available for use in the following year without prejudice to any other arrangements that might be made regarding the provision of further financial assistance to the Administration.

17.   With these objectives in mind and having regard to the likely budgetary position of the Administration in the current financial year, it is proposed to endow the proposed Papua and New Guinea Trust Account with an initial balance of $3 million, this sum to be provided by way of an appropriation from Consolidated Revenue Fund. Provision for such a payment is being made in Additional Estimates this year. The Administration will then be permitted to draw on the balance in this Trust Account to finance its estimated budget deficit in 1969–70 on the understanding that provision will be made in the Territory budget for next year to recoup whatever amount is so used.

RECOMMENDATION

18.   It is recommended that Ministers endorse the arrangements described above.

[NAA: A5869, VOLUME 12]

34   PRESS RELEASE

Port Moresby, 4 April 1970

Police Attacked Near Rabaul

A large group of New Guineans attacked a police detachment near Rabaul last night, injuring nine policemen including two officers.

The Acting Police Commissioner, Mr B. Holloway, said today it was believed the New Guineans had been drinking. He stressed that the incident was not related to the Mataungan Association.[1]

'One of the Mataungan Association's leaders, Mr Daniel Rumet, called at the Rabaul police station early today to say that none of the members of the association were involved in the incident,' he said.

Mr Holloway said about 2 am. today a truck carrying policemen, who had been on routine duty in Rabaul, broke down as it was passing through Malaguna village on its way back to the Tomaringa police camp.

Inspector J. O. Power, and Sub-Inspector J. Ramm, who were in charge of the detachment, and who were following the truck, also stopped.

Most of the policemen were sitting on the side of the road while the officers were attending to the vehicle when a large group of New Guineans attacked them.

The police, who were outnumbered, discharged one teargas grenade in order to get away from the scene.

Mr Holloway said the policemen had been armed with batons, shields, and teargas, but did not carry firearms.

Police succeeded in arresting two men, one of whom jumped from the police vehicle as it moved off.

[NAA: A1838, 936/4/16 PART 3]

---

1   Set up in June 1969 shortly after the elections for the first multi-racial council in the Gazelle Peninsula, the Mataungan Association (MA) had strong support within the Tolai community. It campaigned militantly (and at times violently) for extensive Tolai control over the local area.

35   CABINET DECISION 282

Canberra, 24 April 1970

CONFIDENTIAL

Papua and New Guinea Administration—Revised Estimates 1969/70[1]

The Cabinet endorsed the recommendation of the Treasurer that additional appropriations totalling $124,140,000 be sought for expenditure not approved by the Appropriation Act (No. 1) 1969/70 and the Appropriation Act (No. 2) 1969/70.

2.   This endorsement by the Cabinet carries with it endorsement of Submission No. 213 concerning revised estimates for the Administration of Papua and New Guinea.

[NAA: A5869, VOLUME 12]

36   LETTER FROM BARNES TO GORTON

Canberra, 24 April 1970

I have agreed to open the Annual Congress of the Public Service Association of Papua and New Guinea in Port Moresby on 2nd May next. When Sir Paul Hasluck opened the Congress in 1962 certain assurances were given. These were cleared with the Prime Minister at the time and were given with the authorisation of the Government.

In my opening address I want to try to damp down some of the disquiet now evident in the Territory on the future of overseas staff by analysing the assurances previously given and re-stating them.

I also propose to say the Government is looking into the practicability of some additional arrangements to help meet the needs of the Public Service of the Territory by providing a backing of permanence under the Commonwealth in one form or another for selected experienced personnel now serving in Papua and New Guinea or appointed to serve there in the future.

I think it is important for me to be able to speak about these two critical aspects of the speech with the authority of the Government and I would be grateful if you could clear the […] attached draft paragraphs.[1]

[*matter omitted*]

[NAA: A452, 1970/2031]

---

1   See Document 33.

---

1   Not published. For the full text of Barnes' statement, see Document 38.

37   PRESS RELEASE

Port Moresby, 30 April 1970

Localisation of the Public Service

The Chairman of the Public Service Board, Mr G. Unkles, today commented on the recent statement of the Public Service Association concerning the expression of views to the Select Committee on Constitutional Development.

The statement said that the Association would advise the Committee that, among other things, local officers 'see an indefinite continuance of inadequate efforts to localise the service'. Mr Unkles said he regretted such an irresponsible intention, first because local officers are far from feeling that way, and second because such a view is very far from the facts.

Much has been done in recent years towards localising the service, but the acceleration during the past twelve months has convinced local officers, and others, that a determined and scientific programme is well under way. Although much groundwork had been done, real and obvious results have been seen in the time since the Public Service Board and its Localisation Section came into being.

The Board itself showed the beginnings. Mr Sere Pitoi and Mr Paulus Matane were appointed as Board Members. Both later acted as Departmental Heads and, in the continuing absence on special duty of Mr Grieve, Mr Matane is still directing the Department of Lands, Surveys & Mines. Both of these gentlemen have demonstrated that local officers' abilities are now properly recognised, as have Mr Alkan To Lolo, acting Member of the Board during Mr Matane's absence, and Mr Gabriel Gris, who acted as a Board Member while Mr Pitoi acted as Director of Posts & Telegraphs.

The total picture is very much in line with these beginnings. Between April 1969 and March 1970, local staff increased by more than 1600 while overseas staff increased by less than 350. At 30th June 1969, there were 188 local officers at levels above that of Clerk Class 4. In the relatively short time since then, the number has risen to 233 officers substantively occupying such positions, and there are provisional promotions beyond that number. Provisional promotions for the period 1.7.67 to 30.6.68 stood in the ratio of only 21% for local officers to 79% for overseas officers. For the comparable period July, 1968 to June, 1969 this ratio changed to 30% for local officers and 61% for overseas officers. For the short period since the Board's localisation operations have gained in intensity, say since its Localisation Section began work in November–December, 1969, the ratio has changed still further—47.5% of provisional promotions in 1970 being in respect of local officers as against 52.5% in respect of overseas officers. The actual figures were 172 local officers and 190 overseas.

These figures demonstrate a quite spectacular change. There is a clear and definite acceleration in genuine localisation, dating essentially from the appointment of the Board. This acceleration is only [the] beginning of a scientific localisation programme, but it is quite clear at the same time that it is not being achieved at the expense of advancement of efficient overseas officers.

The essential in accelerated localisation is training. At 31st March 1969, there were 1570 local people in pre-service training, engaged under the Public Service Ordinance. Twelve months later, the figure is 2060, an increase of nearly 500. In addition, in various institutions there are nearly 1400 more local people being trained for Administration service.

At the Public Service Training Centre now, there are nearly 90 more officers receiving specialised training than at this time last year. In addition, the Centre is about to commence an advanced management course for senior local officers.

This year there are 60 cadets in the Public Service. They are officers of the service, receiving full pay, while they study professional courses at IOT[1] and UPNG.[2] On graduation they will be advanced automatically to the appropriate professional classification. They will become architects, engineers, surveyors, lawyers and so on. Next year, the number of cadetships offered is expected to be increased substantially.

Other kinds of training are also under way. Against the time when officers skilled in diplomatic affairs will be needed, two local officers are at this moment ending a specialised course in Canberra, provided by the Department of External Affairs.

Local officers are also broadening their experience by attachment to Commonwealth and State Departments in Australia not as observers only, but actually performing appropriate duties. Five officers have already commenced short term attachments, and ten more are expected to go before the end of June. It is planned that 60 officers will go next financial year.

These facts, Mr Unkles said, give only a brief indication of what has been achieved and what is being done in accelerating localisation. These things in fact, although already impressive, are the results of a year's work and are only the beginning. Local officers are most unlikely to regard them as 'a continuance of inadequate efforts'.

[NAA: A452, 1970/2031]

---

1   The Institute of Technology.

2   The University of Papua and New Guinea (later the University of Papua New Guinea).

38   SPEECH BY BARNES[1]

Port Moresby, 2 May 1970

I am particularly pleased to have the opportunity of speaking to you today and to open your 1970 Congress, because the Government sets great store on the qualities and work of the Public Service.

Public servants have a great responsibility to provide an efficient machinery of administration and one that will adjust smoothly and effectively to whatever constitutional or economic or social changes may take place. You who live and work in this changing Territory scene will appreciate just how important this is.

[*matter omitted*][2]

The Papua and New Guinea Public Service is served by men from all areas who are working towards one end—the effective administration of this country and the service of all the people of the country. Because of this, no other single institution can do so much to promote the sense of nationhood and help towards real national unity. Also, in many ways, the Public Service here in Papua and New Guinea compared with what happens in a more developed country, has a greater opportunity and a greater responsibility.

[*matter omitted*][3]

When Sir Paul Hasluck opened the Association's Congress in 1962, he gave assurances to overseas officers about their future on behalf of the Australian Government. Similarly, when I speak to you today about the future of those officers, I do so on behalf of the Australian Government.

Among the changes since 1962 which are of interest to overseas officers are the amendments have been made to the Papua and New Guinea Act to guarantee rights under the Employment Security Scheme, the Superannuation Scheme and the Retirements Benefits Scheme.

There have also been far reaching developments in the political affairs of this country. In connection with these political changes, the Employment Security Scheme is a very important element in the structure of conditions for permanent overseas officers. In particular, it is designed specifically to reassure those officers about their future so that they may rely—under circumstances that are clearly set out—on being provided with comparable alternative employment or, if this were not possible, reasonable cash compensation.

[*matter omitted*]

The assurances I now give and the guarantees now enjoyed mean that overseas officers serve within the following framework of security:

> (a) all overseas officers are assured it is the Australian Government's intention that the help of Australians should continue to be available in the administration of the government of Papua and New Guinea under conditions which (apart from decisions under Public Service arbitration procedures) are determined by or acceptable to the Australian Government for as long as such help is needed and desired;

1   Barnes delivered the speech to the PNG Public Service Association Congress. External Territories arranged for the printing of 20,000 copies for distribution to all members of the public service in Papua and New Guinea. Note, Sutherland to Warwick Smith, 16 June 1970, NAA: A452, 1970/2031.

2   The omitted material included comments on the roles and responsibilities of public servants.

3   The omitted material reviewed recent developments in the PNG public service, including an increase in numbers, the establishment of a public service board, with two PNG members, in April 1969, the commencement in 1969 of a cadetship for PNG officers, and the introduction in July 1969 of 'equal pay for local women officers'.

(b) permanent overseas officers continuing to serve in the Territory Public Service are assured that the Australian Government will retain effective control of their remuneration and conditions of service subject only to Public Service arbitration processes; and if, for example, at any time before the Territory becomes self-governing the Australian Government determines it can no longer give effect to its assurance that the terms and conditions of their employment will not be altered (otherwise than as a result of Public Service arbitration processes) without its agreement, the Employment Security Scheme applies;

[*matter omitted*]

The Government is not indifferent to the problems confronting overseas officers serving in the Territory or the problems that may face their families. Nor is the Government indifferent to the variety of causes which lead to resignations of permanent overseas officers. Some of these causes are not related to conditions of service.

On the other hand the Government also wishes to maintain the strength of experience that the overseas element in the Territory Public Service can provide. I have already re-stated an assurance of the Government's intention that the help of Australians should continue to be available as long as it is needed and desired. Confidence in the intentions of the Australian Government in this respect will be increasingly important as further intermediate steps are taken towards self-government.

To encourage permanent overseas officers to stay on, suggestions were made earlier to the Government that all permanent overseas officers in the Territory Public Service should be granted permanent status in the Commonwealth Public Service. This course of action was considered in 1965 when the Employment Security Scheme was being worked out. Because of a range of practical difficulties, it was not adopted. To extend the idea now to the appointment of substantial numbers of serving contact officers in order to encourage them as well as permanent overseas officers to stay on for longer periods of service in the Territory would add to these difficulties.

Nevertheless, in recent representations there has been emphasis on the loss of Territory experience when middle ranking and senior overseas officers leave and it has been claimed that the Commonwealth should do more towards meeting the Territory's requirements by providing in some way a greater career security for experienced permanent officers and for experienced contract officers.

The suggestion has been that some status under the Commonwealth is required. Such a Commonwealth status would not be affected by political change in Papua and New Guinea. What is envisaged in this line of approach is a Commonwealth backing for the careers of experienced personnel serving now or who may come to the Territory in the future so that their knowledge and skills and accumulating experience in the Territory will continue to be available to meet the Territory's needs.

The Government is examining the possibility of providing such a backing. Any scheme to give such a backing would be over and above the existing arrangements such as the permanent overseas public service, or the present system of contract engagements, or of secondments from the Commonwealth or States. These would continue to operate and would do so within the present framework of security that I have outlined. Any new scheme, however, might embrace some people from present permanent overseas officers, some from present contract officers, some new appointees. It would not absorb all serving permanent overseas officers or all serving contract officers. The emphasis in any such new arrangements would be on key administrative, professional or technical people.

What is being studied is the possibility of arrangements that would in appropriate cases provide a basic permanence of employment under the Commonwealth. It would be within the

Commonwealth system, though not necessarily within the Commonwealth Public Service. It could possibly also provide medium-term or short-term employment under the Commonwealth for service in Papua and New Guinea.

If practicable proposals of this kind can be developed, the Administrator's Executive Council will be consulted in the course of their development.

The Association will be given the opportunity to comment on them before decisions are taken.

I give no assurance that any such scheme will be found practicable or will be introduced, but the possibility is being investigated.

I might mention one other matter. Your Association has made representations about the superannuation scheme for permanent overseas officers. This has also been raised in the House of Assembly. In view of recent changes in the money market particularly in relation to interest rates I have asked the Superannuation Board to re-examine its recommendations to me following their third quinquennial review.

I turn now to localisation.

The Public Board Service Ordinance makes it clear that the Board is responsible for adequate arrangements for the training of local officers and for their advancement to offices at all levels of the Public Service. Each Department of the Administration has an important role to play. Localisation is being pushed forward subject only to the needs of efficiency and availability of qualified officers [...]

There are now 1200 local officers in the Second Division.[4] Five years ago there were only 140. Progress has been made but a major task still lies ahead. Some areas and some departments of the Public Service have made more progress than others.

Over recent months four local officers have occupied positions at the highest level. They have amply demonstrated their capacity to undertake these responsibilities.

There are, of course, problems that have to be overcome. Some local officers say they are diffident about accepting higher responsibility. Some appear to feel embarrassment about giving instructions. They need not feel this way; with further training and greater experience their confidence will grow.

At the present time a lot of local officers are in training. In teacher training alone there are, this year, 600. In other kinds, there are 277 in the Public Service Training Centre, 25 of whom are doing the Public Administration Diploma course. Under a recently developed cadetship scheme, 60 local officers are doing full-time training at the University or the Institute of Technology. Others are being trained as valuers, technicians, forestry officers, medical officers and so on. Most people in these courses have come straight from secondary school.

[*matter omitted*][5]

Papua and New Guinea is set upon the path towards self-government. I visit many different areas and I talk with many people. It is clear they depend heavily on the Public Service [...] If the Public Service is to continue to meet the demands on it, it needs self-confidence and

4   The PNG public service had three divisions. The 'First Division', which numbered around 20, consisted of the most senior officers. The 'Second Division' comprised senior and mid-range officers, while the 'Third Division' composed officers engaged in support and menial tasks. See also Document 37.

5   The omitted material included reference to further training for 'local officers already in the Public service'; steps to improve the provision of housing for PNG officers; the review of their salary levels by the Arbitration Tribunal; the planned introduction of draft legislation on a superannuation scheme for PNG officers into the House of Assembly later in the year; and the roles of the Public Service Board and the Arbitration Tribunal.

self-respect of a high order. The Public Service Association can play an important role in the achievement of these qualities, and therefore, in the successful progress of this country. This requires that it act always with a high sense of responsibility. I have no doubt that such a high sense of responsibility will inform your proceedings at this Congress.

I declare the Congress open.

[NAA: A452, 1970/2031]

39   MINUTE FROM BALLARD TO HAY

Canberra, 19 May 1970

I hope you received the telex containing extracts of the Prime Minister's letter.[1] I also hope that Kerr brings with him enough material to give you some indication of the thinking of Ministers.[2] I think—but I may be wrong in this—that the significant element in Ministers' thinking is that they do not wish to have to accept responsibility in Parliament for every detail of the activities of the Administration. For example, the leg irons affair[3] is one which is evocative of early Australian history,[4] is judged here in the light of that and should be judged in the context of indigenous opinion in the Territory.

2.   As I understand it Ministers feel that if they are going to be able to say that actions which are taken in the Territory which may not accord with an Australian view of what should be done here are appropriate for the Territory they must be able to say that these are taken on the decision of the elected representatives of the Territory people. For so long as the actions are taken by and in the name of an Administrator who is appointed by and responsible to the Commonwealth the Minister will have to accept responsibility for answering to Parliament in detail for what is done.

•   With the implication that it is difficult to separate a judgement based on Australian pre-conditions from a judgement based on Territory pre-conditions. I am reasonably sure that this is a correct interpretation of the Minister's views—and that as he understands it, it is a correct interpretation of the Prime Minister's view.

3.   I am not sure that the differences between your position and this is necessarily as great as may appear. We do of course envisage new arrangements would contain an ultimate right to over-rule the Ministerial Members (see paragraph 8 of 'Next Steps' paper).[5]

[NAA: A452, 1970/1867]

---

1   Document 15. Ballard had forwarded Hay extracts of the letter. See Telex 4997, Ballard to Hay, 19 May 1970, NAA: A452, 1970/1867.

2   Warwick Smith had forwarded to Hay a copy of the draft Cabinet submission generally referred to as the 'Next Steps' paper and had asked for his comments. Warwick Smith and Hay exchanged terse messages on the draft submission with Warwick Smith refusing to accept many of Hay's suggestions. See, for example, Letter, Warwick Smith to Hay, 13 May 1970, NAA: A452, 1970/1867.

3   In the early months of 1970 controversy had arisen over the use of leg irons to restrain prisoners. In an editorial of 5 May 1970 the *Papua New Guinea Post–Courier* commented that: 'The Controller of Corrective Institutions has acted quickly and wisely in banning the use of leg irons in Territory gaols. This follows the disclosure that such restraining devices were used on prisoners at Kerevat [in New Ireland], on one of them for more than two months.'

4   The reference here is to the use of leg irons to restrain convict and indigenous prisoners in Australia during the colonial era.

5   Not published.

40   LETTER FROM WARWICK SMITH TO HAY

Canberra, 21 May 1970

Constitutional Development

Attached is a copy of a paper prepared in the Department on further steps in constitutional development for Papua and New Guinea.[1] This paper covers steps in constitutional development which can be made without amendment to the Papua and New Guinea Act. It is being considered by an inter-departmental committee of Commonwealth Departments of the Treasury, Prime Minister's and Attorney-General's with a view to a submission being made to Cabinet in June seeking approval of the proposed changes.

2.   The powers or functions which it is proposed to be exercised by Ministerial officer holders are still being worked out, but it would appear that in order to properly give effect to these changes there will need to be a reshuffle of portfolios.

3.   [...] It is felt that the portfolios should be re-arranged so that there are no Assistant Ministerial Members in the same Departments as Ministerial Members and that portfolios could be established for Local Government (the Minister has written separately to the Administrator in this particular case), Police and Corrective Institutions. A schedule setting out a suggested re-arrangement is attached.[2]

4.   The Prime Minister is due to visit the Territory in July and proposes to announce these changes during that visit. I would be grateful therefore for your early comments on the proposed changes and re-arrangements of portfolios for Ministerial office holders.

[NAA: A452, 1970/1867]

---

1   Not published. The paper's title was 'Next Steps in Constitutional Development'.

2   Not published. The schedule proposed that ministerial members be appointed for Agriculture, Stock and Fisheries; Education; Labour; Posts and Telegraphs; Public Health; Local Government; and Trade and Industry; and that assistant ministerial members be appointed for Public Works; the Treasury; Police; Transport; Forests; Lands, Surveys and Mines; Corrective Institutions; Social Development and Home Affairs; and Information.

41   MINUTE FROM KERR TO BALLARD

Canberra, 26 May 1970

Discussions with Secretary Designate¹—Constitutional Development

[*matter omitted*]

During our (Kerr and Hay) discussions² the following points emerged:
–   He saw the 'Next Steps'³ in the light of the Prime Minister's direction to decentralise the decision making process. He felt that whether this was done by giving power to the Administrator rather than to Ministerial Members was not of much substance.
–   He did not agree with the machinery, i.e. using the Approved Arrangements under Section 25 and he did not agree with the 'Split Budget'⁴ concept.
–   When I pointed out that in our opinion the Minister could only duck the issue of responsibility if he could point to the decision being made by the elected members of the territory House of Assembly, Mr Hay replied that he felt that it was the department's fault that things are as they are because it has for too long insisted that the Minister make all the decisions. The Minister for a long time past should have been saying in Parliament—this decision was made in the Territory and either—I have every faith in the Administrator or I do not have faith in the Administrator, or I have written to him to criticise his decision or propose to sack him.

The department is under a misconception if it thinks officials are reluctant to hand over authority.

[*matter omitted*]

As I understand it Hay's approach is for a transfer of authority *to the Territory*—how you do this, that is, whether it is exercised by the Administrator or the Ministerial Members, does not really matter. You simply say—the transfer of power will take place in that Canberra will no longer have a say in a specified list of areas of government.⁵ This transfer of decision making has financial consequences—after the Budget and Development Programme have been agreed then if the territory wants to spend more money in any area which has been transferred to it, then it has to renegotiate priorities [in] the budget or raise the revenues locally.

[*matter omitted*]

Hay did not see any problems about some Ministerial Members having more authority than others. He said the AEC would soon let him know if it did not agree to this and he said he was open to argument about giving defined powers across the board rather than in only a number of areas.

His impression was that the Prime Minister was upset after the 4 March statement because authority was not transferred to the Territory then. This step should have been done then and in his opinion would have caused far less problems than it will cause now.⁶

1   Gorton had approached Hay in late March or early April 1970 to offer him the post of DET Secretary. Hay accepted on 7 April 1970.
2   The discussions between Kerr and Hay took place on 20, 21 & 22 May 1970.
3   The Department of External Territories had under preparation two draft Cabinet Submissions: 'Next Steps in Constitutional Development' and 'Implications of Early Self-Government'.
4   See Documents 31 & 32.
5   Hay had identified the possible functional areas to be transferred as immigration and citizenship, local government, health, education, land, field administration and law and order.
6   Document 26.

Mr Hay relied heavily on the statement in the Prime Minister's letter as follows:

> 'If we believe that we have a good Administrator and good Ministerial Members, then now is the time to decentralise a great deal of decision making, now is the time to allow some mistakes to be made if that should happen, now is the time to move closer to the position which an efficient Head office of an international company would take in allowing its offices in other countries autonomy—subject to periodic reports on progress and the reserve power to interfere if those reports were not satisfactory.'[7]

He does not think the other statements in the Prime Minister's and our Minister's letter about transfer of responsibility to the Ministerial Members alters what he sees as the basic point of the Prime Minister's proposal.

[*matter omitted*]

[NAA: A452, 1970/1867]

---

7   See Document 15.

42   TELEX FROM HAY TO WARWICK SMITH

Port Moresby, 2 June 1970

9100. CONFIDENTIAL

I should be glad if you would place before the Minister my strongly held view that before any decision is taken on stage two paper there should be substantial consultations with elected Members of the House.[1] The effect of the proposals taken as a whole will be profound. They go further than I myself had envisaged, particularly in reducing the role of official members of the AEC and the extent to which Ministerial Members are given authority individually rather than collectively (though Curtis's[2] amendments may go some way towards remedying this). Minister and Prime Minister need to satisfy themselves that change of this magnitude will not give rise to concern that Government is abandoning the Territory and create serious uncertainty in the rural areas and in the business and public service expatriate communities. This could be avoided if there is, and is seen to be, a very full consultation before decisions are taken and before the Prime Minister leaves for the Territory. In my view, the AEC could well be invited to Canberra immediately after the conclusion of the House of Assembly—in the main for budget discussions but also for consultation on the stage two paper. A similar invitation could be issued to the Select Committee, or at any rate its Chairman and Vice Chairman and one or two representative Members (for example Somare) immediately thereafter.

2.   I have discussed this matter confidentially with Tom Leahy (without going into the details of stage two paper) and it is his suggestions on consultation which are incorporated in this message.

[NAA: A452, 1970/2570]

---

1   The 'stage two' paper was the draft of a cabinet submission which was presented to Cabinet on 9 June 1970 (Document 48). In another telex of 2 June 1970 to Warwick Smith, Hay commented on the accompanying 'Implications Paper' submission (Document 47) as follows: 'With reference to [the] Implications Paper, I maintain position previously expressed to yourself and Minister that paper of this nature should not now be presented to Government. It is quite impossible to do justice to the many fundamental policy issues involved in a short time and without full and detailed discussion with a number of departments. The Prime Minister's letter speaks of a "full study". The timing of this ought to be later in the year so that the government is in a position to indicate its view on any fundamental constitutional question that may be raised in the final report of the Select Committee. In saying this, I do not disagree with the tenor of final paragraphs in present draft. However, these do not rest on the implications so much as on the immediate political repercussions and possible law and order problems which premature self-government would involve. These could be indicated quite clearly in the submission which the minister proposes to make to the government covering the stage two paper'. Warwick Smith replied by telex on 2 June that 'Minister has noted your views but as he indicated to you in discussion last week he considers the paper must be presented now'. Telex 9099, Hay to Warwick Smith, 2 June 1970; and Telex 5496, Warwick Smith to Hay, 2 June 1970, both in NAA: A452, 1970/3045.

2   L. J. (Lindsay) Curtis, Secretary for Law in the PNG Administration.

43   TELEX FROM HAY TO WARWICK SMITH

Port Moresby, 5 June 1970

9318. CONFIDENTIAL

Implications

I do not have any comment on paper as an analysis of early self-government on the basis of stated assumptions, particularly paras 2 and 18.[1] Perhaps the prerequisites could include citizenship, currency and banking and the treatment of others, such as the assumption in the Territory of responsibility for civil aviation and law and order, could be more fully treated. But I have no quarrel with conclusions.

2.   From the Territory point of view, main implication of early self-government is the need to set the shortest possible time for completing prerequisites (which in turn need to be analysed). As I see them, prerequisites and relevant timing can be set out as follows:

Political and Constitutional

(a) Adequate constitutional framework (written constitution not necessary). Certain basic decisions necessary for this (broadly those listed in Select Committee questions) and they may well follow from Select Committee report and could be taken within the next twelve months.

(b) Adequate and stable political leadership. Nucleus of leaders with experience is emerging but base is narrow and, in absence of party or spoils system, is inherently unstable. More would be known after 1972 election.

(c) Stable and experienced judiciary and public service. On basis that Australia will pay for expatriate element, this is available and does not constitute limiting factor. But its stability is precarious. Widespread localisation not likely before early to mid-1980s.

(d) Forces of Law and Order and control. Again adequate on assumption that leadership will be largely expatriate. But question of control and use of armed services must be solved.

Economic

(e) Adequate revenue through local resources or overseas aid. No problem seen provided Australia accepts continuance of aid obligations, and Territory accepts some shortfall in full financial autonomy. If Australia takes negative position on aid the key issue is development of adequate local, but not necessarily, indigenous tax base. This is not so far off as before CRA[2] but is still more than ten years away.

(f)   National banking and currency. These are a long way off.

(g) Foreign investment.

---

1   The paper referred to is likely to be a draft version of the report included in Cabinet Submission 327 (Document 47), presented to cabinet on 9 June 1970.

2   Conzinc Riotinto of Australia (CRA) operated the Panguna mine in Bougainville.

Social

(h) Citizenship legislation an essential. This will take time and has to be considered against possible effects on retention of expatriate public servants and of foreign investment.

National Unity and Mutual Confidence

(i)   In the absence of any strong feeling of unity, some means would have to be found to create a degree of mutual confidence between main groupings. As an interim measure, safeguards might be provided through agreed proportional representation of main groupings in Territory Cabinet with understanding that before independence there would be full enquiry as to whether the various parts want to remain together.

3.   If however Commonwealth were, as a matter of broad policy, to favour early self-government while retaining its commitment to its treaty obligations, implications would need to be somewhat differently treated.

4.   Main implication of early self-government would be that Australia would have to be prepared to underpin Papua and New Guinea Government more or less indefinitely, both as to finance and as to manpower in circumstances where it could not control policies on major issues such as land, human rights and freedoms, the Constitution, administration of the law, and so on, although it could expect a good deal of broad and some particular influence on economic policies. Position would be more akin to that of French territories in West Africa than to that of British territories. In short, the assumptions for early self-government, if this is to become the Commonwealth's objective, would have to be different from e.g. paras 18(B) and 18(C) and this would involve significant policy considerations for Australia. These considerations would have to be identified and analyzed and recommendations would need to flow from them.

[NAA: A452, 1970/3045]

44   TELEX FROM HAY TO WARWICK SMITH

Port Moresby, 5 June 1970

9336. Confidential

Stage Two—Consultations with the Select Committee

Further to my 9100.[1] Select Committee is meeting later today to decide on whether it should formally request a full meeting in Canberra with the Minister and Prime Minister very quickly. Middleton has seen me privately this morning with concurrence of Arek and suggested that it would be highly desirable if a small group of two or three could come to Canberra almost immediately for talks with Minister and Prime Minister in order to clarify whether or not the proposals forecast in the Minister's 4 March speech[2] and apparently going to be announced by the Prime Minister during his visit, cut across the work of the Select Committee. Middleton says Committee is seriously concerned about this possibility and hopes that prior consultation can satisfactorily resolve doubts.

2.   Middleton indicates following areas in which Committee was very much concerned and which they fear might be the subject of decisions without consultations:

(A) Public Service—Are any major policy changes contemplated?

(B) AEC—Are any immediate changes proposed in the functions, composition, membership or powers?

(C) Ministerial Members and Assistant Ministerial Members—what immediate changes (if any) are contemplated in functions. Powers and numbers of Ministerial Members? Any changes in Assistant Ministerial Member system? If any changes are made, what will be structure etc. of AEC? Will present Assistant Ministerial Members remain?

(D) Official Members—is there any intention to altering number and/or status of official members?

[matter omitted]

[NAA: A452, 1970/1825]

---

1   Document 42.

2   Document 26.

45   TELEX FROM HAY TO WARWICK SMITH

Port Moresby, 6 June 1970

9352. UNCLASSIFIED

My 9336[1]—Consultations with Select Committee.

Full Committee meeting late yesterday afternoon passed following resolution.

> That the Committee seeks an assurance that any constitutional changes will be within the framework of the Governor General's speech on the 3rd March 1970[2] and the Minister's statement to the House of Representatives on 4th March 1970;[3] and further to endeavour to ascertain from the Prime Minister and the Minister the changes he may wish to make within those terms.

2.   It then appointed sub-committee consisting of Arek, Middleton, Somare and Giregire and formally asks that it be received by Minister and Prime Minister in Canberra on Monday or Tuesday.

3.   Later date would not be possible because Committee has to return on Wednesday in order to enable it to hold meeting on Wednesday night and prepare a report for submission to House on Thursday. House meeting may conclude Thursday night.

4.   Glad early confirmation that at any rate Minister would be prepared to see the Committee and speak to them in relation to above mentioned resolution.

[NAA: A452, 1970/1825]

---

1   Document 44.

2   Document 25.

3   Document 26.

46   RECORD OF MEETING BETWEEN BARNES AND SELECT COMMITTEE MEMBERS

Canberra, 9 June 1970

Messrs Arek and Middleton stated that the purpose of their visit was to obtain an assurance that any changes proposed by the Government (and which might be announced to the Prime Minister during his visit to the Territory) would not cut across the work of the Select Committee nor go beyond the framework of the Governor-General's speech of 3rd March, 1970, and the Minister's statement of 4th March, 1970.[1]

Rumours of considerably greater changes than encompassed by these statements were rife in the Territory. The Committee was concerned to know if the changes proposed encompassed any major changes in Public Service; in the functions, composition and powers of the AEC; in the powers of Ministerial Members and Assistant Ministerial Members; or in the role and status of Official Members.

The Minister expressed surprise and concern at the rumours and gave a full assurance that no major changes were contemplated. He assured Messrs Arek and Middleton that there would be no major changes in the Papua and New Guinea Act until the Select Committee's report has been considered—and it was noted that to change many matters, e.g., number of Ministerial Members, would require amendment of the Act. He also said that any changes in the numbers of Official Members or their role in the House of Assembly was something which would not be considered until the Select Committee expressed itself on the matter.

The Minister said that, whilst he could not go into detail as Cabinet had yet to consider the proposals, the changes contemplated were fully in harmony with the March statements and with the Prime Minister's remarks to the Committee in February. They represented further steps in the Government's approach of transferring responsibility progressively to the Territory's elected representatives.

As for any changes in the Public Service, the Minister said that those contemplated followed from the Committee's concern at the loss of experienced overseas officers and were along the lines outlined in his address to the PSA[2] Conference.[3]

The Minister reiterated the Government's policy that changes in the status of the Territory such as a move to self government or independence would not be forced on the people against their wishes.

Mr Arek thanked the Minister for his assurance and stated that he now considered he could assure the Committee that their fears are groundless.

[NAA: A452, 1970/2570]

---

1   Documents 25 & 26 (respectively).

2   Public Service Association.

3   Document 38.

47   CABINET SUBMISSION 327[1]

Canberra, 9 June 1970

CONFIDENTIAL

Papua and New Guinea—Implications of Early Self-Government

This submission presents a study by Departments of the implications of early self-government in Papua and New Guinea and proposes some points for action suggested by the study.[2]

2.   The report has been prepared by the Department of External Territories after discussion with Prime Minister's Department, the Treasury, the Attorney-General's Department, the Department of External Affairs and Defence and some Departments with special interests and is circulated now in connection with proposals separately submitted for constitutional change in Papua and New Guinea.[3]

3.   'Self-government' as a term has emotional connotations in the Territory particularly in the Highlands. It is feared that Australia and Australians would withdraw leaving the local people under the control of more advanced coastal people. At present those coastal people who do seek early self-government (and many do not) are a small part of the Territory population.

4.   I infer from the report it would be more desirable to proceed by way of intermediate steps rather than by a jump to self-government. It also seems that without some continuing Australian Government presence in the territory early self-government would not have good prospects of success. The corollary is that if the Australian aim is to reduce the extent of the Commonwealth Government's involvement then this is more likely to be achieved by the step by step approach which gives better prospects for the Territory to achieve political, social and economic viability and gives the native people better opportunities for controlling their own destinies.

5.   It is suggested in the report (paragraph 49) that if the policy objective is to be early self-government the decision should be taken now and some particular measures should also be taken. Paragraph 50 suggests that if the policy is to proceed by a process of intermediate steps there are a set of similar measures to be taken but less dramatically.

6.   The report is circulated in connection with the submission regarding constitutional changes in Papua and New Guinea. Those proposals do not preclude a decision, say in 1971, in favour of early self-government e.g. 1972; but they do reflect a quickening of the pace at which intermediate steps are to be taken now and in the future.

7.   What the report points out is that if the decision for early self-government were to be taken the measures referred to in paragraph 5 would have to be taken at a faster pace than otherwise and might be difficult for the native people to absorb.

8.   Independently of that decision, however, it emerges from the report that the existing policy of increasing the extent to which native people participate in political, social and economic affairs needs to be given a great deal more bite. It also needs to be repeatedly made plain that constitutional progress towards self-government will not alter Australia's intention to assist the political, social and economic advancement of the Territory and that the Government will seek to maintain sufficient numbers of Australian officers in the Territory and will continue aid on a large scale.

---

1   Submitted by Barnes.

2   See Attachment below.

3   Document 48.

9.   The position of those Commonwealth Departments and agencies now performing functions of internal self-government (i.e. excluding Defence Forces) outside the aegis of the Administration should be reviewed so that a sensible programme for their absorption in appropriate cases into the Territory Administration may be prepared. This ought to be done I suggest by a Committee consisting of the Department of External Territories, Prime Minister's Department, Public Service Board, the Treasury, and each particular Department or agency in turn. Moreover a special study of the situation in relation to internal security ought to be prepared by the Departments of External Territories and Defence.

RECOMMENDATION
10.   I recommend that Cabinet endorse the measures proposed in paragraphs 8 and 9.

Attachment
Report on Papua and New Guinea—Implications of Early Self-Government
The purpose of this report is to submit some Departmental comments on the implications of the early achievement of self-government in the Territory of Papua and New Guinea. The report has been prepared by the Department of External Territories after discussion with Prime Minister's Department, the Treasury, the Attorney-General's Department, the Departments of External Affairs and Defence and some departments with specific interests.

What is meant by Self-Government?
2.   Self-government as it might be attained by Papua and New Guinea in the near future is taken for present purposes to mean a situation in which the Commonwealth of Australia has ceased to have any executive or legislative part in the administration of the Territory in relation to its internal affairs. This assumes that internal security would be the responsibility of the local authorities, but that the Commonwealth would retain responsibility for the external affairs and defence of the Territory.
[*matter omitted*]

Implications of Self-Government Generally
13.   Before the implications of early as opposed to later self-government are discussed it may be helpful to consider the implications of self-government as such.
14.   For Papua and New Guinea to move from its present dependent status to the stage of self-government would represent a major step in its constitutional development. Everything before self-government is predicated upon the ultimate responsibility of the Commonwealth Minister to the Federal Parliament. At the stage of self-government (assuming a Parliamentary or Westminster system of government were to apply) responsibility for internal affairs will be exercised by local Ministers responsible to the House of Assembly in lieu of the Commonwealth Minister responsible to the Australian Parliament.
15.   Whilst many people in the Territory think of self-government as a lengthy period on the road to independence experience elsewhere suggests that the period of self-government tends to be brief (e.g. Algeria, Kenya, Sierra Leone, Somalia, Tanganyika, Uganda, Zambia). Self-government as a stage in constitutional development has on occasions been omitted altogether because of pressures both in the dependent Territory and in the metropolitan government (e.g. Chad, Congo-Republic, Malawi, Morocco). In theory the time of self-government as a prelude to independence is one in which indigenous politicians and bureaucrats gain experience in government. In recent practice when time has been provided for self-government it has been

only as long as is needed to draw up a constitution, arrange for self-determination, and make the necessary administrative change for independence.

16. In the case however of Papua and New Guinea when the stage of self-government has been reached there might be no broadly-based pressure in the Territory to move on from self-government to self-determination (independence). Yet a lengthy period of self-government as a stage towards self-determination might not be acceptable to the Australian Government. At self-government Australia would remain formally internationally responsible under the Trusteeship Agreement for local developments in New Guinea whether or not it was in control of them. It could be held similarly responsible by the United Nations in regard to Papua. Additionally while responsible for the Territory's international relations, Australia could find its own relations with Indonesia affected by acts of the local authorities—there is some sympathy particularly in Papua with West Irian dissidents.

17. Even within Australia it is doubtful whether the Government could avoid having some responsibility attributed to it for an adverse or deteriorating situation in Papua and New Guinea.

18. If however the people of Papua and New Guinea make it clear that they favour a lengthy or indefinite period of internal self-government and if the Government of the day considers that to do otherwise might lead to serious unrest in the Territory and possibly secession of major areas or even fragmentation, it might feel it desirable to meet those wishes. Some of the unsatisfactory aspects of the Commonwealth's position in this situation might be mitigated if self-government resulted from a referendum by which the people had opted for this status, although given the choice of immediate independence.

19. Advantages of this arrangement would be:

(1) the status would have been chosen by Territory people and not conferred solely by Australia;

(2) it would be explicitly recognised that the Territory could opt at any time for full independence;

(3) Australia's responsibilities would have been delineated;

(4) the international responsibility would be reduced;

(5) some of the difficulties flowing from the different international status of Papua and New Guinea would be reduced if not overcome.

There would be difficulties, including that of international acceptance, if such a status were arrived at as a result of an initiative from Australia. This course might however be a possible reaction to a request by the Territory people for a lengthy period of self-government. But it is likely that the United National General Assembly would not endorse the arrangement as an acceptable outcome to an Act of Self Determination. This would leave Australia's responsibilities to the United Nations unmodified as far as the United Nations General Assembly was concerned. (See paragraphs 21–24, United Nations Implications).

20. No matter what the constitutional position may be, Australia will always have a close interest in whatever happens in Papua and New Guinea. No matter how reluctant an Australian Government of the future may be to contemplate intervening to maintain order or to protect Australian interests, the possibility cannot be ruled out of its being requested to do so or of circumstances in which it would feel compelled to do so even if the Territory had attained full independence.

United Nations Implications

21. The undertakings Australia has made to the United Nations concerning the constitutional development of the Territory are contained in Article 73(b) of the United Nations Charter in respect of Papua, and in Article 76(b) of the Charter and Article 3 of the Trusteeship Agreement in respect of New Guinea. (The texts are attached as Appendix 'C')[4]. The responsibility was accepted in each case to develop the Territory for self-government in accordance with the wishes of the peoples. There were difficulties in the United Nations from the outset in interpreting the term 'self-government' but it is clear that the General Assembly has taken the view in recent years that the manner in which territories become 'self-governing' is primarily through the attainment of independence after an act of self-determination. There is a provision for territories to achieve 'associated status' on self-determination but the association must be on the basis of absolute equality and more closely resembles independence than self-government as it is generally understood.

22. Early self-government for Papua and New Guinea could be granted as an interim constitutional step under the Papua and New Guinea Act, with the Australian Parliament retaining the ultimate power to legislate for the Territory's affairs; there being no separate constitution for Papua and New Guinea, and the external affairs and defence powers, legislative and executive, remaining with the Commonwealth. Current political views in the United Nations and its past practice make it unlikely that the General Assembly would agree to endorse those arrangements as an acceptable outcome of an act of self-determination but the same effective results may be able to be attained by a treaty after self-determination. Australian responsibilities to the United Nations would remain unaltered from the viewpoint of the General Assembly.

23. While the grant of early self-government is unlikely to lead to any modification of Australian obligations it seems certain to lead to a sharp increase in United Nations pressure for the immediate granting of full independence to the Territory. The argument will be advanced that if the Territory is judged capable of accepting responsibility for its self-government then it cannot be maintained that the granting of full independence should be postponed for any lengthy period. Suspicions may also be expressed by our more extreme critics that the form of self-government granted was a ploy to avoid carrying out our UN obligations. The United Nations may even express the wish to study the new constitutional arrangements through a special Visiting Mission. These pressures are likely to be unleashed by the fact of a grant of self-government and other administering powers have sought to minimise the problem by granting self-government to their territories shortly before final self-determination. The problems associated with the meaning of 'self-government' could be avoided by proceeding directly to self-determination through a process of devolution of power which did not identify a point at which 'self-government' obtained.

24. A devolution of power upon elected representatives in the Territory which was obvious and rapid would cause fewer problems from the viewpoint of relations with the United Nations and is likely to be accepted as a responsible and appropriate policy by all but our most extreme international critics.

Some Particular Implications

(a) *Defence*. The Defence Department is at present conducting a comprehensive review of Papua/New Guinea defence, including its future importance to Australia, the size and shape of the local defence forces, the nature of the command and defence organisation to be developed, and ways and means of promoting closer contact and understanding between Australian

---

4   Not published.

defence authorities and Papua/New Guinean authorities. This study is not yet complete and the following brief observations on some implications of the granting of internal self-government to Papua/New Guinea are of a preliminary nature only.

Until independence Australia will be responsible for the external defence of Papua/New Guinea and must be prepared to cope with an emergency threat to the Territory. Following independence Australia could also be required to continue some form of responsibility for defence.

Papua/New Guinea still lacks balanced and adequate defence forces, and their development will take time having regard to manpower problems, scarce resources, the need for trained indigene officers and NCO's and other factors. The earlier that internal self-government is introduced, the greater would be the need for Papua/New Guinea forces to be supported by Australian regular service personnel if they are to be maintained at an efficient level.

It could also be accepted that in a period of internal self-government there would be an increasing demand by local authorities for a 'voice' on defence matters. The promotion of closer understanding and education in defence matters is therefore important both for Australian and Papua/New Guinea interests, and consideration is being given to this aspect in the Defence study referred to above.

(b) *Military Assistance in Internal Security.* A particular problem which will require close examination in relation to a grant of internal self-government will be the question of the availability of military assistance in a deteriorating internal security situation which develops beyond the control of local police forces. In a period of internal self-government internal security will presumably be the responsibility of the local authorities, while on the other hand the defence forces will be under Australian control. They will however no doubt be viewed by local authorities as a possible back-up for the police forces in an emergency situation.

Australian Government policy is that the defence forces should only be used for internal security purposes as a last resort. Australian and Papua/New Guinean views in this regard may not however always coincide. It would be essential that there should be a clear definition where responsibility lay for requesting and approving the employment of defence forces in an internal security situation and this is likely to require the setting up of particular machinery to develop procedures and advise authorities in this sensitive and complicated field.

(c) *External Affairs.* If early self-government (which might be expected to be followed by independence soon afterwards) is contemplated, further consideration would be necessary of the Territory's needs to administer its external relations.

Under self-government the conduct of treaty relations would of course remain with the Australian Government, although arrangements might be made in relation to matters relating to the Territory under which the local administration was authorised to deal with particular matters (e.g. postal and trade matters). The discharge of treaty obligations is another situation in which it may be necessary to retain a right of intervention by Australia.

(d) *Trade.* Australia is an important market for the Territory: in 1968/69 39% ($29.6M) of the Territory's exports went to Australia. Australia is also an important source of goods for Papua and New Guinea—55% (worth $82M) of the Territory's imports came from Australia in 1968/69. Australia is of course a more important market for the Territory than the Territory is for Australia.

In addition to taking Territory interests into account in its Trade Agreements, Australia accords the Territory a preferred tariff position on a number of items of significance in the Territory's economy. These include copra, groundnuts, raw coffee, natural rubber and plywood which account for a substantial proportion of the Territory's exports to Australia. The preferences were provided either by existing legislation dating back to 1926 or through use of a waiver agreed to by the GATT.[5] In addition the Territory is eligible to participate in the Australian system of preferences for less developed countries. Territory products are not subject to primage duties in Australia. The preferences given to the Territory are summarised in Appendix 'D'.[6] Australia does not have any tariff preferences in the Territory.

Should the Territory move to self-government (with the prospect of early independence following) Australia would need to examine the new situation. The examination would look towards such factors as:

– likely Territory's attitude to accession to GATT;
– arrangements to ensure reasonable access to the Territory for Australian products;
– whether Australia should continue to give the Territory preferential treatment without reciprocal concessions;
– the ultimate form and conditions applied thereto of any preference scheme for developing countries that may evolve from current international discussions;
– likely Territory participation in International Commodity Agreements. (At present Australia negotiates on behalf of the Territory.)

(e) *Civil Aviation.* At the stage of internal self-government it could be expected that Australia would retain responsibility for agreements and arrangements governing the provision of international air services and for other international aspects of civil aviation.

Responsibility for the provision and administration of services between Australia and Papua and New Guinea would also be reserved to the Commonwealth.

[*matter omitted*]

(f) *Citizenship.* At present Papuans are Australian citizens and British subjects; New Guineans are Australian protected persons. Neither Papuans nor New Guineans have an automatic right of residence in Australia. They may travel abroad on Australian passports. Some mixed race Territory residents have the status of Australian citizen with the right of residence in Australia. Certain Asians in the Territory have the right to opt for Australian citizenship with the right of entry for permanent residence in Australia. If PNG becomes self-governing *before* an act of self-determination, these citizenship arrangements may continue until independence. If self-government results *from* an act of self-determination and the Trusteeship Agreement is terminated, new Commonwealth (and PNG) legislation may be desirable to create and confer PNG citizenship. There may be no impediment to the creation of a common Papua and New Guinea status for internal purposes only.

(g) *Australian representative: position of Administrator.* The Administrator at present is charged with the duty of administering the Territory on behalf of the Commonwealth. The Territory is building up its own body politic, and in the process of evolution there will be a separation of the functions of head of government and possibly head of state and Australian representative. At self-government an Australian representative as such would no doubt be appointed in Papua and New Guinea.

(h) *Aid arrangements.* Under present arrangements and until 1972/73 Australian aid to the Territory will conform with the Five Year Development Programme. The Government is committed to continuing large scale aid after self-government. The aid arrangements would be a matter for negotiation with the government of the self-governing Territory.

---

5   General Agreement on Tariffs and Trade.
6   Not published.

Disengagement

26.[7] In order that Australia may disengage smoothly when the time comes, the following matters need to be considered well ahead of that time:

(a) It will be necessary to make before self-government appropriate arrangements to protect after self-government any Australians or Australian interests that the Government of the day considers ought to be protected. For example the Government might think that Australian settlers under the Ex-servicemen's Credit Scheme had a special claim. Another aspect of this matter as indicated in paragraph 31 below, is that some Australians are apprehensive that when self-government comes expatriate-owned plantations, urban houses and other property will be peacefully but illegally taken over by the natives or worse, that there may be violence.

(b) Commonwealth legislation applying in the Territory may require amendment. New Territory legislation may be needed also to ensure continuity in the arrangements presently provided for under Commonwealth legislation.

(c) The relationship of the Supreme Court of the Self-governing Territory to the High Court of Australia will have to be defined before self-government and necessary administrative changes made.

(d) The Commonwealth's responsibility for the Territory's public borrowing, including international borrowing, and the existing monetary arrangements would need to be considered.

(e) To the extent that functions of internal government (works, meteorological services, civil aviation, shipping, broadcasting) carried out by the Commonwealth Departments and agencies have not been absorbed into the Administration, their transfer would need to be provided for. This would include not only the formal administrative arrangements but steps to ensure the provision of key technical personnel for as long as they may be needed (e.g. for some positions of DCA).[8]

(f) *Constitutional Aspects.* Any necessary Commonwealth legislation to implement self-government would, of course, need to be related to available legislative powers under the Australian Constitution. Complex questions could arise in the case of self-government which takes the form of a free association with metropolitan Australia (see paras 18 and 19). It is believed, however, that there would be no fundamental constitutional obstacles in the way of implementation.

Territory Interests

27. (a) It is a *sine qua non* for the transfer of power at the time of self-government that there exist a leader, group or party to whom Australia can hand over power and the responsibility of government with reasonable assurance that support will be forthcoming on a sufficiently wide basis to sustain viable government.

(b) It would be desirable for the self-governing Territory to have a public service which has its key policy and administrative positions predominantly staffed by indigenous people. This is a situation for the Administering Authority to promote before disengagement.

(c) It would also be desirable for the politicians and the public to become accustomed to the basic elements of responsible government such as the principle that those who make policy decisions are responsible for finding the money for their execution. At the time

---

7   There is no paragraph 25 in the original document.

8   Department of Civil Aviation.

of self-government local revenue ought to provide the greater part of the budget (This does not exclude external aid as a source of funds, but it means the acceptance of the responsibility of governing oneself primarily from one's own resources.)

Implication of Early Self-Government (say 1972) Compared with Later

28. The Government's policy has been one of balanced development with the nature and pace of development determined in harmony with the wishes of the majority of the Territory people. Concerning the status of the Territory, the Government has stated on many occasions that changes which the majority of the people do not want will not be imposed on the Territory.

29. The majority have claimed and are likely to continue to claim that they are not yet prepared sufficiently in terms of financial and human resources for self-government. Spokesmen for the Highlands have expressed fear of early change. They say they would resist this. With more than half of the indigenous population of the Territory living in less developed Highlands and Sepik districts a 'self-government' which meant in effect government by coastal Papuans and Tolais might well face active resistance or attempts to secede. On the other hand there are some Papuans and some New Guineans e.g. many Tolais who maintain that they are now ready for self-government. These groups are, however, only a small minority (e.g. Tolais number 70,000 in a total population of 2 1/4 million).

30. At no time will all views coincide but the Government has indicated it will not allow a small minority even if vocal to determine the future of the majority.

31. The implications of self-government are not well understood, even by the more sophisticated minority. Some think it means the withdrawal of all Australians. Some think it means access to 'cargo'.[9] Some apparently believe that when Australian administration is withdrawn plantations and freehold land in European hands will revert to native people. This belief seems to be held not only in the less sophisticated Highlands but also among the more advanced Tolai and Bougainville people. There is also a belief widely held among *Europeans* in the Territory that on achievement of self-government there will be outbreaks of native violence against Europeans, (or if this does not happen there will be peaceful but illegal occupation by natives of European plantations and property).

32. In 1972 the gaps in self-sufficiency will still be large, and there will still be disparate levels of social and economic development. Highlanders, Sepiks and the people of Buin in Bougainville have said that if early self-government occurred they would secede from the self-governing country and perhaps seek to retain association with Australia. Papuans stress their present Australian citizenship. During the recent tour of the Select Committee on Constitutional Development, the majority of the people indicated clearly that they did not consider the Territory was yet ready for self-government.

33. In terms of economic development early self-government would probably mean some check to the pace of development generally and perhaps some slackening in the general effectiveness of the Administration drive for economic development.

34. Future relations between Papua and New Guinea and Australia need to be considered in the light of the actual circumstances of the two countries. Over simplified analogies with the withdrawal of European powers from Africa are misleading.

35. The pressures for early self-government in some part of the Territory and pressures for a slow pace of constitutional change elsewhere give rise to problems. These pressures manifest themselves in quite a different way in the Territory from the way they are presented in the Australian press. The press tends to highlight spokesmen for small minorities who seek early

9   The reference here is to the hoped-for provision of large volumes of material goods—'cargo'—by supernatural means.

change and to give a much exaggerated picture to the pressure for self-government in the Territory. The possible consequences of moving too slowly towards self-government need to be set against the possible consequences of moving too fast. In the former case the strength of support for early self-government and the degree to which violence is likely has to be assessed; in the latter case assessment is needed of the prospects of a running down in the efficiency of the Administration or of centrifugal tendencies leading to secession, fragmentation or disintegration within a short period of the achievement of self-government.

36. Australia's long term interests will be best served by a peaceful and well-ordered Papua and New Guinea well disposed towards Australia. It is probable that in 1972 the majority of Papuans and New Guineans will not wish to move to internal self-government. If Australia withdraws to meet the wishes of a vocal minority the result could be violence, possibly secession and possibly even civil war. Australia may then be asked to intervene to sustain the self-governing authorities. The other side of the coin is that if Australia by being too hesitant stays on too long it may be faced with frequent disorders reflecting the acute pressure of rapid social and economic transition. In the extreme this could involve the Government in a decision however reluctant to call out military forces to aid the Administration.

37. If it is correct that to get out too quickly could raise serious problems, it may also be correct that to stay too long could have serious effects. Clearly the objective should be to time disengagement so that it most nearly corresponds with the overall reality of Territory conditions. This entails judgements made in the light of Territory factors rather than in the light of reaction in Australia. Situations may frequently arise where possible courses of action would be acceptable in Papua and New Guinea (e.g. law and order) which would not be acceptable in Australia: and similarly situations arise in the Territory (e.g. acquisition of land) which cannot be resolved by applying there measures which may be acceptable in Australia.

38. There are real difficulties of striking such a balance. In the past years the Government's policy of determining changes in harmony with the wishes of the majority of the people has been interpreted by some as being synonymous with moving at the pace of the slowest— including those expatriates who have a vested interest in making no change at all; yet in fact the Government has taken the initiative in constitutional change, and has been somewhat ahead of the majority Territory view. These difficulties may be able to be reduced in a number of ways e.g.

(i) by pressing authority on to native members of the House of Assembly and native public servants.

(ii) different measures of authority in different local government areas.

While such measures accord with existing policy it will be necessary to press them at the local and the district levels as well as in Port Moresby; and to seek a situation in which changes are made before pressure arises for them. In this way it can be made clear that the Commonwealth's purpose is to advance the native people and not to preserve the position of Australians in the Territory. Policies on these lines have perhaps in the past been applied somewhat hesitantly because of resistance by those Australians—both in private enterprise and in the public service—who exercise the authority which would be transferred to native hands. If the objective described above is to be achieved, these policies will need to be pressed whether such opposition is encountered or not.

39. As more responsibility is given to native representatives it is axiomatic that the officials of the Administration should cooperate to the full in ensuring that elected native people carry their full responsibility.

40. The Cabinet paper being submitted in parallel with this paper suggests further substantial steps along the road to self-government. Its proposals represent a move along a course that might avoid the worst of either of the extremes indicated above. This middle course would

involve pushing the devolution of political authority on to the people's elected representatives—and on native leaders at all levels—just as fast as (or indeed a little faster than) it could be readily digested or would be understood in the more conservative areas. The intention would be to achieve self-determination as soon as practicable in a climate in which the people of the Territory would feel that Australia was anxious to promote their autonomy yet continue to assist them.

Conclusions

41. The implications of early self-government against later self-government are considered in relation to the assumption that:

It is Australia's objective to disengage from Papua and New Guinea in a way which promotes a peaceful, economically and politically viable state well disposed towards Australia and receptive to Australian influence.

42. A basic requisite for self-government is the existence of a leader group or party to whom power and the responsibility of government can be given with reasonable assurance of sufficient local support to ensure effective government. A highly localised public service would be helpful but is probably not a pre-requisite.

43. Immediate problems are:

(i)   widely differing political views in different parts;

(ii) differing levels of development;

(iii) A pronounced lack of internal unity;

(iv) an adherence to customs some of which are incompatible with self-government (e.g. the pronounced unwillingness to make land available for the public benefit).

44. What unity there is has been imposed by the Administration. Withdrawal of outside authority could lead to pressures for Australian intervention to maintain law and order or to prevent secession.

45. On the other hand if withdrawal is delayed too long there could be localised disorder directed against the Administration. The incidents on Bougainville and the Gazelle Peninsula, whilst greatly exaggerated in the Australian press, are an indication of types of events which may recur in the coastal area. There is however no real likelihood of the sort of serious deterioration of the kind experienced in Malaya or Kenya.

46. Whether the move to self-government is taken early or late may make little difference in money or aid terms. Australian officials would continue to be available even though working for native Ministers. Technical assistance would continue to be provided. It is unlikely, however, that self-government (as a stage on the road to independence with a continued Australian responsibility for external affairs and defence) would last for long.

47. It is clear that the great majority of Territory people are opposed to early self-government. Many of them have said they will resist it to the point of fighting or secession. Without firm reassurance of a continued Australian presence after self-government it could not be expected that they would change their views by 1972.

48. There are advantages and disadvantages in whichever course is chosen.

49. If a move to early self-government is favoured the following steps would be necessary:

(a) it would be desirable that the decision be taken now;

(b) responsibility would need to be handed over progressively to elected representatives—not only from Canberra to Port Moresby but also from Port Moresby to local government bodies;

(c) a massive communications effort would be necessary;

> (i) to dispel notions that self-government means a withdrawal of Australian support—the continued presence of Australians and assistance from Australia would need to be stressed;

> (ii) to try to promote national unity.

(d) the pace of localisation of the public service would need to be stepped up;

(e) positive action would need to be taken to help to retain the services of experienced expatriate public servants;

(f) the position regarding confidence of overseas investors would need to be kept under review.

50. The objective might be more nearly realised by a process of intermediate steps. On this basis similar action to that suggested in para. 49 will be necessary but would be taken in a less dramatic way. Action might include in particular

(a) stronger emphasis on indigenous participation (at territorial and local level), in the society and the economy of the Territory;

(b) pressing responsibility on to elected representatives at a faster rate than they may wish, including the exercise of additional responsibilities by local government bodies in different parts of the Territory;

(c) the progressive transfer to Territory control of those internal functions of government presently controlled and operated by the Commonwealth, e.g. civil aviation, works.

Essentially it would be a course which hastens the development of those matters basic to effective self-government.

51. There is no need for an early Government decision unless a deadline for self-government such as 1972 is adopted. A practicable course would be to move ahead on the basis proposed in the accompanying Cabinet paper (increased responsibility) and for the Government to assess the situation in the Territory from time to time. It is clear, however, that during this period a policy which forces indigenous participation at all levels will be critical.

[NAA: A5869, VOLUME 19]

48   CABINET SUBMISSION 328[1]

Canberra, 9 June 1970

CONFIDENTIAL

Papua and New Guinea
Increased Responsibility for Ministerial Members and
Assistant Ministerial Members

Purpose

In the statement to Parliament on 4th March 1970 the Minister for External Territories announced increased authority for Ministerial Members of the Papua and New Guinea House of Assembly and foreshadowed further constitutional changes later in the year.[2]

2.   The purpose of this submission is to put before Ministers proposals to transfer to the Administrator's Executive Council Ministerial Members and Assistant Ministerial Members in Papua and New Guinea final authority in certain defined fields of government or on specified subjects with a corresponding change in the legislative area and with some complementary rearrangements in the Commonwealth Estimates of the way in which Commonwealth aid to the Territory is represented.

Background

3.   The proposal for action of this kind arises out of consideration that the Government's stance in relation to Papua and New Guinea should be one which encourages rather than discourages progress towards self-government. Moreover it appears that if real progress is to be made in that direction intermediate steps towards self-government should be taken and that now is the time to take them.

4.   The proposals are set out in detail in the attached draft statement prepared by the Department of External Territories in consultation with the AG's Department,[3] Prime Minister's Department and Treasury.[4] The draft statement has the broad support of Prime Minister's Department and AG's see no objection from a legal point of view. Treasury is in general agreement with the broad objectives but has reservations about suggesting [...] that the costs of the New Guinea Constabulary and Judiciary should come under the aid item ('Development Grant') for which in general it is contemplated the Commonwealth would bear all or most of the cost. Other Treasury points of difference are recorded in paragraph 17 below.

5.   A separate submission has been circulated regarding the implications of the early achievement of internal self-government in Papua and New Guinea.[5] This provides Ministers with some Departmental views on this question which may help in assessing the timing and appropriateness of the action proposed below and in placing the proposals in perspective as intermediate steps in the process of constitutional change towards self-government or independence.

---

1   Submitted by Barnes.

2   Document 26.

3   Attorney-General's Department.

4   Not published.

5   Document 47.

6.   If the proposals set out in this submission are adopted they should be presented in such a way as not to alienate or excite the predominant body of opinion against early self-government notably in the Highlands, the Sepik area and some parts of the Islands and perhaps in some parts of Papua. However it should be possible to present them in a way which avoids undue adverse reaction of this kind whilst making it clear to the Territory as a whole and to the Australian public and to countries overseas that Australia is encouraging the political as well as the economic development of Papua and New Guinea.

7.   It is proposed these changes be discussed with Ministerial Members and with the House of Assembly Select Committee on Constitutional Development. Subject to those discussions it is envisaged that they will be announced by the Prime Minister during his proposed visit to Papua and New Guinea in July.

8.   The Administrator has suggested that the Administrator's Executive Council may oppose the proposal for the withdrawal of official members from the Administrator's Executive Council when decisions are taken in specified matters. However in the light of the principles in paragraph 15 below and as officials may attend meetings as departmental advisers it is considered desirable to retain this aspect.

The Proposal

9.   In essence the proposal provides for a transfer of powers of final decision in specified fields or subjects to Ministerial Members and Assistant Ministerial Members acting individually or collectively. In so far as Ministerial office holders take final decisions individually on these matters they will be subject to the authority of the Administrator's Executive Council. Ministerial office holders will be in roughly the same relationship to the Administrator's Executive Council as Commonwealth Ministers to the Cabinet.

10.   The present arrangements approved by the Minister for External Territories under section 25(1) of the Papua and New Guinea Act provide that subject to the overall responsibility of the Minister for External Territories (acting through the Administrator) Ministerial Members are fully responsible to the Administrator's Executive Council for the day to day running of their Departments.

11.   It is proposed that this overall responsibility continue to be maintained and that Assistant Ministerial Members who have hitherto had no specific responsibilities should have the same kind of day-to-day responsibility with regard to their allotted areas of operation. For Ministerial Members it is additionally now proposed that subject to the general surveillance and over-riding authority of the Administrator's Executive Council, they exercise full responsibility (i.e. they take final decisions) in respect of specified areas or subjects. Their scope of final decision-making will be the subjects listed under each portfolio in a determination by the Minister and will be additional to their day-to-day responsibilities for the running of their respective Departments. Illustrative lists of subjects in which they could have that additional power to take final decisions are shown in Annex A.[6] Similarly, it is proposed that Assistant Ministerial Members will not only have broad day-to-day responsibilities for the running of the division or part of a Department assigned to them but additionally in respect of certain matters specified in the Minister's determination they will have authority (under the Administrator's Executive Council) to take final decisions. Illustrative lists of subjects in which they will have such full authority (smaller in total than for Ministerial Members) are shown in Annex B.[7]

---

6   The various 'matters or subjects' to be transferred to ministerial members were education, public health, trade and industry, labour, public works, and posts and telegraphs. See also the extracts from Annex A included with this document.

7   The new responsibilities for assistant ministerial members were treasury, transport, local government, lands, surveys and mines, social development and home affairs, forests, information and extension services, and corrective institutions. See also the extracts from Annex B included with this document.

12. The illustrative lists for Ministerial Members and Assistant Ministerial Members do not of course show all the other matters for which they have general responsibility subject to the Administrator. The lists will be firmed up after consultation with Ministerial Members and Assistant Ministerial Members.

13. The proposed additional power to take final decisions on specified matters will be exercised within the agreed development programme and also within the annually agreed financial provisions of the Territory budget.

14. The Commonwealth remains ultimately responsible for the whole of the government of the Territory and all the proposed arrangements including the authority for Ministerial office holders to take final decisions on some of the matters they handle would therefore operate within that overall responsibility. It is expected that in practice the need for Commonwealth intervention will not arise in relation to specified subjects (i.e. the area in which the Ministerial office holders have power to take final decisions). It is proposed however that in the unlikely event of the Commonwealth deciding that it needs to intervene in a particular decision of that kind a statement of the circumstance will be tabled in the Commonwealth Parliament and will also be tabled for information in the Territory House of Assembly.

Basic Principles of the Proposal

15. The proposed additional arrangements are based upon the following principles:

(a) The Commonwealth remains ultimately responsible for the whole of the government of the Territory and the new arrangements therefore apply within that broad responsibility;

(b) The transfer of power contemplated is a transfer from the Minister for External Territories to elected Ministerial office holders in the Territory and not to the Administrator or to officials of the Administration;

(c) as far as practicable, the arrangements will provide that those in the Territory who take final decisions under the new arrangements will be responsible for the financial consequences of those decisions;

(d) to continue to be able to discharge its fundamental overall responsibility the Commonwealth must retain full authority in relation to such matters as the judiciary, law and order, civil rights, internal security and land policy. Also because of its massive aid directed to accelerated economic development the Commonwealth has a special responsibility for the development programme and major development projects. That is, on subjects coming under these headings Ministerial Members and Assistant Ministerial Members would continue as at present to exercise their day-to-day responsibilities subject to the Minister through the Administrator but would not have powers of final decision.

16. The selection of fields or subjects on which Ministerial office holders will exercise final decisions has been based to a considerable extent on the following criteria:

(i) matters of special local interest and matters particularly bound up with the traditions and customs of the peoples of the Territory;

(ii) matters primarily of a social or welfare character without a direct relation to economic development;

(iii) matters with a high degree of political sensitivity.

17. Partly in order to ensure as far as practicable that final decisions will carry their financial consequences with them and partly to give a clearer picture of the purposes for which Australian aid is given to Papua and New Guinea and partly to induce with the Administration as a whole and with the House of Assembly a greater regard for the cost consequences of decisions it is now contemplated that the present single line item in the Division of the Commonwealth

Estimates headed 'Papua and New Guinea—Miscellaneous Services Grant to Administration towards expenses' should be re-defined into several broad categories which would distinguish:

(a) the amount being made available by way of grant-in-aid to help finance recurrent expenditures;

(b) the amount appropriated as grants for development purposes;

(c) allowances and other benefits for expatriate officers of the Papua and New Guinea Public Services, etc;

(d) loans for specific development projects or capital works.

These categories are illustrative only at this stage and may be modified in detail as progress is made in formulating the Estimates in 1970/71. The Department of External Territories proposes a single grant in respect of development projects generally—see (b) above—which would appear under some such description as 'Development Grant'. The Treasury has no objection to this broad category but feels it would be desirable to sub-divide it in some way to provide additional information to Parliament on payments made for specific developmental purposes. However, both Departments are agreed that it will not be possible to take final decisions on these matters until the final shape of the Territory Budget for 1970/71 and the nature and magnitude of the assistance which the Commonwealth is prepared to provide for Papua and New Guinea next year are known. The details of the proposed estimates presentation are set out in paragraphs 21 to 29 of the attached draft statement.

18. In parallel with the changes of the executive government of the Territory it is proposed that the Commonwealth should state its intention not to veto ordinances passed by the House of Assembly relating to the subject or fields that may be specified in harmony with 9 and 15 above. It is also proposed that an elected member of the Administrator's Executive Council instead of an official member should be the spokesman in the House of Assembly for the Administrator's Executive Council when one is required.

19. The proposed changes will not require amendment to the Papua and New Guinea Act. It is envisaged that they be effected by instruments under the Act and by delegation.

20. Decisions taken or measures adopted in 'specified' fields or subjects will be reported to the Minister for External Territories.

21. Apart from the problem of reaction from native opinion in Papua and New Guinea against early self-government that I have referred to in paragraph 6 above two issues of confidence arise when changes of the kind now proposed are contemplated. The first relates to overseas officers of the Territory Public Service and the second relates to the role and confidence of overseas investors in Papua and New Guinea now or in the future.

22. So far as the Territory Public Service is concerned a separate submission has been circulated proposing a new Commonwealth Service to be called the Australian Service for Overseas Cooperation. This is designed to help give effect in a practical way to the Government's intention that Australians should be available to help in the government of Papua and New Guinea so long as they are needed and desired. The scheme proposes to achieve this by giving an assurance of permanence to selected experienced overseas officers now serving in the territory as permanent officers or contract officers and to selected overseas officers who may be appointed to public service positions in the Territory in the future.

23. The other issue of confidence relates to overseas investment.

24. In recent years requests have been received from Territory business interests (especially the New Guinea Planters' Association) for government guarantees of their assets in the Territory. These requests are likely to become more pressing with successive steps towards self-government.

25. There is as yet no evidence of slackening inflow of private investment funds to the Territory. Nor is there any evidence that established investors are anxious to transfer their assets out of the Territory. Deposits with trading and savings banks in the Territory have been rising; most overseas investment is of course in fixed assets but again there is no evidence of owners disinvesting through failure to maintain their assets or of distress sales at sharply reduced prices.

26. In the light of this situation no specific action by the Government is proposed but it is suggested that the position regarding investment confidence in Papua and New Guinea will need to be kept under review. However it might be helpful for a government statement to be made indicating that overseas investors may take renewed confidence from the Government's intention to continue strong financial support of the public sector and to give a Commonwealth guarantee of permanence to key overseas officers of the Territory Public Service.

27. If Ministers approve these new constitutional proposals their substance might be announced by the Prime Minister during his visit to Papua and New Guinea in July. It will also be necessary for them to be the subject of a Parliamentary statement. In view of the changes in the Commonwealth Estimates referred to in paragraph 17 above some explanation will be needed in the Treasurer's budget speech and the comprehensive statement on the constitutional proposals as a whole should therefore be made as soon as practicable after the budget is brought down.

RECOMMENDATION

28. I recommend:

(a) that Australian aid to Papua and New Guinea be presented in the Estimates so as to show in a general way on the lines of paragraph 17 how Australian aid to the Territory is used;

(b) that Ministers

(i) endorse the proposed transfer of authority in defined fields of government to the Administrator's Executive Council, Ministerial Members and Assistant Ministerial Members;

(ii) authorise an announcement by the Prime Minister in July; and

(iii) authorise a Ministerial statement in Parliament on the lines of the attached draft.[8]

Attachment

Attached are illustrative lists of subjects in which Ministerial Members and Assistant Ministerial Members have additional powers to make final decisions. In each case the Ministerial office holder has to day to day responsibilities for the running of his Department of division or part of a Department assigned to him and his scope of final decision making in the subjects listed will be additional to his day to day responsibilities.

The lists are set out in the form they would take as Determinations made by the Minister under section 24(2) of the Papua and New Guinea Act.

The principles on which the lists are based are set out in paragraph 16 of the submission. The lists will be settled after consultation with Ministerial Members and Assistant Ministerial Members.

---

8   Not published. For the final statement, see Document 63.

Annex A
Ministerial Member for Agriculture, Stock and Fisheries:
Department of Agriculture, Stock and Fisheries

All the matters related to the functions of the said Department and for the purposes [...] of the arrangements approved under section 25(1) of the Papua and New Guinea Act the following specified matters:

Agricultural extension services.

Farmer training and institutions.

Technical services in agricultural, pastoral and fishing industries.

Agricultural, pastoral and veterinary training other than agricultural extension and farmer training.

Fishing surveys and training.

Pilot commercial schemes of seeds and planting materials for resale.

Liaison on technical matters with consumers of primary products.

Export quality control.

Marketing services for indigenous producers.

Crop processing facilities for smallholders.

Fauna surveys.

Pilot production of livestock for resale.

Livestock stations.

Abattoirs.

Purchase of cash crops and livestock from indigenous communities.

Introduction and development of new crops.

Disease and pest control.

[*matter omitted*][9]

---

9   The omitted material comprises details of the expanded authority to be exercised by the ministerial members for education, public health, trade and industry, labour, public works, and posts and telegraphs. In each instance these details begin with a general statement saying that the members will be responsible for 'All the matters related to the functions of the said Department and, for the purposes [...] of the arrangements approved under section 25(1) of the Papua and New Guinea Act, the following specified matters'. Then follow a list of specified matters. For the ministerial member for education, for example, the list refers to primary, secondary, vocational and technical education; scholarship allocation for teacher trainees; educational research and teaching methods; provision of school furniture, equipment and teaching aids; and transport of school children.

Annex B
Assistant Ministerial Member for Treasury:
Department of the Treasury

All the matters related to the functions of the said Department and for the purposes […] of the arrangements approved under section 25(1) of the Papua and New Guinea Act the following specified matters:

Financial aspects of Territory/Commonwealth relationships including participation in discussions with the Commonwealth on the formulation of draft estimates.

Financial aspects of powers or functions on which Ministerial Office Holders make final decisions.

Management of the public debt.

Price Control.

Collection of revenue and authorisation of expenditure in accordance with law.

[*matter omitted*][10]

[NAA: A5869, VOLUME 19]

---

10 The omitted material comprises details of the expanded authority to be exercised by the assistant ministerial members for transport, local government, lands, surveys and mines, social development and home affairs, forests, information and extension services, and corrective institutions. In each instance these details begin with a general statement saying that the members will be responsible for 'All the matters related to the functions of the said Department and, for the purposes […] of the arrangements approved under section 25(1) of the Papua and New Guinea Act, the following specified matters'. Then follow a list of specified matters. For the assistant ministerial member for local government, for example, the list refers to town and district advisory councils; establishment, development and extension of local government, including urban local government; local government elections, local government health and education grants, and the remuneration of village officials.

49   TELEX FROM HAY TO WARWICK SMITH

Port Moresby, 13 June 1970

CONFIDENTIAL

Prime Minister to Visit New Guinea[1]

In light of [a] later TIC[2] Report and decision of Prime Minister to visit Rabaul, I have set up a working party to review the situation in depth and come up with an assessment and recommendations which I would send down next weekend and which could be discussed with the Minister and yourself when I come down later in June.

2.   In effect what has been taking place in past four months has been a holding action while moves were encouraged among the Tolais themselves to heal their divisions over the MA[3] and Council issue and create a situation where their long-term problems could be tackled with Administration support. Policy was stated by Johnson[4] over Admin. Radio in February and speech had a good effect and is still referred to. There have been some responses from Council, older men, Warmaram[5] and among individual MA leaders. But none among hard core MA. And the smaller but quite significant Warbete Group[6] (which is anti-Council of any kind) has not changed its attitude. The effects of the considerable restraint exercised by police and field staff have tended to weaken the Council and respect for law generally and to strengthen the MA standing.

3.   Broadly the options seem to be:

(a) To continue the holding action either in present form or on basis of freezing or suspending the Council pending an all Tolai solution which on present indications would be pretty much on MA lines though MA would not have the credit.

(b) Reversion to mono-Council.

(c) Determined, large scale effort to restore Council and uphold MRC[7] concept.

---

1   A press release of 12 June had announced that: 'The Prime Minister, Mr John Gorton, will visit Papua-New Guinea from 5th to 11th July … [H]e will travel extensively, visit a number of key centres, have discussions with elected Members of the House of Assembly, and with the Administration, and meet with representative groups and organisations throughout the Territory. Mr Gorton said today that he wanted to get a first-hand impression of developments in Papua–New Guinea, and to meet and talk with a wide cross-section of the community. Mrs Gorton will be travelling with the Prime Minister, and he will also be accompanied by the Minister for Territories, Mr Barnes, and the retiring Administrator, Mr David Hay, who will become Secretary of the Department of External Territories at the end of July.' Once finalised, the itinerary included Port Moresby, Goroka, Mt Hagen, Mendi, Wewak, Madang, Lae, Rabaul, Kieta and Buka. Press Release, 'Mr Gorton to Visit PNG', 12 June 1970, NAA: A1209, 6723.

2   Territory Intelligence Committee.

3   Set up in June 1969 shortly after the elections for the first multi-racial council in the Gazelle Peninsula, the Mataungan Association (MA) had strong support within the Tolai community. It campaigned militantly (and at times violently) for full local self-government verging on independence.

4   This appears to be a reference to Assistant Administrator (and subsequently Administrator) Les Johnson.

5   Warmaram was a government-approved and supported organisation of Tolai leaders, from the public service and private sector, which sought to mediate in the dispute between the Administration and the Mataungan Association. See Ian Downs, *The Australian Trusteeship: Papua New Guinea, 1945–75*, Australian Government Publishing Service, Canberra, 1980, p. 431.

6   The Warbete Group of villages refused to have local councils or pay council taxes. See ibid., pp. 137, 431.

7   Multi–Racial Council.

4. These options will be examined from the points of view of

(i) Administration's capacity to impose its will and repercussions inside and outside Territory of so doing.

(ii) Effect on Council system elsewhere.

(iii) Effect on developing situation within Gazelle.

[NAA: 452, 1975/105]

50   TELEX TO PORT MORESBY

Canberra, 18 June 1970

6054. CONFIDENTIAL

Gazelle

We have also been giving some thought to the Prime Minister's visit to Rabaul. The PM cannot be left open to the accusation that he made no serious attempt during a visit to Rabaul to resolve differences and we understand from your 9603 of 10 June[1] that this also accords with your view. We appreciate that there may be developments within the next three weeks. If however the Warmaram group[2] have still made no progress and an all-Tolai solution seems as far away as ever we feel that the Prime Minister should be put in a position of being able to announce or effect some Administration initiative which would be put into effect in default of agreement.

We would see the list of options as:

(1) Let things go as they are and wait for something to turn up i.e. give Warmaram more time;

(2) Reversion

(a) to mono-racial council;

(b) to four former councils;

(3) Establishment of more than one council based on existing areas of strength to enable MA[3] Council in MA area and multi-racial council in MRC[4] areas (not necessarily following old councils boundaries) but covering all present council area;

(4) Determined large scale effort to restore council and uphold MRC concept (this is not a realistic alternative if it involves reliance on Army aid to the civil power.

(5) Hold an early election on the basis that the MA may win (in this case we consider that Kokopo and possibly other areas with a substantial non-indigenous population should be excluded).

(6) Hold a referendum on previous alternatives (with questions chosen in advance and announced by PM. This may have much to commend it).

[*matter omitted*]

---

1   Not published.

2   See Document 49, fn. 5.

3   Mataungan Association. See Document 49, fn. 3.

4   Multi-Racial Council.

The working party will need to have regard to previous statements by Ministers. The Prime Minister has said that the government would consider a referendum by secret ballot on the multi-racial issue but that this had not been accepted by the MA. The Minister has said that the government looks to a solution of the Gazelle problems by negotiation among the people themselves, a further test for local opinion to be held by genuinely democratic procedures at an appropriate time. Again in his exchange with Mr Whitlam the Prime Minister stressed the necessity for the government to maintain law and order and to support a legally constituted and elected body. Any policy initiative now taken will need to be capable of reconciliation with those statements.

[NAA: A452, 1975/105]

51 TELEX FROM BALLARD TO WARWICK SMITH

Canberra, 18 June 1970

11359. SECRET

Further to Telex 11353.[1] Re Gazelle situation.

A resolution of the Gazelle Peninsula Council at a meeting on 16th June, 19 Members present voted to cease issue of summons and tax prosecutions until meeting on 8th July between Warmaram, MA and MRC to try to find a solution. In effect this is a partial capitulation by Council which because of lack of finance and public support could lead to early suspension of the Council. This action is likely to strengthen MA determination to continue present policy of civil disobedience. Now becoming clear that opposition to MRC only a pretext to major revolutionary aim to resist all laws which do not suit MA. Indication show a further deterioration in the security situation in Gazelle Peninsula. More aggressive action by the MA in occupying land known as Mandres, Japlik and Vunapalandig took place over the Queen's Birthday weekend.

[*matter omitted*]

Assessment: Indications show a general deterioration in the security situation of the Gazelle Peninsula. An adverse reception of the Prime Minister and party on arrival at Lakunai airstrip[2] by a group in excess of ten thousand, which may constitute a grave security risk, is not unlikely.

[NAA: A1209, 1970/6723]

---

1   Not published.
2   In Rabaul.

52   TELEX FROM HAY TO WARWICK SMITH

Port Moresby, 22 June 1970

9998. CONFIDENTIAL

Stage Two

I have not seen final form of paper which is to go before Cabinet.[1] Minister asked me to let
him have any final comments. Please place the following before him, based on our exchanges
on earlier drafts which have led to broad agreement in many aspects.

(a) I strongly support the general thesis that the area of final decision making in the
Territory should be enlarged

(b) The procedures for taking decisions in the Territory should be suited to local
conditions including inexperience of Ministerial office holders and a natural preference
for collective rather than individual responsibility. Emphasis should be given to the role
of the AEC as a policy making body to which Ministerial office holders are responsible.
It could also have decision making responsibility in areas (e.g. local government) where
responsibility should be taken locally but where there is no Ministerial Member, and in
areas of particular importance such as taxation.

(c) The list of functions in respect of which decision making authority is to be transferred
to the Territory should include some of the more contentious ones such as land and
taxation. Otherwise elected Members will continue to avoid personal involvement in and
responsibility for decisions which, although vitally necessary, may evoke criticism and
possibly physical resistance.

(d) The need to involve elected members in difficult decisions should extend to nominated
functions in which for broad policy reasons it is not proposed to transfer decision-making
authority to the Territory—e.g. law and order, and the development programme. Otherwise
they could be regarded as imposed decisions and could be resisted. This can be achieved
by the Commonwealth agreeing to negotiate with the AEC as distinct from consulting as
at present.

(e) The financial arrangements consequent on the transfer of decision making authority
should retain a degree of flexibility in the early stages.

(f) In general the Commonwealth should lean towards rather than against the early
achievement of internal self-government. The prerequisites, such as citizenship legislation,
should be identified and steps taken to bring policy issues to early consideration.

[NAA: A452, 1970/2570]

---

1   The paper referred to appears to have been a draft of Cabinet Submission 328 (Document 48). Together
     with Cabinet Submission 327 (Document 47), this submission was put before Cabinet the following day,
     23 June 1970 (see Document 53).

53   CABINET DECISION 452

Canberra, 23 June 1970

Submission No. 327:
Papua and New Guinea—Implications of Early Self-Government[1]

The Cabinet noted the Submission and expressed general agreement with the conclusion drawn by the Minister from the report attached that it would be more desirable to proceed to self-government by way of intermediate steps—seeing this as a continuation, though at a faster pace, of present policy.

2.   With this objective, it endorsed the measures as proposed by the Minister in paragraphs 8 and 9 of the Submission.

[*matter omitted*][2]

[NAA A5869, VOLUME 19]

54   CABINET DECISION 453

Canberra, 23 June 1970

Submission No. 328:
Papua and New Guinea—Increased Responsibility for
Ministerial Members and Assistant Ministerial Members[1]

In the context of Decision No. 452,[2] and as recommended by the Minister, the Cabinet:

(a) agreed that Australian aid to Papua and New Guinea should be presented in the Estimates so as to show in a general way, on the lines of paragraph 17 of the Submission, how Australian aid to the Territory is used;

(b) endorsed the proposed transfer of authority in defined fields of government to the Administrator's Executive Council, Ministerial Members and Assistant Ministerial Members;

(c) authorised an announcement of (b) by the Prime Minister in July; and

(d) authorised a Ministerial statement in Parliament on the lines of the draft attached to the Submission.

[NAA: A5869, VOLUME 19]

---

1   Document 47.

2   The omitted matter reiterated paragraphs 8 & 9 of Submission 327 (Document 47).

---

1   Document 48.

2   Document 53.

55   TELEX TO CANBERRA

Port Moresby, 24 June 1970

11392. Secret

Administration's comments on Gazelle Peninsula Sitrep of 10.30AM 24th June[1] are as follows:

It is clear that Kaputin is whipping up opposition to Administration and Prime Minister with good effect and the Waramaram letter[2] has considerably strengthened his position. Irrespective of whether Prime Minister visits Rabaul his visit to the Territory may be used by Mataungan Association to bring matters to a head through large scale confrontation. By midday Friday we should know if any hope of negotiating with Mataungans on Prime Minister's visit is possible and by Monday we should know fairly full details of how Prime Minister's visit will be handled by the Mataungan Association.

It appears likely that confrontation will develop in any event within the next month and we need to prepare for this eventuality. It is considered that the Administrator should make a statement as soon as possible outlining the developments that have led to the situation where we are now faced with a complete breakdown of law and order. It is important that the public be fully prepared before any confrontation takes place. A draft statement is being prepared for further study. If confrontation inevitable it preferable Administration choose time and place by bringing it on through e.g. arresting leaders for tax evasion or taking action to eject trespassers and the advantages of bringing matters to a head will need to be carefully considered. Defence representatives being kept in picture in case of further developments. Please forward copy of this telex and all Sitreps to Hay urgently.

[NAA: A452, 1971/2294]

---

1   Not published.

2   For background on Warmaram, see Document 49, fn. 5. With respect to the 'Warmaram letter', Don Woolford has noted that 'a privately circulated newsletter late in May published a letter sent by the director of information and extension services, Lyall Newby, to the manager of Radio Rabaul. The letter revealed the extent of the Administration's support for Warmaram and, more damagingly, said one of Warmaram's aims was to "destroy Kaputin's standing". The effect of the disclosure was to destroy whatever standing Warmaram might have had and to totally discredit the supposed impartiality of the already highly suspect radio station, which was supposed to be the Administration's chief communication with the Tolais.' Don Woolford, *Papua New Guinea: Initiation and Independence*, University of Queensland Press, Brisbane, 1976, pp. 54–55. See also Hank Nelson, *Papua New Guinea. Black Unity or Black Chaos?*, Penguin Books Australia, Ringwood, Victoria, 1972, pp. 218–219.

56   TELEX TO CANBERRA

Port Moresby, 25 June 1970

11398. CONFIDENTIAL

Please pass to Hay and Warwick Smith urgently.

Special from Rabaul at 1500 hours 25 June.

Reference negotiations with MA Executive concerning PM's visit, discussions between Emanuel and Tammur on 24th and 25th. Tammur emphasised MA will definitely have demonstration and protest march on the 9th July. Although Executive will meet to discuss this on Saturday, his personal opinion is that MA will not repeat not call off demonstration.

Tammur stated he cannot guarantee non-violence, as he is afraid of Kaputin and Tomot,[1] as they are sick of the Government. Tammur stated that Kaputin intended organising a protest march in Pt. Moresby for the PM's visit. No further details available. Tammur himself raised the possibility of him going to Canberra to meet the PM at his own expense, prior to the PM's visit, to obtain the views of the PM on an MA proposal for immediate self-government for the Gazelle Peninsula. He aims to precede the PM to the Gazelle and to announce in advance, the PM's decision on the proposal. As the decisions of the PM would not be favourable, this would exacerbate the situation, and therefore Emanuel is attempting to persuade Tammur to postpone the Canberra visit until after PM's visit to TPNG on the grounds that both he and the PM would have a clearer understanding of the situation after the PM's visit.

Tammur is under pressure by the MA Executive to move a motion in the House of Assembly in August as follows: 'That the Gazelle Peninsula be granted self-government now'. He knows that he will be opposed and the motion lost, but this is what the MA Executive claim the majority of the Tolai people want.

Reference Warmaram.[2] Leaders are agreeable to serious talks with all leaders, and the PM, but Warmaram are unable to communicate with the MA Executive, and any possibility of talks between Warmaram, the Council, Warbete[3] and MA representatives prior to the PM's visit have been blocked by the MA. Emanuel will contact Members of MA Executive today and tomorrow for further discussions.

[NAA: A452, 1970/2973]

---

1   Melkior Tomot, MA Secretary.

2   See Documents 49 (fn. 5) & 55 (fn. 2).

3   See Document 49, fn. 6.

57   MINUTE FROM HORNE[1] TO EASTMAN[2]

Canberra, 26 June 1970

Secret

TPNG—Situation in the Gazelle Peninsula

Secretary[3]—to see

This afternoon I attended a meeting convened by the Department of External Territories, and attended by representatives of several Departments, including Prime Minister's, Defence, and the Services. The meeting was briefed on the general deterioration of the situation in the Rabaul area. There was discussion of the security implications for the Prime Minister's visit to Rabaul on 8/9 July.

TIC[4] Assessment

2.   In its assessment for the week ending 25th July, the TIC, Port Moresby, commented:

' ... It now seems certain that a large, hostile demonstration will be organised against the Prime Minister at the time of his arrival at Rabaul ... There is no indication that the Mataungan Association leaders plan a violent demonstration but the tension and animosity in the Gazelle has reached a stage where the actions of large crowds are unpredictable ... Should a crowd of the size expected (8–12,000 people) get out of hand it would be extremely difficult to guarantee the security of the airport and its access road. The visit of the PM and party could act as a catalyst on an already tense situation.'

[*matter omitted*]

PM's visit

4.   The following points emerged at this afternoon's meeting:

(a) Mr Warwick Smith has written to Mr Hewitt stating that, subject to the PM's clearance, his Minister proposes to authorise a 'swoop' on Monday (29th June) on about 40 Tolais who have warrants out against them. The aim would be to bring a confrontation with the Mataungan Association to a head now rather than have it come to a head of its own accord during the PM's visit.

(b) The Administration would like 2 Hercules to stand-by as from Sunday 28th June until after the PM's visit, in case it may be necessary to airlift 240 police from various parts of TPNG to Rabaul.

(c) With the Germans in mind, Mr Barnes has apparently suggested that a warship in the Rabaul harbour during the visit might help to keep the lid on any trouble.[5]

(d) An Army Guard of Honour of platoon strength was being considered. It could also be used if necessary to protect the PM (I assume this would come from the PIR).

---

1   Donald Horne, Head, Intelligence Coordination Branch, DEA.
2   A. J. (Allan) Eastman, First Assistant Secretary, Division II, DEA.
3   DEA Secretary Keith Waller.
4   Territory Intelligence Committee.
5   This is presumably a reference to a means of imposing order used when New Guinea was a German colony.

DC Meeting

5.   Mr Blakers made it clear that Defence Department and the Defence Committee [DC] could not look at the situation piece-meal. As the DC had made clear previously, an authoritative and carefully considered assessment was needed to accompany any request for assistance from the Services.

[*matter omitted*]

9.   You may wish to raise this with the Secretary.

[NAA: A1838, 689/1 PART 6]

58   TELEX FROM WARWICK SMITH TO NEWMAN

Canberra, 27 June 1970

6410. Secret

1.   Please treat following message with extreme security.

2.   Have passed Prime Minister's views to Minister and have mentioned to him Administrator's and my own views. Following is outcome:

(A) Minister still wishes to go ahead on police action against tax defaulters in respect of whom warrants of arrest are outstanding.

(B) The action he contemplates is restricted to those persons against whom warrants of arrest have been outstanding for some little time i.e. it would not embrace anybody against whom warrants of arrest were issued this weekend or after today.

(C) Planning and preparation should go ahead under strict secrecy over the weekend including consultation with Curtis[1] so that there are no legal flaws in the action but no repeat no action is to be taken until Administrator returns to Port Moresby on Monday and authorises action to be taken.

(D) The whole purpose of the proceeding would be lost if defaulters were gaoled over the whole week thus raising the risk of major demonstration being mounted as a result of this action at the very time of Prime Minister's visit. Hence, no police action should take place after Wednesday.

(E) Planning and preparation referred to above would be conducted on the basis discussed by Ellis and Holloway[2] with Minister of maintaining complete surprise—the idea is the police would pounce on the defaulters. For this reason it is not expected that substantial numbers of police would be flown into Rabaul with the idea of public display of force. Minister leaves number of police to be flown to Rabaul and related questions of maintaining surprise element to Administrator.

[NAA: A452, 1975/105]

---

1   L. J. (Lindsay) Curtis, Secretary for Law in the PNG Administration.

2   Brian Holloway, Assistant Police Commissioner.

59   MEMORANDUM FROM DEPARTMENT OF DEFENCE TO DET

Canberra, 29 June 1970

Secret

Prime Minister's Visit to TPNG—Provision of Service Assistance

With reference to your memorandum of 26th June[1] and in confirmation of verbal advice my Minister has approved the request by your Department that arrangements be made for the provision of a RAAF Hercules from Richmond, and if necessary, Caribous from those already in the Territory, to move 250 police to Rabaul on 29th June, 1970.

2.   It is noted that your Department is examining the more comprehensive measures of assistance foreshadowed in the Administration's message to you of 26th June[2] and that a further approach will be made to this Department shortly.

[NAA: A452, 1970/2973]

---

1   Not published.

2   Not published.

60   MEMORANDUM FROM BALLARD TO HOLT[1]

Canberra, 29 June 1970

Secret

Rabaul Security Situation—Prime Minister's Visit

Further to our memorandum of 26th June 1970[2] the Department has received further reports (copies attached)[3] that state the Mataungan Association objectives are:

- to hold a massive demonstration at Rabaul airport at the time of the arrival of the Prime Minister and to force him to retire from the airport without putting a foot on Tolai soil;
- to damage Council Chambers and other places in Rabaul;
- to move on all available land in defiance of the law;
- to carry out a general civil disobedience campaign through the Gazelle.

2.   In view of the deteriorating situation and the need to have secure reliable communications in Rabaul before and during the Prime Minister's visit it is considered imperative by the Administration that an Army signals unit with cypher equipment be stationed and operating in Rabaul by Wednesday 1st July. This is supported by the Department. We see this as a need at present quite apart from the Prime Minister's visit.

3.   It would be appreciated if you would arrange for the authorisation of the movement of a signal unit to Rabaul on the same basis as the unit sent during the disturbances last December.[4]

[NAA: A452, 1970/2973]

---

1   Not identified. The context indicates that he was a Department of Defence official.

2   Not published, but see Document 57.

3   Not published.

4   For details on the disturbances in December 1969, see Stuart Doran (ed.), *Documents on Australian Foreign Policy: Australia and Papua New Guinea, 1966–1969*, Department of Foreign Affairs and Trade, Canberra, 2006, pp. 954–8 and Documents 333–6, 339–41, 346–8, 350–354.

61   TELEX TO CANBERRA

Port Moresby, 30 June 1970

11432. SECRET

Gazelle

The situation remains tense with opposition to constituted authority increasing as is evidenced by the incidents at Katakati where a police sergeant was prevented from making an arrest, at Vunapalandig where intrusions onto land are becoming more numerous despite notices to quit and at Kerevat where unlawful clearing of land continues.

The Prime Minister's Visit

With the issuing of a press statement by John Kaputin the MA has made public its intention to demonstrate against the Prime Minister.

The moderate tone of the press release in respect of the Prime Minister's visit tends to confirm that violence is not planned.

It should be noted however that

A.   Details of the demonstrations are not known (but should be after the MA meeting on 5 July);

B.   To date the MA has rejected all offers to cooperate with the authorities;

C.   There are strong reasons for believing that the MA will be able to attract very large numbers to the airport; and

D.   Unless the demonstration organisers are prepared to cooperate with the authorities it will be difficult to control a large crowd.

The possibility of incidents either at the airport or in the town has not diminished.

[*matter omitted*]

[NAA: A452, 1970/2973]

62   LETTER FROM TANGE TO HEWITT

Canberra, 2 July 1970

SECRET

I discussed yesterday with the Chiefs of Staff the request from the Department of External Territories, of which you are aware, for a PIR contingent to combine Guard of Honour duty with possible emergency assistance during the Prime Minister's visit to Rabaul. It was the Chiefs of Staff view, on the information then available, that 100 PIR deployed as a guard of honour would add little to the capability of the Constabulary. They might have to resort to substantial use of force which could result in casualties and aggravate the situation and there would be grave danger of their being overwhelmed with undesirable long term implications. In short, if the Government decided to deploy an Army force consideration should be given to its call-out and it should not be provided in the form of a guard of honour. It was also agreed that it would be desirable that the Army commence urgent training and indoctrination for the unaccustomed role of crowd control with minimum force.

My Minister[1] discussed the matter subsequently with the Prime Minister when it was agreed that approval should be withheld from the proposal to provide a guard of honour from the PIR. It was agreed that some training and indoctrination for possible use of the PIR in a crowd control situation should be carried out on a contingency basis.

There is a continuing exchange of signals between Army and the Commander TPNG Command from which information is now coming forward about the police arrangements for crowd control and the protection of the Prime Minister and also the potential which a PIR guard of honour might have in this situation. We are keeping the situation under review and I shall advise you further of developments.

I have forwarded copies of this letter to the Secretaries of the Departments of External Territories and External Affairs, the Attorney General's Department and of the three Service Departments.[2]

[NAA: A1209, 1970/6723]

---

1   Malcolm Fraser.

2   The secretaries referred to were David Hay, Keith Waller, Clarrie Harders, Frederick Green (Air), Bruce White (Army), and Sam Landau (Navy).

63   STATEMENT BY BARNES

Port Moresby, 6 July 1970

Increased Responsibility for Ministerial Members and
Assistant Ministerial Members

In the statement made by me to the Commonwealth Parliament on 4th March 1970[1] new
Approved Arrangements under section 25 of the Papua and New Guinea Act were announced
and changes were outlined in the powers and responsibilities of Ministerial Members.
The statement reaffirmed that the Government's approach was to transfer responsibility
progressively to elected members of the Territory House of Assembly. It was indicated that
further constitutional changes were under examination and that they would be put into effect
later this year.

2.   This statement sets out further intermediate steps in constitutional development in the
Territory which take effect from the date the legal instruments under the Papua and New Guinea
Act are tabled in the Parliament when it resumes in August. Under these further arrangements
Ministerial Members and Assistant Ministerial Members, subject to the Administrator's
Executive Council, exercise full authority in specified subjects or fields of government in
the Territory. Within the overall responsibility of the Commonwealth Government the
purpose of these new arrangements is to bring about a significant transfer of power to elected
representatives of the Territory people.

3.   The proposal consists of the following elements:

First—Under Determinations made by the Minister for External Territories under section
24(2) of the Papua and New Guinea Act certain matters are specified in respect of which
Ministerial Members and Assistant Ministerial Members in practice have full authority to
make decisions subject only to the Administrator's Executive Council.

4.   *Second*—In respect of the specified matters Ministerial office holders are responsible to
the Administrator's Executive Council.

5.   *Third*—In respect of specified matters the Administrator's Executive Council will be in
the same relationship to Ministerial and Assistant Ministerial Members as is the Cabinet to
Commonwealth Ministers. The Administrator's Executive Council will have some additional
responsibilities as explained below.

6.   *Fourth*—At present a number of broad policies in economic and social matters are set
down in the Development Programme which has been endorsed by the Australian Government
and the House of Assembly. Decisions will be taken within that agreed policy framework.
They will also be taken within agreed financial provisions set down in the annual Territory
Budget. As indicated in the statement of 4th March, 1970, the draft Budget will be the subject
of discussion between the Estimates Committee of the Administrator's Executive Council and
the Minister for External Territories.

7.   *Fifth*—In accordance with the normal situation in government, those who are responsible
in Papua and New Guinea for final decisions under these new arrangements will also carry
the responsibility for meeting the financial implications. In these matters the Australian
Government will not be concerned with individual items of expenditure. These will be
a purely local responsibility. In the budget discussions between the Government and the
Administrator's Executive Council, however, the total of the estimated expenditure in respect
of the specified matters will need to enter into the discussions as an element in the total budget.

---

1   Document 26.

Additional expenditures on particular specified matters arising in the course of the financial year could be met by transfers from other heads of expenditure within this broad category. Any addition to the total would in general be financed out of increased Territory revenue or loans.

8.   *Sixth*—The present arrangements approved by the Minister for External Territories under section 25(1) of the Papua and New Guinea Act provide that subject to the overall responsibility of the Minister for External Territories (acting through the Administrator) Ministerial Members are responsible to the Administrator's Executive Council for the day-to-day running of their Departments excepting public service aspects. Ministerial Members will retain this overall responsibility and Assistant Ministerial Members who have not hitherto had similar responsibilities will assume the same kind of day-to-day responsibility with regard to the parts or divisions of departments assigned to them. The new power of Ministerial office holders to make final decisions on specified subjects is additional to their day-to-day responsibility for the running of their respective Departments or parts of Departments.

9.   Under the Papua and New Guinea Act and internationally the Australian Government continues to be responsible for the administration of Papua and New Guinea and therefore on any particular matter the Government will continue to have a formal right to intervene. However, on many matters powers of final decision have been handed over to Ministerial and Assistant Ministerial Members. In future there will be no need to refer these matters to the Commonwealth Government.

10.   These changes represent a definite devolution of authority from the Commonwealth Government to Ministerial office holders in the territory. They will not preclude further constitutional steps forward as may be appropriate in the future for example when the views of the House of Assembly are known about any conclusions reached by the Select Committee on Constitutional Development. The Government reaffirms its policy that it will continue to develop the Territory for self-government and independence but it will not set any arbitrary date or timetable against the wishes of the people of the Territory. Moreover these changes do not in any way affect the Commonwealth's policy on the level of aid to Papua and New Guinea. They do not affect the Government's intention that large-scale aid will be maintained after self-government or independence.

11.   The new arrangements are a significant forward constitutional step. The authority of Ministerial Members is now substantially enlarged. Assistant Ministerial Members are given real authority.

12.   Overseas investment in the Territory has been increasing rapidly under the stimulus of the economic development programme and the heavy Commonwealth aid programme. Overseas investors will take renewed confidence from the Government's declared policy that large-scale Australian aid will continue to be made available to Papua New Guinea after self-government and independence and from the Government's offer to selected experienced overseas officers of the Territory Public Service of a new guarantee of permanence under the Commonwealth.

13.   With regard to the transfer of final authority in certain fields, the allocation of responsibilities now made is considered to fit the stage of the Territory's political development and the financial situation. The size of the Commonwealth's aid programme to the Territory is relevant. In 1969/70 nearly sixty per cent of the Territory Administration's expenditure was financed by Commonwealth grant and if other Commonwealth expenditure is taken into account sixty-three per cent of all government expenditure in the Territory was financed by the Commonwealth. This is $2 out of every $3 spent.

14.   The specified matters or subjects in respect of which Ministerial Members and Assistant Ministerial Members will make final decisions are set out in the Annexe to this statement.[2]

---

2   Not published. For the new responsibilities devolved to Ministerial Members and Assistant Ministerial Members, see Document 48, footnotes 6 & 7.

As already indicated areas of government activity or subjects not specified will remain the responsibility of Ministerial office holders in so far as the day-to-day administration of these matters are concerned subject to the authority of the Commonwealth Government acting through the Administrator as at present.

15. If necessary in the light of practical experience the Government will amend the lists of specified matters or make other changes.

16. As part of its fundamental responsibility the Australian Government will continue to be fully responsible in the same way as now for all other matters principally the judiciary, law and order, internal security, external affairs, international trade relations, defence and some matters which Commonwealth Departments administer directly in the Territory such as civil aviation. The Australian Government will also continue to carry special responsibility for projects necessary to give effect to the Development Programme.

17. It is not necessary to amend the Papua and New Guinea Act to give effect to these changes. They will be effected by Governor-General's instruction under section 15 of the Papua and New Guinea Act, by changes in the Determinations and Approved Arrangements made under the Act, by Regulations under the Act and in certain aspects by delegation or convention.

18. The arrangements outlined increase the authority of the Administrator's Executive Council, Ministerial Members and Assistant Ministerial Members; that is, they give increased power to the executive arm of government in Papua and New Guinea. The changes also enhance the authority of the House of Assembly in that in respect of Ordinances relating to any of the specified matters the right to withhold assent or to disallow will not be employed; that is legislation in the same area as that for which Ministerial Members and Assistant Ministerial Members have powers of final decision will not be blocked by the Commonwealth. Reflecting the greater responsibilities of elected Members of the Administrator's Executive Council it is proposed that one of their number be spokesman for the Council in the House of Assembly. He will assume some of the duties of the Senior Official Member.

[*matter omitted*]

28. To give effect to some aspects of the authority now vested in Ministerial Members and Assistant Ministerial Members in Papua and New Guinea arrangements will be made for the Administrator to delegate to them all appropriate powers and functions under ordinances previously exercised by Administration officials. The Administrator will in practice exercise his authority in respect of specified matters in accordance with the advice of the Administrator's Executive Council and individual Ministerial office holders.

[*matter omitted*]

[NAA: A452, 1970/3718]

64   SPEECH BY GORTON[1]

Port Moresby, 6 July 1970

Your Honour, Members of the Administrator's Executive Council, distinguished guests, ladies and gentlemen.

I think that the Territory of Papua and New Guinea and the other islands which at the moment make up the whole, faces a most difficult period in its evolution towards self-government in the future and towards independence. We have reached a stage of political development inside the Territory at which there are vocal demands for progress, or at least demands for changes in various fields. But such changes are probably more difficult in this Territory than in any other area of which I can think.

We have here in Papua and New Guinea and then across areas of sea, other islands which, as I said, at the moment make up a whole. We have a Territory composed of what are virtually different races, with different languages, with different district loyalties and we have a Territory in which some areas are clamouring for quicker advancement towards self-government and independence and other areas are fearful that the advance is already too swift. And we have a Territory, and I look to the future, which of its very nature is liable to be subject to the dangers of fragmentation.

Those dangers stem partly from different languages, partly from different outlook, partly from different stages of development. They can be reinforced by fallacious argument that if some part of Territory is fortunate enough to discover for example, a copper mine then it would be better off by itself. And if this fallacious argument, and I believe it is a fallacious argument, is accepted then at some stage there would be that fragmentation. If oil were discovered in Papua there could be a danger of fragmentation there, and so it would go on ultimately, I am sure, to the detriment of all the people of the Territory which we would like to see advance as a unit towards nationhood. Talking of advancing as a unit toward nationhood there have been, Sir, as you have said I think, great advances made economically and politically in the Territory since the Second World War.

I think the time has come for further advances to be made along that road. I do not speak of self-government in 1972 or in any calendar year that you may care to mention, because you are on a road towards self-government. You have started on it. There will necessarily be progress along it step by step and anyone who seeks to say that at a given month at a given year a period will have been reached when that can be achieved is, I think, dangerously simplifying the problem and is acting to the detriment of the people for the future.

But there are further steps now short of self-government but towards self-government which I feel should be made and these I wish to outline to you tonight. We believe that the time has come when less should be referred to Canberra for decision and more should be retained for decision by the Administrator's Executive Council and by the Ministerial Members who for the most part make up that Council. What we suggest is this —that there should be negotiated between the Australian Government and the Government here, a sum of money for recurrent expenses and for minor works inside the Territory. And, speaking for the Australian Government, we would expect that there would be more effort on the part of the local peoples to raise revenue inside this Territory, as years go by, for the purpose of this recurrent expenditure and these minor works. But once this sum of money had been negotiated, made up partly by local revenue, partly by what we will call a grant-in-aid for these purposes from the Commonwealth, then that sum of money, we believe, should be divided by the Administrator's

---

Executive Council among the various Ministries up here which will put in claims in the way Ministers put in claims to the Cabinet in Canberra.

So there will be a claim from the Minister of Education, there will be a claim from the Minister of Health, there will be a claim from the Minister of Public Works, and the Administrator's Executive Council—within the sum of money available to it—will apportion to these various Ministers the sums that they can spend. When that has been done, when a Minister, let us say, of Education, has received a sum within the total limits then we believe that he should have authority as to how that money should be spent in the Territory, should be able to make decisions here which now require reference to Canberra before they can be made.

If he has a new programme, he will need to get the agreement of the Administrator's Executive Council. If, as it not unknown in political circles of Canberra, he wishes to get more money in the course of the year for his own portfolio at the expense of somebody else's portfolio—and that is the only way he will get it, he won't get it by additional grant from Australia—then the Administrator's Executive Council can listen to the pleas of the two Ministers concerned and, as a Council, can decide what should be done.

This, I think, will be a great transference, not so much of power, but of administrative power to the elected Members who are Ministerial Members in this Territory and to the Administrator's Executive Council. As there is to be this transference of power and in future, no doubt, other transferences of power, so concommitant with it will there need to be an assumption of responsibility by the Ministerial Members and the House of Assembly in Papua and New Guinea. If there is a requirement for more money to be provided than has been provided by the existing level of local taxes, and what the Australian Government is prepared to provide by a grant-in-aid, then that's fine, it can be provided if the House of Assembly up here is prepared to impose the taxes required to raise it in the same way as the Government of Australia has to impose the taxes required to provide what it wants to do. I hope you won't read into what I have just said any suggestion that Australian aid will cease for Papua and New Guinea. Of course it won't, but I hope you will read into it a realisation that as power is transferred so also must responsibility be transferred and these two things go hand in hand.

That is the first proposition we will make. We will have in the Australian Budget a negotiated amount of money for the Territory called a 'grant-in-aid' added to the sum of money raised by the decision of the local House in the number of taxes they propose to impose, and the rate of taxes they propose to impose, and that will be left to division among the Ministries by the Administrator's Executive Council and for spending by the Ministerial Members concerned.

We will have also in the Australian Budget a development grant. That development grant for the general development of the Papua and New Guinea Territories will remain with, and be negotiated, of course, by the Australian Government and the Government up here, but its expenditure, since it will be provided entirely by the Australian taxpayer, virtually entirely, will remain the responsibility of the Australian Government. In other words, we will want to see that a general development grant is expended on those projects for which it is voted, and we will want to oversee that it is properly expended on those projects.

We propose, this is just a matter I suppose of presentation too, that in future we would have on our Australian Budget an item which is to pay all the overseas allowances of Expatriate and Overseas Officers so that everyone can see that this comes from the Australian Taxpayer and from what is provided in the Territory. The base rates of Public Servants from the Territory and from Australia can of course be the same, but I think it is essential that people should know that the additional allowances paid do come from the Australian taxpayer, are shown in the Australian Budget and are paid to Expatriate Officers.

We have had it brought to our attention that there is fear in the Territory amongst responsible people that key Public Servants may be lost to the future service of this Territory because, if they are Expatriate Officers, they have an insecurity of tenure. A man of 40 or 45 may reach a point where he has a family to educate, responsibilities to take on, and where he says to himself 'Should I remain in the service of the Territory or as a contract officer? Should I continue in this or should I, because I do not know what the future holds for me in case self-government or independence comes, should I at this stage begin to carve some new career for myself?' And it has been put to us that a number of key Public Servants, I mean District Officers, professional officers, sub-professional officers and technical officers, either have resigned or may in the future resign because they do not know what would happen to them when self-government or independence comes.

It has been put to us that this poses a danger to the future development of Papua and New Guinea because these people and their accumulated experience are going to be required when self-government comes or independence comes. And so we have decided to do this. In order to encourage selected key overseas officers to remain in the Service of Papua and New Guinea for the present and future good of the Territory, we propose that those who are permanent officers of the Papua and New Guinea Public Service, some of those who are permanent officers of the Papua and New Guinea Public Service, and some of those who are contract officers, will be offered enlistment in a new Australia-based service. Offers of engagement in this new service (and it will be a selective service), offers of engagement now and in the future will be made to the selected key administrative officers of whom I have spoken, but acceptance of such an offer will be entirely voluntary on the part of any such officers and offers of selection will be decided by the Administration.

At the moment we believe the ceiling of this new Commonwealth based service should be approximately 1,000. It will be additional to the existing arrangements under which officers serve in the permanent service here or in which they serve as contract officers. That is to say permanent officers who are not appointed to the new service will continue as they are at present, losing nothing of what they have achieved. Contract officers who are not offered appointment will continue on their existing contracts. But appointments to the new service will carry a guarantee by the Australian Government that a member appointed will be assured of continued employment in the Public Service of Papua and New Guinea or in the event that he is transferred from that, or displaced from that, in the future, there will be a guarantee that the Commonwealth Government will place him in permanent employment in a like field on a comparable salary. This, we hope, will enable many officers to resolve the dilemma in which perhaps they are at present placed, and will enable them to decide to make their accumulated experience available to the Government of the Territory of Papua and New Guinea while at the same time retaining full confidence in their own future and in their own future employment. Before the details of this approach are settled, overseas officers themselves will be consulted throughout the Territory, as will the Public Service Association. But that is another step which we propose to make which we think will be of assistance to the development of this country in the future and which so many people in this Territory have urged us in one way or another to do.

We propose that the Administrator's Executive Council, as a result of the new responsibilities which it assumes, will have a spokesman for that Council appointed in the House of Assembly to answer questions as to what the Administrator's Executive Council has done and why it had done it. And we also propose that the Parliament of Australia will not exercise its veto power in relation to ordinances if those ordinances affect the actual responsibilities handed over to Ministerial Members.

Now let me indicate to you the kinds of areas which we feel responsibility should be taken by Ministerial Members here and the kinds of areas in which we feel the Commonwealth of Australia should continue to exercise its present authority. These will be delivered later by my colleague, the Minister for External Territories, in more detail but for the moment the subjects on which we think that authority to take decisions should reside in the Ministerial Members or the Administrator's Executive Council are education—primary, secondary, technical, but not tertiary—public health, tourism, cooperatives, business advisory services, workers' compensation, industrial training, posts and telegraphs. [Other subjects for which authority is to be transferred are][2] Territory revenue including taxation (for inherent in what I have said is the need for the House of Assembly to take greater responsibility in the levying of revenue in this Territory), price control, coastal shipping, civil defence, corrective institutions (that's prisons in case anybody's wondering), registration of customary land, land use, leasing of land and town planning and urban development.

The areas in which we wish and must at this stage retain final authority are the judiciary, the enforcement of law and order, internal security, external affairs, external trade and large scale development projects in agriculture, in transport, forestry, … in those things in the five-year development plan which we are now some half-way through and which will for the most part be financed by the Australian taxpayer and therefore overseen by the representatives of the Australian taxpayer rather than the representatives of the Territory.

I may say that other matters such as civil aviation and defence will, as they are at present, be paid for and controlled directly by the Commonwealth Departments concerned.

In the Administrator's Executive Council, when decisions are being arrived at as to proposals put forward by Ministerial Members for authority to spend on this or that, the official members will sit in the Administrator's Council, as they sit at present, and will offer advice to that Council and they will offer their experience to that Council. They will not take part in any vote that Council may have as to what it finally does. I suggest that these are very significant steps forward along the road to transferring power to the representative members of the Territory and to transferring responsibility to the representative members of the Territory.

But I emphasise again that the total sum available for recurrent and minor works will be a total sum, only able to be added to, if the House of Assembly wishes to find some new avenue of expenditure, by imposing taxation to raise the revenue for that new expenditure because as a Territory progresses towards the ability to exercise greater power, so it must accept the greater responsibility for financing the decisions which it makes.

Even when, in the future, self-government comes or independence comes, there will be continuing Australian assistance for this Territory, but the amount of recurrent assistance provided will, to a great extent, depend on the amount of self-help which the Territory is prepared to impose upon itself. The developmental sums made available for development here will continue, but if, as I hope, the Territory develops and has an increased taxable capacity because of such things as the Bougainville copper mining or oil, which may be found in Papua or elsewhere, the industrial development if that happens, then we would expect greater responsibility still to be accepted by the people of Papua and New Guinea, because when you boil it all down I believe that this is the position as far as the Australian people are concerned. We feel we have an obligation and a responsibility to help the development of this country to a stage where it could not only govern itself politically but govern itself economically, and we will accept that responsibility—and this may go on for years.

But I don't think we would want to accept the position where in years to come people from the Territory came to us and said: 'These are our needs, these are our requirements, we don't want to accept the responsibility for taxing to meet them—you tax, you provide them.' At some stage the Australians would say: 'Sorry.' But, if we continue to provide the assistance we are providing and intend to provide in the future, then at some stage there would be no need for the people of the Territory to come to us because, by a joint effort, we would have been able

2   Editorial insertion.

to raise the economic capacity of this country to a stage where the companies that have come in would be taxed, where wealth that flows to individuals would be taxed, where development that have already taken place would lead to developments still in the future, and where the Territory of Papua and New Guinea could probably look after itself.

But for the present and in the foreseeable future we intend to provide that assistance at least which we provide now. And for the present we propose this new step forward towards self-government and responsibility, which I know in some areas of the Territory will be thought to be going too far, which I know in other areas of the Territory will be thought to be going not far enough, but which looked at from either end are, I think, necessary steps towards a future which must, at some time, hold full internal self-government and full independence.

This is as far as we feel we should go now, and I finish as I began by saying that I believe it against all logic and all sense to put a timetable on this. We don't want to remain in the Territory one week against the wishes of the majority of its people. We don't think we ought to get out of the Territory against the wish of the majority of its people. We don't want to rule any peoples without their consent. We don't think it proper to move out and possibly help a vocal minority rule a majority without that majority's consent, and one can't put a timetable on this but one can say these are steps towards the time when this Territory will be self-governing and when its people will express their views. And we will take account of those views instead of imposing our views on them as to a date for self-government and independence.

Your Honour and Members of the Administrator's Executive Council, I hope you will agree that these are significant steps and I hope with all my heart that the people of the Territory and the Members of the House of Assembly and the Members of the Administrator's Executive Council will make the fullest possible use of the opportunities now offered for the advancement of this Territory and the assumption of the responsibilities which must go with them.

Thank you.

[NAA: A1838, 936/13/28]

65   RECORD OF CONVERSATION BETWEEN GORTON, BARNES AND GUISE

Port Moresby, 6 July 1970

[*matter omitted*]

Mr Guise then raised the subject of internal self-government in the Territory. He said that there was a change of attitude taking place and people were becoming more aware and he felt there should be internal self-government sooner rather than later. He himself did not know when but said that a target date should be set so that the resources and minds of the people could be working towards this. He said he thought it was unhealthy not to set a target date. Mr Barnes said he understood that this would be a recommendation of the Select Committee and it was therefore up to the House of Assembly to approve it. Speaker Guise said that he doubted that the Select Committee would make any recommendation for a date although he would not wish to voice that opinion outside his own office.

The Prime Minister said that the Government's attitude is that Papuans and New Guineans are on the road to self-government and independence and that one had to steer a course between those who want self-government quickly and those who don't. It was a difficult problem but there certainly must be steps taken along the road to self-government—there was no turning back. Mr Guise said he did not want a situation to arise where the Territory went along as it was now and then the Government of the day in Canberra said 'independence in two years'. He said that it would be much better to have internal self-government first. The Prime Minister commented that this situation was likely to happen if the Government changed in Canberra. The Prime Minister went on to say that he understood that people in villages were being told that Australia would go away and leave them. The Prime Minister said Australia would not leave, but as self-government and independence comes Australia will not wish to provide as much finance. He said that with power comes responsibility and financial responsibility. The Prime Minister said that he felt however that Australians would feel that while the Territory was another independent country it was one which we would have close ties with into the future. The Prime Minister pointed out to Mr Guise that in the future there will be a complete difference in the approach to the Territory, not the approach his own Government or an alternative Government would take but he said that at some time in the future the Australian taxpayer would query the continuance of large amounts of money to the Territory. However there would always be development funds. The Prime Minister pointed out that the matters Mr Guise had raised himself cost money, things such as tariffs, land settlement and a health scheme. Mr Gorton stressed again that as political powers developed in the Territory so will economic responsibility. Mr Guise said he appreciated the Prime Minister's frankness very much [...]

[*matter omitted*]

The Prime Minister went on to say that he had to take into account the burdens on the Australian people and pointed out that if one got to a situation where radical students said to Australia 'go home' we would go home. The Prime Minister stressed that what he had just said was a private comment to Mr Guise alone.

[*matter omitted*]

The Prime Minister concluded by saying that he was delighted to have had a discussion with Mr Guise and wished it could have been longer. He went on to say that in his belief most of Papua and New Guinea had reached a stage of development which was one of the most difficult for any country to reach. In fact he felt that development in the Territory was more difficult than in other countries because of the different races and languages and the different levels of development such as people from the Highlands contrasted from people from Bougainville or Rabaul. He went on to talk of those who wished to progress towards independence quickly and others who did not and of the problems of burgeoning political power, without that power wanting to take over economic responsibility. He also touched on the problems for the future of disintegration, such as Bougainville, saying that they wished to leave the Territory. The Prime Minister said that this was one of the difficulties this country has to face. The Speaker commented that he felt that in the years to come, and indeed now in his own area (if only [in early][1] formation), a breakaway movement could come. The Prime Minister stated that he felt this was a problem that they must ultimately solve themselves and that he did not believe that Australians could solve it. Speaker Guise agreed that it was a problem they would have to solve and that Australians in his opinion could not, and he quoted Russell Island in his own area as being a problem 'breakaway movement'. The Prime Minister said that he felt that while there were problems in which Australia could advise and help, the ultimate answers lay in the hands of Papuans and New Guineans themselves.

[*matter omitted*]

[NAA: M3787, 14]

---

1   Editorial insertion.

66   LETTER FROM WALLER TO BUNTING

Canberra, 7 July 1970

The Minister for External Affairs[1] has directed that I should raise with you some matters relating to the recent series of Cabinet decisions concerning the future of the Territory of Papua and New Guinea.

The Minister is in general agreement with the broad policy proposed to Cabinet for a significant devolution of responsibility upon elected representatives in the Territory of Papua and New Guinea at this time with associated assurances that Australian aid will continue and that an adequate group of expatriate Australian officers will remain in the Territory to assist the local people.

It seems likely that political development will be accelerated in the Territory as a result of these measures and that it will be necessary for the special problems which will arise to be kept under review and brought to the attention of the Government from time to time as appropriate. The Minister feels that an inter-Departmental Committee should be established to perform this function. Departments represented on the Committee might be External Territories, External Affairs, Defence, Treasury and Prime Minister's.

In the view of the Minister, the paper on 'The Implications of Early Self-Government' is not a satisfactory document for the further guidance of Ministers and requires a good deal of more detailed study by Departments. Its scope should also be broadened to examine the implications of the progress of Papua–New Guinea to a final constitutional status. The task of re-drafting the paper could be given to the inter-Departmental Committee proposed above.

Decision No. 454[2] concerning the proposed establishment of an Australian base service for overseas officers of the Papua and New Guinea public service indicated that there were various points of detail requiring resolution between interested Departments. The Minister has indicated that he wishes this Department to participate in the inter-Departmental discussions envisaged.

In addition to those outlined by you in your letter of 26th June, 1970[3] to Mr Warwick Smith one further point of detail requiring resolution is the title to be given to the proposed service. The title 'Australian service for overseas cooperation' which is employed in the Minister for External Territories' submission (but not in the title of the submission or the Decision) raises some problems since it is an inaccurate description and implies that the service would be responsible for activities beyond Papua and New Guinea.

I am sending copies of this letter to Sir Arthur Tange, Mr G. Warwick Smith, Sir Richard Randall and Mr C.L. Hewitt.

[NAA: A452, 1970/3046]

---

1   Billy McMahon.

2   Not published.

3   Not published.

67   PRESS RELEASE

Goroka, 8 July 1970

Mr Gorton at Goroka

The Prime Minister, Mr Gorton today (July 7) assured highlanders that Australia would not force Papua and New Guinea into self-government against the people's wishes. However he emphasised that Papua and New Guinea was on the road to self-government and there was no turning back.

[*matter omitted*]

Mr Gorton said it would be a betrayal of the Papua and New Guinea people if self-government was forced on them in 1972. He said this talk was utter nonsense. The main point of Mr Gorton's speech on Monday was more power and more responsibility for Ministerial Members in the House of Assembly.

Mr Gorton said this was a good and proper step forward but not self-government.

He told the student teachers that they performed a significant service to their country which would be very dependent on them to get to the stage where it could govern itself properly.

[NAA: A1838, 936/13/28]

68   SPEECH BY GORTON[1]

Rabaul, 9 July 1970

There is division amongst the Tolai people ... brother's hand is raised against brother, and instead of people sitting down to try and reach friendly agreement by discussion, people are hurting and beating those who disagree with them.

Peace is better than that kind of fighting, agreement by discussion is better than name-calling and hurting each other, and yet this happens today in the Peninsula. And why?

There has been some disagreement over whether there should or should not be a Multi-Racial Council or a Local Council. We have said and I have said on behalf of the Australian Government that we wish to discover what it is that most of the people in this Peninsula want by way of a Council.

If most of the Tolai people on the Peninsula wish not to have a Multi-Racial Council, then we would be prepared not to have a Multi-Racial Council. If most of the Tolai people on the Peninsula want a Multi-Racial Council, then we would be prepared to have that. But we need to know what it is that most of the people want.

I said that some months ago to one of the leaders of the Mataungan Association, Mr Kaputin. I said: 'Let us have a referendum. Let the people vote. Let them say what they want.' And I repeat the offer to all the people of this Peninsula today.

But such a vote would need to be a secret one because, when people already are beating each other, some may be frightened to come out openly and say what they think for fear of being hurt. So the best way is a secret vote, and is this not handing over to the Tolai people the solution of this problem? I think it is.

So I would speak not only to the people gathered here but to all those through the length and breadth of this Peninsula. And I would say to each one of them: Sit down in your own house, talk to your neighbours quietly. Ask yourself: 'Would it not be better to have unity than division? Would it not be better to have discussion than fighting? Would it not be better to find out what most want and then agree with what most want?' I ask all those living here to do that.

I have been told by some—I think a minority—but by some, that what is wanted here is self-government now, but self-government for what? For New Britain? Because New Britain has many other races than the Tolai. And if not for New Britain, then for what? For the Gazelle Peninsula only? Is that asked for?

If it means self-government for the Gazelle Peninsula, what will the results be for the people who live here? They will have left the Territory. They will no longer be one unit of what is to be a nation. They will not have the right to share in riches discovered in copper in Bougainville, or riches which may be discovered in oil in Papua or in the industrial development of all the rest of the Territory. They would have no right because they would be gone. Do they want that?

Is it not true that there are many Tolai now who go to Papua, or to New Guinea or to other parts of the Territory and who work to high positions in the Administration or in the Police Force or in industry? Surely Tolais would want that opportunity to continue, would not want to break off from what should be a united nation.

There have already been very great steps towards transferring more power to the people of the Territory, announced less than a week ago, and ultimately there will undoubtedly be self-government for all. But those who tell you the Gazelle Peninsula or the Tolai people would be

---

1   Gorton delivered the speech at Queen Elizabeth Park in Rabaul.

better separate are telling you untruly and would damage your opportunity for work and would damage your opportunity to share in the wealth of the whole nation.

And I would like all the people in the Peninsula quietly, in their own houses, talking to their relatives and their friends, again to consider on this matter whether what I tell you is not true. And if you come to the conclusion that it is true, that it is to your advantage and to the interest of all the Tolai people, then let that voice be known by casting votes for those who agree with you in the House of Assembly, but letting the wishes of the people be known to Councillors and to others who will be influenced by what you say.

So I have spoken to you of the Multi-Racial Council, I have spoken of why I think it would be bad for the people here to have self-government now, if indeed that meant anything for an area of this size, and I know that these are problems and that there are other problems to do with land tenure in the Peninsula.

I have asked the leaders of the Mataungan Society [sic] to come to see me, to talk about these problems, to try to solve them, to see if we can reach agreement. But they have refused to do this. They have refused to exchange ideas. I would like those Tolai who live on this Peninsula to let it be known that most of the people want these things to be discussed in a friendly way, want them to be resolved, want there to be a stop to beatings, to hurtful name-callings, to spitefulness and to divisions.

Do not think that there would be any support from Australia for those who have caused divisions in this country. I know another politician came here some time ago and indicated that there might be such support. This is the Leader of the Opposition. He is not in the Government … he can do nothing. And this should be known to all the people in this Territory.

And for the last things I shall say to you, I say this. We must, while we are here, see that the law is observed for the protection of all people here.

We want to stay and help in the Administration and the Government and the provision of funds to the Territory including the Gazelle Peninsula, for as long as we are wanted . . . and we will do that. When most people wish us to go, which I think would not be until we have helped to build up the industries, to build up the economic capacity of this Peninsula and of all the rest of the Territory, if people then wish us to go, we would be happy to go. For we have no wish to administer or govern one minute after most of the people in the Territory want us to leave.

And for the rest, I hope and I believe that the people here and in the rest of the Territory will for the years ahead want that kind of partnership which has shown such progress in twenty years, will want to have more and more say in the running of their government, as they will. And that when the Tolai can heal the division within themselves, then we can all shake hands as brothers and tackle the task of construction instead of destruction which lies in front of us and which we want to do together.

Thank you for listening, both townspeople who are here and the Tolai who are here. I hope that my words, and my suggestions and requests for peaceful cooperation, will be heard far beyond the confines of this meeting and will help for the future prosperity of the Gazelle Peninsula if the majority of people here agree that what I have said is the best path for us all to follow.

Thank you.

[NAA: A1838, 936/3/21 PART 3]

69   SPEECH BY GORTON[1]

Kieta, 10 July 1970

[*matter omitted*]

I know that there are some people—how many I don't know—but there are some people who wish to secede from the Territory of Papua and New Guinea. I think that it would be bad for the people of Bougainville if this should now happen. I think that as a part of a much bigger unit, the future of the people of Bougainville will be better. There will be bigger markets for the produce of Bougainville, there will be the advantages that the people of Bougainville can go to other parts of the Territory and get work there, join the Administration there. There are all the advantages which a large unit gives to the people as distinct from a smaller unit. Also as the industry of the other part of the Territory grows and develops, as perhaps oil is discovered on the mainland, then while Bougainville remains in the Territory, she will share in all those advantages. And that means her individual people will share in those advantages.

[*matter omitted*]

In any case, I suggest that it is much too early to try and reach any decision on this subject now. I think there should be much more thought given to it by the people of Bougainville, much more discussion, meditation on the advantages of secession, recognition of the disadvantages of secession, talk amongst the older men and the younger people. And that should go on for some long time. Time enough to make significant decisions on something of this kind when the time of independence of the Territory comes. In the meantime, let there be proper discussion among the people of Bougainville.

Meanwhile, Members elected to the House of Assembly from Bougainville will now have much more opportunity to influence decisions, and the Ministerial Members and Assistant Ministerial Members will have much more opportunity to influence decisions. And they can get up when they are elected by their people here, they can get up in the House of Assembly and speak for the people here and they can say 'We want this road' or 'We want that harbour' or 'We want that wharf', and they can put the views of their people in the same way as Members of Parliament from the different States do in Australia.

That does not mean, of course, that every time one of these requests is raised, it will be met. But it does mean that the wishes of the people of Bougainville will be able to be known all throughout the Territory. I know the Members you have elected and they are pretty good Members and they speak out strongly for the people of Bougainville.

So I think it is too soon yet to talk about referendums for secession. I think, as I said before, there should be much more time for discussion amongst the people here. And I say this and you know it is true. It is nothing to me if Bougainville is independent. It is nothing to Australia if Bougainville is independent. I don't say what I say because it is of some advantage to me or to Australia but because I believe it is of advantage to the people of Bougainville, and I want them to have a lot more time to make up their own minds about it.

I think that is all I have to say on those subjects except to express the hope that now that much more authority has been given to Ministerial Members, the Administrator's Executive Council and to the House of Assembly, and decisions that were formerly made in Canberra will now be made in the Territory, that this will help to develop the capacity for running the Territory amongst all the peoples of the Territory and that they will all go forward together, helping each other, and with Australia giving help as long as it's wanted, to build up a better life, a better economic life for all the people.

[NAA: A452, 1961/3329]

---

1   The speech was delivered to the Bougainville Local Government Councils.

70   FAREWELL BROADCAST BY GORTON

Port Moresby, 11 July 1970

Today I leave the Territory. My visit has, of necessity, been all too short. But it has included major announcements of new policy, and I have seen many different places, talked to many different people, and been able to come to some conclusions.

The major policy changes announced are, of course, that there would be a significant transfer of power, power to make decisions, from Canberra to elected representatives of Territory people.

The Administrator's Executive Council will now have authority to allocate money for recurrent expenses in many fields and for minor works—and the House of Assembly will have to be asked to appropriate such monies in the way recommended.

These proposals, which were announced in some detail last Monday, are significant steps along the road to ultimate self-government.

I also re-emphasised that the Australian Government believes the Territory is on the road which leads to full self-government. There can be no turning back from that road. It must be travelled to the end. But it is not for the Australian Government to dictate the speed at which the ultimate goal is reached.

It is not for us to set an arbitrary date and say that on that date we will force full self-government on the people of the Territory whether they want it or not. Instead our attitude is that the majority of the people of the Territory should decide when they wish full self-government— and when they do this they will get what they want.

In the meantime the possibility of different regional responsibilities for regions at different levels of development could well be examined.

It will come as no surprise to the people of the Territory that I found the Highland people, almost to a man, violently opposed to self-government in 1972—or on any fixed date. They do not want this before they feel they are ready for it and of course, the Highlanders make up the majority of the whole population.

In the coastal areas, Wewak, Lae, Madang, opinion was more divided—but there was a strong majority opinion expressed at all the meetings which I attended, that the people did not want full self-government until a time of their own choosing. And in these areas there was for the most part, tolerance and a working together to build a strong edifice on the economic foundations which have been so well laid.

In Bougainville where there has been talk in some quarters of a desire to secede from the Territory I formed the strong impression that the people wished for much more time and thought and discussion on that suggestion before they came to any conclusion.

In the Gazelle Peninsula the sadly divided state of the people was evident. I asked for discussion between the two groups for a cessation of the violence used by the Mautaungans, and for an attempt to arrive at solutions of problems by majority opinion with discussion and without hate and anger. I renewed the offer of a referendum on the multi-racial council and asked the Mautaungans to discuss their problems with me—but they refused. I can only hope that the call for reasonable discussion will bear fruit but, in the meantime, the law must be enforced.

It is impossible for example, to permit land, which has been bought by the Administration for distribution to Tolais, to be illegally occupied by squatters.[1] This illegal squatting is taking place at the very time when the Land Board is considering from Tolai and Bainings people,[2] applications for the 350 blocks available.

If permitted to continue it will retard the chances of orderly economic development in the Gazelle Peninsula, and, indeed, if squatting is permitted on Administration Land bought for distribution to Tolais, what will prevent squatting on land already held by Tolais? This matter is too important to be left undetermined. Illegal occupation of land must and will be stopped.

The future of the Territory as a whole is, at this stage, certain in some way, uncertain in others. It is certain that it will eventually attain self-government and independence. I hope it will remain unfragmented and that different parts of it will not secede. For if it is fragmented then each separate part will be economically and politically less strong than the whole.

And I believe the people in every part, if secession were to take place, would be worse off. But this question is one that will, no doubt, be settled by the local people themselves, perhaps at the time of independence, and the answer to this is not certain.

In the meantime, as new roads are built from the Highlands to the Coast, as new districts are opened up, as more schools are built and staffed, as better agriculture is taught and new crops are tested, as mineral wealth is exploited and as industries arise, I think the Territory will, at an accelerated pace, go forward to that strong independent economic position, which alone can ensure continued economic progress and continued political stability.

There must be and will be more local participation in, and ownership of, businesses and industries—and there should be a continuing partnership between those who live in the Territory and Australians.

I leave with great hope for the future of all the people of this land, and I leave with a feeling that we all owe a great debt of gratitude to those Australians who have selflessly taught in the missions, have selflessly brought law and order and honest administration to what was but yesterday a primitive country—and I think we all owe, too, an equal debt of gratitude to those local people in all regions who have helped in this task—are still helping in it—and are taking more and more responsibility to continue it, for in them lies the hope of the future of the Territory.

[NAA: A432, 1961/3329]

1   Shortage of land resulting from an expanding population and historic grievances over land had encouraged discontent in the Gazelle Peninsula. In the late 1960s, in an effort to allay this discontent, the Administration had purchased some plantations and released some Administration land for the purposes of sub-division into small settler blocks. After completing a survey the Administration had begun allocating the blocks. Many members of the Tolai community, however, did not accept the legitimacy of earlier expatriate acquisition of these and other areas. Much of this acquisition had taken place under German colonial rule, with the land titles later taken over by Australian settlers and the Administration. Dissident Tolai accordingly did not accept that the Administration had a right to allocate what they saw as their land, and the Mataungan Association had accordingly been encouraging its supporters to squat on the land intended for allocation.

2   The Baining people were the original inhabitants of the Gazelle Peninsula. They mainly occupy the mountainous parts of the Peninsula, having largely withdrawn from coastal areas in response to Tolai pressure.

71   LETTER FROM HAY TO BARNES

Port Moresby, 11 July 1970

SECRET

I am writing to confirm the discussion between the Prime Minister, yourself and myself on the illegal occupation of land in the Gazelle Peninsula. The discussion took place on the afternoon of 10th July.

The Prime Minister and yourself, having seen the attached minute to myself from Mr Newman dated 8th July,[1] and in the light of the many requests you had both received while in Rabaul from Tolai leaders, concluded that urgent action should be taken to remove the persons illegally squatting on Administration land. You directed the Administration to draw up the necessary plans and put them into effect without delay.

With respect to the resources available, the Prime Minister informed you that authority had already been given for the Army to train the soldiers of the Pacific Islands Regiment in duties in aid of the civil power. The Prime Minister emphasised that once execution of the plan had started, it must be completed. If, at any stage, it was concluded that police resources could not handle the situation, and it was considered essential to have the support of units of the PIR, then urgent application should be made to yourself and you would discuss it with your colleagues. Consequently I recommend that formal call out takes place now and subsequent action is taken on requisition through yourself in the light of assessments of the developing situation.

The actual timing of action to be taken is to be left to myself in consultation with officers on the spot. You informed me that representatives of the Australian press and possibly of Australian television are likely to remain in the Gazelle for the next few days with the specific object of reporting on developments on the land question. You directed that factors such as presence of press representatives or photographers should not affect the timing of operations to be conducted. On the other hand, it was important that the vital necessity for the action by the Administration should be clearly and frequently stated by all available means, both in the Gazelle and elsewhere in the Territory. The leaders of the Mataungan Association should be specifically and separately informed.

Acting on your directions I have this morning instructed the officers of the Administration and police to draw up detailed plans, including the timetable. As soon as they are completed they will be sent to you for your information.

Attachment
Minute from A. P. J. Newman to the Administrator

The question of whether action should be taken to eject squatters who have recently moved onto Administration land at Mandres, Japlek, Vunapalandig and Kerevat Agricultural Station was discussed by senior officers at a meeting held on the afternoon of Tuesday 7th July.

2.   Indications from SITREPS and newspaper reports are that the Matanguan Association intends to strongly resist any attempts to remove squatters from the land. A showdown is considered to be inevitable at some stage in the near future.

---

1   Newman's report and assessment had been telexed to Canberra on 9 July 1970. See Telex 11501, Newman to Hay, 9 July 1970, NAA: A452, 1971/2294.

3.   Some reservations were expressed regarding the type of distorted publicity that could arise from any attempt to remove landless Tolai intruders from unused Administration land and it was thought it would probably be preferable for confrontation to occur over the tax issue. However, indications are that the Council's request to stay action on tax defaulters will not be varied in the near future and in the meantime the squatter problem is developing further and respect for law and order is rapidly diminishing. It was, therefore, considered that action should be taken within the next fortnight to remove squatters from the Vudal River boundary of Vunapalandig. It is considered that all effort should be concentrated on this one area in the first instance.

4.   In the intervening period a comprehensive public relations campaign should be commenced along the lines proposed earlier when recommendations were made to proceed with the execution of tax warrants before the Prime Minister's visit. Immediate action is being taken to clearly define Vunapalandig boundaries and surveyors already in the area will be instructed to undertake this work, which should be completed in approximately one week.

5.   Ejection of the squatters can be justified on the basis that action is necessary to clear the way for allocation of Administration land to landless Tolais in line with Connolly Report recommendations.[2] The Mataungan leaders should be clearly informed that the squatters are acting illegally by remaining on the land. They should also be advised that it is proposed to evict trespassers from Administration land concerned so that it can be made available for the settlers' purposes. They should be given as much notice as possible.

6.   The Secretary of Law considers that the Administration is clearly entitled to take the proposed self-help action under Section 123 of the Land Ordinance. As there is every possibility that there will be violent resistance to Administration attempts to eject squatters, the Police Commissioner considers that if the proposed action is to be taken, police reinforcements in the Gazelle Peninsula should be increased by 500 to a total of 1250. This will enable him to eject squatters and at the same time protect townships, plantations and isolated business enterprises from likely retaliatory action by Mataungan supporters.

---

2   On 5 September 1969 the House of Assembly had requested the Administration to set up a commission of enquiry into developments in the Gazelle Peninsula. P. D. (Peter) Connolly, QC, was appointed to head the commission. He was a Queensland barrister, the President of the Australian Law Council, and a former Liberal member of the Queensland parliament. The other members were from the Peninsula; they were Bishop Simon Gaius of the Ngatur United Church and Aisea Taviai, a teacher. A leading anthropologist from the Australian National University, Dr T. Scarlett Epstein, was appointed as an adviser; she and Connolly later fell out and the Administration rebuffed her request to submit a minority report. The commission began hearings on 29 September and presented its report to the House on 11 November. A few days before the report was presented Connolly told territories secretary Warwick Smith that 'no really new considerations [had] emerged'. According to Doran, 'The report argued that the proposal for a change to the council had been clearly publicised, contrary to Mataungan claims, and that [Mataungan Association convenor] Tammur had obscured the changes by reference to land alienation and European domination. The report maintained that the current form of local government in the Gazelle was the most appropriate and it recommended that the referendum desired by the Mataungans should not be held but that the new council should be given a "fair trial"'. The report supported the Administration's policy on land issues. Doran notes that Hay was disappointed with the report because he had been hoping 'for a change of course that "would get us out of this painted-in position" while maintaining a strong stand on the rule of law'. Stuart Doran, (ed.), *Documents on Australian Foreign Policy: Australia and Papua New Guinea, 1966–1969*, Australian Department of Foreign Affairs and Trade, Canberra, 2006, pp. 910–911 & 954–955. See also Donald Denoon, *Trial Separation: Australia and the Decolonisation of Papua New Guinea*, Australian National University, Pandanus Books, Canberra, 2005, 63; and Ian Downs, *The Australian Trusteeship: Papua New Guinea, 1945–1975,* Australian Government Publishing Service, Canberra, 1980, pp. 430–31. Doran notes that the report is held on NAA: A1838, 936/4/16, PART 2.

7.   The proposals outlined above may need to be varied as a consequence of developments arising from the Prime Minister's visit to Rabaul and/or Council decision on or about the 11th of this month as to whether it should proceed further with execution of warrants and issues of tax summonses. An early indication of the Administrator's attitude towards the above proposals is essential so that a public relations campaign can be drawn up for movement of police.

8.   It was thought that confrontation might result in an immediate easing of the tensions throughout the Gazelle Peninsula and a return to law and order as has occurred in earlier similar situations. However, the Mataungan movement is wider and larger than any other movement previously encountered in the Gazelle Peninsula and the possibility of continuing guerrilla-type activities following upon a violent confrontation could not be overlooked. Such a development would require the maintenance of additional police strength in the Gazelle Peninsula until the situation returned to normal.

[NAA: A452, 1970/3808]

72   LETTER FROM BALLARD TO TANGE

Canberra, 13 July 1970

SECRET

I have been asked by Mr Warwick Smith, who is out of Canberra following a family bereavement, to write to you about the situation in Rabaul.

As you will be aware the visit of the Prime Minister to Rabaul went off with very little incident. This was to some extent due to the fact that the Papua and New Guinea Administration had not taken up challenges from the Mataungan Association and breaches of the law during the weeks prior to the Prime Minister's visit.

A major cause of discontent in the Gazelle Peninsula is land shortage. Some months ago the Administration purchased a number of plantations and released some Administration land for the purposes of sub-division into 360 small scale settler blocks. These, after survey, are now being allocated. The Mataungan Association have, however, been encouraging its supporters to squat on this land and in his speech to the Prime Minister at Rabaul Airport Kaputin said that their supporters were moving on new land in very much the same way as the first Australian settlers had got new land in Australia.

The matter has subsequently been discussed by the Minister with the Prime Minister and it has been decided that action should be taken as soon as possible to remove these squatters and for this purpose we propose to send an additional 450 police to Rabaul to make up the total police strength there to 1,250. This was specifically mentioned in the Prime Minister's speech in Port Moresby on 11th July last in the following terms:

It is impossible for example to permit land, which has been bought by the Administration for distribution to Tolais, to be illegally occupied by squatters. This illegal squatting is taking place at the very time when the Land Board is considering, from Tolai and Bainings people, applications for the 350 blocks available. If permitted to continue it will retard the chance of orderly economic development in the Gazelle Peninsula, and, indeed, if squatting is permitted on Administration land bought for distribution to Tolai, what will prevent squatting on land already held by Tolai? This matter is too important to be left undetermined. Illegal occupation of land must and will be stopped.

We have reports that some of the squatters may be armed. The Mataungan Association has indicated that it will resist eviction and the possibility of a serious incident which would make it necessary to call out the PIR is very real.

The purpose of this letter is to warn you that it is likely that the Minister for External Territories will be approaching your Minister to seek his concurrence to call-out of the PIR. This would be on the basis that call-out is a precautionary measure and that action would be taken on subsequent requisition with Ministerial approval.

Similar letters are being sent to the Secretaries of Prime Minister's, External Affairs and Army—with a copy to the Secretary of Attorney-General's Department.[1]

[NAA: A452, 1970/3808]

---

1   The departmental secretaries mentioned in this sentence were Lenox Hewitt (Prime Minister's Department), Sir Keith Waller (External Affairs), Bruce White (Army) and John Qualtrough Ewens, who appears to have been acting as the Secretary of Attorney-General's at this time.

73   TELEX FROM BARNES TO FRASER

Brisbane, 14 July 1970

Secret

The situation in Rabaul continues to deteriorate [...] Although the visit of the Prime Minister went off with very little incident that was largely due to the fact that the Administration had not taken up the challenges of the Mataungan Association and breaches of the law during the weeks prior to the Prime Minister's visit.

[*matter omitted*][1]

The Mataungan Association have however been encouraging its supporters to squat on this land [...] It was decided in consultation with the Prime Minister that action should now be taken to remove these squatters and the Prime Minister made this public in a statement he made in Port Moresby on 11 July.

The Mataungan Association has indicated that it intends to advise squatters to resist eviction and to lend its support to those who resist and that they will do this whether or not there is bloodshed. Our information is that the squatters have about six shotguns but they may be able to obtain other weapons.

With the additional police there should be 1,250 police in the area and it is my hope that this will prove sufficient to contain any resistance. The possibility remains that there will be some serious incident where the civil power will be forced to seek assistance from the Army. If this occurs it is likely to happen suddenly and there can be no assurance that there would be time to obtain the formal documents for an order-in-council from the Governor-General for call out.

I am therefore approaching the Prime Minister and Ministers for External Affairs[2] and Army[3] for their concurrence so that if you are in agreement an immediate recommendation may be made to the Governor-General for call out. This would be a preliminary move so that subsequent action would be taken on requisition with the initial requisition approved by Ministers.

I think it highly probable that the Police will be able to cope or that the mere stationing of substantial units of the PIR in the location will be all that is needed. I believe that the larger the force can be seen to exist in the area concerned the less resistance we can expect.

[NAA: A452, 1970/3808]

---

1   The omitted material concerned land tensions in the Gazelle Peninsula and the MA's campaign of land occupation.

2   Billy McMahon.

3   Andrew Peacock.

74   TELEX FROM WALLER TO MCMAHON

Canberra, undated [c. 14 July 1970]

79. CONFIDENTIAL

Following is a note of conversation with Tange today.

Sir Arthur Tange telephoned to say that he had now ascertained the facts about the Gazelle Peninsula.

It had been decided that a confrontation must take place with the Tolai squatters

The law can no longer be defied and it was being claimed that the local government was in danger of collapse.

The Prime Minister had told the Administrator that he agreed the timing was right for confrontation and that the civil power would have the Army behind it.

The Army has no power without a 'callout'.

It was unable for instance to carry out a search.

If they were called out they would not perform Police functions.

The Army say that the options as to how they act are restricted.

They can only act after the Police have failed and the Magistrate has authorised them to restore order.

In other words they would not be called on merely to deal with the squatters.

The scenario is that on Friday the Police will evict the squatters.

There may be a direct confrontation and in the aftermath the Army might be needed to restore law and order.

The Army says that they will act according to regulations.

This will not be by shields and clubs but by establishing a line and shooting anyone who crosses.

We must therefore contemplate bloodshed.

Tange is to discuss this with the Minister for Defence[1] this afternoon to see whether a directive is required.[2]

[NAA: A1838, 936/3/21 PART 2]

---

1   Malcolm Fraser.

2   In response to this telex McMahon's Private Secretary, C. R. (Kim) Jones, advised Waller later that day that: 'Minister made following notation on your teleprinter No. 79 about your conversation with Sir Arthur Tange: (A) Prime Minister has made his decision. (B) I do not know enough about local circumstances. (C) Kent Campus (USA). (D) This is a civil problem. (E) It seems too drastic. (F) This should left to civil police.' Note, Jones to Waller, 14 July 1970, NAA: A1838, 936/3/21 PART 2.

The 'Kent Campus' reference was to a tragic incident on 4 May 1970 at Kent State University in Ohio in the United States in which national guards opened fired on unarmed students demonstrating against the US bombing of neutral Cambodia, killing four students and wounding nine others. The casualties included both demonstrators and bystanders.

75   TELEX FROM WALLER TO MCMAHON

Canberra, 14 July 1970

CONFIDENTIAL

Land Dispute in Rabaul

The Minister for External Territories has informed you today of action to be taken to evict Tolai squatters from land in the Rabaul area.

His message stated that he was seeking your concurrence for making an immediate recommendation to the Governor-General to call out the Pacific Islands Regiment.

Our understanding is that these troops would be moved into the Rabaul area.

2.   There will be a force of 1,250 Police in the area to handle the evictions and it is hoped that the mere presence of the PIR would be sufficient to deter acts of forceful resistance by the Mataungan Association.

[*matter omitted*]

6.   We questioned the Department of External Territories on the evidence available to them of the possible extent of forcible resistance in the light of the confused and incorrect accounts about Tolai demonstrations which preceded the Prime Minister's arrival in Rabaul last week. They admitted that reports had been misleading. However they claimed that this was in part a demonstration of the discipline in the Mataungan Association which in the end had said that the demonstration on the Prime Minister's arrival would be a peaceful one. However, the Mataungan Association has said that they would advise the squatters to resist eviction with force whether or not there was bloodshed involved.

7.   In any case the decision has already been taken to commence the evictions on Friday next with the use of the police.

The question for decision is whether the PIR should be called out and stationed in the area for use should the situation deteriorate.

8.   There was consideration in May 1969 of this same issue of the context in which the PIR might be called out, in this case with regard to the eviction of people from land in Bougainville for the CRA.[1]

On this occasion the situation did not deteriorate to the point where the use of the PIR might have been necessary.

There have been inter-departmental discussions since this time with a view to defining the conditions and the manner in which the PIR might be used but no recommendations have been agreed upon.

The Department of Defence has adopted a very cautious approach to this question indeed and has endeavoured to hold back the Department of External Territories from seeking a ready means by which the PIR might be used.

We also have been concerned as to whether a need could be demonstrated for using the PIR in the Territory in circumstances such as this.

This is apart again from the international concern which would be expressed in the United Nations over any action to use the PIR against the indigenous inhabitants of a Trust Territory.

---

1   Conzinc Riotinto Australia.

9.   We would have this same concern with regard to the PIR in this eviction action in Rabaul.

[*matter omitted*]

In a show of strength it [the Mataungan Association] has refused to negotiate with the Administration and the situation appears to have reached a point where the Administration considers that it must in turn show its own strength against the Mataungan Association by taking these measures against it.

10.   We are not convinced, and this has been demonstrated on previous occasions, that this particular situation cannot be handled by the Police alone.

We would question whether the eviction action could not be combined with action to hasten the work of the Land Board and to ensure that those of the squatters who have any form of customary or other claims will have their cases heard.

There is probably a case also for giving urgent attention to a land policy for the Tolai areas as a whole.

11.   In the last resort the PIR could be used in the military role for which it has been trained.

It has not been trained in a Police role or in a role to supplement the Police, but for use in circumstances directed to fighting and bloodshed.

12.   The Administration states that the squatters have only six shotguns at their disposal.

The Mataungan Association has no access to weapons and has by no means developed into an armed resistance movement.

13.   It is considered that the use of the PIR against the squatters would be wrong unless the situation deteriorated to a point where the Police could no longer maintain order.

We do not believe that this development would be so rapid as not to afford time for Ministers to consider all aspects of the new situation and to decide then whether and under what conditions the PIR should be used.

[NAA: A1838, 936/3/21 PART 2]

•

76   TELEX FROM BARNES TO GORTON

Brisbane, 14 July 1970

SECRET

Following the decision we took during your visit to Port Moresby that action should be taken immediately to remove squatters off Administration land in the Gazelle Peninsula I have authorised an additional 450 Police to be sent to Rabaul

You will be aware that the Mataungan Association has indicated that it intends to advise squatters to resist eviction and to lend its support to those who resist and that they will do this whether or not there is bloodshed. Our information is that the squatters have about six shotguns but they may be able to obtain other weapons.

With the additional Police there should be 1,250 Police in the area and it is my hope that this will prove sufficient to contain any resistance. The possibility remains that there will be some serious incident where the civil power will be forced to seek assistance from the Army. If this occurs it is likely to happen suddenly and there can be no assurance that there would be time to obtain the formal documents for an Order-in-Council from the Governor General for call out

I am therefore approaching the Ministers for Defence, External Affairs and Army for their concurrence so that if you are in agreement an immediate recommendation may be made to the Governor General for call out.[1] This would be a preliminary move so that subsequent action would be taken on requisition with the initial requisition approved by Ministers

I think it highly probable that the Police will be able to cope or that the mere stationing of substantial units of the PIR in the location will be all that is needed. I believe that the larger the force that can be seen to exist in the area concerned the less resistance we can expect.

[NAA: A452, 1970/3808]

---

1   Barnes sent similar messages to Fraser, McMahon and Peacock.

77   PRESS RELEASE

Port Moresby, 14 July 1970

Squatting on Administration Land in the Gazelle Peninsula

The Administrator, Mr D. O. Hay, said today that leaders of the Mataungan Association and their supporters were being warned that the Administration intended to take action to move certain squatters from Administration land in the Gazelle.

[*matter omitted*]

Mr Hay said the Administration, the House of Assembly and other interested groups such as the Warmaram,[1] had, over the past year, made every effort to bring about a peaceful solution to the present conflict in the Gazelle. The Prime Minister himself had sought compromise but had been rebuffed by the Mataungan Association leadership.

It was now evident that the Mataungan Association leaders had adopted an inflexible and unreasonable attitude and would appear to be bent on forcing a confrontation.

The Administration wished to avoid this and for this reason had issued further warnings to the squatters.

The Administration was also prepared to participate in any meaningful discussions or assist in implementing a peaceful settlement of the problems on the Gazelle Peninsula.

However there were indications that, spurred on by Mataungan Association leaders, the squatters would continue to ignore the law.

If this proved to be true, the Administration would have no option other than to remove the squatters.

In enforcing the law the Administration firmly believed that it had tried all other options open.

In the interests of the Tolai and Bainings people, some of whom are themselves leaseholders, and in the interests of the people of the Territory as a whole, the Administration must now act to uphold the law in the Gazelle.

[NAA: A1838, 936/4/13]

---

1   For background on Waramaran, see Document 49, fn. 5.

78   MINUTE FROM BUNTING TO GORTON

Canberra, 14 July 1970

SECRET

The Secretary, Department of External Affairs, has written to me, on behalf of his Minister, about the recent Cabinet discussion and decisions about Papua and New Guinea.[1]

2.   The letter [...] raises two matters.

3.   One is the participation of External Affairs in consultations between the Departments on the detail of the Australian service for the Territory.[2] As to this, I would consider that it flows automatically from the Cabinet discussion that External Affairs should participate, and in any case I assume that you would agree.

4.   The second matter relates to the submission on the implications of early self-government. The Minister sees a need for special problems to be kept under review, and for this purpose he sees a need for an Inter-departmental Committee. Also he considers that the paper is not a satisfactory document for the further guidance of Ministers, and that it requires more detailed study and a broadening of scope. He suggests that the task of re-drafting the paper could be given to the Inter-departmental Committee.

5.   The matter of formal arrangements for a continuing review goes beyond what was discussed at the Cabinet meeting, and I therefore put the External Affairs proposal to you for consideration. You may like to invite the Minister—or alternatively the Minister for External Territories—to raise the matter in Cabinet.

6.   On my own account, I feel that I ought perhaps to mention again a proposal which I made earlier this year when Cabinet Committee formation was under discussion between us. I suggested a Committee on Territory questions. You did not then take the suggestion up beyond saying that it was something to be kept in mind in case a particular need arose. It may now be worth thinking further about it.[3]

[NAA: A452, 1970/3046]

---

1   Document 66.

2   On the proposed 'Australian Service for Overseas Co-operation', see Documents 48 (para. 22) & 64.

3   On 7 August, Bunting advised Waller that 'the Prime Minister has marked the papers to the effect that he sees no need for an inter-departmental committee.' Letter, Bunting to Waller, 7 August 1970, NAA: A452, 1970/3046.

79   NOTE FOR FILE BY WARWICK SMITH

Canberra, 15 July 1970

SECRET

TPNG Aid to the Civil Power

Having been informed by Mr Ballard of the situation in relation to the proposed eviction of squatters from land in the Gazelle and having received a message from Sir Arthur Tange that a meeting of the Defence Committee was proposed to be held this afternoon at 3.30 pm I rang Mr Barnes at about 9.30 am.

I told him about the Defence Committee meeting. I explained we were working on the basis of a preliminary legal move to clear the ground if action became necessary for an initial requisition for the use of PIR personnel on Ministerial authority.

In reply to my question he said he could not say that the proposal had the Prime Minister's agreement. It was his impression that it had been discussed by the Administrator with the Prime Minister and the Prime Minister was in favour.

I asked the Minister whether he would ring the Prime Minister. He did this and rang him about 10 o'clock to say that he had spoken to the Prime Minister who had said that the proposed call out had his full support.

[NAA: A452, 1970/3808]

80   MINUTE BY DEFENCE COMMITTEE[1]

Canberra, 15 July 1970

16/1970. Secret

Possible Call-Out of the Pacific Islands Regiment[2]

The Defence Committee had before it a letter of 13th July 1970[3] from the Department of
External Territories on the possible call-out of the Pacific Islands Regiment in New Guinea. The
Committee also had before it a signal from the Minister for External Territories to the Minister
for Defence advising of an approach to the Prime Minister and other Ministers proposing an
immediate call-out by the Governor-General as a preliminary move so that subsequent action
would be taken on requisition, with the initial requisition approved by Ministers.[4]

---

1   Those present at the meeting were Tange (Chair), General Sir John Wilton, Chairman, Chiefs of Staff,
     Lt General Sir Thomas Daly, Chief of the General Staff, Vice Admiral Sir Victor Smith, Chief of the
     Naval Staff, Air Marshall C. T. Hannah, Chief of the Air Staff. Other participants included Waller, Bunting,
     Warwick Smith, Harders, D. R. Steele-Craik (Treasury) and R. N. Townsend (Prime Minister's Department).

2   On 5 February 1970, the Defence Committee had examined the question of a possible call-out following
     the preparation and revision of a report (dated August 1969) by an inter-departmental committee (IDC)
     formed by Cabinet to review the implications of a deployment of the PIR to assist in the maintenance of
     public order. For details on the IDC, see Stuart Doran, (ed.), *Documents on Australian Foreign Policy:
     Australia and Papua New Guinea, 1966–1969*, Department of Foreign Affairs and Trade, Canberra, 2006,
     pp. xxx, xlviii–l, Documents 46 & 310–313.

     The meeting of 5 February had been unsympathetic to Warwick Smith's request for the deployment of
     the PIR in civil disturbances where there was 'a complete breakdown in law and order'. He had said he
     envisaged 'the PIR acting as a military force and not as a police force', adding 'that the PIR should not
     be trained in the police role nor should they be armed with police equipment such as batons, shields, etc.'
     Instead, in 'a civil disturbance last resort situation the PIR would operate in accordance with their military
     training'. Lt General Thomas Daly, the Chief of the General Staff, felt that 'to discharge the civil role
     meant that soldiers would be employed in circumstances quite the reverse of the role for which they were
     trained. The military role was directed to fighting—to situations of bloodshed, which, he thought, should
     be avoided at all costs in the civil role. To discharge the civil role soldiers had to be trained to cope with
     emotional factors, to remain calm under extreme provocation.' During the meeting it 'was pointed out
     that military forces were just as subject as the police to the overriding principle that in a civil disturbance
     situation minimum necessary force only could be used. This meant that training had to be given in the art
     of graduated response and it meant that the PIR had to be trained in the use of equipment appropriate to
     the purpose.' Warwick Smith also said that 'the military might be asked to take over the whole situation
     in relation to say a town like Rabaul, or even to a small area like a market place. It was pointed out to Mr
     Warwick Smith that as expounded by him, his view appeared to amount to the military forces supplanting,
     not supplementing, the police under circumstances which could have the qualities of a martial law situation.'

     The Committee felt that 'if the PIR were to be used in a civil situation it would be desirable, if not essential,
     to know beforehand the attitude of the PNG House of Assembly'. At the same time, it regarded Warwick
     Smith's views as inconsistent with the IDC report and asked the DET Secretary to refer the matter back to
     the Committee so as 'to identify precisely the circumstances which in its view constituted the last resort
     in which the military would be used and what the role and responsibilities of the military would be'. The
     Committee, therefore remained unconvinced with the basic premise of Warwick Smith's request, adding
     that at the very least a call-out could not be contemplated without a request from the Administrator and
     House of Assembly, and that 'any [such] request should be considered by the Defence Committee and
     [...] should be finally considered by the Prime Minister, Minister for Defence and Minister for External
     Territories and if possible the Minister for External Affairs'. See Defence Committee Meeting, 'Military
     Aid to the Civil Power of Papua New Guinea', 5 February 1970, NAA: A1838, 936/3/21 PART 2.

3   Document 72.

4   Document 73.

2.   The Committee had the benefit of an elaboration by the Secretary, Department of External Territories of present circumstances and of the policies and procedures contemplated by the Papua and New Guinea Administration in respect of the discontent created by the land shortage on the Gazelle Peninsula and the challenge to authority by the Mataungan Association to encourage squatting on Administration land. The Committee also had the assistance of the Secretary, Attorney General's Department in the interpretation of the legal provisions which would govern a recommendation to the Governor-General for the calling-out of the PIR and the subsequent chain of authority and steps which would need to be taken before the PIR would be committed to action. In this regard the Committee noted the distinction between the obtaining of an Order-in-Council for call-out and the act of committing the PIR to action for the restoration of law and order.

3.   The Committee was advised by the Secretary Department of External Territories that all possible action would be taken, not involving the use of the Police initially, to eject and disperse the squatters from the Administration land. If this persuasion fails, use of unarmed general duty police may then be necessary. If that step failed, mobile riot squads may then be required to remove the squatters.

4.   The view was expressed, having regard to the proposal that troops might be called upon, that if there is to be a confrontation, the time and place should be of the Administration's choosing and with the certainty that it would be successful. External Territories' advice is that it is not possible for the Administration to judge at this stage what the reaction or the tactics of the squatters may be. The Committee was further advised that for this reason, it was regarded as prudent by the Administration to seek the assistance of the PIR, even though they would be unlikely to be required; and to have this force as a back-up as a last resort should the situation go beyond the capacity of the Police to handle.

5.   The Committee noted that the use of the PIR in the Gazelle Peninsula would involve three main stages:

    a.   The issue of an Order-in-Council by the Governor-General;

    b.   Deployment of the PIR from Port Moresby and Wewak to Rabaul; and,

    c.   The use of the PIR;

and that within these stages, there were a series of check points before the forces could be finally committed to military action. In respect of the first stage, the Governor-General, on the advice of responsible Ministers, must be satisfied that a state of domestic violence or a clear threat of domestic violence exists before an Order-in-Council is issued. Although there may be some degree of anticipation, the information on which a recommendation is based should be completely current at the time the recommendation is made. In the second stage a requisition from the Administration in writing is then required (Regulation 404) on the Officer commanding the forces. The Commander of the force is then required to meet with a Magistrate (Regulation 405) and then to consult with the Administration and the Police as to the disposition: at this stage it is still merely a call-out, not participation. If a riot situation develops a Commissioned Officer of the Police Force orders the rioters to disperse. If the Magistrate accompanying the Forces concludes that the Police have lost control and the situation demands active participation by the military forces, it is the duty of the Magistrate to request such assistance. This is not the final act of committal of the Forces. The regulations give the Force Commander discretion as to the action he might take—from persuasion to actual use of lethal weapons. Guidance and instructions to the Force Commander would be embodied in his Directive. Subsequent Government instructions to the Force Commander would be issued through the Army chain of command.

6.   The degree of 'domestic violence' necessary legally to justify a call-out was discussed. Although the phrase 'domestic violence' is not specifically defined, the term is used in part 5

of the Military Regulations and the Committee interpreted the phrase to embrace a sizeable and continuing disturbance or a clear danger of such disturbance, by substantial numbers involving violent and armed resistance rather than isolated instances of violence.

7.   The Committee expressed serious concern about the consequences of a call-out and noted the desirability of all steps being justifiable in any subsequent enquiry.

8.   The Committee was advised that the goodwill and confidence which had been built up internationally towards Australian administration of the Trust Territory would be dissipated if recourse were had to the PIR. Moreover, the Committee was informed that, because of past policy, the PIR had had only about two weeks training in the techniques of aid to the civil power and had not been specifically equipped for this role. This will make it more difficult for the Commander to ensure that minimum force would be used and thus increase the risk of casualties.

9.   The Committee concluded that utmost efforts should be made by the Administration to contain the situation with civil power and police resources to its final limits; and that it would be prudent for the Government to proceed with caution before recommending the call out of the PIR. The Committee did not discount the possibility, if an Order-in-Council were issued, that there could be a premature disclosure.

10.   As regards the timetable of action, the desirability of moving elements of the PIR to the Rabaul area as a precautionary measure was discussed. The Army pointed to the undesirability of having Units placed in a situation where, in the absence of a prior call out, they lacked legal power.

11.   The Committee concluded that it would be only in the serious situation where the Police had lost control of law and order or this situation was imminent that a recommendation should be made for the PIR to be called into action.

12.   The Defence Committee concluded that:

a.   it was necessary to demonstrate a sufficient degree of domestic violence or a clear threat of such domestic violence to provide a basis for the issue of an Order-in-Council by the Governor-General;

b.   on the information available at the time of the meeting, and having regard to the legal requirement, it did not appear that the Minister for Defence would be justified in seeking to move the Governor-General to authorise a call-out. In this respect the Secretary of the Department of External Territories expressed the view that the information available justified call-out now, on the basis proposed by the Minister for External Territories, i.e. that any actual subsequent initial requisitioning of PIR personnel would be subject to specific approval of the Prime Minister, Minister for Defence, Minister for External Affairs and the Minister for External Territories;

c.   the situation should be kept under continuous review and that the Minister for External Territories should be invited to take up again the question of call-out at short notice with the Minister for Defence if he judges it necessary, with the expectation that the Minister for Defence could approach the Governor- General rapidly if it were so decided;

d.   there were major policy implications both domestic and international to be considered in any decisions on call-out or on the use of military force by the PIR;

e.   the Committee observed that the deployment of the PIR to take over from the Police, and the use of military force and ultimately lethal weapons, could result in casualties and deaths attributable to the PIR. The Committee noted that the PIR had had only a short period of training, and had not been specifically equipped for other than an orthodox military role;

f.   the utmost use should be made by the Civil Authorities of their civil power and police resources for the preservation of law and order; and that the use of military power be considered only in a situation where it was assessed that it was beyond the capabilities of the civil authorities to prevent a serious breakdown of law and order. The Committee expressed doubts as to whether an Order-in-Council in the circumstances described by Secretary, Department of External Territories would remain undisclosed for any length of time;

g.   in the event of the PIR being used there would be strong adverse public and international reaction to any casualties inflicted by the Army. It felt that all possible measures should be taken to present to the public the Administration's case against the law breakers and the action being taken by the Administration to prevent domestic violence;

h.   it was necessary to provide for a process of continuing consultation between responsible Ministers; and

i.   in the current circumstances [...] the Departments of Defence, Territories, Army, Prime Minister's, External Affairs and Attorney-General's should remain in close contact and keep under review the current threat and the availability of transport capacity with a view to ensuring that possible contingencies can be quickly met. In this connection an RAAF C130 is at present in New Guinea and a second C130 will be positioned there by July 17th and both will remain at least until the present situation is clarified. The Committee noted that a third C130 will be held in Australia at a high state of readiness depending on developments. The Committee also noted that the Army will maintain relevant elements of the PIR on 4 hours notice in hours of daylight from Friday the 17th July.

[NAA: A1838, 936/4/16 PART 3]

81   LETTER FROM TANGE TO WARWICK SMITH

Canberra, 17 July 1970

SECRET

Situation in New Britain

This will serve to confirm my conveyance to you by telephone of the request by my Minister (Mr Fraser), that your Minister consider bringing to the Cabinet, which meets on Monday, the situation which led him to request the Minister for Defence to agree to recommend to the Governor-General a call-out of the Pacific Islands Regiment subject to a joint subsequent Ministerial approval of any actual requisition of the forces.

The Minister for Defence yesterday decided, on the basis of the advice of the Defence Committee[1] and his consultation with certain other colleagues, that he could not in the circumstances existing yesterday, agree that the Governor-General should be asked to approve a call-out.

[NAA: A452, 1970/3808]

---

1   See Document 80.

82   MINUTE FROM KENNETH BAILEY TO HARDERS

Canberra, 17 July 1970

Territory of Papua and New Guinea:
Use of Military Power in aid of the Civil Power

Both from the domestic and from the international point of view, the use by the administering authority in a trust territory of military force in aid of the civil power is one of the gravest political decisions a government may be called on to make.

2.   From the domestic point of view, the legal framework within which such a decision can be taken, and executed, is provided by and under the Defence Act. From the international point of view, the legal framework is provided by the Charter of the United Nations and by the trusteeship agreements made in pursuance of the Charter.

3.   From the domestic point of view, no distinction is to be drawn between Papua and New Guinea. From the international point of view, however, it is to be noted that the Charter provisions regarding trust territories apply to New Guinea but not to Papua.

4.   The relevant provision of the Charter is Article 84. The primary purpose of the Article was to establish the duty of an administering authority to ensure that the trust territory plays its part in the maintenance of international peace and security. (There was no similar provision in the mandate system under the League Covenant). But it does expressly (though perhaps rather inelegantly) permit the use of locally-raised volunteer forces for the 'maintenance of law and order within the trust territory'.

[*matter omitted*]

Whatever the political repercussions both domestic and international of an actual exercise of the power concerned, there is clearly no legal barrier to its exercise.

[NAA: A1838, 936/3/21 PART 2]

83   MEMORANDUM FROM HUGHES TO GORTON

Canberra, 17 July 1970

Secret

Situation in Gazelle Peninsula

I have read a draft report of the meeting of the Defence Committee held on 15th July;[1] I have also read Daily Assessment No. 12,[2] issued by the Department of External Territories at 10.00 a.m. today. My purpose in reading these documents is to assess whether the facts and circumstances presently known to exist would justify the Governor-General in making an Order-in-Council calling out elements of the Pacific Island Regiment for the protection of the Territory of New Guinea against domestic violence.

I accept the proposition that the Governor-General's power to call out the forces for protection against domestic violence is not restricted to cases in which such violence is actually occurring at the time when the question of a call-out is raised. Common-sense and common law clearly indicate that the power is not so restricted. In my opinion, the Governor-General is entitled to call out the forces if there is a *clear* and *strong* probability that the civil police will be unable by themselves to quell a likely disturbance of public order.

The Governor-General is entitled to address his mind to an anticipated emergency; and if he concludes that there is a real danger that public disorder will get out of hand unless the armed forces are made available in aid of the civil authorities, he may act. There is, of course, no legal machinery for challenging his decision in such a case. He can make a decision only on the advice of the Executive Council; and the only check against arbitrary action is the risk of political disapproval, which, in such a case as is being considered, is always likely to be a considerable deterrent, in a domestic as well as in an international context.

Having examined the material to which I have referred I am bound to say—because this is a question not only of fact but of law—that, in my judgment, the evidence presently available does *not* justify the making of an Order-in-Council by the Governor-General.

In considering this problem, all the circumstances must be taken into account. In this connexion, I draw attention to two items on page 1 of today's 'Gazelle Daily Assessment';[3] Mr Beazley,[4] MP, has pleaded with the Mataungan Association to exercise restraint; and Simon Kaumi,[5] Kaputin's brother-in-law, has agreed to lend his good offices in aid of a peaceful solution of the crisis. Until the effect of these two elements in the situation is known, I would say without any hesitation that, quite apart from political considerations (which I leave on one side), it would be legally unjustifiable to take the extreme step of calling-out the troops in aid of the civil authorities.

[NAA: A452, 1961/3329 PART 5]

---

1   For the final report, see Document 80.

2   Not published.

3   Not published.

4   Kim E. Beazley (Snr), Labor MP for Fremantle, was Spokesman on New Guinea Affairs for the Opposition.

5   Simon Kaumi had been appointed Electoral Commissioner in May 1970.

84   LETTER FROM WALLER TO WARWICK SMITH

Canberra, 17 July 1970

S<small>ECRET</small>

The Minister for External Affairs is in Sydney but has asked that the following message be conveyed urgently to the Minister for External Territories.

I am sending a copy of this message to the Secretary, Prime Minister's Department.

'I have the message you sent earlier this week to our colleague, the Minister for Defence, concerning the proposal for an immediate call-out of the PIR for possible use in the Gazelle Peninsula.[1]

'2.   We need first to look to the role that a force might play in the event of a serious deterioration in the situation. But I note that the advice of the Defence Committee is that the legal requirements for a call-out include that there be "… a sizeable and continuing disturbance by substantial numbers involving violent and armed resistance rather than threats to commit violence or isolated instances of violence." My understanding of the current position leads me to conclude that a clear and present threat of these dimensions does not exist. I appreciate nevertheless that a continuing watch must be kept on further developments.

'3.   A decision to employ the army could have serious international repercussions, some of which could follow if it became known that we had taken a first significant step in this direction. I am of the view, therefore, that External Affairs considerations favour not proceeding to a call-out at this point.'

[NAA: A432, 1961/3329 PART 5]

---

1   Document 73.

85   TRANSCRIPT OF TELEVISION INTERVIEW OF GORTON[1]

Sydney, 19 July 1970

Q. Prime Minister, what were your overall impressions of your tour of Papua/New Guinea.

PM: I think the deepest impression one gets is of the great difficulty in advancing a country such as the Territory to full self-government. This is because there are different races, different languages, different levels of development in different regions, different aspirations in different regions and whatever one does would be interpreted by some regions as going too fast towards self-government and in other regions as going too slow. And there are jealousies between the various regions as well. This makes it an extremely difficult exercise. It is one that has got to be carried out gradually but with some regard for the wishes of all the region and for the different levels of development in them and for the growing—what shall I say?—elite as distinct from those who have not yet had full chances of education.

Q. I would like to be a little more specific on some of those particular divisions which you have spoken of. One of the immediate impressions one gets here in Australia is how long can Australia continue as a colonial power in New Guinea?

PM: Well, first of all I reject the concept of Australia being a colonial power. I don't believe she is a colonial power, but we can put that to one side for the moment. And the only answer I can give you is the answer I gave in New Guinea, and that is that we should continue there as long as most of the people want us to continue there and feel they want our help and they want our skills. As an illustration of that I don't know of any section up there, for example, that doesn't want to try and ensure that Australian administrators and technical officers and agricultural officers and surveyors and key people will stay and help even after self-government comes. So the only answer I can give you is I believe we should stay there as long as we are wanted to stay there and no longer.

Q. Now do you think that say, the more advanced people on the coastal fringes ... how long can they wait until the people from the highlands catch up with them?

PM: I would say that you have put your finger on the difficulty which I pointed out at the beginning of this interview. It is a matter surely for arrangement up there. It is not for the Australian Government, I think, to say 'You have got to wait this long' or haven't got to wait that long, and indeed even in the coastal areas, there is by no means a unanimity as to what stage they would like the Australians to go. The Pangu Party, for example, is keen on very quick self-government, but the Pangu Party, as far as one can judge, has not got a very large following. In the highlands, I believe, opinion is unanimous against any early self-government, and the highlands have the majority of the population of the Territory of Papua/New Guinea.

Q. Have you got a sort of twenty-year vacuum here, though, between say, the Tolais who we seem to feel are more educated than the remainder of the indigenous people of New Guinea ... now is there a sort of twenty-year vacuum here where they have had the advantages of say the Germans when they occupied New Guinea, and then the Australian Administration since it has been their area to look after, and the highlands people where there hasn't been a lot of penetration from the white man, have had this sort of twenty-year period...that they have to catch up?

PM: Oh, it is more than twenty years in that sense in that the coastal areas have been subject to European influence for, what, seventy or eighty years, and the highlands for say, twenty, but on

---

1   Gorton was interviewed by John Boland. The interview was recorded on 17 July and screened on the Channel 7 current affairs programme 'This Week' on 19 July 1970.

the other hand, that doesn't mean that the highland people can't catch up quite quickly. And, indeed, I believe they are catching up quite quickly through the provision of primary schools and secondary schools and technical training, teacher training schools at Goroka and things of that kind. But they are still … they believe they still need Australian participation and they need Australian administration. Now, so do a lot of coastal people, so the people around the Sepik and so do, I believe, a lot of the coastal Papuans. But around [Port] Moresby and say Wewak and Madang, there are groups of people who are more eager to move quickly. And it is a matter of the most delicate balance to try and see that one doesn't go too quickly and one doesn't go too slowly, but that all the time one seeks to leave it finally, at any time, to the decision of the people generally. Now it is not easy to arrive at that decision. People have said to me, 'Well, will you come out in favour of a referendum?' I wouldn't be prepared to come out in favour for or against a referendum on that at this time, because that is a possible way of arriving at what they want to do. So is sitting down and arriving at a consensus of opinion by discussion … that is, all areas, perhaps through the House of Assembly. So are expressions of views of the House of Assembly. There are a variety of ways in which I feel this feeling could be discovered. I am not prepared to come out now and say this is the way in which it will be done.'

Q. Now that you have seen it, and had a pretty good look at it, could Papua/New Guinea be self-governing by 1972? This is what Mr Whitlam said.

[*matter omitted*]

PM: I imagine any area can be self-governing if the people who have the responsibility to help it and to advance it move out and say 'Well you are on your own', well, presumably, it has to be self-governing. But I think the things that could flow from that action would be quite dangerous. I think it not putting it too high to say that if one were not careful, something even like a Biafran situation[2] could develop if we just moved out and said, 'Right you are on your own. We wash our hands of you.' I believe it possible.

[*matter omitted*]

PM: I'm sorry, I just think it quite impossible with any responsibility to say a particular date. It can't be too long delayed. I don't myself think it will be too long delayed, because I think the situation will arise, certainly not by 1972 and certainly not by 1973 or 4. I am not going to put on any date at all. All I am going to say is I believe a situation will eventually arise when the people generally there will say, now, we would like to have self-government and then they should have it.

[*matter omitted*]

PM: I see it as a possibility at some stage. In fact, I don't see it as a possibility at some stage, I see it as a certainty at some stage.

[*matter omitted*]

[NAA: A452, 1971/0514]

---

2   Over the period from 1967 to 1970 an attempt by the Ibo (or Igbo) community of south-eastern Nigeria to secede from Nigeria and establish the 'Biafran Republic' was ruthlessly repressed.

86   PAPER FROM HUGHES TO CABINET

Canberra, 19 July 1970

SECRET

Territory of New Guinea: Call-Out of Defence Forces

Following arrangements made at a meeting of Ministers held at the Prime Minister's Lodge on the morning of Saturday, 18th July, I departed by RAAF BAC-111 for Port Moresby at 2.30 p.m. that day. I was accompanied by Mr C. W. Harders, Secretary of my Department. The agreed purpose of my visit was to assess by direct consultation with the Administrator and officials of the Territory Administration the immediately current position in the Gazelle Peninsula and the likely developments should the intended confrontation between Police and members of the Mataungan Association over trespasses to land at Vunapalandig take place as planned on Monday, 20th July. The object of making such an assessment was to form a judgment for the guidance of the Governor-General in Council on the question whether, if violence should break out in the course of the proposed confrontation, there would be a real danger that such a condition of public disorder would arise as would be beyond the capacity of the Police to control. This, as I advised the Prime Minister on 17th July, is the test that must be satisfied in order that the Governor-General may be properly advised to make an Order-in-Council calling out military forces in aid of attempts by the civil authorities to keep the peace.

[*matter omitted*]¹

7.   Rabaul's assessment of police capacity is as follows:

'Police strength and standard of training are capable of handling immediate violent situation. Escalated violence would most likely require assistance from army units.'

[*matter omitted*]²

9.   […] The clear consensus is as follows:

(a) the police will be able to cope with the initial outbreak of violence that is to be expected;

(b) if the initial outbreak should spark off a violent reaction in other areas, then it is unlikely that the police will be able to control the situation without military assistance. This prompted me to ask for an assessment of the degree of risk of a chain reaction. To me, this is the vital question. No one proffered a precise and clear-cut view upon it […]
At all events, everyone agreed using varying forms of expression that there is a real risk of an escalation of disorder after the initial confrontation has occurred. Any escalation would probably occur quickly: news travels fast in the Gazelle.

10.   *My own judgment* therefore is that I would advise the Governor-General that, on the assumption that there is to be a confrontation, it would be proper in the circumstances to make an Order-in-Council calling out the defence forces to assist in the maintenance of public order against domestic violence reasonably anticipated as likely to occur.³

---

1   The omitted material provides details of Hughes' meetings with senior officials and senior police and military officers during his visit to Port Moresby.

2   The omitted material said that 100 further police could be deployed to Rabaul 'provided that no major threat to public order were to develop elsewhere in the Territory'. It also said that the large police deployment in the Gazelle Peninsula meant that police resources were 'already thinly spread elsewhere'.

3   Hughes had earlier displayed caution (Document 83), but it appears that he changed his position on the basis of the 'clear consensus' of discussions in Port Moresby.

11. *The Army's role and the limitations upon its availability*:

(a) There are two PIR companies on stand-by and one reserve in Port Moresby; and two on stand-by in Wewak. Four companies amount to 350 officers and men. The addition of the reserve company would increase the available strength to 440. These men are armed with standard infantry weapons; they lack riot-control equipment. Their training and indoctrination in the techniques of riot control has been commenced only in the last two weeks.

(b) I am advised by the Army Commander[4] that the time required from his receipt of a requisition by the Administration to get his 4 stand-by companies to Rabaul would be 4 hours. It would take 1 to 1½ hours to transport them to the disputed area of land. But it is more likely than not that troops would in the first instance be deployed in defence of installations in Rabaul town. Fast water transport would be available to transport detachments to other parts of the Peninsula as necessary.

(c) The airport at Rabaul has limitations in relation to incoming military traffic: unless take-off from Port Moresby or Wewak is prior to 4 p.m., a landing cannot be made at Rabaul before first light the following day.

(d) The Administrator (but he was alone in this) urged that consideration be given to a call-out by the Governor-General and a consequent requisition by the Administration to the Army Commander both being effected today, so as to enable soldiers to be air-lifted to Rabaul before any confrontation starts. The Military Commander expressed his strong opposition to this proposal. Mr Ellis supports the view of the Military Commander and thinks that it will be sufficient if the army forces are available at Rabaul town p.m. Monday.

[*matter omitted*]

[NAA: A432, 1961/3329 ATTACHMENT]

---

4   Brigadier R. T. Eldridge.

87   LETTER FROM HUGHES TO HASLUCK

Canberra, 19 July 1970

You have requested my advice on the law, both international and municipal, that is applicable in relation to the use of native forces in aid of the civil power for the control of domestic violence in the Territory of New Guinea.

2.   Part I of this memorandum deals with matters of international law; Part II deals with matters of municipal or domestic law.

Part I: International Law

3.   The Territory of New Guinea is a Trust Territory within the United Nations trusteeship system and is administered by Australia pursuant to a Trusteeship Agreement approved by the General Assembly of the United Nations on 13 December, 1946 (see Fourth Schedule to Papua and New Guinea Act 1949–1968).

4.   From the international point of view, the legal framework within which any decision to use native forces in aid of the civil power in the Territory of New Guinea is provided by the Charter of the United Nations and by the Trusteeship Agreement referred to in the last preceding paragraph.

5.   The relevant provision of the Charter of the United Nations is Article 84, which reads as follows:

> '84. It shall be the duty of the administering authority to ensure that the trust territory shall play its part in the maintenance of international peace and security. To this end, the administering authority may make use of volunteer forces, facilities, and assistance from the trust territory in carrying out the obligations towards the Security Council undertaken in this regard by the administering authority, as well as for local defence and the maintenance of law and order within the trust territory.'

6.   The primary purpose of Article 84 was to establish the duty of an administering authority to ensure that each trust territory would play its part in the maintenance of international security. The Article does, however, expressly permit the use of locally-raised volunteer forces for 'the maintenance of law and order within the trust territory'.

7.   The right of an administering authority to use locally-raised volunteer forces, in proper cases and at its discretion, for the maintenance of law and order in a trust territory is expressly recognized by the two leading commentaries on the Charter, namely, the commentaries by Goodrich and Hambro and by Kelsen.[1] I do not think that this right can be disputed. In my opinion the right extends to the use of locally-raised volunteer forces in aid of the civil power for the suppression of domestic violence.

8.   For the reasons set out in paragraph 25 of Part II of this memorandum, I am satisfied that the Pacific Island Regiment, in so far as it consists of indigenous people of the Territory of New Guinea, is a locally-raised volunteer force. Accordingly, I am of the view that the use of the Pacific Islands Regiment in aid of the civil power for the suppression of domestic violence in the Territory of New Guinea would be entirely consistent with Australia's international obligations.

---

1   That is, Leland M. Goodrich and Edvard Hambro, *Charter of the United Nations: Charter and Documents*, World Peace Foundation, Boston, 1946; and Hans Kelsen, *The Law of the United Nations*, Frederick A. Praeger, New York, 1950.

9.   For the sake of completeness, I should perhaps say that I have not considered and would wish to reserve my opinion on the question whether the Pacific Islands Regiment could lawfully be used for the maintenance of law and order in the Territory of Papua (which is not a trust territory). I understand, however, that Your Excellency does not wish me to advise on that question at this time.

Part II: Municipal or Domestic Law

10.   By section 119 of the Constitution, the Commonwealth is under and obligation to 'protect every *State* against invasion and, on the application of the Executive Government of a State, against domestic violence'.

11.   Section 51 of the Defence Act 1903–1966 is as follows:

'51.   Where the Governor of a State has proclaimed that domestic violence exists therein, the Governor-General, upon the application of the Executive Government of the State, may, by proclamation, declare that domestic violence exists in that State, and may call out the Permanent Forces (other than Reserve Forces) and in the event of their numbers being insufficient may also call out such of the Reserve Forces and the Citizen Forces as may be necessary for the protection of that State, and the services of the Forces so called out may be utilized accordingly for the protection of that State against domestic violence:

'Provided always that the Reserve Forces or the Citizen Forces shall not be called out or utilised in connexion with an industrial dispute.'

12.   Section 5A of the Defence Act provides that the Act shall extend to the Territories of the Commonwealth as if each of those Territories were part of the Commonwealth but that Part IV of the Act (which deals with liability to serve in the Defence Force in time of war) does not extend to, or in relation to, the aboriginal inhabitants of a Territory of the Commonwealth governed by the Commonwealth under a Trusteeship Agreement.

13.   Section 124 of the Defence Act authorises the Governor-General to make regulations, not inconsistent with the Act, prescribing all matters which by the Act are required or permitted to be prescribed, or which are necessary or convenient to be prescribed, for securing the discipline and good government of the Defence Force and for certain other specified purposes that are not relevant for present purposes.

14.   Regulations governing the use of the Defence Force in aid of the civil power during domestic violence have been made under section 124 and appear as Part V (regs. 398–415) of the Australian Military Regulations.

15.   Although Part V of the Australian Military Regulations is, perhaps, directed primarily to the use of the Defence Force against domestic violence at the request of a State, my own view (which is shared by my departmental advisers) is that the regulations in that Part apply according to their tenor also to the use of the Defence Force against domestic violence in a Commonwealth Territory, whether internal or external.

16.   The Australian Capital Territory and the Northern Territory are expressly mentioned in at least two regulations in Part V (regs. 398 and 407) and there can I think be no doubt that such of the regulations in Part V as are capable of applying in relation to those Territories do apply.

17.   None of the external Territories of the Commonwealth is expressly mentioned in Part V but, having regard to the provisions of section 5A of the Defence Act (see para.12 above), my own view (which is shared by present and past departmental advisers) is that those provisions on Part V that apply to the internal Territories apply also to the external Territories, including the trust territory of New Guinea. I should add that there may conceivably be circumstances in which Part V would not need to be strictly observed in employing military forces against domestic violence but these would be cases in which the emergency was so grave as to evoke

powers of a quite exceptional character arising from the principle commonly referred to as *salus populi suprema lex*.[2]

17. Whilst there are some provisions in Part V of the Australian Military Regulations that clearly could not apply in relation to a Territory (as, for example, regs. 400(1), 401 and 402), major substantive provisions of Part V pre-suppose that any military forces to be used in aid of the civil power to suppress domestic violence will have been 'called out'—for example, regulation 404(1).

18. In relation to domestic violence in a State, the reference in that regulation is to forces that have been 'called out' by the Governor-General under section 51 of the Defence Act. In relation to a Territory, although there is no counterpart of section 51, the Regulations should nevertheless be construed as contemplating action on the part of the Governor-General similar to that under section 51.

19. As the Governor-General would, in 'calling out' the military forces, represent the civil power, this construction is in accord with the basic principle of our constitutional law that the civil power is at all times supreme.

20. Subject to the possible exception referred to in the concluding sentence of paragraph 17 above, Part V, with the consequential necessity of 'call out' by the Governor-General, must be read as setting out exhaustively the circumstances in which military forces may be used to aid the civil power against domestic violence.

21. In the absence of any statutory provision that prescribes directly the procedure to be followed in 'calling out' the Defence Force for protection against domestic violence in a Territory, I am of opinion that the procedure to be followed should be similar to that prescribed by section 51 of the Defence Act. In my view, the 'call-out' should be effected by the Governor-General acting with the advice of the Federal Executive Council. However, a preceding proclamation that a state of domestic violence exists in the Territory, analogous to the proclamation by the Governor of a State envisaged under section 51, is not required either expressly or impliedly by Part V of the Regulations and would not be necessary. Nor would it be necessary for the Governor-General to proclaim that a state of domestic violence exists. The only essential prerequisite would be, in the light of the basic principle of the primacy of the civil power, a request for 'call out' by the relevant civil authorities. This request could be made by the Administrator or by the Minister for External Territories.

22. Although the instrument by which a call-out is to be effected under section 51 of the Defence Act is a Proclamation, I see no reason to conclude that, as a matter of law, a Proclamation is necessary in those cases where there is no statutory provision authorizing and requiring a Proclamation. The primacy of the civil power would be maintained if the 'call-out' were effected by an Order-in-Council, which has the added advantage that it need not before becoming effective be published. In my view, the appropriate instrument for 'call-out' of the Defence Force against domestic violence in a Territory is an Order-in-Council.

23. An Order-in-Council 'calling-out' those members of the Defence Force who are for the time being serving in that Territory or in the Territory of Papua (including members of any Reserve or of any Citizen Forces who are for the time being rendering continuous full-time service in either of those Territories) would, in my view, be effective to 'call-out' all members of the Defence Force in the territory of Papua or the Territory of New Guinea at the time the Order was made and would operate (until revoked) to call out additional members of the Defence Force as and when they arrived in either Territory. More specifically it would operate effectively and lawfully to 'call-out' the Pacific Islands Regiment including those members who are indigenous people of the trust territory of New Guinea.

---

2   'Let the good (or safety) of the people be the supreme (or highest) law'.

24. I turn now to consider the circumstances that would justify a recommendation by the Executive Council for the issue of an Order-in-Council 'calling out' elements of the Defence Force for the suppression of domestic violence in New Guinea. There is no statutory provision that is directly applicable. In this situation, I have concluded that the fundamental constitutional principle of the primacy of the civil authority requires that military forces should not be called out to assist in the suppression of domestic violence or of imminent domestic violence unless the civil arm of Government is reasonably satisfied on the basis of cogent intelligence that the civil authority cannot or may not be able to cope with an existing or imminent state of domestic violence. I do not think that the power to 'call-out' the Defence Force is restricted to cases in which domestic violence is actually occurring when the question of call-out is raised. In my opinion, the Executive Council would be justified in recommending the issue of an Order-in-Council and the Governor-General would be required to follow a recommendation by the Executive Council if a situation exists in which there is a clear and strong probability that civil policy will be unable by themselves to quell a likely disturbance of public order of a serious character in a Territory of the Commonwealth.

25. With regard to the projected use of the Pacific Islands Regiment in aid of the civil power to suppress domestic violence in the trust territory of New Guinea, I am satisfied that there can be no legal objection to this course. I am informed that all members of the Pacific Islands Regiment are enlisted as volunteers under section 36 of the Defence Act. The period of their enlistment, is a period of four years which, by regulation 135 of the Australian Military Regulations is the period of enlistment appropriate for a soldier in a native force. As so enlisted, they are members of the Defence Force (Defence Act, s.30).

[NAA: A452, 1961/3329 PART 5]

88   RECORD OF CABINET MEETING[1]

Canberra, 19 July 1970

CONFIDENTIAL

Subject: New Guinea Situation and the Use of the PIR

Gorton:

Will give you run-down on situation before inviting Attorney-General to speak. Background is that Mataungan Group—Tolais—not recognising Government or any laws except their own. Intent on violence. Bringing on episode of force—i.e. on their part—to occupy land bought by Administration for re-allotment. View from Administration and the Minister and bound to say I fully agree that we must not allow this— if we back down, further episodes of land occupancy illegally. So necessary to use police to evict. But question is whether police—about 1000—able to deal with the situation satisfactorily. Admin[istrator] feels probably but by no means certain. Therefore the question of back-up arises—i.e. back up by the PIR. If yes, the question of preliminary measures—which means Order-in-Council to call out the PIR. Minister for ET [External Territories] asked the Minister for D [Defence] in this [sense][2]—referred to Defence Committee which advised for legal and other reasons that not prepared to recommend. Min[ister] for Defence accepted this advice and therefore didn't sign order. I had not come in to this up to this point.

Fraser:

But I sent message through Secretary your Department and position was 'as situation then was, no basis' and in any case best made a matter for Cabinet discussion.

Gorton:

Well, however that was, I am only reporting matter as it comes [sic] to me. My information later was that legal basis for call-out satisfied and I therefore had Order-in-Council prepared and signed. But in meantime letter from Attorney saying still not satisfied. So I have sent Attorney to Port Moresby who will report. But want to refer to intransigence and threats of violence of Kaputin and Tammur. Invite Hughes to report.

Hughes:

Reads from report—to be circulated later.[3] Refers to meetings held— preparations of Tolais (i.e. Mataungans)—plans of Administration. Views given to me that police will be able to withstand initial outbreak but any escalation, including spread elsewhere will require military intervention. References made to risk of *Mau Mau* type outbreak.[4] Re degree of risk of chain reaction. No clear views expressed on this—it is intuitive matter anyway but it was agreed that there is real risk of disorder after initial confront[ation]. Escalation, if it is to occur, will

1   In addition to Prime Minister Gorton, those present were McMahon, Barnes, Fraser, Hughes, Bowen, Bury, Snedden, Doug Anthony, Senator Ken Anderson (Supply), and Peter Nixon (Interior). Officials present were Bunting and Lenox Hewitt.

2   Editorial insertion. Word in original illegible

3   This is presumably a reference to Document 86. See also Document 87.

4   The violent *Mau Mau* uprising took place from 1952 to 1960 in Kenya, at that time a British colony, and was ruthlessly suppressed. *Mau Mau* was the name of the secret society which led the uprising.

probably occur quickly. Reads judgement reached if to be asked (by GG) [Governor-General] whether all requirements preparatory to call out satisfied—in summary, my view is that it would be proper to move to call out—on assumption that police are to move on the land occupied as discussed. Refers to Army strength and training and timetable—4 hours from time of signal receipt at Port Moresby—plus 1½ hours if to be deployed at the land, but more likely to be deployed in Rabaul.

Administrator asked for call-out order today and move to Rabaul today. But military commander prefers not to be requisitioned until there is an occurrence requiring it. He believes sufficient to have PIR in Rabaul by Monday pm. Magistrate available to accompany forces to authorise particular actions as required. Would say that if Order-in-Council made, this be announced immediately.

Gorton: That satisfies the legal step which is one factor. Our concerns are these:

(1) Take no action and let M. [Mataungan] occupy the land—but believe this would be disastrous—may as well leave Territory.

(2) Take police action—but [defer]⁵ indefinitely.

(3) Take action now—i.e. tomorrow. This the only real concern.

(4) This being so, do we make contingency plans and call out PIR to be used in case of need.

Realise all kinds of international and local repercussions and accept it could lead to bloodshed. But on the other hand, if situation got out of hand, in sense of life, property etc., we would have no possible defence in face of strongest rec[ommendation] of Minister, Administrator and senior officials. Not a situation we can get ourselves into.

Barnes: All the more in that law and order, under the new regime, remains A/n [Australian] responsibility.

Hughes: Refers to exercise of allocating land.

Barnes: This being speeded up—mostly a question of interviewing—will be hastening it.

McMahon: My first doubts on hearing of this were on legal side—these resolved.

On political side, certainly accept PM's view, especially as metropolitan power remains responsible for law and order. But [...]⁶ would prefer to proceed by steps—first see if the police can handle—if not then withdraw and at that time, go to Order-in-Council. Don't let them say we are provoking them—call would provoke. No doubt we will end up with use of PIR now or later but proceed slowly and without provocation. Also would like to raise question of whether we get expression of view of Assembly and Council.

Gorton: Note this—but feel sure we must have police action now and call-out now—leave the requisitioning till later.

Barnes: Re Council—two recent meetings with them—unanimous in saying that law and order must be upheld.

---

5   Editorial insertion. Word in original illegible.
6   Word in original illegible.

Fraser:	What are prospects and wisdom of charging Kaputin and others for incitement—not yet advocating but interested to know.
Gorton:	This is good point—our laws seem inadequate but if there is an incitement charge opportunity, we should take it.
Hughes:	Law office has this in mind.
Anthony:	My view is clear that we are to uphold the law—having been advised of risk of chain reaction and risk to life and property we must take the contingency action. Would take the military advice of not moving the force today. But otherwise get the force there as soon as possible in case needed for protection of property and life.
McMahon:	So you would go to call-out now.
Anthony:	Yes.
Fraser:	Now accept that the legal basis now satisfied and in situation as it exists, we need to go ahead. Would prefer not to move [troops]⁷ yet until requisition made and would prefer no announcement of issue of order. Next, we should realise that this is the substantive decision, i.e., if requisition made it will come to Ministers but will be virtual formality only.
Gorton:	Agree.
Fraser:	That being so, we can speed up by allowing military commander to get his troops into the air as soon as requisition request made—not wait till the answer given.
Gorton:	Agree.
Fraser:	Next—would hope that matters could be contrived so that first violence is by Mataungans.
Anderson:	No doubt in my mind we need the Order-in-Council today. Have a question about withholding announcement.
Hughes:	This is already in mind.
Snedden:	Have real difficulty—an Order-in-Council, if it becomes known, will be seen as putting us on the path of resorting to troops—a continuing basis of enforcement of law and order. So searching for whether it is possible that escalation of violence instead of leading to requisition leads to Order-in-Council. These may be questions of timetable and other uncertainties.
Gorton:	There are uncertainties—plus emotions up there—including the position of our officials charged with responsibility.
Anthony:	Support Gorton—extreme emotionalism.
Fraser:	The Attorney's report means that there is sufficient threat—that is all that is required—doesn't have to be active situation. And given all the advice we've been given by the responsible authorities, don't see that we can fail to act now to [approve an] Order-in-Council. We would be more culpable in that failure than in going to call-out.
Snedden:	My search is for a course which would go ahead to all our planning but stop short of call-out at present.

---

7   Editorial insertion. Word in original illegible.

Gorton:	Don't think that practicable.
Nixon:	Had concern earlier about a too heavy-handed response—but especially now—in light of recent visit agree necessary to act now and situation could too quickly get out of hand otherwise—bit concerned re small size of PIR.
Bowen:	Believe we should go ahead and get the order—but see risk in provoking international opinion and provoking situation in NG [New Guinea]. Also concerned at level of force—not sure it is strong enough—if it had overwhelming strength it would stop violence. But equal strength could imply [or] mean it would be fought out. Could we supplement from A/a [Australia].
Gorton:	Don't know—but not practicable immediately.
Fraser:	Can speak to that.
Bury:	Agree we must all have regard to reports received. Refers to announcement of Order-in-Council.
Gorton:	There is a general view we go to Order-in-Council and allow Administrator to use his judgement re requisitioning.
Bury:	One more point—we should make Kaputin's backg[round] known publicly.
Gorton:	There is overwhelming view in NG [New Guinea] that we should uphold law and order.
Nixon:	Agree—great fear if we don't.
McMahon:	Strong view that we should get order but still for myself say delay—have it all ready—but not provoke. If issues, not announced.
Anderson:	Want to take that up.
Fraser:	Want requisition sent to Canberra immediately and not sent subsequently—even though automatic reply.
Gorton:	Yes. But they can assume concurrence.
Fraser:	For practical purposes, yes. But not for [forms].[8]
Anderson:	Fear the proposal to stifle fact of issue of order—first it will get known anyway and second, it has its own deterrent effect.
McMahon:	Agree it will be difficult to contain.
Nixon:	I feel that too—would prefer to see announcement by PM.
Hughes:	Also wouldn't feel we could successfully hold it secure—I suppose my visit to NG [New Guinea] already noticed.
Gorton:	That as may be—we can return to this issue.
Fraser:	Refers to various details—some elements of PIR new and untrained—couldn't use. Could be some transport aircraft problems. Regulations for aid to civil powers—should we discuss.
Gorton:	Think not.
Fraser:	So Army follows ordinary course.
Gorton:	That's it.

---

8 Editorial insertion. Word in original illegible.

Fraser:	Re publicity—quite apart from order in council, could PM make a statement to announce today's cabinet meeting. Prefer not to mention Order-in-Council.
Gorton:	That's my view re Order-in-Council—but do I say anything about today's meeting.
Anthony:	Yes. Announce today's meeting—that we considered situation—taken steps to protect law and order—i.e. do all that is necessary. Not name O.in C. [Order-in-Council].
McMahon:	We shouldn't be caught in deceit.
Gorton:	No, of course. But equally not inflame.
McMahon:	We want to include in what we say is [sic] reference to Assembly and need to mention law and order.
Snedden:	Agree to Anthony's formulation—but refer also to the Administrator's request for support by A/n [Australian] Government.
Gorton:	Canvasses words—we discussed Gazelle Peninsula situation and will support by all means.
Anthony:	I would like it in tomorrow's press.
Gorton	)
Snedden:	) Discuss words [sic].
McMahon:	Couldn't give assurance of backing of *all* measures. Use 'in proportion to the danger'.
Gorton:	Suggest Hughes and I draft—but dubious about announcing the Order-in-Council—it is covered by 'all means'.
Snedden:	Greatly prefer not say 'Order-in-Council'.
Gorton:	It is covered by statement that we are back[ing] up.
Anthony:	Yes. But I'm sure we're going to have to put the troops over there.
Gorton:	Feel sure yes—in fact we are probably entering on a classical African situation.
Bowen:	Returns to question of Australian troops to supplement.
Fraser:	Military commander believes not necessary.
Anthony:	[Important][9] thing is that we win—expect bad situation tomorrow—and the Administration's force must be seen to win. Natives will go with the strength.
Bowen:	That's why I mention the A/n [Australian] force.
Anthony:	But I don't see the troops fighting. They only [shoot].[10] Police do the fighting—Army for protection of property.
Gorton:	Chain of command—this must be sorted out.
Fraser:	Yes, believe it is clear—but I will work out with Hughes.

[NAA: A11099, 1/111]

---

9   Editorial insertion. Word in original illegible.
10   Editorial insertion. Word in original illegible.

89   CABINET DECISION 484

Canberra, 19 July 1970

SECRET

Without Submission: Military Aid to the Civil Power in Papua and New Guinea—Call-out of the Pacific Island Regiment

As background, the Prime Minister referred to the challenge of the Mataungan Association to the authority of the Administration and to law and order generally, and mentioned in particular the occupation by Mataungan supporters of land bought by the Administration for allotment to indigenous people, including Tolai, and to the threats by the Mataungans to resist eviction, including to the point of violence.

2.   He informed the Cabinet that the Minister for External Territories had on 14 July sought the concurrence of the Minister for Defence in the 'call-out' of the Pacific Island Regiment— as a formal step in case of need for the Regiment to assist the Police if a situation beyond the capacity of the Police to control should develop—and that the Minister for Defence, acting with the advice of the Defence Committee, had indicated that it did not appear that at that time he would be justified in recommending to the Governor-General in Council that a call-out Order should be signed.

3.   The Prime Minister then indicated that he had asked the Attorney-General to visit the Territory in the past twenty-four hours to form a judgment whether the Governor-General may be properly advised to make an Order-in-Council calling out military forces in aid of attempts by the civil authorities to maintain law and order. It was noted that an Order-in-Council would require a condition of domestic violence, or a real danger that such a condition would arise, beyond the capacity of the Police to control.

4.   The Attorney-General informed the Cabinet that on the basis of his consultations his judgment was—on the assumption that there is to be a confrontation—that it would be proper to make an Order-in-Council calling out the defence forces to assist in the maintenance of public order against domestic violence reasonably anticipated as likely to occur.

5.   The Cabinet noted that on present plans the Administration would, on Monday next, take action, using the Police if necessary, directed to removing the persons occupying the Administration land. The Cabinet agreed that these plans should proceed and agreed further, having regard to the risk that the situation would then develop beyond the capacity of the Police to contain, that the PIR should be available to assist in the event of need. For this purpose, it agreed that the precautionary step of an Order-in-Council calling out the Regiment should be taken forthwith—on the footing that the Regiment would not be brought into use unless the necessary requisition by the Administrator is placed and approved.

6.   It was understood that the approval of a requisition would be a matter for the Australian Government but it was agreed that the Administrator could initiate action without delay at the time of placing a requisition on the basis that approval would be forthcoming. It was further understood that a requisition would be placed only on a confrontation or serious incident or development which, in the Administrator's judgment, threatens or shows loss of control of the situation by the Police.

7.   Against the possibility that the Regiment is brought into use, the Cabinet asked that command arrangements be settled and made clear.

8.   The Cabinet recognised that if military force is used, it can be expected to produce some adverse reaction, including internationally, but it felt—in its total assessment, and taking into account the advice of the Administration—that there was no responsible alternative to

its present decisions. It was noted in this connection that the House of Assembly and the Administrator's Executive Council stood firmly for the preservation of law and order.

9.   It was agreed that the Prime Minister would that day issue a statement announcing that Cabinet had met to consider the situation and that it was expressing to the Administrator the support and backing of the Australian Government for the steps necessary to maintain law and order. It was agreed that the Prime Minister and the Attorney-General would settle the text of the statement, it being in mind that reference need not be made, in terms, to the issue of an Order-in-Council.

[NAA: A5873, 484]

90   PRESS RELEASE

Canberra, 19 July 1970

Cabinet Meets to Consider Gazelle Situation
Statement by the Prime Minister, Mr John Gorton

Federal Cabinet met today to consider a series of reports from the Administrator of Papua and New Guinea.

The reports indicated that the Administrator faced a serious, potentially dangerous situation on the Gazelle Peninsula in New Britain.

The situation has come about in the following way. The Administration bought land on the Gazelle Peninsula in order to subdivide it and distribute it among Tolai and Bainings indigenous people.[1] A section of the Tolai, called Mataungans,[2] had sent squatters onto this land and had stated that they were going to occupy it and distribute it themselves and that they recognised no title and no law but their own will.

The Mataungans had made it clear that they would resist any attempt at removing their illegal squatters and had massed twelve to fifteen hundred persons on the site to resist by violence any attempted removal.

The persons gathered were armed with spears, bows and arrows, sling shots, rocks, bottles, bush knives and axes.

It was clear that if the police carried out their duty and removed those in illegal occupation of the land there was a strong risk of a major clash, of riot and of extreme violence.

After considering these reports, and bearing in mind the expressed wish of the Administrator's Executive Council and of the Tolai opposed to the Mataungans, that the law should be enforced, Cabinet decided that it was essential that law and order should be maintained in the Territory.

Cabinet decided that the Government fully agreed with the Administrator and would fully support the Administrator in carrying out measures which the Administrator had advised the Government he felt to be necessary in the present circumstances, to remove squatters.

The Administrator has been so informed. It is hoped the leaders of the Mataungan section of the Tolais will not incite their followers to the violence they have threatened; but if they do so the responsibility for any consequences will rest upon them alone.

[NAA: A452, 1971/2294]

---

1   The large, self-confident Tolai community numbered around 70,000 and comprised a large majority of the population of the Gazelle Peninsula. The Baining people were the original inhabitants of the Gazelle Peninsula. They mainly occupied the mountainous parts of the Peninsula, after having largely withdrawn from coastal areas in response to Tolai pressure.

2   For background on the Mataungan Association, see Document 49, fn. 3.

91   TELEX FROM WARWICK SMITH TO HAY

Canberra, 19 July 1970

7132. SECRET

Governor-General has signed an Order-in-Council calling out for the protection of the Territory of New Guinea against domestic violence those members of the Defence Force who are for the time being serving in that Territory or in the Territory of Papua (including members of any reserve or of any citizen forces who are for the time being rendering continuous full-time service in either of those Territories).

2.   Signature of this Order-in-Council is secret and is not to be divulged without Ministerial authority.

3.   Signature of Order-in-Council does not repeat not authorise movement or deployment of troops (but see paragraph 5 below).

4.   Before troops are moved from present location a requisition will need to be made on the Force Commander PNG Command by the Administrator.

5.   Such a requisition should not be made until after a confrontation or serious incident which, in the Administrator's judgment, threatens or shows loss of control of the situation by the Police. The requisition will require the authority of Ministers here. However, the Administrator may, in his discretion, anticipate approval of such a request for authority and act without waiting for formal approval. The Force Commander is being similarly advised. The authority should be sought through this Department when desired.

6.   When seeking authority to make such a requisition the request to Ministers should set out all the circumstances considered to make military aid necessary.

7.   A description should also be supplied of the proposed broad general framework of cooperation between Administrator, police and military forces including such matters as arrangements for consultation and coordination on the ground in Rabaul (eg by the establishment of a District Security Committee consisting of the District Commissioner, officer commanding troops and the officer commanding police: military/police command posts etc).

8.   My later message[1] sets out the sequences of steps necessary for the actual employment of military personnel.

9.   If because of developments any major change becomes necessary in the nature of military involvement from that proposed at the time the approval was sought, Ministers should be informed in advance if at all practicable.

10.   In view of government decision in paragraph 1 above action may be taken at your discretion to put up road blocks as discussed with Attorney-General.[2] This could be done immediately if you consider appropriate.

11.   A separate departmental message will be sent tomorrow about possible changes in Territory law relating to preservation of law and order with a view to changes being introduced at the next meeting of the House of Assembly.

12.   This message is being copied by Army to Commander PNG Command.[3]

[NAA: A452, 1970/3808]

---

1   Not published.
2   Tom Hughes.
3   Brigadier Ralph Eldridge.

92   NOTE BY HASLUCK

Canberra, undated [c. late July 1970][1]

Events Associated with Proposal to Use Defence Forces to Maintain Civil Order in Papua New Guinea, July 1970

On the morning of Thursday July 16, 1970, I received by telephone a request by the Minister of Defence, Mr Malcolm Fraser that he might call on me.[2] I suggested that he might come to Government House about noon and stay to lunch. I had an inkling of what he might want to discuss. On the previous day, at the presentation of credentials by the new Soviet Ambassador, the Secretary of the Department of External Affairs, Sir Keith Waller, who was representing his Minister, mentioned to me in a private conversation that the Defence Committee was arguing over the problem of whether Pacific Islands Regiment should be called out to quell civil disorder if the current dispute over land in the Rabaul district resulted in violence. He expressed his own strong doubts about the wisdom of such a course and said that Defence and the service chiefs were also strongly against it but the Prime Minister's Department and the Department of External Territories were pressing strongly for such a course. This proved to be the subject on which Mr Fraser wished to talk. He commenced by saying that as this subject was likely to be presented to me, I should be forewarned so that I was not taken by surprise. He said that the Defence Department was strongly opposed to the use of troops in civil disorder. They thought, in the first place, that the Department of External Territories was greatly exaggerating the risk of violence. Secondly he could not understand why they were trying to force a confrontation. It seemed to him that they had created the situation in which violence was likely to be used and from the start had been planning for a call-out of the troops to crush opposition and 'prove something to themselves'. He objected to the Army being 'planned into' a difficult and unwelcome situation in this way. Now Territories had got the support of the Prime Minister who, without consulting Defence and without referring the matter to Cabinet, had minuted a letter from the Minister for External Territories to the effect that he (the Prime Minister) agreed to the use of troops.[3] Mr Fraser felt strongly that it was improper that a matter of this kind should be handled in this way. It should be taken to Cabinet. There should have been a submission giving full information about the present and prospective situation so that Cabinet could decide whether the facts justified the use of troops and so that Cabinet could decide whether troops should be used and, if so, in what circumstances. Mr Fraser saw strong arguments of both domestic and international politics against the use of troops against natives. He then discussed the unsuitability of the PIR for this type of action. They had not been trained for police duty. If attacked they had been taught to shoot and he feared heavy and unnecessary casualties if they were used in civil disorder any police role. He feared too that such a clash would have serious and lasting ill effects on the future of the defence services in New Guinea. The Defence Committee had discussed the matter and had recommended strongly against the use of troops. Nevertheless he feared the Prime Minister would go ahead regardless of the fact that Cabinet had never discussed the matter and that [the] Defence Committee were against it. In answer to a question he said that, in conversation with him, both the Minister for External Affairs and the Attorney-General had expressed views against calling out troops but he could not rely on what the Minister for External Affairs would do in a 'show down'. Mr

---

1   No date provided. Presumably Hasluck prepared it not long after 19 July.

2   We only have Hasluck's version of his conversations with Fraser, Waller, Barnes and Gorton but what he says of their views is consistent with evidence from other sources. See especially the contents of Documents 72–73, 75, 80–81 & 88–89.

3   Not published.

Fraser felt very warmly about the Prime Minister's failure to take the matter to Cabinet before the proposal had reached its present advanced stage. When I asked him if he had approached the Prime Minister, he conveyed rather tactfully the impression firstly that the Prime Minister was inaccessible, that he would not listen and that unfortunately Fraser had been having many clashes with him in similar situations.[4] Rather more openly he said that there had been frequent situations in which the Prime Minister had decided matters which should have gone to Cabinet. He then asked if he could put an awkward question to me. With permission granted, he sought advice on how he could bring matters to a head. I suggested that he and the Ministers interested should ask to discuss the matters with the Prime Minister. He thought this would be difficult. As his thoughts seem to be turning towards some argument in Cabinet, I said to him that while a Minister might raise a question in Cabinet for discussion he would have to use some care how he did it. No Minister could make a direct challenge to a Prime Minister unless he was trying to replace him. Other Ministers, indeed all Ministers, were bound to support a Prime Minister in the event of a direct challenge unless they were prepared either to leave Cabinet themselves or to unseat the Prime Minister. Mr Fraser accepted the point and said he did not wish to make a challenge in that way and saw my point that if he raised the question in Cabinet he would have to do so with strong care. Unfortunately, he said, Mr McEwen, who was the only strong man in Cabinet, was overseas. He sighed and said he dreaded the effects on Cabinet of the impending retirement of McEwen.[5] Mr Fraser said that he thought the whole matter ought to be discussed by ministers directly concerned before a decision was made. In view of the Defence Committee's report against the proposal he himself would refuse to sign any recommendation to Executive Council. In answer to questions, Mr Fraser could give little information to me on the legal authority for the Governor-General to take action. I said that there seemed to me to be two aspects of the matter. One was the political judgement on the wisdom of the action proposed. The other was the constitutional authority for the action to be taken and the procedures to be adopted. In the final resort I could not refuse to accept the political judgement of my advisers although I had a right to be informed about the facts and arguments on which it was made. I had a responsibility to ensure that any powers I exercised were properly exercised and on that I would need legal advice.

Following Mr Fraser's visit, but without further reference to him, I received from the Secretary of the Department, Sir Arthur Tange, copies of some papers, dated in February, 1962, and in June and July, 1966, containing advice by the Secretary of the Attorney-General's Department to the Department of Defence regarding the legal authority and sources of power governing a call-out by the Governor-General of the Pacific Islands Regiment. I studied these privately. Later I asked the Secretary of the Department of External Affairs, Sir Keith Waller, what was the departmental view of the effect of Section 8 of the Defence Act No 2 of 1951 (No 59 of 1951) inserting a new section 35a into the Defence Act and limiting the use of 'a native force' raised in a Trust Territory. Later I received a paper giving their view.[6]

On Friday, July 17, the new Administrator of the Territory of Papua New Guinea, Mr Johnson, was to be sworn in and the Minister for External Territories, Mr Barnes, called on me to be present at the ceremony.[7] I took the opportunity to have a brief conversation with Barnes in

---

4 The relationship between Gorton and Fraser worsened throughout 1970 and 1971. Although initially supportive of Gorton, Fraser was increasingly critical of Gorton's autocratic approach in Cabinet. Fraser's opposition to Gorton's plans to ensure Commonwealth control over off-shore mining led to a rupture of the relationship that contributed to Fraser's eventual resignation as Minister for Defence in March 1971. See Philip Ayres, *Malcolm Fraser: A Biography*, William Heinemann, Richmond, Vic., 1987, pp. 166–70.

5 McEwen retired six months later, on 5 February 1971.

6 Not published.

7 For the views of Barnes, see Documents 73, 75 & 76.

private. He seemed to be sure that there would be violence, that troops must be called out, that the men concerned were 'unscrupulous', 'full of hatred', and 'dangerous people' and that 'they must not be allowed to get away with it.' He did not appear to have given much thought to anything except the need to 'stand up to them' and to call out the troops for that purpose so I saw no value in pursuing the conversation for more than four or five minutes.

About the middle of the afternoon I had a message from the Assistant Official Secretary, Mr Thompson (the Official Secretary being absent on leave) that the Secretary of the Executive Council, Mr Grigg,[8] was trying to fix a time for an Executive Council and asking if I would be available about 5.45 p.m. As I could not rely on Thompson to handle a matter of which he was ignorant, I asked him to ask Mr Grigg to call me on a direct line. When Grigg telephoned I asked him what was the business for the Council and which Ministers were attending. He said the only line of business concerned the trouble at Rabaul and the Ministers attending would be the Prime Minister and Mr Barnes. In answer to a question he said that at the moment the Prime Minister was tied up in Budget talks at the Treasury. I asked him to give a message for either the Prime Minister or the Secretary of the Department, Mr Hewitt, to telephone to me on my direct line.

Mr Hewitt telephoned about ten minutes later. I said, after preliminary conversation, that the matter proposed to be placed before the Council was a major one. There were some points on which I would need special advice, including advice from the Attorney-General. When Mr Hewitt said that the Prime Minister regarded the matter as urgent and that there were no other Ministers in Canberra, I said that I would be available for a meeting at any time during the week-end and, if necessary, would postpone my planned departure on Monday for a northern tour. I suggested that before any Executive Council meeting was held the Prime Minister and I should have a private talk. Mr Hewitt agreed that would be a good idea.

At that stage I feared that the Prime Minister might want to insist on having his own way and that I might be obliged to resist him. This fear seemed to be justified when, shortly before 5.45, Mr Hewitt telephoned to me again to say that the Prime Minister agreed that we should have a private talk first, that he and Mr Barnes were about to leave for Government House, travelling in the same car, and perhaps on arrival the Prime Minister might be shown to my study on his own while Mr Barnes waited in the drawing room. When the Prime Minister was announced, however, it soon appeared to me that he might not be as difficult as feared and there would be room for persuasion. He commenced by reading messages and other bits of paper about the situation in Rabaul in support of a general proposal that quick action was necessary. In the course of it, however, he mentioned that a message calling for restraint had been sent to the Mataungans by Mr K. E. Beazley as Spokesmen on New Guinea affairs for the Opposition. Finally he came to a short paper he had received, apparently only shortly before coming to Government House, from the Attorney-General, Mr T. F. Hughes. After reviewing the facts, Mr Hughes expressed the opinion that the calling out of troops was not justified in his opinion. The Prime Minister had with him a Minute Paper for the Executive Council containing a recommendation for the making of an Order-in-Council [with] the spaces left blank for his signature.

I had received a copy of these two papers and of the customary 'Explanatory Memorandum',[9] which is attached to Executive Council minute papers, from the Clerk to Council by special delivery in a sealed envelope about half an hour before the Prime Minister's arrival.

At this point, I asked the Prime Minister, who had been standing and moving about the room, to take an easy chair and sat down myself. I said that this was a serious problem. If the troops

8   I. F. (Ian) Grigg, Secretary to the Federal Executive Council, Parliamentary and Government Division, PMD.

9   Document 83.

were called out there would be sure to be a public post-mortem debate, regardless of whether the troops were used. If the troops are used and there was bloodshed the debate would be more critical and heated and would be international as well as domestic; but, even if no violence ensued, there would be debate and in that debate strong points could be made against him if it could be shown that his action had not been fully considered. Suppose it could be shown that the Government had decided to call out troops before they heard the result of the appeal for restraint by Mr Beazley on behalf of the Opposition. Suppose it could be shown that the Government rejected the opinion of its Attorney-General. Suppose it could be shown that the Government had taken no notice of the advice of its Defence Committee.

As the Prime Minister appeared to recognise these points, I said that, as Governor-General I saw two separate aspects of the matter. One was the wisdom of the political judgement to call out troops, the other was legal authority and source of power for the Governor-General to do so. [As to] the first aspect, [I] recognised that in the final issue I could not put my political judgement against the political judgement of my advisers but I hoped he would let me make a few observations about the political factors. I could not contribute any facts to the discussion of the situation existing in Rabaul and, though I might have personal views about the wisdom of using troops in that kind of situation if the Executive Councillors advised me to take action I could not, in the last resort, say that I preferred my own opinion. Because of the seriousness of the action proposed, however, I should like to be reassured that the advice given to me was the result of full consideration and was widely shared by Ministers. Although an Executive Council meeting usually consisted of the Governor-General and two Ministers it had been customary on certain major matters for either the Governor-General or the Prime Minister to ask for a fuller attendance. In this case I would certainly like to have the Attorney-General present at any meeting of the Executive Council and if possible the Minister for External Affairs and Minister for Defence. Moreover, if the Prime Minister would let me speak [with] personal friendliness to him, I thought this would be in his own interest. In any post-mortem debate there would be sections of opinion which would love to represent the decision as one for which the Prime Minister alone was responsible [and] one that he had taken in disregard of the views of his senior Ministers. This would not help him. It would not help the Government. Indeed it might cause serious trouble and, as Governor-General, I had a reasonable interest in the stability of the Government. I put it to him in his own interest that when the debate took place on the calling out of troops, especially if there had been loss of life, he himself and his Government would be in the worst possible position if the Opposition or any other critics were able to say that the opinion that troops were needed was formed only by Gorton and Barnes; that the Prime Minister himself and not the Minister for Defence had signed the minute recommending the call up; that he had signed it at a time when no reply has been received to the Opposition's message appealing to the Mautaugans to exercise restraint; that he had signed it in disregard of any advice the Defence Committee had given, for I understood the Defence Committee had discussed the proposal at length; that he had signed it in disregard of the opinion of the Attorney-General that the calling out of troops was not justified; that he had signed it without having any consultation with the Minister for External Affairs and Minister for Defence (if that were indeed the case); and that on this evidence it appeared that the Prime Minister was taking it on himself to decide what the Government should do. The Prime Minister said that 'it would look like that'. I said that the whole responsibility would be put on the Prime Minister himself. I knew that he was ready to face the blame and had never lacked courage to take the blame, whether or not he were responsible for an action, but he knew that he had already been the subject of this line of criticism and he knew the dangers of separating a Prime Minister from his supporters. In his own interest and in the interest of the stability of his Government he had to be exceptionally careful not to expose himself to attack for 'trying to run the nation himself'. The Prime Minister appeared to accept the political wisdom of what I said. He did not contest my line of argument, but commented on some of the points. He said the Mautaugans would 'take no notice of Beazley'. He said that both Frazer [sic] and McMahon were trying to keep themselves out of it so that 'they would not get any mud on their feet'. He could not understand the Attorney-General, who could not claim to know more about the facts of the situation than the people on the spot. He would have to get him 'to change his mind'. So long as the Attorney-General had put in writing his opinion that the calling out of troops was not justified he could scarcely go ahead. The written opinion of the Attorney-General seemed to have had tremendous influence on the Prime Minister. He had received it only shortly before coming to see me and my impression—only an impression— is that if he had not received it, he might have been less receptive to my views. As for the Defence Committee, the Prime Minister said at first that 'it was none of their business.' I said that the Defence Committee could give advice on defence matters. It could not make political judgements or presume to set itself up against the Cabinet in the making of any political decisions. It did have a responsibility to advise on the military aspects of any proposal—for example, in the present case, it should give the government its advice on what troops were available, with information on any problems or limitations regarding the use of those troops, and it should also give its advice on their suitability for the role of maintaining civil order or any consequences of their use in that role. The Prime Minister appeared to concede the point.

I tried to draw together this phase of our discussion by suggesting that a matter such as this should be considered at an augmented meeting of the Executive Council and that, if it were necessary to do so, there should be some preliminary discussion by the Prime Minister with the Ministers primarily concerned, if not with Cabinet. I again mentioned particularly the Ministers for Defence and External Affairs and the Attorney-General. The Prime Minister said briefly: 'Fraser goes around saying he's against it.' And after a gloomy interval of quiet thought: 'That little bastard McMahon won't come. He'll run away out of reach.'

I then passed to the other aspect of the matter, saying that, after I had satisfied myself that the political advice had been given to me after full consideration, I had a responsibility as Governor-General concerning the legal authority and source of the powers I exercised as Governor-General-in-Council. While in the final issue I could not contest the political judgement of my Executive Councillors I thought I had to bear a large measure of responsibility for the legality of any action taken by the Governor-General-in-Council. I was not sure, from the Minute Paper and the Explanatory Memorandum accompanying it what statute or what constitutional power was being relied upon for the recommended course of action. I had read Section 51 of the Defence Act. This seemed to require a request by the equivalent in the Trust Territory of New Guinea to the Executive Government in a State for the calling out of forces. Could I assume that this was either the Administrator of the Territory or the Minister for External Territories? The Prime Minister said quickly: 'We've got the request all right. They asked me to do it.' I then said that Section 51 also seemed to envisage two steps—a proclamation declaring that domestic violence exists, and a calling out of the forces. I needed advice whether each step had to be taken in sequence and what was the required procedure. I understood that the use of an Order-in-Council linked with Part V of the Australian Military Regulations was the preferred method. I could understand some of the advantages of using this procedure. I also thought there was some value in linking the calling out of troops with the procedures governing their use as laid down in the Regulations. The Prime Minister interrupted that he 'had never seen anything so silly as the Regulations. You call out the troops and then every obstacle in the world is put in the way of using them.' I remarked on the need for safeguards and for limiting the use of troops in [a] civil disturbance. The Prime Minister continued to remark on 'all this nonsense about reading out a piece of paper before you start shooting them.' When he had calmed down I said that while I myself thought these safeguards on military action in civil disorder were necessary, it was also advisable to remember that the existence of such safeguards was [sic] necessary to make the calling out of troops acceptable to public opinion. The Prime Minister said he saw that and, in fact, if troops were called out he would see that the request for their use was referred to a Committee of Ministers. He was strongly of the opinion, however, that the people on the spot were the best people to know whether troops were needed. I resumed the discussion of the legal authority for the proposed action by the Governor-General-in-Council, saying that at present I could not understand the way in which Part V of the Australian Military Regulations was made to apply to a Trust Territory or whether the Regulations contained the legal authority for making an Order-in-Council calling out troops. The Prime Minister apparently had not given much thought personally to this aspect of the matter. He agreed that the Attorney-General should give advice on these matters and had better be at the Executive Council meeting for that purpose. I also drew his attention to Defence Act No 2 of 1951 (No 59 of 1951) inserting Section 35(a) into the Principal Act to the effect that a native force raised in a Trust Territory should not be required to serve except as permitted under Article 84 of the Charter of the United Nations. He said this would be looked at. By this stage it was clear that, without any clash between us, the Prime Minister had given up the idea of an Executive Council meeting attended only by himself and Mr Barnes. I asked specifically for an augmented Council meeting and for fuller legal advice to me from the Attorney-General and suggested to the Prime Minister that before the Executive Council meeting was held, he should get together with the Ministers mainly concerned to ensure that the advice given in Executive Council would be advice which the Government would stand by. I said that it would be difficult for the Governor-General to take action as head of the Executive only to find later that the action was the cause of a division of opinion or a dispute inside the Executive. I said that I would be available all the weekend and would also postpone my departure on Monday on a northern tour if that were necessary. The Prime Minister said: 'We must get it fixed before Monday.' We agreed to make the objective a meeting of Executive Council at noon on Saturday.

Mr Barnes was then called into my study. The Prime Minister said: 'We think it best not to have a meeting now. The Governor-General has a few legal points and I've got this awkward letter from Tom Hughes.' He showed Mr Barnes the passage in the Attorney-General's advice saying that in his opinion the proposed action was not justified, and added: 'I've only just got it. It seems silly to me but I don't see how I can do it when the Attorney-General says I cannot.' Barnes shrugged. The Prime Minister continued: 'We'll fix it up and His Excellency and I have agreed to have a meeting at noon tomorrow. We might call in a few others.'

There was no further substantial discussion. My impression—which I emphasise is only an impression—is that the Prime Minister may have led Mr Barnes to believe that quick action was going to be taken, and perhaps even that he would see that the Governor-General did what he was advised to do; and hence that he was more willing to present the chief obstacle as the advice of the Attorney-General than to traverse any of the matters we had discussed in private.

We then had a drink together, all three, Martinis for the Prime Minister and myself and whisky for Barnes. Our informal conversation over drinks was mainly along the lines that the Prime Minister had promised the people 'up there' that he would back them and he couldn't let them down now; that 'the people on the spot' were the best ones to judge how serious the situation was; and that they were entitled to know where the Australian Government stood. The main contribution by Barnes was that 'if we do not do something now we might as well give the game away.' Gorton could not understand 'some of our colleagues'. They had 'white livers' and they 'dodged the issue'. We parted in a friendly mood, leaving me just over ten minutes to change into evening dress to meet guests for a farewell dinner for the New Zealand High Commissioner and his wife.

Shortly before noon on Saturday I received a telephone call from the Prime Minister on my direct line saying that 'some Ministers' had been having a talk at The Lodge and they had agreed that the Attorney-General should fly up to Port Moresby that afternoon for discussion of the situation on the spot.[10] His report should be received by Sunday morning and Hughes himself should be back for a further meeting of Ministers. They could come out for an Executive Council meeting at noon on Sunday. I said that I would be available. I also said that I was glad that the Prime Minister was trying to settle the matter with his Ministers. The Prime Minister observed: 'It will come out all right. Fraser's talking a lot but doesn't know anything about it. Once we get Hughes up there the local people will convince him. In any case it won't be a bad public appearance to know that we flew him up there on a special mission before we decided to call out the troops. It will look better.' I said I would be ready at any time on Sunday. I then asked if the Attorney-General had cleared up the points I had raised. The Prime Minister said he would refer them to him. About ten minutes later the Attorney-General telephoned me on my direct line. I said that I needed advice on the legal authority and the source of the Governor-General's power for the action proposed and mentioned the matters I had mentioned to the Prime Minister. I could not venture a legal interpretation myself but wished to have his opinion. I then understood the Attorney-General to say that Section 51 of the Defence Act did not come into the argument and that full authority was contained in the Australian Military Regulations. He promised that he would let me have an opinion in writing.

On Sunday morning, the Official Secretary to the Governor-General, Sir Murray Tyrrell, returned to duty. I gave him, in strict confidence, an account of what had transpired. The Assistant Official Secretary and the Private Secretary, who had been twittering in doorways at all the comings and goings since Thursday, had not been taken into my confidence and had not handled any matter related to the discussions.

Shortly before noon on Sunday, Tyrrell reported to me that the Secretary of Executive Council, Grigg, who had come out to await a noon meeting had said that as he passed The Lodge he noticed a congregation of Government cars, indicating that a meeting of Ministers was still in progress. Up to 1 p.m. we had received no message. During the lunch-hour the Secretary of the Prime Minister's Department, Mr Hewitt, telephoned to the Official Secretary, Sir Murray Tyrrell, requesting a meeting of Executive Council at 2 o'clock. After ascertaining that four Ministers would be attending and that other Ministers had previously taken part in discussion, Tyrrell agreed on my behalf. Shortly before 2 o'clock I received a telephone call on my direct line from Mr Hewitt, who informed me that at a discussion in the morning all Cabinet Ministers had attended with the exception of Mr Sinclair, Mr Hume and Mr Swartz, who was overseas. Mr Hughes reported on his visit to Port Moresby and said that in his opinion action was necessary. There was a long discussion and a common view was reached. The Ministers attending the Executive Council would thus be expressing a Cabinet decision. The Executive Council meeting was held at 2 o'clock and a decision recorded to approve a minute signed by the Minister for Defence recommending the issuing of an Order-in-Council calling out the defence forces. The Order-in-Council was also counter-signed by the Minister for Defence. At the meeting the Attorney-General submitted to me a signed opinion on questions of legal authority.[11] I received an assurance from the Prime Minister that the recommendation expressed a decision of Cabinet and, as Commander-in-Chief I sought and obtained an assurance from the Minister for Defence that, so far as could be foreseen, the task likely to be allotted to the available forces was within the capacity of the forces available and the equipment issued to them. In this connection some doubt arose whether the Order-in-Council would cover the Navy. It was agreed that the Attorney-General should examine this question and if the services of the Navy should be required in dealing with civil disorder he should ensure that there was full legal authority so to employ them.

[NAA: M1767, 3]

---

10   See Document 86.

11   Ibid.

93   TELEX FROM HAY TO WARWICK SMITH

Port Moresby, 20 July 1970

11604. CONFIDENTIAL

Gazelle situation reviewed at 3.00 PM by myself and senior officers. Latest information is that three formed bodies of Mataungans, each of one thousand strong approximately, are marching on police positions in Vunapalandig/Kerevat Forest area. Reports are that Mataungans are not repeat not armed. We do not repeat do not know their intentions but it is possible that they will try to spread out and occupy the Vunapalandig/Kerevat land and provoke police to throw them off.

2.   In the circumstances I am not able to certify that a confrontation or serious incident has occurred which in my judgment threatens or shows loss of control of the situation by the police. Senior Police Officer here and other senior officers concur. Have discussed with Brigadier Eldridge who also concurs. Deadline for requisition today is therefore now past. There will be a further review later this evening.[1]

[NAA A1838, 936/3/21 PART 3]

---

1   During much of July 1970 the Administration provided External Territories and other interested departments with assessments of developments in the Gazelle Peninsula on at least a daily basis, and at times did this two or three times a day.

94   LETTER FROM WARWICK SMITH TO JOHNSON[1]

Canberra, 21 July 1970

In connection with your assumption of the Office of Administrator of Papua and New Guinea this week I write to inform you of Government decisions taken at the same time as the decisions concerning increased responsibility for Ministerial office holders announced by the Prime Minister.

As a background approach to policy generally the Government considers that the existing policy of increasing the extent to which native people participate in political, social and economic affairs needs to be given a great deal more bite; it also needs to be repeatedly made plain that constitutional progress towards self-government will not alter Australia's intention to assist the political, social and economic advancement of the Territory and that the Government will seek to maintain sufficient numbers of Australian officers in the Territory and will continue aid on a large scale.

The Government has also directed that the position of those Commonwealth Departments and agencies now performing functions of internal self-government (i.e., excluding Defence Forces) outside the aegis of the Administration should be reviewed so that a sensible programme for their absorption in appropriate cases into the Territory Administration may be prepared. This is to be done by a Committee located in Canberra consisting of the Department of External Territories, Prime Minister's Department, Public Service Board, the Treasury, and each particular Department or agency in turn. Similarly a special study of the situation in relation to internal security is to be prepared by the Departments of External Territories and Defence.

The Department should of course consult the Administration and the Public Service Board on these matters.

[NAA: A452, 1970/3046]

---

1   On 17 July 1970, Les Johnson was sworn in as Administrator, taking up the appointment on 23 July. Hay's term as Administrator concluded on 22 July. Soon afterwards he replaced George Warwick Smith as Secretary of the Department of External Territories, with Warwick Smith taking up the position of Secretary of the Department of the Interior.

95   TELEX FROM HAY TO WARWICK SMITH

Port Moresby, 21 July 1970

11621. CONFIDENTIAL

Meeting of senior officers reviewed situation at 1400 hours and concluded that situation requiring use of armed forces was not imminent. In view reports of assembly of Mataungans on Administration land at Vudal College,[1] instructions are being issued to DC[2] and Police to eject on grounds of illegal occupation. Emphasis is also to be maintained on road blocks in order to cut off food supplies where possible. This will all maintain pressure on Mataungans. Police are preparing camp at Vunapaladig to facilitate occupation overnight. Possible initiatives (my 11614, para 3)[3]—a list of possibilities under Territory ordinances has been forwarded to Crown Law in Rabaul. In addition police and legal officers will be examining past statements by Kaputin and others for possible offenses under Crimes Act and other acts. Grateful if television interviews could be recorded at Departmental end and examined for possible breaches. District staff will also be instructed to patrol villages which Mataungans have left in order to go to Vunapaladig in order to increase family pressures on squatters to return home.

[NAA: A452, 1971/2342]

---

1   The PNG Administration's Department of Agriculture, Stock and Fisheries established the Vudal Agricultural College (VAC) in 1965. In its early years a male-only college, VAC enrolled its first female students in 1975.

2   District Commissioner

3   Not published.

96   CABLEGRAM TO NEW YORK

Canberra, 21 July 1970

826. UNCLASSIFIED

Prime Minister's Statement on Gazelle Situation

Further to his statement of the 19th July, which was cabled to you, the Prime Minister made the following statement on 20th July in response to press inquiries:

'The Government was advised by the Administration that it would be prudent to arrange for troops of the PIR to be available for use in the Gazelle Peninsula in case a situation developed which police on the spot were not numerous enough to handle.

'The Government accepted this advice and has taken the necessary steps to this end.

'The Administrator is empowered to call on the assistance of the PIR to protect lives and property should the situation require it. It is not believed that this will be necessary but it is believed that if it should prove to be necessary it should be done.'

[NAA: A1838, 936/3/21]

97   CABINET DECISION 539(M)

Canberra, 23 July 1970

Submission 410—Aid to Papua and New Guinea Administration in 1970/71[1]

The Ministry:

[*matter omitted*]

(c) agreed that grants for Papua and New Guinea for 1970/71 should total $100 million,[2] including an amount of $32.3 million for allowances and other benefits of overseas officers of the Papua and New Guinea Public Service with the division of balance between grant-in-aid and grant for development purposes being settled between the Treasurer and the Minister following further consultation with the Estimates Committee of the Administrator's Executive Council;

(d) agreed that the Administrator's Executive Council be informed that the Administration will be allowed some flexibility, subject to the approval of the Minister for External Territories and the Treasurer, to offer more liberal terms and conditions than at present to borrow up to a total of $27.5 million in the Territory, and in certain circumstances as the need arises, in Australia in 1970/71.

[NAA: A5873, VOLUME 2]

---

1   Not published.

2   See also Documents 18–19, 33 & 35. The figure given in this Document presumably refers only to the direct grant to the Territory, and not to funds administered by departments, agencies and authorities other than the Department of Territories. See Ian Downs, *The Australian Trusteeship: Papua New Guinea, 1945–75*, Australian Government Publishing Service, Canberra, 1980, p. xiv.

98   PRESS RELEASE

Port Moresby, 27 July 1970

Statement on Gazelle Peninsula

The Administrator, Mr L. W. Johnson, said today he had examined the present situation in the Gazelle Peninsula at the weekend.

'I have noted that the leaders of the Mataungan Association have emphasised the non-violent nature of their movement,' he said.

'I now propose the following actions:

'The strength of the police in Rabaul will be reduced immediately. One hundred police will be withdrawn today or tomorrow and a further reduction will be made later this week.

'An immediate appointment of a Mataungan Association member will be made to the vacant position on the Special Land Board considering applications for land on Vunapaladig, Japlik, Mandres and Buri.

'This will mean that the Special Land Board will now consist of: the Chairman; two members representing the Baining people; and four members representing the Tolai people, two of whom are Mataungan Association sympathisers.

'It seems to me that this Board thus fully and fairly represents the interests of the people involved.

'An investigation is currently under way to see if further purchases of freehold properties are possible in the Gazelle Peninsula and every effort will be made to make additional land available to landless people in the area.

'Allocation of blocks from Matanatar and Revalien Plantations, previously purchased, will begin as soon as possible.

'I have noted the ideas put forward by various Tolai groups for economic development in the area.

'The Administration will fully support any economic initiatives by groups of Tolais, irrespective of their political sympathies, provided that viable propositions are put forward.

'I propose to visit the Gazelle Peninsula myself next week and I would hope to have discussions with the representatives of the various Tolai interests including the Executive and prominent members of the Mataungan Association.

'I feel confident that the leaders of the Mataungan Association will respond with frank and open discussion.'

[NAA: A452, 1971/2342]

99   PRESS RELEASE

Port Moresby, 29 July [1970][1]

Administration Taking New Initiatives on Gazelle Peninsula

The Administrator, Mr L. W. Johnson, said today that he had noted the expressed intention of the Mataungan Association leaders to try to achieve their objectives by peaceful means.

Mr Johnson emphasised the Administration's firm intention to require that all citizens observed the laws of the land.

He also said that the Administration remained deeply concerned at the continued divisions among the Tolai people and that a significant proportion of the people on the Gazelle Peninsula were still alienated from their Government.

In the circumstances the Administration proposed to seek further advice from an impartial and informed source as to what additional measures might be considered to solve the existing problem.

Professor R. F. Salisbury, Professor of Anthropology at McGill University in Canada, had been asked for his advice and he hoped to spend a month, in August, on the Gazelle Peninsula. Professor Salisbury was well known in Papua New Guinea and had done a great deal of anthropological work here in the past.

He is the author of two authoritative books on this country—'From Stone to Steel' dealing with the economic consequences of technological change in New Guinea, and first published in 1962; and more recently, 'Vunamami' dealing with the economic transformation in traditional society, published in 1970. He is the author of numerous articles on Papua New Guinea published in various learned journals.

Mr Johnson said that Professor Salisbury's background and experience assured that his advice would be objective and he expected that valuable and constructive proposals would be put forward.

[NAA: A 1838, 936/4/16 PART 5]

---

1   The document is dated 29 July 1971, but accompanying documents and the context confirm that the press release was issued on 29 July 1970.

100   REPORT BY JOINT PLANNING COMMITTEE

Canberra, 30 July 1970

17/1970. Secret

Review of Defence Forces in Papua/New Guinea

[*matter omitted*]

Introduction

Following consideration in 1968 of the future size, role, rate of development and disposition of the Pacific Islands Regiment, the Defence Committee[1] directed that a review be undertaken of the structure of the Papua/New Guinea defence forces having regard to the country's future needs and circumstances. The Defence Committee desired that the review should take into account Papua/New Guinea's economic and social conditions, strategic conditions affecting Australia, the future relationship between the Papua/New Guinea forces and the Australian Defence structure, and the desirability of developing a unified defence force.

Australian Policy towards Papua/New Guinea

2.   The Government's policy is to assist Papua/New Guinea to become a self-governing country developed for independence when it is demonstrated that this is what is wanted. The Government has stated it will continue to help the acceleration of economic growth and the development of greater economic self-reliance in the Territory. It is clear that Papua/New Guinea's dependence on external aid will continue into the future and that Australia will need to continue making substantial financial contributions for this purpose, though as a declining proportion of total expenditure, if Papua/New Guinea's essential services and prospects for economic viability are to be sustained and developed. Australia at present meets all the costs of the Papua/New Guinea defence forces.

3.   Australia's economic interest in Papua/New Guinea, although increasing in terms of trade and investment, is not a decisive factor in assessing Australia's own defence interests in the Territory. Except perhaps for rubber there is at present no items of local production of strategic importance to Australia. The Territory could increase in value as an outlet for our exports, although it is more likely Australia will become a vital market for Papua/New Guinea. Moreover, the contribution made by Australia to Territory's budget is greater than the economic value of Papua/New Guinea to Australia.

4.   At least until independence, the defence of Papua/New Guinea will remain an Australian commitment. It has been our policy to develop progressively the Papua/New Guinea defence forces and their local infrastructure as a supplement to our own defence efforts within the Territory and because Papua/New Guinea will require its own defence capability on independence. Moreover in an emergency requiring the use of military forces, it would be most desirable for indigenous forces to be deployed first, as the introduction of Australian units would almost certainly become the subject of international political controversy. In situations affecting internal security, we would wish to deploy Australian forces only as a last resort. The local forces should therefore continue to be developed to extent of available resources. This policy is consistent with our defence and other obligations under the United Nations for the Trust Territory of New Guinea.

---

1   Here an original footnote referred to 'Minute No. 42/1968'.

5.   Constitutional development in the Territory and how long Australia will retain complete responsibility for defence cannot be precisely forecast, but progress towards self-government and independence is expected to quicken. An independent Papua/New Guinea might wish to leave the responsibility for defence and external affairs with Australia. It might wish however to negotiate a shared defence relationship with us or even assume full responsibility for its own defence and external relations with no treaty link with Australia. Its continuing dependence on Australia could provide us with opportunities to encourage Papua/New Guinea to retain a defence relationship with us should we consider it in our interests to do so.

6.   What sort of defence undertaking, if any, Australia would seek cannot be determined at this stage, but decisions taken now on the size and shape of Papua/New Guinea's defence forces will have a considerable bearing on what the Territory might desire from us at self-determination and on the obligations we might be prepared to undertake.

Current Threat Assessments

7.   The following assessment of the threat to Papua/New Guinea during the period to 1979 has been made by the National Intelligence Committee for this paper. It assesses that a government of the present type will continue in Indonesia for some years and while it does limited war between Indonesia and Australia or confrontation-type activity against Papua/New Guinea is unlikely. Minor incidents could occur in the border area but major clashes are unlikely. Indonesia (and Australia) would use great restraint to prevent the escalation of minor incidents.

8.   The achievement of independence, or possibly internal self-government, by Papua/New Guinea would introduce new factors. Indonesia might exercise less restraint against a small, weak, independent nation, although she would take into account the nature and extent of defence support expected from Australia. Given continuation of a moderate government in Indonesia and responsible behaviour by the government of an independent Papua/New Guinea, relations between the countries are expected to be friendly.

9.   The emergence of an extremist regime in Indonesia cannot be ruled out completely later in the decade arising from a failure of economic policies or a coup. The motivation for the latter would build up gradually, probably over several years. If the regime were hostile to Papua/New Guinea, Indonesia could, up to 1979, with little or no foreign military aid, engage in confrontation-type operations with up to 12 battalions. Not more than six of these are likely to be engaged in operations at any one time. The emergence of a regime which had these intentions is assessed, however, as unlikely.

10.   The emergence of an extremist regime which received massive military aid is unlikely, although it is possible after 1972 if an extremist government came to power in Indonesia. There would be warning of such a development. Indonesia could with such aid undertake a relatively large ground force effort against Papua/New Guinea, and naval and air operations against major targets there. It would take time for the build-up of aid to become effective and such a threat is very unlikely to emerge before 1979.

Internal Threat to Papua/New Guinea

11.   Within Papua/New Guinea frustrated political ambitions or dissatisfaction with the nature of political progress or with economic and social conditions, as well as regional and tribal differences, could lead to the emergence of subversive movements. There is no evidence of a subversive threat in Papua/New Guinea at present, although in the Gazelle Peninsula strong local dissatisfaction exists and there has been a defiance of authority that could ultimately lead to the emergence of subversive movements. In the period before Papua/New Guinea independence, subversive elements would be unlikely to attract support from Indonesia under

her present government, but they might conceivably do so after independence (see paragraph 8). An extremist Indonesian government, might, however, be interested in exploiting subversive movements from the time of its accession to power. Even without a well-organised subversive organisation, local threats to internal security in Papua/New Guinea are likely to arise from a variety of causes, e.g. secessionist movements, a deterioration in race relationships, particularly as a result of disparity in living standards or financial conditions, disputes over land ownership, or from inter-tribal or inter-regional disputes generated by uneven economic development or political progress. The existence of subversive elements within Papua/New Guinea or localised unrest would provide opportunities for communist exploitation.

[*matter omitted*]

The Strategic Significance of Papua/New Guinea

14. Papua/New Guinea is of abiding strategic interest to Australia because of its geographic position astride our military and trade lines of communication from our eastern seaboard to South-East Asia, Japan, and United States bases in the Western Pacific; because of its common border with Indonesia; and because of its potential as a base for the conduct of operations inimical to Australian security and [other][2] interests. In addition, we are responsible for its defence as long as it remains a dependent Territory, and could be involved in arrangements for its defence after self-determination.

15. If the direct air route to South-East Asia via Indonesian airfields were denied to us, and the alternative route via Cocos Island made untenable, our military aircraft other than F-111, Hercules, Neptune and Orion would need to transit through Papua/New Guinea airfields. In addition there is a continuing requirement for unrestricted passage for our military shipping through New Guinea waters in support of our regional security arrangements. This requires the maintenance of a re-fuelling facility for naval escorts in the area.

16. The land frontier with West Irian could provide a hostile Indonesia with opportunities to threaten the security of Papua/New Guinea and thereby embarrass Australia. Should this occur we would require base facilities in Papua/New Guinea to fulfil any defence obligations we might have. Access to bases there would also be important in the event of limited war involving Australia and Indonesia.

17. In the very long term, given the continuance of a world nuclear balance, it has been assessed that it is from or through Indonesia that the possibility of hostile action against Australia or its Territories is most likely to arise. In this event attacks on northern Australia would not depend on an enemy possessing bases in Papua/New Guinea. On the other hand should Papua/New Guinea be taken over, or come under the influence of a power unfriendly or hostile to Australia, this would open up the way for further penetration of the south-west Pacific, facilitate military operations down the eastern Australian coast and expose our important trade routes with Asia to interruption.

18. We conclude from the foregoing that should Papua/New Guinea become unfriendly or hostile to Australia there would be serious deterioration of our strategic situation. It is therefore highly desirable that Papua/New Guinea should not come under the dominance of hostile influences.

The Defence and Security Needs of Papua/New Guinea

19. The following paragraphs assess the type of tasks which the Papua/New Guinea defence forces could be required to undertake in the defence of the Territory and, if necessary, its internal security.

---

2   Editorial insertion.

Border Control

20. The task of control and surveillance of the West Irian border and adjacent coastal areas and waters basically involves routine immigration, quarantine and customs matters. Because of the political situation in West Irian, refugee control measures are likely to continue for some time and armed pursuit of refugees by Indonesian security forces could arise. The Administration is responsible for dealing with these matters and police rather than military action is required.

Internal Security

21. Preservation of law and order is a primary function of Government and dealing with internal disorder is essentially a matter for the police. The defence forces however provide a backup for the police forces and could be made available, if authorised, to assist in internal security situations should they develop beyond the control of the police.

22. Australian Government policy is that defence forces are used in internal security situations only as a last resort, i.e. when a confrontation or serious incident has occurred which threatens or shows loss of control of the situation by the police. We would hope that this view would be adopted by the Papua/New Guinea Government in its turn. The basic function of the military forces is the defence of the Territory. They should not be raised solely on the basis of possible internal security needs.

23. An essential requirement to deal adequately with internal security problems is an organisation with responsibility for intelligence on internal security matters, complemented by an adequate civil communications system to support the police. A separate study of intelligence requirements for Papua/New Guinea is being made.

[*matter omitted*]³

Border Operations

[*matter omitted*]⁴

29. Highly mobile, suitably trained and equipped ground forces and maritime patrol elements would be necessary to deal with even the initial stages of such attacks. Because of the difficult nature of the terrain and length of the border, tactical air transport and air reconnaissance elements would be essential if effective use were to be made of the small ground forces likely to be available.

Roles

30. From the foregoing, we assess the roles of the Papua/New Guinea defence forces to be:

    a.   To keep under surveillance and defend the land border and the coastal areas particularly those adjacent to West Irian.

    b.   To assist the civil administration in maritime surveillance throughout the island area.

    c.   To contribute, if authorised, to the internal security of Papua/New Guinea.

---

3   The omitted material assessed defence tasks with respect to the surveillance of territorial waters and the declared 12-mile fishing zone.

4   The omitted material reviewed what Indonesian operations in the border region could involve, and how such operations could be addressed.

The Basis for Development of Papua/New Guinea Defence Forces

31. A Papua/New Guinea defence force capable of meeting the needs outlined in the previous section would take a considerable time to develop. The absence of a current threat to the Territory, however, provides us with the opportunity to undertake such a development on a gradual basis within available resources.

Limiting Factors

32. The development of the forces will be influenced not only by military factors but also by political and international considerations, by future defence relationships with Australia, and by the extent to which resources of finance and manpower can be made available by Papua New Guinea and Australia.

33. The present economic position of Papua/New Guinea is such that in 1969/70 the estimated local revenue, $58m, provided less than one-third of the estimated total Government expenditure of $188m. This expenditure included direct expenditure by Commonwealth Departments, $22m. of which defence expenditure amounted to $10.2m (excluding a relevant portion of major supporting defence overheads borne by Australia which would have to be provided for an independent defence force).

34. An approximate projection based on the programme for economic development, and taking into account the CRA enterprise in Bougainville, shows that by 1972/73 Australian aid (excluding defence expenditure) will still represent more than half of Administration receipts. By the second half of the 1970's the impact of the Bougainville operations should be very significant, and Australian aid may be less than one third of Administration receipts by 1980. But expectations are beginning to run ahead of what can be provided, and greater pressure can be expected for expenditure on social services, development works and equity in major externally-controlled enterprises.

35. All the policies for development are projected upon a unitary territory where the profits of one part are used for services in another, and take no account of the possibility that the most developed areas (e.g. Bougainville and the Gazelle Peninsula) may seek a degree of autonomy in order to retain for themselves some or all of the profits of development in their own area.

36. The Territory will continue to look to Australia for aid after independence, and will it be our aim to ensure that such aid is directed to appropriate areas, including defence. At the same time we will have a responsibility to ensure that the amount of expenditure on the defence forces of Papua/New Guinea does not take up an unreasonable proportion of total Papua/New Guinea expenditure and would be acceptable to the Government of Papua/New Guinea [...]

37. An examination of the manpower considerations indicates that a limiting factor on the development of the defence force, if the contribution of Australian personnel is to be kept to a minimum, will be the rate at which indigenous officers and NCOs can be produced. There are advantages in adjusting progress in the development of the defence force so that it is compatible with the production of local key personnel.

[*matter omitted*]

Command and Administration of the Defence Forces

39. The present trend, particularly in small countries where reduced overheads are important and skilled manpower and other resources scarce, is towards centralised control and administration of a single defence organisation. Given the size and shape of the limited forces Papua/New Guinea is likely to have over the next decade, and taking into account the type of operations they could be engaged in, a unified defence force based principally on the Army, with maritime patrol and air transport support wings, appears attractive. It can also be argued

that if unification is what the Papua/New Guinea Government of the future would want for its defence force, now is the time to introduce it. The results, however, in terms of greater efficiency and economy of the Services have yet to be proved, and many of the advantages claimed for unification may be gained through a centralised defence organisation with a common administrative system and common logistic support organisation. Furthermore we consider there could be dangers in an emerging country in building up a monolithic defence force based primarily on a single service.

40. There are, moreover sizeable practical difficulties, which suggest it would be premature to decide now that a unified Service could be set up and operated efficiently. Some of these difficulties are as follows:

•   The Papua/New Guinea defence force will continue to develop in close relationship with the three separate Australian Services and it will be easier for us to train them if they are organised as separate Services. A higher degree of professionalism would be developed by retaining the identity of the individual services.

•   Imposition of a unified force concept in the Papua/New Guinea defence force at too early a stage would undoubtedly increase the problems and difficulties of indigenous officers in command and administration.

41. It is our view that, in the first instance, we should aim at establishing a centralised command and defence organisation with a common administrative system and common logistic support arrangements, while retaining the separate identity of the separate identity of the individual Service components. This would place a future Papua/New Guinea Government in a favourable position to further integrate or unify the Services if it should so desire.

Future Organisation

[*matter omitted*]

43. It will be important that control of the future Papua/New Guinea defence organisation eventually be vested in a local Minister. The establishment of a centralised Defence Department in support of the Minister is therefore an essential objective. To this end the defence headquarters organisation should comprise an integrated military and civilian staff responsible to the Minister for advice on defence policy, administration, the command and control of the forces and their logistic support, and for liaison and coordination with other departments and authorities.

[*matter omitted*]

Measures to foster in Papua/New Guinea an Informed Understanding in Defence Matters

49. It is desirable to foster with the Territory at the legislative and administrative level, a knowledge of and expertise in defence matters [...]

[*matter omitted*]

51. Progressively as the above procedures develop understanding the thinking of the Administrator's Executive Council could be canvassed when major changes are in prospect; another advance could be the appointment eventually of a Ministerial officer holder with a watching brief but without formal responsibility.

[*matter omitted*]

THE GROUND FORCE

Existing Forces

53. The ceiling strength of the Army in Papua/New Guinea is 2,559 Pacific Islanders and 650 Australian Regular Army, a total of 3,209. Command and control is exercised from Headquarters, Papua/New Guinea Command. The force has been trained for operations in the border area and organised into two battalions, each approximately the same size as an Australian infantry battalion [...]

The Requirement

54. The ground forces required for border operations would need to be capable of patrolling in the border area to gather information and establish a presence in support of the police, of conducting operations against incursions, and of providing for the security of administration centres and their own forward bases [...]

[*matter omitted*]

56. The central mountain range in Papua/New Guinea divides the Territory into two clearly defined and almost completely physically isolated regions. There are approximately ten border crossing places from West Irian, five to the north of the range and five to the south, the majority of which consist of a complex system of trails. Effective operations in the border area would require at least one battalion on either side of the mountain range.

57. In a deteriorating situation, any enemy would have the initiative in deciding which of the crossings, over a wide area, he would use for armed incursion. In this event operational flexibility would be achieved with a mobile battalion held in reserve and available to reinforce the forward units. In a protracted situation a reserve battalion would be necessary to allow rotation of the deployed units.

58. In view of the foregoing we conclude that a three battalion force is the minimum required for the Papua/New Guinea Ground Force. This conclusion is based on the assumption that some air transport and air surveillance will continue to be available to the force. In addition to its training for its purely military tasks, the force should be trained to support the police in internal security duties.

Development of the Ground Force

59. Three possible courses of action for developing the infantry element have been examined.

[*matter omitted*][5]

62. The third course 'c' [of developing three smaller-sized battalions][6] is favoured as it could be carried out with only a modest increase in indigenous manpower, and with a progressive reduction in seconded Australian personnel. The preliminary estimate is an increase from the present manpower figure of 3,209 (paragraph 53) to 3,460 by 1974/75. This course would meet the requirements of three readily available battalions and ensure that the structure and majority of key officers and NCOs were available should expansion to three larger battalions be necessary. Moreover, smaller compact battalions may well prove to be more suitable for indigenous officers to command and control.

[*matter omitted*]

---

5   The material omitted considered various options for developing a three-battalion force, concluding that the best option was the establishment of three battalions 'which are smaller in size than the present battalions'.

6   Editorial insertion.

64. In the meantime, the existing two battalion structure should be retained until the change can be made without increasing the numbers of Australian personnel. Preliminary planning indicates the change could be introduced about 1971/72.

Combat support

65. The operations likely to be undertaken by ground forces would not demand that armour and artillery be available, indeed the problems of employment of this support in the border area could outweigh any tactical advantage. Fire support would be provided by mortars and rockets […][7]

THE MARITIME FORCE

[*matter omitted*]

70. The Papua/New Guinea area has some 2,000 miles of mainland coastland and some hundreds of islands. To provide for sustained operations at either end of the border, surveillance elsewhere, coast watching support, training, search and rescue, and miscellaneous tasks, and allowing for refit and maintenance periods, it is assessed that a minimum force of 10 patrol boats is required.

[*matter omitted*]

Development

72. The existing force [of five patrol boats][8] is barely adequate to meet present peacetime needs, but given the current assessed threat to the Territory there is no immediate need for expansion. However, the provision of trained manpower is a lengthy process, and the development of infrastructure and the provision of additional boats have long lead times. A phased programme of development is therefore required.

[*matter omitted*]

Implementation

76. Because of recruiting and training lead-times early expansion of the force is not possible. It is assessed that, financial considerations aside, the force could be expanded to 10 patrol boats and almost completely indigenised by 1980.

THE AIR FORCE

Existing Force

77. There is no indigenous military air capability in Papua/New Guinea. The PIR requirement for transport, surveillance, reconnaissance, etc. is met by a RAAF detachment of three Caribou, and Australian Army Aviation of two light fixed-winged aircraft and four Sioux helicopters, civilian charter, and occasional use of other RAAF aircraft. The Caribou also move units of the police force when the use of Service aircraft is approved.

The Requirement

78. The effective employment of the Papua/New Guinea infantry battalions will depend on the availability of tactical air transport for deployment, logistic support and casualty

---

7   The omitted material referred to the provision of additional combat support by assault pioneer platoons.

8   Editorial insertion.

evacuation, and light reconnaissance aircraft for effective patrolling and other operations. The maritime force could perform its surveillance task more effectively with assistance from aircraft. Furthermore, if aircraft were provided for military purposes in this way, then they could also be made available to transport police units.

[*matter omitted*][9]

83. We therefore consider that the realistic approach at this stage is to recommend progressive indigenisation of the three Caribou aircraft plus a communication flight of four small fixed-wing aircraft as rapidly as can be reasonably expected, i.e. within about five years of the decision to start. Whilst such a course only results in one quarter of the minimum force [of 28 aircraft][10] we considered desirable and is not initially cost effective in manpower,[11] it does provide a means of acquiring experience and expertise, and it does not prevent Papua/New Guinea from developing to the more mature force at a later stage should it so desire.

84.   From initial studies an optimum plan [would be] for the development of a force of three Caribou and three light-fixed aircraft with maximum indigenisation [...]

[*matter omitted*]

The Mature Force

85. Training lead-times will inhibit rapid expansion of the initial force to its desirable complement of 28 aircraft. If the period of partial RAAF manning is extended it is assessed that, ignoring financial considerations, the force could be expanded to 28 aircraft and almost completely indigenised in about 16 years after the decision to start.

SUPPORTING ORGANISATIONS

[*matter omitted*][12]

Australian Infrastructure Requirements in Papua/New Guinea

91. The infrastructure required in Papua/New Guinea by the Australian Services falls into two main categories, namely the transit facilities required to enable deployments of our forces through Papua/New Guinea to South-East Asia, and the access to facilities required if our forces are introduced to support Papua/New Guinea forces in operations.

[*matter omitted*]

RAN Requirements

93. The present RAN requirements are for refuelling facilities for our own and allied ships on passage to and from South-East Asia and for ships that might be deployed in support of Papua/New Guinea forces on the north and south coasts [...]

94. If Madang is developed as the base for the Papua/New Guinea maritime force we would expect to have access to the facilities there. Manus, however, is the most suitable location for our purposes and we would wish to retain its use as a refuelling facility as long as possible.

---

9   The omitted material discussed the development of the air force, concluding that in the longer term 22 fixed-wing aircraft and 6 light helicopters would be required.

10   Editorial insertion.

11   Presumably a reference to the deployment of more expensive Australian personnel in the early stages of the development process.

12   The omitted material discussed requirements for administrative, logistical, technical and communications support, proposing that these be the subjects of further studies.

Army Requirements

95. There are no particular Australian Army infrastructure requirements in Papua/New Guinea [...]

RAAF Requirements

96. Transit Facilities—Nadzab,[13] which was rehabilitated some years ago, is adequate for staging Mirage type aircraft and should be maintained until other suitable civil or military facilities are available.

97. Transport Support—The existing network of airfields in Papua/New Guinea is generally adequate for air transport operations support of the Army [...]

98. Combat Air Support Operation—No suitable airfield is available for this purpose in the border area. Ideally, two airfields should be available, one to the north of the mountain spine and one to the south [...]

Indicative Costs and Manpower Implications

99. It is emphasised that the costs below are tentative and meant to provide a broad indication of the likely magnitude of costs for development of the forces proposed in this review.

[*matter omitted*][14]

Conclusions

108. We have an obligation to develop for Papua/New Guinea a defence force appropriate to its needs and circumstances, bearing in mind the prospects of early independence and the considerable time it takes to develop defence forces. There is no current threat to the Territory which demands a substantial and immediate increase in its defence forces. The current threat assessment also indicates that we have time to undertake development of the forces on a gradual basis consistent with the above factors.

---

13   Nadzab is located near Lae.

14   The omitted material contained over five pages of detail, including tables on costs and manpower requirements. It noted: 'Costs are based on the assumption that there will be no increase in Australian personnel in the ground and maritime forces and that indigenisation will be achieved as soon as possible'. In the material the indicative costs for 'developing a ground force of three mini-battalions' over the five years from 1970/71 to 1974/75 were an average of 10.58 million dollars a year. Over the same period, indicative costs for the maritime force were an average of 3.97 million dollars a year. For the air force, over the five-year period from 1971/2 to 1975/76, indicative costs were an average of 0.75 million a year under the seven aircraft plan, and an average of 1.23 million dollars a year for the early stages of the 28 aircraft plan. In terms of indicative manpower planning, it was envisaged that the ground force would number 3,209 in 1970/71, including 650 Australian regular army personnel, and would increase to 3,460 in 1974/75, but with a decrease of Australian regular army personnel to 375. In the maritime force there were 371 PNG personnel and 35 Australian personnel in 1970, with it envisaged that there would be 460 PNG personnel and 54 Australian personnel in 1976.

In the air force, under the seven aircraft plan, no figures were given for the number of Australian personnel over the 1971/72 to 1975/76 period, but during that period the number of PNG personnel was expected to increase from 37 to 158. It was envisaged that in 1976/77 the air component would comprise 219 PNG personnel and 75 Australian personnel. Under the more ambitious 28 aircraft plan, again no figures were given for the number of Australian personnel over the 1971/72 to 1975/76 period, but during that period the number of PNG personnel was expected to increase from 43 to 203. It was envisaged, under this plan, that in 1976/77 the air component would comprise 401 PNG personnel and 95 Australian personnel.

109. Papua/New Guinea is of abiding strategic interest to Australia and should it become unfriendly or hostile, there would be a serious deterioration of our strategic situation. For this reason, and because we may have a defence obligation to the Territory after independence, it is in our own interests that indigenous forces be developed which will form the first line of defence for the Territory. In these circumstances and in view of Papua/New Guinea's economic limitations, it seems likely that Australia will need to bear the main burden of defence expenditure in the Territory for some years to come.

110. The following proposals provide an outline plan suitable for the development of the Papua/New Guinea defence force.

111. *Centralised Defence Organisation, Common Administrative System and Common Logistic Support Arrangement*. It should be an essential objective that the control of the defence force should eventually be vested in a local Minister supported by a centralised defence department.

[*matter omitted*]

113. *Ground Forces*. The PIR should be re-organised into three small battalions by 1974/75. This will involve manpower of about 3,460 of which the infantry element comprises about 1,890 [...]

114. *Maritime Force*. This should be established with the existing five patrol boats and expanded to a force of 10 patrol boats by 1980. A main base needs to be developed (probably at Madang, subject to approval of the recommendations of the naval study) with forward operating base facilities at Port Moresby and Manus and one place in the Bismarck Archipelago.

115. *Air Force*. The Air Force should be developed by 1976 to a force of three short-range transport aircraft (Caribou type) and four small fixed-wing aircraft, with appropriate supporting elements, at an air base at a site to be selected.

[*matter omitted*][15]

116. *Development*. In the development of the defence forces and their infrastructure full account should be taken of civil development to avoid duplication. Due regard should be taken of the Australian infrastructure requirements in Papua/New Guinea and as such continuing administrative and technical assistance should be provided by Australia.

117. *Studies*. If the initial objectives for the central defence organisation and ground, maritime and air forces proposed in paragraphs 111 to 115 above are approved the following action is required:

    a.   Establish a joint military/civil study group to investigate and recommend the type of centralised organisation including the common administrative system and common logistic support arrangements best suited to the needs of Papua/New Guinea.[...] The Study Group should also propose the phasing of the transition period from the present to the future organisation and provide estimates of the financial and manpower implications.

    b.   Army to plan and propose the action necessary to re-organise the PIR in accordance with paragraph 113.

    c.   Navy to plan and propose the continued development of the existing Papua/New Guinea Division of the RAN in accordance with paragraph 114.

    d.   RAAF to plan and propose the development of an air force in accordance with paragraph 115.

---

15   The omitted material referred to the longer-term development of the more ambitious, and unrealistic, 28 aircraft plan.

e.   Pending completion of the study in a., a separate study should examine whether there would be advantage in setting up a Joint Force Headquarters, with appropriate civilian elements, as a first step.[16]

Recommendations

118. It is recommended that:

a.   The Conclusions in paragraphs 108 to 116 be endorsed as an outline plan for the development of the Papua /New Guinea defence force; and

b.   subject to approval of the outline plan the studies proposed in paragraph 17a. to d. be undertaken.

[NAA: A452, 1970/4193]

---

16   As the planning process moved forward, it became more complex, with additional studies undertaken.

101   TELEX FROM JOHNSON TO HAY

Port Moresby, 3 August 1970

CONFIDENTIAL

[*matter omitted*]

My personal view follows. There is no great risk of an uncontrollable situation but the elements for serious disturbance still remain and there could be a flare up at very short notice. In the circumstances, I would prefer the call out order to remain in force as if it became necessary to ask for military aid after its cancellation presumably we would again require Cabinet approval. I discussed this matter with Minister for Army[1] and Secretary[2] this morning. I see no local difficulty for order remaining in force and this need not interfere with normal PIR training programme as Commander[3] advised that two companies would be available even when training patrols are fully resumed.

I propose further reduction in police strength this week by withdrawing fifty on Wednesday but police strength will remain well above normal indefinitely as will warder strength. In my view situation remains about amber plus.[4]

[NAA: A452, 1970/ 3199]

---

1   Andrew Peacock, Minister for the Army, 1969–72, who was visiting the Territory at the time.

2   Probably Secretary of the Department of the Army, Bruce White, who was accompanying Peacock.

3   Brigadier R. T. (Ralph) Eldridge, Commander PNG Command, February 1969–January 1972; Commander Joint Task Force, January–April 1972.

4   A reference to the colour-coded schema to indicate the level of seriousness of the security situation, ranging from a low at green through amber to a high at red.

102   LETTER FROM JOHNSON TO HAY

Port Moresby, 10 August 1970

I set [out] below a summary of my experiences in the Gazelle Peninsula during my recent visit, 5th to 7th August.

Council

I saw the Council on two occasions, each time for about two hours. I had been led to believe that Council attitude was tending towards dissolution with possible reversion to the four original councils. There was absolutely no indication of this at all. […]. In general, it could be said the Council's views are firm for the maintenance for the existing arrangement. No doubt their attitude has been influenced by the police strength in the Gazelle Peninsula, by the fact that tax prosecutions have been resumed and by the fact that some tax evaders have been jailed. […]

[*matter omitted*]

Mataungan Association

After much dithering, the MA decided that they would have a meeting with me and present were Daniel Rumet[1] and eight Executive members … It must be remembered that the Mataungan Executive consists of two representatives from each of the constituted villages and there are sixty or more Executive members. The eight men who came in were villagers […] and Rumet claimed he was there as an observer. He did, however, occasionally participate in the discussions and clearly was managing the whole show. […] I think the whole point of this discussion was that although there were clear statements from the Mataungan Executive that discussions would follow the revocation of the proclamation, there was and is no indication that their fundamental attitudes have changed. In short, I suspect that when discussions did begin, they would simply insist that they were quite capable of governing the affairs of the Gazelle Peninsula themselves on their own ideas and principles and discussions would break down on that particular issue.

[*matter omitted*][2]

Warmaram Association

I met the Warmarams who will present a formal report next week. In their view a revocation of the proclamation is necessary and they recommend a reversion to the four original Councils. They were unable to have any worthwhile discussions with the Mataungan leadership or the Mataungan Executive but claim to have spent a great deal of time talking to people in villages and consider that they have influenced opinion towards some sort of settlement of the dispute. How true this is I do not know.

[*matter omitted*]

---

1   Deputy-Chairman, Mataungan Association.

2   In the omitted material Johnson noted that senior MA figures Kaputin, Kereku and Tammur did not take up the opportunity to engage in the discussion.

Expatriate Community

The meeting with the expatriate community was not particularly useful as there was no consensus of opinion as to what should be done. If anything, the community would welcome any solution irrespective of what it was provided peace was restored to the Gazelle Peninsula. However, there were a number of hard-liners who wanted force used and, of course, a number who supported the continued existence of the multi-racial Council. In general, I thought, the opinion was one of disengagement by the expatriate community. The view really is that this is an Administration/Tolai problem and the expatriates did not want to be involved in it if they can keep out.

Warbete Association

I met the Warbete who simply reiterated their well-known views that they did not want to be involved in any council at all. When pressed a little further, they said that if there was a reversion to the four original Councils, they would still want to be excluded but would manage their own affairs [...] and would be quite happy to pay tax to support their own social services, etc., within their own particular area. I think this was a perfectly genuine proposition and, indeed, if there is a reversion to the original Council system, some such possibility should be explored.

[*matter omitted*]

Conclusions

In my view the only possibility of a solution within the relatively near future would be the revocation of the proclamation establishing the multi-racial Council. In view of the strong Council attitude however, I would not like to exert undue pressure on the Council to reach the same conclusion themselves but rely upon the pressure of public opinion in the Gazelle Peninsula, which seems to be tending in this direction. However, one should not be too optimistic about what might happen once the proclamation is revoked. There would certainly be strong pressure on the Mataungans to assist in coming to some sort of satisfactory solution but their intransigence in the past does not suggest that they would be likely to budge if indeed a conference did eventuate. The most promising initiative would seem to be by getting the big men of the villages together, who might come to the same conclusion. Their prestige would undoubtedly have a strong bearing on the attitude of both the Council and the Mataungans. Meanwhile, I propose to proceed with the establishment of committees which might provide some useful guidance in any case and hope that this attack on a number of different fronts might ultimately result in a solution. I am not optimistic of much immediate significant improvement.

[NAA A452, 1970/3536]

103   LETTER FROM WALLER TO HAY

Canberra, 13 August 1970

CONFIDENTIAL

We have been giving some further thought to possible ways in which this Department might assist, if so desired, in meeting the eventual requirements of Papua-New Guinea, post-independence, for a Foreign Affairs Department or Branch and for modest overseas representation, as well as the need for Australian diplomatic representation in Port Moresby.

It seems to me that our possible role might be considered under two headings:

(a) the training of suitable indigenes, both in the period leading up to independence and perhaps also afterwards, by inclusion in our annual Foreign Service training course, by in-Service training in this Department and by attachment to our overseas posts; and

(b) assistance, both by the provisions of personnel and otherwise, in the setting up in Port Moresby of a modest Foreign Affairs cell which could, inter alia, collect and collate documents and other information of foreign political relevance to the Territory and continue the in-Service experience of trainees who had already passed through our Foreign Service course; such a cell might provide the nucleus, in both personnel and reference material, for the Foreign Affairs Department or Branch which would be required after independence.

As you will know, there has already been some limited progress in this field. Apart from the attachment of a number of indigenous political figures to appropriate delegations to the United Nations, two indigenous graduates were nominated for our 1970 Foreign Service training course and are at present training with us. In addition officers of this Department had a useful preliminary discussion on 12th February with Mr Unkles and Mr Granger which explored, without commitment, possible future targets for training and also touched, to a lesser extent, on the possible scale of the future requirement for a Foreign Affairs Department and for a modest overseas representation.

There is also the question of the eventual requirement for an Australian diplomatic mission in Port Moresby. This would not, of course, need to be established until the date of independence but some forward planning would seem to be desirable on the questions of staffing, the training of personnel and, in particular, the reservation of appropriate sites for both Chancery and Residence and the planning of suitable buildings.

I feel that a suitable stage may now have been reached for further discussion between our Departments on the above questions in greater depth and on a more definitive basis. If you agree, I would be ready to make appropriate officers available for a meeting at a time suitable to you.

[NAA: A452, 1971/0729]

104   LETTER FROM FURLONGER TO WALLER

Canberra, 16 August 1970

SECRET

I thought you might like to look at the attached report on my visit to Papua/New Guinea since some of the matters covered are relevant to papers which will be coming before the Defence Committee. The report has not been distributed outside this Department.

Attachment
Visit to Papua-New Guinea by the Director, Joint Intelligence Organisation
I visited Papua-New Guinea between 19 July and 1 August 1970 to address the annual District Commissioners Conference in Port Moresby and to make a familiarisation tour through the Territory.

2.   We are, I think, as Australians, too ready to excuse the present state of development in Papua-New Guinea by arguing that we have not had long enough there. In reality, however, the Territory has been exposed to Western influence for as long as many other more advanced ex-colonial territories. German and British control in New Guinea dates from the 1880s —not very different in time from Burma (1885), Vietnam (1884) and earlier than, for example, Northern Nigeria (where the British protectorate dated from 1900).

3.   More valid reasons for the current backwardness of the Territory lie in the shortage of resources which were suitable for colonial exploitation, the ruggedness of its terrain, and apathy and limited finance during much of the period of Australian rule. Until the Hasluck reforms in education and agriculture in the early fifties, we ran the Territory on a shoestring. There was little forward thinking or planning. In Papua, even the famed regime of Hubert Murray,[1] while benevolent and enlightened on such matters as land ownership, was essentially paternalistic and politically static. Murray had no real concept of preparing the local people to govern themselves as a modern community. In New Guinea, before 1941, we merely continued the German administration, but without its worst excesses. For the most part of the first postwar decade, despite the sentimentalism towards the local people which grew out of the Second World War, we did little more than re-establish the rough and ready pre-war administration in both Papua and New Guinea. This had largely been staffed—with notable exceptions —by people who could not make the grade in Australia.

4.   It is only really in the last decade or so that Papua-New Guinea has begun to be much more than a series of coastal enclaves linked only by the sea and aeroplane, with thin lines of administration running inland from these settled coastal strips. Even now, you cannot drive from Lae to Madang and Wewak; although these towns are quite large, and each has its area of settlement around it, the habit of wider contact, and the broadening of horizons which a coastal road link would help produce, are still to come. (There is, however, now a road from Lae to the Highlands which promises to break down some of the latter's traditional isolation.) There remains no road link between Papua and New Guinea.

5.   In the Highlands, which comprise over 40% of the Territory's population, the first white patrol dates only from the thirties, and administrative control from only after the war. Serious development in the Highlands has occurred only in the last decade, although the progress

---

1   Lieutenant-Governor of Papua, 1908–40.

made, and the Highlander's receptivity in this period, are impressive. But I fear that it has not been long enough.

6.   In the island groups—which comprise an eighth of the total population but produce 60% of the export income (this figure will rise to 90% when the Bougainville Copper project begins production in 1972), the gaps in understanding and contact are even wider. In the case of Bougainville, there is even a racial barrier; the coal-black Bougainvillean characterises the other inhabitants of the Territory as 'red-skins'. The Tolai in the Rabaul area—who has some of the characteristics of the Ibo[2] or the Bengali[3]—considers himself superior to most other New Guineans. Both Tolais and Bougainvilleans seize avidly on education and are more advanced in this regard than the mainlanders. Secessionism, whether jointly or, more probably, separately, is growing in both New Britain and Bougainville.

7.   In this situation, there cannot yet be, and may never be, any deeply rooted sense of New Guinea nationalism. Kinship—the 'one-talk'[4] system which entails binding social and economic obligations on members of the group or tribe—is the determining factor for most people.

8.   Another persistent popular influence is cargo cultism. I had expected to find the traditional Melanesian attraction to millenary [millenarian] movements displaced by more developed political concepts, but the tendency survives in politically significant ways. In the popular mind, which is much given to sorcery and magic, the source of the power and wealth of the European is occult and miraculous: it is not seen as the product of long and painfully exercised effort, knowledge and technology. It follows that there is a magic key which the indigene only need to find to cause a transformation in his own less privileged state and to admit him to the material wealth of the European and to equality with him. There is a tendency in some areas to look at independence as such a key: the local people will then, as effortlessly as the Europeans seem to do, enjoy the fruits of Western influence. There are echoes of these beliefs in the Mataungan movement, where Kaputin claims his proposed Development Corporation already has ships in Japan and the United States, loaded and ready to leave; and that it will be the fault of the Administration if they do not come. Political attitudes based not on cultural and other affinities, but on delusions such as these, provide an insecure basis for both an independence movement and for understanding between governors and governed after independence as well. They provide fruitful soil, as Peter Hastings[5] comments, for the elitist manipulation of irrational mass hopes and expectations.

9.   It is true that there is emerging a new and more enlightened elite in politics, education, the Universities and the Army, but the process is very slow. Unifying institutions like political parties and trade unions are still in their infancy. The possibilities of radio as a unifying force are largely undeveloped: the ABC's concept of its role does not extend much beyond serving the expatriate. The first local university graduates—a mere handful—will come out this month.

---

2   The Igbo (or Ibo) community of south-eastern Nigeria has a reputation for confidence and enterprise. From 1967 to 1970 an attempt by the Igbo to secede from Nigeria and establish the 'Biafran Republic' was ruthlessly repressed.

3   Here Furlonger appeared to be expressing the view that the Western-educated middle class in West Bengal was notable for political sophistication and a tendency to political militancy and radicalism.

4   *Wantok*, or 'one-talk', refers in a literal sense to those speaking the same language. It can also refer to members of a wider group whose members have developed a sense of common identity.

5   Peter Hastings was the foreign affairs writer for *The Australian* (1966–70) and *The Sydney Morning Herald* (1970–74), the executive officer of the Council on New Guinea Affairs, which he had helped establish, the editor of the council's journal, *New Guinea and Australia, the Pacific and South-East Asia*, and the author of *New Guinea: Problems & Prospects*, Cheshire for the Australian Institute of International Affairs, Melbourne, 1973 (first published 1969).

Although the Army has been more far-sighted in its planning, and will have 31 local officers at the end of this year and will be totally indigenised before the end of the seventies, there will, by late in this decade, be only several hundred professionally trained people available for Government and other jobs. An indigenous industrial middle-class is hardly beginning; business and industry remain expatriate. I understand that none of the large Territory concerns have yet admitted New Guineans to share in ownership. The 'crash' economic development programme now under way will increase the expatriate sector in future years: the present European population of 30,000 is expected to be more than doubled by 1976. Australia will then have a large economic investment in the territory and a vociferous, and largely new, Australian minority to demand its protection.

10. Both political and economic development, as they have so far progressed, have been gifts from the white man. They lack indigenous roots. There is no tradition of political leadership and no native aristocracy or other traditional elite. Our legal system, with its involved procedural tangles, complicated rules of evidence and Government acceptance of adverse court decisions, is not widely understood; the native has his own rough concept of 'pay-back' justice. There were three major cases of this in the Highlands while I was in New Guinea, each involving 'pay-back' killings—generally over disputed land.

11. Our political system seems hardly destined to last in its present form. One perhaps un-intended effect of the recently approved devolution of power in the Territory is likely to be the building up of the role of the Administrator, who will need to act as the arbiter between the various local Ministers in the exercise of their powers, particularly over finance. The Secretary for Law sees the Administrator as gradually acquiring a quasi-presidential position. Experience with this kind of executive may well dispose the New Guineans towards a presidential-type system—probably no bad thing. The Secretary for Law added that he thought it likely that the real political issue of the future would lie less between Westminster and non-Westminster government than between a multi- or one-party state; perhaps the best we could hope for was a one-party state, with room within it for the expression of differing views. Such a party, however, is not yet in prospect.

12. There are, of course, more hopeful aspects of the New Guinea problem. Present and prospective mineral and timber developments open up the possibility of ultimate economic viability—which seemed out of the question only a few years ago. The Bougainville Copper project alone will increase the local GNP by 50%, and there are five or six other large projects under advanced examination. One of them (the Kennecot copper project near the West Irian border) could be larger than Bougainville—it may be the biggest copper find in the world. Fortunately, too, the Territory has escaped some of the problems which plague other Afro-Asian countries. Apart from isolated areas (such as the Gazelle Peninsula and the Chimbu region in the Highlands) there is no population or land pressure. There is no starvation and no absentee landlord problem. Australian land policies have generally been benevolent—almost, in some cases, to the point of impracticality, in view of the obstacles they place in the way of economic development. Anti-European feeling, though undoubtedly widespread and growing, is probably not as deep-seated as in some other countries—although it would be easy to be complacent in this regard, and we probably have some unpleasant shocks ahead. (One of the best academics in New Guinea—Charles Rowley—told me that, whenever the word *kiap*[6] (synonymous with the white administrator) was mentioned to his students, it always produced an outburst of laughter.)

13. Furthermore, the common view of the warlike tendencies of the New Guinea tribes seems exaggerated. Fighting between New Guinea tribesmen tends, from what I heard, to be a comic

---

6   Patrol officer.

opera affair, and generally stops after a killing or two, with a ritual exchange of gifts. Bitterness may deepen as regional feelings grow, but, so far, fighting to exhaustion or near annihilation, as in Nigeria, does not seem to be in the New Guinea tradition.

14. One is nevertheless left with some pessimism regarding the permanence of the Australian achievement. The fragility and shallowness of it all are much too evident, and there is not enough indigenous contribution. What we are doing tends too much to be made in our own image: education, politics, the law, the civil service, the Army (although the Army recognises this better than most and is doing something about it.) We have taught the local people to live beyond their means: medical and dental attention is almost free, and housing policy for civil servants is generous to a fault. The lesson that these things can be financed only by production and exports has not sunk in. I suspect that we made a mistake in abolishing pidgin as a medium of lower education: English is less suited as a *lingua franca* and the effect will be to increase the already wide generational gap.

15. Moreover, we cannot have much time left. There has just been one substantial devolution of power, and a further stage must come after the Select Committee on Constitutional Development reports later this year. Self-government is likely to be an issue in the House of Assembly election in 1972; and there must be a real prospect that the 1976 election will either be for, or about, independence. Even the Highlanders, who are asking us to stay, do so only because they want more time to be able to compete with the lowlands; not out of affection for us.

16. Bearing in mind also, the almost invariable tendency of colonially-sponsored island groupings or mainland federations to break up after independence, one must seriously question whether the objective conditions for continued unity exist in Papua-New Guinea. The main exception to the long catalogue of post-colonial disintegration that comes to mind is Indonesia; but Indonesia had a well-developed Malay civilization, a strong sense of nationalism, and, most important, a large Army. Even then, Indonesia might have fallen apart in the fifties. It is, I suppose, possible that eventually the New Guinea armed forces might discharge the unifying role the Army has played in Indonesia; but the New Guinea armed forces will be about one hundredth the size of those in Indonesia, and the problems of unity much more difficult.

17. If New Guinea were to disintegrate, it would by no means follow that it would remain a sphere of Australian influence. The Japanese are now coming into the Territory in a big way. They are already second to Australia as a market for the Territory; the Toyota is the most widely marketed car, produced, unlike the Holden, in a multitude of models; the Japanese will take more than half the copper from Bougainville; and they are prospecting vigorously for timber and raw materials. Economically, Japan could soon become as important to New Guinea as it is already to Australia. The political leverage which Japan would have in an independent Bougainville, because of its copper market, is not hard to see.

18. One other significant factor in the current situation is the declining quality of the expatriate civil service in the Territory. The Economic Adviser used the word 'disintegration' to describe their developing condition; the Chairman of the local Public Service Board (himself a controversial figure) was scathing in his comments on much of the human material available to him. The quality of expatriates has always been a problem, but it has declined further, except at senior levels, with the cessation of permanent recruitment. The recently introduced ASOC[7] scheme seems unlikely to reverse the trend. The universal view I found was that the thousand people guaranteed employment gained little they did not already have, whilst the several thousand who are the real problem get nothing new. (I comment separately in para. 47 below on the critical state of the police).

---

7   Australia Service for Overseas Co-operation. See Documents 48 & 64. In the event, Cabinet decided not to proceed with the establishment of this body (Documents 394 & 395).

19. The above comments are an attempt to present a realistic, if gloomy, sketch of the problem we face in trying to bring into the independent world a united, stable, progressive and friendly New Guinea. These observations do not, of course, provide any reason for not continuing our present efforts. But we need to consider possible 'fall-back' positions if we cannot achieve all we hope for; our policies should seek to maximise our future options. The currently greater interest in creating institutions between the local councils and the central government level, and the recognition of the possibility of differing rates of regional development, seem to be steps in the right direction. Centrifugal tendencies are already there, and cannot be ignored; the existence of intermediate administrative machinery will provide something to build on if our hopes for a unified New Guinea prove unattainable.

Pre-Independence Problems

20. If the long-term prospects for New Guinea are cloudy, this is equally the case for the pre-independence period. Events are accelerating, and problems still unseen undoubtedly lie ahead. Some likely problem areas, however, are already identifiable and are sketched out in the paragraphs that follow.

Land

21. The significance of land for the New Guinea villager (who still constitutes over 95% of the total population) is described by Charles Rowley as follows:

> 'The New Guinea villager shares with most others that special attachment to the land characteristic of those whose land rights are their hold on life itself. These rights are based on the tradition of inheritance, which may be matrilineal or patrilineal ... Before the European came, there was no concept of individual ownership, nor of land as a commodity. Land belongs to the whole group, and the villager's rights are those of user only. This relationship involves the most deep-seated emotions, and is different from that of the owner to his personal property. No right of a person to dispose of land was recognised; for the ancestral spirits must have their place, and the unborn generations must be provided for.'

22. All land in Papua-New Guinea belongs to one tribe or another, with overlapping areas often in dispute; under the shifting subsistence cultivation system, there may be long periods when land is unexploited but its ownership does not change. The land alienated to Europeans was, in the native view, made available to that generation of Europeans only, and he sees the payment made as in the nature of rent; the New Guinean does not therefore feel a compulsion to compensate present generations of expatriate landowners for land which he regards as only hired to their forbears. Thus, Kaputin says that plantations in the Gazelle Peninsula must be restored to the Tolai without compensation, and most Tolais would agree with him.

23. Despite the reputed benevolence of Australian land policy, Rowley estimates that the proportion of arable land alienated to expatriates may be over ten percent (most of it during the period of German control and subsequently expropriated by Australia as enemy property). In the Gazelle peninsula, 40% of Tolai land is in the possession of expatriates. Significant alienated areas exist in other parts of former German New Guinea, particularly near Madang; large areas, there and elsewhere, are in the possession of Christian missions. Troubles over plantations are bound to become more serious, and expatriate owners would do well to begin switching from cultivation to processing.

24. There are other problems flowing from the traditional native attitude to land, which is now enshrined in Territory law. There are local groups (e.g. the Tolai and the Chimbu) where there is heavy population pressure, but the tribal groups will not move elsewhere; their resentment is

more likely, as in the Gazelle peninsula, to be turned against the expatriate, or the Government as preventing them from occupying 'their' land. Furthermore, since the group's agreement is normally needed before an individual can alienate any piece of land, the process of acquiring land for developmental urban or national needs is protracted and complex. I heard of one case where land was needed for a copper project in the Sepik region; court hearings to establish ownership had to be deferred indefinitely because a previously unknown nomadic tribe, which might conceivably have a claim to the land, had just been discovered, and the existence of another was suspected.

25. In many of the problems that lie ahead, land is certain to be involved—often not very obviously. The new land legislation just introduced deals only with a small part of the total problem; I heard the view expressed that it would probably take a strong, progressive but ruthless indigenous Government to get at the root of the matter. Land always lay, for example, at the base of the opposition to the Multi-Racial Council in Rabaul. The Council broadly represented the 'haves', and the Mataungan Association the 'have-nots'; the Council was also a symbol of the foreign authority that denies the Tolai the land that he regards as his.

26. In areas where a system of matrilineal inheritance applies, as in Rabaul and Bougainville, land problems become even more complex. The matrilineal system is particularly unsuited to the needs of a modern economy, since the fact that ownership does not pass from a father to his sons acts as a large disincentive.

Rabaul

27. The general view in New Guinea was that the Mataungan problem would drag on, and that the basis for any viable settlement could not yet be discerned. The incoming Administrator said that he did not think Kaputin wanted a solution; the maintenance of his position in the Mataungan Association (which is not unchallenged) required a continuance of tension and crisis. The District Commissioner in Rabaul[8] said that he believed that the Mataungans would go on playing cat and mouse with the Administration; that there was ample evidence in recent Tolai history to justify the belief that the Mataungans will not run out of unity, stamina or local support; and that they have the capability of holding out at a price the Administration will ultimately find insupportable. He sees a decade of trouble with the Tolais. There seems little doubt that they could apply more pressure than they do now; new tactics such as boycotts would be hard to counter.

28. As for the support which the Mataungan leadership are getting from the Tolais, the local Special Branch representative estimated that 30% of the Tolai actively support the Mataungan Association and 30% passively, while only 5% are actively opposed.

29. There has been a notable escalation of MA aims as the dispute has progressed: these now include an economic programme and a demand for self-government either for the island groups as a whole or for the Tolais alone. The MA is the first genuine mass movement the Territory has produced, and it looks durable.

30. It is hard to see any permanent outcome of the dispute that would not involve acceptance of many of the Tolai demands. The problem for the Government is that recognition of Tolai political demands would encourage separatism; a government back down now would affect its credit elsewhere in the Territory; and acceptance of the Tolai attitude towards land ownership would throw all alienated land in dispute. The Administration plans gradually to re-purchase alienated land, but the cost is high, and even the return of all alienated land would not satisfy

---

8   H. W. (Harry) West, District Commissioner, East New Britain. In December 1970 West was appointed as Assistant Director of Native Affairs in the Department of the Administration, with Jack Emanuel succeeding him as East New Britain's District Commissioner.

the Tolai land hunger. The population will rapidly get worse since the Tolai are growing at nearly 4% a year; their population nearly quintupled in the last 80 years.

31. It is likely that the Mataungans will continue to maintain pressure but avoid initiating violence (they may well want to *provoke* it), whilst relying on [the] Opposition and radical opinion in Australia to assist their cause. Although the situation will remain volatile, I think the Administration could, without serious risk, reduce the police strength below the figure of 700 the Administrator was talking of keeping there when I saw him on 31st July. (The maximum figure was about 1050.)

32. It is hard to be certain about the repercussions of the Mataungan movement elsewhere in the Territory. The Mataungans are trying to use migrant plantation labour in Rabaul to spread their cause elsewhere, but have not had much success. Associations with comparable aims are beginning to emerge in New Ireland and Chimbu (in both of which there is population pressure), Bougainville (see below), Lae, Milne Bay and the Western District. The potential for development in these bodies is still hard to estimate.

Bougainville

33. The Army Commander[9] (a knowledgeable officer on his second tour of duty in New Guinea) told me that he thought Bougainville would eventually develop into a bigger problem than Rabaul. Bougainville has had a long and unhappy contact with the West. It was a blackbirding source in the last century; it was traded between the British and the Germans; and it is now the scene of the first exposure to large-scale Western enterprise.

34. The huge Bougainville Copper project is very impressive. It will cost $400 million before an ounce of copper is produced; it will, from 1972, produce an export income of $100 million a year; and, as stated above, this one project will increase the local GNP by 50%. There are many sources of potential trouble: labour disputes (over the next two years the work force will drop 2/3 while the percentage of expatriates will be increasing); tribal problems (90% of the labour comes from elsewhere in the Territory); racial conflict (there is a large unskilled Australian labour force working and living with relatively underpaid, but in some respects pampered, indigenous migrant labour); and further possible land problems (not all the land needed has yet been purchased). Inflated land prices and the possibility of too high a local wage-level could have wide repercussions elsewhere in the Territory. The diversion of Administration resources—the township of Arawa alone will cost them $40 millions—is also producing short-term economic distortions and dissatisfaction elsewhere in the Territory.

35. The Company and the Administration are working closely together, but serious problems will be hard to avoid. Bougainville will be the pace-setter for other large new projects as they develop, and it will cast ripples through the whole economy and society.

36. There are other problems in Bougainville. Secessionism is a growing movement, and is fed by students (Bougainvilleans are very education-conscious). It is also, I was told, encouraged by some American missions. Bougainvilleans will be increasingly loath to share their new-found wealth with the mainland—or even with the racially akin Solomon Islanders. In the south of the island, there is also the beginning of a Mataungan-type cooperative movement, lead by a 'drop-out' from legal training in Australia, and which seeks the removal of expatriates from the local administration. As in Rabaul, it is opposed by the local elected Council.

---

9   Brigadier Ralph Eldridge.

Urban Squatters

37. There are growing up around the main cities—particularly Port Moresby, Rabaul and Wewak—vagrant squatter communities attracted by urban life and wealth. In Port Moresby, squatters and vagrant labour living with kinsmen ('one-talks') make up over a quarter of the population. Many of the older squatters have been there for years and are not a serious problem, but the vagrant 'one-talks' and the often uneducated second generation of squatter children are a present source of petty crime and a possible basis for mob violence, tribal conflict and political exploitation. 'Second Form drop-outs', i.e. boys who fail in the early stages of secondary education, are also beginning to be a problem: they have lost contact with village life, regard themselves as educated, but cannot do responsible jobs. The unemployable younger generation around the cities is expected to double within five years and will require special handling.

Trade Unions

38. The trade unions are developing only slowly and are not at present a significant problem. The Pangu Pati is attempting to organize the unions but has not yet got very far. The ACTU[10] seems generally to have played a constructive and responsible advisory role in the union field. I was told, for example, that they recognise the undesirability of forcing local wages to an uneconomic level and are being cautious in promoting a central trade union federation, since they argue that the foundation of a sound union movement lies in specialised unions being able to demonstrate to their followers their ability to gain benefits for them. In Bougainville, the Company has reached what it considers a satisfactory wage agreement with local labour.

Students

39. Students of the Territory's two tertiary institutions the university in Port Moresby and the technical college at Lae—are generally quiet. In Port Moresby most are inactive, conservative and troubled by recent developments. There is, however, a beginning of political activism in the person of a student named Kasaipwalova,[11] an intelligent young man but one who failed at an Australian university and who seems likely to become a drop-out in Port Moresby as well, because of his concentration on politics. He is active in promoting a political club at the university. Encouragement of 'protest' politics in both Lae and Port Moresby comes from some university staff.

40. There are some interesting matters deserving comment in the student field.

(a) The role which educated 'drop-outs' are beginning to play politically.

[*matter omitted*]

(b) New Guinea students at Australian and other universities are being exposed to the whole range of radical anti-establishment ideas—Che Guevara, Mao, Marcuse, Black Power, SDS,[12] etc. Australian Communist party publications have recently begun actively to deal with New Guinea (although the Party is not at present active in the Territory).

[*matter omitted*]

---

10 Australian Council of Trade Unions.

11 John Kasaipwalova, from Kiriwina Island in the Trobriand Islands in Milne Bay District, had become involved in radical politics as a student on scholarship at the University of Queensland. See Donald Denoon, *Trial Separation: Australia and the Decolonisation of Papua New Guinea*, Australian National University, Pandanus Books, Canberra, 2005, pp. 77, 78 and Don Woolford, *Papua New Guinea: Initiation and Independence*, University of Queensland Press, Brisbane, 1976, pp. 185, 198.

12 Students for a Democratic Society.

Their intellectual beliefs tend to be a confused mix of anarchism, Black Power and national pride. Their tactics seem also to be influenced by those of the protest movement, whose publications are freely available from Australia.

[*matter omitted*]

Violence would thus have played into Tolai hands. (One senior Administration officer in Rabaul, in evident recognition of this, commented to me: 'One shot, and that is the end of it.')

(c)   There are elements in the New Guinea situation which could be ripe for exploitation by the protest movement in Australia, with Vietnam beginning to lose its force as an issue.

New Guinea Border

41.   It is a relief to be able to say, after this catalogue of potential problems, that the New Guinea border remains very quiet. The District Commissioner at Vanimo[13] (who has a 'hot-line' to Djajapura which is used daily) said that the local tribal people have drawn the moral from harsh reprisals by Indonesia against their kin across the border, and are now disinclined to meddle or even to live in West Irian (where some of them still have tribal land). Those who still trickle across—and there is still a sizeable refugee camp near Vanimo—tend to be urban malcontents from the Djajapura region.

42.   Two possible developments which might, in time, affect the border problem are:

(a)   the planned mining of nickel near Djajapura. (Nickel is also being prospected on the Australian side of the border.) The Indonesians say that they intend to bring in labour from Biak and Ambon, and this could possibly produce social problems, with repercussions in East New Guinea;

(b)   the huge Kennecot copper project in the Star Mountains. It will probably be at least two years before development begins. If the project develops, it will undoubtedly attract considerable cross-border movement, with the possibility of tribal movements and other frictions as well as considerable economic dislocation in the general region.

Other Problems

43.   There are other sources of possible future trouble in the Territory.

(a)   *The Nationality Problem.* Papuans have Australian nationality but are not admitted to Australia for permanent residence. It is not hard to visualize situations (e.g., the expulsion of a Papuan student in Australia) which could lead to strong reactions, and perhaps racial violence, in the Territory.

(b)   *The Chinese Minority.* The Chinese middleman behaves as elsewhere and is strongly disliked. Some have plantations in the Gazelle Peninsula. Unlike the indigenes, Chinese with Australian nationality (and most have) can settle freely in Australia. Frustrated nationalists could easily turn on the Chinese without much, if any, notice.

(c)   *Public Service.* There is still a good deal of indigenous discontent about discriminatory wage levels. Indigenisation has also not progressed much.

(d)   *Tribalism in Army and Police.* This has not yet been a problem but might become so in certain circumstances. The Army has already had one mutiny.

(e)   *Organised Political Agitation.* This has hardly yet begun.

---

13   J. E. (John) Wakeford was District Commissioner for the West Sepik District from the late 1960s to mid–1971.

The Administration's Ability to Cope

44. I do not mean to be prophet of doom. The above possibilities, if they eventuate, will not all do so simultaneously; some may never occur. There have, however, in the last year, been three major crises in Bougainville and Rabaul. Fortunately, none coincided with each other. Two of them produced a request to the Defence Committee for military support.

45. We must recognise the possibility that comparable problems will arise more frequently; and that more than one may occur at the same time; and that there may be less warning.

Intelligence problems

46. I was in Port Moresby on the day the initial confrontation with the Mataungan Association over land issues occurred, and in Rabaul a week later. I was thus able to see the handling of the problems at both ends. Even after allowances are made for the difficulties which the Administration has in grappling with new and uncertain issues, there are a number of aspects of the Rabaul affair, and of the general intelligence problem, that give rise to concern.

(a) First, although I cannot document it in detail, I believe that there is a widening communication gap between the Administration and the local people. This was generally acknowledged by those expatriate officers whose opinions I felt most inclined to value. One of the most knowledgeable and experienced senior Administration officers whom I spoke to said that he doubted if the Europeans knew 95% of what went on in the indigenous community.

(b) Second, the traditionally monolithic nature of the *kiap* system is an obstacle to present understanding: everything in the district has traditionally passed through the *kiap*, and he does not readily take to the concept that the new and changing situation requires objective assessments by intelligence specialists without a vested interest in policy. One key obstacle in this regard has been the Secretary of the Administrator's Department (Ellis). His technique in each crisis has been to go to the trouble spot and take over, as the District officer has traditionally done. Ellis is a second generation expatriate who was born in Rabaul. He cannot escape his background: he is the embodiment of the *kiap* and a believer in the strongarm methods that have always worked in the past. (The Army Commander told me that Ellis had even wanted to 'teach the Indonesians a lesson' in one of the past border situations.) Ellis also has what amounts to his own private intelligence service through a system of District Inspectors responsible to him. (I was told that those positions had originally been intended for Special Branch.)

(c) Third, the Special Branch is too thin on the ground (it is represented in only 6 of the 18 districts) and is retrogressing. Its best officers are leaving it, and some posts have had to be closed because of the staff problem. Even in districts where it is represented, the single European Special Branch officer has only a handful of uneducated local constables (occasionally a sergeant) who are not suited to move along the semi-intelligentsia from whom the future problems are likely to emerge. This situation is well known to Mr Hay and Mr Barbour,[14] and I am hopeful that it will soon be changed. It is, however, a key part of the general intelligence problem, and I do not think the Defence Committee can ignore the matter. The Special Branch needs, as a minimum, to be removed from the Police, thoroughly re-organised and stiffened by generous assistance from ASIO. The new Administrator would also like to send people to Special Branch in Singapore for training in Asian-type security operations, but he said that he had not been encouraged in Canberra to do this. I think he should be.

---

14   Peter Barbour, Director-General, Australian Security Intelligence Organisation (ASIO).

(d) Fourth, the Territory Intelligence Committee is not serving the Administrator and the Defence Committee as intended. Under direction from the previous Secretary of the External Territories Department,[15] the flow of information to the committee was carefully controlled, and it was kept ignorant of policy. It has not been the real adviser on intelligence and there is no point in reforming it unless it is accorded this role. My visit confirmed me in the general proposals included in the report submitted in April[16] (which I will be revising in consultation with Mr Hay who, I believe, unlike his predecessor, broadly agrees with it.)

(e) Fifth, security is rudimentary in the Territory. The standard safe in most offices has a key lock. Rapid and secret civil and police communications generally do not exist; the Army is well equipped, however, and its facilities need to be more widely used. In the Mataungan confrontation, communication between Rabaul and Port Moresby was by unclassified police radio link or by open telephone. There was an Army classified radio link, but it was not used since it was claimed to be too slow. Since then, I understand that the Administration has decided to put in scrambler phones between Moresby, Rabaul, Kieta and Vanimo, but Army informants doubt that the units used are really secure. Security needs to be improved quickly; there has already been one security breach which had important political effects (the Warmaram leak).[17]

(f) Sixth, the intelligence aspects of the Rabaul operation left much to be desired. On the day of the confrontation, progressive spot reports were going to Port Moresby, but there was so little assessment that the Administrator sent over a special intelligence team the next morning. The main reason for the lack of assessments, I was told, was that the two key officers on the special intelligence unit which had been set up, were diverted to operational tasks. This probably contributed to the over-reaction which occurred during the afternoon when, on the basis of reports later found to be false, Ellis and others recommended a state of 'Red Plus', which, if accepted, would have involved flying troops immediately to Rabaul. This recommendation was not endorsed by the Army Commander in Port Moresby (who had to monitor the Police radio to keep up with the play) and was over-ruled by the Administrator.

Although it is easy for an outsider without responsibility to criticise, I think there was in fact a degree of over-reaction in the whole affair that it might have been possible to avoid if there had been in Port Moresby a skilled intelligence body in which there was high-level confidence.

The Police

47. There is one final matter I want to touch on briefly in this already over-lengthy report, namely the critical state of the police. This is not directly the responsibility of the Defence

---

15 Warwick Smith.

16 Not published.

17 Warmaram was a government-approved and supported organisation of Tolai leaders, from the public service and private sector, who sought to mediate in the dispute between the Administration and the Mataungan Association. See Ian Downs, *The Australian Trusteeship: Papua New Guinea, 1945–75*, Australian Government Publishing Service, Canberra, 1980, p. 431. The reference to 'the Warmaram leak' refers to the leaking of a letter from an Australian official. Don Woolford has noted that '... a privately circulated newsletter late in May published a letter sent by the director of information and extension services, Lyall Newby, to the manager of Radio Rabaul. The letter revealed the extent of the Administration's support for Warmaram and, more damagingly, said one of Warmaram's aims was to "destroy Kaputin's standing". The effect of the disclosure was to destroy whatever standing Warmaram might have had and to totally discredit the supposed impartiality of the already highly suspect radio station, which was supposed to be the Administration's chief communication with the Tolais'. Woolford, *Initiation and Independence*, pp. 54–55.

Committee but the police situation has such serious implications for future public order, and hence for Defence Committee involvement, that it cannot be ignored. It is relevant to the Defence Forces paper to come before the Defence Committee; if there is present competition for finance and resources between the Armed Forces and the police, I would say unhesitatingly that improvement of the police should come first. (This is not to say that the Armed Forces do not need the expansion which is recommended).

48. The Army Commander described the police to me as 'badly led, badly administrated and badly trained', and I think he is entirely right. The police have traditionally been treated as a 'poor relation' (I was told that before World War II policemen were not given commissioned rank, which was reserved for the *kiap*) and they are wrongly equated with Southern police forces for pay and conditions of service. Their salary levels are three grades below comparable levels in the civil service (one of the reasons why the Special Branch, now staffed by the police, is in such poor shape). There are too many commissioned officers who were un-commissioned misfits in State Police forces; too many racist ex-policemen from Africa; I was told that there is even a former mercenary from Katanga.

49. Police officer strength is inadequate in numbers as well as quality. At the scene of the confrontation with the Mataungans, the police officer in charge said that he had 11 officers to 600 men; since he could not rely on his NCOs in this situation, he really needed 1 officer to no more than 30 men to be reasonably sure that his force would not crack under pressure. The general officer ratio in the force as a whole is also too low.

50. Nor are the police adequately trained or equipped for the mobile role they are increasingly being required to fulfil. Very little was done between the two Rabaul crises to improve glaring deficiencies. I visited two police camps in the disputed area in Rabaul: they were makeshift in the extreme. Communication was by insecure taxi-type radios; the police Superintendent depended on a hired helicopter to keep track of the situation on the ground. Equipment and training inadequacies contribute to the excessive number of police that have been deployed in emergencies: nearly a third of the total Territory force was in Rabaul when I was there. I do not think this kind of deployment can, or should, go on. The cost is enormous and reduces money available for other urgent Administration needs. In the last financial year, the Territory was 'in the red' to Treasury by $3 millions. Much of this must be accountable to the cost of meeting three major crises in a year by massive movement of police and other emergency measures.

51. The police system might well be unable to cope if there were simultaneous crises in two or more parts of the country. There is already too much inclination to look to the PIR to get them out of trouble. The whole police problem needs fundamental review, and the new police commissioner[18] requires the full support of the Government in urgent measures flowing from such a review. Something like the Malaysian police force is one thing worth looking at; but so are means of getting more and better officers whilst local officers are being trained.

Prospects

52. Fortunately, the recent administration changes in Port Moresby and Canberra have produced an environment favourable to change. Control from Canberra will be much less constrictive, and, on the matters of concern to the Defence Committee, there should be fewer differences with the Department of Territories. There remain, however, basic problems that will tax our ingenuity, foresight and patience in the years ahead.

[Prepared] 13 August 1970.

[NAA: A1838, 689/1 PART 6]

---

18 Norman Allan Mark Nicholls was appointed Police Commissioner on 14 August 1970. Until then Brian Holloway had been acting in the role since the departure of R. W. (Ray) Whitrod in March 1970.

105 INSTRUCTIONS UNDER PAPUA NEW GUINEA ACT

Canberra, 20 August 1970

Governor-General's Instructions to Administrator

Commonwealth of Australia

By His Excellency the Governor-General in and over the Commonwealth of Australia

to wit PAUL HASLUCK Governor-General

WHEREAS it is provided by section 15 of the *Papua and New Guinea Act* 1949–1968 that the Administrator of the Territory of Papua and New Guinea shall exercise and perform all powers and functions that belong to his office in accordance with the tenor of his Commission and in accordance with such instructions as are given to him by the Governor-General:

AND WHEREAS my Government has decided on new arrangements in relation to the government of the said Territory for the purpose of bringing about a significant transfer of power to elected representatives of the people of the Territory:

AND WHEREAS it is intended that, under the said arrangements, the Ministerial Members, and Assistant Ministerial Members, of the House of Assembly of the said Territory will exercise full authority, and accept full responsibility, in relation to certain matters and that the powers and functions of the Administrator of the said Territory will be exercised consistently with the said arrangements:

NOW THEREFORE I, SIR PAUL MEERNAA CAEDWALLA HASLUCK, the Governor-General aforesaid, acting with the advice of the Federal Executive Council, hereby give the following instructions to the person from time to time holding the office of Administrator of the Territory of Papua and New Guinea or exercising and performing the powers and functions that belong to that office:

(1) Subject to your duty to act in accordance with law, in the exercise of your powers and functions in relation to a matter that is included in the matters that are specified, for the purposes of arrangements for the time being approved in accordance with section 25 of the *Papua and New Guinea Act 1949–1968*, matters in respect of which a Ministerial Member or Assistant Ministerial Member is to have full authority:

(a) you shall act in accordance with any advice given to you by the Administrator's Executive Council; and

(b) in the case of a matter with respect of which it is not legally necessary for you to obtain the advice of the Administrator's Executive Council and in respect of which advice is tendered to you by the Ministerial Member or Assistant Ministerial Member concerned without the matter having been considered by the Administrator's Executive Council, you shall either act in accordance with that advice or refer the matter to the Administrator's Executive Council.

(2) You shall cause a record to be made of the decision of the Administrator's Executive Council as to the advice to be given in relation to a matter referred to in the foregoing instruction that has been considered by the Council and shall forward to the Minister of State for External Territories, as soon as practicable, a copy of the papers submitted to the Council for the purposes of its consideration of any such matter and of the record so made of the decision of the Council.

Given under my Hand and the Great Seal
of the Commonwealth this twentieth
day of August in the year of Our Lord,
One thousand nine hundred and seventy
and in the nineteenth year of Her Majesty's reign.

[*matter omitted*]

Commonwealth of Australia
Papua and New Guinea Act 1949–1968
Determination Under Section 24

WHEREAS paragraph (a) of sub-section (1.) of section 24 of the Papua and New Guinea Act 1949–1968 provides that there shall be seven offices of ministerial member of the House of Assembly, of such respective designations as the Minister of State for External Territories determines;

AND WHEREAS paragraph (b) of the said sub-section provides that there shall be such number, being not more than ten, of offices of assistant ministerial member of the House of Assembly, and of such respective designations as the Minister of State for External Territories determines;

AND WHEREAS sub-section (2.) of the said section provides that in respect of each ministerial office, the Minister of State for External Territories shall determine the matters in respect of which the holder of the office is to perform the functions of a ministerial member or assistant ministerial member, as the case requires, being all or any of the matters to which the functions of a specified department of the Public Service relate:

Now therefore I, *CHARLES EDWARD BARNES*, Minister of State for External Territories, pursuant to the power conferred upon me by sub-section (1.) of section 24 of the Papua and New Guinea Act 1949–1968 HEREBY DETERMINE the seven offices of ministerial member shall have the respective designations as set out in column 1 of Annexe A attached hereto and that there shall be eight offices of assistant ministerial member which shall have the respective designations as set out in column 1 of Annexe B attached hereto AND pursuant to the power conferred upon me by sub-section (2.) of the said section I HEREBY DETERMINE that the functions of the specified departments for which the ministerial members and assistant ministerial members will be responsible in so far as the day-to-day administration of those matters are concerned shall be as set out in column 2 of Annexes A and B respectively.[1]

I HEREBY REVOKE all prior determinations made pursuant to the powers conferred by section 24 of the Papua and New Guinea Act 1949–1968.

Dated this twenty-first day of August 1970.

C. E. BARNES
Minister of State for External Territories

[*matter omitted*]

---

1   Annexes A and B not published. For information on the powers transferred, see Document 65.

A. *Responsibilities in connection with the Department*

(1) In accordance with the Governor-General's Instructions given to the Administrator, pursuant to the powers conferred by section 15 of the Papua and New Guinea Act 1949-1968, a Ministerial member or Assistant Ministerial Member shall exercise full authority, and accept full responsibility, in relation to the matters specified for the respective designations in the Annexe attached hereto. In so doing a Ministerial or Assistant Ministerial member shall not act inconsistently with:

(a) The programmes and policies of development from time to time agreed upon by the Commonwealth of Australia and the House of Assembly or the Administrator's Executive Council, as the case may be;

or

(b) Any lawful agreement or obligation entered into by the Administration of Papua and New Guinea or by the Commonwealth of Australia in respect of the Territory of Papua and New Guinea.

(2) In respect of those matters not specified in the Annexe, a Ministerial or Assistant Ministerial Member shall:

(a) Be responsible within the framework of broader government policy for decisions regarding policy and for administrative actions of the department, or part of the department as may be determined, in its day-to-day activities (other than management and Public Service aspects);

(b) Be responsible for the formulation of plans and proposals for departmental, or part of the Department as may be determined, expenditure including the formulation of draft departmental estimates.

(3) In carrying out his functions, a Ministerial or Assistant Ministerial Member shall:

(a) Refer policy decisions or other matters to the Administrator's Executive Council where

(i)   He considers it necessary to do so;

or

(ii)   The Administrator's Executive Council or the Administrator directs;

(b) considers papers and recommendations submitted to him by the department and his decisions shall be retained as part of the records of the department;

(c) receive advice in all matters relating to the exercise of his functions from the departmental head of the relevant department who is responsible for the general working of the department.

B. *Responsibilities in connection with the Administrator's Executive Council*

(1) Except as may be otherwise arranged in any particular instance a Ministerial or Assistant Ministerial Member shall in relation to matters within his competence:

(a) Introduce submissions into the Council including proposals for legislation;

(b) Present draft estimates of annual expenditure;

(c) Give effect to decisions made by the Minister or the Administrator after consideration of the advice of the Administrator's Executive Council.

(2) A Ministerial member shall participate in the general functioning of the Council under section 19 of the Papua and New Guinea Act.

(3) With respect to the Administrator's Executive Council an Assistant Ministerial Member may, with the agreement of the Administrator, attend a meeting of the Council, when matters in respect of which he is performing the functions of an Assistant Ministerial Member are under discussion, and may be heard at the meeting.

C. *Responsibilities in connection with the House of Assembly*

A Ministerial or Assistant Ministerial Member shall generally be responsible in the House of Assembly for matters within his competence and in particular:

(a) He shall answer questions and make official statements concerning those matters and by arrangement other matters; and

(b) He shall introduce legislation concerning those matters and by arrangement other matters, being legislation approved by the Administrator's Executive Council or the Minister for External Territories as the case may be, and shall guide the legislation through the proceedings in the House.

[*matter omitted*]

[NAA: A452, 1970/3961]

106   LETTER FROM WALLER TO FURLONGER

Canberra, 21 August 1970

Secret

I have had three or four officers read your paper on New Guinea.[1] Two of them have produced commentaries on it and I attach copies which I think you will find interesting.[2]

I have also read the JPC draft[3] for the Defence Committee. I find it difficult to pinpoint my unhappiness with it. At the same time, I have an uneasy feeling that we have not completely come to grips with what is likely to happen. I suppose the Belgian Congo is the closest analogy and yet, after a period of bloodshed and despite the lack of educated Congolese, the Congo seems to be working reasonably well.

[NAA: A1838, 689/1 PART 6]

---

1   Document 104.

2   For one of these 'commentaries' see Document 107. The substance of the other commentary, by M. W. (Max) Hughes (Acting Head of the DEA Dependent Territories Section), was as follows: 'Mr Furlonger has brought together some of the main problems we face in Papua/New Guinea and this paper contains some perceptive comments on developments there. His general impression seems to be that the Australian Administration has created nothing more than a fragile superstructure which it seems will disintegrate as Australia disengages. I think this an unlikely outcome for the short term although the political structure we will leave behind at independence could collapse later. The assessment that political development is ephemeral and shallow is excessively pessimistic I think. We probably cannot expect anything more than a national political system based on an educated politically-conscious section of the population in the foreseeable future in TPNG. The system will no doubt have undemocratic features and be influenced at the local level by cargo cultism, regionalist feelings and the lack of widespread nationalism as is the case in other countries. But something which is at least workable should emerge. My guess is that the expatriates will build up their "independent" coalition with the indigenous Highland representatives in the House of Assembly into a majority grouping and that power will be transferred to them on self-government. That coalition arrangement should hold together in the short term and provide a majority against the small radical parties which will develop. One can visualise some stability for a period until political opinion comes more under the influence of ideology and the Highlanders decide to go it alone in pursuing their objectives. After that, a breakdown in the political structure, one-party systems, military take-overs etc. seem real possibilities.' Minute, Max Hughes to Waller, 20 August 1970, NAA, A1838, 689/1 Part 6.

3   For the JIC paper, see Document 100.

107   MINUTE FROM BOURCHIER[1] TO WALLER

Canberra, 21 August 1970

SECRET

You asked me to comment on the attached paper.[2]

2.   Mr Furlonger has concluded that much is wrong in TPNG, some of it alarmingly so. I find myself in general agreement.

3.   Although Mr Furlonger would not wish us to draw immediate particularised conclusions from what he has set down, I believe he has provided us with valuable insights of which this Department should take practical account.

4.   In a paper[3] which you saw earlier this year I proposed that the Department of External Affairs might concern itself more closely than it has in the past with Australian Government policy towards TPNG and, in proper cases, with its application. The reasoning of that paper was, briefly, that External Affairs has a strong present interest in PNG because the PNG situation will in due course become a wholly foreign affairs matter. When that happens, all the shortcomings of which we are presently aware will, insofar as they have remained unamended up to independence, carry their adverse influence into the situation with which this Department will then be confronted. In the worst cases, the prospective international relationship is even now being severely prejudiced thereby. It seems reasonable that the Department of External Affairs for this reason, and because its accumulated knowledge of diverse political and social situations is available and at the disposal of the Government, should participate in formulating policy in respect of PNG to the extent that it would be useful to do so. Most of the subjects covered by Mr Furlonger appear to be subjects of legitimate interest to External Affairs, at least to some extent, and would be proper subjects for discussion with the Department of External Territories.

5.   I believe we should seek to establish full and harmonious cooperation between External Affairs and External Territories. This would not only introduce an External Affairs voice into policy formation, as I believe to be essential, but [would also ensure] that a policy impetus [would be][4] greater than that achievable by the two Departments acting individually.

[*matter omitted*][5]

[NAA: A1838, 689/1 PART 6]

---

1   M. G. M. (Murray) Bourchier, Head, Malaysia and Indonesia Section DEA.

2   Document 104.

3   Not published.

4   Editorial insertion.

5   The omitted material contained Bourchier's further observations on Furlonger's paper, including recommendations for the simplification of the PNG legal system; the disadvantages of a presidential system of government; the need to 'ensure that the independent PNG government is capable of looking after itself' and able to prevent PNG 'being plundered' by foreign interests; land issues and expatriate investment; the risks to democratic government posed by low levels of education and awareness; the negative impact of bureaucratic rivalry on the Australian 'intelligence effort' and the need to address this; the potential usefulness of advice and training on special branch functions from Singaporean officials; and the value of training 'senior indigenous officers to as high a degree of sophistication as that of the [indigenous] regular officers in the Pacific Islands Regiment, who are really quite impressive.' With respect to political education, he remarked that 'The "education and hope for the best" principle is largely what it comes down to, and of course a well-educated oligarchy is better than an ill-educated one.' He also remarked that: 'I wonder … whether it might not be worthwhile aiming [for] a crash programme for PNG women—trying for instance to place PNG girls of the prospective ruling class at Australian boarding schools in large numbers—if one accepts the proposition that in any society social change is solidly established only when its women are induced to adopt it.'

108   PRESS RELEASE

Canberra, 23 August 1970

Papua and New Guinea Constitutional Arrangements Now Effective
Statement by the Minister for External Territories, the Hon. C. E. Barnes, MP

The Minister for External Territories, Mr Barnes, today announced that legal instruments giving additional powers to ministerial office holders of the House of Assembly of Papua and New Guinea had been signed and were in effect from 21st August.[1]

Mr Barnes said that the Government's decision to devolve these powers to elected Ministerial and Assistant Ministerial Members had been announced in Port Moresby by the Prime Minister on 6th July.[2]

The instruments are Governor-General's instructions to the Administrator under Section 15 of the Papua and New Guinea Act; a determination under Section 24 by the Minister for External Territories setting out the designations of the offices and the matters in respect of which the ministerial office holders are to perform their functions; and arrangements approved by the Minister under Section 25 detailing the extent to and manner in which the ministerial office holders are to assist in the administration of the government of the Territory.

Mr Barnes said that the instructions to the Administrator provided that in those areas where ministerial office holders have full authority, the Administrator is to act in accordance with the advice tendered to him by the Administrator's Executive Council or a ministerial office holder. Where the advice is tendered by a ministerial office holder the Administrator can accept such advice or ask that the matter be referred to the Administrator's Executive Council for consideration.

The new approved arrangements specify the matters over which the responsible Ministerial or Assistant Ministerial Members exercises full authority.

The arrangements have been prepared on the basis of the illustrative lists in the statement issued by the Minister in the Territory on 6th July[3] and after consultation between the Administration and the Department of External Territories. They were considered, and endorsed, by the Administrator's Executive Council, at a meeting on 19th August.

The Minister stressed that the making of the determination and approved arrangements did not preclude further changes being made in the areas of final authority or re-allocation of offices.

[*matter omitted*]

[NAA: A452, 1970/1716]

---

1   Document 105.

2   See Document 64.

3   For the nature and scope of these additional powers, see Document 48, footnotes 6 & 7.

109   PRESS RELEASE

Port Moresby, 31 August 1970

Statement on Constitutional Change by the Senior Official Member

In the House of Assembly today the Senior Official Member, Mr A. P. J. Newman, made the following statement on constitutional changes in the Territory:

The Prime Minister of Australia in a speech in Port Moresby on 6 July said 'We believe that the time has come when less should be referred to Canberra for decision and more should be retained for decision by the Administrator's Executive Council and by the Ministerial Members who for the most part make up that Council.'[1] Aspects of the Prime Minister's speech have now materialised in the form of:

1.   Governor-General's Instructions to Administrator;

2.   Determination Under Section 24 of Papua and New Guinea Act 1949–1968;

3.   Approved Arrangements Under Section 25 of Papua and New Guinea Act 1949–1968;[2]

Copies of which I now table for the information of Honourable members.

Reference to the Governor-General's instructions to the Administrator makes it clear that under new arrangements Ministerial Members and Assistant Ministerial Members will exercise full authority and accept full responsibility in relation to certain matters and that the powers and functions of the Administrator will be exercised consistently with the said arrangements. It will be further noted that the Administrator is required to act in accordance with any advice given to him by the Administrator's Executive Council in respect of matters on which a Ministerial Member or Assistant Ministerial Member has full responsibility. Further the Administrator in the case of a matter where it is not legally necessary for him to obtain the advice of the Administrator's Executive Council shall either act in accord with any advice tendered to him by Ministerial Members or Assistant Ministerial members or refer the matter to the Administrator's Executive Council. The fact that the Administrator is now required to act in accord with advice given him by the Administrator's Executive Council is illustrative of the emerging authority of that Council.

The Determination under Section 24 of the Papua and new Guinea Act highlights the functions of the specified departments for which Ministerial Members and Assistant Ministerial members will be responsible insofar as the day-to-day administration of those matters are concerned. Again in the approved arrangements under Section 25 of the Papua and New Guinea Act it emerges that a Ministerial Member or Assistant Ministerial Member shall exercise full authority and accept full responsibility in relation to the matters specified in the schedule attached to the document.

The determination goes on to make it clear that in respect of matters not specified in the attachments, a Ministerial Member or Assistant Ministerial Member shall:

(a) be responsible within the framework of broader government policy for decisions regarding policy and for administrative actions of the department or part of the department as may be determined in its day-to-day activities (other than management and public service aspects);

(b) be responsible for the formulation of plans and proposals for departmental, or part of the department as may be determined, expenditure including the formulation of draft departmental estimates.

---

1   See Document 64.

2   See Documents 105 & 108.

It is a requirement of a Ministerial Member or Assistant Ministerial Member that in the performance of his functions he shall refer policy decisions or other matters to the Administrator's Executive Council where he considers it necessary to do so, or the Administrator's Executive Council or the Administrator so directs [*sic*]. Further, he is required to record on papers and recommendations submitted to him by the Department his decisions in writing. Insofar as advice, recommendations, etc. the Ministerial Member or Assistant Ministerial Member in all matters relating to the exercise of his functions shall be advised by the appropriate departmental head.

[*matter omitted*]

What I have just said illustrates in clear terms that Ministerial Members and Assistant Ministerial Members will exercise final authority in many respects and quite clearly emerge as responsible office holders to whom departmental heads are subordinate. It also makes clear that the Administrator's Executive Council in many respects is a responsible body with important final decision and policy making functions. It is also clear that the Official Members of the Administrator's Executive Council are there solely in an advisory role.

[*matter omitted*]

[NAA: A452, 1970/3961]

110   STATEMENT BY BARNES

Canberra, 3 September 1970

Commonwealth Departments and
Instrumentalities in Papua and New Guinea

The Australian Government has begun reviewing the position of Commonwealth departments and instrumentalities performing functions of internal self-government in Papua and New Guinea outside the aegis of the Administration.[1]

The purpose of the review is to prepare a programme for the absorption of their Territory activities in appropriate cases into the PNG Administration.

The review follows on major constitutional changes announced by the Prime Minister, in Port Moresby on 6 July.[2]

The Minister for External Territories, Mr Barnes, said today that an Interdepartmental Committee had been established to undertake the review. The core members of the Committee are representatives of the Department of External Territories, Prime Minister's Department, Public Service Board and the Treasury. At a later date it will include a representative from each particular department or instrumentality in turn when aspects of their activities in the Territory are being considered.

The views of the Administrator's Executive Council would also be sought in the process of the review.

In 1970/71 expenditure by Commonwealth departments and instrumentalities of an economic nature in the Territory is estimated at $14.5m.

[NAA: A452, 1970/3823]

---

1   See Documents 47 (para. 9), 53 & 94.

2   Document 64.

111   LETTER FROM JOHNSON TO HAY

Port Moresby, 9 September 1970

SECRET

I refer to papers relating to the Call Out.[1] The present situation is such that the civil power is well able to cope with any disturbance which seems likely in the immediate future. However, the situation remains such that a future occasion could arise in which military assistance is necessary.

In terms of principle, I believe that the Administrator should have the right to call for assistance from the Army if there is a danger that the civil authority cannot or may not be able to cope with an existing or imminent state of domestic violence. Naturally, such an authority would only be used subject to adequate notification to the Australian Government, but I believe that reference to Cabinet on each such occasion should not be required.

If, however, there are legal problems associated with the continuation of this authority, I would be content if any further recommendation for the use of military forces could be dealt with at very short notice.

[NAA: A452, 1970/4297]

---

1   For background on the call-out question, see especially Documents 79–81, 86–89 & 101.

112   MINUTE FROM COOK[1] TO WALLER

Canberra, 10 September 1970

SECRET

Defence Committee Agendum No. 14/1970:
Review of Defence Forces in Papua/New Guinea

The argument in the JPC paper[2] is developed in this way.

a.   PNG is of abiding strategic significance to Australia and we should consequently aim to ensure that PNG does not come under the dominance of hostile influences.

b.   In this decade, the only possible threat—and it is a very remote one—to PNG and Australia is from or through Indonesia. Nevertheless, it would be imprudent to conclude on the basis of that assessment that the matter of PNG's defence can be left on one side.

c.   It would be possible to defend PNG with Australian forces should a threat develop. But both before and after independence, and in both external aggression and internal security situations, it is to Australia's interest that indigenous forces be deployed first with Australian forces being used only as a last resort.

d.   PNG's own defence forces should accordingly continue to be developed. But development must be modest, having regard to financial and manpower restrictions, and can afford to be deliberate, having regard to the unlikelihood of a threat developing suddenly.

e.   This leads to the conclusion that PNG should have a defence force, with the roles set out at paragraph 30 of the paper, consisting of:

a ground force capable of limited border operations (three mini-battalions, requiring an increase of less than eight per cent on the existing ceiling strength, by about 1975);

a small maritime force (10 patrol boats, a doubling of the number stationed in PNG at present, by about 1980);

and a small tactical transport air force (three Caribous and a communications flight of four small fixed wing aircraft—approximately what the RAAF now has in PNG—by about 1977, with another three Caribous and eighteen helicopters being added in the longer term).

The Threat

2.   Paragraphs 7–13 of the paper were supplied by the NIC.[3] The JPC can challenge NIC's intelligence assessments but in the end is bound by NIC's view. This is to prevent the planners tailoring threat assessments to suit their own needs.

3.   You were, I think, concerned that the internal security threat was under-played. There will be an opportunity to take up this matter in the Defence Committee, which will have before it a longer Intelligence paper.

---

1   M. J. (Michael) Cook, Assistant Secretary, Defence Liaison Branch, DEA.

2   Document 100.

3   National Intelligence Committee.

Internal Security

4.   The JPC worked on the following assumptions.

a.   Primary responsibility for coping with internal security situations should continue to rest with the police.

b.   Consideration of the size and shape of the defence forces should accordingly not be influenced by the internal security threat.

c.   Nevertheless, the defence forces must be available in case of need to back up the police. For that reason, the defence forces—especially the army—should be trained in appropriate techniques, including those not involving the use of firearms.

d.   It was not for the JPC to attempt to determine priorities of finance and manpower as between the defence forces and police. (My own view is that for the time being at least the police should have the higher priority, though not to the extent of doing nothing to develop the ground forces.) Nor was it for the JPC to determine priorities between the development of the defence forces and the development of the economy and social infrastructure of PNG (e.g. education).

e.   Nevertheless, the JPC had regard to PNG's limited resources and competing demands in reaching judgments about the desirable size and shape of the defence forces.

5.   The Defence Committee will have before it a separate paper on internal security. This is not yet available. When it is, I shall do a separate briefing note.

Role of Australia

6.   The JPC did not find it necessary to forecast the formal defence relationship, if any, between Australia and an independent PNG. Nevertheless, we assumed that Australia would go on providing aid to PNG after independence, and that this aid would have a bearing on PNG's ability to maintain defence forces, whether because some Australian aid was earmarked for that purpose or because 'civilian' aid freed PNG's own resources for spending on defence.

7.   It was further recognised in the JPC that it could well be regarded as appropriate for Australian aid to have a special defence component, whether or not publicly so earmarked, because the defence of PNG will continue to be in Australia's direct defence interest even after the achievement of independence and the relinquishment of Australia's legal responsibility for PNG's defence.

Unified Defence Force

8.   The JPC did not think it right to recommend a unified defence force on the Singapore or Canadian model. Nevertheless, the solution put forward by the JPC is a radical departure from the Australian system of separate Services, each with its own Department. That solution is that there should be a centralised command and defence organisation with a common administrative system and common logistic support arrangements, while retaining the separate identity of the individual Service components.

Cost

9.   From the section on Indicative Costs (paragraphs 99–107), it would seem that the total annual cost (maintenance and capital) of the recommended defence forces (with an air-force of 7 aircraft) would be about $15 m.—more in some years, less in others—which is 8% of what was spent in PNG in 1969/70 by the Administration and Commonwealth Departments. This is a high percentage; but by the time of independence it will have been reduced by increases in the PNG Budget. Nevertheless, it is apparent that Australia will need to subsidise the cost

*Top: Malcolm Fraser, the Minister for Defence, 1969–71, and Arthur Tange,
the Secretary of the Defence Department, 1970–79.*

*Bottom: Sir Paul Hasluck, the Governor-General, 1969–74; and
Robert (Bob) Furlonger, Director of the Joint Intelligence Organisation, 1969–72,
and Ambassador to Indonesia, 1972–75.*

[NAA]

Troops of the Australian-led, PNG-recruited Pacific Islands Regiment march through Port Moresby in the late 1960s.

[AUSTRALIAN ARMY INFANTRY MUSEUM/CHIN H. MEEN]

*Members of the Royal Papua New Guinea Constabulary,
the Territory's police force, on parade in the early 1960s.*

[NAA]

Paulias Matane and Philip Bouraga. In October 1970 Matane was appointed as Head of the Department of Business Development, thus becoming the first Papua New Guinean to hold such a position. Also in October 1970, Bouraga became the first Papua New Guinean to attain the rank of District Officer. In March 1972 he became the first Papua New Guinean to serve as a District Commissioner.

These and other appointments of Papua New Guineans to senior roles were part of an effort to speed up the localisation of public sector positions.

[PAPUA NEW GUINEA POST-COURIER]

Dirona Abe, a member of the 1964 House of Assembly and the President of the Rigo Local Government Council, speaks during the visit by the Select Committee on Constitutional Development to Kwikila in February 1971.

[PAPUA NEW GUINEA POST-COURIER]

Top: PNG representatives at the United Nations in 1971. Clockwise from centre: Members of the PNG Administrative Executive Council, Angmai Bilas and Tom Leahy, and Australian officials Richard Rowe, J. Brown and Robin Ashwin. On the left is Ms Eda Weiss, the Committee of 24 representative from Austria.

Bottom: Select Committee members consider designs for the PNG flag in early 1971.

[PHOTOS COURTESY OF DIANNE McINNES]

*Governor-General Sir Paul Hasluck with the new Prime Minister,
William (Billy) McMahon, after the swearing in of the McMahon Ministry
in March 1971. Before replacing Gorton as Prime Minister, McMahon had
served as Minister for Foreign Affairs.*

[NAA]

*PNG officials receiving training in Australia pictured in Canberra in 1972 with, in the
centre, Sere Pitoi, Chairman of the PNG Public Service Board. From the left the trainees
are: Dominic Diya (Foreign Service); John Balagetuna (Foreign Service);
Andrew Yavaib, Forestry; and Benais (Ben) Sabumei, Foreign Service.*

[DFAT]

Top: Oscar Tammur, MHA for Kokopo and the Convenor of the Mataungan Association addresses supporters in the Gazelle Peninsula in early 1971.

Bottom: Also in early 1971, police seek to restrain Mataungan Association protesters.

[PAPUA NEW GUINEA POST-COURIER]

Andrew Peacock replaced Charles Barnes as Minister for External Territories in early February 1972. From left: Andrew Wabiria, MHA for Koroba and Assistant Ministerial Member for Lands, Surveys and Mines; Andrew Peacock; and a third Andrew, Andrew Andaja, President of the Tari Council and a candidate in the House of Assembly elections, during a visit by Peacock to Koroba.

[PAPUA NEW GUINEA POST-COURIER]

Peacock at a coastal village near Wewak in 1972.

[DFAT]

of the PNG defence forces either directly or indirectly. (At present all defence forces costs in PNG—including the PIR—are borne on the Australian budget.)

[NAA: A1838, 936/4/16 PART 5]

113   MEMORANDUM FROM HARDERS TO DEFENCE

Canberra, 11 September 1970

SECRET

Territory of Papua and New Guinea: Call-Out of Defence Force

I refer to your memorandum dated 9 September, 1970,[1] concerning revocation of the Order-in-Council dated 19 July, 1970, by which elements of the Defence Force were called out for the protection of the Territory of Papua and New Guinea against domestic violence. You have asked for guidance as to the criteria to be applied in deciding whether the Order of 19 July should be revoked.

2.   The continued operation of the Order-in-Council and the timing of the revocation of the Order involve very important considerations of policy. The sanctions that would apply, if the Order is to continue in force, would be political, rather than legal, in the sense that the legal validity of the Order or of action taken under it could not, in my view, be impugned in a Court. Nevertheless, there are some basic matters of constitutional principle that I think should be noted. These matters were described in a memorandum of advice given by the Attorney-General to His Excellency, the Governor-General, at the time of consideration of the recommendation made by your Minister to the Executive Council for the calling-out of elements of the Defence Force in aid of the civil power in the Territory of New Guinea.[2] The Attorney-General's memorandum included a paragraph reading as follows:

'I turn now to consider the circumstances that would justify a recommendation by the Executive Council for the issue of an Order-in-Council "calling out" elements of the Defence Force for the suppression of domestic violence in New Guinea. There is no statutory provision that is directly applicable. In this situation, I have concluded that the fundamental constitutional principle of the primacy of the civil authority requires that military forces should not be called out to assist in the suppression of domestic violence or of imminent domestic violence unless the civil arm of Government is reasonably satisfied on the basis of cogent intelligence that the civil authority cannot or may not be able to cope with an existing or imminent state of domestic violence. I do not think that the power to "call-out" the Defence Force is restricted to cases in which domestic violence is actually occurring when the question of call-out is raised. In my opinion, the Executive Council would be justified in recommending the issue of an Order-in-Council and the Governor-General would be required to follow a recommendation by the Executive Council if a situation exists in which there is a clear and strong probability that civil police will be unable by themselves to quell a likely disturbance of public order of a serious character in a Territory of the Commonwealth.'

---

1   Not published. For a list of documents on the call-out question, see Document 111, fn. 1.

2   Document 87.

3.   It would be desirable for you to note carefully the terms in which the Order-in-Council was framed and the circumstances in which it was made, as these were explained in the Explanatory Statement included with the papers submitted to the Governor-General in Council.

4.   The Order called out certain members of the Defence Force 'for the protection of the Territory of New Guinea against domestic violence'. It is relevant to consider therefore, from the point of view both of the terms of the Order and of the rule of constitutional principle (with which the Order, when made, was consistent), whether the risk of domestic violence then foreseen continues to exist, or whether that risk has passed.

5.   Turning to the Explanatory Statement, it is apparent that the making of the Order-in-Council was recommended against the clear risk of violence from a *particular* situation, namely, the squatting of Tolai people on Administration land and the likelihood of violent resistance to efforts by the civil authorities to remove them. You will wish to consider whether that particular situation still exists. If it does not, then the proper course would be revocation of the Order, unless a new, and similarly dangerous, situation has since developed. Even in that case, you would probably wish, having regard to the fact that the original circumstances were placed before Cabinet, to consider with your Minister whether any such new circumstances should not likewise be brought to the attention of Cabinet.

[NAA: A432, 1961/3329 PART 6]

114   LETTER FROM BARNES TO GORTON

Canberra, 16 September 1970

CONFIDENTIAL

I refer to Cabinet Decision No. 484 of 19th July, 1970[1] which authorised a recommendation to be made to the Governor-General for call-out of the defence forces in New Guinea.

The Administrator now advises that the civil police power is well able to cope with any disturbance which seems likely in the immediate future.[2] Accordingly, I consider that it would be appropriate for a further recommendation to be put to the Governor-General revoking the Order-in-Council.

The Administrator has also advised that the situation remains such that a future occasion could arise in which military assistance is necessary.

I am sending a copy of this letter to our colleagues the Minister for Defence, Minister for External Affairs and the Attorney-General.[3]

[NAA: A1838, 689/2 PART 7]

---

1   Document 89.

2   See Document 111.

3   The ministers referred to were Fraser, McMahon and Hughes. Gorton, for his part, replied on 9 October, asking that Barnes 'advise the Administrator that, in the current circumstances, the Government's approval of a requisition should no longer be anticipated in the manner authorised [...] If it should become necessary to requisition the forces, then the approval of the Government should be sought prior to the Administrator's initiating action'. Letter, Gorton to Barnes, 9 October 1970, NAA: A452, 1970/4297.

115   MINUTE FROM ANDERSON TO WALLER

Canberra, 16 September 1970

SECRET

Defence Committee: Report for Cabinet on the Implications of the Use of Military Aid to the Civil Power in Papua/New Guinea

The Report of the Inter-Departmental Committee established by Cabinet to study this question has been completed (Annex 'A')[1] and is to be considered by the Defence Committee on Thursday, 17th September, 1970.

Background

2.   The Report was first considered by the Defence Committee on 5th February, 1970.[2] At that time the Defence Committee felt it could not give adequate consideration to the paper until the Department of External Territories had clarified its attitude on certain points of policy. The Defence Committee also set down its views on some policy considerations relating to the paper (Annex 'B').[3]

3.   Further work on the IDC Report was overtaken by the request for a call-out of the PIR for possible use in the Gazelle Peninsula. The comments of the Defence Committee (Annex 'C')[4] and the text of the Cabinet decision (Annex D)[5] concerning that request are attached. At the request of the Minister for Defence, the IDC has since reconvened and revised the Report in the light of the Defence Committee's comments and the Government's decision to move to a call-out of the PIR on 19th July, 1970. Defence and External Territories have in mind that the Report will be taken to Cabinet by the Minister for External Territories for consideration together with the comments of the Defence Committee.

The Report

4.   As members of the Interdepartmental Committee, we agreed to the Report as it satisfactorily presents the major External Affairs considerations (paragraph 9) and emphasises military and legal difficulties standing in the way of the use of the military forces except in a last resort situation in the Territory.

5.   The Report recommends that requests for call-out and requisitions should be forwarded to the Prime Minister, the Minister for Defence and the Minister for External Affairs jointly (paragraph 47). The previous Report (and the Defence Committee) stopped short of a clear recommendation that our Minister should be among Ministers consulted as a matter of course on proposals to use the military forces, and we considered securing a recommendation for his inclusion to be an important objective in the Committee. Now that the Government has shown itself prepared to authorise the use of the PIR in one instance, we feel that it will be important to ensure that the Minister has an opportunity to consider other requests at an early stage.

6.   In the matter of associating any decision taken with local opinion in the Territory, we have included a new paragraph 12 in the Report, which is also reflected in the recommendation on

---

1   Not published.
2   See Document 80, fn. 2.
3   Not published.
4   Document 80.
5   Document 89.

procedures to authorise the use of troops in paragraph 47. This formula varies slightly from the Defence Committee's recommendation (5th February Meeting—paragraph 10(e)). We think that the Administrator's Executive Council is the appropriate representative body in the Territory (representing the executive arm of Government) rather than the House of Assembly.

7.   A basic issue upon which Departments disagree underlies the Report, but is not highlighted. External Territories takes the view that the PIR would be something of a luxury for the Territory if it performed only pure military functions. They feel that it could legitimately be called upon to support the police in internal security situations where such interventions might not be acceptable in developed countries such as Australia. External Territories argue that armies have this role in other developing countries and that the alternative is expenditure on developing the police which would be excessive in terms of the capacity of Papua/New Guinea. They do, however, agree that the PIR's prime role is external defence and that its use in internal security situations should be as a last resort. This question will be thrown up in another submission to the Defence Committee on proposals to increase the size of the defence forces in the Territory, but it is closely related to the present Report.

8.   We doubt the wisdom of involving the PIR too far in internal security matters. The existence of an adequate defence force to provide against external security threats will contribute to political stability in TPNG and further Australia's own defence interests. A defence force with day-to-day responsibilities for maintaining internal order could itself be unstable and more prone to look to an internal political role at some stage. In our view, the police should be the force to be developed to deal with foreseeable internal security problems short of serious insurgencies or riots; and the PIR should only be called on in emergencies.

9.   Should you wish to emphasise further the serious international implications of the use of the PIR in a civil role in TPNG, you could develop the point in the Report that the PIR is legally constituted as part of the Australian Army. As long as Australia retains responsibility for the defence and internal security of Papua/New Guinea, a PIR intervention is likely to be seen internationally as an Australian initiative. Afro-Asian opinion is particularly sensitive in the matter of military activities by the Administering powers in dependent territories. There is a standing sub-committee of the Committee of twenty-four which is concerned exclusively with the subject. It could also be noted that when criticising our administration at the United Nations, the Russians have made a point of attempting to demonstrate that military installations in Papua/New Guinea serve sinister colonial purposes.

[NAA: A1838, 936/3/21 PART 4]

116   MINUTE BY PMD[1]

Canberra, 16 September 1970

Secret

Defence Committee Agendum 14/1970
Review of Defence Forces in Papua/New Guinea

In accordance with the decision (flagged on file herewith) by the Defence Committee in 1968 the Joint Planning Committee has reviewed the structure of the Papua/New Guinea Defence Forces having regard to the country's future needs and circumstances.[2] The Defence Committee desired that the review take into account Papua/New Guinea's economic and social conditions, strategic considerations affecting Australia, the future relationships between Papua/New Guinea Forces and the Australian Defence structure and the desirability of developing unified defence forces.

2.   The Joint Planning Committee has agreed (see paras 108 and 109) that there is no current threat to the Territory which demands the substantial and immediate increase in its Defence Forces, but points out that because of Australia's strategic interest in Papua/New Guinea, the prospect of early independence and the probability that we will have a defence obligation after independence, it is in our interests that the indigenous forces be developed as they would be the first line of defence of the Territory. The Committee recognises that it is likely that Australia will have to bear the main burden of defence expenditure for the Territory for some years to come.

[*matter omitted*]

Departmental View

5.   We are in agreement with the general direction of the recommendations made by the Joint Planning Committee. However, we feel they need to be qualified in some respects especially having in mind the additional (and probably understated) costs involved, the possible future relationship of the Australian defence forces to those of Papua/New Guinea and the desirability of adequate access for Australian forces to the defence infrastructure of Papua/New Guinea. An important priority now is to establish the necessary infrastructure—logistics, command and training—to enable Australia to maintain an effective support of the Territory defence forces.

6.   We favour the proposals in paragraphs 49–52 to foster within the Territory the knowledge of and expertise in defence matters at the legislative and administrative levels and suggest that a beginning should be made on this at an early date. In this respect it would also seem to be desirable that there should be appropriate consultation with the Territory authorities as the new defence proposals are developed and implemented.

7.   We support the objective of developing the indigenous forces of the Territory. However we would caution that we should not hasten this too quickly if it should involve a significant reduction in the opportunities for training and experience of Australian personnel in Territory conditions.

8.   The proposal in regard to the PIR has our support; and we see merit in the mini-airforce proposal. However, we suggest that any expansion beyond a force of seven aircraft should be

---

1   Author not identified.

2   Document 100.

reconsidered again say in 1974/75. We do, however, support any necessary action on airforce infrastructure e.g. upgrading at Wewak (paragraph 97). Similarly, the Navy has not made a clear cut case for the doubling of its fleet by 1980. In fact, in paragraph 72 it is stated that there is no immediate need for expansion. Some increase will no doubt be justified over this period so perhaps in this regard approval in principle could be given with the proviso that detailed cases must be presented before the purchase and manning of any additional vessels will be approved. In this situation the proposed development of naval bases would perhaps also deserve some closer study especially in regard to the possible value of the bases for the RAN,[3] if it should become involved in the defence of the Territory (and indirectly Australia).

9.   The timing of independence could still be some years off and as indicated in paragraph 5 of the report the nature of the defence relationship with Australia after independence cannot be clearly foreseen. However, having regard to the economic situation likely to then obtain in the Territory and the almost certain continuing reliance on Australia for significant financial aid for many years, it seems that, provided our general relationship with the people of the Territory continues on a reasonably cordial basis, we should be in a position to considerably influence the nature of their defence arrangements if we so desire. In this situation we believe the defence interests of Australia would best be served—at least into the 80's—if the defence policy of the Territory is tied in with that of Australia as far as practicable and our forces continue to be involved with the forces of the Territory. This would provide a continuing operational relationship between the two forces and excellent training opportunities for Australian personnel which would be most beneficial directly if Australia should be called upon to support the defence of Papua/New Guinea and perhaps more importantly as a means of providing a more effective forward defence for Australia. It should also be possible in these circumstances to play a more direct role in ensuring that the necessary infrastructure requirements are maintained in the Territory to meet our overall needs.

10.   The Committee does not seem to have given adequate consideration to the future working relationship between the Australian and Territory forces. This is a most important matter and one on which we should have or be developing a clear line. It is true that anticipating the future in this regard is by no means easy but we cannot use this as an excuse. We have a responsibility to the people both of the Territory and Australia in this area and our future defence relationship with the Territory will probably be all the more satisfactory if we give a strong lead.

[NAA: A1209, 1969/9045]

---

3   Royal Australian Navy.

117   MINUTE BY DEFENCE COMMITTEE[1]

Canberra, 21 September 1970

19/1970. SECRET

Review of Defence Forces in Papua/New Guinea

The Defence Committee had for consideration Joint Planning Committee Report No. 17/1970[2] which had been prepared in accordance with a request by the Defence Committee in Minute 42 of 1968.

2.   The Committee did not address itself to the detailed analysis in the paper but confined its discussion to broad policies and principles, to general observations, and to the practical steps which might be taken immediately for the development of an indigenous defence force in Papua/New Guinea after independence which would be suitable to its internal and external requirements.

3.   The Committee noted that the paper assumed a high degree of cooperation by the Government of independent Papua/New Guinea towards Australia, and that this could not be taken for granted.

4.   The Committee also recognised that we do not have any indication of what level or kind of force indigenous opinion would want as there had not been any consultation. The Committee considered that it would be premature to accept at this stage the arguments for three independent Services and the kind of organisation recommended. Ideas in the JPC report could be considered later as indigenous attitudes emerged, and as the requirements and economic capabilities of the Territory and the priority to be given to Armed Services became clearer. Nevertheless the size of the force proposed by the JPC does give perspective to the requirement in terms of orders of cost and of the training which should be carried out before independence. Assuming that TPNG would continue to look at Australia for help after independence, the Committee considered that a reasonable amount of training should be commenced now.

5.   A view was expressed that any contribution that Australia may make in the future by way of training and in respect of the shape, size and organisation of a defence force for TPNG would be increasingly influenced by indigenous thought as they move towards independence. Attempts to offer them a mirror image of our three Services and Defence Organisation may not be in the best interests of Papua and New Guinea and planners should not be burdened with preconceived ideas. It was also pointed out that, after independence, the Papua/New Guinea Government will decide the way the Army will be used for internal security and its views on legal and other aspects may not remain identified with those of the Australian Government now. Whatever the answers to these questions may be the role of the Police will be vital.

6.   The Committee agreed that the extent of financial contribution by Australia after independence is crucial. It will presumably affect the priority the Papua/New Guinea Government will give to defence spending. It was the view of the Secretary, Department of External Territories that if the Territory were to be left to finance a defence force from its own limited resources, the role of the Army in internal security would become a major issue; the Territory could not afford both a Police force and a Defence force from within its own resources.

---

1   Those present were Tange, General Sir John Wilton, Chair of the Chiefs of Staff, Lt General Sir Thomas Daly, Chief of the General Staff, Vice Admiral Sir Victor Smith, Chief of Naval Staff, Air Marshal C. T. Hannah, Chief of the Air Staff. Also in attendance were Hay, Waller and D. R. S. Craik (Deputy Secretary, the Treasury.

2   Document 100.

7.   The Committee agreed that the strategic importance of TPNG to Australia was not in question and generally endorsed paras 14–18 of the JPC report. It is in Australia's interest that an independent TPNG should remain well disposed towards Australia. It would serve our defence interests if TPNG should seek an understanding or an arrangement on defence matters. Although Australia has no legal obligation to give to Papua/New Guinea a defence capability, there is a general expectation that we should. In this regard it is important that the PIR should be seen as identified with TPNG and Australia should endeavour to develop a great indigenous awareness of the need for defence preparation and expenditure.

8.   For the reasons set out in previous paragraphs a start should be made in the direction of consulting indigenous opinion. It would be helpful to bring both the Administration Council and TPNG public servants into the study process. As consultation with TPNG leaders would imply Australian Government financial assistance post independence, and as discussion of possible levels of Papua/New Guinea forces and equipment post independence would arouse public interest and discussion of Australian Government intentions, Ministerial approval would be required.

9.   The Committee decided that in the light of its discussion and the propositions canvassed to remit the JPC paper to a Working Group which should:-

(a) prepare proposals for further training of indigenes in some areas of military capability, such as air transport, operation of naval patrol boats, and intelligence. It should also indicate what flexibility is needed in the limitations laid down by Cabinet in respect of the manpower ceiling for the PIR to enable the recruitment of more indigenes for preparatory training and the further indigenisation of the PIR;

(b) consider the extent and methods of consultation with local TPNG opinion on the matters referred to in paragraph 8 above; and,

(c) present the currently approved statement of the strategic importance of New Guinea to demonstrate that any military capability possessed by Papua/New Guinea would serve the defence interests of Australia.

10. On the basis of the foregoing a paper should be submitted to the Minister for Defence, after consultation with the Services, recommending the lines of an approach to the Cabinet on the foregoing matters.

11. The Working Group which should undertake this study should comprise:

Director Joint Staff, or his representative
Defence Planning
Department of External Territories
Army

Navy and Air representatives are to be consulted when matters affecting their particular Service are being considered.

12. At the request of the Secretary, Department of External Territories the Committee also recommended that the Group should examine the potentialities, having regard to the law and other aspects, of arriving at an arrangement whereby a Ministerial office holder in TPNG could be given some functions in relation to military activities and intentions in Papua/New Guinea. The Committee recognised that at the time deemed appropriate it will be desirable, with Government approval, to institute a process of association of a responsible indigene Minister with Service activities in the Territory and with Defence policy and the objectives that both are serving. It was realised, however, that this involved constitutional and political questions needing careful consideration before submission to the Government.

[NAA: A1209, 1969/9045]

118   LETTER FROM HAY TO JOHNSON

Canberra, 23 September 1970

CONFIDENTIAL

Papua and New Guinea Domestic Citizenship

There has been considerable attention paid recently to citizenship matters. Mr Olewale has called on Australia to spell out its policies on the rights and privileges of Papuans. A recent question in the House of Assembly asked the Administration to take steps to make Papuans aware of their citizenship status and what rights and privileges this entitled them to. Another question in the House of Assembly asked whether consideration had been given to the establishment of a citizenship status which could be enjoyed equally by Papuans and New Guineans and could be conferred on non-indigenes wishing to remain permanently in this country and become citizens of it. In a recent letter, the Speaker of the House, Dr Guise, mentioned the political headaches which could result from Papuans seeking to clarify their rights as Australian citizens. Another aspect of citizenship was raised in representations by the Highland Farmers' and Settlers' Association and Dr Guise which sought to establish whether Australians in the Territory after Independence could retain their Australian citizenship while at the same time taking on the citizenship of the new country.

2.   Two basic problems seem to be involved; the position of Papuans as Australian citizens and the place of non-indigenous people in Territory society after Independence. About five years ago much work was done here and in the Territory on the possibility of introducing a domestic Papua and New Guinea citizenship as a means of overcoming such difficulties. In view of recent developments it seems timely to look at this possibility afresh.

3.   A working paper was forwarded with departmental memorandum 61/2457 of 17th February 1964 and detailed comments were made by the Territory's Legislative Draftsman, Mr C. J. Lynch, contained in CLO 2-9-163 of 3rd March 1964, which was conveyed to the Department under cover of a memorandum from the Administrator dated 6th March 1964.[1] Comments were also obtained from the Department of Immigration and the Attorney-General's Department.

4.   It seems from the advising given by the Attorney-General's Department that the House of Assembly has the power to initiate legislation to provide for a separate Papua and New Guinea citizenship of a domestic kind which would not affect the present citizenship status of the inhabitants of the Territory in international law. The advising also confirmed that Australians could acquire a Territory domestic citizenship without losing their Australian citizenship. There are a number of precedents for citizenship of this kind being established for the people of non-self-governing territories, e.g., the Rhodesias and Singapore.

Arguments in Favour of Creating Domestic Citizenship

5.   There would seem to be some important advantages in creating a domestic citizenship. Depending partly on the type of citizenship proposed, it could be expected to contribute in some measure to developing national consciousness. Although it would not alter the position of Papuans as Australian citizens in international law, it could be valuable as a means of playing down the separateness of Papuans. Potentially, it would give non-indigenous people a means of identifying themselves with the Territory as a first step towards gaining recognition

---

1   These documents not published.

as true members of the future independent New Guinea state. It would be a further sign of Australia's intention to develop the Territory for independence.

6.   The degree to which a domestic citizenship would give these advantages would depend of course on the nature of the citizenship but whatever its nature it would have to be recognised that it would be impossible to meet all anticipated needs. It would not really resolve the position of Papuans as Australian citizens since, unless their position as Australian citizen was changed to that of Australian Protected Person by amendments to the Nationality and Citizenship Act (a move which would be likely to create far more problems than it would solve), they would remain Australian citizens under international law. It would not change the requirement that Papuans and New Guineans must obtain permission to enter Australia. Nor would it really satisfy the European settlers who are looking for an assurance that their Australian citizenship will continue after independence irrespective of the citizenship arrangements which are made by the independent government. Nevertheless, if properly handled the introduction of domestic citizenship would, it is thought, be valuable in promoting national unity and preparing the ground for citizenship arrangements which would take care of the problem envisaged above.

7.   It might also have other less important but valuable advantages such as providing a means of defining who is eligible for permanent appointment to the Territory Public Service, to stand for public office or to vote.

8.   Some thought has been given to whether a domestic citizenship could be used to define who is eligible to take up special share issues such as the 20% equity held by the Administration in BCPL[2] or the proposed placement by Bougainville Mining Ltd in about March 1971 of a limited number of shares in the Territory. If it is decided to limit share issues associated with the Administration's 20% equity in BCPL to Papuans and New Guineans, the proposed citizenship would not provide an appropriate definition of eligibility since it is envisaged that the citizenship would be open to expatriates as well as indigenes. It may be that the citizenship would provide an appropriate definition of eligibility for the purpose of any Bougainville Mining Ltd shares which might be made available to Territory residents as it is understood that the Company is considering making the Territory parcel of shares available to a limited number of expatriates as well as indigenes. These are questions which need not be resolved immediately but might be borne in mind in considering the nature of any Territory citizenship.

9.   It would seem important to associate significant rights and privileges with the new citizenship and to provide clearly for some form of preference for local citizens or non-citizens. As Mr Lynch suggested in his paper, to do otherwise would be to make the new citizenship quite meaningless. In addition it seems desirable to make the domestic citizenship something that a non-indigenous person cannot obtain too easily and must consciously take steps to acquire rather than acquire automatically. It is suggested that this would give the new citizenship a meaning and a prestige which it might not otherwise have, and would increase the likelihood of a future independent government recognising expatriate holders of the domestic citizenship as having a permanent place in the Territory.

10. In line with the thinking above, it is suggested that the new citizenship should be conferred *automatically* only on people born in the Territory and there should be provision for the automatic loss of the citizenship in cases where people leave the Territory to reside permanently elsewhere, e.g. children born in the Territory of immigrant parentage who move permanently to Australia or elsewhere. It is further suggested that immigrants should be able to acquire the new citizenship only after continuous residence in the territory, of, say, seven years (including leave, education outside Territory, etc.) by making application to the responsible Ministerial Member who would decide on the granting of citizenship according to criteria laid down in the Territory legislation.

---

2   Bougainville Copper Pty Ltd.

Passports

11. In his paper Mr Lynch drew attention to the fact that the Citizenship of Western Samoa Ordinance 1959 provided for the issuing of Western Samoan passports while Western Samoa was still a dependent Territory.

12. It is suggested that there might be administrative and presentational advantages in providing for the issue of Territory passports. It is understood that it is proposed shortly to issue a 'Declaration as to Status' in similar form to a passport to give effect to the Voutas amendments to the Migration Ordinance. It seems that only minor amendments would be needed to convert this document into a passport which could be used not only for entry to Australia but also for international visits. To get over the problem of the citizens of a dependent territory travelling abroad on their own passports it could be made clear in the passport that they are travelling under the protection of the Australian Government. The issuing of Territory passports would be a further indication of Australia's intention to develop the Territory for Independence. It would also provide a convenient and logical document for travel to Australia which would emphasise the separateness of the Territory and its people from Australia.

Next Steps

13. It is suggested that the next step towards the consideration of a Territory domestic citizenship might be a meeting in Canberra between officers of the Administration, External Territories, Immigration and Attorney-General's Department. If you agree, a paper comprising Administration and Departmental thoughts and proposals could be circulated to the Commonwealth authorities involved. The next step would then be a paper to the AEC. Approval for the drafting of a Territory Citizenship Ordinance not inconsistent with the Australian Act could then be sought from the Ministers of External Territories and Immigration to the full Cabinet.

14. Your comments would be appreciated.

[NAA: A452, 1970/1453]

119   MINUTE BY DEFENCE COMMITTEE[1]

Canberra, 24 September 1970

20/1970. Secret

Military Aid to the Civil Power in the Territory of Papua and New Guinea

The Defence Committee had before it an analysis by an inter-departmental Committee set up by Cabinet Decision No. 1044 of 20 May 1969[2] to report on the implications of the deployment of the PIR to guard important points or as a last resort to back up the Royal Papua/New Guinea Constabulatory if this should become necessary to maintain public order.

2.   The Defence Committee emphasised that fundamental to any consideration of the use of the PIR in aid of the civil power is the fact that the responsibility for law enforcement in the Territory is with the Police. The Police force should be given the capability of containing most internal security situations. The main emphasis should therefore be on building up an efficient Police force as quickly as possible to reduce to the minimum any requirement for the use of the PIR.

3.   Internationally, as well as domestically, it could be embarrassing for Australia to have a Defence force, controlled and paid for by Australia, involved in a situation of violence in Papua/New Guinea. Nevertheless, as a practical matter, the prevention of bloodshed, and prevention of spread of violence, is also important for domestic and international reasons. Having this in mind, the Committee could envisage a variety of circumstances where the PIR might justifiably be used to aid the civil power. For example, if the Police were deployed to one area, thus leaving other areas relatively unprotected, the PIR could be used without a call-out. At the other end of the scale, the PIR could, in a dire emergency, be called out (after due legal process) for the suppression of domestic violence. This could involve the use of lethal weapons. There are various intermediate situations—e.g. guarding of key points—and the question is whether provision should be made to enable the PIR to be used in circumstances short of call-out.

4.   In circumstances short of a call-out, the legal rights of a soldier are no more than those of a private citizen. Therefore if a soldier takes action involving the use of force, he could be liable for action in the civil courts. For example, he would be limited legally, if an unruly group began damaging property, to calling the Police. A Policeman could call on the soldier to assist him in making arrests. In a cordon and search operation where the Army provide a cordon while the Police conduct the search, members of the PIR could not legally detain a person attempting to break the cordon. The Committee could envisage some situations, such as logistic support, where legal backing would not be necessary. There could also be circumstances such as a guard duty or crowd control when the mere presence of the PIR would act as a deterrent. It could not be assumed however that an incident would not occur, calling for a forcible reaction, nor could it be assumed that a Policeman would always be available to make an arrest. Additional legal provision is therefore required if the PIR is to carry out such ancillary tasks in circumstances short of a call-out. In this regard the suggestion was made

---

1   Those present were Tange (Chair), General Sir John Wilton, Chair, Chiefs of Staff, Lt General Sir Thomas Daly, Chief of the General Staff, Vice Admiral Sir Victor Smith, Chief of the Naval Staff and Air Marshal C. T. Hannah, Chief of the Air Staff. Also in attendance were Hay, Waller, Bunting, Harders and Craik. The meeting was actually held on 17 September.

2   See Stuart Doran, (ed.), *Documents on Australian Foreign Policy: Australia and Papua New Guinea, 1966–1969*, Department of Foreign Affairs and Trade, Canberra, 2006, Document 273.

that it may be possible, with existing legislation, to swear in members of the PIR as special constables, and thus overcome the legal obstacles. If the use of the PIR for these purposes is approved, it would be important for the role and legal status of the PIR to be publicly defined.

5.   The Committee agreed that whatever the circumstances, with or without a call-out, the principle of a graduated response with minimum force should apply. The Chief of the General Staff [CGS] expressed the view that, in the absence of legal backing, in situations short of domestic violence, it would be preferable to use the PIR in conjunction with the Police, who would possess the necessary powers of arrest, search etc., thus enabling some Police to be released for duty elsewhere. If a graduated response were needed, the Police because of the numbers, training and equipment, would be better suited for this role, than the PIR. The CGS expressed reservations with regard to employing the PIR in any situation without first investing them with the legal powers needed to enable them to deal with all likely developments.

6.   The Committee agreed that the PIR would need to be provided with riot control equipment and trained properly for these tasks.

[*matter omitted*]

9.   The Defence Committee endorsed the broad principles set out in the inter-departmental Committee analysis, and:

a.   recognised that provided adequate new steps are taken to furnish forces with legal powers, and provided the necessary measures are taken in respect of training, circumstances are conceivable, before a call-out, in which the PIR might be made available, with proper authority and control, to support the civil power. These potentialities, which are analysed in the report by the inter-departmental Committee, are subject to the amendments and reservations referred to in para 7 f. above;

b.   emphasised the view that the Constabulary of the Territory, and any developments there may be in its organisation, weapons and training, should continue to be the principal means of maintaining law and order in the Territory. In this connection the Defence Committee noted that the use of a well trained, well equipped and disciplined Police force in an internal security situation of graduated response, up to and including the use of lethal weapons would carry with it other advantages. It would avoid the risk that the first lethal action would be by the PIR and the consequent domestic and international opinion which would inevitably be aroused;

c.   emphasised that its discussion and comments and observations were addressed to the pre-independence situation; and

d.   suggested that the Secretary, Department of External Territories and the Secretary, Department of Defence, discuss procedures for bringing these views before Cabinet.

[NAA: A1838, 689/2 PART 7]

120   MINUTE BY DEFENCE COMMITTEE[1]

Canberra, 25 September 1970

18/1970. SECRET

Intelligence in New Guinea

The Defence Committee had before it a report[2] submitted by the Director JIO on the degree to which the Defence Committee's need for intelligence in Papua/New Guinea is being met.

2.   The Committee expressed general agreement with the recommendations in the report subject to the following observations and qualifications.

The need for a strong intelligence committee in Papua/New Guinea is not in question, but equally important is the requirement for skilled supporting staff with the ability to collate and assess intelligence;

All sources of raw intelligence must be exploited to make the intelligence staff fully effective. Collecting agencies should be so directed and the Chairman of the Intelligence Committee should be given authority for this purpose;

Communications in the Territory should be developed to improve the security, speed and the inter-change of information;

There was a need for weekly assessments and for as much continuity in membership as possible [...];

[*matter omitted*]

3.   The Defence Committee:

a. noted the situation in paragraph 11 of the report regarding the Special Branch and endorsed the need for urgent agreement between the Department of External Territories and ASIO on its re-structuring and strengthening;

b. endorsed the following proposals in relation to the Territory Intelligence Committee:

(i)   the change in its title to 'Papua New Guinea Intelligence Committee' [PNGIC];

(ii) the continuance of the existing Terms of Reference *mutatis mutandis*;[3]

---

1   Those present were Tange (Chair), Furlonger, General Sir John Wilton, Chair, Chiefs of Staff, Lt General Sir Thomas Daly, Chief of the General Staff, Vice Admiral Sir Victor Smith, Chief of the Naval Staff and Air Marshal C. T. Hannah, Chief of the Air Staff. Also in attendance were Hay, Waller, Craik and Director-General of the Australian Security Intelligence Organisation (ASIO) Peter Barbour. The meeting was held on 17 September.

2   The report reviewed arrangements for intelligence in the Territory, and recommended that the Defence Committee note the need for urgent agreement between the departments and agencies concerned on the restructuring of the Special Branch. It added that the 'Special Branch needs to be reconstructed and expanded, both in respect to its staff and its functions'. It also recommended changing the title of the Committee to 'Administrator's Intelligence Committee (AIC)'; that the Committee retain, with some minor adjustments, the terms of reference which had been approved by Ministers in 1964; that the full-time Committee Chairman be a senior officer with wide PNG experience and direct access to the Administrator, and with sufficient authority to ensure that the various Commonwealth and Administration departments and agencies engaged in the Territory would 'pass to him and his staff all relevant intelligence information'; that the staff of the Committee be strengthened to comprise five professional staff, seconded for two year periods from Australia, and three support staff; and that the Committee henceforth produce two weekly reports, one highly classified for a senior audience and one less highly-classified intended 'for more general purposes'. JIO, 'Intelligence in Papua–New Guinea', 14 September 1970, NAA: A452, 1970/4671.

3   'with things changed that must be changed'.

[*matter omitted*]

> (v) the production by the PNGIC of a brief weekly report for high level audiences in Canberra and Port Moresby, and a less highly classified report for more general purposes (paragraph 16 of the report);
>
> c. noted the concept […] set out in paragraph 22 of the report in relation to the future development of the intelligence system in PNG;
>
> d. observed that organisations in Australia with expertise in intelligence matters should place at the disposal of the PNGIC training and other facilities which they may have available; and
>
> e. emphasised the need for the provision to the PNGIC of all relevant information collected by the various intelligence and other agencies in the Territory.

[NAA: A452, 1970/4671]

121   TELEX FROM HAY TO JOHNSON

Canberra, 20 October 1970

10319. SECRET

Your secret LH149 of 9th September 1970[1] refers. The Prime Minister has asked the Minister for External Territories to advise you that, in the current circumstances, the Government's approval of a requisition should no longer be anticipated in the manner authorised by Cabinet on 19th July 1970[2] and set down in paragraph 5 of our secret 7132 of same date.[3]

This means that for the time being the Order-in-Council will not be revoked but if it should become necessary to requisition forces the approval of Ministers should be obtained before you issue any requisition on the Commander, PNG Command.

[*matter omitted*]

[NAA: A452, 1970/4297]

---

1   Document 111.

2   Document 89.

3   Document 91.

122   LETTER FROM FRASER TO BARNES

Canberra, 10 November 1970

SECRET

The Defence Committee recently considered and broadly endorsed the analysis by the Inter-departmental Committee set up by Cabinet Decision No. 1044 of 20th May, 1969 to report on the implications of the use of the PIR to guard important points or as a last resort to back up the Royal Papuan and New Guinea Constabulary if this should become necessary to maintain public order.[1]

I understand that the report of the Inter-departmental Committee is now being amended in the light of some particular suggestions by the Defence Committee. As to the further handling of the report, I see no current need to bring the matter before Cabinet, but I suggest we review the position again early in the New Year. I hope you can agree to this.

There are however two aspects arising from the report which I consider need not await its final clearance. These are the training and equipping of the Pacific Islands Regiment to fulfil its role of contributing, if authorised, to the internal security of the Territory of Papua and New Guinea.

Prior to the Prime Minister's recent visit to Rabaul the Army had no authority to train the Regiment in this role nor does it have stocks of special riot control equipment. Following discussions which I had with the Prime Minister before his visit to Papua and New Guinea, it was agreed that the Army should be authorised to carry out some training and indoctrination of elements of the Pacific Islands Regiment for possible use in a crowd control situation in Rabaul on the basis that such training for this limited role should not be taken to preclude training for the exercise of their normal capabilities. This training has continued, of course, following the call-out Order of 19th July, 1970.[2]

In its consideration of the report of the Inter-departmental Committee, the Defence Committee emphasised that fundamental to any consideration of the use of the PIR in aid of the civil power is the fact that the responsibility for law enforcement in the Territory is with the Police. Nevertheless the Defence Committee envisages a variety of circumstances where the PIR might justifiably be used to aid the civil power. In agreeing that the PIR would need to be provided with riot control equipment and trained properly for such tasks the Defence Committee has observed that:

'A situation can be contemplated in which the PIR would use, subject to some important stipulations, riot control weapons rather than lethal weapons. The stipulations are the existence of adequate legal power and procedures covering the use of weapons, and adequate prior training in the use of such weapons and in techniques. The military officer in command on the spot must make the decision as to the weapons to be used subject to the principle of minimum force appropriate to the situation.'

In order to remove any doubt as to the authority of the Army to do so I have approved the continuation of training for the PIR in its internal security role including the use of riot control weapons and techniques and the procurement by the Army of adequate stocks of appropriate riot control equipment for the PIR.

---

1   See Document 119.

2   See Documents 88, 89 & 90.

In informing the Minister for the Army of this approval, I have stressed that this training should take the form of a carefully prepared programme phased in with the normal training of the PIR. It should be carried out without publicity but in the event of the programme attracting public interest I would envisage that enquiries would be handled by Army in low-key along the following lines.

> 'Training in crowd control methods is being undertaken by elements of the Pacific Islands Regiment. It is in keeping with the maintenance of a well-balanced force so that both Police, and Army if required, will have members available who are trained in techniques of maintaining order with a minimum of disruption to the safety of people and property.'

[NAA: A452, 1970/4297]

123   MINUTE FROM GREENWELL TO HAY

Canberra, 13 November 1970

UNCLASSIFIED

New Constitutional Arrangements

We have attempted to set out the new constitutional arrangements in chart form. Chart 1 deals with the Administration proper; Chart 2 with special groupings in the Territory.

Notes

A. *Specified Matters*

(1) The effect of the Governor-General's instruction to the Administrator[1] is that in the specified matters the AEC acts in a similar role to the Cabinet/Executive Council. Thus the Administrator accepts the advice tendered to him in the same way as, for example, the Governor-General accepts the Minister's recommendation on the appointment of a Judge. The only limitation would be if the Governor-General gave a special instruction to the Administrator that he was not to accept the advice tendered to him.

(2) In specified matters the role of the Department is substantially changed. In future it should act as a channel between the Administration and the Commonwealth or States and to keep itself briefed so as to be able to keep the Minister informed and advise at the time of the annual budgetary negotiations. The Department would give the Administration assistance on request.

(3) If it is proposed that a matter in the area of final local responsibility should be financed from the development grant, then Ministerial approval is required and the 'oversight' provisions set out in the Finance paper apply.

B. *Other Matters*

(4) In non-specified areas the functions of the AEC remain as in section 19 of the Papua and New Guinea Act. This draws a distinction between giving advice on matters referred to the Council by the Administrator (or in accordance with an Ordinance) and the discussion of matters submitted to it.

Introduction for discussion is designed to enable the Administrator to sound out the views of the Council as part of the process of formulating policy. Prior clearance with the Minister is not a requirement.

Advice should not however be sought from the Council on any matter of policy without prior approval from the Minister. Otherwise the Minister may be faced with advice from the AEC which he does not wish to accept and in circumstances where the full implications of non-acceptance have not been considered by him.

(5) While the new constitutional arrangements involve no basic change in the respective functions of the Department and the Administration in matters in which the Commonwealth retains final responsibility, working arrangements need to have regard inter alia to:

(a) the views of the AEC;

(b) the views of a ministerial office holder who has day-to-day (as opposed to final) responsibility.

---

1   See Document 105.

It is expected that in placing policy recommendations before the Minister his Department will have regard to the views and opinions of the Commonwealth Departments and Ministers. As stated in Secretary's message to officers the Department's object will be to work towards joint submissions by the Department and Administration.

General

(6) Chart 1 sets out the lines of responsibility of Departmental Heads, Ministerial Office Holders and the AEC. In specified matters a Departmental Head works to the Ministerial Office Holder as the Permanent Head of a Commonwealth Department works to his Minister (i.e. he is responsible for advising the Ministerial Office Holder). A Departmental Head has to accept the decision of his Minister; the Administrator may, however, have the matter referred to the AEC.

In non-specific matters, where there is a Ministerial office holder with day-to-day responsibility, the Administrator, in making his decision, is not prevented from asking to see the advice of the Departmental Head and any other relevant advice on the matter. This action should result from the initiative of the Administrator and should not be construed as permitting the Departmental Head whose advice has been overruled by the Ministerial office holder, to approach the Administrator.

(7) The Treasurer has a unique role. Since he is responsible for the expenditure of so much money provided by the Commonwealth it remains appropriate for this function to continue to be held by an official. At the same time an essential part of the present arrangements is that, in the matters not financed from the Development Grant, Territory politicians should decide whether they want increased taxes to provide increased services. Taxation is therefore a matter for local decision on the basis that if taxation is not raised increased services will not be provided.

(8) The Economic Adviser is an adviser to the Administrator regardless of whether any matter on which he might advise is a specified matter. He does not advise the Commonwealth but to ensure a smooth working relationship the principle in para. 5 applies to his functions.

(9) Chart 2 refers to statutory authorities. Only the Liquor Licencing Commission has been placed under final local control so far but further proposals will be worked out with the Administration so that the Secretary can discuss with the Administrator next week and firm proposals be put to the Minister before he visits the Territory at the end of November.

If you agree with the above I will get it run off and circulated for discussion at Senior Officers Meeting next Monday.

[NAA: A452, 1970/5267]

CHART ONE

THE ADMINISTRATION

SPECIFIED MATTERS   NON SPECIFIED MATTERS

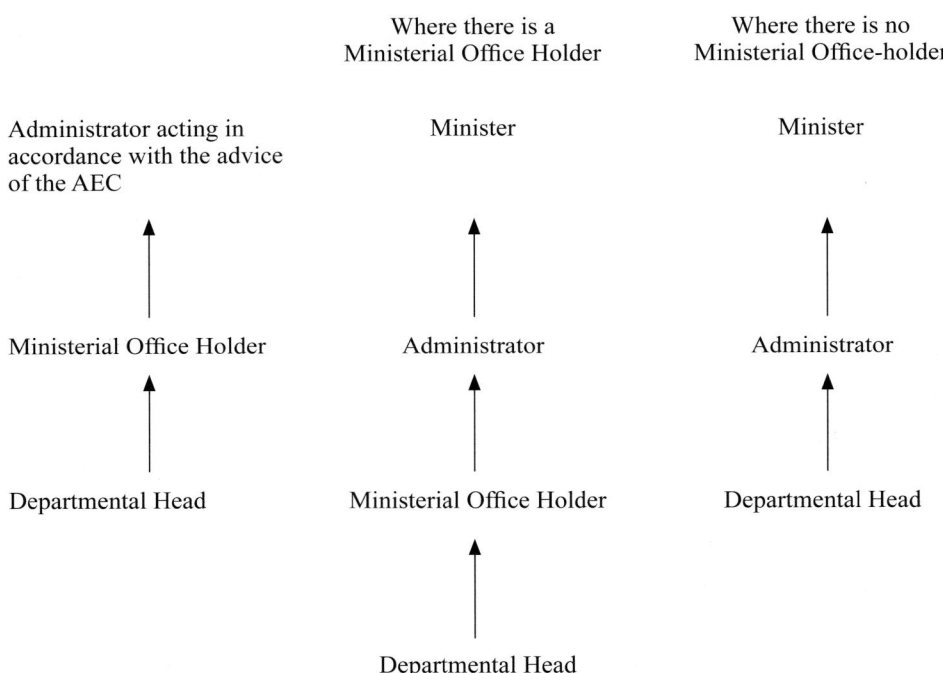

	Where there is a Ministerial Office Holder	Where there is no Ministerial Office-holder
Administrator acting in accordance with the advice of the AEC	Minister	Minister
↑	↑	↑
Ministerial Office Holder	Administrator	Administrator
↑	↑	↑
Departmental Head	Ministerial Office Holder	Departmental Head
	↑	
	Departmental Head	

Under the Governor-General's instruction the Administrator is bound to accept the advice of the Ministerial Office Holder or the AEC.

The Administrator may seek advice from the AEC at his discretion. He is not bound to accept the views of the Ministerial Office Holder and in reaching his own conclusion there would be nothing to prevent the Administrator asking to see the advice given by the Departmental Head.

CHART TWO

SPECIAL GROUPS

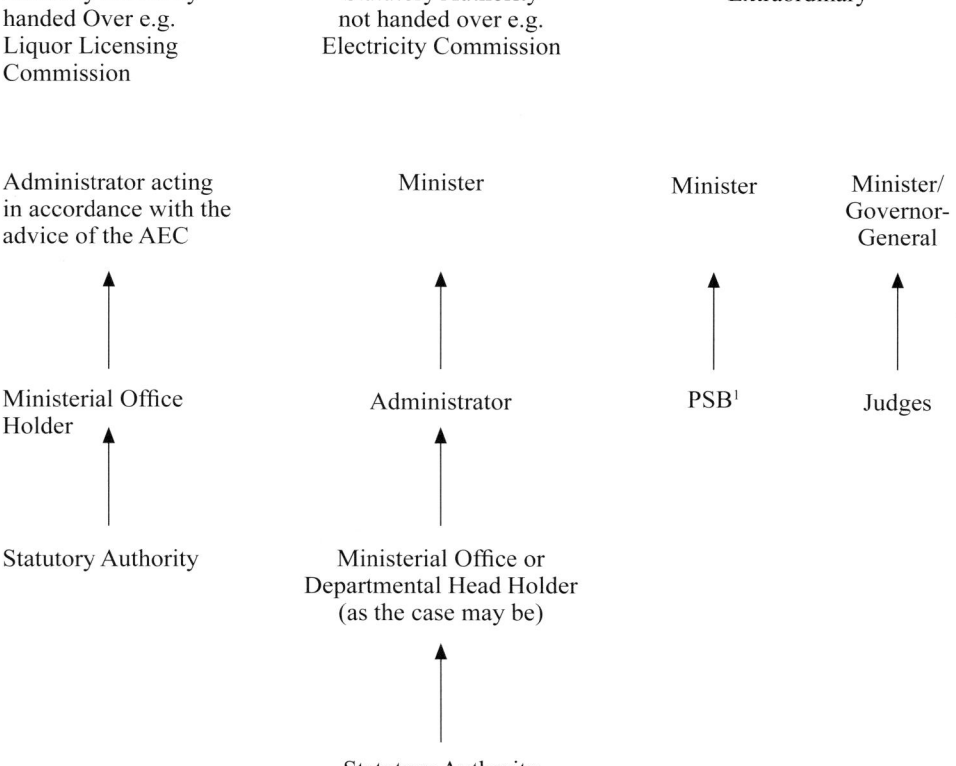

| Statutory Authority handed Over e.g. Liquor Licensing Commission | Statutory Authority not handed over e.g. Electricity Commission | Extraordinary | |

Statutory Authority handed Over e.g. Liquor Licensing Commission

Statutory Authority not handed over e.g. Electricity Commission

Extraordinary

Administrator acting in accordance with the advice of the AEC

Minister

Minister

Minister/ Governor- General

Ministerial Office Holder

Administrator

PSB[1]

Judges

Statutory Authority

Ministerial Office or Departmental Head Holder (as the case may be)

Statutory Authority

The purpose of this example is to show the similarity of the roles of the Governor General in appointing judges and the Administrators in respect of specified matters.

---

1 Public Service Board.

124   CABLEGRAM TO NEW YORK

Canberra, 15 December 1970

1619. Unclassified

UNGA Resolution on TPNG[1]

Following is text of press release issued this evening 15th December AEST:

Begins:

'The Minister for Foreign Affairs, The Rt Hon. William McMahon, MP, said today that the resolution on the Territory of Papua and New Guinea, adopted by the United Nations General Assembly on 14 December 1970, showed that the United Nations had approached the resolution concerning Australia's Administration of the Territory with moderation.

'The resolution was adopted by a vote of 98 in favour, with 0 against and 5 abstentions, including Australia.

'The Government noted that the resolution adopted at the twenty-fourth session in 1969 represented a movement away from the extreme position adopted in previous resolutions on the Territory. While earlier resolutions reflected adversely on the Territory House of Assembly by, for example, calling for fresh elections in a year when free elections had been held, the 1969 resolution had called for the transfer of full executive and legislative powers to elected representatives in accordance with the freely expressed wishes of the people. Australia was able to vote in favour of that resolution, which the General Assembly had adopted without a negative vote being cast. It was pleasing, Mr McMahon said, to see the same general approach repeated this year.

'However, Australia had basic objections to one aspect of this year's resolution and had accordingly felt bound to abstain on it.'[2]

[NAA: A452, 1970/4769]

---

1   The resolution, passed in the United Nations General Assembly (UNGA), not only invited 'the administering Power to cooperate fully with the visiting mission and to provide it with the necessary facilities and assistance in the performance of its tasks' but also called upon Australia 'to prescribe, in consultation with the freely elected representatives of the people, a specific timetable for the free exercise by the people of Papua and the Trust Territory of New Guinea of their right to self-determination and independence, and to report to the Trusteeship Council and to the Special Committee on the action taken in this regard'. It also requested that Australia 'intensify and accelerate the education and technical and administrative training of the indigenous peoples of the Territories and the localisation of the public service'. UNGA Resolution 2700(XXV), 'Question of Papua and the Trust Territory of New Guinea', 14 December 1970, A/RES/2700 (XXV).

2   Presumably a reference to the demand for 'a specific timetable' for self-determination. An annotation by an unidentified DET officer dated 18 December noted: 'Minister cleared text and decided he would rather not buy in—rather let Mr McMahon issue statement'.

125   MINUTE FROM GALVIN TO BARNES

Canberra, 21 December 1970

Papua and New Guinea—Status of Papua

You asked the Secretary if the status of Papua could be examined in the light of the recent statements by the Speaker of the House and other Papuans.

2.   Present Status

The Territory of Papua is administered in union with the Trust Territory of New Guinea under the Territory of Papua and New Guinea Act, 1949–1968. The Act provides for the maintenance of the identity and status of Papua as a possession of the Crown. The national status of persons born in Papua is defined by the Nationality and Citizenship Act 1948.[1] Persons born in the Territory of Papua are Australian citizens by birth, and by virtue of that citizenship are British subjects. Non-indigenes born in Papua retain individual national status. This is in contrast to persons born in the Trust Territory of New Guinea, where, under the Citizenship Regulations under the Nationality and Citizenship Act, persons born who are not British subjects are Australian Protected Persons. Those born of British subject parentage may register as British subjects. Australian citizenship may be obtained by Australian Protected Persons by application for naturalisation.

3.   Government Position

The difference in status has been examined before and the Government's view (considered by Cabinet and expressed by Ministers to the Select Committee on Constitutional Development in 1966)[2] has been that the effect on people of Papua and of New Guinea of the difference in status (e.g. Australian Territory and Trust Territory) is of little consequence now. Territory people, whether Papuans or New Guineans, who travel abroad do so on Australian passports and are entitled equally to the protection of the Australian Government. Further, in the Government's view the difference in nationality between Papuans and New Guineans would not lead to Papuans having a preferred position over New Guineans at the time of self-determination. Ministers were of the opinion then that it would be undesirable to seek any variation in the Trusteeship Agreement until such time as the Trust is discharged. Ministers gave an assurance that there is no intention to change the status of either Papua or New Guinea except in accordance with the wishes of the people of the respective Territory.

4.   Trusteeship Status

The Papua and New Guinea Act affirms the status of Papua as a possession of the Crown, and distinctly affirms the difference in status from the Trust Territory of New Guinea, whose integrity as a Trust Territory it maintains. It also provides for both the Territory of Papua and the Trust Territory of New Guinea to be governed in an administrative union. Government policy is for the development of PNG for self-determination as a single unit. The Department of Foreign Affairs has in the past been of the view that the United Nations would not agree to a change in the status of the Trust Territory of New Guinea, other than to independence, nor would it accept the Territory of Papua as a Trust Territory, given their current stage of development. This has prevented consideration of action which would lead to the abolition of separate status, and hence, complete union of both Territories prior to self-determination.

---

1   This Act came into force in 1949, and was renamed the *Australian Citizenship Act* in 1973.

2   See Stuart Doran, (ed.), *Documents on Australian Foreign Policy: Australia and Papua New Guinea, 1966–1969*, Canberra, Department of Foreign Affairs and Trade, Canberra, 2006, Documents 25 & 38.

5.   It is our view that an application for Papua to be a Trust Territory would lead to immediate calls in the United Nations for a UN supervised plebiscite or for a special visiting Mission to determine the wishes on independence of the majority of Papuans and New Guineans. As Papua is amongst those non-self governing territories within the purview of the Committee of 24, such a request would involve consideration and recommendation by that Committee whose membership has not shown great propensities for realistic assessment.

6.   General Considerations

Whilst the Government's past position can still be considered appropriate, it would seem desirable to bring home to Papuans from time to time the point that they are neither discriminated for nor against in development planning and general policies. An important element here may be the early introduction of a common internal citizenship (which is presently under consideration).[3] It seems also important to let it be well known from time to time that United Nations interest in the Territory lies in both Territories and that Fourth Committee consideration and General Assembly Resolutions apply to both equally. The continuation of past practice by inviting the Members of the coming United Nations Visiting Mission to pay a visit to Papua would be in keeping with this approach.

7.   Submitted for your information.

[NAA: A452, 1970/5535]

---

3   Document 118.

126 MINUTE FROM HAY TO GALVIN

Canberra, 22 December 1970

Status of Papua

This will confirm that the Minister wishes the Department to consider the possibility of some change in the status of Papua which would bring it more in line with the Trust Territory of New Guinea. The Minister no doubt had in mind that one of the arguments used by Guise and others in criticising the Government, is that because New Guinea is a Trust Territory, the interest of the United Nations ensures that Australia will put ample investment and other aid funds there. Another factor is that while Papua remains a dependent Territory under Australia's sovereignty the Papuan people retain a sense of difference with the New Guineans and also a sense of grievance against Australia because they do not get the full benefits which they believe attached to Australian citizenship.

No doubt this matter has been considered in the Department before. In getting your thoughts together, would you please consult with Foreign Affairs and see what their approach is. Please emphasise, in doing so, that this is a preliminary study only and that we will not necessarily be submitting a paper to the Minister on the substance.[1]

[NAA: A452, 1970/5535]

---

1 An annotation by a non-identified DET official on the original of this document indicates that Hay signed it before he had seen the minute that Galvin submitted on 21 December (Document 125). The annotation accordingly suggested that there be no further action on this matter at present.

Part 2

Documents, January–December 1971

'Sooner rather than later': Key Developments in 1971

In 1971, Minister for External Territories Charles Barnes remained concerned about the challenges of preparing Papua New Guinea for self-government and uneasy with the pace of change. In February, he wrote to the Prime Minister noting that 'every year counts', but Gorton was not swayed (Documents 137 & 140).

During the year officials from the Department of External Territories (DET) took forward the transfer of its own powers and responsibilities and coordinated transfers from other civilian departments, agencies and instrumentalities. In February 1971 the DET-led committee working on this task agreed that 'so far as it is a function of self-government, every case is appropriate for transfer in the long run'. It decided that immediate staff localisation was not essential because the PNG Government could assume responsibility while Australia continued to provide personnel. If Australia was presented with any choice over timing, 'it should be sooner rather than later' (Documents 138 & 143). Barnes gained Cabinet agreement in late 1971 to the transfer of the work of number of bodies 'outside the aegis of the Administration' subject to consultations with the Administrator's Executive Council on timing (Document 250).

In March the Select Committee proposed in its final report that preparations be made for a transition to self-government in the term of the next House of Assembly—that is, between 1972 and 1976. It also proposed the expansion of the legislature, the continuation of a single chamber—rather than the addition of an upper house—and a national crest and flag (Document 142). The House agreed with all the Committee's proposals, except with the re-naming of the Territory as 'Niu Gini', agreeing instead to omit the 'and' from 'Papua and New Guinea'. Henceforth, 'Papua New Guinea' was the Territory's name (Documents 155, 159 & 160).

Also in March, William 'Billy' McMahon, formerly the Foreign Affairs Minister, replaced Gorton as prime minister. The change had a PNG connection. Among the grievances raised by Malcolm Fraser, a leading figure in the push against Gorton, was his claim that in July 1970 Gorton had tried 'to prevent a Cabinet discussion of the proposed call-out' of the PNG defence force.[1]

After a visit from late January to early March a United Nations Trusteeship Council Mission commented favourably on the success of 'Recent advancements involving substantial transfer of authority to local ministerial members' (Document 169).

In April the Commonwealth Government revoked, without any publicity, the order authorising a call-out (Document 156). In the event, despite the challenge posed by the Mataungan Association in the Gazelle Peninsula, implementing a call-out had not been necessary.

Localisation continued to move forward slowly. Following a visit in July a senior DFA official commented: 'In some fields, e.g. health and education, localisation has progressed quite well. However, where it counts most, localisation has progressed least, namely, in the formation of a solid cadre of middle and senior level administrators' (Document 201).

In August the Department of External Territories prepared a detailed critical path plan mapping out the complex constitutional, legal and administrative changes involved in 'gearing up' to implement self-government in the Territory (Document 209).

---

1   Ian Hancock, *John Gorton. He Did It His Way*, Hodder, Sydney, 2002, pp. 321–24.

Australia continued to provide substantial financial support. Barnes told Parliament in September 1971 that Australian 'aid of an economic nature' would amount to nearly $131 million in the 1971–72 financial year, and that over the eight years to 1970–71 total economic aid had amounted to $716 million. He highlighted some progress towards greater self-reliance: in 1971–72 internal revenue would provide 'about 36 per cent of total Administration expenditure in Papua New Guinea compared with about 25 per cent in 1963/64' (Document 214).

During the year Papuan representatives expressed their sense of a separate Papuan identity, based in part on their status as Australian citizens, whereas the inhabitants of New Guinea, a UN trust territory, were 'Australian Protected Persons'. Australian ministers and officials were concerned lest the Papuans demand a separate referendum (Documents 171, 223, 226, & 228–229). Nonetheless, a visit to Canberra in October by a delegation of Papuan representatives from the House of Assembly caused no great difficulty; the Papuans expressed support for PNG's 'national unity' (Documents 230).

127   TELEX TO CANBERRA

Port Moresby, 3 January 1971

7550. Unclassified

Following is text of statement issued by Whitlam yesterday, Sunday, after his arrival in Port Moresby.

This visit has two chief aims: to widen personal contacts between this country and the Australian Labor Party; and to widen the debate on issues about this country's future.

Since my last visit one year ago, the problems of Papua–New Guinea have achieved greater prominence in the Australian Parliament and the Australian press than ever before. More Papuans and New Guineans than ever before have been prepared to speak freely and vigorously about the future of their own country. In both countries, there is a growing consciousness of the identity of Papua-New Guinea as a genuine, distinct and distinctive nation.

The basic political question—the question of self-government and independence—is by no means the hardest problem facing this nation. The present and future leaders of Papua–New Guinea are faced with far more difficult problems concerning development, education, the distribution of wealth and ownership, land reforms, regional cooperation and race relations. Discussion and decision on these matters are now urgent in the very short time remaining for Australian rule in this country.

Despite the Australian Government's present official attitude, a majority of the members of the Australian House of Representatives would now personally favour immediate self-government for Papua-New Guinea.

The United Nations General Assembly has again called upon Australia to prescribe a specific timetable for self-determination and independence. The 98-nil vote (with 5 abstentions) included all the near neighbours of Papua-New Guinea and Australia.[1]

It is an error to suppose that decisions about the political future of this territory rest solely here. Australia has to decide whether or not she is willing to continue as a colonial power. This is a decision by Australians about Australia's place in the world.

It is increasingly likely that the next government of Australia will be a Labor government. The Australian Labor Party will not accept a colonial role on Australia's behalf. We have many moral and material responsibilities to the people of Papua-New Guinea, and inescapable responsibilities for our own nationals in Papua-New Guinea. Ruling is not one of those responsibilities.

My basic proposition is that none of the real problems of Papua–New Guinea come nearer to solution by continuing Australian rule. On the contrary, Australia's false position as a ruling colonial power detracts from the ability of Australia and individual Australians to help Papua–New Guinea.

One of the most distressing trends in Papua-New Guinea is towards separation. Every year that independence is delayed, the more the focus of national identity is blurred and the more powerful such movements are likely to grow. This is a clear example of how external rule sharpens internal difficulties.

I should make it absolutely clear that the Australian Labor Party has no wish or intention to form a branch or sponsor any party in Papua–New Guinea. Political parties in Papua–

---

1   See Document 124, fn. 1.

New Guinea must grow in response to the needs and circumstances of this nation, just as the Australian political parties grew in response to the needs and circumstances of the Australian nation.

The presence with me of Labor officials as well as parliamentarians[2] is a sign of our deep and continuing interest in the welfare of this country, as a neighbour nation, not as a colony.

[NAA: A452, 1971/4741]

---

2   Whitlam was accompanied by Bill Morrison, MP for St George, Paul Keating, MP for Blaxland, Clyde Cameron, MP for Hindmarsh, ALP Federal President Tom Burns, and ALP Federal Secretary Mick Young. After Labor won power in December 1972 Whitlam appointed Morrison as Minister for External Territories.

128   TELEX TO CANBERRA

Port Moresby, 17 January 1971

437. Unclassified

Following is text of press statement issued by Whitlam prior to departure today. He did not hold a press conference. Statement begins:

In the past year the political climate of Papua-New Guinea has been transformed. A year ago proposals for early self-government were met with official hostility and public dismay. Some elementary truths about the early and inevitable end of colonialism Papua-New Guinea held the terror of the novel and the unknown. Now the most significant leaders of Papua-New Guinea and significant sections of the population accept that they must shortly come to terms with their own future as a self-governing nation. It has been a remarkable proof of the power of an idea. There can be no turning back now.

For the past fortnight my colleagues and I have met and talked with some hundreds of the present and future leaders of Papua-New Guinea. Despite the vast improvement in the level of political debate in every part of the territory, it is clear that political education has been woefully deficient. Again and again we asked the people if they had ever heard the Administration explain the advantages of self-government. Invariably, the answer was 'no'. With the shining exception of the new Administrator himself,[1] it would seem that practically nothing has been done to dispel confusion and fear about the meaning and consequences of self-government. On the contrary needless anxiety and false fears have been planted and nourished. Consequently my colleagues and I found that in many parts of the territory our visit became a mission of reassurance that Australia's contribution to the welfare of Papua-New Guinea would be enhanced and expanded after self-government and later after independence.

There can be no qualification about the depth of the commitment of the Australian Labor Party in this matter. The representative nature of the colleagues who have been with me in the territory would alone ensure that, beyond personal commitment, the Labor Party as a whole finds its most deeply-held conscientious convictions affronted in Papua-New Guinea. It would be impossible for a party like ours to condone or connive at vast inequalities, entrenched privilege, blatant exploitation and racial discrimination. These inescapable attributes of colonialism disfigure life in this colony, as in all other colonies. They debase the dedication, enterprise and energy devoted over the years by the many thousands of fine Australians who have worked in this territory.

Australia's role as a colonial power is a wrong thing in itself. It would be bad for us as a nation, even if we were able to isolate ourselves from the pressures and opinions of all other countries, but we enjoy no such luxury of isolation. In particular, we live in a region in which every one of our neighbours for thousands of miles around were former colonies, each detests colonialism. To all these neighbours and all our fellow members of the Commonwealth of Nations every justification the Australian Government makes for dragging its feet in Papua-New Guinea, every argument about the inability of native peoples to govern themselves smacks of racial superiority.

Australia's major diplomatic effort, not only at the United Nations but in most world capitals, is devoted to justifying the official position on Papua-New Guinea. This is a sterile exercise. It cripples our power for any constructive diplomatic initiative. We are needlessly placed on

---

1   Les Johnson.

the defensive, it needlessly complicates our relations with our neighbours and our friends, including our chief ally, the United States, which possesses the world's most powerful black community.

All Australians must now realise how damaging and dangerous a reputation Australia's present policies produce. We are a European nation on the fringe of the most populous and deprived coloured nations in the world. What the world sees about Australia is that we have an aboriginal population with the highest infant mortality rate on Earth, that we have eagerly supported the most unpopular war in modern times on the ground that Asia should be a battleground of our freedom, that we fail to oppose the sale of arms to South Africa, that the whole world believes that our immigration policy is based on colour and that we run one of the world's last colonies. We may rightly profess our good intentions and feel that we are merely the victims of special circumstances, but the combination of such policies leans heavily indeed on the world's goodwill and on Australia's credibility. The true patriot therefore will not seek to justify and prolong these policies but will seek to change them.

In Papua-New Guinea, it will be found increasingly that the question for the timing of self-government involves a quibble about the matter of 2 or 3 years. Even if the Gorton Government were to survive, self-government will come in the lifetime of the next House of Representatives. The Australian Government has a clear duty to speed up preparations for the inevitable day. Target dates for self-government and independence should be set now, as we are obliged to do by the unopposed decision of the United Nations General Assembly.

The official members of the House of Assembly should be removed now. Elected ministers should be made responsible to the House of Assembly in fact, political education should receive top priority. The Australian Parliament should immediately ratify the International Labour Organization conventions on plantation workers and on race relations. A new set of labour laws and ordinances should be drafted and approved to make labour laws and conditions conform with these conventions. Employment preference should be given to unionists. The Australian Government should spell out clearly the entitlements of Australian public servants and should make it plain that it accepts responsibility for their future welfare, both in the Territory and in Australia. Only if this is done can localisation of the public service proceed speedily and smoothly. There is no need to wait until 1972 for these things to be done. They constitute in themselves the essence of self-government.

Australian businessmen and the Australian companies have a particular interest in the establishment of a self-governing New Guinea.

By its very nature, an Australian administration committed to its own eventual abdication cannot guarantee the validity or permanency of business and investment arrangements it may make.

The best safeguard against expropriation is that an indigenous independent government should accept responsibility for the laws and arrangements under which prosperity is held and capital invested.

There are clear statistics in the present situation in which all employers and businessmen are expatriates while New Guineans are only employees and customers.

In the final analysis the attitudes of the Australian Labor Party to Papua-New Guinea involve a convinced judgement about the very nature of man, we cannot accept that nations should be ruled by other nations, we cannot accept that we do not wish to be free, we cannot accept that the people of Papua-New Guinea are some special exception in a world where millions have died for national independence. It may be true that we cannot be forced to be free, it is certainly true that men cannot be forced to rule others. An Australian Labor Government will not be blackmailed into accepting an unnatural role as rulers over those who have had no say and can have no say in electing us. Australia's obligation in the United Nations is to hand over

Papua-New Guinea as a single entity as soon as possible. Papua-New Guinea has a chance of remaining united only if self-government comes quickly. Self-government in itself will be the real unifying force in this country. To delay self-government is to promote separatism. Self-government must be given quickly to the people as a whole, otherwise section after section will seize with anger and bitterness towards us what we should grant wholly and wholeheartedly.

[NAA: A452, 1971/0004]

129   PRESS RELEASE BY BARNES

Canberra, 17 January 1971

Minister Deplores Labor Interference in Territory Internal Politics

The Labor leader, Mr Whitlam, had shown contempt for the standing of the Papua and New Guinea House of Assembly in trying to impose his own arbitrary timetable for internal self-government and independence on the Territory.

The Minister for External Territories, Mr Barnes, said this today in commenting on a statement issued by Mr Whitlam in Port Moresby today.

Mr Barnes also accused members of the Labor Party of undermining the confidence of overseas businessmen and public servants whose presence in the Territory was essential to aid the transition of the Territory to nationhood.

Mr Barnes said that the question of how quickly the Territory should move towards the final stages of internal self-government was even now a matter of consultation with the people of the Territory. It was the first among a number of constitutional questions on which the people were being asked at public meetings in every district of Papua and New Guinea to give their views to the Select Committee on Constitutional Development. The Committee was also explaining to the people the meaning of self-government.

Mr Barnes said the select committee would report to the House of Assembly in March, and the Australian Government would wish to have before it the views of the House of Assembly on the committee's report when considering possible amendments to the Papua and New Guinea Act before the 1972 House of Assembly elections in the Territory. To do otherwise would be to ignore the authentic voice of the Territory people expressed after full consultation with them.

Mr Barnes said that Labor spokesmen had belittled the very considerable powers already transferred to elected Ministers in the Territory. They covered matters like education, public health, local government, and the whole field of taxation. In all these matters, the Territory House of Assembly had the full rights of legislation without disallowance from the Commonwealth.

Mr Barnes said the involvement of Papuans and New Guineans in determining their own destiny had dramatically increased in the last 12 months.

The Government, however, could not ignore the fact that, in some areas of the Territory, these steps had been thought too far reaching and precipitate.

The Government's policy was that there should be continuous progress on the road to internal self-government as a matter of course and in an atmosphere of confidence.

When the final steps were taken, the foundations of government and of an advanced economy would have been laid and Papuans and New Guineans would be able to build on them structures of their own choosing.

The measures needed at this time were being taken with a sense of urgency, but the supply of skilled and experienced manpower, both indigenous and expatriate, was still perilously small in many key areas, and it was folly to conduct a debate about the date of self-government without regard to factors such as these.

Mr Barnes emphasised that accelerated development was only possible if overseas investors and public servants were confident that their presence in the Territory was supported by both the Commonwealth Government and Territory political leaders. To try to undermine this confidence was a disservice to the people of the Territory.

Mr Barnes said that statements such as those attributed to Mr Cameron[1] that 'anyone who defended all that was happening in Papua and New Guinea was a "mongrel"' were extravagant and almost hysterical. If they had been made other than by a shadow Minister of the Federal ALP, they should deserve to be ignored.

Mr Barnes said: 'They are not only a reflection on the many thousands of Australians who are bringing a better life to the people of Papua and New Guinea, but they are grossly untrue.'

[NAA: A452, 1971/297]

130   MINUTE FROM HAY TO GREENWELL

Canberra, 18 January 1971

CONFIDENTIAL

Question of Target Dates

The Minister has twice emphasised in conversations with me that he feels that it is up to the Select Committee[1] to ensure that it covers the question of target dates and time-tables in its report to the House of Assembly. He said that the Government needs to have the views of the House of Assembly on this matter. He asked that we ensure that this be brought before the Select Committee.

I spoke to the Administrator and asked him to arrange this. He said that quite apart from the fact that there was a relevant question in the group of questions to be asked of the people by the Committee as it did its final tour, there was some opinion (Arek, for instance), which wanted to have references to targets and time-tables in the Report. However, people like Arek had to consider the effect that this might have on Highland's opinion in the House of Assembly. Their fear is that too much reference to targets etc. or too forward a time-table might cause the House of Assembly to throw out the whole report. Against this background the Administrator thought that it might not be as easy as the Minister hoped to get the Committee to address itself to this question and to report formally on it. However, he will see what he can do.

The matter should be followed up from time to time. I noticed that it does figure in the District Assessments and because of this is ought to figure some way in the Committee's report to the House, without too much pushing on our part.

[NAA: A452, 1970/4962]

---

1   Clyde Cameron, Labor Member for Hindmarsh.

---

1   The House of Assembly Select Committee on Constitutional Development.

131   SUBMISSION FROM HAY TO BARNES

Canberra, 20 January 1971

Policy Brief for UN Visiting Mission

The Visiting Mission will be in Papua and New Guinea from 24th January to 6th March.[1] They will then spend a few days of the following week in Canberra.

2.   The Mission comprises representatives of UK and France, both of which are members of the Trusteeship Council, and of Iraq and Sierra Leone, for the first time representatives of countries not members of the Trusteeship Council—and both members of the Committee of 24 and representatives of the Afro-Asian bloc.[2]

3.   A policy brief[3] has been prepared in the form of a letter to the Administrator of Papua and New Guinea for his reference and that of senior officers in their discussions with the Mission. It would form the basis for your own discussions with the Mission in Canberra.

4.   It is *recommended* that you approve the brief which you may like to discuss when you are in Canberra on Friday.

[NAA: A452, 1971/0268]

---

1   The mission travelled extensively in Papua and New Guinea, visiting Port Moresby, Goroka, Kainantu, Lae, Finschhafen, Hoskins, Kimbe, Rabaul, Buka, Kieta, Buin, Panguna, Kavieng, Manus, Vanimo, Telefomin, Aitape, Lumi, Maprik, Wewak, Ambunti, Angoram, Madang, Bundi, Mendi, Kundiawa, Kerowagi, Banz, Mt Hagen, Wabag, Wapenamanda and Daru. It then travelled to Canberra for meetings with ministers, senior officials (Document 145) and the Leader of the Opposition (Document 147). It submitted its report to the UN Secretary-General on 19 April 1971.

2   Sir Denis Allen, a senior British official, chaired the mission. The other members were Paul Blanc (Counsellor of the Permanent Mission of France to the United Nations), Adnan Raouf (Deputy Permanent Representative of Iraq to the United Nations), and Charles E. Wyse (First Secretary of the Permanent Mission of Sierra Leone to the United Nations).

3   See Document 132.

132   LETTER FROM HAY TO JOHNSON

Canberra, 20 January 1971

Discussions between Departmental and Administration officers on preparations for the reception of the United Nations visiting mission have already taken place. There is evidently agreement on how best to apply the lessons derived from experience with the last visiting mission.[1]

In this letter I am writing about the more general points of policy on which you and senior officers may be asked by the visiting mission to express Government views in the first few days after the mission arrives in Port Moresby. It is essential that you speak from the same brief which will be used by the Minister when he talks to the Mission, as the Minister responsible in the Australian Government, on completion of the Mission's visit to the Territory. It is to be hoped that this will lead to a sympathetic understanding on the part of the Mission, and also to an accurate statement of the Government's policies in their report. Reference to the 1968 report will indicate that extensive changes are necessary to bring its descriptions of government policy up to date.

I have consulted the Minister on this matter and he has asked that the following points be emphasised:

(a) The policy of the Government was stated by the then Governor-General to the Australian House of Representatives and again on 4th June 1968 to the present House of Assembly in the Territory at its first meeting in the following terms:

'It is that the destiny of Papua and New Guinea is to become a self-governing country developed for independence if and when it is clearly demonstrated by the majority of the indigenous population that this is what they wish …'

(b) So far as the pace of development is concerned, the Minister for External Territories said on 21st March 1968 in the Australian House of Representatives:

'It is the expressed intention of the Commonwealth to help the inhabitants of the Territory to become self-governing as soon as possible and to ensure that when this aim is reached the Territory will, to the greatest extent feasible, be able to stand on its own feet economically.'

(c) The Government favours and aims to foster the development of national unity. It believes that the interests of the people of the Territory are best served by National Unity and endorses the House of Assembly Resolution of November 1968 supporting National Unity and the development of Papua and New Guinea as a single country.[2]

(d) The preparation of Papua and New Guinea for internal self-government is and has been for a number of years, a matter of urgency. This policy has been carried out in a number of ways, through intensified training of public servants to take on higher responsibilities, through the efforts of the Development Bank and the Business Advisory Service and the Department of Agriculture, to provide economic and business training and opportunities as well as credit for Papuans and New Guineans, and above all through the steadily increasing responsibility being placed in the hands of elected Members of the House of Assembly.

---

1   The previous UN mission visited PNG from 24 February to 7 April 1968. The Trusteeship Council issued the mission's report in late May 1968. See Stuart Doran (ed.), *Documents on Australian Foreign Policy: Australia and Papua New Guinea, 1966–1969*, Department of Foreign Affairs and Trade, Canberra, 2006, pp. 446–47, 682 and Document 252.

2   Ibid., Documents 239 & 242.

(e) The year 1970 has seen a considerable advance towards internal self-government announced by the Prime Minister in Port Moresby on 6th July last.[3] The effect of this announcement has been to transfer final authority for decision-making over a large and important area of government to elected Ministerial office holders in the Territory. Instruments bringing these changes into effect, particularly the Governor-General's Instruction to you,[4] should be referred to in this context.

(f) Decision-making authority runs with increasing financial responsibility and this has been reflected in the revised budget arrangements first agreed upon for the 1970/71 Australian and Territory Budgets. Under these arrangements Commonwealth aid to the Territory is shown in four parts:

(i)   The amount intended for development purposes

(ii) Grant-in-aid

(iii) Allowances and other benefits for expatriate officers of the Public Service.

(iv) Loans for special development projects.

(g) The amendments to the Papua and New Guinea Act which were passed in 1968 give authority to the Minister for External Territories to continue the process of handing over decision-making authority and taking further steps toward internal self-government. However, the Government has had to take account of the fact that the steps already taken are in some areas of the Territory thought to be going too far, although in other areas of the Territory they are thought to be not going far enough. In the light of this difference of opinion, the Commonwealth, as announced by the Prime Minister, has not agreed to put a time-table on progress towards internal self-government and eventual independence. In respect of independence he has said that:

> 'We don't want to remain in the Territory one week against the wishes of the majority of the people. We don't think we ought to get out of the Territory against the wish of the majority of its people. We don't want to rule any peoples without their consent. We don't think it proper to move out and possibly help a vocal minority to rule a majority without that majority's consent, and one can't put a time-table on this but one can say these are steps towards the time when this Territory will be self-governing and when its people will express their views. And we take account of those views instead of imposing our views on them as to a date for self-government and independence.'[5]

(h) This statement does not affect the urgency with which preparations for internal self-government are going ahead. One of the important questions which is now the subject of consultation with the people through the Select Committee of the House of Assembly on Constitutional Development is: 'When would you like to see internal self-government in Papua and New Guinea'?

The visiting mission could be assured that if the Select Committee recommends and the House of Assembly endorses an increase in the rate of movement towards internal self-government that will meet with a sympathetic response from the Commonwealth.

(i) In the meantime the Government also recognises the need to meet a situation in which the people of different areas of the Territory may wish to exercise differing degrees of regional responsibility. Legislation to meet this has been introduced into the House of Assembly by this Administration and is now before the House.

3   Document 64.

4   Document 105.

5   See Document 64. See also Document 25.

(j) These points are made in order to demonstrate that the stance on which the Government is operating is one which encourages rather than discourages the early achievement of self-government. Opportunity could be taken to describe the efforts which you yourself and the Administration is [sic] making to this end through, for example, the political education programs. However, it is important that the mission should be aware that these are matters on which the House of Assembly itself is very sensitive. The attitude of the House towards the last report of the Select Committee, should be mentioned in this context. This also is relevant in pointing out that the steps already implemented have in the view of some members gone too far too soon.

(k) The Government's policy is to accelerate the pace of economic development in line with the changing political situation.

(l) The five year development programme is being revised to take account of the impact of the Bougainville copper project, the changes which have occurred in market opportunities and their need to accelerate indigenous participation in the economy;

(m) The problems of reconciling customary usage of land with the need to bring land into economic production has been under consideration in the light of experience in other developing countries. The House of Assembly has been kept informed of progress and the Administration will introduce proposals in the form of Bills at the March meeting of the House. These Bills, if passed, would modernise traditional tenures and stimulate indigenous economic development in the areas in which, with the consent of the people of a locality, they are applied.

(n) A study is being undertaken with a view to formulating a long-term policy on taxation. The study will consider in particular the ways by which the Territory can increase its financial self-reliance.

(o) Increasing attention is being given to indigenous involvement in economic activity. Government guidelines on investment encourage overseas investors to provide opportunities for Papuans and New Guineans to participate in ownership and management and to provide employment and training opportunities. An Investment Corporation is being established to take up equity in major projects in the Territory to be held for future sale to the local people.[6] A new Department of Business Development has been established to concentrate efforts to accelerate indigenous participation in business activity. The Development Bank has established regional offices and representatives in outlying centres as part of the drive for indigenous development. Major emphasis is being given to the advancement of indigenes through secondary and higher education. Further measures will be taken after the examination of a report expected shortly from a UNIDO[7] expert who recently completed a six month's study on methods of promoting indigenous business enterprise in the Territory.

(p) The Territory stands to suffer not only the loss of existing preferences in the traditional United Kingdom Market in the event of British entry to the EEC but also in some cases to encounter a tariff providing reverse preferences to competitive Associated Territories. A Papua and New Guinea Delegation led by the Ministerial member for Trade and Industry last year secured from the British an undertaking to raise the Papua and New Guinea problem with the Six. Although the Territory may suffer as a result it will be unable to take counter-preferential treatment because of Article 76(d) of the UN Charter.

---

6   Les Johnson describes this body as the 'coping stone' of the Administration's economic actions. It served as the vehicle whereby the Administration acquired equity in various enterprises and industries, including oil palm plantations and the copper mine being developed in Bougainville. See L. W. Johnson, *Colonial Sunset: Australia and Papua New Guinea 1970–74*, University of Queensland Press, St. Lucia, 1983, p. 80.

7   United Nations Industrial Development Organization.

(q) Integration of pupils and teachers in schools is being furthered wherever this can be done without educational disadvantage to the children concerned. Common curricula are being used or developed as far as possible. Mission and Administration schools have been merged into a single education system with greater local participation in planning and administration. Mission and Administration teachers have been merged into a single teaching service paid at the same basic salary rates. Enrolments have greatly expanded at the secondary and post secondary level, and a number of higher level institutions including the University and Institute of Technology have produced their first graduates. A committee of enquiry has been appointed to advise on the future development of higher education and on the means of coordinating the activities of the various institutions.

(r) The new employment code being drafted will take account of the recommendations of a Board of Inquiry into rural wages. A Bureau of Industrial Organizations is to be established representative of employers, employees, and Administration, and its functions could be outlined to the Mission.

(s) All positions in the Public Service now carry the local salary classification which is paid from the Territory Budget. Overseas officers receive direct from the Commonwealth an overseas allowance to bring their total remuneration to the Australian level plus a Territory allowance. Local female officers receive equal pay. A new structure of family needs allowances for local officers has been introduced.

(t) The Public Service Board currently comprises an Indigenous Chairman, one indigenous and two expatriate members. As well as its general role in relation to the Public Service, the Board is specifically charged with responsibility for 'adequate arrangements for the training of local officers and for their advancement to offices at all levels of the Public Service, ensuring, as far as possible, a uniform approach to the question of standards'. A localisation section coordinates the localisation effort and generally advises the Board. Current policy is to promote the advancement of local officers at all levels rather than to localise from the bottom up. Local officers are increasingly attaining senior status in government employment. Training assistance for local officers comprises scholarships, cadetships and financial assistance and study leave for *professional*, sub-professional and technical training at Territory and Australian institutions. Local officers and employees also participate in the Commonwealth Government sponsored practical training in Australia scheme for Papuans and New Guineans.[8]

[NAA: A452, 1971/0268]

---

8   The brief was approved by Barnes on 21 January 1971.

133   NOTE FOR FILE BY GREENWELL

Canberra, 26 January 1971

Discussions with Minister

On Thursday 20 December Mr Kearney[1] had a brief discussion with the Minister. The Minister felt that perhaps a new stage had been reached and that having [introduced political] development, education [and][2] economic development, there was a need to direct attention to the legal system. He said he was concerned at the deterioration in order in Papua New Guinea and indicated that perhaps we had not previously emphasised the importance of this because it was assumed that law and order would continue.

2.   Mr Kearney emphasised a basic difficulty in that the people would not accept the decisions of the Courts and after extensive appeals would continue to dispute the matter. He referred particularly to land disputes.

3.   The Minister felt that some difficulty was being caused in the villages by the younger men returning. The older men remembered the old days and knew the advantage of imposed law and order. He felt that there should be some need to recapture the authority of the older men in the villages.

[NAA: A452, 1972/0588]

---

1   Bill Kearney, Secretary for Law in the Administration in Port Moresby.
2   Editorial insertions.

134   MINUTE FROM HAY TO GREENWELL

Canberra, 27 January 1971

CONFIDENTIAL

Constitutional Development

I discussed with the Minister this afternoon the Administrator's letter LH. 434 of 9th January 1971.[1]

With reference to the paragraphs on pages 1 and 2 on movement towards self-government, the Minister expressed himself very firmly as opposed to the naming of a date by the Australian Government. He felt to do so would rest heavily on his own conscience in view of the grave risk that the Territory would not have a sure enough foundation to run its own affairs without unrest or violence.

I said to the Minister that the present assessment of the likely outcome of the consideration by the Select Committee of the question of how quickly the people want self-government to come to the Territory was an expression of view favouring either the period 1972 to 1976 or the period 1976 to 1980. The Minister said that he would not feel obliged to react against such an expression of view if it came out of consideration by the House of Assembly. I suggested that it might be wise, if a recommendation in these terms came to the House of Assembly, for official Members to ensure that the House had before it the factors without which consideration of the question of a date would be meaningless, for example, the factor of manpower shortage. I said that it would be possible for an official Member to indicate, if the House came out, for example, in favour of the period 1972 to 1976, the kind of steps which the Australian Government would feel it necessary to take in order to have the process of moving towards self-government completed by 1976.

We discussed without going into too much detail what steps would be involved. I put it to the Minister that it would be possible to take a fairly important step early in the period by creating a position of Chief Minister as Deputy Chairman of the Administrator's Executive Council. This could be done without at that time handing over powers such as internal security, police etc., for which the Territory was not yet ready. The Minister saw some difficulty in this and at this stage he favours a situation in which the institution of a position of Chief Minister would not precede the handing over of law and order powers. In effect, he was indicating a view that a Chief Minister would be one of the last steps to be taken in the time scale.

However, the Minister said that we needed a paper on this general matter in order to clarify our own thinking and to place the issues clearly before him.

The Minister will wish to hear, from Kerr directly, an assessment of how the Select Committee is getting on. I have arranged an appointment for 9:30 a.m. tomorrow.

[NAA: A452, 1970/4962]

---

1   Not published.

135   LETTER FROM HAY TO JOHNSON

Canberra, 27 January 1971

CONFIDENTIAL

I am writing to raise with you three inter-related subjects, domestic citizenship, selective entry for employment and immigration policy.

In a memorandum dated 23rd September[1] I proposed a domestic citizenship which would not affect present citizenship status in international law but would confer important privileges such as the right to vote and stand for public office. I had in mind that people born in the Territory would automatically acquire the citizenship and immigrants would become eligible to apply after some years in the Territory e.g. seven years. I see such citizenship arrangements as an important means of encouraging a feeling of national identity, overcoming the artificial and misleading distinction between Papuans and New Guineans and enabling immigrants to identify themselves with the Territory.

Domestic citizenship seems to be inseparably linked with immigration policy. According to an advising from Attorney-General's Department no immigrant to the Territory has an unqualified right of permanent residence as the law now stands i.e. an immigrant can always be deported under certain conditions. The granting of domestic citizenship would presumably carry with it the right of permanent residence.

I see a good deal of merit in considering the introduction, concurrently with domestic citizenship, of new immigration policies and procedures designed to make the permits system less obviously racially discriminatory. At the same time we might consider liberalising the conditions of entry of non-Europeans with skills in short supply in the Territory. Proposals along these lines are set out in a separate memorandum.[2]

Selective entry for employment (work permits administered through the immigration system) is also linked to immigration policy because in addition to assisting localisation it would make the immigration policy less obviously discriminatory by applying the test of skill to Europeans as well as non Europeans.

Late last year the AEC considered the question of work permits and decided against them. Earlier, however, the Minister had indicated that he was very much in favour of a system of work permits which would be introduced gradually so as to avoid raising unnecessary fears and to minimise the administration involved.

Following the AEC's consideration the question was again raised with the Minister and he reaffirmed his earlier view in favour of work permits. The Department will be sending a memorandum separately outlining the considerations put to the Minister.

Unfortunately in raising the matter with the Minister again it was overlooked that you had not put your own views as distinct from those of the AEC. I would like to raise the matter with the Minister again so that he may consider your views alongside those of the AEC.

I would be grateful for your views on these related subjects. You might care to discuss them when you are in Canberra next week.

[NAA: A452, 1970/1453]

---

1   See Document 118.

2   Not published.

136   LETTER FROM JOHNSON TO HAY

Port Moresby, 11 February 1971

CONFIDENTIAL

I refer to the draft letter[1] from the Minister to the Prime Minister seeking agreement to the broad lines of Australian policy in Papua-New Guinea.

My assessment of the situation remains the same. I think it likely that the Select Committee on Constitutional Development will advocate either a target date for self-government or advert to self-government in such a way that its views on the timing of it will be evident. The date is likely to be in the range 1974/76 and will probably be accepted by the House of Assembly, though possibly not unanimously. Failure of the House to agree to a target date and the reluctance of the Australian Government to impose one would cause serious problems for us here. There would be a total alienation of the educated youth of the community and increased strength of dissident movements. A degree of civil disobedience could be expected to eventuate.

The likely situation in the House of Assembly is that the Select Committee Report will be presented at 8:00 p.m. on Thursday, March 4th, and the debate adjourned till the following week. It would be inadvisable for Official Members to intervene in the debate until the trend of House opinion became clear. Australian Government policy has always been that it will conform to the clearly expressed wishes of the people. An attempt to lead House opinion by anticipating debate would be inappropriate. I should think that the Senior Official Member could arrange to speak after four or five elected Members have had the floor. Once the Report has been adopted by the House then it would be appropriate to have a clear Australian Government reaction and perhaps this might come from the Prime Minister or the Minister.

I have no substantial points of disagreement with the content of the draft letter. I have already drawn your attention to the possible need to redraft a part of page 3(c) (i), '. . . as though he were the Chief Minister.' In (c) (ii) you refer definitely to the Chief Minister. I think that we would need to have a hard look at writing a Chief Minister into amendments to the Papua-New Guinea Act at this stage.

I have made my own views known to you in that I prefer the road upon which we are already travelling in the progressive transfer of powers. Radical amendment of the Papua-New Guinea Act as the first step removes all our bargaining power and would be likely to make for difficult relationships between the Chief Minister and the Administrator. On page 4(f) you refer to an independence date being set by an expression of public opinion through an election, referendum or consensus. I can see the dangers of reliance on a House of Assembly resolution but by such a time I should think that internal events in Papua-New Guinea will not be within Australia's control and a referendum for instance would have to emerge from a House of Assembly action in any case.

Your draft also outlines some of the difficulties associated with handing over control of law and order to a self-governing Papua-New Guinea. I cannot imagine any circumstances in which the retention of law and order by the Australian Government would be tolerated for long by a Papua-New Guinea Cabinet. Here again, your use of the term Chief Minister may have misled me as to your projected timing. I think that law and order can be a withheld power until shortly before the final step to self-government is taken. An earlier minor problem for consideration is the access of the person acting in the capacity of Chief Minister to intelligence and security files.

[NAA: A452, 1970/5267]

---

1   Not published. For the final version of the letter, see Document 137.

137   LETTER FROM BARNES TO GORTON

Canberra, 11 February 1971

In this letter, I set out for your information the broad lines which I propose to take up with the United Nations Visiting Mission when, on completion of its visit to PNG it comes to Canberra in March. Statements of policy will also be required:

   a.   for the Territory House of Assembly in March, since the Select Committee on Constitutional Development presents its report to the House that month;

   b.   for the Australian Parliament in the event that policy matters are debated as a result of the recent visit to the Territory of the Leader of the Opposition.

The main elements of current policy are set out in the attachment to this letter in note form. If a statement (e.g. in the Australian House) is necessary in the later part of February I will, of course, draw on this.

The position may, however, change in the early part of March because by then the Territory Select Committee on Constitutional Development should have presented its report to the House of Assembly. I do not anticipate that the House will complete its consideration of the report before June but Official Members will need guidance on the attitudes they should take to the report in the interim, and the Visiting Mission will probably seek a preliminary reaction from the Government.

The Administrator has in January reported that the transfer of decision-making power to Ministerial office holders which you announced in July, 1970, has been 'central to a number of other events of political significance.' Among them, in his opinion, has been an 'obvious fore-shortening in the independence time-scale'. It is too early to say whether this will be reflected in the report of the Select Committee, and in the views of the majority of the House. But early reports from districts visited by the Committee, and some reports of opinion in the Highlands expressed to the UN Visiting Mission indicate that it will. I would not be surprised if the House of Assembly were obliged at least to debate a proposal that full internal self-government be achieved in the period 1972–76 (the life of the next House of Assembly, for which elections take place in 1972) or the period 1976–1980.

In order to ensure, so far as possible, that such a debate takes place with some knowledge of the likely reaction of the Commonwealth to a House of Assembly resolution supporting the achievement of internal self-government in either of these two periods, I propose to authorise the senior Official Member to make a statement covering the following points:

   (a) The Commonwealth does not abdicate from its responsibility to make the final decisions on the future of the Territory, but it will not impose an outside view. If the House wishes, after due consideration, to recommend a timetable for internal self-government, the Commonwealth will be well disposed towards it;

   (b) if the timetable were to envisage movement to full internal self-government in 1972–76, then

      i)   the Commonwealth would, once the new House had settled down and shown that a group of Ministers under their own leader had the majority backing, act towards its leader as though he were Chief Minister and his colleagues as though they were a government. The Administrator would progressively cease to chair the AEC when matters affecting transferred powers were discussed. His authority would be confined to matters within Commonwealth responsibility. District Commissioners would become the personal representatives of the Chief Minister and would be appointed by him. This process could be well advanced by early 1973;

ii)   the Chief Minister would negotiate with the Commonwealth for the handing over of further powers, as he felt in a position to accept added responsibility. The hand-over could if necessary be spread out over the period to 1975;

iii)   by 1975 the process would be complete and the Commonwealth would legislate accordingly by amending the Papua and New Guinea Act to formalise the steps already taken by establishing a system of responsible government;

iv)   while the powers to be handed over would be a matter for negotiation, the Commonwealth would expect to retain until independence the responsibility for defence, foreign affairs, foreign trade negotiations, currency and international loans (for both of which it would continue to stand as guarantor) and the Supreme Court (but not law and order). It would retain responsibility for the public service and the Magistracy until 1975.

(c)   Reaffirm the Government's long-term position on economic aid as stated during your visit to Port Moresby in July, 1970.

(d)   The date for independence could be set after full self-government on request of the Chief Minister and on the basis of an expression of public opinion through an election in which the date of independence was in issue, a referendum or a consensus.

If the House were to favour internal self-government in the period 1976–80, the steps described above would be spread out over a longer period but would still start in the period 1972–76.

The alternative approach to that described above would be to have the Papua and New Guinea Act amended to introduce responsible government as a first step rather than a final one. This would reduce the flexibility left by the other approach in the hands of the Commonwealth and would over-dramatise the issue at a time when what is needed is continuous progress towards self-government as a matter of course and in an atmosphere of confidence. It would also be likely to accelerate the existing tendency of key Australian public servants to withdraw. I do not therefore favour it.

I have not been specific as to when the responsibility for law and order should be handed over. My preference is to delay that until the later stages, i.e. until well after a Chief Minister has taken office. The reasons for this are the heavy dependence of the Police on Australian officers, the need for time to build an indigenous foundation for the public service, and the need to retain the confidence of the expatriate communities in Papua and New Guinea. This could lead to a situation where the Australian Government had to take responsibility for picking the Chief Minister's chestnuts (e.g. forceful quelling of a Bougainville secessionist movement) out of the fire. But there is, I believe, sufficient flexibility in my proposed procedures to permit this problem to be resolved later on.

What I have suggested above is consistent with the present policies (Cabinet Decision 452 of 1970).[1] What will be required is increased speed in pursuing the preparatory measures therein envisaged.

The fore-shortening of the independence time-scale reported by the Administrator has caused me apprehension because the public debate on the time-scale has so far been conducted with very little regard to such crucial factors as:

   Quality of leadership: Is there likely to develop early in the life of the new House a cohesive grouping able to command a majority in the House, and in turn to support a leadership capable of governing and coping with e.g. dissidence and separatism?

---

1   Document 53.

Quality of executive support: The public service, with existing largely expatriate leadership, is barely able to cope with rapidly expanding requirements. The results of indigenisation, now being accelerated, could be chaotic if the key expatriates leave. The retention of expatriates depends on personal decisions which will be affected by anticipated social conditions not under Commonwealth control as such by financial and service conditions which are within Commonwealth control.

National unity: There are difficulties in balancing the demands for local autonomy against the need for a strong central government necessary for national unity.

Law and order capacity: This is not high at present. The police officer component[2] is largely expatriate and not well trained. A build-up will take up to 5 years.

Limited capacity to raise internal revenue: Internal revenue from all sources provided 39.7% of the budget in 1970–71. If Commonwealth direct expenditure on defence, civil aviation Commonwealth works which does not now appear in the budget but which would do so on or before independence is added to the budget total, the percentage is only 29.8. Of this amount, the greater part comes from expatriates either corporately or individually. Experience in other countries has shown a heavy decline in expatriate presence after independence if the standard of Administration deteriorates sharply or if the security of the expatriates is swept away. The measures being carried out, and others being set in train, to broaden the indigenous economic base will take some years to show effective results.

Inadequate constitutional and legal foundation for self-government: The Commonwealth has never planned on building in TPNG an exact replica of its own political and legal systems. But if by the time of full internal self-government there is not an adequate foundation, in terms of the systems themselves and of public support for them, the orderly development of a modern society could be jeopardised.

It is not possible to put a figure on the time required for this, but every year counts. I regard it as a folly to conduct a debate about the date of self-government or independence without reference to such factors as these, and I propose, in addition to the statement to be made by the senior Official Member, to ask the Administrator to have these factors brought into the debate in the Territory House of Assembly.

Once the House has decided its attitude to the report of the Select Committee I shall make a submission to Cabinet. In the meantime I propose to act on the lines set out in above in respect of the debate in the Territory House of Assembly and of discussions with the UN Visiting Mission in Canberra.

Attachment
Summary of Current Policy in Papua and New Guinea

(a) The destiny of Papua and New Guinea is to become a self-governing country developed for independence if and when it is clearly demonstrated by the majority of the indigenous population that this is what they wish.

(b) The Commonwealth intends to help the inhabitants of the Territory to become self-governing as soon as possible and to ensure that when this aim is reached the Territory will, to the greatest extent feasible, be able to stand on its own feet economically.

(c) The Government favours and aims to foster the development of national unity.

---

2   Presumably a reference to senior and mid-ranking police officers, rather than to the indigenous rank and file members of the PNG police.

(d) Decision-making authority runs with increasing financial responsibility.

(e) A time-table for progress towards internal self-government and eventual independence will not be imposed by the Government. This does not affect the urgency with which preparations for self-government are going ahead.

(f) The need to meet a situation in which the people of different areas of the Territory may wish to exercise differing degrees of regional responsibility is recognised and legislation to meet this has been introduced into the House of Assembly.

(g) The Government continues to support the economic development of the Territory through substantial contributions to the five year development programme on the basis that the House of Assembly will contribute by raising the maximum practicable finance from internal revenue. The programme is being revised to take account of the impact of the Bougainville copper project, the changes which have occurred in market opportunities and the need to accelerate indigenous participation in the economy.

(h) Bills to reconcile customary usage of land with the need to bring land into economic production will be introduced at the March meeting of the House.

(i) A long term policy on taxation is being formulated designed to increase [the] Territory's financial self-reliance.

(j) Integration of pupils and teachers in schools is being furthered wherever this can be done without educational disadvantage to the children concerned.

(k) In the public service policy is to promote the advancement of local officers at all levels rather than to localise from the bottom up.

[NAA: A452, 1971/0268]

138   MINUTES OF IDC MEETING

Canberra, 12 February 1971

Absorption of Functions Now Undertaken by
Commonwealth Departments and Instrumentalities in PNG

The second meeting of the core members of the inter-departmental committee was held on Friday, 12th February 1971. Those present were:

Prime Minister's Department	Mr J. Taylor
Public Service Board	Mr H. B. MacDonald, Mr J. Dick
Treasury	Mr H. G. Heinrich, Mr J. O'Neill
External Territories	Mr M. A. Besley, Mr C. E. Reseigh, Miss J. Prior

The Chairman opened the meeting with an outline of the approach of the Department of External Territories to the appropriateness of transfer of functions:

(i)   so far as it is a function of self-government, every case is appropriate for transfer in the long run;

(ii)   localisation is not essential; the Territory can assume responsibility for a function while the Commonwealth continues to provide staff—as in the case of BMR[1] at present;

(iii) between now and the period of transfer, the Territory should be consulted by Commonwealth Departments and Instrumentalities which have plans for expansion (e.g. Bureau of Meteorology). The standard of services should not build up to an extent that makes them prohibitively expensive for financial control by the Territory Administration;

(iv) a list of Departments and Instrumentalities in order of policy content has been distributed to members;

(v)   even in the case of those instrumentalities whose transfer is likely only at independence, e.g. OTC[2] and QANTAS, something can be done now so that there are in the Territory people familiar with the operations of international organisations in, for example, OTC.

The meeting was in agreement with this approach and note was taken that a function could be transferred irrespective of adequacy of local staff.

The feeling of the meeting was that if there were any choice over the timing of transferred responsibility, it should be sooner rather than later.

Mr MacDonald agreed that the Department of National Development could appropriately be considered first, as the staffing arrangements peculiar to it could be a useful reference for staffing other bodies.

Mr Reseigh listed the information sought and received. No replies have been received from the Department of Civil Aviation or the Department of Works; however it is expected that this will be discussed next week at permanent head level.

[*matter omitted*]

Mr MacDonald suggested that the Committee could go back to Cabinet with a programme for some of the instrumentalities while those which required more protracted consideration were still being discussed. This was agreed.

---

1   Bureau of Mineral Resources.

2   Overseas Telecommunications Commission.

Mr Heinrich's suggestion that Shipping and Transport should be tacked as well as National Development was accepted; the impression of progress had to be created.

[*matter omitted*]

Mr Taylor said that Departments would have to be imbued with the political will to overcome problems. Mr Besley cited DCA[3] as an example where it would probably be inappropriate to load the Territory with the sort of standards now imposed by DCA—present day Australian standards should not be the criteria.

Mr Taylor said that it could be borne in mind that if any information requested was not forthcoming Prime Minister's Department would be happy for Minister for External Territories to write to the Minister concerned, and the Prime Minister would support this.

Mr Heinrich pointed out that the financial implications of the Territory's assumption of responsibility for functions could affect the level of the Development Grant to the Territory. Possibly there could be an arrangement whereby, over a certain number of years, the level of Commonwealth aid would reflect assistance for the running of organisations, and such assistance would gradually be phased out.

Consideration would have to be given to whether this assistance would be tied to specific functions or whether, once given, it was up to the Territory to determine how it should be spent.

[*matter omitted*]

Four further meetings were agreed upon, on 18th and 19th February, to meet Shipping and Transport and National Development, and on 24th and 25th February to meet Interior and CSIRO.[4]

[NAA: A452, 1971/0674]

---

3   Department of Civil Aviation.

4   Commonwealth Scientific and Industrial Research Organisation.

139   LETTER FROM HAY TO JOHNSON

Canberra, 22 February 1971

CONFIDENTIAL

When I was in Port Moresby last week, we discussed your letter LH. 514 of 11th February[1] concerning the Minister's letter to the Prime Minister about constitutional advance.

This letter will confirm that the Minister's intention is to avoid fundamental changes in the Papua and New Guinea Act until virtually the last stage of movement towards internal self-government. There would be no early amendment, for example, to introduce the concept (and name) of 'Chief Minister'. This would be a de facto arrangement. The legal situation would remain, as now, that the Administrator is formally responsible to the Commonwealth for the administration of the Territory. The effect of the existing Instruction from the Governor-General would be widened as more powers were placed under local control.

What is contemplated is very much the continuation of the step by step approach to which you refer in your fifth paragraph, with the legislation conferring the formality of internal self-government coming at the end and not the beginning.

The timing of the intervention of the senior Official Member in the debate in the House of Assembly is, of course, for determination at your end. The point made in the Minister's letter is the need to ensure that the House when coming to its conclusion on the Select Committee's report (and it may wish to defer this in respect of the major constitutional matters until the June session) is not in doubt on the Commonwealth's broad approach. There may be some members who think that the Commonwealth would oppose a timetable set by the House. What the Commonwealth is opposed to is imposing a timetable itself.

What the Commonwealth would do if the House fails to agree (an eventuality referred to in your second paragraph) will need to be looked at in the light of all the circumstances at the time. We agree it would be a delicate situation.

We shall be giving early consideration to your final sentence, namely, access to classified intelligence and security files by a de facto Chief Minister.

[NAA: A452, 1970/5267]

---

1   Document 136.

140   LETTER FROM GORTON TO BARNES

Canberra, 22 February 1971

I have your letter of 11 February 1971[1] in which you told me of the broad lines which you propose to take with the UN Mission to TPNG when it visits Canberra.

I believe that we should, as far as possible, move with any fore-shortening of the independence time-scale. I think that it is important both in the discussions with the UN Mission and the debate in the Territory House of Assembly to avoid giving any impression that the Government is attempting to delay the achievement of internal self-government. In fact, the existence of some of the problems which you have raised to early self-government, such as the quality of leadership, the quality of executive support and the law and order capacity, could well be interpreted by our critics as being of our own making. Under these circumstances I believe that it would be advisable to avoid nominating time-scales for the retention of certain powers, such as retaining responsibility for the public service and the Magistracy until 1975. I think that the intermediate step of promoting indigene participation in all aspects of government should be accelerated. In particular, if the police officer component is largely expatriate[2] and not well-trained, increasing emphasis should be placed on training programmes for indigenous officers.

As far as the proposition that the Commonwealth should retain until independence the responsibility for foreign trade negotiations is concerned, we could well be accused of protecting Australia's trade interests by keeping this control. I am inclined to the view that it would be in our own long-term interests to provide all help and assistance but to bring on indigene participation in a direct way at an early date. While these two propositions are not mutually exclusive, I would not consider it to be essential that we should retain full control in this area until independence.

I note that you will make a submission to the Cabinet when the House has decided its attitude to the report of the Select Committee. Your Department has raised with my Department the possibility of the UN Mission having a brief meeting with me on its visit to Canberra in March. I would be happy to meet the Mission if you wish and suggest that our Private Secretaries arrange the details.

[NAA: A452, 1970/5267]

---

1   Document 137.

2   Presumably a reference to senior and mid-ranking police officers, rather than to the indigenous rank and file members of the police.

141   EXTRACT FROM REPORT OF ANZUS OFFICIALS MEETING[1]

Canberra, 1–2 March 1971

SECRET

Defence Developments, Papua/New Guinea

54. Mr Poyser said that Australia was responsible for the defence of Papua/New Guinea until independence. We had unreservedly accepted this obligation and had devoted considerable effort towards building up local forces—both as a supplement to our own forces there and as a nucleus for the indigenes own force. We had spent about $100 million on local forces and infrastructure, but the forces were still modest. The Army had two battalions plus supporting troops, and was known as the Pacific Islands Regiment; there was a division of the Navy built round five patrol boats; and a small RAAF detachment of transport aircraft.

55. A comprehensive review of forces against the growing movement to independence had just taken place. It had recommended that the Army be increased slightly, that Navy strength be doubled and that a start be made on the Air Force. However, this study had been done without any real indication of the levels and types of forces which the indigenes would want. It had therefore been decided to look at methods of consultation with the local people and of making them more aware of defence issues.

56. We did not know how long Australia would remain responsible for defence matters and there appeared to have been little consideration of this question by local leaders in Papua/New Guinea. There seemed to be a vague hope that Australia would continue to make some provision for defence or at least pay for it. However, we should not assume that Papua/New Guinea would always remain amenable to Australian guidance or even continue to want financial support for defence forces.

57. Australia could maintain the situation without outside help before independence. The main threat after independence would come from a possible breakdown in law and order from secessionist movements. Trouble might also arise from an immoderate reaction by a Papua/New Guinea government to incidents on the West Irian border.

58. Whatever the formal defence relationship after independence, Australian interests would lie in affording a P/NG Government of reasonable prospects of military assistance in case of emergency.

59. Papua/New Guinea's role in regional defence affairs had not been given much thought in the Territory.

60. Mr Shann said that the Australian assessment was that the main threat was internal, coming from law and order problems, secessionist movements, and the richer areas wanting to keep their wealth to themselves. But this had not always been the only potential threat. In the days of Sukarno's Indonesia, we had been afraid that Indonesia might make trouble. Sometimes we worried about the problems which might arise out of the fact that Papua/New Guinea was developing at a faster rate than Indonesia could afford in West Irian— this might also cause problems if Papua/New Guinea acted as a magnet for West Irianese. We assessed that under the present Indonesian regime, which we did not see disappearing in the near

1   The meeting was attended by over forty officials. The delegation leaders were Keith Waller (Australia); L. C. Larkin (Assistant Secretary, NZ Ministry of Foreign Affairs); and Winthrop G. Brown (Deputy Assistant Secretary for East Asian and Pacific Affairs, US State Department).

future, serious problems would not arise. After independence, if problems did arise, the United Nations would take an interest and this interest would probably not be favourable to Indonesia. Some United Nations members were not happy with aspects of the Indonesian acquisition of West Irian.

61. Mr Galvin said that, just as West Irian was becoming more Indonesian, Papua/New Guinea was becoming less Australian. The pace of development in Papua/New Guinea had quickened greatly over the last year. He expected that the Select Committee on Constitutional Development would table, and the House of Assembly would endorse, a timetable for self-government. It would then be for the Australian Government to decide what to do. It would be consistent with the Government's stated policy and actions to accept the recommended timetable. We did not know exactly what timetable would be recommended because there would be a delicate balance needed between the wishes of the conservative highlanders and of the progressives. However, it might be noted that three years ago the highlanders would not even talk about self-government; now the most conservative of them were talking about 1980. The only question was 'when'? He believed the Select Committee would most likely suggest that self-government should come during the life of the next House of Assembly, i.e. 1976–1980. Self-government would mean control over internal affairs. Australia would continue to look after foreign affairs and defence, and Australian forms and legislation would still apply. Independence would then be a matter for negotiation between the Papua/New Guinea Government and the Australian Government.

62. Mr Mullins (NZ)[2] asked about recruiting and localisation policy in the armed services, particularly officers.

63. Mr Poyser said that recruits were selected from all over the Territory. The training of officers was a slow and difficult business. There were now about 20 Papua/New Guinea officers, 12 in the PIR and 8 in the Navy. Training was carried out in Australia, and often some basic general education had to be given first. A more conscious effort had been made over the last year to expand officer training and the position should improve steadily from now on.

64. Mr Martin (US)[3] asked whether Australia had had any indication of the views of the Trusteeship Council Visiting Mission.

65. Mr Galvin said that the Mission would be in Canberra next week. It consisted of two Trusteeship Council members and, for the first time, two members of the Committee of Twenty–Four (Iraq and Sierra Leone). The general opinion of officials in TPNG was that this was one of the best quality Missions to have visited the Territory. One could not tell how much colour the Committee of Twenty-Four would want to add, but whatever report the Mission produced should be a sound document. The two Committee of Twenty–Four members were serious and questioning. Some of their remarks were unexpectedly frank and helpful, e.g., the Iraqi told a questioner in Bougainville that independence did not necessarily give the right to secede.

66. Mr Galvin said that his impression was that the Visiting Mission would be looking to provide some sort of timetable, but he hoped the Select Committee might pre-empt them on this. They would probably criticise the Australian administration on a few things such as land, political education and provision of secondary education facilities. In general, Australia could afford to be more confident because of the action the House of Assembly was expected to take.

---

2   R. M. Mullins, Head, Defence Division, NZ Ministry of External Affairs.

3   James V. Martin, Jr, Country Director, Australia, New Zealand and Pacific Affairs, US State Department.

67. In reply to a question from Mr Mullins (NZ), Mr Galvin said that he expected the House of Assembly to propose a time range rather than a specific date for self-government. This would probably be during the life of the next House of Assembly, 1976–1980.

68. Mr Martin (US) asked whether there had been any developments in regard to West Irian. Had any border problems similar to those that had occurred in the past been encountered?

69. Mr Shann said that Australia did not have anything like the problems it had had some time ago. There had been visits to Papua/New Guinea by the Indonesian Military Commander in West Irian and by Australian officials to West Irian. There was a clear intent by both governments to deal with problems as sensibly as possible. There would continue to be some movement across the border. The border was not yet clearly marked. The Papua/New Guinea Administration had had occasional problems with people who had crossed the border and claimed that they should not be sent back because they would suffer from their political activities in West Irian […]

70. Mr Galvin […] agreed and added two further examples of cooperation:

(a) the Administrator of Papua/New Guinea had accepted an invitation to visit West Irian in the next few months; and

(b) in the near future, the Speaker of the House of Assembly, Mr John Guise, would lead a Parliamentary Delegation to Djakarta at the invitation of the Indonesian Parliament.

[NAA: A1838, 936/30/2 PART 1]

142   FINAL REPORT OF THE SELECT COMMITTEE

Port Moresby, 4 March 1971

CHAPTER I

Introduction

1.   The Select Committee on Constitutional Development was appointed by resolution of the House of Assembly on 24 June, 1969.[1] Its terms of reference were:

'... To consider ways and means of preparing and presenting, and to draft for the consideration of this House, a set of constitutional proposals to serve as a guide for future constitutional development in the Territory ...'

2.   Your Committee has presented three interim reports. The first, on 17 November 1969, reported on the matters being examined by the Committee and outlined its proposals to tour the Territory to ascertain the views of the people on various aspects of its work. The second, on 12 March, 1970, concerned certain questions the Committee was considering and the course of action it intended to follow. The third, on 3 September, 1970, described your Committee's visit to countries in the Pacific, Indian Sub-continent and Africa, recommended certain constitutional changes and outlined matters being considered by the Committee. The Committee's recommendations contained in its third interim report were adopted by the House of Assembly on 24 September, 1970.

3.   Your Committee made two extensive tours of the Territory in April/May 1970 and January/February, 1971. In its tours your Committee visited each district twice and held a total of 236 meetings with the people.[2]

CHAPTER II

Internal Self Government

4.   On the evidence submitted to the Committee during its tour in 1970 the majority of the people of Papua and New Guinea expressed opposition to early internal self-government. The Committee also noted that there was a widespread lack of appreciation and understanding of the meaning and implication of internal self-government.

5.   Before your Committee made its recent tour of the Territory the Chairman outlined to the House your Committee's understanding of the sort of arrangements which will probably exist in Papua and New Guinea during internal self-government. The Deputy Administrator in a statement to the House of Assembly in November indicated that the Government agreed with the Committee's concept of arrangements regarding areas of Government being negotiated between the Territory Government and the Australian Government at the time of internal

---

1   For insights into Australian Government thinking on the formation and role of the 1969 Select Committee, see Stuart Doran (ed.), *Documents on Australian Foreign Policy: Australia and Papua New Guinea, 1966–1969*, Department of Foreign Affairs and Trade, Canberra, 2006, Documents 261, 263 (paras 24 & 25), 273, 275–276, 283 & 284.

2   For details on the Select Committee's work, see the bulletin circulated by the Committee in early 1971 entitled *Tour by Select Committee on Constitutional Development, 4 January to 19 February, 1971*, Select Committee on Constitutional Development, Port Moresby, 1971. For views expressed to the Committee during its 1971 tour, see also Minutes, Kerr to Barnes, 28 January and 23 February 1971, NAA: A452, 1970/5345.

self-government. The Deputy Administrator also indicated that the Government welcomed the Committee's definition as it would help to clarify the issues facing this country on the road to self-government and independence.

6.   Your Committee's understanding of the position at internal self-government was put to the people of the Territory before your Committee toured this year.

7.   The majority of the people of Papua and New Guinea again expressed their opposition to early internal self-government during your Committee's tour. However, while in the first tour the majority of the people were not prepared to consider when internal self-government should come about in Papua and New Guinea, your Committee found in its recent tour that the response of the people to this question had changed. Most people are now prepared to discuss when they feel the time would be appropriate for internal self-government to come to Papua and New Guinea.

8.   At the moment the majority of the people of Papua and New Guinea feel that internal self-government should come about no sooner than during the life of the 1976–1980 House of Assembly. Many people, particularly those of the Western and Southern Highlands, oppose early internal self-government. Those who oppose early internal self-government feel that there is a need for much economic, social and educational development and that there is a need for skilled local manpower in all aspects and areas of government before internal self-government can become a reality for the Territory. On the other hand, there are a number of people who feel that the time is now ready for internal self-government to come about in Papua and New Guinea.

9.   Your Committee believes that the rate of political development and awareness in Papua and New Guinea is accelerating. Your Committee is aware that the policy of the Australian Government is for the steady advancement of Papua and New Guinea along the road to self-government under the terms of the Papua and New Guinea Act. The changes announced by the Rt Hon. the Prime Minister in July, 1970,[3] have resulted in an acceleration in the advancement of this country towards internal self-government. Because of this rate of advance the possibility may exist that the majority of the people of the Territory may request that the country move to internal self-government before the end of the life of the next House of Assembly. Also your Committee is aware that there could be a change of Government in Australia which could result in internal self-government becoming a reality before the majority of the people are prepared to accept it.

10. Your Committee therefore recommends that the development of the Territory be geared to preparing the country for internal self-government during the life of the next House of Assembly so that should it become a reality earlier than expected or if it is in fact requested by the people then, then the move to internal self-government can be made at that time with the least possible amount of administrative disruption.

11. Your Committee is concerned that attention be given to the sort of economic and political arrangements and relationships which might be developed between Papua and New Guinea and Australia at internal self-government and recommends that these be considered as part of the programme of development towards internal self-government.

12. Your Committee feels that target dates for internal self-government and independence should not be arbitrarily set. Your Committee, nevertheless, believes that an approximate timetable, such as it now recommends, will provide a sense of direction to the development of Papua and New Guinea for internal self-government.

---

3   See Document 64.

13. If programmes are developed now with the view that the Territory may become internally self-governing during the life of the 1972–1976 House, your Committee feels this should ensure a smooth transition to internal self-government when the people are ready for it.

14. Your Committee believes in the planned gradual development of Papua and New Guinea for internal self-government and believes that the attainment of internal self-government should merely be a further step in an orderly process of development.

CHAPTER III

System of Government

15. During the November, 1970, meeting of the House of Assembly the Chairman of the your Committee outlined certain suggestions of the Committee regarding constitutional change in Papua and New Guinea short of internal self-government. These suggestions were discussed with the people during the Committee's recent tour and the people's reaction and attitude to them is outlined below.

16. The majority of the people of the Territory have requested that the system of government for the Territory be one single central Government, as at present. There was some call for a system of State Governments for the four main regions of Papua and New Guinea, but most people calling for this, when questioned, indicated that they would be satisfied with a single central Government, provided a good deal of authority and autonomy was given to the districts.

17. Your Committee recommends that the system of government for Papua and New Guinea be a single central Government as at present.

18. Your Committee has already recommended the establishment of area authorities to provide autonomy to the districts, but it is apparent on the evidence presented to the Committee that area authorities will need to be able to exercise real authority and responsibility if they are to satisfy the aspirations of the people.

19. The patron of the Mataungan Association, Mr O. Tammur, indicated to the Committee that the Association would not be satisfied with the proposed area authority concept. The Committee understands that his submission was for an independent government for the Gazelle Peninsula. Mr Tammur requested your Committee to record in this report that the Association and its followers would break away from the Territory of Papua and New Guinea if its wishes were not satisfied. Your Committee therefore records the Association's wishes for the information of the House of Assembly. From the submission it is not clear to the Committee whether a united self-governing Papua and New Guinea would in fact satisfy the aspirations of the Mataungan Association. Whether the Association would be any more satisfied with a united Papua and New Guinea central Government than it is with the present central Government is not clear to the Committee. As its wishes seem to run contrary to the [wishes of the][4] vast majority of the people of Papua and New Guinea who have expressed a desire for a strong central Government and a united country, the Committee cannot recommend any particular course of action which would meet with the Association's approval at this time.

20. Your Committee was advised in Southern Bougainville that the people wish to have an official referendum regarding the question of Bougainville seceding from the Territory before they would consider the matters outlined by the Committee. Your Committee indicated to the people of South Bougainville that it could not recommend that a referendum be held on the question, but that it would record this wish this report.

---

4   Editorial insertion.

21. During its tour the Committee received representations from certain Papuan people that Papua should be treated separately from New Guinea on the question of internal self-government – that is, it should be granted internal self-government when it wanted it and not have to take it when New Guinea becomes internally self-governing. There was also a call from certain Papuan people for the question of their status and citizenship rights to be clarified before internal self-government, and a call from some people in New Guinea to have Papua brought under the United Nations International Trusteeship system and administered by Australia as a trust territory along with New Guinea. Your Committee understands that the United Nations would not be prepared to have another territory brought under the trusteeship system and points out that generally Papua representatives are against Papua becoming a trust territory.

22. Your Committee believes it would not be in the best interests of the Territory as a whole for separate groups to break away and become self-governing before the whole.

CHAPTER IV

Structure of Legislature

23. Your Committee suggested that there be one House of Parliament at this stage of the Territory's development. The Committee believes that one House of Parliament—as at present—ensures the best use of the country's manpower and economic resources.

24. Some people felt that two Houses of Parliament would mean better consideration of legislation and some, while agreeing that there should be one House of Parliament at the moment, suggested that this could be reviewed after internal self-government had come to the Territory.

25. The majority of people, however, are in favour of one House of Parliament and your Committee recommends that the Legislature comprise one House of Parliament as at present.

[*matter omitted*][5]

44. Your Committee therefore recommends the following representation in the 1972–1976 House of Assembly:

18 persons elected by the people to represent Regional electorates;

82 persons elected by the people to represent Open electorates;

up to 3 Nominated Members, nominated by the House of Assembly for special purposes;[6] and

4 Official Members.

This structure would provide a legislature of 100 members elected by the people, provision for up to 3 Nominated members if considered necessary by the House and 4 Official Members.

---

5   The omitted material included discussion of views on representation, regional electorates, open electorates and nominated members.

6   The purpose of nominated members was to represent special groups and interests, including women. It appears that no women contested the elections in 1964 to the House of Assembly. One woman contested the elections in 1968 but was unsuccessful.

Structure of the Administrator's Executive Council

45. Your Committee has considered this and now recommends that the composition of the Administrator's Executive Council at the start of the 1972–1976 House of Assembly be as follows:

Administrator; 3 Official Members; 10 Ministers.

The Ministry

[*matter omitted*]

47. The Committee also recommends that following nomination of the Ministers in the 1972 House of Assembly by a Ministerial Nominations Committee composed of seven members of the House, the Ministers should choose one of their number to be the Deputy Chairman of the Administrator's Executive Council. The Ministers' choice for Deputy Chairman of the Council should be approved by the House of Assembly.

CHAPTER VII

National Unity

48. Your Committee recognises that a unified country and people is of the utmost importance in the move forward to internal self-government and later to independence and during the Committee's tours many people called for unity in Papua and New Guinea. One name, our own flag and crest will help to create a feeling of national identify for our nation.

49. The majority of the people have asked that our country be given the name Niugini and our people be called Niuginians. During your Committee's tours it noted strong support in Papua for retaining the name Papua and New Guinea but removing the 'and' between the two words. However, your Committee also noted in its recent tour that a growing number of people in Papua were now favouring the name Niugini for our country. The House is aware that the name Niugini has significant meaning in the Motu language and that our country is generally called New Guinea by people overseas. Your Committee recommends that our country be called Niugini and our people Niuginians.[7]

50. The crest suggested by your Committee is acceptable to the majority of the people. Many groups, particularly in the New Guinea Islands Region, submitted that some object representing their particular area be represented on the crest, but it would not be practicable to include a representation of all the areas on it. As there was widespread support for the crest as it stands, your Committee recommends that it be adopted.

---

7   Don Woolford has recalled that: 'There were plenty of suggestions for a new name. Niugini—a Pidgin spelling of New Guinea which also, in Motu, meant coconut stand and had gained some currency since winning a newspaper competition in 1968—had plenty of supporters. But many Papuans wanted Papua retained. Pagini was a compromise which received some backing, and another relatively popular choice was Paradesia'. Don Woolford, *Papua New Guinea: Initiation and Independence*, University of Queensland Press, Brisbane, 1976, p. 96.

The Motu language is spoken by communities in and around Port Moresby. Hiri Motu, also known as Police Motu, is a simplified version of Motu which was widely used in Papua in the colonial period. Hank Nelson has noted that at first there was support for the names 'Pagini' and 'Paginians'. This support, however, 'died quickly after Pidgin speakers who replace the "p" with an "f" demonstrated that to them "Pagini" sounded like a most improper suggestion.' Hank Nelson, *Papua New Guinea: Black Unity or Black Chaos?*, Penguin Australia, Ringwood, Victoria, 1972, pp. 163.

51. The Committee suggested a flag for the country and showed it to the people on its recent tour. Your Committee received numerous representations to either alter the suggested flag or replace it. Because of the wide variety of views about the colour and design of the suggested flag, your Committee has decided to choose one of the submissions made to it on its recent tour.

52. The Committee has chosen a design submitted by a young Papuan girl named Susan Kanike. In her submission to the Committee, Susan described the colours of the flag as being those most commonly used by our people in their traditional ceremonies. The Committee recommends that this flag be adopted as the flag for Niugini.

CHAPTER VIII

General

53. The Committee recognises that a strong and efficient Public Service is essential if Papua and New Guinea is to have meaningful self-government. The Committee and the people appreciate that there will be a need for expert officers to serve in the Public Service and private sector of the country for an appreciable number of years.

54. Your Committee is concerned at the disquiet among expatriate Public Servants which continues despite planning for an Australian overseas service into which they could be incorporated, and the existence of an Employment Security Scheme for permanent officers to be implemented on redundancy, or when the Australian Government itself is no longer able to ensure the maintenance of satisfactory terms of employment for these officers.

55. The Committee feels that it is now time for the Government to define precisely the terms under which the Employment Security Scheme will be implemented. The Committee hopes that when the time comes for this scheme to be implemented, then the provisions of the scheme will also be implemented generously. However, your Committee also hopes that all officers essential for the continuing development of Papua and New Guinea will remain in the future national Public Service.

56. In its third interim report your Committee indicated that it felt a statement of fundamental rights of individuals, that is, a Bill of Rights, was most desirable for Papua and New Guinea, but that it was giving this matter further consideration before making a recommendation.

57. Your Committee believes that a Bill of Rights drawn up now and enacted in the normal Territory legislation would not be in the country's best interests and your Committee therefore recommends that the drafting of a statement be considered by a committee of a subsequent House of Assembly, and that such a statement be embodied in a proposed Constitution for an independent Papua and New Guinea.

Recommendations

58. Your Committee recommends

(A) That the development of the territory be geared to preparing the country for internal self-government during the life of the next House of Assembly so that should it become a reality earlier than expected or if it is in fact requested by the people then, then the move internal self-government can be made at that time with the least possible amount of administrative disruption. (Paragraph 10).

(B) That the sort of economic and political arrangements and relationships which might be developed between Papua and New Guinea and Australia at internal self-government be considered as part of the programme of development towards internal self-government. (Paragraph 11).

(C) That the system of government for Papua and New Guinea be a single Central Government as at present. (Paragraph 17).

(D) That the Legislature comprise one House of Parliament as at present. (Paragraph 25).

(E) That 18 Regional electorates be created for the elections for the 1972–1976 House of Assembly. (Paragraph 30).

(F) An increase of 13 in the number of Open electorates, making the number of Open electorates in the 1972–1976 House, 82. (Paragraph 34).

(G) That the number of Nominated Members be not more than 3, to be nominated for special purposes, only if the House considers it necessary. (Paragraph 36).

[*matter omitted*]

(M) That four Official Members be appointed in the 1972–1976 House of Assembly. (Paragraph 43).

(N) That representation in the 1972–1976 House of Assembly shall consist of:

18 persons elected by the people to represent Regional electorates;

82 persons elected by the people to represent Open electorates;

Up to 3 Nominated members, nominated by the house of Assembly for special purposes; and

4 Official Members. (Paragraphs 30, 34, 36, 43, 44).

(O) That the composition of the Administrator's Executive Council at the start of the 1972–1976 House of Assembly be as follows:

Administrator

10 Ministers

3 Official Members. (Paragraph 45).

(P) That the Ministry should be chosen wholly from the Legislature (which may comprise Nominated as well as Elected Members), but that although the three Nominated Members may be appointed as Ministers, not more than two of them should be Members of the Administrator's Executive Council. (Paragraph 46).

(Q) That following nomination of the Ministers in the 1972 House of Assembly by a Ministerial Nominations Committee composed of seven Members of the House, the Ministers should choose one of their number to be the Deputy Chairman of the Administrator's Executive Council. The Ministers' choice for Deputy Chairman of the Council should be approved by the House of Assembly. (Paragraph 47).

(R) That our country be called Niugini and our people Niuginians. (Paragraph 49).

(S) That the crest shown by the Committee on its recent tour of the Territory be adopted. (Paragraph 50).

(T) That the flag based on a design submitted by Susan Kanike and shown to this House be adopted. (Paragraph 52).

(U) That the drafting of a Bill of Rights be considered by a committee of a subsequent House of Assembly and that such a statement be embodied in a proposed Constitution for an independent Papua and New Guinea. (Paragraph 57).

[NAA: A1838, 936/4/17 PART 1]

143   MINUTES OF IDC MEETING[1]

Canberra, 5 March 1971

Absorption into PNG Administration of Functions of Internal Self-Government

[*matter omitted*]

Mr Besley said that the Committee's approach was that it would be appropriate to transfer all functions of internal self-government sooner or later and that there was a strong presumption in favour of the transfer as soon as possible of all functions which would normally be exercised by a self-governing State. The absence of indigenes with the necessary skills was not regarded as preventing this, provided arrangements could be made under which the outgoing Australian Department would support the Papua New Guinea Department until it had the necessary number of skilled staff, e.g. by accepting a responsibility to second staff to the Papua New Guinea organisation or by undertaking work on an agency basis. The Committee had put these views to other Departments with whom it had had discussions and they had moved from a position of some doubts to one of general cooperation.

If an early transfer was not thought likely in a particular case the committee would be looking to the Department concerned to provide reasons. The committee would comment on those reasons and let the Department see the comments.

[*matter omitted*]

[NAA: A452, 1971/2647]

---

1   Hay chaired the meeting.

144   PRESS RELEASE BY BARNES

Canberra, 7 March 1971

Final Report by Select Committee on Constitutional Development

The Minister for External Territories, Mr Barnes, said today that he had read with great interest the final report of the Select Committee on Constitutional Development tabled in the House of Assembly, Port Moresby, on 4 March.[1]

The attitude of the Commonwealth to the Report will be determined when the House of Assembly has debated the Report and reached its conclusions on the recommendations in it. The Government attached great importance to the views of the House on major constitutional matters, the more so when they followed such an exhaustive enquiry into the wishes of the people as that conducted by the Select Committee.

Referring to the paragraphs in the Report which mention an 'approximate timetable' for the achievement of internal self-government, Mr Barnes said that reservations about a timetable expressed by the Government in response to a UN resolution in December last year were based on objections to a timetable being imposed by an outside authority.

Such reservations would not apply in the event that the House of Assembly on the basis of enquiries by the Select Committee were to recommend a timetable of its own choosing.

[NAA: A1838, 936/4/17 PART 1]

---

1   Document 142.

145   RECORD OF DISCUSSION WITH UN VISITING MISSION

Canberra, 8 March 1971

Members of the Mission[1] and its staff were present, the Secretary and senior officers of the Department of External Territories,[2] and Mr Ashwin of [the] Foreign Affairs Department. After exchange of courtesies it was decided to discuss first political then economic and then social (including educational) matters.

Political

The Secretary said that conferring increased power on local political leaders by the modification of constitutional relationships announced in July–August 1970 had been a real change. A second crucial development was the report of the Select Committee[3] tabled in the House of Assembly in the previous week and the Minister's statements of 7th March; in particular, his reference to the accountability to the Government of a timetable for constitutional development if recommended by the House of Assembly.

What might come out of the 1972 House of Assembly elections was a cohesive group of Ministers electing a spokesman of the AEC. If this were to happen they would have the power and there would be the machinery to negotiate transfer to them of the remaining powers to complete internal self-government. The only problems would be those of detail— e.g. responsibility for the functions now carried out by the Commonwealth Department of Civil Aviation. How far and how fast the transfer can progress will be for decision by the Government.

Sir Denis Allen commented that there might be need for provision of stimulus from the Australian end. The Secretary agreed; it would be by dialogue; the Government already had an inter-departmental Committee working in this field and the Minister had made a statement on it.

Sir Denis asked whether de facto the Administrator as a constitutional figure would as it were be replaced. The Secretary replied that this may happen imperceptibly. The approach would be flexible—a gradual withdrawal. In reply to the further question whether the withdrawal of powers would include the Australian power to veto legislation the Secretary said the final act would be an amendment of Australian legislation—but it could be that this was merely formal recognition of an already existing situation.

Sir Denis next asked what change in financial arrangements would be involved and the Secretary's reply was that there is need to think these out, but that they should be purely formal.

Sir Denis asked whether it was possible to forecast developments beyond self-government to independence. The Secretary said it is still a bit premature. The Prime Minister had outlined three possible methods of discovering the wishes of the majority on the issue of further constitutional development. He stated the Government's views on the television current affairs programme 'This Week', screened on July 19.[4]

---

1   Sir Denis Allen, a senior British official, chaired the Visiting Mission. The other members were Paul Blanc (Counsellor of the Permanent Mission of France to the United Nations), Adnan Raouf (Deputy Permanent Representative of Iraq to the United Nations), and Charles E. Wyse (First Secretary of the Permanent Mission of Sierra Leone to the United Nations).

2   Apart from Hay and Bill Granger (the note-taker), other DET officers present were not identified.

3   Document 142.

4   These were: a referendum, arrival at a consensus through discussion, or through 'expressions of views' by the House of Assembly. See Document 85.

Sir Denis commented that precedents show that independence usually comes very quickly after self-government and the Secretary said the Department was very conscious of this.

M. Blanc asked why there should not be created a position of Deputy Chairman of the AEC which would be the precursor to the position of first Minister.

The Secretary said this corresponded closely to the development of the de facto status he had described.

Sir Denis said he could see that development depended on personalities—the emergence of a charismatic figure: he is not immediately apparent.

The Secretary commented that mention of a Deputy Chairman in the Select Committee's Report (paragraph 47) had been a very big step forward.

Mr Raouf referred back to the Government's power to veto territory legislation. The Secretary said this was scarcely now exercised (it has not been used during the past three years), and progressively as powers were transferred was less and less likely to be invoked. Mr Raouf said he thought another aspect of the acceptance of and exercise of power by leaders in the Territory was to have indigenes facing the people in the exercise of executive authority under the elected indigenous leaders. This was particularly so in the position of District Commissioner. There didn't seem to be enough indigenes in senior field positions in the Department of the Administrator.

The Secretary said problems had been encountered and asked Mr Besley to discuss them.

Mr Besley referred to the position of the PSA[5] and to Section 49 of the Public Service (Papua and New Guinea) Ordinance 1963–1970. In answer to a question by Sir Denis as to why action was not taken under that Section he explained there is not as yet a Compensation Scheme. Discussions now in progress between the PSA and PSB should overcome the problems. Training of indigenes to accept senior positions is an important aspect. The Administrative College is important for this purpose and it is planned to use other facilities too; e.g., ASOPA.[6] Localisation needs speeding up on all grounds.

Mr Raouf expressed the view that to rely only on the Administrative College would be too slow and he thought that ASOPA provided training only for expatriates and only at patrol officer level, but surely locals could take over at all levels.

Mr Besley said it was a question of providing higher training away from the job for them.

Mr Raouf observed that it was to be expected that ASOPA would reduce its functions in training expatriates. Mr Besley said this would happen and the school would be re-oriented to training indigenes. It would however, continue to train expatriate teachers—these are required so that all indigenous teachers would not be engaged in teaching and some would be available for training and promotion to senior positions.

The Secretary said that the phrase '… the Territory be geared to preparing the country for internal self-government' (Select Committee Report para 58 (a)) was an apt phrase. Expert attention was being given to this.

Sir Denis said there appeared to be a deadlock in staff matters; the Mission had encountered demand for a published plan on indigenisation and redundancy of expatriates; it seemed as though the Government was waiting on the progress of negotiations for transfer of powers as described by the Secretary.

Mr Besley said that one factor was that the Public Service of the Territory was expanding; there had been delay also until the Select Committee addressed itself to the problem.

5   Public Service Association.

6   Australian School of Pacific Administration.

M. Blanc said experience is that it is useful to develop plans as soon as possible; it helps expatriates to plan and improves morale if they know their options. The question of localisation of District Commissioners is political rather than, as in the case of teachers, technical.

Mr Besley said that up till now the whole question had been ethereal—if a timetable is adopted as a result of the Select Committee's report it will help a great deal. There will be a series of options tied to different events, and the total plan will need to proceed hand in hand with local events. Expatriates needed to be retained as advisors but the policy adopted some seven or eight years ago of developing a unified service has created dissension. Creation of a pool of advisers would diminish this.

M. Blanc expressed the view that some heat could be taken out of the situation if the Commonwealth paid direct, and not partly through the Territory Budget, the whole of expatriate's allowances and salaries. He did not express himself very clearly, and I think Mr Besley missed the point. Mr Besley explained the rationale of the current system which M. Blanc already knew from earlier discussions.

The Secretary observed that it was logical that the advisory service should manifestly be provided wholly by the Commonwealth, and M. Blanc reiterated that he considered this would remove a cause of friction.

[*matter omitted*][7]

Sir Denis wished to discuss the question of allowing local public servants to engage in politics.

Mr Besley summarised the views in the Minister's statement on the subject, made in an address at the opening of the Public Service Association Congress, Port Moresby, 2 May 1970.[8]

The Secretary said a particular aspect of the whole question arises from the situation that the local Ministers are not yet used to being Ministers, and Departmental Heads are not used to working for Ministers. A senior officer from the Australian Cabinet Office is acting as advisor to help correct this.

Sir Denis said this was a particularly important question where there were illiterate Ministers. He said a number of senior officers had told the Mission that they would like a non-political Public Service.

Mr Raouf said this problem arose when there were party politics; it was a question of allegiance when there was a change in government.

Both Sir Denis and M. Blanc spoke about disparities in housing and general conditions provided for expatriate officers and local officers. They referred to this as the greatest cause of ill will, not the less important because it was essentially emotional.

[*matter omitted*]

Sir Denis said that the Mission had encountered the feeling that there was not enough consultation, e.g. local officers were not convinced that their views on mosquito screening and on the need for privacy in their houses were taken into account.

The Secretary said that this is now a problem for the Territory, and referred to the establishment of the Housing Commission and its powers, and added that cost is a major problem.

Mr Raouf asked why accommodation to expatriates should be subsidised.

---

7   The omitted material referred, among other things, to PSA 'complaints about control of the Public Service Board from Canberra'; to the powers of statutory authorities; and to the question of ministerial control of public service matters.

8   In that speech Barnes had underlined the importance of an apolitical public service. See Document 38.

The Secretary said that this was a part of the terms and conditions which were necessary to attract expatriates to work in the Territory; to that extent it was a passing phase. Charging expatriates economic rents would be impossible.

Sir Denis said he thought it important that as many frictions as possible should be removed because expatriate services would be needed in the Territory for a long time.

Mr Raouf said he would like to refer back to constitutional questions. What would be the position of the Papua New Guinea/Queensland border at independence?

Mr Ballard said that on the Australian side of the border close to the Papuan coast are three populated islands. Ethnologically the people were mostly Papuan, but they do not want to transfer from Queensland to Papua New Guinea. The Queensland Premier[9] is opposed to their transfer. The attitude of the Commonwealth is to keep the matter under review. The boundary does not seriously affect the international aspects of fishing. The territorial waters extend three miles from the coast, and outside these limits fishing rights have been declared to extend for a further nine miles. Papuans are allowed to fish in Australian waters equally with Australians. (No mention was made by Ballard of the situation after independence.) In connection with offshore oil a median line has not been drawn to delimit the Papuan and Australian share of the Continental shelf but as compensation an area has been left with Papua, and it so happens that this particular area has good prospects.

The Secretary pointed out that the question is not at present a problem but obviously the Government has to consider its position before independence.

Mr Ballard commented that the Federal structure in Australia complicates the question.

Mr Raouf said he would like [to have][10] discussed the status of Australians in regard to citizenship of Papua and New Guinea, particularly as it affects eligibility for election as Member of the House of Assembly.

Mr Besley said that Australians received citizenship of the Territory and the status of citizenship was currently under discussion. Mr Raouf asked what significance the line between Papua and New Guinea had, and Mr Besley replied that the Government treats people on each side equally.

The Secretary said it would be necessary to ensure that whatever was done in this connection was done with the approval of the people of Papua and New Guinea.

M. Blanc raised the question of common citizenship.

Mr Ballard said these are bread and butter issues within the Territory; they are not matters of international significance [...]

Sir Denis said that nevertheless a lot of people in the Territory are concerned with these questions, and particularly with the relationship of Papua to the United Nations. Some suggestions have been received that Papua should be placed under trusteeship before self-government or any rate independence.

Mr Ballard said that the views of the Papuans would be important in his connection, and Sir Denis acknowledged this.

Mr Raouf said he had the impression that Papuans did not want to give up their status of Australians until they were confident that there was going to be an independent Papua and New Guinea. The Mission had encountered allegations from both Papuans and New Guineans that the Government was favouring the other.

9   Joh Bjelke-Petersen, Premier of Queensland, 1968–87.
10   Editorial insertion.

Sir Denis said he would like to raise the question of defence and the role of the Army in defence and internal security. First, there is the question of external threat and the possibility of protection against external aggression at various stages up to and after independence. Secondly, there is the question of internal security and the fact that there are many precedents for coups by the Army. It seems necessary to inculcate allegiance to local authorities. The question is whether a military board should be established in the Territory to control the Army. Another question which has been raised is that one Minister should have some obvious link with the Army and be able to answer questions on the Army in the House of Assembly.

Mr Ballard said that is PIR is maintained purely for defence. It patrols the border and undertakes duties of that kind. He referred to Articles 4 & 7 of the Trusteeship Agreement which charge the administering authority to take measures to provide for the defence of the Territory. The Army may used to give aid to the civil power if necessary; it has not been so used but is appropriately trained and is on call if necessary. He would expect the Army to remain under Commonwealth control until independence and that there would be negotiations between Australia and a self-governing New Guinea for a defence treaty which would become operable on independence. There is now under consideration the question of how to rationalise this situation in relation to the House of Assembly. Cost is a big factor. New Guinea can not at present afford to maintain an Army from its own Budget. There is an arrangement for answering questions about the Army in the House of Assembly.

[*matter omitted*]

M. Blanc asked when the new flag will be adopted formally. Mr Ballard told him the flag would be used in the Territory before self-government but it would not have international status.

Mr Raouf referred to the attitudes the Mission had encountered that the UN was 'pushing' the Territory to self-government and independence. He said sight was lost of the qualification 'in accordance with the freely expressed views of the people' contained in Article 76(b) of the UN Charter. He asked if some effort could not be made to explain at least to Members of the House of Assembly the thinking behind the relevant UN resolution.

The Secretary said he thought that as a practice members of the House who attended meetings at the United Nations should report to the House on their return.

[*matter omitted*]

Economic

M. Blanc said that the first question which he would like to raise was that of lack of development in remote areas.

Mr Gutman said that this concept has arisen from the recommendations of the Economic Survey Mission of the IBRD.[11] They had recommended that the criteria for investment should be firstly to concentrate where there are best prospects for an economic return; secondly to

---

11   International Bank for Reconstruction and Development, an organisation which is part of the World Bank group. At the invitation of the Commonwealth Government a ten-member IBRD economic survey team had visited Papua and New Guinea from June to September 1963 and delivered its report in June 1964. The report recommended concentrating resources on areas which would bring rapid growth, helping the Territory increase its economic self-reliance. It also supported the expansion of education. See Ian Downs, *The Australian Trusteeship: Papua New Guinea, 1945–75*, Australian Government Publishing Service, Canberra, 1980, pp. 253–56. See also Stuart Doran (ed.), *Documents on Australian Foreign Policy: Australia and Papua New Guinea, 1966–1969*, Department of Foreign Affairs and Trade, Canberra, 2006, p. xxi; and Donald Denoon, *Trial Separation: Australia and the Decolonisation of Papua New Guinea*, Australian National University, Pandanus Books, Canberra, 2005, p. 30.

involve the locals; and thirdly that standards in the provision of housing, medical services and the like should be such that the Territory would subsequently be able to support them.

Mr Gutman went on to say that the Government and the Administration were not committed unequivocally to this concept. In any case investment in many development projects depended upon the grant of foreign aid and therefore on the criteria of the lenders or donors. District funds were made available to each district and there was a great deal of local discussion on their allocation. There were social as well as economic aspects. As a major source of funds the attitude of the World Bank was important, and it did not completely follow the concept which its Survey Mission recommended. The availability of land both physically and in regard to the people's willingness to make it available was an important determinant of where investment may be made [...]

[*matter omitted*]

[NAA: A1838, 689/1 PART 6]

146   RECORD OF DISCUSSION WITH UN VISITING MISSION[1]

Canberra, 8 March 1971

In Secretary's Office

The Mission first was received by the Secretary, Sir Keith Waller, in his office. There was an exchange of courtesies and a brief discussion—five minutes in all.

Sir Denis said the Mission had been impressed by the resources of the Territory, but they were not such as to provide for any easy pattern of economic development.

On 'Foreign Affairs matters' the question of national unity was in many people's minds—there was concern that both Papua and New Guinea should be committed to unity as soon as possible, even before self-government or independence. The Mission had attempted re-assurance, saying that both the UN and the Australian Government thought of the Territory as an entity and that at this advanced stage of evolution to self-government it is unnecessary and possibly would be delaying to attempt other changes in constitutional status. The matter of unity would easily be solved as self-government was achieved.

There were encouraging developments that earlier Missions had probably not encountered—the quality of the emerging senior public servants and of the bright young people undertaking tertiary education. One thing these people were thinking about was their place in the world—not just in relation to Australia, but also particularly to other countries in the South Pacific and in South East Asia. In the Melanesian and South Pacific communities Papua and New Guinea was something of a whale among minnows.

Sir Keith said in a sense the Territory was developing a foot in both camps—e.g., membership of the SPC[2] and of ECAFE.[3]

Sir Denis said a special topic in the foreign affairs field was the relationship with Indonesia; on the one had there was a feeling of brotherhood with West Irianese; on the other, a fear of being vulnerable after independence.

In Conference Room

As well as the Mission, Messrs Ashwin and Granger, there were present from the Foreign Affairs Department Messrs Harry (in chair), Moodie, Borthwick, Bailey,[4] Petherbridge,[5] Hogue and Dan.[6]

Sir Denis was invited to open. He said the Mission would like to know how the Foreign Affairs Department see Papua and New Guinea's emerging place in the world. Contacts with Australia had set high standards, and people were acquiring high standards through travel and seemed particularly interested in Africa. There was concern about Indonesia, and some suspicion of the UN in the light of the history of West Irian. The status of Papua in relation to the UN has

---

1   This meeting was held between DFA officials and members of the Visiting Mission. For details on the members of the Mission, see Document 146, fn. 1.

2   South Pacific Commission.

3   Economic Commission for Asia and the Far East.

4   Kenneth Bailey.

5   John Douglas Petherbridge, Assistant Secretary, UN and International Agencies, DFA.

6   Malcolm John Dan, Acting Head, UN Political Section, DFA. Dan was the Australian representative who accompanied the UN Mission on its visit to Papua and New Guinea in early 1971.

been raised—the Mission had expressed the view that the UN regarded the Territory as in effect a single country and was in favour of unity.

Mr Harry said that familiarisation with the UN had begun several years ago when indigenes began attending the General Assembly. He wouldn't know which way they turn their eyes— probably they would turn them all ways. Sir Denis had mentioned political matters; are they interested also in economic matters, e.g., do they appreciate the significance of membership of ECAFE, ADB,[7] etc.?

Sir Denis said they were extremely interested in assurances that Australia will continue aid, and that they will continue to receive UNDP[8] assistance. In fact they were interested in aid from all sources; e.g., in securing the services of Philippine school teachers.

Mr Harry asked the Mission's views on the employment of volunteers—and their utility. Sir Denis said that volunteers can do very useful work; also they act as contacts with the world generally.

Monsieur Blanc said that volunteers are probably most useful when they are attached to Missions.

In agreeing, Sir Denis commented that the missions probably have a more pervading influence in Papua and New Guinea than in most countries […]

Mr Harry observed that the standard of living seems lower in West Irian and asked if the PNG people were aware of and interested in this.

Sir Denis said that most of their information about West Irian came from 'refugees', and may therefore be coloured by biased sources. He agreed that there was greater consciousness of West Irian in areas nearer the border, but it is encountered in other regions possibly due to movement out into the community of permissive residents. Even on Bougainville, the possibility of instability in the relationship between Indonesia and independent New Guinea had been mentioned as a reason why Bougainville should secede.

In reply to a question about relationships along the border, Sir Denis said he assumed that perhaps there would be a future defence agreement to regulate this. Mr Harry said that what was in mind was more in the nature of a 'frontier regime'.

Sir Denis commended the liaison between the DC Vanimo[9] and the authorities in Djajapura.[10]

Mr Harry referred to the forthcoming visit of a party from the House of Assembly to Djkarta.[11] He said there had been several instances of cooperation between both parties and referred to the border mapping and marking. With further reference to establishment of a border regime, he said that both parties were beginning to understand the problems involved. In the meantime, the handling of refugees has been such as strictly to keep heat out of the question.

Mr Harry and Professor Bailey referred to the delineation of the continental shelf between Indonesia on the one hand and New Guinea and Papua on the other [sic]. They said there was hope for a firm inter-governmental agreement this year.

Sir Denis commented that it would be useful if all these things could be tidied up as soon as possible.

---

7   Asian Development Bank.

8   United Nations Development Programme.

9   This is a reference to the District Commissioner for the West Sepik District, J. E. (John) Wakeford. Vanimo is located on the north-west coast of Papua New Guinea, close to the border with Indonesia.

10 Jayapura.

11 Jakarta.

After Professor Bailey had commented that the AEC had been brought into the continental shelf discussions, Mr Moodie said that this led on to the question of training people in international relations to serve independent New Guinea. It was obvious that some people in the Territory would need training; Foreign Affairs could give assistance. Had the Mission any ideas?

Sir Denis said that this would be obviously useful, but at present highly qualified men for such training were very scarce. He thought the addition of Papuans and New Guineans to delegations travelling overseas was useful training.

It was not constitutionally possible to have a New Guinea delegation to the UN, but he was pleased to see that they were given opportunities to speak.

Monsieur Blanc commented that the extent to which the people could be used depended on their personalities. He said that maybe the special representative should be an indigene (the UK and France had sent indigenes as special representatives for a year or two before trust territories became independent). For the present he hadn't encountered any individual indigenes in the Territory who he though could handle this but it would come.

Mr Harry commented that the Government would look forward to giving indigenes a greater role from when self-government is granted.

Sir Denis said he thought this would be appropriate; they could then speak generally on the exercise of powers by the self-governing country.

Monsieur Blanc said he thought that more requests could be made to the United Nations for scholarships for travel by Papuans and New Guineans to learn more about the world; especially should these opportunities be given to young students—it would open windows for them.

Mr Raouf said that it was also important to create in the Territory a good image of the outside world. This includes an image of the United Nations organisation.

[*matter omitted*][12]

Mr Moodie raised the question of aid. He commented that receiving aid requires a redoubled effort on the part of the recipients. Sir Denis said […] aid tends to be taken for granted. Some of the young people had spoken about the need for hard work and self-help; also the local government councils are developing a realistic approach as the result of programming funds, and the MHAs and the Administrator's Executive Council also received valuable training in budgeting and supervising expenditure.

Mr Wyse said it is a fact, however, that the Papuans and New Guineans don't realise that aid is no substitute for self-help; that it is at best only a supplement.

Sir Denis said he thought the people of Papua and New Guinea do not realise how lucky they are—what a large amount of aid they receive per capita relative to other developing countries.

Mr Harry said that not much thought had been given to institutional arrangements when eventually the Australian aid is given on a State to State basis.

Sir Denis commented that separation of the Budget into several elements just recently had been a first step; maybe something more visible will be needed soon.

[NAA: A452, 1971/1981]

---

12   The omitted material contained a discussion of how to ensure that members of the House of Assembly were
     kept informed of UN discussions concerning the Territory.

147   RECORD OF DISCUSSION WITH UN VISITING MISSION[1]

Canberra, 10 March 1971

[*matter omitted*]

Mr Whitlam agreed that the mission should take notes and volunteered that they could refer to the discussions in their report. On his part, he would not make any public reference to what the Mission might say.

I did not take notes during the discussion and the following points are from recollection only, and are not in the sequence in which they arose.

Most of the time (say an hour) was occupied by Mr Whitlam presenting his views in a discursive way to the mission. Sir Denis commented or led the course of the discussion to some extent. During the final half hour Mr Whitlam answered questions, but his answers were generally lengthy, so that a number of questions which the Mission had in mind were not put. The whole exercise was not so much a discussion, as a presentation of his views by Mr Whitlam.

Mr Whitlam said that it was somewhat ironic that the mission should be seeing him just when the Select Committee Report had appeared, on major issues recommending what he had advocated.

He himself was very interested in Papua and New Guinea and had paid six visits there since becoming a Member of Parliament in 1952, compared with few or none by other political leaders. He knew many of the indigenous leaders, and was able to have dialogues with them.

He would refer to the Trust Territory and the Colony as an entity. This is how it should evolve.

Mr Whitlam did not think there was much political mileage for any of the Australian political parties in Papua and New Guinea as a political issue, and this was not the basis of his interest. It was even money whether a political party taking a stand on any Territory issue would gain or lose votes in the Australian electorate. At another point he said he could well be embarrassed ultimately by disappointment of 'cargo' expectations associated with his discussions with the Mataungans, his views about early self-government, and other measures with which he was becoming identified.

The Territory is, however, politically important to Australia:

(a) Principally it is a matter of Australia being seen to take positive action to disengage from a colonial relationship which is harmful to Australia's international standing—particularly to its standing with its neighbours in South East Asia and the Pacific which with one exception have themselves experienced colonial status. He wanted to see Foreign Affairs Department engaged not in apologies for delay in winding up Australia's colonial administration, but in cooperating with the Committee of Twenty-four.

(b) Also the Territory is close to Australia geographically and while it is a colony its problems are right on the doorstep, in distinction to the case where colonies were distant from metropolitan powers.

(c) In a positive way Australia wanted to have good relation with an independent New Guinea, and of course Australians had genuine good-will (not to be confused with paternalism) towards Papuans and New Guineans.

---

1   Those present at the meeting included the four members of the UN Visiting Mission (for details, see Document 145, fn. 1); Whitlam and his Press Secretary Graham Freudenberg; Robin Ashwin; and Bill Granger, who was the note-taker. Also present were Messrs Zollner and Abebe, UN staff members supporting the Visiting Mission.

His second last visit about eighteen months ago had had a great deal of publicity.[2] He had not particularly sought it or expected it, but it was during a silly season when there was not much news and had been greatly played up by the press. In the event, it had developed into probably the greatest single act of political education in the history of the Territory.

The general topic of timing for self-government was dealt with by Mr Whitlam a couple of times in his presentation to the Mission and in reply to questions. Mr Whitlam's theme was that grant of self-government is now simply a matter of timing. The demand for speed will be greater after the next elections; for the present candidates are soft-peddling in order not to alienate conservative electors. After the elections many members who have electioneered on parochial issues will link up with Pangu on the question of timing. Sir Denis referred to the Compass Party[3] proposal then before the Assembly to retard the timing proposed by the Select Committee; he thought no encouragement should be given to timing becoming a divisive issue which could cause a split out of proportion to its importance. It was quite apparent that self-government was on its way; it should progress under its own momentum—better to come by a steady progression as fast as assimilable, rather than by a series of jerky steps during which at times, in terms of practical arrangements, powers and responsibilities could pass prematurely to the government of the Territory.

Mr Whitlam acknowledged this in a non-committal matter.

On the question of determining the will of the people Mr Whitlam thought the Select Committee examination, its discussions throughout the Territory, and a House of Assembly debate and resolution on its report a satisfactory process for determining the will of the majority of the people. He passed the opinion that the Select Committee report was an excellent one for this purpose.[4]

A member of the Mission raised the question of absence of a nationalistic political party which could serve as a focus for, and a force motivating, a popular movement for self-government and eventually provide a governing group. Mr Whitlam acknowledged the deficiency, and in reply to a question said he thought the indigenised Public Service and the House of Assembly had to provide this stimulus and leadership until such a force emerges.

He thought that there would be a big change in the membership of the new House. There would also be wastage of some experienced political figures at the forthcoming election because they had become identified with unpopular policies of the Administration; for example, Toua Kapena loyally had had to announce an unpopular policy on wages (with which privately he probably did not agree), and Matthias Toliman had become identified with fees for education—this was particularly tough, because the local people recognised that it was practical for their children to undertake secondary education only as boarders where they had conditions conducive to study out of school hours.

In connection with readiness for self-government, Mr Whitlam said the local people were not lacking in ability, but confidence. He would have no doubts about appointing as Administrator the first medical graduate (Reuben Taureka) or John Guise. This was the only reference during the tour to the possibility of an expatriate Administrator being followed by an Australian-appointed indigenous Administrator rather than by a Chief Minister or the like selected by the AEC or the House.

---

2   This comment refers to Whitlam's visit to the Territory in late December 1969 and early 1970. See Documents 1, 3–10.

3   See also Document 148. The name 'Compass' was a contraction of 'combined political associations'. Compass supporters opposed a swift transition to self-government. The group later evolved into the United Party.

4   See Document 142.

Mr Whitlam said that the process of granting self-government would need some positive action by Australia. He did not discuss this in a context in which it was not clear that a majority of the people wanted self-government, and the Mission did not put questions on this, although a main purpose in seeking a discussion had been to determine the philosophy behind Mr Whitlam's 'coming ready or not' statements about self-government.

He stated his reasons for wanting early self-government as [follows:][5] to forestall separatist movements by creating a single Territory, to negotiate before Australia and the Territory grew apart, and to pass executive authority to the local people while they (and particularly the young educated ones) were willing to lean on Australia for advice, and there were Australian officers with Territory experience available to participate in Australian aid programmes to the Territory.

In the course of his comments on self-government Mr Whitlam commented on political education. He said it had not gone well because mostly it was in the hands of immature young men. He said he had had several complaints too about local government council advisers, youths who treated mature councillors with scant courtesy—making up agenda, writing letters in the name of the council, and carrying on council business without reference to the councillors. The absence of political parties to lead political thinking among the people had been noted, and it was rather left up in the air who would handle political education if not the Administration.

A question was asked on the negative side; what were the retarding influences?

Mr Whitlam placed the Administration first. He considered some District Commissioners [DC], and identified Mr Ellis with them, to secure their own positions played on the people's fears about self-government instead of endeavouring to allay them. Self-government was translated in pidgin by a phrase that implied Australia would withdraw personnel and funds. On the other hand, some District Commissioners are progressive. The retired DC of Manus had taken some delight that because Paliau[6] had been a problem to the Administration in the early days after the Second World War, Manus had maximum educational facilities, almost 100% literacy in the rising generation. Manus people were in important positions throughout the Territory, and Paliau himself was an MHA with the incongruous distinction of an award of the order of the British Empire.

A further retarding influence was the attitude of private enterprise. Planters and others endeavoured to keep wages down and did nothing to assist political education or entry to the economy of competing indigenous entrepreneurs.

He said wages were miserably low. When Labor was in office before, it had reformed the conditions of indenture principally by abolishing the penal clauses. Planters and others had said that this would be the ruin of the country but the Territory had survived and the economy had improved, and there was scope for Labor to make further reforms in industrial conditions in the Territory. The Government had been very remiss in applying ILO[7] Conventions to the Territory. This was a matter which he was following up by means of questions and he would keep at it. He attributed delay to pressure from planters. Mr Whitlam supplied the Mission with copies of about a hundred questions which he had on the notice paper.

---

5   Editorial insertion.

6   Paliau Maloat, formerly a police sergeant, formed the Paliau movement in the late 1940s, gaining thousands of adherents in the south of the Manus District. He was elected as member for Manus to the 1968 House of Assembly. According to Downs the movement 'blended the activities of a religious sect […] with elements of orthodox village administration'. See Ian Downs, *The Australian Trusteeship. Papua New Guinea 1945–75*, Australian Government Publishing Service, Canberra, 1980, p. 63.

7   International Labour Organization. The meaning here is presumably that the Commonwealth Government had been remiss in failing to apply ILO Conventions to Papua and New Guinea.

Mr Whitlam had expected the Christian Missions to be conservative to the point of retarding political advancement but had found this not to be so and expressed admiration for the progressive attitude which generally they took.

The Highlanders, Mr Whitlam said, were not as conservative as they appeared. They had capacity for self-government as evidenced by their handling of local government councils. They were standing out in order to try and gain provision of roads, schools, etc. Some of them under the influence of their educated children were fairly progressive in political thinking—e.g. Kofikai.[8]

Mr Whitlam or his Secretary asked whether the Mission had encountered the 'West Irian threat'. The answer was only from people who had had immediate contact with refugees who probably were not objective in their accounts of life in West Irian. Mr Whitlam said he considered it a phony scare.

On language Mr Whitlam said multiplicity of local languages was a handicap in some respects, but in a broader view by imposing the necessity for a lingua franca it was unifying. If there were only two or three languages throughout the Territory this could, as in the case of India, be a divisive influence.

On the question of Bougainville separatism Mr Whitlam said he thought that if Australia could do a deal with the United Kingdom, with the consent of the people, to take BSIP[9] into the Territory of Papua and New Guinea this would tend to remove some of the motivation for secession by the people of Bougainville who feel strong bonds with other Solomon islanders. He considered this would be preferable too to BSIP becoming yet another mini-State.

In reply to a question Mr Whitlam said he feared the area authorities proposals at this stage in political evolution could be divisive; for the present the priority is to establish and consolidate strong central government making its presence felt at district level through indigenous DC's and magistrates.

Mr Whitlam said he considered localisation was lagging badly. External Territories Department and the Administration were not prestigious services and too many jobs which indigenes could handle adequately were filled by young, just-average Australians who travelled to the Territory on first class air tickets and remitted a good deal of their salary to Australia for holidays, amenities of living, school fees for their children, etc. A lot of the Australian aid funds was thus diverted from the Territory economy.

Out of [a] comment by Sir Denis emerged views that the greatest lag in indigenisation was in district administration (DC's etc.) and justice (Magistrates) where the visible manifestation of district administration of indigenous central government was most important. Mr Whitlam commented that health, agriculture and education departments were doing quite well in indigenisation and maybe DC's—who really have a coordinating rather than a technical function—should be pulled in from whatever departments could best provide them. *Obiter Dicta*[10] by Mr Whitlam: the Supreme Court of the Territory is excellent; the Magistrates are very poor.

Mr Whitlam cited some newly independent countries which employed more expatriates than before independence. But they were employed in technical and advisory functions. In expert fields and in tertiary education particularly employment should be cosmopolitan. The important thing is that the employers and the decision makers should be Papuans and New Guineans.

---

8   Sabumei Kofikai, MHA for Goroka.

9   British Solomon Islands Protectorate.

10   A magisterial comment in passing.

Mr Whitlam said he thought it was necessary to have satisfactory schemes for secondment of experts from Australia, and satisfactory conditions for re-absorbing into Australia professionals who stayed on in the Papua and New Guinea services while required—both to induce them to stay on and to avoid creation in the metropolitan country of a disaffected group which would tend to sour the spirit of the handover. The problem of providing for these officers congenial alternative employment utilising overseas know-how was rather more difficult for Australia than for England and France.

As referred to earlier, Mr Whitlam, expressed the view that private enterprise in the Territory was doing little to assist indigenous entrepreneurs to enter the economy. He considered it a sad commentary that the private enterprise sector was entirely in the hands of expatriates, Caucasian or Chinese. He said that even prior to the war indigenes had had such businesses as taxis, but that now there were none of these. He referred to reports of the Mission's comments that there were no indigenous members of the Chamber of Commerce in Rabaul.

In connection with both this and political education he said that at his meetings in the Territory there had always been Europeans who wanted to dominate. In a number of cases be had found it necessary to ask that Europeans withdraw from his meetings in order to induce frank expressions of views by the native people. He seemed surprised when the Mission told him that only at Madang had Europeans played a significant part in its public meetings.

Mr Whitlam said that his party was akin to the socialist-democratic parties in a number of continental countries. He considered that socialism had probably a greater part to play in developing countries than in the developed ones, and that joint ventures between Government and private enterprise on the line of Commonwealth New Guinea Timbers and the Oil Palm Project were desirable. In answer to a comment that this would require considerable Government funds he said this was understood; he would like to see the Government saving money in some directions, principally by localisation, and spending it in more constructive ways; he considered that the Government should spend up to 1% of GNP in the Territory.

Mr Whitlam conceded that there was at present a lack of managerial skill among indigenes and that a number of enterprises to be successful had to employ European managers at this point of time. He did not deplore this, providing the managers were employed by the native people. He considered that cooperatives had great scope.

He said that individual entrepreneurs were emerging, but that very often the Administration did not give them much encouragement. He instanced the case of a man who learnt from an Administration officer how to make very good metal furniture. This man had received loans from the Development Bank to acquire premises and to tool up. Unfortunately when tenders were let for furniture, they were for such quantities and the delay in payment was such that this man found it impossible to do business with the Government and therefore furniture of this kind was imported from the South instead of being obtained through him. If the stores and tender procedure were more flexible, it would have been possible for him satisfactorily to have contracted to supply the requirements.

Mr Whitlam said the troubles on the Gazelle were deep-seated and not of recent origin but there had been provocation by the Administration. Basically the Mataungans are non-violent. Oscar Tammur in particular is anxious to avoid violence. The Mataungans are winning their points (change in nature of local government Council; transfer of [the] DC; transfer of Magistrates) and therefore, despite the hopes of the Administrator which he shared, it is unlikely they will participate in the forthcoming Council elections and by electoral success find scope for their influence within existing institutions. The long term outcome is hard to foresee. Their economic aspirations are unlikely to be realised because of limited managerial capacity (I think it was here that Mr Whitlam said that because of his contact with Mataungan leaders he was in risk of being embarrassed when eventually it became apparent the cargo will not eventuate). On purely political and industrial issues the Association could last a long time. In Rabaul they have a wing of the Association with membership of Sepiks[11] and this is a unifying influence: to the contrary, the Administration's contemplated strike-breaking action by using Sepik labour in Rabaul would have had a strongly divisive effect.

Re-location of the boundary between the mainland of Australia and Papua should be effected before there was danger of it becoming a subject of dispute between Australia and the self-governing Territory. Mr Whitlam's main concern was the question of territorial waters in relation to passage by ships engaged in ordinary coastal traffic, but reference was made also to fisheries and to off-shore minerals and oils. Olewale's representations received mention. The delineation of the continental shelf boundaries should be by one of the internationally recognised techniques which could ultimately be accepted as an international boundary by the Australian and the Papua and New Guinea Governments. The complication raised by the inhabited islands where people have been under the jurisdiction of Queensland was mentioned but not discussed.

Mr Whitlam questioned whether an army was needed at all in Papua and New Guinea: certainly it should not be larger than the present two battalions. Relativity with the police had raised problems; apart from questions of pay, allowances and housing, the army tended to work and live together and to develop an esprit de corps and high standards in sport and the like—on the face of it to outclass the police. If the army ever had to be employed within the Territory, it would be a shocking thing if it were not commanded exclusively by indigenes. Most importantly, machinery is needed to bring the army under local (i.e. indigenous) civil control. Mr Whitlam referred to the 'call out' but did not discuss it.

[*matter omitted*]

[NAA: A452, 1971/1003]

---

11   People from the Districts of East Sepik and West Sepik who had migrated to East New Britain.

148   NOTE BY JOHNSON

Canberra, 11 March 1971

Political Development—Parties

Representatives of the Compass Party[1] saw me on March 10th, 1971, to discuss their future relationships with the Government. The following were present:

His Honour the Administrator
Deputy Administrator, Mr Newman
Mr Tei Abal, Chairman of Compass
Mr Sinake Giregire, Deputy Chairman of Compass
Mr Anton Parao,[2] Organising Secretary
Mr Ron Neville.[3]

The representatives said that their organisation had reached such a stage that they now urgently required a floor leader in the House of Assembly and that leader had to be a man of both status and experience. A European would be unacceptable. However, all of those with leadership qualities were members of the Ministry and, consequently, the Party posed the following questions to the Government:

1.   If the leader selected were already a Minister, could he remain one after taking up his party post, though sitting in the front bench of his party group?

2.   If not, would the Government agree to a Minister resigning to take up party leadership?

3.   In the event of 2, would the Government make a special allowance to the leader of the majority party to compensate him for the financial loss suffered through his resignation from the Ministry?

I replied that a Government could only operate effectively if it could be assured of the support and loyalty of the Ministers, who could contest issues as strongly as they liked in AEC and within the Ministry but were bound thereafter to support the decisions reached in AEC or Ministerial Conference. Thus a Compass Minister would be bound to support Government decisions even though at times such decisions might differ from those pursued by Compass. In such cases the Minister would have no choice but to resign from either the Ministry or the party.

I pointed out that the next constitutional development could well be a form of party government which would ensure the coincidence of Government and Party views so that conflict would not take place but in my view the Party was still a good long way from having the policies, organisation and discipline to do this.

---

1   For background on Compass see James Griffin, Hank Nelson and Stewart Firth, *Papua New Guinea. A Political History*, Heinemann Educational, Richmond, 1979, pp. 168–69.

2   Anton Parao, a teachers' college student and student leader who had advocated for 'no independence for at least 35 years', was elected as the Western Highlands regional MHA in the 1972 elections. See R. S. Parker, 'Papua New Guinea', in Gordon Greenwood and Norman Harper (eds), *Australia in World Affairs, 1966–1970*, Cheshire for the Australian Institute of International Affairs, Melbourne, 1974, pp. 393–424, 417–8

3   MHA for the Southern Highlands regional electorate. Downs has described Neville as 'an aggressive conservative who relied heavily on the advice of T. W. Ellis, the Director of District Administration, better known as the former District Commissioner at Mt Hagen in the Western Highlands'. Ian Downs, *The Australian Trusteeship: Papua New Guinea 1945–75*, Australian Government Publishing Service, Canberra, 1980, p. 393.

To the second and third questions, I told the representatives that this was their decision but that the matter of additional allowances was for the Minister for External Territories to decide and it might not be reasonable to consider this until the new House of Assembly came into being in 1972.

Comment

It is now quite apparent that the 1972 House of Assembly will see the introduction of party-type government if any one political party, or group of political parties, obtains a firm majority in the elections. At least for some time to come party organisation will be inadequate and amorphous, while party discipline will be poor. The very fact that a majority party will have large numbers means that its task in organising its members, who see each other infrequently, may well be beyond its capacity. The development of policies based on a political philosophy is also unlikely and party attitudes may lack consistency. Ad hoc decisions will be taken on many issues.

For the first two years of its existence it seems likely that the House and the Ministry will continue to be strongly influenced by the views of senior expatriate public servants, though it would be rash to assume that this will prevail in all cases. The presence of the Administrator and three Officials in the AEC will be a stabilising influence during this period. If a well organised majority party emerges in 1972 it is unlikely that the full self-government could be delayed beyond mid-1974.

[NAA: A452, 1970/4963]

149 LETTER FROM JOHNSON TO HAY

Port Moresby, 15 March 1971

Recent events have again caused renewed discussion on the question of the Papuan and New Guinean citizenship. When we considered this earlier[1] it was agreed that, although there may be some legal problems, these would not be insurmountable and that it would be advantageous to introduce a local citizenship some time prior to self-government.

My preliminary thoughts are that citizenship would be conferred automatically on all indigenous inhabitants and that it would be available on application for those of non-indigenous origin who have been born here or who have fulfilled a residential qualification of, say, five or seven years and were resident at the time of application. As I recall, most of these suggestions have been canvassed recently.

Such action would in part meet the desires of those who wish to abolish the distinction between Papua and New Guinea and would provide a further unifying factor for nationalist sentiment.

I recommend early action to create a citizenship status for residents of Papua-New Guinea. I believe that there would be strongly favourable reaction over most of Papua-New Guinea for such action and suggest that, if possible, legislation be prepared for presentation to the June meeting of the House of Assembly.

[NAA: A452, 1970/1453]

---

1   See Document 135.

150   MINUTE BY GALVIN

Canberra, 15 March 1971

S<small>ECRET</small>

TPNG—Review of Defence Forces

The Defence Committee considered a paper, prepared by the JPC,[1] in September last year. The Committee decided to remit the paper to a Working Group which should:

(a) prepare proposals for further training of indigenes; indicate what flexibility is needed on manpower ceilings for the PIR to enable greater localisation of the PIR;

(b) consider the extent and methods of consultation with local TPNG opinion on defence matters;

(c) re-state the approved statement of the strategic importance of New Guinea to point up that any military capability possessed by Papua and New Guinea serves the defence interests of Australia;

(d) examine the potentiality of involving the Ministerial office holder in defence matters.

2.   The Working Group has now virtually completed its task and the final draft of the paper will be sent to Departments for final clearance this week.

3.   The paper recommends inter alia:

(a) consultation to be carried out through the AEC;

(b) papers to be presented to the AEC by the Administrator over a period of time in order to involve the AEC in the process of defence planning;

(c) an existing Ministerial office holder be allocated the task of spokesman in the House on defence matters;

(d) greater flexibility in PIR ceilings to increase training and localisation of PIR army procedures in the Territory;

(e) a group of officers within the Administration to be established now to handle defence matters for the Administrator—training to be provided where appropriate by the Defence Group;

(f) the feasibility of turning the existing PNG Command Headquarters into a centralised Defence Organisation be examined;

(g) compatibility of existing Service procedures with those of the Administration be examined;

(h) flying and aircraft maintenance training to commence;

(i) naval ceilings to be adjusted to ensure greater localisation;

(j) an early matter for consultation to be the future of the naval base at Manus and the proposal to establish a patrol boat base at Madang;

(k) as part of the consultative and educative process a paper be prepared for presentation by the defence spokesman Ministerial office holder to the next meeting of the House of Assembly.

---

1   Document 100.

4.   As soon as the paper has been cleared by Departments it will be passed to the Secretary, Department of Defence.[2] In view of the Defence Committee minute attached there would seem no need to remit it to the Defence Committee again. Rather the next move would be the preparation of a Cabinet Submission for early submission by the Minister for Defence.

[NAA: A452, 1970/4193]

151   PAPER BY DFA[1]

Canberra, 19 March 1971

SECRET

Implications for Department of Foreign Affairs of Early Self-Government and Independence for Papua and New Guinea

I.   Time Scale

With the exception of the proposed name of 'Niugini' for an independent state of Papua and New Guinea (PNG), the PNG House of Assembly has now adopted the Final Report of its Select Committee on Constitutional Development.[2] That report recommended, *inter alia*, an approximate time-table for the achievement of internal self-government during the life of the next House of Assembly (1972–1976). The Australian Government had already foreshadowed its support for the recommendations of the Select Committee, when the Minister for External Territories said on 7 March 1971, that Australian Government reservations about a time-table for independence 'would not apply in the event that the House of Assembly, on the basis of enquiries by the Select Committee, were to recommend a timetable of its own choosing'.[3] The House has recommended such a time-table.

2.   While the precise date for full independence remains unstated, we can no longer assume that final transfer of powers will occur at some distant point in the future. Once internal self-government is achieved, possibly as early as 1973, independence will follow quickly. And even before full independence, PNG Ministers will need to be consulted, briefed and educated, on foreign affairs issues. For planning purposes and in order to achieve our long-term objectives in PNG, we must now work within a minimum time scale for full independence during the life of the next House of Assembly (1972–76). Should independence come later, and this seems unlikely, we will have lost nothing by being prepared to relinquish control by an earlier date. Recent political developments in PNG have demonstrated that the political climate is changing more quickly than many had expected and that the desire for self-government is accelerating among the leaders of PNG.

3.   The main consideration that should influence the sense of urgency with which Australia acts in this matter, is a crucial one that can be expected to make or break our immediate post-

---

2   Arthur Tange.

---

1   It appears that this paper was circulated only within the DFA. The author is not identified but it may be a revised version of the paper earlier prepared by Murray Bourchier which is referred to in Document 107, para. 4. See also Document 153.

2   The House of Assembly adopted the report on 11 March 1970.

3   Document 144.

independence relations with PNG. In order to establish healthy post-independence relations, Australia should seek to leave PNG with some measure of dignity, goodwill and the capacity in the future to further its own interests there. Otherwise we run the risk of being represented as having been forced out reluctantly, with much residual bitterness, economic uncertainty and political instability.

II   Australia's Objectives in PNG

4.   Australia's national interest requires a peaceful transition to internal self-government and independence of a united PNG with strong economic and political ties, and favourable historical ties, to Australia. These must be seen by PNG as being to its advantage. They should be such that PNG would actively wish to continue to seek our guidance and help in developing its relations with the outside world. In order to realise these objectives, much will depend on how and at what pace we handle the transfer of sovereign powers to a PNG Government.

5.   The potential for separatism in PNG is already high. The Select Committee's Report has drawn attention to the positions adopted by the Mataungan Association, which has demanded independence for the Gazelle Peninsula, and by the people of Southern Bougainville, who seek a referendum regarding the secession of Bougainville. These demands are not likely to be met by the House of Assembly, but it is clear that in the next few years the radical, politically-conscious activists in New Britain, Bougainville and Papua will continue to force the pace of self-government and independence. We need to take this into account and we shall need to bend before it, at least to some degree, if we are to preserve a viable PNG with prospects for good relations with Australia.

6.   Under its Trusteeship obligations Australia is obliged to assist PNG in developing its relations with the outside world. Because of the expense involved and also because of the lack of adequate trained personnel in PNG, we should encourage PNG initially to establish only a limited number of embassies and to further its interests in other countries through the Australian missions there, supplemented as necessary (e.g. in conference posts) by visits by PNG officers based in Port Moresby. We should urge PNG to establish overseas missions in areas of maximum economic and political importance, and to concentrate in the first instance on creating an effective home office. This would logically mean representation in the first instance in only four capitals—Canberra, Djakarta, New York (United Nations) and Tokyo, though PNG might well decide on more than this (including, perhaps, Honiara, Djajapura[4] and Fiji.) In assisting TPNG into these relationships our primary effort should be directed at Indonesia. Possible problems and pinpricks should be removed before independence and it would be essential to associate Territory leaders and the embryo PNG Foreign Ministry in the international discussion about these problems. Delimitation of the border, offshore rights, border crossings, refugees, health, quarantine, customs and immigration problems with Indonesia should all be settled before independence. Most importantly, however, PNG in general but its leaders in particular must be brought to accept that West Irian is a Province of Indonesia—a fact that currently enjoys only tenuous acknowledgement in the Territory. Conversely, we should seek to encourage the Indonesians to underline their support for PNG's independence, sovereignty and territorial integrity.

7.   In the United Nations and elsewhere we can expect PNG to diverge from us on many international issues that currently divide the races and rich and poor. We must accept that for a time PNG will probably hate us a little. Indeed, the growth of a sense of national identity and a desire for independence are virtually synonymous with the development of differing

---

4   Jayapura, the largest centre in the Indonesian part of the island of New Guinea. Its name was changed from Djajapura to Jayapura in 1973.

attitudes between the ex-colonial power and the ex-colony. We should not be deterred by this, nor should we seek to impose our views. Of far greater and lasting importance will be PNG's attitudes towards the larger strategic and political issues on which we might expect to influence their views. With far-sighted, sensitive handling, there is no reason why PNG, Australia and Indonesia should not develop a common fundamental outlook on their respective interests in this region.

8.   If PNG's international relations evolve smoothly and logically, they could probably eventually be expected to extend to modest representation in Bangkok (to cover ECAFE and other regional developments—ASEAN, ASPAC and perhaps, too, the ADB)[5], Noumea (the South Pacific)[6] and possibly Brussels (the EEC[7] and aid). For the time being, however, we should encourage this sort of international organisations work on an *ad hoc* basis from Port Moresby; it would for some clearly be extravagant to send abroad on [a] long term [basis] anyone able enough to do this work.

9.   PNG relations with the United States, Britain and other countries could be handled by Australia.

10. It is in our and PNG's interests to encourage this sort of evolution, although there are limits to what we can in this respect.

11. In short, therefore, we wish to see the creation of a united, independent PNG, which shares some at least of our own international attitudes and which understands the reasons behind those which it does not share. We wish to exclude inimical influences, especially those of the PRC[8] and Soviet Union, and to ensure that PNG avoids disputes which could embroil us in conflict with Indonesia. We wish to see a PNG which retains friendly ties, including defence ties, with Australia and which automatically turns to us for assistance and guidance. We wish to protect Australian commercial and investment interests. We wish to ensure that so far as possible the evolution of PNG's international relations is smooth and logical. We have a very limited amount of time available either to create the machinery for PNG to conduct its own foreign affairs or to achieve the atmosphere that we would like to exist at independence.

III How Do We Achieve These Objectives?

12. Within a few years the Department of Foreign Affairs will be the principal point of contact between Australia and PNG, bearing primary responsibility for the state of relations between the two. If the present Australian departmental arrangements for relations with PNG are continued until independence, the ground on which Foreign Affairs will have to build— the state of Australian relations with PNG at the date of independence—will depend almost entirely on the performance of those departments now principally responsible for the Territory: External Territories, Defence, Trade, Civil Aviation, Works and Housing. We cannot be sure that this will produce the best long-term results for Australia. Foreign Affairs must, therefore, begin to take up its responsibilities immediately, in order to ensure that Australian actions in PNG before independence do not sow seeds of hostility or resentment towards Australia; that Australia, while remaining the major aid donor in PNG, is seen not simply as a source of cargo,

---

5   The organisations referred to were the UN Economic Commission for Asia and the Far East (ECAFE) —which later became the UN Economic and Social Commission for Asia and the Pacific (ESCAP); the Association of Southeast Asian Nations (ASEAN); the Asian and Pacific Council (ASCAP); and the Asian Development Bank (ADB).

6   Presumably Noumea was referred to as a possible locale for PNG representation because it hosted the headquarters of the South Pacific Commission (SPC).

7   The European Economic Community (EEC).

8   Peoples Republic of China (PRC).

but in context, as a state like many others, with interests of its own spreading far further afield than PNG; that the Department is prepared both physically and in terms of knowledge and wisdom, to assume primary responsibility for relations with PNG. All three tasks are urgent, and share a high priority; because they must be undertaken in a bureaucratic framework which is necessarily slow-moving, they should be commenced without delay if they are to be done effectively. In undertaking them, we should take into account the experience in this field of countries—especially Britain—experienced in the art of decolonisation.[9]

13. The basic task—ensuring that Australian actions now do not prejudice Australia's standing later—is in many ways the most intricate. It goes beyond seeking a Foreign Affairs voice in policy decisions. In bald terms, it involves participating in the formulation and implementation of the policies of other departments. It means persuading External Territories—along with Trade, Defence and the service departments—not only to bear in mind, in a general sense, the international ramifications of their actions in PNG, but to seek and heed Foreign Affairs advice on specific issues apparently lying entirely within their competence. This might best be achieved—having convinced other Departments of the legitimacy of the Foreign Affairs interest in their business—through a series of interdepartmental committees and sub-committees, chaired in each case by the Department bearing responsibility, under a Permanent Heads' Committee chaired by the Secretary of the Department of Foreign Affairs or of the Prime Minister's Department.

14. The other chief tasks facing the Department of Foreign Affairs are partly educational and partly organisational. The educational aspect involves the creation and rapid development of awareness of the world beyond PNG and of international relationships between PNG, Australia and the United Nations, both among the potential leaders and administrators and among the population at large. The organisational aspect involves the creation and development within PNG of a core of professional expertise in the foreign affairs field, together with appropriate administrative machinery [...]

[*matter omitted*][10]

[NAA: A1838, 936/1/3/1 PART 1]

---

9   A marginal note on this paragraph says 'rephrase'. Possibly a senior DFA officer thought the points made about DFA's role should be expressed more diplomatically.

10 The issues discussed in the omitted text included 'Creation of International Awareness in PNG', 'Departmental Structure and Representation' of a PNG foreign affairs department, a projected Australian mission in PNG and machinery for the conduct of PNG foreign affairs.

152   LETTER FROM HAY TO JOHNSON

Canberra, 24 March 1971

Thank you for your letter LH.572 of 15th March[1] about a Papuan and New Guinean citizenship.

Your thoughts on this subject accord entirely with our own. I am arranging for discussions with the Department of Immigration on the proposals, particularly our earlier proposal that Territory passports should be issued.

A submission will then be put to the Minister recommending that legislation be introduced into the House of Assembly providing for a domestic citizenship along the lines suggested in our memorandum to you of 23rd September[2] on this subject.

I hope this can be done in time for the introduction of the legislation at the June meeting of the House of Assembly. You will be informed of the outcome as soon as possible.

[NAA: A452, 1970/1453]

---

1   Document 149.

2   Document 118.

153   LETTER FROM WALLER TO HAY

Canberra, 24 March 1971

CONFIDENTIAL

Some time ago, we discussed the desirability of close cooperation between our two Departments as Papua-New Guinea moves into a new political phase.

I have had my Policy-Planning Group examine some of the issues as they appear on the basis of our limited knowledge of the problem and I attach a copy of their paper.[1] Discussion may reveal that many of the points raised have already been the subject of decisions.

However, perhaps the paper will be useful in identifying areas in which we can help.

If you agree with this approach, perhaps Shann and I could come to see you and go through the list with you. If your discussion reveals areas in which Foreign Affairs should be active, we might perhaps agree on an informal working party to plan a scheme of action.[2]

Attachment
Papua New Guinea: Subjects for Possible Discussion between the Secretaries of the Departments of Foreign Affairs and External Territories

The following notes are based on the assumption that PNG could well achieve independence during the life of the next House of Assembly, i.e. in the period 1972–76.

2.   By the time PNG becomes independent, we would like to ensure that PNG leaders possessed sufficient knowledge of international affairs to be able to form their own opinions on international relations, and that suitable machinery existed for the carrying forward of their policies. If possible, we would like PNG to share some of our international attitudes and to be able to understand the reasons behind those which it did not share. We would like inimical influences excluded from PNG, especially those of the PRC[3] and Soviet Union, and to ensure that PNG avoided disputes that could embroil Australia in conflict with Indonesia. We would hope that PNG would retain its friendly ties, including defence ties, with Australia, and that it would automatically turn to us for assistance and guidance. We wish to protect Australian commercial and investment interests. We would like to see a smooth and logical evolution of PNG's international relations. We have a limited amount of time available to create the machinery for PNG to conduct its own foreign affairs, to break down the insularity of the leaders and the people and to educate them in international affairs.

3.   These general aims suggest various tasks for the Department of Foreign Affairs, some organisational, the others educational.

---

1   See Document 151.

2   Waller and Shann called on Hay on 8 April 1971. Also present were Besley and Ralph Harry (Deputy Secretary B, DFA). The discussion covered the organisation of an international relations section in the Administration, a Commonwealth Office in Port Moresby, an education program to introduce Papua New Guineans to the concepts behind international relations, the establishment of consulates and the creation of a PNG foreign ministry. For details, see Record of Conversation between Waller and Hay, 8 April 1971, NAA: A452, 1971/0729.

3   People's Republic of China.

Organisation

(a) The creation of the nucleus of a PNG Foreign Ministry which will permit PNG to take its own decisions, in its own interests, in an informed manner.

(b) The establishment in PNG of a Foreign Affairs Office that could with independence become the Australian High Commission or Embassy there.

(c) The planning of an eventual PNG diplomatic mission in Canberra.

(d) The acquisition within the Department of Foreign Affairs of a wide expertise in PNG, so that we will be able at independence to conduct Australia's foreign relations with PNG in much the same way as we conduct Australia's foreign relations with other countries.

Education

In PNG there is little interest in and understanding of broader international issues and how they relate to PNG. We need to help in creating such an awareness, chiefly so that PNG will have a basis of knowledge from which it can form its own foreign policies and judge the foreign policies of others; but also to enable it to avoid possible pressures from the Soviet Union, China and others which seek to 'use' newly independent states for their own purposes.

4.   Some of the problems that these tasks imply are set out below.

Education: The Creation of International Awareness in PNG

5.   The educational process should no doubt be aimed at as wide an audience as possible, with the major effort focussed on the politicians and public servants. How can this be done?

(a) Can the TPNG Administration officers be briefed to talk to people about international affairs, to conduct seminars and discussion groups throughout the country? Special attention would probably need to be given to attitudes towards Indonesia by the United Nations. Can the press and radio be asked to help in this?

(b) Would it be possible and useful to encourage schools and the University to form international affairs societies and United Nations Associations?

(c) Would the formation of a House of Assembly Foreign Affairs Committee be of use? If so, how can this be done? What servicing will be needed by the TPNG Administration and the Department of Foreign Affairs? What can actually be given?

(d) Consideration might be given to the establishment of an Institute of International Affairs, to be addressed from time to time by Government leaders and senior officials, as well as academics. Would it be useful to encourage foreign (e.g. Indonesian) Government leaders and officials to address such a body? What financial and other help should the Commonwealth give? How can indigenous people be encouraged to participate?

(e) Would there be value in encouraging friendly countries (Indonesia, New Zealand, Japan, Germany) with interests in PNG to establish career consulates there? This might have three possible advantages—it might help in the process of political education; it could provide experience for the embryo PNG Foreign Ministry in dealing with foreign missions; and it should enable the beginning of a build-up in other countries of officials with first-hand experience of PNG.

(f) What attitude should we adopt towards Soviet desires or attempts to develop links with PNG? Should we permit official Soviet visits? Should we allow the establishment of a Soviet consulate? If so, when? Would a Soviet presence have a useful educative role? If so, would that role outweigh the disruptive effect of probable Soviet interference in PNG politics? In this we must remember that on independence PNG will have to have some dealings with the USSR.

6.   In all of these educational functions, officers of Foreign Affairs could probably give considerable assistance, both in speaking to local groups and politicians and public servants, and in briefing Administration officers and providing written briefing material. Indeed, this educational function could be a major part of the duties of those Foreign Affairs officers who might be sent to PNG to establish a Foreign Ministry nucleus. To a lesser extent they could also be part of the functions of a later Australian mission to PNG.

Creation of a PNG Foreign Ministry

7.   The basic problem here is the availability of suitable PNG personnel for training into a foreign service cadre in the limited time available. To some extent this could be overcome by reducing entry standards and by concentrating on training administrative staff, clerks, accountants, security officers and communications officers, rather than diplomatic officers. We will need to train some of the latter, but it is more important that we have a Foreign Ministry that can run itself than a top-heavy and administratively weak Ministry.

8.   What training can be given in Canberra? What types of trainee should we be looking for? How many can be found and spared for clerical/administrative training? Can we obtain at least two or three diplomatic trainees—not necessarily graduates—for training within the Department's regular Foreign Service Training Course, as well as others who might be trained in specially arranged courses? Can some of these trainees be spared for short-term attachments to selected Australian missions? Can we find the required numbers of instructors?

9.   What training can be given in PNG?

10.   We need to consider establishing a Foreign Affairs presence within the Administration in Port Moresby, specifically to set up the nucleus of a PNG Foreign Ministry, but also to assist in training and to carry out some of the education functions mentioned above. How many and what grades of staff can be spared for this? What will be their terms and conditions of service? To whom should they be responsible? When should they be sent to PNG?

11.   As independence approaches, the character of the Foreign Ministry nucleus could be expected to change from one with a primarily training emphasis to one that was increasingly a functioning foreign affairs advisory Department, offering advice on foreign policy to the PNG Government. With independence the Australian officers would presumably be withdrawn, leaving the field open to senior indigenous public servants.

Australian High Commission in PNG

12.   The need for a separate Foreign Affairs Office in PNG, responsible directly to this Department in Canberra, and eventually to become the Australian High Commission in PNG, will emerge more clearly as the advisory functions of the Foreign Ministry nucleus grow. The proposed Australian mission in PNG would carry heavier staffing implications for the Department of Foreign Affairs than does the establishment of most new overseas posts, because our diplomatic mission in PNG will necessarily be larger than most new missions that we are likely to establish. We need to look very carefully into the question of housing such a mission. At first it would probably be best to house it temporarily within an existing Administration building. However, we would probably eventually need to build a Chancery and residences. Should we do this before or after independence? If before, should we not at the same time construct a number of administration buildings for PNG? How big should the Chancery be? Is it to be in effect a large Commonwealth centre or will such a centre be separate from the Chancery? Should we construct a small building before independence,

leaving the major construction work until after independence? We should not assume that we can keep the Administrator's residence as a Head of Mission residence; this could be expected to go to the Head of State of an independence [*sic*] PNG. We should, therefore, plan to build a new Head of Mission residence, probably before independence. Should this form part of a staff-residence compound, and, if so, what other residences should we begin building before independence?

13. Some of these questions are already under study within the Department of Foreign Affairs and between Departments. However, decisions of principle must be taken before firm planning can be begun.

PNG Mission in Australia

14. We need to consider the eventual establishment of a PNG mission in Australia. Such a mission will need to be planned, established, operated and treated in a very special manner from the point of view of both Port Moresby and Canberra. It will need to cover a very comprehensive range of interests, among them: trade, supply, university and scientific liaison, civil aviation, quarantine, tourism, social services (including pensions of expatriate officials), investment and defence. This matter will need to receive full examination within the Department and between departments.

Aid

15. As well as the implications for the Department of Foreign Affairs in staffing a Section to deal with the political and economic aspects of Papua and New Guinea, there is also the problem of establishing in Australia machinery to administer a large aid programme to an independent PNG. The principal issues are:

(a) Who shall have responsibility for the administration of aid to PNG?

(b) If this is to be the Department of External Territories, or an agency under its auspices, how much staff will be required and what coordination is to be established between the Department of External Territories and the Department of Foreign Affairs?

(c) Should consideration be given to the feasibility of seconding one or two officers of the Department of External Territories to the Trusteeship Section and/or the Aid Branch of the Department of Foreign Affairs to work in the coordination of PNG aid matters?

(d) Can we maintain one set of policies and machinery for aid to Asia and a quite different set for PNG?

(e) What sort of machinery, if any, might we envisage for coordination of possible multilateral aid to PNG?

[NAA: A452, 1971/0729]

154   LETTER FROM HAY TO TANGE

Canberra, 6 April 1971

SECRET

You will by now have seen the Report of the Inter-Departmental Committee on Aid to the Civil Power.[1] In your letter of the 18th May, 1970[2] to my predecessor you said that you did not feel that the report should be settled by the group of officials who comprised the Inter-departmental Committee but that it should receive some further consideration either by Permanent Heads or in the Defence Committee. I would be glad to know if this remains your opinion.

In my view, whilst the Report has usually brought together many of the relevant matters it has not resolved the inadequacies in the current position.

There is, I believe, every possibility of emergencies such as that which caused the Minister for External Territories to request the call-out of the PIR last July continuing during the transitional period to internal self-government and independence. Whilst the Report puts forward certain useful and simplified procedures in the case of 'call out' I question whether these and the additional powers proposed to be conferred by Territory Ordinance are sufficient.

If it be accepted that there exists in the Territory an internal security problem of a continuing nature quite unlike that which applies in Australia it is, in my view, inappropriate that the use of the army should be governed by provisions and procedures which were prescribed primarily for the stabler conditions prevailing within the Commonwealth.

There is the further and important consideration of the quickening pace of constitutional change in the Territory. The Report of the Select Committee on Constitutional Development, adopted by the House of Assembly and shortly to go before the Government, recommends that the development of the Territory be geared to preparing the country for internal self-government during the life of the next House of Assembly (1972–1976) if in fact this is requested by the people at that time.

We are thus dealing with a Territory which could be self-governing within that period. The next stage of independence would then be within sight. Against this foreshortened timescale I am struck by the need not only to consider questions of internal security in a different (i.e. not necessarily Australian) frame of reference, but also to open up for consideration by the Government the question of the establishment of a Papua-New Guinea defence [force] no longer part of the Commonwealth defence forces.

If, for the broad reasons I have referred to, it were decided that the Territory defence forces were to be established separately from those of Australia, legislative change to this effect would enable the special security situation in the Territory to be separately dealt with also. If such a suggestion were accepted it may be appropriate to effect it by legislation through the House of Assembly with corresponding amendments to the Defence Act and related legislation. The mechanics of such a change would of course have to be worked out but in this regard it may be desirable to have a look at the legislative position which obtained in Fiji and Singapore prior to independence.

There are other difficulties arising from the integration of the Territory's defence forces with the Australian services which tend to strengthen this suggestion. In the discussion in the Defence Committee on the future development of the Territory's defence forces on 17th September,

---

1   Not published.

2   Not published.

1970[3] I referred to the Territory's limited resources and said that it would not be able to afford both a police force capable of dealing with all internal security situations and a defence force freed from that responsibility. There have been discussions between my Department and the Department of the Army about the provision of logistic support for the Police from the Army. We have sought their help in the provision of field equipment (tents and catering equipment, additional rifles, transport, communications, and first aid). There is however the difficulty that money which has been voted by the Commonwealth Parliament to the Army should not be spent for other purposes.

Moreover, there is likely to be greater pressures for parity of conditions of service between expatriate and indigenous members of the PIR in an integrated service than if separate services were adopted to the separate needs and capabilities of Australia and PNG.

I am not of course suggesting that the Commonwealth should cease to be responsible for external defence before independence, or that authority over the Territory defence forces which goes with it, should be transferred from the Minister for Defence. I believe, however, that it is possible to retain this through the Administrator and at the same time bring the evolving Territory Government into defence matters, particularly as they are related to the Police and internal security. The working out of these objectives is a separate undertaking which may be assisted by the legislation I have suggested. It is however, I believe becoming an increasingly urgent undertaking.

At present there is a joint study of internal security at the stage of self-government (Cabinet Decision No. 452 of 23rd June, 1970)[4] and on the Review of the PNG Defence Forces (Defence Committee Decision No. 42 of 1968).[5] I understand that the Working Group established by the Defence Committee has almost completed its task. I have instructed officers of my Department to press forward [with] their study of the internal security situation at self-government. What concerns me somewhat, in the light of the Territory's present stage of development, is that these interrelated matters should be proceeding separately. I have in mind also the position of the police.

As I have previously indicated the Territory's limited financial resources could make it necessary for its own authorities in due course to consider a rationalisation of funds to be expended on the PIR and the police to avoid uneconomical allocation of expenditure which is likely to occur if their finances are considered separately. I should add that a review of the size and organisation of the Royal Papua and New Guinea Constabulary has recently been completed and has been approved in principle by the Minister for External Territories but for which funds have not yet been provided.

I would appreciate the opportunity of an early discussion of these matters with you.

[NAA: A452, 1971/1619]

---

3   Document 119.

4   Document 53.

5   Stuart Doran (ed.), *Documents on Australian Foreign Policy: Australia and Papua New Guinea, 1966– 1969*, Department of Foreign Affairs and Trade, Canberra, 2006, Document 190.

155   CABINET SUBMISSION 45[1]

Canberra, 7 April 1971

CONFIDENTIAL

Papua and New Guinea Constitutional Development

The purpose of this submission is to seek Cabinet endorsement of recommendations in the Territory House of Assembly Select Committee Report on Constitutional Development[2] agreed upon by the House on 11 March, 1971.

2.   In summary, the recommendations fall into three groups:

(a) The first foreshadows an approximate timetable for the further transfer of authority from the Commonwealth to elected political leaders in Papua and New Guinea by a gradual process which could lead to full internal self-government in the period 1972–1976 if it is in fact requested by the people at that time. Acceptance of these recommendations will require the Commonwealth on the one hand to play its part in gearing the development of the Territory to this approximate timetable so as to ensure a smooth transition; and on the other hand to consult with the leadership group after the 1972 elections, if in fact a cohesive group emerges, on a programme for the handing over of authority and on the kinds of political and economic relations which should exist with Australia at internal self-government.

(b) The second group mainly confirms certain characteristics of the present constitution, such as a unitary, unicameral system of government. They are consistent with the Papua and New Guinea Act.

(c) The third group, of a more detailed constitutional character, mainly concerns changes in the House of Assembly and the Administrator's Executive Council. If accepted, these recommendations will require amendments to the Papua and New Guinea Act. The changes in the House of Assembly need to be made well before the next House elections in March/April 1972 to enable the Territory's Chief Electoral Officer to undertake his re-distribution work and this submission seeks Cabinet authority for drafting of the necessary amendments as a matter of urgency for introduction in the present sittings of Parliament.

3.   The recommendations reflect a recent report to me by the Administrator of an 'obvious foreshortening in the independence time scale' in Papua and New Guinea. They conform to the Government's policies of encouraging progress towards internal self-government and of looking to the elected members of the House of Assembly to represent the wishes of the majority of the people and to take the initiative in such matters as the pace and nature of constitutional development.

Government Decisions in 1970

4.   In Decision No. 453 of 23rd June, 1970[3] Cabinet endorsed a transfer of authority in defined fields of government to the Administrator's Executive Council and Ministerial Office Holders in the Territory. The decision was announced in Port Moresby on 6th July, 1970[4] and the formal

---

1   Submitted by Barnes.
2   Document 142.
3   Document 54.
4   Document 64.

documents giving effect to it were promulgated on 21st August, 1970.[5] The decision was taken in response to clear indications from the Select Committee and from the Administrator that an early transfer of some real power was essential in order to involve Territory political leaders in important decisions affecting the Territory's stability and development. The Government undertook, however, because this was also the wish of the Committee, to stand short of constitutional changes requiring amendment to the Papua and New Guinea Act until such time as the House of Assembly had considered the Committee's report. The 1970 changes received a mixed reception in the Territory, some opinion being that they went too far, but generally they were welcomed.

House of Assembly Select Committee on Constitutional Development

5.   The Select Committee was set up on 24th June, 1969, its terms of reference being:

'to consider ways and means of preparing and presenting, and to draft for the consideration of this House a set of constitutional proposals to serve as a guide for future constitutional development in the Territory'.

6.   The Committee toured the Territory twice to explain the issues and to discuss its proposals with the people at the village level. It also made an overseas visit to study constitutional development in recently independent countries. It presented three interim reports. It made its final report to the House on 4th March, 1971. Both the third interim report presented on 3rd September, 1970 and the final report contained recommendations for constitutional change. With the exception of one recommendation which was rejected and one recommendation which was deferred the House adopted the Committee's recommendations. Most of the large number of members who took part in the debate on the final report agreed with the report, the only successful amendment being the rejection of the proposed name of 'Niugini'.[6] Of the other two amendments moved, one, to abolish regional electorates, was defeated 47/17, while the other, to defer consideration of the flag, was rejected on the Speaker's casting vote. The report, as amended, was accepted on the voices on 11th March. Copies of the third and final reports of the Committee are attached.

7.   Certain recommendations in the third interim report have already been effected by administrative action or Territory Ordinance. These are that wide publicity be given to the 1970 constitutional changes, that public service heads of the Department of Administration be redesignated and that local governing authorities be set up in each district in the Territory.

Timing of Internal Self-Government

8.   Recommendations (A) and (B) of the final report deal with the timing of internal self-government and the kinds of relationships which might exist between Australia and the Territory at internal self-government. The recommendations are:

(A) That the development of the Territory be geared to preparing the country for internal self-government during the life of the next House of Assembly (1972–1976) so that should it become a reality earlier than expected or if it is in fact required by the people then, then the move to internal self-government can be made at that time with the least possible amount of administrative disruption.

(B) That the sort of economic and political arrangements and relationships which might be developed between Papua and New Guinea and Australia at internal self-government be considered as part of the programme of development towards internal self-government.

5   See Documents 105 & 108.
6   See Document 142, fn. 7.

The Committee explained (paras. 7 and 8 of the report) that on its first tour of the Territory the majority of the people were against early internal self-government, and were not prepared to discuss when it should come about, but that during its second tour most people were prepared to consider when internal self-government should occur. The majority opinion favoured internal self-government no sooner than the life of the 1976–80 House of Assembly.

9.   However, because of the evident acceleration in the rate of political development and awareness, the Committee recommended the gearing of development to allow for internal self-government during the life of the 1972–76 House in case this became a reality earlier than expected or was requested by the people at that time.

10. In effect these recommendations set, in the Committee's words, 'an approximate timetable', which is somewhat in advance of the wishes of the majority of the people. In accepting them the Government will need to adopt a flexible attitude. It will need to prepare a programme for movement to full internal self-government in the period 1972–76, but the execution of that programme will need to have regard to the state of opinion as it develops after the 1972 elections and to the policies of the political leaders who have emerged.

11. The recommendations reflect a foreshortening of the independence time scale. I believe the Government should move with this. In adopting the flexible attitude described above it would be acting in conformity with its policies of encouraging progress towards internal self-government and of looking to the House of Assembly to represent the wishes of the majority of the people. The reservations about a timetable which the Government has expressed from time to time particularly in response to United Nations resolutions have been based on objections to an externally imposed or arbitrary timetable. Such reservations do not apply to a timetable of the Territory's own choosing in circumstances where the House must be regarded as the authentic voice of the people.

12. There are certain critical and possibly limiting factors to a foreshortening of the time scale. Perhaps the most important of these is the quality and stability of leadership. It is by no means certain that there will develop early in the life of the 1972–76 House a cohesive grouping able to command a majority in the House and in turn to support a leadership capable of governing effectively. Other limiting factors are the lack of skilled indigenous manpower, the lack of national unity, the capacity to maintain law and order, the present limited capacity to raise internal revenue and the need to attract private investment to maintain the continued momentum of the economic development programme.

13. The gearing up process will need to concentrate on these factors and ensure that continuing priority is given to localisation and training programmes to minimise any disruptive effect the factors may have on a smooth transition to internal self-government. The continuation of positive action to maintain sufficient numbers of expatriate officers in the Territory public service is essential to this process.

14. With reference to the gearing up process Ministers will recall that in an earlier submission to Cabinet (No. 327 of 1970)[7] I indicated the need to step up the existing policy of indigenous participation in political, social and economic affairs. I also recommended the establishment of an interdepartmental committee to deal with the preparation of a sensible programme for the absorption, where appropriate, into the Territory Administration of those Commonwealth Departments and agencies now performing functions of internal self-government outside the aegis of the Administration and a special study of the situation in relation to internal security. Cabinet endorsed both these measures (Decision No. 452 of 23rd June);[8] they are being implemented and a report will be made to Cabinet in due course.

7   Document 47.

8   Document 53.

15. The existing policy of indigenous participation in political, social and economic affairs has been stepped up. Localisation objectives and programmes for the Public Service are being prepared, legislation to establish an Investment Corporation has been passed by the House, a Department of Business Development has been established, powers have been transferred to Ministerial office holders, the present development programme is being revised and the revision will include more emphasis on indigenisation. Steps are also being taken to ensure that in the preparation of the new five-year development programme consideration is given to the desirability of a more aggressive attitude towards indigenisation, greater emphasis on agricultural small-holder development, greater attention to education especially secondary and technical, and measures to attract and retain suitable expatriates where trained indigenes are not yet available. The structure of the Department of External Territories is being streamlined to take account of the movement towards self-government in the Territory.

16. A programme for further movement towards internal self-government will require consultations with the Territory leadership group after the 1972 elections. Given that a cohesive group emerges, with a majority backing in the House, I envisage:

(a) that the Commonwealth might in practice regard the group as constituting a government, with the authority of the Administrator gradually becoming confined to matters remaining within Commonwealth responsibility;

(b) that the Commonwealth would negotiate with the leader of the group for the handing over of further authority step by step as he felt in a position to accept added responsibility;

(c) that when the above process is complete the Commonwealth would amend the Papua and New Guinea Act to establish formally a system of responsible government;

(d) that the kinds of economic and political relationships which might be developed between the Territory and Australia at internal self-government would be considered as part of this process.

17. As a basis for the consultations outlined above I propose that the Department of External Territories in consultation with the Administration and other Departments and Authorities concerned draw up a flexible programme of movement towards full internal self-government which includes the kinds of political and economic relations which should exist with Australia at internal self-government for consideration by Cabinet at an early date.

Broad Constitutional Recommendations

18. Recommendations (C) and (D) of the final report confirm characteristics of the present constitution. These recommendations read as follows.

(C) That the system of government for Papua and New Guinea be a single central government as at present.

(D) That the legislature comprise one house of parliament as at present.

No legislative action is required in regard to these recommendations and I support them.

19. Recommendation (U) of the final report concerns a Bill of Rights and reads as follows:

(U) That the drafting of a Bill of Rights be considered by a committee of a subsequent House of Assembly and that such a statement be embodied in a proposed constitution for an independent Papua and New Guinea.

This recommendation has been deferred until the House deals with a private member's Bill of Rights which is before it. If the House rejects the private member's Bill I consider that a Bill of Rights is a matter for the Territory to decide upon at independence.

20. In its final report the Committee also recommended particular designs for a Territory flag and coat of arms as an incentive to national unity. There appears to be no legal or

constitutional objection to the adoption by Territory Ordinance of a flag and a coat of arms with the exception that the flag probably could not be flown on ships registered in the Territory. The Commonwealth Flags Act which prescribes the national flag would continue to extend to the Territory however and it is proper that the Australian flag should continue to be flown until independence and take precedence over the Territory flag on official and similar occasions. I support this recommendation.

Recommendations requiring amendment to the Papua and New Guinea Act
The Legislature

21. Recommendations (E) and (F) of the final report read as follows:

   (E) That 18 regional electorates be created for the elections for the 1972–1976 House of Assembly.

   (F) An increase of 13 in the number of open electorates, making the number of open electorates in the 1972–1976 House 82.

At present the House consists of 15 regional electorates and 69 open electorates. During its 1971 tour the Committee met with an overwhelming request for increased representation and it based its recommendations on one regional member for each district in the Territory and one open member to approximately 30,000 people. It was made clear to the Committee by the Government that the costs of additional representation in the House would have to be met from Territory revenues.

22. Regional electorates were recommended by the previous Committee on Constitutional Development as a means of ensuring that there was some degree of expertise and competence in the House. A candidate for a regional electorate must have as a minimum educational qualifications the Intermediate Certificate or its equivalent. This requirement tends to act in favour of non-indigenous persons and a recommendation to abolish regional electorates would have been consistent with the policy of increased indigenous involvement in the political development of the Territory. However the majority opinion favoured their retention considering that there would be a lack of expertise and competency in the House if there was not the requirement of an educational standard for at least some of the elected members. The Committee noted (para. 29 of the final report) that regional electorates could be reviewed in the 1972–76 House but that it might be necessary to consider some minimum qualification for open members such as the ability to read and write if regional electorates were to be replaced or abolished. There could be dangers in accepting this recommendation.

23. In its third interim report the Committee recommended the creation of positions of nominated members in the House. This is a new concept in the type of representation in the House and arose in conjunction with the Committee's wish to reduce official members in the House. The Committee recommended the abolition of the 10 positions of official member and their replacement by 10 nominated members an unspecific number of whom to be nominated official members (recommendation No. 6—third interim report). As a result of its 1971 Territory tour the Committee altered its recommendation to a reduction in official members and the creation of not more than 3 nominated members.

24. The terms of recommendations (G) to (L) in the final report are:

   (G) That the number of nominated members be not more than 3, to be nominated for special purposes, only if the House considers it necessary.

   (H) The following method of appointing nominated members:

   If the House feels there is a need for a nominated member or members to be appointed, then a two-thirds vote of the total members of the House of Assembly should be required to agree to the setting up of a seven-man select committee of the House to be known as the Nominated Members Selection Committee to choose the Member or Members concerned. After the Nominated Members Selection Committee has chosen a person or persons in consultation with the Administrator, then their choice should be endorsed by a simple majority of the Members of the House of Assembly present and voting and the Selection Committee would cease to operate after it had chosen the person or persons concerned.

(I)   That to be eligible for selection as a Nominated Member a person must have lived in the Territory continuously for not less than five years.

(J)   That a defeated candidate at the general elections for the House to which Members are to be nominated should not be eligible for nomination.

(K) That should a nominated member chosen by the Nominated Members Selection Committee be a public servant he must resign his public service position to accept appointment.

(L)   That once a person has been nominated to the House then he should hold office on the same basis as if he was an elected member of the House.

25.   The inclusion of non-elected members in the popular house of a parliament is a departure from the Westminster system of government but there is a widespread feeling in the Territory of the need to provide a means for persons representing special groups, for example, women, or persons having a special expertise to take their place in the legislature. The recommendation allows the House to decide itself whether these positions should be filled.

26.   The recommendation dealing with the selection of nominated members is similar to the existing method of selecting ministerial office holders. The eligibility provision and the limit to the number of people able to be nominated are reasonable precautions.

27.   As there could be a lack of suitably qualified people in the 1972–76 House I think this proposal could meet a real need and I therefore support it.

28.   In its final report the Committee recommended:

(M) that four Official Members be appointed in the 1972–1976 House of Assembly.

29.   At present the Papua and New Guinea Act provides for 10 positions of official member in the House. A reduction in their number accords with the transfer of authority to political leaders in the Territory, but their role will not change; they remain responsible for the carriage of government business in the House. Thus the number needed is a matter for the Committee and the Committee was advised that a minimum of three official members was necessary for the conduct of government business.

30.   Summing up, the total picture of the composition of the 1972–76 House as recommended by the Committee is as follows:

18 persons elected by the people to represent regional electorates;

82 persons elected by the people to represent open electorates;

up to 3 nominated members, nominated by the House of Assembly for special purposes; and

4 official members.

I support the Committee's recommendations.

The Executive

31. Recommendation No.2 of the third interim report reads as follows:

'That the offices of Ministerial Member and Assistant Ministerial Member be abolished and replaced by up to seventeen (17) offices of Ministers of the House of Assembly of such respective designations as the Minister for External Territories from time to time determines'.

In 1966 the previous Committee on Constitutional Development recommended the creation of Ministers and Assistant Ministers. The Government did not agree to the proposed titles because the office holders were not to exercise full executive authority nor take final decisions in respect of their areas of responsibility. It was therefore decided that the titles should be Ministerial Members and Assistant Ministerial Members. However since August 1970 all ministerial office holders now exercise final responsibility in respect of matters specified in the arrangements approved under section 25 of the Papua and New Guinea Act. Thus the adoption of the term Minister would be consistent with their responsibilities and duties and I support this recommendation.

32. Recommendations (O), (P) and (Q) in the final report are as follows:

(O) That the composition of the Administrator's Executive Council at the start of the 1972–1976 House of Assembly be as follows:

Administrator:

3 Official Members;

10 Ministers.

(P) That the Ministry should be chosen from the Legislature (which may comprise nominated as well as elected Members), but that although the three nominated members may be appointed as Ministers, not more than two of them should be members of the Administrator's Executive Council.

(Q) That following nomination of the Ministers in the 1972 House of Assembly by a Ministerial Nominations Committee composed of seven Members of the House, the Ministers should choose one of their number to be the Deputy Chairman of the Administrator's Executive Council. The Ministers' choice for Deputy Chairman of the Council should be approved by the House of Assembly.

If recommendation (O) is accepted the structure of the Administrator's Executive Council would be changed by the addition of three Ministers and the removal of the position of an elevated member of the House nominated by the Administrator. I support the recommendations.

33. The report is silent on the method of choice of Ministers to sit on the AEC with the exception of the Deputy Chairman who would be a member. I propose therefore that the choice be a matter for the Minister for External Territories on the advice of the Administrator, who would consult the Deputy Chairman.

34. The recommendation for a name for the Territory was rejected by the House. At a later sitting however the House unanimously adopted a private member's motion that the word 'and' be deleted from Papua and New Guinea: the Territory to be known as Papua New Guinea. I support the recommendation.

35. I propose that the Territory be described in the Act as Papua New Guinea rather than the Territory of Papua New Guinea. Norfolk Island is described as such in the Norfolk Island Act and the removal of the word Territory from the name of the administrative union would help to promote the concept of an emerging self-governing Papua New Guinea. The Territory of New Guinea and the Territory of Papua would of course remain as such until independence.

36. The Administrator of Papua and New Guinea has indicated that he supports the Committee's recommendations as amended by the House.

RECOMMENDATION

37. I recommend that Ministers:

(a) agree to the recommendations in the Committee's report concerning the development of the Territory towards internal self-government and adopt these as a basis for planning by the Commonwealth (paras 8, 10, and 11);

(b) authorise the Department of External Territories in consultation with the Administration and other Departments and authorities concerned, to draw up a flexible programme of movement towards full internal self-government which includes the kinds of political and economic relations which should exist within Australia at internal self-government for consideration by Cabinet at an early date as a basis for negotiations with the leadership group emerging from the 1972 elections (para 17);

(c) authorise the planning of legislative and administrative steps necessary to ensure that the Commonwealth is in a position to conform to such a programme, if agreed upon (paras. 13 and 16);

(d) agree to the constitutional changes short of internal self-government recommended by the Committee in its third and final reports and adopted by the House and authorise the drafting of the necessary amendments to the Papua and New Guinea Act as a matter of urgency (paras. 21–33);

(e) agree to the name of the Territory being altered by amendment to the Papua and New Guinea Act to Papua New Guinea and described in the Act as Papua New Guinea rather than the Territory of Papua New Guinea and to the adoption of the Territory of a flag and coat of arms (paras. 34, 35 and 20).

[NAA: A5908, VOLUME 45]

156   LETTER FROM PETER BAILEY TO CURTIS[1]

Canberra, 16 April 1971

CONFIDENTIAL

This is to confirm my telephone advice to the effect that the Prime Minister would like the Order authorising call-out of elements of the defence forces in Papua and New Guinea to be revoked.

The Prime Minister understands that it will be necessary for the revoking Order to be signed by the Acting Minister for Defence, and I have spoken to him to that effect.

The next meeting of the Executive Council will be on Thursday, 22 April.

The Prime Minister indicated that he sees no need for the revocation to have publicity.[2]

[*matter omitted*]

[NAA: A452, 1971/3329 PART 6]

---

1   W. J. Curtis, Deputy Secretary, Department of Defence.

2   The order was accordingly revoked on 22 April. The question of revoking the call-out had been under review for six months. On 9 October 1970, Gorton had advised Barnes, who had in turn advised Hay, that the Government's approval of a requisition should no longer be anticipated in the manner authorised by paragraph 6 of Cabinet Decision No. 484 of 19 July, 1970, whereby 'the Administrator could initiate action without delay at the time of placing a requisition on the basis that approval would be forthcoming' (Document 89). Henceforth, in contrast, if it should become necessary to requisition the forces, then the approval of the Government should be sought prior to the Administrator initiating action. Letter, Gorton to Barnes, 9 October 1970, NAA: A452, 1970/4297. See also Document 121.

On 12 March 1971 Cabinet noted that it was in mind to revoke the call-out order. A few days later, however, following discussions with Fraser and Barnes in response to heightened tensions in the Gazelle Peninsula, McMahon decided that for the time being the rescinding order would not be put to the Executive Council. Cabinet Decision 11, 12 March 1971; and Letter, Bunting to Harders, 17 March 1971, NAA: 432, 1961/3329 PART 7.

157   SUBMISSION FROM HAY TO BARNES

Canberra, 17 April 1971

TPNG—Cabinet Submission on Constitutional Development

Attached is a schedule of possible questions which might be put during the Cabinet discussions on the above submission[1] together with suggested answers for your consideration.

You asked me to consider whether we should not seek in the Cabinet submission or in the associated discussion in Cabinet a formal Cabinet view on whether the Government should continue to look to the House of Assembly as the guide to public opinion on constitutional advance, having in mind particularly the possibility that at some stage there will be a difference between the view of the majority in the House of Assembly and what we know of public opinion in the country at large.

There are two separate issues. The first relates to constitutional advance on the present pattern and the achievement of internal self-government. The second relates to the actual timing of independence.

As to independence, there has been always an assumption that there would be some formal expression of majority opinion before Australia finally gave up its responsibility for the Territory. This has been emphasised in statements by yourself and by the former Prime Minister. It is in connection with this formal expression of majority opinion that reference has been made to such methods as referenda, consensus or resolution of the House of Assembly.[2] It seems to us that it is too early yet to seek a firm view from the Government on this. We have been in touch with Foreign Affairs Department who are of the same mind. They point out that the United Nations will have an interest, and we need to consider how that interest might be attended to. It could be that there will be so little doubt about the matter when the time comes that the United Nations will be quite content, without even sending an observation team, to accept a majority opinion of the House of Assembly. However, if there is a strong opinion against independence at the time, then the situation could be different, the UN may wish to be involved and it may be necessary to consider some other means of ascertaining public opinion.

In relation to further movement towards and the achievement of internal self-government, which is distinct from and short of independence, I do not myself see any reason for seeking Cabinet endorsement of the policy which is incorporated in paragraph 3 of the submission namely:

'looking to the elected members of the House of Assembly to represent the wishes of the majority of the people and to take the initiative in such matters as the pace and nature of constitutional development'.

Because this is the policy you are already following.

If in discussions you are asked what our attitude would be in the event that the House of Assembly seemed to be taking a view which did not accord with what you believed to be the majority opinion in the country, you could say that the House has always in the past satisfied itself through the medium of select committees that it is acting in accordance with the wishes of the majority of the people. You would not therefore expect the problem to arise. But if it did, you would want to consider all the circumstances at the time rather than seek a commitment

1   Document 155.

2   In a television interview aired on 19 July 1970 Gorton had told John Boland of Channel 7 that there were three options for assessing support for further constitutional development—a referendum, arrival at a consensus of opinion by discussion, or an expression of views by the House of Assembly (Document 85).

now to a particular course of action such as asking for a 2/3 majority vote in the House or the setting up of a new Select Committee to test public opinion.

[*matter omitted*]

Possible Questions	Suggested Answers
Why can't the Select Committee on Constitutional Development undertake this programme? (paragraph 17)	The Select Committee has placed the onus on the Government and the Administration to propose the programme. It would not be competent to do it itself. The AEC would be very much involved in the preparation of the programme.
A rigid programme is necessary so we are sure of where we are going. (paragraph 17)	No. Keynote is flexibility—speed and nature of programme depends on: (a) emergency of a cohesive leadership group after 1972; (b) political attitude of that group & degree of support in the House (c) mechanics of transfer of functions
Doesn't a 'timetable' bind the Commonwealth? (paragraph 11)	Not in the way it is recommended by the Committee. This allows flexibility for both Commonwealth and Territory.
Limiting factors should not be used as a means of delaying progression. (paragraph 12)	They won't be; they are included to point up the kinds of things the gearing process should concentrate on.
Will the programme cost anything? (paragraph 17)	It may be that there will be a need for a special grant to finance the programme of movement towards internal self-government. This would be fully brought out in the Cabinet submission at that time.
How is the Department being streamlined? (paragraph 15)	There has been a slight overall reduction in establishment which has been made possible by redeploying staff resources from areas where decision making authority has been transferred to areas where the work load has remained high.
What is being done about localisation training and the future of overseas officers? (paragraph 15)	See attached briefing note.[3]

---

3   Not published.

What about secession movements in the Territory?	The Government endorses the House of Assembly resolution that national unity is essential to the progress of the Territory and the objective of the Government's policy for constitutional, economic and social development is the development of the country as a whole.

[NAA: A452, 1971/3543]

158   MINUTE FROM TANGE TO HUGHES[1]

Canberra, 19 April 1971

Comments on Working Party Paper[2] on Development of Defence Forces in PNG

I am not satisfied with progress on this subject—nor with the quality of this material.

2.   Please discuss with me the selection of personnel to write a perceptive analysis of what PNG needs *post-independence*. This material shows some fatal signs of independent Army/Navy/RAAF[3] drafting that cannot be added together.

3.   There is a lot of windiness in the material p. 13 *et seq.*[4]—yet I cannot see treatment of:

(a) the idea of making forces responsible to the Administrator as British colonies did;

(b) any evidence in text of study of precedents in the history of steps taken before independence in dozens of other British colonies;

(c) what independent PNG will need forces to *do*, what will be the main tasks and what capabilities will they need for *PNG purposes*. You won't get the answer by asking Army, Navy and RAAF to describe *their* ideas about the future of *their* forces in PNG prior to independence and to *project* them into the post-independence period. Our present forces there are to protect Australia. The task is to describe what forces *PNG will need* for its purposes after independence. One can see the confusion in the recurring phrase '*future* PNG forces'. State unambiguously whether pre or post-independence.

4.   Where is the treatment of how to provide the PNG Army with air and sea lift—and how to prepare? Where is the treatment of how to provide the PNG Government with coastal patrol?

5.   Start the relevant Chapter with the answer to this—and subsequently indicate whether present manpower and training will provide this—and show Australian equipment (e.g. Navy patrol boats) as only illustrating what is sustained, by given manpower in present circumstances.

6.   Where is a table showing annually, the capability of PIR officering and NCOing,[5] its formation with locals?

7.   Where is the treatment in the text of the relations of soldiers and politicians? Are Working Party studying the various writings on this subject, and experiences in Africa? Is *Army* teaching the indigenes anything about *politics*? If so—what? Is [*sic*] not—why not?[6]

8.   Please see me on this, with appropriate officers.

[NAA: A452, 1971/1619]

---

1   Major General Ron Hughes, Director, Joint Staff, Department of Defence.

2   See Documents 100, 112 & 116.

3   At the time Australia had separate defence, army, navy, and air force departments. These departments were combined in 1973.

4   'and what follows'.

5   NCO: Non-commissioned officer.

6   Tange was apparently not aware that the Army was providing civic education to PIR soldiers, in an effort 'to create a national Papua New Guinean military'. Tristan Moss, ' "Taking Itself Out of a Political Future": Education and Australian Army Engagement with Papua New Guinean Independence, 1966–72', *Journal of Pacific History*, 54 (2), 2019, pp. 149–65.

159   CABINET DECISION 89

Canberra, 20 April 1971

CONFIDENTIAL

Submission No. 45—Papua and New Guinea—Constitutional Development[1]

As recommended by the Minister, the Cabinet:

(a) agreed to the recommendations in the Committee's report concerning the development of the Territory towards internal self-government and adopted these as a basis for planning by the Commonwealth;

(b) authorised the Department of External Territories, in consultation with the Administration and other Departments and authorities concerned, to draw up a flexible programme of movement towards full internal self-government, which includes the kinds of political and economic relations which should exist with Australia at internal self-government, for consideration by Cabinet at an early date as a basis for negotiation with the leadership group emerging from the 1972 elections;

(c) authorised the planning of legislative and administrative steps necessary to ensure that the Commonwealth is in a position to conform to such a programme;

(d) agreed to the constitutional changes short of internal self-government recommended by the Committee in its third and final reports and adopted by the House and authorised the drafting of the necessary amendments to the Papua and New Guinea Act as a matter of urgency; and

(e) agreed to the name of the Territory being altered by amendment to the Papua and New Guinea Act to Papua New Guinea and described in the Act as Papua New Guinea rather than the Territory of Papua New Guinea and to the adoption by the Territory of a flag and coat of arms.

2.   It noted that the recommendations of the Select Committee envisaged a unicameral system of government. It felt that, having regard to the circumstances in Papua and New Guinea, there could be advantages in the bicameral system under which the interests of regional and other groups could be given recognition through the membership of a second chamber. Moreover, such a system would be likely to promote a more considered approach to legislative action. It left this matter as one which the Minister might, as he considered appropriate, pursue further at some later stage.

[NAA: A5908, VOLUME 45]

---

1   Document 155.

160   STATEMENT BY BARNES[1]

Canberra, 27 April 1971

Papua New Guinea—Constitutional Development

I wish to inform the House that the Government has accepted the recommendations of the Papua New Guinea House of Assembly Select Committee on Constitutional Development as agreed upon by that House on 11th March, 1971. I propose to summarise the recommendations and to explain what action is required as a result of the Government's acceptance.

Government Decisions in 1970

2.   During the Committee's deliberations the Government, in July 1970, announced a transfer of authority in defined fields of government to the Administrator's Executive Council and ministerial office holders in the Territory. This decision was taken after discussions with the Committee. The Government undertook, however, because this was also the wish of the Committee, to stand short of constitutional changes requiring amendment to the Papua and New Guinea Act until such time as the House of Assembly had considered the Committee's report.

House of Assembly Select Committee on Constitutional Development

3.   The Select Committee was set up on 24th June, 1969, its terms of reference being:

'to consider ways and means of preparing and presenting, and to draft for the consideration of this House, a set of constitutional proposals to serve as a guide for future constitutional development in the Territory'.

4.   The Committee toured the Territory twice to explain the issues and to discuss its proposals with the people at the village level. It also made an overseas visit to study constitutional development in recently independent countries. It presented three interim reports. It made its final report to the House on 4th March, 1971. Both the third interim report presented on 3rd September, 1970 and the final report contained recommendations for constitutional change. With the exception of one recommendation which was rejected and one recommendation which was deferred, the House adopted the Committee's recommendations. Most of the large number of members who took part in the debate on the final report agreed with the report, the only successful amendment being the rejection of the proposed name of 'Niugini'. Of the other two amendments moved, one, to abolish regional electorates, was defeated 47/17, while the other, to defer consideration of the flag, was rejected on the Speaker's casting vote. The report, as amended, was accepted on the voices on 11th March. Copies of the third and final reports of the Committee are available to Members.

Timing of Internal Self-Government

5.   The first two recommendations of the final report deal with the timing of internal self-government and the kinds of relationships which might exist between Australia and the Territory at internal self-government. The recommendations are:

(a) that the development of the Territory be geared to preparing the country for internal self-government during the life of the next House of Assembly (1972–1976) so that should it become a reality earlier than expected or if it is in fact requested by the people then, then the move to internal self-government can be made at that time with the least possible amount of administrative disruption;

---

1   The statement was made in the House of Representatives.

(b) that the sort of economic and political arrangements and relationships which might be developed between Papua and New Guinea and Australia at internal self-government be considered as part of the programme of development towards internal self-government.

The Committee explained that on its first tour of the Territory the majority of the people were against early internal self-government, and were not prepared to discuss when it should come about, but that during its second tour most people were prepared to consider when internal self-government should occur. The majority opinion favoured internal self-government no sooner than the life of the 1976-80 House of Assembly. However, because of the evident acceleration in the rate of political development and awareness, the Committee recommended the gearing of development to allow for internal self-government during the life of the 1972–76 House in case this became a reality earlier than expected or was requested by the people at that time.

6.   In effect, these recommendations set, in the Committee's words, 'an approximate timetable', which is somewhat in advance of the wishes of the majority of the people as reported by the Committee. In accepting them the Government will adopt a flexible attitude. It will prepare a programme for movement to full internal self-government in the period 1972–76, but the execution of that programme will have regard to the state of opinion as it develops after the 1972 House of Assembly elections and to the policies of the political leaders who then emerge. This attitude accords with the Government's policies of encouraging progress towards internal self-government and of looking to the elected members of the House of Assembly to represent the wishes of the majority of the people, and to take the initiative in such matters as the pace and nature of constitutional development. The reservations about a timetable which the Government has previously expressed from time to time, particularly in response to United Nations' resolutions, have been based on objections to an externally imposed or arbitrary timetable. Such reservations do not apply to a timetable of Papua New Guinea's own choosing.

7.   The Government's response to the recommendation that the development of Papua New Guinea be geared to preparing for internal self-government in the period 1972–76 will include giving continuing priority to localisation through a stepped-up training effort. At the same time, positive action will be taken to maintain sufficient numbers of expatriate officers in the Papua New Guinea public service not only by recruitment but also by ensuring confidence in a rewarding career to serving officers. A new look has recently been taken at localisation in the public service. Discussions have been held between the Administration, the Papua New Guinea Public Service Board and my own officers. There have also been discussions with the Papua New Guinea Public Service Association. The results of these discussions will, I believe, lead to important advances which will recognise the real problems now faced by expatriate officers in the Territory as localisation gathers momentum.

8.   No less importance will be attached to the more complex task of indigenous involvement in the economic development of Papua New Guinea. Important progress has been made recently. A Department of Business Development has been established. Legislation to set up an Investment Corporation which will take up equity in business ventures on behalf of the people was passed by the House of Assembly in March. The Administrator's Executive Council has decided to introduce legislation providing for preference to Papuans and New Guineans in the issue of trade store and similar licences to conduct small businesses. It has also decided to legislate to prohibit the employment of overseas workers in certain occupations requiring little or no skills. The present development programme is being revised. Preparation of a new five year development programme will begin shortly. This will be weighted towards indigenisation, including greater emphasis on agricultural smallholder development, greater attention to education especially secondary and technical, and measures to attract and retain suitable expatriates where trained indigenes are not yet available.

9. The problems facing Papua New Guinea should not be overlooked. There are still obstacles to national unity. The capacity to raise internal revenue is limited. Skilled indigenous manpower is in short supply. But Papuan and New Guinean leaders are already more fully involved than ever before in solving these problems in a way best suited to their own circumstances, and I have every confidence in their judgment. The programme for further movement towards internal self-government will require consultations with the Territory leadership group after the 1972 elections. Given that a cohesive group of Ministers emerges, with a majority backing in the House, I envisage that the Commonwealth would in practice regard this group as constituting a government, with the authority of the Administrator gradually becoming confined to matters remaining within Commonwealth responsibility. The Commonwealth would negotiate with the leader of the group for the handing over of further authority step by step as he felt in a position, with the support of the House of Assembly, to accept added responsibility. When this process is complete the Commonwealth would amend the Papua and New Guinea Act to give formal recognition to the attainment of full internal self-government. The kinds of economic and political relationships which might be developed between the Territory and Australia at internal self-government would be considered as part of this process.

Constitutional Recommendations

10. A second group of recommendations in the Select Committee's Report confirms certain characteristics of the present constitution. These recommendations read as follows:

> that the system of government for Papua and New Guinea be a single central government as at present;

> that the legislature comprise one house of parliament as at present.

No legislative action is required in regard to these recommendations.

The report also has a recommendation on a Bill of Rights, as follows:

> that the drafting of a Bill of Rights be considered by a committee of a subsequent House of Assembly and that such a statement be embodied in a proposed constitution for an independent Papua and New Guinea.

This recommendation has been deferred by the House pending consideration of a private member's Bill of Rights which is before it.

In its final report the Committee also recommended particular designs for a Papua New Guinea flag and coat of arms as an incentive to national unity. The Government has agreed to the adoption by Papua New Guinea of a flag and coat of arms and necessary legislation will be considered by the House of Assembly. The Commonwealth Flags Act which prescribes the national flag will continue to extend to Papua New Guinea.

11. I now turn to a third group of recommendations which require amendment to the Papua and New Guinea Act. Two of them are matters of urgency, because they affect preparations for the 1972 elections in Papua New Guinea. They are:

> (a) that 18 regional electorates be created for the elections for the 1972–76 House of Assembly;

> (b) an increase of 13 in the number of open electorates, making the number of open electorates in the 1972–76 House 82.

At present the elected membership of the House represents 15 regional electorates and 69 open electorates. During its 1971 tour the Committee met with an overwhelming request for increased representation and it based its recommendations on one regional member for each district in the Territory and one open member to approximately 30,000 people. The costs of additional representation in the House will be met from locally-raised revenue.

12. I shall be presenting a Bill within the next few days to give effect to these recommendations in order that a sufficient period will be available in Papua New Guinea for the necessary preparations to be made for the 1972 elections.

The remaining recommendations in this group will be the subject of amending legislation in the budget session. A full explanation of them will be provided at that time. In summary, what is involved is:

(a) the creation of not more than 3 positions of nominated Member of the House to represent special groups, such as women, or to enable persons with special knowledge to take their place in the legislature;

(b) the reduction of the number of official members in the House from 10 to 4;

(c) the abolition of the offices of Ministerial Member and Assistant Ministerial Member and the creation of up to 17 offices of Minister of the House of Assembly;

(d) a change in the composition of the Administrator's Executive Council which would comprise the Administrator, 3 Official Members and 10 Ministers;

(e) a change in the name. In accordance with the terms of a resolution of the House of Assembly the Territory of Papua and New Guinea will be described simply as Papua New Guinea.

13. The House of Assembly Select Committee on Constitutional Development has played a great and important role in the political development of Papua New Guinea. The many weeks of discussions, explanations and questions and answers by Councils and individuals with the Committee all over Papua New Guinea have been the most important factor in the growing political awareness to which the Committee's report refers. The Government welcomes the responsibility taken by the Committee and the House in Papua New Guinea's political progress. The Government, having accepted the report of the Select Committee as agreed to by the House, will proceed to draw up a flexible programme of movement towards full internal self-government which will include the kinds of political and economic relations which might exist between Papua New Guinea and Australia at internal self-government as a basis for negotiations with the leadership group emerging from the 1972 elections in Papua New Guinea.

[*CPD*, HR, vol. 72, 27 April 1971, pp. 2049–52]

161   LETTER FROM HAY TO WALLER

Canberra, 27 April 1971

You were kind enough to send me a copy of the record of the discussions which took place in my office on 8th April.[1] I agree generally with it and to complete your records enclose a copy of a note[2] of the discussions which Mr Besley had also prepared. I write now to suggest certain follow-up action.

On the question of building up a nucleus of a Papua New Guinea Foreign Ministry we agreed that there would be advantage in the Territory making use of your Department's training facilities. It was also suggested that we look into the possibilities of Foreign Affairs sponsoring cadetships at the University of Papua and New Guinea. On this I shall have information prepared and send it over to Mr Harry. You will recall that we stressed the shortage of suitably qualified manpower coming through the education system which could be made available to a Foreign Ministry nucleus as such. However we appreciate that a sufficient priority will have to be attached to building up the nucleus and I shall seek early nominations for training.

I also mentioned that there is not yet an agreed definition of functions of a new department, as required by the Public Service Ordinance. International trade negotiations, for example, are going to loom large in Papua New Guinea's foreign relations and, given likely staff shortages, it might be desirable to include these in the new department's functions.[3] It is likely that this matter will be moved ahead soon after the Administrator returns from leave at the end of this month. We shall also be wanting to discuss this with the Trade Department here who may well have assistance to offer.

We discussed the possible early establishment of an office of your Department in the Territory—the office to be a base for assistance to a Papua New Guinea Foreign Ministry nucleus, for the educational activities referred to in your paper, and, in the long-term, for the eventual Australian diplomatic mission which would need to be a going concern at independence.

My own preference is for your assistance to be given in the short term by seconding one or two officers to established positions in the Administration. This would be clearly useful from the Territory's own point of view. There are precedents for this sort of thing. While it would mean that the officers were directly responsible to the officer in charge of the office and through him to the Administrator it would not mean that direct communications between the officers as individuals and your own Department would be ruled out. Common sense would rule what was appropriate for this and what was not. As officers working within the administrative set-up it would be quite easy for the persons concerned to travel widely in the Territory and talk to selected groups about foreign policy issues likely to be of importance. As their prime task, however, would be to assist in the development of the office, its functions and staff, it would be important in arranging their posting to ensure well beforehand that serving officers of the Administration recognised the need for this assistance.

So far as a future Mission is concerned, I have for some time been convinced of the need for a Commonwealth office for officers of the many Commonwealth departments that will have dealings with their opposite numbers in the Territory and/or carry direct responsibility for certain

---

1   Not published. For details of the meeting, see Document 153, fn. 2.

2   Not published.

3   On trade issues, see also Letter, Johnson to Hay, 6 January 1971; and Letter, Hay to Johnson, 18 January 1971, both in NAA: A452, 1971/0729.

government functions in the period leading to internal self-government and independence. I am anxious also to move the communications system out of the Administration and into a Commonwealth office as soon as possible. Provision would need to be made for housing of these Commonwealth officers, with an eye of course to the needs of a future Head of Mission and diplomatic staff. Some discussions on this have already been held between officers of your Department and mine, as well as with the Defence Department. Land is available in Port Moresby.

The important consideration will be to plan this office so that it can be merged into the future diplomatic mission at the appropriate time. To facilitate this, it will be important to work to an agreed concept of the nature and size of the future mission.

Our discussions revealed two approaches. Mr Shann had in mind that there should be a conventional mission, in its own building, and that any special aid component ought to be separately identified as such, and separately housed.

My own view was that we should plan for a larger and more comprehensive mission with a resident staff capable of consultation and advice over a wide range of government activity in addition to the normal activity of a diplomatic mission. This is partly because it will not be possible to cut off at any given point of time the network of relationships built up over the years in such matters as finance, civil aviation, defence and trade. Nor do I imagine that it is desirable for us to bring this about. There is no attempt in this to keep a flame of paternalism burning after independence. It seems rather a matter of prudence, and in the Australian interest just as much as it is in our interest that Papua New Guinea should 'automatically turn to us for assistance and guidance' in foreign affairs. Here I am quoting from paragraph 2 of your own paper, with which I agree. If this approach is adopted then we will need quite a sizable office.

We discussed the question of education of key groups in foreign affairs issues. I referred to the heavy pressure from many sides that is being put upon Territory leaders now. The time may be more opportune after the 1972 election, and I think we should look at particular suggestions e.g. a House of Assembly Foreign Affairs Committee, then. Another reason for suggesting caution is that there is already something being done to educate the public through the senior forms in the schools and through the radio in basic foreign affairs matters. Whoever takes on a special education programme would need to be familiar with what is being done. I suggest that an officer of yours who goes to TIC[4] meetings might at a convenient time spend a few extra days in the Territory checking out the details of this. It would be readily available from the Education Department, from the Department of Information and Extension Services, and no doubt from the ABC[5] also. It would be possible as well to talk to the University and to the executives of societies such as the New Guinea Society in Port Moresby.

You mentioned the possibility of establishing certain career consulates from friendly countries in the reasonably near future. I see no objection to this but we would need to check it out with the Administrator's Executive Council and the Administrator. Perhaps your Department could let me have a more detailed note which described what might be expected from consulates from the countries which you have in mind, in a form which would make it easy to present it to the Administrator's Executive Council.

You also raised the question of Soviet officials visiting the Territory. I do not raise objection from the Territory's point of view to lifting the ban, provided the AEC are happy to do so. The objection in the past has always been of a broader nature, namely, that no matter what the Russians saw it would not affect what they said at the UN and elsewhere and that for this reason we ought not to give up this particular stand without some quid pro quo. You will no

---

4   Territory Intelligence Committee.

5   Australian Broadcasting Commission.

doubt have heard of my discussion with Blakeney on these lines late last year.[6] If therefore you would like this pursued, perhaps again your Department could advise us accordingly and I will ask the Administrator to consult the AEC and then place the matter before my Minister.

The Administrator and I are anxious for you, Mick Shann or Ralph Harry to visit Papua New Guinea and have a personal look. Indeed I think this should take place soon and before we move too far on the questions of the shape of the future foreign ministry and the posting of your officers to assist in its development. If you would let me know what dates would suit you, I will take the matter up with the Administrator.

[NAA: A452, 1971/0729]

---

6   Not published. F. J. (Fred) Blakeney was Ambassador in Moscow, 1968–71.

162   STATEMENT BY BARNES[1]

Canberra, 29 April 1971

Papua New Guinea Bill 1971

[*matter omitted*]

The purpose of this Bill is to give effect to certain recommendations made by the Papua New Guinea House of Assembly Select Committee on Constitutional Development and agreed to by that House.

In a statement I made to this House on 27 April[2] I indicated that the Government had accepted the Select Committee's recommendations as adopted by the House of Assembly and I foreshadowed the early introduction of legislation to deal with those recommendations concerning a change in the elected representation in the House of Assembly.

At the present time the House of Assembly consists of 94 members of whom 84 are elected and 10 are official members. The 84 elected members are returned from 69 open electorates and 15 regional electorates. Candidates nominating for regional electorates must have an educational qualification equivalent to the Intermediate Certificate. There are no education qualifications for candidates nominating for open electorates.

In its final report the Committee recommended that the number of open electorates be increased from 69 to 82 and the number of regional electorates be increased from 15 to 18. During its 1971 tour of Papua and New Guinea the Committee meet with an overwhelming request for increased representation in the 1972–1976 House of Assembly. It based its recommendations on one regional member for each of the 18 districts in Papua New Guinea and one open member to approximately 30,000 people.

Although the Committee found some call on its tour for regional electorates to be abolished the majority opinion favoured their retention. The Committee felt hat it was necessary that there be a guaranteed standard of education in the House. The Committee noted in its final report that regional electorates could be reviewed during the 1972–1976 House but that it might be necessary to consider some minimum qualifications for open members such as the ability to read and write if regional electorates were to be replaced or abolished. When the Committee's report was being debated in the House of Assembly an amendment was moved to abolish regional electorates. This amendment was defeated by 47 votes to 17.

The Bill provides in Clause 3 for the recommended increase in the number of open and regional members of the House, Clause 4 adjusts the quorum figure for the House and Clause 5 that the amendments are to apply from the date of the completion of the next general election in Papua New Guinea.

The elections for the 1972–1976 House of Assembly will commence in March/April 1972. Under the Papua New Guinea Electoral Ordinance a redistribution committee must redistribute boundaries following a change in the composition of the House. Its report must be made public for three months and then be adopted by the House of Assembly. If the report is adopted the Administrator may proclaim the new boundaries.

The Government is anxious that the amendments to the Papua and New Guinea Act contained in this Bill are made as soon as possible so that sufficient time will be available for the necessary redistribution action to be completed and in operation for the 1972 House of Assembly elections in Papua New Guinea.

[*CPD*, HR, vol. 72, 29 April 1971, p. 2251]

---

1   Barnes delivered the statement to the House of Representatives.

2   Document 160.

163   SAVINGRAM TO ALL POSTS

Canberra, 3 May 1971

65. CONFIDENTIAL

Constitutional Developments in Papua New Guinea

The situation in Papua/New Guinea has changed markedly over the last few months and the Administrator has reported an 'obvious foreshortening of the independence timescale'. Internal self-government is likely to be achieved between 1972 and 1976 and full independence will then be a matter for the Papua New Guinea Government to negotiate with the Australian Government.

2.   This Savingram attempts to put recent developments in context and to give posts guidance on handling questions and press reports.

Constitutional Developments

3.   On 24 June 1969 the House of Assembly appointed a Select Committee on Constitutional Development:

> 'To consider ways and means of preparing and presenting, and to draft for the consideration of this House, a set of constitutional proposals to serve as a guide for future constitutional development in the Territory ...'

4.   The Committee presented three interim reports on 17 November 1969, 12 March 1970 and 3 September 1970. Its final report was presented on 4 March 1971 and, except for one clause, was approved by the House of Assembly on 11 March 1971. The Committee made two extensive tours of the Territory to ascertain the people's wishes, and travelled abroad to examine practice in countries in Africa, the Pacific and the Indian sub-continent.

5.   The Report's most important recommendation was that the Territory should be prepared for internal self-Government 'during the life of the next House of Assembly', i.e., 1972–1976. It noted that at present a majority of people would prefer self-government to come during the 1976–1980 House of Assembly, but it felt that the rate of advance was accelerating and that by 1972–1976 a majority might well be in favour of self-government. The Committee said it was also 'aware that there could be a change of Government in Australia which could result in internal self-government becoming a reality before the majority of the people are prepared to accept it'.

6.   The Committee's other recommendations have the effect of giving greater power to indigenous politicians by changing the composition of the Administrator's Executive Council and by varying the numbers of different types of electorates. They confirmed some existing practices, e.g., a unicameral legislature, and suggested that a bill of rights be embodied in the constitution of an independent Papua/New Guinea. They recommended a flag and a crest (the flag has since been flown at ECAFE[1] and ADB[2] meetings). Their recommendation that the country should be called 'Niugini' was the only recommendation to be rejected by the House. The House decided that it be known as Papua New Guinea.

7.   In a statement on 7 March 1971, the Minister for External Territories, Mr Barnes, said that the attitude of the Commonwealth Government would be determined when the House of Assembly had reached its conclusions.[3] However, he noted that the Australian Government

---

1   United Nations Economic Commission for Asia and the Far East.

2   Asian Development Bank.

3   Document 144.

'attached great importance to the views of the House on major constitutional matters, the more so when they followed such an exhaustive enquiry into the wishes of the people as that conducted by the Select Committee'. Mr Barnes also made it clear that the reservations expressed by the Government about 'timetables' in response to a UN resolution last December, did not apply to the 'approximate timetable' proposed in the Report. Our reservations had been based on objections to the imposition of a timetable by an outside authority and not to timetables chosen by the House of Assembly.

8.   On 27 April 1971 this approach was confirmed when the Minister for External Territories made the attached statement to Parliament.[4] In summary, he said that the Government accepted and would implement the Committee's Report as endorsed by the House of Assembly, and that it would negotiate the attainment of formal self-government with the leadership group which emerged from the 1972 elections in Papua New Guinea.

9.   Within the Territory, two political parties have emerged which could hope to gain a majority in the House. These are the somewhat radical urban-based Pangu[5] Pati [Party] which advocates immediate self-government, and the more conservative and rurally oriented Compass Party,[6] recently re-named the United Party, whose policy is to slow down the movement towards self-government.

Guidance

10. In the past we have tended to take a somewhat defensive approach towards our role in Papua/New Guinea, stressing our efforts and achievements and providing evidence that the local people did not yet want self-government. Following the Government's endorsement of the Select Committee's recommendations, posts might now take a more positive attitude towards the Territory. We are naturally still anxious to avoid uninformed criticism and would hope that posts would continue to counter any such criticism, but we would also like now to place stress on Papua/New Guinea as a country rapidly approaching self-government and one which will soon take its place in the world.

11. In discussions or public statements, you could draw on the following points:

(a) Australia has always said that the people of Papua New Guinea could have self-government or independence when they wanted it. Now that the people have expressed their wishes, through the House of Assembly, the Australian Government is taking the necessary steps to put these into practice.

(b) Once formal self-government is attained, the question of independence will be up to the Government of Papua New Guinea. Australian control will in any case be minimal and we will show the same regard for the freely expressed wishes of the people as before.

(c) Our objections to 'timetable' provisions in UN resolutions were objections to the attempt to impose one, and do not apply to a timetable proposed by the people themselves.

(d) PNG will require outside economic and technical help for some time to come. We will continue to give aid and assistance after independence if this is desired by the Government of PNG.

(e) We will continue to observe our obligations under the Trust Agreement until these cease to exist, i.e., on independence.

[NAA: A1209, 1968/9698 PART 3]

---

4   Document 160.

5   Pangu stood for 'Papua and New Guinea Union'.

6   The name 'Compass' was a contraction of 'combined political associations'.

164   LETTER FROM KERR TO JOHNSON

Canberra, 4 May 1971

Changing of Official Name of the Territory of Papua and New Guinea

I refer to your memorandum of 21st April, 1971, reference 35–4–137,[1] concerning the form of reply to be made to the resolution of the House of Assembly requesting a change of name for Papua and New Guinea.

2.   The Australian Government has agreed to the change of name requested and the forthcoming amendments to the Papua and New Guinea Act will include provisions to alter 'Territory of Papua and New Guinea' to 'Papua New Guinea'. It is suggested that the Senior Official Member might make a statement on the Government's acceptance of the recommendations of the Select Committee as endorsed by the House at the June meeting and a draft statement is being prepared for your consideration. This statement will include a reference to the acceptance of the change in the name to Papua New Guinea.

3.   However, as the request for a change of name was embodied in a motion separate from that endorsing the Select Committee's recommendations, it is agreed that normal practice should be followed and a separate letter of reply forwarded to the Speaker. A suggested form of reply is set out hereunder.

Dear Mr Speaker,

I refer to the motion of Mr Chatterton[2] which was passed during the March 1971 meeting of the House of Assembly.

The motion reads as follows:

'That this House requests the Government of Australia to change the official name of the Territory from "Papua and New Guinea" to "Papua New Guinea".'

The Australian Government has considered the resolution in conjunction with the recommendations of the Select Committee on Constitutional Development and has agreed to the change of name requested by the House. This will be included in the amendments to the Papua and New Guinea Act to be put before the Commonwealth Parliament later this year.

[NAA: A452, 1970/4523 PART 8]

---

1   Not published.

2   The Reverend Percy Chatterton, a retired Congregationalist missionary and minister, and a prominent social reformer, was the MHA for Port Moresby.

165   PRESS RELEASE

Port Moresby, 5 May 1971

'Government' Not 'Administration'

The Administrator, Mr L. W. Johnson said in Lae today that the time had come to drop the term 'Administration', in favour of the word 'Government'.

He said the Territory no longer had a colonial Administration but the Papua New Guinea Government.

He said the Administrator's Executive Council Ministers were Ministers of that Government.

Mr Johnson was speaking to 300 students at the Institute of Technology in Lae at the beginning of the AEC tour of the Morobe District.

He said the reason for adopting the term 'Government' was that most of the important decisions were made by the AEC, and the Administrator was bound to accept the advice of the AEC in most matters.

Throughout, Mr Johnson used the term 'Ministers' rather than Ministerial Members or Assistant Ministerial Members.

The Ministerial Member for Health, also a member of the AEC Finance Sub-Committee, Mr Tore Lokoloko, gave a warning of financial stringency next year. He said the Australian Government, which was suffering from inflation problems, has asked Papua New Guinea to do everything possible to meet more of its needs from internal revenue.

'Australia cannot keep spending money on us. We have to find our own money before we ask for more from Australia.'

He also said that the AEC would be careful to make sure that the tax burden did not fall too heavily on the 'small men back in the villages'.

Mr Johnson added that if it were a choice between cutting growth and higher taxation the usual answer was to find more money.

[NAA: A452, 1971/888]

166 SUBMISSION FROM GREENWELL TO BARNES

Canberra, 7 May 1971

Papua and New Guinea—Administrative Arrangements (Vesting of Powers) Ordinance 1971

The attached *Administrative Arrangements (Vesting of Powers) Ordinance* 1971,[1] which originated as an Administration Bill, was passed without amendment on 18 March 1971 and was reserved by the Acting Administrator on 30 March 1971 for the Governor-General's pleasure.

2.   This submission recommends action for assent to the Ordinance.

3.   The purpose of this Ordinance is to enable powers given under other legislation to the Administrator and public servants to be transferred to Ministerial office-holders. The Ordinance is thus complementary to recent determinations under the Papua and New Guinea Act 1949—1968 conferring final responsibility in certain areas of government to Ministerial office-holders.

4.   Section 25 of the Papua and New Guinea Act provides that the House of Assembly may not make Ordinances conferring powers directly upon Ministerial office-holders but that such powers may be delegated to them by the Administrator. This Ordinance enables powers of public servants to be transferred by the Administrator to himself, and for the Administrator to delegate these and others of his powers to Ministerial office-holders or to public servants. Under section 10 of the Ordinance certain powers are excluded from delegation under the Ordinance; these include the Administrator's powers under Commonwealth Acts.

5.   There is no difference of view between the Department and the Administration regarding the provisions of this Ordinance.

RECOMMENDATION

6.   It is recommended that the Governor-General be advised to assent to the *Administrative Arrangements (Vesting of Powers Ordinance)* 1971, which provides for the vesting of certain statutory powers in the Administrator and for the delegation of certain powers and functions of the Administrator to Ministerial office-holders.[2]

[NAA: A452, 1971/1169]

---

1   Not published.
2   Barnes approved the recommendation on 12 May 1971.

167   RECORD OF DISCUSSION BETWEEN HAY AND TANGE[1]

Canberra, 12 May 1971

Record of Discussions in Department of Defence

At Sir Arthur Tange's invitation the Secretary opened the discussion by referring to the Government's recent decision under which the Department was required to draw up a programme so as to be ready for self-government in Papua New Guinea if it comes during the life of the 1972/76 House.[2] Movements towards self-government would depend upon firstly, whether a cohesive majority emerged after the April 1972 elections and secondly, if such a majority did emerge and formed a 'government' with whom the Australian Government could negotiate the attitudes (i.e. either conservative or progressive) which such a majority group might have. [sic] In essence programming had to be flexible but it had to be done.

2.   The Secretary indicated that his letter of 6th April[3] to Sir Arthur had raised two points. The first was the possibility of opening up now for consideration by the Government the question of establishing a New Guinea defence force separate from the Commonwealth Defence Forces.[4] The second was the need to isolate those points on which discussions had been proceeding and which were now agreed for decision by the appropriate authorities and at the same time to list outstanding issues so that these can be properly coordinated and brought to a decision as early as is practicable.

3.   The idea of a move towards a separate defence force which the Secretary saw being done in such a way that it would not derogate from the Minister for Defence's responsibility for external defence (and therefore the shape and size of the force) would have the advantage of inculcating the idea that the force would ultimately belong to the Territory. It would also have the advantage that it might make easier the machinery for invoking aid to the civil power in light of the particular circumstances in Papua New Guinea.

4.   On the question of the numerous studies the Secretary felt that there was some vagueness about the terms of reference for the internal security study group and that these ought to be amended and no doubt would be from a settling of the issues on which agreement had already been reached. He also thought it would be appropriate for a new study on the question of a separate defence to be put in hand right away.

5.   The Secretary indicated that he had not discussed the issues with the Minister for External Territories but that the Minister was aware he had written to the Secretary for Defence to open up these questions for inter-departmental discussion.

6.   Sir Arthur indicated that the Defence group would endeavour to be responsive to the Secretary's proposals. He said he was somewhat concerned himself about the need to bring together the differences in judgement from the Territory and Defence sides on some particular issues e.g. the size and role of the PIR and also that he felt there had perhaps been too much

---

1   The final version of this record has not been found. Although a draft, the document is sufficiently important to include in the volume. Apart from Hay and Tange, others present at the meeting were Besley, Admiral Sir Victor Smith, Chair of the Chiefs of Staff Committee, and Major General R. L. (Ron) Hughes, Director, Joint Staff.

2   Document 159.

3   Document 154.

4   At the time Australia had separate defence, army, navy, and air force departments. These departments were combined in 1973.

thinking that future arrangements for the Territory would simply be a projection of the past. He wondered whether decisions could be made on some quite practical matters without knowing what the local viewpoint is in Papua New Guinea. He asked whether there was an informed public opinion on these matters.

7.   The Secretary said that it would be difficult now to obtain a Papua New Guinea viewpoint since the present House of Assembly was coming to a close and people were beginning to become pre-occupied with the 1972 elections. In these circumstances it would probably be necessary to settle such questions as the size of the Force by making a judgment now so that the outstanding studies could proceed on a reasonable basis.

8.   Sir Arthur agreed that it would be appropriate to isolate the points on which decisions could now be made and that there was a need to amend the terms of reference for the internal security study group. In his view the present terms of reference were not only vague but perhaps contradictory. A fundamental question is who is responsible for internal security now?

9.   Sir Arthur said that he felt there was an area of neglected work in that there had been no studies of the potential legal/constitutional processes by which progressive delegation of control and command could be passed over from Australia to Papua New Guinea. This would involve some amendments to the law in Australia and the introduction of appropriate legislation in the Territory. It would be necessary to define the most practicable way in which this could be done having regard to the experience of other countries and to the views of the Chiefs of Staff on the size of the Force—the size would have to comprehend not only the strategic and military aspects but the economic as well. On the role of the PIR it would be necessary to examine where it would fit into the Papua New Guinea society and what inbuilt checks and restrictions might be appropriate.

10. Sir Arthur said he did not propose to discuss the question of aid to the civil power in detail but he wanted to stress the point that the Defence attitude will continue to be a very cautious one. There was also the question of what power a soldier has in such circumstances and what are his legal rights in the event that a person is killed. He suggested that there could well be a good deal more thought given to the development of a new set of procedures perhaps not so restrictive in Papua New Guinea. But it would be necessary to inter-weave this with due consideration to such things as the rule of law and the implications of a possible future government ruling by force and so on.

11. The Secretary said he felt that enough had been done at the present on call-out. The procedures as developed, though restrictive, were satisfactory and were ones with which we could live so long as there was a range of responses which the military forces could use on the basis that the force used was the minimum necessary to maintain law and order. This for example would involve the use by soldiers of batons and shields. The adoption of these procedures for the present would not preclude the commencement of studies right away on what it is that is appropriate for Papua New Guinea in this respect. He would like to see the internal security group address itself to the question of when responsibility for internal security should pass to the Territory. He indicated that self-government had not been defined. It was something which would emerge with time and may or may not include responsibility for internal law and order.

12. Sir Arthur felt it important to gather up in the studies a thorough review of the organisational arrangements relating to the use of the PIR in support of the civil power in the period before responsibility for internal law and order passed to the Territory. There were also some machinery problems which needed settling, for example, training of soldiers in the use of batons and shields.

13. The Chairman, Chiefs of Staff, said that it had been his impression that soldiers were to be trained in the use of batons and shields. The Director, Joint Staff, said in his view it

was not appropriate to train soldiers in this way. He favoured the use of the army in such circumstances as an ultimate power in which to maintain law and order it may be necessary to shoot someone. He also referred to the difference between the training of a policeman who was trained to act as an individual whereas a soldier is trained to operate as part of a team. The soldier's legal power is also different. He therefore favoured the use of the army either in its ultimate sense or to guard key points and man radio blocks but not in an intermediate role involving, for example, batons and shields as had been suggested. He said he doubted whether the legal position of a soldier even in respect of guard type duties was clear and that probably some Territory legislation was needed.

14. The Secretary said he thought that there would be problems in this which led him to the view that we should not pursue for the time being the question of legislating in the Territory to clarify the legal position of members of the Forces. He also pointed out that there is a substantial number of the police force trained to act as team members and that the riot squads are very much like a military platoon. They are also trained to kill if necessary. In his view there would be great value in a show of force by a formed and disciplined body of troops being available and on many occasions the mere show of force would be sufficient to restore law and order. He also said he thought that the training of troops in riot techniques had been authorised and was in hand.

15. The Director, Joint Staff, said that troops were being trained but that the training was in traditional riot control methods. He did not favour the use of batons and said that he could not see how a contingent of the PIR which would in all probability be smaller than the police could, with batons and shields, achieve something which the riot control police had failed to do. He mentioned that the Force Commander was looking at some of the newer techniques such as gas projectors and rubber bullets.

16. Sir Arthur said that he was confident the uniform people could develop new methods appropriate to the Territory's needs.

17. The Director, Joint Staff, said that a point of concern to him was that in the size and role days [sic]5 both External Territories and Foreign Affairs had insisted that the functions of border control and internal security be omitted from the role of the PIR for the purpose of that exercise. He himself saw merit in accepting a border control role and that if this were done he understood it would release some 300 odd policemen held in the Mt Hagen area to look after any problem which might arise on the border.

18. Sir Arthur said that in his experience it was normal to have a buffer zone of police so as to avoid a possible confrontation between opposing military forces. The role of the PIR would need to be settled but in his view it ought not to be primarily shaped for internal security.

19. The Secretary suggested that the useful role which the PIR might undertake would be that of civil defence since it was well equipped to handle the kind of operation which a civil defence normally undertook.

20. Sir Arthur said he was somewhat concerned at the organisational arrangements in Papua New Guinea. There was a need for some form of Security Committee in which the Force Commander could be involved so that there could be an appropriate dialogue between himself and the Administrator and others on the available intelligence.

21. The Secretary said that there was a Security Committee but that it did not appear to be operating satisfactorily and that this was something which the internal security study group might look into. It would be useful for the Committee to take a look into had been done in such

---

5   The wording of 'size and role days' may be a reference to planning days during which officials considered the respective sizes and roles of the defence and police forces in Papua New Guinea.

places as Fiji and Tanzania. So far as the role of the PIR was concerned he thought this ought to be defined in a Territory ordinance at the earliest practicable time.

22. Sir Arthur again referred to the legal aspects which required further study and said that as he understood it there were constitutional barriers to the raising of an army in Papua New Guinea since Attorney-General's seemed to believe that Section 114 of the Constitution which prohibited such action within a State also applied to the Territory. It was agreed that it would be necessary to clarify the legal position.

23. The Secretary suggested that perhaps the appropriate kind of machinery would be similar to that which had been established in Malaysia with Australia retaining some form of control. He thought that the study group ought to address itself to the time of handover of responsibility for internal security. This was related to the broader issue of citizenship which was now receiving some attention.[6] The group would also need to bear in mind and examine the implications of the possibility of a self-governing government of Papua New Guinea in some way committing Australia by exercising its part of responsibility for the Papua New Guinea defence.

24. It was agreed to set up a working party at a senior level (not below FAS)[7] since the Chiefs of Staff would be involved. The working party's task would be to isolate those issues on which a decision could now be made and to draw up a desirable list of further studies. The working party should also suggest which departments ought to be involved with further studies and propose terms of reference for carrying these studies forward. Those items on which agreement had been reached and for which there was some pressure to reach a decision because of time factors would need to be identified. Further studies would include as a priority item the role and authority of the Defence Forces both before and after [the] handover of [the] internal security function and would need to look [into] what additional check[s and balances][8] machinery might be [made] necessary by the coming into existence ultimately of a responsible ministry in Papua New Guinea but before the actual act of transfer of full responsibility for internal security.

[NAA: A452, 1971/2828]

---

6   See Documents 118, 149 & 152.

7   First Assistant Secretary.

8   Editorial insertion.

168   PRESS RELEASE

Canberra, 13 May 1971

Department of External Territories: Changes in Organisational Structure

The Minister for External Territories, Mr Barnes, today announced changes in the organisational structure of the Department of External Territories.

Mr Barnes said that the changes were consequent on recent constitutional developments in Papua New Guinea. In June last year the Government decided to transfer powers to Papua New Guinea Ministerial Members over a wide range of areas.[1] In April this year it accepted an 'approximate timetable' for self-government which had been proposed by the Papua New Guinea House of Assembly.[2]

The overall effect of the organisational changes was to introduce a three-divisional structure for the Department of External Territories. Adjustments of workloads between branches and sections had been effected. Staff had been redeployed as necessary from areas where the work load had been reduced to areas where it had increased. The Department now had the capacity to form 'task forces' to undertake special assignments on behalf of Papua New Guinea. A separate section devoted to the smaller Territories (Norfolk, Cocos (Keeling) and Christmas Islands)[3] had been created.

Mr Barnes said that the Government's decision on constitutional changes had significantly changed the function of the Department of External Territories, especially in relation to those activities for which decision-making authority had been transferred to Papua New Guinea.

'While these changes of functions have reduced work loads of certain branches, the Government's decision involves an intensification of the Department's responsibilities in the preparatory work necessary for internal self-government of Papua New Guinea, and in economic development', the Minister said.

In those areas of responsibility which had been transferred to Papua New Guinea, the Department would continue to keep the Minister informed of development, particularly in relation to Australia's international obligations, to oversight expenditure from the Development Grant, and to assist Administration departments as required.

The Department would continue to initiate policy recommendations and to review policies and policy recommendations initiated by the Papua New Guinea Administration in matters for which the Commonwealth retained financial responsibility. Its responsibilities in respect of the Territories of Norfolk Island, Cocos (Keeling) and Christmas Islands and the Coral Sea Islands would continue.[4]

---

1   See Documents 48 & 54.

2   See Document 142.

3   In 1914 Norfolk Island, which is located east of Sydney and north of New Zealand, became Australia's second external territory (after Papua). The Cocos (Keeling) Islands, which are 2,950 kilometres north-west of Perth, were transferred from the United Kingdom to Australia, at Australia's request, in 1955. Christmas Island, located 2,650 kilometres north-west of Perth, was transferred from United Kingdom to Australia, again at Australia's request, in 1958. See Alan Kerr, *A Federation In These Seas: An Account of the Acquisition by Australia of its External Territories*, Attorney-General's Department, Barton, 2009, pp. 121, 267, 316, 327–28.

4   The Coral Seas Islands are a group of small and uninhabited islands (including reefs and sand cays) to the north-east of Queensland. In 1969 Australia incorporated these islands into the Coral Seas Islands Territory. See ibid., p. 365.

The Department would also retain its secretariat function and its agency functions on behalf of all the Administrations. It would remain the channel of communication between the Administration and authorities outside Papua New Guinea.

Mr Barnes said the reorganisation involved the redeployment of resources on a relatively small scale in areas where the functions of the Department had changed. In all, the establishment has been reduced by 10 positions (all of which are at present unoccupied) and the number of officers who will, in fact, be [re]deployed is 20, out of a total of some 470.

A feature of the new arrangements would be the avoidance of duplication between the work of departmental and Administration staff.

'The Department will continue to have an important part to play in Papua New Guinea's transition to self-government. In particular, there is a need to provide forward planning for the future', Mr Barnes said.

[NAA: A1838, 936/3/5 PART 2]

169   CABLEGRAM TO CANBERRA¹

New York, 14 May 1971

338. Unclassified

Papua and New Guinea—Visiting Mission Report

(A) Political Advancement

468. Recent advancements involving substantial transfer of authority to local ministerial members seem to be working well. The process of transfer will need to be continued, especially in the fields of internal administration and economic development. (Paragraphs 282 to 284).

469. The lack of political parties with a solid nation-wide base is a source of weakness in the House of Assembly. Consideration should be given to possible means for encouraging existing parties to establish a truly national organisation (Paragraphs 286 to 289).

[*matter omitted*]²

(E) Future of the Territory

497. The Mission endorses the findings of the Select Committee on Constitutional Development. In particular it agrees with the Committee that since the rate of political development is accelerating there may be a majority demand for internal self-government before the end of the 1972–1976 House of Assembly, and that, in consequence the development of the Territory should be geared to preparing it for self-government during the life of the next House (Paragraph 460).

498. The Mission considers it important that progress towards full self-government should be seen to continue without interruption. There are matters in the fields of localisation, economic development and political education which, in its opinion, will merit particularly close attention in the years ahead (Paragraph 461).

499. While the chief responsibility for setting a date for independence should rest with the government of a self-governing Papua and New Guinea, the Mission believes that it would be both prudent and realistic to assume for planning purposes that independence will be achieved during the life of the fourth House of Assembly (Paragraph 463).

500. The Mission recommends that, since the vast majority of the people desire a strong central government and a united country, separatism should be discouraged, that a single citizenship law should be established soon for internal purposes for the whole territory, and that appropriate opportunities should be taken to emphasise publicly that the destiny of Papua and New Guinea is to move on to full self-government and independence as a single, united country (Paragraphs 464 to 466).

501. The Mission considers that in the interest of future good relations between Australian and the Territory, the question of the border with Queensland should be kept under constant review (Paragraph 467).

[NAA: A452, 1971/1077]

---

1   This cable reported the conclusions and recommendations of the UN Mission report.

2   The omitted matter included comments on the localisation of the judiciary, local government and the public service; economic development; social development; defence; international relations; and the role of the United Nations.

170   LETTER FROM WALLER TO HAY

Canberra, 17 May 1971

CONFIDENTIAL

Thank you for your letter of 27 April 1971[1] [...] I would like to take up the points made in your letter so that we may go ahead where we agree, and resolve our differences where we may not. I am attaching, for your information, a paper setting out where this Department stands on the major issues.[2]

I appreciate your offer to provide material on the possibilities for sponsoring cadetships for potential diplomats at the University of Papua and New Guinea and your seeking [of] early nominations for training. When a senior Foreign Services Officer pays his projected visit to Papua New Guinea he might discuss with the University the possibility of providing one or two year cadetships along the lines of the old External Affairs Cadet Scheme. This might help overcome the shortage of graduates.

I agree that trade should be included amongst the functions of the Foreign Ministry and that this should be taken into account in training. Because of the overall shortage of trained manpower, it would be wise to avoid duplication of effort and such matters as immigration and negotiation of international civil aviation matters might also be included. I look forward to hearing from you after you have discussed the matter with the Administrator.

I agree that one or two officers from the Department of Foreign Affairs should be sent to work with the Officer-in-Charge of the International Affairs Branch, and I suggest that an FAO[3] Class 4 and an FAO Class 2 would be suitable levels. We might perhaps plan on sending them late this year, if you agree that this would be the best timing?

I do, however, have some reservations on the suggestion that an officer might be seconded to the Administration. This would require him to take leave without pay and, apart from the possible effect on the officer's promotion prospects and other conditions, raises a number of complications from our own staffing point of view. Perhaps your preference could be met by establishing positions in the Department of Foreign Affairs in Canberra and posting men as Commonwealth Officers. They would, of course, be instructed to place themselves at the disposal of the Head of the International Affairs Branch and work under his direction, but would retain the right of direct communication with this Department.

On the question of a Commonwealth office during the pre-independence period, I see no difficulty in using the future Australian High Commission building to house all officers concerned with matters still handled by Australia. There is certainly no need at this stage for a purely Foreign Affairs building, so long as its construction takes account of its long term use. The main problem we face in this context is to estimate the likely requirements for the eventual High Commission.

I think you agree in principle that after independence the High Commission must not appear to be taking a major part in the running of the new country. Although we shall almost certainly need a large Australian establishment under the general responsibility of the High Commissioner, some of these could be separately grouped as an aid mission separate from, though under the 'umbrella' of the High Commission. There will no doubt also be a Defence

---

1   Document 161.

2   Not published. For a developed version of the main themes of this paper, see Document 187.

3   Foreign Affairs Officer.

staffed military mission with a training and advisory role. I assume there will be a separate category of Australians on contract or seconded to the PNG Government for whom the Mission would have no direct administrative responsibility. If separate accommodation is provided for the operating staff of the military and aid missions, the High Commission staff itself could be relatively compact and engaged essentially with its diplomatic functions, extensive though these may be.

On the question of education of key groups on the nature of international relations, I believe your suggestion that we examine carefully what is being done is a sound one. I will arrange for an officer to do this soon. However, I feel that an effort to reach the wider community is a lesser priority. The immediately important requirement would seem to be to give a small group of leaders, i.e., politicians, administrators and academics etc., a thorough understanding of the problems and pressures they will face in the period following self-government and independence. This goes well beyond the kind of thing envisaged by the present Territory political education programme as we understand it—valuable though this is. It would cover topics such as the strings which may be attached to aid, the activities of Communist diplomats, the cost of overseas representation, the realities of international power relations, international trade arrangements and the activities and uses of international organisations. Help in creating more of this more sophisticated awareness, including the necessary administrative arrangements and their costs could be given by officers of this Department visiting PNG and through contacts made by the Foreign Affairs officers posted to Port Moresby in the International Affairs branch. It will be slow and informal and will be supplemented by talks to university groups and others. Stimulation of members of the Assembly to set up a Committee on Foreign Affairs, and the encouragement of a Papua/New Guinea equivalent of the Australian Institute of International Affairs would be other possibilities.

I agree with your remarks on foreign consulates and Soviet visits and my Department is taking these matters up in the way you suggested. The German Ambassador, who visited PNG recently, has already mentioned that his Government may wish to appoint an honorary consul.

I shall be in touch with you again very soon in connection with your suggestion that a senior Foreign Affairs officer should visit PNG. I hope this will be possible before the end of June.

[NAA: A452, 1971/0729]

171   LETTER FROM BARNES TO MCMAHON[1]

Canberra, 17 May 1971

Recently the Administrator of Papua New Guinea and Mr Tom Leahy, the spokesman for the Administrator's Executive Council, expressed their concern to me at moves by certain Members of the House of Assembly from electorates in Papua to seek some form of permanent, special treatment for Papua before independence. Notice has been given of three motions in this tenor which could lead to heated and divisive debate in the June meeting of the House of Assembly.

The Administrator and Mr Leahy suggested that the former be given discretion to issue a public statement, before the House meets, reiterating the Government's policy on this issue. I agree with them, provided the agreement and support of the Administrator's Executive Council is first obtained.

I attach for your information the text which I propose to authorise.[2] It may well be that the Administrator's Executive Council will wish to add to the statement details of certain supporting measures within its own competence, such as the removal of the boundary line between Papua and New Guinea on maps in schools, and the refusal to agree to proposals for early referenda on separate status for part or regions of the country.

The statement contains no new policy. The Government has previously placed on record its intention to advance Papua New Guinea to nationhood as a single unit (a view echoed recently by the Leader of the Opposition in Parliament). Requests for referenda in both Bougainville and Papua were refused in 1970.

As long ago as April 1966 I told the then Select Committee of the House of Assembly on Constitutional Development that the difference in status between Papua and New Guinea was of little consequence, and I so informed the Parliament on 21st April, 1966.

But some Papuans because Papua is technically a Crown colony still claim that Papuans are entitled to special consideration such as, for example, an act of free choice before they finally join, as a minority element with New Guinea as a single nation. I do not rule out the possibility of an ascertainment of their views at or about the time of independence, but given that the only practical alternative would be continued association with Australia, I believe no encouragement should be given to any expectation of special consideration.

I am hopeful that another firm statement, appropriately timed, will discourage those now, for various reasons, aiming to promote divisions among the people of Papua New Guinea. If however separatist sentiment either in Papua or elsewhere should in the period between now and self-government increase in strength to the degree where it poses a law and order problem, I shall bring the matter to your notice.

[NAA: A1209, 1971/9229]

---

1   McMahon was now Prime Minister, having replaced Gorton following a leadership challenge on 10 March 1971.

2   Not published. The final statement is at Document 173.

172   NOTE FOR FILE BY BESLEY

Canberra, 19 May 1971

CONFIDENTIAL

Unity Statement

I have had a number of discussions with Mr Bailey[1] of [the] Prime Minister's Department about the proposed press release on unity in Papua New Guinea. The only issues which PM&C[2] would wish to discuss with the Prime Minister were firstly the tone of the submission, i.e. was it too hard, and secondly the question of keeping open the option of an ascertainment of the wishes of the people of Papua later by way perhaps of a referendum.[3]

2.   Mr Bailey subsequently reluctantly accepted the view I put to him that the statement needed to be fairly hard hitting. I told him that this was readily accepted by senior people in Papua New Guinea, some of whom thought that the statement was perhaps too mild. So far as the second issue was concerned, Mr Bailey agreed that the statement as prepared did not foreclose on the option of a referendum if thought appropriate later. He also accepted the view I put to him which I said was firmly held by the Secretary, that to mention a referendum or the possibility of a referendum in the statement would serve only to cause some to seek it now even if only for political motives.

3.   Following a telephone call from the Administrator early on the afternoon of the 19th I informed Mr Bailey that the AEC, including the only Papuan member present, had accepted the statement. I said that the Administrator proposed to release it at 9.00 a.m. on Thursday 20th and that if there were any difficulties from his point of view he would need to know about them now. He said that there would be none and that from his point of view there was no impediment to us going ahead as planned. I informed the Administrator of this.

[NAA: A452, 1971/1995]

---

1   Peter Bailey.

2   After becoming Prime Minister in March 1971, McMahon had united the Prime Minister's Department and the Department of the Cabinet Office into the Department of the Prime Minister and Cabinet (PM&C). His predecessor, John Gorton, had created these two departments by dividing the Prime Minister's Department, which had been operation since 1911.

3   In a television interview aired on July 1970 Gorton had told John Boland of Channel 7 there were three options for assessing support for further constitutional development—a referendum, arrival at a consensus of opinion by discussion, or an expression of views by the House of Assembly (Document 85).

173   PRESS RELEASE

Port Moresby, 20 May 1971

National Unity

The Administrator, Mr L. W. Johnson, today issued the following statement.

I am authorised by the Minister for External Territories Mr C. E. Barnes, to reaffirm that it is the policy of the Australian Government to advance Papua New Guinea to internal self-government and independence as a united country.

In particular I am authorised to say that, in the Government's view, there is no ground for any people of Papua New Guinea to expect, as self-government and independence approach, that their present legal status will lead to any difference in their treatment by the Australian Government or the Administration or in their rights. In practice the difference of legal status between the inhabitants of Papua on the one hand, and New Guinea on the other has been of little consequence since the approval by the United Nations of the Administrative Union in 1947. The Government sees no other long term course for Papua and for New Guinea than one directed towards internal self-government and independence for the country as a whole.

I can see how some elected leaders, in their anxiety to obtain benefits for their electors, might see advantage in pressing for some form of separate treatment. This might be particularly true of less populous and less developed areas.

I wish to say two things about the concern of those people who press for separate treatment—and here again I have the Minister's authority and also the full agreement of the AEC.

The first is that so far as the Administration is concerned the principle of fair treatment for all areas is firmly established. It is true that as a matter of sound economic policy and in accordance with the best economic advice available, we have supported the principle of investing money and resources where they will give the best return. But this has certainly not meant the neglect of the needs of other areas. Funds have been and will continue to be devoted to development in areas where there is a prospect of economic return only in the very long term future.

The second thing is that there will be the opportunity in the lifetime of the next House to look more deeply into the problem of the relationship between the future central government and its constituent elements and the means by which the interests of the less populous and less developed areas can best be protected. Even now, through the regional member system, the less densely populated areas have more representation per person than the populous areas. This difference is obscured by the fact that they all sit in the one House. It is also highly relevant that membership of the AEC and the Ministry as a whole is broadly representative of the regions within Papua New Guinea. Of the elected members of the AEC, two come from Papua, two from the Highlands, two from the Islands and two from the coastal areas of New Guinea. There is a precedent of the utmost importance and I am confident that similar principles will apply to future Ministries but it is also possible for appropriate safe-guards to be incorporated in the Constitution either before self-government by an amendment to the Papua New Guinea Act or in the Papua New Guinea Constitution of an independent country. The AEC has always taken a broad national view of its responsibilities and I am confident that it will continue to do so.

The Australian Government's firm attitude on this subject is based on its conviction that Papua New Guinea can only prosper and promote the welfare of its people as a unified nation. There are 700 different languages in this country and a very large number of tribal groups, none of which can successfully run its own affairs in isolation from the rest. The benefits of national development can best be provided if the whole country goes forward together. Otherwise, it will inevitably break down into a collection of tiny, hostile fragments which will not be able to meet the aspirations of the people.

I call upon all who fill positions of leadership in the House of Assembly, in Local Government and elsewhere to recognise the grave dangers which disunity threatens. We need above all the united efforts of all of the people of Papua New Guinea to develop a nation which can hold its own in the wider world of the future.

[NAA: A1209, 1971/9229]

174   MINUTE FROM BAILEY[1] TO MCMAHON

Canberra, 21 May 1971

Unity in Papua New Guinea

In the attached letter[2] the Minister advises you of his intention to authorise a statement by the Administrator which is designed to damp down motions in the House of Assembly designed to promote divisions among the people of Papua New Guinea.

2.   When the Department of External Territories gave us a copy of the letter earlier in the week, we expressed to them our anxiety about a statement as firm as that proposed by the Minister. However, in the light of advice from Port Moresby that the Administrator's Executive Council, and the Administrator himself, were firmly in favour of the statement, we indicated that we would not raise objections to it. However, we said that we felt we should bring to your notice the issue which concerns us.

3.   The issue is that separatism is a recurring feature in the political developments of the Territory. It is not at all impossible that, if the Australian Government stands flat-footed behind unity, it will find itself opposed to steadily rising internal pressures. In short, the Government could find itself, on this issue, in as much difficulty as it would have been had it not taken the line in relation to self-government and independence that it would be guided by the views of the people themselves.

4.   This is an issue that we feel needs careful watching, and we therefore alert you to it. However, as the Minister's letter is 'for information', we do not feel it necessary to suggest a reply, unless you so desire.

5.   I should perhaps add that to a considerable extent External Territories are relying on a statement[3] by Mr Gorton when he was in the Territory last July. He told Territory Members of the House of Assembly and Local Government Councillors that it would be 'a very retrograde step' for Papua to be independent of New Guinea. He said that [the] Government 'would do what we could to prevent that happening and to persuade Papuans from doing it, but if and when self-government comes and ultimately independence should come then that would be a matter for decision by those who were then fully responsible for the running of this Territory'. You will see that Mr Gorton himself did in effect leave some ultimate room for review in the light of expressions of opinion in the Territory.

[NAA: A1209, 1971/9229]

---

1   Peter Bailey.

2   Document 171. See also Document 172.

3   Not published. For Gorton's statements during his visit to PNG in July 1970, see Documents 69 & 70.

175 MEMORANDUM FROM MCINTRYE TO WALLER

New York, 21 May 1971

Papua New Guinea: Observation of 1972 Elections

United Nations Visiting Missions have coincided with elections in Papua New Guinea only in 1968. On that occasion the Mission arrived while polling was in progress, saw voting at three centres in Madang and Western Highland Districts and counting in Rabaul.

2.   It appears that the elections next year will almost certainly produce the House of Assembly and the Ministry that will preside over the establishment of full internal self-government, and possibly also over the attainment of independence. The elections will consequently be of great importance in United Nations consideration of Papua New Guinea in the next few years.

3.   In previous reports from this Mission we have from time to time spoken of the difficulties in and the need for convincing UN members that the House of Assembly really does represent the vox populi.[1] I refer particularly to the Delegation Report on the thirty-sixth session of the Council. With the Select Committee Report, the last Visiting Mission Report and the changing nature of the political party system in Papua New Guinea, some of these problems have disappeared. Nevertheless, I think we ought not to pass up an opportunity to have some UN members see and report on this next election and thereby strengthen general respect among missions here for the House of Assembly that the election is going to produce.

4.   The obverse of this is more important. It will, I believe, strengthen the position of PNG Ministers in their external dealings over the next few years if they are able to say that the election that produced their Ministry was observed by a UN group.

5.   With these considerations in mind, I should like to recommend that the Government invite a UN group drawn from the Trusteeship Council and the Committee of Twenty-four to go to Papua New Guinea next year for a period of two to three weeks specifically to observe last-minute electoral arrangements, polling and, if possible, counting in selected electorates.

[*matter omitted*]

18.   We have made considerable progress in Papua New Guinea (from the UN point of view as from others) in the last two years and I doubt whether we will have a difficult road in the Assembly this year. Nevertheless members will be conscious of the importance of the forthcoming elections and may well wish to seek something on the above lines. The best way of avoiding this is, I believe, to get in before them and place in the hands of the Trusteeship Council (where it belongs) an invitation of the sort I have described. At the same time I stress that, while avoiding being put in a disadvantageous position later in the year is a consideration of the importance, I make the proposal primarily for the reasons set out in paragraphs 3 and 4 above.

19.   If you were to agree to the proposal, the invitation could I believe be handled by the Council President out of session, i.e., after mid-June. It would of course be preferable at least to submit an invitation while the Council is in session, if this is feasible. I appreciate that the Ministers for Foreign Affairs and External Territories would have to be consulted, and I imagine it would be necessary also to put the question before the Administrator's Executive Council. If you agree with the idea, and if it were possible to do all this and advise us before, say, 16th June, it would I think be helpful from all our points of view.

[NAA: A452, 1971/2303]

---

1   *Vox populi* literally means 'voice of the people'. In English it means: 'the view or the opinion of the people' or 'the view of the majority of the people'.

176   LETTER FROM BARNES TO MCMAHON

Canberra, 24 May 1971

Citizenship has long been a subject of concern in Papua New Guinea.[1]

Papuans have to some extent relied on their Australian citizenship status to press claims that they should be treated differently from New Guineans in regard to progress towards internal self-government. I have written separately about the attitude which the Government might take about Papuan and other types of separatism.[2]

Australians living in Papua New Guinea, some of them born there, probably wish to retain their Australian citizenship status even when Papua New Guinea becomes independent.

I propose that, as part of the programme for movement to full internal self-government in the period 1972–76, as approved by Cabinet recently,[3] consideration should be given to establishing a common citizenship status for Papuans and New Guineans. This citizenship would, if the House of Assembly supported it, also provide for Australians and other overseas people who satisfy the criteria to take Papua New Guinea citizenship. For the present I am thinking of a form of citizenship that would not affect the international status of Papuans as Australian citizens (conferred under the Nationality and Citizenship Act) nor of Australians living in Papua New Guinea. It might well be the first stage of a move towards a true international citizenship and I would hope that, through the Administrator's Executive Council and the House of Assembly, it would be possible to establish a citizenship now that the country could feel it could adopt.

There is a need to consider citizenship now because some Papuans may want to cite their Australian citizenship status in support of seventh state or separatist demands. A common citizenship would confirm our intention to develop Papua New Guinea as a unified nation. Also Australians living in Papua New Guinea are anxious to know what their rights will be with internal self-government and independence. My own feeling is that while we obviously cannot pre-determine this, it would be preferable to test Papua New Guinean leaders now on the extent to which they would be prepared to allow expatriates to participate in the affairs of their country. Expatriates would then have early notice of local feelings in this respect.

I would like to introduce this subject by means of a statement by the Senior Official Member to the House of Assembly at its meeting next month. Such a statement would help blunt [the] Papuans' separatist moves and would retain the initiative for the Government. There is a possibility of a private member's bill on citizenship.

I am attaching a draft statement[4] which, if you concur, would be made by the Senior Official Member at the June meeting of the House of Assembly.[5] The Administrator has informed me

---

1   See Documents 118 & 149.

2   Document 171.

3   See Document 159.

4   Not published.

5   The senior official member of the AEC was A. P. J. (Tony) Newman. In the event, however, the final statement was delivered to the House on 8 June 1971 (Document 182) by the AEC's spokesman—Tom Leahy, the MHA for Markham. Leahy was a farmer from Morobe District and a leading member of a long-established expatriate family with agricultural and other business interests. Hay had appointed Leahy to the AEC following the 1968 elections and the formation of the second House of Assembly. In mid–1970 the AEC elected Leahy as its spokesman, with the official AEC members abstaining from the vote, by five votes to three, defeating Tore Lokoloko, the MHA for Kerema and ministerial member for public health, who accordingly became the AEC's deputy-spokesman. See Ian Downs, *The Australian Trusteeship: Papua New Guinea, 1945–75*, Australian Government Publishing Service, Canberra, 1980, pp. 391, 393–5; and James Griffin, Hank Nelson and Stewart Firth, *Papua New Guinea: A Political History*, Heinemann Educational Australia, Richmond, Victoria, 1979, pp. 166–67.

that he agreed generally with the draft statement and that he intended to place it before the Administrator's Executive Council at its meeting on Thursday 20th May. I have not yet heard the result of Council's deliberations. As the House of Assembly meets on 31st May, however, I am seeking your concurrence to the statement beforehand. The views of the Administrator's Executive Council would be fully taken into account in drawing up the final version.

I would of course propose that any firm proposals on citizenship would be a matter for Cabinet consideration. It would be desirable that the Cabinet have the views of the House of Assembly and reactions of the people before considering this matter and I would therefore envisage Cabinet consideration later this year.

I am sending a similar letter to the Minister for Immigration.[6]

[*matter omitted*]

[NAA: A1209, 1971/9229]

177   CABLEGRAM TO NEW YORK

Canberra, 28 May 1971

512. CONFIDENTIAL

Visiting Mission Report

Following are comments on the visiting mission report[1] which you may draw on as required. They do not represent the Government's formal response to the report.

[*matter omitted*]

Political Advancement

(A) Political advancement—some general comments.

The Government is concerned to ensure that the transfer of authority to ministerial office holders works well. The process of transfer is a continuing one. On 27th April, 1971, the Minister for External Territories said that the Government 'will prepare a programme for movement to full internal self-government in the period 1972–76, but the execution of that programme will have regard to the state of opinion as it develops after the 1972 House of Assembly elections and to the policies of the political leaders who then emerge.'[2]

The people of Papua New Guinea are perfectly free to form political parties and associations and the Government welcomes their formation.

A complete review of local government is being undertaken—this will affect local government development and financial requirements. New arrangements for the provision, control and training of Council staff are also under consideration. Action is in hand regarding the establishment of area authorities and the Government agrees with the principle spelt out in the report of the need for them to exercise real responsibility within the framework of national unity.

---

6   Jim Forbes, who agreed to the text of the draft statement; McMahon acknowledged the letter on 7 June. See Letter, Forbes to Barnes, 31 May 1971, NAA: A452, 1971/1916; and Letter, McMahon to Barnes, 7 June 1971, NAA: A1209, 1971/9229.

---

1   Not published. The conclusions of the report were cabled from New York to Canberra on 14 May 1971 (Document 169).

2   See Document 160.

The administration conducts an extensive programme of political education which provides information for village people, local government councillors, town people, school and tertiary students and indigenous officers of the public service. There are obvious limitations, however, to the extent that public servants can be political educators, for not all political education comes from lectures on institutions, but through political participation. Local government councils have been providing this for many years. Emergence of political parties takes this further.

[*matter omitted*]

With the presentation of the final report of the Select Committee on Constitutional Development, an important phase of the political education programme is now directed to allaying the fears and misconceptions relating to self-government and independence which have become apparent, and pointing out the inevitability of self-government and independence.

The whole tenor of the programme is consequently based on the recommendation of the Select Committee, adopted by both the House of Assembly and agreed to by the Commonwealth Government 'that the development of the Territory be geared to preparing the country for internal self-government during the life of the next House of Assembly so that should it become a reality earlier than expected or if it is in fact requested by the people then, then the move to internal self-government can be made at that time with the least possible amount of administrative disruption'.[3]

[NAA: A452, 1971/1981]

---

3   Document 142, para. 10.

178   CABLEGRAM TO NEW YORK

Canberra, 31 May 1971

525. UNCLASSIFIED

Development Planning in Papua New Guinea

The Minister for External Territories, Mr Barnes today announced new arrangements for development planning in Papua New Guinea.

These involve:

> The setting up of a committee of the Administrator's Executive Council to accept overall responsibility for development planning:
>
> The creation of a new office of programming and coordination which will come under the control of a ministerial member.

Mr Barnes said that decisions concerning development were so interwoven with the entire complex of government policies that they should be made by those responsible for final policies.

The move would involve ministerial members directly with the planning process and would place responsibility for development planning decisions with a committee of the Administrator's Executive Council.

The arrangements also accord with recommendations made by the 1971 United Nations visiting mission to Papua New Guinea in its report to the Trusteeship Council, Mr Barnes said. The mission recommended that economic policy and development planning should be brought into the ambit of the ministerial system.

Mr Barnes said that the Committee of the AEC would be serviced by a committee of officials chaired by the Director of the new Office of Programming and Coordination.

He said the main function of the new office would be to recommend a coordinated development programme for Papua New Guinea taking into account financial, natural and human resources.

It would undertake in conjunction with the Public Service Board and the Treasury an annual review of functions and priorities of departments and agencies.

> Other functions included:
>
> Periodic reporting and evaluation of the progress of the development programme:
>
> Coordinating and stimulating planning activities of departments and agencies:
>
> Submitting advice on economic problems and economic aspects of major policy questions:
>
> Advising and assisting with regional and local development planning:
>
> Coordinating administration interest in private sector major projects:
>
> Identifying projects which can attract international development finance:
>
> Working up detailed plans for such projects in consultation as necessary with appropriate departments and agencies:
>
> Collecting and publishing statistics.

[NAA A452, 1971/2098]

179   CABINET SUBMISSION 116[1]

Canberra, 1 June 1971

CONFIDENTIAL

Papua New Guinea:
Employment Security Scheme for Permanent Overseas Officers

This submission seeks Cabinet agreement to an amendment to the Employment Security Scheme for permanent overseas officers in Papua New Guinea to permit them, after a date to be fixed by the Commonwealth, to terminate their service at a time of their own choosing without prejudice to their eligibility for benefits under the scheme.

2.   The present scheme, which offers to displaced permanent officers either suitable government employment in Australia or, if this is not available, a lump sum for loss of career, plus certain general re-establishment benefits, affords no such option. The decision as to when the scheme comes into operation remains with the Commonwealth as it is the Minister who decides when the services of an officer are to be terminated. (A general background to the scheme as it now stands is given at Appendix 1—pages 8 to 12.)[2]

3.   The amendment to the Employment Security Scheme proposed in this submission is in part a response to the unfavourable reaction by permanent overseas officers to the Government's decision (No. 454) of 23rd June, 1970[3] to the principle of establishing an Australian Service for Overseas Cooperation to provide key and essential staff for Papua New Guinea on a long-term basis. ASOC has by no means been rejected, and I foresee it playing an important part in attracting to long-term service in Papua New Guinea both new officers and a relatively small number of key staff now engaged on contract (as distinct from permanent officers). But I have reluctantly come to the conclusion that ASOC will not be a factor in influencing permanent staff to stay on.

4.   The amendment is also a response to the increasing emphasis on localisation which must accompany the Government's decision (No. 89) of 20th April, 1971,[4] to move with the

---

1   Submitted by Barnes.

2   The Appendix noted that in Decision 8 of 3 February 1966 Cabinet had approved the Employment Security Scheme in order to encourage permanent overseas officers to continue to serve in the Territory. It recalled that in 1963 the Australian Government had stopped offering permanent appointments to Australians and other eligible expatriates as part of its commitment to the long-term localisation of public service positions in the Territory. In the mid-1960s expatriate officers 'had expressed an uncertainty about their future, particularly the security of their employment, on the ground that either their jobs could be expected to be progressively taken over by persons serving under local terms and conditions or that their careers could be interrupted by political developments in the Territory'. In response Cabinet had 'accepted that uncertainty about the future was not unnatural in the particular circumstances of the Territory where the aim was the economic, social and political advancement of its people to the stage where they would be able to manage their own affairs, and which required, amongst other things, the building up of an efficient public service staffed by well-trained and competent local officers'.

The Appendix also noted that when the scheme was announced in June 1966 about 2,300 officers were eligible. By June 1971 this number had declined to 1,580, comprising 1,510 in the public service and teaching service, 50 in the police, and 20 in the Electricity Commission. It was envisaged that the scheme would become applicable to all eligible officers in 1976, at which time it was expected that these officers would number 1,200. (Presumably 1976 was chosen for planning purposes because it was assumed that self-government would be attained in that year.)

3   See Documents 36, 38 & 64.

4   Document 159.

foreshortening independence time-scale in Papua New Guinea. We have to move from the long-standing policy under which permanent overseas officers have a long-term career in Papua New Guinea in competition with indigenous permanent officers. Increased emphasis on localisation requires deliberate preference for indigenous officers for promotion at all levels. Although this will be selective, as a consequence the promotional and career prospects of permanent overseas officers will be adversely affected.

5.   It may seem paradoxical that I am proposing an option to leave the Public Service for key permanent overseas officers when the need for the continuing presence of a good number of them up to and beyond independence is no less patent than it was a year ago. Indeed, it could be argued that such a proposal will expose the Government to domestic and international criticism on the grounds that it will weaken the Public Service at a critical period.

6.   My judgment is that the risk of losing officers after the chosen date is worth taking. No doubt a number of officers will leave. But there is an even greater risk of many leaving in the immediate period ahead, albeit without benefit of either alternative employment or compensation, because of the officers' present uncertainty about their future. I believe that removal of this uncertainty will result in substantial numbers of officers electing to continue to serve, particularly key personnel who are now within sight of completing their careers in Papua New Guinea. This is also the view of the Administrator, the Administrator's Executive Council and the Papua New Guinea Public Service Board and is in line with the tenor of advice to me from the recent UN Visiting Mission. In its official report the Mission has referred specifically to the urgent need to establish a clear programme for retention of experienced expatriate officers with special skills and for adequate compensation for those displaced, as well as the need for a new impetus to localisation.

7.   Details of the proposed amendment to the Employment Security Scheme, which is supported by the Public Service Association [...] In short, the amendment:

(a) gives permanent overseas officers an option to terminate their careers on or after a date to be fixed by the Commonwealth;

(b) at the same time provides an incentive for officers to continue to serve beyond the fixed date —if they leave after serving an additional three years they will have the choice of full financial compensation for loss of career (calculated at the most advantageous point of their additional service) or alternative employment; and

(c) provides for payment of any compensation for loss of career (i.e. in the event that there is no alternative employment) to be phased over five years instead of in a lump sum at present.

8.   The proposed date on which officers could take up their option to terminate their careers in Papua New Guinea is the date on which responsibility for all public service matters is handed over to a Papua New Guinea government. I foresee this being at or shortly before, and certainly no later than, internal self-government—perhaps in 1975. I expect the attractions for officers to stay on after that date (point (b) in the preceding paragraph) to be a powerful factor in retaining the services of many, perhaps the most useful, of them. Although these attractions would accrue after a minimum period of three years' service subsequent to the chosen date, I would not expect this to influence officers immediately at that time, although again this is a matter of judgment. As stated previously, I believe that removal of uncertainty about their future will encourage officers to remain and there will still be a need for numbers of them for years to come.

9.   The proposal has been placed before the departments most concerned, namely, Treasury, Prime Minister and Cabinet, Public Service Board and Labour and National Service. Full agreement with or between departments has not been reached because the proposal and the implications of it are largely a matter of judgment. Both the Departments of Treasury and

Labour and National Service agree that permanent overseas officers should be able to exercise an option to terminate their careers in Papua New Guinea but have reservations about the non-application of alternative employment provisions to those officers who continue service for a minimum period of three years. The Department of the Prime Minister and Cabinet and the Public Service Board have general reservations about the judgement on which the proposal is based. All departments agree, however, that, because of the policy issue involved, it is essentially a matter for political decision.

Financial Implications

10. Responsibility for the payment of benefits under the Employment Security Scheme rests with Papua New Guinea, with the Commonwealth as guarantor. The Administrator's Executive Council accepts this liability but is concerned about its possible effects on the finances of Papua New Guinea. The Council wishes to pursue with the Commonwealth Government the possibility of a cost-sharing arrangement which could be embodied in a formal agreement with the future Papua New Guinea government.

11. The estimated maximum contingent liability if the scheme had to be applied to all eligible officers in, say, five years and on the basis that no alternative government employment could be found for any of them could be as much as $53m. Such a situation is most unlikely and in any case the actual liability would be spread over a number of years.

12. Of the estimated amount of $53m, $21.6m is attributable to payments in respect of superannuation retrenchment benefits, resettlement grant, and fares and removal expenses to Australia. These payments would have to be made whether or not alternative employment provisions of the scheme were applied to some or all officers. The changes now proposed therefore, have significance only in relation to the $31.6m representing compensation for loss of career (see Appendix 3[5]—page 16). If waivure [waiver] of the alternative employment provisions in the manner proposed encourages officers to serve for a minimum period of three years after the chosen date, any savings that might accrue through total application of the alternative employment provisions at that time must be considered against the value of having the services of the officers for that period alone, and, as I expect, for longer periods.

13. I recommend that Cabinet:

(1) agree that the Employment Security Scheme be amended to incorporate an option for eligible officers to terminate their careers in Papua New Guinea after the date on which responsibility for the Public Service Board is transferred from the Commonwealth to local executive authority [...];

(2) approve the introduction of legislation into the House of Assembly to give effect to the amendment;

(3) enter into no commitment at this stage to assist with the financing of the scheme, but authorise me to continue discussions with the Administrator's Executive Council on this; and

(4) authorise me to announce this decision.[6]

[NAA: A5908, 116]

---

5   Not published.

6   While agreeing on 'the need to retain as far as possible the service of permanent overseas officers up to and beyond independence', Cabinet 'did not feel able to agree with the particularly recommendations for the amendment of the Employment Security Scheme put forward'. With that in mind, 'it was decided that the matter should be referred for urgent examination and report by an interdepartmental committee' consisting of DET, Treasury, Prime Minister and Cabinet, Labour and National Service, and the Public Service Board. Cabinet Decision 199, 'Papua and New Guinea Employment Security for Permanent Overseas Officers', 8 June 1971, NAA: A5908, 116.

180   SPEECH BY BARNES[1]

Brisbane, 1 June 1971

Australia's Relations with Papua New Guinea After Independence

I commend the associated Chambers of Commerce of Australia for arranging the seminar on 'Australia's Relations with Papua New Guinea After Independence'.

The topics have been well chosen. Subsequent speakers will give you a good insight into the problems facing us and the aspirations of the people of Papua New Guinea at this time of change. For my part, I would like—with the support of the film to follow—to set the scene for your discussions and to offer some observations on future relations between Australia and Papua New Guinea.

Even now these relations are being conducted with an eye to the development of Papua New Guinea as a nation.

The Government's policy is to encourage the progress of Papua New Guinea towards internal self-government and independence. Internal self-government is a stage of political development short of independence in which elected political leaders in Papua New Guinea will have full authority over a wide area, but not the full area of government. They will not, for instance, have full control over defence and foreign affairs before independence.

Already there has been quite considerable movement along the road to internal self-government. In 1970 the Commonwealth decided to transfer to elected ministerial office holders authority to make final decisions on a number of important matters, such as taxation, local government, health [and] primary and secondary education. With that authority went responsibility for financing some local decisions through locally raised revenue. The Administrator has described the present situation as more than half-way to internal self-government. This step-by-step progress is likely to continue.

The Papua New Guinea House of Assembly has recently agreed to a number of recommendations by a Select Committee on Constitutional Development. The Australian Government has accepted these recommendations.

In effect these recommendations set, for the first time, an approximate timetable. This will require the Commonwealth and the Administration to prepare a programme for full internal self-government in the period 1972–76, but the execution of that programme will have regard to the state of opinion as it develops after the 1972 House of Assembly elections and to the policies of the political leaders who then emerge. At present majority opinion in Papua New Guinea favours a later period—1976–80, but opinion has been changing and there could be full internal self-government within the next five years. How long an interval there would be between that stage, and the next, and final stage of independence will depend on the wishes of the elected leaders of the time. The Commonwealth looks to the elected members of the House of Assembly to represent the wishes of the majority of the people and to take the initiative in such matters as the pace and nature of constitutional development.

There are two important implications in these developments for Australian businessmen: firstly, they mean that in matters of trade and investment you will deal increasingly with elected political leaders in Papua New Guinea.

Secondly, I believe that it is in the long term interests of overseas companies trading with or investing in Papua New Guinea that opportunities should be given for Papua New Guinea to participate in business ventures at all levels. One of the main sources of dissatisfaction

---

1   Barnes delivered the speech to the Associated Chambers of Commerce.

in emergent countries is the foreign domination of their economies and the consequent marked disparity in living standards between indigenes and expatriates. For this reason the Government encourages investment in the Territory which involves Papua New Guineans not only as unskilled, semi-skilled and skilled employees, but as part owners and managers. Our policy is to involve the people of Papua New Guinea in the sharing of the benefits of economic development. They are growing with their country.

The complex task of increasing the indigenous involvement in the economic development of Papua New Guinea is one for the Government also. Important progress has been made recently. A Department of Business Development has been established. Legislation to set up an investment corporation which will take up equity in business ventures on behalf of the people was passed by the House of Assembly in March. The Administrator's Executive Council has decided to introduce legislation providing for preference to Papua New Guineans in the issue of trade store and similar licences to conduct small businesses. It has also decided to legislate to prohibit the employment of overseas workers in certain occupations requiring little or no skills.

A cornerstone of economic development in Papua New Guinea has been to reconcile this need for more and more Papua New Guinean businessmen with the need for overseas investment.

For their part, the elected members of the Papua New Guinea House of Assembly are on record as supporting a rapid rate of economic growth, a favourable investment climate and a flow of outside capital. This attitude is reflected in the House of Assembly's 'Development Capital Guarantee Declaration', which is aimed at safeguarding the interests of private investors.

At independence, Australia's legal obligations towards Papua New Guinea deriving from the United Nations Charter will expire. Papua New Guinea will take its place as a member of the international community. Any special relations between Australia and Papua New Guinea, on defence, for example, will be the subject of negotiations between the governments of the day. I am confident that Australia will want to maintain close and friendly relations with an independent Papua New Guinea. We would want to preserve the bonds which have already been established over the years, deriving from war-time associations and personal contacts, from interest in the work of the missions and from a certain pride in doing a job which needs to be done.

We do not intend to leave it to the last minute to work out our future relations. In this we are acting in accord with the wishes of the House of Assembly. In appraising the report of the Select Committee on Constitutional Development the House specifically asked that consideration be given in the transitional period to the kinds of economic and political relationships which might be developed between Papua New Guinea and Australia at internal self-government. This will be done.

A constant feature in future relationships between the two countries will be economic aid. As the then Prime Minister said last July, 'Even when, in the future, self-government comes or independence comes there will be continuing Australian assistance' for Papua New Guinea. We have an obligation and responsibility to help the development of this country to a stage where it can not only govern itself politically but govern itself economically. We accept that responsibility—and this may go on for years. As the then Prime Minister also said, the amount of recurrent assistance provided will, to a great extent, depend on the amount of self-help which Papua New Guinea is prepared to impose on itself.

In 1969–70, Australian aid to Papua New Guinea amounted to almost $115 million and the estimate for the current financial year is more than $130 million. This is slightly more than half Papua New Guinea's total public finance. Economic aid to Papua New Guinea forms the major part of Australia's total foreign aid.

Naturally Papua New Guinea will have to find more funds from its internal revenue. Indeed, it is already doing this. The percentage of locally-raised revenue as compared with funds from Australia in total Administration spending has been growing in recent years. This is evidence of the effectiveness of the Administration's economic policies which are designed to reduce Papua New Guinea's long term dependence on external aid.

I hope, too, that indirect assistance to Papua New Guinea's developing economy will continue after independence in the form of special arrangements which facilitate Papua New Guinea's access to the Australian market. There are already a number of arrangements which facilitate Papua New Guinea's access to the Australian market. These cover such commodities as timber and logs, plywood, passionfruit juice and pulp, desiccated coconut, natural rubber, and coffee. Papua New Guinea is also eligible to benefit from the Australian system of tariff preferences for developing countries.

This is, of course, a two-way understanding, and I look forward to increasing trade in both directions after independence.

In 1969–70 Papua New Guinea imported $114 million or 54 per cent of its total imports from Australia and exported commodities valued at $41 million or 44 per cent of its total exports to Australia. Australian policy has encouraged trade between the countries. In 1969–70, Papua New Guinea was Australia's fifth largest export market after New Zealand.

Australian exporters are well placed to supply Papua New Guinea. For some time to come Australia will continue to supply gaps in Papua New Guinea's production of foodstuffs, particularly of meat, dairy products, rice, sugar and some other staples. There are opportunities also for Australian manufacturers to establish pioneer industries in Papua New Guinea with the cooperation of Papua New Guineans as equity partners, managers and employees of new enterprises. To cite one example, an Australian clothing manufacturer is using Papua New Guinea as a base for export production and to compete more strategically for the Papua New Guinea market.

I commend this sort of partnership to you, to aid investment in Papua New Guinea, to help the people along the road to independence, to develop its infant economy and to assist the Australian Government in its trusteeship obligations, and when these expire.

[NAA: A452, 1971/2098]

181   MINUTE FROM BAILEY[1] TO MCMAHON

Canberra, 3 June 1971

CONFIDENTIAL

Citizenship in Papua New Guinea

Attached is a copy of a letter the Minister for External Territories sent you on 24 May.[2] We have been unable to trace the original, but, having obtained a copy from the Department, feel we should provide you with a comment as we understand the Senior Official Member may be making a statement in the House of Assembly in the next day or so.[3]

2.   The Minister seeks your concurrence to a statement which would set out some of the possible arrangements for common citizenship for the Territory and would include a statement that

> 'The Government's policy is to develop Papua New Guinea as a unified nation and its people should therefore have a common citizenship and common rights and obligations as citizens … The Australian Government would not wish, on the other hand, to take decisions now which would commit a future government along lines which are clearly not in accord with the wishes of the majority of the people.'

3.   There have been Papuan objections to the proposal to adopt a joint citizenship for the Territory because, Papuans being in a minority, any vote in the House or among the people at large is likely to leave them in a minority. This is one illustration of the kind of difficulties that [the] Government will continue to face if it wishes to maintain the unity of the whole Territory, a point which I raised with you recently in connection with a statement to be made by the Administrator about unity in the Territory.

4.   The Minister says in his letter that he will bring any firm proposals on Territory citizenship before Cabinet. Ahead of this, we doubt whether you need feel obliged to give your concurrence to any particular statement made in the House of Assembly, and the attached draft reply to the Minister is based on this view.[4] Perhaps I should add that we understand that the Minister for Immigration[5] has indicated that he sees no problem in the proposed statement, particularly as it relates to the future position of expatriate Australians. The Administrator's Executive Council has also approved the statement.

[NAA: A1209, 1971/9229]

---

1   Peter Bailey.

2   Document 176.

3   Tom Leahy, the spokesman for the Administrator's Executive Council (AEC), presented the statement on 8 June (Document 182). For background on Leahy and his presentation of the statement, see Document 176, fn. 5.

4   Not published. However, McMahon replied to Barnes on 7 June 1971 noting the proposed statement and Barnes' intention to bring forward a Cabinet submission on citizenship issues. Letter, McMahon to Barnes, 7 June 1971, NAA: A1209, 1971/9229.

5   Jim Forbes.

182   STATEMENT BY LEAHY[1]

Port Moresby, 8 June 1971

Papua New Guinea Citizenship

The AEC announced recently that it would be giving consideration to the matter of citizenship and that the subject would be introduced into the House for preliminary discussion. The purpose of this statement is to open up the subject in a preliminary way and indicate the lines of government thinking.

The Australian Government accepted the recommendations of the Select Committee on Constitutional Development and has undertaken to prepare a programme for movement to full internal self-government in the period 1972–76. It has said that the execution of that programme will have regard to the state of opinion as it develops after the 1972 House of Assembly elections and to the policies of the political leaders who then emerge.

One matter to be considered in the programme of preparing for internal self-government is citizenship. The Government's policy is to develop Papua New Guinea as a unified nation and its people should therefore have a common citizenship and common rights and obligations as citizens.[2]

Papua New Guinea does not yet have its own citizenship. It is proposed that attention be given to citizenship now so that a sound foundation is laid for a future national government. The Australian Government would not wish on the other hand, to take decisions now which would commit a future government along lines which are clearly not in accord with the wishes of the majority of the people. It would wish to have full discussion on the issues so that any citizenship prepared now in the period before self-government would have wide support and could appropriately be continued beyond that time. A future Papua New Guinea government would of course be free to legislate for citizenship as it saw fit.

Citizenship is basic to the idea of a nation. It defines those people who are members of the nation. In most countries, citizenship establishes a person's rights as a member of the country and his obligations to the country. A person may for instance obtain the right to vote and to stand for election because he is a citizen. At the same time citizenship may impose upon him an obligation to defend his country in a time of need. At the very least the holding of citizenship would indicate which people have a right to be regarded as permanent residents of a country and cannot for instance, be deported for criminal offences. Citizenship would not normally be conferred on people who are tourists, transients or who are residing in a country for a limited period of time.

In developing countries citizenship has commonly been used to identify the original and permanent residents of the country with rights to full participation in the country's affairs. These have often been economic and social rights as well as political rights. This is one basic issue which will need to be considered for Papua New Guinea—whether citizenship should have attached to it economic rights and privileges such as preference for citizens over non-citizens in the issuing of licences.

Our thinking is that if the House of Assembly wishes to establish a form of citizenship now which would be appropriate at the time of internal self-government and later, independence, it would be desirable to attach all the rights and obligations which seem appropriate to a developing country. This might or might not include economic rights. We would want to be

---

1   The statement was delivered in the PNG House of Assembly. For background on Leahy, see Document 176, fn. 5.

2   See Documents 118, 149, 152, 176 & 181.

sure however, that any provision for economic rights to be attached to citizenship did not conflict with its established policies of promoting localisation and indigenous participation in industry, business and commerce. A need for a clear policy of preference for indigenes in seen for some time to come.

It would be envisaged that political rights such as the right to vote and to stand for election would be attached to citizenship. However, time would not permit such changes to be introduced so as to affect the 1972 elections.

The next question would be 'Who should be citizens?' Obviously all Papuans and New Guineans should automatically be citizens. We would hope that establishing a common citizenship status for Papuans and New Guineans would clarify their status and remove some differences which are now seen to exist. Papuans have the international status of Australian citizens and New Guineans the international status of Australian protected persons. For practical purposes, both within and without Papua New Guinea, there is no difference between the rights of Papuans and the rights of New Guineans. Neither the Australian citizenship of Papuans nor the Australian protected person status of New Guineans enables them to settle in Australia.

Australia has a separate law, as had Papua New Guinea, to determine who may or may not enter the country and settle there.

Our attitude then is that both Papuans and New Guineans should look to the future and create the kind of citizenship that they would want to have at self-government and independence.

One reason for considering the question of citizenship now is that Australians and other overseas people who have been living and working in Papua New Guinea would like to know whether they can become citizens of Papua New Guinea.

Numbers of Australians came to Papua New Guinea many years ago and many were born here. They regard themselves as members of the Papua New Guinea community and see their future in this country. They can of course return to Australia or their homelands at any time but numbers would like to live in Papua New Guinea permanently. We would think that a citizenship law could include provision for these people to become citizens.

There would be an obvious difference between expatriate and indigenous citizens because the expatriates came from overseas or were born of overseas parents. It would be proposed therefore that they would not become citizens automatically but would have to apply for Papua New Guinea citizenship. It would be proposed too that Papua New Guinea citizenship could be acquired only by non-indigenous persons who had been born here or had lived here for many years. It would be a matter of judgment how long this period should be but a period of say at least 7 years or even 10 years would seem appropriate.

Furthermore, it would be envisaged that a non-indigenous citizen who settled permanently outside Papua New Guinea would automatically lose his citizenship after a certain time.

An important question for Australians would be whether they would have to lose their Australian citizenship when they applied for Papua New Guinea citizenship. So long as Papua New Guinea citizenship did not have international status—because Papua New Guinea was not yet independent— Australians could become citizens of Papua New Guinea without losing their Australian citizenship.

Australia would expect that the final arrangements for citizenship, affecting the international citizenship status of Australians, could only be made at the time of independence by the Papua New Guinea national government after consultation with the Australian Government. It would be desirable however that the form of citizenship established now be as nearly as possible the citizenship established at the time of independence. In this way Australians and other non-indigenous people of long standing in Papua New Guinea could associate themselves with the country now with some assurance that they could hold Papua New Guinea citizenship status in the future. Their Australian or other citizenship status would obviously be affected if they had to choose between Papua New Guinea international citizenship and another. Other citizenship would not be affected if Papua New Guinea citizenship were established now and continued into independence, that is, if the international citizenship were automatically conferred on those who held the pre-independence citizenship.

The AEC considers that now that Papua New Guinea has the one name, its own flag and emblem, it is appropriate that it should have the one citizenship. The AEC is concerned that the people of Papua New Guinea do not yet think of themselves as one people and proposes that the House of Assembly should now give consideration to citizenship so that Papua New Guineans will begin thinking of themselves as citizens of one country. The AEC does not believe that this consideration should be deferred to some later time but would like to see a wide debate on the sort of citizenship that should be enacted. It has instructed the Administration to survey the citizenship legislation of other countries and in the light of the House's reaction and that of people generally, to begin preparing appropriate legislation for further consideration.

[NAA: A452, 1971/888]

183   CABLEGRAM TO NEW YORK

Canberra, 10 June 1971

586. CONFIDENTIAL

TPNG—Observation of 1972 Elections

Please issue invitation for the Trusteeship Council to observe the 1972 House of Assembly elections as proposed in your Memorandum 749.[1] The Mission may contain representatives of the Committee of Twenty-Four.

2.   The following points are made for your guidance:

A.   The Mission should have an observing role only.

B.   Its itinerary should include Papua as well as New Guinea.

C.   Members should, as far as possible, be selected to our advantage.

D.   The visit should be for two weeks only—one week before and one week after the elections, i.e. before and after closing polling day.

E.   In planning the itinerary it will be necessary to ensure that areas of some sensitivity be visited [after] and not before the elections.

F.   We will need to have firm assurances that the Mission will not allow itself to be used for political purposes by any candidates, parties or other groups.

3.   The decision to include Papua will apply also to future Trusteeship Council visiting missions. This follows from the Government's long standing policy, recently reaffirmed, of treating Papua and New Guinea as a single unit.

4.   Timing of invitation is at your discretion. Please let us know in time to advise the Administrator when the invitation will be formally issued.[2]

[NAA: A452, 1971/1076]

---

1   Document 175.

2   See Document 184.

184   LETTER FROM MCINTYRE TO DAVID LANE[1]

New York, 11 June 1971

Elections will be held in Papua New Guinea in the period March/April 1972 to elect representatives to the Third Papua New Guinea House of Assembly.

My Government considers it would be valuable for Papua New Guinea, and for future consideration in the United Nations of questions relating to the Territory, if the Trusteeship Council were to decide to send a Visiting Mission to Papua New Guinea for the purpose of observing these elections. I am therefore authorised to extend an invitation through you to the Council to send such a Mission.

If the Trusteeship Council is prepared to agree in principle, my Government suggests that the composition of the Mission be determined in the manner requested by the General Assembly in operative paragraph 5 of resolution 2590 (XXIV) of 16 December 1969: namely, that in deciding to send a Mission to Papua New Guinea for this purpose the Trusteeship Council should decide also to include in the Mission non-members of the Council, who should be chosen on the basis of consultations between the Council, the Special Committee on the Situation with regard to the Implementation of the Declaration on the Granting of Independence to Colonial Countries and Peoples,[2] and the Administering Authority. There is of course a precedent for this in the procedure adopted for selecting the members of the 1971 Visiting Mission.

My Government envisages that the Mission which it now invites should comprise the traditional number of four members, and it suggests that the precedent established for the 1971 Mission of two members chosen from the Trusteeship Council and two chosen on the basis of consultation with the Special Committee might be followed.

My Government hopes the Mission would be able to remain in Papua New Guinea for a period of two weeks. It suggests that it arrive in the Territory one week before the closing polling day and remain for one week after that day to observe counting and the declaration of polls.

The itinerary for the Mission would be so arranged as to provide it with a sampling of electoral arrangements, candidate and party activities, polling and counting in a broad cross-section of the Territory as a whole. We would intend that the Mission's itinerary include visits to places in Papua as well as in the Trust Territory of New Guinea.

While the Mission will be most welcome to take the opportunity of its presence in the Territory to see something of political, economic and social development generally, my Government would emphasise that it invites the Council to send a Mission for the specific purpose of observing the House of Assembly elections and it therefore suggests that the Mission's terms of reference might be worded with this in mind.

I note in conclusion that it will be important to ensure that the presence of the Mission in Papua New Guinea during the election does not lend itself to use by contending candidates as an issue to their advantage. I am confident that the Trusteeship Council and the Special Committee are fully cognizant of this need.

My Government would greatly welcome a decision by the Council to accept this invitation and expresses the hope that such a decision can be reached at its current session.[3]

[NAA: A452, 1971/2292]

---

1   David N. Lane (United Kingdom), President of the Trusteeship Council, May 1971 to May 1972.

2   Otherwise known as the Committee of Twenty-four.

3   The Council Secretariat circulated this letter to Council members on 11 June 1971. The invitation was accepted.

185   MINUTE FROM HAY TO BESLEY

Canberra, 15 June 1971

Pace of Movement towards Self-Government

I have had some indications from the Administrator that the AEC is somewhat concerned that the Government here may be taking steps towards self-government over and above what has been involved in the acceptance of the report of the Select Committee on Constitutional Development and the Commonwealth Government's statement thereon.

For example the Administrator has commented to me privately that he thinks it would be premature to press on with the establishment of consulates in the immediate future. Also, I see in the latest list of AEC decisions that the Council noted the timetable of the IDC[1] on the handing over of Commonwealth functions to the Administration [and noted] 'it would like to examine the possibility of phasing the transfer over a longer period'. (Conclusion No. 153/71).

The Administrator describes the AEC as being 'very hesitant to agree to steps which makes self-government look to be just around the corner'. This attitude should be noted for general background by Branch Heads over the next year or so.

[NAA: A452, 1971/888]

---

1   Inter-Departmental Committee.

186   MEMORANDUM FROM MOODIE TO DET

Canberra, 18 June 1971

Papua-New Guinea Citizenship

I refer to the copy of the draft statement on citizenship referred to us on June 2, which with some minor editorial changes, was subsequently made in the House of Assembly on 8 June[1] by Mr T. J. Leahy in his capacity as spokesman for the Administrator's Executive Council.

2.   It may be helpful to place on record our own comments on this text, to confirm those already conveyed to you.

3.   We agree of course with the proposition in paragraph 3 [...] that the people of the Territory should have a common citizenship and common rights and obligations as citizens.[2]

4.   We would regard it as regrettable if citizenship were established in Papua–New Guinea on a strictly racial basis. The House of Assembly may of course insist on a system in which birth in the Territory, and continued residence thereafter, would not entitle a person to citizenship if his own skin—or that of his parents—were yellow or white, rather than brown. But it is matter for consideration whether the administration should itself be concerned to promote legislation along these lines (paragraphs 6–12 of the statement, especially paragraphs 6 and 11). We are not sure if any special provision would be necessary to ensure that for international purposes the present law would remain until Papua-New Guinea becomes independent, although we would not think so.

5.   Paragraph 13 makes the point that, because PNG is not yet independent, Australian citizens could become citizens of PNG without losing their Australian citizenship. We would make the further point that in our understanding there is nothing in international law to prevent dual citizenship even [after] independence; this would be a matter for the two legislatures respectively. If paragraph 13 is intended to imply the contrary view, we would be inclined to disagree. Paragraph 14 may well be intended to make precisely this point, namely that dual citizenship could be a matter of arrangement between the two countries at the time of independence. You may wish to consider this aspect in the light of further developments.[3]

[NAA: A452, 1971/1916]

---

1   Document 182.

2   See Documents 118, 149, 152, 176 & 181.

3   Annotations on the original indicate that DET officials discussed this letter, and decided that 'No reply seems needed at present'.

187 INFORMATION PAPER BY DFA[1]

Canberra, 23 June 1971

RESTRICTED

The Future of Papua New Guinea: The Implications for Foreign Affairs

As you will know, the Select Committee on Constitutional Development of the House of Assembly of Papua New Guinea presented its report on 4th March, 1971.[2] The Report called for self-government within the life of the next House of Assembly, which will sit from 1972–76. This recommendation was adopted by the House of Assembly and accepted by the Australian Government. It has also been endorsed by the United Nations Visiting Mission.

2.   The report was a watershed in the development of Papua New Guinea. The people of Papua New Guinea, through their elected representatives, had themselves chosen the direction and the pace of their political development. With a target date for self-government established, the Administration in the Territory and the Government in Canberra is now giving new impetus to the process of bringing Papua New Guinea into the international system.

3.   This process has already gained some momentum. Papua New Guinea is now associated with the ADB[3] and ECAFE[4] and is playing a role in those organisations. It is also broadening its activities in the Pacific and we hope to see PNG participate in the Pacific Forum. We are seeking the appointment of Oala Oala Rarua as Secretary-General of the SPC[5] and attempting to obtain an agreement for PNG with the EEC.[6] Recently, a Parliamentary delegation led by the Speaker of the PNG House of Assembly, John Guise, paid a successful visit to Indonesia. All of these developments are important steps in bringing PNG into the international arena, but more will need to be done during the period of self-government.

4.   Developmentally, we are, as you will know from Policy Information Reports, now working on the premise that Papua New Guinea will become a self-governing territory early after the March 1972 House of Assembly elections and independent fairly soon thereafter. Although the Australian Government will retain certain powers, including the foreign affairs and defence powers, after the date of internal self-government and until Papua New Guinea becomes fully independent, in practice, these powers will need to be exercised in close consultation with the Government of Papua New Guinea. We must, therefore, begin to prepare now for the transfer of responsibilities in the field of foreign affairs and, as a Department, play an active role in the transfer. To this end, the Department has been examining the areas in which we will be involved, such as the creation of a foreign service for PNG, the establishment of an Australian High Commission there, and international political education for the people of PNG.

---

1   This paper was circulated in Canberra and sent to all DFA posts.

2   Document 142.

3   Asian Development Bank.

4   United Nations Economic Commission for Asia and the Far East.

5   South Pacific Commission, a regional organisation based in Noumea, New Caledonia, which had been established to support social and economic development in the Pacific Islands region. In the event Oala-Rarua withdrew his candidacy for the SPC position. He later became PNG's official representative in Australia, and its first High Commissioner there following independence in September 1975.

6   European Economic Community.

Development of a Foreign Ministry and Foreign Service

5.   Our priority task is to establish a Foreign Office for PNG and to train its staff. Even at the self-government stage there will be a need for a Foreign Office in PNG to assist the Australian Government to exercise the foreign affairs power on behalf of PNG. We have, therefore, initiated discussions with the Department of External Territories with a view to advancing the establishment and training of a PNG Foreign Office this year.[7]

6.   Territories have suggested, and we have agreed, that the International Affairs Branch in the Department of the Administrator should be the nucleus of the new office. The Minister has approved the posting of two Foreign Affairs Officers to the Territory (one FA04 and one FA02), as Commonwealth officers responsible to the Head of the Branch.

7.   The Foreign Affairs Officers in PNG will discharge a twofold responsibility. First, they will advise the Administration on the organisation and functioning of the Foreign Office. The second task will be to train recruits in the work of the foreign service.

8.   We take the view that the organisation of the Foreign Office should be simple and flexible and that the administrative arrangements for the service should be developed according to need rather than modelled on our own systems. We expect also to plan in the first instance for a comprehensive range of functions including the international aspects of such matters as trade, civil aviation and immigration, for the office, and a flexible staff trained in all aspects of foreign service work, including administration.

9.   Three local University graduates have been recruited to work initially in the International Affairs Branch. It is hoped to recruit at least another three at the end of the year. In view of the shortage of graduates, we expect to take some older people with the lower educational standards, e.g. thirty-year olds with Matriculation equivalent.

10.   The training programme for recruits will need to be extensive and varied. The Foreign Affairs Officers in PNG will have the primary responsibility for training the recruits at their desks in the Foreign Office there. In addition, as many as possible of the recruits should receive training in Australia in trade promotion, immigration and administration and accounting procedures and attend the Foreign Service Training Course. We would also intend to attach the recruits to desks in Canberra and posts abroad for practical on-the-job training.

11.   We regard it as essential to the success of this operation for the Officers posted to PNG to be largely independent of the Department in Canberra. Their task is to assist in the development of the Office, its functions and staff for PNG, and not to prosecute particular interests for Australia.

Establishment of an Australian High Commission

12.   It will clearly be necessary for an Australian diplomatic mission (presumably a High Commission on the assumption that Papua New Guinea will wish to remain in the Commonwealth) to be established in Port Moresby by the time of independence. We will also need a Commission during the self-government period. We are, therefore, actively engaged in discussions with the relevant Departments regarding property requirements and the future role of the mission.

13.   We regard it as essential that after independence the High Commission must not appear to be taking a major part in running the country. It should, therefore, function as a normal diplomatic mission and should not take over functions which are properly those of the PNG Government. We will need to demonstrate the reality of independence by making a clear distinction between continuing friendly help and advice and the previous colonial relationship.

---

7   See Documents 153, 161 & 170.

Because there will probably be on-going projects and wide-ranging contacts between the two Governments, we will need to take particular care to avoid any suggestion that independence is not complete. For this reason, it is desirable to refrain from including in the High Commission staff, except in specialised positions, former officers of the PNG Public Service. Also, although we shall almost certainly need a large Australian establishment under the general responsibility of the High Commissioner, consideration is being given to the possibility that some of its components could be separately grouped as an aid mission separate from, though under the 'umbrella' of, the High Commission. In addition, there will probably be a Defence-staffed military mission with a training and advisory role. We would intend for this mission to be separately housed. Other Departments with interest in PNG would be included in the High Commission on the Washington pattern.

14.   There will, of course, be a very large consular problem with a large Australian community in the Territory. We take the view that Australians whose job is to advise, assist or work for the PNG Government should be quite divorced from the High Commission. However, we shall need to establish consulates in the main centres at an early stage.

15.   There are a number of problems which will need to be resolved before the High Commission can be established. Not the least of these are the practical ones of finding a suitable site, choosing a flexible design and finding housing for the staff. One problem which may not be resolved until after independence is the site of the capital. The Administration is strongly of the opinion that Port Moresby should be the capital and points out that it would be enormously expensive to move it at this stage. Nevertheless, it is difficult to predict what an independent government concerned with national prestige and the need to place the capital in a 'neutral' area will do. For planning purposes, our premise must remain that the capital will be in Port Moresby but we will ensure that our plans are flexible enough to cope with a decision to move it.

Political Education

16.   In addition to setting up the formal organisation necessary to conduct the country's foreign relations, we need to create an awareness of the facts of international life in the community. This education programme would not be aimed at the population at large, since even in advanced countries many people do not have a great deal of interest in or knowledge of foreign affairs. Instead it would be directed towards a target group of leaders within the community. This group would include politicians, administrators, journalists, academics, businessmen and the educated class generally.

17.   Some foreign affairs content could be injected into the existing programme of political education, but this would be fairly basic and is perhaps not relevant to our main purpose. The makers of foreign policy decisions will come from a relatively small group, and although individuals cannot yet be identified, it is in the area of the informed and relatively well educated that there is most prospect of developing relations sufficient to ensure a realistic and balanced foreign policy for PNG, including a balanced policy towards Australia. They must also be aware of the kinds of pressures to which a newly independent country may be subject, and how to handle these pressures.

18.   This process will not be an easy one. It will depend to some extent on the Foreign Affairs Officers in PNG, through their public and private contacts with leaders in the community. They may also find it possible to encourage the establishment and guide the development of organisations such as an Institute of International Affairs.

19.   At this stage, we are not in a position to plan a political education programme including these various elements. After the Foreign Affairs Officers have been appointed and can assess the needs and possibilities, we will examine the role which Foreign Affairs might play in such

a programme.

20. The implications for Foreign Affairs are wider than the three points canvassed here. We have, for example, already examined the question of Foreign Consulates being established in PNG before independence. We have informed the Department of External Territories that we would see positive advantages in the establishment of Japanese and Indonesian Consulates and have suggested that these might be discreetly encouraged. However, the Administrator feels that this should be postponed till after the 1972 elections because the Administrator's Executive Council is becoming increasingly concerned at the way in which self-government is being forced.

21. Other questions of this sort will continue to arise as PNG moves towards self-government and thereafter to independence and we will need to be in a position to cope with them departmentally. To do so, we need to establish a presence in PNG now and ensure that we play an influential role in the transfer of power. To this end we are bolstering our establishment in Canberra dealing with these matters and are establishing the machinery for consultation both within the Department and with other Departments on matters related to the transfer of power with implications for foreign affairs.

[NAA: A1838, 689/1 PART 6]

188   LETTER FROM JOHNSON TO HAY

Port Moresby, 25 June 1971

CONFIDENTIAL

I refer to three motions passed during the last meeting of the House of Assembly relating to unity, two of them with specific reference to special consultation with Papua. The texts of the motions follow:

1.   That this House requests the Australian Government to appoint a Commonwealth Parliamentary Committee comprising representatives of all political parties to make an early visit to Papua to determine the wishes of the Papuan people and to learn of their concern at first hand.

2.   That this House requests the Australian Government not to take any action that would alter the existing status and rights of Papua and Papuans without the express approval of the Papuan people or their elected representatives.

3   a.   That this House, believing that the best future for the country lies in a united Papua and New Guinea, and believing that unity must be physical as well as administrative to be accepted by the people, and noting the precedent set in the Chimbu District, requests the Administration, as the quickest practical means of beginning to develop such unity, to change district boundaries so that some districts encompass part of both New Guinea and Papua, particularly where ethnic groups at present are divided by the Territory boundary.

   b.   That this House calls upon the Administration, the Australian Government and the United Nations to find a way to abolish the present boundary between Papua and New Guinea.

You will also recall an earlier motion passed by the House:

4.   That this House directs the Select Committee on Constitutional Development to tour the entire Territory again seeking the true consensus of opinion of the people of this Territory on vital issues, especially that of self-government, before it tables any further reports on constitutional development in this House and, further, that this tour should be undertaken early in 1971; and further, that any future transfers of power or constitutional changes, whether requiring amendments to the Papua and New Guinea Act or not, will be unacceptable to the House unless such changes have been agreed to by a majority of Members of this House.

It appears that the only clear pattern emerging from all of these is the expressed desire of the House that consultation and consent should precede further constitutional change. I think that it is inadvisable to consult Papuans alone about their future and the Australian Government could be faced with an insoluble problem if, on consultation, there was wide support for separation. I do not believe that the majority of Papuans have given serious thought to the matter and I am sure that most sensible leaders of the Papuan community see their future as part of a Papua New Guinean nation. Nonetheless, a concerted campaign based on emotion rather than reason could probably arouse uninformed opinion and present any formal enquiry committee with quite unacceptable propositions.

In general terms, I think that we should firmly maintain our previous position—that Australian policy is for a united Papua New Guinea, that this policy has been consistently supported by the House of Assembly and, in particular, by the Select Committee on Constitutional Development, and that the Australian Government will continue to seek the views of the House of Assembly before constitutional changes are initiated.

You might give some thought to the possibility of a Ministerial statement timed for the November meeting of the House of Assembly outlining a little more clearly the constitutional position in the early months of our new House of Assembly. The recommendations of the Select Committee on Constitutional Development have been accepted but they did not bear upon any increase in power of the Ministers or of the Administrator's Executive Council. It is axiomatic that the AEC jurisdiction will expand over a wider area as, presumably, the seventeen Ministers will exercise more final powers—at any rate they will in those Departments which have not previously had Ministerial representation.

The AEC has not yet considered the resolutions referred to in the earlier part of this letter and I seek your views before introducing the matter for consideration.

My recommendations at this stage are:

i.   That the Australian Government does not appoint the Parliamentary Committee proposed.

ii.   That the Australian Government re-affirm its position on unity and on consultation with the people through their representatives in the House of Assembly as a whole and not with any one section of those representatives.

iii. That attention be drawn to resolution (3) above which seems to indicate majority House support for unity.

iv.   That the Australian Government consider a statement later in the year outlining its proposals for Ministerial and AEC responsibility in the new House of Assembly after the election.

[NAA: A452, 1971/2441]

189   LETTER FROM TANGE TO HAY

Canberra, 28 June 1971

CONFIDENTIAL

I have examined the joint submission[1] by the Steering Group which we established to formulate a programme of future work relating to defence and internal security requirements in Papua New Guinea.

I approve the programme in its present form and the Chairman, Chiefs of Staff Committee,[2] is also in agreement with it. My staff is already taking action on some of the items in Section I, and it is important that we proceed forthwith with the remaining matters, particularly the studies in Section II.

There are several outstanding questions which we could resolve in a short meeting at your convenience:

•   We should consider the need to list a study of the additional legal powers that would be required by military forces if they were to be used in roles short of direct intervention in a riot situation. You will recall the Defence Committee last September expressed the view that the PIR might be made available before call-out to support the civil power *provided* new steps were taken to furnish the forces with adequate legal powers.[3]

•   We should finalise the planning assumptions relative to constitutional advancement in Papua New Guinea for use in planning studies […]

•   We should discuss whether there would be advantage in some of the studies, e.g. Serials 13 and 15, being undertaken in Port Moresby rather than Canberra to maximise the contribution that could be made by officers, directly or through consultation, on the basis of their practical experience in Papua New Guinea.

I propose to bring the Chairman, Chiefs of Staff Committee and Mr Poyser to the meeting. Would you contact me about dates please.

[NAA: A452, 1971/2828]

---

1   Not published. See Document 150.

2   Vice-Admiral Sir Victor Smith.

3   See Document 119.

190   TELEX TO CANBERRA

Port Moresby, 1 July 1971

13815. CONFIDENTIAL

Gazelle Peninsula Sitrep

1.   At 0535 hours this morning police in strength moved into Matupit Village[1] and served the summons on Peter Urami.[2] Villagers attacked the police and tear gas was used. Trees were cut down across road and chainsaws used to clear. Withdrawing police continued to be attacked by villagers and more tear gas used. By 0645 all police withdrawn from Matupit and deployed around airstrip to protect aircraft. Airstrip was closed and by 0650 Tolais withdrew to Matupit side of airstrip. One [Tolai] arrested and charged with assault. Airstrip opened at 0730 to limited traffic. From 0730 to 0750 tear gas used on Matupit side of airstrip. Situation described as quiet at 0800.

2.   During confrontation in Matupit villagers requested medical aid for children allegedly affected by gas. Ambulance proceeded to Matupit but was delayed at road block mentioned above. It completed its mission.

[NAA: A452, 1971/2629]

---

1   Matupit village is located on an island adjacent to Rabaul.

2   Peter Urami, of Matupit village, was a vice-president of the Mataungan Association (MA). The summons concerned a charge that 'he had hindered a member of the police force in the execution of his duty'. See Ian Downs, *The Australian Trusteeship: Papua New Guinea, 1945–75*, Australian Government Publishing Service, Canberra, 1980, p. 517.

191   LETTER FROM HAY TO TANGE

Canberra, 1 July 1971

CONFIDENTIAL

You will be aware from Situation Reports[1] and other papers which have been forwarded to you today that there have been a series of confrontations at the Rabaul airstrip between the Territory Constabulary and members of the Mataungan Association. A copy of the latest Situation Report as at 1145 hours this morning is also attached.[2]

Altogether five police have been injured together with two officers and a sergeant who was stabbed with a knife. The police have been obliged to use tear gas and riot guns.

The Administrator has telephoned requesting the approval to fly sixty additional police from Port Moresby to Rabaul today by RAAF[3] aircraft. The Administrator stated that private aircraft were not available to carry out this task. He added that the native children who have been examined for eye trouble as a result of the use of tear gas had not been harmed in any way, but it is believed that a number of Mataungans would have been injured by the pellets fired from the riot guns.

I should be glad if you would take the necessary action to authorise, as a matter of urgency, the use of RAAF aircraft for this purpose today.

[NAA: A452, 1971/2629]

---

1   See, for example, Document 190.

2   Not published.

3   Royal Australian Air Force.

192   TELEX TO CANBERRA

Port Moresby, 2 July 1971

13852. SECRET

Gazelle Peninsula

1) Events during the week have indicated determination by at least some Mataungan Association (MA) members of resisting the service of summonses. The degree of general MA support for this action is not yet clear. In so far as Matupit Village is concerned, it is anticipated that resistance will continue although other courses of action are open to the villagers.[1]

2) The amount of active support for Matupit from other areas is uncertain, at the time of writing, but it is a distinct possibility that MA extremists from other areas in the Gazelle could rally to the support of the Matupit people should they have sufficient forewarning.

3) What does seem clear is that once the Administration embarks on a course of action, failure to carry it through to a successful conclusion will provide powerful encouragement to the MA and create very serious disillusionment among Administration and Council supporters.

[NAA: A1838, 936/4/16 PART 5]

---

1   See Documents 190 & 191.

193   LETTER FROM JOHNSON TO PITOI[1]

Port Moresby, 5 July 1971

I am concerned that localisation of senior positions may not proceed fast enough to meet our needs on the advent of self-government. It is reasonable to expect self-government no later than 1975 and perhaps earlier, particularly if a Labour Government is in power in Australia. Independence will surely follow a few years later. Experience in other countries points to the strong possibility that a timetable for self-government and independence is almost invariably foreshortened by events.

It may not be desirable or necessary for all senior posts to be localised on independence but by this time I think it essential that all Heads of Departments and all District Commissioners and other senior representatives of central government should be Papua New Guinean, while positions other than purely technical/professional should be filled mostly by Papua New Guineans.

This seems to mean that substantial progress towards this objective should be made by 1975. In short, within four years we should have men already taking over a considerable proportion of these key posts.

I do not see how this can be achieved without special measures over and above those now being implemented. To begin with, I think that measures must be extra-departmental in that we should pre-select positions to be localised and after a suitable period of training and experience make an appointment from a pool of officers irrespective of the departmental origins of that officer. It is the management positions that must be filled first and this does not necessarily require a high degree of competence in the technical operations of the Department concerned, particularly if it is possible to retain the services of experienced and technically competent expatriate officers. There is of course also the device used in Malaysia of retaining technically competent Departmental Heads but having them subordinate to permanent Under-Secretaries of the Ministries.

Already there are many local officers of ability and experience filling professional/technical posts and it seems axiomatic that we must draw upon these to fill positions of greater management sensitivity.

I believe that special measures are necessary and that such measures may be difficult to implement within the confines of the present Public Service Ordinance and Regulations. It may be necessary to introduce an amendment to the Public Service Ordinance which exempts from its provisions certain positions declared by the Board as essential to the localisation of senior posts. I appreciate that this may be a radical departure from present practice but it seems to me that radical measures are now required.

My preliminary thinking would be:

    1.   Set up a special cell with a senior indigenous officer in charge (Mr Vincent Eri[2] occurs to me as having a suitably creative mind for this).

---

1   Johnson sent Hay a copy of his letter to Pitoi under a covering letter in which he commented: 'I cannot stress too strongly the urgency of doing something pretty radical' about the localisation of senior posts 'if we are to be anywhere near prepared for self-government'. He suggested early discussions between Hay, Pitoi and himself. Letter, Johnson to Hay, 2 July 1971, NAA: A452, 1971/3947. (The date of 2 July on the letter to Hay predates that of the letter sent to Pitoi; it appears that by an oversight the date on a draft of the letter to Hay was not amended before its despatch.)

2   Born in 1936 and one of the first graduates of the University of Papua New Guinea, Vincent Eri became a school teacher and then a public servant. He wrote the first novel by a PNG author, *The Crocodile: A Novel of Papua New Guinea*, published by Jacaranda Press, Milton, Queensland in 1970.

2.   The committee to recommend senior positions for the special localisation programme.

3.   The committee to nominate a group of officers from whom those to fill the positions should be chosen.

4.   After appropriate experience and training these promotions should be made and not subject to appeal.

I know that the Board already has comprehensive plans but I would appreciate an opportunity to discuss a special accelerated programme with you, perhaps after the Commonwealth Inter-Departmental Committee has left Papua New Guinea.[3]

[NAA: A452, 1971/3947]

---

3   Probably a reference to the IDC made up of representatives from External Territories, Labour and National Service, the Treasury and the (Australian) Public Service Board which had 'been examining the alternative employment provisions of the scheme with a view to ascertaining the general prospects of placing redundant Territory officers in alternative Commonwealth or State employment and the conditions that would apply to them for entry into such employment'. For details of the IDC, see Attachment in Cabinet Submission 116, 'Papua New Guinea—Employment Security for Permanent Overseas Officers', 1 June 1971, NAA: A5908, 116.

194   LETTER FROM TANGE TO GREEN[1]

Canberra, 8 July 1971

S<small>ECRET</small>

Papua/New Guinea: Aid to the Civil Power: Provision of RAAF Assistance

The following is an extract from the report of the Interdepartmental Committee on military aid to the civil power in Papua/New Guinea; the broad principles of which were endorsed by the Defence Committee in Minute No. 20/1970:

> 'Any use of the military forces in an internal security role involves a policy decision which would have to be taken in the light of all the circumstances, domestic and international, at the time. In all cases an approach to the Minister for Defence for his approval is required. In the case of the provision of logistic, administrative or transport assistance to the police in which there is no real possibility of violent confrontation an approval by the Minister for Defence only may be sufficient. If the use of military forces without call out were contemplated in other than these circumstances e.g. guarding key installations, this would require consultation by the Minister for External Territories with at least the Prime Minister, the Minister for Defence and the Minister for Foreign Affairs, with legal advice from the Commonwealth Law Officers. It is important that a situation should not be created in which such a decision by Ministers might be pre-empted, inadvertently or otherwise, by administration action.'[2]

2.   These procedures are a continuation of those observed during earlier disturbances on the Gazelle Peninsula and it will be noted that they make no provision for blanket clearance for Service assistance in such circumstances or for anticipation of ministerial authorities.

3.   In the context of the recent request by the Department of External Territories for RAAF assistance to deploy police to the Rabaul area the Minister for Defence expressly indicated his desire to approve each such flight before the mission is commenced. This does not, of course, preclude the initiation of precautionary measures in consultation with this department to facilitate a prompt response once Ministerial approval has been given.

4.   These procedures are related to internal security situations in Papua/New Guinea and do not vary the existing Service arrangements for the provision of military assistance to the Administration in respect of natural disasters, mercy flights and other such occurrences.

5.   Would you please promulgate the foregoing to those concerned.[3]

[NAA: A452, 1971/2828]

---

1   F. J. Green, Secretary, Department of Air, 1968–71. At the time Australia had separate defence, army, navy and air force departments. They were combined in 1973.

2   See Document 119.

3   A copy of the letter was sent to Hay 'for your information in connection with verbal discussion with your department'.

195   LETTER FROM HAY TO WALLER

Canberra, 14 July 1971

The purpose of this letter, following on our discussions and exchange of letters in April and May,[1] is to record the action that has been taken so far to obtain land and to plan the construction or purchase of office buildings, residences etc. for your Department and other Commonwealth Departments in Papua New Guinea and to propose a course of action for the future.

The sort of timetable I have in mind for completing at any rate the main office building and the residence is that following agreement by our Ministers concerning the sites and uses of the various buildings required we should be in a position by November 1971 to ask the Department of Works formally to provide broad cost estimates for the purpose of a joint Cabinet submission which I would propose would be circulated in January 1972. Assuming an early favourable decision I would see the project proceeding through the stages of design listing and examination by the Parliamentary Public Works Committee so that the buildings would be constructed by the end of 1974 or early in 1975.

I see the project as a joint venture by our two Departments. However, as far as works programming is concerned I feel in present circumstances it would be preferable for the project to be included in the works programme of the Department of External Territories which department should have the coordinating function with the Commonwealth Department of Works. It is, of course, our intention to continue to work in full accord with your Department. In fact the preparation of the detailed statement of requirements for the chancery and other buildings would be in your hands entirely.

To maintain the timetable suggested above the urgent need at present is to determine the uses to which various buildings required would be put and their location. In this connection we would welcome an early visit to Papua New Guinea by yourself or one of your senior officers, both to look at sites and to have discussions with the Administrator. The Administration will give full cooperation.

[NAA: A452, 1971/2802]

---

1   Documents 161 & 170.

196   LETTER FROM HAY TO JOHNSON

Canberra, 15 July 1971

CONFIDENTIAL

You will have been informed that Mr L. H. Border, Deputy Secretary, Foreign Affairs Department, is to visit Papua New Guinea from 22nd to 30th July.

Mr Border will be having detailed discussions with the Department here before he leaves. However the main purposes of his visit are:

(a) to discuss with Administration officers the question of land for a future diplomatic mission and if possible to reach a firm conclusion thereon;

(b) to discuss with you and your officers the question of training for the future Papua New Guinea foreign office;

(c) to discuss with you the role of Foreign Affairs Department officers in the running of the future foreign office in its early stages and in the training of Papua New Guinea officers;

(d) to acquaint himself generally with the problems of the Territory by discussions in Port Moresby and, if time permits, visits to a limited number of other centres.

As for the future foreign office of Papua New Guinea, we understand that the Administration and the Public Service Board are preparing a base paper which would cover the broad concept of a future office and would contain initial establishment and training proposals for submission to the Minister for External Territories.

An important element in the total set of recommendations to the Minister will need to be the timing of the build-up of a foreign office. This should perhaps be a matter for consideration by the AEC. For one thing, the foreign office will be competing with other departments for personnel. In addition there is some risk of the function of conducting international affairs moving ahead more quickly than some of the other functions of government. Papua New Guinea is already an Associate Member of ECAFE[1] and a member of the Asian Development Bank. It conducts on a day to day basis liaison with the Indonesian authorities over West Irian border matters. Unless there was a major policy conflict which I cannot foresee at present it is unlikely that an Australian Government would wish to move on any international matter directly of concern to Papua New Guinea against the wishes of its elected representatives.

In short we could well be faced with a situation in which, de facto, foreign affairs were handled by the Papua New Guinea Administration before internal self-government, let alone before independence. We do not necessarily see this as a bad thing but we need to watch the pace of development and to make sure that it accords with the wishes of the political leaders. It may well be that we should hasten the whole process fairly slowly until the new AEC comes into office in early 1972.

Another matter for decision which has been raised in discussions between officials is that of ministerial responsibility in the pre-independence period. Given the interest of political leaders in foreign affairs, and in particular in trade negotiations, it would seem impossible in practice to avoid some form of ministerial supervision [of] international relations generally. We are working on this matter in the Department but it may be that, for example, a senior minister in the 1972 AEC might exercise supervision over matters like international affairs, foreign trade and defence with some such title as Assistant Chairman of the AEC.

[NAA: A452, 1971/2802]

---

1   UN Economic Commission for Asia and the Far East.

197   LETTER FROM HAY TO JOHNSON

Canberra, 16 July 1971

CONFIDENTIAL

I wish to bring to your attention the result of discussions which have taken place between myself, the Secretary for Defence, and Chairman Chiefs of Staff Committee, and the Director, Joint Staff on the problem of future defence arrangements in Papua New Guinea.[1] You have of course in your letter of 15th June raised for consideration some of the matters involved in the problem.[2]

You will recall that an Inter-Departmental Committee [IDC] had reported earlier this year on the aid which the PIR could and should extend in aid of the civil power in internal security situations in Papua New Guinea.[3] It was evident that this report did not provide solutions to many of the important questions relating to defence if only because of the foreshortened independence time scale implicit in Cabinet's approval of the Select Committee report. As a result I initiated discussions with the Secretary for Defence. This resulted in the preparation by officers of both Departments of a Programme for Future Work.

[*matter omitted*]

We agreed, and Sir Arthur Tange was quite emphatic in his view on this, that the Administration must be closely involved in the work of these Study Groups[4] and that much of their work should be carried out in Papua New Guinea. Where the document shows this Department as having a role, it is to be taken as meaning the Department jointly with the Administration. We did not of course define with precision the circumstances, in relation to any group, when or if it should work in the Territory. This is left to the common sense of the members. Arrangements in this regard would need to be flexible. Study Groups 1, 4, 9, 10, 11 and 14 in particular are among groups which should or may have to work frequently in Papua New Guinea. Indeed I would have thought studies 4 and 9, for example, would carry out most, if not all, of their work there.

In addition Sir Arthur and I are to receive a two-monthly report which I will discuss with you on receipt.

It is of course also necessary that there should be Administration representation on many of the proposed groups.

You might also let me have your views on the Administration representation you think appropriate. I should add that Study No 1 (the IDC on Internal Security) held one meeting earlier this year which the Commissioner of Police[5] attended, and it was thought appropriate that he should attend the second meeting which is due to be convened this week when as you know he is visiting the Department. Study No 4 relating to localisation is very much a matter for the Territory Public Service and I would have thought Study No 9 will require close involvement of Departments of the Administration.

I might add in connection with Study No 1 (internal security) that the terms of reference cover intelligence and it may be necessary for the group to link up with the Security Committee, which will come into operation under the new Intelligence arrangements.

---

1   See Document 167.
2   Not published.
3   See Documents 119 & 194.
4   See Document 100, para. 117.
5   Brigadier N. A. M. Nicholls.

The matter of timing was dealt with. It was agreed that all the studies should proceed concurrently in so far as manpower permits. In particular it was agreed that Studies 1, 10, 13 and 14 were of prime importance and should get under way forthwith.

Sir Arthur Tange felt that it was basic to the work of Study 13 that the group work from an agreed statement of the Government's broad philosophy of the role which it is thought the military should play in the future Papua New Guinea security. I have asked officers in my Department to prepare a draft of such a statement and I will be in touch with you further when it is completed with a view to submitting an agreed final version to the Minister.

I might add that Defence thinking with respect to the Commonwealth's future financial policy seems to accord substantially with that expressed in your letter. At all events it was felt necessary for the Commonwealth to form some broad judgement at this stage as to the financial commitment which the Commonwealth is prepared to undertake.

All of these studies are to be carried out upon the basis of agreed planning assumptions as to constitutional development. These relate to the time scale for self-government and independence which it was thought ought to be defined with some precision solely for planning purposes.

On this quite hypothetical basis it was assumed that internal self-government would come about in 1975/76 with independence in 1979. However, as a matter of contingency a short-term possibility was put forward as an alternative assumption—internal self-government in 1973 with independence in 1976.

I will be in touch with you further as to these matters generally but would be pleased to have any views which you might have.

May I suggest that a point of future day-to-day contact in the Administration would seem to be necessary and, if you agree, I would be pleased if you could advise me of the officer nominated. This Department's officer directly responsible will be Mr Galvin, but Mr Greenwell will have the carriage of policy matters and will represent the Department personally on certain groups.

I would prefer to reserve for later comment the question of Army taking over border surveillance. I acknowledge the weight of the consideration advanced in your letter.

[NAA: A452, 1971/2828]

198   SAVINGRAM TO ALL POSTS

Canberra, 19 July 1971

88. CONFIDENTIAL

Recent Developments in Papua New Guinea

This savingram is concerned with developments arising out of the Report of the 1971 UN Visiting Mission and the Thirty-eighth Session of the Trusteeship Council, and the recent meeting of the House of Assembly. It follows on from our AP65 of 3 May 1971 which described recent constitutional developments.[1]

Visiting Mission

2.   The Trusteeship Council sends a visiting mission to the Trust Territory of New Guinea every three years. The 1971 Mission visited New Guinea and, very briefly Papua, during January/March 1971 and presented its Report to the Council in May. For the first time two members of the Committee of Twenty-four were invited. To avoid any suggestion that the Committee of Twenty-four had any rights in Papua New Guinea, they were invited by name and as General Assembly members after the President of the Trusteeship Council had consulted the Chairman of the Committee of Twenty-four. The members were UK (Chairman), France, Iraq and Sierra Leone.

3.   We consider the Mission's Report to be a very reasonable one. Criticism was generally muted and tended to point to areas where we might be doing more rather than accusing us of being on the wrong track. The Mission supported our policy of giving independence to a unified Papua New Guinea and agreed with the conclusions of the Select Committee Report. The Mission suggested it would be sensible to plan on self-government during the period 1972–1976 and full independence during 1976–1980.

4.   Posts have received a summary of the Mission's Report[2] and the full Report will be sent when copies come to hand. Enquirers may be told that the Australian Government believes the Report to have been a fair and generally accurate document.

Trusteeship Council

5.   The regular annual session of the Trusteeship Council was held in New York from 25 May to 18 June 1971. The two indigenous special advisers to the Australian Delegation were the Ministerial Member for Public Health, Mr Tore Lokoloko, MHA and Mr Yakob Talis, MHA.[3]

6.   Debates in the Council followed the usual pattern and gave us no cause for concern. The Soviet delegate made an ill-informed and therefore not very effective attack on our administration and intentions in Papua New Guinea.

The recommendations of the Council followed the general lines of the Visiting Mission's Report and do not pose any serious problems for us. The Council endorsed our policies and actions in the field of constitutional development and agreed with 'the stated policy of the Administrating Authority that it is for the elected leaders of a self-governing Papua New Guinea to determine when independence is to be achieved'.

---

1   Document 163.

2   See Document 169.

3   Yacob Talis, MHA for Wapei-Nuku.

8.   Consistent with our efforts to promote unity in Papua New Guinea, the Australian delegate proposed informally to members of the Council, after the Session, that a single report on Papua New Guinea should in future replace the present two separate reports.

UN Observation of 1972 Elections

9.   Towards the end of the Trusteeship Council Session, the Australian Representative invited the Council to appoint a special mission to observe the 1972 House of Assembly elections in New Guinea and in Papua.[4] He indicated that we intended that Papua should be included in the itineraries of future visiting missions as well. It was suggested that the composition of the mission might be decided in accordance with General Assembly resolution 2590 (XXIV), i.e. two members of the Trusteeship Council and two others selected by the President of the Council after consultation with the Chairman of the Committee of Twenty-four.

10.   As the 1972 House of Assembly is likely to lead Papua New Guinea into full internal self-government and might even lead it to independence, we considered it important for it to be endorsed by the UN as fully representing the people. Such endorsement will strengthen its hand in dealing with other Governments and possibly also with its own people. In view of the recent unrest amongst Papuan politicians, we insisted that Papua be included so that Papuans could not claim they were being discriminated against.

11.   Following negotiations with the Chairman of the Committee of Twenty-four, the Council agreed to a resolution deciding to despatch a mission of four—UK, USA and two others to be designated by the President on the basis of continuing consultations with the Committee of Twenty-four, members of the Council and the Administering Authority. At this stage, it seems likely that the other two members will be Yugoslavia and Afghanistan, although Fiji might take the place of Afghanistan.

12.   We hope by this move to have headed off moves by the Committee of Twenty-four to try and visit the Territory and also to have avoided the possibility of the Council or the General Assembly asking to send a mission later in the year when Communist China might be a member of the Trusteeship Council.

Papuan Separatism

13.   During the recent session of the PNG House of Assembly,[5] a number of members complained that Papuans were not being consulted about their future and that a referendum should be held to see whether Papuans wished union with New Guinea. The House passed a motion calling on Australia not to take any action that would alter the existing status of Papua without the express permission of the Papuan people or their representatives. Then, on June 3, Mr Momei Pangial[6] gave notice that he would move that afternoon:

    'that this House requests the Australian Government to invite the United Nations to make an early visit to Papua to determine the wishes of the Papuan people and to learn of their concerns at first hand'.

14.   This motion was amended by substituting 'a Commonwealth Parliamentary Committee' for 'the United Nations', and passed as amended.

15.   The Administrator had earlier made a strong statement of unity in which he pointed out that the administrative union had been approved by a resolution of the General Assembly

---

4   See Document 184.

5   See Document 188.

6   MHA for Mendi.

and that the report of the recent UN Visiting Mission had agreed with the policy of unity.[7] Furthermore, the Select Committee on Constitutional Development had ascertained that a majority of Papuans as well as New Guineans favoured unity. He made it clear that Papuans' Australian citizenship did not put them, in practice, in a different position from New Guineans who were legally Australian protected persons.

16. We cannot be certain why this discontent should have been expressed at this time. Most probably it was an attempt to show the Australian Government that the House was independent and cannot be taken for granted. Some of the Papuan politicians may feel that Papua has been neglected and wished to bring pressure on the Australian Government, or at least—with an election next year—to make it clear to their voters that they were standing up for Papua. The New Guineans who voted for the motions were presumably motivated solely by the desire to cock a snook at the Administration, and show that the House was not just a rubber stamp for Australian-imposed policies. Some expatriate members representing Papua electorates (e.g. Counsel)[8] appear to have a naïve belief that Papua might become the seventh state of Australia or that it is in some way entitled to something special because of its people's legal status as Australian citizens. More trouble can be expected from these people who are more Papuan than the Papuans, but we are hopeful that serious moves away from unity will not arise in Papua.

[NAA: A452, 1971/2292]

7   See Document 169.
8   V. B. (Bert) Counsel, MHA for Gulf regional.

199   LETTER FROM BESLEY TO JOHNSON

Canberra, 4 August 1971

I refer to the Secretary's A.141 of 3rd of May about[1] citizenship and earlier correspondence.[2]

We had earlier thought it might be possible to introduce citizenship legislation during the August sitting of the House of Assembly so that it could pass all stages during the life of the present House of Assembly. This now looks out of the question as we still have to obtain the considered reactions of the House on the opening statement on citizenship made at the June Sitting.[3]

One particular issue which has been exercising our minds here is whether the proposed citizenship should provide citizens with certain economic rights and privileges including rights to any preferential treatment that the Papua New Guinea government might give in economic affairs. This question arises because I believe it was our common feeling that the proposed citizenship provisions should so far as possible resemble those which would be appropriate at self-government. Some other developing countries have created preference to citizens in such matters as trade store licensing and permanent employment in the Public Service or confined such entitlements entirely to citizens. Mr Leahy has strongly advocated that overseas people of long standing in the Papua New Guinea community should have the opportunity to become citizens of the country and that there should be no discrimination between black and white citizens in economic matters.

We have some sympathy with this principle but applying it does impose certain difficulties. There is little doubt in my mind that a policy of non-discrimination between black and white citizens in such matters as licensing for trade stores would detract from the Government's policy of promoting the economic participation and advancement of the indigenous people.

It has been suggested that an acceptable alternative would be to provide for preference in economic affairs to citizens who stand in need of special assistance or support, that is, there would be no discrimination on the grounds of race but the same result would be achieved by a sort of means test. If that were our conclusion however, I suggest that we would only be imposing legislative and administrative difficulties upon ourselves. The reality would be that black citizens would continue to have preferences which were not available to white citizens.

The basic thought on the part of the expatriate community has been that a citizenship which provides for economic rights as well as political rights could protect their interests at a later time. I would be doubtful that we could successfully legislate to secure this end. Our thinking here therefore leans to the view that citizenship should be introduced as a means of defining political rights in the community, and hopefully, encouraging national thinking, and should not be linked with the question of the economic security of expatriates.

I should be glad of your reactions.

[NAA: A452, 1971/1916]

---

1   Not published. Besley referred incorrectly to letter A.141 of 3 May; it was actually dated 10 May. In it Hay referred to recent discussions 'with Mr Leahy and departmental officers in Canberra' where it had been agreed that legislation for a PNG domestic citizenship should not be introduced into the June session of the House of Assembly. Instead, 'a statement would be made during the June session'. The letter attached a draft statement and sought Johnson's views (see Document 188). Letter, Hay to Johnson, 10 May 1971, NAA: 452, 1971/1916.

2   See, for example, Documents 118, 149, 152, 176, 181, 182 & 186.

3   Document 182.

200   LETTER FROM WALLER TO HAY

Canberra, 6 August 1971

RESTRICTED

As planned, Mr L. H. Border, Deputy Secretary of this Department, visited New Guinea from 22 to 30 July 1971 for exploratory talks on the Territory's needs for the development of a foreign service and on Australia's property requirements when Independence is achieved. He had discussions with the Administrator and his officials, the Public Service Board and visited Kieta, Rabaul, Lae and Goroka. I would like in this letter to offer some suggestions arising from Mr Border's visit and to seek your confirmation that the proposed arrangements are acceptable to you.

Papua New Guinea Foreign Service

2.   Scarce resources notwithstanding, there is a clear and urgent need for a group of Papuans and New Guineans to be trained in foreign service work; it is equally clear that this should involve training in Papua New Guinea, in Australia and at Australian overseas posts. The International Affairs Branch of the Department of the Administrator is the logical focal point for this training, and could provide the base for the future Papua New Guinea Foreign Office—whatever form that Office might eventually take. I understand that both the Administrator and Mr Border felt it was most likely that, initially at least, the Office would form part of the Prime Minister's Department. Its location, however, is not the matter of greatest importance; the pressing need is that—somewhere in the public service—a body of people should be found, trained and organised to be ready to give policy advice to ministers on the handling of Papua New Guinea's international relations as soon as self-government and/or Independence is achieved. It will take time for this to be done and it is a task which can only be done by the indigenes themselves.

3.   Another basic point—accepted, I understand, by the Administrator and the Chairman of the Public Service Board—is that a country of the size and resources of Papua New Guinea must have a 'generalised' foreign service which would handle foreign trade, migration and all international negotiations and consultations. Separate services, especially at this stage, would be an unwarranted expense.

4.   I am pleased therefore to learn that discussions are now taking place between the Public Service Board and the Department of the Administrator on the reorganisation and establishment required for the new concept of the International Affairs Branch and on the recruitments of officers to undergo foreign service training and fill the new positions. Two young men have already been recruited; I think the objective should be to bring in people at the rate of about six a year, so that the Territory would have about twenty trained officers by 1975. This would indeed seem to be the minimum if there is to be a functioning foreign office by the time of internal self-government—assuming, for the sake of planning a programme, that this might be achieved in, say, 1975. It would also allow for some people to be attached to Australian overseas posts at that time, and for one or two very small missions to be established overseas, should Independence have occurred by then. (In view of cost and other difficulties we do not envisage the opening of overseas missions on anything but a very small scale for some time after Independence.)

5.   I suggest a total training period of about two years. It would include attendance at the Foreign Service training course in Canberra (three months); three months working in the Department of Foreign Affairs in Canberra; six months at an overseas post; six months in the

International Affairs Branch before undertaking the above training, and a further six months there at the end (or else some specialised training e.g. in trade promotion). Where possible, wives would accompany their husbands to Australia and overseas, and special efforts would be made to help them overcome the problems of adjusting to the burdens placed on them by this career.

6.   Regarding the proposal to send to Foreign Affairs officers to Port Moresby at the end of this year, I suggest now that a Foreign Affairs Officer [FAO] Class 4 be posted to Port Moresby around December/January to act as adviser to the Administration—on establishment, training and substantive matters—under the conditions set out in the draft directive sent to you on 8 July 1971. (The Administrator has indicated that this was acceptable to him with one minor change, which we have accepted). However, because of work and space considerations, the FAO Class 2 should *not* be posted for the time being. Instead, he should work in the Department of Foreign Affairs in Canberra and travel to Port Moresby, as required, for special jobs. We could then decide, in the light of experience, whether to post him permanently to Port Moresby.

Future Australian Representation

7.   Mr Border examined a number of possible sites for the future Australian High Commission and staff residences. He had discussions with officials from the Administration and the Commonwealth Department of Works, and with Mr Wood of your Department.[1]

8.   There are three matters to be resolved:

(a) siting of the offices;

(b) siting of staff housing;

(c) accommodation needs outside Port Moresby.

9.   The siting of the Chancery will depend largely on the location of Government offices. Under the proposed town plan, it is intended that several government departments will be established in the new Town Centre in the June Valley/Waigani area. The Administrator seems to think, however, that the key policy departments—Prime Ministers, Defence, Foreign Affairs, Law and Treasury, for example—will remain in the present buildings in the Konedobu area. Since these are the departments with which the High Commission staff will deal on a daily basis it seems that the Chancery would be better located close to Konedobu than to the new Town Centre. Access to commercial and banking houses will be important, and these are located (and seem likely to remain) in the port area not far from Konedobu. Although we have suggested that several sites near the Town Centre area be earmarked for possible Chancery and Official Residence sites, I feel we should explore fully the possibility of sites in the general area of Konedobu/Harbour/Administrator's residence or in the region of the proposed new road through to Waigani. The advantage of the last mentioned area is that it would have good access to the new Town Centre when the new road is finished, and would also give good access to Konedobu both now and later. The Administrator has undertaken to have an examination made of what land is available in this general area and the possibility of building there, and I should be most interested in his views on this.

10.   Mr Border did not feel that the old Cemetery and the Museum sites were suitable; if we had to build in that general area it would be best to go to a site on the present golf course nearer the proposed Supreme Court. This would also be a fine site for a small diplomatic enclave, provided that road development were undertaken in such a way as to ensure easy access from that area to the main government offices and commercial buildings.

---

1   This officer was probably E. J. Wood, Assistant Secretary, Special Projects No. 2 in DET.

11. Another matter which requires early resolution is the size of the future High Commission. I understand that Mr Wood will, in consultation with Works Department and Mr Marshall of this Department,[2] arrange for interdepartmental meetings to determine what departments will want to be represented and what staff they will want in the High Commission. I fully appreciate the need for urgency if the Chancery is to be completed before Independence, but equally the building must be well-sited and big enough to hold all the staff working there.

12. Staff housing depends to some extent on the location of the Chancery. The High Commissioner's residence could be next to the Chancery, but we would not aim for a large residential compound. Ideally the Residence should have harbour views. The number of staff houses required will depend on the results of the investigations on staffing referred to in paragraph 11 above. Mr Border examined a number of sites with Mr Wood, and felt that suitable sites might be found in the Gerehu area, in Gordons 5 and possibly on Tuaguba Hill. It will also be necessary to consider what existing housing the Australian Government might expect to keep after Independence. My own feeling is that we should not count on being able to use existing housing, the bulk of which will presumably be taken over by local officials or used for expatriate advisers and experts. I understand that some housing sites will be temporarily earmarked for us.

13. Mr Border considered the question of Australian representation outside Port Moresby. Since Lae will remain an important centre, with a significant Australian community, we shall need to set up an office there and should ask the Administration to set land aside. We would want a central location and envisage a total of up to 10 officers. Rabaul is another probable site, and the land problem there seems to be a complex one. No more than 5 officers would be needed. Other possibilities are a small office in the highlands (largely because of highlanders' susceptibilities) and Kieta (to cater for the Australians connected with the Mine). The latter two would probably contain no more than 3 officers.

14. I would appreciate your comments on the possibility of acquiring property in these places—whether by rental or building.

Transitional Arrangements

15. The Department of Foreign Affairs will be concerned to ensure that, in foreign policy matters, future relations between Australia and the Territory are not prejudiced by the development of conflicts or mistrust in the pre-Independence period. However, the only officers we would expect to post to Papua New Guinea before Independence are:

   (a) those advising on the establishment of a PNG Foreign Office and Foreign Service;

   (b) officers who may be sent to work on the Papua New Guinea Intelligence Committee;

   (c) officers to advise the Australian Representative on foreign affairs during self-government, if required;

   (d) officers sent a few months before formal independence to carry out the housekeeping chores necessary if the High Commission is to be functioning on the day of Independence.

At this stage, therefore, it seems that there will be no Foreign Affairs requirement for separate temporary office space before independence. However, if space is required (to cater—for example—for an adviser to the Representative) it could perhaps be made available in any temporary building which may be contemplated for the Commonwealth representatives in the interim period.

---

2   This officer was probably Harold Marshall, Assistant Secretary, Services, DFA.

16. As understood by Mr Border, the Administrator believes that Australian and PNG interests should be kept separate during self-government and that Commonwealth Government officials would be better located separately from those working for the Papua New Guinea Government. This seems sound in principle; I think all Commonwealth representatives working in PNG during self-government should come under the jurisdiction of the Australian Representative, just as they would under a High Commissioner later, so that Commonwealth policy and action can be unified and coordinated in a vital period of the Territory's development.

Conclusions

17. As I see it, action on the following lines is required:

(a) the Administration and the Public Service Board to finalise an establishment for a re-organised International Affairs Branch and to recruit local trainees to fill the positions and undertake foreign service training. Foreign Affairs to make places available on its Foreign Service Training Course and, in concert with the International Affairs Branch, to arrange training in Australia and at overseas posts. About 6 trainees a year are required;

(b) the Department of Foreign Affairs to post a Foreign Affairs Officer Class 4 to Port Moresby around the end of this year. An FAO Class 2 working in the Trusteeship Section of Foreign Affairs to be available to go to Papua New Guinea for brief periods if required;

(c) A study to be made of the possibility of siting the Australian High Commission (Chancery and Official Residence) as indicated in paragraphs 9, 10 and 12;

(d) the Department of External Territories, in consultation with the Departments of Works and Foreign Affairs, to seek advice from other departments on their likely requirements in the future High Commission. These numbers are to be used as a basis for planning the size of the High Commission building and the numbers and standards of staff housing, taking into account accommodation (if any) likely to be retained by the Commonwealth;

(e) the Administration to be asked to suggest a suitable site for an Australian office and Residence after Independence in Lae, Rabaul and—tentatively—Kieta and Mount Hagen;

(f) the Department of Foreign Affairs to be kept closely in touch with any developments which might have some bearing on Australia's future relations with an independent Papua New Guinea.

18. I suggest that Mr Border discuss these matters with you when you have [had] a chance to consider this letter.[3]

[NAA: A452, 1971/2802]

---

3   For Hay's response, see Letter, Hay to Waller, 18 August 1971, NAA: A1838, 936/3/24 PART 1.

201   REPORT FROM BORDER TO WALLER

Canberra, undated [c. early August 1971]

SECRET

Report on Visit to Papua New Guinea

My visit to Papua New Guinea from 22 to 30 July 1971, accompanied by Mr C. Hogue, covered Port Moresby, Bougainville (Kieta and Panguna Mine), Rabaul, Lae and Goroka. Its purpose was to have exploratory talks on the formation of a Papua New Guinea Foreign Office and Foreign Service and to examine possible sites for a future Australian diplomatic mission. My recommendations for action are contained in a letter dated 6 August 1971 from Sir Keith Waller to Mr D. O. Hay, Secretary of the Department of External Territories.[1] Some general impressions are recorded below.

Localisation

2.   It is difficult not to feel some sense of unease about the progress made in preparing the indigenes for self-government and independence. The extreme social and linguistic fragmentation of the people, their retarded material and political development, the nature of the terrain, poor communications etc.—all these are well known. Equally the achievements in building up an economic and educational infrastructure are impressive. It is evident, however, that much of this development has benefited the expatriate community more than the native. For example, an excellent air network exists, but railways are non-existent and road communications are generally poor. Most of the commercial houses and much of the industry and large scale agriculture does not basically serve the native community.

3.   Social integration is minimal and localisation of the public service and private enterprise has only been undertaken in the last few years. In some fields, e.g. health and education, localisation has progressed quite well. However, where it counts most, localisation has progressed least, namely, in the formation of a solid cadre of middle and senior level administrators. Technical men, including doctors and even teachers, can be hired from overseas. Policy advisers on sensitive matters of a national character should ideally be the natives of the country. But even today, localisation is proceeding slowly, partly because of a shortage of skilled and experienced local people but largely—one suspects—because of a general unwillingness or hesitation on the part of expatriates to give real responsibility to the natives. A very strong paternal outlook persists even in the 'liberal' expatriates. Most are unwilling to sacrifice efficiency by delegating authority (they have their jobs to consider and there is a pride-of-work element also involved), and the local officers know that there is always an Australian lurking in the background to pick up the pieces when the local makes a mess of things. It is hardly surprising that many local officers lack confidence in themselves and find it difficult to assume real authority and responsibility.

4.   In fairness to the expatriates, it might be noted that, in the absence of a scheme to compensate them for loss of jobs and promotion opportunities caused by localisation, there is little incentive for them to train locals to take over. Furthermore, it must be very hard for people who have given orders for up to 20 years suddenly to turn round and become advisers. But the net effect is that the locals are not occupying positions and exercising the responsibilities in the administration that might now be expected, and to me this is a matter of concern.

---

1   Document 200.

Law and Order

5.   Most people to whom I spoke, both in Port Moresby and outside the capital, believe that there is a steady deterioration in law and order (fighting, civil disobedience, drunkenness, ordinary criminality etc.) which the colonial regime is powerless to stop.

6.   The Administrator thought that the police were badly officered and were not a very effective force, a comment which is not inconsistent with the reports from the districts that law and order are not being maintained. The main reason for this deterioration apparently is that officials including police are not allowed now to be tough enough—they cannot quieten things down by 'breaking a few heads' as they did in the old days. The Administrator felt that the PIR was generally effective and should be used as an internal security force. In particular, he wanted to use the PIR on border patrolling to bolster the confidence of the local people who were showing fear of Indonesian soldiers. This would require some rethinking on the part of Australian defence officials who thought of the PIR as having a traditional military role.

Progress to self-government and independence

7.   The belief seems to be growing in the Territory that, despite all the difficulties involved, the granting of self-government should take place as soon as possible, since antagonism will swell with delays. Thus it is argued that:

(a) law and order is breaking down and the ability of the Administration to prevent this is decreasing. The necessary measures could be taken, however, by an independent government;

(b) there is increasing resentment of Australians in general and white people in particular, born partly from envy of the superior conditions enjoyed by expatriates and partly from resentment of the racial attitudes of many expatriates. This will worsen the longer self-government is delayed;

(c) the expatriate public servants are unwilling or unable to train people to take their place. Self-government would open the way for the government to phase out the incompetents and the unwilling, and hire those who are effective, and would enable the locals to exercise real responsibility;

(d) many of the institutions being imposed on the people are unfamiliar and unsuited to them, and the process of modifying them to suit local conditions should be initiated as soon as possible;

(e) independence could help unify the country e.g. by taking the sting out of the Mataungan situation, especially if the Tolai were given some limited form of local authority.

8.   The Administrator said he thought that self-government and independence will be affected by the composition of the House of Assembly to be elected early in 1972; it is widely believed that the members returned will be better educated and more radical than the present.

PNG Foreign Relations

9.   I discussed the handling of Papua New Guinea's foreign relations with the Administrator, the PNG Public Service Board, Mr Stan Pearsall (First Assistant Secretary, Department of the Administrator) and Mr John Brown (Head of International Affairs Branch). Both Mr Pearsall and Mr Brown seemed to understand what was needed and to be personally in favour of the establishment of a PNG Foreign Office together with the training of Papuans and New Guineans in foreign service work. The Chairman of the Public Service Board (Mr Pitoi) also accepted the need for a Foreign Office, but was wary of the expense involved in setting up missions abroad. I suggested that this Office might remain within the Prime Minister's Department, at least in the early stages.

398 [early August 1971]

10. The Administrator seemed, rather grudgingly, to accept the inevitable, but argued that people should be trained as generalist administrators rather than as diplomats as such. He agreed that the training should take place, but reserved the right to pull trained people out of the foreign affairs field and put them into some other policy area if the need arose. I accepted that this might be justified in an emergency given the dearth of administrative skill, but if it were done too often the effectiveness of the foreign office would decline. In any case, our own experience had been that public servants who went into foreign service work tended to stay there, for a variety of personal and official reasons, and that he would probably find a de facto diplomatic service developing willy nilly.

11. The International Affairs Branch now has two local trainees and hopes to recruit more at the end of the year. Mr Brown had considerable difficulty getting these two, but this was for bureaucratic reasons rather than through a shortage of volunteers. The Administrator said that the problem was not that people would not volunteer for the foreign service, but rather that it would prove so attractive that other branches of the service would be denuded of capable people unless restraints were imposed.[2]

12. I have suggested that a small pamphlet be produced in the Department explaining the need for, and functions of, a foreign service—for the instruction of the Administration and the people themselves, especially those in the University and the educational institutes.

Transitional Period

13. Everyone from the Administrator down took a great interest in what would happen during the interim period of internal self-government. They wondered what would be the status and powers of the Governor—or whatever he was called—and how he would exercise his foreign affairs and defence powers, if these areas were retained by Australia. I had the impression that they thought Foreign Affairs to be more intimately involved in this phase than we would be. I pointed out that our interest was more logically related to the independence phase. We would want to be consulted in the interim period on policies which would have implications for Australia's future relations with Papua New Guinea, and we would also expect to be involved in providing expertise for the establishment of a foreign service. We would of course play a major part in the design of the future Australian High Commission. However, the transitional arrangements would be made by the House of Assembly and the Australian Government, acting largely on the advice of the Minister for External Territories. I thought the Governor might want one or two advisors on Foreign Affairs during self-government if this power were reserved. I also threw in the thought that it might be possible for the Governor (or Representative) to live in the present Administrator's house and to have a small annex built in the grounds for use as an office, rather than take an office in the proposed temporary office for Commonwealth representatives. This could become a State Guest House on Independence.

14. I suspect that the PNG Government will in fact seek to take over all functions during self-government and that, even if defence and foreign affairs are reserved, will try to move into these fields whatever the formal relationship might be. It will be important at self-government to separate what belongs to the PNG Government and what belongs to Australia, and no doubt External Territories is now giving thought to the role and functions of the Governor/High Commissioner/representative—whatever he is—during self-government.

---

2   On 12 August 1971 Border, accompanied by other DFA officers, called on Hay to discuss the establishment of a PNG Foreign Office and a training program for its staff.

Future Australian Representation

15. Australia will need to have a High Commission in Port Moresby (assuming PNG stays in the Commonwealth) and I examined a number of possible sites. My views have been expressed in the Secretary's letter to Mr Hay following my visit.

16. I also considered the question of a consular representation. Lae is a natural site for a consulate to cover the New Guinea mainland. Communications with the highlands are good, it is a large centre with some light industry, and there is likely to be a fairly large Australian community. It might be necessary also to establish a consulate in the highlands—Goroka or Mount Hagen—if only for political reasons. The highlanders might actively resent not having Australian representation in their area. Such an office need not be very big.

17. Another possibility is Rabaul. The Australian community on independence may not be as large as it is now, but Rabaul is likely to remain the focal point of important political development. It might be possible to cover Bougainville from Rabaul, although the number of Australians connected with Panguna mine might necessitate a resident consular office there. Alternatively, Lae might cover both these places.

18. Particularly in Lae and Rabaul land will be a problem and we will indicate our possible needs to the Administration.

Bougainville Copper

19. The Bougainville Copper Mine is an impressive venture. The investment of $400 million will do much for PNG's economic development; the company has also offered shares to the PNG Government and to individuals and has embarked on an ambitious programme to train locals in all phases of the Company's work.

[NAA: A1838, 936/13/29 PART 1]

202   LETTER FROM JOHNSON TO HAY

Port Moresby, 12 August 1971

I refer to Mr Besley's A.199 of the 4th August, 1971, concerning citizenship.[1]

When the concept of Papuan New Guinean citizenship first arose we had in mind its symbolic significance rather than attaching to it any specific advantages. Used merely as a factor in unity it had obvious advantages without being controversial. However, informed discussion has introduced a number of new elements which make any legislative action undesirable, at least for the time being.

Adverse reaction from the Papua Group is obvious but this has not been the principal point of criticism. Interest has centred on the qualifications for citizenship and the rights conferred by such citizenship. It has been said at the outset that there cannot be first class and second class citizens and those privileges extended to indigenous citizens should also be extended to non-indigenous citizens. You have alluded to the problems arising from this approach in your letter.[2]

However, indigenous politicians have pointed out that citizenship now would give non-indigenous citizens—Australians at any rate—the best of both worlds. They would probably be able to hold dual citizenship or, at worst, revert to Australian citizenship as well. There appears to be a fairly strong current of indigenous opinion that vexed issues of this nature would be better deferred until independence.

The more progressive MHAs see citizenship as a right involving privileges, duties and obligations. One of the obligations is primary loyalty to Papua New Guinea and not to a foreign country. Another is to live within a local wage scale. On such bases then the privileges of citizenship which might involve various sorts of preferences could be extended to all who meet the qualifications.

There is an obvious desire for the present that indigenous inhabitants should enjoy preference in various forms of development—business licences, land leases, scholarships, University entry, and so on—but there appears to be an equally clear intention that when citizenship is conferred all citizens should be equal, both within Papua New Guinea and in their relationships with other countries.

Indigenous thinking on the citizenship issue is rather more sophisticated than I had expected and I now feel that we should not attempt to make the pace in this matter but leave it to further initiatives from within the House of Assembly.[3]

[NAA: A452, 1971/1916]

---

1   Document 199.

2   Not published.

3   After seeking Barnes' approval to endorse Johnson's approach, Hay replied on 12 October indicating that 'I agree with your suggestion that the Government should not attempt to set the pace in this matter but should leave it to further initiatives from within the House of Assembly'. He adjudged it 'unlikely that there will be any need to consider further action in this field before the 1972 elections'. Letter, Hay to Johnson, 12 October 1971, NAA: A452, 1971/1916.

203 MINUTE FROM GREENWELL TO DET BRANCH HEADS

Canberra, 16 August 1971

CONFIDENTIAL

Papua New Guinea—Gearing up Procedures for Self-Government

The Select Committee on Constitutional Development, in its final report to the House of Assembly on 4th March, 1971, recommended, inter alia, that:

'the development of the Territory be geared to preparing the country for internal self-government during the life of the next House of Assembly so that should it become a reality earlier than expected or if it is in fact requested by the people then, then the move to internal self-government can be made at that time with the least possible amount of administrative disruption'.[1]

The Minister for External Territories, in a statement to Parliament on 27th April, 1971,[2] said that the Government had accepted the recommendations of the Select Committee. In referring to the approximate timetable and 'gearing up' mentioned in Select Committee's report, the Minister said:

'... the Government will adopt a flexible attitude. It will prepare a programme for movement to full internal self-government in the period 1972–76, but the execution of that programme will have regard to the state of opinion as it develops after the 1972 House of Assembly elections and to the policies of the political leaders who then emerge'.

2. In accordance with the Government's policy, the Department is planning a programme for full internal self-government in Papua New Guinea. For the purposes of this programme, full internal self-government is defined as the Papua New Guinea Government having executive authority and responsibility for internal affairs of government, while Australia would remain responsible for Defence and External Affairs (including perhaps international trade, foreign aid and investment, currency and immigration). This programme will involve the development of detailed forward planning in all areas of government and administration, from which a realistic critical path or mainstream plan can be identified. For the purposes of the programme only, December, 1975, has been chosen arbitrarily as the date of full internal self-government. It should be kept in mind that the selected date is a flexible one, and can move either forward or backwards as circumstances and events permit or require. The date has its advantages in that it occurs towards the end of the period 1972–76, which the Select Committee on Constitutional Development has referred to as the 'gearing up' period. It has its disadvantages in that Australian general elections are currently scheduled for that time and, in addition, it occurs almost at the end of the term of office of the next House of Assembly.

3. The programme should be seen as serving a twofold purpose. In the first place, it will allow the Department to define what needs to be done, when it needs to be done, and the inter-relatedness and inter-dependence of various activities before internal self-government can be granted. Secondly, the programme plan will serve to protect the Australian Government. In the event of unforeseen circumstances, or the need for rapid acceleration because of an earlier than expected date for the granting of internal self-government, a contingency plan exists that can quickly be adapted to requirements.

4. Political and constitutional activities will be the main contributors to the critical path. Other important factors will need to be taken into account.

---

1   Document 142.

2   Document 160.

5.   Attached you will find the papers showing how a plan for the implementation of internal self-government, dealing with only political and constitutional movements, might look.[3] Again I emphasise that the draft plan is arbitrary, and will no doubt be amended with changing events and circumstances. It would be appreciated if you would study the attached papers to assess what still needs to be done in your area before internal self-government can be achieved in Papua New Guinea. I would be grateful if you would then submit to me a working list showing all aspects that will have to be dealt with in your area, the step-by-step activities that will need to be taken in each case, and time-scales and projections for these activities. In some cases you may have to list matters which you regard as essential to be dealt with before self-government and others that it is merely desirable that they should be dealt with. It is not expected that these working lists will be final ones. Unforeseen circumstances and events will no doubt change any projections made at this stage, and they will be considered at the appropriate time. Upon receipt of the working lists from all branches, the Government Branch will then construct a draft master plan. This master plan will show, against a time scale, the events and activities that will need to take place before internal self-government can be granted and also show which events and activities are critical to the plan. It is further intended that when agreement on the plan is reached within the Department, it be discussed with the Administration with a view to seeking Cabinet approval for the plan no later than April, 1972.

6.   I need not stress the urgency involved in moving quickly in developing the master plan, and I would appreciate the return of your initial working lists and any other comments to me by no later than c.o.b.[4] 25th August. Security is important and at this stage only Branch and Section Heads should be involved.

[*matter omitted*]

[NAA: A452, 1971/2739]

---

3   Not published. A version of the document is provided with Document 209. On the 'gearing-up' process, see also Ian Downs, *The Australian Trusteeship: Papua New Guinea, 1945-75*, Australian Government Publishing Service, Canberra, 1980, p. 490; and Donald Denoon, *A Trial Separation: Australia and the Decolonisation of Papua New Guinea*, Pandanus Books, Canberra, 2005, pp. 93–4, 107–108.

4   Close of business.

204   CABINET SUBMISSION 294¹

Canberra, undated [c. mid-August 1971]

CONFIDENTIAL

Papua New Guinea—Retention of Permanent
Oversea Officers of the Public Service

In Decision No. 199 of 8 June 1971² Cabinet appointed an inter-departmental Committee consisting of the Departments of External Territories, the Treasury, the Prime Minister and Cabinet, Labour and National Service and the Public Service Board to examine and report urgently on the most effective means of retaining, as far as possible and at a reasonable cost, the services of permanent overseas officers up to and beyond independence. Appointment of the Committee followed Cabinet's not being able to agree with the particular recommendations for an amendment to the Employment Security Scheme which I put forward in Submission No 116.³

[*matter omitted*]

3.   The committee's major proposals are as follows:

(1) A range of alternatives under which an officer can make a choice about his future. The choices are:

— to continue as a permanent overseas officer on the basis that at independence an officer may terminate voluntarily his career (an officer exercising this choice would have the further option of electing to retire on full pension after self-government at the age of 50 years or over, subject to payment by him of additional contributions in a lump sum);

OR

— to terminate voluntarily his career at self-government or when the Public Service becomes responsible to local executive authority, with certain limited benefits;

OR

— to continue to serve on a contract basis.

(2) The establishment of a tribunal to which an officer may appeal in respect of certain aspects of the operation of the Employment Security Scheme, the tribunal to advise the Minister.

The committee also sees the need for the strengthening of Commonwealth guarantees in respect of employment security, superannuation and retirement benefits schemes and for formal agreements between the Australian Government and the future Papua New Guinea government in respect of benefits and payments under those schemes, and terms and conditions of employment. There are also several supplementary proposals.

[*matter omitted*]

5.   I support the committee's conclusions and proposals and subject to Ministers' acceptance of them I am proposing that I be authorised to announce the decision pending introduction of enabling legislation.

---

1   Submitted by Barnes.

2   Not published. See Document 179, fn. 6.

3   Document 179.

6.   As part of that announcement I would propose to release plans for accelerated localisation and the stepping-up of the training of local officers for this purpose. These plans have been settled and, amongst other things, will involve the deliberate but selective use of provisions in the Public Service legislation under which preference in selection for promotion to a position may be given to a local officer over an overseas officer. These provisions, however, will be applied in such a way that permanent overseas officers whose services are clearly needed will still have an opportunity for promotion within the Papua New Guinea Service. (Those officers who are no longer needed will have their services terminated under the Employment Security Scheme).

7.   The announcement would be in line with my statement on constitutional development to the House of Representatives on 27 April 1971.[4]

[*matter omitted*]

Recommendation

I recommend that:

(1)   The committee's conclusions and proposals as set out in the schedule to this submission (pages 5 to 8)[5] be accepted;

(2)   Enabling legislation be introduced into the Commonwealth parliament and the Papua New Guinea House of Assembly , as the case may be, as soon as practicable; and

(3)   I be authorised to make an announcement in line with paragraphs 5 to 8 above.[6]

[NAA: A5908, 294]

---

4   Document 160.

5   Not published.

6   Cabinet broadly endorsed the recommendations in this submission but did not commit itself to the guarantees referred to in the attached schedule and asked that they be further examined. See Cabinet Decision 361, 16 August 1971, NAA: A5908, 294.

205   SUBMISSION FROM WALLER TO BOWEN[1]

Canberra, 16 August 1971

CONFIDENTIAL

Papua New Guinea—Employment of Expatriates

The Department of External Territories has forwarded the attached copy of a Cabinet submission[2] on this topic, prepared after proposals made in an earlier one had proved unacceptable.

[*matter omitted*]

2.   The recommendations are designed to clarify the terms which expatriate officers of the Papua New Guinea Public Service are to be dealt with as a consequence of approaching political and constitutional changes. The changes involve a need, on the one hand, to accelerate the replacement of the expatriates by local officers and, on the other, to preserve as far as possible the services of those expatriates likely to be needed in the changeover period surrounding the attainment of self-government and eventually independence. The proposals are seen as serving both of these purposes in that they make provision for expatriate officers, whose careers are affected by accelerated promotion of locals, in the form of alternative employment and compensation where appropriate, while preserving opportunities for those whose services are still required.

3.   From the point of view of this Department it does not seem necessary to analyse in detail the recommendations in the submission. They appear to go quite a distance towards meeting the claims of the expatriate staff associations having regard to the availability of funds for the purpose.

4.   Departmentally, however, we support most strongly the localisation objective, which has been the subject of specific comment by successive UN Visiting Missions to the Territory and which is underlined in paragraph 6 of the submission. The change in the pace of constitutional development has to a considerable extent found Papua New Guinea unprepared in this respect, and there is an urgent need to act now. To move in this direction without injuring the prospects of continued cooperation of expatriate staff, which would itself damage the effectiveness of the Administration, involves a prior decision on the arrangements to govern their future employment. The recommendations made by the Inter-Departmental Committee and included in this submission represent to us the best that can be made in the circumstances, and I would recommend their support and adoption accordingly.

[NAA: A1838, 936/5/5]

---

1   Nigel Bowen succeeded Les Bury as Minister for Foreign Affairs on 2 August 1971.

2   Document 204.

206   LETTER FROM BARNES TO MCMAHON

Canberra, 19 August 1971

CONFIDENTIAL

I am writing to inform you of the action I propose to take in respect of two Papua New Guinea House of Assembly resolutions affecting the question of unity.[1]

At the June meeting of the Papua New Guinea House of Assembly two resolutions were passed asking the Australian Government to take special action in relation to Papua as distinct from New Guinea. The first called upon the Government not to take any action that would alter the existing status and rights of Papua and Papuans without the express approval of the Papuan people or their elected representatives. The second asked the Government to appoint a Commonwealth Parliamentary Committee, representative of all parties, to make an early visit to Papua 'to determine the wishes of the Papuan people and to learn of their concern at first hand'.

The course of Australian policy has been firmly in the direction of bringing Papua New Guinea to internal self-government and independence as a single country and as I mentioned to you in my letter of 17th May I authorised the Administrator to reaffirm Australian policy on unity for Papua New Guinea which he did on 20th May last. The text of the statement is attached.[2] Since that time the Trusteeship Council has supported the Government's policy. The following is an extract from their conclusions and recommendations dated June, 1971:

'... the Council, taking note of the recommendation of the Visiting Mission that separatism must be discouraged and that appropriate opportunity should be taken to emphasise publicly that the destiny of Papua and New Guinea was to move to self-government and independence as a single country, notes with the [sic] interest the statement of the Special Representative that it was the policy of Australia to advance Papua New Guinea to internal self-government and independence as a united country and that one of the main features of the political education programme now under formulation is to stress national unity ...'

Very similar statements have been made by the Leader of the Opposition, the last occasion being his address at Monash University on 29th July[3] in the course of the seminar, in which I myself took part, in which he said, in part:

'the most worrying political problem in Papua New Guinea at the moment is the growth of separatism. There can be nothing more destructive, more weakening or more self-defeating. With the exception of events in the Gazelle, I do not blame the Administration for this disturbing development. The Australian Government has always made it clear that its responsibility is to hand over independence to a single government of Papua New Guinea and that Papua and New Guinea as well as all regions of New Guinea must march to independence together'.

I see nothing in the two resolutions from the House of Assembly which should cause the Government to reconsider its long-standing policy. The House of Assembly and the procedure of ascertaining the wishes of the people on constitutional matters through select committees provide a safeguard for the Papuans. No constitutional change affecting the status of the whole country will take place without their representatives having an opportunity to state their views. But to accede now to the demand for a separate ascertainment of the wishes of the Papuans

---

1   See Document 188.

2   Document 173.

3   Not published.

and particularly to do so by means of an all-party Commonwealth Parliamentary Committee, would only serve to strengthen separatist forces and give prominence and importance to an issue which has in all probability been exaggerated by certain interested parties.

This is the view of the Administrator also.

I therefore propose to inform the Administrator and ask him to notify the Speaker of the House of Assembly in appropriate terms.[4]

[NAA: A1209, 1971/9229]

---

4   For McMahon's reply, which acknowledged the letter without substantive comment, see Letter, McMahon to Barnes, 3 September 1971, NAA: A1209, 1971/9229.

207   PRESS RELEASE

Port Moresby, 19 August 1971

The Administrator of Papua New Guinea has just made an announcement of extreme gravity.

Mr Emanuel,[1] District Commissioner, East New Britain, has been killed. Murder is suspected and the area is cordoned off by police.

Mr Emanuel was last seen alive with one man in the Kabaira area.

[NAA: A1838, 936/4/16 PART 6]

---

1   Errol John (Jack) Emanuel had been appointed District Commissioner of East New Britain on special
     duties in 1970. He had extensive earlier experience in East New Britain and the highlands region. In 1972
     he was posthumously awarded the George Cross in recognition of the bravery he had shown in negotiations
     directed to resolving disputes and reducing tensions in East New Britain.

208 CABLEGRAM TO CANBERRA

Port Moresby, 20 August 1971

14331. CONFIDENTIAL

Gazelle Peninsula: Murder of District Commissioner Emanuel

1. The land which comprises Kabaira Plantation, about 20 miles from Rabaul, has been under dispute for some year. Over the last few months squatters have been encroaching more and more upon the Plantation. They cleared land and erected dwellings. On 11th August these squatters were removed by police in the presence of the District Commissioner.

2. On the morning of 19th August 1971, the District Commissioner (DC) of East New Britain, E. J. Emanuel, was murdered at Kabaira Plantation. The incident occurred following a discussion involving Police Superintendent Feeney,[1] the DC and some 30 ritualistically-attired Tolais.[2] The DC was murdered while talking privately to one of the group out of sight of the police party.

3. The identity and place of origin of the Tolais involved in the incident is not yet clear. They may have come from local villages or possibly further afield. Their ritual attire, related to magic and sorcery, and the evacuation of local villages by women and children, suggests that an incident of some kind was anticipated.

4. Emanuel's life has been threatened on a number of occasions. The most recent reported was connected with steps to remove squatters from the Kabaira Plantation late in July. Initial questioning indicates that the murder was probably premeditated and organised by five men and that the Rabaul Police Superintendent Feeney has also been marked for murder. Specific threats have also been made against the life of Deputy District Commissioner Walsh[3] and Police Superintendent Hoeter.[4]

5. Reports from the Highlands area indicate a significant degree of concern amongst Highlanders in areas where Emanuel has served, over his death.

6. It is probable that the murder of the DC was pre-planned although for what reason and by whom is unknown. However because of the fact that some members of the Mataungan Association (MA)[5] have been threatening to take the DCs life for some time, it can be assumed that if the MA was not directly involved it must bear at least an indirect responsibility for creating an atmosphere encouraging violence.

7. From this it is clear that threats against Walsh, Feeney and Hoeter should be taken seriously. It can be expected that elements in the Gazelle could take advantage of a field situation, in particular an emotionally charged one, in an effort to kill any administration or police officer who they have marked for death or who presents an opportune target.

8. There are indications that some Highlanders could react strongly to this murder of a person they regarded as an old friend. Any reaction will probably be directed against Tolais in the Highlands area.

---

1 District Police Superintendent Greville (Grev) Feeney.

2 The large, self-confident Tolai community numbered around 70,000 and comprised a large majority of the population of the Gazelle Peninsula.

3 John Walsh, formerly the Principal of the Vunadidir Local Government Training Centre in the East New Britain District, had been serving as Deputy District Commissioner in the district since January 1970.

4 Superintendent Frank Hoeter.

5 For background on the Mataungan Association see Document 49, fn. 3.

9. This incident could heighten expected tension at the Mt Hagen show.

10. Should the perpetrator of this crime not be apprehended and brought to justice quickly then an adverse effect on the morale of police and field staff can be expected. At the same time malcontents and discontents elsewhere in PNG, could be encouraged to seriously consider violence as a panacea for their dissidence.[6]

[NAA: A1838, 936/4/16 PART 6]

---

6 After a police investigation and committal proceedings, fourteen men were committed for trial. Held in Rabaul, the trial ran from February 1972 to the following June. William Taupa and Anton ToWaliria were sentenced respectively to 14 and 11 years. Three other men received shorter sentences while the other defendants were acquitted. No evidence emerged linking the leadership of the Mataungan Association with the murder. See Ian Downs, *The Australian Trusteeship: Papua New Guinea 1945–75*, Australian Government Publishing Service, Canberra, 1980, pp. 520–24.

209   NOTES FOR DET MEETING

Canberra, 20 August 1971

Papua New Guinea—Gearing Up Procedures for Self-Government

This is a gearing-up operation.[1] Purpose of exercise is to determine what steps need to be taken, examine constraints (such as time factor involved in training, negotiations, etc.), fit programmes to a time scale that might be either expanded or contracted, examine links with other activities, and take steps necessary to put an approval plan into operation. It is not merely a study—it is a blueprint for action. Government Branch will endeavour to ensure proper integration of all activities and, in consultation with other branches, and later the Administration, arrive at a working programme. The programme will provide means for the Government to react swiftly to changing situations.

Numbers of comments from functional areas to date state that certain matters will be examined or reviewed 'as matters become clearer'. A different outlook is needed. We need to take the initiative and make positive plans.

In general, notes received from functional areas to date list numbers of discrete items—matters to be resolved before or at self-government. In most cases it is obvious that a series of steps would be involved. What we need is a statement of the steps involved and a time scale. In the case of such matters as treaties and conventions, or the application of legislation, it could be helpful to consider whether they could be grouped and dealt with group by group.

We also need to have links indicated and whether these are necessary or merely desirable—it may not be possible for certain events to occur until others in another functional area have occurred. Desirable links should certainly be indicated. For example, should handing over of final responsibility for territory education be linked to handing over of other powers.

Where a policy decision is to be made, the most likely decision (as it appears at this stage) should be shown. For example, the Papua/Queensland border question should indicate successive steps of consultation with Queensland Government and Papua New Guinea, Cabinet submission, likely Cabinet decision, and legislation.

All matters that are likely to require Cabinet decision should be clearly indicated (with time scale and links) so that we can examine, for example, the possibility of consolidating Cabinet submissions.

Branches should examine any major regular or recurring activities to determine if, in the light of the present draft plan, any of these should be varied. For example, UN Missions are expected in 1972 (to observe elections) and 1974 (regular Visiting Mission). Because it is possible that there will be a UN observation team for the period leading to internal self-government, should it be suggested to the UN that the 1974 Mission be brought forward to 1973 or eliminated.

Where it may be necessary for a matter to be studied in some detail, times for the beginning and [end] of the study should be indicated, as well as action likely to arise from the study.

Although present planning is towards internal self-government, some studies at least should be examining the independence situation.

---

1   See Document 203. Information has not been located on who was to be invited, but on the basis of Document 203, especially para. 6, it is likely that the proposed participants would have been senior and mid-ranking DET officials.

Attachment

Diagram on constitutional steps[2]

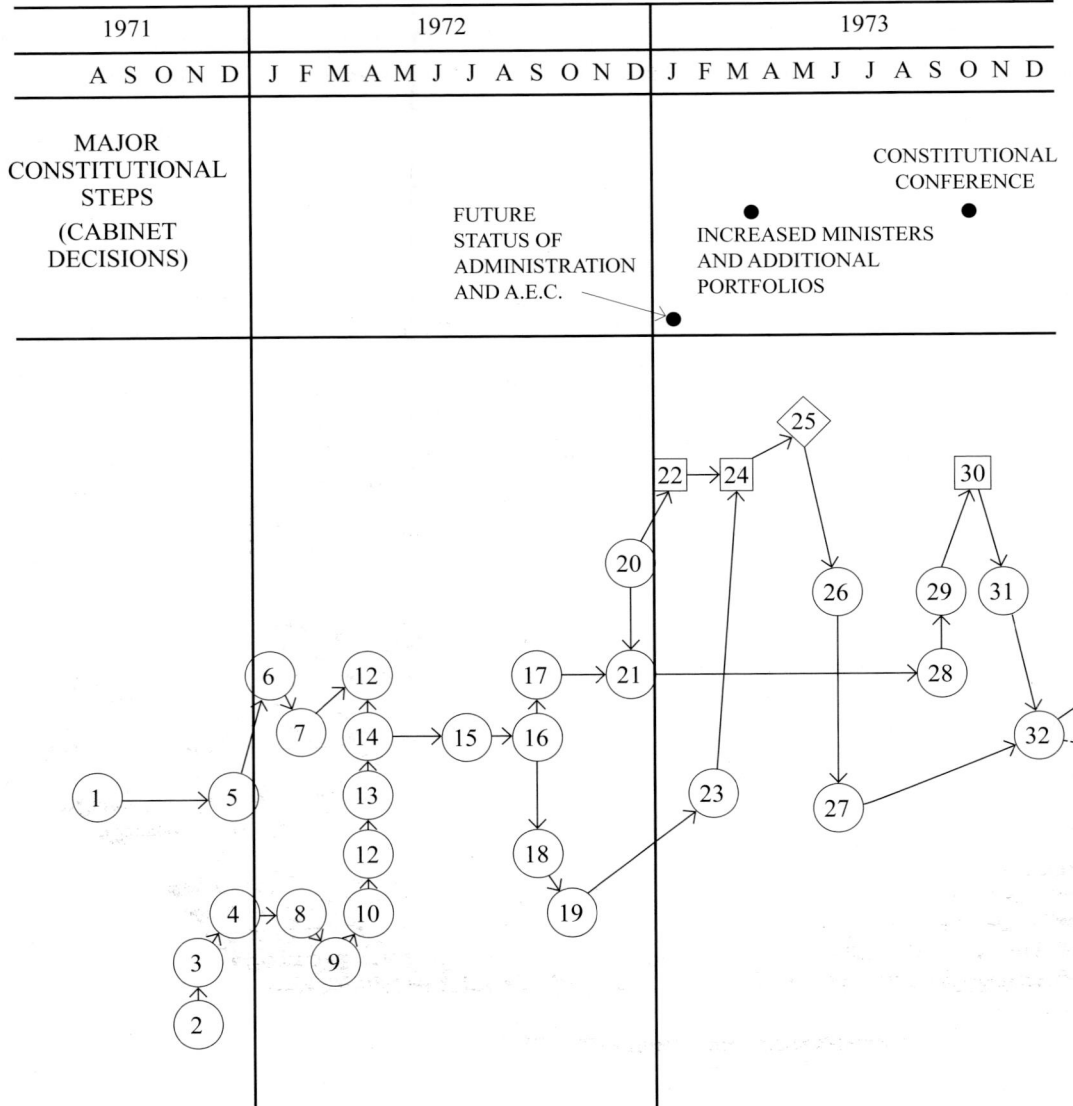

1971	1972	1973
A S O N D	J F M A M J J A S O N D	J F M A M J J A S O N D

MAJOR
CONSTITUTIONAL
STEPS

(CABINET
DECISIONS)

FUTURE
STATUS OF
ADMINISTRATION
AND A.E.C.

INCREASED MINISTERS
AND ADDITIONAL
PORTFOLIOS

CONSTITUTIONAL
CONFERENCE

---

2   In this early version of the diagram, presumably by mistake, the number '11' has been omitted whereas the number '12' appears twice.

1974	1975
J F M A M J J A S O N D	J F M A M J J A S O N D

HANDOVER
COMMONWEALTH
FUNCTIONS

●

●

RATIFICATION OF
CONSTITUTIONAL
CONFERENCE
FINDINGS

● P-DAY

Key to Diagram[3]

Number	Date	Activity
1	Aug 71	Start study ministerial portfolios and Approved Arrangements 1972 House of Assembly (based on present powers).
2	Nov 71	Writs issued for House of Assembly elections.
3	Nov 71	Nominations open for House of Assembly elections.
4	Dec 71	Nominations close for House of Assembly elections.
5	Dec 71	Complete study ministerial portfolios and Approved Arrangements 1972 House of Assembly.
6	Jan 72	Dept. approaches Admin to settle final draft of study ministerial portfolios and Approved Arrangements 1972 House of Assembly.
7	Feb 72	Agreement reached on ministerial portfolios and Approved Arrangements 1972 House of Assembly.
8	Feb 72	Voting begins in House of Assembly elections.
9	Mar 72	Voting ends in House of Assembly elections. Declaration of polls.
10	Apr 72	Return of Writs for House of Assembly elections.
11	Apr 72	Termination appointments of Official Members 1968–72 House. Appoint new Official members.
12	Apr 72	House of Assembly meets for inaugural session. Terms of office ends for Ministerial Office holders.
13	Apr 72	House of Assembly appoints Ministerial Nominations Committee. Committee nominates Members to fill (15) Ministerial positions.... Administrator submits recommendations to Minister.
14	Apr 72	Minister [for External Territories] signs instruments appointing Ministers and 10 elected and 3 official members of AEC; and determining functions and approved arrangements. Ministry and AEC sworn in.
15	Jul 72	Preliminary discussions with leadership group on gearing up plans for self-government, and whether group wants to accept more authority at this stage.
16	Sept 72	Deputy Chairman informs House of Assembly of outcome of discussions of planning for self-government. Minister releases similar statement.
17	Sept 72	Following debate on Deputy Chairman's' statement, House of Assembly decides to set up (1) a Select Committee on Constitutional Development; or (2) a Constitutional Commission; or (3) both.

3   Over the months that followed, further detail was progressively added to the diagram and key.

Number	Date	Activity
[*matter omitted*]		
20	Dec 72	Cabinet submission on future status of Administrator and Administrator's Executive Council. [Decision in January 73].
[*matter omitted*]		
23	Feb 73	Cabinet submission to amend PNG Act to increase size of Ministry and additional portfolios. [Decision in March 72]
[*matter omitted*]		
25	May 73	Parliament passes amending legislation to increase Ministry and portfolios. Assented to by Governor-General.
[*matter omitted*]		
28	Sept 73	Select committee reports to House of Assembly.
29	Sept 73	Leadership group approach Australian Government for holding of Constitutional Conference, arising from Select Committee's report.
30	Oct 73	Cabinet agrees to constitutional conference.
[*matter omitted*]		
32	Dec 73	Constitutional Conference held. Date for self-government set agreed upon.
33	Feb 74	Cabinet ratifies Constitutional Conference agreements.
34	Mar 74	Papua New Guinea appoints Committee to plan ceremonial arrangements for P-Day.
35	Apr 74	Relevant Commonwealth Depts and Dept. of External Territories plan coordination handover of remaining functions.
[*matter omitted*]		
38	Oct 74	Cabinet submission on handover of remaining Commonwealth functions and other proposals for final handover of self-governing powers.
39	Dec 74	Cabinet decision on handover of Commonwealth functions, etc.
40	Feb 75	Final functions not requiring amendment to Act are passed over to local ministerial control by approved arrangements.
41	May 75	PNG Act amended to allow for internal self-government, but to operate from a date to be fixed. Legislation also included for handover of remaining Commonwealth functions, etc. Assented to by Governor-General
42	Jun 75	Aust Govt finalises arrangements for P-Day[4]
43	Jul 75	PNG Committee finalises arrangements for P-Day
44	Sept 75	P-Day

[NAA: A452, 1972/763]

---

4   DET referred to the target date as Proclamation Day, abbreviated as 'P-day', because self-government would be proclaimed on this date.

210 MINUTE FROM HAY TO GREENWELL

Canberra, 29 August 1971

Delineation of Responsibilities for Law and Order Function

The Minister in his conversation with me last evening said that he would like us to advise him on whether the line should be drawn between the Commonwealth Government and the Administration on questions of law and order. This is a function in which the ultimate decision-making remains with the Commonwealth. However, the Minister seemed to be reluctant to have the Commonwealth intervene beyond a certain limit. He appeared to be of the view that we should not intervene for instance in the action to be taken by the AEC and the House of Assembly in respect of the new Public Order Legislation.

The Minister was also concerned to ensure that the Commonwealth retention of ultimate responsibility did not prevent the problem of law and order being seen as a Territory one which required measures which were not necessarily of the same kind as would be suitable in the circumstances of the Commonwealth where the tradition of respect for law has of course longer history.

Please consider this and advise in the form of a draft minute to the Minister.

[NAA: A452, 1971/888]

211   MINUTE FROM HAY TO GREENWELL

Canberra, 31 August 1971

CONFIDENTIAL

Policy on Unity for PNG

I spoke to Mr Bailey[1] in Prime Minister's Department this morning. He said that his doubts were not so much as to the substance of the policy but as to the extent to which the Prime Minister should at this stage commit himself publicly to it without seeking the advice of his Cabinet colleagues.[2] The alternative was not to raise an objection to the Minister proceeding as he intended but simply to avoid the Prime Minister at this stage committing himself personally to the policy without further thought and, if he so wished, reference to his colleagues.

I suggested to Mr Bailey that the policy as stated to the Prime Minister in an earlier letter[3] (preparatory to the statement to the Papua New Guinea House of Assembly authorised by the Minister in May of this year)[4] was not one to which the Government ought to be bound at all costs and in all situations. His letter had said that if in the future a situation arose in which the carrying out of the policy might involve the extensive use of force, including the use of Australian troops, then that policy would need to be reviewed. Mr Bailey said that he recalled this expression of the Minister's views. All he was interested in was protecting the Prime Minister from a personal commitment at this stage when he might later wish to consult his colleagues on it.

I went on to say that the consideration of this issue could be separated from the consideration of whether or not an all-party Commonwealth Parliamentary Committee should go to Papua New Guinea to ascertain the wishes of the Papuan people. There were many obvious disadvantages to such a course of action and I thought they stood on their own feet without reference to the unity policy. Mr Bailey said he appreciated this and thought that the decision might be taken on this basis.

In a later conversation, Mr Bailey said that in his view the issues of citizenship and unity were very closely connected, and that when the time came to place proposals on citizenship before Cabinet, the policy on unity should then also be placed explicitly before Cabinet.

[NAA: A452, 1971/2323]

---

1   Peter Bailey.
2   For background on Bailey's concerns, see Documents 172 & 174.
3   Document 176.
4   Document 182.

212   TELEX TO CANBERRA

Port Moresby, 3 September 1971

7371. UNCLASSIFIED

Oala-Rarua expected to move this afternoon Friday 3 September the following motion.[1]

1.   That in view of the obvious need for problems of constitutional and political development in Papua New Guinea and related matters to be investigated in depth and with more expertise and technical knowledge than a series of part-time select committees of this House can be expected to be able to do in the future, this House requests his Honour the Administrator to set up as soon as possible an independent commission with appropriate powers and wide terms of reference to investigate and report to this House from time to time, with recommendations, on possible forms of constitutional and political development, bearing in mind the expressed wishes of the people of Papua New Guinea and of this House;

2.   That the Commission also be empowered to investigate and report to this House on such related matters (such as, for example, the problem of citizenship, the recent human rights bill and the proposed public officers integrity bill) as are referred to it by the Administrator or by this House, and that it act as a kind of constitutional watchdog over parliamentary procedures and legislative, political and administrative developments in Papua New Guinea;

3.   That the Commission be constituted on a semi-permanent basis to continue working until a final constitution evolves (say, until the time of self-determination) and that it be provided with all facilities and resources necessary for his purposes; [and]

4.   That the Commission consists not only of people with an understanding of the problems and aspirations of Papua New Guinea but more importantly of people with personal and intimate experience and technical knowledge of constitution making and constitutional and political developments and other developing and newly independent countries, especially in the Pacific area.

[NAA: A452, 1971/888]

---

1   In the event, Oala-Rarua tabled the motion on 7 September 1971. See PNG House of Assembly, *Debates*, 7 September 1971, Port Moresby, pp. 4691–94.

213   TELEX FROM HAY TO JOHNSON

Canberra, 9 September 1971

9125. Confidential

Your 14484[1]—Oala Rarua's Motion on Constitutional Commission[2]

1.   We agree that the essential principle is that the House of Assembly accept responsibility for decisions on fundamental constitutional issues and does not hand that responsibility to an outside body.

2.   Government policy as stated by Minister in Parliament on 27th April[3] when he said that Commonwealth 'looks to the elected members of the House of Assembly to represent the wishes of the majority of the people, and to take the initiative in such matters as the pace and nature of constitutional development'.

3.   Main objective should be to avoid action before 1972 elections and establishment of new AEC. Important argument against a Commission being appointed before then is that Administration would be exposed to criticism that, however indirectly, it attempted to influence House decisions on fundamental constitutional matters. This would not apply if decision were made on advice new AEC.

4.   We see role of official members as being to reiterate Commonwealth policy as stated by Minister and to draw the attention of the House to possibility mentioned in para. 1. Beyond that we do not see requirement to participate in debate or the vote.

[*matter omitted*]

[NAA: A452, 1972/3878]

---

1   Not published. In it, Johnson had pointed out that the House of Assembly to be formed after the April 1972 elections would establish a select committee on the constitution and would employ professional advisers. He went on to suggest that if instead a committee were established now then the Administration could select 'reputable and well informed' advisers who could be employed periodically to examine specific issues. Telex 14484, Johnson to Hay, 8 September 1971, NAA A452, 1972/3878.

2   Document 212.

3   Document 160.

214   STATEMENT BY BARNES[1]

Canberra, 14 September 1971

Papua New Guinea—Economic Prospects and Development

This year's Budget makes provision for Commonwealth aid of an economic nature to Papua New Guinea amounting to nearly $131 million. This aid will enable the Government to meet Australia's obligations for the economic development of Papua New Guinea.

It has become fashionable to emphasise political development as Australia's main task in Papua New Guinea. In many ways this is understandable. It is an area in which everyone regards himself as an expert. But in the long-term Australia will be judged by the way it has performed the more complex task of economic development.

When I became Minister eight years ago and paid my first visit to Papua New Guinea I concluded that we would have to do more towards economic development and do it quickly. An education system was well on the way. Many of the country's health problems were being met. A system of local government was drawing the people into active political participation. The course was already set which was to lead the House of Assembly to its present position as the authentic voice of the people. All this was gratifying.

But I took the view then, as I do today, that if self-government and independence were to mean anything at all to the people of Papua New Guinea they must not be too dependent economically on Australia and other countries. The country had to build up its capacity to pay its own way.

A World Bank Mission reported in 1964. The Australian Government accepted the Mission's production programmes as a working basis for planning. It formulated plans to increase Papua New Guinea's productive capacity. These plans have since been incorporated in a development programme published in 1968 and revised this year.

As I told the people then I was guided by a sincere desire to do everything I could that would best further the progress and prosperity of the country.

At that time agriculture was the chief activity. The economy was to a large extent dependent on the production of copra, rubber, coffee and cocoa. The timber industry was in the early stages of development. Manufacturing industries were of minor significance. Mining was declining. Commercial fishing was insignificant. Telecommunications were unsophisticated, if not primitive. The people relied heavily on costly air transport for freight. Revenue collected by the Administration was low—less than half the amount of the Commonwealth grant.

Rightly, I think, we gave a new direction to Papua New Guinea's progress to nationhood. In the last eight years economic progress there has been nothing less than remarkable. There have been substantial increases in primary production. The basis range of agricultural crops has been extended. Rural production has been diversified. A whole range of new industries has been introduced.

These new industries have included:

Oil Palm which is expected to generate exports valued at $7 million a year by 1976/77.

Tea production which is expected to exceed $6 million by 1974/75.

Cattle which has been made substantial progress over the last 5 years. The national cattle herd increased by 15,000 head last year to 103,000 of which 14,000 are owned by indigenous farmers. These figures will be doubled in the next 4 to 5 years.

---

1   The statement was delivered to the House of Representatives.

Rice which is making steady progress and will continue to develop under the stimulus of a seed improvement programme and improved storage and pest control measures.

Papua New Guinea's forestry and fishery resources have been researched and promising new large-scale industries are now in sight. Only last month an agreement was signed for the establishment of a $12 million forest products industry in Madang. Papua New Guinea waters have substantial resources of skipjack tuna. They hold out the promise of an integrated industry involving catcher boats, shore-based freezers and a cannery processing complex.

Manufacturing has been one of the fastest growing sectors of the economy. In the past seven years manufacturing output has more than trebled. New industries now make glass bottles, fibreboard containers, cigarettes, fiberglass products and metal roofing.

Mining is now becoming a prime source of export income and public revenue. Exports of copper concentrates from the huge Bougainville project will more than double Papua New Guinea's exports in 1973/74—the first full year of concentrated production. Total Administration revenue from the project is expected to amount to between $200 million and $300 million during the first ten years of exports.

At the same time Papua New Guinea's economic infrastructure is being strengthened and expanded. The provision of transport and communications services is costly and must therefore be carefully planned. The Administration has been assisted by international consultants under contract to the World Bank and the United Nations Development Programme and by loans from the Bank. As a result many major road projects have been undertaken or are under way. When the present stage of the telecommunications programme is completed in June next year, Papua New Guinea should have a system that will cater for all traffic offering at that time, and be a sound foundation for future growth.

On top of this the Administration has established the necessary institutional framework for promoting economic development. There is a development bank, institutions for tertiary and technological training, and machinery for planning and coordinating the country's economic development programmes.

Large scale foreign investment has been essential to the development of Papua New Guinea. The indigenous people simply have not had the savings to act on their own. Everywhere I have been in Papua New Guinea I have heard the same plea for economic development—for more roads, new businesses, new crops to make rising standards of living possible. Without overseas investment there would not have been any modern economy for the people of Papua New Guinea to participate in.

This foreign investment has been subject to policy guidelines. It has also been associated with the increasing participation of Papuans and New Guineans in the economy at all levels. They have derived many advantages—through employment, the contribution of taxes to administration revenue, training and the ownership of equity. The participation of Papuans and New Guineans in economic development has been a cardinal point in our policy.

The proportion of commercial, agricultural and pastoral production controlled by Papuans and New Guineans is increasing and is expected to reach 46% by 1974/75. At present the Department of Business Development is giving regular assistance to 300 indigenous businesses. New fishing projects will provide an important new base for training Papuans and New Guineans and for servicing indigenous fishing activities. The Development Bank has an active policy of seeking indigenous borrowers. The number of Development Bank loans to indigenes increased from 422 in 1967/68 to almost 2,000 in 1970/71. The amount of indigenous loans increased from $678,000 in 1967/68 to $2.4 million in 1970/71.

A Bill before the House of Assembly will authorise Local Government Councils to give preference to indigenous applicants for trade store and similar licences to conduct small businesses. Legislation to restrict the entry of certain categories of non-indigenous workers is also before the House of Assembly.

The investment corporation will acquire equity for the people of the country in selected major overseas business enterprises operating in Papua New Guinea.

Business concerns themselves are responding to the Government's wish for greater indigenous participation in the economy. The record of Bougainville copper is but one example. On behalf of the people of Papua New Guinea the Administration has acquired a 20% equity interest in the Bougainville project. In addition, 14,000 shares in the company are held by landowners in the area. The recent share issue of Bougainville Mining Ltd. of one million shares offered in Papua New Guinea was 300 percent over-subscribed. More significantly, however, 75 percent of these shares were allocated to indigenous people and organisations.

In short indigenous participation in economic as well as social and political aspects of the development of Papua New Guinea has increased significantly. Policies designed to further increase such participation will continue to be implemented.

Our record in Papua New Guinea has been a proud one. The Commonwealth contribution has been generous and well directed. Total economic aid over the eight years to 1970/71 was $716 million. The advice of recognised international experts has been sought at every stage.

The result has been an increase in Papua New Guinea's financial self-reliance. Internal revenue in 1971/72 will provide about 36 percent of total Administration expenditure in Papua New Guinea compared with about 25 percent in 1963/64.

From a country almost entirely dependent on a limited range of agricultural crops Papua New Guinea has been transformed into a country which in the period 1965–66 to 1969–70 had a rate of growth of 10% per annum for the whole of the economy—an achievement equalled by very few other countries. Gross monetary sector product increased from $142 million in 1963–64 to $450 million in 1970–71.

I would be the last to deny that Papua New Guinea, like all developing countries, still faces many problems. But I have confidence in its capacity to overcome them. We can see beyond the problems of today in the broader prospects ahead.

It is unfortunate that the enthusiasm and energy of the people are not being accurately depicted. Much of what we read about Papua New Guinea is clouded by pessimism. Such a view is not only harmful. It is incorrect. Papuans and New Guineans everywhere are participating in and, indeed, taking increasing responsibility for their own affairs and they are truly shaping their own destiny. The record of achievement in economic development shows how they are doing so. It is an achievement that should give every reason for confidence in the future.

[*CPD*, HR, vol. 73, 14 September 1971, pp. 1277–79]

215 NOTES OF MEETING WITH POYSER[1]

Canberra, 20 September 1971

SECRET

At the request of the Chairman[2] Mr Greenwell gave a report on the progress made with the various studies required by the Programme for Future Work. He said that a first draft of the report on study 1 would be ready shortly. Consultations would then be held with the PNG Administration. A preliminary meeting had been held on study 15 but difficulties had been experienced as so many of the studies were inter-related. Study 16 was starting and the Department of Defence had asked the Department of the Army for confirmation of the powers the army required if it was to aid the civil power.

Mr Johnson said that he gathered from the brief that it was not intended to transfer control of the PIR to Papua New Guinea until independence. *Mr Poyser* said that no decision had been made yet and Mr Hay remarked that he interpreted the terms of reference of study 10 as possibly envisaging the transfer of some control over the PIR before independence.

Mr Johnson asked whether the transfer of the PIR and the defence of PNG could be separated. *Mr Poyser* replied that there would be difficulties if control of the forces and responsibility for defence were split. There were other responsibilities besides ultimate control which could be transferred and study 10 would deal with these.

On study 2 *Mr Poyser* said that consideration of the training programme and equipment for the PIR in relation to internal security duties was going ahead. Only one problem had arisen. The PIR wished to get supplies of a cluster tear gas bomb which could be dropped from a light aircraft and on impact would break into some 30 small tear gas bombs. It would saturate the areas with gas. The Department of Defence thought that this might be rather too drastic for an internal security situation and also it might contravene the Geneva Convention. The matter was still being considered.

Mr Johnson stressed the need for compatibility between the Police and the PIR riot equipment and training.

Mr Poyser agreed and said that this was approved but opportunity for actual training between the Police and the PIR had been limited so far. The list of riot equipment desired by the PIR would be sent to the Department of External Territories for comment.

Mr Johnson pointed out that the PNG Administration would also want to comment. It was desirable too for the Police to be able to borrow equipment from the PIR.

Mr Poyser said that he had a few comments to make on studies 15 and 16. Study 15 was looking at the procedures used in other countries and he gathered that the committee on study 1 favoured the Singapore model for its purposes. A list of the army's requirements for use in study 16 had only just been received. Basically the army wanted the same powers as were granted to the army in Malaya during the emergency. It was debatable whether it was necessary to go quite as far as this.

Mr Johnson reviewed the present internal security situation in PNG. He said that the situation was not critical at the moment but could become so at any time. He felt that the only area where control might break down within the next six months was the Gazelle Peninsula. The only reason that the Gazelle was under control now was because there were 600 police there.

---

1 As well as Poyser, those present from the DET were Hay, Johnson, Besley, Greenwell, Galvin, G. Baird, B. Bray and G. Cowap.

2 Presumably Hay.

Two other areas, the Western Highlands and Chimbu, could cause trouble at any time and could need three to four squads each to maintain order. This would be beyond the resources of the police force which, in addition, was weak and poorly officered. He could not guarantee to control the situation in PNG with the present police force. To be able to offer an assurance to the Commonwealth that control would be maintained in all circumstances he must be able to call on the army if necessary. A graduated response was also needed. He wished to be able to call on the army *before* a crisis situation had arisen. He understood that at present the army could only be made available *after* a crisis had developed. It was also urgent that he be able to call on the army without too much red tape—in short, that he have some delegated authority to act without having to refer beforehand to Commonwealth Ministers. In a pre-crisis situation he saw the following roles for the army:

1.   As a presence. The mere presence of an army sub-unit could be a restraining influence.

2.   To supplement police equipment.

3.   To supplement police transport. Trucks should preferably have army drivers but if this could involve army personnel in a confrontation with dissidents then the police could supply drivers.

4.   To guard sensitive areas.

5.   To form and man roadblocks.

He wondered whether this was going further than the Department of Defence would approve.

Mr Poyser said that it was not Defence so much as the Service Departments[3] which were dubious. They argued that service personnel must have adequate legal powers to protect them before taking on such duties. As far as Defence were concerned there was no difficulty in the proposals and he agreed that the Services ought to have the capacity to carry out these tasks. This was the reason for study 16. In fact the Services already could carry out some of the tasks in a pre-call-out situation.

The Chairman asked that these tasks be identified.

Mr Poyser said that the Services were already able to provide the following support to the police in a pre-call-out situation:

Logistic, Administrative and Transport support;

Guarding of key installations and controlled areas;

Cordoning in passing support of the police.

It would be necessary to get the approval of the Minister for Defence. *The Chairman* remarked that an army presence could be provided simply by the movement of a company and *Mr Johnson* said that he could need an army presence in the Gazelle.

There was discussion on whether increased legal authority for the Services should be provided by Commonwealth Act or PNG Ordinance. It was pointed out that the House of Assembly would not be able to consider such legislation before June 1972 at earliest. *Mr Johnson* asked for a minute to be sent to him giving the existing powers of the army in a pre-call-out situation.

The committee paper on internal security and intelligence organisation prepared for study 1 was discussed.

Mr Johnson said that the important question was how much the local cabinet became involved and how much should be kept separate in Australia's interests.

---

3   At this time Australia had separate defence, army, navy and air force departments. They were combined in 1973.

Mr Greenwell said that before self-government it was proposed that the Chief Minister be the Police Spokesman in the House of Assembly and be involved in meetings of the Internal Security Committee, and have some acquaintance with intelligence work. At self-government he would have the Administrator's present powers over the Police. The proposal was that there would be a policy and an executive security council and that Australian representatives would be on the policy council to exercise control.

Mr Johnson said that the intelligence function did not seem to interest the local politicians much. They were interested in the army and the policy and by transfer of police powers they meant the power the give orders to the police.

The Chairman said that at internal self-government intelligence and security would both be localised. The internal security committee would be localised to some degree. However, the PNGIC[4] would never be localised and would work to the Administrator. Mr Galvin pointed out that if politicians and officials were on the same committee there could be personality difficulties and has asked whether the AEC had not discussed the Gazelle and were not thus already being progressively involved in internal security matters and expressing views to the Administrator. In this case by June 1972 they would be wanting more power in fact if not in form.

Mr Johnson said that all matters went to the AEC. If a matter was within the final powers of the Administrator the AEC was asked for its 'concurrence' and not 'approval' as in the case of matters within its power. The AEC already considered internal security matters but did not see intelligence reports.

Mr Poyser raised the subject of the establishment of a Defence Department in PNG. Should it be developed out of the joint force HQ which was being established or should a defence cell be set up in say the Administrator's Department which could combine with the joint force HQ in due course to become the Defence Department. After discussion opinion was that civilian paramountcy would be better upheld if even a very small cell could be established to deal with defence matters and later merged with the joint force HQ. Officers could be seconded from Canberra to start the defence cell and then some local officers could be introduced. Also once there was some civilian departmental defence organisation it would be easier to appoint a Minister.

Mr Johnson thought that the majority of members of the new House of Assembly would probably favour a go-slow on self-government, and would not wish to consider self-government legislation seriously until 1973. He felt that even if a Labour Government was elected in Australia in 1972 self-government for PNG would not come before 1974. The tolerances were mid-1974 to 1976 and as a guess he would suggest National Day 1975. Independence would be about two years later. If in fact the next House of Assembly had a larger proportion of activists then this prediction would have to be reviewed.

It was agreed that on the basis of this forecast there should be a discussion on whether the present early and late dates for self-government and independence given in the programme of future work could be reduced to one set of dates.

[NAA: A452, 1971/2828]

---

4   Papua New Guinea Intelligence Committee.

216   NOTES OF DET MEETING[1]

Canberra, 20 September 1971

Secret

The Chairman[2] confirmed the conclusion of the previous day that responsibility for law and order should be handed over to the local government at self-government and not before. Everything depended on the maintenance of law and order. Once responsibility for them were handed over, it was inevitable that other powers would go over too—in fact internal self-government had to follow. In addition the Australian Government would be criticised internationally if it handed over law and order too early and the local government enforced it with undue severity.

Mr Greenwell opened the discussion on the Police Force.

Recruitment

It appeared that limitations of accommodation and training facilities at the Bomana Training Centre were preventing an expansion in the recruitment of police. *Mr Greenwell* drew attention to the discussion paper 'Law and Order—Police' and particularly to paragraph 3 which suggested that an endeavour should be made to increase the annual intake to a level which would produce a regular increase of 184 per year. This would require a recruitment intake of 500 a year and would involve an extra 50-man barrack room, ablutions, etc. and an extra class room. He said he thought the matter should be considered carefully when reviewing the estimates.

Special Duty Squads

The Review had recommended 14 squads on the basis that there would be 4 in the Gazelle. As it now appeared that 6 to 8 squads would be needed there for the indefinite future there might be a case for increasing the number of squads to 18. Mr Greenwell remarked that they seemed to have been effective in the Highlands.

Mr Johnson said that the squads had been reasonably effective in Mt Hagen town but had not been of much use in stopping tribal clashes although their presence had presumably been of some help. He said that a decision on increasing the number of squads must depend on what use could be made of the army and on the Defence Minister's views and what he would permit.

The Chairman agreed that the use that could be made of the army must be clarified first and said that he would try to get a letter to the Administrator within a week informing him exactly of the respects in which the army could be made available to him at the present time in a pre-call-out situation.

It was agreed that if the uses to which the army could be put were not adequate for the Administration's purpose in maintaining law and order then arrangements should be made to have an additional 4 squads.

Mr Greenwell referred to para. 4 of the discussion paper[3] and said that accommodation would have to be provided. Accommodation for additional squads at Port Moresby and Lae […]

---

1   As well as Poyser, those present from the DET were Hay, Johnson, Besley, Greenwell, Galvin, G. Baird, B. Bray and G. Cowap.

2   Presumably Hay.

3   Not published.

could cost about $60,000. Such accommodation should have high priority and the availability of funds could be assessed when reviewing the estimates.

Mr Besley raised the possibility of having an Australian Police Contingent in PNG on the lines of the Cyprus Police Contingent. It was agreed that it would not be possible for such a contingent to work as a squad in PNG and so such a contingent would not be very practical.

Localisation and Officer Training

Mr Besley said that there should be a localisation committee for every statutory body including the Police. Places could be made available for officers at ASOPA[4] and probably at the Manly Police College.

Mr Johnson said he had suggested to the Police Commissioner the possibility of using Singapore and Malaysian training facilities.

The Chairman suggested that it might be possible to get police officers from other countries than Australia e.g. Singapore or India. The Commissioner should be encouraged to improve the quality of the Force by any means. The recruitment of specialist officers from overseas and training overseas should help.

Mr Sutherland asked whether the introduction of foreign police might not cause a violent reaction.

Mr Johnson said that he thought not as long as they were employed in fairly backroom jobs such as fingerprints, CIB[5] etc. There would be trouble if they were put in charge of a squad. He also felt, like the Commissioner, that the Reserve Constabulary was of little use and the resources used on it would be better put into the regular force. The quality of the Police officers was also low and he would like to see the senior police officer level strengthened by the transfer of a few DDA[6] officers. There would however be opposition both from the DDA and the Police Commissioner.

Mr Sutherland said that the Commissioner had a plan for the promotion of local officers but he felt that the Commissioner was too optimistic in his prediction that it would be readily accepted by the expatriate officers.

Law and Order at Village Level

Mr Johnson said that a start had been made on the appointment of village constables and magistrates. If the DDA supervised them the Police Commissioner might be against such an expansion of the DDA role. Also the DDA were short of men. However there were not enough good Police officers to supervise either.

Mr Greenwell said that the name 'village officer' had been suggested rather than village constable. There was the question of the numbers to be appointed. He suggested 500 and that they work under the central administration rather than the local councils. He thought that their powers should include limited powers of arrest, the service of summons, assisting police officers and general reporting of disturbances. Their work would be part-time and if they were paid $5 per week it would cost $125,000 p.a. for 500.

Mr Johnson said that village officers should be all right if they were associated with village magistrates. He favoured trying the scheme out bit by bit to see if it was valuable rather than appointing 500 all at once. He said that the Area Councils would want police powers and perhaps they could be given control of the village officers.

4   The Australian School of Pacific Administration located at Middle Head, Sydney.

5   Criminal Investigation Branch.

6   PNG Department of District Administration.

Mr Greenwell said that the Department had been doubtful of this idea.

Mr Johnson agreed that it would be better for the village officers to be under the Administration to start with but perhaps the question of their transfer could be raised at a later date. He added that the village officers' powers would depend on the village magistrates' powers.

There was discussion of the powers of village magistrates and powers to impose fines of up to $100 or 5 days hard labour were canvassed. It was agreed that a White Paper on the subject should be prepared for the November meeting of the House of Assembly.

[NAA: A452, 1971/2828]

217   NOTE ON MEETING BETWEEN BARNES, HAY AND JOHNSON

Canberra, 21 September 1971

CONFIDENTIAL

(1) *1972 Elections and likely attitude of House of Assembly*

1.   The Administrator indicated that in his view only some 20 to 30 of existing MHA's could be confident of being returned at next year's elections. This would be a minimum number and it could be expected that some others who may be considered doubtful would win their seats again. He felt that a somewhat higher percentage of Ministerial office holders would be re-elected. So far as parties are concerned he expected that some 20 to 30 Pangu supporters might be elected, 40 to 50 United Party [UP] supporters, 120 Peoples Progress Party [PPP] with the remainder coming in as independents. He felt that some people who campaigned on an independents ticket may subsequently join parties after the elections when Ministerial prospects were clearer to them.

2.   So far as the formation of a government is concerned the Administrator thought that there might be two alternatives. First a coalition between the UP and the PPP and secondly an all-party government. On the first possibility he did not think that it would be a stable and cohesive majority. The second alternative also had problems. The possibilities would need to be considered in light of the election results.

3.   The Administrator considered that a good number of members of the House apart from United Party supporters would be elected on the basis of 'don't hurry with self-government' and it would therefore be necessary to be cautious about moving on constitutional issues at least for the first 2 or 3 meetings of the new House.

4.   The Governor-General had informed the Minister that he would be willing to open the next House subject to receipt of a formal request from the Minister.

5.   There was some discussion on the setting up of the Ministerial Nomination Committee and the leadership which it might be given. The Administrator expected to be in a position to provide an advance assessment of possibilities fairly soon after the elections and before the House met to elect the Nomination Committee. It was agreed that it would be important to bear in mind regional distribution and unity aspects in shaping the Ministry in so far as it was going to be possible for the Administrator to influence the outcome.

6.   On the question of a Deputy Chairman[1] on the AEC the Administrator saw three prospects namely, Messrs Lokoloko, Giregire and Abal. The former was probably the most qualified but

---

1   With the Administrator as Chair, the Deputy Chairman would be the senior elected representative on the AEC.

the least likely. Mr Giregire, who is probably most likely to actively seek the position, could be the most difficult to handle. Mr Abal, who would not seek it but who would probably respond if asked to take the position, would be a good person to deal with. But both he and Mr Giregire could not speak or read English and this would cause some little difficulty.

7.   So far as the Administrator's role is concerned in relation to the next House the Administrator saw 1972 as a year of more of the same kind of thing that happens now. The Deputy Chairman would gradually assume a more positive role in press conferences and the making of 'national' statements and with the Administrator would begin to adopt a 'low posture'.

(2) *Papuan Delegation*

8.   The Administrator indicated that the AEC would decide tomorrow whether or not to press for the inclusion of Dr Guise in the delegation. The Minister saw some problems with this even though the Speaker is basically a confessed nationalist.

9.   Two of the issues likely to arise are citizenship, and even the Papuan nationalists have strong views on this, and the Papuan share of development funds. Leading Papuans have been told on a number of occasions that their Australian citizenship does not confer any particular rights on them and that on the basis of statistics the Papuan share of development monies is a reasonable one. But they still continue to press the issues.

10.   There was some discussion on the kinds of major projects which might come to fruition in Papua and these included the Sagarai Timber proposal, the Purari hydro development and the Kennecott Copper Mine. All of these were however fairly long term.

11.   There was also some discussion on possible road developments in Papua. But all these [options were][2] very costly.

12.   As to the line which the Minister might take it was agreed that it would be appropriate for there to be a session during which the Minister listened to the Delegation's views following by a recess and a further discussion at which it would most likely be necessary for the Minister to take a firm line. No good purpose was seen in arranging for a specific agenda for discussions.

[*matter omitted*]

(4) *Gazelle situation generally*

15.   The Administrator indicated that he saw the Administration's role as one of sitting on the lid. No quick solution appeared practicable. In the main Salisbury's ideas were not new.[3]

16.   It is proposed to proceed with local government elections towards the end of the year but it is doubtful that there will be a very widespread participation. The Administrator did not think that the Town Council elections at the end of next month would greatly affect the situation. In order to maintain the present position on the Gazelle it would be necessary to retain the same police strength on the peninsula and the same firm hand. The Administrator expressed his doubts about the ability of the police to continue at the same level of activity and indicated that he did not think he would be able to hold the situation if there were two or three incidents in other areas while the Gazelle remained tense. The only way in which he could give an assurance to the Government that he could hold the situation would be if he could readily use the Army in a number of situations short of actual call-out.

---

2   Editorial insertion.

3   In the latter part of 1970 Professor R. F. Salisbury, Professor of Anthropology at McGill University in Canada and a PNG specialist, had undertaken a study and prepared a report on the issues in the Gazelle Peninsula (Document 99).

17. There was some discussion on the possible use of the Army ahead of a call-out. The Administrator is keen to see arrangements develop which would lead to an acceptance that the Army could be used as a general rule in a number of responses long before a crisis situation developed.[4] It was agreed that the Department would press ahead with the studies with Defence and submit proposals along these lines to the appropriate authorities.

(5) *Bougainville*

18. The Administrator indicated that the next House would be likely to contain 3 Bougainvilleans who were committed to secession against only one likely to be for unity; even the latter would need to support to some extent the concept of an independent Bougainville to be re-elected. He saw this as one of the greatest long-term problems for government. The Bougainvilleans feel different, have money and see no advantage in staying with Papua New Guinea. In the Administrator's view it could ultimately come to the question 'how much force would be used to hold Bougainville in Papua New Guinea?' Though this would be a question for a future independent government it would raise an issue for Australia as to whether or not it could stand aside in such circumstances.

19. A further point about Bougainville was a concern which the Bougainvilleans had about the disorderliness of foreigners working on the copper project. This includes people from other areas in PNG as well as Europeans. The Minister indicated that this might be a very good argument for the introduction of Asian employees in similar large ventures.

20. The Administrator informed the Minister that all of the first leases in Arawa township had gone to Papuans and New Guineans or two joint venture operations with Papuans or New Guineans in partnership with Europeans.

(6) *Law and Order*

21. The Minister indicated he had previously thought it appropriate to hand over law and order at an early date. But he had been advised against it both by the Administration and the Department and did not wish to press it for the time being. He added however that in the handover from the Kiap rule law and order enforcement was just not working and asked what progress had been made on consideration of the introduction of village constables. Results of the study to-date were outlined and the proposal to introduce a White Paper into the November House of Assembly was discussed. The Minister thought these arrangements appropriate.

22. On the broader question of the role of the police force the Administrator referred to the weakness in leadership and to the difficulty of recruiting suitable officers from Australia. The Commissioner had decided not to recruit any further expatriates and until local officers could be groomed there would be a fall-off and the quality and quantity of officers would continue to decline for a while. This again raised the question 'what use can be made of the Army?' (See Section (4) above.)

23. It was agreed that progress in localisation along the lines of the recent White Paper would assist the position so far as the police force was concerned.

24. The decisions in the Liquor Licensing Commission could also have some effect in reducing lawlessness.

[*matter omitted*]

---

4   See also Documents 215 & 216.

(9) *Reaction to Localisation plans and ESS⁵ modifications*

29. The Administrator said that the permanent officers were concerned at the Government's proposals and that as a result their morale were [*sic*] low. He added that their expectations were unreal and that the Government's proposals were reasonable.

30. There was some discussion on whether it would be helpful to send a mission around Papua New Guinea to explain the proposals. The Administrator felt that a prepared question and answer paper might serve a more useful purpose.

31. It was agreed to consider the matter again following the PSA⁶ Congress. Items for consideration would be the attitude which official members should take in the House on Commonwealth guarantees and as to whether or not any proposals directed towards increasing the resignation payments could be held to be out of order as they would in effect be money bills which could not be introduced without a message to the Speaker from the Administrator. It was agreed that the Department would take a look at the possibilities.

[*matter omitted*]

[NAA: A452, 1971/3543]

5   Employment Security Scheme. For brief details of the scheme, see Document 179, para. 2.
6   Public Service Association.

218   PRESS RELEASE

Port Moresby, 21 September 1971

Banking in Papua New Guinea

[*matter omitted*]

It was announced today that the Treasurer, Mr B. M. Snedden, and the Minister for External Territories, Mr C. E. Barnes, had agreed that an inter-departmental committee be set up to examine further arrangements for banking in Papua New Guinea.

The Ministers pointed out that the Select Committee on Constitutional Development had recommended that the Government should take steps to gear up for the possibility of self-government being achieved in Papua New Guinea in the period 1972 to 1976. In response to that recommendation, the Government had already stated that it will prepare a programme for movement to full internal self-government in the period 1972–76, but the execution of that programme will have regard to the state of opinion as it develops after the 1972 House of Assembly elections, and to the policies of the political leaders who then emerge.[1]

The Ministers said that banking matters in Papua New Guinea are at present subject to Australian banking legislation. At the stage of independence or even earlier, Papua New Guinea would need to assume the relevant powers.

To ensure smooth transition and avoid the possibility of inconvenience to this important industry and the general public, a committee of officers has been set up to examine and make recommendations about a suitable structure for banking in Papua New Guinea in the future. The committee would then be chaired by the Department of External Territories, and comprise officers of the Papua New Guinea Administration, the Treasury and the Reserve Bank.

[NAA: A452, 1972/2704]

---

1   See Document 160.

219   MEMORANDUM FROM DET TO AGD

Canberra, 28 September 1971

SECRET

Pacific Islands Regiment—Aid to the Civil Power

In a recent visit to the Department the Administrator made clear the Administration's very real difficulties in maintaining order in Papua New Guinea. He sought in the first instance, as a matter of urgency, clarification of the legal powers at present vested in the Pacific Islands Regiment to assist in a pre-call out situation.[1]

2.   The Administrator feels that it is necessary that he should be able to call upon the Army to provide increased support in situations before they have reached crisis proportions, i.e. before they can be termed 'situations of domestic violence' in respect of which a call-out order would be appropriate. He instanced the need for the Army to provide the Police with transport assistance and equipment, and to move Army units into the neighbourhood of disturbed areas to deter by their mere presence as well as more active roles such as the guarding of sensitive areas and the manning of roadblocks.

3.   The achievement of this ultimate objective would require both an extension of the powers of the Army in Papua New Guinea in a pre-call out situation and a relaxation of the procedures under which the Administrator can be authorised to invoke the assistance of the Army.

4.   As you are aware these matters are at present the subject of an inter-departmental study and clearly any extension of power or modification of current procedures will require some further time. However it is becoming increasingly clear in the light of the deteriorating law and order situation in PNG that they should be completed speedily. A first step is to give the Administrator the clearest possible advice as to the current legal powers of the Pacific Islands Regiment to aid the Police if the requisite authority is given.

5.   You will recall that this matter was considered by an inter-departmental committee set up by Cabinet Decision No. 1044 of 20 May 1969[2] which received legal advice from officers of the Attorney-General's Department. In the course of the Report (at paragraph 35) illustrations of measures in which the Armed Forces might render assistance were set out. The suggested measures were as follows:

(a)   the provision of logistic, administrative and transport assistance to the police;

(b)   guarding of Commonwealth or Administration property;

(c)   guarding of civil key installations: e.g. electricity generating plant, petroleum refineries and storages;

(d)   assisting police at places or areas declared to be controlled, restricted or prohibited places or areas;

(e)   cordoning off areas in passive support of the police or by establishing save areas;

(f)   armed intervention, whether with conventional lethal weapons or riot control equipment.

6.   There is however some difficulty in determining the precise ambit of the assistance which the Armed Forces can give in these situations. This question was dealt with in paragraphs 41–44 of the Report. It is understood that the power of the Armed Forces to assist depends

---

1   See Documents 215 & 217.

2   See Stuart Doran (ed.), *Documents on Australian Foreign Policy: Australia and Papua New Guinea, 1966–1969*, Department of Foreign Affairs and Trade, Canberra, 2006, Document 273.

upon their being vested with the same power as ordinary citizens. Paragraph 42 indicates that there is no limitation on the power of the Defence forces to provide logistic, administrative and transport assistance, nor for units of military forces to be used to deter unlawful activities by their mere presence provided at all events that this did not require their involvement in violence. We would also assume that the use of Army equipment by the Police does not entail any legal restriction other than of course obtaining the necessary authority.

7.   Guarding of Commonwealth property, Administration property, key installations and the like and the provision by military forces of assistance to the Police in controlled areas would seem to be limited to the powers given in the legislation set out in paragraph 43.

8.   As the matter is urgent it may be helpful if an officer of this Department is available to consult with any officer you depute to prepare the advising. Accordingly Mr Greenwell of this Department would be available for any consultation if this is thought necessary.

[NAA: A452, 1971/2828]

220   MINUTE FROM MENTZ TO HAY

Canberra, 29 September 1971

Constitutional Development—Currency

I refer to our discussion this afternoon in which you expressed the view that we should accept the approach of the Banking Committee and confine our study of currency to the preparation of a simple information paper for the Administrator.

2.   Mr Gutman and I tried to convince the Committee that it was necessary to go further than this. It was in fact agreed that a working group of officers from the Reserve Bank, Treasury and this Department should be set up to prepare a paper which would set out the alternative arrangements possible in the currency field and the advantages and disadvantages of each. We are in some discussion with the members of the Committee at the moment as to whether the paper produced for this purpose should be examined by the Committee or not. There seem to be prospects of an agreement that the paper should be examined after the formal meeting of the Banking Committee has closed, by the same officers.

3.   I realise that any discussions of currency runs the risk of giving rise to rumours and a consequent panic among people in Papua New Guinea. As against this our experience in the past seems to show that such panics start from time to time and it is then necessary to issue a statement designed to restrain them. In the past it has been possible to base such statements on the fact that the Australian Government is not contemplating any change in the existing currency arrangements.

4.   The situation will, I think, be different in the future because any further discussion of currency issues is bound to focus around constitutional development, i.e. as soon as currency becomes a matter of public discussion people will want to know what is the attitude of the Government to currency in relation to self-government and independence.

5.   If the question should arise at the moment it would really be necessary to say that the Government has not considered the matter. Such a statement is in my view not going to do anything to restore confidence. In the first place the public will find it hard to believe that when we have embarked on an intensive programme of preparation for self-government we have not given consideration to the question of whether a separate currency should be a part of self-government or not. If, on the other hand, the investing public accepts the fact that we

have not given the matter consideration it is unlikely that their confidence will be restored by this evidence of lack of foresight.

6.   The situation could of course be met by issuing a statement saying that a separate currency was a matter for independence and not self-government. Such a statement however obviously cannot be issued when the Government does not have a policy on the question. Unless we are willing to decide this important question without consideration there would seem to be no escape from studying the question and preparing a reasoned position on it.

7.   It would seem in any case to be necessary to have a view about currency and self-government to be put to Cabinet as part of the submission on the nature, timing etc. of self-government. As I understand it this submission is seen as the first step towards negotiations with the leadership group in Papua New Guinea. That group will naturally want to know how the Australian Government sees the content of self-government i.e. what subjects should be included and what subjects are excluded. I do not see how we are to give them an answer in respect of currency without having a Cabinet Decision on the subject. In view of these considerations, I think we should try to have a paper prepared by the working group, cleared by the Reserve Bank and the Treasury and the most convenient way to do this is to have it considered by the members of the Banking Committee—outside their formal meeting to meet the scruples expressed by this point. Once this is done we have a fairly authoritative paper which will meet the Administrator's request for basic information. We also have a paper on the basis of which we can come to a conclusion about the recommendations we put to Cabinet on currency in relation to self-government. The Cabinet submission would of course have to be cleared with Treasury and probably with the Reserve Bank but this will be facilitated if the recommendation is based on a paper already cleared by their senior officers.

[NAA: A452, 1970/2505]

221   LETTER FROM WHITE TO HAY

Canberra, 30 September 1971

Last week I visited Port Moresby to examine at first hand the progress and problems in building up a local department staff for immediate Army functions and as the nucleus of an eventual Territory Defence Forces Department.

For various reasons, our entry into the field of localisation of departmental staff has been somewhat belated and is at present confined, with one or two exceptions, to the clerical assistant and base grade clerk areas. While we will continue to press on with localisation from this base, I fear that the process will be much too slow unless there is some injection of more senior experienced or well-trained local officers.

I discussed our problems at considerable length with the members of the Territory Public Service Board, who proved most understanding and helpful despite the serious and challenging difficulties they themselves are encountering in their own task of localisation of the Administration generally.

The most urgent need is for a reasonably senior experienced local officer who can understudy the present Australian Command Secretary, participate from the outset in the transfer of functions from Australia and the reshaping of procedures to fit those followed in the Administration Service generally, and desirably would possess the potential for development for senior office, up to Permanent Head level, in the ultimate Territory Defence Forces Department.

The Public Service Board members suggested that their Senior Administrative Programme will produce the sort of specially selected well trained officer who appeared to be required. While this Programme will not, for some time, meet the needs of the Administration Service itself, the Board members saw the particular problems of the evolution of a Defence Forces Department. They agreed to give consideration to the tentative allocation of one of the officers who would become available from the Senior Administrative Programme in October 1972. If this were finally agreed, the training of the individual selected could be progressively oriented towards Defence administration.

Another area which was discussed was the possible use of University cadetships. I proposed that Army should sponsor six of these University cadetships and, subject to wastage, etc., receive the appropriate number of graduate officers in due course. The Board undertook, however, to examine the possibility of diverting to Army one of those graduating at the end of 1971 as an advanced product from the Army sponsored cadetships.

These measures would be of very considerable assistance to the task of transferring functions now carried out in Australia to the Departmental Administration in the Territory, revising Australian procedures to bring them into line with Administration practice and accelerating the development of a localised Defence Forces Department. I would greatly appreciate approval to the measures proposed, subject to detailed arrangements being worked out with the Public Service Board of the Territory.

[NAA A452, 1971/1664]

222   LETTER FROM JOHNSON TO HAY

Konedobu, 5 October 1971

I know that you share my concern at the weakness of the administrative structure of the Royal Papua New Guinea Constabulary, and you know of our attempts to strengthen it by recruitment and secondment. Neither of these measures has achieved much success and I wonder whether some of the short term projects and studies which are necessary could be undertaken by officers of your Department.

I appreciate that you are fully taxed as it is but I attach a memo from the Police Commissioner[1] listing some of the things which he is unable to do. You might be good enough to have a look at it to see if it is possible to help.

Attachment

Police Staff Projects

1.   You asked that I provide you with details of the urgent tasks and projects which could be performed by attached officers.

Review of the Establishment of Police Headquarters

In April, after considerable delay, the Public Service Board approved an establishment for the Public Service element of Police Headquarters. The concept of the Headquarters was an integrated public service/police staff. Since then several of the public service appointments have had to be allocated to key individuals in order to retain their services within the Department. Additionally, it is now quite clear that police officers will not be available to fill a number of appointments previously allocated to them, with the result that to the extent possible their duties will have to be performed by members of the Public Service.

Lack of sufficient and skilled staff at Police Headquarters is one of the biggest burdens which the Constabulary has to carry. It is due almost entirely to this that the Force is virtually administratively bankrupt.

I consider that an examination of the functions, structure and composition of the Headquarters is, at least in the initial stages, not a task for an examiner of establishments. It requires one or more persons with the requisite skill and experience to appreciate what is needed to enable the Headquarters to meet its current and future commitments while, at the same time, taking into account the need for localization which, as far as the Administration of the Force is concerned, has hardly begun. This might well be a task for consultants.

Leave

Following the Arbitration decision in relation to local public service members of the PSA,[2] the Police Association has asked that these provisions plus others which apply in the Army be extended to the Police by 1 January, 1972. This will necessitate the drawing up of a complete comparison of the Police, Public Service and Army leave provisions, and the preparation of an AEC submission. This would require a class 8/9 officer for about two weeks.

1   N. A. M. Nicholls.
2   Public Service Association.

Trade Pay

Late last year approval was given to the payment of trade pay to indigenous policemen. So far the only action taken has been to reduce the period of probation for constables from three to two years. To be able to implement the scheme fully, trade training, trade qualifications and trade tests must be drawn up. Other details to be decided and written into instructions include the conditions of eligibility for trade pay, effective dates for its payment, relinquishment, etc. This would require a class 8/9 officer for up to three months.

Women Police

We need a study of the introduction of Women Police to be developed to the stage where we could make the major decisions and secure the services of a female police officer from Australia to develop the scheme in detail. The requirement is a class 9 officer for about two months.

Review of Land Holdings

We need a complete study of the Land required for police purposes during the next five years. This would require the preparation of an inventory of all land allocated to the Police, plus a forecast of future land requirements. A class 5/6 officer would be required for about six weeks.

2.   If we are to expend the funds allocated this year, one of the most pressing tasks is to draw up a 'shopping list' of equipment. If, on my visit to Canberra on 6/7 October I find that a seconded officer is not likely to be immediately available, special arrangements will have to be made to secure the services of an experienced man for at least three months.

[NAA: A452, 1971/3941]

223   NOTE FOR FILE

Canberra, 5 October 1971

Papua and New Guinea—Right of Papua to
Separate Self-Determination—Note of Oral Advice

Messrs A. Kerr and A. Dyster,[1] Department of External Territories, attended on Messrs Body, Brennan[2] and Johnston of this Department on 30 September 1971.

2.   Mr Kerr explained that local feeling had developed amongst various persons in Papua adverse to automatic union with New Guinea at Independence. This had culminated in a motion in the House of Assembly to get a UN delegation to investigate the matter: this had been amended to request a delegation of the joint Houses of Parliament of the Commonwealth to visit the Territory to assess the matter.[3] This had been passed but rejected by the Government which had agreed instead to allow a delegation of Papuan members of the Administration's Executive Council to wait on the Minister in Canberra in a couple of weeks' time. With that in mind, Mr Kerr requested advice[4] as to the legal aspects of separate Papuan self-determination. Could and if so, how could Papuans assert a legal right to decide (a) whether or not they should be granted independence (b) whether Papua should be linked with a future New Guinea? Matters in which the Papuan delegation would probably be interested would be whether Papua would be given constitutional guarantees against New Guinean domination in any emerging Constitution; the provision of special grants for Papuan development; a road from Pt. Moresby to Lae. Underlying all this was a belief that Papuans enjoy a special status with respect to citizenship, even though they are excluded from entry into Australia.

3.   It was pointed out that, with respect to the possibility of asserting that Papua has a right to self-determination, independently of New Guinea, this could be viewed from the point of domestic law and international law. From the point of domestic law, it was hard to see how a Papuan could assert, by right of his Australian citizenship, or as a subject of a previously British territory, that he could not be divested of his present nationality if Australia were to pass an Act establishing an independent Papua, joined with New Guinea or not. It was noted that the situation was somewhat unique in that usually most 'colonies' were seeking a break away from their dominant country, whereas here it was a case of the nationals having, perhaps, an interest in continuing in association with Australia.

4.   From an international standpoint, the position was far from clear. Though the United Nations Charter did not treat territories such as Papua in identical terms to trust territories such as New Guinea, in that the principal nation was not obliged to lead the former to 'independence', that of itself was no reason for suggesting Papua had to be given different and separate treatment from New Guinea. Mr Brennan pointed out, however, that some account should be taken of the practice of the United Nations, particularly as shown in resolutions. An examination might indicate that there had been a development towards the acceptance of the idea that a plebiscite was appropriate in establishing the wishes of a territory with regard to the form of self-determination. If so, it would be difficult for Australia to justify not holding one if the Papuans requested one. The terms of such a plebiscite would have to be settled at

---

1   Dyster's position and role in DET has not been established.

2   G. A. Brennan, Special Assistant in Public International Law, AGD.

3   See Document 188.

4   An annotation by Body noted that Johnston's comment that Kerr had requested advice was put too strongly. Rather, Body said that Kerr had said these were matters that 'were bothering him'. Kerr had also indicated, Body said, that the discussion should be regarded as a 'preliminary exchange of views' rather than comprising a more formal meeting.

the time. It would be relevant to see if Australia, in supporting past resolutions, had virtually stopped itself from denying that a plebiscite should be held. It was recognised that politically, Australia would be placed in difficulty if it was likely that a plebiscite indicated the majority of Papuans desired to stay with Australia, or wanted independence apart from New Guinea.[5]

[NAA: A432, 1971/3353]

---

5   An unidentified officer noted at the end of this document: 'This is a very interesting and difficult question, and obviously a lot of work wld. [would] be required before we cld. [could] propose an answer'.

224   LETTER FROM BARNES TO MCMAHON[1]

Canberra, 7 October 1971

The Treasurer recently concurred in my proposal that a committee be set up under the Chairmanship of the Department of External Territories, including representatives of the Treasury, the Reserve Bank and the Papua New Guinea Administration, to examine the development of the banking system in Papua New Guinea preparatory to self-government and eventual independence.[2]

Before the Committee commenced its operations the Administrator of Papua New Guinea suggested that the Committee's work ought to be extended to embrace also an examination of future currency arrangements for Papua New Guinea because of its close connection with banking and because both subjects have significant political implications. The Administrator felt that the Administrator's Executive Council would expect to be advised on the currency question when it considers the Committee's report on banking.

I am in full agreement with the Administrator's view that there is a need to examine the future currency arrangements for Papua New Guinea. The climate of opinion is changing rapidly and it is likely that before long the elected representatives of Papua New Guinea will look to us for advice on future currency arrangements. I think it is important that we should have formulated clear views on future currency arrangements by the time we commence negotiations for self-government with the Papua New Guinea authorities. As the currency question is a complex one, I feel that the study should be commenced at an early date.

I therefore asked officers of the Department of External Territories at the first meeting of the Committee on Banking to seek the views of the other members on the desirability of extending the terms of reference to include the question of currency. The Committee acknowledged the need to provide the Administrator's Executive Council with some material on alternative currency arrangements open to Papua New Guinea but favoured a study separate from the banking study and outside the formal framework of the Committee. The suggestion was made that the Reserve Bank could prepare a suitable background paper setting out the advantages and disadvantages of various alternative currency arrangements open to Papua New Guinea.

I accept this proposal by the Committee and suggest that in the first instance, authority be given for the Reserve Bank to prepare a paper, in consultation with the Treasury and the Department of External Territories. After clearance with these Departments the paper could be made available to the Administrator. This will meet the Council's requirement in its consideration of the banking report. The question of formulation of appropriate currency policies for Papua New Guinea and steps needed to implement these could then be further reviewed in the light of the Administrator's Executive Council.

[NAA: A452, 1971/4971]

---

1   McMahon was Acting Treasurer in Snedden's absence.

2   See Document 218.

225   LETTER FROM WALLER TO HAY

Canberra, 8 October 1971

I wish to raise with you, and with our colleagues from the other major Departments concerned, what I regard as important and pressing matters arising from our earlier correspondence on future Commonwealth interests and representation in Papua New Guinea.[1] Senior officers of our Departments recently initiated inter-departmental discussions on these matters and have carried out relevant visits to the Territory.

The matters are as follows and I shall deal with each in turn although all are very closely related:

   i)   the immediate need for Commonwealth offices in Papua New Guinea;

   ii) the future High Commission in the capital of an independent Papua New Guinea; and

   iii) the policy machinery for preparing for the transition of responsibility from the Commonwealth to, first, a self-governing and then an independent Papua New Guinea.

[*matter omitted*][2]

The Policy Machinery for Future Commonwealth/Papua New Guinea Relations

This brings me to the wider question of what existing Commonwealth machinery there may be or ought to be for considering all the major policy aspects of the Commonwealth's future relationships with an independent Papua New Guinea. There is already certain machinery set up, some of it dealing with principal matters such as the transfer of Commonwealth assets, banking and so on. My Department's participation has been limited to the property consideration in so far as they relate to our future diplomatic establishment in Papua New Guinea.

I am concerned about two things. First, it would be unwise for the Commonwealth to handle all the facets of its future relations with Papua New Guinea—and in this I include all the preparations that must necessarily go on well before the event of independence—in an isolated and piecemeal fashion. There must, I suggest, be a comprehensive and coordinated approach, because obviously what is done in any one field—defence, banking, property, aid, etc.—could have repercussions on many other fields and will form part of the framework and the climate of our overall relations with the independent country. I appreciate that major matters come before Cabinet but this is too late a stage for any single Department concerned to have its real interests taken properly into account.

The second point is that, whatever Departments have an interest in this period before independence, and whatever these interests may be, my Department will ultimately have the overall responsibility for dealing with the independent government and coping with results of the earlier action and decisions. You will appreciate that the sooner Foreign Affairs is involved with all the relevant actions and decisions, the simpler will be our task after independence.

I conclude, therefore, that, in this very complex and difficult exercise of preparing to transfer responsibility from the Commonwealth to Papua New Guinea and laying the foundations for a fruitful and cooperative relationship with it as an independent country, we should aim for a basic policy committee in Canberra at the very senior Departmental level. This could be akin

1   See Documents 151, 153, 161, 170, 187 & 201 (paras 9–12).

2   The omitted matter concerned the immediate need for Commonwealth offices and the future High Commission in Port Moresby.

to the Japan Committee.[3] Such a committee should perhaps set out the guidelines as to the kind of treaty relationship that should exist between Australia and Papua New Guinea. Through machinery such as this we can ensure, as the Government would wish, that all Commonwealth interests are properly examined and coordinated and the bases for recommendations are sound. My own Department's interest in any such machinery needs no underlining.

I should like to have your reactions to this suggestion which I also propose to place before my Minister.

To sum up: I see your own Department as having the primary responsibility for setting up some sort of immediate 'Commonwealth' office in Port Moresby and we shall be most happy to work closely with you on this. So far as the future High Commission is concerned, the most workable arrangement would be to make my own Department responsible for this from the beginning and take the lead in coordinating action with other Departments. All Departments with existing and likely future interests in Papua New Guinea have a concern in part or all [with] the inter-departmental machinery that exists or needs to be established, and I suggest thought be given to meeting the Commonwealth policy requirements by the establishment of a very senior inter-departmental coordinating committee under your chairmanship.

I am sending copies of this letter to our colleagues Sir John Bunting Sir Arthur Tange, Sir Frederick Wheeler, Sir Richard Randall and Mr Reiher whose views I would also welcome.

[NAA: A452, 1972/4041]

---

3 A standing committee of senior officials who coordinated Australian policies on Japan.

226   NOTE FOR FILE

Canberra, 12 October 1971

Papua New Guinea: Right of Papuans to Independent Self-Determination[1]

Mr Johnston and I [A. H. Body] attended a meeting this morning at the Department of External Territories. Mr Greenwell (First Assistant Secretary, External Territories) was in the chair and the other Departments represented were Foreign Affairs and Immigration. There were a number of officers of the Department of External Territories also present.[2]

2.   The meeting was rather discursive and partook of a general, and far from conclusive, discussion about several of the problems that might arise during the forthcoming visit of a Papua delegation to Canberra—particularly the likelihood that the delegation would raise questions about Australia's powers to divest Papuans of Australian citizenship and unite Papua with New Guinea at independence, against the wishes of a substantial number of Papuans.

[*matter omitted*]

4.   At this stage, Territories circulated a confidential 12 page paper headed 'Papuan Delegation—Legal Issues'.[3] Of course, there was no chance to digest this properly and the discussion turned only to the first question on page 1—whether Australia was obliged, as a matter of law, to hold a referendum (or otherwise to ascertain the wish of the people) in relation to independence and, if so, what form the referendum should take. It was recognised that the matter was not simply one of law and the United Nations practice in other cases and the terms of the United Nations resolutions and declarations (and Australia's voting position in relation to these) would have to be considered. Foreign Affairs hoped to be able to get information relating to the practice adopted in the United Nations in the case of each of the Trust Territories that had attained independence and they also undertook to explore whether there were any cases where separatist demands had been raised and, if so, whether any special action was taken in relation to these demands. It was also felt necessary to obtain the texts of important United Nations declarations and resolutions in relation to dependent territories—both Trust Territories and colonial territories.

5.   The view was put by Mr Borthwick (Foreign Affairs) on a personal basis that, if a referendum were held throughout the Trust Territory and Papua (without any separate referendum in Papua), this would pass muster in the United Nations, so long as there was no substantial indication from the people of New Guinea that they supported Papuan demands for a separate referendum. He said, however, that if such a course were to produce friction in the two Territories, it could jeopardise Australia's relations with them and also stimulate opposition in Australia to the Government's plans. It would be particularly embarrassing if Australia had to participate in a 'security situation' stimulated by local opposition. Finally, it was noted that it could not be assumed, by any means, that New Guineans would wish to impose unity upon Papuans against their wishes.

6.   The meeting adjourned on the above note, but Mr Greenwell said that the Secretary to his Department had asked several officers to join him at a working lunch, later in the day, at which he wanted to talk around the general issues. I attended this working lunch.

7.   Mr Hay opened the discussion at the lunch (which was also attended by Sir Kenneth Bailey, Mr Brennan (Foreign Affairs)[4] and several senior Territories officers) by saying that he

---

1   See Document 223.

2   The DFA official was Alexander Borthwick, while the Immigration and 'other' DET officials were not identified.

3   Not published.

4   Keith Brennan, Senior Assistant Secretary, International Legal Division, DFA.

was apprehensive as to two matters with legal implications that the Papuan delegation might raise, to the Government's embarrassment, in connexion with the present Government policy of future national unity for New Guinea. These were:

(1) Whether Papuans have any right to a *separate* act of self-determination with respect to their future political status (separate, that is, from New Guinea).

(2) Whether Australia is under any special obligations to Papuans because of their being Australian citizens, and, in particular, whether it can deprive them of that citizenship against their will (or at least the will of the majority).

In fact time did not permit any discussion of (2).

8.   Mr Hay went on to refer to a statement by the Minister for External Territories in the House of Representatives on 21 April 1966[5] to the effect that the Government had no intention of changing the status of Papua or New Guinea except in accordance with the wishes of the people of the separate territories. He noted that this might be interpreted as an agreement to separate referenda, but said that the Government now wished to take the line that it was its policy to bring the two Territories to a separate united country. This course had the blessing of a recent United Nations visiting mission as well as the Trusteeship Council earlier this year.

9.   Mr Hay then asked Sir Kenneth Bailey for his views. Sir Kenneth said that he would like first to have more information as to what Territories had in mind—in particular, whether they proposed to have a separate act of self-determination of one form or another. Mr Hay replied that Territories would like to stand on the view that the House of Assembly expressed the views of the peoples of the two Territories and that referenda in the two Territories (or a single referendum) were not necessary.

10. Sir Kenneth commented that, although he had, of course, not had an opportunity to consider the point in any depth, his first reaction was to doubt that the law required any formal act of self-determination by the people as such. He did not think that there was anything in the Trusteeship Agreement to that effect, but he added that this may not be the only source of international law by which Australia was bound. He referred in particular to the Friendly Relations Declaration of 1970 but said that no one had yet really determined the legal status of these principles. However, as they had been adopted unanimously, he thought that Australia might find it awkward to say that they were not part of the law. (Australia had not expressed any qualification to them at the time of the vote.)

11. Mr Greenwell referred to Article 73 b. of the Charter with its reference (in relation to Papua) to the 'aspirations of the peoples'. He wondered whether, if the people of Papua said they wanted a referendum, this could be avoided, or whether it might not still be possible to maintain that the House of Assembly could give adequate expression to the people's view. Sir Kenneth's reply was that these propositions were not capable of a 'Yes' or 'No' answer. He felt, however, that there was no legal obligation to hold a referendum or to ascertain the views of the two Territories separately or, for that matter, to ascertain the views of the peoples in any particular manner. So far as Papua was concerned, Australia's legal authority did not come from any United Nations instrument—it was a sovereign authority based on sound constitutional grounds. He repeated that he felt that there was nothing in the Charter, the Trusteeship Agreement or the Declaration on Friendly Relations that, as a matter of fact, required any particular act of self-determination—he saw no reason why the wishes of the people could not be ascertained by decision of the House of Assembly. I commented that while, as a matter of law, it might be possible to argue for the correctness of these views, there would appear to be a body of international practice in these fields that probably could not be

---

5   See Stuart Doran (ed.), *Documents on Australian Foreign Policy: Australia and Papua New Guinea, 1966–1969*, Department of Foreign Affairs and Trade, Canberra, 2006, pp. xxiii-xxvii and Document 34.

ignored, at least in actual practice. I said that I felt that some account should be paid to this and suggested that Foreign Affairs might make an analysis of this, so far as it might apply to the Papua-New Guinea question.

12. Mr Greenwell then raised the question whether, if the House of Assembly's view was that there should be separate referenda, that could be avoided. It was recognised that, of course, this would have to be considered further if matters developed in that direction—it was thought that, if the issue were raised, it might be difficult to avoid the conclusion that separate referenda were required. Mr Hay repeated, however, that, from a policy view, his Minister would be reluctant to agree to separate referenda.

13. It was left that Territories would prepare a briefing note for their Minister which they would circulate. Sir Kenneth said that he thought that the Minister for External Territories might wish to have the backing of the Attorney-General and perhaps the Prime Minister, for the line that he proposed to take. Meanwhile, it was considered that, before the delegation arrived, the legal implications should be analysed.

14. In conclusion, Mr Hay repeated that his Minister 'does not wish to depart from the policy' referred to above.

[NAA: A432, 1971/3353]

227   LETTER FROM HAY TO WALLER

Canberra, 20 October 1971

I refer to your letter of 8th October (your file 1428/117).[1]

Your letter referred to three matters namely:

(i)   the immediate need for Commonwealth offices in Papua New Guinea;

(ii) the future High Commission in the capital of an independent Papua New Guinea; and

(iii) the policy machinery for preparing for the transition of responsibility from the Commonwealth to, first, a self-governing and then an independent Papua New Guinea.

I propose to deal with the first two of three matters in this letter. The third is a separate matter and I shall write to you separately about it.

In brief, I see no problem in your proposals about handling the immediate need for Commonwealth offices in Papua New Guinea and the future High Commission. It is best that this Department takes the running so far as the first is concerned and that your Department takes the running so far as the second is concerned. In other words the High Commission buildings will be on your work programme, and the Commonwealth offices on this Department's appropriation.

However I see advantage in the Cabinet submission being made jointly. This would not so far as the construction of a High Commission is concerned impede your Department's proper role of preparing the brief and seeking funds from the Commonwealth. However there may be issues which ought to be in the Cabinet submission on which the views of the Minister for External Territories will be essential. For example the location of the capital is a matter of judgement on which the Minister would wish to express an opinion. Other issues may arise in the course of preparation of the submission which make desirable the 'joint venture' approach already suggested by me in earlier correspondence. For example Cabinet will need to be satisfied that in the event of independence occurring substantially earlier than currently anticipated there was some adequate plan for provision of temporary office space. Similarly Cabinet might wish to have a view from the Administrator as to the political effects on an essentially conservative minded House of Assembly (should that be the complexion of the House after the 1972 elections) of the construction of a building so clearly designed to provide against independence. Likewise we shall need to consider the implications for opinion in Papua New Guinea of the expected wish of other governments to be constructing embassy buildings well before the date of independence.

A further consideration which would no doubt need to be placed before Cabinet and on which the views of the Minister for External Territories would be relevant is the concept of the mission stated in your letter. You have previously discussed with me the alternatives of a relatively small or 'normal' diplomatic mission with, as an adjunct but not in the same compound, provision of office space for a substantial aid mission which presumably would tend to run down over the years with its office space being taken up in all probability by non-government organisations. You had also envisaged the possibility of separate accommodation for the staff of a military mission. Your letter of 17th May[2] refers.

Your present letter points towards a concept based on the special characteristics which it would be advantageous to develop in relations between Australia and Papua New Guinea. This would involve representation in Papua New Guinea by a number of Commonwealth departments

---

1   Document 225.

2   Document 170.

which need to have direct contact, as part of the High Commission, with their opposite numbers in Papua New Guinea departments. The relationships between the Commonwealth departmental representatives and their opposite numbers will no doubt vary in particular cases. In short there would be a broad range of relationships with the network differing from department to department. A larger building would clearly be necessary for this concept. Your letter does not indicate your current thinking on whether space for an aid mission and/or a military mission would be separately provided.

These are matters on which the Minister for External Territories would wish to place his views before the Government and he would prefer to do this in the form of joint submission rather than a separate one, with your Department taking the initiative in preparation of a draft, in consultation with such other departments as is necessary. Decisions on these matters are also relevant to the kind and size of the interim Commonwealth offices.

[NAA: A452, 1971/3880 PART 1]

228   BRIEFING NOTE BY KENNETH BAILEY

Canberra, 20 October 1971

Papua: Right to Separate Act of Self-Determination[1]

In preparation for discussion with Papuan leaders, the Department of External Territories has asked whether the people of Papua have a legal right to make (if they so wish) a separate 'act of self-determination': independently, that is, of the people of the Trust Territory of New Guinea.

2.   The broad answer seems to be that the relevant law is in general terms which neither require nor forbid a separate act of self-determination by the people of Papua. It appears, therefore, that the question whether or not there should be such a separate act is largely a matter of policy, so long as the future status of Papua is in accordance with the freely expressed wishes of its people. The appropriate arrangements would basically be a matter for agreement between the Government of Australia, as the administering authority, and the people concerned. But in the special circumstances of Papua the United Nations will probably also be involved.

3.   The law applicable is:

(a) International law: the United Nations Charter, the Trusteeship Agreement in respect of the Trust Territory of New Guinea, and perhaps also the Declaration on the Principles of International Law concerning Friendly Relations and Cooperation among States (1970);

(b) Australian constitutional law: in particular, Constitution, s.122;

(c) Australian statute law; in particular the Papua and New Guinea Act.

4.   The concepts in the field of self-determination are by no means strictly defined or universally agreed. In the United Nations context, the accepted view seems however to be that 'self-determination' is an act by which a people indicates its own choice of future status. The 1970 Declaration embodies the substance of UNGA Res. 1541 (1961), as follows:

'The establishment of a sovereign and independent State, the free association or integration with an independent State or the emergence into any other political status freely determined by a people constitute modes of implementing the right of self-determination by that people'.

This text clearly envisages self-determination as an act of choice between various options, including independence. On that view, the question of 'self-determination' would strictly not arise during the earlier stages of constitutional development—the stages, for instance, of evolving self-government.

5.   As a matter of law, it is Chapter XI of the Charter that applies to Papua, and not the trusteeship provisions of Chapters XII and XIII. Art.73 does not specifically mention either 'self-determination' or 'independence'. Administering authorities do however accept the obligation:

'to develop self-government, to take due account of the political aspirations of the people, and to assist them in the progressive development of their free political institutions'.

Australia has accepted, moreover, provisions of the 1970 Declaration which apply to colonies and non-self-governing territories generally the concept of self-determination. The relevant provision is:

---

1   See Document 226.

'The territory of a colony or other non-self-governing territory has, under the Charter, a status separate and distinct from the territory of the State administering it; and such separate and distinct status under the Charter shall exist until the people of the colony or non-self-governing territory have exercised their right of self-determination in accordance with the Charter, and particularly its Purposes and Principles".

6.   Since 1945, too, Australia has governed Papua in full administrative union with the Trust Territory of New Guinea. I do not suppose, therefore, that Australia would wish for a moment to contend that as a matter of international law the people of Papua have no right to make any 'act of self-determination' at all. It is clear nevertheless that international law does not prescribe the form of such an act, but leaves it to the decision of Australia as administering authority.

7.   Section 122 of the Australian Constitution vests in the Commonwealth Parliament plenary legislative power in relation to the Territory of Papua. Continued government as a separate Territory is neither required nor forbidden. The power to govern Papua in administrative union with the Trust Territory is derived not from the Trusteeship Agreement but from s.122 itself. The Constitution therefore supplies no answers to the question now raised, and leaves wholly open all questions of the Territory's future status.

8.   The same is true, in my view, of s.8 of the Papua New Guinea Act, which declares that 'the identity and status of the Territory of Papua as a Possession of the Crown and the identity and status of the Territory of New Guinea as a Trust Territory shall continue to be maintained'. This declaration of intention must be read as subject to the immediately following provisions, which establish the administrative union between the two Territories concerned. The High Court of Australia has emphasised the comprehensiveness of the union thus established (*Fishwick v. Cleland*, (1960) 106 CLR[2] 186, esp. at pp. 194–196). It is a union for all the purposes of government. There is nothing in the Act, in my opinion, which in law would require two separate eventual 'acts of self-determination' in respect of the two Territories, or would preclude Australia from pursuing its present policy of preparing the united Territory for self-government and eventual independence.

9.   What the relevant law does seem to me to require is that any eventual decision by Australia to provide for the establishment of Papua New Guinea as a single independent state should reflect the freely-expressed determination of the people of Papua, as well as of the people of the Trust Territory. This determination could quite properly be expressed, so far as the law is concerned, by a resolution of the House of Assembly. It would be necessary, however, that the resolution should at least have the concurrence of a majority of the members of the House who represent Papuan constituencies.

10. Present views in the United Nations seem definitely to favour evolution towards independence in Papua New Guinea as a single entity. Australia's decision to link the future of Papua with that of the Trust Territory gives necessarily to United Nations views a significant role, since the termination of the Trusteeship Agreement will be an integral part of the process of establishing the independence of the Trust Territory itself. If the consenting majority in Papua were to be very narrow, or if the freedom of the vote in the House were to be challenged, there could be a demand for the holding of something in the way of a plebiscite under some international authority. In view of considerations such as these, the Minister for External Territories will no doubt wish at the forthcoming meetings to keep all Australia's options open, as indeed he did in his statement in the House of Representatives on 21 April, 1966.[3]

[NAA: A1838, 3080/1/2/3 PART 1]

2   Commonwealth Law Reports.

3   See Stuart Doran (ed.), *Documents on Australian Foreign Policy: Australia and Papua New Guinea, 1966–1969*, Department of Foreign Affairs and Trade, Canberra, 2006, pp. xxiii-xxvii and Document 34.

229   OPINION PAPER BY AGD

Canberra, 20 October 1971

CONFIDENTIAL

The Question of the Right of Papua to Determine
Its Political Future Legal Aspects

An examination has been made whether there are any legal considerations of an international or domestic character that would lay open to challenge the Government's expressed policy of bringing Papua and New Guinea to independence as a single entity.[1] As a result of that examination, which was carried out by the Attorney-General's Department and the Department of Foreign Affairs, in consultation with the Special Adviser on International Law to those two Departments, Sir Kenneth Bailey, the following notes have been prepared in case the Papuan delegation should claim a right on the part of Papua to choose a separate status for the Territory at the stage of independence.

2.   In very summary form, the relevant legal considerations may be stated as follows:

•   Australia's legal authority with respect to the Territory of Papua is a sovereign authority based on sound constitutional grounds.
•   There are no domestic legal considerations that would prevent that sovereign authority being exercised to bring Papua to independence along with New Guinea as a single entity.
•   Also, there are no international legal considerations that would prevent the firm pursuit by the Government of that policy at the present stage.
•   There is nothing in the relevant international instruments that, as a matter of law, would require that the act of self-determination for Papua must take one particular form, such as a plebiscite of the people of the Territory.
•   In pursuit of the Government's policy, the House of Assembly, elected by adult suffrage of the 'administrative union' constituted by the two territories, can properly be looked to, at this stage as being the organ for expressing the wishes of the peoples to have independent status, as a single national unit.
•   The ultimate acceptability of such arrangements could, however, depend upon the approval of the United Nations General Assembly when the matter is presented to it. As a matter of law, that approval would only be required so far as the arrangements affected the status of the Trust Territory of New Guinea. But almost inevitably the General Assembly would also take note of the effect of the arrangements on Papua.

3.   It is to be noted that there are two possible variables in the situation to which the present policy is addressed, one being the attitude in the House of Assembly and the other being the attitude within the United Nations. Present thinking in both bodies, as evidenced by [the] resolution in the House of Assembly and by the conclusions of the Trusteeship Council in 1971, is to favour the national unity of the two Territories. These matters could be drawn upon by the Minister in justifying the maintenance of the policy of the Government.

4.   But if a situation were to develop in which, e.g. the House of Assembly voted by majority for independence against a highly vocal dissent by the Papuan members, United Nations thinking could change. In cases of self-determination, the General Assembly is committed by its own resolutions to give effect to 'the fully expressed wishes of the people concerned'. As a matter of practice, it has sought to do this by United Nations supervised plebiscites, where

---

1   Documents 226 and 228.

there has been a question as to what these wishes were. Whether in the circumstances posed the General Assembly could, as a matter of law, insist upon a plebiscite for Papua would be highly arguable, but the practical effect in the circumstances might be much the same.

5.   Such a possibility indicates that it would be unwise in any discussion with the Papuan declaration to state that the Government will not under any circumstances hold a separate plebiscite for Papua. Rather, if a right to a plebiscite is asserted, it might fairly be observed by the Minister that no one specific form of self-determination is required as a matter of law.

6.   The fact that Papuans are Australian citizens and British subjects does not affect the foregoing legal considerations.

[NAA: A432, 1971/3353]

230   PRESS RELEASE

Canberra, 22 October 1971

Statement by the Minister for External Territories at the Conclusions of His Discussions with a Group of Papuan Parliamentarians

The Minister for External Territories, Mr Barnes, said today that agreement had been reached with a group of Papuan Parliamentarians on the approach to social, economic and political implications for Papua.

One important result of the talks will be a visit to Papua New Guinea by a consultant who will make a study of problems in less developed areas with a view to drawing up a programme of special measures and report to the Administrator's Executive Council and the Minister.

The group consisted of Messrs Oala-Rarua (Assistant Ministerial Member for Treasury), Kapena (Ministerial Member for Labour), Lokoloko (Ministerial Member for Health), Watson (Assistant Ministerial Member for Business Development)[1] and Wabiria (Assistant Ministerial Member for Lands and Surveys).[2]

Mr Barnes had agreed to the visit following a request by the Administrator's Executive Council for discussions about the economic, social and political implications for Papua and Papuans in the movement towards self-government for Papua New Guinea.

Mr Barnes said that the discussions had been very frank and wide-ranging. The main purpose of the group's visit had been to secure special consideration from the Commonwealth for the economic development of Papua. The Commonwealth was asked amongst other things to provide a special development fund for Papua, and to finance a special survey of Papuan resources. The question of constitutional safeguards for Papua in a future independent country was also touched upon and it was agreed that this was an important matter for consideration by a Constitutional Development Select Committee of the next House of Assembly.

The Minister said that the group had gone on record in favour of national unity for Papua New Guinea. In doing so they had confirmed views expressed by the House of Assembly in the past, and by members of the group individually. The talks had therefore taken place against a background of full agreement on the principle of national unity.

The group expressed the view that the people of Papua had not been fully consulted on the future of Papua New Guinea. In particular it was felt that conclusions in the United Nations had been arrived at on the basis of reports of Visiting Missions which had only been to New Guinea. It appeared that this question of consultation had been the basis for the request by the House of Assembly for a Joint Parliamentary Committee to visit Papua.

The Minister assured the group that when considering recent constitutional changes the Government had before it the report of a Select Committee which had visited the whole of Papua New Guinea and which had reported the views of the people in Papua as well as New Guinea. The same would apply before any future constitutional decisions were made.

The Minister acknowledged that the Government was aware that so far as United Nations Missions were concerned the impression could have been created that Papuans were not being fully consulted since the Mission's itineraries were largely confined to the Trust Territory. The Government had agreed in light of this and opinion expressed in the House of Assembly that future Visiting Missions would be invited to visit Papua New Guinea as a whole and report thereon to the General Assembly. In addition, in early 1972 a mission comprising members

---

1   Lepani Watson, MHA for Kula.

2   Andrew Andagari Wabiria, MHA for Koroba.

of the Trusteeship Council and the Committee of 24 will visit Papua New Guinea during the course of the elections. In the light of this the Minister felt that no purpose could be served by the visit of a Parliamentary Committee, but he pointed out that individual members of the Commonwealth Parliament make frequent visits to Papua New Guinea. He believed that these visits should include Papuan areas so that members could learn at first hand from discussion in the villages what the people thought about the future of their country.

The group had raised the question of regional authorities for Papua New Guinea which it felt would help to protect minority groups and through which local government could make its demands known to the central government. The Minister noted the views of the group and it was agreed that this was a matter for a select committee on constitutional development of the next House.

The group had drawn to his attention what they believed to be the economic disadvantages suffered by Papuans in the allocation of resources under the 5 year development programme.

This was the reason for the proposed special development fund for Papua. Members of the group submitted details of projects which they thought suitable for financing from such a fund, emphasising that in their view decisions should not be made solely on economic criteria but should also take political and social considerations into account. Amongst the projects were a road link between Papua and New Guinea, the development of the forestry, fish and cattle industries. The group also enquired about an air service between Australia and Daru. The Minister said he anticipated an announcement on this in the next few weeks.

The group discussed the enormous hydro-electric potential of the Purari River system. The exploitation of this potential was presently under serious consideration. The power which could be produced would be in excess of 6,000 mw., which in terms of the amount of the power would be larger than the Snowy River Scheme. The project was still under investigation. The cost of developing it is very substantial but it could fairly be said that if it eventuates the portion of Papua would be revolutionised economically by attracting industrial and manufacturing development in the area. The group also discussed a possible substantial copper mining project developing in the Western District. It was also noted in the discussions that the Cape Rodney timber venture was proving a successful enterprise.

These indicate that the medium and long-term prospects were most encouraging and the group expressed a hope that the question of developing these projects would be a high priority.

The Minister assured the group that while the Administration accepted the responsibility of ensuring that less well-endowed areas did not suffer in the allocation of development funds this question involved budgetary implications and in this field the Administrator's Executive Council was accepting an increasing responsibility. The Minister agreed that in any developing country the advancement of the less developed areas was a special and difficult problem.

He therefore agreed that a special study will be made, by a consultant, of the problem of these areas in Papua New Guinea with a view to drawing up a programme of special measures to assist them and to report to the Administrator's Executive Council and the Minister.

In addition the Minister said he would ask the Administrator to carry out an examination of the ways of enlarging the scope of the Rural Development Programme to give special consideration to the less well-endowed and remote districts of Papua New Guinea. The examination agreed to by the Minister would include the possibility of the fund being applied in under-privileged areas on social projects and other items which may not be of a predominantly economic character. The Minister would look to the Administrator's Executive Council for recommendations on this matter.

In respect of economic development broadly and of the development of national institutions the Minister emphasised the need for decisions to be taken by a central government in the light of a national development plan based on national aspirations.

On the question of a special resources survey for Papua, the Minister said that much work had been done already with the preparation of draft Development Programmes for each district. At the request of the group he would ask the Administration to ensure that this was brought to notice in Local Government Councils and in Area Authorities so that grass roots views could be brought to bear and he pointed out that a full scale resources survey would be given consideration in the light of the costs.

The group indicated that it was in favour of foreign investment in accordance with existing policy in the development of Papua and the Minister welcomes their attitude.

[NAA: A1838, 3080/1/2/3 PART 1A]

231   LETTER FROM WHEELER TO SHANN

Canberra, 27 October 1971

I refer to Sir Keith Waller's letter 1428/117 of 8 October 1971[1] addressed to Mr Hay, concerning the future arrangements in relation to Papua/New Guinea as it moves towards self-government and independence. A copy of the letter was forwarded to me for my views on the several matters discussed in it.

The most important matter raised in the letter seems to be the question of the policy machinery for future Commonwealth/Papua/New Guinea relations. I am in full agreement with the view expressed in the letter that there must be a coordinated approach so that there is a smooth transition from one stage to the next. In the period leading up to independence, the prime responsibility rests with the Department of External Territories while after independence your Department will assume its customary role of dealing with the independent government. There will, of necessity, have to be close consultation, as I understand has already been the case, between the Department of External Territories and your Department and with other interested parties. I am not sure, however, that a high level policy committee of the type I imagine Sir Keith has in mind would necessarily be the best way to achieve the desired result.

The interests of the various departments and other organisations concerned are quite different and will wax and wane according to the stage reached in the movement towards an independent Papua/New Guinea. The Board, for example, is vitally interested in such matters as machinery of government and the organisational arrangements for the departments involved in Papua/New Guinea both before and after independence. It is not, on the other hand, directly concerned with such issues as the kind of treaty relationship which might exist between the two countries. In these circumstances to establish a continuing high-powered committee akin to the Japan Committee could be wasteful of resources. It would seem to me that full and complete consultations could be arranged with the particular departments directly involved on an ad hoc basis without the need for formal committee machinery. The Board and its officers would, of course, be available to participate in such consultations as the occasion demanded.

With regard to the two related accommodation matters to which Sir Keith referred, I agree with the basic division of responsibility he has suggested and with the need for early planning. My only comment is to suggest that at an appropriate stage you will need to involve the Overseas Property Bureau in the planning and acquisition of the future High Commission.

[NAA: A1838, 3080/10/2 PART 1]

---

1   Document 225.

232   LETTER FROM JOSEPH[1] TO WALLER

New York, 2 November 1971

SECRET

Australian Aid Policies

In memorandum No. 1781[2] we referred to some aspects of Australian contributions to multilateral aid agencies. The following supplements that memorandum but is forwarded separately since it reflects primarily the views of the undersigned. On the other hand, the view—that the allocation of more than three-quarters of Australian bilateral aid to Papua New Guinea represents a major distortion in Australian aid patterns—was expressed independently to the undersigned by Mr Bowen during a discussion at a social function last month when the Minister was here for the United Nations General Assembly.

2.   The historical reasons for the existing allocations are recognised and there is the fact of our colonial presence in PNG and the concomitant obligation Australia feels to fulfil its 'special responsibilities' towards the territory. Russell Hill[3] papers on PNG also stress the defence and strategic importance of PNG to Australia. However, we also have the impression that the case for the proportion of assistance going to PNG has never been carefully argued, at least in terms of what interests might be served by an alternative allocation under which other countries, of existing and certainly potentially more importance to us, would receive a greater share of Australian aid resources. Such a distribution could be achieved by levelling off the assistance provided to PNG at its existing level or if this is politically impractical, limiting the annual increases of assistance to PNG to say 4%–5% in lieu of the 10% annual increment which has become a norm in recent years. In the view of the undersigned, it is a truism that Indonesia, Malaysia, Thailand, and probably Singapore and even perhaps the Philippines, are all intrinsically more important to Australia's long term political and strategic interests than PNG, with its small population, but which happens to be a colonial territory and which occupies a position close to the Northern Queensland coast.

3.   As to the question of Australia's special responsibility, why should it be more special to assist people of PNG rather than the equally poor people, indeed poorer people, of Indonesia? [What of the views of][4] the United Nations? It is recognised that in relation to its administration of Papua New Guinea Australia finally seems to have won the UN on side; and it would be a pity to erode this sympathy now as a result of shortfalls in Australia's financial assistance for economic and social progress in PNG. However, as will be seen from the attached table,[5] PNG already receives assistance per capita almost double that of the next ranking country. Indeed, with the possible exception of American Micronesia, it is difficult to think of any country in the world which has had proportionately the amount of internal help which Australia has lavished on PNG in recent years. This fact, of course, is no guarantee of an easy passage for Australia in the UN. But it does place us in a strong position to answer charges about our performance, and there would seem to be scope for easing PNG down a few notches in the scale of aid priorities without necessarily provoking criticism at the UN. In any case, over

---

1   Lance Joseph, Counsellor, Australian Mission to the United Nations, New York.

2   Not published.

3   That is, the Australian Department of Defence, which has its headquarters in the Canberra suburb of Russell.

4   Editorial insertion.

5   Not published.

the longer term it is the opinion of the countries like Indonesia, Malaysia and Thailand which we should most value, and not those of the countries who stage-manage the Committee of Twenty-four in New York.

4.   What about the defence argument? Papers prepared for the Defence Committee in 1968 on the strategic importance of PNG to Australia emphasised two points. One was that PNG provided a base for Australian military operations and that this was important in carrying out our defence obligations to the territory. Need one comment on the circular nature of this line of reasoning? The second argument was based on the threat concept that a PNG in hostile hands would provide a jumping off point from which to strike against Australia. Even if it is accepted that this scenario has some semblance of credibility, one can question whether such large allocations of Australian aid will secure a well-disposed government in an independent PNG. However, one also needs to question whether it is likely that PNG could be used as a platform from which to launch attacks against Australia. The idea of invasion fleets crossing the ocean or bomber squadrons launching long range attacks against the sinews of Australian defence production seems far-fetched. A major deterrent to such action would be ANZUS. And while the alliance has been questioned in response to the obvious signs of military fatigue in the United States, it has also been accepted that this fatigue relates primarily to the commitment by the United States of ground forces to new military actions, rather than the deployment of air/sea forces. This emerges clearly from the public pronouncements about the Guam Doctrine.[6] But, even ignoring ANZUS, it can be argued that a hostile power could inflict equal damage on Australia by launching an attack from Merauke or other West Irian centres as from Pt. Moresby so that on this argument we have no less reason to support the independent government of President Soeharto than our charges in PNG. The strategic advantages of helping the former is that Indonesia could offer a bulwark in a way that PNG could never do, against penetration from hostile forces located farther north.

5.   One might add that in terms of Australia's defence posture it is precisely the presence in PNG where we are most over-exposed. Whereas amphibious and air invasions seem a thing of the past, this is not the case with regard to land conflicts in Asia where the exact degree of overt aggression can be blurred and where the difficulty of the terrain makes it particularly hard for regular forces to counter guerrilla-type activities or forays by lightly armed irregulars. It is, of course, precisely that kind of terrain that we have on the PNG/West Irian border, and the undersigned for one, has always had a nagging doubt that an independent government in Pt. Moresby might drag Australia into some new confrontation with Indonesia through troubles on the border. No doubt one of the most controversial matters during the negotiation of PNG's final independence will be whether Australia will provide an open-ended defence guarantee. If political considerations, both domestic and in the territory, force this on Australia, it may be possible to reduce the dangers by seeking to involve Indonesia in some way with the guarantee, perhaps through some tripartite consultative arrangement. Apart from thereby recognising Indonesia's interest in the security of PNG, it could be a useful way of ensuring

---

6   The Guam Doctrine—also known as the Nixon Doctrine—was promulgated by US President Richard Nixon in mid–1969 and established that the United States would help with 'the defense and development of allies and friends' but 'cannot—and will not—conceive of all the plans, design all the programs, execute all the decisions and undertake all the defense of the free nations of the world'. At the time, the DEA recognised that Washington had 'downgraded the threat of Communist-inspired expansion in Asia ... and that the United States military and economic involvement in the region will also be sharply downgraded on the list of United States foreign policy priorities'. It concluded that Asian and Pacific nations—including Australia—'will be left progressively more to their own resources'. Cited in Neville Meaney, 'The United States', in W. J. Hudson (ed.), *Australia in World Affairs, 1971–1975*, George Allen and Unwin, Sydney, 1980, p. 164.

that the Papuans could not invoke an automatic clause in a treaty whereby Australia would be obligated to move in support of PNG's defence in any troubles which may erupt with their large neighbour.

6.   But this, of course, is another matter. Here the point to underline is that an allocation of Australian assistance which provides $140 million to a country of 2½ million people and only $20 million to an enormously more important country of 120 million people is on the surface a distortion of aid priorities. It is worth asking the question how much aid would the territory receive from Australian sources if its history had been different and it had remained a British colony. Yet it would be occupying precisely the same geographic strategic location as it does today.

7.   As I say, I have been led to advance these observations since the Minister also apparently shares some of the feeling behind them. The Minister would no doubt also accept, however, that political realities make it unlikely that much can in fact be done to correct the imbalance in aid allocations in the short-term. The fact that the Government has endorsed the 1968 New Guinea development plan means that we are already inescapably committed to a rising level of financial support for the territory. And it is probably wishful thinking to believe that this support will do other than generate continuing requirements in the future. At some time PNG may develop a viable and self-contained economy, but all recent projections indicate that it will remain a substantial burden on the Australian taxpayer for years to come, including in the period after independence.

8.   It should be reiterated that the purpose of this memorandum is not to advocate a reduction in the existing level of economic assistance to PNG but rather a levelling off in the annual rate of increase, and a corresponding increase in the amounts of aid provided to Australia's other near neighbours, particularly Indonesia. Despite the obvious political obstacles, we need to guard against allowing PNG to become a sacred cow. This used to be the way that the British Government looked on their military base in Singapore. Yet, after a few calculations of costs and benefits, the British were able, almost overnight, to overturn Singapore in their scale of military priorities. It would be a pity if Australia were not prepared to be equally flexible in its thinking about PNG. At the very least, since we choose to present internationally our assistance to PNG and assistance elsewhere as one, it would be logical and legitimate that the Department of External Territories should be required to bid against our own Department for its share in the overall aid cake. Such recourse may not result in any immediate benefits for the independent countries of South East Asia, but the discipline imposed, and the need to provide cogent arguments in support of various aid allocations, could lead within a few years to a point where the allocation of Australian aid and assistance was more neatly tailored to Australia's overall political and strategic objectives.

[NAA: A1838, 689/1 PART 6]

233   RECORD OF MEETING

Canberra, 3 November 1971

Papua New Guinea—Programme of Future Work

Record of main points arising from a meeting between Permanent Heads of Defence, External Territories and Army on Wednesday, 3rd November, 1971.

In attendance

Sir Arthur Tange,	Secretary, Department of Defence
Mr D. O. Hay,	Secretary, Department of External Territories
Mr B. White,	Secretary, Department of the Army
Admiral Sir Victor Smith,	Chairman, Chiefs of Staff Committee
Major General R.L. Hughes,	Director, Joint Staff, Department of Defence
Mr P. J. Galvin,	Assistant Secretary, Department of External Territories
Mr R. W. Law-Smith,	Chief Executive Officer, Defence Planning Division, Department of Defence

Subjects discussed were planning assumptions for constitutional development in Papua New Guinea; establishment and terms of reference for a working party to consider future defence departmental organisations in PNG (Study No. 12) and outline guidance for a study of the future role and employment of PNG forces (Study No. 13).

Assumptions for constitutional development

2.   Sir Arthur Tange directed attention to the existing assumptions for use in all studies under the programme.

3.   Mr Hay explained that Territories' planning was proceeding on the departmental assumption (noted by the Minister) that self-government would occur during 1975. A flexible planning programme capable of adjustment in response to local wishes was in preparation. A submission would be made to Cabinet early in 1972 scheduling tasks to be accomplished to permit self-government by that time. The elections would be held in February/March 1972 (again in 1976) and a new Administrator's Executive Council will be established in April/May 1972. The Administrator expects the return of a majority of conservatively inclined members and that, in practice, local Ministers will not wish actively to discuss self-government with the Commonwealth until after a settling-in period of about twelve months duration.

4.   Territories had no clear assumption about a date for independence but they were proposing to suggest to the European Economic Community 1977/78 as a possible period for termination of existing rates of entry to the British market of tropical products from Papua New Guinea. While 1977/78 seemed a reasonable guess at a date for independence, it was generally recognised that the period between self-government and independence is likely to be short.

5.   Sir Arthur Tange said that preparatory work in the defence field was directed toward independence and that that date, rather than the date of self-government, was the significant one for defence planners and defence decisions. Australia would necessarily retain responsibility for defence and control of forces up to independence day. In the absence of a clear assumption by Territories, Defence would have to make one, without commitment to the Government.

We would need to inform the Minister for Defence accordingly. He remarked also on the inevitability, sooner or later, of this assumption being leaked and of the Government having to face up to public scrutiny, possibly misinformed or even mischievous, of its timetable for constitutional change in PNG.

6.   Following discussion of possible time tables it was agreed that at least for the programme of PNG studies the following should be assumed

- • Self Government in 1975
- • Independence in 1976/77

The time span of twenty four months implicit in the dates assumed for independence was clearly necessary because we can only guess at what responsible PNG opinion and Australian Parliamentary attitudes will be at that time towards independence.

7.   Sir Arthur Tange observed that flexible interpretation and application of these guidelines was essential. He suggested also that consideration be given to preparation of a statement for public use by Ministers and others in replies to any questioning. This might take the form of a statement of dates being used by officials but with the qualification, clearly stated, that assumptions are being made, without commitment, for essential planning purposes, about decisions clearly the prerogative of, and to be taken by, elected PNG leaders. The assumptions would be varied as experience and indications of emerging local views dictated. But the subject of public handling is difficult and needs more thought.

[*matter omitted*]

15. Sir Arthur Tange suggested that in addressing ourselves to the questions raised we should not be impressed by a belief that the Australian system was necessarily appropriate to PNG.[1] We must ask ourselves, what does PNG require for good government and administration and what concessions may have to be made to the peculiarities of the PNG situation? For instance, what will be the relative ages, experience and capabilities, in 1976/77, of contenders for the top military and civilian positions in the Department?

[*matter omitted*]

[NAA: A452, 1972/1111]

---

1   See also Documents 158 & 167.

234   STATEMENT BY BARNES[1]

Canberra, 4 November 1971

Papua New Guinea Bill 1971

[*matter omitted*]

The purpose of this Bill is to give effect to certain recommendations made by the Papua New Guinea House of Assembly Select Committee on Constitutional Development and agreed to by that House.

The Select Committee on Constitutional Development was set up by the Papua New Guinea House of Assembly on 24th June, 1969.[2] Its task was to draft a set of constitutional proposals as a guide for future constitutional development in Papua New Guinea. The Committee presented three interim reports, and made its final report to the House of Assembly on 4th March, 1971.[3] Both the final report, and the third interim report presented on 3rd September, 1970, contained recommendations for constitutional change. The Committee's recommendations were adopted by the House on 11th March, 1971, with the exception of the proposed name of 'Niugini', which was later amended, and the drafting of a Bill of Rights, which was deferred.

In a statement to this House on 27th April, 1971,[4] I outlined the recommendations of the Select Committee. I also informed the House that the Government had accepted these recommendations.

As a result, the Government is now preparing a programme for movement to full internal self-government in the period 1972–76. The execution of this programme will have regard to the state of opinion as it develops after the 1972 House of Assembly elections and to the policies of the political leaders who then emerge.

The Government also placed before this House in May 1971, amendments to the Papua and New Guinea Act which gave effect to the Select Committee's recommendations or changes in the elected representation in the House of Assembly.[5] The amendment to the Papua and New Guinea Act at that time provided for the recommended increases in the number of open and regional electorates for the House of Assembly from 69 to 82 and from 15 to 18 respectively, and was introduced in advance of the present proposals to allow the necessary electoral redistribution to be carried out before the elections for the 1972–76 House of Assembly in February–March, 1972.[6]

In my statement on 27th April, 1971, I referred to a further group of recommendations which would be the subject of later amending legislation. These I will deal with now. One recommendation in this group is for a change in the name of the Territory. The Select Committee recommended the name 'Niugini'. This was rejected by the House, and at a later sitting the House unanimously adopted a private member's motion that the word 'and' be deleted from 'Papua and New Guinea'. The Territory would be then known as 'Papua New Guinea'. Clause 5 of the Bill provides that the Territory of Papua and the Territory of New Guinea shall be together described in the Act, and in other laws and instruments, as 'Papua

---

1   The statement was made in the House of Representatives.

2   See Stuart Doran (ed.), *Documents on Australian Foreign Policy: Australia and Papua New Guinea, 1966–1969*, Australian Department of Foreign Affairs and Trade, Canberra, 2006, Documents 261, 263, 269–270, 275–276, 283 & 289.

3   Document 142.

4   Document 160.

5   The amendments were actually placed before the House in April. See Document 162.

6   This amendment was passed by the Australian Parliament and then assented to in May 1971.

New Guinea' rather than the 'Territory of Papua and New Guinea' and other amendments also effect this change of name.[7]

Clause 10 of the Bill gives effect to recommendations on the composition of the Administrator's Executive Council. It will be composed of the Administrator, 10 Ministers and three official members. The effect of this change is to add three Ministers to the seven previously in the Council and to eliminate the one member previously nominated by the Administrator without reference to the House of Assembly. The seventeen Ministers of the House of Assembly will choose one of their number to be the Deputy Chairman of the Administrator's Executive Council, this choice to be approved by the House of Assembly. Although nominated members of the House of Assembly may be appointed as Ministers, not more than two such members may be members of the Administrator's Executive Council.

The Select Committee report was silent on the method of choosing the Ministers to sit on the Administrator's Executive Council, with the exception of the Deputy Chairman. The Bill provides that this will be a matter for the Minister for External Territories to determine on the advice of the Administrator, who will consult the Deputy Chairman.

I propose, in addition, to consult with the Deputy Chairman through the Administrator in the allocation of the portfolios to the Ministers, and in any subsequent changes in portfolios that may be necessary.

These provisions will give the Deputy Chairman an important part in the selection of members of the Administrator's Executive Council and in the allocation of Ministerial responsibilities.

Clauses 12–15 deal with Ministers and Ministerial offices.

In its third interim report of September, 1970, the Select Committee recommended 'that the offices of Ministerial Member and Assistant Ministerial Member be abolished and replaced by up to seventeen offices of Ministers of the House of Assembly of such respective designations as the Minister for External Territories from time to time determines'.

The titles 'Ministerial Member' and 'Assistant Ministerial Member' were used because the office holders did not when first appointed in 1968 exercise full executive authority nor take final decisions in respect of their areas of responsibility. However, since August 1970, all ministerial office holders have exercised final responsibility in respect of a wide range of governmental matters specified in the arrangements approved under section 25 of the Papua and New Guinea Act. The change of name therefore reflects a change of function already introduced.

Clause 13 of the Bill provides for the replacement of the offices of ministerial member, and assistant ministerial member, with up to seventeen offices of Minister of the House of Assembly.

The Select Committee recommended that the House of Assembly should, after the next elections, be composed of not less than 104 members and not more than 107 members, as follows:

    18 persons elected by the people to represent regional electorates;

    82 persons elected by the people to represent open electorates;

    up to 3 nominated members, nominated by the House of Assembly for special purposes; and

    four official members, appointed by the Governor-General on the Administrator's nomination;

---

7   This amendment was passed by the Australian Parliament and then assented to in December 1971.

and Clause 16 of the Bill so provides. The recommended increase in the elected membership from 84 to 100 was provided for in the amendments to the Papua and New Guinea Act earlier this year and these provisions are merely re-enacted now. At the time of the earlier amendment no change was made in the number of official members in the House nor was provision made for nominated members.

Another of the Committee's recommendations is the creation of not more than three positions of nominated member of the House of Assembly which is provided under Clause 17 of the Bill. The inclusion of non-elected nominated members in the House is a new concept in Papua New Guinea but there is a widespread feeling in Papua New Guinea of the need to provide a means for the representation of special groups, for example, women, or persons having a special expertise, in the legislature.[8] As recommended by the Committee the Bill provides for the House to decide itself whether these positions should be filled. A two-thirds vote of the total members of the House is required to agree to the setting up of a seven-man committee of the House to choose the nominated member or members. When the committee in consultation with the Administrator, has chosen a person or persons, their choice must be endorsed by a simple majority of the Members of the House present and voting. The committee would cease to operate after it had chosen the person or persons concerned. The procedure of selecting nominated members is similar to the existing method of selecting ministerial office holders.

The Bill also sets out in clauses 17 to 19 the conditions of eligibility for nominated members. To qualify for appointment as a nominated member, a person must have lived in Papua New Guinea for not less than five years. A defeated candidate at the general elections for the House to which members are to be nominated is not eligible for nomination. Should a nominated member chosen by the committee be a public servant or a holder of a statutory office he must resign his position to accept appointment. Once a person has accepted nomination to the House, he will hold office on the same basis as if he were an elected Member of the House. These provisions accord with the recommendations of the Select Committee.

The Committee's recommendation to create the positions of nominated member arose in conjunction with its wish to reduce the number of official members in the House from 10 to 4, who are appointed by the Governor-General on the nomination of the Administrator.

The reduction in the number of official members from 10 to 4 is effected by clause 16 of the Bill and is in keeping with the responsibilities of Ministerial office holders. Four official members remain to ensure that Government business regarding matters still under the control of the Commonwealth is introduced in the House, and to explain Commonwealth Government matters to the members.

The other clauses of the Bill are of a machinery nature and arise from the creation of the position of Deputy Chairman, the change in name and the provisions for nominated members and Ministers of the House of Assembly.

Clause 27 of the Bill validates the National Identity Ordinance 1971 to remove beyond doubt the validity of that legislation. On 18 June 1971, the House of Assembly made the National Identity Ordinance 1971 which provides among other things, for the name of the administrative union of the Territory of Papua and the Territory of New Guinea to be known as Papua New Guinea. As the name for the administrative union is provided for under the Papua and New Guinea Act the National Identity Ordinance, in so far as it purports to alter the name, could be invalid. Likewise publication of notices in the Papua New Guinea Government Gazette could be ineffective. This validation clause has therefore been inserted to remove all possible doubt.

---

8   For background on this proposal, see Document 142, fn. 6 & Document 155, paras 23–27. In the event, no
     nominated members were appointed.

The purpose of the Bill, as I have indicated to honourable members, is to give effect to the remaining recommendations of the House of Assembly Select Committee on Constitutional Development as approved by that House. The amendments contained in this Bill give legislative effect to the request by the House of Assembly for changes in the constitutional framework for Papua New Guinea.

I commend the Bill to honourable members.[9]

[*CPD*, HR, vol. 74, 4 November 1971, pp. 3033–35]

235   TELEX FROM HAY TO JOHNSON

Canberra, 4 November 1971

Unclassified

Last week you asked me whether the Minister would wish to address a final message to the coming meeting of the House of Assembly.

I have discussed the matter with the Minister. He does not wish to have a separate personal message delivered. He is content that you should address the House in appropriate terms and that you should include in your address a message of appreciation on behalf of the Government, broadly in terms of the immediately following text.

'The Minister has asked me to convey to you his very deep appreciation for the work of the House of Assembly over the past four years. He made particular mention of some of the more important highlights of this very busy and productive period for which all members deserve great credit. The establishment of the Administrator's Executive Council and the appointment of Ministerial office holders together with the subsequent transfer to them of final authority over a wide range of very important areas of government was a most significant step, as was the report of the Select Committee on Constitutional Development whose recommendations have led to a programme of development to prepare Papua New Guinea for internal self-government during 1972–76 if this is in fact wanted by the people at this time, and to amendments to the Papua New Guinea Act to provide the structure for the next House and its executive.

'The Australian Government is most gratified that the people of Papua New Guinea, through their democratically elected representatives in the House of Assembly, are able to take such initiatives and make such progress.

'Papua New Guinea is now indeed well along the road towards full internal self-government, and on behalf of the Australian Government and the Australian people the Minister wishes you every success in the future, when the crucial issues concerning the emergence of Papua New Guinea as a united country and independent nation will have to be considered and determined by the House.'

The Minister would like you to consider including in your own address, and not as part of a government message, one or two themes that have been uppermost in his mind over the past four years. One such theme would be the need for members of the House, both those holding ministerial office and others, on occasion to take the lead in standing out for a national approach to issues even when this conflicted with local interests of their electorates. Another theme might be the necessity for the House of Assembly to bear responsibility in the future

---

9   Parliament passed the bill later in 1971 without any significant changes.

for constitutional development, as it has in the past. A possible draft of what might be said on these two themes [is] in the following text:

'For my part, I must again stress the necessity for the House of Assembly to continue to bear responsibility in the future for constitutional development. The relationship between the future central government of Papua New Guinea and its constituent parts will have to be given the closest attention in the life of the next House as will the means by which the interests of the less populous and less developed areas can be adequately protected.

'The matters will require all members of the House, both those holding ministerial office and others, to take the lead in standing out for a national approach to issues even when this conflicts with the local interests of their electorates.

'It will be of the utmost importance that not only the AEC and the ministry, but the House as a whole continue to maintain a broad national view and I am confident that this is what it will continue to do. In establishing the foundations for democratic self-government Papuans and New Guineans will, by united effort and determination, go forward to build a nation which can take its place in the world at large.'

[NAA: A452, 1971/3543]

236   LETTER FROM HAY TO WHITE

Canberra, 5 November 1971

I regret that your letter of 30th September[1] regarding your visit to Port Moresby to examine the progress and problems in building up a local departmental staff for Army functions has not been acknowledged earlier.

Your comments on the need for localisation of Army departmental staff are of great interest to me in view of the recent announcement of an accelerated localisation training plan for the Papua New Guinea Public Service. In most areas of Commonwealth interest the need for localisation will parallel that of the Administration and your proposals are timely.

I would agree that your proposal to secure a reasonably senior, experienced local officer to understudy the Command Secretary must be accorded a high priority in your localisation efforts and I would support the line of your discussions with officers of the Public Service Board that a member of the first Senior Executive Programme might be allocated to the Department of the Army. I would also support your proposal to sponsor local undergraduates under the cadetship scheme.

Both these steps can play a part in making a start to localise higher level positions. At the same time the effort has to continue at all levels according to priorities resolved by your Department and I do most strongly approve of your movements towards localisation at all levels.

I would be pleased to offer the assistance of officers of my Department in pursuing the arrangements you have discussed with the Papua New Guinea Public Service Board and in formulating your overall localisation plans. Mr L. F. Hennessy, Assistant Secretary, Social Development Branch and Mr A. J. Sutherland, Assistant Secretary, Public Employment Branch, would be available to work with your officers on these matters.

Following discussions in Canberra last week between the Commonwealth Public Service Board, the Papua New Guinea Public Service Board and this Department it is proposed to hold a meeting later this month with representatives of Commonwealth departments to discuss the present situation regarding the absorption of Commonwealth local employees into the Papua New Guinea Public Service. Localisation and intensified training measures including cadetships will be discussed at the meeting. We will be in touch with your Department shortly about representation and the timing of the meeting.

I will be writing to you separately regarding the development of the Australian School of Pacific Administration to support the localisation training effort in Papua New Guinea and possible cooperation between the Army and the Department to achieve this end.

[NAA: A452, 1971/1664]

---

1   Document 221.

237   LETTER FROM SNEDDEN TO BARNES

Canberra, 9 November 1971

I concur in the proposal set out in your letter of 7 October 1971[1] that the Administrator of Papua New Guinea be provided with some background material to be cleared by representatives of our two Departments as well as the Reserve Bank—which would enable him to answer any questions that might be put to him by indigenous members of his Executive Council regarding possible future currency arrangements for the Territory when it becomes independent.

The question of currency is, as I feel sure you would agree, a delicate one with important political and psychological ramifications not just for the local and overseas businessmen who have invested in Papua New Guinea in the past or who might be contemplating such action in the future but also for the indigenous people themselves, many of whom, so I understand, are a little wary of Australia's future intentions in the light of recent political developments in the Territory.

For these reasons, I believe that we should be careful not to seek to influence the wishes of the local people on this particular question one way or the other at the present time although I would agree with you that we ought to stand ready to respond fairly quickly to any widely based desire on the part of members of the new House of Assembly that Papua New Guinea should have a separate currency in the future.

[NAA: A452, 1971/4971

---

1   Document 224. See also Document 220.

238   LETTER FROM BORDER TO HAY

Canberra, 10 November 1971

UN Mission to Observe 1972 Elections in Papua New Guinea

Please refer to our memorandum 909/8/7 of 14th September 1971 from New York attaching memo 1395 and your reply of 11th October 1971.[1]

2.   We strongly support the Ambassador's proposal that the UN Visiting Mission should spend longer than two weeks in Papua New Guinea [...][2]

3.   Since the Ambassador wrote, there have been developments which reinforce his case. The Peoples Republic of China (PRC) has replaced the Republic of China (ROC) in the United Nations, and therefore PRC will have taken the place of the ROC when the Trusteeship Council meets next year to consider the report of the Visiting Mission. He will appreciate that the PRC might subject us to a more rigorous examination than we have had in recent years. It is doubly important therefore not to leave any loopholes.

4.   In view of the important decisions which will be taken by the Third House of Assembly it is important to Papua New Guinea and to Australia that the House be accepted internationally as truly representative of the people of Papua New Guinea. If the Mission is not in Papua New

---

1   Not published.

2   In his memorandum of 21 May (Document 175), McIntyre had referred to a visit 'of two to three weeks'. DFA replied that the UN mission 'should be in Papua New Guinea for about one week before and one week after' the day on which polling closed, and McIntyre had extended the invitation on this basis. A number of delegations had responded that this would allow insufficient time, so McIntyre then proposed, subject to confirmation by Canberra, that the mission arrive ten days to a fortnight before the final day of polling. McIntyre's thinking had then evolved following the announcement of election dates, with polling to begin on 12 February and finish on 11 March. As set out in a memorandum of 8 September 1971, he had come to the view that it would be better not 'to restrict the visiting mission's presence … to a period of half or less of the voting time'. He noted that Australia had gained 'considerable goodwill here [New York]' from the invitation, and argued that 'it would be a pity if some of this, and some of the international standing we seek to obtain for the House which will be elected next year, is lost through a report which might begin: "The Mission arrived in Papua New Guinea when the elections to the House of Assembly were more than half completed"'.

McIntyre noted there were two main reasons why Canberra might wish to restrict the time spent by the mission in Papua New Guinea. One reason was 'the fear that the mission might in some way interfere in the election'. He did not regard this as a serious problem, noting that 'we put to the Council and the Special Committee your warnings about interference, and these were accepted fully'. The mission would comprise officials from the United States and the United Kingdom, representing the members of the Trusteeship Council, and from Afghanistan and Yugoslavia, informally representing the members of the Committee of Twenty-Four. McIntyre noted that the 'likely Afghan nominee' and the 'probable Yugoslav nominee' were both 'well-disposed towards us and will I feel sure seek to be as fair and objective as were Raouf and Wyse this year' (see Documents 145 & 146). He did not comment on the UK and US representatives, presumably because they could be expected to support Australia.

The second possible reason for a shorter rather than a longer visit concerned the 'great deal of work involved for Administration officers in preparing itineraries and briefing papers, setting up appointments and then handling the mission after arrival'. He pointed out, however, that much of the work would be done in advance of the mission's arrival, and that the disruption to normal activities in each location visited would only last for two or three days, concluding that 'it should not be proportionately more arduous to arrange and carry out a five-week visit than a three-week one'. See Memorandum 1395, McIntyre to DFA, 8 September 1971, NAA: A452, 1971/2303.

Guinea for the whole period of the elections, it might take the line that it cannot unreservedly endorse the new House of Assembly. We believe this should be avoided by every possible means.

5.   We appreciate that it will not be possible to draw up a firm itinerary until the end of November. However, if the members of the Mission are to plan on a five week visit, rather than a two week one, they will need notice in order to make the necessary arrangements.

6.   I therefore suggest that the Australian Ambassador to the United Nations be authorised as soon as possible to invite the Mission to observe the whole election, involving a visit of approximately 5 weeks. The detailed itinerary and final arrival and departure times could be advised later. Since less than three months are left before the Mission is due to arrive, urgent agreement to this proposal would be appreciated.[3]

[NAA: A452, 1971/2303]

---

3   The UN visit went ahead over a longer period in accordance with DFA's recommendation to DET.

239   SUBMISSION FROM HAY TO BARNES

Canberra, 17 November 1971

CONFIDENTIAL

Suggestion by Foreign Affairs Department for Inter-Departmental Committee on Policy towards Papua New Guinea

Before he left for overseas last month, Sir Keith Waller wrote to me[1] suggesting, amongst other things, 'a basic policy committee in Canberra at the very senior departmental level ...', under the chairmanship of this Department. The purpose of the committee would be to ensure that policies in relation to developments in Papua New Guinea were coordinated and also that Foreign Affairs had the opportunity, as a member of the committee, for early involvement in decisions the results of which, as Sir Keith puts it, they would have to cope with after independence.

2.   Sir Keith said he wished to place the matter before his Minister[2] and has sought my reactions. I have at this stage only acknowledged his proposal.[3]

3.   Sir Keith gave two reasons for his proposal.

4.   The first is the need for coordination and 'a comprehensive approach'. He implies that such an approach has not been forthcoming under this Department's planning so far. The second reason is that Foreign Affairs will ultimately have overall responsibility for dealing with an independent government and 'the sooner Foreign Affairs is involved with all the relevant actions and decisions, the simpler will be our task after independence'.

5.   Neither reason is very convincing. Foreign Affairs overlook the fact that coordination and planning are precisely the responsibility of this Department, under your direction. They make no reference to Cabinet's approval of the report of the Select Committee on the Constitution which specifically:

'authorised the Department of External Territories, in consultation with the Administration and other Departments and Authorities concerned, to draw up a flexible programme of movement towards internal [full] self-government, [which includes] the kinds of political and economic relations which should exist with Australia [at] internal self-government, for consideration by Cabinet at an early date as a basis for negotiation with the leadership group emerging from the 1972 elections'.[4]

The Department has been heavily engaged in preparing the programme and we have made considerable progress, in consultation with the Administration. In short we are at the point now where we are able to submit outline plans to interested departments for their comments. We have in mind to do this between now and the end of the year, with the object of preparing final draft submissions for discussion with you and, if you are in agreement, for submission to Cabinet in January, 1972.

6.   The programme is being prepared and will be presented in such a way that Cabinet will be able to consider as a whole, and in perspective, all the steps which will have to be taken by the Commonwealth and by the Administration before internal self-government.

---

1   Document 225.

2   Nigel Bowen.

3   Document 227.

4   See Document 159.

7.   The programme is to include reference to 'the kind of political and economic relations which should exist with Australia at self-government'. We have in mind suggesting to you that this would be the subject of a separate submission which would set out current decisions and policies and seek Cabinet endorsement of broad guidelines against which the various steps in the programme would be taken.

8.   The second reason given by Sir Keith is a somewhat specious one. While it may be said that Foreign Affairs has an interest in being involved in matters which will affect Australia's future relationships with Papua New Guinea, it has no need to become involved in the many decisions which are of an internal character, such as banking, broadcasting, etc.

9.   My first reaction is therefore that no encouragement should be given to the idea of a formal inter-departmental committee with a very broad range of functions suggested by Sir Keith Waller. However you will recall that in the middle of 1970 Sir Keith put a somewhat similar proposal to Sir John Bunting as Secretary to the Cabinet and through him, with his then Minister's concurrence, to the then Prime Minister. Mr Gorton gave a very firm refusal.[5] However Sir John Bunting himself was in favour of some such body. It could well be therefore that the Prime Minister himself, the head of his Department, and the Minister and Secretary of Foreign Affairs will be of one mind in relation to Sir Keith's present proposal.

10. Given the background as stated above, my disposition is to recommend your agreement to our proceeding with what is our normal practice where policy matters arise which are of interest to other departments, and ourselves calling together representatives of those interested departments and consult them. This process would in any event have been necessary in relation to the 'gearing-up' submission, and particularly so far as Foreign Affairs is concerned, in relation to the submission on future political and economic relations.

11. I therefore propose to proceed with the calling together of groups of departments on an ad hoc basis during the final stages of the drafting of the submissions which this Department has been authorised to prepare for you to present to Cabinet in relation to the report of the Select Committee on Constitutional Development. This should to an extent satisfy the interests of Foreign Affairs. It should also confirm that this Department is carrying out the responsibility given it by Cabinet to conduct a coordinated planning task in consultation with other departments.

12. It is also relevant that other studies are proceeding by means of inter-departmental committees, consequent upon earlier Cabinet decisions. These are:

(a) Transfer of Commonwealth functions. Cabinet directed in June 1970 (Decision No. 452)[6] that a committee, consisting of External Territories, Prime Minister's, Public Service Board and Treasury, with particular departments coopted as required, be set up to consider and report on 'a sensible programme' for the absorption into the Administration of functions, now performed as Audit, Commonwealth Works, now performed in PNG by Commonwealth Departments.

(b) Internal Security. By the same decision, Cabinet directed that this be the subject of a special study by External Territories and Defence.

13. In addition and arising from (b), the Defence Department, in consultation with this Department, is engaged in a series of studies[7] relating to the future of the defence forces in Papua New Guinea. The purpose of these studies is to relate planning being done by Defence to the 'gearing-up' planning being done by this Department.

---

5   See Document 78, fn. 3.

6   See Document 53.

7   See Documents 150, 158, 167, 189 & 197.

14. I should be glad to know whether the course of action proposed in paragraphs 10 and 11 which I would put to Sir Keith Waller in reply to his letter has your approval.[8]

[NAA: A452, 1972/4041]

240   LETTER FROM FAIRBAIRN TO MCMAHON

Canberra, 29 November 1971

Secret

Because of the quickening pace of constitutional development in Papua New Guinea my Department has commenced a comprehensive programme of studies of future Papua New Guinea defence and security requirements and of appropriate means of transferring responsibilities to local authorities in areas touching on defence policy, administration and control of forces.

While it is intended that the Commonwealth will retain ultimate responsibility for defence and control of forces until independence day it is important that Papua New Guinea's elected leaders; senior administrators and indigenous service officers adequately are prepared, before then, for exercise of whatever defence responsibilities the independent Papua New Guinea decides to accept, either alone or in association with Australia.

A list of subjects currently under study within my Department and jointly or separately, as appropriate, with the Department of External Territories; Army, Navy, Air, the Treasury and some of the Attorney General's Department, is attached. Some of the studies are already nearing conclusion and I would expect the whole programme to have been traversed before the elections in Papua New Guinea in February/March 1972. Studies are likely to continue thereafter.

From time to time I shall, in consultation with the Minister for External Territories, and other colleagues, be making submissions to Cabinet on matters arising from the studies.

You will appreciate that a practical matter central to all the studies is the question of when independence and self-government are likely to occur. In the absence of any clear or agreed expression of local views on these dates the Secretary of my Department in consultation with the Secretary, Department of External Territories has had to make certain assumptions. They are that self-government will be granted in 1975 and that independence will occur in the time span 1976/77.[1]

I have agreed that these assumptions may be used as a working hypothesis for defence planning for Papua New Guinea on the proviso that they shall be without any commitment to Government. I understand that a similar working hypothesis, without commitment, has been adopted by the Department of External Territories for their planning.

These assumptions are, of course, politically very sensitive. Although they are being treated with special care and their existence limited to those with a need to know it seems to me probable that, sooner or later, their existence will become known to the news media.

---

8   Barnes approved Hay's approach.

---

1   See Documents 189 & 233.

Complete discretion and avoidance of revelations cannot be assured. My officers are therefore considering, together with the Department of External Territories and Foreign Affairs, the preparation of a statement for public use by Ministers and others should the need arise. My feeling is that such a statement should explain that assumptions are necessary for the central planning purposes recognising that decisions on the constitutional state of Papua New Guinea will involve the appropriate constitutional bodies in Papua New Guinea and Australia, and the interest of the United Nations in the termination of the Trust agreement.

I have sent a copy of this letter to the Minister for External Territories.

Programme of Defence Studies Related to Papua New Guinea

1.   Study of arrangements necessary at internal self-government for maintenance of internal security as a local responsibility.

2.   Consideration of the training programme and of equipment acquisitions for the Pacific Islands Regiment to enable it to render aid to the civil power.

3.   Review of communication arrangements in Papua New Guinea.

4.   Study of localisation of civilian positions in Papua New Guinea Command.

5.   Review of the need to vary, on a temporary basis, the existing manpower ceilings of Papua New Guinea forces in order to facilitate more rapid indigenisation.

6.   Study of arrangements to achieve compatibility of standards and administrative procedures in the Territory between the defence forces and the civil service.

7.   Further examination of requests for Service personnel and logistic support for the Royal Papua and New Guinea Constabulary.

8.   Study of expansion of information, public relations and civic action activities of the Papua New Guinea forces.

9.   Consideration of organisation, training, and other matters relative to PNG forces which could be accomplished now without prejudice to their ultimate shape and size.

10.   Study of consultations with, and increased responsibilities by PNG authorities in defence matters up to the time of independence.

11.   Consideration of establishment of a Joint Force Headquarters in Papua New Guinea.

12.   Enquiry into composition, location, in terms of reference of a Working Party to develop and plan for the establishment of a 'Department of Defence Forces' in Papua New Guinea.

13.   Study of the concept for the future role and employment of the PNG forces post-independence.

14.   Consideration of financial arrangements on Defence between Papua New Guinea and Australia in the period of internal self-government and at independence.

15.   Examination of possible procedures for the employment of Papua New Guinea Defence Forces in aid of the civil power.

16.   Examination of legal powers required by military forces if employed in roles short of direct intervention in a riot situation.

17.   Study of policy for provision of communications security assistance to PNG forces and Civil Administration.

[NAA: A1209, 1969/9045]

241   LETTER FROM HAY TO TANGE

Canberra, 30 November 1971

SECRET

I am writing to you with respect to the desirability of involving other departments at this stage in the deliberations of Study No 1 of the Programme of Defence Studies. As you are aware this Study relates to internal security. The question of involving other departments has been discussed previously by officers of our Departments and as a result we had adopted the view that the Programme should not require consultation with departments other than those specified in the Programme until the Study in question was approaching finality.

I am informed that the officers engaged in Study No 1 are at present engaged in drafting a report which they hope to complete at an early date.

The completion of this study has in my view some urgency. The Minister for External Territories intends early next year to place before Cabinet a number of submissions relating to constitutional development in Papua New Guinea. This follows from the Government's acceptance early this year of the reports of the Select Committee on Constitutional Development as adopted by the House of Assembly and in particular the recommendation which authorised the Department of External Territories to prepare, in consultation with the Administration and other Commonwealth departments, a flexible programme for the movement of Papua New Guinea to self-government during the period 1972/1976. In view of the significance of internal security to any process of constitutional change in Papua New Guinea it seems necessary that a submission relating to it should go forward at the same time. It would be appropriate that such a submission should deal with the recommendations contained in the Report of Study No 1.

This would seem particularly so having regard to the fact that this particular study derives from a Cabinet Decision No 452 of 23 June, 1970,[1] in which Cabinet directed a special study of the situation in relation to internal security. The implementation of the study was deferred whilst the Interdepartmental Committee on Aid to Civil Power completed its report.

All of these considerations suggest the desirability of bringing other departments in at this stage if the Report is to be speedily finalised. It would seem to me appropriate that the Department of Foreign Affairs should be consulted on the question of transferring power in respect of internal security as it bears upon Australia's international obligations and its international standing. I think also that the Department of the Prime Minister and Cabinet should be consulted and perhaps the Department of the Army and Attorney-General's Department. It is to be noted that in establishing an Interdepartmental Committee on Aid to Civil Power Cabinet in Decision No 1044 of 1969[2] expressly included Foreign Affairs, Prime Minister's, Army and Attorney-General's as well as the Departments of Defence and External Territories.

It is against this background that I would suggest that we direct the officers concerned with this particular study to complete their report by 13 December and commence interdepartmental discussions with the Department of Foreign Affairs and Department of the Prime Minister and Cabinet and the following week on the basis that interdepartmental consideration would be concluded in early January.

---

1   Document 53.

2   See Stuart Doran (ed.), *Documents on Australian Foreign Policy: Australia and Papua New Guinea, 1966–1969*, Department of Foreign Affairs and Trade, Canberra, 2006, Document 273.

For our own part I would have in mind that you and I have preliminary discussions on the Report in the week commencing 13 December so that officers concerned can have an indication of our own thinking on the subject.

I should be glad of your comments on these suggestions.

[NAA: A452, 1971/280]

242   LETTER FROM HAY TO SHANN

Canberra, 30 November 1971

CONFIDENTIAL

I refer to Sir Keith Waller's letter of 8th October and to my reply of 20th October,[1] on future Commonwealth representation in Papua New Guinea.

In this letter I address myself to your suggestion that there should be 'a basic policy committee in Canberra at the very senior departmental level', in relation to preparation 'for the transition of responsibility from the Commonwealth to, first, a self-governing and then an independent Papua New Guinea.'

Your letter advances two reasons for the suggestion. The first is that there should be a comprehensive and coordinated approach to government planning. The second relates only to your own Department in which you argue that because of your Department's overall responsibility in the post-independence period, it should be involved in 'all relevant actions and decisions' so that your task will be 'simpler' after independence.

I agree that comprehensive and coordinated planning for the transition of Papua New Guinea to self-government and independence is needed. This is already, of course, a responsibility of this Department. In exercising this responsibility it consults fully with other departments and authorities. I draw your attention to the fact that, following the Government's approval of the report of the House of Assembly Select Committee in April, it:

'authorised the Department of External Territories in the consultation with the Administration and other Departments and Authorities concerned, to draw up a flexible programme of movement towards internal self-government, including the kinds of political and economic relations which should exist with Australia at internal self-government, for consideration by Cabinet at an early date as a basis for negotiations with the leadership group emerging from the 1972 elections.'[2]

A considerable amount of preliminary work has been done, together with the Administration, in accordance with the abovementioned decision. The point has now been reached where detailed discussions with other interested departments are in train with a view to ensuring that their views are taken into account before final submissions to Cabinet are drawn up. Several separate, but related, submissions are envisaged. One would describe the 'flexible programme' which is being drawn up as a basis for negotiations with the leadership group emerging from the 1972 elections. Another would deal with 'the kinds of political and economic relations which should exist with Australia at internal self-government'. A third would deal with the question of national unity. A fourth submission may be necessary in order to deal with certain

---

1   Documents 225 & 227 (respectively). See also Documents 231 & 239.
2   Document 159.

constraints (such as law and order, manpower, the considerable legislative programme) which may affect the negotiations with Papua New Guinea leaders.

The submission on the programme will comprehensively review *all* the steps being taken and planned, and will put in perspective for Cabinet the activities of other groups, whether constituted by Cabinet itself (such as the IDC on transfer of Commonwealth functions, and the IDC on internal security) or by agreement between Ministers such as the Committee on Banking, or at departmental level, such as the groups of officers working on the future of Papua New Guinea's defence forces. Reports or recommendations resulting from the work of such groups may well be put to Cabinet in separate submissions by my Minister or other Ministers at the appropriate time. But in all cases, coordination is assured through my department's membership and through regular reporting of the total programme to Cabinet, after consultation with other departments concerned.

It is my Minister's wish that there be full discussion on these matters with interested departments, as enjoined by the Government. These discussions will ensure that your Department's views will be taken fully into account at an early stage. It goes without saying that a submission on future political and economic relations with PNG would not be placed before Ministers unless it reflected the views of Foreign Affairs, and also other departments such as Treasury, Defence and Trade and Industry.

So far as the special interest of your Department is concerned, deriving from what you say will be its responsibilities after independence, it seems to me that this will be satisfied by the full consultation envisaged and described in this letter relating to general policies and guidelines. But this is a matter which I would be happy to discuss further with you or your officers.

I am sending a copy of this letter to those of our colleagues named in Sir Keith Waller's letter of 8th October.

[NAA: A1838, 3080/10/2 PART 1]

243 LETTER FROM POYSER TO MOODIE

Canberra, 6 December 1971

Secret

With the quickening pace of constitutional development in Papua New Guinea, this Department in conjunction with the Department of External Territories has commenced a programme of studies of future defence and security requirements in PNG and of appropriate means of transferring responsibilities to local authorities in areas touching on Defence/Service matters.[1] When these studies have been further developed, I will be in touch with you about those aspects likely to affect your department's responsibilities.

2.   A practical matter central to all these studies is the possible dates of self-government and independence, and on these Mr Hay and I have had to make assumptions. We have agreed that the planning assumptions to be used should be that self-government will be granted in 1975 and independence will occur in the time-span 1976/77. The Ministers for Defence and for External Territories have agreed that these assumptions may be used as a working hypothesis for defence planning studies for Papua New Guinea on the proviso, of course, that they are without commitment to Government.

3.   As the assumptions are politically sensitive, despite their hypothetical nature, they are being treated with special discretion. Their existence is being limited to those with a strict need to know, but it seems probable that sooner or later they will become known.

4.   With this in mind we have been giving consideration to the line to be adopted publicly by Ministers and others if the need arises to comment in Parliament or to the press. We suggest the following, to be drawn on as appropriate:

In April 1971 the Australian Government announced its acceptance of the recommendation of the Papua New Guinea House of Assembly Select Committee on Constitutional Development that the Development of the Territory be geared to preparing the country for internal self-government during the life of the next House of Assembly (1972–1976) so that if it is in fact requested by the people, then the transition to internal self-government could be made with the least administrative disruption.

Studies and planning for this purpose are being undertaken by appropriate Departments, and it is, of course, necessary to employ planning assumptions about the actual timing of self-government and independence. These assumptions are adopted as a working hypothesis for planning only and without commitment to the Australian Government or to the elected representatives of the people of Papua New Guinea. It is fully recognised and understood that decisions on the constitutional advancement of Papua New Guinea will involve not only the appropriate bodies in PNG and in Australia but also the interests of the United Nations in the termination of the Trust Agreement. The assumptions and the planning that flows from them can and will be adjusted if necessary.

5.   I should be pleased to know whether this statement would have your endorsement from the Foreign Affairs viewpoint.

6.   When we have arrived at an agreed text, steps will be taken to bring the statement to the notice of Ministers and others for use as appropriate if the assumptions become known to the media. I am also seeking the views of the Department of External Territories.

[NAA: A1838, 3080/10/1 PART 1]

---

1   See Documents 189, 233 & 240.

244   RECORD OF CONVERSATION BETWEEN SHANN AND VAN LAETHEM[1]

Canberra, 7 December 1971

CONFIDENTIAL

The French Ambassador has recently been to Papua New Guinea and at my house the other evening we began a most interesting conversation about his reactions to his visit. I invited him to come to the Department and talk about it in more detail, which he did this morning.[2]

2.   The Ambassador began by saying that he had been the recipient in Indo-China, Morocco and Algeria of a great deal of unsolicited and occasionally unwanted advice. He therefore approached the subject with some diffidence, but he had been so impressed by the problem that we faced nationally in New Guinea that he wanted to speak to us about them frankly. I said that I hoped he would tell me exactly what was in his mind and that he could assume at the outset that I was not going to get prickly about it.

3.   Van Laethem said that in all his experience he had not encountered a place which had so many weaknesses as it approached independence. He thought that perhaps it did not have as many immediate dangers as others, where there had been predominant tribes which proceeded immediately to take the country over for their own short term power and advantage. He thought, however, that PNG had grave weaknesses in the light of the assumed timetable for self-government and perhaps independence during the term of the next House of Assembly. He described them as follows:

(a) He had been unable to perceive any general national urge for self-government or independence. There was some localised interest in these matters at the local council level, usually for selfish and short term reasons. The political elite was undeveloped, and there was no obvious national leader at all. Political consciousness was localised.

(b) The lack of English as a national language was potentially disastrous. It was true that about one third of the time of students in schools and the University was taken up with the study of English, but this would not become useful in a national sense for many years. Those graduates of Australian universities and the University of Papua New Guinea who had English were inclined at the moment, with understandable modesty, to believe that their contribution could best be made in minor administrative positions. Those people without it had different ambitions unlikely to be productive of good government. Pidgin, which we had unwisely allowed to become the currency of communication between the majority of the Members of the House of Assembly, was so clumsy as to make it impossible for the consideration of either national or international problems.

(c) He had observed with distaste and some fear the existence of a lot of advisers standing behind the pidgin-speaking politicians, none of whose tenure was likely to be substantial because of the egalitarian tendencies in TPNG to change representatives as often as possible. These 'advisers' were expatriate and English-speaking, young and inexperienced, and were not engaged in an exercise which bore any relationship to the national interest of Australia or PNG. They regarded themselves as participants in socialist or anti-colonialist experiments. He had seen this in Algeria with Ben Bella, who had been

---

1   Gabriel Van Laethem, French Ambassador to Australia, 1971–74.

2   Given the tragic history, for both France and its colonies, of French decolonisation, it may seem surprising that Van Laethem's views were accorded close attention. He was, however, an impressive individual who was highly regarded by Australian officials.

surrounded by young Frenchmen preying on his absolute inexperience of government and who had been described in France, accurately he thought, as the 'talons rouges'.[3] These young men in PNG were interested basically only in fat jobs. They put up most of the ideas and questions which were propounded by the Members of the House of Assembly.

(d) On the security side, and this seemed to concern the Ambassador more than anything else, he found a police force, not all that well trained, of some 3,000 and an army of a similar number. The latter could not be used in what the Ambassador regards as the inevitable local security problems, without the authority of Canberra, and indeed the authority of Cabinet. He reminded me that Marshal Lyautey[4] had said that one 'must show force in order not to use it'. Van Laethem said that it is known in New Guinea that army force cannot be used immediately, and his view is that it should be known in New Guinea that it can be used at once if necessary, and that its availability and strengthening will become known to those who might trade on the present fragility of needed force behind the Administrator at the moment, and the new Government when it comes into existence.

(e) There is in the Territory at the moment a substantial body of Australian land-owners who cannot sell their land because of uncertainty, and because of the lack of local resources to buy it. They feel in relation to PNG both impermanent and let down by Australia. If they go, as they well may, the economy and its productive capacity will suffer a major setback. In this context (and see below) the Japanese will need watching.

(f) The University and the other institutions of higher learning are, because of the inadequacy of courses that they provide and the substantial number of drop-outs, producing in those who attend them 'ambition rather than knowledge'. This again the Ambassador regards as dangerous. The drop-outs themselves are a problem conducive of instability.

4.   He regards the senior District Commissioners whom he met as of the highest calibre and people devoted to the future of Papua New Guinea. His experience of the middle and lower groups in the Administration led him to conclude that they were very weak. Not only had they no feeling of dedication to their tasks, but they had 'one hand on their suit-cases'. Moreover, there appears to be a substantial group of foreigners from Europe, particularly Central Europe, and colonial administrators, also foreign, who were the 'remnants of Africa', who were doing the territory no good, and whose hands were similarly 'on their suit-cases'.

5.   The climate for private investment in the country was of enormous importance to Papua New Guinea. But the big companies involved in the territory had middle grade representatives who regarded their stay in the territory as temporary, and the work that they were doing just a job. If our companies do not do the work a Japanese take-over, already a danger, could quite easily become a fact.

6.   The Ambassador tried to convey that many of the expatriates in Papua New Guinea were either not interested in what they were doing except for what they could earn from it or, if they were interested, had a feeling of being deserted by Australia. His view was that they must have a more substantial national backing from Australia, particularly from Canberra.

7.   He was especially worried by the system of 'pay-back'. In Lae he had seen a car knock down a native girl. Within an hour between 800 and 1000 of the thousands of de-tribalized natives, who live aimlessly around most of the big settlements throughout the country, were

3   Literally *talons rouges* means 'red heels'. The term was at first used to refer to aristocrats, and later was also used to refer to pretentious people. Presumably Van Laethem intended this latter meaning.

4   Hubert Lyautey (1854–1934) was a French general and colonial administrator renowned for the 'pacification' of colonial territories by a combination of ruthless military force and political finesse.

stoning all the cars of Europeans in the streets of Lae. The system of 'pay-back' has, in the Ambassador's view, affected the usefulness and proper severity of the whole legal system in that penalties are not imposed because of the tradition of retribution.

8.   He fears that very easily, as self-government approaches or on its attainment, or particularly with independence, a situation of 'panic' could develop where, practically all of the people useful to the development of the country would go, taking with them wherever they could their assets, and producing a situation where further private Australian investment in the Territory would cease. The resultant burden on Australia would be intolerable, and indeed on the United Nations which must bear part of the responsibility for the situation in PNG.

9.   The Ambassador anticipates that a United Party will win the next elections from the Pangu Party, but that the United Party will be afraid to state its real views about the speed of self-government or independence because it will be accused by the Pangu Party of being no more than a stooge of Australia. The Pangu Party itself will, badly advised by the young English-speaking 'hippie' types behind it, promote exactly the panic situation that the Ambassador most fears. Should this happen everything that we have tried to do in New Guinea will be undone. The climate for the kind of investment like that in Bougainville, with all its potential for the budget of the new country, will have gone. Van Laethem feels that it is essential that the speed of movement to self-government and independence be held down until conditions of confidence and national support from Australia have been created. It would be desirable for us to have 25 years, but this is clearly impracticable. If, as is probable, we are committed to a time scale perhaps leading to independence by 1975, then it is the question of the buttressing of confidence that we must attack.

10.   Finally, he wondered whether there was anything that he could recommend to his Government to alleviate what he regards as a most dangerous situation. He noted that the United Nations would be sending a Committee to observe the elections, with membership from Britain, the United States, Yugoslavia and he thought an African. (It is I think an Afghan, not an African.) Could the French Government urge on the governments providing members of this Committee caution in encouraging the advance to self-government? He would be very glad to recommend this if Australia thought this would be a useful move. He thought his Government would agree, and would be listened to by those concerned.

11.   I said to the Ambassador that I hoped he would excuse me if I declined to offer comments on his suggestion. I said that I was grateful for the way in which he had talked about his impressions of the Territory, and that I was sure that when I reported his comments, as I would, there would be neither irritation nor resentment at them, because they had been offered in an attempt to be as helpful as possible. I could not comment personally on such an important proposition. It would be necessary to consult the Department of Territories, and I would certainly want to refer what he had said to the Minister, as I imagined they would to theirs. I undertook to let him have a reaction within the next couple of weeks. He said that until then he would delay writing to Paris about his impressions.

12.   There can be no doubt of Van Laethem's credentials in relation to the problems of countries reaching independence. Neither is there of his brains. He is probably the best Ambassador we have. He served as Number 2 in Saigon when the French still controlled Indo-China, and was Legal Adviser to the French authorities in Hanoi at the time of the hand over to the Viet Minh. He was in Morocco when the King returned, and he spent five years in Algeria during the whole of the troubles between France and that country. His views are certainly worth thinking about.

13. The Ambassador expressed warm thanks for the way he had been looked after in PNG. He had been treated with great courtesy and informed of the situation with frankness. If the visit had not filled him with such foreboding he would have enjoyed it thoroughly.[5]

[NAA: A1838, 3080/10/1 PART 1]

---

5   On 13 December DFA Deputy Secretary Border commented: 'Many of the British colonies in Africa were brought to independence by a small, educated elite in an apathetic mass and this will happen in PNG. The desire for self-government is growing rapidly and if we hold out too long, we will be pushed out instead of getting out while we are still friends. I agree there is no obvious national leader, but is this necessary? Potential leaders exist, e.g. Michael Somare, Oala Oala Rarua'. Border also noted that 'Pidgin' (Tok Pisin) was widely used and an effective means of communication. Minute, Border to Shann, 'Papua New Guinea—Views of French Ambassador', 13 December 1971, NAA: A1838/3080/10/1 PART 1.

On 20 December Robin Ashwin, Minister in Australia's Mission to the United Nations, commented that: 'Van Laethem is clearly a very experienced and sophisticated observer. His gloomy forebodings need to be borne seriously in mind. They do appear to us, however, to be a little exaggerated and, of course, French. We cannot expect Papua New Guinea to become another Ivory Coast or Niger. Nor is the situation really in any significant way comparable to that which existed in Algeria.' Ashwin noted the utility of Tok Pisin, and commented on Van Laethem's views on expatriate advisers as follows: 'While there is some point in this, the Ambassador seems to be drawing too heavily on his Algerian experience. Neither Crocombe nor Voutas (to take two cases) can be fairly described as "talons rouges" or after fat jobs'. Dr Ron Crocombe had served as the Director of the Australian National University's New Guinea Research Unit in Port Moresby from 1962 to 1969. Tony Voutas, a former patrol officer, served as the MHA for Morobe regional from 1968 to 1972 and was the leading adviser to Pangu leader Michael Somare.

Aswhin also noted that '[Rabbie] Namaliu, a UPNG graduate currently studying at Victoria University, was an example of a graduate with knowledge and intelligence with ambitions for his country'. Memorandum, Ashwin to DFA, 20 December 1971, NAA: A1838/3080/10/1 PART 1.

245   LETTER FROM BARNES TO BEAZLEY

Canberra, 8 December 1971

I refer to my letter of 14th October[1] in which I indicated that I had asked the Administrator of Papua New Guinea for a report on the social and labour problems around the Bougainville mining sites.

The Administrator, on the advice of the Ministerial Member for Labour and the Assistant Ministerial Member for Social Development and Home Affairs in the House of Assembly for Papua New Guinea, has informed me that while there is some truth in the information provided by the mission authority, there are some points which need to be clarified.

In the twelve month period up to 15th October, 1971 there have been four unlawful killings in the project area. The victims were all indigenous persons and the deaths in each case occurred as the result of incidents in which prior excessive drinking was a major contributing factor. There have been 14 traffic accidents which resulted in the death of 20 persons. Police investigations revealed that the contributory factors to the accidents were vehicle mechanical failure (3), unstable road conditions (5), driving under the influence (3) and driving error not associated with any of these causes (3).

There is little doubt that drunkenness has become more prevalent in the area as a result of the existence of the project and because the local people have more money to spend. This type of social problem is inevitable in an area where a $400 million construction programme is utilising in excess of 10,500 employees.

While there are social problems associated with drinking at various mining camps they are not apparent in the local village communities. It has been established that at the villages near the project, particularly Rorovana, traditional social controls are effective and the situation is under control.

On one occasion two seven year old children were found to be intoxicated but they were not on a public road as reported by the mission informant. Police investigations were instituted but the children's source of liquor supply was not located.

With regard to the matters of the importation of labour and repatriation, there are industrial rules operating which incorporate industrial agreements registered under the Industrial Relations Ordinance 1962–1971. These rules bind all employees of sub-contractors to Bechtel–WKE,[2] the managing authority for Bougainville Copper Pty Ltd. They specifically provide for payment of award wages to both expatriate and indigenous workers as well as laying down the terms and conditions under which repatriation will take place.

The project industrial rules associated with the mining and construction workers cover two situations: those engaged at the mining site and those engaged elsewhere in Papua New Guinea. There is no doubt that for indigenous employees engaged other than at the site the contractors are obliged to repatriate them. However, for those engaged at the site, contractors are obliged to repatriate only if they have served a period of 12 months or if the contract is completed at an earlier time or if they become redundant at any time. In addition under the rules applying to mining workers there is provision for repatriation of dependents if such dependents are recognised as such by the employer.

---

1   Not published. This was an interim response to an earlier letter from Beazley which raised concerns about the impact of the Bougainville copper mine on nearby indigenous communities. Here Barnes has provided a point by point response to Beazley's concerns.

2   An American entity, Bechtel–WKE was a joint venture of the Bechtel Corporation and Western Knapp Engineering which in turn was a component of Arthur G. McKee & Company.

Should the indigenous employees resign, or have employment terminated for misconduct, then employers are not compelled to repatriate them. Employees in this category are nonetheless encouraged to avail themselves of the cheaper fares available on charter aircraft which frequently go to other centres in Papua New Guinea. They may also apply for funds from the District Commissioner at Bougainville which are provided for the repatriation of destitute persons.

The Papua New Guinea Administration foresaw the likelihood of problems of this nature arising and prior to any phasing downward of the construction programme, came to an agreement with BCPL[3] and BWKE for procedures to be followed in connection with the repatriation of indigenous workers.

The case of repatriation of expatriate workers is different as the Migration Ordinance 1963–1969 compels either the worker or the employer to lodge a bond with the Administration on arrival in Papua New Guinea to an amount equal to the cost of an air fare to Australia. Any Administration expenditure involved in repatriating expatriates is therefore recovered from the bond lodged by the employer or employee.

More generally the Administrator has advised that the problems of unemployment or vagrancy which have arisen have not been associated with workers 'imported' by employers at the project but with those people who have arrived in the area at their own expense looking for work. In such cases the Bougainville Unemployment Committee (comprising representatives from various Administration Departments, BCPL and BWKE) has taken several measures to discourage people from going to Bougainville unless employment had been pre-arranged.

These measures have included the following: radio broadcasts requesting people to complete employment arrangements prior to leaving their home districts; requests to airline authorities to refer obvious job seekers purchasing tickets to Bougainville to the nearest employment office for advice; circulars to all District Commissioners requesting district publicity to discourage movement of people to Bougainville seeking employment; and announcements by the Ministerial Member for Labour.

On the matter of squatter settlements around the mining sites, the Administrator advises that there are no problems at present. Those people who attempt to settle on Administration land in the area are fully accounted for by procedures established for this purpose.

Your informant also mentioned an attack upon a nun at the Tonuru Mission. This incident was regrettable and the two men involved in the assault, who were employed workers and not displaced persons, were captured and charged by the police. They were convicted of assault and sentenced to six months' imprisonment.

In regard to the usage of the term 'redskins' I should like to mention that this is not a new development caused by the mining project. It is a term that has been used for many years by the Bougainville people. As you would appreciate it has been most difficult to prevent the usage of the term which has been applied as far back as the German administration era.

You may have noticed from a press report in the 'Post Courier' of 18th October that more police are being sent to Arawa but that the numbers are regulated by the availability of accommodation. It is intended that the [police establishment] in the project area will keep pace with the population expansion. It should be recognised, of course, that the problems are more than law and order issues and require people experienced in community development and social work to assist in the development of new communities.

Finally may I assure you that the Government has been most conscious of the likely effects of the mining project on the traditional way of life since the planning stage of the project with

---

3   Bougainville Copper Proprietary Limited.

the result that committees have been established which have considered matters relating to the likely social, cultural and labour problems arising out of the project.

The Administration continues to be aware of its responsibilities towards the welfare of the people living and working on the project and is keeping in close touch with the situation through its Bougainville Unemployment Committee and its representatives who are in close touch with the people of the area meet weekly with BCPL on the mining site.

[*matter omitted*]

[NAA: A452, 1971/3895]

246   LETTER FROM WALLER TO HAY

Canberra, 14 December 1971

CONFIDENTIAL

I have sent you a copy of a record of conversation[1] between Shann and the French Ambassador on 7 December, containing the Ambassador's impressions of his recent visit to Papua New Guinea.

Although the Ambassador seems to be both apprehensive and pessimistic in a number of his observations, I believe there is something in what he has to say. Indeed, he came away from the Territory with a general feeling of unease which a number of my own officers have experienced as a result of their own visits to the Territory. Many of the factors making up this sense of unease are not hard to pinpoint, as Van Laethem has done—the absence of a widespread urge for self-determination and of an extensive political elite, the deficiencies of pidgin as a national language, the adequacy of security forces and of the major educational institutions, the insecurity of some of the expatriates and the uncertain future of the economy, the clear interest of the Japanese in the area, and the oddities of the 'legal' system, and so on. Some of the advice offered is sound and sensible.

In my view, however, it would be wrong to conclude—as the Ambassador has done—that it would be in the best interests of both Australia and the Territory to slow down the move towards self-government. The longer we delay independence the harder it may become to grant it, not least because of the separatist tendencies already apparent within the Territory. Anything short of independence, for example, would seem to be a palliative only in the resolution of the situation in the Gazelle Peninsula, and there is growing pressure from the rapidly increasing educated elite for self-government. The longer we stay in PNG the more we will become disliked and the more difficult it will be for us to control a law and order situation which has already shown signs of strain. It is in our interest to give the natives a sense of self-confidence, to encourage them to build up their own institutions and take the strong measures to preserve law and order that can only be taken by a native government, and to persuade the better and more dedicated expatriates to stay on after Independence. The essential fact seems to me to be that the pressure for self-government no longer comes primarily from the United Nations but from within Papua New Guinea; it is the people of the Territory who will decide the pace of progress towards self-government.

[*matter omitted*]

I should be grateful for your advice as to how we might proceed.[2]

[NAA: A1838, 3080/10/1 PART 1]

---

1   Document 244.

2   Lew Border had given a draft of this letter to Waller on 8 December. On the covering note to the draft Waller had written 'How do we discuss this with Territories? There is much in what Van Laethem says. But the longer we delay independence, the harder it may become because of separatist tendencies within PNG. I am sure that what he says about expatriates is very true.' Waller, annotation on covering note, 8 December 1972, NAA: A1838, 3080/10/1 PART 1.

247   SAVINGRAM TO ALL POSTS

Canberra, 15 December 1971

167. CONFIDENTIAL

Recent Developments in Papua New Guinea

This savingram reports on political developments in Papua New Guinea (PNG) since our savingram AP88 of 19 July 1971.[1] The topics discussed are:

- Second House of Assembly
- 1972 Elections
- Third House of Assembly
- Unity in PNG

Second House of Assembly

2.   The Second House of Assembly concluded its final session on 26 November 1971. The final week of the Second House's sitting was marked by an unusual display of cohesion on the part of elected members of all parties when the House rejected bills introduced by the Administration to implement the compensation scheme for permanent overseas officers in the public service. A motion strongly criticising the compensation provisions as inadequate and urging the Australian Government to revise its policy had been passed a few days earlier. Members claimed that they were protesting against the Administration's persistence in trying to force through legislation for which the House had already expressed its disapproval. Having made its point, the House approved one bill the next day which abolished the 'appeals' system. It had previously agreed to bills speeding up localisation of the public service and apparently accepted the argument that failure to abolish the appeals system would seriously hamper the progress of localisation.

[*matter omitted*]

3.   It is fair to say that the Second House was characterised by a marked increase in the powers given to the House and to ministers, and by an increasing willingness on the part of Ministers to exercise those powers.

1972 Elections

4.   This trend towards a greater self-assurance will almost certainly be carried a stage further in the Third House of Assembly to be elected in February/March 1972. In addition to the constitutional developments which have increased the powers of the executive and the House, the steady development of political parties should have a marked effect on the attitudes taken by Members. Most voters still vote for the man, but increasingly parties are becoming known and are influencing voters even if only to a limited extent. Party discipline, particularly within the United Party is still fragile, but there are now three major political parties which show some degree of cohesion:

    (a)   The United Party (UP—formerly Compass Party) will seek to widen its support and of the three parties will field the greatest number of candidates in electorates throughout Papua New Guinea. It will seek blanket coverage in the Highlands where its strength lies. It advocated a conservative approach to self-government and is often accused of being dominated by expatriates.

1   Document 198.

(b) A relatively new party, the People's Progress Party (PPP), which claimed the support of up to eleven members in the old House, will contest approximately 30 seats throughout PNG, and not simply in the New Guinea islands where it has so far attracted most support. Its views on self-government are quite close to those of the United Party.

(c) Pangu Party has so far endorsed thirty-five candidates but could field as many as seventy. The Party's platform, which includes a plank demanding immediate self-government, appeals mainly to urban voters and some coastal Papuans, i.e. the more sophisticated. Pangu spokesmen recently have spoken of the Party's aim to win a majority of seats in the next House, but such a result would surprise most observers.

5.   Australia has invited a UN mission to observe the elections.[2] It will consist of two members of the Trusteeship Council (UK and USA) and two from the Committee of Twenty-Four (Yugoslavia and Afghanistan). It was invited to include Papua in its formal itinerary. We hope the mission will report that the elections were fairly conducted and that the members elected truly represent the people of both Papua and New Guinea.

Third House of Assembly

6.   The Australian Government has agreed to prepare PNG for internal self-government during the life of the Third House of Assembly, 1972–76, if this is wanted at that time, and to negotiate with any leadership group which might emerge from the 1972 elections. Thus, it will be open to any party or group which can command a majority in the House to set the pace for self-government and subsequent independence.

7.   Irrespective of how quickly the House wishes to move to formal, internal self-government, the powers which have been devolved on to Ministers will ensure that elected representatives will continue to have a very high degree of de facto control over the internal affairs of Papua New Guinea. The principal member of the leadership group will be called Deputy Chairman of the Administrator's Executive Council and will be, in effect, a Chief Minister. The Administrator will be bound to accept the advice of the Ministers in areas under their control.

8.   The House will also probably decide on the form of Government to be adopted possibly through the use of a Select Committee. Although formal development to date has been along Westminster lines, weak parties and incompatible local traditions have hindered the emergence of a really effective Westminster system. Australian policy is to let the House work out its own system. Important decisions which will have to be taken include the role of the Head of Government (e.g. President or Prime Minister) and the question of to what degree power should be devolved to regional authorities or assemblies. (Area authorities are being developed at present but in an experimental way).

Unity

9.   *Papua.* The separatist tendencies in the Gazelle Peninsula and in Bougainville remain a source of friction. Recently, Papuan secession became an issue temporarily overshadowing these two. Papuans claim that the Australian Government has neglected them and that major economic development projects have gone to New Guinea because it is a Trust territory and therefore under the eye of the United Nations. Some MHAs, largely expatriates who are more Papuan than Papuans, have claimed that Papuans' Australian citizenship gives them special rights (New Guineans are Australian-protected persons). In October 1971 a delegation of Papuan parliamentarians visited Canberra to put their case. In the event, it became fairly clear that they were not seriously interested in secession, but would be satisfied if greater attention

---

2   See Document 238.

were paid to the economic development of Papua. The Minister for External Territories promised to have a special examination made by a consultant of the problems of comparatively less developed areas of Papua and New Guinea. Work has now started on this study.[3]

10. *United Nations.* The Australian policy of unity has always received general support in the United Nations. In its Report dated 17 November 1971, the Committee of Twenty-Four noted Australia's statement on the existence of separatist tendencies in several regions of Papua New Guinea. The Committee strongly urged the administering power to discourage these movements. It welcomed moves to establish a common PNG citizenship and, 'in its desire to avoid any fragmentation of Papua New Guinea', urges the intensification of the new campaign to promote national unity. It is therefore clear that separatist movements in PNG cannot expect any support from the UN.

11. We have reason to believe that Papuans may complain to members of the 1972 Visiting Mission, but we would expect the Mission to discourage any expressions of separatist tendencies.

Guidance

12. Posts should continue to stress the rapid constitutional development of Papua New Guinea and the degree to which Ministers will exercise de facto control over its internal affairs in discussions with local officials or others. The importance of the forthcoming elections should be underlined. We are anxious that the new House of Assembly should be accepted internationally as a valid body to represent the people of PNG and to take important decisions on their behalf. We also wish to make it clear that major constitutional decisions will continue to originate in PNG. It is up to the House of Assembly when self-government comes and what form it should take. Similarly, once self-government has been achieved, the Australian Government will be guided by the wishes of the PNG Government on the timing and form of independence.

We also wish our policy of unity to be endorsed. It is possible that adverse reactions could arise if there were further trouble, requiring the use of force, in for example the Gazelle Peninsula. Posts could draw on the Committee of Twenty-Four's strong endorsement of unity and indicate that it is our firm belief that there is no viable future for a series of mini-states in Papua New Guinea.

[*matter omitted*]

[NAA: A1838, 3080/1/1/1 PART 1]

---

3   Document 230.

248   LETTER FROM HAY TO WALLER

Canberra, 16 December 1971

Personal and Confidential

Thank you for your letter of 14th December[1] about the impressions of the French Ambassador following the latter's recent visit to Papua New Guinea.

I agree with you that it would be preferable if the French Ambassador were dissuaded from recommending to his Government that it should urge on other governments caution in encouraging the advance to self-government.

The Commonwealth has a publicly expressed policy of:

'encouraging progress towards internal self-government and of looking to the elected members of the House of Assembly to represent the wishes of the majority of the people and to take the initiative in such matters as the pace and nature of constitutional development'.

It is now preparing a programme for movement to full internal self-government in the period 1972–76, but the execution of that programme will have regard to the state of opinion as it develops in Papua New Guinea after the 1972 House of Assembly elections and to the policies of the political leaders who then emerge. This policy involves a number of obvious risks, many of them having been pinpointed by the Ambassador. But the Government has been aware of this all along (see paragraph 12 of the Minister's submission to Cabinet dated 7th April, 1971,[2] and also paragraph 9 of his public statement in the House of Representatives on Papua New Guinea constitutional development dated 27th April, 1971,[3] for example). I would not therefore see any reason to be diverted from existing policy because of the French Ambassador's observations, however pertinent.

I have discussed this attitude with Mr Barnes who fully agrees. He has only one point of disagreement with the observations of the Ambassador, a point to which you refer in your letter. Mr Barnes does not agree that pressure from the United Nations has in recent years weighed heavily with the Government or political leaders in Papua New Guinea.

You suggest in your letter I might take some part in further talks with the French Ambassador. Following our telephone conversation, I am agreeable to seeing him myself. I will let you have a note of the discussion.[4]

More generally, with regard to the considerations you have included in your third paragraph, you might care to see the observations in the submission Mr Barnes put to Cabinet on 7th April on the question of constitutional development. In particular paragraphs 4–17 are relevant. Our tentative planning date for internal self-government is 1975. That could have to be moved forward or backwards depending on the views of the political leaders who emerge after the

---

1   Document 246.

2   Document 155.

3   Document 160.

4   Hay met Van Laethem on 21 December 1971 and began the conversation by saying that 'a change in existing government policy was not likely'. As a result, 'the Ambassador did not pursue as he had in his conversation with Mick Shann the idea that France should take any particular steps on a government basis such as urging caution on visiting representatives of other countries'. See Letter, Hay to Waller, 4 January 1972; and DET, 'Notes of discussion between Ambassador for France and the Secretary, Department of External Territories', 21 September 1971, both in NAA: A1838/3080/10/1 PART 1.

next elections. The latter factor will also affect the independence date. Here for planning purposes we have assumed a date early in the lifetime of the next House of Assembly but one, and are also assuming that whatever the date we choose the reality will probably be somewhat in advance of it.

[NAA: A1838, 3080/10/1 PART 1]

Cartoonist John Keith McCarthy highlights the range of views in Papua New Guinea in mid-1972. McCarthy had earlier been a senior official in the PNG Administration, and then a member of the 1964 House of Assembly.

[PAPUA NEW GUINEA POST-COURIER]

MR TEI ABAL
National Leader
Minister
Member for 8 years.

MR SEVESE MOREA
ABC Announcer
Businessman

MR SINAKE GIREGIRE
Deputy Leader
Minister
Member for 8 years

MR SHONG BABOB
Printer, Educated
Australia, Winner
Churchill Scholarship

United Party

MR TOM LEAHY
Senior Member
Administrator's
Executive Council

MR McKENZIE DAUGI
Teacher, Lectured
Geelong Grammar

MR M. TOLIMAN, MBE
Minister, Member
Executive Council

MR ROBERT SEETO
President Territory
Council Association
Namatanai
Businessman

men

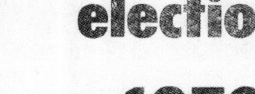

elections

MR TORE LOKOLOKO
Minister, Member
Executive Council

MR MICHAEL AIGAL
Teacher 9 years
Town Councillor

1972

MR ANGMAI BILAS
Minister, Member
Executive Council

MR APASAI SIRENDA
Cocoa Planter
Member Kiviens
Building Board

experience

ability

MR ANDREW WABIRIA
Assistant Minister
for Lands

MR SAM WINGEN
President Kiunga
Council

MR MECK SINGILIONG
Assistant Minister
Corrective Institutions

MR TOM GUMWASEVA
Trobriand Islands
Council Clerk

(Authorised by Vince Nielsen, Hubert Murray Highway, Port Moresby)

United Party election advertisement, February 1972.

[PAPUA NEW GUINEA POST-COURIER]

Polling goes ahead in Hanuabada village, Port Moresby, in February 1972.

[PAPUA NEW GUINEA POST-COURIER]

Josephine Abaijah and Father John Momis.

As a result of her election in early 1972 as the member for Central regional, Abaijah became the first women to be elected to a PNG House of Assembly. Momis, a proponent of Bougainville separatism, was elected as MHA for Bougainville regional in 1972. In June 1972 he was appointed as the Deputy Chairman of the Constitutional Planning Committee.

[DFAT]

Michael Somare with members of his National Coalition Government.
John Guise is on Somare's right, and Julius Chan is on his left.

[PHOTO COURTESY OF DIANNE McINNES]

Senior Australian figures pictured on the occasion of the opening of the new
House of Assembly in April 1972. Standing from left: Les Johnson, Andrew Peacock,
Charles Barnes and David Hay. Sitting: Jack Keith Murray (provisional PNG
Administrator and then Administrator, 1945–52), Sir Paul Hasluck, and Donald
Cleland (PNG Administrator, 1953–67).

[DFAT]

Top: Nigel Bowen, Minister for Foreign Affairs, August 1971–December 1972;
and Sir James Plimsoll, Secretary of the Department of External Affairs, 1965–70
and Ambassador to the United States, 1970–74.

Bottom: Sir Keith Waller, Secretary of the Department of Foreign Affairs, 1970–74;
and Sir Laurence McIntyre, Australia's Permanent Representative to the United Nations,
1970–75.

Supported by their officials, Bowen and his predecessors in the foreign affairs portfolio—
William (Billy) McMahon, 1969–71 and Leslie (Les) Bury, March–August 1971—favoured
a prompt transition to self-government.

[NAA]

*Senior Department of Foreign Affairs officials Lewis (Lew) Border
and David Anderson*

[NAA]

*Sir John Bunting, Secretary, Department
of the Cabinet Office, 1968–71, and
Secretary of the Department of Prime
Minister and Cabinet, 1971–74.*

[NAA]

*Jack Emanuel, District Commissioner,
East New Britain, from 1969 until his
violent death in 1971.*

[DFAT]

Top: Paulus Arek, MHA for Ijivitari and Chair of the Select Committee on Constitutional Development, 1969–72; and Julius Chan, MHA for Namatanai and leader of the People's Progress Party.

Bottom: Ebia Olewale, MHA for South Fly; and Anthony (Tony) Voutas, a former patrol officer and member of the 1964 House of Assembly who became Somare's leading adviser.

[DFAT]

Chief Minister Michael Somare meets Dr H. Roelan Abdulgani, the former Indonesian Permanent Representative at the United Nations, during Dr Abdulgani's visit to Papua New Guinea in September 1972. The Commonwealth Government encouraged good relations between Papua New Guinea and its large neighbour.

[DFAT]

Andrew Peacock and Michael Somare at a meeting in 1972.

[PHOTOGRAPH COURTESY OF ALAN KERR]

249 SAVINGRAM TO ALL POSTS

Canberra, undated [c. mid-December 1971]

170. Unclassified

UN Fourth Committee Resolution on PNG

The following is the text of the resolution adopted unanimously by the Fourth Committee on 14 December, 1971.

Begins:

[*matter omitted*]

6.   Noting in particular the express desire of the people of Papua and the Trust Territory of New Guinea for national unity and independence as a single political and territorial entity.

7.   Taking note of the decision of the House of Assembly of Papua and the Trust Territory of New Guinea that the territory formed from the administrative union of those two territories should be named Papua New Guinea,

8.   Bearing in mind the decisions taken during 1971 by the House of Assembly of Papua and the Trust Territory of New Guinea and the administering power with regard to the attainment of full internal self-government during the period 1972–1976, and the affirmation by the administering power that the interval between the attainment of full self-government and independence will be a matter to be determined by the then Government of Papua and the Trust Territory of New Guinea,

[*matter omitted*]

3.   Calls upon the administering power to take all necessary steps to ensure the speedy attainment by Papua New Guinea of self-government and independence as a single political and territorial entity and in that regard to establish in consultation with the freely elected representatives of the people, a specific time-table for the free exercise by the people of Papua New Guinea for their right to self-determination and independence,

4.   Urges the administering power to discourage separatist movements and to ensure that the unity of Papua New Guinea is preserved throughout the period leading up to independence.

5.   Requests the Trusteeship Council, while continuing to exercise its specific responsibilities towards the Trust Territory of New Guinea, and the Special Committee, to bear in mind the need to consider Papua New Guinea as a single political and territorial entity and to take account of this when determining the itineraries of future visiting missions in consultation with the administering power.

[*matter omitted*][1]

[NAA: A1209, 1971/9229]

---

1   The UN General Assembly, after noting the Fourth Committee's 'conclusions and recommendations', endorsed the essential elements of the resolution on 20 December. It also welcomed 'the invitation extended by the administering Power to the Trusteeship Council to dispatch a special mission to observe the elections to the Papua New Guinea House of Assembly'; urged Australia 'to intensify its programme of political education in Papua New Guinea and to expedite the implementation of the programme for accelerated localization of the Papua New Guinea public service'; and requested the extension of educational services in the territory and that 'the administering Power continue to expand the measures being taken to promote ownership, management and participation by the inhabitants of Papua New Guinea in enterprises throughout all sectors of the economy'. UN General Assembly Resolution 2865(XXVI), 'Question of Papua New Guinea', 20 December 1971, A/RES/2865(XXVI).

250   CABINET SUBMISSION 471[1]

Canberra, undated [c. mid-December 1971]

Papua New Guinea—Transfer of Functions of Internal Self-Government

This submission presents for Cabinet's consideration the recommendations of an Inter-Departmental Committee which it established (Decision No. 452 of 23rd June, 1970)[2] to review the position of Commonwealth departments and agencies now performing functions of internal self-government in Papua New Guinea outside the aegis of the Administration so that a sensible programme for their absorption in appropriate cases into the Papua New Guinea Administration might be prepared.

2.   The Committee consists of the Department of External Territories, the Department of the Prime Minister and Cabinet, the Public Service Board, the Treasury and each of the particular Departments or agencies concerned in turn.

3.   The report is an interim one since the Committee has not completed its review. The Committee states that it is making the interim report in the belief that Ministers may wish to consider an early start being made with the transfer of activities and that Departments and agencies should commence early preparations to that end. A copy of this interim report is attached as Appendix 'A'.[3]

4.   The following bodies have been reviewed by the Committee:

   (i)   Bureau of Mineral Resources
   (ii)   Commonwealth Scientific and Industrial Research Organisation
   (iii)   Department of Shipping and Transport
   (iv)   Department of Works.
   (v)   Bureau of Meteorology
   (vi)   Division of National Mapping
   (vii)   Auditor-General's Office

5.   Consideration of the following bodies has yet to be finalised:

   (i)   Department of Civil Aviation
   (ii)   TAA[4]
   (iii)   Postmaster-General's Department
   (iv)   Overseas Telecommunications Commission
   (v)   ABC[5]
   (vi)   Commonwealth Actuary
   (vii)   Department of External Territories (recruitment and procurement activities)
   (viii)   National Biological Standards Laboratory

---

1   Submitted by Barnes.
2   Document 53.
3   Not published.
4   Trans Australia Airlines.
5   Australian Broadcasting Commission.

6.   The Committee's basic approach has been that every function of internal self-government is appropriate for transfer in readiness for self-government and that in view of Government policy that Papua New Guinea can have self-government whenever the people say they want it, the Government should be prepared for the transfers of the Administration to take place at the earliest practicable time.

7.   In taking this view the Committee states that it had in mind that one of the assumptions of the Submission which led to the Government's decision that this Committee should be established was that while political powers were being transferred to Papua New Guinea as part of the progress towards self-government, steps in relation to administration should also be taken to ensure the smooth transition to internal self-government.

8.   The Committee also had in mind Cabinet Decision No. 89 of 20th April 1971[6] which, on the suggestion of the Select Committee of the Second House of Assembly, approved the drawing up of a time-table for internal self-government. The Select Committee had recommended 'that the development of the Territory be geared to preparing the country for internal self-government during the life of the next House of Assembly (1972–1976) so that should it become a reality earlier than expected and if it is in fact requested by the people then, then the move to internal self-government can be made at that time with the least possible amount of disruption'.

9.   The Committee took the view that, while localisation of staff must be pressed, responsibility for a function can be transferred irrespective of the availability of local staff provided that suitable arrangements for the continued supply of the necessary expatriate staff are made. The Committee recommends that Cabinet approve arrangements to ensure that suitable expatriate staff are available to the Administration as needed to undertake the functions transferred from the Commonwealth.

10. The Committee recommends financial arrangements to facilitate the take-over of functions by the Administration. These would need to be flexible so as to take account of the particular circumstances of each function; a good case would exist for the Commonwealth Government to increase, in the financial year of take-over of a function its total assistance to the Administration by at least the same amount as the Department or agency was spending in Papua New Guinea. Commonwealth Departments or agencies would need to be compensated for any back-up or agency services they were called upon to provide, this cost being taken into account in determining the total amount of assistance to be provided to Papua New Guinea by the Commonwealth. The assistance provided in years subsequent to take-over would be determined in the light of Papua New Guinea needs and the total amount provided in the preceding year. In some cases it might be appropriate for Commonwealth capital assets to be 'sold' to the Administration and in this event some special financial arrangements could be necessary to ease the burden on the Administration's limited resources.

[*matter omitted*]

12. The Committee has developed the following general and tentative time-table it thinks should be aimed at in respect of certain activities so far examined:

1971–72

  Bureau of Mineral Resources (Geological and Vulcanological Branch

  Department of Shipping and Transport (lighthouse services)

  Department of Works (supervision/control of the PNG Administration Works programme; day labour, maintenance and operation)

---

6   Document 159.

1972–73

Bureau of Meteorology

[*matter omitted*]

18. The Committee has recommended that:

(i)   Cabinet endorse the general approach that responsibility for every function of internal self-government now being undertaken by a Commonwealth Department or agency in Papua New Guinea is appropriate for transfer to the Administration in readiness for self-government.

(ii) The Government express its intention that the transfers take place at the earliest practicable dates.

(iii) Lack of suitable local staff should not be allowed to delay transfer. Arrangements for expatriate staff should be made to assist in enabling the Administration to perform the functions transferred to it.

(iv) Cabinet endorse the view that the Commonwealth Departments whose functions in Papua New Guinea are transferred to the Administration should make every effort in conjunction with the Commonwealth Public Service Board to ensure that suitable expatriate staff are available to the Administration, as needed, to undertake the functions transferred from the Commonwealth and that agencies involved should make similar efforts. The heads of the Departments and agencies concerned should for a time accept an obligation to help the Administration to meet its staffing requirements on the basis of equal priority with their own staffing obligations in Australia.

(v)   Upon transfer of a function appropriate arrangements should be made by agreement between the relevant Commonwealth department or agency and the Administration, for necessary specialised services to continue to be rendered on an agency basis.

(vi) Appropriate financial arrangements should be made under which:

(a)   the assets relating to transferred functions which are owned by Commonwealth departments or agencies in Papua New Guinea would be transferred to the Administration;

(b)   the Administration would be required to make an appropriate payment for any services rendered by the Commonwealth department or agency after transfer of the function.

(vii) While it will become the responsibility of the Administration to determine after transfer the level at which the function in question is to be maintained, the Administration should be provided with additional financial assistance in the first year of take-over of any function equal to that which would otherwise have been spent by the Commonwealth. In subsequent years the costs incurred by the Administration in undertaking the function should be taken into account along with other Administration expenditures and revenues in determining the total level of assistance to be provided by the Commonwealth.

(viii) The following be accepted as a target programme for transfer of the functions shown:

1971–72

Bureau of Mineral Resources (Geological and Vulcanological Branch)

Department of Shipping and Transport (Lighthouse Services)

Department of Works (Supervision/control; day labour; maintenance)

1972–73

Bureau of Meteorology

[*matter omitted*]

19. When I announced the establishment of the Inter-departmental Committee I said that the views of the Administrator's Executive Council would be sought in the process of the review. The Administrator's Executive Council noted the time-table suggested by the Committee with interest, but indicated it would like to examine the possibility of phasing the transfer over a longer period. Council saw merit in coming to an early agreement with the Commonwealth on the terms and conditions under which the responsibility for the recurrent financing of such functions would be gradually transferred.

20. Elections are to be held in Papua New Guinea in March/April, 1972 following which a new Administrator's Executive Council will be appointed. I propose that the position regarding transfer of functions be reviewed in, say, July/August, 1972 by which time it would be expected that the new House will have settled down and the attitude of the majority group would be beginning to emerge:

21. I would therefore recommend:

(1) Acceptance of the recommendations of the Report, subject to further consultation with the Administrator's Executive Council about the timing of the proposed transfers and about the arrangements for staffing, finance and the transfer of assets being used in the function; any matters arising from this consultation to be settled between the Treasurer, the Minister concerned and myself;

(2) that when the Committee has formulated views on the second round of functions it is to consider, the views be sought of the Administrator's Executive Council elected from the 1971 House of Assembly before reporting to Cabinet; and

(3) that working parties be set up to effect the proposed transfers. The working parties should consist of a member of the department concerned, the Papua New Guinea Administration, the Department of External Territories, the Department of the Treasury and the Public Service Board.[7]

[NAA: A5908, 471]

---

7   Cabinet endorsed all three recommendations. See Cabinet Decision 674, 'Papua New Guinea—Transfer of Functions of Internal Self-Government', 21 December 1971, NAA: A5908, 471.

251   LETTER FROM WALLER TO HAY

Canberra, 20 December 1971

Thank you for your letter of 30th November[1] addressed to Mr K. C. O. Shann. It is clear from your letter that you feel the Department of Foreign Affairs is endeavouring to intrude into areas which are your responsibility. This was not our intention.

Under the circumstances, I believe that in the period prior to independence, this Department need not concern itself with Papua-New Guinea which as you rightly point out is the responsibility of your Department. It shall so inform my officers.

I am sending copies of this letter to the addressees of my letter of 8th October 1971.[2]

[NAA: A452, 1972/4041]

---

1   Document 242.

2   Document 225.

252   LETTER FROM JOHNSON TO BARNES

Port Moresby, 28 December 1971

CONFIDENTIAL

As the year closes it may be useful if I set down my view of the broad developments of 1971 and try to draw some conclusions as to likely trends in 1972. Although there have been notable developments in politics, in the Public Service and in the economy of Papua New Guinea, the salient feature of the year has been the nature and extent of social change. Social change is the product of many factors: the introduction of a cash economy and the consequent expansion of horizons; national politics; roads and the changed nature of contacts those roads bring; education; radio; improved health; these are but a few of those factors. They have made a dramatic impact on the minds and lives of the people. Even where the outward manifestations of change are hardly apparent, men and women are trying to cope with new concepts and re-arranging their thoughts and their lives accordingly. Often this leads to uncertainty and confusion, to the breakdown of social controls before the new kind of society has its own established mores. It leads to a search for explanations which often results in bizarre beliefs and practices.

Arising from this situation there has been a growing disregard for the established law and for those administering it, which has resulted in a substantial increase in violent crime. The excessive social strains seem likely to continue for this decade and beyond. During that time the law enforcement agencies will have a crucial role to play. Maintaining and increasing their strength and effectiveness is one of the important priorities for 1972 and I have in other correspondence often referred to the need to supplement the Police effort with the almost totally unused capacity of the Army.[1]

It is perhaps invidious to commence this survey by emphasising the need to strengthen the Police, but our new society is fragile indeed, and any serious failure to maintain firmly a coherent body of law would result in either the fragmentation of that society or the alienation of most of its members.

Another of the obvious results of social change has been the changed nature of race relations: some would call it a deterioration, but I think that this would be a misinterpretation of what is happening. The master/servant relationship—or, in the more enlightened section of the community, that of tutor/student—is no longer tenable as a means of social differentiation. Those who persist in regarding Papuans and New Guineans in this light provoke anger, resentment and rejection. In general, race relations remain amicable, but there are tensions which occasionally result in expressions or demonstrations of antipathy. Papuans and New Guineans do not resent expatriates with high levels of skills, nor is there much criticism of the pay they get, but increasingly there is criticism and jealousy of unskilled and semi-skilled young expatriates enjoying a standard of living far above that of their Papuan and New Guinean colleagues. The repatriation of this class of European is unlikely to proceed fast enough to avoid numbers of unpleasant incidents in the next year or two. In particular this will remain a constant source of irritation to the young educated Papuans and New Guineans.

The more apparent expressions of the tensions referred to above have been the subject of earlier surveys: the continuing intransigence of the Mataungan Association;[2] the various

---

1   For Johnson's views on this matter, see Documents 215, 217 (paras 17 & 22) & 219.
2   For background on the Mataungan Association, see Document 49, fn. 3.

cargo-cult movements, most notably the Yeliwan-led cult in the Sepik; the incidents of violence in the Highlands; and the proliferation of movements which are in part a search for identity and in part designed to tap the material riches of modern society: Napidakoe Navitu,[3] Nemea, Damuni, Tutukuvul Kapkapis Association (TKA) and the Mataungan Association are examples. The growth of understanding the development of more logical patterns of thought may transmute all of these into movements working through normal political and economic channels to attain legitimate ends. (Napidakoe has already gone this way). Most of the groups mentioned appear to be moving in this direction in that they are nominating candidates for the 1972 elections, though it must be understood that participation in a national election does not necessarily mean the acceptance of the other trappings of government. At least for the time being most of these movements will preach a disregard for the law—or some of it—and maintain anti-government stances.

The search for identity on a national scale took a long step forward with the acceptance of the recommendations of the Select Committee on Constitutional Development and public opinion moved, perhaps rather grudgingly, to the point of view that self-government would come, if not before 1976, then shortly after. The outward symbols of that identity, name, flag, and crest, were adopted albeit somewhat reluctantly but the whole thing reached a rousing climax with a tumultuous celebration of National Day throughout Papua New Guinea.

As might be expected, these newfound feelings of unity are subject to the pressures of self-interest and in this respect Papua and Bougainville exhibited respectively noisy and strong separatist tendencies. Without discounting the fact that the pre-War Administration in Papua have developed some sense of Papuan unity, the clamour of the Papuans was largely generated by hopes of obtaining some economic advantage. They wanted a greater share of the national resources diverted to their districts and they clung to the possibility that their nominal Australian citizenship might be a further bargaining point. Papuan politicians with an eye to the next elections used separatism to burnish their electoral images. Ultimately, all of the more responsible Papuan leaders accepted the goal of national unity.

Bougainville, however, is and will remain genuinely secessionist and the reasons for this have been traversed previously. At present the strength of the movement is in the centre and south with the north speaking for unity, but this is rather more an indication of internal political rivalries than fundamentally opposed feelings. Almost all of the people of Bougainville are basically secessionist and at this point it is hard to see what courses of action are likely to change them. It is not a problem which causes much administrative difficultly now, but most certainly it is a grave problem for the future.

If Bougainville is excluded, I do not regard the talk of the likely fragmentation of Papua New Guinea as soundly based. There is as yet only a very tenuous feeling of unity, but there is a national parliament and there is a pervasive national Public Service. There is a national education system and a national broadcasting system. So [I am] confident that given a firm Public Service framework supported by an efficient law enforcement body [we] can build a united Papua New Guinea.

The pace of economic development slackened somewhat during the year. The reduction in real terms of the Commonwealth grant coupled with low prices for our export crops meant a check in the growth rate. Nonetheless, there were some encouraging developments. The West New Britain Oil Palm project began producing earlier and more vigorously than the

---

3   The Nasioi people of Bougainville formed *Napidakoe Navitu* in 1969 to oppose land acquisitions and seek compensation. The movement later broadened its support base and supported Bougainville's secession from Papua New Guinea. Ian Downs, *The Australian Trusteeship: Papua New Guinea, 1945–75*, Australian Government Publishing Service, Canberra, 1980, pp. 440, 478; and R. J. May, *State and Society in Papua New Guinea: The First Twenty-Five Years*, Crawford House Publishing, Adelaide, 2001, pp. 60–61.

most optimistic forecasts and generated considerable international interest in adjacent areas. At least two promising occurrences of copper were delineated and it is possible that both may ultimately be producers. Construction began on the Ramu hydro-electric scheme and large financial interests began a study of the vast power potential of the Purari River. The Bougainville copper mine is almost at the production stage. Mineral exploration was pursued vigorously over most of Papua New Guinea and, indeed, exploration reached the proportion of a significant industry in itself. There seem to be good prospects of the establishment of a major fishing industry on the New Guinea coast, while the first agreement to establish a wood chip industry was signed.

These developments or possible developments are meaningless if they do not benefit the people of Papua New Guinea and although they may do so in the future there remain serious problems of under-employment and unemployment and of low productivity and low wages. We are presently at the stage where we have a vast deficiency in skilled workers of all kinds which looks likely to continue for at least some years while the numbers of unskilled seeking work continues to grow. Most of our consultants in these areas propose heroic measures involving adult training programmes, vastly increased resources for education of workers and so on, to overcome the gaps. The simple fact is that we do not have the resources to embark on programmes of sufficient scope to make an early impression on the problem if we are to continue to advance our present broad front. There will need to be some hard choices made, and our third House of Assembly and [Administrator's] Executive Council will be faced with these early in its life when development options and their consequences are placed before them in mid-1972.

Although rapid by any standards, our economic growth has not generated sufficient work opportunities for young men and women leaving school without specific skills or for the unskilled migrants from rural villages. This underemployed group is presently a problem of minor proportions but it may grow to become quite unmanageable and form a disaffected group which would be very easy prey to agitators. The next year and those that follow must see a greater effort to find productive occupations for this group.

I cannot leave this subject of economic development without recording my view that many town residents who are fully employed are not in receipt of an adequate living wage. It is essential that 1972 should see an upwards movement in the base pay for unskilled and semi-skilled workers. Unionism still has little coherence and strength which is to be deplored in the dangerous situation which may result should there be determined employer attempts to hold wages down. Firm unionism can hold its members to reasonable agreements and can prevent erratic and irrational demands. To date our labour problems have been small ones but there is an increasing tendency for workers to make absurd demands and when these are not met to vent their frustrations in threats and violence. I believe that we need to encourage the presentation of a wages case to the Minimum Wages board at an early date in the New Year.

The framing of policy and its execution is in the hands of parliament and the Public Service. During 1971 parliament grew largely in self-confidence though not notably in its perception of the significance of issues, but the public service declined in strength and efficiency though not in actual numbers. The perceptible weakening of the Public Service probably presents 1972 with its gravest problem.

It is unreasonable to expect highly qualified expatriates to choose employment in Papua New Guinea when only short-term contracts are offered and when it is obvious that promotional preferences will favour Papuans and New Guineans. Also, those already employed are seeking the greater security offered in Australia. It is the best qualified of the middle range officers who may be termed well qualified, and the number of young Papuans and New Guineans entering the service with an adequate educational preparation is still very small. For possibly the next five years the Public Service vacancies may be filled, but in very many cases by officers of lesser skill and experience than those they replace. Our attack on this problem must be on two fronts: first with intensive programmes of training for local officers; and, at the same time, by a more determined effort to hold those expatriate officers who are central to continued stability and progress. The first of these measures is already developing well, but today we have been notably unsuccessful in persuading key expatriate officers that their best interests are served by staying, manifestly they are not. It seems that special inducements will have to be offered selectively. Any principle of selectivity is difficult to introduce into an egalitarian public service but it is time that Australian public service practices were discarded. Papua New Guinea development, and perhaps even survival, depends on maintaining the Public Service is a firm national framework.

In the preceding paragraph I have not referred specifically to localisation but when the new promotional measures are implemented in the New Year satisfactory progress should be made. Despite the above remarks concerning the retention of expatriate officers, I regard it as completely essential that Papuan and New Guinean officers should move quickly into decision making posts. However, we cannot afford to lose the experienced officers they may replace and the approved policy of retaining these officers in other roles is essential to progress—though persuading them to stay is another matter. In this context, our judgement of the [acceptability] of the Employment Security Scheme was at fault. What seemed to me to be a reasonably generous approach was vilified as niggardly. Perhaps the real problem is the sense of insecurity engendered by the proposals and by confrontation with the fact that self-government is approaching rapidly. Assuming that the basic financial provisions are unlikely to be changed appreciably, the only other measure which may change attitudes is the Australian Government taking direct responsibility for compensation payments and pensions.

I referred previously to the growth in self-confidence of the House of Assembly, but it was used more often to promote individual or group interests than for national purposes. There was little evidence of the developing political parties trying to promote any consistent policies. In general, policy initiatives came from the Administration; the AEC and the House of Assembly reacted to those initiatives. It is hardly to be expected that national initiatives would come from poorly informed politicians with no defined central executive body to shape ideas. There has, however, been some growth in political party coherence in that each of the three major parties is attempting to establish working executive committees serviced by full-time employees. Presently it is convenient and makes for more efficient government for initiatives to arise from within a Public Service still Australian in outlook and still largely subject to Australian direction, but whether or not this is in the best interests of the future for Papua New Guinea is quite another matter. The strengthening of the executives of the political parties, so that the operation of government more closely resembles that in Australia or the United Kingdom, is one way of ensuring that policies are made in Papua New Guinea, though I have always had some doubt as to whether such a system is particularly suited to Papua New Guinea society. If indeed the party system solidifies and party government becomes established, there may be merit in setting up what might be called a National Advisory Council, including representatives of all parties, which could be a sounding board for broad policy proposals.

As I have observed above, not much in the way of policy initiative comes from the AEC but individually and as a group they developed a high degree of confidence in their judgements and were much firmer in their advocacy of particular courses of action. In the House of Assembly Ministers generally performed poorly in defending AEC policy decisions unless that decision directly touched their own portfolios and the burden of advocacy and defence continued to fall on Official Members. This support will largely disappear in the 1972 House—Ministers will be forced to accept public responsibility for both their individual and collective decisions. It must be said that the AEC reacts conservatively in most instances. It adopts a hard line on law and order, would apply very restrictive measures to migrants and summarily terminate the residence permits of those it considered trouble makers. In general, it views wage rises with caution. It wants to ensure the retention of expatriate skills and to continue to hold and attract large scale overseas capital movement. In this latter regard, it has moved quite markedly to an acceptance of Japanese investment. It very strongly favours the development of indigenous business enterprise, possibly at the expense of the small scale Australian or Asian entrepreneur. In general, its policy orientation is towards economic development as a priority, though during the latter part of the year social issues assumed more prominence in discussions. There is no reason to think that the new Ministry in 1972 will be much different from the present one.

I should like to conclude this over-long document by summarising the important objectives for 1972 as I see them:

1.   Continue the present measures and implement new ones to preserve the strength and efficiency of the Public Service.

2.   Appreciably strengthen our capacity to preserve law and order and concurrently embark on a programme to develop a greater sense of civic responsibility among the people of Papua New Guinea.

3.   Take strong measures to upgrade the quality of the indigenous work force.

4.   Ameliorate the unemployment problem for youth in urban areas.

5.   Continue programmes designed to create a national consciousness and promote national unity.

6.   Bear in mind that individual objectives serve a common end—a better Papua New Guinea society.

May I express my warm appreciation, both as Administrator and personally, for the firm guidance and support you have given us and for the help provided by the Department of External Territories. The cooperation between the Department and the Administration has been both harmonious and productive.[4]

[NAA A452, 1972/0932]

---

4   In January 1972, Barnes replied: 'I am myself very happy with the way things are developing in Papua New Guinea from the Government's point of view. Clearly the Administration is in very good hands and I record in this letter my appreciation of your own achievements and those of your officers in the past year.' Letter, Barnes to Johnson, undated (c. early January 1972), NAA: A 452, 1972/0932.

253   LETTER FROM BILAS TO MCMAHON

Port Moresby, 31 December 1971

CONFIDENTIAL

I refer to the statement you made in the House of Representatives on 25th November[1] last informing the House about the successful conclusion of negotiations with Britain and the European Economic Community on behalf of Papua New Guinea.

I have been asked by the Administrator's Executive Council to convey to you our sincere appreciation for the efforts that the Australian Government made on our behalf to bring this matter to a satisfactory conclusion. We believe that the outcome announced in Brussels on the 24th November, 1971 is most satisfactory for Papua New Guinea in view of our very heavy dependence upon the British market for the sale of many of our exports.[2]

When I visited Britain and the member countries of the European Economic Community as leader of a Papua New Guinea Delegation in October/November, 1970, I was very aware that the success of the visit was largely due to the strenuous efforts by officers of the Commonwealth Departments of Foreign Affairs and Trade and Industry. These officers had made representations on Papua New Guinea's behalf long before my Delegation's visit and these representations were carefully followed up throughout 1971 by Ambassadors and Trade Officers in the foreign capitals. Officers of the Departments of External Territories have, of course, facilitated all these arrangements and representations over the long period of the negotiations.

I am very mindful of the personal interest that you took in this matter and of your representations to the British Prime Minister[3] and Mr Rippon[4] when you visited London in November last.

I am also aware of the personal efforts of the Deputy Prime Minister and Minister for Trade and Industry—in the early stages Mr McEwen and then subsequently Mr Anthony—who, on several occasions, made representations on our behalf.

Would you please pass on to the relevant Ministers this word of thanks and appreciation for a long and strenuous combined effort which has resulted in a favourable conclusion which I believe will be of great benefit to the future development of Papua New Guinea.[5]

[NAA: A452, 1972/0235]

---

1   In the statement McMahon said negotiations had been successfully concluded, with it agreed that PNG's exports would 'be able to enter the United Kingdom until 1 January 1978, under the conditions which apply at the time of British accession to the Community'. The agreement allowed 'for the review of these arrangements' and the British Government had 'expressed its confidence that the Community would make reasonable arrangements for Papua/New Guinea in the context of any review'. Statement by McMahon, 'Papua/New Guinea and the European Economic Community', 25 November 1971, A452, 1972/0235.

2   Papua New Guinea exported coconut oil, copra, cocoa, tea and pyrethrum to the United Kingdom. In early 1972 a DET brief noted that if appropriate arrangements to protect PNG interests had not been made then 'some $18M worth of exports; i.e. about a quarter of PNG's export trade, would have been at risk'. Notes on two Cabinet submissions on Australia and the Enlarged EEC, undated [February?] 1972, NAA: A452, 1972/0235.

3   Edward (Ted) Heath, UK Prime Minister, 1970–74.

4   Geoffrey Rippon, UK Chancellor of the Duchy of Lancaster and Chief Negotiator with EEC, 1970–72.

5   McMahon replied to Bilas on 20 January 1972. He thanked him and said he was sending copies of Bilas's letter to those of his ministerial colleagues who had been 'engaged in this matter'. Letter, McMahon to Bilas, NAA: 1972/0235.

Part 3

Documents, January–December 1972

'Most important: establishment of relations of mutual confidence between our governments': Key Developments in 1972

In January, Territories Minister Charles Barnes resigned and was succeeded by Andrew Peacock, formerly Minister for the Army, who brought a new energy to the role. Peacock visited Papua New Guinea as soon as he had been appointed, and visited several more times before the change of government in December 1972. He made it clear to his officials that he wanted to move ahead promptly towards self-government for the Territory and to build rapport with PNG leaders. He noted on a submission from Hay in February that: 'Most important: establishment of relations of mutual confidence between our two governments' (Document 260).

Elections for the expanded House of Assembly took place from February to March 1972. The conservative, Highlands-based United Party (UP) won 42 seats; Michael Somare's nationalist Pangu Pati (Papua and New Guinea Union Party) won around 24 seats; and Julius Chan's moderate, business-oriented People's Progress Party (PPP) won 10 seats.[1] Of the four women candidates, one was successful—Josephine Abaijah, who won the Central regional seat and thus became the first women elected to a House of Assembly.[2]

Officials expected the UP to form a government, slowing the momentum towards self-government (Documents 217, 275 & 310). Michael Somare and his colleagues, however, manoeuvred effectively to form a National Coalition Government (NCG), based on Pangu and the PPP, with Somare emerging as Chief Minister of Papua New Guinea.

At the opening of the new House on 20 April Governor-General Sir Paul Hasluck said it was government policy 'to encourage the movement towards self-government but not to impose self-government upon Papua New Guinea.' The Australian Government looked to the House 'to represent the wishes of the majority of the people and to take the initiative on the pace and nature of constitutional development' (Document 281).

In June, Somare established a cross-party Constitutional Planning Committee, tasked to recommend 'on a constitution for full internal self-government' (Document 317). In late June he announced a target date for self-government of December 1973, which Peacock accepted (Documents 318 & 336). In the course of the year Peacock established a strong rapport with Somare, including during talks held in July and August.

Peacock reported to Cabinet on the outcome of the talks on 30 August, noting Somare's wish to have authority in all areas transferred as soon as practicable. He said Somare and his colleagues were not distinguishing between self-government powers and those more appropriate to a state of independence. Papua New Guinea could thus find itself virtually independent at the time when internal self-government was attained (Document 361).

Cabinet endorsed Peacock's approach and—while recognising the likelihood of a shortened interval between self-government and independence—expressed a preference for the transition to independence to take place in the term of the next House of Assembly, that is, in the four years from April 1976 (Document 370).

During the year senior figures addressed the challenge posed by the departure of key expatriates from public service positions. Many expatriate public servants were concerned that, should

---

1   James Griffin, Hank Nelson and Stewart Firth, *Papua New Guinea. A Political History*, Heinemann Educational Australia, Richmond, 1979, pp. 182–3.

2   Ian Downs, *The Australian Trusteeship: Papua New Guinea, 1945–75*, Australian Government Publishing Service, Canberra, 1980, p. 486.

they opt to stay on after Papua New Guinea's transition to self-government, their conditions of service and job security could be at risk. In December 1971 the Administrator, Les Johnson, had said that probably 'the gravest problem' for the year ahead was the 'perceptible weakening' of the public service because it was hard to retain key expatriates while young educated Papua New Guineans to take up positions were in scarce supply (Document 252). In February 1972, a senior official advised Peacock that many expatriates were 'not in the mood to stay on' (Document 260). In October, the Cabinet agreed in principle to arrangements whereby Australian officers could be deemed to be Commonwealth employees when responsibility for the public service was transferred to the PNG Government (Documents 394 & 395).

The victory of the Australian Labor Party in Australia's national elections on 2 December 1972 marked the beginning of a new phase in Australia's relations with Papua New Guinea. Soon afterwards Whitlam declared: 'It is altogether probable that Papua New Guinea will be fully independent and, one trusts, admitted to both the United Nations and the Commonwealth of Nations ... no more than two years from now (Document 412).'

254   LETTER FROM BARNES TO MCMAHON

Canberra, 6 January 1972

Last May I forwarded for your comment a proposed paper on domestic citizenship which had been drafted for consideration by the Papua New Guinea House of Assembly.[1] In your reply of 7th June[2] you noted the statement and my intention that, when firm proposals on citizenship were developed they would be brought forward for consideration by Cabinet. This letter will bring you up to date on the present situation.

A statement on citizenship was tabled in the House of Assembly in June and debated in September.[3] The debate was adjourned and is not likely to be resumed until after a new House is elected in February/March [...] However, it seems from speeches by Papuan and New Guinean members that, although there is some support for the creation of a domestic citizenship, most members are opposed to any arrangement under which Australians could obtain the benefits of domestic citizenship without committing themselves in any definite way to Papua New Guinea or foregoing any benefits of Australian citizenship. Some members were of the opinion that it would be premature to create a domestic citizenship ahead of self-government.

The Administrator of Papua New Guinea has suggested that, in the light of the attitudes expressed during the debate, the Government should not attempt to set the pace in this field but should leave it to the House of Assembly.[4] I have accepted the Administrator's advice and I will keep you informed of any important decisions made by the House.

I am sending a letter in similar terms to the Minister for Immigration[5] for his information.[6]

[NAA: A452, 1971/4011]

---

1   Document 176.
2   Not published.
3   Document 182.
4   See Document 202.
5   Jim Forbes.
6   McMahon acknowledged receipt of the letter on 10 January 1972.

255   STATEMENT BY BARNES

Canberra, 12 January 1972

Papua New Guinea House of Assembly Elections

On the eve of the Papua New Guinea House of Assembly elections, the Minister for External Territories, Mr Barnes, has emphasised the importance of the elections in the constitutional development of Papua New Guinea. Mr Barnes said the elections were vital because the transition to internal self-government could occur during the period of the next House of Assembly.

Mr Barnes said that the fact that more than 600 people had nominated for the elections to begin on 19 February demonstrated that the people of Papua New Guinea recognised the importance of the House of Assembly in the movement of their country to nationhood.

The candidates represented a wide cross-section of the Papua New Guinea community and gave the people of Papua New Guinea a broad choice for the future progress of their country.

The significance of the next House of Assembly and the people who compose it stemmed from the report of the House of Assembly's Select Committee on Constitutional Development.[1]

Mr Barnes said: 'Last year, in response to the request by the House of Assembly, the Australian Government undertook to prepare a programme for movement to full internal self-government during the life-time of the 1972–76 House of Assembly should the people want it at that time. Preliminary work is proceeding in readiness for negotiations with Papua New Guinea political leaders after the elections.

'The programme will, in effect, be a list of the legislative and administrative actions which will have to be taken in Australia and Papua New Guinea before internal self-government.

'It is being prepared in consultation with the Administration and Commonwealth departments concerned, for consideration by the Government. The programme will necessarily be flexible because its execution will have to have regard to the state of opinion as it develops after the 1972 elections and to the policies of Papua New Guinea's political leaders.

'As so many candidates representing such a wide range of interests have nominated and as the elections are of such critical importance to Papua New Guinea, I hope that all eligible people will now exercise their responsibilities and will go to the polls aware of the issues and their candidate's attitudes towards them.'

[NAA: A452, 1971/3550]

1   Document 142.

256   MINUTE FROM HAY TO GREENWELL

Canberra, 12 January 1972

CONFIDENTIAL

Relevance of Decision on Citizenship to Programme of Movement towards Internal Self-Government

I have been giving some thought to this matter and am forming the view that the Government should not be in a position of having to take a decision on a fundamental matter such as the date of internal self-government or the main elements of a programme of movement towards it unless it is satisfied that the political leaders with whom it is dealing have been selected by citizens of Papua New Guinea.

In short, I am concerned lest decisions may be influenced by persons who do have not a long-term stake in Papua New Guinea and who could cause decisions to be made to serve relatively short-term interests on the understanding that if the results were not palatable then those responsible could fall back on their Australian or other expatriate citizenship.

This suggests that at the talks with the Papua New Guinea leadership in mid-1972 we should place fairly high on the agenda the resolution of the citizenship question and should at least consider beforehand whether it should not be a government position, stated to the PNG leadership, that we will only deal with Papua New Guinea citizens on important matters including the handing over of power.

If this becomes a departmental view then I think we would need to consider including it in the 'programme' submission and asking for some government reaction to it.[1]

Please give this some thought and advise your views, in consultation with FAS (CS)[2] and Asst. Sec. (SD).[3]

[NAA: A452, 1971/4011]

---

1   DET was preparing a Cabinet submission focusing on PNG's 'Programme of Movement Towards Internal Self-Government'. See Documents 278 & 283.

2   Tim Besley.

3   L. F. Hennessy, Assistant Secretary, Social Development Branch, DET.

257   MINUTE FROM BESLEY TO HAY

Canberra, 25 January 1972

CONFIDENTIAL

Relevance of Decision on Citizenship to Programme
of Movement towards Internal Self-Government

I share the concern expressed in your minute of 12 January 1972.[1]

2.   During my visit to Port Moresby last week I gained the impression that small sectional interests are if anything stepping up their campaign to influence the course of constitutional development for their own short term benefit.[2] I think this coupled with the views expressed in the House when the citizenship issue was discussed point to the need to ensure that important issues should be settled between the Australian Government and bona fide Papua New Guinea citizens.

3.   I therefore see merit in including this concept in the gearing up programme and in pursuing the question of citizenship early in the life of the next House of Assembly so that those expatriates who are eligible and who wish to opt for Papua New Guinea citizenship can do so at the earliest practicable time.

[NAA: A452, 1971/4011]

---

1   Document 256.

2   Hay and Besley appear to have been concerned about the activities of some expatriate businessmen in PNG. See also Document 260, section (b) (vii).

258   NATIONAL BROADCAST BY PEACOCK[1]

Port Moresby, 4 February 1972

I am pleased to be with you on this my first visit to Papua New Guinea as Minister for External Territories.

I have been here a number of times before and so I know something of the developments taking place and of the problems too. But this time I look at Papua New Guinea with new eyes—the eyes of the Minister who must speak for you in the Australian Parliament and the Minister who is responsible in that Parliament for Australia's work in Papua New Guinea.

I cannot do this job unless you and I know each other very well. It is not enough that I hear of your problems and read about them, I must see them for myself and I must hear your voices telling me about them. I need to know your minds and your hearts too.

I plan to begin this now. I have already had personal discussions with many different people— with political leaders, with Administration officers, with community leaders and with men and women from many different jobs and many different places. Next week I plan to come again and to meet you and see and hear you in as many districts as I can visit in the short time I will have. I plan to make frequent visits to Papua New Guinea and I hope to get to know many of you personally. Very many of you are not town dwellers, so I will see you in the villages.

I come to my new work at an important time in the history of your country for you are on the road to self-government and independence. The Australian Government is there to help you carry out your wishes. The people of Papua New Guinea and the people of Australia have been partners now for a long time. In that time we have got to know each other well and to trust each other too. Now Papua New Guinea is increasingly managing its own affairs. Our wish is that we can help you to do so. In so doing we look to the House of Assembly to speak for you and to speak clearly as to the pace and nature of constitutional development. On the recommendation of the Select Committee on Constitutional Development the Australian Government has prepared a programme for movement to full internal self-government in the life of the 1972/76 House of Assembly should the people want it during that time. Preliminary work is underway in readiness for negotiations with your political leaders after the elections.

There can be no doubt that these are testing and demanding times and it may be that many of you have doubts and fears. The road ahead is not an easy one. You are building a nation and this is a task which will take all of your strength, courage and endurance and all of your political and administrative skills. It requires, in particular, a new bond among the people of this country. It calls for loyalty to a nation stretching far beyond the family, clan and village to the whole of Papua New Guinea.

I can only guess what it means to you to accept this new and additional allegiance. It may often mean confusion but it is nonetheless absolutely essential if the fullest scope is to be given to the development of Papua New Guinea and to the creative energy of its people. Only thus can you establish a Papua New Guinea nation that will stand in pride among the nations of the world.

The House of Assembly is the voice of Papua New Guinea. It is heard in Australia and far beyond. That voice has said that Papua New Guinea shall be one country, one people, one nation. Through the members of the House of Assembly you speak to the world and through

---

1   Andrew Peacock, MP for Kooyong, was sworn in as the Minister for External Territories on 2 February after Barnes retired on 25 January. Peacock immediately left for his first visit to Port Moresby in his new capacity. He had previously visited as Minister for the Army.

the House you make the great decisions about your future. Let me say that you make these decisions with the best wishes of the Australian people. We are your partner at the moment and as partners we can help one another by talking freely and being open with our thoughts.

I look forward to meeting you and to seeing a great deal of you and your beautiful country.

[NAA: A1838, 3080/1/6 PART 1]

259   LETTER FROM PEACOCK TO MCMAHON

Canberra, 9 February 1972

You recently arranged for the South Australian Police Commissioner, Brigadier J. C. McKinna, to visit Papua New Guinea to report on a request for special assistance from the Commonwealth to strengthen the officer component of the Royal Papua New Guinea Constabulary.

Brigadier McKinna presented his report[1] to me on 2nd February. He fully supports the assessment made by the Administrator and the Papua New Guinea Police Commissioner[2] that the Constabulary has a critical shortage of commissioned officers. This situation has arisen at a time when the Constabulary is not only facing an increasing crime rate, especially in urban areas, but is also being called upon to meet more frequently and deal with situations of emergency which are not uncommon as an underdeveloped country moves towards self-government and independence as Papua New Guinea is doing. The assessment of the Administrator, supported by Brigadier McKinna is that the Constabulary is unable to meet the challenges before it due to the serious shortage of commissioned officers.

Brigadier McKinna also agrees that the request by the Papua New Guinea Police Commissioner for the secondment of experienced police from the Australian Police Force is the only satisfactory means of overcoming immediately the shortage of commissioned officers until sufficient indigenous officers can be trained to fill the gap. Brigadier McKinna has urged that action be taken as soon as possible.

I agree with Brigadier McKinna's report, and my own discussion in Port Moresby last week with the Administrator, the Police Commissioner and other senior officers leaves no doubt in my mind that there is an urgent need for immediate remedial action with the full support of the Commonwealth.

I am therefore writing to ask that you seek the agreement of State Premiers to the secondment of members of Australian Police Forces to a special contingent of up to 30 police for service in Papua New Guinea. It is proposed that the term of secondment for the contingent would be two years and that it should assemble in Port Moresby in August 1972. I am anxious that the agreement of State Premiers be secured in time for their Police Commissioners to be prepared to discuss details of the proposal at their conference in Perth on 9th April and, if possible, arrive at agreed conclusions.

I enclose a suggested draft letter to the State Premiers.[3] This stresses the fundamental importance of the maintenance of stability based upon law and order as Papua New Guinea makes the transition to internal self-government and independence.

If you agree, I propose to write to the Attorney-General[4] and the Minister for the Interior[5] in similar terms, requesting their assistance in arranging the secondment of officers of the Commonwealth Police Force to the proposed contingent.

I attach for your information a copy of Brigadier McKinna's report.

[NAA: A452, 1972/1079]

---

1   Not published.
2   Norman Allan Mark Nichols, OBE.
3   Not published.
4   Ivor Greenwood.
5   Ralph Hunt.

260   SUBMISSION FROM HAY TO PEACOCK

Canberra, 18 February 1972

CONFIDENTIAL

Papua New Guinea—General Assessment

I have set down in this note some observations which you may wish to discuss.

(a) You have taken office at a time when a basic change of direction has been taken by the Commonwealth and broad lines of policy set by the government. The change originated with initiatives by the former PM in early 1970 which led to major policy decisions in mid-1970 (as a result of which for the first time some power of decision was given to political leaders in PNG) and early 1971 (as a result of which the possibility of a timetable for movement to full internal self-government by 1976 was accepted). Several important consequential policy decisions were taken in 1971 on, for example, localisation, expanded training for public servants, and retention of key expatriates. Accompanying these political and administrative decisions there has been a conscious policy of placing more financial responsibility on Papua New Guinea—both for revenue and for deciding on expenditure.

(b) Within this policy framework there are many critical areas, some of which will require government policy decisions, and others of which will require decision by you in consultation with PNG leaders. I list these below:

(i)   Definition of Australia's national interest against the time when PNG becomes independent. At present the UN Charter sets out our obligations. These will, formally, be discharged at independence.

(ii)   National unity. The government has not taken a formal stand on what it would do if, e.g. Bougainville sought to secede.

(iii) Planning of and preparation for the hand-over of the remaining powers.

(iv)   The timetable of movement to internal self-government.

(v)   The judiciary and court systems.

(vi)   The strengthening of the police force, and the role of the Army in internal security.

(vii) Citizenship. There is no Papua New Guinea citizenship. Expatriates, who may have no long term intention of staying in Papua New Guinea, are able to exercise considerable political and economic influence.

(viii) The structure of government in PNG—in particular, the distribution of power between the centre and the Districts.

(ix)   Commonwealth aid policy.

(x)   The setting of goals for national development, and the preparation of a national development programme to be put into effect when the present five year programme ends in 1973.

(xi)   The social problems consequent upon economic development

E.g. urban drift

school dropouts

(xii) The preservation of PNG's cultural and natural heritage.

(xiii) Relations with Japan and other foreign investors. Australia's future role in investment.

(c) Apart from these general problems, particular issues will arise, e.g.

Police officer strength

Excess coffee production

Retention of expatriate public servants

Papuan and Bougainville separatism

Effectiveness of training programmes, particularly the proposed training of Papua New Guineans at ASOPA.[1]

(d) The machinery at your disposal consists of:

a Department which has responsibilities to advise and inform the Minister, assist the Administration and, with the Administration, carry out government policies;

an Administration headed by an Administrator whose duty it is to administer the government of Papua New Guinea on behalf of the Commonwealth, and various departments and statutory organisations. Of these the Public Service Board and the Judiciary occupy special positions. Both have a direct link with you deriving from responsibilities of the Commonwealth contained in the Papua New Guinea Act. In all cases the normal channel of communications to you is through the Department, but this is without prejudice to the right of the Administrator, the Chief Justice and the Chairman of the Public Service Board to communicate direct with you. Relations with the Administration are complicated by the fact that some departmental heads, though still appointed by you and under direction of the Administrator, advise Papua New Guinea Ministers who exercise independent powers of decision.

(e) The system has been working reasonably well, for two reasons:

(i)   There is much more latitude in the hands of the Administrator than before, even in areas which are still within Commonwealth responsibility; and

(ii)   There is good cooperation and teamwork between the Administrator and the Department.

(f) Nevertheless the outlook is, in my view, at best uncertain, for the following reasons:

(i)   There are few accepted leaders prepared to accept the responsibility of exercising power nationally;

(ii)   Modern ways in relation to local government, paying tax, the law, disposal of land have not yet generally taken root. Their continuance still depends on the Administration. There are no indigenous equivalents on which to fall back;

(iii)   The administrative framework of government still depends on expatriates (though much less so than five years ago). Those expatriates are feeling the strain and many of them are not in the mood to stay on if, for instance, social conditions for their families and their own financial futures are not secure;

(iv)   The economy still heavily depends on expatriates—for investment, production, distribution, training and the paying of taxes. In the few industries (e.g. coffee) where Papua New Guineans predominate, any difficulties could lead to demands that the expatriates bear the brunt of any unpleasant remedies;

1   Australian School of Pacific Administration located at Middle Head, Sydney.

(v)   The economy is also heavily dependent on an increasing annual Australian grant. There is resistance to this within the Commonwealth Government. As the movement towards internal self-government proceeds, there will be pressure to do away with the special aid status which Papua New Guinea now enjoys and put her on the same footing as other recipients;

(vi)   Even though Australia and Papua New Guinea are so mutually dependent, it is likely that areas of difference will emerge and be publicly debated. The current difference on oil drilling in the Gulf of Papua is an example. The Papua Queensland border is another. Trade interest may well diverge. Australia may expect to receive greater protection in the Papua New Guinea market. In particular, Papua New Guinea leaders may wish to deal with lawlessness and dissidence with a degree of force which may not be well received in Australia. These factors are likely to make for earlier separation than otherwise would be considered feasible.

(g) In these circumstances, much is going to depend on the quality of decisions taken by the Commonwealth over the next few months and years. But perhaps more will depend on the establishment of relationships of mutual confidence between the Commonwealth and Papua New Guinea governments. In this, your own role will be critically important. If you succeed, then Papua New Guinea leaders will look to you and consult you on all important decisions. They will ring you up or ask to see you frequently. This will do much to ensure a smooth transition and a friendly relationship thereafter. It is hardly necessary to emphasise the importance for building up a relationship of confidence of your knowing the country and its people as intimately as possible.[2]

[NAA: A452, 1972/0932]

---

2   Peacock annotated the submission: 'Most imp[ortant]: Establishment of relations of mutual confidence between our governments'.

261   NOTE FOR FILE BY DRAKE-BROCKMAN[1]

Canberra, 25 February 1972

Minister's Comments on Self-Government/Independence[2]

The Minister was generally cautious and non-committal on the question of self-government and constantly returned to the theme that the people of PNG themselves must decide. At this stage, he was mainly interested in hearing their views.

The Minister put great emphasis on the House of Assembly as the means of gauging opinion on the question of self-government. He said that the Australian Government's policy was:

'to await the elections themselves, then to await the determinations of the Members of the House of Assembly ... and their recommendations ... in regard to any gearing up programme as such. The pace at which it should develop would be largely determined by them, but within the time frame recommended of course by the (Select) Committee' (Press Conference, Port Moresby, 3/2).

Though he most often stressed the pivotal role of the House of Assembly, the Minister suggested (15/2) that there were various alternative methods of determining when the people were ready for self-government 'a referendum, consensus, the viewpoint of the House of Assembly' (*Age* 15/2). However, on his first visit he stated that the pace would be set by those elected, rather than by referendum (Press Conference, Port Moresby, 3/2).

The Minister was particularly taken by the 'extraordinarily strong opposition to self-government' in Highland areas—'put with greater force than I would have perhaps anticipated' (Press Conference, 15/2). The contrast between this and the sentiment in coastal regions prompted the Minister to remark:

Self-government [is seen] by some groups as a panacea, by others as the great barrier to all problems. They are going to have to show an understanding of one another's views which you won't get at this stage during an election campaign. They need an awareness that this is a great national issue which is going to have a tremendous impact' (*Age* 15/2).

When asked whether Australia would push PNG towards self-government, the Minister replied:

'In neither way would I rush them at all ... We have made it clear that we will be looking to them to express a view. My predecessor has made this clear, and others have' (Press Conference, Port Moresby, 3/2).

He added that the pace of development so far had been satisfactory. When asked on his next visit whether Australia would wait indefinitely for PNG to arrive at self-government, the Minister said:

'To answer this would cut right across our stated policy to be guided by the House of Assembly. Of course an important consideration is the manner in which this advice is tendered—whether it is an overwhelming vote' (*Age*, 15/2)

The Minister confirmed a reporter's assertion that there were various legal and administrative hurdles to be overcome before self-government could be attained. He added that revenue raising was another vital prerequisite (Press Conference, Port Moresby, 3/2).

---

1   The role and position of this DET official has not been established.

2   The document records Peacock's comments during his first two visits as Minister for External Territories to Papua New Guinea on 3 and 15 February 1972.

Asked if he envisaged any alteration [to]the Westminster-type system in PNG the Minister replied that he had a 'natural bias' towards a political structure which mirrored, that of Australia; but he added: 'I would have to look at any request that were made to amend the system with the utmost seriousness' (Press Conference, Port Moresby, 3/2).

The Minister said little about the question of independence: 'I don't envisage in the short term at all, New Guinea being primarily responsible for her own defence; I don't think many would' (Press Conference, Port Moresby, 3/2).

[NAA: A452, 1971/0514]

262   SUBMISSION FROM HAY TO PEACOCK

Canberra, 1 March 1972

CONFIDENTIAL

Papua New Guinea—Cabinet Submission on 'Gearing Up'

By decision No 89 of 20 April 1971[1] Cabinet accepted, inter alia, those recommendations of the Select Committee on Constitutional Development which had been endorsed by the House of Assembly. In doing so Cabinet agreed with the first recommendation in the Select Committee's report that:

'the development of the Territory be geared to preparing the country for internal self-government during the life of the next House of Assembly so that it should become a reality earlier than expected or if it is in fact requested by the people then, then the move to internal self-government can be made at that time with the least possible amount of administrative disruption'.

Cabinet authorised the drafting of a flexible programme of movement towards internal self-government, to include the kinds of political and economic relations which should exist between Australia and Papua New Guinea at internal self-government. The Submission to Cabinet and the Decision are attached.[2]

The then Minister for External Territories, in a statement to parliament on 27 April 1971 (copy attached)[3] referring to the approximate timetable and 'gearing up' mentioned in the Select Committee's report, said

'... the Government will adopt a flexible attitude. It will prepare a programme for movement to full internal self-government in the period 1972–1976, but the execution of that programme will have regard to the state of opinion as it develops after the 1972 House of Assembly elections and to the policies of the political leaders who then emerge.'[4]

Accordingly the Department, in consultation with the Administration and other Commonwealth Departments who have a major interest in the developing of Papua New Guinea (Prime Minister's, Foreign Affairs, Attorney-General's, Defence, Trade and Industry and Treasury) has prepared a draft programme for movement to full internal self-government in Papua New

---

1   Document 159.

2   For the Cabinet Submission and Decision, see Documents 155 & 159.

3   For the statement, see Document 160.

4   Although presented as a verbatim record, this is rather a very close paraphrase of the wording of the statement.

Guinea. This programme has involved the development of detailed forward planning in all areas of government and administration.

For the purposes of this programme only, September 1975 has been chosen arbitrarily as the date for granting full internal self-government. The selected date is a flexible one, and can be moved either forwards or backwards as circumstances and events permit or require. The date has its advantages in that it occurs towards the end of the period 1972–1976, which the Select Committee on Constitutional Development has referred to as the 'gearing-up' period and appropriately September is the month during which National Day is celebrated in Papua New Guinea. On the other hand Australian elections are currently scheduled for about that period (the end of 1975) and, in addition, it occurs almost at the end of the term of office of the next House of Assembly.

As previously mentioned the programme has been discussed only with certain Commonwealth Departments with a view to having the papers in a sufficiently agreed form so as to be able to submit them to you.

[*matter omitted*]

The programme is the central core of the Government's planning for movement to internal self-government, but it is not the only element in the planning. There are other essential steps which are necessary to ensure the country's readiness for internal self-government such as the stepping-up of localisation in the Public Service, the retention of key expatriate officers, the complex task of achieving more indigenous involvement in the economic sector of Papua New Guinea and the settling of such things as control over internal security during the period. On this last matter a study has been completed and will be the subject of a separate draft Cabinet submission to be put before you shortly.

In the past couple of years the Department of Foreign Affairs both at Ministerial and Permanent Head level, has suggested that a permanent head level inter-departmental committee be established to ensure coordination of all policy aspects of Papua New Guinea's development.[5] This has been resisted by this Department as well as the other Departments concerned. The suggestion for a permanent head policy committee on Papua New Guinea may be raised again when Cabinet considers this submission and briefing material will be prepared for you at that time. I mention this now only as background for your consideration of the attached papers.

[*matter omitted*]

The programme serves a twofold purpose. In the first place, it defines what needs to be done, it plans the timing of such needs and points up possible relationships between the various activities which may be necessary before internal self-government can come about. Secondly, the programme will help to ensure that the wishes of the people are carried out with the least amount of administrative disruption.

[*matter omitted*]

[NAA: A452, 1972/811]

---

5   See especially Documents 225, 239, 242 & 251.

263   LETTER FROM PEACOCK TO JOHNSON

Canberra, 7 March 1972

CONFIDENTIAL

The purpose of this letter is to inform you of the Government's thinking on some of the constitutional issues which are likely to arise in Papua New Guinea in the period immediately after the 1972 elections. In drawing up this letter I have had the benefit of your own views, conveyed to me directly and through the Department.

My understanding of the likely course of events after the elections is that once the state of the parties can be assessed (even in a preliminary way) you will be giving thought to the composition of the Ministry and the Administrator's Executive Council with a view to discussions with the Ministerial Nominations Committee once elected on or about 20th April.

In the present state of Papua New Guinea's development an all-party government has attractions, and you should feel free to test attitudes towards this.

I might say initially that I would hope that if possible the Speaker of the third House would be a Papua New Guinean.

The next matter to which I should refer is the question of Ministers in the new House, the allocation of their portfolios and the approved arrangements. Whilst there may need to be revision in the light of the actual election results and your assessment, it does seem probable that there will be many new members in the House, many of whom will be reluctant to support any early moves to internal self-government.

It would also accord with the planned approach of movement towards self-government if both the new House and the Administrator's Executive Council were given time to settle down.

Although I do not anticipate a demand for additional ministers or transfer of increased power immediately on the election of the new House it is necessary to have regard to the possibility that the contrary is the case and bear this in mind. Also it will be necessary to have regard to possible requests that spokesmen for the Administrator's Executive Council on Defence and Police matters be appointed.

Accordingly as soon as this Deputy Chairman is elected it will be necessary for you to raise these matters with him. If there is a request for increased power you will have to engage in discussions at this early point on that subject. Before the discussions go very far, I would wish to discuss the matter personally with you and with the Deputy Chairman.

It is desirable that the Ministerial Nominations Committee, the Ministry and the Administrator's Executive Council should be as geographically representative in membership of the various areas in the country as is consistent with effective government and I would hope that you may be able to influence their composition to this end. It is also desirable that Papuans and New Guineans not only predominate overwhelmingly in numbers, but also occupy key portfolios. Although the Government is committed to negotiate with the leadership group I would be extremely reluctant to negotiate the handing over the additional powers with a leadership group in which an important part is played by an expatriate with less than a life time interest in Papua New Guinea.

I should also wish you to consult with and accept the advice of the Deputy Chairman on the composition of the Administrator's Executive Council and the recommendations to myself on the allocation of Ministerial portfolios. Thus although the Deputy Chairman would have no say in the choosing of the Ministry as a whole he would, in fact, be able to choose his Cabinet. I would not envisage the process being completed necessarily during the April meeting of the new House.

The new House will include four official members only. The Deputy Administrator will initially remain in the House. If, as I would hope, the Deputy Chairman comes increasingly to assume the role of Chief Minister it may be necessary for the Deputy Administrator to take a less prominent part at a later stage. The Secretary for Law and the Treasurer will also both continue to sit in the House of Assembly. The Governor-General has appointed the Secretary of the Administrator's Department as the remaining official member but this position may need to be reviewed when the Deputy Chairman adopts the role of a Chief Minister.

I intend to appoint Messrs. Newman, Ellis and Ritchie[1] to be the official members on the Administrator's Executive Council until 20th April, 1972 when new appointments will need to be made.

As far as the timing of my discussions with the leadership group on the gearing up programme is concerned I would envisage that when the Administrator's Executive Council Budget Committee visits Canberra in May I would take up the matter of the programme in a preliminary way to settle on procedures and an agenda and timing for a meeting about the middle of the year. I would present the group with the programme and suggest that substantive talks be arranged at their convenience.

I now turn to the position after these initial steps have been taken. It is apparent that any views on this are to a degree speculative depending on the state of the new House, and your assessment of it.

As you know, since the report of the Select Committee was approved by the House my predecessor announced that the Government had agreed to the approximate timetable as endorsed by the House. Accordingly, my department is preparing, in conjunction with the Administration, a programme to develop Papua New Guinea for internal self-government during the period 1972/1976 if the people request this at that time. The programme will be placed before the Commonwealth Government this month and will be discussed with the leadership group which emerges following the 1972 House of Assembly elections.

If the result of the election is that there is no group in the House which is both in command of the House and will generally act together in respect of decisions it may prove to be necessary to reconsider the situation in the light of the circumstances at that time. If, as you have suggested, the likelihood is a very cautious leadership group which needs a period in which to gain confidence, then the programme may have to be adjusted to avoid an appearance of pressure for early decisions on the transfer of additional powers. This however must be reconciled with the Government's policy of encouraging progress to self-government. Whilst I wish to avoid pressure which may result in an adverse reaction I do not see this as inconsistent with making it clear that the government is willing to accede to a request for additional powers.

A final decision will have to await the election and your own assessment of the outlook after the new Administrator's Executive Council takes office. Would you please provide this assessment, in a formal letter to myself, early in May, 1972.[2]

In this assessment you should comment at large on the political and constitutional position as you see it at that time bearing in mind that it is the government's policy to encourage the movement to self-government and comment in particular on such things as:
   —   whether a leadership group exists;
   —   the ability of such a group to hold together and to command support in the House of Assembly;
   —   the Deputy Chairman's ability to assume a leadership role in the House and in the country generally;

–   the likely adherence of the leadership group to the government's policy of bringing Papua New Guinea to self-government as a single entity;
–   the regional groupings and affiliations among the newly elected members, and their attitude towards the development of a strong central government;
–   the anticipated attitude to the timing of internal self-government on the part of the assumed leadership group and the House generally.

Although I have reached a view that any transfer of power might have to be deferred until early 1973 I would hope that consultations could be initiated with the leadership group in the middle of the year on this aspect and the programme of movement to internal self-government generally.

As was mentioned in my predecessor's statement to the House of Representatives on 27th April[3] the Commonwealth would negotiate with the Deputy Chairman, and those of his colleagues whom he wishes to take part, for the handing over of future authority step by step as the leader felt in a position with the support of the House to accept added responsibility.

As I have mentioned, the consultations with this group, would be held by the Minister for External Territories. Officials from both sides would of course advise and in fact there will be negotiation groups of officials at all stages, but the consultations must clearly be seen to be at Ministerial level. Although I will have the benefit of your advice and assessment regarding the pace at which the leadership group and the House will wish to move constitutionally it will be necessary for me to be informed of this by the Deputy Chairman himself.

Despite the prospect that initially the assumed leadership group will wish to move cautiously I would hope that as soon as practicable in the life of the third House the Deputy Chairman would begin to as assume the role of Chief Minister and the Administrator's Executive Council would increasingly assume the functions of a Cabinet. This process would, as I envisage it, be progressive but it may not be possible for major changes to take place until 1973. Nevertheless certain steps need to be taken from the outset to give the holder of that office, and his Ministerial colleagues, the opportunity of becoming truly national leaders. This could involve the Deputy Chairman for example, holding press conferences, issuing news releases concerning Papua New Guinea Government attitudes, visiting areas of Papua New Guinea for important occasions, and making the main broadcast on National Day.

As the Deputy Chairman assumes responsibility it will be necessary for him to be able to change his Ministry if he feels this is necessary. If groups he led were threatened with defeat in the House on a major issue it would be necessary for him to be able to seek an election to obtain this majority. Accordingly the Administrator as head of state may in these circumstances be obliged to direct the holding of a general election should the Chief Minister indicate to the Administrator's satisfaction that it was not possible for him, or for the members of his ministry to command the necessary majority in the House. The Administrator would of course have available to him the range of options available to the Governor-General in this sort of situation and a decision to hold a general election would only be a last resort after it was obvious that no one else in the House could form a government.

Although the timing of these changes will have to turn upon events I think it is necessary that the Deputy Chairman quite early in the piece be seen to be, in practice, the leader of the Government.

All this will of course require a changed role for you as Administrator and for the Administrator's Executive Council. Initially it would involve you assuming a lower profile particularly in relation to the Deputy Chairman. As Administrator you would gradually cease to chair the

---

3   Document 160.

Administrator's Executive Council when matters of final local responsibility were being discussed and determined. The officials, who would in any case sit only as advisers would also withdraw when matters of final local responsibility were being discussed unless of course they were requested by the Ministers to attend in an advisory capacity. The Administrator would gradually move to a position where his authority was confined to matters within Commonwealth responsibility.

During this period he would in relation to matters of local responsibility perform a 'Head of State' role and formally endorse legislation, Cabinet and other papers in much the same way as the Governor-General does in Australia.

A committee of the Administrator's Executive Council should be established to deal with statutory business in the same way as the Executive Council deals with statutory business in Australia. In this way the Administrator's Executive Council in the year or so following the House of Assembly elections in 1972 could gradually evolve itself into a Cabinet.

In the interval between internal self-government and independence the Commonwealth may wish to appoint a separate officer—an Australian High Commissioner—to conduct day-to-day relations with the Papua New Guinea government. That is for later decision. Up to self-government you would assume that the Administrator will remain for all purposes, the Commonwealth's link with the Papua New Guinea government.

At independence the position of the Administrator could possibly become that of governor acting on the advice of the Ministers as Papua New Guinea's Head of State. A High Commissioner would be appointed to take over the Commonwealth's responsibilities.

A Commonwealth Office is being established through which communication would be made with the Australian Government. It will be a liaison point between the Department and yourself and all its papers will be available to you.

I see it as important that the Deputy Chairman or Chief Minister have control or be able to exercise close supervision over the areas of local government and economic planning which he could do with help of Ministers assisting. District Commissioners should come under his direct control and in this way he could have effective control over central and local government and the economic planning policy of the country.

I envisage that by these sorts of practical steps Papua New Guinea can be placed in a position of exercising de facto responsible Government according to a timetable to be agreed upon with the leadership group. When this position is reached then the Papua New Guinea Act would be amended to give formal effect to it. Of course I recognise that insofar as this letter has dealt with the more distant future its proposals are contingent upon events and the attitudes of the Australian Government and of the people of Papua New Guinea to the form of government they desire.

[NAA: A452, 1972/0932]

264   RECORD OF CONVERSATION BETWEEN BORDER AND NORRIE

Canberra, 15 March 1972

CONFIDENTIAL

The Military in Papua New Guinea

Brigadier Norrie called prior to taking up his new position as commander of the newly established Joint Force Headquarters in Papua New Guinea. He said he preferred to speak bluntly and personally, and proceeded to do so. He said he had served previously in the PIR and had just made a short visit to PNG to orientate himself.

2.   Brigadier Norrie thought his most important task was to leave to independent PNG an effective military force organised as simply as possible. He hoped to streamline all procedures and make them relevant to PNG where conditions were completely different from those in Australia. He would introduce a single uniform and ensure that the naval and air components of the joint force were completely integrated. He said he had already rejected a plan for a task force headquarters as unnecessary and impractical. This was before he even arrived.

3.   Mr Border referred to the Army's role and wondered whether some kind of police field force might be preferable to traditional military forces, given that an external threat was slight and that law and order would be the chief concern of the Government. Brigadier Norrie felt that, whatever they were called, two forces were required—one for ordinary police duties and the other for border patrolling and perhaps for backup (as a last resort only) to the police. He saw two main problems with the concept of a unified police field force:

(a) the different types of training required.

(b) the danger of dictatorship if all armed forces were put under the control of one Minister.

4.   Brigadier Norrie thought it was vital to have an efficient, well trained, well equipped and widely respected police force. The present force was none of these. He would do everything he could to help improve the police by offering use of military training facilities and any kind of cooperation they wanted. He thought the military might be able to provide logistic and signals back-up to the police, particularly in internal security situations. He recognised that urgent action was required, and that the time remaining to set up systems and effect improvements was running out quickly.

[matter omitted][1]

7.   Brigadier Norrie said he was anxious to cooperate with Foreign Affairs, as he had in Vietnam, and hoped that Mr Colin McDonald[2] in Port Moresby would exchange views with him regularly and frankly. Mr Border agreed that there were common problems and that this kind of cooperation would be useful. He said he would speak to McDonald. Brigadier Norrie said he would like to see visiting Foreign Affairs officials when they were in PNG.

[NAA: A1838, 689/3/1 PART 7]

---

1   The omitted matter contained Norrie's comments on intelligence arrangements in Papua New Guinea, which he described as 'poor'. Along with other remarks, Norrie reportedly said: 'Information was kept back by the various branches of the Administration who were jealous of each other and whose officers would, in many cases, be out of a job anywhere else. He made it clear that any of his officers who did not measure up would be sent back to Australia'.

2   From early 1972 to 1974 DFA officer C. E. (Colin) McDonald served in Port Moresby as a foreign affairs adviser and head of the DFA section.

265   MINUTE BY DEFENCE COMMITTEE[1]

Canberra, 16 March 1972

5/1972. Secret Austeo

Papua New Guinea—Measures for associating PNG Authorities with Defence matters and for Transfer of Functions

The Defence Committee had before it a report,[2] prepared by an interdepartmental study group comprising representatives of the Defence, External Territories and Attorney General's Departments, on measures for progressive consultation in defence matters with Papua New Guinea authorities and for the transfer of defence functions up to the time of independence, including the need for and requirements of legislation.

2.   The report proposed a series of measures, to commence in mid–1972, including consultations with the Administrator's Executive Council (AEC); appointment of a local Minister as a spokesman on Defence matters; establishment of a local defence section; creation of a PNG Advisory Committee on Defence and preparation of Australian legislation to permit the establishment of a separate Papua New Guinea Defence Force.

3.   The Defence Committee was informed that the forces in Papua New Guinea comprise about 4000 men, cost about $14m annually to maintain and require an annual capital expenditure currently of $2m. These orders of magnitude and the practical problems of military administration that they represent will be of increasing concern to the Papua New Guinea authorities as the country approached independence. It was suggested in discussion that measures implemented now must lead to the emergence of a simple and practical defence organisation and force structure without unnecessary duplication and proliferation of personnel and staffs.

4.   The view was expressed that the interdepartmental study report rested on a major, but unstated, assumption that Papua New Guinea at independence will need and accept military forces in the traditional sense and that alternatives, such as para-military grouping of forces and the police, were in danger of being overlooked or prejudiced. It would be unwise to commence work on legislation relating to Papua New Guinea forces until all options as to their roles and composition had been fully investigated.

5.   The Committee as a whole felt that an independent Papua New Guinea with a frontier with an alien state would see the need for an orthodox military force the size and composition and role being a matter yet to be discussed. It was argued that it was in Australia's interest that Papua New Guinea should have such a force. It was observed also that the size, role and composition of forces in Papua New Guinea are being studied interdepartmentally and that the consultation with local authorities, foreshadowed in the present report, will provide an indication of local wishes as to the nature and size of the force they require. It was felt that consideration and further development of the present report would be without prejudice to full examination of all options.

6.   The Committee was advised by the Administrator of Papua New Guinea that the broad assumptions as to constitutional advance contained in the report are probably unaffected by the

---

1   Members of the Defence Committee present for the meeting were Tange, Bunting, Waller, Wheeler, Admiral Sir Victor Smith (Chair, Chiefs of Staff Committee), Air Marshal Sir Colin Hannah (Chief of the Air Staff), Vice Admiral Sir Richard Peek (Chief of Naval Staff) and Lt General M. F. Brogan (Chief of the General Staff). Also present were Hay, Johnson and Harders.

2   Not published.

outcome of the elections. It is more apparent, however, that independence will follow shortly after self-government. While there is at present no strong demand in Papua New Guinea for defence consultations the Commonwealth would be wise voluntarily to initiate defence discussions with the AEC as soon as it is formally constituted in July. The Administrator favoured early appointment, at the request of the Commonwealth Government, of a local Minister to act as spokesman for the defence forces and supported the related proposals for creation of a PNG defence section and establishment of a local Advisory Committee on defence.

7.   While appreciating the factors which led to the proposal for appointment of a local defence spokesman the Committee observed that difficulties will arise in ensuring appropriate control and coordination between statements by the local Ministerial spokesman and those by responsible Australian Ministers. Answers to parliamentary questions are a case in point. The potentially complex and contradictory considerations inherent in the proposal needed to be spelt out with workable suggestions as to their reconciliation. Rapid and effective means of communication between Canberra and Port Moresby will obviously be required.

8.   Accepting that the Administrator and the local Ministerial spokesman on defence will require locally oriented civil advice on defence matters the Committee considered, without reaching any firm conclusion, options for the location of the proposed Papua New Guinea defence section. While there appeared to be some practical considerations tending to support location in the Joint Force Headquarters there were points of principle—notably the demonstration of the primacy of civil authority—in suggesting that it be located in the Department of the Administrator. The section will be an embryo policy advising body which will need to develop a capability for counsel in relation to higher direction and control of Papua New Guinea forces. It was suggested there is a qualitative difference in function between it and the Command Secretary's office. The defence section might well belong in close physical proximity to the principal local representative of the civil authority. The psychological and political importance of demonstrating, in practical terms, the Administrator's authority in relation to the forces should not be discounted. In light of this discussion, the Committee felt that the question of location needed closer investigation. The decision will rest as much on points of principle as on practical considerations.

9.   The Committee stressed however the need for constant and close liaison between the defence section and the Joint Force Headquarters. They observed also that the Joint Force Commander must have direct personal access to the Administrator at all times to enable him effectively to discharge his given responsibilities as adviser on matters relating to his Force.

10.   The Committee accepted, in principle, the case for a PNG Advisory Committee in Defence but noted again that the practical implications were insufficiently canvassed in the report. The Advisory Committee would be a mixed body of local Ministers and Australian officials. There were potentialities for embarrassment to the Australian government in this and in the fact that they and the AEC might simultaneously be considering contentious matters of defence importance. There was also the question to consider of how the power to initiate matters for advice is to be exercised.

11.   There will clearly need to be appropriate coordination and sharing of responsibility between the Commonwealth Ministers for Defence and External Territories in considering and acting on advice emanating from the Advisory Committee. This aspect will be further discussed between the Secretary of the Department of Defence and the Secretary of the Department of External Territories.

12.   It was noted that the proposals for Australian legislation leading to establishment of a separate new Papua New Guinea Defence Force were intended, in advance of independence, to consolidate into a manageable package all the disparate elements involved in preparing

local authorities for exercise of defence functions. It might permit graduated and selective delegations prior to independence and obviate hasty implementation of measures on the eve of independence.

13.   On the other hand the legislative approach is likely to be slow, difficult and contentious. The proposal amounts to a significant re-organisation of elements of Australia's own defence organisation and systems in the interests, essentially, of Papua New Guinea requirements. A more pragmatic and less sweeping approach to the problem of developing management and policy links between the dispersed Australian defence structure[3] and the relatively small Papua New Guinea unified force should be fully explored. One such possibility would be to have policy control of the Papua New Guinea Joint Force exercised by the Minister of Defence acting through Chairman, Chiefs of Staff with practical military administration matters being handled by one Service Department and Minister acting as agent for the other two Services. Such a course of action might be less disruptive of accepted Australian processes including the parliamentary responsibilities of Australian Service Ministers. In the meantime, legislation necessary at or about the time of Papua New Guinea's independence should be fully investigated and alternative drafts prepared in readiness.

14.   The Committee was of the opinion that these aspects merited further consideration.

[NAA: A1838, 3080/4/4]

---

3   At the time Australia had separate defence, army, navy and air force departments. They were combined in 1973.

266   MINUTE BY DEFENCE COMMITTEE[1]

Canberra, 16 March 1972

7/1972. Secret

Procedures for the employment of PNG Defence forces in Aid of the Civil Power

The Defence Committee had before it a report[2] on the above subject by an interdepartmental study group comprising representatives from the Defence, External Territories, Army and Attorney-General's Departments.

2.   The Committee noted that the study group had examined possible procedures for the employment of defence forces in PNG in aid of the civil power in the periods:

(i) between the assumption by PNG of responsibility for internal security and independence; and

(ii) after independence.

3.   The Committee also noted that the study was not limited to procedures relating to employment of the forces in a situation of the type to which Section 51 of the Defence Act applies, i.e. a state of domestic violence. The study also covered the wider spectrum of possible assistance in lesser situations, ranging from the provision of minor logistic support to the provision of personnel for a wide variety of tasks in support of the police where a state of violence does not exist.

4.   The Committee refrained from detailed consideration of the report in the absence of the Secretary, Department of External Territories and the Administrator, Papua and New Guinea who were unable to be present.

5.   Nevertheless, the Committee, having noted that the paper needed further development, canvassed questions of policy and principle during which the following views were expressed:

Call-out is a very serious step which must be capable of public explanation by Ministers. Therefore the request by the civil authority to the military should be made at the highest level of civil authority, i.e. the Governor-General, placing beyond doubt the authority to call-out. The majority of the Committee was opposed to any change from the present procedure for call-out.

Traditionally the Australian Services have not favoured aid to the civil power which involved a policy type role and accordingly consider that the tightest possible control of the use of the forces should be retained.

Authorisation for the use of the forces in aid of the civil power by the Minister for Defence, on the recommendation of the Minister for External Territories, contemplates substantial discussion with Ministers such as Foreign Affairs and with the Prime Minister and possibly Cabinet. The additional step of authorisation by the Governor-General in Council would not be time consuming. Hence the Committee questioned the practical advantages, apart from any principles involved, of the assumption of such power by the Minister for Defence as foreshadowed in the report.

---

1   Members of the Defence Committee present for the meeting were Tange, Bunting, Wheeler, Admiral Sir Victor Smith (Chair, Chiefs of Staff Committee), Air Marshal Sir Colin Hannah (Chief of the Air Staff), Vice Admiral Sir Richard Peek (Chief of Naval Staff) and Lt General M. F. Brogan (Chief of the General Staff). Also present were Harders and Mick Shann, who sat in for Waller.

2   Not published.

There do not appear to be any serious Service objections to the Administrator, after consultation and agreement with the Force Commander, using Service transport and communications facilities, which could not otherwise be available, in circumstances where a state of violence clearly does not exist.

The question of giving a delegation to the Administrator in respect of the use of the forces for logistic purposes was deferred for further discussion with the Department of [External] Territories on the practical situations foreseen which could make such a delegation desirable.

Increase in flexibility in relation to the use of the forces could lead to the Services being drawn into riot situations unwittingly. Therefore proposals to simplify procedures to obtain Service support should be carefully weighed. Judgements on whether situations appeared likely to lead to the firing of weapons would be difficult.

There could be a feeling in Papua New Guinea that the procedures open to the Administrator to seek the assistance from the Forces are cumbersome and time consuming and that this situation gives a certain amount of encouragement to dissidents in the creation of disturbances. Therefore, for psychological reasons, it would be advantageous if the procedures open to the Administrator should *seem* to have been speeded up.

In the circumstances of a call-out authorised by the Governor-General, the Committee sought advice from the study group on the question of the duration of the instrument of call-out and the circumstances for seeking revocation.

A limited instrument of call-out specifying the type of support required (referred to in the Report) may not be a practical proposition as circumstances can change rapidly and the instrument could be challenged legally.

The position of seconded Australian personnel after independence should be examined.

6.   The Committee agreed that the foregoing comments should be taken into account by the study group in the further development of the proposed procedures. The further development should consider in more detail both the legal and practical aspects, and be coordinated with related studies already in progress.

[NAA: A452, 1973/470]

267   BRIEFING NOTE FOR PEACOCK

Canberra, undated [c. mid-March 1972]

Localisation in Papua New Guinea

1. *Background and Problems of Localisation*

In April, 1971 the Government announced that Papua New Guinea would be geared to self-government in the period 1972–76 and that as part of the gearing up programme continuing priority would be given to localisation.[1] On 30th August, 1971 the Papua New Guinea Public Service Board issued a White Paper describing plans for an accelerated localisation and training programme. A copy of the White Paper is attached.[2] The plans aim to provide the future government of Papua New Guinea with a strong, stable and efficient Public Service staffed as far as possible by Papuans and New Guineans. There are three basic problems:

(i)   Firstly there is the shortage of experienced local officers and of officers educationally equipped to undertake appropriate level training. There are three divisions of the Papua New Guinea Public Service. In the Third Division of the Service there has been considerable localisation over a long period of time and there are now approximately 12,500 local officers of permanent or temporary status. In the Second Division there are over 8,000 established positions of which approximately 6,500 are staffed at present. Local officers occupy only about 1,700 of these positions. One Departmental Head is a local officer.

(ii) The second problem is to ensure that the trained local officers are, through experience and responsibility, genuinely capable of replacing expatriates without a serious loss of efficiency, requiring in many cases a handover period of guidance by the experienced or professionally qualified expatriates.

(iii) Thirdly is the problem of personal difficulties for both local and expatriate officers to cope with very significant changes in their lives; local officers being rapidly promoted to positions of responsibility and expatriates returning to Australia after long periods of service in Papua New Guinea.

The localisation plans for the Public Service aim to solve these problems.

2. *Measures to Accelerate Localisation*

(i)   An ordinance passed by the House of Assembly provides more effective procedures for the advancement of efficient local officers. Expatriate officers who are no longer needed will have their services terminated under an Employment Security Scheme. Overseas contract officers whose services are no longer needed will not be offered a renewal of contract.

(ii) Priority positions are being determined. Highest priority is being given to First Division and senior Second Division positions in politically sensitive areas.

(iii) Localisation plans are being developed on a departmental basis through localisation committees charged with detailed planning and implementation of localisation policy.

(iv) Training activities for local officers are being expanded. A ten-stage Executive Development Scheme provides opportunities for training at all levels and attention is being given to the upgrading of skills of local officers throughout the Service.

---

1   See Document 160, para. 7.

2   Not published.

(v) Work simplification measures designed to more fully utilise the skills of local officers, are being studied.

(vi) Establishment reviews will be undertaken of career streams in certain branches of administration with the aim of assisting career path planning for local officers.

3. *The Present Stage of Development of Localisation Plans*

(i) There has been a strong reaction to some proposals of the Employment Security Scheme and in the House of Assembly a motion has been passed calling on the Government to review the proposals. This is now being done.

(ii) A small number of priority positions are now localised and at the top end of the Executive Development Scheme, a Senior Executive Programme has been developed to prepare a corps of senior officers for localisation of further priority positions.

(iii) Assessments have been made of the potential of Second Division local officers and the Board's training effort has been greatly accelerated at all levels in order to develop the potential of the maximum number of officers. In 1971, 347 officers undertook short courses of training and 277 undertook long courses. In 1972 there will be 1,040 undertaking short courses and 358 attending long courses, a total of 1,398 compared to 624 in 1971.

Plans are being considered for the financing of regional training centres but at present most of the training will take place at the Administrative College in Port Moresby. At least 160 Papuans and New Guineans will be brought to Australia in 1972 for training at ASOPA[3] and a further 150 officers will receive on-the-job training in Australia under the Commonwealth Practical Training Scheme. These programmes will be developed to the extent of available resources in future years.

4. *Future Development of Localisation*

350 school leavers were recruited to the Public Service from the 1971 school output. Most of these recruits will continue their education in various training institutions. 1,700 recent recruits are already in training. If the 1972 level of recruitment is maintained for 5 years the number of local officers appears sufficient to replace most of the expatriate personnel at present in the Second Division. However this projection does not take account of growth of the Public Service or attrition. More importantly it does not take account of the quality of the Service. Most of these newly trained recruits will occupy the lower level positions and only a proportion of them will have the potential to advance to higher levels. Significant numbers of professionally qualified and experienced expatriates will be required particularly in middle and higher level positions who will in fact be responsible for the development of the local staff on the job as well as for the actual duties of the position. The continuing training effort can only be maintained if the services of these expatriates are retained or new expatriates are recruited for the positions.

[NAA: A452, 1972/3694]

---

3   Australian School of Pacific Administration located at Middle Head, Sydney.

268   BRIEFING NOTE FOR PEACOCK

Canberra, 17 March 1972

Papua New Guinea—Public Service—Localisation

A. *Size of Public Service (Including Teachers in Teaching Service) at December,
1971*

		1st Div.	*2nd Div.*	*3rd Div.*	*Total*
Local Staff	—Permanent	1	1388	7846	9235
	—Temporary	–	507	6556	7063
	—Cadets and Trainees	_	–	–	1762
Overseas Staff	—Permanent	13	1074	263	1350
	—Contract	6	2402	952	3360
	—Temporary	–	1128	1718	2846
			Total		25,616

B. *Localisation Measures*

On 30th August, 1971 the Public Service Board announced special measures designed to
accelerate the rate of localisation and training in the Public Service in line with the pace of
constitutional development. A copy of the white paper 'Accelerated Localisation and Training'
issued by the Board is attached.[1]

Measures taken since the publication of the white paper include:
   –   The establishment of a localisation committee in each Department (Appendix 1 of
   the white paper refers).
   –   Substantial increases in enrolments for courses of training under the Executive
   Development Scheme at the Papua New Guinea Administrative College.

      Figures are:

	1971	*1972*	
Long courses	277	358	(forecast)
Short courses	347	1040	(forecast)
	624	1398	

   –   Development of a Regional Training Centre at Port Moresby.
   –   Conversion from 1972 of the Australian School of Pacific Administration (ASOPA)
   at Mosman, Sydney, from the role of training Australians for service in Papua New Guinea
   and the Northern Territory to the training of Papuans and New Guineans. ASOPA will
   supplement training and undertake specially structured training which cannot be better or
   more conveniently provided in Papua New Guinea or elsewhere in Australia. Up to 200
   Papuans and New Guineans are expected to attend training courses at ASOPA in 1972.

---

1   Not published.

Additional facilities for training at ASOPA will become available in 1975 when existing courses for Australians at the school have been phased out (copy of announcement on 3.11.71 by the Minister for External Territories attached).

— Increased numbers of Papuans and New Guineans being sent to Australia under the Commonwealth Practical Training Scheme for on-the-job training where suitable training opportunities are not available in Papua New Guinea or the training can be better provided in Australia.[2] From the inception of the Scheme in March 1970 to 30.6.71, 76 Papuans and New Guineans were sponsored for training under the Scheme. In the 12 months to 30.6.72 it is expected that over 160 will commence training in Australia under the Scheme (copy of brochure on the Scheme attached).[3]

— Amendments to certain provisions of the Public Service Ordinance will be brought into operation shortly. These provide for the filling of vacancies by a Selection Committee system instead of under the promotions and appeals system formerly in use. The new system is designed to speed up localisation and incorporates procedures for local officers to be advanced solely on the basis of their efficiency to fill positions at higher levels without the requirement to win promotion in competition with overseas officers.

C. *Progress in Localisation*

The Second Division of the Public Service is the key area for localisation of the Public Service. The proportion of local officers in this Division is increasing progressively. For example, between June, 1969 and June, 1971 local staff in the Second Division increased from 849 to 1777, which is 23.7 per cent of all staff in the Division. This increase comprised 346 in Manpower Class B and 582 in Manpower Class C.

The proportion of local officers in the Third Division increased from 80 per cent in June 1969 to 82 per cent in June 1971 and the rate of growth of overseas Third Division staff has fallen sharply over the past two years.

Future progress in localisation will depend upon:

• the effectiveness of the stepped-up training effort
• the impact of future output from post-secondary institutions
• future trends in the growth of the Public Service
• the attraction of sufficient numbers of school leavers from secondary schools
• rates of wastage from the Public Service and training institutions.

[NAA: A452, 1972/3694]

---

2   See Documents 21 & 22.

3   Not published.

269   MINUTE FROM MOODIE TO SHANN

Canberra, 20 March 1972

CONFIDENTIAL

Papua New Guinea

I had an informal word with Mr David Hay yesterday about the elections and the future.

2.   He was inclined to think that the new Government to be formed might be something more than a coalition between the United Party and the Progressive Party plus a few Independents. He apparently did not exclude participation by individual members of the Pangu Party. However, he emphasised that it would be foolish to make predictions.

3.   He also expressed some concern that the likely line up of Parties in the new Assembly could mean that there was an inter-play on the question of self-government and independence with the result that the more conservative members might feel more inclined to hurry things along than they had been previously. Mr Hay thought it was a fair prospect that this could lead to a demand by whatever leadership group finally emerged for earlier self-government. This, in turn, would have an effect on the Government's gearing-up programme and things would have to move faster.

4.   Mr Hay did not seem to anticipate any fundamental difficulty about moving faster although he acknowledged practical problems in such matters as getting decisions from our Ministers during the next few months and getting the requisite legislation drafted by Parliamentary Counsel. He was inclined to doubt whether there was any alternative to a step-by-step process in putting matters up to Australian Ministers for their consideration (although he also said that there might be an increasing disposition on the part of our Ministers to 'get quit of it all'). His Minister was keen to get on with talks with the leadership group and recognised the high importance of establishing easy personal relations with them all and not relying too much on paper and legalism. However, Hay could foresee difficulties with individual Ministers and Departments who would be reluctant to make adjustments and would want to cling to their existing authorities as long as they could. This might constitute an even greater problem than dealing with Papua New Guinean politicians.

5.   Hay seems to be envisaging a situation in which Mr Peacock, with the support of other Ministers, depending upon the particular topics discussed, would conduct discussions with the leadership group. He made it clear that so far as he was concerned he was not thinking of this being conducted as an exercise by the Minister for External Territories and his Department. For example, he thought it would be a very good thing indeed if Mr Bowen would be able to devote time to studying the problems which affected this Department and join with Mr Peacock in negotiations.

[*matter omitted*]

[NAA A1838, 3080/10/1 PART 1]

270   LETTER FROM PEACOCK TO MCMAHON

Canberra, 21 March 1972

The purpose of this letter is to seek your approval to certain Ministers examining the problem raised by the proximity to the Papuan coast of certain islands in the Torres Strait which are at present part of the State of Queensland. I would hope that the Ministers, could, after consultation with their colleagues, recommend what attitude and action, if any, the Commonwealth should take. I am attaching to this letter a paper which covers some of the detail regarding this problem.

Quite briefly the position is that a number of islands which form part of the State of Queensland lie within a few miles of the Papuan coastline. Included in these islands are three which are inhabited (Saibai, Boigu and Dauan). Apart from their proximity, the Queensland territorial rights on these islands leaves Papua New Guinea with a relatively small area of the continental shelf. In addition, Papuan fishermen may be excluded from certain reefs from which they have fished traditionally for many years and more recently through commercial operations.

The presence of these islands in such close proximity to the Papuan coastline could become a potential source of friction between Australia and an emerging self-governing Papua New Guinea, jeopardising relations between the two countries generally and, in particular, in such fields as fisheries, off-shore oil and mineral developments and navigation in Torres Strait.

I should add that this question has already been the subject of discussions and complaint by Papuan members of the House of Assembly. It has been specifically raised with me when visiting Papua New Guinea.

The present position has attracted international comment. In 1971, the United Nations Visiting Mission to Papua New Guinea reported that it considered 'that in the interest of future good relations between Australia and the Territory, the question of the border with Queensland should be kept under constant review'. The Visiting Mission drew attention to the matter following strong representations from Papuan politicians, although an examination of conditions in Papua was not included in its brief. This aspect of the Mission's report may arise in the United Nations next year and in any event the 1974 visit by the Mission will embrace both the Territory of Papua and the Territory of New Guinea.

In June 1971 the Premier of Queensland[1] drew your attention to the fact that Papuan fishermen were carrying out commercial fishing operations in Torres Strait waters where until recently their activities were confined to traditional subsistence fishing only. Discussions are to take place on this subject but it is evident that ultimately boundary considerations will become involved.

I have in mind, and I submit for your consideration, that a group of Ministers comprising the Minister for Foreign Affairs,[2] the Attorney-General,[3] the Minister for National Development[4] and myself examine in detail all matters relevant to this question. This group would of course consult closely with other interested Ministers. The object of the examination would be to make recommendations defining the stand the Commonwealth Government should adopt. I would then envisage that a personal approach of an exploratory nature be made by yourself to the Queensland Premier to ascertain the Government's attitudes. What course should then be followed would depend upon those discussions.

1   Joh Bjelke-Petersen, Premier of Queensland, 1968–87.

2   Nigel Bowen.

3   Ivor Greenwood

4   Reginald (Curly) Swartz.

The procedure I have suggested has in part been dictated by the practical impossibility of readjusting the boundary without the concurrence of the Queensland Government. It is for that reason that I favour a cautious approach by the Commonwealth and think that personal and private discussions between yourself and the Queensland Premier in which the international aspects are presented would be the most appropriate way of broaching the subject.

I am aware of course of the need for the matter to be placed before Cabinet at an early stage but it appears to me that until the examinations which I have suggested are concluded and possibly the suggested discussions with the Queensland Premier have taken place, it would be difficult to present to Cabinet any clear proposals as to the stand which the Commonwealth should adopt and the action which should be taken.[5]

[NAA A1838, 3080/11/2/1]

---

5   McMahon replied to Peacock on 6 April 1972 (Document 274).

271   LETTER FROM TANGE TO HAY

Canberra, 23 March 1972

CONFIDENTIAL

PNG—Police

I refer to the programme of studies agreed between us relating to the future defence and internal security requirements in PNG.[1] As you know, a major part of the studies relates to the nature and scope of the assistance which the defence forces might provide to the police in maintaining law and order, and to the various legal, administrative and practical aspects of the arrangements necessary. A number of the agreed studies are directed specifically to these matters, but all are affected to some extent by assumptions as to the role of the forces in assistance to the police.

In addition the future size and shape of the defence forces in PNG and their role must be considered in relation to the organisation and functions of the police. The need is obvious to coordinate concepts for the development of the two forces and avoid duplication of activity with consequent waste of scarce manpower and other resources.

It has become increasingly apparent that to enable the studies to proceed on a firm basis, we need authoritative information in regard to the PNG police, including their present capabilities and existing plans for their development. This information is critical if we are to ensure that future developments and arrangements that might be proposed for the forces will be coordinated with and complementary to developments in regard to the police, to meet the total PNG requirement.

For these purposes, we need a comprehensive statement relating to the PNG police. In the first place this statement should show the present strength, organisation and control arrangements, a summary of present tasks in relation to internal security, and of changes, if any, foreseen in these tasks as self-government and independence approach. It should include an assessment of the extent to which the present organisation and strength is adequate for tasks foreseen, and details of any approved proposals for future development, either in regard to 'teeth' or to support elements. The annual cost and how this is provided should also be shown.

In regard to equipment, it would be desirable to indicate the major types currently held, including weapons, communications and transport equipment, together with major proposals for new additional equipment.

An important need is an assessment of the future attitudes and loyalties of the police. This should consider such factors as the attitudes of the people (overall and in regions) towards the police, the attitude of the police themselves towards the administration, local political parties, indigenous or expatriate officers, and the Australian armed services. Any regional patterns in recruiting, strengths and outlook, or any political aspirations or sympathies should also be shown.

A related factor is morale, which will depend to a considerable extent on conditions of services, pay etc. and general levels of education, and on the standards of leadership, both expatriate and indigene.

It will be important to indicate any notable limitations and weaknesses current or foreseen in the future, of the police as an effective force including any restrictions, legal or otherwise which might apply to their use in any particular roles. Finally we would wish to know of any

---

1   See Document 240.

assumptions of support by the defence forces either in general or for particular tasks, which may have been made in considering proposals for the development of the police force or for its equipment.

I am aware that the terms of reference of the current study of future internal security arrangements require the Inter-Departmental Committee to take into account the projected capabilities of the Police Force. In my view however, the need for an authoritative and comprehensive statement covering the aspects outlined is much wider, and is an essential basis for the major part of the programme of work we have undertaken. I would be glad therefore if you would arrange for preparation of an authoritative statement covering the above matters. Your early advice would be appreciated.

[NAA: A452, 1972/1111]

272   LETTER FROM HAY TO TANGE

Canberra, 29 March 1972

SECRET

I have read the draft minutes of the Defence Committee's meeting of 16th March.[1] I have had no comment to make on them but the meeting itself has prompted me to offer the following general observations.

I am struck, even more forcibly than when I wrote to you on 6th April last year,[2] by the need to move very soon toward the establishment in Papua New Guinea of its own Defence Forces within the framework of Papua New Guinea legislation. I question whether some of the security problems facing Papua New Guinea in the period to independence can be dealt with adequately in any other way. Apart from that it is becoming increasingly important that the Papua New Guinea Defence Forces become more closely identified with that country well before independence. In my view this in itself requires an initial move towards separation from the Australian Defence Forces, whilst, of course, maintaining the responsibility of the Commonwealth, through the Minister for Defence, for the external defence of Papua New Guinea.

I was concerned to note that the Committee contemplated the possibility of policy control of the Papua New Guinea Joint Forces being exercised in the way proposed in paragraph 13 upon the supposition that legislation could conveniently be deferred until independence.

The lack of progress at the meeting, together with my own belief that the time scale is contracting, causes me to stress the urgency. I am pleased to note that the Study Group has been reconvened. I would suggest that it should aim at having a revised report by the second week in April so that we may take steps to resolve the position. The immediate urgency arises from the desirability of the Administrator being in a position by 20th April if possible to discuss with the leadership group the immediate appointment of a spokesman for Defence matters. Accordingly I think that the Study Group should in the first place direct its attention to spelling out the practical implications of the appointment of a Defence spokesman and the establishment of a Defence Advisory Committee.

If possible I would also hope that the Study Group could report speedily on the suggestion that there may be a means other than separate legislation to deal adequately with the devolution of power. I would suggest that it should bear in mind the possibility that if legislation establishing the force in Papua New Guinea as a separate entity is deferred until independence Australia may be confronted with attempts to initiate legislation in the House of Assembly.

I am also writing to you in response to the suggestion that we should discuss the appropriate coordination and sharing of responsibility between our respective Ministers. I would be pleased to meet with you on this aspect as soon as possible. We might consider whether [...] the question of the Administrator being authorised to engage in discussions on the basis that the Commonwealth Government would view favourably the appointment of a Defence Spokesman, might be resolved at Ministerial as distinct from Cabinet level.

In addition I think it may be useful to discuss with you soon the question of early moves towards the establishment of separate defence forces in Papua New Guinea.

[NAA: A452, 1972/1111]

---

1   Documents 265 & 266.

2   Document 154.

273   BRIEFING NOTES BY NUTTER[1]

Canberra, 4 April 1972

CONFIDENTIAL

Attached are briefing notes prepared in this Branch.

2.   The suggestion in Part II for tightening up procedures for handling border crossers is not a firm proposal. Rather it is illustrative of the type of measure that might be useful in administrative terms. Whether such a procedure would be politically advisable would depend on our assessment of likely reactions in Australia, PNG and Indonesia to a more public process and our assessment of the likely attitude of the AEC—e.g. would it be too lenient towards applicants for permissive residence?[2]

3.   You will be able to form an idea of some of these considerations during your visit.

[*matter omitted*]

5.   Finally, the main point of concern to this Branch is this Department's lack of full information and effective control over PNG's relations with Indonesia in these matters. During your visit you may be able to consider ways in which this problem can be solved. Perhaps it will be necessary to raise the matter at Ministerial level in order to re-affirm the primacy of our function in respect of PNG relations with Indonesia. Clearly there is a pressing need for an educational programme amongst Administration officials and leading indigenous personalities about the facts of life with regard to international relations and particularly to Indonesia.

Attachment

I PNG and Indonesia

Basic Principles

There does not appear to be any authoritative statement of our broad policy objectives in all dealings with the Indonesians on border and related questions; however, it seems clear that these should be:

(i)   to lay the foundations for a peaceful and mutually satisfactory relationship between an independent PNG and Indonesia;

(ii) to preserve our own relationship with Indonesia;

(iii) to protect legitimate PNG interests (no competing, distinctly Australian interests have been identified).

We have sought to advance these objectives by seeking to be kept fully informed of developments relevant to Indonesia (particularly, to date, relations along the border and refugee questions) and by tendering advice to the Department of External Territories which alone is in a position to issue instructions to the Administration.

---

1   D. G. (Gerry) Nutter, Assistant Secretary, South East Asia, DFA. The notes were prepared for Lew Border's visit to Papua New Guinea on 5–13 April 1972. Border had first visited PNG from 22 to 30 July 1971 (see Documents 196, 200 and 201).

2   'Permissive residence' referred to the arrangement under the UN Convention on the Status of Refugees and by accepted international practice whereby a residence permit was given to persons judged to have 'a well-grounded fear of persecution because of their political beliefs'. The Administrator's Executive Council had the delegated authority to refuse an application for permissive residence.

Problems

As a general rule, the Administration reports promptly on day-to-day developments. In recent months however its reporting has been unsatisfactory on three important cases: minor border incidents in the Pagei area, the decision to discontinue rations to refugees on Manus,[3] and the Indey-Maury affair.[4] A brief outline of each of these cases is in Part III of this brief. In all three cases no report reached Canberra until it was too late for any advice of ours to be taken into consideration by the Administration; in the case of Indey and Maury the Administration's reporting was incomplete, evasive and misleading. More generally, we are, despite our constant efforts, unable to maintain a satisfactory dialogue with the Administration on the many matters affecting Indonesia. Our ability to affect the Administration's actions in these matters is very limited.

The inadequacies in the Administration's reporting clearly arise in part from physical problems of communication and from inefficiencies in the Administration. But it is also clear that a very large factor is a conscious attempt on the part of the Administration to deny to Canberra Departments an opportunity to meddle in what Konedobu sees as its own business.

This attitude is boldly stated in a recent memorandum from Mr Webb, Head of Security Branch which reads in part: 'It is essential at this time that Foreign Affairs should realise that in many instances they are not dealing with Australian Public Servants but with a Public Service of a country quickly gaining more autonomy and with the possibility of local political involvement which makes quick consultation more difficult.'

This situation is unsatisfactory on several grounds:

(a) This Department is still responsible—and is held accountable both inside Australia and abroad—for the Administration's actions in relation to Indonesia and people of West Irian. For Australia, relations with Indonesia are as important, if not more so, than relations with an independent PNG;

(b) We therefore need to learn in useful time of significant developments with a view to preparing ourselves and relevant overseas posts (Djakarta, The Hague, UN New York, and Geneva for the UNHCR)[5] to meet or head off possible adverse reactions to the Administration's actions;

3   In late 1971 there had been 74 permissive residents at the holding camp at Salasia on Manus Island, of whom 62 had been drawing Government rations. The 'breadwinners' among them had 'refused offers of employment arranged by the Administration'. The Administration had responded by terminating 'the issue of rations to permissive residents capable of taking employment, who have been at Salasia for more than three months'. DFA endorsed the Administration's policy on this issue, but regretted that it had taken the Administration two months to advise DFA of the policy, as it 'would have liked earlier advice to equip overseas posts (The Hague, Djakarta, UN New York and Geneva—for the UNHCR)'. Briefing Notes for your visit to PNG', 4 April 1972, III, (2), NAA: A1838, 3036/10/6/5, PART 1.

4   Amos Indey (a former Deputy Governor of West Irian) and Stevanus Maury had crossed the border in October 1971 and sought permissive residence. At a meeting with Australian and Indonesian officials on 29 November they had agreed to return to Indonesia, but subsequently changed their minds. An Administration official decided that 'economic considerations were their real reasons for wanting to stay in PNG and accordingly that they should be sent back'. On 8 December the two men, with three companions, walked out of the holding camp at Yako, located near Vanimo on the north-west coast of Papua New Guinea. Indey and Stevanus were later thought to have joined the 'rebel headquarters' in a remote area on the PNG side of the border. DFA officials were concerned that the official's 'decision to send the men back was *ultra vires* [that is, beyond the powers of the official concerned] because these powers "rested with the AEC"'. Moreover, the decision exposed the Australian Government 'to accusations of breaching the "non-refoulement" clauses of the Status of Refugees Convention'. As far as DFA officials were concerned, 'The Administration's reporting to Canberra on this case was tardy, evasive and in several respects misleading.' Briefing Notes for your visit to PNG, III, (1), 4 April 1972, NAA: A1838, 3036/10/6/5, PART 1.

5   United Nations High Commissioner for Refugees.

(c) The Administration's decisions in these matters are not always wise. Proper consultations, before actions are undertaken, would enable us to draw attention to international considerations which are not always evident to the Administration;

(d) It is important for PNG's own sake, as well as Australia's that the administrative process to be inherited by an independent PNG should include a habit of calling for expert advice on the international considerations relevant to projected decisions, before action is taken in matters where these are likely to be important.

Recommendations

At present, all border and refugee questions are the responsibility of the Administration's Security Branch, headed by Mr R. Webb. It appears highly desirable that carriage of these questions should be transferred to the International Affairs Branch as soon as the latter is capable of handling them. This would give International Affairs Branch early experience with practical international relations; it should also help International Affairs Branch establish its proper, post-independence role within the Administration.

In addition, whichever Branch of the Administration is responsible for these matters, there is a clear need to establish firmly as a working rule that this Department must be fully and promptly informed and consulted on all matters relevant to dealings with Indonesia and Indonesians.

You may have occasion to raise these matters in Port Moresby. Opportunities may also arise during your visit to attempt to convince people in PNG:

(i)   that, as long as PNG is not independent, this Department has a legitimate right to be informed and consulted before the Administration takes decisions relevant to Indonesia;

(ii) that we are not unmindful of PNG interests; indeed one of our prime policy objectives is to protect and promote them;

(iii) that we are in a position to be useful to PNG, through our expertise and our machinery for dealing with other governments.

II PNG and Indonesia—the Permissive Residents Problem

[*matter omitted*]

All these questions are complex. Essentially, the Administration seeks to handle them by administrative actions on an ad hoc basis. [...] its record is not up to the standards we think necessary in view of the international considerations. Even if the Administration itself is satisfied with its own performance, we think that to leave these matters on this basis as PNG moves towards localisation and independence would be to court serious trouble.

Ideally we would like to see legislation that would give the Administration clear cut powers and obligations in these matters. We would like to know that there were procedures, carefully worked out in consultation with us and effectively applied in the field.

For instance the procedure could be:

(a) all illegal immigrants[6] would be charged and held until either granted permissive residence or handed back at the border;

(b) in the case of applicants for permissive residence the court would allow a stay of proceedings while the case was referred to the AEC for political decision. This Department would have a voice in the submission to the AEC.

---

6   A footnote to the original documents notes that this would not, of course, apply to 'border residents on legitimate visits to PNG or casual crossers who are met in the field and told to go home'.

Such a procedure would deter much border crossing. It would finally resolve questions such as whether restrictions can be placed on the political activities and resettlement of permissive residents (if the AEC were not prepared to make these enforceable, the Administration could refrain from trying to apply them). We do not expect it to appeal to the Administration because as individuals they have a strong attachment to their traditional way of handling all questions on an ad hoc basis, being guided only by the judgement of the kiap[7] on the spot.

After looking at the problem first hand, you may be able to form an opinion on whether we should try for a solution of this type.

[*matter omitted*][8]

[NAA: A1838, 3036/10/6/5 PART 1]

---

7   Patrol officer.

8   The omitted material, which contains Part III of the brief, provides background on nine 'current problem' cases. For brief details of two of these cases see footnotes 3 & 4 above.

274   LETTER FROM MCMAHON TO PEACOCK

Canberra, 6 April 1972

I refer to your letter of 21 March 1972[1] regarding the problem raised by the proximity to the Papuan coast of certain islands in the Torres Strait which are at present part of the State of Queensland. You have suggested the establishment of a Ministerial Committee to examine in details all matters relevant to this question preparatory to discussion with the Queensland Premier and Cabinet consideration of the issues involved.

I agree with you on the importance of this matter and its potentialities as a source of friction between Australia and an emerging self-governing Papua New Guinea. At the same time, I recognize the need for a cautious approach in respect of Queensland's interest.

In the circumstances I think the proper course would, in the first instance, be to refer the question to a high level inter-departmental committee for examination and report. This committee would comprise representations of the following Departments—Attorney-General's (Chair), External Territories, Primary Industry, National Development, Shipping and Transport and Foreign Affairs. Other Departments would be brought into the discussions as appropriate.

On receipt of the report, I would, in the light of the conclusions reached, consider the Cabinet and other action required.

Copies of this correspondence are being sent to our colleagues the Deputy Prime Minister, the Ministers for Primary Industry, National Development, Foreign Affairs and Shipping and Transport and to the Attorney-General and the Treasurer.[2]

[NAA: A1838, 3080/11/2/1]

---

1   Document 270.

2   The ministers listed were Doug Anthony, Ian Sinclair, Reg Swartz, Nigel Bowen, Peter Nixon, Ivor Greenwood and Billy Snedden.

275   LETTER FROM JOHNSON TO HAY

Port Moresby, 6 April 1972

I have again had conversations with political leaders concerning the establishment of the Government but it is as yet not possible to foresee the course of events.[1] Neither of the major parties has a majority, nor would alliance with the People's Progress Party [PPP] ensure one. Both the United and Pangu parties are wooing the PPP and also endeavouring to recruit uncommitted Members but to date most of the large group of independents remain unaffiliated. Dr Guise is endeavouring to muster what he calls a third force which, if large enough, would be in a strong position to bargain with either the United Party [UP] or Pangu. Dr Guise's own preferences lie within the Pangu Party. To date he has been unable to gather more than three or four adherents and any such alliance would be essentially unstable.

It is unlikely that any clear patterns will emerge before Members gather in Port Moresby in the week preceding the opening of the House of Assembly and it may be that the first time there is any definition of party sympathies will be when a vote is taken on the composition of the Ministerial Nominations Committee. This will probably be on Friday, April 21st.

There are elements in both the Pangu and United Parties who would accept a national or all-party Government but at present this is a minority attitude. When it becomes clear that one or other party is unable to muster a majority there may be a change of heart but as of now this appears unlikely.

The most likely possibility appears to be a Government based on the United Party and PPP, with sufficient independent support to provide an uncertain majority. The alternative is a Government based on Pangu and progressive independents with a PPP alliance. This would also have an uncertain majority. Either Government would be in a weak position, and prone to modify policies to placate minority groups on whose support they were dependent. Frequent defeats on the floor of the House could be anticipated and one of the early tasks of the House would be to establish conventions as to when a motion was one of confidence and could cause the fall of the Government. I would expect opinion to move to the left during the life of the

---

1   The national elections, the third to be based on a common roll, ran from 19 February to 11 March 1972. The minimum voting age was 18 and the number of enrolled voters was around 1.5 million. There were 533 candidates for the eighty-one open electorates and 58 for the eighteen regional electorates. Voters were entitled to vote twice: once for a candidate in their local or 'open' electorate and once for a candidate in their regional electorate. The regional electorates were aligned with PNG's administrative districts and candidates were required to have a PNG Intermediate Certificate or its equivalent. This educational qualification made it easier for expatriate candidates to gain election. Expatriates had comprised 30 per cent of those elected in 1964 and 20 per cent in 1968. Their level of representation declined further to 8.6 per cent in 1972. Four women contested the election, with one of them, Josephine Abaijah, elected. One woman had unsuccessfully contested the 1968 elections. A four-member UN Mission observed the 1972 elections. According to Downs: 'Their report to the UN stated that the conduct of the elections had been "thorough, comprehensive and fair".' Ian Downs, *The Australian Trusteeship: Papua New Guinea, 1945–1975,* Australian Government Publishing Service, Canberra, 1980, pp. 486–488.

Party organisation and affiliation remained weak, and there were varying assessments of the number of successful candidates supporting particular parties. Griffin has noted that: 'The final result seemed to show— for the depth of commitment was often far from clear—that the United Party had won 42 [seats], Pangu 24, People's Progress Party 11, [and the] National Party seven, while the radical Mataungan Association took three out of the four seats in East New Britain'. Negotiations to form a government continued until the eve of the first sitting of the new House of Assembly on 20 April. James Griffin, 'Papua New Guinea', in W. J. Hudson (ed.), *Australia in World Affairs, 1971–75*, George Allen & Unwin, Sydney, 1980, p. 353.

House and that a Pangu opposition would find increasing support as time went by. A scenario would be a UP-based Government with a narrow but eroding majority being supplanted eventually by a Pangu-based Government.

Should the parties fail to agree on the formation of a national Government, I believe it will be necessary to set up a national consultative body with representatives from all political groups. Major policy issues would be discussed by this body and there would be an attempt to reach a consensus on important issues. Such a body could be called the National Advisory Council or the National Consultative Council and could also include some who are not actively involved in politics. Such a body could be set up either informally or by Papua New Guinea legislation provided that it did not intrude upon the Papua New Guinea Act. I would appreciate any views you may have on this suggestion.

I regret the highly speculative nature of this communication.

[NAA: A452, 1970/4963]

276   LETTER FROM JOHNSON TO HAY

Port Moresby, 7 April 1972

I refer to earlier discussions on the possible appointment of a Minister of the Papua New Guinea House of Assembly to be Spokesman for Police.

Most of the issues are dealt with in the Inter-Departmental paper on Internal Security and I have conveyed my general agreement to the conclusions of this paper to the Departmental representative in Port Moresby. However, it may be useful if I summarise my views on the specific question of a Spokesman for Police.

1.   I believe that a Spokesman for Police should be appointed when the Ministerial portfolios are being allocated in late April.

2.   This Spokesman should be the Deputy Chairman of the AEC, who may or may not have another Ministerial portfolio.

3.   Initially no final powers should be conferred upon the Spokesman but he should be consulted on policy issues. He and the Administrator should consider issues jointly.

4.   Subject to Parliamentary or AEC pressures and the wishes of the Deputy Chairman, action should be taken at an appropriate date to delegate the Administrator's police powers to the Deputy Chairman.

5.   These delegated powers should be revokable in clearly delineated circumstances.

At this stage I am unable to offer a possible timetable for the processes suggested above. Dr Guise has already indicated to me his interest in Police matters and it can be assumed that any Ministry of which he is a member would press for an early transfer of decision making powers. The attitude of a more conservative Government is less predictable but you will know that suggestions that Police control should pass to a local Minister have been widely canvassed here and particularly in the Highlands.

[NAA: A452, 1972/2841]

277   REPORT BY BORDER

Canberra, undated [c. mid-April 1972]

Visit to Papua New Guinea, 5–13 April 1972[1]

[*matter omitted*][2]

Political Developments

3.   The elections for the House of Assembly had not produced a clear cut result at the time of my visit. A common view was that, had they been held a year earlier, United Party would probably have easily formed a government: a year later, and Pangu could form one. The odds were generally considered to be slightly in favour of United Party, but nobody thought a UP Government would last long, and Pangu would succeed. The Administrator was of this view and said that the tide was swinging against the UP towards the 'radicals'. If a Pangu-based government were formed however, it would have a much greater chance of success. It might be wobbly at the start but some UP members and independents would be likely to join Pangu, and within a year it should be fairly secure. Pangu's main danger lies in internal fights for power. It has been disciplined to date, but the new House contains a number of Pangu members and probable supporters of high intellectual calibre and considerable ambition e.g. Somare, Kiki, Guise, Kaputin. This may lead to party in-fighting.

4.   A government of national unity is not considered likely and, if formed, would not last. Both major parties have indicated they are not in favour of such an arrangement.

5.   The mood of the House will be rather different from that of the old one. It was relatively easy for the Administration to get its proposals through the House and, as a rule, Ministers accepted the advice of their public service advisers. The new Ministry is likely to be much more independent, especially if it is a Pangu one. Pangu will scrutinise public service proposals much more carefully and will apply the principles in its party platform. It is also likely to receive advice from the University with which it has close contacts.

6.   The impression I gained was of a rising nationalism and increasing resentment of white domination, together with an increased willingness to accept responsibility. It could be that Australia will be faced with a demand for (or proposal of) self-government even by the end of this year. As the Administrator pointed out, practical self-government could be given to PNG in a week. The Governor-General has only to instruct the Administrator to delegate certain powers, i.e. to accept the advice of his Ministers on certain topics, and effective self-government would have been achieved. Admittedly the legal arrangements for the formal granting of self-government would then take six months to a year, but the Administrator felt that the politicians would be content in the meantime with the practical exercise of power. Once self-government comes, independence seems likely to be about a year away. This means that independence could come within two to three years from now. There is no doubt that the House elected in 1976 will form the Government of an independent state.

---

1   Border was accompanied by Cavan Hogue. For details of Border's previous visit to Papua New Guinea, see Document 273, fn. 1.

2   The omitted matter provides details of Border's itinerary and of the people with whom he spoke. He and Hogue visited Port Moresby and East and West Sepik, including Vanimo, Wutung, Green River, Imonda, Amanab, Telefomin, Wewak and Maprik, along the way meeting 'local and expatriate officials, army officers and politicians'.

Internal Security

7.   There is some cause for concern over internal security. The electoral victory of the Mataungan Association[3] on the Gazelle Peninsula, and of the separatists on Bougainville, will give rise to pressure for greater regional autonomy. If this is granted, then other groups will want it too, e.g. Papua, the Highlands. Mr Tom Ellis thought the potential for real trouble was in the Highlands where the people felt keenly that they had been discriminated against, especially in education. The police and, if necessary the Army, could handle 75,000 people on the Gazelle. But a million highlanders would be a different situation. If the highlanders felt they were being dominated, there would be trouble.

8.   Rising urban unemployment and squatter settlements are another possible cause of trouble. The poor quality of the police does not help matters. Senior officials admitted that the expatriate police officers were of a low standard and that police standards generally were falling off. Mr Simon Kaumi[4] said people were afraid of the police, and Mr Tom Ellis said the police had lost contact with people at the grass roots level. They came in when there was trouble instead of nipping it in the bud. He felt that the proposal to make respected local identities low level magistrates in villages would help.

The Border

9.   One of the main purposes of my visit was to see what problems might arise in border negotiations with Indonesia and get an impression of the situation on the ground.

[*matter omitted*]

12.   Most of the officers we met, both in the field and in Wewak and Port Moresby, were at pains to point out that their relations with the Indonesians were good. There was quite a lot of informal cooperation, and as far as possible they both preferred to work things out themselves instead of getting enmeshed with the bureaucrats in Canberra and Djakarta. All agreed that the Indonesians' only real interest was to capture or kill the dissidents. When they talked to us of 'cooperation', this is what they meant. They were fairly relaxed about what we did with border crossers unconnected with the dissidents.

13.   The dissidents numbered about 30–40 and had a camp called Markas Victoria somewhere in the border area. The country is thick jungle and mountainous and it is easy to see how the dissidents could hide and move freely across the border. They managed to get food and some cooperation from villagers through terrorist tactics. They were not related to the local people and received no voluntary support.

14.   We inspected Yako camp, which is some 20 kilometres from the border and about half that distance from Vanimo. It is just a collection of tents divided by an imaginary line into quarantine and non-quarantine areas. There is a police post on the other side of the road and medical attention is provided from Vanimo if necessary.

15.   Crossers are put into quarantine for 14 days, but after that the Administration has no power to hold them unless they are charged. It is obviously quite easy to escape from Yako. The Secretary for Law advised that any crosssers could be charged as illegal entrants and given up to six months jail and then [be] deported. If we wish to hold them pending consideration of an application for permissive residence—which was a decision for the executive—they could be remanded and held. The district officials preferred the present informal arrangements whereby applicants for permissive residency are kept at Yako pending consideration of their

---

3   For background on the Mataungan Association, see Document 49, fn. 3.

4   PNG Electoral Commissioner.

application. Since they are not formally charged they cannot legally be held [...] Mr Webb[5] [...] felt that the advantages of the present system were that it did not commit anyone formally to a course of action, did not bring cases to the attention of the United Nations High Commissioner for Refugees and, by implication at least, kept things out of the clutches of officials in Port Moresby and Canberra who did not 'understand' the local situation. They claimed that the Indonesian officials in Djajapura also preferred this kind of arrangement. I suggested that a more formal arrangement—without undue rigidity—might be preferable in the future, and the border study group in Port Moresby said they would study this subject.

16. It was generally believed that the Indonesians were inclined to take a different view from us on rights across the border. We recognised traditional land rights on both sides of the border and were prepared to let Indonesians come across to our side to make use of such land. The Indonesians were not keen for them to do so and told them the Australians would put them in jail if they did [...]

17. Mr Bunting[6] suggested that if we denied people rights to move over the border as they did at present, this would be accepted by the people. Mr Webb disagreed and his view seemed to be the one accepted by others to whom we spoke. He said that people would be angry if they could not visit relatives on the other side or work their gardens. He thought that politicians would take up their cause in Port Moresby and there would be trouble. It was therefore necessary to work out a border regime which allowed people within a determined area to move freely across the border. These people could be given special passes. Anyone without such a pass would go through the normal entry procedures. The concept would be easily grasped by the people since it fitted in with their traditional patterns of land usage.

18. There would probably be about 5,000 to 6,000 people involved in this arrangement and a strip about 5 miles either side of the border would probably be effective.

[*matter omitted*][7]

20. A committee is meeting in Port Moresby to present a report detailing PNG's interests in delineation of the border and the desirable elements in a border regime. It will cover questions of river navigation, access to land, control of crossing, and anything else which seems relevant [...]

21. It is clear that Administration Officers want to handle border matters themselves as much as possible and it may be that we will gain more information and better results if we establish more personal contacts with them. (For example, Mr Webb gave us two reports which the Department [of Foreign Affairs] had not received.) The standard answer on reports not received by us is always that they have been sent to the Department of External Territories. I suggested to Mr Webb that if he wanted a quick Foreign Affairs reaction he should feel free to call on Mr Colin McDonald [...]

22. There was a general feeling that the AEC needed to be consulted on permissive residency but that it was likely to be sympathetic to border crossers. [...]

23. Wherever we discussed border matters, we were told that the real border issue was the Papua/Queensland border. It was felt that this issue would be raised early in the life of the new House of Assembly, and that Australia would be under pressure to do something very soon.

---

5   Royce Webb, Assistant Secretary, Security Branch, Department of the Administrator.

6   R. (Bob) Bunting, District Commissioner for West Sepik District.

7   In the omitted material Border comments on the views of Australian officials on the management of border crossers.

Defence

24. We spent a day at Moem Barracks in Wewak where we had informal discussions with Australian and Pacific Islander officers. We inspected the base and also visited the out-station at Vanimo where we spoke to Major Lowa[8] who was in command. In Port Moresby we spoke to Brigadier Eldridge. We also discussed defence and security matters with civilian officials and politicians.

25. It was generally agreed that if something were not done very soon to simplify the PIR administrative procedures and make them more suitable for PNG, the PIR would rapidly disintegrate after independence. Proposals had been submitted but no reaction had been received. If something were not done very soon it would be too late to train people in the new procedures. Some concern was also expressed over the PIR's ability to maintain some of the more sophisticated equipment they now had. Elementary maintenance would not be a problem but far too much equipment depended on Australian maintenance and was unsuited to PNG conditions.

26. It was also clear that the role of the PIR after independence would be given a different emphasis. There was a general consensus that the PIR would have to justify its cost, and that the politicians would not accept arguments based on external threats as justification. Some people thought it could be reorganised as a para-military police force (mostly civilians) while others thought it ought to maintain its military identity (mostly servicemen). But whatever its organisation, most people were inclined to agree that the role of the defence force should embrace:

   a.   major civic action, e.g. road building;

   b.   aid to the civil power in major disturbances;

   c.   border and maritime patrolling;

   d.   nation building;

   e.   basic infantry training, concentrating on counter-insurgency techniques.

27. Papua New Guineans showed some concern at the PIR remaining 'an Australian Army'. They wanted to get some control over it as soon as possible. Michael Somare indicated that Pangu Pati would be raising this issue.

28. Generally speaking, the PIR seemed to be popular among the people. There was some jealousy, however, among public servants of the generally superior conditions enjoyed by the PIR and some intellectuals were afraid of the possibility of a military takeover.

29. The attitudes I encountered make me believe that we need to work out quickly the kind of defence agreement we want with Papua New Guinea. From this will flow, probably, the nature of the security force the country should have. The kind of forces likely to emerge will want assistance in engineering maintenance and some simple infantry tactics, but they are likely to find most of our sophistication and expertise irrelevant to their problems. Some degree of cooperation between the two forces can no doubt be kept, but their roles will increasingly diverge and we should not delude ourselves that the present relationship will be maintained.

30. The only way a traditional, Australian-style military force could be maintained would be if Australia were to pay for it. I doubt whether this would be politically acceptable to an independent PNG Government, and for us it could raise the problem of supporting forces being used (as is highly likely) in a law and order role. Another problem, raised by the failure of the RAAF to train Papuans and New Guineans as pilots or mechanics, is that the small transport

---

8   Major Patterson Lowa, a company commander in the second battalion of the Pacific Islands Regiment, was one of the two most senior indigenous officers in the PIR. The other was Major Ted Diro.

force will have to be maintained by Australia and staffed by Australian personnel for some time. Since one of its roles will be to transport troops or police in case of civil disturbance, Australian servicemen could well find themselves in an awkward position. (It might be noted in this context that Brigadier Eldridge thought PNG should have one integrated force and not a separate army, navy and air force. This view seemed to be widespread and would make a completely Australian air element even more of an anomaly).

31. Since defence arrangements are going to have political implications for Australia's relations with Papua New Guinea, I believe it important that a Foreign Affairs view be formulated and injected into defence planning at as early a stage as possible. I have the impression that much of the planning now going on—insofar as I am aware of its content—is tardy and theoretical. One important feature in any defence agreement will be to ensure Australian rights on navigation through PNG claimed waters if, as seems probable, PNG takes an archipelagic approach to law of the sea matters.

East Sepik District

32. We visited Wewak and Maprik in the East Sepik District. Maprik sub-district is the centre of the Peli Association Cargo Cult. Its leader, Mr Matias Yeliwan, was elected to the House Assembly at the last elections. He is considered by district officials to be quite mad. From a practical point of view, his activities will be harmful because the money which people have contributed to his Association (in order to assure themselves of fantastic returns later) will not be available to the local council for education and crop improvements. There is also a tendency for people not to work hard while awaiting the imminent arrival of the millennium.

[*matter omitted*]

Aid

35. In one sense, the present Administration can be seen as a large, aid-giving body. There could be a tendency after independence to preserve the patterns and practices already established. I therefore tried to get some impression of how effectively Australian money was being spent in PNG—in terms of developing the country—and whether there were lessons to be learned by us in our aid planning.

36. The present system is geared very much to Australia and Australian ways of doing things. Much of this will disappear after independence and this is not necessarily a bad thing. The administrative systems used by the public service and the army are lifted from Australian practice and need to be drastically simplified and improved. They are not efficient in the PNG context. Much of the economic development benefits the rich. There is an excellent network of air services—almost entirely run by Australians—but only a poor road system and no railways. Food patterns are Australian to the extent that people import foodstuffs from Australia and ignore the local products.

37. A strong paternalistic attitude is obvious throughout the Territory. Australians prefer to do themselves things they are convinced the natives cannot do or will not do as well. Australians are imported and paid high salaries for relatively simple jobs. (They are never sacked.) Often if a relatively simple machine like an air conditioner breaks down, there is nobody to fix it except an Australian who may live in the next town. There has been a general disinclination to give real authority or responsibility to natives. The relatively low level of localisation is a reflection of this approach. For the District Administration field service which does not demand high educational qualities nor specialist knowledge, only about one third are local officers and most of them are junior. This helps maintain the mystique of white superiority in the villages.

38. In our programme instruction and guidance must be the keynote. With expertise will come confidence. We should be very wary of employing expatriates with long years of service in the Territory. Those expatriates who are needed and wanted will be offered contracts by the Papua New Guinea Government. Many others will come to us asking to be taken on as experts. Some might be suitable but we should not employ the people Papua New Guinea has rejected. To this end, our aid might best be largely in the form of budget subsidy. In the early days of independence the number of Australians present in Papua New Guinea should be kept to a minimum. (Mr Michael Somare, MHA made it clear that he wanted foreigners to work for the Papua New Guinea Government so they could be sacked if they were not suitable.) Inevitably PNG will change things, will make a mess of things, and will improve things. They will do things in their own, un-Australian way. This should not worry us. If we are to establish and maintain an effective relationship with PNG, it has to be on a new basis—and be seen to be on a new basis. This means no more paternalism.

39. This is not to say that some project aid will not be useful. We might undertake projects requiring capital and expertise which PNG does not have. These should be carefully selected, large projects involving expenditure of the order of $100,000 upwards. They should be basic, infrastructure projects or the setting up of an industry which will benefit a wide area. Political factors will have to be taken into consideration in selecting projects e.g. is it in an area which is relatively well developed and will this give rise to complaints from other lesser developed areas?

40. One idea I would like to see studied is the possibility of aid in the form of a Development Bank. I appreciate that there is a PNG Development Bank and that PNG has access to international credit sources such as the Asian Development Bank. But an Australian Development Bank, lending at low rates of interest, might be a useful supplement. It would have the advantages of getting away from the kind of thing we have been doing before—giving everything and doing the job ourselves.

41. I had an interesting conversation with a young Patrol Officer who had worked in the Telefomin area.[9] He saw the role of the expatriate 'kiap'[10] as that of an adviser. He should spend most of his time in community development and be available for advice. He would not spend his time, as he did now, taking decisions and burying himself in paper.

42. Another valid point was made by an Australian Captain in the PIR. He thought that, at least in the early stages, experienced expatriates could be available to advise, but the power and responsibility should be given immediately to the local officer. This was far better than having local officers understudy an Australian. He quoted an example of an Australian Staff Sergeant who recently handed over to a local Sergeant. The Australian simply walked out 3 or 4 weeks before he was due to leave and handed over to the local sergeant. Every few days he dropped by to see how things were going and to answer questions. But he took no further decisions and accepted no further responsibility. This seemed to me to be the right approach.

43. In the light of the above comments we should oppose moves, which may be made, to convert External Territories to a Department of Overseas Aid and/or to employ large numbers of ex-Administration Australians.

PNG Foreign Service

44. I saw Mr Colin McDonald and met the five trainees to come to Canberra for training in May. Mr McDonald seems to be settling in well and I was impressed by the quality of the

---

9   Telefomin is located on the border between West Sepik and the (then) Western District.

10   Patrol officer.

trainees. So far, it has not been possible to implement fully the proposals for re-organising the International Affairs Branch into an embryo Foreign Office, but Mr McDonald has some plans worked up and is talking with the PNG Public Service Board. This Department should keep in close touch with him and be ready to help him in any possible.

45. Mr McDonald said that recruiting of trainees had to be done through the PNG Public Service machinery, and it was likely that the Branch would get about eight people a year. They might not always come evenly, and it could be that they would six in one group and two in another, for example. Whatever happens, the Department should accept all trainees proposed and make sure they are given as much training as possible. In terms of our Foreign Service Training Programme, Papua New Guinea should be given the highest priority. At the rate of eight people a year we will have some thirty trained men by the end of 1975. Allowing for drop-outs this will provide the bare minimum of trained personnel. We should take a similar approach to any other requests for training from PNG.

46. Mr Pearsall, FAS,[11] Central Secretariat, Department of the Administrator, said that the PNG Department of Trade would soon be sending two officers on the Foreign Service Training Course. He seemed to think that the Department recognised the need for a single office to handle PNG's international relations. I said we would be happy to take these officers and thought that this was a step in the right direction.

Property

47. I spoke briefly to Mr Boyce of the Commonwealth Department of Works. He showed me a proposed site for the commercial building to be used as a temporary Chancery. He said that timing previously given us was not accurate and that building time would be some seventy-two weeks. He estimated that it would take three years from the time a decision was taken to the time the building was ready. We must therefore move quickly.

[*matter omitted*]

Japanese Interests

48. There was evidence of a growing Japanese presence in Papua New Guinea. A short walk through the shops showed a great variety of Japanese consumer goods and the only non-Japanese cars to be seen on the streets seemed to be the official Administration Holdens.[12] The District Commissioner in Wewak said there were large numbers of Japanese passing through the district on all kinds of ostensible missions. Many claimed to be anthropologists and there was a steady stream of Japanese ex-servicemen groups visiting memorials and battlefields. It was hard to be sure how many of these were genuine, but many were obviously businessmen who were keeping their eyes open.

49. The Administrator said that although the Japanese were very active, so far their actual investment was limited. They had some fishing and timber projects going and were interested in oil palms. It was obvious, however, that there was great potential for Japanese capital in developing mining and other natural resources. Mr Michael Somare, MHA, has visited Japan and been given some expensive presents by the Japanese. He appears to be quite pro-Japanese and talks of getting capital and expertise from countries other than Australia.

50. I do not see that this interest is necessarily contrary to Australia's interests, nor to PNG's interests. Even if it were, it is hard to see what we could do about it. Unless we see Japan as a potential aggressor, a strong Japanese presence in PNG could be a stabilising factor in the

---

11   First Assistant Secretary. It appears Pearsall was acting in this role at the time of Border's visit.

12   Holden was an Australian-manufactured motor car.

region. The main danger is commercial. We may lose some of our markets there, and Japan might develop mineral deposits in PNG which would compete directly with Australian exports to Japan.

Conclusions

51. I have recorded separately a summary of my conclusions and recommendations for action by Foreign Affairs. My overall conclusion is that Papua New Guinea is moving very rapidly indeed to self-government and independence. The Administration is more aware of this now and is gearing itself for action. There is a growing nationalism particularly among the younger, better educated people. There is also a growing impatience with Australian direction and what is seen as Australian paternalism and self-interest. We must give more thought to ensuring that we leave PNG on amicable terms, and to establishing a new kind of relationship. I wonder how many people in the Administration, and even more so in some Departments in Canberra, really understand how different the relationship could be. The people of PNG are not necessarily going to thank us and feel beholden to us for our bounty. We need to assess carefully PNG's importance to us, and our importance to PNG. The new relationship must be based on a realistic and unemotional assessment of Australia's interests and of PNG's interests.

[*matter omitted*]

[NAA: A1838, 3036/10/6/5 PART 1]

278   CABINET SUBMISSION 627[1]

Canberra, 17 April 1972

CONFIDENTIAL

Papua New Guinea
Programme of Movement towards Internal Self Government

Purpose

This submission places before Cabinet a programme of movement towards internal self-government in Papua New Guinea (defined in Annexe 'A'—supplied to the Cabinet Secretariat) during the period 1972–76 as a basis for negotiations by the Minister for External Territories with the leadership group which emerges from the 1972–1976 Papua New Guinea House of Assembly. Further submissions will be made after the negotiations have taken place, and before final commitments are entered into.

2.   In addition the submission seeks the views of Cabinet, as requested by the Papua New Guinea House of Assembly, on the political and economic relations which might exist between Australia and Papua New Guinea at the time of internal self-government. For this purpose a summary of the main obligations of a political, economic and defence character now in operation and, in the terms of this submission, likely to be in operation at the date of internal self-government has been supplied to the Cabinet Secretariat as Annexe 'B' to this submission.

3.   Broadly, it is not the date of internal self-government but the date of independence which will be the watershed in relations between the two countries. At internal self-government, Australia's obligations under the Trusteeship Agreement (in respect of New Guinea) and the Charter of the United Nations (in respect of both Papua and New Guinea), and those we have undertaken unilaterally in the light of those obligations will continue to apply.

4.   At independence Australia's United Nations obligations will be discharged, and a new set of relations will need to be developed. This submission recommends that this fact be made known in the course of the negotiations which will take place with the leadership group and that the group be informed also that discussions on post-independence relations would be envisaged well before the date of independence.

5.   This submission further recommends that a study be made of Australia's national interest in relation to an independent Papua New Guinea. The conclusions of such a study would be placed before Cabinet which may wish to direct that certain of them be used as guidelines in the consideration of policy issues arising as the result of movement towards internal self-government and the subsequent movement towards independence.

6.   The submission also explores the administrative implications of implementing the programme for Papua New Guinea.

The Programme

7.   Cabinet, in Decision No. 89 of 20th April, 1971 (Submission No. 45)[2] 'authorised the Department of External Territories, in consultation with the Administration and other Commonwealth Departments and authorities concerned, to draw up a flexible programme of movement towards full internal self-government which includes the kinds of political

---

1   Submitted by Peacock.
2   Documents 155 & 159.

and economic relations which should exist with Australia at internal self-government for consideration by Cabinet at an early date as a basis for negotiations with the leadership group emerging from the 1972 elections'. It also 'authorised the planning of legislative and administrative steps necessary to ensure that the Commonwealth is in a position to conform to such a programme'.

8.   Accordingly the Department of External Territories has prepared a programme in consultation with the Administration and Commonwealth Departments and Instrumentalities involved. The formulation of such a programme required an assumed date for internal self-government and September, 1975 has been adopted. This date has been chosen as it allows a reasonable time for the execution of the necessary steps and still falls within the lifetime of the Third House of Assembly. September is appropriate as it is the month during which National Day is celebrated in Papua New Guinea. A framework of possible constitutional development has been supplied to the Cabinet Secretariat as Annexe B to the submission. Details of the programme and the programme itself are attached to this submission.

9.   The programme is essentially a list of the issues which need to be resolved before internal self-government in relation to each activity of government specified in the programme against a framework of possible constitutional development. It is made up of statements of the preliminary administrative and legislative steps which must be taken if the timing of preparation of Papua New Guinea for internal self-government during the life of the Third House of Assembly is to be adhered to.

10.   It does not address itself to the substance of the alternative policy issues which will arise from time to time although for planning purposes it makes a number of assumptions about what the policy decisions are likely to be.

11.   It is flexible. Its execution will depend on the state of opinion in Papua New Guinea and the policies of Papua New Guinea's political leaders.

Related Studies

12.   There are a number of related studies regarding the transfer to Papua New Guinea of functions of internal self-government now carried out by Commonwealth Departments and Instrumentalities, and the questions of internal security and defence. These are set out in Annexe 'C'[3] to this submission which has been supplied to the Cabinet Secretariat.

13.   The programme as such does not deal with defence. Commonwealth control in this field will continue beyond internal self-government to independence. Nevertheless attention is drawn to the fact that decisions as to future defence arrangements and the organisation, development and roles of the forces in Papua New Guinea, and a major programme of action in accordance with those decisions, will also be necessary. These decisions and the consequent programme of work will have a lasting relevance beyond independence for Australia. Separate submissions will be made to Ministers as necessary.

Post-Independence Situation

14.   While in formal terms the change to a new basis of relations between Australia and Papua New Guinea will take place on the date of independence, I believe that in practice our relations in the pre-independence period should be conducted at least with an eye to the post-independence situation. For this reason, as well as the need to prepare for the pre-independence negotiations referred to in paragraph 5 it is necessary to study in depth the requirements of Australia's long term national interests in its relations with an independent Papua New Guinea.

---

3   Not published.

The current formula to the effect that decisions should be taken on the basis that Australia's long term interests will be best served by a peaceful and well-ordered independent Papua New Guinea well-disposed towards Australia, while serving a useful purpose, is not adequate as a long-term guide.

Implications of administering the Programme

15. Work done, money spent and measures taken now and in the immediate future could have a long lasting impact on relationships between Australia and a self-governing Papua New Guinea in the years to come. Because of the Government's commitment to preparing the programme and the fact that developments in all fields in Papua New Guinea are moving at a rapid pace it is essential that there be sufficient numbers of experienced qualified public servants both in the Administration and the Department of External Territories to ensure the smoothest possible transition to internal self-government during perhaps the most critical period in Papua New Guinea's development. The implications of administering the programme are set out in Annexe 'D' which has been supplied to the Cabinet Secretariat.

Recommendations

16. It is recommended:

(a) that Cabinet note the draft programme for presentation by the Minister for External Territories to the 1972 leadership group and endorse its use as a basis for initial negotiations, with that group at Ministerial level, and later at Departmental level, on further progress towards internal self-government;

(b) that, at the appropriate time, the leadership group be informed that the achievement of internal self-government by Papua New Guinea will not affect Australia's obligations undertaken with the United Nations and its continuing commitment to provide aid and assistance to Papua New Guinea, but that at independence a new set of relations will need to be developed and that it is envisaged that discussions on post-independence relations would take place well before the date of independence;

(c) that the Department of External Territories in conjunction with the Department of Foreign Affairs initiate as soon as possible a study in consultation with other Commonwealth Departments to define Australia's national interests in relation to an independent Papua New Guinea and the arrangements between it and Australia which ought to be entered into in the light of these interests. The conclusions of such a study would be placed before Cabinet with a view to recommending that certain of them be used as guidelines in the consideration of policy issues in the period up to independence and as the basis for discussions on the post-independence relations between Australia and Papua New Guinea;

(d) that the staffing implications of the programme be the subject of priority consideration by the Minister for External Territories, and the Treasurer, who would seek the approval of the Prime Minister to their recommendations.

Attachment

Introductory Note

The attached programme lists the activities which require legislative action before internal self-government. It describes in the case of each activity the legislative and administrative steps which will be necessary or desirable in Papua New Guinea and Australia to enable the move to internal self-government to take place with the least amount of administrative disruption.

The programme points up the procedures by which policies will be referred for government decision at the appropriate times and indicates those actions which will be necessary if administrative disruption is to be avoided.

It has been necessary in some instances to assume a specific decision but it should be made clear that this action has been taken for programming purposes only and in no way should it be construed as attempting to dictate the course of action on any policy issue.

Most issues will require policy decisions by both the Commonwealth Government and the Government of Papua New Guinea.

It should be noted that the last House of Assembly resolved in September 1970 that 'any further transfer of power or constitutional change would be unacceptable to the House unless agreed to by a majority of members'.

In almost all instances it is envisaged that the final goal sought to be achieved is an administrative structure operating in Papua New Guinea (which in many instances already exists) within the framework of legislation passed by the House of Assembly and subject to executive authority vested in a Minister of the Government of Papua New Guinea. In such a case this will ordinarily require amending Commonwealth legislation and the enactment of Papua New Guinea legislation. Before this legislation can be drafted and enacted a decision by Cabinet and by the government in Papua New Guinea (The Administrator's Executive Council) will be necessary.

It will frequently be the case before either Cabinet or the Administrator's Executive Council make a decision that a study and recommendation will have to take place. The study can be done either by an interdepartmental committee/Administration joint report, or by a Department of External Territories/Administrations Committee report, or by a separate Department of External Territories or Administration report depending upon the circumstances and importance of each issue. In order to formulate the programme it has been necessary to assume certain specific decisions involving policy in the light of these considerations. It should be stressed, however, that the programme does not purport to determine in advance the policy involved or to imply in any way that the decision specified will in fact be made.

In so far as steps in the programme require a decision on policy they are to be treated as merely hypothetical. They have been specified in the programme in order to indicate the administrative consequences if such decisions should in fact be taken. Accordingly they represent only possible decisions which may be made and the administrative "flow on" which will be necessary if they should occur. If the programme were to omit all decisions of a policy nature it would fail in its endeavour to specify the administrative steps necessary to avoid administrative disruption.

It will be necessary when making future policy decisions in the course of implanting the programme for Ministers to give consideration to the staffing and financial requirements of the administrative structures envisaged.

INDEX OF ACTIVITIES

Air Navigation, DCA and Airlines

ASOPA[4]

Banking

Broadcasting

International Trade

Investment Guidelines and Investment Code

Investment Insurance and Guarantee

Law, Department of

---

4   Australian School of Pacific Administration located at Middle Head, Sydney.

Commonwealth Aid

Commonwealth Property and Liabilities in PNG

Commonwealth Teaching Service

Courts

Cultural Development

Currency

Custodian

Ex-Servicemens Credit Scheme

External Publicity

Fisheries

Foreign Office and Foreign Activities

Higher Education

ILO[5] Conventions

Immigration

Insurance

International Organisations, PNG Membership of

Marine Navigation Aids

Mining Legislation and Mines Department

Offshore Oil

Overseas Staff

Overseas Telecommunications Commission

Overseas Trade Promotion

Papua/Queensland Border

PNG Loans

PNG Statutory Authorities

PNG/West Irian Border

Police

Public Service and Statutory Authorities

Public Service Legislation

Shipping Legislation

Transfer of Commonwealth Functions

Volunteers

Wages and Wage Rates Policy

[*matter omitted*]

Annex A
Definition of Internal Self Government

Stated broadly, internal self-government means a situation in which the Commonwealth has ceased to exercise executive control in the administration of Papua New Guinea in respect of its internal affairs. External Affairs and Defence would remain a Commonwealth responsibility. Self-government is not an inflexible term. For instance the retention of the control of internal security and even the public service by the metropolitan power has been regarded as constituent with it. The outward sign of internal self-government will be the formal divesting by Australia of its powers by amendment to the Papua New Guinea Act. This would take place in the final stages of an orderly progression and possibly be subject to consultation with the UN. The scope of power conferred at internal self-government may need to reflect Australia's continuing obligations under the Trusteeship Agreement. By the time of this divesting of powers under the Papua New Guinea Act other Commonwealth legislation affecting the bulk of Papua New Guinea's internal affairs would have ceased to be applicable to Papua New Guinea.

Annex B
Basis of Australian/Papua New Guinea Relations at Internal Self Government

Current Australian policy towards Papua New Guinea is based on the obligations accepted under the United Nations charter and the Trusteeship Agreement. This is to promote the

---

5   International Labour Organization.

political, social, economic and educational advancement of Papua New Guinea and its progressive development towards internal self-government and ultimate independence in accordance with the freely expressed wishes of its people. It is implicit in the terms of the Trusteeship Agreement, that Australia's obligations include the defence of Papua New Guinea, and the government's policy has been to defend the integrity of Papua New Guinea's boundaries as though they were Australia's.

2. These obligations do not as a matter of law, expire on the achievement of internal self-government. They persist until independence.

3. In the context of these obligations certain decisions governing present relationships have been taken which place Papua New Guinea in a special and advantageous position compared with Australia's independent neighbours. To modify them at internal self-government would raise the question of Australia's intention to continue to meet its charter obligations. But it is to be expected that they would require review and possible renegotiation before independence.

4. The following is a summary of the decisions.

A. General

In Cabinet Decision No 138 of 24th/29th March 1966[6] (Submission No 71—Papua New Guinea—Ultimate Status) Cabinet agreed:

> 'That the Government ... will assist towards financial independence by progressively giving the Territory more financial autonomy as its capacity to contribute to its own revenue increases ... finally, still in the terms of give and take of counsel, it might be said that Australia would think that whatever the political status of New Guinea may be at any time, there would be, as a matter of mutual self-interest, a defence relationship and also a trade relationship of mutual advantage. The defence relationship would derive from the territory's need of Australian aid in defence, and from Australia's interest, from a defence point of view, in New Guinea.'

B. Economic and Financial Assistance

> (i) In Cabinet Decision No 452 of 23rd June, 1970 (Submission No 327) (Implications of early self-government for Papua New Guinea)[7] Cabinet endorsed the measure that '... the Government will seek to maintain sufficient numbers of Australian officers in the Territory and will continue aid on a large scale ...'

> (ii) In Cabinet Decision No 1002 of 9th June, 1965 (Submission No 821) Cabinet endorsed certain broad policy objectives and in relation to Papua New Guinea decided that for purposes of public presentation, the grant to Papua New Guinea might be included with external aid expenditure but Papua New Guinea is an Australian responsibility and the determination of its grant is to be treated as a separate matter.

> (iii) In Cabinet Decision No 890 of 11th February, 1969 (Submission No 449) Cabinet endorsed '... a policy that, in furtherance of Australia's responsibilities to develop the economy of the Territory of Papua and New Guinea, every effort be made to supplement Australia's existing aid by seeking to assist the development of Territory exports to Australia by appropriate measures consistent with Australia's international commitments and the need to maintain protection to Australia's own industries.'[8]

---

6   See Stuart Doran (ed.), *Documents on Australian Foreign Policy: Australia and Papua New Guinea, 1966–1969*, Department of Foreign Affairs and Trade, Canberra, 2006, Document 34.

7   Documents 47 & 53.

8   See Doran (ed.), *Australia and Papua New Guinea*, Document 251.

(iv) Under section 75A of the Papua New Guinea Act when the Administration borrows any moneys by way of public loan the Commonwealth guarantees the due payment of all moneys (including interest) payable by the Administration under the terms and conditions of the public loan.

[*matter omitted*]

Annex D
Implications of Administering the Programme

The administration of the programme will impose increased demands on staff and finance. In the case of most activities of government specified in the programme a major examination of the administrative structure is required. In many instances it will be necessary to determine not only the machinery of transfer but along with it the appropriate institutions for a new country as for example the reorganisation of the public service and the Court structure. This will throw up important policy questions and it will be noted that in many instances a decision by Cabinet will be required before the programme can be implemented. In addition the approval of the Administrator's Executive Council of Papua New Guinea as its embryo Cabinet, must be secured. The carrying out of the necessary examinations, and the preparation of the numerous submissions will add greatly to the already heavy demands on administration. In the case of the Administrator's Executive Council it will be necessary to explain fully to Ministers of the House of Assembly fields of government which are novel and complex.

As appears from the programme itself the process of transfer and the administrative reorganisation required will produce a marked increase in substantial legislation. This will impose demands on the Office of the Parliamentary Counsel insofar as Commonwealth legislation has to be prepared. At present, in Papua New Guinea, the drafting of Bills for introduction into the House of Assembly is carried out by a small section of the Department of Law. The large amount of legislation required to implement the programme will impose a heavier burden upon the draftsmen. In addition there are numerous Commonwealth Acts extending to Papua New Guinea. Much of this legislation will need to be incorporated in the law of Papua New Guinea. In many instances it will require prior adaptation and the drafting of the resulting legislation.

These administrative demands will be made against a background of staff shortages in the Administration which are already acute in key areas such as general administration in the field, special land duties and political education. These shortages have arisen as a result of demands on these areas of administration as a result of rapid economic developments in recent years. In some instances this has required the formation of new Departments within the Administration. In other instances it has produced a need for increased staff.

The Papua New Guinea Public Service Board is at present implementing an accelerated training programme to speed up the process of localisation at all levels of the Public Service. Progress in localisation has been considerable in lower level positions but the availability of Papuans and New Guineans with required educational qualifications has limited the numbers in middle and upper levels of the Public Service. Special attention is being given to the implementation of priority positions for localisation at the senior administrative, policy and planning levels and to the provision of intensive training to groom local officers for those positions.

Notwithstanding the measures being taken to accelerate localisation at all levels the experience and expertise of a large number of overseas officers will continue to be needed in Papua New Guinea for a considerable time to come.

[*matter omitted*]

[NAA: A1838, 3080/10/1 PART 2]

## 279	CABINET SUBMISSION 638[1]

Canberra, undated [c. mid-April 1972]

CONFIDENTIAL

Papua New Guinea:
Future Security of Permanent Overseas Officers of the Public Service

This submission seeks Cabinet's authority to discuss with the incoming Papua New Guinea Administrator's Executive Council a proposal for the future security of permanent overseas officers. The proposal is to establish a separate Commonwealth service to which overseas officers would be appointed for the purpose of secondment to the Papua New Guinea government.

Background

2.	In Decision No. 361 of 16 August 1971 Cabinet approved certain modifications and additions to the Employment Security Scheme (ESS) for permanent overseas officers. (Annex 'A' available from the Cabinet Secretariat).[2]

3.	The decision was announced on 30 August 1971, and was poorly received. The interdepartmental committee which had prepared the report on which the decision was based agreed that, without departing from approved basic principles, some marginal adjustments could be made in order to assist the passage of implementing legislation through the House. (Annex 'B' available from the Cabinet Secretariat.)[3] However the adjustments were not introduced because the final advice of the Administrator was that they would have no effect on the attitude of Members of the House of Assembly in the light of intense pressures from members of the Public Service Association [PSA]. After passing a motion which, in effect, called on the Australian Government to reconsider its proposals the House of Assembly refused leave for the introduction of the implementing legislation.

4.	Since taking office I have received further representations about the future security of permanent overseas officers both from the PSA and from individual (and responsible) officers.

5.	In the light of the attitude of the House and further representations the Department of External Territories has made a comprehensive review of the ESS and the future position of permanent and contract overseas officers. It has concluded that, in order to achieve the Commonwealth's objective of retaining the services of key expatriate officers while localisation and the building of an indigenous public service proceed, a separate Commonwealth service should be established. This would preserve beyond doubt, under Commonwealth legislation, the conditions of service for overseas officers. It would involve transferring the present Superannuation Scheme and the Employment Security Scheme from a Papua New Guinea ordinance to an Act of the Commonwealth Parliament. In the case of contract officers it would involve transferring the present Contract Officers Retirement Benefits Fund from a Papua New Guinea Ordinance to an Act of the Commonwealth Parliament. Future overseas staff recruited by the Australian Government would also be included in the new service under conditions identical to those now applying to contract staff.

6.	The new service would exist only for as long as overseas staff were needed and desired by the Papua New Guinea government. It would in effect be a 'holding ground' for Australian-

---

1	Submitted by Peacock.

2	Document 204.

3	Not published.

recruited overseas staff who would be formally seconded to the Papua New Guinea government. It would do more than preserve to Commonwealth officers, under Commonwealth legislation, their present entitlements and those already agreed to by Cabinet and further adjustments agreed to by the interdepartmental committee. It would encompass the proposed Australian Service for Overseas Cooperation (ASOC) which was approved in principle by Cabinet in Decision No. 329 of 9 June 1970.[4]

7.   From the point of view of the Australian Government there are advantages in that there would be no question of the Commonwealth losing effective control over officers' terms and conditions of employment; the issue of Commonwealth guarantees, which was to be further examined under the terms of Cabinet's decision of 16 August 1971, would be solved and the transfer of responsibility for the Public Service to local executive authority could take place without raising any legal or constitutional issues on which a challenge affecting the legal basis of the Employment Security Scheme could be made.

8.   Insofar as overseas officers are concerned the main advantage would be that the Government would be seen to be honouring in a positive way the assurances that have been given to them over the years. In addition, the problem of guarantees now seen by overseas officers as to their entitlements under the Superannuation, Contract Officers Retirement Benefits and Employment Security Schemes, [and the questions of] the currency in which their entitlements would be paid, and the taxation on those entitlements, would not arise.

Departmental Attitudes

9.   The Treasury considered that if permanent overseas officers were brought directly under Commonwealth legislation they should not carry with them certain benefits approved by Cabinet in Decision No. 361 of August 1971 and the further marginal adjustments agreed to by the interdepartmental committee, and saw problems in permanent overseas officers becoming Commonwealth employees with more favourable superannuation provisions than other Commonwealth employees. The Department of External Territories considered it would be undesirable to withdraw options that have already been publicly offered and that the preservation of existing superannuation provisions would be an essential ingredient in its approach. In any event, permanent appointments to the Papua New Guinea Public Service ceased in 1963 and the Papua New Guinea Superannuation Fund had therefore become a 'closed' fund for over 8 years and would be unlikely to create a difficult precedent for the Commonwealth.

10.   The Treasury felt that an attempt should be made to persuade the new Administrator's Executive Council to accept the proposals approved by Cabinet's Decision No. 361 of 16 August 1971 subject to those marginal adjustments subsequently agreed to by the interdepartmental committee.

11.   The Department of the Prime Minister and Cabinet and the Department of Labour and National Service were not opposed to the concept of a separate Commonwealth Service. The Public Service Board questioned the need to go this far, its view being that it should suffice to strengthen the existing Commonwealth guarantees. These departments considered however that the first step should be to try to gain acceptance of the original proposals of August 1971 with the marginal adjustments agreed to later.

12.   All departments were unanimous that the approach adopted should first be discussed with and have the full support of the incoming Administrator's Executive Council before any new public announcement.

---

4   Not published. See Documents 36 & 38.

13. The modified August 1971 proposals plus strengthened guarantees would go a good distance towards meeting the Government's objectives and the reasonable representations of the Association and its members. But in my view they would not go far enough. Furthermore the question of strengthening guarantees in Commonwealth legislation of obligations in Papua New Guinea ordinances is not a straightforward matter. The proposal to introduce a separate Commonwealth service on the other hand has the advantage of putting beyond doubt the preservation of the conditions of service of overseas officers and of settling the question of Commonwealth guarantees.

Views of the Public Service Association

14. The Public Service Association of Papua New Guinea has recently made a detailed submission to me. (Annex 'C' available from the Cabinet Secretariat.)[5] The Association believes, as it has from the start, that a date should be set which should be as soon as possible at which permanent overseas officers should have the choice of whether to resign with full

---

5   In its submission, dated 21 March 1972, the PNG Public Service Association (PSA) argued that the Employment Security Scheme had failed to encourage 'permanent overseas officers to remain in the Territory' and had failed to provide 'adequate compensation for those officers forced to leave the Territory or suffer limitations in their career prospects due to changed conditions'. It said that because of the high resignation rate among permanent officers the Australian Government was failing 'to meet its obligation to promote steady development in the Territory as a preliminary to the granting of Independence' and to ensure that 'skilled expatriate officers' remained in the Territory 'to train an efficient and stable indigenous Public Service, which will enable PNG to cope with the responsibilities of independent nationhood'. It proposed several amendments to the scheme, namely that the Commonwealth Government should specify a date on which the scheme would come into operation; accept full and direct responsibility for the scheme; guarantee all pension rights for all officers who retired under the scheme; make special provision for enforced early retirements of expatriate officers; and pay interest on compensation payments to public servants who remained in Papua New Guinea for the period between self-government and independence.

Under the established arrangements, the scheme would have come into operation at independence. The PSA argued that the more appropriate date at which the full benefits available under the scheme would become available would be the date when Papua New Guinea attained self-government, or—should it occur sooner—the date when control of the PNG public service was transferred to local executive government. It added: 'The Government has stated that the Scheme will begin operating "upon Independence". But nobody knows when Independence will be granted or whether it will come about through peaceful constitutional change, by unilateral action on the part of Territory political leaders or in other ways which may prevent the Australian Government from ensuring that expatriate public servants' rights are preserved'. Referring to the 'Master-Servant Relationship', the PSA pointed out that at around the time of self-government, with the transfer of control over the public service, there would 'be a "change of master" for permanent expatriate public servants, and that it was 'at least morally wrong that a group of individuals should be forced, without compensation, to choose between accepting a change of master-servant relationship about which they have no control, or to abandon their legitimate career expectations'.

The PSA was particularly concerned that the Commonwealth wanted the new Territory Government to accept responsibility for the Employment Security Scheme, a proposal which, it said, had 'caused very great concern and disillusionment among overseas officers in the Territory'. It pointed out that no-one could predict whether the Territory would 'have sufficient resources to meet the cost of the Scheme' or whether 'a new Territory Government would feel itself obliged to carry out responsibilities imposed on it by the Australian Government'.

The PSA attached to its submission a letter providing an opinion in favour of its proposed starting date for the scheme from Geoffrey Sawer, Professor of Law in the Research School of Social Science at the Australian National University. It also attached extracts from the House of Assembly debate in November 1971 on the scheme, in which MHAs expressed concern at an apparent attempt to shift the burden of the costs of the Employment Security Scheme to Papua New Guinea; and letters from PSA members expressing concerns about career uncertainties and increasing crime and unrest. Letter, PSA President T. C. Jackson to Peacock, and attached Submission, 21 March 1972, NAA: A5908, 638.

ESS benefits or stay on. Cabinet has previously rejected this. I do not discount the possibility of the matter being taken before the Courts. The Attorney-General's Department has indicated that any such action is unlikely to succeed.

15. The Association's representatives have raised other issues such as deteriorating health and education services and a concern at law and order problems. However I do not believe that it is appropriate even if it were practicable to attempt to respond to representations in these fields.

Cost of Proposal

16. The costs arising under the proposal are payments under the ESS, the Superannuation Scheme and the Contract Officers Retirement Benefits Scheme. They would be the same under this proposal as would be the case under existing provisions including Cabinet's Decision No. 361 of 16 August 1971 and the further marginal adjustments agreed to by the interdepartmental committee. Costs at present are a matter for the Papua New Guinea budget but there is a guarantee embodied in Commonwealth legislation which places on the Commonwealth a contingent liability to meet those costs. Under the new proposal the costs would be a direct charge against the Commonwealth in the context of its total aid to Papua New Guinea. But I would propose a cost sharing arrangement in terms of a government-to-government agreement along the lines of British practice in these matters. Cabinet's decision of August 1971 provided that the Treasurer and I were to have discussions in consultation as necessary with the Administrator's Executive Council on this aspect and this will be done.

Recommendation

16. I seek Cabinet's authorisation

(a) to put to the Administrator's Executive Council and seek its support for a proposal to establish a separate Commonwealth service to which all permanent and contract overseas officers would be appointed as described in paragraphs 5 and 6 above; and;

(b) if the Council supports the proposal, to proceed to a conclusion subject to confirmation of details in consultation with the Prime Minister, the Treasurer and the Minister for Labour and National Service.[6]

[NAA: A5908, 638]

---

6   In response to this submission, Cabinet noted that Decision 361 of 16 August 1971 (Document 204, fn. 6) on arrangements for overseas officers in the Territory had been poorly received by the PNG Public Service Association, and by individual officers, and that the inter-departmental committee addressing the question had 'felt unable to support the further suggestions received from the Association'. Expatriate officers had been concerned about the increased uncertainty of their employment security and prospects and about what they regarded as insufficient guarantees for the protection of their entitlements. On 18 May 1972, Cabinet 'concluded that the best course was for the Minister to seek agreement to the appointment of an independent enquiry into the total arrangements to be made for the future security of permanent overseas officers'. Decision 981, 'Papua New Guinea: Future Security of Permanent Overseas Officers of the Public Service', 18 May 1972, NAA: A5908, 638. See also Document 179.

280   TELEX FROM HAY TO JOHNSON

Canberra, 18 April 1972

3643. CONFIDENTIAL

Re Police Spokesman

In reference to your letter of 7 April[1] I note your views.

1.   They accord with our thinking and those presented in the interdepartmental paper.[2]

2.   Whilst we agree that police powers should be conferred upon Deputy Chairman at an early stage we would prefer it if this question could be deferred from your initial discussions with the Deputy Chairman in April. We think that it would be preferable to discuss this along with other transfers of additional power in say May–July. However, if the matter is raised we suggest you engage in discussions on the basis that no Commonwealth Government commitment is involved.

3.   The only further point which I would mention concerns the view that delegated powers should be revocable in clearly delineated circumstances. This view has been remitted to the Interdepartmental Committee for further consideration but we see some difficulty in defining in advance specific circumstances when the power ought to be revoked.

[NAA: A452, 1972/1079]

---

1   Document 276.
2   Not published.

281   SPEECH BY HASLUCK[1]

Port Moresby, 20 April 1972

Members of the House of Assembly, today marks another stage in the progressive development of the Papua New Guinea legislature from a body composed mainly of appointed members into an elected parliament with full authority to make laws and to vote its executive into and out of office.

The Legislative Council and the first and second Houses of Assembly have all contributed to this development. Select Committees appointed by them have consulted the people and have prepared reports which reflect the wishes of the people. The reports have been debated, and the recommendations endorsed by Members have been put into effect by the Australian Parliament. This House, more than any other, bears the imprint of opinion in Papua New Guinea.

The policy of the Australian Government towards Papua New Guinea has been declared to the second House of Assembly as well as in the Australian Parliament and in the United Nations.

Australia will continue to observe its obligations under the United Nations Charter—to promote the political, economic, educational and social advancement of Papua New Guinea in accordance with the freely expressed wishes of the people.

It is the policy of my Government to encourage the movement towards self-government but not to impose self-government upon Papua New Guinea. To this end my Government looks to this House to represent the wishes of the majority of the people and to take the initiative on the pace and nature of constitutional development.

My Government responded to the recommendation of the Select Committee on Constitutional Development, endorsed by the second House of Assembly, that the development of Papua New Guinea be geared to the achievement of self-government in the lifetime of the third House of Assembly. To this end, a growing number of Papuan and New Guinean public servants is being trained in special courses both here and in Australia to fit them for important positions at all levels of the Public Service.

The retention of expatriate staff for as long as their assistance is required is receiving further attention and will be discussed with the Administrator's Executive Council before being placed before the House. A programme has been prepared of the legislative and administrative actions which will have to be taken by Australia and by Papua New Guinea by the time of self-government.

My Government intends to invite Papua New Guinea's political leaders, once they have taken office, to join in early discussions about these matters.

This House will be asked to consider before long many important policy matters. Some of these still fall within the responsibility of the Australian Government. On others, this House already has the authority to make the final decision.

The examination of the legal system may well be one of the most important tasks of the House. The judges and magistrates and their courts are essential for maintaining the rule of law and protection of the rights of the individual. It is also necessary that they apply laws which will take root in this country.

My Government will encourage the House of Assembly to give attention to the question of citizenship.

---

1   Hasluck delivered the speech when opening the Third House of Assembly.

The prosperity of Papua New Guinea as a whole and the well-being of individuals and small communities depend to a large extent on making productive use of land. Members will be asked to consider legislation to give greater security in land ownership and thus encourage better use of the country's land resources.

This House will be in a position to assess present policies on education, urban development and conservation, and to contribute to the solution of social problems normal in a rapidly changing society, including the effect of development on traditional customs and culture.

My Government has contributed very large resources of money and skilled men and women to Papua New Guinea's economic advancement in order to put its people more firmly in control of their own affairs and, in time, to reduce its dependence on outside aid.

This House is well fitted to decide the form of development best suited to the needs and wishes of the people in the future. The Administration will table in the House this year a White Paper on the strategies for a new national development programme to be introduced in 1973.

This will enable the House to discuss the main issues fully before the programme is drawn up. It is the hope of my advisers that this programme will be shaped by, and bear the clear imprint of, this House and will win, through the efforts of Members in their own electorates, the support of the people.

The new programme will depend heavily on outside aid. My Government confirms its undertaking that the movement to self-government will not affect its intention to continue to provide large scale aid.

Papua New Guinea and Australia share responsibility for the Public Service. My Government is undertaking a review of the Public Service Ordinance. Amending legislation will be placed before the House of Assembly which in respect of this important area of Government also will be in a position to examine the principles on which the present ordinance is based.

Australia is responsible for the defence of Papua New Guinea and accepts that obligation. The Pacific Islands Regiment and the Papua New Guinea division of the Royal Australian Navy are being steadily developed, including the necessary personnel, organisational and administrative requirements, to meet the needs of an emerging independent nation. Australian support in matters of defence will continue.

In its resolution on Papua New Guinea in December 1971 the General Assembly of the United Nations stressed the development of Papua New Guinea as a single political and territorial entity. It urged further that separatist movements be discouraged and the unity of the country preserved through the period leading up to independence.

In the eyes of the world outside, Papua New Guinea already has a distinctive character as a developing nation. The last House of Assembly showed its concern for national unity by declaring that unity is essential to the progress of Papua New Guinea as a modern state, with enough resources and population to sustain a developing economy. My Government holds the same view.

Members of the House of Assembly, the decisions which will shape the destiny of Papua New Guinea are largely in your hands. I leave you to your deliberations.

[NAA: A 452, 1972/1668]

282   LETTER FROM JOHNSON TO SOMARE[1]

Port Moresby, 26 April 1972

On the assumption that the House of Assembly endorses the Ministerial list we have agreed upon, I hope that we may proceed to the election of the Deputy Chairman of the AEC on Thursday morning, April 27th. I will today give notice to Ministers of this meeting.

The constitutional position as per the Papua New Guinea Act Section 20 (i)(c) is that Ministers are then appointed to portfolios and the nine places in the AEC by the Minister for External Territories on the nomination of the Administrator, after consultation with the Deputy Chairman.

Let me say right away that I have no intention of disputing AEC membership. I am happy to nominate for AEC membership those Ministers put forward by the Deputy Chairman. However, I am 'charged with the duty of administering the government of the Territory on behalf of the Commonwealth' under Section 13 of the Papua New Guinea Act, and I offer some comments on portfolio allocation for your consideration before we begin discussion.

In the first place I believe that it is a good principle to have the AEC Ministers responsible for the most important policy portfolios. This, of course, is not essential and there may be good reason to include in the AEC a man who by reasons of particular talents is best placed in charge of a relatively less important portfolio. But on the assumption that this latter circumstance is likely to be unusual, I list below those portfolios which I consider to be most important:

Lands

Education

Transport

Health

Agriculture

Internal Finance

Interior

Labour

Trade

Public Works is a technical service Department and has little involvement in major policy. I prefer Trade to Business Development because of the major role Trade plays in the important commodity agreements for coffee, cocoa and other agricultural products and for that Department's responsibility for attracting large scale industrial development. Transport is vital to our whole development programme and involves planning for land, sea and air. Labour in its influence on industrial relations and wages policy is more significant than Mines,

---

1   According to Downs, 'when the election results became known in March, no party had a majority; but the United Party with 40 members was expected to form a Government'. A period of intense political manoeuvring began, with the conservative United Party and the nationalist Pangu Party competing to form a coalition. The breakthrough came shortly before the new House was due to convene, when the ten members of Julius Chan's business-oriented People's Progress Party agreed to join Somare's Pangu in a national coalition. On this basis, with the addition of the highlands-based New Guinea National Party, the Mataungan Association members and independents, Somare was able to form government. His first ministry comprised ministers from the Pangu Party (7), the People's Progress Party (4), the New Guinea National Party (4), and two independents. Ian Downs, *The Australian Trusteeship: Papua New Guinea, 1945–1975,* Australian Government Publishing Service, Canberra, 1980, pp. 488–89. For background on the elections, see Document 275, fn. 1.

though Mines may assume increasing importance if there are additional significant mineral discoveries.

A second principle I put forward is that the most experienced and able Ministers should handle the most important portfolios. I think that it is sometimes a positive disadvantage for a Minister to have had a close inside knowledge of the Department he takes charge of. Inevitably he interferes with the internal management of the Department, which is the business of the Director. The Minister's task is to guide policy and ensure that his Department's actions conform to political realities. He is concerned with broad issues and not Departmental minutiae. A Minister who has worked as a member of a Department too is subject to pressures from those with whom he has worked and may well have developed personal prejudices and antipathies that may render him less than dispassionate in his guidance of the Department. If a Minister is able, there is much to be said for appointing an outsider to a particular portfolio so that new points of view may be injected into the Department's thinking.

In my view, the Ministries of greatest importance after the position of Deputy Chairman are those of Lands, Internal Finance, Education and Agriculture. I would hope that you would suggest men of special abilities to fill these posts.

Lands requires a man who will have to make some tough decisions and risk unpopularity for the good of his country. Agriculture is presently in a state of depression and important policy decisions on assistance proposals will need early consideration. Education has the biggest share of our budget and holds the key to our future. The importance of Internal Finance is self-evident.

I look forward to substantive discussion on portfolios as soon as the Ministry has elected the Deputy Chairman.

[NAA: A452, 1972/0932]

283   SUBMISSION FROM WALLER TO BOWEN

Canberra, 26 April 1972

CONFIDENTIAL

Cabinet Submission—Papua New Guinea:
Programme of Movement towards Internal Self-Government[1]

The attached Cabinet Submission from the Minister for External Territories aims to establish a general framework for the conduct of negotiations on self-government between the Papua New Guinea leaders and the Australian Government. I see no basic objection to the general approach from a Foreign Affairs viewpoint, but one or two points might be clarified and spelt out in any Cabinet decision. The first—and major—point is that the target date of September 1975 for full self-government as set out in the Submission is almost certainly unreal in the light of recent developments. Admittedly the Submission stresses that it is indicative only but the whole moderately leisurely approach envisaged in the Submission as worded may well have to be scrapped. The Minister for External Territories will no doubt speak to this.

2.   Recommendation (a) proposes that the draft programme attached to the submission be used as a 'basis for initial discussions' initially at Ministerial, and later at Departmental level. The programme is said to be flexible, to be 'essentially a list of issues which need to be resolved before self-government' and not to address itself to 'alternative policy issues which will arise from time to time'. The programme seems in parts to lack coordination and some of the specific proposals could lend themselves to undesirable interpretations, e.g. No. 17 'Foreign Office and Foreign Activities' states that Foreign Affairs will assist to develop a 'Foreign Office' until independence when Foreign Affairs officers will be withdrawn. This may well be so, but if the Papua New Guinea Government wants advisers after independence I imagine we would be prepared to provide them. Rather than go through the 45 items one by one, it might be sufficient if Cabinet were to note that the Programme was indicative only, and that its endorsement by Cabinet did not necessarily imply acceptance of all details or policy in respect of each item. It would be desirable to record in the Cabinet decision that relevant Ministers and their Departments are to be consulted on matters in their fields, and where necessary participate in discussions. We understand that it is the Department of External Territories' intention to do this, but a formal record to this effect is preferable.

3.   Recommendation (b) is that Papua New Guinea leaders be told that although there would be no basic changes at self-government, the relationship between Australia and Papua New Guinea would obviously be different after independence, and that talks with the Papua New Guinea leaders on post-independence relations should take place well before independence. I see no objection to this, and assume that you would wish to have a substantial role in any such talks. The submission leaves open how and by whom these talks are to be conducted.

4.   I suggest you strongly support recommendation (c) which proposes that Foreign Affairs and External Territories prepare a paper for Cabinet on Australia's national interests in Papua New Guinea. This will form an essential base for a wide range of planning Australian/PNG relations.

5.   Recommendation (d) proposes a priority study on staffing implications, to be submitted to the Prime Minister by the Minister for External Territories and the Treasurer. Staffing will be important and I see advantage in the proposal.

[NAA: A1838, 3080/10/1 PART 1]

---

1   Document 278.

284   LETTER FROM BUNTING TO HOLTEN[1]

Canberra, 27 April 1972

CONFIDENTIAL

The Prime Minister has decided to establish a Standing Committee of the Cabinet to deal with matters affecting Papua New Guinea.

This recognises that developments in the Territory, in the period ahead, will bring forward complex and sensitive issues and will bear upon the long term relationship between Australia and Papua New Guinea.

The Prime Minister wishes the recent Submissions by the Minister for External Territories— No. 627, Papua New Guinea: Programme for Movement towards Internal Self Government[2] and No. 638, Separate Commonwealth Service for non-indigenous Public Servants in Papua New Guinea[3]—to be taken by this Committee.

The membership of the Committee will comprise the Prime Minister, the Minister for External Territories Mr Peacock, Mr Anthony, Mr Snedden, Sir Kenneth Anderson, Mr Bowen, Mr Fairbairn and Senator Greenwood.

The Prime Minister has asked that an early meeting of the Committee be arranged to consider the two Submissions mentioned above. Thereafter it will meet periodically as the need arises.

I am writing similarly to all Ministers.

[NAA: A452, 1972/1506]

285   MINUTE FROM BESLEY TO HAY

Canberra, 27 April 1972

Australian/PNG Relationships

As I mentioned to you the Minister discussed last night in a general way the question of long term relationships between Australia and Papua New Guinea. He seemed very much in favour of a special relationship and of the need to settle this as a policy base at the earliest practicable time. We discussed this in relation to future aid arrangements and the Minister indicated his willingness to pursue vigorously a line that Papua New Guinea should continue to be given special treatment in this respect and not be simply equated with other foreign aid recipients.

[*matter omitted*]

[NAA: A452, 1972/0932]

---

1   Rendle McNeilage Holten, Minister for Repatriation, 1969–72.

2   Document 278.

3   Document 279. This submission was put up to Cabinet by Peacock on 18 May 1972 with the revised title of 'Papua New Guinea: Future Security of Permanent Overseas Officers of the Public Service'.

286   INSTRUCTIONS FROM PEACOCK TO PNG MINISTERS

Canberra, 28 April 1972

Commonwealth of Australia—Papua New Guinea Act 1949–1971
Approved Arrangements under Section 25

[*matter omitted*]

NOW THEREFORE I, ANDREW SHARP PEACOCK, Minister of State for External Territories, DO HEREBY APPROVE the following arrangements applicable to each office of Minister;

A. *Responsibilities in connection with the Department*

(1) In accordance with the Governor-General's instructions given to the Administrator, pursuant to the powers conferred by section 15 of the Papua New Guinea Act 1949–1971, a Minister shall exercise full authority, and accept full responsibility, in relation to the matters specified for the respective designations in the annexe attached hereto.[1] In so doing a Minister shall not act inconsistently with:

(a) the programmes and polices of development from time to time agreed upon by the Commonwealth of Australia and the House of Assembly or the Administrator's Executive Council, as the case may be;

or

(b) any lawful agreement or obligation entered into by the Administration of Papua New Guinea or by the Commonwealth of Australia in respect of Papua New Guinea.

(2) In respect of those matters not specified in the Annexe, a Minister shall:

(a) be responsible within the framework of broad government policy for decisions regarding policy and for administrative actions of the department, or part of the department as may be determined, in its day-to-day activities other than aspects which are concerned with Public Service matters, terms and conditions of service;

(b) be responsible for the formulation of plans and proposals for departmental expenditure (or part of the department as may be determined) including the formulation of draft departmental estimates.

(3) In carrying out his functions, a Minister shall:

(a) refer policy decisions or other matters to the Administrator's Executive Council where:

(i)   he considers it necessary to do so;

or

(ii) the Administrator's Executive Council or the Administrator so directs;

(b) consider papers and recommendations submitted to him by the department and his decisions shall be recorded in writing and shall be retained as part of the records of the department;

(c) receive advice in all matters relating to the exercise of his functions from the departmental head of the relevant department who is responsible for the general working of that department.

---

1   Not published.

B. *Responsibilities in connection with the Administrator's Executive Council*

(1) Except as may be otherwise arranged in any particular instance a Minister shall in relation to matters within his competence:

(a) introduce submissions into the Council including proposals for legislation;

(b) present draft estimates of annual expenditures;

(c) give effect to decisions made by the Minister for External Territories or the Administrator after consideration of the advice of the Administrator's Executive Council;

(2) A Minister appointed to the Administrator's Executive Council pursuant to paragraph (c) of sub-section (1) of section 20 of the Papua New Guinea Act shall participate in the general functioning of the Council under section 19 of the said Act.

(3) A Minister not appointed to the Administrator's Executive Council may, with the agreement of the person for the time being presiding at a meeting of the Administrator's Executive Council attend that meeting of the Council when matters in respect of which he is performing the functions of a Minister are under discussion, and may be heard at the meeting.

C. *Responsibilities in connection with the House of Assembly*

A Minister shall generally be responsible in the House of Assembly for matters within his competence and in particular:

(a) he shall answer questions and make official statements concerning those matters and by arrangement other matters; and

(b) he shall introduce legislation concerning those matters and by arrangement other matters, being legislation approved by the Administrator's Executive Council or the Minister for External Territories as the case may be, and shall guide the legislation through proceedings in the House.

In addition to the foregoing in the performance of their functions under section 25 of the Act Ministers should conform with the accepted code of conduct applicable to holders of ministerial office, notes on which are attached. They should also respect the convention that they will not publicly oppose opinions of the Administrator's Executive Council.

I HEREBY REVOKE all prior approved arrangements made pursuant to the powers conferred by section 25 of the Papua New Guinea Act 1949–1971.

[NAA: A1838, 3080/11/1/2 PART 1]

287   SPEECH BY PEACOCK[1]

Port Moresby, 30 April 1972

Development will clearly be one of the main interests of the new Government and the House of Assembly. The present five year programme will be completed in 1973 and a new five year national development programme is being prepared.

Later this year the Administration will set out the main issues as it sees them in a white paper to the House. The preparation of the programme can then be guided by what is said in the House and the plan itself will be fully debated in the House before any final decisions are made.

The aim is to produce a plan that reflects technical expertise and experience from both inside and outside Papua New Guinea and at the same time is fully endorsed by the House of Assembly whose members will be prepared to explain and advocate it to their people.

We believe that the movement to internal self-government will be completed in the lifetime of the plan and for this reason the plan, from its inception, must bear the stamp of the leaders of Papua New Guinea. To this end the Commonwealth will be looking primarily to the ministers and the House of Assembly, but it will also be looking to informed public discussion in the villages and towns no less than in the University.

There are certain basic criteria which the new national development programme will need to satisfy. In the first instance, it must be a programme which expresses, in a practical way, the aspirations of the widest possible cross-section of Papua New Guinea's people as defined by their representatives.

Only if it does this can it become a national plan with which people other than its creators will identify and which will command the hard work and sacrifices in terms of income contributed for taxation and consumption foregone in order to set aside savings for investment, which an ambitious and thrusting national programme requires for its success.

In order to be realistic and practical, such a programme must, of course, be within the capacity of the people of Papua New Guinea to implement and to finance with their own resources and those that can be made available from outside the country.

To the extent that the success of the plan depends on contributions by Australia and by other foreign aid givers and on savings to be provided by foreign private investors, the national programme in addition to being acceptable to the people of Papua New Guinea must also inspire confidence and attract support from those sectors.

This is a situation which can sometimes raise difficulties, although I see no evidence that any conflict of interest is likely to arise. The situation does suggest, however, that the new Development Programme must aim at creating in Papua New Guinea the economic base which will enable the country to rely increasingly on its own domestic effort for mobilising the resources for continuing economic development.

I think that this would generally be accepted as being clearly in the interest of Papua New Guinea. It should also be acceptable to foreign aid givers and investors who tend to be vitally interested in the extent to which the resources contributed by them are channelled into productive uses in the receiving country.

Putting a national development programme into effect will require wisdom combined with strong and convincing leadership. The Commonwealth and the Administration, with its experts,

---

1   The speech was delivered at the sixth Waigani seminar, a forum established at the University of Papua and New Guinea in 1966 for public discussion of issues relevant to PNG's history, politics and development.

can say a good deal about means towards ends. We can say a lot about desirable priorities. We can make resources available. But in Papua New Guinea's current circumstances it is not for us to define national goals although we can make some assumptions in the light of our understanding of the mood and temper of the people. Nor is it for us to go to the villages and the towns to get support. These vital responsibilities must rest in the main in the hands of the elected leaders of Papua New Guinea, and their Papua New Guinea officers.

I propose to say something today about the kinds of decisions which must be faced by Papua New Guinea's leaders if such a national plan is to succeed in giving economic substance to the political development of the country.

The first, and in a sense basic, decision which must be faced is this: are the people of Papua New Guinea prepared to face the implications of moving from a subsistence to a modern cash economy.

The development of Papua New Guinea as a modern nation requires that more and more people earn cash income. Agricultural producers will do this by producing crops for the market and use the money they earn to purchase the goods which they cannot produce. Other people will leave the agricultural economy for industrial, commercial or governmental occupations. They will produce goods and services on which the rural community will spend its cash income.

It seems to me that this goal of development is widely accepted by Papuans and New Guineans. In my travels I have found that most people in this country want more roads, schools and aid posts, more opportunities to earn a cash income and more of the goods which that income can buy. This is what development means to individual people—a rising standard of living. But while the overall goal of development is widely accepted, there very often seems to be a lack of urgency or drive to achieve it. 'Kamapim kantri'[2] has become a common phrase but it is unusually associated with demands for more government expenditures in the speaker's district.

The leaders of this country—and this means the members of the House of Assembly, operating at grass roots level—will have to decide whether to confront their people with some hard questions. Should they decide to do so, I presume they would ask, for example: you want more goods. Are you prepared to earn the money to pay for them by working harder and more consistently?

Roads, schools, aid posts, law and order and government services generally, all cost money. In the long run a government can provide and expand these services only if more revenue is collected from the people. In Papua New Guinea much of the cost of development has been met by the Australian Government. This aid will continue but it has always been accepted that Papua New Guinea must progressively increase its financial self-reliance and that the pace of progress will finally depend on the efforts of Papuans and New Guineans themselves.

There are other demands of economic development which may impose certain social strains because they require adjustments to old established patterns of life and work in the community. In particular, the getting and spending of money by means of productive effort and division of labour will tend to change the atmosphere of villages. Inevitably, more importance will be placed on the efforts of enterprising individuals and groups throughout the country, and there will also be a growing realisation of membership of a much more extensive and independent unit than the village.

At times, these influences may be or seem to be in conflict with the traditional approach to living. In short, it is not possible to modernise the economy and preserve traditional social structures and social values unchanged. These structures and values may well be inconsistent

---

2   This translates as 'improve or develop the country'.

with development and an obstacle to it. A commitment to development involves a commitment to changing them, but not to uprooting them.

Social attitudes, such as those stemming from the extended family system and the mutual obligations of village life, can be adapted and mobilised to this end. The mutual social obligations of village life can mean support for the aged and the infirm and help in times of crisis. They can ease the strains of transition from a rural to an urban environment. But they can also prevent the enterprising man from doing more than his fellows in the village. They can place an impossible burden on people in urban employment to support unemployed kinsmen, raising the possibility of nepotism and corruption.

This system of obligations needs to be adapted to changing conditions. The formation of land-holding groups for more effective use of the land is one such adaptation. The activities of local government are also strengthened when they can draw on such foundations. At the same time, those aspects of the traditional system, which curb individual initiative and freedom, need to be modified if they are not to continue to obstruct development and create tensions. The path to success in this field of social and economic adjustment will not be easy, and it will take time and great effort. This has been the common experience of all countries in the course of their development.

For as long as one can see ahead, the great majority of the people will depend on the land for their livelihood, and the further development of agricultural enterprise is therefore fundamental.

Many rural enterprises are already conducted with marked efficiency and success. In other cases much remains to be done to make agriculture more efficient and productive. There are many instances, too, where production and living standards could be greatly increased by using idle lands for productive purposes and by more diligent husbandry and marketing of established tree crops.

One particular difficulty remaining unresolved is that of land tenure. Uncertainty of tenure clearly prevents some people from expanding their plantings because they have no certainty of enjoying the proceeds. Land tenure problems have also made it difficult both to provide land for potentially major development projects and to carry on with land settlement schemes. They have also, of course, impeded other vital developments including the provision of essential community services.

Legislation to overcome land tenure problems while at the same time ensuring maximum protection for existing land rights was introduced in the last House of Assembly but was not passed. It will be necessary for the new House of Assembly to face up to the conflict between traditional and modern ideas on this subject and to adopt legislation which endeavours to resolve it. More important, perhaps, having made up their mind on the legislation they will accept, Members would have to explain it to the people and urge them to make use of it.

Effective agricultural development requires the guidance of skilled technical staff. Such staff, whether expatriate or local, cost money. The people will have to decide how much they are willing to pay, through their taxes, for such guidance.

There are some forms of agriculture, such as oil palm, which currently can only be developed in partnership with foreign investors. These investors have the technical knowledge, the understanding of world markets and the capital which Papuans and New Guineans lack. To succeed leaders of Papua New Guinea will need to encourage such investment and technical knowledge as they have done in the past and, I believe, will continue to do. Mr Somare's statement to the House of Assembly last Monday recognising the importance of attracting overseas capital is most welcome in this context.

It is apparent that urban life even under conditions of a fringe settlement must in the eyes of those who come to live there be in some ways more attractive than rural life. It seems inevitable that increasing numbers of younger people will seek to escape from the constraints and tensions of rural life by migrating to the towns which in any case they find more attractive. To provide for this influx by creating more employment opportunities in the towns is a most difficult task for a developing country. It will therefore be necessary to try to restrain and direct the urban drift by promoting the improvement of rural life, especially by encouraging people to earn larger cash incomes from agriculture and to develop useful occupations in rural centres.

Such measures cannot, however, be expected to prevent the rapid growth of urban population. Papua New Guinea's leaders will have to face up to the problems of urbanisation and decide what proportion of their limited resources they are prepared to devote to their solution.

Concentration on the towns could well mean neglect of the rural areas where the bulk of the people will continue to live. Neglect of the towns could lead to worsening urban living conditions and heightened social tensions. Somehow or other, a balance must be struck.

The problem has also arisen of inequalities in development between different parts of the country. This is an inescapable consequence of the unequal distribution of resources, which is purely a matter of chance and economic geography. It is impossible to take the resources, whether they be minerals, agricultural land or fishing resources to the people somewhere else in the country. They must be developed where they exist. As a consequence the wealth of any country will not be produced uniformly throughout the country but in a relatively few growth areas. This means that the money and manpower for development will be distributed according to the pattern of available resources. However, the whole nation stands to gain by this approach, and the wealth so produced becomes a basis for the provision of services, employment opportunities, and social development on a national basis.

It is therefore fully consistent with this policy to endeavour to assist and encourage the people of the less developed areas to make the greatest possible use of the resources available to them, earn a larger cash income and thereby contribute to the general wealth of the country. There is a great deal that the people in these areas, as elsewhere in this country, can do to help themselves. Within the limits of the resources available the Government will do all it can to support these efforts.

There is another sort of inequality which can develop within Papua New Guinea if steps are not taken to guard against it. In many poor countries development has created a cap between a mass of impoverished peasant producers and a small but relatively prosperous modern sector. This provides the setting for the development of a self-regarding class without commitment to the welfare of the great mass of the populations.

As the distinguished economist Harry G. Johnson writes:

Those who have had a political claim on the development process—the educated, the 'middle class', the established native capitalists, and the minority of labour employed in industrial establishments, not to speak of the politicians themselves—have done very well out of development policy as it has been executed in practice, regardless of its efficiency or otherwise at the level of economic aggregates and averages. The rest of the population has not done well. For it, the visible economic development that has enabled the minority to regard itself as 'modernised' and able to deal with other national elites on equal terms has been achieved by a process of forced income transfer, not of shared economic progress.

Unless there are institutions which lead this small prosperous group to see their own interests as consistent with those of the people, adequate linkages between the rural and urban environment, and exchanges of goods and services and a flow on of ideas and benefits from the more advanced to the less advanced sectors, the development of such a group in the more advanced sector is probably inevitable. A society of this nature apart from failing to meet welfare goals is inherently unstable.

The leaders of Papua New Guinea will have to face up to the challenge of maintaining a real commitment to the welfare of their people and a real understanding of their condition and their needs.

I have spoken about the problems that have to be faced, and the decisions that must be taken, because I think that this seminar can make a valuable contribution to public discussion, to the clarification of issues and the deepening of understanding. But when the discussion is finished the decisions will have to be taken by the leaders of Papua New Guinea in the Administrator's Executive Council and in the House of Assembly. Australia will continue to assist, as it has done in the past. But increasingly the brunt of decision-making must fall on Papua New Guinea's own leaders. It will be a most exacting job but I am confident they will prove equal to the challenge.

[NAA: A452, 1972/1169]

288   LETTER FROM WALLER TO DET

Canberra, 1 May 1972

SECRET

I refer to the report of the Inter-Departmental Committee, set up by Cabinet Decision No. 452,[1] on internal security in Papua New Guinea, upon which our comments have been sought.

2.   We recognise that a great deal will depend upon a relationship of trust and confidence being developed between the Administration and the Chief Minister. We support the concept that until independence ultimate control of the armed forces and responsibility for defence (and for that matter for foreign affairs) should remain with Australian Ministers answerable to the Australian Parliament. At the same time we believe that this power should be exercised with the fullest possible degree of consultation and collaboration with indigenous leaders and accepted by the latter in the spirit.

3.   We appreciate your feeling that to confer the role of 'spokesman' upon a Minister in the House of Assembly may involve the frustration of holding apparent responsibility with little effective power. On the other hand it is open to question whether the devolution of power on a revocable basis would not run the considerable risk of friction arising in any possible emergency. Might it not appear that at the very time when the exercise of authority involves local issues of the highest sensitivity and importance, the position of Chief Minister would be seen to be weakened by the recall of power to act into the hands of the Administration, representing a government in Canberra?

4.   It seems to us desirable that because of their obvious interrelationship the control and deployment of military forces should be dealt with on the same basis as the police. If it should be decided that power over the military forces is not to be delegated, and if this arrangement proves acceptable to indigenous leadership, there would not seem to be any pressing necessity to go further so far as the police are concerned. We believe the two forces should be dealt with on a compatible basis. We understand that consultation is proceeding between your Department and the Department of Defence regarding use of military forces within Papua New Guinea. We believe that submissions regarding these two cases should go to the government for consideration at the same time.

5.   In view of the comparative shortness of the time-scale likely to be involved before self-government we hope that it may be possible to avoid these issues becoming the cause of major difficulties with elected Ministers in Papua New Guinea. If it were to become evident that they wanted to be given power over the police now, then the matter can be reconsidered. When the time comes to legislate for self-government experience of working with elected Ministers may perhaps also justify a more flexible approach.

6.   A lesser issue would seem involved in the appointment of a Papua New Guinea Police Commissioner. If in practice no suitable indigene is likely to be available to fill this position in the next two or three years, there seems no occasion specifically to assert a necessity to retain this position in expatriate hands, in any discussion with local leaders. To do so would seem to introduce an element of political controversy.

7.   These comments are put forward on a Departmental basis only, but they are being brought to our Minister's attention.

8.   A copy of this memorandum is being sent also to the Secretary, Department of Defence.[2]

[NAA: A452, 1972/1079]

---

1   Document 53.
2   Sir Arthur Tange.

289   LETTER FROM JOHNSON TO PEACOCK

Port Moresby, 5 May 1972

CONFIDENTIAL

Your letter to me of 7th March asks me to comment at large on the political and constitutional position as I see it at present.[1]

You are familiar with the developments which have produced a coalition group which commands a majority in the House of Assembly, currently about 54 or 55 votes of the 99 elected Members on the floor of the House. I think this support is likely to be maintained or even increased unless the Peoples Progress Party [PPP] finds that it is being drawn into measures contrary to its policies. There is no doubt that the dominant partner is the Pangu Pati and that this party will be active and vigorous in promoting its policies. It has a strong extra-parliamentary party advisory group which is responsible for the proposals that the Deputy Chairman of the AEC should have a large personal staff so that the fusion of party and government can develop. Although it is a far cry from it yet, this points towards the development of a one party state, perhaps on the Tanzanian pattern. I regard the proposal with concern and consider that although some personal staff are justified, caution should be exercised in acceding to the demands. The key man on the personal staff must be the link between the party, the Deputy Chairman and the Public Service. If he is not acceptable to senior public servants he will be ineffective. He will need to be conscious of the administrative problems of a public service in implementing party programmes. Clearly the best man for the job would be a senior and experienced man from within the Public Service. I believe that this viewpoint should be pressed strongly.

It can be expected that, from the party advisers referred to above, a positive programme of legislation will emanate, some of it probably ill-considered, and that the existing restraints of Commonwealth controls will be cast off as soon as practicable. How soon this might be, is discussed further below.

Opinion is likely to move more strongly in the direction of self-government and any attempts by the Commonwealth to influence legislation which it might not favour will be resented and possibly diminish Australian influence in the longer term.

The public attitude of the coalition towards self-government was set out by Mr Somare in his first speech to the new parliament.[2] In effect the coalition accepted the Peoples Progress Party's policy in this matter. I think that there is no doubt at all that most of the supporters of the coalition, with the exception of course of PPP, do not accept it and will work to achieve a parliamentary majority which will permit them to fulfil their policy to early self-government. However, I believe that the party leadership now recognises that there are some substantial obstacles to be overcome before all of the requirements of a self-governing Papua New Guinea can be met. The party may be satisfied with a large degree of de facto self-government if this is conceded at a reasonably early date while the larger obstacles are being overcome.

---

1   Document 263.

2   Speaking in the House of Assembly on 24 April 1972, Somare said: 'The Australian government has drawn up a plan of movement towards self-government. This coalition will examine the Australian plan carefully and guarantees not to accept the plan just for the sake of getting self-government quickly. The coalition accepts the People's Progress Party platform that the timing of self-government is not as important as the type of self-government best suited for this country. Sir, there is a difference between formal legal steps towards self-government and real movement towards self-government.' PNG House of Assembly, *Debates*, Third House, III, 1, Port Moresby, 1972, pp. 21–24.

However, I have this week discussed with Mr Somare and Mr Chan the coalition attitude towards constitutional development. Mr Somare asserts that his statement in the House of Assembly is a proper reflection of the opinion of his followers at this point in time. Both Mr Somare and Mr Chan agreed that the coalition would be satisfied to institute constitutional discussions with the Australian Government after the June meeting of the House of Assembly. They agreed that they understood the Australian Government's position that any further constitutional advances that might be agreed upon by the coalition and the Australian Government would need House of Assembly endorsement. I pointed out that this would mean that endorsement could not take place until August/September and that further action required by the Australian Government, such as amendment of the Papua New Guinea Act to increase the size of the Ministry, would probably be affected by the imminence of an Australian election. They said that they appreciated the nature of this difficulty.

The general expectations of the adherents to the coalition were then discussed and I set out below what seemed to be an agreed position between the two leaders, though there could be no assurance the party members would support it.

Arising from the July meeting with the Australian Government and subsequent House of Assembly endorsement, there could be extension of Ministerial final powers in portfolios already held and up to three new Ministries created. Two that have been specifically mentioned are Economic Planning and Urban Development. Given the likely long delays in amending the Papua New Guinea Act to create additional Ministries, it might be possible to appoint some MHAs as 'Members assisting the Minister of …' and means of providing special allowances for these will be investigated.

Up to the present there has been no mention of assuming powers in such sensitive areas as Internal Security but I believe that a July meeting should plan for this during 1973 on the basis of delegation of powers as was previously discussed. The larger problems of achieving total self-government was [sic] referred to briefly: e.g.

- long term financial arrangements with the Commonwealth;
- Banking;
- DCA;[3]
- and others

There is at present no obvious intention of the coalition, or of the Pangu Pati for that matter, to rush its fences but it will have to show its members substantial actual progress towards its self-government objective at an early date with longer term plans also outlined. The People's Progress Party through its leader is much more cautious but may find it difficult to act as an effective brake.

Might I suggest that the Australian Government consider the following broad time-table:

Stage I
Notionally
Jul/Dec 72

1. An agreed definition of self-government.

2. Extension of final powers of Ministers in existing portfolios.

3. Creation of new Ministries with final powers in areas outside of those considered sensitive, e.g. exclude internal security and law.

---

3   Department of Civil Aviation.

4.   Initiate planning for orderly transmission of powers in sensitive areas and agree upon an approximate time-table.

5.   Arising out of current planning for the development of a Department of Law with a Papua New Guinea Minister exercising final powers, the initial drafting of legislation to insulate from political pressures Crown Solicitor, Public Prosecutor and Electoral Office.

6.   Consideration of changing role and powers of Administration.

7.   Commence border negotiations: PNG/Indonesia; PNG/Australia.

8.   Establishment of Constitutional Commission.

Stage II

1.   Delegation of Police and other internal security powers.

2.   Commence substantive discussion on Defence arrangements.

3.   Passage of legislation referred to in Stage I.

Stage III

1.   Consideration of recommendations of Constitutional Commission.

2.   Banking legislation—Currency.

3.   Local control of Public Service Board.

4.   Finalisation of borders' negotiations.

Stage IV

1.   Implementation of agreed recommendations of Constitutional Commission.

2.   Final legislation for complete self-government.

I appreciate that the 'gearing up' programme takes account of all eventualities and in the above outline I have confined myself to the issues which are of direct significance to the exercise of effective self-government. I have not attempted to indicate dates for the Stages but in view of the nature of some of the changes to be made it would be optimistic to think that the programme could be concluded before the end of 1974.

[NAA: A452, 1972/0932]

290   RECORD OF MEETING BETWEEN MCMAHON, PEACOCK AND PNG MINISTERS[1]

Canberra, 10 May 1972

RESTRICTED

Mr Peacock introduced the delegation.

Mr Somare said that it was known that the Commonwealth had accepted a commitment to give financial assistance to Papua New Guinea. The new administration would be preparing its own Budget and will be raising extra revenue in Papua New Guinea. But it needs to know what the Commonwealth will give and where the Commonwealth stands. This was the first time that the new administration had had to work on a budgetary programme.

The Prime Minister mentioned the Australian Government's normal Budget timetable and asked whether the request was that this timetable should be brought forward. *Mr Somare* said that this was not being sought.

Mr Chan supplemented Mr Somare's remarks by commenting that the Australian Government had invested a great deal to bring Papua New Guinea towards self-government. It now had a Government that appeared to be on that road. But there was uncertainty. The people of Papua New Guinea needed to have confidence in the Government, but this could be jeopardised if it were to set about raising local taxes. A grant was needed to relieve the extent of the call on taxpayers in Papua New Guinea. The main problem was with the expatriates; the Government had to be wary of imposing additional taxes on them, because this would affect their confidence and readiness to invest in Papua New Guinea.

Mr Peacock explained that if taxes had to be increased significantly, a significant burden would fall on expatriates.

Dr Guise commented that a spokesman for the Opposition in the last Parliament had given warning in relation to this taxation issue because if the burden fell on expatriates, it could turn into a question with racial overtones.

The Prime Minister said that he felt a need to restrain himself from offering advice, but nevertheless he understood the sensitivity of the problem. The Minister for External Territories would be bringing his recommendations to Cabinet but he hoped not to be asked for a commitment before the normal Budget time. The Australian Government would want to be as helpful as it could and would, on this significant occasion of the first Budget of a new Government, watch the position carefully.

Mr Somare turning to another matter said that Papua New Guinea had had visits from a number of highly placed dignitaries. The Minister had visited the Territory frequently. They would nevertheless greatly welcome a visit from the Prime Minister and he wished officially to extent the invitation. A visit would help the new Government's image and the image of Australian/Papua New Guinea relationships.

The Prime Minister responded that he wanted to come and felt he had an obligation to come. Because of commitments, he would not be able to do this before the Budget, but he would certainly talk to the Minister for External Territories about a visit after that. Sir John Bunting would take note of his intention. *Mr Peacock* emphasised the pleasure with which the delegation received this indication from the Prime Minister.

---

1   Those present included McMahon, Peacock, Hay, Bunting, Michael Somare, John Guise, Julius Chan, Thomas Kavali, Ebia Olewale and Leo Morgan.

Mr Olewale referred to the border issue between Papua New Guinea and Queensland and asked the Prime Minister about his attitude on a redrawing of the boundary.

Mr Peacock intervened to say that Queensland's responsibility in this was central, but there were inter-departmental discussions taking place to help define the Commonwealth's attitude. It was not regarded as a matter for unilateral action by any of the parties involved. The Commonwealth would invite discussion with all those interested before acting. This included the Queensland Government and the Administrator's Executive Council. The position of the people in the Islands would also be borne in mind.

The Prime Minister referred to the constitutional position. A change in the boundaries required the consent of the Queensland Government and a referendum, and therefore the Commonwealth could not act on its own. In any case, a significant consideration was what the people on the islands affected would want. But he was only able to speak for the moment of the constitutional position. He looked to Mr Peacock to state the views of the Commonwealth Government.

Mr Olewale continued that if a Government official wished to sail along the Papua New Guinea coast he, at present, had to sail through Queensland waters. He hoped the border problem would soon be solved. But he would rest on what the Prime Minister had said.

The Prime Minister concluded the discussion by undertaking to give Mr Somare a copy of a note that had been prepared concerning the constitutional position.[2]

[NAA: A1838, 3080/11/1 PART 1]

2   Not published.

291   RECORD OF DISCUSSION BETWEEN HAY AND DET OFFICIALS[1]

Canberra, 11 May 1972

Extension of Powers of PNG Ministers

Mr Johnson said that in the next months Pangu may be able to muster a majority without People's Progress support. The distinction between the [PNG] Coalition's views and Pangu's views on self-government may then emerge. In any case it is important that Pangu leaders are not challenged for breaking down on Pangu policies. At present Somare is maintaining a public position of not hastening constitutional development, although expecting that further transfers will take place this year. In the light of this it is desirable for the Australian Government to take some positive steps towards increasing powers and to be seen to be moving towards self-government.

Mr Greenwell said that to extend the number of Ministers required amendment to the Papua New Guinea Act, but that if a decision were made early enough this could be done in the Budget session. Apart from creating new ministries there could be further transfers of matters such as Higher Education, Registered Land, Area Authorities, and Industrial Relations (though care was needed here because of public service implications). These transfers could be authorised now under the PNG Act as it now stands.

In the light of the Government's intention to invite PNG leadership group to discuss the question of movement to self-government, the meeting:

(a)   Agreed that immediate action should be taken to authorise an amendment to the PNG Act in the Budget session to remove the ceiling on the number of PNG Ministers.

(b)   Discussed the following other steps which might be taken in the near future:

(i)   Transfer of additional powers, of a routine nature, to PNG Ministers under existing legislation. It was agreed that this would in any event be on the agenda for the constitutional discussions with PNG Ministers, but should be further studied in the basis of a complete list of non-transferred powers being prepared by the Administration.

(ii) Removal, by additional amendments to the PNG Act of the Minister from constitutional procedures (e.g. appointment of Ministers), and of such bodies as the Ministerial Nominations Committee. It was agreed that these steps would need further study before conclusions could be reached.

(iii) Substitution, in relation to transferred powers, of 'Administrator' for Minister of External Territories in PNG legislation.

(iv) Possible amendment of the PNG Act to take away from Ministerial Nominations Committee their role in removal of Ministers.

[*matter omitted*]

[NAA: A452, 1972/0932]

---

1   Along with Hay, those present included Johnson, Besley, Greenwell, Gutman and Galvin. Tos Barnett was also present. Downs has noted that Barnett, formerly a senior lecturer in law at the University of Papua New Guinea, had been appointed in February 1972 to advise the PNG Administration on 'a program of legislative and administrative actions relating to self-government and a national constitution'. Ian Downs, *The Australian Trusteeship: Papua New Guinea, 1945–75*, Australian Government Publishing Service, Canberra, 1980, pp. 490–91.

292   LETTER FROM PEACOCK TO SOMARE

Canberra, 11 May 1972

In our talks in the past few days, which were mainly directed towards the 1972–73 Papua New Guinea budget, we had a preliminary discussion about the question of further movement towards self-government. I think it would be useful if I set out in writing the views which I expressed during this preliminary discussion.

I opened the discussion by recalling the Commonwealth's decision in July, 1970 to hand full and final responsibility for a number of functions of government to Papua New Guinea Ministers, and the Commonwealth's policy on the further movement towards internal self-government which was stated by the Governor-General on 20th April in opening the House of Assembly, in the following words:

'It is the policy of my Government to encourage the movement towards self-government but not to impose self-government upon Papua New Guinea. To this end my Government looks to this House to represent the wishes of the majority of the people and to take the initiative on the pace and nature of constitutional development.'[1]

I said that the Commonwealth Government stood ready to enter into discussions on the question when you and your Ministerial colleagues are ready. In doing so I stressed that there were really two things involved—the handing over to Papua New Guinea Ministers of further powers now exercised by the Commonwealth; and the withdrawal of the Minister for External Territories from the constitutional process. As I understand it, for the immediate future, your preference was that Ministers address themselves to urgent questions of policy and organisation which could be done in your view within the present constitutional framework.

As to the date, we agreed to a meeting in July. You indicated you would like to make an announcement to this effect later in the next meeting of the House of Assembly. Perhaps you could discuss this further with the Administrator who will act on my behalf in deciding both date and location of the meeting.

In discussing this matter with your own government, it might be helpful for you to know the kind of things which the Commonwealth would feel it appropriate to include in an agenda:

Identification of main functions of government which remain in Commonwealth hands.

In respect of each of these functions:

The factors involved in setting a date for partial or complete transfer, such as the time required for legislation in Australia and in Papua New Guinea; the extent to which you would want to have indigenous public servants occupying key positions by the hand-over date; financing of the budget.

Identification of main constitutional steps to be taken in Papua New Guinea and here in carrying out the final stages of the movement to self-government. I mentioned for example the need for an agreed constitution and an agreed structure of government, and the timing of amendments to the Papua New Guinea Act to remove the Minister for External Territories from the process of appointing and discharging Ministers of the House of Assembly.

Establishment of such working parties as may be required to give effect to agreed decisions.

Procedure for reference of conclusions to the House of Assembly as representing the wishes of the majority of the people.

---

1   See Document 281.

I am sending a copy of this letter to the Administrator.

[NAA: A452, 1972/0932]

293   LETTER FROM PEACOCK TO FAIRBAIRN

Canberra, 17 May 1972

SECRET

I refer to your letter of 5 May 1972[1] which relates to your proposed visit to Papua New Guinea in June.

[*matter omitted*]

I should perhaps take this opportunity to refer to your meeting with the Administrator's Executive Council. As you are aware a Report has been prepared after study by our Departments and other Departments on the matter of devolving Defence power to Papua New Guinea which has been approved in principle by the Secretaries. I am informed that in the course of it the early appointment of a defence spokesman was recommended if it should be sought and that you might possibly announce the Government's willingness to appoint a defence spokesman during your forthcoming visit. I have not yet studied the report. I am in agreement in principle with the appointment of a Defence Spokesman and I consider that a question such as this could properly be decided by yourself and myself on behalf of the Government.

I have however some reservations concerning the making of such an announcement during your visit. In the first place it will tend to produce claims at the June meeting of the House for a police spokesman and it may not be possible to obtain a decision on this question before your visit. In addition that announcement of the possible appointment of a Defence Spokesman in advance of additional powers may generate strains within the [PNG] Coalition. As you are aware I am to hold discussions with the Chief Minister in July and I would prefer the question of a defence spokesman to be considered along with other matters. Of course you would be brought into our discussions if any matter concerning defence were raised.

The question remains as to what could appropriately be the subject of your address to the Administrator's Executive Council. No doubt your advisers will assist you in this connection but the following observations might be of assistance. It may be useful for you to mention the matter of the Defence Spokesman and indicate that it is being sympathetically considered by the Government but that you understand that there will be talks on a range of subjects concerning additional powers in the near future. It may also be appropriate to give a brief outline of the defence studies which are now taking place with an indication of their progress. Other topics may usefully include the role of the Defence Forces in Papua New Guinea and the implications of Commonwealth Defence responsibility. In the latter respect it might be useful to emphasise the distinction from other powers which can be handed over absolutely at self-government.

Finally the Administrator's Executive Council is likely to enquire from you on the question of financing the defence forces and may not be satisfied with the statement that it is under study. It may be useful if officers of your Department and the Department of External Territories were to consult on this aspect to arrive at an agreed position.

[NAA: A452, 1975/108]

---

1   Not published.

294   SPEECH BY PEACOCK[1]

Sydney, 18 May 1972

The recent elections for the third House of Assembly in Papua New Guinea were of historic importance to that country. The result of the most exceptional organisational and logistic effort that is required to conduct an election in that country has been the formation of the first Government of Papua New Guinea.

No one party which contested the elections obtained a majority in the House of Assembly but shortly before the House sat on 20 April the Pangu Pati was able to form a coalition government with the People's Progress Party, the New Guinea National Party, a group of independents and the elected representatives of the Mataungan Association.[2]

This coalition group which commands a majority in the House of Assembly succeeded in having the House endorse its proposed ministry. Acting on the recommendation of the Administrator who had held discussions with the leader of the coalition, Mr Michael Somare, I approved the allocation of portfolios and the membership of the Administrator's Executive Council. Mr Somare became Deputy Chairman of the Administrator's Executive Council, in effect the Chief Minister of Papua New Guinea.

The coalition has a ministry consisting of seventeen ministers, ten of whom together with three officials and the Administrator form the membership of the Administrator's Executive Council, the Papua New Guinea Cabinet.

The Cabinet has been quick to get down to the business of Government. Many of you will have seen reports of the visit to Canberra last week by the Papua New Guinea Ministers who came as members of the Finance and Works Committee to negotiate with me the 1972–73 Budget for Papua New Guinea.[3] I have also held informal discussions with the Chief Minister both in Port Moresby and in Canberra on a number of other topics. The Government in Papua New Guinea has started work in earnest.

It is a Government that will have greater significance both in the executive and in the House of Assembly as a result of devolution of powers previously exercised by the Minister for External Territories. The key difference between this House of Assembly and the last is the greater exercise of powers by Ministers as a result of this continuing and growing devolution which began in 1970. Each Minister has final powers over a wide range of internal government. These powers are subject only to the collective responsibility of his cabinet colleagues. In areas such as internal finance, works, health, business development, labour, local government, agriculture and transport all seventeen ministers can make important decisions on the development and governing of Papua New Guinea.

As a result, ministers in Papua New Guinea will not only be governing but will be seen to be doing so; it is they who will be making the decisions and they are the ones who will take the credit or the blame for the results of their actions. They will work out the national priorities in various fields; whether it be the demands of education as against social services, those in Posts and Telegraph against those in Information, the policies on land use, and development of forest and mining resources against policies in the Trade and Industry portfolio. The Chief Minister and his colleagues will be governing in these areas and accepting the final responsibility for the decisions made, experiencing the difficulties as well as the satisfactions of government.

---

1   The speech was delivered to the Australian Universities Liberal Federation.

2   For background on the Mataungan Association see Document 50, fn. 3.

3   See Documents 290 & 292.

The official members of the House of Assembly will also have a reduced role and will not vote on any matters for which Papua New Guinea Ministers are finally responsible. Their role now is advisory plus a responsibility to explain policy on matters for which the Commonwealth continues to have final responsibility.

Thus we now have a situation in Papua New Guinea in which Ministers who are part of an elected executive will formulate and determine policy over a wide range of government activities. Together with this goes the responsibility of the Government of Papua New Guinea as a whole for translating the decisions of the executive into legislation or other action in this House.

There are, of course, the number of areas of government where the Commonwealth retains final responsibility —for example the judiciary, internal security, defence, international trade, foreign affairs and civil aviation. It is not the intention of the Commonwealth Government to exercise these residual responsibilities exclusively. For some time now the policy of the Commonwealth has been to take part in full consultations with the AEC on decisions in these areas. Wherever the Administrator thinks it in the public interest he is empowered to submit a matter for discussion to the AEC. In this way the Australian Government has sought the views of the AEC on all important policy matters since 1970 and will continue to give increasing weight to its views and advice in such areas. The result of this policy will be apparent by the degree to which the AEC in future influences the Commonwealth's attitude on important issues.

It may be that the Government of PNG would like some closer connection with all areas of government still retained by Australia. Should this be the case the Australian Government would welcome a request for a connection closer than that which currently operates and it would be a subject that could then be discussed when talks are held between the Commonwealth and the PNG Government.

The effect would be that the PNG Cabinet would be involved in the full spectrum of government activities and not just in those areas where PNG Ministers exercise full responsibilities. The Commonwealth has followed this approach in the past and considers it vital to the present given the emerging-nation status of Papua New Guinea.

This is the general framework therefore within which the Government of Papua New Guinea will operate.

This situation has come about not as a result of recent and radical change in Papua New Guinea but as a result of a continuing and accelerating movement, a movement which started in 1967.

In that year, on the recommendation of its Select Committee on Constitutional Development the first House recommended that Ministerial office holders be appointed from the House and that arrangements to allow for the development of a system of ministerial responsibility be provided for. In 1968 the Papua New Guinea Act was amended to give effect to this request and in 1969 and 1970 Ministerial office holders gradually assumed responsibility and became more involved in governing Papua New Guinea. In July 1970 final powers over wide areas of internal government were devolved to Ministers.[4] The initiative for this devolution of authority and responsibility, which is a continuing one, rests with the Papua New Guinea Ministers with the support of the House. Australian Government policy has been and is, that the initiatives for constitutional development should come from Papua New Guinea—we will not impose constitutional changes regardless of the wishes of the people.

Likewise we will not impose self-government in Papua New Guinea. The Australian Government stands ready to give self-government to Papua New Guinea and its aim is to help

---

4   See Documents 63–64, 67 & 70.

and encourage Papua New Guinea towards self-government. But the decision to accept self-government is one for the House of Assembly to speak about or to indicate the way in which the wishes of Papua New Guinea on this question can be clearly seen.

The Commonwealth has already announced its intention of holding discussions with the Papua New Guinea Government on further moves towards self-government. No doubt a timetable will be discussed. The Australian Government has already prepared a programme, at the request of the second House of Assembly, which lists the legislative and administrative actions which will be required before self-government.[5]

I should point out in this context that the move to self-government is not something to be accomplished at a single step—a sudden jump from one status and set of responsibilities to another; self-government should be seen as emerging from a series of steps which are agreed upon in advance by both Papua New Guinea and Commonwealth Governments.

All further steps to be taken, however, cannot be put into an acceptable timetable without a good deal of mutual discussion and consequent action both in Papua New Guinea and in Australia. I would envisage that in respect of each function of government, Commonwealth and the Papua New Guinea representatives would need to discuss in some detail such matters as the necessary legislation required in Papua New Guinea and in Australia and any administrative problems that might arise.

The legislative requirements alone will in many cases be formidable at both ends. Joint working parties may be needed and further Ministerial meetings called to consider the results. The question of a constitution for Papua New Guinea will need to be considered.

There is much to be discussed and negotiated, but I have no intention of letting progress to self-government be impeded by the complicated nature of the matters with which we will have to deal. Nor will decisions that can be made rapidly be held up because there are others that cannot be made quickly. In this field there is one overriding concern—it is not the timing of self-government or even the act of self-government itself that is of prime importance. The aim must be to achieve a self-governing country and not just a legal facade. As the Chief Minister, Mr Somare, said in his coalition's policy speech in the House of Assembly—'the timing of self-government is not as important as the type of self-government best suited to this country. There is a difference between the formal legal steps towards self-government and real movement towards self-government.'

Within Papua New Guinea there are many matters that will require the attention of the Papua New Guinea Government. These would include the question of citizenship, productive land use, the most appropriate legal system for Papua New Guinea. Others such as the role of and the function of the public service, the defence forces, the national development programme and the training and localisation programmes are matters for Papua New Guinea to determine with our help and assistance. In all these matters the Australian Government will encourage and assist in the development of the necessary measures. We will continue to provide large scale aid to Papua New Guinea and implement measures to retain expatriate staff for as long as their assistance is requested. The initiative and moves for change and development will come from Papua New Guinea, not from Australia. In many cases the Papua New Guinea House is uniquely qualified to provide the solutions and we would welcome such action.

Australia continues to have international obligations for Papua New Guinea under the United Nations Charter. These are to promote the political, economic, educational and social advancement of Papua New Guinea in accordance with the freely expressed wishes of the people and we will retain such an obligation until independence. We will therefore do all

5   See Document 278.

we can to assist the Papua New Guinea Government to govern effectively and implement its policies. We will assist in overcoming the difficulties that exist in Papua New Guinea such as lack of indigenous participation in business and economic life and the small number of Papuans and New Guineans in the senior managerial and executive areas of Government, private enterprise and the professions but we will not treat these realities as being constraints on the movement towards self-government. Rather they will act as an incentive to action on our part as well as on the part of the Papua New Guinea Government.

In response to some of these difficulties the Commonwealth has already set investment guidelines for Papua New Guinea which are designed to encourage investment which assists in developing Papua New Guinea on a sound and balanced basis, providing opportunities for significant local equity participation, making provision for employment and training opportunities for local people, and involving maximum processing of products and the provision of common user facilities. The establishment of the Investment Corporation earlier this year was another important move to ensure the people of Papua New Guinea have a healthy participation in the major enterprises in their country. These measures are designed to encourage the economic development that gives substance to self-government and to do so in a way that is consistent with the changing status of Papua New Guinea.

Australia's relationship with Papua New Guinea is in the process of changing fundamentally. In working towards self-government and later independence we are discarding the former relationship of administering authority and administered country. So far this process has been achieved without bitterness or recriminations from either party. On the contrary, the relations between our two countries at the moment are soundly based on goodwill and mutual trust. Speaking personally, I value greatly my own close personal relations with the Chief Minister and his Ministers and with a number of other Papua New Guinea leaders throughout the country. Close personal contact we have with Papua New Guinea at all levels of Government is something that will stand both countries in good stead; it is something that will minimise the scope for misunderstandings and provide the positive basis on which the future relations between our two countries will be built.

It is an exciting possibility to imagine a situation some time in the future in which Papua New Guinea, independent and developing, has close and friendly relations with Australia that have stabilised into a permanent reality.

The association between our two countries cannot end at independence. Events of history and factors of geography have dictated that our two countries must have a close relationship—we are too important to each other for it to be otherwise and not be to the detriment of both countries. I am confident that with the efforts of men of goodwill in both Papua New Guinea and Australia we can achieve this goal.

[NAA: A1838, 3080/10/1 PART 2]

295   CABINET SUBMISSION 655[1]

Canberra, undated [c. mid-May 1972]

<small>CONFIDENTIAL</small>

Papua New Guinea—Creation of Ministerial Offices

The purpose of this submission is to seek the agreement of Cabinet to an amendment of the Papua New Guinea Act 1949–1971 to remove the limit on the number of offices of Minister of the House of Assembly that the Minister for External Territories may create, and to provide for the creation of offices of Assistant Minister of the House of Assembly. The Act at present provides for not more than seventeen Ministers in conformity with a recommendation of the Second House of Assembly.

The Administrator's Executive Council of Papua New Guinea has, through its Deputy Chairman, foreshadowed a request for the appointment of additional Ministers and a need for the creation of offices of Assistant Minister. The Administrator of Papua New Guinea has recommended that this request be agreed to.

The House of Assembly on 22nd September, 1970 resolved that any further transfer of power or constitutional changes will be unacceptable to the House unless such changes have been agreed to by a majority of its members. The Administrator's Executive Council will therefore seek the House of Assembly's agreement to the proposed amendment in June.

It would enable time schedules both in Australia and Papua New Guinea to be met if the approval of the House of Assembly was anticipated and Cabinet agreed to the amendment at this stage so that a Bill could be drafted for introduction in the first week of the Budget session.

It would assist the development of executive government in Papua New Guinea if the Minister for External Territories was able to create such Ministries and Assistant Ministries as the Administrator, after consultation with the Deputy Chairman of the Administrator's Executive Council, recommended.

RECOMMENDATION

I recommended that Ministers:

(a) agree to the removal of the limit on the number of offices of Minister of the House of Assembly that the Minister for External Territories may from time to time determine;

(b) agree to the creation of such number of offices of Assistant Ministers of the House of Assembly that the Minister for External Territories may from time to time determine;

(c) authorise the drafting of the necessary amendments to the Papua New Guinea Act as a matter of urgency.[2]

[NAA: A5908, 655]

---

1   Submitted by Peacock.

2   Cabinet endorsed these recommendations. See Cabinet Decision 979 (PNG), 'Papua New Guinea: Creation of Ministerial Offices', 18 May 1972, NAA: A5908, 655.

296   CABINET DECISION 980 (PNG)

Canberra, 18 May 1972

Submission No. 627—Papua New Guinea:
Programme of Movement towards Internal Self Government[1]

The Committee, accepting the recommendations by the Minister at paragraph 16 of the Submission:

(a) noted the draft programme (see attachment to the Submission) for presentation by the Minister for External Territories to the 1972 leadership group and endorsed its use as a basis for initial discussions, with that group at Ministerial level, and later at Departmental level, on further progress towards internal self-government;

(b) agreed that, at the appropriate time, the leadership group be informed that the achievement of internal self-government by Papua New Guinea will not affect Australia's obligations undertaken with the United Nations and its continuing commitment to provide aid and assistance to Papua New Guinea, but that at independence a new set of relations will need to be developed and that it is envisaged that discussions on post-independence relations would take place well before the date of independence;

(c) decided that the Department of External Territories, in conjunction with the Department of Foreign Affairs, initiate as soon as possible a study in consultation with other Commonwealth Departments to define Australia's national interests in relation to an independent Papua New Guinea and the arrangements between it and Australia which ought to be entered into in the light of these interests: the conclusions to be placed before Cabinet with a view to recommending that certain of them be used as guidelines in the consideration of policy issues in the period up to independence and as the basis for discussions on the post-independence relations between Australia and Papua New Guinea; and

(d) agreed that the staffing implications of the programme be the subject of priority consideration by the Minister for External Territories, and the Treasurer, who would seek the approval of the Prime Minister to their recommendations.

2.   In the course of considering the Submission and accepting the recommendations the Committee also:

(a) noted the advice of the Minister that planning for the establishment of internal self government should proceed on the basis that it might be expected to come into effect in 1974 (rather than in 1975 as suggested in the Submission) but emphasised that the new Government should be encouraged to comprehend the need for sound groundwork and be brought to an appreciation of the complexity of the steps involved;

(b) noted that the position of the Departments and Agencies now performing functions of internal self-government (Annex C to the Submission) and matters falling within the responsibility of other Ministers (paragraph 13 of the Submission) would need to be the subject of careful examination as the programme of movement towards internal self-government developed;

(c) noted that there may need to be consultation with [the] United Nations before the establishment of internal self-government;

---

1   Document 278.

(d) while recognising the need to deal fully and frankly with the new Ministry, and the sensitivities involved, felt that every effort should be made by the Minister, after full consultation with the Chief Minister and his senior colleagues, to involve the non-Government party leaders in discussions of basic developments towards self-government and independence so that Australia's position is as far as possible accepted by all sections of political opinion in the Territory;

(e) saw a particular need for sensitive and careful handling, in close consultation with the Minister for Foreign Affairs, of relationships with Indonesia—particularly on matters relating to the land border with West Irian and the Papua New Guinea/West Irian sea bed;

(f) emphasised that the question of the border between Queensland and Papua must be delicately handled and that any position taken by the Commonwealth should take full account of the Constitutional position as set out in Section 123 of the Constitution; and;

(g) established a standing interdepartmental committee on Papua New Guinea consisting of representatives of the Departments of External Territories (Chairman), Foreign Affairs, Treasury, Defence, Trade and Industry and Prime Minister and Cabinet with representatives of other departments being coopted as necessary; the Committee is entrusted with coordination of departmental activities comprehended by the recommendations in the Submission but is not to derogate from the full and joint responsibility of the Departments of External Territories and Foreign Affairs for the study authorised in paragraph 1(c) above.

[NAA: A5908, 627]

297   NOTE FROM BORDER TO WALLER

Canberra, 24 May 1972

When Peter Hastings[1] called on me yesterday afternoon he spoke in general terms about the need for an Interdepartmental Committee to look at the overall Australian policy on PNG matters, and said that he would be talking to Mr Peacock about it that afternoon. (I suspect that he had got wind of earlier suggestions for such a committee.) I said that there would be great merit in such a committee and that the only policy coordination of this type at present probably lay in the Cabinet itself or in its committees on PNG.

This morning Hastings rang to say that he had in fact raised the matter with Mr Peacock and that Mr Peacock had said that he proposed to have an Interdepartmental Committee established 'next month', for this purpose, at a high level under the chairmanship of External Territories. He asked Hastings not to write the story for a couple of weeks until he had made all arrangements and he said he would keep other papers off the story in the meantime. The Departments concerned, according to Hastings, will be Foreign Affairs, Defence, Prime Minister's, Trade, Attorney-General's, Treasury and possibly Primary Industry. Mr Peacock also spoke to him about an Interdepartmental Committee on the border problems; he told Hastings that he expected the Queensland border problem to be resolved within six months.

To my question, he said he got the impression that Mr Peacock was well aware of the many pressing problems involved in the new PNG–Australian relationship, and that he was anxious to 'keep things moving' rather than to allow them to develop in a leisurely manner.[2]

[NAA: A1838, 3080/10/1 PART 2]

---

1 Peter Hastings had been the foreign affairs writer (and a leader writer) for *The Australian* from 1966 to 1970 and then took up these roles at *The Sydney Morning Herald*. He was also executive officer of the Council on New Guinea Affairs, a 'think tank' he had helped establish, editor of the Council's journal, *New Guinea and Australia, the Pacific and South-East Asia*, and author of *New Guinea: Problems & Prospects*, Cheshire for the Australian Institute of International Affairs, Melbourne, 1969.

2 Waller initialled the note from Border on 24 May; it was circulated to several senior DFA officials who initialled it on either 24 or 25 May. The brief marginal comments made by Waller and his colleagues give no indication that at this stage they had learnt of the Cabinet decision of 18 May to set up an interdepartmental committee (Document 296). The fact that senior DFA officials had not yet learned of the Cabinet decision several days after it was made, combined with Border's somewhat plaintive attempt to seek an insight into Peacock's intentions from someone outside Australian government circles, would suggest that the DET (and possibly also the Department of Prime Minister and Cabinet) was not giving a high priority to keeping the DFA informed of developments. Hay only informed Waller of the Cabinet decision on 29 May (see Document 304).

298   LETTER FROM WHEELER TO HAY

Canberra, 24 May 1972

On 22 May we despatched to you copies of a background paper,[1] which was prepared by a working group of officers from our two departments and from the Reserve Bank, concerning currency arrangements for Papua New Guinea. I understand that after clearance with all concerned the paper will be given to the Administrator of Papua New Guinea for his information.

As you are aware the attitude of this department and more importantly of the Treasurer has been that the complex question of currency arrangements for Papua New Guinea should not be dealt with in a precipitate fashion. In particular we have been concerned that the work of the Committee on Banking in Papua New Guinea should not become bogged down in the broader issues relating to currency.

However, we are now I think reaching a position where the currency question can be considered more closely. In the first place completion of the background paper on currency provides a basis for discussion and for exploration of the whole problem in more depth. Secondly, the work of the Banking Committee is now well underway and its Interim Report should be submitted to Cabinet within the next few days. Finally, with the formation of a ruling coalition within the new House of Assembly there is now an indigenous leadership group with whom more permanent solutions to the currency question can be discussed.

I therefore believe it is time that we considered the arrangements for future examination of the currency question with a view to devising some detailed and practical proposals which can be discussed with the Papua New Guinea authorities.

I believe that we need to establish a committee to carry out this examination and I assume that its composition could very well be the same as that for the committee on banking. Currency questions go to the heart of Treasury business and I hope you would agree that the prime responsibility for overseeing the work of this committee should rest with the Commonwealth Treasury. You will recall that the Treasurer has already expressed some views on this point to your Minister.

I should be grateful for any comments you may have to offer before I take this matter up again with the Treasurer.

[NAA: A452, 1972/3607]

---

1   Not published. For background on the currency issue, see Documents 220, 224 & 237.

299   LETTER FROM GREENWELL TO HAY

New York, 26 May 1972

CONFIDENTIAL

I had discussions with Mr Tang Ming Chao, the Under-Secretary-General, Department of Trusteeship and Non-Self-Governing Territories, Mr Refei, Director, Department of Trusteeship and Non-Self Governing Territories and Mr Pradas who is Head of the Trusteeship Division in the Secretariat. Mr Ashwin attended the discussions.

[*matter omitted*]

3.   It was explained, by way of background, that the talks were informal, but that departmentally we would be interested in UN thinking as to the manner in which the Trusteeship agreement might be discharged and what, in the UN view, would constitute an act of 'self-determination'. Reference was made to the quickening pace of constitutional change and also to the relationship between the mode of self-determination to the question of national unity which had been specifically referred to in the resolution of the General Assembly. (In this connection I pointed out that there were elements in Papua which could seek to take advantage of the possibility of a separate act of self-determination either from political motives or to extract a greater and possibly unfair economic contribution as a condition of unity with New Guinea. Such a movement might gain greatly if on purely formal grounds the UN felt it was obliged to ascertain the wishes of the people of Papua *separately*. Accordingly, we would hope that there would be no requirement of a separate plebiscite in Papua.) I also referred to the division between the people of Papua New Guinea over the timing of self-government and independence and suggested that we would hope that a national attitude on this might be established. For this reason we would hope that any means of doing so should accord with what the UN might require.

4.   The UN said that a resolution of the General Assembly would be required. Mr Refei was rather reluctant to adopt the suggestion of a House of Assembly resolution supported by a Papuan majority—I had pointed out that there were about thirty open and regional Papuan electorates. He rather favoured a national plebiscite. He acknowledged this and the possibility of a resolution passed by the House but my impression is that something more than this is likely to be required—if not a referendum a resolution of the House after elections.

5.   He was firm, however, that there would be no need of a separate plebiscite applicable to both Papua and New Guinea. He had in mind one plebiscite in which the majority of the people would be asked whether they wish to have independence in the united country of PNG. I did not press him on possible legal objections to this because he seemed to accept that they had separate status internationally but he accepted the fact that they had been administered as one for 23 years and that the UN had called frequently for unity. It was suggested that possibly the elections in 1976 adopting a constitution providing for independence on a particular date (if supervised by UN observers) could constitute an act of self-determination. This may be a possibility (judging on the Administrator's present views as to the acceleration of timing by one year and provided that agreement had been reached between the two main parties.) I pointed out to him that there were a number of precedents where resolutions of the legislative assembly had been accepted—the Cameroons, Tanganyika and Togo and that the only reason it had not in the case of Western Samoa was because the legislature was thought to be unrepresentative.

6.   Mr Refei suggested that a UN Mission should examine the facts and report on the appropriate mode of self-determination. I pointed out that a motion specifically for this purpose

might only generate separatist demands. He appeared to fully understand our difficulties (it occurred to me later that next year's visiting mission could less obtrusively have this as one of its terms of reference).

7.   Turning to Bougainville I pointed out the distinctive regional feeling there, the ethnic differences of the people, the existence of the copper project and further that there might be a motion calling for a separate referendum on Bougainville at the next meeting of the House. Would the UN countenance a separate act of self-determination for Bougainville? The whole approach of the UN was that there would not be. Mr Refei said there was no precedent for a separate act of self-determination (I should add the questions asked of the northern and southern provinces of the British Cameroons came over rather close to it). Certainly we would have the support of the UN if we were to reject any resolution by the House of Assembly which called for a referendum for Bougainville. I took up the question of agreements between the Commonwealth and PNG before independence. He explained that these were discouraged prior to independence but could be negotiated before and entered into immediately after independence. After my discussion it emerged during the examination of the TTPI[1] that the desire of the Marianas Islands to negotiate a separate act of self-determination had similarities with what could occur in Bougainville. I will report on this later.

[*matter omitted*]

[NAA: A452, 1972/0932]

---

1   Trust Territory of the Pacific Islands. This territory, located in the northern Pacific, had been administered by the United States under a UN trusteeship since the end of the Second World War; previously, its various components were under Japanese rule. These culturally-distinct and geographically-scattered components lacked a sense of common identity. In the 1970s and 1980s, in a process of partial decolonisation, four new entities emerged. Three of these entities (the Republic of the Marshall Islands, the Federated States of Micronesia and the Republic of Palau) are quasi-independent states linked to the United States in Compacts of Free Association. The fourth entity, namely the Commonwealth of the Northern Mariana Islands, is a Commonwealth 'in political union' with the United States.

300   LETTER FROM HAY TO JOHNSON

Canberra, 29 May 1972

I refer to our discussions recently about the possibility that the [PNG] Coalition may need to take the initiative on the question of a Constitutional Commission if there was a move in the June House of Assembly to set up a Select Committee on Constitutional Development.

We have been giving some thought to this question and attached is a suggested proposal which you may wish to consider.[1] I suggest that if you are in general agreement with it that we could then place it before the Minister for his consideration and following this you might discuss it with Mr Somare before the June House meets.

Our feeling is that a Commission consisting only of Members of the House should be established and be removed from the House in the sense that it would not be a Select or Standing Committee of the House. When Ratu Sir Kamisese Mara[2] was in Canberra recently the Minister raised with him the question of a Constitutional Commission. Ratu Mara was also firmly of the opinion that such a Commission should comprise parliamentarians and that academics should not be appointed to it.

The Commission will, of course, require the services of advisers and we would propose that constitutional or other specialist experts would be appointed part-time to advise the Commission on matters before it and that one of the constitutional advisers should be a senior Commonwealth officer, possibly from the Attorney-General's Department. The Commission would therefore be a parliamentary one removed from the parliamentary scene but able to have the advice of constitutional and other specialist experts when required.

The Commission may also be able to perform some of the functions as outlined by Mr Oala-Rarua in speaking to his motion in the November 1971 House of Assembly, and it may also be able to fulfil a role along the lines envisaged by you in your LH4063 of 4 April 1972[3] regarding the possible need for a national consultative body with representatives from all political groups.

It may be that you feel that the suggested Commission is too unwieldy or insufficiently representative of political groups but on the basis that it is put up as a suggestion only, I would be grateful for your comments.

[NAA: A452, 1972/3878]

---

1   Not published.
2   Prime Minister of Fiji, 1970–87.
3   Not published.

301   LETTER FROM HAY TO JOHNSON

Canberra, undated [c. mid-May 1972]

During a recent discussion with Sir Keith Waller the question was raised of whether or not to allow consulates from friendly foreign nations permanent representation in the Territory. In the past we have approached this rather cautiously and whilst agreeing to the appointment of honorary consuls in one or two cases have not encouraged the establishment of career consulates. I think we have probably reached the time when we should review this approach.

Any request to establish a particular consulate should be considered on its merits as is normal practice. Those most likely to want consulates are Indonesia and Japan, both of whom expressed interest in 1970. They were discouraged at the time and have not raised the matter formally since then. However, as the Territory moves towards independence and as Japanese investment increases, it is quite probable that they will raise the matter again. Whether or not they do, we and Foreign Affairs see some positive advantages in the presence of a Japanese and an Indonesian Consul.

Japan

Japanese investment and business activity in Papua New Guinea is increasing and is generally welcome. There is some tourism and this could be developed further. Japan is a world power with special interests and influence in the Pacific region, of which Papua New Guinea forms part. It is important that relations with Japan should be good and that misunderstandings should be cleared up quickly. It is probable that Japan will want to establish an Embassy when PNG becomes independent.

A Japanese Consul would help stimulate investment and would provide consular services for the Japanese citizens resident in Papua New Guinea. He would also be able to give information and advice to people in PNG who wished to know more about Japan or to trade with Japan. At the same time he would be able to keep the Japanese Government informed of developments in PNG and of the PNG Government's views and interests.

Indonesia

Indonesia is PNG's nearest neighbour with whom PNG shares a common border. It is also a large and potentially powerful country. Following the visit of the PNG Parliamentary Delegation led by the Speaker, Dr Guise, many people in Indonesia and New Guinea have expressed interest in increasing direct contacts between the two countries. Indonesia will want to establish an Embassy when PNG becomes independent.

An Indonesian Consul would act as a point of contact for those who wished to learn more about Indonesia and would be able to explain developments in PNG to his own Government. He would be of assistance in helping to solve any particular problems which might arise. His presence would make it easier for PNG people to go to Indonesia and he might be able to promote cultural exchanges and offer some scholarships for study.

As the Papua New Guinea Foreign Office develops, contact with career consuls will give them valuable experience in dealing with foreign missions and will expose them to new ideas and practices. Thus, when independence comes, they will have developed procedures for handling foreign missions and should be able to avoid embarrassing mistakes when the first foreign embassies arrive.

It should be kept in mind that the acceptance of consuls from some countries does not commit PNG to admit consuls from other countries which they may not wish to see represented there.

In the light of the rapid approach of self-government, I feel that our attitude towards consular representation could well be received and relaxed. In particular because we have actively discouraged them in the past it might now be advisable to indicate discreetly that they would now be welcome should they so decide.

If you agree, I should be glad if you would consult the AEC on the matter. I would then take it up with the Minister.

[NAA: A452, 1972/2310]

302   LETTER FROM HAY TO WHEELER

Canberra, 31 May 1972

Thank you for your letter 71/5881 of 24th May[1] on the question of currency for Papua New Guinea.

I am in full agreement that arrangements for the future examination of the currency question need to be made without delay. It is likely in fact that the discussions on constitutional and other matters with Papua New Guinea's Chief Minister tentatively set down for July will require at least some reference to currency including the steps that are contemplated by the Commonwealth to consider jointly with Papua New Guinea authorities the issues involved in a separate currency for Papua New Guinea and the steps to be taken to give effect to a decision on a separate currency. This was, of course, forecast in item No. 12 of the programme of movement towards self-government submitted to Cabinet (Submission No. 627 of 17th April 1972).[2]

This is why this Department has been pressing the need to move ahead and has in fact sent over to Treasury the draft of a Cabinet Submission seeking certain broad authorities from Cabinet. I have no objection to Treasury making the running in further studies. But I hope you share my view as to the urgency of moving ahead. As I see it, the immediate need is for a paper to go to Cabinet to cover the July meeting with the Chief Minister. A preliminary to this, in terms of Decision No. 980 (PNG) of 18th May 1972,[3] will be discussion in the IDC[4] which is now being set up. I suggest our officers get together on the basis of the present draft and work it into an acceptable submission to go to the IDC within the next week or so. I appreciate that this timing is tight but I am afraid that the demands of the movement towards self-government leave us no further option. I hope therefore that the Treasury will be able to assist us in meeting this timetable.

[NAA: A452, 1972/3607]

---

1   Document 298.

2   Document 278.

3   Document 296.

4   A reference to the standing interdepartmental committee (IDC) established by Cabinet on 18 May (see Document 296).

303   LETTER FROM JOHNSON TO HAY

Port Moresby, 31 May 1972

CONFIDENTIAL

I have not yet had an opportunity to consider the issues raised in your A.323 of the 29th May, 1972.[1] There is, however, one salient fact which must be taken into consideration and that is that the executive of the Pangu Pati is unlikely to be awaiting initiatives from the Commonwealth Government or from me but is certain to be preparing its own plans, which could differ substantially from those suggested in your memo.

I am seeking preliminary constitutional discussions with the [PNG] Coalition Leaders but feel that it would be improper for me to make concrete proposals at these discussions. I see them as merely indicating what needs to be accomplished in the achievement of self-government and the possible alternative methods by which this might be accomplished.

The Pangu Pati is likely to be particularly sensitive on this issue and, provided that I feel that sensible proposals will eventuate, I think that I should not seek to take any initiatives. I believe that responsible propositions will be presented, though they may not be entirely in accordance with our own views.

I will comment in greater detail on your proposals in due course.

[NAA: A452, 1972/3878]

---

1   Document 300.

304   LETTER FROM WALLER TO HAY

Canberra, 1 June 1972

CONFIDENTIAL

Thank you for your letter of 29 May 1972[1] concerning Cabinet's decision to establish an interdepartmental committee to coordinate departmental activities comprehended by the recommendations in Cabinet Submission 627—Programme of Movement Towards Internal Self-Government in Papua New Guinea.[2]

As many of the matters with which the interdepartmental committee will be dealing will play an important part in shaping the nature of Australia's future relationship with an independent Papua New Guinea, its establishment is a welcome development from our point of view. I hope the committee will not adopt too restrictive an approach to its task and will also embrace the question of policy formulation. The committee can make a significant contribution towards cocoordinating Australia's approach to Papua New Guinea through the period leading up to independence and I think it important therefore that it should be at an appropriately high level.

On this assumption I propose to nominate Mr L. H. Border, Deputy Secretary (B), as the Foreign Affairs representative on the interdepartmental committee. I think you know that Mr Border is responsible for the general oversight of Papua New Guinea matters in this Department and is familiar with the Territory and many of its problems.

I am copying this letter to Sir John Bunting, Sir Frederick Wheeler, Sir Arthur Tange and Mr D. H. McKay.

[NAA: A1838, 3080/11/1/2 PART 1]

1   Not published.
2   Documents 278 & 296. See also Document 283.

305   EXTRACT OF MINUTE FROM KERR TO GREENWELL

Canberra, 6 June 1972

Papua New Guinea—AEC Procedures

We are trying to develop a Papua New Guinea Public Service which serves an emerging Papua New Guinea Government and any actions which highlight a remaining responsibility on the part of the Public Service towards the Australian Government will tend to exacerbate the underlying mistrust which exists at the moment between the Coalition Government and the Public Service.

I suggest therefore that it would be in our interests if we could move as quickly as possible to the separation of the Administrator and his small Australian component on the one hand and the Administration as a whole on the other but short of this do nothing to discourage a Papua New Guinea Minister's involvement in areas within his portfolio but not yet within his final responsibility.

It would seem to me that we could live with Papua New Guinea Ministers expressing an opinion before the Minister had determined his position provided that the procedures as outlined in the AEC Booklet[1] as amended by the revised telex[2] are applied.

[NAA: A452, 1971/1463]

---

1   Not published.
2   Not published.

306   MEMORANDUM FROM GREENWELL TO DFA

New York, 6 June 1972

CONFIDENTIAL

The Question of an Act of Self-Determination for Papua New Guinea

It is clear that a resolution of the General Assembly is required if the termination of the Trust Agreement between Australia and the United Nations is to be internationally acceptable. During the period I was in New York I had discussions on the kind of act of self-determination and related procedures necessary for this.

2.   This included a joint discussion with the Under-Secretary-General for Trust and Non-Self Governing Territories, Mr Tang, the director of the Department, Mr Rifai, the Head of the Trust Section in the Department, Mr Pradas, and the Australian representatives on the Trusteeship Council, Mr Ashwin.[1] In Washington I spoke briefly on the matter with Sir James Plimsoll.[2]

3.   By way of preliminary comment it is evident that strictly formal or legal considerations, whilst not irrelevant, are of secondary importance. Political conditions in Papua New Guinea as interpreted in the Trusteeship Council, the Special Committee and the General Assembly and international positions will determine United Nations attitudes and, in this latter respect, the overriding factor is that trust and non-self-governing territories should achieve independence as soon as possible. The other matter to be mentioned of a preliminary nature is that it will be evident that these comments must as a result be provisional and speculative.

THE KIND OF ACT OF SELF-DETERMINATION

Generally

4.   Looking at the question apart from Papua, we had received advice from Sir Kenneth Bailey and the Attorney-General's Department that no specific requirements as to the nature of the 'act' required had been laid down either by law or previous practice.[3] Nothing arose in the course of my discussions to reflect on the accuracy of these views.

5.   It is true that Mr Rifai expressed a preference for a national plebiscite but it was no more than that. A legislative resolution was acceptable in Italian Somaliland, Tanganyika and Rwanda-Urundi. In the case of Western Samoa a plebiscite had been insisted upon by the United Nations but that was because, as I understand it, the legislature as then constituted in Western Samoa, was not regarded as representative. In my view, short of a requirement by the House of Assembly or unexpected developments in Papua New Guinea we can assume no plebiscite would be required.

6.   It is necessary to note that the kind of act of self-determination had in most if not all cases been the subject of prior recommendations by a visiting mission to the Trust Territory concerned, followed by a resolution on those recommendations in the General Assembly. In one instance—the British Cameroons—the General Assembly modified the recommendations of a visiting mission to require a plebiscite in the northern province.

---

1   See Document 299.

2   Australian Ambassador to the United States, 1970–74. For Plimsoll's comments to Greenwell, see para. 18 below.

3   See Documents 226 (para. 11), 228 & 229.

Papua

7.   At the time of the administrative union the separate identity and status of Papua as a non-self-governing territory was preserved and the obligations in respect of a trust territory (Art 76) and a non-self-governing territory (Art 73) differ. Although the establishment of single national institutions under the administrative union has rendered this distinction largely formal and Australian policy has accepted the more onerous obligations under the Trust Agreement as applicable to the whole, the question is whether this formal distinction requires some separate identification of the wishes of the people of Papua to unite with New Guinea as an independent country.

8.   Sir Kenneth Bailey has advised that if a House of Assembly resolution were to be relied upon it 'should at least have the concurrence of a majority of members of the House who represent Papua constituencies'. In the case of two other administrative unions, the British Togoland/the Gold Coast and the British Cameroons/Nigeria, a separate plebiscite was held in the Trust Territory to determine whether unity was desired. (In the latter case there were separate plebiscites in each of the northern and southern provinces.) France as always opposed the assimilation of non-self-governing territory obligations to trust obligations and it was because of the identification of Papua with New Guinea in the resolution on the Trusteeship Council's Report before the last General Assembly that France abstained.

9.   M. Blanc, who had been a member of the Visiting Mission, believes his country's attitude is changing. He is pressing the view that, having regard to the General Assembly resolution at the time of the administrative union, Papua New Guinea can be distinguished from territories in which France has an interest. In his address to the Trusteeship Council during the present session he went out of his way to indicate the reality of the union. Nobody else with whom I spoke suggested that 'Papua' as a separate entity presented any problem.

10.   I have not discussed the matter with the Legal Department at the United Nations partly for the obvious reason of not wishing to produce a problem where there may be none, but also because political considerations would in any event seem to be predominant. It is to be noted that Papua New Guinea was, as a unity, permitted to join ECAFE[4] and WHO[5] and nobody at the United Nations regarded the separate identity of Papua as a matter of consequence in the case of these applications. Thus, the long history of the administrative union, the calls for national unity in the General Assembly resolution, the single flag, the advice to the United Nations of the passage of the National Identity Act,[6] the composite reporting on the two territories and the impossibility of the two territories functioning as independent entities, all suggest that the United Nations would not of its own volition create any difficulties with regard to Papua. It would however be useful to secure France's support for our position.

Bougainville and Procedures

11.   It is necessary to deal both with the procedures and the separate problem of Bougainville.

12.   The general practice has been broadly as follows:

(i)   A Visiting Mission makes recommendations as to the appropriate act of self-determination;

(ii)   The General Assembly considers its proposals;

---

4   The United Nations Economic Commission for Asia and the Far East.

5   The World Health Organisation.

6   The National Identity Act, passed by the House of Assembly in 1971, contained provisions on the use of the PNG national flag and other symbols of national identity, including the PNG crest and the National Pledge of Papua New Guinea.

(iii) The act of self-determination is then implemented;

(iv) It is adopted by resolution of the General Assembly and the Trusteeship Agreement is discharged.

13. It appears to me that a Visiting Mission to Papua New Guinea specifically charged with advising on the appropriate act of self-determination would be divisive. I do not envisage that the kind of act would be arrived at without prior consultation with Papua New Guinea leaders, but if a Visiting Mission has to report (as to which see below) it would be preferable if that could be done unobtrusively.

14. The next Visiting Mission is due to arrive in January/February 1974. This may be too early to ask it to consider that appropriate act of self-determination but if a Mission has to report, it would be best done by a regular Visiting Mission as part of its ordinary duties. As its views would become public by May/June 1974, it would follow that the act of self-determination recommended by it would become a political issue in Papua New Guinea from that point onwards and no doubt the political reaction to the Mission's recommendations would become an issue in the General Assembly's consideration of the matter in November 1974. Nevertheless it may avoid the issue 'blowing up' whilst the Mission was visiting Papua New Guinea.

15. I would only envisage that taking action to secure prior endorsement by the United Nations of the appropriate act would take place as early as the next Visiting Mission in the following eventualities:

(i) If an agreed national attitude within Papua New Guinea as to the appropriate act of self-determination and timing had been previously arrived at;

(ii) If the Pangu-led coalition should press very strongly for independence;

(iii) If separatism in Papua New Guinea intensified to a point where it was felt early self-determination was more likely to produce unity;

(iv) A change of government in Australia.

As to these, (i) appears unlikely; (ii) is beyond anything that the Coalition has yet sought, and (iii) and (iv) are speculative.

[*matter omitted*][7]

18. Sir James Plimsoll was of the view that the present temper in the United Nations would be to accept a firm majority resolution of the House of Assembly. Having regard to the endorsement of the electoral procedures in Papua New Guinea by the recent Visiting Mission it would seem that such a resolution if it provided some basis for indicating Papua support and did not generate too much opposition within any parts of Papua New Guinea, would effectively present the General Assembly with a fait accompli without going through immediate steps of seeking prior United Nations approval which might generate conflict. This may be an appropriate course but it would depend perhaps on a greater measure of agreement within Papua New Guinea than presently exists.

Bougainville

19. There remains the question of Bougainville. It would seem quite unlikely that the House would pass a resolution permitting Bougainville to determine its own future, but of course such a motion may be moved and may be supported by Bougainville members in the House. In the light of the House's expressed view in favour of national unity and the coalition's policy

---

7   The omitted matter includes information on the constitutional arrangements made for Rwanda–Urundi and the Northern Marianas Islands. On the latter, see Document 299, fn. 1.

one could only expect acceptance of such a resolution as deriving from internal party politics. What should happen if such a resolution were passed in anything like the near future would no doubt be a matter for government policy at the time. So far as the United Nations is concerned it is clear enough that at present it could be disregarded. It might be added, as this point was not covered earlier, that it is clear both from the general attitude here and the General Assembly resolution 'to discourage separatist movements' that the Commonwealth Government could similarly reject any demands for a separate ascertainment of Papua sentiment.

20.   There is only one difference, in United Nations terms, between Papua and Bougainville. In the former instance there is legal justification for Papuan demands. In the case of Bougainville, as part of the Trust Territory, no legal obligation for a separate act of self-determination would be justified.

21.   The question of a separate act of self-determination for Bougainville turns entirely on political considerations and would only be contemplated after all endeavours to keep it with the rest of Papua New Guinea have failed. Separatist feeling would have to go far beyond what presently exists for a separatist act of self-determination to be contemplated. There are however instances where separation becomes inevitable.

[*matter omitted*]

Conclusions

(a)   If the House of Assembly were to resolve on either a referendum or a Select Committee as the appropriate mode of self-determination, it would be obligatory to follow this request.

(b)   If the House of Assembly were simply to resolve upon independence for a united Papua New Guinea that would be acceptable unless possibly it stimulated widespread unrest in any area. Prior United Nations endorsement through a recommendation by a Visiting Mission would of course make this more certain but in my opinion prior approval would not be essential.

(c)   In the event of either (a) or (b) my interpretation is that the United Nations might look to some minimal requirement 'to set the record straight' on Papua but it would be satisfied with anything Australia recommended in this regard. In the case of a simple resolution it may be, as Sir Kenneth Bailey suggests, a majority of the Papuan members in the House or alternatively it may be the support of the (a) members representing a majority of the people in Papuan electorates or (b) the support of a majority of Papuan members. In the case of a referendum or a Select Committee, the question asked of all the people could be perhaps whether they are in favour of national unity; a question with which they have become familiar through visits of the Select Committee and resolutions of the House.

(d)   A separate act of self-determination for Bougainville would only be permitted as a last resort.

(e)   So far as immediate government policy is concerned the expression of policy outlines in the Administrator's statement of May 1971 would have full United Nations backing and, if government policy should otherwise dictate, this would include a rejection of demands for separate plebiscites.

(f)   A plebiscite will not be insisted upon but would of course be acceptable.

[NAA: A452, 1972/2015]

307   LETTER FROM GREENWELL TO HAY[1]

New York, 6 June 1972

CONFIDENTIAL

I flew to Washington on Friday as that was the only day Sir James Plimsoll was available. He was interested in our projections on timing and I told him of the Administrator's view that the result of the elections was probably to hasten things by about a year. He was rather strongly of the view that from all his experience these things gather momentum and he expected self-government sooner. He considered there would be no difficulty in our relying solely on a House of Assembly resolution as an act of self-determination.

[*matter omitted*]

You have mentioned the question of amendments to the Papua New Guinea Act, and I think your concern is to maintain a step by step momentum in constitutional development. One possibility which might be considered is the modification of the veto provisions in the Papua New Guinea Act eliminating the powers at present invested in the Governor-General. Of course the Administrator would still retain the power of assent or refusal to assent and it would need to be clear in the amendments of the legislation that in reserved areas the right of assent could still be exercised substantively. I have in mind, of course, defence, international relations, the public service and internal security. We have to make these amendments at some stage and at present it would be true to say that reference to the Governor-General is largely formal. As long as I have been in the Department no ordinances have been disallowed and no assent in reserved areas has been refused.

[*matter omitted*]

[DFAT: Historical Research Section]

---

1   John Greenwell kindly made this letter from his private papers available to Bruce Hunt. A copy is held in the Historical Research Section, DFAT.

308   EXTRACT OF RECORD OF CONVERSATION BETWEEN BOWEN AND MALIK[1]

Djakarta, 8 June 1972

CONFIDENTIAL

Papua-New Guinea

Malik raised the question of future relations between West Irian and Papua-New Guinea. The Minister said that Papua-New Guinea was moving rapidly towards self-government. It would be some time before it reached full independence and Australia would remain responsible in the meantime for defence and foreign policy.

In the interim, we were helping train a future foreign service for Papua-New Guinea. We wanted to move forward as quickly as possible and not to slow down the development towards independence.

At the same time we would assist in whatever ways we could to see that the new country had good solid contacts with Indonesia. If Indonesia was interested in opening a consulate in Port Moresby, Australia would recommend it to the Administrator's Executive Council. Malik said that this would be very useful and expressed appreciation.

[NAA: A452, 1972/2310]

1   Adam Malik, Indonesian Minister for Foreign Affairs, 1966–77. Bowen accompanied Prime Minister McMahon on a visit to Jakarta from 5 to 8 June, 1972. *Current Notes on International Affairs*, 43 (6), June 1972, p. 269.

309   SPEECH BY PEACOCK

Sydney, 8 June 1972

Future Relations between Australia and Papua New Guinea

I am very pleased to address the [Australian] Institute of International Affairs tonight on future relations between Australia and Papua New Guinea. This is an important and timely subject. Australians need to adjust to the likelihood that Papua New Guinea, more quickly than many people expect, will cease to be a dependent Territory under Australia's ultimate legal responsibility. Instead it will be our nearest independent neighbour. In the eyes of the world and particularly the nations in the Pacific, Papua New Guinea, with its $2^1/_2$ million inhabitants and its economic potential, will be a nation of consequence. I am taking this opportunity to offer some observations on future relations between our countries. In doing so I hope that informed discussions will be stimulated.

Recent political development in Papua New Guinea has seen the country moving rapidly to self-government and independence. Even now our relations with Papua New Guinea are being, and for some time have been, conducted with an eye to the development of Papua New Guinea as an independent nation.

[*matter omitted*]

The transfer of all powers at independence will mark a watershed in our relationship with Papua New Guinea. At this time our United Nations obligations will be discharged and Papua New Guinea will take its place as a member of the international community. A new set of relations based on respective national interests and taking into account political and geographical factors affecting both countries, will need to be established. The terms of this relationship will, I hope, be planned and some elements of it negotiated between our governments before the actual date of independence. We would be remiss if we found ourselves completing the independence of Papua New Guinea without adequate preparation for the post-independence period.

Independence should not represent a sudden break from one status to another. The Commonwealth has long held the view that there should be a smooth and orderly transition which establishes Papua New Guinea by the time of independence as a state able to manage its own affairs with a government responsive to the wishes of the people. There is a need to plan ahead to avoid the hangover that so often follows the intoxication of an emotional independence celebration.

[*matter omitted*]

In the areas of government where the Commonwealth thus retains responsibility up to self-government and perhaps afterwards—for example defence and international relations—it will not exercise these residual responsibilities exclusively. Indeed, for some time now the Australian Government has been seeking the views of the Papua New Guinea Government on all important policy matters. It may be that the Government of Papua New Guinea would like to be more closely involved in the exercise of some or all of the powers still retained by Australia, perhaps by the use of non-official spokesmen in the House of Assembly or by the creation of Parliamentary Subject Committees in these areas. Should this be the case the Australian Government would welcome such a request. Such a request could be discussed when talks are held between the Commonwealth and the Papua New Guinea Government later in the year. The effect would be that the Papua New Guinea Government would be involved well before independence in the full spectrum of government and not just in those areas for which it has final responsibility. This would facilitate the orderly and peaceful transition to which I have referred.

[*matter omitted*]

I do not expect that the discharge of our international obligations at independence will result in a total reorientation of our relations with Papua New Guinea. True, we will no longer be legally responsible for the economic, social, political and educational advancement of the country, but our links are such that independence, arriving as a result of an orderly transition, at a time mutually agreed upon need not mean sudden severance or destruction of existing relations and the need to re-build from the ground up.

[*matter omitted*]

While Australia will remain important to Papua New Guinea, we should not seek to build an exclusive relationship based on a mistaken belief that past assistance places Papua New Guinea under an obligation to us. Looked at from Papua New Guinea's point of view, Indonesia, Singapore, Malaysia, the Philippines and Japan, as well as the island nations of the Pacific, will have important places in the eyes of Papua New Guinea Governments. Other Governments will be seeking to assist Papua New Guinea. We will do well to recognise this. Not to do so might adversely affect both our and Papua New Guinea's relations with third countries.

I cannot anticipate that there will be no divergences of interest after independence and that Papua New Guinea will not grow away from Australia. It may turn to other models of government, administrative organisation and even economic organisation.

Independence will not change some underlying factors affecting our future relations. Geography is one of them. Papua New Guinea is our closest neighbour and on independence will be our closest foreign neighbour. It is only natural that both our countries should want to be friendly with each other, because the actions of each are bound in important respects to affect the interests of the other.

Another factor in relations between Australia and Papua New Guinea is Australia's aid contribution. The Commonwealth has given assurances that large-scale aid will continue after independence if it is requested.

[*matter omitted*]

If there are to be changes in Australia's aid pattern after independence these need to be considered and agreed to before then. Some of the questions to be answered include: the extent to which financial aid should be fully on a project basis, or whether as now some of it should be devoted to supporting an annual or multi-annual programme of expenditure, whether there should continue to be oversight of project aid, whether Papua New Guinea products will continue to have preferential access to the Australian market, and whether Commonwealth assistance by way of guarantee of Papua New Guinea's international loans and through encouragement of investment will continue. Until such time as Papua New Guinea becomes a full member in its own rights of international bodies which provide assistance to developing countries, such as the IBRD[1] and the IDA,[2] Australia will continue to act as guarantor for Papua New Guinea. This will be the case even for loans entered into now and extended beyond independence.

In my view, it could not be contemplated that the formal termination of Australia's obligations to Papua New Guinea under the UN Charter when Papua New Guinea becomes independent will mean that Papua New Guinea will cease to occupy a somewhat special position in Australian eyes. At the same time the Australian Government has made it clear that it looks to Papua New Guinea to progressively increase its financial self-reliance by raising the level

---

1   International Bank for Reconstruction and Development.

2   International Development Authority, the concessional loan facility of the International Bank for Reconstruction and Development (IBRD). The IBRD and IDA are referred to collectively as the World Bank.

of its domestic revenue. In this connection Australia's aim in Papua New Guinea has been to maintain or increase the pace of economic development so as to increase the country's financial self-reliance and build up its capacity to pay its own way and reduce its dependence on outside aid. We will continue to do this, but despite our best efforts Papua New Guinea is likely to be heavily dependent on foreign aid after independence.

[*matter omitted*]

As present the Australian Government is conducting a comprehensive review of Papua New Guinea defence, including the size and shape of the local defence forces, the nature of the command and defence organisation to be developed, and ways and means of promoting closer contact and understanding between Australia and Papua New Guinean defence authorities.

The Commonwealth will give every assistance to ensure that the establishment of Papua New Guinea Forces is kept at a level suitable to the needs of Papua New Guinea and Australian support in matters of defence will continue. In the meantime, the PIR and the Papua New Guinea Division of the Royal Australian Navy are being steadily prepared, including the necessary personnel, organisational and administrative requirements, to meet the needs of Papua New Guinea.

[*matter omitted*]

It is necessary to distinguish between Australia's relations with Papua New Guinea and Papua New Guinea's own foreign relations. We have to determine our relations with Papua New Guinea with proper regard to Australia's own national interests. We should expect Papua New Guinea to do the same. In particular, we should not expect Papua New Guinea to look to us to decide what her national interests are. Nor as I have said earlier should we expect that Papua New Guinea's national interests will not over the years, as they are better defined and as Papua New Guinean political leaders become more conscious of them, more and more diverge from Australia's. There will undoubtedly be a residual common interest. If mutual respect accompanies it, if we can succeed in avoiding gratuitous insults to Papua New Guinea's nationhood and sovereignty, then that residual common interest will be of great importance.

It will I hope be clear to you that in my view Australia should seek a longer term relationship of a special quality, a relationship between two independent countries which is based on friendliness, informality, mutual respect and understanding and a breadth of contact, not just one confined to diplomatic channels—a relationship which recognises the depth of our common national interests and which will be enriched by the loosening of legal ties.

[NAA: A1838, 3080/10/1 PART 2]

310   REPORT BY MCDONALD

Port Moresby, 8 June 1972

Papua New Guinea: Developments since formation of the National Coalition

As you will be aware from news reports, the pace of constitutional developments here have [sic] begun to snowball since the formation of the National Coalition just prior to the new House of Assembly commencing for the first time in the latter part of April. The actual developments have been pretty much along predictable lines, some encouraging and some disappointing.

The Administration

Perhaps the most notable feature of recent weeks has been the lack of anticipation or preparation for demands for change in the higher levels and much of the middle ranks of the Administration. Few senior officials seemed to realise that the United Party had lost the elections even when all the results were known; few could conceive of any group but the old pidgin speaking nucleus of Abel [sic],[1] Giregire and Bilas reconstituting the Cabinet. Even now, some seem unable to comprehend the realities of the new situation and the desire for a new order. Most do not seem to appreciate that anything is basically amiss with the old order—where salaries take up to three months to be paid and officers of Assistant Secretary rank cannot compose comprehensive English.

Within the sensitive Intelligence and Security bureaucracy (at best a rather clumsy structure of in-fighting expatriates with little idea of their purpose other than notions based on popular fiction) a request by the new Chief Ministers to see their reports caused compounded confusion and distress. It seems that its Administration staff must have never expected to be employing indigenous people above menial levels, and certainly never to be asked to submit their product to indigenous holders of office. It is equally obvious that some of the field officers supplying a mixture of pompous and stuttered reports into the organisation have not realised what changes are taking place. The whole Intelligence and Security organisation is already a subject of deep suspicion outside of the inner Administration circles, and the current uncertainties hanging over it are doing nothing to improve its reputation.

Further afield in the Administration the response has generally not been so obtuse, but some sectors have been caught badly on the outer.

Probably the worst off [are] in the District Administration establishment, where much of the trouble stems from the character and past alliances of its top men.

However the general antipathy of professional and academic people (from Dr Gunther[2] down) towards the 'kiap'[3] system is also contributing. There is a real chance that the existing district administration system will be disbanded, or made totally ineffective, while the local

---

1   The context indicates that the person referred to was not Cecil (later Sir Cecil) Abel, but Tei Abal, MHA for Wabag, 1968–72.

2   J. T. (John) Gunther (later Sir John), Foundation Vice-Chancellor, University of Papua New Guinea, 1966–72. Earlier, Gunther had served as PNG's Director of Public Health (1949–66); as Assistant Administrator (1957–66); as chairman of the select committee which recommended the formation of the first House of Assembly; and as an appointed member of the AEC and senior government member in the House (1964–66).

3   Patrol Officer.

government network and functional organisations are promoted. Irrespective of the mixed quality of many of the present District Commissioners, I would, on the basis of what I have seen of the district administration systems in India and Western and Eastern Malaysia, consider it highly desirable to retain the kiap apparatus as the paramount instrument for economic and social development programmes of the future. The ranks of district officers are, in relative terms, well localised, and are an area of service where retaining expatriates in non-technical positions could be of marked value to the country (unlike the multitude of clerks and clerical assistants holding positions well in excess of what they could obtain in Australia). Morale in the district administration service is low and this could lead to serious breakdowns in administration outside Port Moresby prior to independence and could cause confusion over who is responsible for whom.

Political Parties

It seems that the people who were most surprised by the formation of the National Coalition were the leaders and organisers of the United Party. Suddenly, the former Ministers are nobodies, forced to give up their ministerial houses and cars, no longer pampered and feeling betrayed by the groups which have associated with Pangu. Their initial reactions have largely reflected their shock; but the failure to win over Coalition supporters or to arouse massive protests against 'turncoats' like Kavali (the Leader of the National Party—the Pangu ally in the Highlands) must be beginning to take root throughout the party. Although I have not heard of any deliberate efforts to woo them since April, a number of members of the opposition must be ready to change sides. The United Party's expatriate elements have been notably quiet.

A major threat of regional politics gaining in strength rather than abating nevertheless continues to exist. Anton Parao, the Secretary, had been blatant in referring to the United Party as the party of the Highlanders—thereby ignoring Toliman, who has replaced [Abal] as parliamentary leader—disregarding the important Madang bloc as well as the handful of other parliamentary supporters. Giregire has attempted to play on highlanders' sensitivities.

At the same time, the Gazelle problem is far from resolved, although Somare has moved to bring the different parties to a conference table. (In this he is being helped by Toliman). He has not yet found a breakthrough for the apparent intractable irrationality of Kaputin, Kereku[4] and Tammur.[5]

A number of Papuans are still not happy over the union with New Guinea; and the risk of separateness regenerating in the Solomons[6] has not yet passed completely.

On the other hand, Somare's recent statements about future overseas representation and Papua New Guinea's place in the South Pacific and the reports of the UN Visiting Mission and the Trusteeship Council, have all helped to focus people's attention on their national identity. There can be little doubt that the movement towards independence will add to the forces which could be marshalled to engender national unity, provided dispirited politicians can see beyond widening the gap between the people of the hinterland and those of the coast and islands.

Another encouraging development in this direction was the somewhat sudden emergence of the National Party as a force within the House of Assembly. Only one or two of the eight parliamentary members gave any notification prior to the election of having any affiliation with the party, apart from Thomas Kavali, its leader. It has now been accepted as the Highlands'

---

4   Damien Kereku, MHA for the East New Britain regional electorate.
5   All three men (Kaputin, Kereku and Tammur) were leading figures in the Mataungan Association (MA). For background on the MA, see Document 49, fn. 3.
6   Presumably a reference to Bougainville.

chapter of the progressive movement, but will probably maintain a separate identity in recognition of its supporters' wariness of lowland domination.

The Ministry

In addition, Somare's success in finding places in his Ministry for representatives of three of the four Highlands' districts must be commended and his ability to exclude loyal Pangu members from office in order to do this was a further display of competence.

The most marked weakness of the new Ministry is the possible dissatisfaction of Guise. He is ambitious and although he may be bought off with promises of the Presidency or a well-paid High Commissionership in Canberra in the future, he must see his chance for glory and his desire for personal vindication as fading. He nearly frustrated formation of the Coalition at the last moment by holding out for the leadership; and some of his actions since have rather emphasised his discomfort in the second position. Certainly he looks odd in the company of Somare, Olewale, Kavali and Chan—all about twenty years his junior. He is shrewd and widely respected in Papua, but I think he is too old and lacking in intelligence to represent a real challenge to Somare any more.

I should however sound a word of caution to balance my enthusiasm for Somare. I think he is an able politician and is developing as an astute leader. He has progressive and sensible ideals and has succeeded in placing himself in firm command of his party. Nevertheless he has some weaknesses. He wavers at times. He is over prone to the influence of hangers-on and depends too much on a band of young expatriates for inspiration and company. He is completely lacking in arrogance, somewhat in ruthlessness. (He is no Lee Kuan Yew).[7] But there can be little doubt that he is the best man available for his position at the moment.

Constitutional Development

There are at present still differences within the Coalition over issues such as the timing of self-government and independence. Somare back-tracked on Pangu's platform of immediate self-government to appease the People's Progressive Party and Paulus Arek (who was Chairman of the last Constitutional Committee) but in return obtained agreement to push out a number of senior expatriate officials (notably Ellis). He has since begun to bring the target dates for both self-government and independence forward again in his public statements but has not yet tackled the issue in his Cabinet. He apparently proposes to do so within the next week or so.

While he was in Western Samoa, Somare's personal staff (a group of expatriates, headed by Tony Voutas and Voutas' wife)[8] and a small Constitutional Development Branch have been preparing papers for him to present to the Ministry on the subject of self-government. His staff still see Chan as not yet committed to early constitutional changes, but I doubt that any members of the Coalition Ministry will hold out against self-government next year and independence during 1975. The proposals include a request for the immediate creation of a body to examine and draw up a constitution.

---

7   Lee Kuan Yew, Prime Minister of Singapore, 1959–90.

8   Shelley (Warner) Voutas.

9   Probably John Ley, a former Deputy Solicitor-General who became Counsel to the Speaker and members of the House of Assembly from 1968. See Donald Denoon, *A Trial Separation: Australia and the Decolonisation of Papua New Guinea*, Australian National University, Pandanus Books, Canberra, 2005, pp. 75–77.

10   Assistant Executive Officer, AEC, 1972.

As a first step of an administrative nature, an Office of the Chief Minister is in the process of being created. It will consist of three or four units—a research unit (the Voutas couple, Leahy [sic][9] and some other expatriates), a cabinet secretariat (probably headed by Leo Morgan,[10] a Bougainvillean who was a diplomatic trainee with Foreign Affairs in 1970) the Constitutional Development Branch and possibly a political education section. The Office will be headed by Paul Ryan who at present is in charge of the AEC Secretariat; but the key figure in the group is likely to be 'Tos' Barnett, a lawyer in his mid-thirties who goes to some length to identify himself with indigenous interests.[11] Far too many of the people in the Office will be expatriates, and many of the personal appointees lack administrative experience and in some cases may be wrongly motivated. I think we must expect the inexperience and immaturity to show up at times—and at the same time realise that the outside appointments will free Somare from the set lines of thought which established civil servants would offer him.

[NAA: A1838, 3036/10/6/5 PART 7]

---

11   Thomas E. (Tos) Barnett, formerly a senior lecturer in law at the University of Papua New Guinea, was appointed as a First Assistant Secretary in the PNG Administration in March 1972 to advise on 'a program of legislative and administrative actions relating to self-government and a national constitution'. Ian Downs, *The Australian Trusteeship: Papua New Guinea, 1945–75*, Australian Government Publishing Service, Canberra, 1980, pp. 490–91. Following the formation of Somare's National Coalition Government, Barnett was tasked with advising and reporting directly to Somare, under the oversight of Johnson. Denoon, *Trial Separation*, p. 107.

311   STATEMENT BY FAIRBAIRN[1]

Port Moresby, 15 June 1972

Australia is responsible for the defence of Papua New Guinea and until independence will continue to fulfil this obligation.

[*matter omitted*]

Looking to the future, as Papua New Guinea approaches self-government and independence, we must increasingly shape the further development of the defence force towards post independence needs. Decisions taken now regarding training and accommodation facilities, equipment and so on will all have very long term effects. It is therefore desirable that there should be close consultation with and involvement of Papua New Guinea Ministers' opinion in defence matters. The Administrator's Executive Council will clearly be a focal point of this consultation. I regard these discussions today as a start point of what I hope will be a continuing and growing exchange of views between senior Australian Defence authorities and the Papua New Guinea authorities on Papua New Guinea defence matters.

[*matter omitted*]

For our part we are actively considering what machinery is required, both in Papua New Guinea, and in Canberra, to ensure that views can be sought and exchanged as necessary and that prompt and sufficient account is taken of your views. At the Papua New Guinea end we are studying the possible appointment, should you so desire, of a Defence Spokesman in your House of Assembly. You will of course understand that this cannot be decided in isolation from the talks on a range of subjects concerning additional powers which are to be held with you in the near future by the Minister for External Territories.

[*matter omitted*]

We would see a Defence Spokesman in the Papua New Guinea House of Assembly as fulfilling a most useful and important function. This would include answering Parliamentary Questions and making statements on defence matters, consulting the Administrator and leading discussions in the Administrator's Executive Council in regard to the development of the Papua New Guinea forces, and undertaking ceremonial duties.

Should it be decided to appoint a Defence Spokesman, there would be advantage if he had a small advisory and supporting section available to assist him. To meet this requirement we have in mind the possible establishment within the Department of the Administrator of a small Defence Section.

[*matter omitted*]

Ultimately there will be a need for Papua New Guinea to build up its own defence department organisation, to administer effectively the Defence forces and provide advice to Ministers on policy issues. We would see the nucleus of this Department growing out of the proposed Advisory Defence Section within the Department of the Administrator, together with elements of the Joint Force Headquarters.

[NAA: A452, 1972/4109]

---

1   Fairbairn delivered the statement to the AEC during his visit to PNG from 15–16 June.

312   TELEX TO CANBERRA[1]

Port Moresby, 15 June 1972

11590. UNCLASSIFIED

[*matter omitted*]

Press:

Apart from covering the possibility of Military aid from Aust[ralia] to the Civil Power in PNG, do you see the likelihood of long-term pacts for Aust[ralian] use of Defence Installations in an Independent PNG? Like Manus Island?

Minister:

Yes, I think if we required to maintain Manus as an Australian Naval Base it would need to have the agreement of the Local Government here for that to proceed.

Press:

Do you think it is likely that you would wish to?

Minister:

This is something for the Navy to determine whether, in the light of whatever was happening at the time, whether they needed that base to continue. It has been a very useful refuelling base but it would be an assessment of the Navy at the time whether they desired still to use the facilities.

[*matter omitted*]

[NAA: A452, 1972/1993]

---

1   The telex provided a transcript of a press conference given by Fairbairn in Port Moresby on 15 June.

313   TELEX TO CANBERRA[1]

Port Moresby, 16 June 1972

291. UNCLASSIFIED

Ashton:

Is PNG still important to Australian Defence thinking in view of what the Director of the Institute of Defence and Strategic Studies,[2] Dr Robert O'Neil, had said on 'Contact' in April. Here again is Dr O'Neil:

The old role of New Guinea as a shield in Australia's defence in the missile age now I think is quite unimportant. Of course it does remain of importance to Australia that there be a Government in New Guinea which is friendly to Australia. That permits Australian airlines to overfly New Guinea and permits Australian shipping to fly through New Guinean waters. But once that state of affairs is guaranteed and I see no prospect that it won't be guaranteed, Australia's most substantial defence interest is the Manus Island base and this does facilitate the operations of the Royal Australian Navy in Northern Australian and South East Asian waters tremendously.

Minister:

I think it is correct to say that just from the point of view of a base for Australia or denying a base to the enemy that PNG has lost its importance. On the other hand it is extremely important to us that PNG, our nearest neighbour, should be friendly and should not be taken over by an enemy.

Ashton:

Australian defence thinking then envisages the continuance of an Australian military presence in PNG subject to negotiation with an independent PNG after independence.

Minister:

What we envisage is that as PNG moves towards independence which it is doing and undoubtedly it will become independent in the not too distant future, it will then be in control of its own forces but these forces I would think would obviously need to be supported by Australia and by this I mean we would make available as required and as requested Australian technicians and Australian senior officers who would become part of the PIR or whatever unit they join.

[*matter omitted*]

[NAA: A452, 1972/1993]

---

1   This is an extract from a telexed transcript of an interview of David Fairbairn by Chris Ashton, an Australian Broadcasting Commission (ABC) journalist based in Port Moresby. The interview took place on 15 June.

2   Based at the Australian National University.

314   SUBMISSION FROM HAY TO PEACOCK

Canberra, undated [c. mid-June 1972][1]

CONFIDENTIAL

Papua New Guinea—The Timing and Planning of Self-Government

The Papua New Guinea Chief Minister intends to place before the AEC a submission on the timing and planning of self-government in Papua New Guinea (copy attached).[2]

2.   The Chief Minister proposes to make his submission on Wednesday 21st June for resolution on that date and the Administrator has asked for the Minister's views on the submission before there is a full discussion in the AEC.

3.   The purpose of this submission is to indicate the main proposals in the Chief Minister's submission and to comment on them. This submission recommends that certain parts of these comments be passed to the Administrator for his guidance in the AEC discussion.

The Chief Minister's Submission

4.   The submission covers two matters:

    1.   The timing of self-government;

    2.   The establishment of a constitutional planning committee.

5.   The submission has been discussed with the leaders of the coalition parties and as a result certain modifications have been made. It is proposed that it be discussed with the Leader of the Opposition (Mr Toliman) before submission to the House.

Timing of Self-Government

6.   The submission proposes that self-government come about on 1st December 1973 or as soon as possible thereafter. Originally it was proposed that the date for self government should fall between 1st September 1973 and 31st December 1973 but it is understood that the final proposal was agreed upon as a compromise between the attitudes of the PPP[3] and the MA.[4]

7.   The submission suggests that the interim period to 1st December 1973 will provide sufficient time to:

    (a)   develop a constitution suited to PNG's needs;

    (b)   accelerate political education;

    (c)   allow Ministers to establish their roles;

    and give the coalition two years of self-government before the next elections.

8.   The submission proposes that the date be ratified by the House and offers two alternative methods of approach with respect to timing:

    1.   Chief Minister introduces a motion at the end of the June meeting of the House seeking its approval of the timing. The debate is adjourned until the September meeting and voted on before the conclusion of the September meeting.

---

1   The date of this submission is not clear but its contents suggest it was prepared in the second or third week of June.

2   Not published. See Document 292.

3   People's Progress Party.

4   Mataungan Association (MA).

2.   Chief Minister introduces a motion early in the September meeting seeking approval of the timing. This is adjourned until the latter part of the September meeting and voted on before its conclusion.

It is understood that the latter method will be recommended.

Constitutional Planning Committee

9.   The submission proposes that the AEC appoint a Committee to determine the nature of PNG's constitution.

[*matter omitted*]

14.   The Committee's terms of reference are as follows:

To make recommendations for a constitution for full self-government in Papua New Guinea with a view to eventual independence. Without limiting the power of the committee to make any investigation or recommendation which it deems relevant to this objective, matters to be considered by the committee for possible incorporation into these constitution-related instruments should include the following:

(1)   the system of government; executive legislature and judiciary;

(2)   central–regional–local government relations and district administration;

(3)   relations with Australia;

(4)   defence and external affairs (transitional provision);

(5)   the machinery of government—control, organisation and structure of the public service;

(6)   a Director of Public Prosecutions and the Public Solicitor;

(7)   an ombudsman and tribunals of administrative review;

(8)   protection of minority rights;

(9)   A Bill of Rights;

(10) emergency powers;

(11) citizenship;

(12) procedure for amendment of the Constitution;

(13) judicial review (the power of a court to decide whether or not any action by government or law passed by parliament is in accordance with the constitution).

In addition, the Committee should be asked to consider the mechanism for implementing the constitution, including the possibility of holding a constitutional convention, and to make recommendations.

[*matter omitted*]

Comment

18.   Generally the timing and approach suggested by the submission is responsible and acceptable. The desire to have a constitution which suits the needs of Papua New Guinea accords with Government policy. Apart from the tightness of the timing, the date proposed for self-government is a reasonable one. Whether the Coalition can persuade the House of the reasonableness of its proposals both to time and the establishment of the Committee remains to be seen and this submission recommends that the Administrator point out to the AEC the Australian Government's attitude to the role of the House of Assembly in the constitutional process.

[*matter omitted*]

29. The Committee may be criticised for not getting the views of the people as it only proposes to visit District headquarters and discuss certain topics. This submission recommends that bearing in mind the Commonwealth's policy of looking to the House to represent the wishes of the people and that the UN would need to be satisfied that the proposals had the support of the majority of the people the Administrator be requested to suggest that the Committee tries to ensure as far as possible that Local Government Councils are kept informed of the Committee's work and invited to send representatives to give Council views when the Committee visits Districts. In this way it could be fairly said that the people had been consulted. The method was proved successful when the Select Committee on Constitutional Development of the 2nd House toured Papua New Guinea.

RECOMMENDATION

30. I recommend that you agree that the Administrator be advised that:

(a) In general you agree to the proposed timing for self-government, bearing in mind that some functions may not be able to be transferred by that date, and the constraints of securing amendments to Commonwealth legislature, if these are necessary;

(b) You agree to the proposed Constitutional Planning Committee but suggest that the views of the leader of the opposition as to the UP[5] representatives be accepted if possible and that it looks for an adviser with Melanesian experience and one with practical experience;

(c) You suggest that the Committee bear in mind Commonwealth policy regarding the role of the House of Assembly and the UN attitude in its discussions with the people and that it might look to Local Government Councils to put forward views.[6]

[NAA: A452, 1972/0932]

---

5   United Party.

6   It is not known whether Peacock provided an official ruling, but his subsequent comments and actions suggest that he agreed.

315   CABINET SUBMISSION 728[1]

Canberra, 21 June 1972

CONFIDENTIAL

Aid to Papua New Guinea 1972/73

The purpose of this submission is to seek Commonwealth aid to Papua New Guinea for 1972/73 of $132.5M compared with $120.0M in 1971/72, as follows:

	1971/72 Actual	1972/73 Estimate
	$M	$M
Normal Grant Aid	108.3	126.0
Special Aid	11.7	6.5

(For details see Annexure A to this Submission available from the Cabinet Secretariat.)[2]

Of the special aid of $6.5M, $6M will be paid to the Commonwealth in 1972/73 for the purchase of Commonwealth assets.

Political Considerations

2.   It is the Australian Government's policy to encourage the movement towards self-government in Papua New Guinea. This cannot be achieved unless there is a stable Papua New Guinea Government. I believe that the present coalition can be regarded as such, provided it receives adequate support from the Commonwealth.

3.   I have had several discussions with Papua New Guinean Ministers on aid proposals for 1972/73. Initially the figures presented to me involved aid proposals totalling $136M normal grant aid which meant a total, including special aid, of $142.5M. At the same time the Papua New Guinean Government was reluctant to increase revenue by new measures because it feared that these measures would affect mainly the expatriate sector whose confidence in the new government was regarded as vital. This was quite acceptable and I so informed the Chief Minister.

4.   The Papua New Guinean Government has now decided, as a result of my request, to introduce new revenue measures of $4M and also to reduce expenditure and to reduce their bid for grant aid to $126M.

5.   There can be no doubt that the next few years are going to be most important to the future of Papua New Guinea. It is the time of decision and of actions that set the course of a new society. The coalition Government in Papua New Guinea is in my view a Government with which Australia can work with mutual confidence and respect towards the common goal of a smooth transition through self-government to independence. I consider that the new Government needs special consideration to set it on its course to achieve these objectives in accordance with Commonwealth policies and the aid figure I propose represents the measure of assistance I consider necessary at this critical time of Papua New Guinea's history.

---

1   Submitted by Peacock.

2   Not published.

The Papua New Guinea Economy

6.   Particular difficulties confront Papua New Guinea in preparing its 1972/73 budget. These include:

   (a) extremely depressed export prices for agricultural products;

   (b) rising import prices—largely as a result of Australian and Japanese inflation and currency re-valuation;

   (c) the expectation of no increase in the rate of private investment—quite apart from the decline due to the completion of the Bougainville construction phase;

   (d) the problem of significant and increasing unemployment, particularly among unskilled groups.

Commonwealth Responsibility

7.   The Commonwealth Government has a long standing policy objective of development for Papua New Guinea which will ensure that to the greatest extent practicable that country is able to stand on its own feet in an economic sense by the time it achieves self-government. Specifically in terms of the current development programme the Commonwealth has undertaken to provide increased financial support. There are corresponding obligations which have been accepted by the Papua New Guinea Government.

Papua New Guinea Responsibility

8.   The Papua New Guinean Government is responsible for preparation of a budget which will implement policies agreed upon with the Commonwealth and other policies for which it is fully functionally responsible. It must also progressively increase the degree of financial self-reliance by raising the level of revenue and loan receipts as much as practicable as its own contribution to financing the proposed budget.

Papua New Guinea Estimates

9.   The Papua New Guinea Administrator's Executive Council estimates expenditures at $264.2M in 1972/73 compared with $240.5M (including $11.7M of special loans on the Bougainville project) in 1971/72. The public sector in Papua New Guinea is responsible for a high proportion of national expenditure and is therefore a principal generator of economic activity, employment and taxes. To avoid aggravating the problems caused by conditions in other sectors of the economy I consider there should be a reasonable increase in public expenditure in 1972/73.

10. The functional classification of estimated expenditure 1972/73 shows approximately the same balance between economic development and other expenditure as for 1971/72.

11. Because of the state of the economy the increase in revenue from natural growth is only $4M in 1972/73 compared with about $7M in 1971/72. The AEC has agreed to raise $4M by new revenue measures in 1972/73 even though the political climate for such action is not good.

12. The loan estimate for 1972/73 is $43.1M compared with $35.6M for 1971/72. This is a significant increase in the level of borrowing and I consider that because of the cost of debt servicing the Papua New Guinea Government should not be advised to increase the level still further.

Consideration of the House of Assembly

13.   Commonwealth grants have been provided on the basis that in the event of the House of Assembly (on whose adoption the PNG budget depends) seeking to vary the budget in a way unacceptable to the Government the amount and the arrangements for Australian aid would need to be reviewed (Cabinet Decision No. 417M of 19th July, 1967).[3] It is proposed that this proviso be retained for 1972/73.

Recommendations

14.   I recommend:

    (a)   aid to PNG for 1972/73 amounting to $132.5M for:

	$M
Normal Grant Aid	
Grant-in-Aid	30.0
Development Grant	54.3
Allowances etc. of overseas officers	41.7
	126.0
Special Aid	
Loans	
Purchase of Commonwealth interest in CNGT[4]	3.0
Grants in respect of Commonwealth functions transferred to PNG	
– for purchase of Commonwealth assets	3.0
– for maintenance, operation and administration	.5
	132.5

    (b)   the proviso to Commonwealth aid to the PNG budget (see para 13) to be endorsed.

[NAA: A5908, 728]

---

3   See Stuart Doran (ed.), *Documents on Australian Foreign Policy: Australia and Papua New Guinea, 1966–1969*, Department of Foreign Affairs and Trade, Canberra, 2006, Document 136.

4   Commonwealth New Guinea Timber Limited.

316   PRESS RELEASE

Port Moresby, 21 June 1972

Legal Transfer of Powers to Ministers

The Administrator, Mr L. W. Johnson, said today that he had yesterday signed over to the Ministers of the Papua New Guinea Government a great majority of the powers previously held by himself and by Departmental Heads.

Mr Johnson said that this was the legal transfer of powers that had, in fact, been held by members of the Ministry since its establishment.

He said that he and the Departmental Heads had retained a limited number of powers only.

Mr Johnson said that the Ministers could sub-delegate authority to their Departmental staff to ensure the continuing smooth operation of their Departments.

[NAA: A452, 1971/1169]

317   STATEMENT BY SOMARE[1]

Port Moresby, 23 June 1972

Establishment of a Constitutional Planning Committee

In the past, the House of Assembly has set up Select Committees on Constitutional Development. Much of the attention of these Committees and of the people of our country has been directed towards the timing of self-government.

The Government feels strongly that the issue of the timing of self-government should be completely separated from the planning of a constitution for self-government.

The Government recognises the right of the Members of this House, as representatives of our people, to decide on the date for self-government, and my Government will accept the date so decided.

Whatever date is finally agreed upon, it is important that the fullest consideration be given to the kind of future government we shall have. It is for our people that a constitution will be made. It is our people that will have to live under the system of government that is established. We must therefore ensure that the constitution is suited to the needs and circumstances of Papua New Guinea and is not imposed from outside. In short, it should be a home-grown constitution.

This view has been supported by the Minister for External Territories, Mr Peacock, when he said on 7th April, 1972:

> 'It is the policy of the Australian Government that the choice of the system of government to be ultimately adopted in Papua New Guinea is one for the people of that country.'

To meet this objective my Government proposes to establish a Constitutional Planning Committee made up of members of the House of Assembly, representatives of the various regions of the country, and of political parties and groups in the House.

The basic reason for this Committee being established by the Government instead of being a Select Committee of the House, is to allow the Committee maximum flexibility. The Committee will be able to consult progressively with the Commonwealth Government and with the Administrator's Executive Council which will *not* have regular representatives on the Committee. Under this arrangement, the Committee may submit draft sections of its report to the Administrator's Executive Council and to the Commonwealth for comment. Upon receipt of any comment, the Committee may or may not wish to reconsider some of its proposals before making its final report. In addition, the Committee would in no way be restricted in seeking public reaction to sections of its draft proposals before completion of its final report.

My Government will table the Committee's final report in the House of Assembly for its consideration. My Government also undertakes to accept whatever decisions are reached by this House on the final report.

COMPOSITION OF THE COMMITTEE

Although Ministers will be keenly interested in the work of this Committee, they will not have sufficient time to attend Committee meetings regularly, with the exceptions referred to in the next paragraph, [and] it is therefore intended that Ministers do not become members of the Committee.

---

1   The statement was delivered in the PNG House of Assembly.

It is proposed that I, as Chief Minister, be Chairman of the Committee *ex officio*, and that the chairmen of the two previous Select Committees on Constitutional Development be included as members in recognition of the value of their experience. However, our Ministerial duties will mean that we can only attend from time to time.

The position of Deputy Chairman of the Committee will be virtually a full-time job between meetings of the House. The Government intends to nominate the Chairman of Committees of this House, Father John Momis, for this position.

All appointments to the Committee will be made by His Honour the Administrator, on my recommendation as Chief Minister, after full consideration with the leaders of the parties and groups represented in this House.

The following composition is proposed:

Chairman *ex officio*	Mr Michael Somare
Previous Chairmen of Select Committees	Dr John Guise and Mr Paulus Arek
Pangu Pati	Three members, including Father Momis (Deputy Chairman)
People's Progress Party	One member
National Party	One member
Mataungan Association	One member
United Party	Five members
Independents	One member.

TERMS OF REFERENCE

The terms of reference of the Committee [will] be:

'To make recommendations for a constitution for full internal self-government in a united Papua New Guinea with a view to eventual independence. Without limiting the power of the Committee to make any investigation or recommendation which it deems relevant to this objective, matters to be considered by the Committee for possible incorporation into the constitution or related documents should include the following:

(a) the system of government; executive, legislature and judiciary;

(b) central–regional–local government relations and district administration;

(c) relations with Australia;

(d) defence and external affairs (transitional provisions);

(e) the machinery of government; control, organisation and structure of the public service;

(f) a Director of Public Prosecutions and the Public Solicitor;

(g) an Ombudsman and tribunals of administrative review;

(h) protection of minority rights;

(i) a Bill of Rights;

(j) emergency powers;

(k) citizenship;

(l) procedure for amendment of the constitution;

(m) judicial review (the power of a court to decide whether or not any action by the government or law passed by Parliament is in accordance with the constitution).

'In addition the Committee should be asked to consider the mechanism for implementing the constitution, including the possibility of holding a Constitutional Convention and to make recommendations.'

[*matter omitted*][2]

[NAA: A452, 1972/3878]

318   STATEMENT BY SOMARE

Port Moresby, 27 June 1972

I wish to refer to the important question of the timetable for self-government. On what date should our country achieve self-government? My Government realises that this is an important issue and that the people themselves must be consulted. For this reason, Sir, we have no intention of rushing our decision. In August I will be having talks in Port Moresby with the Minister for External Territories and the question of the date for self-government will be discussed then. It is my intention to invite the Leader of the Opposition to participate in those talks.

Meanwhile I ask all members of this House to consult with the people of their electorates because when the House reconvenes in September it is my intention to seek approval of a date for self-government. Whatever date this House approves will be given to the Constitutional Planning Committee as its target date. The target date is essential to enable detailed plans to be drawn up and implemented.

Sir, the view of my Government is that self-government should not occur before December 1, 1973, but that it should come as soon as possible after that. I emphasise that is the view of the National Coalition Government—but we will respect the decision of this House when it sits in September this year.

[*PNG Parliamentary Debates*, Third House, III, 4, Port Moresby, 27 June 1972, p. 386.]

---

2   The omitted material set out the staffing and administrative arrangements for the committee, and noted it would invite submissions and consult and travel widely.

319   LETTER FROM PEACOCK TO FAIRBAIRN

Canberra, 3 July 1972

SECRET

I wrote to you on 17 May 1972[1] regarding the question of the appointment of a Defence Spokesman in Papua New Guinea. I stated that while I had not at that time studied the report prepared by our Departments on arrangements for associating PNG authorities with defence matters, I agreed in principle with the particular recommendation that such an appointment be made.

I have now had the opportunity to examine the report of the study group, which recommended that there be:

 — continuing consultations with the Administrator's Executive Council on defence matters;
 — the appointment of a Defence Spokesman;
 — the establishment of a small Defence Section in the Department of the Administrator; and
 — further study on the question of the establishment, composition and functions of a PNG Advisory Committee on Defence.

I now advise that I agree with the recommendations made in the report. I assume, having seen the text of your statement to the AEC[2] in Port Moresby—opening discussions which were themselves the first of those envisaged by the study group—that you will have no difficulty in agreeing with the suggestions. However, I would be grateful for your confirmation of this.

I propose to visit Papua New Guinea in the first week of August to undertake discussions with the Chief Minister and his colleagues regarding further progress towards self-government. As to the defence aspects in this movement I would seek to reach agreement, based on the recommendations set out in the study groups report, with the Ministers on the appointment of a Defence Spokesman and the establishment of a Defence Section in the Department of the Administrator. If such agreement is obtained I would not expect to refer the matter back to you before formally signifying the Government's agreement to such arrangements. Your responses to press enquiries in Port Moresby were consistent with this approach but again I would like confirmation of your viewpoint before I commence these discussions.

[NAA A452, 1972/448]

1   Document 293.
2   See Document 311.

320   SPEECH BY PEACOCK[1]

Melbourne, 4 July 1972

Independence—Papua New Guinea Style

The title of my address today implies an exercise in prophecy—always a dangerous exercise in the field of politics. The development of society has a way of bringing surprises to even the most imaginative and far-seeing of those foolhardy enough to forecast the future. We can see now the forces and factors which made the United States the economic and technological power it is today, but who at the end of the eighteenth century could possibly have foreseen such a future for the rural communities, on the frontier of civilisation, which had just won their independence and formed the new republic?

At the same time Australia's close association with Papua New Guinea over most of this century and the forthright expression of opinion by Papua New Guinea leaders themselves does enable something to be said about the sort of independence which Papua New Guinea will experience and I can say something about the process leading up to that period.

Papua New Guinea will soon be fully and effectively self-governing. Indeed it is virtually that now. The achievement of this status by the people of Papua New Guinea will be the culmination of a steady process of development in which each step has been brought about by cooperation and, in later years, mutual agreement.

Originally the impulse for development inevitably had to come from Australia, the administering authority. Over the last ten years however, the initiative for constitutional change has come from committees of the country's own legislature. Before formulating their proposals, these committees conducted extensive surveys of public opinion through meetings in every part of Papua New Guinea. The Commonwealth has accepted, and put into effect, those suggestions endorsed by the legislature, with little if any, modification.

Today Papua New Guinea Ministers are responsible for final decision in many areas of the Government of Papua New Guinea. Less than two years ago some people in many areas of the country believed that self-government and independence were at least two generations away. Yet last week the Chief Minister, Mr Somare, gave the Pangu Pati's view on the timing of self-government which he saw as no earlier than 1st December 1973, but as soon as possible thereafter. I will be having discussions on this question with Papua New Guinea leaders in Port Moresby at the end of this month. We will be discussing then the sequence and timing of the handover of the various powers that Australia still retains. The Commonwealth has already indicated that it welcomes an indication from the PNG Government on the timing of self-government and that it stands ready to act on that indication.

This is all part of the process of a gradual independence—gradual not in the sense that it is necessarily slow, but that it is smooth and not a sudden break from one status and set of responsibilities to another. Papua New Guinea independence when it comes will, as a result, signify that the last step in a long process has been taken and not that a whole series of changes have occurred overnight.

In this way we believe that the actual movement towards independence will contribute greatly to the post-independence period by establishing a government that is practised in governing and can call upon the resources, human and otherwise, that are a necessary part of an orderly and developing nation.

---

1   The speech was delivered to the Australian-American Association.

What shape will an independent Papua New Guinea take? On a general level, it can be expected an independent Papua New Guinea will continue to bear the imprint of the formative Australian influence. This is simply the obvious fact that Papua New Guinea will be a different country in many ways from what it might have been if governed by, say, France, the United Kingdom or the United States. But it is inevitable, and therefore predictable, that the people of Papua New Guinea will make their own society, in their own way and will develop and assert their own distinctive identity.

Pride in the diversified traditions of the country is already being asserted. The evolution of attitudes in this area has been rapid—from the initial shocks and disorientation on contact with Europeans through unquestioning acceptance of Western influences to a determination to maintain continuity with their own past while respecting the many advantages introduced by the foreign civilisation.

In all parts of Papua New Guinea I have found a realisation of the need for a distinctively Papua New Guinean approach to the questions and problems posed by the changes taking place in the traditional societies. This is an eminently sensible approach on their part. From widely separated parts of the country there are calls to preserve and encourage tradition in the schools and concern that the education system be oriented towards producing people both aware of their own culture and capable of making a worthwhile contribution to Papua New Guinea.

This process of change is national development in the widest sense of the term; it is being carried out with energy and understanding, not on any negative basis of removing Australians or the Australian way of life, but in the positive approach of producing the nation of Papua New Guinea. It is not a process that is being whipped along on some tide of xenophobic fervour as has happened in other countries in similar situation, and I cite in support of this the statement of the Papua New Guinea government that they were not so much concerned with the timing of self-government as the type of self-government best suited to Papua New Guinea.

An example of the Papua New Guinea approach to a problem is the law enforcement and court system which has hitherto been an imposition of essentially Australian concepts and practice. With the decline in the role of the District Officer with judicial powers there has been a vacuum in law enforcement at village level. This need to resolve local disputes in a way acceptable to villagers has led now to a review of the courts system to deal with those matters where more elaborate machinery is just not needed. The aim of the review is to find a simple workable system at village level that will recognise and resolve the tenets of village custom and the law of the government.

This need for a distinctly Papua New Guinea approach is also reflected in the attitude of Papua New Guinea leaders to foreign investment. There is a very real and widespread recognition of the importance of foreign investment so that the country may realise its economic potential and establish its financial self-reliance. At the same time many political leaders are beginning to call for greater local effort to provide an ever increasing share of the capital required to meet the aspirations of the people and to satisfy the widespread desire for the development of local commerce and industry.

While the need for foreign investment is widely appreciated, there is no attitude of indiscriminate welcome, but concern as to its nature and direction. The type of investment and company policy which will maximise the benefits to Papua New Guinea is naturally encouraged.

From this it can be expected that while an independent Papua New Guinea will actively seek overseas investment, it will be guided by hard-headed calculations of its own interests, and will bargain for maximum advantage with ability and skill and be prepared to shop around until it gets the best deal possible. There have already been indications that, in this and related economic matters, an independent Papua New Guinea will be influenced neither by ties of sentiment nor by self-conscious feelings of inadequacy. I mean by this latter point that I expect there to be less of the phenomenon familiar in recent times of some newly independent countries dramatising their freedom by deliberately preferring less advantageous contracts and arrangements with third parties than those offered by the former administering power or by its agencies and firms.

Discussing Papua New Guinea's future economic relations at a recent seminar, Mr Somare, the Chief Minister, expressed his view that:

> 'There is no doubt that after independence we will continue to trade with Australia, but we will certainly look around us for the best offers. Australia is geographically close to us and should be able to compete very strongly with our other neighbours because of this ... Australia will be just one of our trading partners ... Papua New Guinea must not allow any country to retain a stranglehold on its future trade relations.'

In the sphere of foreign relations, less can be said with any degree of certainty simply because there is less factual evidence to go on. For example, except in relation to the United Nations, only occasionally have matters involving foreign relations arisen as issues. It is the transfer of these areas of responsibility to Papua New Guinea, however, which will form part of the act of formal independence for that country as a sovereign nation.

But in the area of foreign relations Australia is following its policy in all areas of residual powers of ensuring as far as possible that no decision affecting Papua New Guinea is taken without full consultation with its government. Australia hopes to arrive, in this way, at a situation prior to independence where, because of the progressive involvement of Papua New Guinea leaders in the whole range of government activities and responsibilities, there is no sphere in which the newly independent country will find itself unfamiliar and lacking experience.

I doubt if many people would question that Australia and an independent Papua New Guinea will have a mutual interest in maintaining what is a unique and special relationship. The government has announced Australia's intention to continue to aid an independent Papua New Guinea for the foreseeable future, both financially and by the provision of experts and training, if this is requested by Papua New Guinea.

Factors of geography alone have dictated that our two countries are too important each to the other to ignore the historical links that have been forged in the course of our Administration of Papua New Guinea. Papua New Guinea will be our closest foreign neighbour; we will be her closest source of aid and expertise.

Until the recent past Papua New Guinea has been, except for coastal areas, free from outside contacts and influence. Ethnically however, the country is related to, and during more recent years has been historically oriented towards, the islanders in the adjoining areas of the Pacific.

There must however be increasing interest in developments in South-East Asia—to an extent even greater than Australia's—in that to the west of Papua New Guinea and sharing a common land border is part of the largest of the countries of that region. For this if for no other reason, relations with Indonesia will inevitably occupy a special place for Papua New Guinea.

Another country with a role to play in Papua New Guinea's future is Japan, which has shown a ready recognition of the vast economic potential of the country coupled with a willingness to invest in new projects. Japan's need for natural resources of various sorts and Papua New Guinea's supply of them must mean a degree of cooperation between the two countries that may well grow to be considerable. There is no reason why Papua New Guinea could not have a similar relationship with other developed nations of the world in North America or Europe for instance.

I have mentioned a number of areas as examples of the special character Papua New Guinea is injecting into its approach to self-government and independence. Independence Papua New Guinea style must mean that the social structures and institutions, indeed the whole direction of that developing society, should bear the stamp of the Papua New Guinea people. Independence Papua New Guinea style is coming gradually, smoothly and with a great deal of goodwill on both sides. With this goodwill and our residue of common interests I am confident that the excesses of nationalism and bitterness will be avoided and that when the final seal is set on this process of independence, Papua New Guinea will be ready to govern itself and govern itself capably.

[NAA: A1838, 3080/11/1/2 PART 1]

321   LETTER FROM WHITELAW TO GUTMAN

Canberra, 5 July 1972

CONFIDENTIAL

Future Currency Arrangements for Papua New Guinea

I refer to your memorandum of 19 May 1972 on this subject and the draft Cabinet Submission attached thereto.[1]

2.   We have taken the opportunity to solicit the views of the Reserve Bank on this question since it obviously impinges on the responsibilities and present functions of the Bank. You may be interested to know that, in reply, the Reserve Bank made the following main points:

(a)   The Bank sees no insuperable *technical* difficulties in Papua New Guinea continuing to use Australian currency after independence, if the authorities so desire, although the Bank recognises that when one country uses the currency of another country, administrative complications (if not policy frictions) can (and frequently do) arise from time to time between the two governments concerned and/or their respective central monetary authorities in the fields of exchange control and monetary policy.

(b)   The Bank shares the view that if Papua New Guinea is likely to wish to introduce its own currency within the next five years then the sooner it decides to do so the better, given the unavoidable delays (of up to two years) involved in the manufacture of new notes and coin, and the many other problems with which the local authorities in Papua New Guinea will perforce have to wrestle at the time of full internal self-government, much less independence.

(c)   If such a decision were taken, the Bank would be prepared to offer its services to the authorities in Papua New Guinea to help with the design and production (either in Australia or overseas) of the new notes and coins required.

3.   We for our part would not take issue with the above comments by the Reserve Bank although we would qualify (a) by saying that, while the Treasury would probably not object if Papua New Guinea wished to continue to use Australian currency for a time after it becomes independent—provided, of course, the Papua New Guinea authorities were prepared to accept the limitations on their freedom of action in certain fields of economic policy making that this would necessarily entail—we find it difficult to conceive that the Commonwealth Government would agree to such an arrangement continuing indefinitely into the future.

---

1   Not published. See Document 302.

4.   As to the draft Cabinet Submission on this subject which your Department has prepared, there is much in it with which we can fairly readily agree and would support. However, we consider that it goes too far in a number of places, with the result that we could not recommend to the Treasurer that he agrees to co-sponsor a Submission to Cabinet along the lines of your draft at the present juncture.

5.   We recognise that your own Minister must be able to respond in a meaningful way if the indigenous leaders of the new government in Papua New Guinea should raise the question of currency with him during the proposed Ministerial discussions next month—as we have been given to understand by you that they most certainly will. However, as already explained to you, we believe that sufficient authority for your Minister to do so already exists in the form of the correspondence on this subject between the Treasurer and the previous Minister for External Territories—see in particular paragraph 2 of the Treasurer's letter of 19 January 1972.

6.   Apart from the general consideration—to which we in the Treasury continue to attach some importance—that the Commonwealth ought not to press, or appear to press, the indigenous leaders in Papua New Guinea at the present time to decide to introduce a separate currency any earlier than they might otherwise feel inclined to do themselves, there are a number of practical issues that we would wish to examine carefully in regard to such questions as what, if any, formal backing we should provide for a separate currency in Papua New Guinea and for how long, etc., before we could agree to the Commonwealth taking any initiative in this field.

7.   On the assumption that, notwithstanding the above comments, you may still wish to refer this matter to Cabinet for consideration before the forthcoming Ministerial discussions with leaders of the new government in Papua New Guinea, we have modified your draft Submission in a manner that would make it acceptable to us.

8.   If this re-draft should meet with your approval, we would have no objections to the substance of it being cleared with other members of the newly established high level inter-departmental coordinating committee on Papua New Guinea. In that event, however, I would emphasise that we have not yet cleared this revised text with the Treasurer and that it must accordingly remain subject to amendment, if necessary.

9.   I look forward to receiving your further comments on this matter.

[NAA: A452, 1972/3607]

322   MINUTE BY DET[1]

Canberra, 7 July 1972

Secret

Mr Somare's Statement on Internal Security Powers

The media have reported Mr Somare's press conference in Port Moresby on 29 June, where he is said to have stated:

'I envisage that the responsibility of internal security will be handed over at self-government and not at independence.'

2.   The Minister's comments on this statement were sought by journalists in Port Moresby last week. The Minister was noncommittal, saying that he had always anticipated this to be an item for discussion.

3.   The question of timing and extent of the transfer of responsibility for internal security has, as you know, been examined by the Interdepartmental Committee [IDC] set up by Cabinet Decision 452.[2] In studying the matter, the Committee acknowledged the Administrator's view that the leadership will accept, in the first instance, the appointment of a spokesman as an interim measure, and felt that demands for some positive authority would arise within 12 months i.e. by late 1973.

4.   The IDC, whose report must, of course, pass through a number of stages of consideration before it is accepted, envisages that the Government might agree to delegate actual authority over the police to the Deputy Chairman or other Minister. The Committee further envisages that the Department of the Administrator, which includes internal security functions such as DDA[3] and the Division of Intelligence and Security (including the Internal Security structure) might be transferred at or around the same time, but in any case a little before self-government. *Important factors in these recommendations are that the delegation is to be revocable, and that the Administrator retains the right to address the AEC on internal security matters.*

5.   The Committee envisages that at internal self-government, the Commonwealth Act conferring internal self-government, should reserve responsibility for internal security measures *to the Administrator*. The Administrator would as before (and if the IDC Report is approved) delegate his powers to a Minister but, as before, the delegation would be revocable. The Administrator would, moreover, retain the right of access to the AEC and the ISC[4] on internal security matters as well as to refuse assent to Bills on internal security matters.

6.   The Committee's recommendations do not, therefore, appear to be inconsistent with the publicly stated (though admittedly in general and sketchy terms) aims of the Chief Minister. There is no indication in any statements of his views on whether any delegation of authority and power might or might not be revocable.

[NAA: A452, 1972/1079]

---

1   Author not identified.

2   Document 53.

3   Department of District Administration.

4   Internal Security Committee.

323   CABINET SUBMISSION 727[1]

Canberra, undated [c. 10 July 1972]

<small>CONFIDENTIAL</small>

Banking in Papua New Guinea

Purpose

The purpose of this Submission is to seek Cabinet endorsement of recommendations on future arrangements for banking in Papua New Guinea, contained in the Interim Report of the Interdepartmental Committee on Banking in Papua New Guinea. This paper is available as Annex 'A' from the Cabinet Office.[2]

Background

The Committee on Banking was set up by the Minister for External Territories and the Treasurer in September 1971 to examine and advise on the development of the banking system in Papua New Guinea preparatory to self-government and eventual independence.[3] The Committee includes representatives from the Department of External Territories, the Treasury, the Reserve Bank of Australia and the Papua New Guinea Administration.

The decision to set up such a Committee followed the presentation in March 1971 of the Papua New Guinea Select Committee on Constitutional Development which recommended that the development of Papua New Guinea should be geared to preparing the country for internal self-government during the life of the new House of Assembly (i.e. during the period 1972/76).

We considered that banking should be regarded as one of the areas in which appropriate arrangements should be developed by the time of self-government.

The Committee's terms of reference are as follows:

• 'to set out and advise on the major elements of a framework appropriate to banking in Papua New Guinea at the stage of self-government and at the stage of independence giving special attention to the part which Australian, overseas and Papua New Guinea institutions should play in this system;
• 'to consider and make recommendations as to the lines along which the Papua New Guinea banking system should be developed over the next few years;
• 'to consider and make recommendations on the nature and the timing of the various steps for setting up of an appropriate banking system in Papua New Guinea, taking account for that purpose of any legislative changes that may be needed in Papua New Guinea and in Australia.'

Interim Report

The Committee's Report covers its investigations to date and recommends the acceptance of certain principles on which the Committee has already reached agreement.

The Committee considers that the present situation in which banking in Papua New Guinea is under the control of Australian authorities would not be compatible with self-government, much less with independence. It suggests that the control of banking should be passed over to

---

1   Submitted by Snedden and Peacock.
2   Not published.
3   Document 218.

Papua New Guinea authorities not later than the date on which it achieves [self-]government, and preferably earlier. This would enable the Papua New Guinea authorities to gain experience in the operation of the new powers under the guidance of the Australian authorities.

The timing of the actual transfer of banking powers would depend largely on the establishment of the necessary legal and administrative machinery to enable them to be accepted. Legislation would be required to exclude Papua New Guinea from the operation of the relevant Commonwealth legislation, in particular the Reserve Bank Act and the Banking Act; and appropriate local legislation would need to be enacted in Papua New Guinea.

The Committee while recognising some shortcomings in the range of existing facilities considers that there is a sufficient range of banks and other financial institutions operating in Papua New Guinea to provide the foundations for a separate banking system.

The Committee recommends the establishment of a separate Papua New Guinea central bank based on the Port Moresby office of the Reserve Bank and adapted to local needs, which would be responsible for the administration of banking controls and bank supervision. The Committee is examining further the question of the central bank's functions embracing some controls of non-bank financial institutions.

The Committee also recommends that the Papua New Guinea business of the Commonwealth Banking Corporation should be transferred to some form of Papua New Guinea ownership. The Committee considers that for the Corporation to continue operating in Papua New Guinea in its present form could well be unacceptable on political grounds and would, in any case, conflict with the principle that Papua New Guinea should have a separate banking system under its own control. The Committee proposes to consider further the timing of the transfer and the precise form of future ownership of the Corporation.

Although the Committee's investigations have not yet been completed it sees advantages in early decisions being taken in respect of the broad proposals referred to above so that its investigations can proceed on matters of detail in the knowledge that its general approach is acceptable to Government.

We endorse the Committee's conclusions and the specific recommendations contained in the Interim Report. If Cabinet accepts these recommendations it is proposed to refer the Committee's report to the Administrator's Executive Council and seek Council's concurrence to the recommendations so that the necessary follow-up action could be set in train as soon as possible.

Currency

The question of a separate currency for PNG was not included in the Banking Committee's terms of reference, but has been under examination by a separate working group of officers of the Department of External Territories, the Treasury and the Reserve Bank. Recent changes in the Papua New Guinea leadership group have made it more likely that self-government will come at a somewhat earlier stage than had been assumed at the time the present programme for gearing-up was formulated. The Administration of Papua New Guinea has strongly put the view that the gearing-up programme on currency matters should be progressed in such a way that substantial powers in this field can be handed over, if desirable, at the time of self-government. This matter may well be raised by the Papua New Guinea leadership group in their discussion with the Minister for External Territories which are now scheduled to take place in August. It is therefore proposed at an early date to submit a separate paper on the question of Papua New Guinea currency.[4]

---

4   See Document 321.

RECOMMENDATION

It is recommended that:

(1) Cabinet endorse the following specific recommendations contained in the Banking Committee's Interim Report:

(a) that responsibility for control of banking in Papua New Guinea be passed to Papua New Guinea as soon as this is practicable;

(b) that a central bank be established in Papua New Guinea on the basis of the Port Moresby office of the Reserve Bank of Australia with full powers to act as a central monetary authority for a separate banking system; and

(c) that the business of the Commonwealth Banking Corporation in Papua New Guinea be transferred to some form of Papua New Guinea ownership; the timing of the transfer and the precise form of future ownership (and the question of whether and to what extent the Corporation should continue to maintain a presence in Papua New Guinea) to be a matter for consideration in the light of the Committee's deliberations on the appropriate form of overall financial structure.

(2) The Minister for External Territories be authorised to seek the concurrence of the Administrator's Executive Council to the above recommendations.[5]

[NAA: A5908, 727]

---

5   Cabinet endorsed all four recommendations. See Cabinet Decision 1055, 'Banking in Papua New Guinea', 10 July 1972, NAA: A5908, 727.

324   NOTE BY DET

Canberra, 10 July 1972

Transfer of Migration Policy

•   Present position is that Minister for Trade and Industry is responsible for 'entry or deportation (except cases involving security considerations) under the Migration Ordinance and within the framework of approved government policy'.

•   This has been a sensitive area in the past. Controversy over entry of Indian academics reached the point where it became the subject of an urgency debate in the House of Representatives.

•   Present formula has worked well but we cannot escape the fact that Minister is still responsible for immigration policy. He could become involved in further controversy if anyone wanted to debate the question of policy rather than an individual case.

•   PNG Minister has always acted responsibly in considering individual cases and has never sought to adopt questionable practices (e.g. refusing entry on purely political grounds), even though it would be difficult to prevent him if he chose to do so.

•   Practice has been to consult Administrator's Executive Council on all policy issues and it seems unlikely that Minister would overrule them.

•   Latest policy amendments (yet to be approved by AEC) are designed to remove differences in *administrative* arrangements for entry and stay of non-Europeans and Europeans. Discrimination against entry of non-Europeans remains. Policy has been to maintain racial composition until self-governing PNG can determine its own policies. This policy is likely to be blurred in future by:

    —   Selective Entry for Employment which provides for prohibition or restriction of people seeking employment in certain categories, regardless of race;
    —   engagement of Filipinos and other non-Europeans in hard to fill categories.

•   Seems appropriate time to give PNG full control over immigration policy.

•   Study of British practice has shown that it was their practice to hand over immigration before or at self-government—i.e. they did not treat it as part of external affairs function.

•   Only doubt about handing over immigration policy immediately is number of amendments and reforms that are still in the pipeline. These include abolition of exit permits and creation of 'declaration as to status' documents, establishment of a Commonwealth Immigration Office in Port Moresby, amendment of policy to place all future immigrants on temporary entry permits indefinitely, issue of two-year extensions to permits irrespective of race, revision of Consular Instructions and the final steps necessary on the immigration side to implement Selective Entry for Employment. There could possibly be a case for delaying handing over responsibility for policy until these projects are further advanced.

•   On balance however, it is considered that migration policy should be transferred to local control immediately. This would remove Minister and Department from area [is necessarily for PNG itself to decide].[1]

•   Security aspect will be the subject of separate consideration. If this aspect is to continue to be reserved, some form of words would need to be devised to limit the immigration function accordingly.

---

1   Inserted by hand.

•   Department would still be available to assist PNG authorities. In view of good relations between officers concerned, it is expected that such assistance would be welcomed by PNG authorities.

[NAA: A452, 1970/3202]

325   MINUTE FROM ANDERSON TO WALLER

Canberra, 11 July 1972

SECRET

PNG: Border Crossers

We have been disturbed by the continuing lack of consultation by the PNG Administration with us on questions affecting Australian relations with Indonesia.

2.   In January Mr Shann wrote to Mr Hay bringing this to his attention and a reply was received from Mr Hay saying that he would remind officers of the importance of these matters within the framework of Australian–PNG–Indonesian relations. Since then there has been no improvement, and as the situation with the rebels on the Indonesian side of the border has deteriorated we can foresee the possibility of major difficulties arising with the Indonesians. [The Administration's practice of giving medical treatment to known rebels, and then allowing them to return freely to their bases, is a cause for particular concern.][1]

3.   I have therefore had this letter to Mr Hay drafted for your signature, if you agree. The main purpose of the letter is to recommend that a meeting take place as soon as possible between the Department of Foreign Affairs and the Department of External Territories at First Assistant Secretary level to consider ways and means of improving consultations on these matters.[2]

[*matter omitted*]

Attachment
Letter from Waller to Hay

As you know, my Department has for some time been concerned with the manner in which the Administration of Papua New Guinea has dealt with matters affecting our relations with Indonesia.

Mr Shann wrote to you on 7 January 1972[3] about the case of Amos Indey and Stevanus Maury, in which we were disturbed by inadequacies in the Administration's reporting and consultation and concerned that actions taken by Administration officials could give rise to problems in Australian–Indonesian relations. In your reply of 12 January 1972,[4] you said that you shared our concern at anything that might tend to affect relations with Indonesia on West Irian border matters. You said that you would ask the Administration to remind the officers concerned with these matters of their importance in the total framework of Australian, Papua New Guinean

---

1   This sentence was added inserted by hand.

2   On 11 July 1972 Waller annotated this minute: 'This record is quite dreadful. We must press on.'

3   Not published.

4   Not published.

and Indonesian relations, and that you had sought a full report on the particular case of Indey and Maury.

We have not been informed of the outcome of your request for a full report from the Administration on these men. We have, however, learnt that Indey and Maury, and Maury's brother who accompanied them, are with the rebels at their mobile headquarters [known as] Markas Victoria. The case has received press publicity in the Netherlands, and this led our officers to seek further information from your Department on 9 May. No reply has been received to date. The Foreign Minister expressed his continuing interest in this case once again on 26 May.

My Department has experienced continuing difficulty in its attempts to obtain information and to maintain effective consultation with the Administration, via your Department, on matters of this kind.

One case in point is that of Wellyp,[5] a young member of the rebel band, who crossed into PNG on 22 January 1972 with a letter from a rebel leader asking that he be given medical treatment. We were informed on 6 March that the Administration proposed to give him the medical treatment he required and return him to West Irian thereafter. We replied on 16 March[6] that this raised a basic point of policy, namely that for the Administration to give food, shelter and medical treatment to rebels and to allow them to return to the fray in West Irian would constitute material aid to the rebels. In the particular case of Wellyp we suggested that he should not be allowed to go back freely to the rebels; if he did not apply for permissive residence, he should be formally handed over to Indonesian authorities. After receiving contradictory reports from the Administration on 2 and 4 May, we were finally informed that Wellyp had been returned to West Irian. On 27 June we were informed that he had been taken on 28 April to a point within half a mile of the border and there allowed to go free. Our understanding is that this was contrary to your Department's wishes as conveyed to the Administration.

The Government's interest in these matters has also increased since our exchange of letters concerning the Indey/Maury case. Cabinet Decision No. 980 (PNG) of 18 May, on Papua New Guinea's programme of movement towards internal Self-Government, draws attention to the need for sensitive and careful handling, in close connection with the Minister for Foreign Affairs, of relations with Indonesia, particularly in matters relating to Papua New Guinea's border with Indonesia.[7] During the Prime Minister's visit to Indonesia, he and President Soeharto made special mention of their desire to resolve potential sources of friction in these matters.[8]

A number of problems requiring urgent decision have been raised by the recent outbreak of fighting between the rebels and Indonesian forces in West Irian near the border. As you know, the Indonesians believe that the rebels have made use of Papua New Guinea in support of their activities.

I therefore propose that a meeting be held as soon as possible between our two Departments at First Assistant Secretary level (assisted by the officers directly concerned in these matters)

---

5   Andreas Wellyp

6   Not published.

7   Document 296, para 2(e).

8   During their conversation, McMahon mentioned 'developments in Papua New Guinea, with the associated problems of the land and sea frontiers with West Irian'. After emphasising 'the importance of examining the long term relationships between the two countries with a view to avoiding potential disagreements', McMahon promised to take the matter up with Bowen after returning to Australia. Extract of Discussion between McMahon and Soeharto, 6 June 1972, NAA: A1838, 3036/10/6/5 PART 1.

to consider ways and means of improving consultations between us on these matters and to examine some of the immediate practical questions we now face.

The following is a list of subjects that might be discussed. Some explanatory comment on these is contained in the attachment to this letter.[9]

1. Improved consultation in general
2. Coordination of Public Statements
3. Preventing the rebels from using PNG in support of their activities
4. What to do with rebels found on our side of the border
5. Internment of rebels
6. Procedures for return to West Irian
7. Treatment of captured rebels
8. Intelligence exchanges
9. Attitudes in PNG

[NAA: A1838, 3036/10/6/5 PART 1]

---

9   The final version of this letter has not been located, but it appears that the meeting it proposed went ahead (Document 330). The attachment is not published.

326   LETTER FROM GUTMAN TO HEINRICH[1]

Canberra, 14 July 1972

Future Currency Arrangements for Papua New Guinea

Further to your memorandum 71/5881 of 5 July[2] it seems we are not now far apart in our views and should be able to reach calm agreement on a Submission to put before Ministers. There are three points we would wish to see revised in your draft submission:

(a)   We are unable to agree that the initiative in this matter must remain entirely with the leadership group in Papua New Guinea. As we have explained this is contrary to the general approach which our Minister has taken to the question of self-government and indeed to the Government's general approach of actively preparing Papua New Guinea for self-government. We could not therefore recommend to our Minister that he accept a submission saying that 'for a variety of reasons we believe that it would be undesirable for the Commonwealth to take any initiative in regard to this matter at the present juncture'.

We appreciate the force of the points in paragraph 6 of your memorandum but to our mind they indicate not that the Commonwealth should refrain from taking any initiative in principle but rather that consideration of these matters should be hastened.

(b)   Paragraph 3 of your memorandum makes it clear that you find it difficult to conceive that the Government would agree to a common currency arrangement continuing indefinitely into the future. I understand that in discussion with Mr Kelloway[3] you have placed some stress on the fact that you are talking about an indefinite continuation and that you would not necessarily see obstacles in continuation for a period after independence. Even allowing for this qualification it seems to us important that the Papua New Guinea Government should be put on notice that the option of using Australian currency indefinitely may not be open to them.

(c)   Also we would prefer to see some indication of the major policy issues which need to be considered as listed in paragraph 15 of our draft.

It now seems probable that the Papua New Guinea Government will raise the currency issue at their discussions with the Minister later this month. You may have noted a report in the *Financial Review* of 12 July, where Mr Somare is quoted as having said that it would take Papua New Guinea two or three years to develop its own currency and until then it would continue to depend on Australian currency. It seems the submission could be re-drafted on the assumption that the Papua New Guinea Government will in fact raise the issue and without stressing the point of difference between us on whether or not an initiative by our Minister would be appropriate.

We would appreciate your early reaction to these suggestions as we are anxious to finalise a submission with the least possible further delay.

[NAA: A452, 1971/4971]

---

1   H. G. Heinrech, Assistant Secretary, International Relations, Treasury.

2   Document 321.

3   Paul Kelloway, Assistant Secretary, Economic Policy and Research, DET.

327   LETTER FROM BESLEY TO PITOI[1]

Canberra, 14 July 1972

Officers of the Department have had useful discussions in the last few days with Mr Baker, head of the Localisation Branch of the Public Service Board. Mr Baker brought with him for discussion drafts of two papers[2] which will be the subject of consideration by the Board for presentation to the AEC and the House of Assembly.

In looking at the drafts we have been mindful that with the pace of constitutional development, a decisive stage has been reached in reviewing localisation objectives.[3] Against this background, I am taking this opportunity to give you our general reactions to the papers and to make some particular suggestions on how they might be put to the AEC and the House of Assembly respectively.

Firstly, I should say that we were appreciative of this opportunity for consultation. As the Board put it itself in the white paper of August 1971[4] on accelerated localisation and training, a total operation is involved which depends on cooperation between the Board, departmental heads and overseas and local officers. I confirm the interest of the Minister and the Department in the progress of the accelerated localisation and training programme. Without wanting to restate the obvious, we are interested in being involved not only because localisation affects the futures of overseas officers but because it is so vital to the achievement of the Australian Government's objectives in Papua New Guinea.

Our basic reaction to the draft AEC paper is that we would like to see it go further in a number of respects. As presently drafted, it informs the AEC of the progress made in localisation and training and notes a number of problems in the way of further progress. I suggest that the paper could more directly spell out the problems with a view to seeking AEC guidance and in some respects seeking AEC endorsement of the Board's proposed solutions.

I would not be at all reluctant to seek such guidance. Generally, while we are conscious that management of the Public Service should be free from political interference, localisation must be regarded as something of a special case. The basic motivation for localisation is political— that the Public Service should be as rapidly as possible staffed by Papua New Guineans, it is being prepared for its new role in a self-governing Papua New Guinea. I suggest that it is reasonable then to seek guidance from our political masters as to how they wish to see this process of localisation handled and the rate at which they wish to move. (On the other hand of course, I am not suggesting that we should be seeking AEC guidance on who gets what position, other than departmental head and other statutory appointments on which it is normal practice to consult them.)

In particular I suggest that we obtain from the AEC an indication of their thinking on the positions which have top priority for localisation and the rate at which they would hope to see them filled. As I see it, we need especially to focus on the next 18 months or so, the period up to and including self-government. By then, it could be expected that most if not all of the 80 positions which have been designated as top priority for localisation (the Board's memorandum 19–1–16 of 13th March)[5] would have been localised. Is this the way the AEC

1   Sere Pitoi, Chairman of the PNG Public Service Board.

2   Not published.

3   For background on localisation see, among others, Documents 266 & 267.

4   Not published.

5   Not published.

sees it? Do we have the resources, of qualified or experienced local officers, to achieve such an objective? What of the problems of maintaining standards—is this rate too fast or too slow? Are the positions which the Board has proposed as top priority, with major policy and administrative content (and not professional and technical positions), the ones that the AEC also see as top priority?

The AEC also needs to be told of the impediments to localisation—competition between local and overseas officers and the feelings of overseas officers about their futures and sideways movement. I suggest however that one of the purposes of the paper should be to remove blockages as well as identifying them. In particular, we need to grapple with the issue raised in the paper of the adverse psychological effects on local officers of their being promoted as 'second choice'. Are there any new proposals or modifications of existing selection procedures to meet this problem?

From what I have already said, I think it can be inferred that I would look for the reports to both the AEC and the House to be as frank and open as possible. I suggest that we expose fully to them the magnitude of the localisation task quantitatively as well as qualitatively. We perhaps need to promote the notion of selective localisation to dispose of any view that we should be working towards total localisation within the next few years or even within the next decade—unless of course the country is prepared to pay the price of a less efficient Public Service and a slowing down in the rate of development and growth of services.

I suggest then that both the AEC paper and the eventual report to the House of Assembly need to be covered by short papers which give an 'overview' of the magnitude of the tasks, the major indicators of progress and the major restraints to further progress and action under way or proposed to undo them. The summary paper for the House of Assembly could be prepared with an eye to publication.

Finally, I would feel that there is a need to strengthen the machinery for putting into operation the new programmes for accelerated localisation and training. While localisation committees can prepare programmes internal to their departments, there will obviously need to be movement between departments to even up the whole process and to head people towards priority positions. There is a need both to coordinate programmes so that they are prepared on a contingent basis (a responsibility of the Board) and to integrate them into a total programme which has the endorsement of all the authorities concerned and I would hope, the AEC. Until an overall programme with targets and timetables is settled, there will be continuing difficulties for the trainers in seeing just what they should be training people for.

I see a need then for some new machinery. Possibly this could be of the sort adopted in some African countries—a statutory Localisation Office reporting directly to the Chief Minister. I would be inclined myself to favour a more consultative arrangement such as a Localisation Coordination Committee consisting of the personal nominees of the Administrator, the Chairman and the Secretary to review regularly and report to the AEC and the Minister for External Territories on progress with accelerated localisation and training. I would have in mind that the Committee operate on the basis of meeting quarterly and with the representation not to be below say, First Assistant Secretary level in the case of the Administration and Department, and Board Member in the case of the Board.

A most immediate task of the Committee would be to review the Senior Executive Programme and determine the priority positions that the participants should be groomed for.

Within the Department we have recently taken steps to bring together the localisation and training functions within the one Branch (the Social Development Branch). Equally, you might wish to consider a greater integration of the Board's activities in localisation and training.

I should be glad if you take these suggestions into account in preparing final drafts of the papers for the AEC and the House of Assembly. When you have put them to the AEC I would like to have the opportunity to place the final draft with the AEC comments or endorsement before the Minister for his consideration prior to tabling in the House of Assembly. I should be glad also if you could respond directly to me on the proposal for a Localisation Coordination Committee bringing together the Board, the Administration and the Department in a regular and formal way on this most important subject.

I am sending a copy of this letter to the Administrator.

[NAA: A452, 1971/3947]

328   SUBMISSION FROM GREENWELL TO PEACOCK

Canberra, 14 July 1972

SECRET

Police Spokesman

Following Cabinet Decision No. 452 of 23 June, 1970[1] an inter-departmental committee comprising officers of the Departments of External Territories and Defence has considered the question of internal security in Papua New Guinea. Its report[2] has already been passed to you for information but it is felt that it ought not to be submitted to Cabinet until after your August talks.

2.   One recommendation, that a *Police Spokesman* be appointed, ought, however, to be resolved *before* your arrival in Port Moresby. There has already been public speculation on the matter, including some public comment by Mr Somare. Furthermore, interest has increased since the Minister for Defence intimated the possible appointment of a Defence Spokesman.[3] In view of the fact that you will be in a position to respond positively and affirmatively to any request for a Defence Spokesman, it is important that you are able to be similarly positive, without the necessity of further consideration in Canberra, in the likely event that the Chief Minister seeks a Police Spokesman appointment.

3.   Agreement to the appointment of a Defence Spokesman was reached between the Minister for Defence and yourself. Defence officials agree with those of this Department that, similarly, the question of a Police Spokesman (which does not involve the transfer of any powers) might be resolved by you as the Minister responsible for the Police Force functions.

[*matter omitted*]

7.   It is *recommended* that you agree in principle that a Police Spokesman (with the functions set out in paragraph 49 of the extract) be appointed by the Administrator, after consultation with the Deputy Chairman of the AEC should the leadership group request such an appointment.[4]

[NAA: A452, 1972/2841]

---

1   Document 53.

2   Not published.

3   Document 319.

4   Peacock annotated this submission as follows: 'Approved—please ensure I have the attached papers when I leave for POM [Port Moresby]. It is my view that I should make an announcement of both Police and Defence Spokesman after the initial discussion.'

329   CABINET SUBMISSION 781[1]

Canberra, 16 July 1972

Treasury Analysis of Submission No. 728:
Aid to Papua New Guinea, 1972/73[2]

In Submission No.728 (including the Addendum thereto) the Minister for External Territories seeks approval for an increase of $19 million, or 17.5 per cent, in normal grant aid to Papua New Guinea—from $108.3 million in 1971/72 to $127.3 million in 1972/73—made up as follows:

	1971/72 Actual	1972/73 'Bid'	Increase	
	$ million	$ million	$ million	Per cent
Grant in Aid	30.0	30.0	–	–
Development Grant	39.9	54.3	+ 14.4	+ 36.1
Allowances, etc. for Expatriates	38.4	43.0	+ 4.6	+ 12.0
Total	108.3	127.3	+ 19.0	+ 17.5

Note: In order to make a valid comparison, the final drawings of $11.7 million made in 1971/72 on the special non-recurring Arawa loan have been excluded. Similarly, the 1972/73 figures do not include the special financial assistance (which could total as much as $6.5 million) which the Government has agreed to provide to the Administration to enable it to purchase certain Commonwealth assets in Papua New Guinea (e.g. the equity interest in Commonwealth New Guinea Timbers Ltd.).

Papua New Guinea Budget

2.   As shown in Attachment A,[3] an increase of $24 million, or 10 per cent, is proposed in total expenditures by the Administration in 1972/73.

3.   However, if we exclude the abnormal expenditures, estimated at $16 million, on the Bougainville copper project in 1971/72 which will not be repeated in 1972/73 since the mine is now operational, it appears that the increase in what might be called 'normal' expenditures in 1972/73 will be of the order of $40 million, or 18 per cent.

4.   I have the strongest doubts whether such a large increase is in the longer-run best interests of the Territory and in any event, I do not believe it can be justified, insofar as its implications of the present and future financial and other relationships between Papua New Guinea and Australia are concerned.

5.   In saying this, I have particularly in mind that, to meet the increase in expenditure which it proposes in 1972/73, the Administration expects local revenues to increase by $8.1 million only, including $4 million from new (and as yet unspecified) tax measures.

---

1   Submitted by Snedden.

2   Document 315.

3   Not published.

6.   Thus, the Commonwealth is being asked, in effect, to finance nearly 80 per cent of the proposed increase in expenditures by the Administration in 1972/73. That does not seem reasonable to me.

Trends in Commonwealth Aid

7.   The most disturbing feature of the Minister's proposals is that they envisage an *increase* from 45 per cent in 1971/72 to 48 per cent in 1972/73 in the proportion of the Papua New Guinea Budget which is financed by the Commonwealth.

8.   In line with our established policies designed to prepare the Territory to face up to the realities of the post-independence period, Papua New Guinea's dependence on assistance from the Commonwealth has been *declining* relatively in recent years. I believe that this trend must be continued in Papua New Guinea is to be expected to stand on its own feet in future.

9.   As further powers are transferred by Australia to Papua New Guinea, the indigenous leaders must face up to the financial consequences of the decisions they take under those powers. There can be no question of simply cutting off our assistance to Papua New Guinea as independence day arrives. But equally there can be no question of our simply standing ready to finance whatever schemes of expenditure the indigenous government feels moved to embark upon. In short, the proportion of expenditures to be financed by the Commonwealth must continue to be reduced.

10.   While I am conscious of the problems confronting the new Coalition Government in Papua New Guinea at the present time, I believe that it would be short-sighted to relax this principle.

11.   It will not assist Papua New Guinea to become independent in future to increase its dependence on financial assistance from the Commonwealth in 1972/73.

Future Developments

12.   The question of *standards* is important here. In my opinion, we would be doing Papua New Guinea a grave disservice in the longer run by trying too hard to cast it in our own image. The local people there simply will not be able to sustain such standards in future when they become independent. To delay recognition of this inescapable fact, and worse to heighten expectations in Papua New Guinea by agreeing to over-generous increases in Commonwealth assistance before independence, seems bound to lead to resentment in the future.

13.   In this regard, I am particularly concerned about the intention of the Administration to recruit an additional 300 odd *expatriate* officers in 1972/73. One would expect the present localisation programme (to assist which it has been agreed to provide approximately $1 million in 1972/73 for the training of Papuans and New Guineans in Australia) to produce a move in the opposite direction.

14.   I have been informed of criticism developing that most of Australia's aid to Papua New Guinea goes to benefit expatriates (the great majority of whom will eventually leave the Territory) rather than indigenes, and that too much is being spent in Port Moresby at the expense of outlying rural areas where the great bulk of the population lives.

15.   On the figures there seems some basis for these criticisms. It would seem to me to be in Australia's interests to blunt them as soon as possible by seeking to reduce the existing large disparities between urban and rural development and in the standards of living of expatriate and local officers in Papua New Guinea.

My Own Views

16. In the light of the foregoing considerations, I believe that Papua New Guinea's financial dependence on Australia should *not* be increased in 1972/73. By this, I do not mean that the absolute level of Australia's aid to Papua New Guinea should be reduced. Some increase is clearly warranted. However, I believe that the *proportion* of Papua New Guinea's Budget which is financed by the Commonwealth should *decline* in 1972–73. The consequences of such a decision are illustrated below:

Proposed Papua New Guinea Budget for 1972–73	
(see Attachment A)—	$265.5 million
Proposed to be financed by the Commonwealth:	
43 per cent—	$114.0 million
44 per cent—	$116.7 million
45 per cent (i.e. the same proportion as in 1971-72)—	$119.3 million
48 per cent (as suggested by the Minister)—	$127.3 million

17. If the Minister's bids were to be reduced along the lines suggested above, the effects on the Papua New Guinea Budget for 1972–73 could, I believe, be offset by a combination of greater local revenue raising efforts by the Administration and some reduction in the present extremely high (18 per cent) rate of increase proposed for non-Bougainville expenditures.

18. In this latter connexion I mention that a reduced rate of increase in expenditures would have the effect of increasing the proportion of the Budget financed by the Commonwealth. That is, in effect, another reason for pitching our own 'proportion' figure lower rather than higher. For example if we were not to go beyond the figure of $114 million mentioned above it would amount to some 43 per cent of a budget totalling $265.5 million, but a higher proportion than that of any budget of somewhat more modest shape.

19. As to the revenue-increasing possibility, it is relevant to mention that rates of both direct and indirect taxation in Papua New Guinea are considerably lower than they are in Australia— personal income tax rates, etc. are approximately one half; company tax is 25 per cent as against 47½ per cent; and sales taxes and customs and excise duties, etc. are also generally much lower.

20. It is no coincidence that Papua New Guinea currently receives more (in most cases, many times more) aid per capita than practically every other developing country in the world and also has one of the lowest tax burdens.

Recommendation

21. In the light of the foregoing, and as a means of encouraging the Administration to do more to help itself in future consistent with the move towards independence, I believe that, as a matter of principle, the Commonwealth should decide to finance a *lower* proportion of the proposed Papua New Guinea Budget for 1972–73 than it did in 1971–72 (i.e. 45 per cent).

22. In this regard, 43 per cent, which in money terms amounts to $114 million, would still be $5.7 million greater than the comparable amount provided in 1971–72.

23. If the amount of the bid is reduced, it might be left to the Minister from External Territories and myself to work out how the cut should be apportioned.

[NAA: A5908, 781]

330   RECORD OF CONVERSATION BETWEEN ANDERSON AND GREENWELL[1]

Canberra, 18 July 1972

CONFIDENTIAL

PNG and West Irian Rebels

Mr Anderson explained that we had been concerned for quite some time about reporting from PNG on the Administration's dealings with matters affecting Indonesia and with its arrangements for handling rebels who crossed the border, political activities by permissive residents etc. These questions had become urgent because of indications that the Indonesians believed the rebels were using our territory and had shown concern over our treatment of rebels and permissive residents.

Mr Greenwell said that the standing instructions to officers in the field for handling border crossers could be reviewed if necessary. It was agreed that they would be examined again; but DFA's present concern was mainly with matters not covered therein. *Mr Granger* said that the record was not as bad as suggested—most cases did not give rise to problems.

Mr Greenwell could offer no explanation for the Wellyp case[2] in which his Department's direction to the Administration had not been followed. (Comment: The Department of External Territories told us in May that they were asking the Administration to explain its actions— apparently no report has been received).

Internment of Rebels

Mr Greenwell argued that if inmates of Yako[3] returned to West Irian, it was not because they had been 'allowed' to do so—they were under no restraint and were free to do so any time. *Mr Anderson* explained that the Indonesians would not appreciate this semantic difference.

Applicants for Permissive Residence

The Department of External Territories officials were adamant that

(a) There was no prospect of the AEC agreeing to any changes in legislation or practice that would enable applicants for permissive residence to be held securely while their case was being considered (They are currently subject to no restriction. They are free to receive correspondence and funds, to receive visitors, or after a 2 weeks period of quarantine to go back clandestinely to West Irian).

---

1 Along with Anderson and Greenwell, those present were Gerry Nutter, Cavan Hogue, Bill Granger, Ronald Walker (Director, Indonesia-Philippines Section, DFA), John Monfries (Indonesia-Philippines Section DFA) and G. Baird (Head, International Relations and Defence Branch, DET). Walker prepared the record of conversation.

2 For background on this case, see Document 325, Attachment.

3 Yako near Vanimo in the West Sepik District was a holding camp for border crossers.

(b) if any applicant were charged with illegal entry and brought before a magistrate it would be politically impossible to send him back to West Irian.

(c) If any one were transferred away from the border area—e.g. to the camp at Manus—it would be politically very difficult to send him back.

Mr Greenwell proposed, and it was agreed, that the possibility of moving the holding camp to a point, still in the vicinity of Vanimo, but further from the border, should be examined, so that it would be more difficult for the residents to go back and forth.

Mr Greenwell also said that the problems would be much reduced if applications would be concluded quickly, so that border crossers spent a minimum time at the camp. *Mr Granger* argued that this was already being done. It was pointed out to him that the only case referred to Ministers in 1972 was that of a rebel leader who had been at Yako for 9 months and that several applicants now at the camp had been there for several months. It was agreed that a statistical report would be made showing, for the past 18 months, how many applicants had been in the camp, for what periods and how many had been returned in consultation with the Indonesians, and how many had returned clandestinely.

Mr Greenwell said that many of these problems would be resolved when a border regime agreement was concluded. (Comment: The problems in fact are in the area of PNG's own legislation and administrative practice). He noted that Foreign Affairs officers have participated in the Port Moresby committee considering the issues involved in such an agreement. He thought these questions were of special interest, particularly if—as some people were proposing—Australia were to retain responsibility for border matters after PNG's independence. *Mr Anderson* said that he had not heard of this proposal, but his first reaction was that it was a very bad idea.

Applications for Permissive Residence

Mr Anderson referred to the distinction that had been drawn by Sir Kenneth Bailey between political refugees (e.g. Moses Weror) who had committed no civil crimes and active rebels (e.g. the two Bonsapias) who had been responsible for acts of violence and, in some cases, killings in West Irian. *Mr Greenwell* thought that the AEC would not be less sympathetic, or less inclined to favour granting temporary residence, to active rebels than to people with purely political motivations.

Political Activities by Permissive Residents and their Passing Correspondence and Funds to the Rebels in West Irian

The Department of External Territories officials thought that nothing could be done about this, because of PNG sympathy for the rebels.

Rebel Sanctuaries in PNG

The Department of External Territories officials had been assured by the head of Security Branch of the Administration that rebels did not have sanctuaries in PNG. They accepted these assurances. It was pointed out to them that Administration officials had consistently told us that it was physically impossible to police the area effectively. *Mr Granger* said that any movement in the area would be reported to the Administration by local villagers. (Comment: The District Commander at Vanimo reported in June 1972 that 'there is quite probably justification in the opinions expressed by the Indonesians that insurgents are repeatedly and illegally crossing into PNG. It is some time since a systematic patrol was conducted of the border area.') In response to Mr Anderson's enquiry about the possibility of increased patrolling, *Mr Greenwell* said that the police were already overstretched and the Administrator was opposed to using the

Army in the border area. (Comment: On 21 July the Administrator told Sir Keith Waller that he wanted to use the Army for border patrolling. You could not stop border crossing, he said, but tighter control could be exercised.)

Coordination of Public Statements

It was agreed that this would be done.[4] Formal points of contact would be Mr Hogue for Foreign Affairs and the External Territories Director of Information and Publicity for that Department. Copies of Administration public statements affecting Australia's international relations would be made available to this Department. The case was mentioned of a recent encounter between an Administration patrol and some Indonesians near Lake Murray. A report had been supplied by the Administration, in response to our request, some ten days after the *Post Courier* had published an account of the official report. *Mr Granger* said that this was unexceptionable.

List of Permissive Residents

Mr Anderson asked whether the Department of External Territories had yet decided whether it agreed to the list being passed to the Indonesians. Mr Walker said that the Administration had told the Indonesian Embassy that it was agreeable to handing over the list but was awaiting the approval of Foreign Affairs. Mr Granger said that External Territories had informed us that they agreed to the list being handed over but we had asked if this meant that they were satisfied that there would be no unmanageable political reactions in PNG. They could not provide such an assessment. They would have to ask the AEC and that would take a long time. Mr Anderson said, and Mr Greenwell agreed, that it would be undesirable to consult the AEC; all we wished to know was whether or not the Department of Territories was concerned about likely reactions in PNG if the fact that the list had been passed became known there. Mr Greenwell undertook to look into the matter.

Attitudes in PNG

Mr Anderson said that the attitudes of PNG politicians and public opinion to these questions was clearly crucial. We would be interested in reports on these attitudes. *Mr Greenwell* said that the Department of External Territories was basing itself on a brief exchange in the House of Assembly in February 1970. They thought that attitudes then expressed would still be current. If we wanted a more up-to-date assessment we should ask the Papua New Guinea Intelligence Committee. *Mr Hogue* informed Mr Greenwell of the current reorganisation of PNGIC and the changes in its functions. *Mr Greenwell* said that he had been unaware of this. He would ask the Administrator for a report.[5]

[NAA: A1838, 3036/10/6/5 PART 1]

---

4   The original document contained the following footnote: 'The Department of External Territories had a grievance of its own. The Foreign Affairs PIO [Public Information Officer] had made public the fact that Indonesia had been invited to open a Consulate in Port Moresby.'

5   Here Waller annotated: 'This is pretty unsatisfactory.'

331   BRIEF FOR MINISTER[1]

Canberra, 18 July 1972

Involvement of AEC in Matters of Commonwealth Responsibility

1.   In the areas where the Commonwealth Government retains final responsibility, it does not intend to exercise its powers exclusively.
    –   In March 1970 when announcing transfers of final powers to Ministers, the then Minister for External Territories spoke of the enlarged role of the AEC.
    –   From that time the AEC has been consulted on all important issues; not only has it been consulted, but its views have been given full weight and have influenced the Australian Government's decisions.
    –   The Minister has on a number of occasions publicly stressed the importance the Australian Government attaches to the policy of full consultation with the AEC on matters of Commonwealth responsibility.

2.   The consultation is not a mere formality. It is significant involvement in policy-making. To make the involvement of the Papua New Guinea Government fuller, the appointment of Spokesmen in certain areas has been suggested. As part of their consultative and advisory functions, Spokesmen could suggest reference of matters to the AEC, would themselves introduce such submissions and would make any public statements or announcements.

3.   Certain procedures for the AEC have been suggested in view of the present constitutional situation. As far as PNG final powers are concerned, it is suggested that the AEC Secretariat make available to the Department the agenda of all AEC meetings, but that it is not necessary for all submissions and decisions to be seen. The Minister will however reserve the right to ask the Administrator for a report together with a copy of the submission and the decision reached on any matter if it becomes of importance in Australia. It should be stressed that this procedure would be exercised very rarely if at all.

4.   In the area of non-final PNG powers it has been agreed that AEC Ministers should forward each submission on such a matter to the Administrator, asking him to obtain the Minister's comments before it is put to the AEC, and that until such comments are received the submission should not be circulated.

5.   The AEC in the time to self-government is undertaking a critical task. It is regarded essentially as the executive, decision-making and policy-forming body in the Papua New Guinea Government—the highest point of reference. Self-government will largely be as shaped by decisions and views of the AEC.

6.   It is clear from the points made about involvement of the AEC in all aspects of government, that the Australian Government is placing a high value on mutual cooperation. On its side it will do all possible to inform and consult with the Papua New Guinea Government. Cooperation needs to be two-way: the Minister (and thus the Australian Government) needs to be kept fully informed of decisions and developments in the areas where final powers are transferred. The government of a country cannot be divided into compartments: a decision on one matter inevitably affects decisions in other matters. Hence the need for full information to be available to all those concerned with governing Papua New Guinea.

[NAA: A452, 1971/1463]

---

1   The brief was prepared in advance of Peacock's visit to Papua New Guinea in late July.

332   STATEMENT BY PEACOCK

Canberra,[1] 20 July 1972

Secondment of State Police Officers to Papua New Guinea

Arrangements have been made to second a contingent of Australian police for service in Papua New Guinea.

The contingent of 31 men is expected to arrive in Papua New Guinea in two groups—the first of 21 on 2 September and the second of 10 from New South Wales early next January.

They will be attached to the Royal Papua New Guinea Constabulary for two years, to supplement the force.

The Minister for External Territories, Mr Andrew Peacock, who announced the arrangements today, said he appreciated the help of the Australian police forces in providing assistance for Papua New Guinea.

Mr Peacock said the Royal Papua New Guinea Constabulary did not at present have sufficient resources. In particular there was a shortage of trained, experienced commissioned officers.

Papua New Guineans were rapidly being trained to meet the officer requirements of the Papua New Guinea police force, but it would not be possible to look to them to meet all of the demands for commissioned officers for some time. The force did not have enough expatriate officers to fill the gap, and the Australian contingent would help to overcome the problem.

The seconded officers would enable existing officers to be used more effectively and would have special responsibility for training Papua New Guinean members of the Constabulary. Their presence also would enable local officers to be released from routine police duties to undergo formal training.

Mr Peacock said that arrangements to second officers of State police forces flowed from a report of the former South Australian Police Commissioner, Brigadier J. G. McKinna, who made a special investigation for the Australian Government.[2]

The police officers on secondment to Papua New Guinea are selected, experienced men. After an initial orientation period, they will be assigned to police duties.

Mr Peacock said that five State police officers seconded early in 1972 from Australian police forces were already undertaking specialised roles.

The infusion of officers which the contingent will provide will be a major contribution both to the Constabulary's capacity to meet its present commitments and its ability to provide adequate training for its Papua New Guinean members.

Mr Peacock said that the secondment of these officers would not affect the promotion aspects of those officers who are already serving in the Constabulary.

[NAA: A452, 1972/2263]

---

1   The statement was also released in Port Moresby.

2   See Document 259.

333   CABINET DECISION 1176 (BRE)

Canberra, 21 July 1972

CONFIDENTIAL

Submission No. 728—Aid to Papua New Guinea 1972/73[1]
Submission No. 781—Treasury Analysis of Submission No. 728[2]

The Committee confirmed the agreement between the Treasurer and the Minister for External Territories that:

(a)   aid to Papua/New Guinea for 1972/73 be provided on the following basis:

$ million

Normal grant aid	121.3
Special aid	6.5
giving a Grand Total of	127.8[3]

(b)   in the event of the House of Assembly seeking to vary the Papua/New Guinea Budget in a way unacceptable to the Government, the amount and the arrangements for Australian aid would need to be reviewed.

[NAA: A5908, 781]

---

1   Document 315.

2   Document 329.

3   Treasury's strong reservations about the DET's proposed level of spending on PNG in 1972/73 (Document 329) appears to have resulted in Cabinet approving an amount of $121.3 million in normal grant aid for 1972/73 instead of the $126 million proposed by Peacock (Document 315). However the amount of special aid proposed by Peacock—$6.5 million—was approved.

334   RECORD OF MEETING BETWEEN WALLER AND JOHNSON[1]

Canberra, 24 July 1972

CONFIDENTIAL

Papua New Guinea

Mr Johnson called on the Secretary on 24 July 1972 at the Secretary's request.

[*matter omitted*]

Handover Procedures

7.   The Administrator saw his role at self-government as threefold:

(a) representing the Australian Government and acting as a channel of communication and liaison;

(b) exercising certain reserved powers on behalf of the Australian Government;

(c) acting as a constitutional Head of State on the advice of his PNG Ministers.

8.   He had now changed his earlier view and thought that, the move to independence having begun, the sooner it came, the better. If it were quick there was a better chance of retaining needed expatriates and relations between Australia and PNG were likely to be better because there was less time for resentments to grow. Probably, it would be better to go directly to independence without first passing through a self-government phase, but this seemed unlikely to happen because of practical and political difficulties e.g. the conservatives were making enough fuss over self-government and independence would be too much for them to take.

Defence Forces and Internal Security

9.   The Administrator said that, at present, PIR soldiers were indoctrinated with the view that their role is to resist external aggression and to keep out of politics and internal disorders. This would change as the Government discovered how ineffective the police were and wanted to use the Army in an internal security role. To this end, there should be joint police/army groups learning the same techniques and working out ways of quelling internal disorder without too much shooting—which is presently the only way the Army is trained to act.

10. The Army should also be used in border patrolling to release police for other tasks and to provide a more effective border control. You could never stop border crossing, but tighter control could be exercised.

[*matter omitted*]

12. Mr Johnson thought that internal security would be delegated by the Administrator to the Chief Minister at self-government. In theory, if the PNG Government could not control widespread disorders the powers would be taken back. In practice, the Administrator doubted that it would be possible to take them back. There was, however, the formal problem of our obligations in respect of New Guinea under the Trusteeship Agreement. We might feel obliged to make at least a pretence of keeping some control.

Indonesia

13. The Administrator raised the problem of border crossers.[2] He asked what should be done when West Irianese crossed the border—as we all knew they did—and were caught. The

---

1   Also present were Lew Border and Cavan Hogue.

2   See Documents 273, 277, 325 & 330.

problem in simply handing them back to the Indonesians was that there was a certain sympathy for the West Irianese in PNG, including the Government (he cited Mr Maori Kiki). This made it hard for the Government to be tough and send back any but the most blatant cases. He agreed it would not be difficult to move the holding camp further away from the border. He accepted the Secretary's views on the need for the government to learn to be tough in the interests of its relations with Indonesia, and agreed with Mr Border that once an Indonesian consulate was established in Port Moresby, it would be hard to keep up the present ad hoc arrangements at the border. However, he kept coming back to the political problems in PNG and gave the impression that they would not be easy to resolve.

14. A similar problem arose with outspoken statements by permissive residents. Following recent political statements by Mr Moses Weror[3] he had sent a letter to all permissive residents reminding them of their obligations. Weror was reprimanded. However, the problem really was they could not be sent back to Indonesia; what else in practice could be done? He thought that to send one back, as an example to the others, would raise the same sort of political problems.

15. The AEC had discussed the possibility of an Indonesian consulate recently, and had shown some concern that this might open the way to entry of many foreign representatives in Port Moresby. The AEC was not sure it could handle this situation. They were concerned about Taiwan in particular and did not want to commit themselves on such things until independence. They were well disposed to Japan and he saw no difficulties with a Japanese consulate. The Secretary explained that, if they did not intend to open a post in another country, there was no need to accept a mission from that country in PNG. They could refuse on the grounds that PNG could not reciprocate.

[NAA: A1838, 3080/10/4/7 PART 1]

---

3   Moses Weror, a former member of the diplomatic staff of the Indonesian Embassy in Canberra, had crossed the border in 1971 and had been granted permissive residence. He found employment in Mount Hagen but in March 1972 had moved to Madang.

335   LETTER FROM WALLER TO HAY

Canberra, 25 July 1972

CONFIDENTIAL

As you will know, I had a talk on 24 July[1] with the Administrator on the general question of the Foreign Affairs role in pre-independence Papua New Guinea. Having also the views of the Foreign Minister on this matter I have, as a result, made some tentative staffing plans which would be acceptable to my Minister and to the Administrator. If you concur, I propose to implement them immediately.

The Administrator thought it probable that the functions of the present Department of the Administrator would have been fused into the Chief Minister's Department by April/May 1973 and that by then, it was quite likely that a Foreign Affairs Spokesman would have been appointed. He agreed that it would be appropriate for an experienced Foreign Affairs officer to head the embryo Foreign Office. He proposed, therefore, at a suitable time, to split the present International Affairs Branch and have a Foreign Affairs officer in charge of the Foreign Office part. The Administrator felt, and I agreed, that if a Commonwealth officer were to be formally in charge of a Branch of the PNG Public Service, then he should be formally seconded to that Service.

To this end, I propose to leave Mr McDonald in his present position for the time being. When the Administrator splits the present International Affairs Branch, I will arrange to have Mr McDonald—or possibly a more senior officer—seconded to the Papua New Guinea Public Service to head the embryo Foreign Office, and to leave this officer there as long as his services are required by the PNG Government. The existing Foreign Affairs Officer Class 2 position within the International Affairs Branch will be filled as required and, if desirable, I would be prepared to arrange for an officer to be seconded. Should other officers be required I would consider providing them, but our aim should be to localise the Office as quickly as possible.

Consideration has also been given to meeting Australian Foreign Affairs needs in a rapidly changing situation. The Administrator saw no need for a Foreign Affairs adviser on his personal staff so long as he could draw on advice from the officer in the International Affairs Branch (or its successor) and a Foreign Affairs officer working for the Commonwealth. He had no objection to our appointing a Foreign Affairs officer responsible to me and working physically in the Commonwealth Office. He would, however, like to be shown copies of this officer's reports and to have an overall disciplinary power should this be necessary.

I therefore propose to transfer Mr Burns from the PNGIC[2] Secretariat to a new position of Foreign Affairs Liaison Officer. I would hope that he might be located in the External Territories office in Port Moresby and receive some administrative support from Mr Galvin. Burns would report to this Department, showing copies of his reports to the Administrator, and would undertake duties given him by this Department. I have in mind appointing a more senior officer as Foreign Affairs representative in the future, in which case Mr Burns would probably work to this officer.

[*matter omitted*]

I have also been giving some thought to the form of Australian diplomatic representation in an independent Papua New Guinea and how best this might be phased in. It may be a little premature to raise this in detail, but I feel that we should now be looking at all Commonwealth staffing arrangements in PNG in the light of the likely situation at independence.

[NAA: A1838, 3080/10/4/7 PART 1]

---

1   Document 334.

2   Papua New Guinea Intelligence Committee.

336   STATEMENT BY PEACOCK[1]

Port Moresby, 27 July 1972

Constitutional Talks

I see these discussions as one event in the continuing process of development towards self-government. However, because of their nature, they are probably the most important discussions yet held. This meeting will of course be the first of a number of meetings between our Governments. It arises from the recommendation of the last Select Committee on Constitutional Development which suggested that there should be preparation for internal self-government in Papua New Guinea during the life of the 1972–76 House of Assembly.[2] In response to this recommendation, the Australian Government approved the preparation of a programme of movement towards full internal self-government as a basis for discussions with the political leaders of Papua New Guinea. A programme which lists all necessary administrative and legislative changes has been drawn up. It is flexible. After this meeting it will be redrawn in the light of our conclusions.

Our main purpose as I see it is to discuss in concrete terms the transfer of further powers from Australia to Papua New Guinea. We are beginning to see a framework in which to operate. You have agreed to the appointment of a Constitutional Planning Committee. The Coalition has also put forward to the House of Assembly a target date for self-government. I should be very happy if we could finish this meeting with at any rate a provisional or tentative timetable for the transfer of further powers and an agreed list of the administrative and legislative steps which have to be taken by the Commonwealth and the Papua New Guinea Governments in order to give effect to that timetable. It will, of course, be necessary to refer the revised timetable to the Commonwealth Government before a final commitment is made.

There is no universally accepted definition of self-government. It is therefore up to this meeting—of representatives of both Papua New Guinea and Australia—to begin to discuss the powers which will be controlled completely by Papua New Guinea at the time of self-government, and those which will remain in Commonwealth hands until independence. Once this has begun we will be closer to a definition of Papua New Guinea self-government which subsequent meetings will be able to take further.

In statements from time to time, members of the Coalition Government have indicated some of the areas where they see control as essential for self-government. In line with the last Select Committee report my department, in consultation with relevant Commonwealth Departments and authorities and with Papua New Guinea officials has been preparing a programme listing all the administrative and legislative changes necessary for full transfer of power in all areas. The programme originally was prepared in line with the Committee's recommendations to allow for self-government *within the life of the third House of Assembly*, i.e. about mid–1975. A change in date say to December 1973 does not really affect the programme; the same number of administrative and legislative changes are necessary. What it *does* do however is to reduce the time available to pass all the legislation and make all the administrative changes. So that in making arrangements for self-government, there may need to be an understanding that while

---

1   The statement was delivered at the opening session of constitutional talks between Peacock and PNG ministers held on 27–28 July and again on 7 August 1972. In addition to Somare, the PNG representatives present were Paulus Arek, Julius Chan, John Guise, Bruce Jephcott, Ebia Olewale, Reuben Taureka, Matthias Toliman, John Maxwell Middleton, John Momis and John Kaputin. Somare, Olewale, Guise and Chan were members of the AEC. Following the discussions, a communiqué was issued on 8 August 1972 (Document 347)

2   See Documents 142 (paras 7–10) & 155 (paras 8–11).

in practice a transfer of power has taken place in the areas you specify, allowances will have to be made for some delay while the loose ends are tied up, and the situation adjusted in law. The Chief Minister in his statement to the House of Assembly foresaw this problem when in stating the projected target date of December 1973 he added 'or as soon as possible thereafter'. As I said before, I hope that as a result of this meeting the programme will be redrawn after discussion between us. I think this will accord with your view that it is not merely the *timing*, but the *type* of self-government which is important.

While the Australian Government looks to Papua New Guinea to indicate the areas which are considered essential to self-government, I feel that I should mention those matters which I see Australia continuing to be responsible for until independence. People speak very often of *internal* self-government. It therefore makes sense that in external affairs, such as defence and foreign relationships Australia's role should continue. But the extent of Australia's involvement in those areas will vary; Papua New Guinea will have its own case to state and its own interests to serve. Full consultations will be necessary on any international arrangement to ensure that those interests are served in a manner not contrary to Australia's international obligations. Perhaps it should be stated here too that part of Australia's continuing role will be a supply of aid and personnel. The Commonwealth as you know has given assurance that large-scale aid will continue beyond self-government and after independence.

Once we have defined areas which you see as essential to self-government, we can consider changes which must take place between now and self-government. As I see it there can be some immediate transfer of further powers which we can discuss in detail shortly. These transfers can be made under existing legislation. Different arrangements for Ministerial portfolios can be made with my approval, and the Governor-General can issue new instructions to the Administrator to accord with the changed situation. The arrangements and instructions will clarify relations between Papua New Guinea and the Commonwealth, and spell out the increased role of the AEC. In addition in other areas—e.g. those which may not be transferred until independence—the Australian Government wants to involve the Papua New Guinea Government as far as possible. Arrangements for spokesmen with a consultative and advisory function might be made in these areas.

Your involvement in these matters where I retain responsibility is only one side of the picture—I trust that in areas where you have responsibility that I will be kept informed, both because of the need to have all the facts when making decisions on any matter; and because of my obligation to keep the Australian Government informed of developments in Papua New Guinea.

It is clear that more than ever from now on there is a need for mutual effort and mutual cooperation. Some matters will raise problems for both Papua New Guinea and Australia, and they can only be faced jointly. Australia on its part is seeking to involve Papua New Guinea fully in areas where Australia retains responsibility. It is not possible to divide government into compartments. A decision on one matter inevitably affects decisions in other areas. Therefore I trust that information will flow two ways.

Australia has for many years looked to the wishes of the majority of the people of Papua New Guinea to determine constitutional changes. It would wish to do so particularly in the case of a decision on the timing of self-government; moreover it is obliged to do so under the United Nations Charter and Trusteeship Agreement. Therefore I am very pleased that Mr Toliman as Leader of the Opposition is participating in these discussions. I see this both as valuable because of his personal abilities and experience, and as necessary because of his position as leader and spokesman for a significant proportion of Papua New Guineans. The importance of seeking a majority view leads me to hope that the House of Assembly will continue to be involved as fully as possible in ratifying transfers of powers. Mr Somare has indicated on several occasions that it is his intention to consult the House fully, and that he would seek more than a narrow majority on these major issues. This is consistent with Australia's policy of looking to the House of Assembly to represent the wishes of the majority of the people.

The AEC will of course be more closely involved, discussing in detail such things as progressive transfers. It will also be in a position to assess the operation of new arrangements and to make recommendations accordingly. I trust that some conventions can be developed which ensure that the Leader of the Opposition continues to be consulted and informed. The role of the Administrator might also be mentioned. His position is changing and he will on the one hand continue his administration on behalf of the Australian Government, while on the other he will progressively withdraw from his active role in the Papua New Guinea Government. More than ever he will carry out a liaison role; on my behalf he will be discussing and dealing with the Papua New Guinea Government, and you on your part must feel free to use him as your contact point with me. Because of the involvement of the Administrator in both the Australian and Papua New Guinean sides of government, and because of his knowledge of and experience in Papua New Guinea, he will be able to provide valuable counsel.

Perhaps before ending I should point out that Australia's obligations to the United Nations to develop Papua New Guinea will continue after self-government. By the time of independence a new set of relations between our countries needs to have been developed. We would hope that discussions on post-independence relations would take place well before the date of independence.

I have mentioned frequently the need for liaison, mutual experience and cooperation in talking about constitutional changes. I trust both these discussions and those to be held in the future will be marked by frankness and friendliness.

The Australian Government agrees with the views of the Papua New Guinea Government that a smooth transition to self-government is essential. Mutual confidence will go a long way to ensuring this but it is also essential that there is a proper and full comprehension by all parties concerned of the need for sound ground work and a full understanding and appreciation of the complexity of the steps involved in the transition.

I see it as a future aim of both your Government and the Australian Government to establish in Papua New Guinea a viable government practised in governing and calling on all its available resources—human and otherwise. To this end all of us involved in planning for self-government in Papua New Guinea will do our utmost to ensure that Papua New Guinea builds a solid foundation for its own future and for future cordial contact with Australia.

[NAA: A1838, 3080/11/1/2 PART 1]

337   STATEMENT BY SOMARE[1]

Port Moresby, 27 July 1972

Constitutional Talks

Self-government is coming and we want it as soon as practicable. The time has come when our educated and capable men are ready to accept responsibility and once they get it and are seen to be doing the job the remaining people who have doubts will take confidence and support their leaders. If the handover of responsibility is too long delayed, however, the present climate of goodwill between ourselves and Australia could rapidly change under pressure of frustration. We are glad that our views on this issue seem to be shared by a progressive Minister for External Territories and by his departmental officers.

This is the first in a proposed series of constitutional talks. At the outset I wish to state the principles which my Government proposes to follow during these discussions.

(1) As the Government, we shall take the initiative in preparing the country to accept the idea of self-government and independence and shall not press for the final legal handover until this step is in accordance with the will of our country's elected representatives in the House of Assembly.

(2) Prior to the handover to a legally recognised state of self-government there must be the maximum possible involvement of Papua New Guineans in the policy making for, and the practical administration of, every single part of government and semi-government machinery. This means that all practical day-to-day administrative decisions must be made here. Unless there is an absolutely vital Australian interest involved, the *policy* should be decided here also by my Government. Given the present friendly relations with the Commonwealth, Australia's advice on policy will be carefully considered. We must get used to making our own decisions and it is my belief that it is we, who must live with the results, who will make the best decisions. I feel the Commonwealth should be prepared to hand over final power in nearly all matters concerning internal self-government within the timetable agreed to by our governments and that Commonwealth efforts should now be directed towards ensuring that the best possible advice is put before us to help us make our own policy decisions. I ask the Commonwealth Minister before deciding to retain final power over something to consider whether it is vital to Australia's interests to retain it. If not, then Australia's obligations to Papua New Guinea and to the United Nations would probably be best served by handing it over now to let us decide what sort of institutional or other arrangements need to be made.

(3) In all matters where formal handover is not immediately possible either because of temporary machinery or policy considerations the policy nevertheless should be as much involvement of Papua New Guinea Ministers and officials as possible.

(4) These are really preliminary talks and it will not be possible to reach final agreement on many issues, especially as there has so far been insufficient time for us to work out our own policy on all matters. For instance, we have not yet considered all aspects of the future electoral machinery, or the economic development planning structure. On such matters as these we hope to have preliminary talks to sort out the issues and to determine which issues require AEC policy determinations and which issues fall within the terms of the Constitutional Planning Committee. During these talks we shall work out procedures and sort out issues to enable our officials to continue the handover operation. At the next talks, probably in October,

---

1   The statement was delivered at the opening session of constitutional talks between Peacock and PNG ministers held on 27–28 July and again on 7 August 1972.

we should be in a position to ratify the actual handover of substantial powers and the creation of new portfolios and institutions after the House of Assembly has had a chance to debate proposed changes. At that time it is hoped that the Constitutional Planning Committee will be in full operation and a target date for self-government will have been agreed to by the House of Assembly.

A smooth transition to self-government will require from Australia a great deal of tolerance, sensitivity and understanding.

Sir, my Government is grateful for what Australia has done and we think you will continue to give us the support we need. We are prepared to do much more to help ourselves, however, we need special help to get over the last few hurdles. With that help our future is assured and Australia has discharged its trust.

[NAA: A1838, 3080/11/1/2 PART 1]

338   LETTER FROM SOMARE TO PEACOCK

Konedobu, 28 July 1972

My government has authorised me to formally request that the Papua New Guinea Act be amended so as to permit the creation of additional offices of Minister of the House of Assembly.

As there is a need to have flexible arrangements in relation to the creation of such offices it would be appreciated if this change could be brought about as soon as possible.

Such a change would permit the implementation of certain proposals which the Papua New Guinea Government is at present considering.

The House of Assembly will of course be involved, through its Ministerial Nominations Committee, in the choosing of the new offices.

I am sending a copy of this letter to His Honour the Administrator.[1]

[NAA: A452, 1972/1220]

---

1   See Document 295.

339   TELEX TO CANBERRA

Port Moresby, 31 July 1972[1]

430. Confidential

Report of Private Discussion between Peacock and Somare

Intelligence Arrangements

Mr Somare said he had had discussions from time to time with the Administrator on this matter. At his request the Administrator outlined the present plans for the re-organisation of the intelligence machinery in order to adjust it to the developing situation in Papua New Guinea [...] The Chief Minister said he was going to set up a group of Ministers to be interested in intelligence matters [...].

I [Hay] mentioned that the head of the Intelligence Branch would become the Chief Minister's direct adviser on intelligence matters and it would be this officer to whom he would turn if he needed information or intelligence advice at short notice.

[matter omitted]

Mr Barnett then enquired as to when responsibility for intelligence would be transferred to Papua New Guinea. I said that this was a matter that went with responsibility for internal security. So long as the Commonwealth maintained an internal security responsibility it would need to have access to the necessary intelligence to enable it to exercise this responsibility.

There was some discussion on the localisation of the Intelligence Branch but this did not proceed beyond indicating the name of one of the officers of the Branch who had been a university student.

Internal Security

There was an interchange of views on this on the basis that the Minister had not yet had brought close before him the recommendations being prepared in Australia in consultation with other interested departments. Until he had seen [these] recommendations he was not in a position to make any firm commitment. Barnett indicated that they would like to be in a position to make decisions in Papua New Guinea even though Australia decided to retain final authority in a formal sense until independence. It was agreed that it was not possible in this case to indicate a firm target date for a handover but I said that we envisaged a situation in which the first step would be a police spokesman (this could be agreed upon immediately). A later step would be a delegation of authority by the Administrator to a PNG Minister who would to the extent of the delegation have a relationship to the police akin to the present relationship to the Administrator and the police.

It was agreed that this would be a matter for further discussion when the Minister was in a position to indicate his decision.

---

1   The discussion actually took place on 28 July. Hay prepared the record. In addition to Peacock, Somare and Hay, those present included Les Johnson, Tony Voutas and Tos Barnett. Voutas was Principal Adviser in the Chief Minister's Office. Barnett, a senior official in the PNG Administration, was the legal and constitutional adviser to Somare.

DDA

It was agreed that the responsibility for the Division of District Administration could be handed over to the Chief Minister at the end of the year or early in 1973, subject to the Administrator's responsibilities for internal security.

The Gazelle

The Chief Minister spoke at some length on this. He said that he saw no immediate solution. The intention of his Ministry was to throw the question of a solution back to the Tolais on the basis that this was where a solution must come from. They did not wish to force them into any decision. It was an extremely difficult situation because they had told him plainly that they did not want to have anything to do with the central government. He had discussed this in some detail in seeking to see what they meant. He asked them, for example, did this mean taking out the police. In such an event who would look after them in the event of disorders? He said that they were clearly not talking in specific terms and there was no clear idea of what they meant by what they call a district government or self-government for the Gazelle. Anything which bore a name reminding them of a body set up under Papua New Guinea Ordinance (for example, a Council or an Area Authority) would not satisfy them. He and his colleagues were therefore looking at ways of introducing a form of authority under some other name, for example a group of Commissioners under the same idea as the Arawa Commission. The disposition of the Ministry was to agree to a good deal of what the Mataungan Association wanted in the way of self-government. This was why they had asked to discuss with the Minster the question of relations between the central and regional governments. What they needed was some authority to act on this matter of handing over power to a regional government without having to refer it to Canberra.

The Administrator said that if the Ministry agreed now to hand over power to the Gazelle, it would pre-empt the whole basis of the work of the Constitutional Committee. If the Tolais were given the degree of autonomy apparently [being considered] then the Hulis and the Engans[2] and other tribal groups might demand the same. On the other hand, he saw no difficulty in some special ordinance to cover what the Chief Minister was thinking about although there was ample room under the existing Local Government Ordinance and the Area Authorities Ordinance.

[*matter omitted*]

The Chief Minister then said that one idea in his mind was to make the existing leaders commissioners with their own 'kivung'.[3] It would be necessary to recognise, for example, on the legal side, the extent to which already the Mataungan Association was exercising authority of a governmental character. For example, it in fact had its own courts.

Barnett said that the best thing seemed to be to start on land which was functional, a matter close to the hearts of all parties to the differences of opinion within the Tolai people. Other things which it might be possible to do would be for the central government to assist the Tolai Development Corporation to get on to its feet and perhaps to combine with the successor to the Tolai Cocoa Project.

It was agreed that this whole matter would be discussed further with the Minister on 7th or 8th August in another private meeting.

[*matter omitted*]

---

2   The Hulis and the Engans are large ethnic groups in the PNG highlands region.

3   Local council or association.

The Minister said he hoped that although the matter would not be taken further until 7th or 8th, the Chief Minister would tell the Prime Minister personally his feelings on the matter when they had their private meeting next week.[4] The Minister then raised the question of his own presence at such private talks and it was readily agreed by the Chief Minister that he should be present, but that no officials on either side should be present.

Amendment to the Papua New Guinea Act

It was agreed that the Act would be amended as requested so that the Ministry could be increased and, if necessary, Assistant Ministers appointed. There was no discussion of the new portfolios because the Chief Minister had not yet made up his mind what they should be. He did indicate however his preference for having a certain number of Ministers without portfolio. The Minister encouraged him in this and said it would help lighten his own burden. At the same time, the Minister indicated that he felt responsibilities relating to security such as police spokesman should come under the authority of the Chief Minister. The Chief Minister was clearly in agreement with this. The discussion did not however extend to the identity of the Defence spokesman.

[NAA: A452, 1972/2801]

---

4   Prime Minister McMahon had planned to visit Papua New Guinea in late July/early August 1972 but cancelled his visit at a late hour because of major industrial relations problems in Australia.

340   PRESS STATEMENT BY SOMARE

Port Moresby, 31 July 1972

The following article by the Chief Minister, Mr M. T. Somare, appeared in *The Age* newspaper, Melbourne on July 31, 1972

Papua New Guinea is a country facing a critical time in her history. Although no final dates have been set we know that this country faces home rule and nationhood in the immediate future.

We as a people have to 'go it alone' and even though it may seem like an anomaly, there is no doubt that in order to go it alone, we will need help from wherever we can get it.

In the past the trend has been for the administering country to cut back aid and assistance when the developing country obtains self-government and independence. I believe there are many Australians who think that once Papua New Guinea has achieved self-government, and later independence, Australia's responsibility will end in most fields. We have had promises of continuing long term aid, but is this enough?

I know that in Australia the people tend to get the impression that Papuans and New Guineans are only too anxious to shrug off their Australian associations.

However, despite the press reports that reach Australia, there is in Papua New Guinea an enormous amount of goodwill between my people and Australians. This may be partly a case of 'the devil we know' but nevertheless it exists. It is a fact that we know Australians, and some of us might even think we understand them. Under these circumstances I believe it is important that Australia should not destroy that goodwill, just to save a few dollars.

Papua New Guinea has gained many advantages under Australian administration, but it has also inherited many Australian made problems. It will not be enough for Australians to sit back when Papua New Guinea becomes a nation and say—'well considering all the problems, I don't think we did a bad job'. Australia will never be able to sit back contentedly while Papua New Guinea lies at its northern doorstep.

Our political development since the first House of Assembly in 1964 has been rapid, and the pace is continuing. It has been uneven development because Papua New Guinea is such a geographically and ethnically diversified country. Some people believe they have been left behind both economically and politically, others can't wait to get on with the job of governing themselves. But our hopes for the future political and economic development of our country cannot be achieved without help from Australia, which in some cases has left us with legacies of its own failures as a colonial administrator.

[*matter omitted*]

Australia has also given us an Army—but the question which faces Papua New Guinea leaders today is, who is going to pay for it?

Australia never really considered whether an Army was a necessary expense in this country. There are almost certainly more essential services to be provided before we as a nation start spending our money on the maintenance of an armed service. At this stage we do not even know how much it costs to maintain the Pacific Islands Regiment, and it seems unlikely we are going to need a defence force completely our own for many years. It may be necessary for Australia to continue to provide the means of maintaining the army, without destroying the revenue needed for so many other services in a developing Papua New Guinea.

The failure to implement a speedy localisation programme until the early 1960s has left Papua New Guinea with a large European component within the Public Service for a country facing self-government and independence. Had Australia moved 15 years earlier in Papua New

Guinea my country would probably have inherited only about ten per cent of the problem as it now stands. Australia will have to think very carefully in the coming months about 'paying off' some of these white public servants that are still with us. Certainly Australia cannot hope to dump in the lap of my government an annual wage bill of about $36 million, without some strong resistance from us.

These are some of the problems that Papua New Guinea faces, and in the extremely delicate period of home rule, Australia can only help us if it thinks carefully about its position in relation to Papua New Guinea, and in some areas re-thinks its position.

I believe Papua New Guinea has a bright future, because I believe in its people and in our land. Australia has helped us along the road to nationhood, but our hopes for the future stable development cannot be realised unless Australia walks with us in these vital final stages of the road.

[NAA: A1838, 3081/1/11]

341   LETTER FROM PEACOCK TO MCMAHON

Canberra, 1 August 1972

CONFIDENTIAL

Earlier this year the Papua New Guinea Committee of Cabinet authorised the drafting of amendments to the Papua New Guinea Act to remove the limit on the number of offices of Minister of the House of Assembly that may be created and, secondly, to allow for the creation of offices of Assistant Ministers of the House of Assembly (Decision No. 979 (PNG) of 18 May, 1972 refers.)[1]

The Submission seeking the authorisation for these amendments to the Papua New Guinea Act envisaged ratification of such changes by the House of Assembly at its June Meeting but the Papua New Guinea Coalition Government was not able to put the proposal to the House as planned. You will be aware however that the Papua New Guinea Chief Minister announced a suggested date for the attainment of internal self-government and the appointment of a Constitutional Planning Committee to make recommendations for a Constitution for Papua New Guinea.[2]

The Chief Minister has now requested that the amendments to the Papua New Guinea Act regarding additional Ministers be limited to cover only the removal of the limitation on the creation of Ministers of the House of Assembly; in other words he does not wish to appoint Assistant Ministers.[3]

In the light of the expressed wishes of the Chief Minister therefore I seek your agreement to vary Cabinet Decision No. 979 of 18 May, 1972.

I would stress that additional Ministries are not created by the amendments; rather the amendments are in the nature of enabling machinery. Most importantly, no additional Ministers can be created by the Minister for External Territories without the House of Assembly taking part in the process through its Ministerial Nominations Committee.

Although the House of Assembly has not yet given its views on the requested amendments to the Papua New Guinea Act it will be necessary for me to introduce the legislation as planned early in the Budget Session so that the machinery for the creation of the additional offices is available when the House of Assembly requests them.

I have sought the agreement of the Chairman of the Legislation and Parliamentary Programming Committee of Cabinet to this, should you concur.

[NAA: A452, 1972/1220]

1   See Document 295, fn. 2.

2   See Document 337.

3   See Document 338.

342   LETTER FROM SOMARE TO MCMAHON

Konedobu, 2 August 1972

I would like to express my personal regret that you were unable to visit us this week as earlier proposed.[1] I fully understand that you had no alternative other than to cancel your visit on this occasion and I would like to assure you that my Government would welcome a visit in the future.

I am very appreciative of the sentiments expressed in the draft of your major speech which you were to have made in Papua New Guinea tonight. The assurances of continued future support from Australia are welcomed by my Ministry. I am particularly grateful for your reference to a special grant of $5 million to support our cultural development programme. As you may know, I am still Chairman of the Board of Trustees of the Papua New Guinea Museum and I have been deeply concerned that we have never had the resources necessary to do anything worthwhile in the cultural development field. There could be no gift more welcome to my Government than the special grant you were to have offered us.[2]

I did hope to raise with you two matters which are of the deepest concern to my Government. The first is related to the Employment Security Scheme which until it is resolved satisfactorily makes the movement to self-government far more difficult and unsatisfactory than is really necessary.[3] The second problem relates to land matters. Land is the most important factor in the lives of our people and wrongful acquisition of some land in German times and the failure of Australia to find a solution to date, leaves us with scars that cannot heal until these problems are resolved. I am writing to the Minister for External Territories, Mr Peacock, in detail on these matters but as I intended to mention them to you in private talks here I thought I should draw your attention to the two major problems which face my Government.

You will always be welcome to visit us and I would hope that when you do come you can spend a week or more in our country. There is much to see and you would find real evidence of the high regard we have for the help given to us by Australia and Australians.

[NAA: A452, 1972/3207]

1   McMahon had planned to visit Papua New Guinea in late July/early August 1972 but cancelled at the last minute because of major industrial relations problems in Australia.

2   David Hay noted on this letter, in reference to the draft speech: 'I have not approved of a draft!?? Did I give approval for this [i.e. the draft speech] to go on to Somare?' Peter Bailey of PM&C wrote to Hay to express strong concern that a copy of the speech had reached Somare in spite of the visit not having gone ahead. Officials noted that no clearance had been given in Canberra, and expressed the view that the wording in the speech did not imply a commitment to provide a cultural grant. Treasury was opposed to the idea of a 'special grant', that is a grant involving funding additional to that already planned for allocation to Papua New Guinea. In mid-September, Treasury asserted that 'the Treasurer never approved the speech, the visit did not come off, and therefore all bets are off'. By late November DET had decided, after consultations with Treasury, that it was not 'feasible or wise to proceed with this matter on the basis of seeking an additional special grant of $5m for cultural development'. It proposed that instead the $5 million be found, over a three year period, from within existing planned allocations. See Letter, Bailey to Hay, 11 August 1972; Minute Besley to Peacock, 15 September 1972; Submission, Hay to Peacock, 24 November 1972; Letter, Bunting to Hay, 19 December 1972; all in NAA: A452; 1972/3207.

3   It appears likely Somare's concerns about the Employment Security Scheme related to the potential impact on the PNG budget of the costs of the scheme. See Documents 340 & 389.

343   LETTER FROM BOWEN TO PEACOCK

Canberra, 3 August 1972

As you are aware, the Indonesian Government has expressed interest in establishing a consular post in Port Moresby. We have now received a formal request to this effect from the Indonesian Embassy in Canberra.[1]

The establishment of an Indonesian Consulate in Port Moresby would, I believe, be in the best interests of Papua New Guinea/Indonesian relations, and would be a useful way of improving each country's knowledge of, and interest in, the policies and attitudes of the other. The two countries share a common border and common problems of economic and social development. The early establishment of an Indonesian mission in Port Moresby should contribute to the development of the close and relaxed bilateral relations which will be important to both countries. Such representation will also help to ensure that those problems which do arise between Papua New Guinea and Indonesia are resolved in as understanding and amicable a way as possible.

If you agree, I suggest you might wish to seek the endorsement of the Administrator's Executive Council.

You may also wish to advise the AEC that the United States, the United Kingdom, Japan, New Zealand and the Federal Republic of Germany have also made informal enquiries about the establishment of consulates in Papua New Guinea. Perhaps the AEC could be asked at the same time to consider giving its concurrence to the establishment of consular missions by these Governments in advance of their lodging the necessary formal proposals.

It might also be useful to inform the AEC that the usual practice is for a country's Minister for Foreign Affairs, rather than for its Cabinet, to approve requests from foreign governments for the setting up of diplomatic and consular missions. The AEC, therefore, might wish to delegate to the Chief Minister the responsibility for approving such applications in the future.

[NAA: A452, 1972/2310]

---

1   Not published. For background, see Documents 301 & 308.

344   PRESS RELEASE BY PEACOCK

Canberra, 3 August 1972

Independent Enquiry into Future of Overseas Officers in Papua New Guinea

The Minister for External Territories, Mr Andrew Peacock, announced today the appointment of an independent enquiry into arrangements concerning the security of overseas officers of the Public Service of Papua New Guinea.

The enquiry is to be carried out by Mr A. M. Simpson, CMG, and will begin next month.

Mr Simpson, who was educated at Adelaide University, is Chairman of Simpson Pope Ltd and a director of several leading South Australian companies. He is a member of the Council of Flinders University and is the South Australian representative on the National Steering Committee on training. Mr Simpson last visited Papua New Guinea in 1968 as a member of the Tripartite Labour Mission.

Mr Peacock said that the Australian Government had reviewed the particular situation of permanent overseas officers last year, and in August 1971 had announced some proposed changes to the scheme providing for their future security in the event of enforced premature retirement, as well as some proposed additional arrangements to give them certain options about the basis of their future service in Papua New Guinea.[1]

These proposals, however, had not been well received by the officers concerned or their staff associations and the House of Assembly had, in effect, asked the Australian Government to reconsider them. The Government had again reviewed the whole matter and in doing so had given very careful consideration to a detailed submission put forward in March 1972 by the Public Service Association.[2] While the Commonwealth Government stood ready to implement the August 1971 proposals it had decided that because there was such a difference on fundamental issues between its position and that of the Public Service Association an independent enquiry should be made. Papua New Guinea Ministers had been consulted and agreed with the enquiry and its terms of reference.

The terms of reference are:

Having regard to the various assurances given by the Australian Government to overseas officers about their future security and to the wishes of the Papua New Guinea Government:

(1) to enquire into the arrangements that could be appropriate now and in the future for the security of overseas officers, and in particular into:

(a) the respective roles and obligations of both the Australian and Papua New Guinea Governments in the provision and retention of overseas staff;

(b) the efficacy and reasonableness of the Employment Security Scheme, including the improvements proposed to it in August 1971;

(c) the desirability of introducing arrangements along the lines proposed in August 1971, additional to and separate from the Employment Security Scheme, under which officers who are eligible under that scheme would have a choice about the basis of their future service in Papua New Guinea; and

(d) the form of guarantee which the Commonwealth should give in respect of payments due to overseas officers under certain Papua New Guinea ordinances; and

---

1   See Documents 204, 205 & 279.

2   Not published.

(2) to advise the Minister for External Territories and the Papua New Guinea Chief Minister on these matters.

Mr Peacock said that Mr Simpson had been asked to submit his report in the shortest practicable time. Mr Simpson would visit Papua New Guinea in the course of the enquiry and overseas officers and staff associations would have the opportunity of expressing their views to him.

Mr Simpson will announce shortly his itinerary and the manner in which he proposes to conduct the enquiry.

[NAA: A452, 1972/2883]

345   RECORD OF MEETING BETWEEN PEACOCK AND SOMARE[1]

Port Moresby, 6 August 1972

CONFIDENTIAL

Persons Present

The Minister for External Territories, the Chief Minister, the Administrator, Mr Hay, Mr Barnett, Mr Voutas, Mr Ryan[2] and Mr Leo Morgan.

The *Chief Minister* opened by referring to the Police and Defence spokesmen.

Police Spokesman

The Chief Minister said he wanted the Police Commissioner[3] to be able to deal with the spokesman direct.

Mr Voutas questioned whether this arrangement would really cover the main interest of the Papua New Guinea Government which was to be consulted on major policy decisions. He instanced the creation of a third battalion for the PIR. Could this be decided by the Australian Government without consultation with the AEC? Mr Voutas was assured that it was most unlikely that the Commonwealth by reason of its general approach to these matters would take such a step without consultation.

Mr Voutas then asked whether a Papua New Guinea Government representative could actually take part in the discussions, which he understood were now going on on defence policy matters, and be fully involved before consideration had gone too far.

The Minister for External Territories said he was sympathetic to this approach. He explained that it was not appropriate, in the Australian system, for Ministers to be personally involved in the work of Committees of this kind. Normally the Committees completed their work and then reported to Ministers. It was at that stage that the political and policy considerations which Ministers wished to bring forward were considered by them. It was only after this had been done that decisions at Ministerial level were taken. The Minister felt that this point may not have been quite clear during the discussions of a week ago when for example Dr Guise had indicated an interest in having political representation on the Banking Committee. He felt it preferable for this policy element, which he agreed was clearly the responsibility of Ministers, to be brought in when final consideration was being given to the reports. He would be prepared to discuss with Mr Fairbairn, his opposite number, the interest of Papua New Guinea in being directly represented by officials on the Committees at present studying defence policy matters. In any event he saw nothing but good in Papua New Guinea officials and politicians addressing themselves to defence questions and clarifying their own ideas.

Mr Barnett suggested that in order to do this effectively they should be able to call upon Papua New Guinea officers in the PIR to participate. Would there be any objection to this? *The Minister* said he would want to reflect on this. He was seeking, in this as in other things,

---

1   The author of the record was not identified.

2   Paul Ryan, Director of the Office of the Chief Minister and Secretary to Cabinet, 1972–73

3   N. A. M. Nicholls.

to strike a balance which would enable Papua New Guinea to have full involvement but at the same time to protect the Commonwealth's responsibility where that was retained.[4]

The Chief Minister then confirmed that he would like 'Area Command' to be involved in the defence studies. This would ensure that local knowledge was brought to bear. The same requirement for local knowledge was also to be seen in the appointment of the officer to head the embryo defence cell in the Administrator's Department.

The Administrator assured the Chief Minister that the officer concerned would be a senior officer probably of Level I rank and well experienced.

The Administrator then sought clarification from the Chief Minister as to whether:

(a) he was agreed on the appointment of an officer to head the defence cell concurrently with the appointment of a spokesman. The *Chief Minister* gave the impression that he would prefer to discuss this in more detail later.

(b) he was of a mind to assume the responsibility of spokesman of defence himself. The *Chief Minister* indicated that he was.

Intelligence and Internal Security

The discussion then turned to intelligence and internal security. Both *Mr Barnett* and *Mr Voutas* pressed for early transfer of responsibility for these functions.

Mr Hay recalled what had been said during the earlier discussion about this, namely, that so long as the responsibility for internal security rested in Australian hands, a certain degree of control over intelligence should also be retained. This however had not prevented a reorganisation going ahead of the present intelligence system to ensure that it would be suited to Papua New Guinea needs and its product available to the Chief Minister and such Ministers as he wished in addition to the Administrator.

Mr Voutas then turned to the question of who would be the officer responsible for intelligence matters. He asked that the Chief Minister be consulted on the appointment and that the person be acceptable to the Chief Minister. This was an important appointment since whoever it was they would have to live with him for some time. The Administrator said that it was a well understood practice that important appointments such as this were subject to consultation with the Chief Minister before they were made. In any event he would not expect the duration of the first appointment to be more than, say, two years.

---

4   In the text (which was later removed) of a draft version of the record of the meeting, Barnett is reported to have argued strongly for greater consultation with the PNG Government in all of its areas of responsibility. 'He instanced in particular the Kennecott negotiations. He felt that [the] Papua New Guinea Government should be involved from the very start. He was concerned that Papua New Guinea should not find itself in the position, as it now did with the Bougainville agreement, of regretting some of the provisions and feeling that a more advantageous arrangement could have been negotiated. In the case of Kennecott, the Papua New Guinea Government might well want to hire its own consultant to advise it on important aspects. Would the Commonwealth object to this? The Administrator explained that there had been no negotiations with Kennecott to this point and that the Administration was in fact fully involved. No difficulty was seen if the Papua New Guinea Government wished to hire its own consultant. The Chief Minister supported Mr Barnett's remarks and said that in the Sepik an American-Australian Company was exploring and even building a road without the people knowing anything about the reasons for it. There was a good deal of disquiet.' See Minute (Draft), 'Note of Private Meeting between Minister and Chief Minister', August 1972, NAA: A452, 1972/2801.

Downs has noted that Kennecott Explorations (Australia) Proprietary Limited had undertaken test drilling of copper deposits in Madang District and at Ok Tedi in Papua and had also taken out options on other copper-gold prospects. Ian Downs, *The Australian Trusteeship: Papua New Guinea, 1945–75*, Australian Government Publishing Service, Canberra, 1980, p. 301.

Mr Barnett then reiterated that what they were seeking was total involvement in these matters which up to now had remained mysteries. It was not only a question of being involved but of Papua New Guinean Ministers being seen to be involved.

Land

The Chief Minister then mentioned the subject of land. He said he would not want to pursue it during the present talks. As a result of the previous talk with the Minister he and his staff were considering in more detail the ideas discussed with a view to putting them into the form of a proposal which could at a later stage be discussed with the Minister.

The matter had been mentioned in a letter which the Chief Minister had just written to the Prime Minister in relation to his postponement of his visit to Papua New Guinea.[5]

[*matter omitted*][6]

[NAA: A452, 1972/2841]

346   EXTRACT OF MEETING BETWEEN PEACOCK AND SOMARE[1]

Port Moresby, 7 August 1972

CONFIDENTIAL

Constitutional Conference: Record of Ministerial Discussions

The Commonwealth's Continuing Responsibilities

The *Minister for External Territories* reminded the meeting of Australia's continuing responsibilities after self-government, notably its international obligations derived from the UN charter and the Trusteeship Agreement. Just as Australia would be consulting with PNG on the matters for which it retained responsibility, he hoped that PNG would agree to consult with Australia, where a matter might affect Australia's international obligations.

The Significance of Self-Government and Independence in Relations between Australia and PNG

The *Minister for External Territories* further stated that, from Australia's point of view, it was not the date of internal self-government but that of independence which will be the watershed in relations between the two countries. The achievement of self-government will not affect Australia's obligations undertaken with the United Nations and its continuing commitment to provide aid and assistance. At independence a new set of relations will need to be developed and discussions on post-independence arrangements will need to take place well before the date of independence.

[NAA: A452, 1972/0932]

---

5   Document 342.

6   Among other things, the omitted material indicated that the Somare government had decided to undertake a new initiative by sending officials to the Gazelle Peninsula for discussions on how to resolve ongoing problems with the MA.

---

1   The author of the record was not identified.

347   JOINT STATEMENT BY PEACOCK AND SOMARE

Port Moresby, 8 August 1972

Constitutional Talks

The Minister for External Territories met with the Chief Minister, Papua New Guinea Ministers,[1] the Deputy Chairman of the Constitutional Planning Committee,[2] the leader of the Papua New Guinea Opposition[3] and members of the United Party initially on 27 and 28 July to discuss the transfer of further powers to the Papua New Guinea Government, the timing of such transfers and the necessary administrative and legislative steps.

The leader of the Opposition made it clear at the outset that decisions reached at these talks would in no way bind the United Party.

During the week 31 July to 4 August, officials of both the Commonwealth and the Papua New Guinea Governments examined in detail matters referred to them by Ministers. The Deputy Chairman of the Constitutional Planning Committee participated in a number of these discussions between officials.

On 7 August, the Minister for External Territories met again with Coalition leaders including a representative from the Mataungan Association[4] and the Opposition leader to consider the report of officials. A large measure of agreement was reached. Ministers directed that certain matters should be set aside for further study and discussed again at the next round of constitutional talks.

Discussions throughout were frank. A few earlier disagreements were resolved to mutual satisfaction as the talks proceeded. For example the Chief Minister had drawn attention to the misunderstanding caused in the House by the practice of Official Members leaving the House when a vote is taken on matters within the final responsibility of Papua New Guinea Ministers. The Minister for External Territories, on the understanding that it is the Commonwealth's wish to phase out Official Members altogether, agreed, as an interim measure, that Official Members may vote on matters within the final responsibility of the Papua New Guinea Government as well as within Commonwealth responsibility. It was also agreed that, as in the previous House, Official Members would not vote on constitutional matters and the timing of self-government nor would they vote on matters of no-confidence.

Although some matters remain unresolved all parties were satisfied with the honest exercise of two-way consultation.

Among other things it was agreed to create a position of Ministerial Spokesman for Defence. This had been foreshadowed by the Commonwealth Minister for Defence during his discussions in Port Moresby in June. The Minister for External Territories had also agreed to the creation of a Ministerial Spokesman for Police. Initially the Chief Minister will assume these responsibilities.

Both Papua New Guinea and Commonwealth representatives agreed that the proposed transfer of further final powers to the Papua New Guinea Government would not be effective until the House of Assembly had been given an opportunity to consider proposed changes. If the House of Assembly objected on a majority vote to any of the proposed changes, then these would not be implemented.

---

1   The PNG ministers who took part in the discussions were Paulus Arek; Julius Chan; John Guise; Ebia Olewale; Bruce Jephcott; and Reuben Taureka.

2   Father John Momis.

3   Matthias Toliman.

4   John Kaputin.

It was also understood that the Minister for External Territories would place the results of these discussions before his Ministerial colleagues.

Those involved in the discussions kept in mind that some matters might properly fall within the terms of reference of the Constitutional Planning Committee.

The Chief Minister indicated that he would ask the House of Assembly at its Budget sitting to agree to the appointment of a small number of additional Ministers. The Minister for External Territories agreed to seek an amendment of the Papua New Guinea Act to permit this.

It was agreed that following reference to the House of Assembly a number of matters could be transferred to the Papua New Guinea Government immediately. These matters include wages and industrial relations policy and training and localisation in the private sector, migration policy and land settlement and development policy.

Other matters, such as Area Authorities and the Tariff Advisory Committee could be transferred as soon as the necessary Papua New Guinea legislation had been passed.

It was agreed that continued close consultation would be necessary between Papua New Guinea and Australia on such matters as development planning and major development projects. This would not preclude final responsibility being handed over as soon as suitable executive arrangements had been settled.

Responsibility for control over the Public Service was discussed at length and although there are still some unresolved difficulties, it was agreed that transfer could occur near to the date of full internal self-government. The difficulties have been referred to a study group for further examination.

It was also agreed that Civil Aviation, which is a complex and expensive operation, could not be the subject of an early handover. However planning for the eventual handover would be accelerated.

While it was agreed that some matters such as foreign relationships and defence would remain the final responsibility of Australia until independence, the need for full involvement of the Papua New Guinea Government in these matters was recognised and the means of doing so will be further studied.

It was also agreed that there would be a further round of similar discussions in October 1972.

[NAA: A452, 1972/2841]

348   RECORD OF CONVERSATION BETWEEN HOGUE AND KERR

Canberra, 9 August 1972

CONFIDENTIAL

Constitutional Talks in PNG

I called on Mr Kerr to discuss the recent discussions with PNG on Constitutional development. Following is the gist of his comments.

2.   The PNG leaders have not thought things through in many areas and are not really sure what they want. However, they are quite sure that they want progress and they will not be put off. They are clear that they want a labour intensive development programme and that they want the Australian subsidy to continue at its present level. They are serious in their desire to be involved in everything and to take a real part in decisions affecting them. The distinction between independence and self-government is being blurred and there is every indication that independence will follow very quickly after self-government. Despite the general confusion, present indications are that the transfer of power will be orderly. A lot of work is being done in External Territories and by some PNG officials. This will help fill in the detail.

3.   A major problem is that the PNG Ministry is suspicious of the public servants and vice versa. Neither the public servants (black or white) nor the Ministers have a clear idea of how a public service works and what it is supposed to do. Public servants do not brief their Ministers properly nor even keep them informed. Ministers therefore tend to look for advice outside the ranks of the Public Service and tend to rely increasingly on a small group of expatriate advisers (e.g. Tos Barnett, Constitutional adviser and Paul Ryan, AEC Office). These advisers are not in a position to give them sound advice on all matters—particularly technical issues— and their advice is seldom cleared with the relevant Public Service departments.

4.   Things change quickly and something which is required now may not be wanted in three months. It is hard to keep up with the pace of change and great flexibility is needed.

5.   Mr Somare got manoeuvred into saying that the date for self-government would have to be approved by 75 (out of 100) members of the House of Assembly. He originally said that proposals of the Constitutional Committee would need a 75% majority of members present. In a talk in the Highlands in Pidgin, because of translation problems, this came out as 75 members. When pressed by journalists on his return to Port Moresby, he said that this applied to the self-government date too. He has since shown signs of trying to get out of this commitment and in his last press conference refused to be drawn on what he considered to be a 'substantial' majority. He seems confident that he can get the 75 members with defections from the Opposition, but still may try to blur the issue. Mr Peacock and the External Territories officials took the view that this was an internal political matter in which they had no part.

6.   The Opposition, particularly in the person of Mr Toliman (Leader of the Opposition) started off reasonably enough but seemed to get 'stiffened' by its white backers into taking a more intransigent approach. There was a general feeling that the Commonwealth was trying to get out quickly and this view was put by the Opposition.

7.   The PNG Government has made a real attempt to involve the Opposition and smaller groups in the process. Mataungan Association representatives were present, for example, and Mr Kaputin attended the final day of the Ministerial talks. The Government will have to work out its tactics now on its approach to self-government. It may spell out to the Opposition exactly what it proposes to take over and try and convince them that self-government is not such an evil after all, or it may keep things to itself and try to use its numbers to force things through.

8.   The Constitutional Committee has been given an impossible task and is unlikely to produce what its terms of reference require of it in time. It is supposed to produce a PNG Constitution by next June, but if it does it will be a very superficial document. Its Chairman, Father John Momis, is an able man but has strong views and favours Bougainville separatism. There are other strong minded members whose views conflict, e.g. Dr Guise, the Mataungans. All members of the Committee are inexperienced backbenchers. What will probably happen is that the Government will continue to pass ordinances and just move steadily forward to self-government shortly followed by independence, leaving the formal side to catch up later. They are already, for example, talking about establishing an 'international' citizenship and about negotiating their own trade agreements.

9.   There was a general feeling among PNG Ministers and officials that it was time they got their hands on Civil Aviation and that DCA[1] had fiddled about too long.

10. The reference in the communiqué[2] to 'Migration' should not worry us. It was clearly recorded that the immediate transfer of migration power would exclude two areas:

    a.   international relations aspects, especially those concerning Indonesia and border relations; and

    b.   security.

11. Mr Kerr suggested that I discuss Foreign Affairs matters with Mr Greenwell (FAS) who was better informed. I spoke briefly to Mr Greenwell who said we would be getting the full record of the talks in a few days. He said that officials had raised the Foreign Affairs spokesman question and had put certain proposals. He would send these to us. He thought we would need to show by October that some progress was being made, but did not see any need to finalise things there. More important, he thought we should have some talks before October on the Foreign Affairs Department which would support the Spokesman. He would take this up with us later. Other matters of interest to us were raised, mainly concerning representation at international conferences and negotiations for loans and trade matters. These were covered in the record.

[*matter omitted*]

[NAA: A1838, 689/1 PART 6]

---

1   Department of Civil Aviation.

2   Document 347.

349   LETTER FROM JOCKEL[1] TO BESLEY

Canberra, 9 August 1972

SECRET

You may remember I promised to give you an outline of my ideas at the discussion we had on the paper on Australia's National Interests in an Independent PNG.[2]

Somewhat belatedly, I am giving you the attached small paper and I am sending copies to Percival[3] and Hogue.

JIO could take on the work on paragraph 4 and help you with the work on paragraph 3 at the initial drafting stages, and we would no doubt have views on some of the other aspects as the paper developed.

Attachment
Australia's National Interests in an Independent PNG

I would think that what Cabinet had in mind was a realistic and critical assessment of our long-term, abiding national interests in an independent PNG. We have currently obligations, and indeed attitudes, to PNG arising out of our responsibilities as the administering power there. But I think Cabinet would not want the thinking on future policy towards an independent PNG simply to flow out of this past and these special associations, but out of a long, cool look at PNG as a foreign country.

2.   Of course, this cannot be done in a vacuum even if we do it in a cool, detached way. The paper should begin with a recapitulation of the policy decisions already taken by Cabinet in respect of an independent PNG. There are probably only a few such statements, e.g. that Australian aid will continue; that in principle we favour national unity; and that we want a peaceful and stable New Guinea in good relations with Australia.

3.   The paper should seek to estimate how important an independent PNG will be to Australia. This covers such questions as:

(i)   its size, resources, population;

(ii) its geographical position in relation to Australian territory, in relation to our off-shore interests, and in relation to our lines of communication (this should be realistic and technically sound, not mere assumption);

(iii) the economic benefits and disadvantages of our economic and financial links with PNG.

4.   The paper should have a concise but detailed account of current and prospective Australian involvement on the ground in PNG—the size of the Australian expatriate community and

---

1   G. A. Jockel, Director, Joint Intelligence Organisation (JIO), Department of Defence.

2   In Cabinet Decision 980 of 18 May 1972 (Document 296) ministers had asked for the preparation of a study on Australia's 'national interests' in relation to an independent Papua New Guinea and the relations which ought to be entered into with it. Over the next eighteen months officials produced several drafts but it seems the study was never finalised. In November 1973, however, the Defence Committee agreed on a form of words to describe the long-term defence relationship with PNG post-independence and define the strategic importance of Papua New Guinea to Australia. See Bruce Hunt, *Australia's Northern Shield. Papua New Guinea and the Defence of Australia since 1880*, Monash University Publishing, Clayton, Victoria, pp. 245–51.

3   R. J. (Ray) Percival, Assistant Secretary, Pacific, DFA.

its activities, the role of the Australian business community in running the modern sector of the economy, the role of Australian agencies in transport, communications, banking and insurance etc. etc. How important is all this on something like the present scale for the economic viability of the country? Is the present profile of Australian involvement likely to change significantly in the foreseeable future? If not, what responsibilities does it imply for an Australian Government?

5.   The paper should study PNG in its regional and international setting. It should look at such questions:

(i)   PNG's likely standing and influence in the region among its neighbouring countries;

(ii) the extent to which PNG may attract the attention of outside powers and the effect of PNG's relations with outside powers on Australia's security interests.

(iii) the degree to which a friendly or an unfriendly PNG could respectively support or harm our strategic and security interests (again this should be a realistic assessment and not merely a traditional response.)

6.   The question should be posed as to how important the stability and national unity of PNG is to Australia. How seriously would Australia be affected if PNG were to deteriorate economically and politically? How important is it for Australia for PNG to retain its national unity as at present constituted? What is the likely effect on regional stability if PNG became unstable?

7.   Some judgment should be made about the place of PNG in our overall foreign policy. What role do our allies and the countries in the region with whom we associate expect us to play in PNG? To what extent will they accept and support the commitments the Australian Government might undertake in respect of PNG?

8.   The guidelines should not be too difficult to formulate. They would be along the following lines:–

(i)   Australia is bound to remain heavily involved in PNG for a good many years to come.

(ii) This should be accepted as a fact of life. We should not seek to create a special regime of relationships and avoid referring to it as a 'special relationship'. Indeed, we should encourage the broadening of PNG's multi-lateral interests and associations, especially with its regional neighbours.

(iii) The growth of political cooperation and common outlook in the immediate neighbourhood to PNG in South East Asia should help to shape PNG's outlook on the world.

(iv) We should encourage the flow of Australian capital and investments, provided it is in the advanced sectors of the economy; at the same time, we should encourage the indigenous government to squeeze out the superfluous numbers of expatriates through its employment policies, etc.

(v)   We should help the indigenous government to press on with the indigenization of basic infrastructure facilities such as airlines, radio etc.

(vi) Later on, our aid should become less generalized and aim at helping the government with key areas of economic and national development.

(vii) We should build up the local military forces so that they become stronger in manpower and capable of greater mobility from their own resources.

(viii) In order to help assure the security of the large expatriate community, we should retain close links with the Army, Police and intelligence, and seek to influence their orientation.

(ix) We should make up our minds whether we should accept formal treaty commitments to the defence of PNG or aim for something less binding. We should make up our minds whether we need defence facilities in PNG.

(x) We should act as if the principle of national unity was important to us (while treading carefully).

9. Nearly all these points are in the Foreign Affairs draft.

[NAA: A452, 1972/1993]

350   TELEX FROM PNG INTELLIGENCE COMMITTEE

Port Moresby, 11 August 1972

17571. CONFIDENTIAL

Bougainville Combined Councils' Conference:
The Question of Constitutional Development

1.   The Bougainville Combined Councils' Conference was held on July 11th and 12th with representatives from all seven Bougainville Local Government Councils attending. A significant topic on the agenda was the future form of government for the Bougainville district. After confused discussion and voting on the issue, the Conference approved a motion calling for a 'referendum to determine the wishes of the Bougainville people'.[1] Although the motion itself was inconclusive, the diverse views expressed during debate illustrate a significant difference of opinion on the issue between Northern and Southern Bougainvilleans.

2.   Initially the Conference had before it two proposed Agenda items: one calling for a 'Bougainville Referendum' and the other for a 'Bougainville Referendum on State Government'. During discussion of these items the three central and southern Bougainville MHAs present, Father John Momis, Paul Lapun and Raphael Bele[2] (the Northern Electorate Representative, Donatus Mola[3] was not present) supported a form of Bougainvillean Statehood within a Federation, with little Central Government control.

3.   During discussion, a clear difference of views emerged between Northern and Southern Delegates over what form of government should be instituted. The Northern Bougainvilleans indicated they would accept a referendum covering the options for a form of area government within the framework of a United PNG. On the other hand the Southern view, as put by Father John Momis (Deputy Chairman of the Constitutional Planning Committee), was Separatist and Ethnocentric, calling for a Bougainville State with powers in the fields of migration policy, police, education, culture and land tenure.

4.   After confused debate and vote, the Conference appears to have approved a vague motion calling for a referendum in general terms.

5.   Subsequent to the Conference the Buka (Northern) Delegates complained to their Council that the Referendum issue had not been clearly stated and that two of the four delegates from Bana Council attended illegally. They therefore considered the resolution invalid and attacked Father Momis and others for 'stage-managing' the debate. They also criticised the presence [at] the Conference of Barry Middlemiss,[4] Secretary of Napidakoe Navitu[5] and his license to speak during the meeting.

---

1   See Documents 299 & 306 (paras. 19–21).

2   Raphael Bele, MHA for Central Bougainville.

3   Donatus Mola, MHA for North Bougainville.

4   Barry Middlemiss was an Australian manager at the Arawa plantation in the late 1960s when it and adjacent areas were resumed as the site of a township and processing plant as part of the Bougainville copper project. He supported protest against land resumption and Bougainville's secession from Papua New Guinea. See Ian Downs, *The Australian Trusteeship: Papua New Guinea, 1945–75*, Australian Government Publishing Service, Canberra, 1980, pp. 355, 359, 440, 478.

5   The Nasioi people of Bougainville formed *Napidakoe Navitu* in 1969 to oppose land acquisitions and seek compensation. The movement later broadened its support base and supported Bougainville's secession from Papua New Guinea. See ibid., pp. 440, 478; and R. J. May, *State and Society in Papua New Guinea: The First Twenty–Five Years*, Crawford House Publishing, Adelaide, 2001, pp. 60–61.

6.   Bougainville separateness is a significant factor in Bougainvillean thinking. A separate regional Government is seen as necessary by the majority of educated Bougainvilleans, the actual form it would take is a matter of dispute. While Southern Bougainvilleans seem set on a Federal relationship with a strong State Government, the Northerners have demonstrated their opposition to such an extreme form of regionalism.

[NAA: A1838, 3080/1/2/3]

351   SUBMISSION FROM HAY TO PEACOCK

Canberra, 14 August 1972

CONFIDENTIAL

Constitutional Talks—Port Moresby

This note brings together some of the impressions and observations which you and I discussed after the Ministerial meeting.

2.   The Coalition leaders clearly want to do things in their own way in the future. Father Momis was the most consistent exponent of this viewpoint. He spoke several times of a specifically New Guinean concept of economic development. In respect of the Public Service he spoke not only of localising the personnel but of localising the thinking. Mr Somare and even Mr Toliman also voiced these sentiments in relation to economic planning. Mr Barnett in your private talks with Mr Somare spoke in the same vein about planning for the future of the Army and Mr Somare seemed to be of one mind with him. There is nothing surprising about this. It accords with the views which you have been stating publicly, notably in your Waigani speech.[1] But we need to bear in mind that the process of consultation on matters like the Development Programme and the future of the Public Service is in all likelihood going to lead to some differences of view and bring us before too long face to face with difficult decisions on such matters as economic aid.

3.   I was impressed by the urgency with which both Mr Somare and, perhaps more particularly his immediate advisers like Mr Voutas and Mr Barnett, were seeking to take over powers not only in the areas normally associated with full internal self-government but in areas related to independence. Julius Chan was, consciously or not, doing the same thing when he sought not only control over the budget but also the right to negotiate international loans. The fact that Coalition leaders want some powers which are really attributes of an independent government does not in my view mean that we should resist handing them over. What it does suggest is that we need at an appropriate time to draw to the attention of the leaders that the process of handing over on the lines discussed at your talks is likely to lead them to independence a good deal before they now appear to think is the desirable date.

4.   There are two aspects of this which suggest some caution on the part of the Commonwealth. The first is that PNG leaders do not appear to have taken into account the constraints on early independence—particularly their administrative capacity and financial resources to administer effectively the powers which they are seeking. You rightly refrained from talking much about capacities of this kind during the meetings. There is a good cause for saying more about them at the next meeting. The second point for concern is that the Commonwealth may be thought, by the Highlanders at any rate, to be deceiving them by only talking of self-government when in fact we are really bringing well forward the date of independence. It would be embarrassing for the Coalition if this were to be said publicly by the Commonwealth before the next meeting of the House of Assembly. However, the Administrator could say it privately as he thinks fit either in the AEC or to individual Ministers. After the September meeting of the House of Assembly you might consider taking the opportunity to bring the facts of the situation to light publicly. In any event, I expect you would wish to inform Cabinet.

5.   Insofar as the drive for the powers associated with independence is coming from Mr Somare's immediate advisers I think we could justifiably discuss it with them without

---

1   Document 287.

delay. There would be one avenue through which Mr Somare himself could be apprised of our concern.

6.   Another area for concern is the speed with which decisions are being taken. There was some frustration I believe amongst Ministers of the Papua New Guinea Government because of the fact that they had only received the papers very shortly before the final meetings. This suggests that in future we should leave a bigger interval between the completion of officials' discussions and the renewing of discussions at Ministerial level with a view to taking decisions. We are of course under pressure from individual Ministers such as Maori Kiki, to come quickly to policy decisions on the Australian side. I doubt whether we can respond as quickly as they wish. Indeed October is too early for the next meetings. We are committed to the October date, but I would not advise you to commit yourself to concluding any discussions in that month. It may be best to let a final Ministerial meeting following official discussions await the aftermath of the elections.

[*matter omitted*]

13.   A Cabinet Submission will of course be necessary in order to inform Cabinet of the results so far and get any clearances necessary. A draft of this will be placed before you tomorrow. It will be necessary to place it before the Inter-departmental Committee before it goes into Cabinet.

14.   I was struck by the competence, poise and charm of Mr Somare in his handling of his colleagues in the Papua New Guinea Cabinet. But some of his colleagues did not seem aware of the considerations behind many issues and are likely to rush into decisions without proper consideration. One way in which we can counter this is to insist, where we are considering the handover of an important power, that the position put forward by the Papua New Guinea Government (e.g. on the Public Service) is considered substantively by the AEC before it is brought into discussions with yourself. The position papers for the last meetings were prepared by a small group of officials and did not necessarily represent a mature and considered viewpoint on the Papua New Guinea side. One other course we can pursue is to invite individual Ministers to Australia ostensibly for consultations but in fact for educational purposes. Two Ministers I had in mind for early visits were Mr Julius Chan and Mr Jephcott. The former is talking about taking the reins in many fields of activity where his expertise is very small. He needs to come and talk to Treasury in detail in Australia about a number of aspects of what a Treasury is and does, and also to have his first introduction into the financial world perhaps through the Reserve Bank. I have mentioned this to the Administrator who agrees. He feels that it is something which could be initiated perhaps by Mr Stone[2] of the Treasury when he visits Papua New Guinea later this month. Mr Jephcott seems to me to be urgently in need of this kind of education. However the Administrator is less keen for him to be invited to Australia because he feels he may not be able to absorb the necessary knowledge down here. He feels that the best introduction to the realities of civil aviation policy will come during the course of Senator Cotton's visit.[3]

15.   If you agree I will send a copy of this Minute to the Administrator.

[NAA: A452, 1971/4151]

---

2   Probably a reference to John Stone, Deputy Secretary, Treasury.

3   Senator Robert Cotton, Minister for Civil Aviation, visited Port Moresby from 3 to 5 September 1972. For the text of Cotton's report to Parliament, see *CPD*, Senate, vol. 53, 19 September 1972, pp. 910–13.

352   MINUTE BY DEFENCE COMMITTEE[1]

Canberra, 14 August 1972

5/1972. CONFIDENTIAL

Comments by Mr Hay

Mr Hay spoke to the Committee on the recently completed constitutional talks held in PNG between the Minister for External Territories (Mr Peacock) and the PNG Chief Minister (Mr Somare).[2] The main points made by Mr Hay are summarised below (Mr Hay indicated he would be forwarding detailed comment through Departmental channels):

a.   There was gathering urgency in PNG for greater involvement in policy and practical day to day decision matters, including in defence matters.

b.   PNG Ministers sought involvement in the studies relating to PNG being undertaken in Canberra. In the case of various defence studies Mr Somare wanted indigenous officers of the PIR involved.

c.   In private discussions Mr Somare gave some indications that he might have in mind a concept of a 'people's army' modelled on the Tanzanian or Chinese experience for PNG; (ie, involving 'youth organization, less barracks orientation of the forces etc.').

d.   Mr Somare accepted with some reluctance the offer of an Australian Defence Officer to head the Defence Section and would have preferred that the Section be headed by an indigenous officer.

e.   Timescales for self-government and independence were accelerating and in practice PNG could find themselves in a virtually independent situation by the time of the granting of self-government. Present timetables may need to be dramatically reduced.

f.   Practical financial and manpower limitations which will require the cooperation of Australia to solve may however in the ultimate event cause PNG to adapt a more pragmatic approach.

g.   In due course some sort of Defence Advisory Committee might be formed within the AEC to advise and assist the Defence Spokesman. At present Mr Somare was relying to a large extent for advice on his small, largely expatriate personal staff.

Questioned on the degree of actual PNG involvement which Mr Somare would seek in the development of defence studies, Mr Hay replied that Mr Somare would probably insist upon 'consultation' as a minimum.

[NAA: A452, 1972/2671]

---

1   Those present for the discussion were Curtis, Blakers, Sir Victor Smith (Chair, Chiefs of Staff Committee), Major-General R. L. (Ron) Hughes (Director, Joint Staff, Department of Defence), Rear Admiral A. M. (Tony) Synnot (Deputy Chief of Naval Staff), Air Vice Marshal G. T. Newstead (Deputy Chief of the Air Staff) and Brigadier J. Whitelaw (Representing Chief of Operations Army). Also in attendance were Hay, Greenwell and Norrie.

2   See Documents 336–37, 345–48 & 351.

353 PRESS STATEMENT BY SOMARE

Port Moresby, 17 August 1972

The Chief Minister, Mr Somare, today reaffirmed his view on the question of West Irianese refugees who were in PNG.

2.   He said any West Irian refugees who cross the border into PNG seeking respite from fights with Indonesian troops and who were members of the Free Papua Movement would be sent back to their own country unless they applied for permissive residence.

3.   'We do not want the members of the Free Papua Movement to cross the border and use PNG as a base for fighting with the Indonesians,' he said.

4.   'Anyone crossing the border for this purpose will be returned to their own country.'

5.   However Mr Somare said that people who applied for permissive residency in PNG were in a different situation.

6.   He said the PNG Government and the Australian Government would return people who crossed the border unless it was shown that they faced persecution on return to their own country.

7.   He said the Australian Government had to be satisfied that this was so before a West Irianese would be granted permissive residency.

8.   Permissive residency would not be granted to criminals, spies or those using PNG as a base for operations against Indonesian authorities.

9.   Mr Somare also reiterated the view that those who publicly attack Indonesia or who engage in activities against Indonesia after being granted permissive residency run the risk of losing their permits.

10.   He said this was clearly laid down in the permits issued to those who had successfully applied for permissive residency.

11.   Mr Somare said that no permits had ever been cancelled in the past and it was not expected that any permits would be cancelled for those West Irianese who were presently living in PNG and who had been granted permissive residency.

12.   'The policy and attitude of the Australian and PNG Governments has not changed in the slightest. Anyone who wishes to compare past policy with my statements will find that there are no contradictions.'

Mr Somare said that some of the eight West Irianese who had been returned to West Irian on Wednesday had claimed that they were associated with the Free Papua Movement.

'This had been checked carefully and was proved untrue,' he said. 'They all later admitted that they were not associated with the movement. Because of this it was decided that they ran no risk of persecution on return to West Irian. Since they could not fulfil the necessary qualifications for permissive residency they were returned.'

[NAA: A1838; 3036/10/6/5 PART 1]

354   LETTER FROM HAY TO TANGE

Canberra, 18 August 1972

SECRET

Papua New Guinea: Defence Spokesman and other Defence Aspects of Constitutional Talks with PNG Leadership Group

As recorded in the communiqué issued by the Minister for External Territories and the PNG Chief Minister on 8 August,[1] following the discussions between Mr Peacock and Papua New Guinea Ministers and officials on constitutional development, it has been agreed that a position of Ministerial Spokesman for Defence should be created, as foreshadowed by the Commonwealth Minister for Defence during his discussions in Port Moresby in June,[2] and that initially the Chief Minister should assume this responsibility.

2.   In the course of the discussions it was agreed that the Defence Spokesman should have the functions suggested by Mr Fairbairn during his discussions with the Administrator's Executive Council in June, namely:

(a) answering Parliamentary questions and making statements on defence matters;

(b) consulting the Administrator and leading discussions in the AEC in regard to the development of the PNG forces;

(c) undertaking ceremonial duties.

3.   It was further agreed that a Defence Section (or Branch) should be established within the Department of the Administrator to assist the Defence Spokesman, as foreshadowed by the Minister for Defence. It was agreed that this Branch should preferably be headed initially by an experienced officer of your Department. In his separate, private talks with Mr Peacock, the Chief Minister expressed some reservations about the head of the Defence Section (or Branch) having direct access to Canberra. However, I think that the Chief Minister's view is in accordance with the duty statement for the Head of the Defence Branch that has already been agreed between our Departments. (Attachment 'A').[3] This proceeds on the basis that the head of the Defence Branch will be responsible to the Papua New Guinea Government through the Administrator.

4.   It seems to me that in order to clarify the position of the Head of the Defence Branch it may be desirable to draw up a directive making it quite clear not only to the officer himself but also to Ministers, members of Parliament and officials both in Papua New Guinea and in Australia that he will be a servant of the Papua New Guinea Administration, working through normal Administration channels in all his day-to-day activities, and that his advice is expected to reflect the interests of Papua New Guinea, although it would be given within the framework of Australia's defence policy until independence. It would also draw attention to the need for clearance with the Minister for Defence of public statements and answers to questions by the Defence Spokesman in accordance with the agreed arrangements. I enclose a draft of such a directive for your consideration (Attachment 'B').[4]

[*matter omitted*]

---

1   Document 347.

2   See Document 311.

3   Not published

4   Not published.

7.   During the talks, Papua New Guinea Ministers made clear their concern that there should be a more rapid orientation of the existing Defence Force in PNG and their administrative processes towards the Papua New Guinea Government, and towards the needs of PNG as PNG Ministers see them. They therefore considered it a matter of vital importance that Papua New Guinea Ministers and officials should be more closely involved in planning for the future defence forces of their country. During private discussions with the Chief Minister and his advisers, it was clearly thought to be vital that the PNG Government be consulted in all important policy decisions and the point was also strongly made that Papua New Guinea Government representatives and in some cases officers of the PNG Defence Forces should be directly represented on committees at present studying defence policy matters.[5] This point was obviously directed towards the programme of seventeen studies upon which our Departments and the Service and some other Departments have been engaged for the past year. Administration officers have been consulted in relation to most of these studies. But since many of them discuss policy considerations from an Australian Government viewpoint it may be desirable to institute a series of parallel study groups, perhaps based in Papua New Guinea, so as to involve Papua New Guinea officials.

8.   Throughout the constitutional talks Papua New Guinea Ministers pressed for an acceleration of the pace of constitutional change. This was particularly evident in the private discussions between the Chief Minister and the Minister for External Territories.

[NAA: A452, 1972/2801]

---

5   See Documents 345 & 352.

355   SUBMISSION FROM BORDER TO BOWEN

Canberra, 25 August 1972

CONFIDENTIAL

Papua New Guinea—Constitutional Talks

I attach a copy of the record of the PNG Constitutional talks held recently in Port Moresby between the Minister for External Territories and the PNG Chief Minister.[1]

[*matter omitted*]

2.   There are a number of points of particular foreign affairs interest. We will need to study the implications of some of these and be ready to put a view by the next round of talks which are set down for October 1972.

PNG Role in International Relations

3.   PNG Ministers made clear their determination to take an active part in the decision making process even in reserved areas such as foreign affairs. The final communiqué said: 'the need for full involvement of the Papua New Guinea Government in these matters was recognised and the means of doing so will be further studied'.[2] It was also agreed that the Administrator's Executive Council should be fully involved in any international agreements, including aid ones, before they are negotiated and that PNG should be represented jointly with Australia wherever appropriate. (To this end the PNG Secretary for Law was sent to the Law of the Sea Conference in Geneva 'to ensure that PNG's interests were advanced' in a situation where Australian and PNG interests are likely to diverge.) However, the Minister for External Territories stressed that consultation was a two way process and the PNG Government should also consult Australia where a decision on a matter within PNG jurisdiction might impinge on Australia's international relations. He also made it clear we could not accept any decision which ran counter to our obligations under the Trusteeship Agreement or some other international arrangement to which Australia was a party.

Aid and Economic Matters

4.   PNG representatives, including the Leader of the Opposition, referred to economic planning as a 'foreign concept' which was not always understood and stressed that PNG could not rely on 'imported ideas' imposed by foreign experts but needed to decide itself the 'social goals, standards and society it wanted'. The message, in short, seemed to be that while they wanted us to finance it, they had to work out their own economic development schemes. While accepting the general philosophy, the Minister for External Territories pointed out that Australia, 'like any aid-giver, would reasonably expect that if it were to support a programme to a large extent the programme would need to be acceptable to it'. He suggested therefore that, with the concurrence of their Ministers, PNG and Australian officials might work together on such programmes to avoid a 'confrontation' between the two governments.

5.   The Chief Minister said PNG needed to know some 3 to 5 years in advance what financial aid would be available if it were to plan effectively. This should be discussed in October. (On 16 August he repeated this point publicly.)

---

1   See Documents 345 & 346.

2   Document 347.

6.   There would seem to be a need for Foreign Affairs officials to be closely involved in such discussions if aid is to continue after independence.

Migration

7.   Migration policy is to be transferred immediately except that the transfer must not affect Australia's responsibilities for international relations. Here migration policy impinges on international relations, e.g. in regard to the border with Indonesia, the PNG Government will need to consult the Australian Government. It was further agreed that negotiation of a border agreement with Indonesia, covering border crossers, would involve the participation of both Australian and PNG Governments. Australia will keep control over security aspects as well.

[*matter omitted*]

Defence

9.   It was agreed a Ministerial Spokesman for Defence should be appointed and that an officer of the Department of Defence in Canberra should be seconded to establish a Defence Section of the Administrator's Department. However, the PNG side stressed their wish to keep their options open on defence arrangements and noted that there was a need for a more rapid orientation of the existing Defence Forces in PNG and their administrative processes towards the needs and Government of PNG. There was also a need for PNG officials to take part in discussions and study groups on defence matters which were undertaken by Commonwealth officials.

[*matter omitted*]

Role of the Administrator

11.   It was recommended that the Constitutional Planning Committee should give a high priority to an examination of the role of the Administrator during self-government—assuming self-government and independence were not achieved simultaneously. The Administrator expressed the view that there should not be two Australian representatives, i.e. the Administrator and a diplomatic representative. In the meantime, the Administrator will continue to withdraw gradually from his active role.

Foreign Affairs Spokesman

12.   Although not mentioned in the attached document, we understand that PNG officials raised informally the question of a Foreign Affairs Spokesman and what bureaucratic arrangements might be made to support him, e.g. a Foreign Affairs Department perhaps merged with International Trade.

Conclusions

13.   The main conclusions which emerged from the discussions are:

(a) PNG leaders have not always thought their ideas through in detail, but they intend to push for a rapid transfer of powers and for a close involvement in those powers which are reserved;

(b) independence is likely to come very soon and possibly within two years from now;

(c) Foreign Affairs will need to become much more closely involved with PNG from now on.

Comment

14. It seems to me that if PNG is, albeit under certain constraints, to project a separate international identity and if the PNG Government is to participate in the decision making process, we need to consider whether the present arrangements for contact with PNG on foreign affairs are adequate. There may be advantage in having more direct contact at official level and perhaps, in your taking part in some of the discussions with PNG Ministers. At present all formal contact with PNG Ministers and officials takes place through the Minister and Department of External Territories.

[*matter omitted*]

[NAA: A1838, 3080/5/2 PART 2]

356   LETTER FROM TANGE TO HAY

Canberra, 25 August 1972

CONFIDENTIAL

Thank you for your letter[1] received on 18th August regarding the exchange of letters with the Chief Minister in Papua New Guinea on the appointment of the Ministerial Spokesman on Defence and on the duties and responsibilities of the Head of the Defence Branch to be appointed in the Administrator's Department.

[*matter omitted*]

I expect that the officer would keep my department fully and promptly informed of developments in the defence field as they emerge in the House of Assembly. For my part, my staff stand ready to give assistance and guidance as required, and the necessary administrative arrangements are being activated to ensure that any advice required by the Ministerial Spokesman from this end is available without delay.

I note your observations in the penultimate paragraph of your letter about the desire of PNG Ministers as stated in the recent constitutional talks to be fully consulted and more closely involved at both Ministerial and official levels in planning and decisions concerning the future defence forces. As regards consultation at Ministerial level, my Minister emphasised during his talks in June with the Administrator's Executive Council and publicly that close and continuing consultation was our objective. Once we have the Head of the Defence Branch established in Port Moresby, it would also be possible for PNG officials to be associated in studies and proposals as they are being developed, although the effectiveness of parallel study groups would need to be fully evaluated.

There is one other matter to which I wish to refer. I think it is important that the Australian Parliament should be informed in appropriate terms of the matters relating to the appointment of the Ministerial Spokesman on Defence, as set out in the Administrator's letter to the Chief Minister. The timing of such a statement would presumably need to have regard to the Chief Minister's plans for announcement in the PNG House of Assembly about the recent constitutional talks and to any plans your Minister may have to inform Parliament on the talks. I would appreciate your early views on my proposal.

[NAA: A452, 1972/2801]

---

1   Document 354.

357   MEMORANDUM FROM TANGE TO DET

Canberra, 28 August 1972

CONFIDENTIAL

Papua New Guinea Defence Coordinating Committee (PNG DCC)

The Minister for Defence has approved the establishment within the Department of Defence of a Papua New Guinea Defence Coordinating Committee (PNG DCC) to coordinate and direct the functioning of the PNG Defence Force as PNG approaches self-government and independence. The membership and functions of the committee are set out below.

Membership

The PNG DCC will comprise:

> *Chairman*
>> Chairman, Chiefs of Staff Committee [CCS]
>
> *Members*
>> Deputy Secretary (A), Department of Defence
>>
>> Deputy Secretary (B), Department of Defence
>>
>> Director, Joint Staff, Department of Defence
>>
>> Deputy Chief of Naval Staff
>>
>> Chief of Operations (Army)
>>
>> Deputy Chief of the Air Staff

Representatives from other Departments, including the Department of External Territories, will be co-opted as required.

Functions

The PNG DCC will be responsible for:

(a) coordination and direction of the functioning of the PNG Defence Force, including its organisation, manning, equipment and support needs, to prepare it for independence;

(b) coordinating the various planning activities and studies related to the development of the PNG Defence Force, and to monitor their progress;

(c) consideration of Australian defence requirements in PNG after independence.

The Committee will ensure that necessary decisions are promptly made at whatever level is appropriate.

Secretariat

The Chief Executive Officer (Mr G. R. Marshall) Section D, Defence Planning Division and the Army Member (Colonel I. R. W. Brumfield) of the Joint Policy Staff, working as an integrated team, will be responsible for providing executive and administrative support to the CCS and the PNG DCC in carrying out its function and will be known as the PNG Secretariat. For this purpose they will be responsible directly to the CCS. They will be the point of inter-Service and inter-Departmental contact on matters appropriate to their level.

2.   It would be appreciated if you could nominate an officer from your Department who might be invited to attend meetings of the PNG DCC when subjects of relevance to your Department are to be discussed.

[NAA: A452, 1972/2671]

358   LETTER FROM PEACOCK TO JOHNSON

Canberra, 29 August 1972

CONFIDENTIAL

You will recall that, at my recent Constitutional talks with the Chief Minister, I agreed on behalf of the Commonwealth to the creation of a Ministerial Spokesman for Police.[1]

I have also agreed that this appointment should be made 'by the Administrator after consultation with the Deputy Chairman of the Administrator's Executive Council'. This arrangement is consistent with that covering the Ministerial Spokesman for Defence, to which I refer in my separate letter of today's date.[2]

Since the Chief Minister has already advised that initially he will assume this responsibility, you should proceed with the appointment, to take effect from 28 August, the date on which the appointment of the Ministerial Spokesman for Defence will also take effect.

The role of the Police Spokesman is at the present time analogous with the role of the Defence Spokesman but as I indicated privately to the Chief Minister, the question of greater involvement of the Papua New Guinea Ministry in police and internal security matters is still under study. For the time being, the Commonwealth retains executive authority over the Police.

It is envisaged that the Chief Minister will be informed in writing of the Spokesman's responsibilities and that you and the Commissioner of Police will engage in close consultation with him on police matters generally.

I should be glad if you would write to the Chief Minister in terms of the attached text which sets out the functions of the Ministerial Spokesman for Police. No doubt, you would wish also to discuss the contents of the letter with him personally.

Attachment
Draft letter—Administrator to Chief Minister

At the recent constitutional talks, the Minister for External Territories signified Commonwealth agreement to your request that a Ministerial Spokesman for Police be appointed. The Minister has now authorised me to proceed with your appointment to this office.

You and the Minister have briefly discussed the functions of the Ministerial Spokesman for Police which would be:

(A) answering questions in the House of Assembly and making statements on police matters;

(B) consulting the Administrator (and the Commissioner of Police)[3] on policy decisions related to the basic planning structure, or development of the force, equipment and major expenditure;

(C) presenting submissions to the AEC and leading discussion on major expenditure and equipment proposals involving the Royal Papua New Guinea Constabulary;

(D) attending the invitation meetings of the Internal Security Committee;

---

1   See Document 345.

2   Document 359.

3   N. A. M. Nicholls.

(E) being consulted in respect of an emergency such as civil disturbance or disaster;

(F) submitting recommendations (after consultation with the Administrator) that the AEC approve measures to preserve law and order by bringing into effect the Public Order Ordinance and its provisions relating to restrictions of meetings and processions in defined areas.

After appointment of a Spokesman, Australia will continue for the time being to be fully responsible, as now, for executive authority over the police and matters of internal security. The question of devolving authority over the police and internal security to Ministers of your Government is still under study. The present aim is that you should become closely involved with policy matters relating to the development and functioning of the Constabulatory [sic]. The Commissioner of Police and I will refer to you all major policy matters relating to the police and important questions of internal security. For your part, we hope that you will consult with us about any matters concerning the Constabulatory [sic] which may be raised with your Government. Australia recognises that there are good reasons for assigning a considerable degree of responsibility for internal security to your Government as part of the evolution to self-government.

As Ministerial Spokesman for the Police you will be entitled to make public statements on police matters. Consistent with the fact that the Commonwealth at this time still retains final responsibility for police matters there is a need to arrive at procedures so that there may be prior agreement with me before the issue of public parliamentary statements by the Police Spokesman.

[NAA: A452, 1972/2801]

359   LETTER FROM PEACOCK TO JOHNSON

Canberra, 29 August 1972

CONFIDENTIAL

You will recall that, at my recent constitutional talks with the Chief Minister,[1] I confirmed that the Commonwealth is willing to agree to his request for a Defence Spokesman with functions outlined by the Minister for Defence in his June discussions with the members of the AEC.

The Minister for Defence and I have agreed that the appointment should be made 'by the Administrator, in consultation with the Deputy Chairman of the Administrator's Executive Council'.[2]

Since the Chief Minister has already advised that initially he will assume this responsibility, there is no reason why you should not proceed with the appointment this week.

It is important that the Chief Minister is informed in writing of the Spokesman's responsibilities and the limitations which derive from the Australian Government's intention to continue to be fully responsible, in the same way as now, for the defence of Papua New Guinea. The Spokesman will thus need to operate within the broad Defence policies of the Australian Government.

In order to ensure that there is no misunderstanding in this respect, I should be glad if you would write to the Chief Minister in terms of the attached text. No doubt you would wish also to discuss the contents of the letter with him personally.

Attachment
Draft Letter—Administrator to Chief Minister

At the recent Constitutional talks, the Minister for External Territories signified Commonwealth agreement to your request that a Ministerial Spokesman on Defence be appointed. The Minister has now authorised me to proceed with your appointment to this office.

You and the Minister have already endorsed the conclusions reached by officials that the functions of the Spokesman might be:

(a) Answering Parliamentary questions and making statements on defence matters;

(b) Consulting the Administrator on defence matters;

(c) Presenting submissions to the AEC and leading discussions on the development of the PNG Forces and on defence policies to be evolved for PNG in the future; and

(d) Undertaking ceremonial duties.

After the appointment of a Spokesman, Australia will continue to be fully responsible, as now, for final control over the defence of Papua New Guinea and for the defence forces and equipment deployed within the Territory. For so long as this constitutional position remains, it is important that in the Assembly and publicly the Spokesman states the defence policies for PNG as laid down by the Australian Government. The appointment is designed to further the acquisition of knowledge and expertise of defence matters within the Papua New Guinea ministry. In addition, the Spokesman is free to provide to Australian authorities, on a continuing basis, considered confidential advice on the organisation and management of the defence force

1   See Document 345.
2   See Document 356.

to satisfy Papua New Guinea's present and future defence needs. This function is particularly applicable where you feel that the Australian experience and aims might not be relevant to the needs of the Papua New Guinea situation as you see it. In so doing your Government will need to give close attention to the development of longer term defence policies which have regard to future contingencies which could affect the security of PNG.

The desirability of close consultation with your Ministry in defence decisions was recognised and stated by the Minister for Defence when he addressed the Administrator's Executive Council in June last.[3] As the Commonwealth, and specifically the Minister for Defence, has final responsibility for defence policy, and as the Minister for Defence also directs the Chairman, Chiefs of Staff Committee who in turn controls the three Services in PNG, there is a need for us to arrive at procedures so that there may be prior agreement with Defence authorities in Australia before the issue of public or parliamentary statements by the Defence Spokesman. Likewise the Australian Defence Minister and his Department would seek means of clearing with you statements made by Australian authorities in relation to PNG defence interests. The Department of Defence has undertaken to provide fast and secure channels for such an arrangement. I hope you will agree with me that the Spokesman will comply with a convention that agreement will be reached on the texts of public statements and substantive responses to Parliamentary questions, including any public reference to the nature of advice given to the Australian Minister for Defence. A procedure where the Spokesman might defer responding immediately to questions without notice would be necessary in this context.

You have already endorsed the officials' conclusion that there will be a need for some advisory and supporting staff to advise the Administrator and the Spokesman to carry out his responsibilities. Steps will be taken to second from Australia an official, experienced in defence matters, to take up duty within my Department. Apart from training Papua New Guinea staff to handle matters of a defence policy nature, the official will, as Head of the Defence Branch within the Department of the Administrator, assist the Spokesman in the formulation and development of Papua New Guinea views on future defence requirements. He will work through normal Administration channels in all of his day to day activities, (although where advice of fact or policy is required urgently for responses to Parliamentary questions he may need direct communication with Defence officials in Canberra).

[NAA: A452, 1972/2801]

---

3   Document 311.

360   CABLEGRAM TO CANBERRA[1]

Djakarta, 30 August 1972

3610. CONFIDENTIAL

Official Talks[2]

After a slightly slow start on the first morning, the seven hours of discussion which we had with Foreign Ministry officials on Monday and Tuesday were productive and frank.

The most useful part of them was the exchange on bilateral relations, and in particular on Papua-New Guinea.

2.   On Papua-New Guinea, the rapidity with which events are moving in the Territory has come home to the Foreign Ministry for the first time, as well as the fact that Indonesia has an urgent need not only to get to know Territory leaders better but also to dispel suspicions there about Indonesian motives and actions.[3]

We spoke frankly to them on this last count.

The Indonesians reacted well to the Secretary's observation that they needed the best man they could find for the proposed consular post in Port Moresby.

They are clearly anxious for early agreement to their request to open up there.

Their officials told us later that our presentation to them would generally help the Foreign Ministry in arguing its case on Papua-New Guinea with other Ministries, particularly the Defence establishment.

They left no doubt that the future foreign relations of an independent PNG would be of concern to Indonesia.

The Foreign Ministry is also seized of the desirability of a reasonably early invitation to Somare to visit Indonesia.

3.   There was a useful general discussion on the complexity of border questions—the seabed boundary, the land border in PNG and the question of a possible border regime agreement.

The Indonesians tentatively agreed to 25th September for the seabed talks, the meeting to last perhaps a week.

They are now anxious to push on quickly with the remaining land border issues in New Guinea and would like to have at least a preliminary discussion (and if possible more) of these matters during the 25th September meeting.

---

1   See also Documents 308, 325, 334 (para 15) & 343.

2   Australia–Indonesia Official Talks. Waller led the Australian delegation.

3   Waller made the same point the previous day, telling Indonesian officials that 'constitutional change [in PNG] was proceeding more rapidly than we had previously expected'. He predicted that 'this process would be accelerated and it was now clear that full independence would follow on very rapidly after self-government'. Under these circumstances, Waller felt that 'it was not only important that Indonesia should have a Consul in Port Moresby, but also that it should be able to establish good contact with the indigenous leadership'. Somare, he said, 'was a good man, intelligent and realistic', but had little experience in foreign affairs: 'Indonesia would have to look to building up its own relations and would have to make efforts of its own to convince the people in Papua New Guinea that it was friendly and in no way a threat to Papua New Guinea'. Record of Conversation between Waller and Indonesian Officials, 29 August 1972, NAA: A1838, 3034/10/1/8 PART 2.

We told them that we would have to raise this with you, and that the need to have representation from PNG at such discussions, and to take PNG views into account, might complicate matters in this regard.

[*matter omitted*]⁴

11. In general, we found the talks to be very useful, and we believe that the Indonesians were equally pleased. The highlight is undoubtedly the frank talking on Papua New Guinea and the opening of what can be a real dialogue on this subject.⁵

[NAA: A452, 1972/3137]

---

4   The omitted matter contained an account of discussions on various matters, including the land border issue, Indonesia's 'archipelago and straits policies', its 'approach to ASEAN and neutralisation', defence cooperation, and various regional and international issues.

5   In an annotation dated 31 August 1972, Peacock asked: 'Secretary: Does this Department (DFA) believe it is empowered to "speak frankly" about PNG without close consultation and representation by our Department? Perhaps they would be unusually courteous by advising us fully on their return.' Hay responded by assuring Peacock that Foreign Affairs had consulted the DET fully before the talks and had undertaken to furnish a full record of the discussions relating to PNG. At the same time, he told Peacock that the DET's 'very limited staff resources' on PNG matters constrained the participation of DET officials in talks of this kind and that the DFA 'clearly understood' that External Territories and the PNG Administration would be represented in any technical discussions with the Indonesians on land and sea borders. Hay concluded: 'In my view the Department of Foreign Affairs does not always enable this Department to make the contribution it should to international negotiations. The question of representation at the recent South Pacific Forum is a recent example. However in view of the facts and considerations stated above I submit that it would be unfair to reproach the Department of Foreign Affairs for its handling of the diplomatic negotiations in Djakarta on 28–29 August.' Peacock responded: 'Thank you for the above information [...] I had wished to write to the Foreign Minister but will not do so now'. Minute, Hay to Peacock (containing Peacock's instruction), 11 September 1972, NAA: A452, 1972/3137.

361   CABINET SUBMISSION 863[1]

Canberra, 30 August 1972

CONFIDENTIAL

Papua New Guinea—Programme of Movement towards
Internal Self-Government—Report on Initial Discussions[2]

Purpose

The purpose of this submission is to report to Cabinet on my recent constitutional discussions with the Papua New Guinea leadership group authorised in Decision No. 980 (PNG) of 18 May, 1972.[3]

Background

2.   The discussions took place in Port Moresby on 27 July and 28 July, 1972 and on 7 August, 1972. At the first meeting the entire Ministry was present. Thereafter I met with Coalition leaders. On 7 August, a representative of the Mataungan Association was also present.[4] The Leader of the Opposition, Mr Toliman, was present, at the Chief Minister's invitation, at all meetings. He took an active part in the discussions though from the outset (in his opening statement) he made it clear that the decisions reached during the talks 'in no way bind the Opposition to a future course of action or set of policies'. A record of the discussions (Annex A)[5] including texts of the opening statements of the Chief Minister, the Leader of the Opposition and myself, and of the final communiqué, is available from the Cabinet Secretariat.

3.   The atmosphere throughout was friendly. The Chief Minister was very much in command of his colleagues and presented the Papua New Guinea viewpoint effectively. He left me in no doubt about the wish of the Coalition to have authority in all areas of government transferred as soon as practicable. Even in areas which had been thought likely to remain a Commonwealth responsibility until independence (e.g. defence, internal security, intelligence and representation at international conferences) the Chief Minister, his colleagues and advisers are seeking immediate involvement in terms which indicate that they do not at present distinguish clearly between powers appropriate to self-government and powers more appropriate to a state of independence.

4.   As a result, without pressing for independence as such, the Coalition could well find itself virtually independent by the date set down for internal self-government. Such a situation could lead to political problems in Papua New Guinea, for example, the Highland leaders may claim that they have been deceived by talk of self-government when in fact it is independence which is being planned. In this connection it is understood that the United Party may be preparing a written submission to me giving its considered views. It also raises acutely the question of whether Papua New Guinea is ready as soon as this for full independence. I intend to discuss this aspect with the Coalition leaders during the next series of constitutional talks in October with a view to reaching a clear understanding on what they see as constituting self-government.

---

1   Submitted by Peacock.

2   See also Documents 336–37, 339, 345–48, 351 & 354–55.

3   Document 296.

4   For the PNG participants, see Document 347, fns 1–4.

5   Not published.

5.   In my submission to Cabinet (No. 627 of April 1972)[6] I included the following definition of internal self-government:

'... a situation in which the Commonwealth has ceased to exercise executive or legislative control in the administration of Papua New Guinea in respect of its internal affairs. External Affairs and Defence would remain a Commonwealth responsibility. The outward sign of internal self-government will be the formal divesting by Australia of its powers by amendment to the Papua New Guinea Act. This would take place in the final stages of an orderly progression. The scope of power conferred at internal self-government may need to reflect Australia's continuing obligations under the Trusteeship Agreement. By the time of this divesting of powers under the Papua New Guinea Act other Commonwealth legislation affecting the bulk of Papua New Guinea's internal affairs would have ceased to be applicable to Papua New Guinea.'

Results of the Meeting

6.   The tentative programme endorsed by the Cabinet in Decision No. 980 as a basis for discussions for the transfer of further powers is being re-drawn in the light of the discussions in order to reflect the wishes of the Coalition leaders. This revised programme will be the subject of further discussions in October.

7.   A schedule of powers which are to be transferred in the very near future is attached. Subject to the views of the House of Assembly after consideration of the transfer of these further powers, I propose to take the necessary steps to effect the transfer. It is anticipated that the House of Assembly will consider this matter during its present meeting (August/ September). No substantial administrative or financial commitments are involved for the Commonwealth in respect of those matters listed in paragraph 1 of the schedule for in these cases the administrative machinery already exists in Papua New Guinea.

8.   I would transfer the remaining powers listed in the Schedule (paragraphs 2, 3, and 4) once all the outstanding points have been resolved. The transfer of authority, and its timing, in respect of these matters depend either on the settling of arrangements to provide for the necessary consultation between the Australian and the Papua New Guinea Governments, or, on the allocation of the powers to a particular portfolio, or, on amendment of Papua New Guinea legislation. An example of this first category (matters listed in paragraph 2 of the Schedule) is economic development. The Papua New Guinea Ministers have indicated their desire to have final authority over their development programme and new major development projects. I believe that this authority should be transferred but in view of the possibility that Papua New Guinea may in due course wish to seek Commonwealth financial assistance for some of the projects involved, the transfer should be on the basis that, as in the past, continuing consultation will take place with the Commonwealth, even in the preliminary stages. Papua New Guinea Ministers have already indicated acceptance of this.

9.   Some of the powers referred to in paragraph 8 involve the functions of other Commonwealth Ministers and before any commitment is entered into with the Papua New Guinea Government these Ministers will be fully consulted.

10.   The necessary studies on powers still remaining with the Commonwealth but which are not included in the Schedule were authorised at the discussions. These studies are the preliminary steps to setting target dates at the next meeting in October for the transfer of those powers to Papua New Guinea Ministers. In some cases for example Civil Aviation, the most expeditious procedure is through direct discussions between the Papua New Guinean and the Australian authorities. I have in such cases been in direct touch with the Ministers concerned.

---

6   Document 278.

Consultation with Papua New Guinea Government

11. I have informed the Chief Minister that it is the Government's wish even in matters which are likely to remain a Commonwealth responsibility until independence to consult fully with him before decisions are taken. As a practical means of involving Papua New Guinea authorities at an early stage, I have, with the agreement of the Minister for Defence arranged for the appointment of one of the Papua New Guinea Ministers as a 'Defence Spokesman' with duties mainly related to answering Parliamentary Questions and acting as a point for consultation on policy matters. I have also agreed to the appointment of a Police Spokesman. Initially the Chief Minister will assume both functions himself. I expect to be in touch with the Ministers for Foreign Affairs and Civil Aviation in anticipation of requests for spokesmen in these two areas.

Role of the House of Assembly

12. The Government's policy of looking to the House of Assembly to represent the wishes of the majority of the people is accepted by the Chief Minister. The following procedures were agreed upon:

'Where the Commonwealth and Papua New Guinea Governments agree that power is ready for transfer and the Papua New Guinea Government requests transfer of such a power the Commonwealth shall arrange the transfer as soon as practicable. The Papua New Guinea Government intends to inform the House of Assembly of all proposed transfers before accepting them.

'If a constitutional or important change is involved, both Governments agree that there should be a recorded vote in favour, by a substantial majority of Members, and that the majority should be broadly representative of the country.'

13. None of the proposals for immediate and early transfers of power (paragraphs 7 and 8) are, in my view, in the category of a 'constitutional or important change'.

The Date of Self-government

14. The time-scale for self-government is clearly an 'important change'. The Coalition has before the House of Assembly a recommendation that the date of self-government be 1 December, 1973 or 'as soon as possible thereafter'. This recommendation will be considered by the House at its meeting beginning 28 August, 1972. In my opinion it is probable that the Coalition will achieve a majority on this matter in the House in terms of the agreed procedures. It is desirable that the Australian Government react quickly to a conclusion of the House of Assembly. Given the quality of leadership displayed by the Chief Minister and his Government, I believe the Government should respond favourably and I now seek Cabinet agreement to such a course.

15. In respect of certain other considerations in Cabinet Decision 980 (PNG), I comment as follows:

Paragraph 2(a)—Comprehension of the Need for Sound Groundwork. I am bound to say that it is not likely that Papua New Guinea Ministers will regard the need for sound groundwork as an obstacle to quick movement toward self-government. Nevertheless this aspect has been emphasised by me in my discussions, and my Department has, as a major task, the giving of assistance to Papua New Guinea to establish a sound administrative and financial basis for the exercising of newly transferred powers.

Paragraph 2(b)—Departments and Agencies Performing Functions of Internal Self-Government. Inter-departmental consultations are proceeding.

Paragraph 2(c)—Consultations with the United Nations. My Department and the Department of Foreign Affairs are in agreement that no problem is likely to arise from the United Nations in relation to the programme.

Paragraph 2(d)—Involvement of Non-Government Party Leaders. The Chief Minister has of his own initiative sought to include the Papua New Guinea Leader of the Opposition in constitutional discussions.

The Standing Interdepartmental Committee on Papua New Guinea has raised no objections to this submission.

Interval between Self-Government and Independence

16. Whatever the outcome of the clarification of the Coalition's degree of involvement in matters over which the Commonwealth is finally responsible (paragraph 4 above), the likelihood of a substantial interval between self-government and independence continues to diminish. I believe that we should recognise now the distinct possibility of a short interval between self-government and independence and be prepared to act accordingly.

RECOMMENDATIONS

17. I recommend:

(a) that Cabinet note the results of the discussions held in Port Moresby in July/August;

(b) that Cabinet note the Schedule for further transfer of powers (Attachment);

(c) that Cabinet authorise me to accept a recommendation from the House of Assembly that the date of self-government be 1 December, 1973 or as soon as possible thereafter, on the basis set out in paragraph 12 and to state this publicly at the appropriate time;

(d) that Cabinet note the possibility of the shortened interval between self-government and independence;

(e) that Cabinet note that discussions with the Leadership Group are to continue in October 1972.

Attachment
Schedule for Further Transfer of Powers

1. *Immediately*
    *   Cocoa Appeal Committee
    *   Coffee Appeal Committee
    *   Rubber Board
    *   Supply of Goods and Services
    *   Wages and Industrial Relations Policy in the private sector
    *   Localisation and training in the private sector
    *   Pollution Control
    *   Administration transport fleet policy
    *   Selective entry for employment
    *   Land settlement and development policy

2.   *Subject to the need for consultation taking place (on the specific power or function)*
between the Papua New Guinea and the Commonwealth Governments
   • Migration policy excluding security aspects
   • Volunteer policy
   • Economic Development Programme Structure, including the Office of
Programming and Coordination (suitable arrangements to be settled—see paragraph
8 of Submission)

3.   *Subject to the allocation of the power or function to a Minister of the House of*
Assembly
   • Political Education
   • Parliamentary Drafting
   • Bankruptcy and Insolvency
   • Probate and Administration
   • Registration of Births, Deaths and Marriages
   • Culture

4.   *Subject to the need to amend Papua New Guinea legislation*
   • Arawa Municipal Commission
   • Area Authorities
   • Papua New Guinea Harbours Board
   • Tariff Advisory Committee
   • Income Tax Review Tribunal.

[NAA: A5908, 863]

362   STATEMENT BY SOMARE[1]

Port Moresby, 31 August 1972

I wish to report to this House on the Constitutional talks which were held from 27th July to 7th August last and on matters arising from them.[2]

The talks were attended by the Ministers of this House, the Leader of the Opposition,[3] Father John Momis, as Deputy Chairman of the Constitutional Planning Committee, and the Minister for External Territories. During the closing stages a representative of the Mataungan Association attended.[4]

Like myself, the Leader of the Opposition was assisted by advisers, one of whom was a lawyer provided from the Political Development Division of my own office.

After the first two days of ministerial discussion certain matters were referred to officials of the Australian and Papua New Guinea Governments who discussed and reported on them. Father Momis also participated during these discussions. The ministerial talks were then resumed. Ministers considered the officials' reports and they reached agreement on some of those matters. Other topics were set aside for further study and discussion.

It was agreed that final powers over various matters could be transferred to the Papua New Guinea Ministry now. In practice, both this Government, and the previous Government have been exercising these powers without reference to the Commonwealth for some time. What is about to happen is the step which formalises the Constitutional position. The change will be made simply by the Minister for External Territories altering the Approved Arrangements regarding the powers of the Papua New Guinea Ministers.

Unless this House objects, the matters over which power is to be transferred immediately are:

Cocoa Appeal Committee

Coffee Appeal Committee

Rubber Board

Supply of Goods and Services

Supply and Tender Board

Wages and Industrial Relations Policy (Private Sector)

Pollution etc. Control

Arawa Municipal Commission

Area Authorities

Migration Policy (Excluding Security Aspects)

Papua New Guinea Harbours Board

Administration Fleet Policy

Political Education

Localisation and Training (Private Sector)

Parliamentary Drafting

Bankruptcy and Insolvency

---

1   The statement was delivered in the PNG House of Assembly.

2   See also Documents 336–37, 339, 345–48, 351, 354–55 & 361.

3   Matthias Toliman.

4   John Kaputin.

712 31 August 1972

Probate and Administration

Registration of Births, Deaths and Marriages

Economic Development Programme Structure

Culture

Volunteer Policy

Tariff Advisory Committee

Selective Entry for Employment

Land Settlement and Development Policy

Income Tax Review Tribunal

The proposed new arrangements by which this transfer of further power is to be effected are being prepared by the Commonwealth.

It was stated in the joint statement by the Minister for External Territories and myself, that positions of Spokesman for Defence and Spokesman for the Police should be created.

It was agreed that the function of the Spokesman for Defence will be to:

(a) Answer Parliamentary questions and make statements on Defence matters;

(b) consult the Administrator, present submissions to the Administrator's Executive Council, and lead discussions in the Administrator's Executive Council in regard to the development of the Papua New Guinea forces and Defence policies;

(c) undertake ceremonial duties.[5]

The Commonwealth has undertaken to second a suitably qualified senior Public Servant to head up a Defence Section to be created initially in the Department of the Administrator. This section will support the Spokesman for Defence.

Although Australia will continue to be fully responsible as now for the final control over the defence of Papua New Guinea and for the defence forces employed in Papua New Guinea, the creation of the Ministerial Spokesman for Defence will provide the means for effective consultation which will ensure that the defence forces are trained and developed in ways which will satisfy Papua New Guinea's long term national interests.

With regard to Police the situation is very similar. It is not intended to transfer final power over the Police at this stage and so it is not appropriate to create a ministerial portfolio. A Minister will, however, be appointed as Spokesman for Police and will speak on Police matters in this House and will consult with the Administrator and the Commissioner of Police and will take part in discussions of policy concerning the Police force and Police actions.[6]

Initially I intend to assume responsibility for both these positions myself.

The Minister for External Territories also agreed to my request that the Papua New Guinea Act be amended to remove the then existing restrictions on the number of ministers who can be appointed. The necessary amendment, to section 24 of the Papua New Guinea Act, has now been passed by the Commonwealth.[7] I wish to ask the Minister for External Territories to create three additional positions of Minister but I shall not make this request if the House on resolution objects.

Constitutional talks will be held in October to discuss further Constitutional matters, including future financial arrangements between Australia and Papua New Guinea, and to consider the

---

5   See Document 359.

6   See Document 358.

7   Cabinet had agreed to the amendment on 18 May. See Document 295.

transfer of further power to the Papua New Guinea Government. The Leader of the Opposition, the Deputy Chairman of the Constitutional Planning Committee and a representative of the Mataungan Association will be invited to attend these talks.

[NAA: A452, 1972/2801]

363   LETTER FROM SMITH TO NORRIE

Canberra, 31 August 1972

CONFIDENTIAL

During the Ministerial discussions which were held in July/August 1972 in Port Moresby the point was made by the Chief Minister that PNG soldiers had been developed as members of the Australian Army and it was essential that they were oriented quickly away from Australia to PNG.[1] This view, together with the possibility that independence may be granted earlier than was previously planned, makes it necessary that we should begin considering means of achieving suitable orientation. To this end, it is requested that you forward your views and proposals regarding a common uniform for the PNG Defence Force (working uniforms for each element may have to have regard to the working/environmental conditions of the element) a common system of ranks for all three elements and common badges, except where special badges denoting particular skills or membership of a certain element appear desirable.

This letter has been classified 'CONFIDENTIAL' and it is not wished that information concerning this matter become generally known until the various approvals connected with it have been received.

Any further proposals connected with the objective of establishing a PNG Defence Force identity would be appreciated.

[NAA: A452, 1972/2801]

---

1   See Document 354 (para. 7). See also Document 277, para. 27.

364   SAVINGRAM TO ALL POSTS

Canberra, 4 September 1972

133. CONFIDENTIAL

Political Developments in Papua New Guinea

The rapid pace of political development in Papua New Guinea since the formation of the national coalition Government has continued during the past three months. This savingram examines the changes taking place and in particular, the results of discussions held in Port Moresby during August between the Minister for External Territories, Mr Peacock, and the Papua New Guinea Chief Minister, Mr Somare.

Policies of the National Coalition Government

2.   The hesitancy which seemed at first to characterise Mr Somare's attitude to the speed of movement towards self-government has not been evident in recent months. The Papua New Guinea Government now seems determined to press ahead as quickly as possible with changes in the formal constitutional relationship with Australia and has shown a willingness to exercise full power in those areas of responsibility which have already been passed to it. Furthermore it wishes to be fully involved in decisions even on subjects which remain under Australian control.

3.   As reported in our savingram AP096,[1] Mr Somare announced on 27 June that it was the view of the national coalition government that self-government should come not before, but as soon as possible after, 1 December 1973. The Government would, however, abide by the decision of the House of Assembly in this matter, and would only proceed if a 'substantial majority' of members voted in favour of this timing during the September sitting of the House.

4.   A Constitutional Planning Committee has been set up to 'make recommendations for a constitution for full internal self-government in a united Papua New Guinea with a view to eventual independence'. Father John Momis, a Bougainvillean member of the national coalition, will be Deputy Chairman (and effective head) under the Chief Minister. This appointment is interesting in view of Father Momis' stated sympathy with the autonomist movement on Bougainville.

5.   Despite the Chief Minister's assurances that the Committee will be concerned only with the planning of a future constitution, and is not being set up to pre-empt any decision of the House on the timing of self-government, the opposition United Party has not yet named its members of the Committee. Because of this the Committee will not now hold its first meeting until after the next sitting of the House of Assembly, by which time the United Party is expected to be in a position to name its representatives.

Talks on the Transfer of Power

6.   Between 27 July and 7 August 1972 the Minister for External Territories and the Chief Minister held the first of a series of meetings in Port Moresby to discuss the transfer of further powers to the PNG Government. Mr Matthias Toliman (the Leader of the Opposition), and senior government and opposition members also attended the talks.[2]

7.   The main decisions made at these talks include:

---

1   Not published.

2   See especially Documents 361 & 362.

Defence

8.   It was agreed a Ministerial Spokesman for Defence should be appointed and that an officer of the Department of Defence in Canberra should be seconded to establish a Defence Section of the Administrator's Department. However, the PNG side stressed their wish to keep their options open on defence arrangements and noted that there was a need for a more rapid orientation of the existing Defence Forces in PNG and their administrative processes towards the needs and Government of PNG. There was also a need for PNG officials to take part in discussions and study groups on defence matters which were undertaken by Commonwealth officials.

Aid and Economic Matters

9.   PNG representatives, including the Leader of the Opposition, referred to economic planning as a 'foreign concept' which was not always understood and stressed that PNG could not rely on 'imported ideas' imposed by foreign experts but needed to decide itself the 'social goals, standards and society it wanted'. The message, in short seemed to be that while they wanted Australia to finance it, they had to work out their own economic development schemes. While accepting the general philosophy, the Minister for External Territories pointed out that Australia, 'like any aid-giver, would reasonably expect that if it were to support a programme to a large extent the programme would need to be acceptable to it'. He suggested therefore that, with the concurrence of their Ministers, PNG and Australian officials might work together on such programmes to avoid a 'confrontation' between the two governments.

10.   The Chief Minister said PNG needed to know some 3 to 5 years in advance what financial aid would be available if it were to plan efficiently. This should be discussed in October. (On 16 August he repeated that point publicly).

Migration

11.   Migration policy is now to be transferred immediately except that the transfer must not affect Australia's responsibilities for international relations. Where migration policy impinges on international relations, e.g. in regard to the border with Indonesia, the PNG Government will need to consult the Australian Government. It was further agreed that negotiation of a border agreement with Indonesia, covering border crossers, would involve the participation of both the Australian and PNG Governments. Australia will keep control over security aspects as well.

Role of Administrator

12.   It was recommended that the Constitutional Planning Committee should give a high priority to an examination of the role of the Administrator during self-government— assuming self-government and independence were not achieved simultaneously. The Administrator expressed the view that there should not be two Australian representatives, i.e. the Administrator and a Diplomatic Representative. In the meantime, the Administrator will continue to withdraw gradually from his active role.

Citizenship

13.   There will be an early examination by PNG and Australian officials of the establishment of an 'international citizenship' for PNG.

Other Matters

14. It was agreed that powers over wage and industrial relations policy, training and localisation in the private sector and land settlement and development policy will be transferred immediately to the PNG Government subject to the approval of the House of Assembly. Other matters such as Area Authorities and the Tariff Advisory Committee will be transferred as soon as the necessary PNG legislation has been passed.

15. A further round of similar discussions will be held in October.

16. Mr Toliman stated at the outset that the United Party would not necessarily be bound by any decisions made during the talks.

17. Possibly the most important point to emerge from these talks was the indication they gave of the PNG Government's determination that it should be fully consulted and involved in all matters concerning Papua New Guinea. Mr Somare said at the beginning of the talks that 'all practical day-to-day administrative decisions must be made (in PNG). Unless there is an absolutely vital Australian interest involved, the *policy* should be decided here also by my government'.

PNG Role in International Relations

18. PNG Ministers made clear their determination to take an active part in the decision making process even in reserved areas such as foreign affairs. The final communiqué said: 'the need for full involvement of the Papua New Guinea Government in these matters was recognised and the means of doing so will be further studied'.[3] It was also agreed that the Administrator's Executive Council should be fully involved in any international agreements involving PNG; including aid ones, before they are negotiated and that PNG should be represented jointly with Australia wherever appropriate. (To this end the PNG Secretary for Law was sent to the 4th Seabed Committee Meeting in Geneva 'to ensure that PNG's interests were advanced' in a situation where Australian and PNG interests are likely to diverge.) However, the Minister for External Territories stressed that consultation was a two way process and the PNG Government should also consult Australia where a decision on a matter within PNG jurisdiction might impinge on Australia's international relations. He also made it clear we could not accept any decision which ran counter to our obligations under the Trusteeship Agreement or some other international arrangement to which Australia was a party. These arrangements to some extent blur the distinction between self-government and independence.

19. A proposal to create a position of Foreign Affairs spokesman in the House of Assembly was discussed informally by officials during the talks, but no final decision will be made until the next round of discussions in October. We would not oppose the establishment of such a position, which is in line with our interest in ensuring that the PNG Government is as closely informed as possible on matters of foreign affairs concern to it.

20. Formal responsibility for the conduct of PNG's international relations will, of course, remain with Australia until independence.

21. Few PNG Government leaders yet appear to have given detailed thought to the country's future foreign policy, but interest in the subject is beginning to grow as more ministers and others travel overseas, and as the implications of what independence will mean to the country are better understood.

22. An Indonesian request to set up a consulate in Port Moresby is at present being considered by the Administrator's Executive Council.

---

3   See Document 347.

Guidance

23. In discussions you should stress the degree of control which the PNG Government now exercises over its internal affairs and the pace at which powers are being transferred. The initiative now comes from the PNG Government and Australia is, in principle, handing over power when asked to by the PNG Government. In many cases where legislation causes delays in handing over formal power, effective power is being delegated earlier.

24. Posts should also appreciate the significance of these changes for the Department's relationship to PNG. It is no longer a simple matter of making our wishes known to the Department of External Territories which passes them on to a pliant Administration. Increasingly we are presented with a request—or even a demand—from PNG Ministers which may cause us inconvenience but which we must meet as best we can. We would therefore ask posts to bear with us if difficult requests are made. You may be sure that we will not make them unnecessarily.

25. Posts might also bear in mind PNG needs in their reporting. If the embryo foreign affairs organization in Port Moresby is to prosper it will need to build up information and background files. We will of course provide the major contribution from Canberra, but where practicable, posts might report on matters which seem to be of importance to PNG, even where they might only be of marginal interest to Australia. Equally, it may be possible from time to time to submit reports from a PNG angle which could be passed to Port Moresby. We are not yet in a position to lay down clear guidelines on what reporting PNG wants but will do so as soon as possible. In the meantime we leave it to posts' discretion.

[NAA: A1838, 689/1 PART 6]

365   SUBMISSION FROM BORDER TO ACTING MINISTER[1]

Canberra, 5 September 1972

CONFIDENTIAL

Cabinet Submission 863—PNG Constitutional Talks

In my submission dated 25 August 1972 (copy attached)[2] I informed you of the main points of Foreign Affairs interest arising out of the Constitutional talks held in July/August between the Minister for External Territories and the PNG Chief Minister. The Minister's present submission to Cabinet reports on the talks and seeks Cabinet endorsement for further follow-up action.[3] The following, briefly, are some points of particular interest.

2. The Minister's submission to Cabinet stresses that PNG leaders seem determined to press for a quick devolution of power and that they are not drawing a clear distinction between self-government and independence. They want, for example, to become closely involved even before self-government in areas like foreign affairs and defence. Our own observations tend to support this assessment of the situation. We see no advantage to Australia in trying to slow things down and agree with the line that the Minister has taken with Mr Somare that there should be full consultation with the PNG Government on matters which will remain a Commonwealth responsibility until independence. Whether or not internal political opinion in PNG is ready for the pace being set is, at this stage, a political judgment best made by PNG Ministers.

3. You agreed last July that we should support the appointment of a PNG Spokesman on Foreign Affairs if the PNG Government seek this. (Please see paragraph 11 of the Cabinet Submission.)

4. In paragraph 16 the Minister states that we should recognise the possibility of a short interval between self-government and independence and be prepared to act accordingly. If this is true, and I believe it is, and if self-government is to come around December 1973, that means that independence will probably come during 1974, or at the very latest 1975. This reinforces the desirability of acting in close consultation with the PNG Government in areas such as foreign affairs and defence which will remain a Commonwealth responsibility until independence.

5. It is recommended that you agree to the recommendations of the Minister for External Territories.

[NAA: A1838, 3080/5/2 PART 2]

---

1   Not identified.

2   Document 355.

3   Document 361.

366   LETTER FROM HAY TO SHANN

Canberra, 5 September 1972

CONFIDENTIAL

In Sir Keith Waller's letter of 25th July[1] he referred to his discussions with the Administrator during his last visit and in light of these discussions proposed measures designed to strengthen the Administration's foreign affairs capability. I have discussed his proposals with the Minister and I can say at the outset that broadly he and the Department are in agreement with them.

I would like to thank Sir Keith Waller for his offer to make available as required experienced Foreign Affairs officers on secondment to the Papua New Guinea Administration. It will be particularly important when the main policy element of the Administration International Affairs Branch is separated from the rest of the Branch for it to be headed by an experienced seconded Foreign Affairs Officer responsible initially to the Head of the Administrator's Department and later that Department serving the PNG Minister who becomes the spokesman on foreign affairs matters.

Although the appointment of a Foreign Affairs spokesman was raised by officials during the constitutional talks earlier this month, the proposal was not mentioned in meetings between Ministers. There seems therefore to be no immediate pressure for a Foreign Affairs spokesman but it could be that this position will have changed by the time set for the next round of constitutional talks towards the end of October and we should be ready to respond to that change if it should eventuate.

I think it is for further consideration whether the Chief Minister should be the Foreign Affairs spokesman. I am inclined to think he should not. There are two reasons for this. The first is that I do not think it would be appropriate for the Chief Minister to be too overloaded at this stage and with the decision that he should be spokesman for both Defence and Police matters, his personal commitments are now quite heavy. The second reason is that in our view the needs of Papua New Guinea would be better served by a joint Department of Foreign Affairs and International Trade Policy under a single Minister. The foreign relations that will be important to Papua New Guinea in the next few years are likely to involve international trade and aid more than other matters. As well, a composite Foreign Relations Department would make it possible to better utilise scarce staff resources, a problem which Papua New Guinea is likely to have for some years.

We have already commenced discussions within the Department and with the Administration on the concept of a combined Foreign Relations Department and I shall arrange for officers of my Department to have discussions with your own officers and with those of the Department of Trade to develop the proposal further. If necessary we could then discuss the matter in light of the outcome of these considerations.

I am in agreement with Sir Keith Waller's proposal that a Foreign Affairs officer responsible to your Department be posted to the Commonwealth Office in Port Moresby. In such a posting it would be important for there to be a clear understanding, which I have no doubt will be readily achieved, as to the role which this officer should play. As I see it the Administrator as the Commonwealth's senior representative would have a direct supervisory role and would receive copies of all reports sent to Canberra by your officer.

A question for consideration is the relationships which would need to exist between your officer and the senior External Territories officer in charge of this Department's staff posted to

1   Document 335.

the Commonwealth Office. I would see it as appropriate that there would be an independence of operations except in those areas where by agreement they would work together on matters of broad Commonwealth interest such as intelligence. We would for the time being continue to provide common housekeeping services such as operation of the communications link and upkeep and maintenance of the Commonwealth Office.

Under the present constitutional arrangements it would not be appropriate for the Foreign Affairs officer to conduct relations with Ministers of the Papua New Guinea Government or to represent Australian views to that Government these being the Administrator's responsibility. For the present therefore I would see your officer confining activities to observing and reporting to your own Department.

I appreciate that in anticipation of the independence situation you might want progressively to involve the officer with PNG authorities and I should be glad to discuss with you if you wish the way in which we might work out an acceptable phase-in-phase-out arrangement.

Perhaps you could let me know when it would be convenient for you to take these matters further by discussion between us.

[NAA: A1838, 3080/10/4/7 PART 1]

367   TELEX FROM JOHNSON TO HAY

Port Moresby, 5 September 1972

9686. Unclassified

Somare to move that the following be added to the motion on self-government timetable:

'(A) Requests that constitutional changes necessary for full internal self-government be brought into effect on 1st December, 1973, or as soon as possible thereafter

'(B) Interprets full internal self-government for Papua New Guinea as leaving the Commonwealth of Australia final powers only in the matters of defence and external affairs, which it should exercise in the fullest consultation with the Government of Papua New Guinea.'

I have queried (B) with Chief Minister in respect of external trade and internal security. He considered that external trade should become Papua New Guinea responsibility on self-government but would not seek to define this in debate but leave for discussion at next constitutional talks. In speaking to the amendment he will explain the nature of Australia's legal responsibility for internal security and advance the proposal we have previously discussed that this can be conceded de facto but not de jure.

[NAA: A452, 1972/2640]

368 LETTER FROM WALLER TO HAY

Canberra, 11 September 1972

CONFIDENTIAL

Thank you for your letter of 5 September addressed to Mr Shann[1] in reply to my letter of 25 July about the various measures I had discussed with the Administrator to strengthen the Administration's foreign affairs capability and to provide adequate Foreign Affairs representation in Port Moresby in the pre-independence period. I am very pleased to have your own and your Minister's general agreement with what is proposed.

I assume the Administrator will now be proceeding with his plans to split up the existing International Affairs Branch, putting the seconded officer from this Department (Mr McDonald) in charge of that part of it which will be developed into the future Papua New Guinea Foreign Relations Office. As I indicated in my previous letter this is quite satisfactory from this Department's point of view

[*matter omitted*]

You mentioned your view that the needs of Papua New Guinea will probably best be served by a single Department responsible for foreign relations and international trade matters. I share this view, particularly in terms of making the best use of scarce local staff resources, although I think we cannot be sure that trade and aid are likely to be the aspects of foreign relations of primary interest to Papua New Guinea over the next few years. This would be contrary to what has happened in the case of most other newly independent countries in recent experience. Already there is evidence that Mr Somare and some of his colleagues are keenly interested in a wide range of foreign affairs matters such as relations with Indonesia and Japan, entry into the South Pacific Forum, and Papua New Guinea's future role in the region. In addition we can expect various governments to be represented in Port Moresby before or shortly after independence. These diplomatic missions will naturally generate a need for the Papua New Guinea Government to concern itself with all sorts of foreign policy issues. Again, the new country will be a member of many international bodies requiring special service and attention. I think it would be a serious mistake to develop the future Foreign Relations Office on the basis of a disproportionate weighting towards trade and aid matters.

I would be happy to have officers of my Department discuss, at whatever time is convenient, details of the concept of a combined Foreign Relations Department with your officers and those of the Department of Trade, as you suggest.

As regards the appointment of a Foreign Affairs officer in the Commonwealth office in Port Moresby, I see no difficulties from our point of view in the various matters you mention. The officer's primary role will be to report to this Department on developments in Papua New Guinea of interest to us and to advise the Administrator on Commonwealth views on foreign policy matters. He would also provide a channel for conveying information on international affairs, through the Administrator, to the reorganised International Affairs Branch of the Administration and eventually to the Papua New Guinea Foreign Relations Department. He would operate under the general supervision of the Administrator (in his capacity as senior Commonwealth representative) and we would see no objection to copies of his reports being made available as required to the Administrator. He would, as you say, work alongside your Department's representative in the Commonwealth office but his operations would

---

1 Document 366.

be independent except perhaps for intelligence matters. He would need your Department's administrative support, at least in the initial period.

I agree that the Foreign Affairs representative would not, at this stage of constitutional development, deal directly in any formal sense with the Papua New Guinea Government or its Ministers. As I mentioned above, however, he would be in a position to advise the Administrator and his officers on foreign affairs matters from the Commonwealth viewpoint.

[*matter omitted*]

[NAA: A1838, 3080/10/4/7 PART 1]

369   MINUTE BY PNG DCC[1]

Canberra, 11 September 1972

SECRET

[*matter omitted*]

4.   After a full discussion, the Committee endorsed the following functions and roles for the Police Force and the Defence Force which in their totality will comprise the security forces of PNG.

5.   *Functions*. The functions or broad responsibilities proper to the PNG security forces may be described as follows:

    a.   Under the direction of the legally constituted Government to provide for the enforcement of national laws and processes with particular regard to preservation of internal security and the protection of national resources.

    b.   To contribute as required to economic development and to the promotion of national administration and security.

    c.   To maintain a capability for external defence of the nation.

6.   *Shared or Common Roles*. The shared or common roles of the security forces—embracing all three elements of the Defence Force and the Police—would be:

    a.   to provide forces as authorised for the effective discharge of the common functions of the security forces viewed as a whole (see paragraph above);

    b.   to undertake, as necessary, planning and operations in combination with any or all elements of the security forces and, to this end, to coordinate equipment, communications, administrative processes, logistic facilities, and, where applicable, operational techniques and training methods;

    c.   subject to (b) above, to establish, maintain and operate bases, installations and other appropriate facilities;

    d.   to contribute to the national intelligence organisation and to make available operational intelligence to elements of the security forces as appropriate;

---

1   Defence Coordination Committee. Those present were Admiral Sir Victor Smith, Chair, Chiefs of Staff Committee (Chair); Major-General R. L. (Ron) Hughes, Director Joint Staff, Department of Defence; Air Vice Marshal G. T. Newstead, Deputy Chief of the Air Staff; Major-General S. C. Graham, Chief of Operations (Army); Rear Admiral S. M. (Tony) Synnot, Deputy Chief of Naval Staff; and E. W. Dwyer, representing Curtis. Also present were Blakers, Greenwell and R. N. Hamilton, Assistant Secretary, Department of Defence.

    e.   to provide assistance to civil authorities and organisations as authorised;

    f.   to contribute to the relief of civil disasters as required.

7.   *Police*

    a.   to maintain law and order within police zones and operate urban and rural police stations;

    b.   to organise, train and equip police for the maintenance of law and order in urban centres, townships, rural villages and in all areas determined by the Government;

    c.   to undertake in the areas defined by (b) above the protection of life and property, crowd control, the prevention and detection of crime, prosecutions, liquor, traffic, gambling and firearms control, process serving and law enforcement generally, including exercising the power of arrest;

    d.   to undertake, in concert with the ground element of the PNG Defence Force, the manning of static frontier control posts—particularly on the West Irian border—and liaison at these points with the relevant foreign authorities.

8.   *Ground Element of the PNG Defence Force*

    a.   to engage in patrolling, particularly in remote and/or difficult areas as may be determined by the PNG Government, for the purpose of supporting and extending the presence and authority of the Government; and, so far as circumstances require and allow and as authorised, to assume in these areas the role defined in c above;

    b.   to render support and assistance as necessary to the police in situations of discord and violence in areas defined in b above and to sustain that support, if necessary, for lengthy periods;

    c.   to patrol in frontier regions between established frontier control posts as defined in support of the regime established for the frontier area and for intelligence collection as well as for the purposes identified in d above.

    d.   to conduct as may be required, particularly in and beyond frontier regions, operations to impede and where possible repel armed incursions or attacks by external forces.

    e.   to make available personnel, material and expertise for the planning and execution of civic action tasks, as directed by the government.

9.   *Nature of the Ground Element*. Generally the Ground Element should comprise lightly equipped forces organised, equipped and supported to ensure flexibility of employment and mobility in action. They should be provided with a number of permanent bases throughout the Territory. Members of the Ground Element of appropriate rank should possess general powers of arrest and detention of citizens, including civilians, in accordance with the laws of the independent Papua New Guinea. Under conditions of overt challenges to the integrity of PNG the Ground Element should be capable of operational association with Australian military forces and of receiving Australian logistic support.

[NAA: A452, 1972/1111]

370   CABINET DECISION 1347 (AD HOC)

Canberra, 12 September 1972

CONFIDENTIAL

Submission No. 863—Papua New Guinea Programme of
Movement towards Internal Self-Government—Report on Initial Discussions[1]

The Committee:

(a) noted the results of the discussions held in Port Moresby in July/August;

(b) noted the Schedule—attached to the Submission—for further transfer of powers;

(c) agreed that on receipt of a recommendation from the House of Assembly as to the date of self-government, on the basis set out in paragraph 12 of the Submission, the Minister will consult the Prime Minister as to the terms of a statement to be issued by the Government;

(d) noted the possibility of the shortened interval between self-government and independence; and

(e) noted that discussions with the Leadership Group are to continue in October 1972.

2.   In connection with sub paragraph (d) above, the Committee noted that the broad time-table envisaged by the Government was that the present Parliament in Papua New Guinea, which would normally run until 1976, would see the transfer to self-government and the constitutional preparations for independence and that the next elections would produce the leadership which carried the country to independence. It hoped that this basic concept would not be disturbed but acknowledged that a request for independence might be made by the New Guinea Leadership before the next scheduled elections.

3.   It noted also that the role of the Administrator after the introduction of self-government was under examination in the Constitutional Planning Committee.

[NAA: A5908, 863]

---

1   Document 361.

371   LETTER FROM JOHNSON TO HAY

Port Moresby, 14 September 1972

I set out for your information the emerging views of the Papua New Guinea Ministry on the localisation of the Public Service.

In broad terms the Ministry desires to begin to run down the total number of expatriates in the Public Service. A figure of 15% reduction by the end of 1973 has been suggested as a target and further progressive reduction in the succeeding years. It is however recognised that probably throughout the 70's there will be a considerable expatriate component remaining within the Public Service.

The Ministry wants to begin exploring ways and means of achieving the first stage of this reduction as soon as possible. There appear to be two categories for immediate consideration: those who are useless and can be dispensed with without any significant loss of efficiency and those who are politically unacceptable to the Government, some of whom would leave quite substantial gaps in the system. At a guess this figure might be 300 to 400. Thereafter reductions can only be achieved if there are suitable indigenous replacements or if there is a rigorous re-examination of departmental functions and of the staffing of them. Radical rationalisation of support staff for departmental activities in districts will be necessary.

The Ministry will also shortly turn its attention to departmental heads and is likely to arrive at a list of positions to be localised before the end of 1973.

It is appreciated that as yet these matters fall within the jurisdiction of the Minister for External Territories and I will keep you advised of developments. The Australian Government reaction to the Simpson Report[1] on the Employment Security Scheme will obviously affect the issues.

[NAA: A452, 1972/3694]

---

1   See Document 344.

372   MINUTE FROM GALVIN TO GREENWELL

Port Moresby, 15 September 1972

In recent casual conversation with Ryan (Director, Chief Minister's Office) and Voutas (Chief Minister's personal staff) it became obvious that they remain very wary of the Commonwealth in defence matters and had quite a misunderstanding of the role of the Defence officer seconded to the Administration to develop a Defence Branch.

2.   As a first step in remedying this I had a lengthy conversation with Voutas this morning.

3.   Neither he nor Ryan had seen the papers setting out the duties and terms of reference of the Defence Officer and he was quite heartened when I told him of the relevant sentences concerning the man's role as a servant of Papua New Guinea. I indicated to Voutas that next week Mr Murray[1] intended to have a meeting with a number of people in the Chief Minister's Office and the Administrator's Department in order to talk about the activities to be performed and to expose some of the issues on which a Papua New Guinea view needs to be formulated. I said that I expect that as a result of that meeting some machinery would be developed by which groups of people at this end could commence thinking about defence issues and produce papers for the Administrator and the Chief Minister as the first steps in the development of a defence policy.

4.   He said that he was quite worried that because of the Papua New Guinea lack of preparedness on defence matters the Ministry would be presented with a series of *fait accomplis* similar to the recent Civil Aviation decision which they would find difficult to resist or indeed to understand. He also was concerned that the Australian defence forces in Papua New Guinea continued to be Australian, that the Papua New Guinea servicemen continued to be oriented to Australia and that no means had been found by which PNG servicemen of calibre and intelligence could play a role in the total development of government policy.

5.   He saw no reason for example why men like Major Diro[2] should not take part in defence policy studies and working groups which may be set up nor for that matter why individual officers should not spend time on secondment in civilian administration, e.g. as a District Commissioner.

6.   I think he was somewhat puzzled when I did not react against either suggestion but rather indicated to him that I saw both ventures as quite respectable and indeed not unexpected developments.

7.   Throughout the conversation it was clear that there remains a quite considerable residual doubt about the Commonwealth's intentions and honesty in this area. Part of this is simple misunderstanding which I think will be overcome by Mr Murray and then by Mr Webb[3] (who is well and favourably known to Voutas). But the more important reason is the complete lack of involvement in the past and the fact that although Mr Fairbairn announced some months ago

---

1   Possibly Commodore Brian Stewart (Chick) Murray (later Sir Brian Murray), Director, Joint Operations and Plans, Department of Defence.

2   Edward Ramu (Ted) Diro, from the Central District (now Province), was promoted to Major in 1971. He thus became the first PNG Major in the Pacific Islands Regiment.

3   In mid-September Nick Webb, the Chief Executive Officer, Joint Staff in the Department of Defence, was appointed to the Defence Branch in Port Moresby as an adviser to the Chief Minister on defence policy and planning. It was decided he would take up duty in Port Moresby in November. Letter, Tange to Hay, 18 September 1972, NAA: 1838, 3080/4/5, PART 1.

the process of consultation⁴ nothing really has occurred since then. There have for example been no propositions to the AEC on even small defence matters let alone any information papers to start the ministry thinking about the topics.

8.   It could be argued of course that the consultation process had to await the appointment of a Defence spokesman and the establishment of a Defence Branch. Whilst that argument has logical support it does not really remove the emotional feeling that in the defence area we are 'playing games'.

9.   What must be done if we are to make any impact on Papua New Guinea thinking is to commence rapidly to serve up to the AEC a steady stream of submissions on any aspect of the Defence Forces in Papua New Guinea. Many of these submissions might involve administrative matters which in the future would not go to the full ministry e.g. information submissions about building programmes, housing development, patrol programmes, exercises, etc. Unless this process is well developed over the next few months I foresee difficulties in getting ready acceptance of any major propositions in the coming year.

[NAA: A452, 1972/2801]

---

4   See Document 311.

373   LETTER FROM HAY TO JOHNSON

Canberra, 18 September 1972

The Minister has asked me to take up with you the question of the motion before the House of Assembly regarding the date for self-government.[1]

The Minister has reported to Cabinet on the results of the July/August constitutional talks, at the same time informing it of the [PNG] Coalition's motion regarding the date for self-government.[2] The Minister also advised Cabinet of the procedures agreed upon at the talks regarding the role of the House of Assembly. These were that:

> 'if a constitutional or important change is involved, both Governments agree that there should be a recorded vote in favour by a substantial majority of members, and that the majority should be broadly representative of the country.'

The Minister's view was that a decision on the date of self-government is an important constitutional matter and that the agreed procedure should apply. (The Minister did not refer to the question of the 75% or 75 votes in favour.)

In informing Cabinet of the date the Minister indicated that in his opinion it was probable that the Coalition would achieve a majority on the motion for the date in terms of the above agreed procedures.

The Minister went on to indicate that it was desirable that the Australian Government should react quickly and favourably to a conclusion of the House of Assembly.

Cabinet agreed that on receipt of a recommendation from the House of Assembly as to the date of self-government, on the basis of the agreed procedures the Minister should consult the Prime Minister as to the terms of a statement to be issued by the Government.

It seems likely that when the House of Assembly meets again next week, it will resume debate on the timing of self-government and vote on the date put forward by the Coalition. As soon as possible after the House of Assembly has reached its decision it will be necessary for the Minister to announce the attitude of the Australian Government. Should there be a recorded vote in favour by a substantial [and] broadly representative majority of members, then the Minister will be in a position to respond quickly and favourably.

However, there may be problems in responding quickly and favourably depending on the extent to which the criteria which have been agreed for an acceptable vote have been met.

I should be grateful therefore if you could emphasise to the AEC the importance of the agreed criteria and of the desirability of as many members as possible recording their vote.

I should also be glad for your early views on the attitude you feel should be adopted by the Australian Government as soon as the vote has been taken.

[NAA: A452, 1973/0039]

---

1   See Document 367.

2   Document 361.

374   LETTER FROM HAY TO SCULLY

Canberra, 21 September 1972

I am now in a position to follow up with you some of the matters we discussed with the Administrator on 25 July last. I regret the delay but feel that the further exchanges between our Departments in the interim, and particularly the discussions last week with Messrs Conroy and Joseph[1] from the Papua New Guinea Administration, have assisted considerably in clarifying the issues.

Your suggestion about establishing contact at a technical level between officers of the Department of Trade and Industry and the Papua New Guinea Administration is most welcome and I see no reason why arrangements could not be put in hand almost immediately. The Administration has some difficulties in the next few months due to the absence of key officers on leave but I think the initial contact should proceed. I understand that you propose to send one or two officers at the Class 10 or 11 level and that they will be accompanied by one officer from the Economic Division of this Department. The purpose of the visit would be for all concerned to gain a greater understanding of the procedures and difficulties in handling bilateral trade matters between Australia and Papua New Guinea. In particular, they would look to ways of avoiding the development of misunderstandings between Australia and Papua New Guinea, as was the case in the recent events concerning the export of Australian-made ice cream to Papua New Guinea. My understanding is that they would carefully avoid becoming involved in any way in policy aspects of Papua New Guinea's external trade relations between Australia and a future independent Papua New Guinea.

As you know Ministerial discussions on constitutional development were held in Port Moresby during July and early August, and further discussions are to take place in Australia during October. I enclose a draft of a paper which is being prepared for consideration by Ministers at the October discussions.[2] The purpose of this paper is to outline the interim arrangements which are considered necessary in order to ensure that the Papua New Guinea Government is adequately consulted and represented in matters affecting its external trade in the period before the transfer of the powers for external trade policy. The paper also identifies the major tasks involved in preparation for this hand-over of power.

It is proposed that the draft paper be considered by the Papua New Guinea Committee on Foreign Trade at a meeting in Port Moresby on Friday, 29 September. This Committee has been established by the Papua New Guinea Government and will tender advice to the Chief Minister and the Minister for Trade prior to the October constitutional discussions. Mr Mentz of this Department will be attending the meeting and it would be appreciated if your officers could let him have any comments they may wish to make as soon as possible on Monday 25th. Any arrangements agreed between Mr Peacock and Mr Somare would of course be subject to appropriate endorsements by both the Australian and Papua New Guinea Governments.

One of the points we discussed with Mr Johnson and which is also dealt with in the proposed interim arrangements is the possibility of the Commonwealth Department of Trade and Industry providing assistance in the training of Papua New Guineans in matters related to both the functional and policy areas of trade responsibility. I understand it might also be possible for your Department to arrange a suitable course, similar to the Trainee Trade Commissioner course, but designed specifically to cater for the needs of a group of perhaps ten or twelve Papua New Guineans who would not have the qualifications or experience normally required for your standard courses.

---

1   W. L. (Bill) Conroy was the Director of the Department of Agriculture, Stock and Fisheries. No further details have been located on the position and role of his colleague named 'Joseph'.

2   Not published.

On this training question I feel it would be best if we asked the Papua New Guinea Government to provide a consolidated statement of their requirements. I would propose to do this as soon as appropriate interim arrangements have been agreed between Mr Peacock and Mr Somare, even though the arrangements may still be subject to endorsement by the Australian and Papua New Guinea Governments.

I would also like to take this opportunity to bring you up to date with some important moves concerning the functional organisation of departments within the Papua New Guinea Administration. As part of the programme of preparation for self-government and independence the administrative arrangements in the Papua New Guinea Public Service have been under review. Consideration has also been given to the question of increasing involvement of Papua New Guinea Ministers in all matters of Government, including those over which the Commonwealth will retain final responsibility until independence. This latter development has already led to the establishment of a spokesman on police and defence matters.[3]

The appointment of a spokesman on foreign relations was also raised in the constitutional talks in July/August. In considering this matter we have come to the conclusion that international trade and aid matters will be the dominant area in Papua New Guinea foreign relations for some time to come.[4] For this reason and the necessity to encourage coordination and limit manpower requirements and operational costs we find it difficult to divorce the diplomatic aspects of foreign relations from those of foreign trade. We feel that these two areas could well be combined in the one department under the one Ministerial spokesman.

We are therefore discussing with the Minister for External Territories and the Administrator a proposal to create a single separate department which will have functional responsibility for all matters related to foreign relations. The international trade responsibilities of the existing Department of Trade and Industry and the aid and foreign relations areas of the Administrator's Department would be gathered together under one Minister who would be known as the spokesman on foreign relations. This proposal should be seen as a merging of all responsibilities affecting international relations into a completely new department. The proposal would need to be discussed with, and have the support of, the Papua New Guinea Ministry before a formal recommendation is made to Mr Peacock.

I appreciate that the Department of Trade and Industry has a functional interest in these proposals. If there are any particular aspects which you wish to raise or discuss further I would appreciate your advice as soon as possible.

[NAA: A452, 1972/2640]

---

3   See Documents 358 & 359.

4   This comment suggests that Hay had not been swayed by Waller's views on the importance of the foreign affairs component. See Document 368.

375   LETTER FROM SCULLY TO HAY

Canberra, 28 September 1972

Thank you for your letter of 21st September[1] in which you express your agreement to a visit to Papua New Guinea by two officers from Trade and Industry and one from External Territories for technical level trade discussions.

I regard it as important that we establish working level trade contact with the Administration as soon as possible and accordingly agree that we proceed to organise the visit to take place as soon as possible. I understand that the officials concerned in the Administration will not be available before the next round of Constitutional discussions on 9th October. From this Department's point of view, departure for the Territory on or after 22nd October would be feasible. The two officers who will make the visit from this Department are Mr F. R. Somes, Director, Food Section, Secondary Industry Operations Division and either Mr W. G. McGregor, Director, Asia and Western Pacific Section, Trade Relations Division, or Mr N. J. S. Bayley, Assistant Director, and at present the project officer on Papua New Guinea in our Trade Relations Division.

I see the essential purpose of the visit being an exchange of views in the areas you mention in your letter. At the same time officials might discuss areas where Australian techniques and experience in handling various trade matters might be drawn on by Papua New Guinea. This suggestion emerged from discussion with Mr Joseph. He mentioned that because Papua New Guinea is short of skilled officials it is the intention to prepare an operations manual detailing procedures and factors to be considered in examining various trade matters and problems. This Department would be happy to assist in any way possible with this task and perhaps on this visit we can get as far as defining the areas of interest and then doing some work on the various matters in the Department; with further visits to the Territory by other officers taking place as necessary to follow up the various areas.

I also confirm your understanding that the officers concerned would carefully avoid becoming involved in any way in policy aspects of Papua New Guinea's external trade relations and in particular the shape of trade relations between Australia and a future independent Papua New Guinea.

Against this background perhaps you could inform me of the name of the officer from your Department who will make the visit and with whom the Trade and Industry officers would discuss the necessary arrangements. I think it appropriate that we leave it to you to finally fix the dates and prepare a draft programme in consultation with the Administration. We would see the visit lasting about a week to ten days but again would be guided by your views.

Turning now to the other matters you raised in your letter, officers of our Department passed preliminary comments to Mr Mentz on the interim trade arrangements paper before he left for Papua New Guinea and have arranged to work with Mr Mentz on a further draft when he returns to Australia.

I agree with your suggestion on the question of training and will be happy to make all appropriate arrangements once we have the statement of Papua New Guinea requirements to which you refer.

Thank you for letting me know of the proposals for functional re-organisation in Territory Departments. From our point of view we have had experience in working with this type of structure in a number of countries and I would not expect any major difficulties if we have to deal with Papua New Guinea on this basis.

[NAA: A452, 1972/2640]

---

1   Document 374.

376   REPORT FROM BURNS[1]

Port Moresby, undated [c. September 1972]

CONFIDENTIAL

Post-Election Politics in the Highlands

Introduction

1.   Any attempt to rehearse in detail the physical, cultural and economic background of the highlands would be tedious in the present context. It should be borne in mind, however, that the highlands of eastern New Guinea have served in the past much like a complex of battlements and fortresses, providing its people not only with barriers to outside influence but also with a terrain which discourages internal contact. Inside this geographic maze, enmities were rife and the separation of communities produced by the complex system of valleys and ranges intensified the pattern, almost universal in Melanesian society, of small language groups fragmented by internal rivalries.

2.   The lack of traditional large-scale political units or established leadership systems and the overriding influence of clan loyalties and relationships is the general pattern throughout Melanesian societies. The problems for a modern political leadership which this social and geographic fragmentation present are endemic throughout PNG. In the highlands they have been intensified by the pressure of population, particularly in areas where the effects of migrations and warfare have built up heavy concentrations of people deep inside the secure reaches of the mountain system. Thus the highlanders do not possess unique problems in comparison with other Melanesian groups—they experience the same problems, only more so.

3.   Likewise, in terms of ethnic origin, it would be rash to isolate any unique ethnic blend which would separate highlanders from other Melanesian peoples of PNG. If the whole question of the origin of the so-called Melanesians is insoluble on the present evidence, it would be fruitless to attempt to trace the origins of the highlanders to one or more particular strains in what appears to be an infinitely complex series of migrations and ethnic sources. It can only be concluded that the highlanders reflect a complexity of origins which are as diverse as those of most other peoples of PNG.

4.   If the Highlands are neither in an ethnic nor a cultural sense inherently divided from the rest of PNG, nevertheless recent history has provided the unique element in that the four highlands districts were the last to be contacted and to come under Australian administration. While attempts to reconstruct the pre-contact history of the highlands are still very tentative, it is reasonable to conclude that the introduction of European administration had come at a time when a process of enormous change was under way. The introduction of the sweet potato (which probably occurred only in the three centuries since the earliest Portuguese voyagers touched on the coast of New Guinea) had caused a revolution in agriculture and thus in the whole way of life of societies entirely dependent on subsistence crops. While there is little evidence that wide-spread population movements were still occurring, many areas were, however, in the throes of intensive inter-clan struggles at the time of European entry. This pattern of internecine warfare may indicate that societies were in the midst of a series of struggles for supremacy between clan groups and is not simply proof of a perpetual state of

---

1   The report was dated 'August/September'. It was circulated within DFA and to its overseas posts under cover of a memorandum from Cavan Hogue of 19 October 1972.

anarchy and aimless savagery. This unrest probably foreshadowed the development of more comprehensive political units, rather than the further fragmentation of language groups. This might eventually have preceded the rise of more stabilised societies and brought to an end the disruptive effects of major population shifts.

5.   The past thirty years have thus brought not only immense change in terms of adaptation to an alien administration and economic system but have demanded a precipitate hastening of these processes of transformation which would normally have come to a resolution by internal adjustments over a period of decades or centuries.

6.   As a result of this abrupt introduction of Australian administration and reform, it is not surprising that the highlanders should now show a determination to gain time in order to catch up with the rest of PNG in education and economic development. It is this determination which has led to a distinctive outlook amongst highlanders in national politics. Unfortunately, many observers in the past have created the impression that this 'go-slow' approach to self-government implies a unique way of thought amongst highlanders which pre-determines them to be more conservative than other Papua New Guineans. If this report is able to dispel such illusions it may begin to serve some useful purpose in setting out a more realistic basis for considering the future role of the highlands in national politics.

Political Developments 1971–72

(a) The United Party

7.   Until the February/March 1972 elections, recent political development in the highlands was dominated by the role played by the United Party (UP) (or its predecessors the groupings of highland MHAs known as the Independent Group or the Compass Party).[2] As the party is now undergoing a process of deterioration, its former role and organisation are largely a matter of history and not directly relevant to a consideration of the post-election situation. However the reasons for the party's virtual collapse and the way in which it came about do shed some light on the way in which political activity has recently developed in the highlands.

8.   The difficulty in attempting to describe the UP as it was, is that it never became more than a loose grouping of disparate (and often conflicting) interests which coincided in the cause of opposing early self-government. The pro-UP (and anti-self-government) forces grouped together in order to keep a Pangu-led grouping out of power in the last House, and broadly speaking, reflected three main interest groups:

(a) the expatriate businessmen and planters who saw self-government as a possible threat to their livelihood;

(b) the highlanders who saw that any delay in self-government would allow the gap between levels of development on the coast and in the highlands to be narrowed;

(c) those coastal members whose outlook was basically conservative. Normally older than other coastal members, they were convinced that a gradualist approach to self-government and independence was the only safe course and that expatriate enterprises were basic to economic advancement and continued Australian aid.

On the sidelines, the Administration tacitly allowed some of its senior officials and district administration staff to foster the belief that early self-government would encourage disintegration and result in the precipitate withdrawal of expatriate funds and expertise. The fact that, by default, this came to be commonly received as administration policy meant that

---

2   The name 'Compass' was a contraction of 'combined political associations'.

many administration officials often conducted themselves on the assumption that the UP reflected Australian aims and that Pangu and other seemingly 'radical' groups were a threat to administration.

9.   The UP served as a shaky alliance. Even within each of the three groups outlined above, there was no unanimity of purpose—attitudes amongst expatriate supporters, for example, varied from those who sought a white-dominated society on the lines of Rhodesia, to those who made a more shrewd calculation of their economic interests and genuinely supported a black-led multi-racial society which they hoped would not conflict with their trading or plantation interests. Although UP members, together with a number of independents, generally commanded a majority in the second half of the life of the second House, party discipline and organisation were exercised spasmodically. UP members held a number of ministries but generally failed to use their positions to initiate policies or effectively supervise their departments while they served as rubber stamps for administration policy initiatives.

(b) *1972 Elections*

10. The UP was clearly unprepared for the outcome of the 1972 elections and had seriously under-estimated the organisation and determination of its opposition, particularly the Pangu Party. The party had expected to romp home in the 36 highland seats, pick up a number of coastal seats contested by influential conservative figures and to command the 50 seats necessary for a majority in the House without the need to call upon other parties for support. In fact, when counting ended, the UP could be confident of approximately 42 supporters in the House, a good deal short of a majority.

11. Little or no attempt was made to canvass support amongst the 30% of members who had not committed themselves to either the conservative or progressive forces. While Pangu spent the weeks between the counting of the poll and the crucial first sitting of the House energetically canvassing uncommitted members and parties to join a national coalition, the UP leadership had either failed to recognise the urgency of the issue or had lost heart. The party's expatriate leadership was drastically weakened during and shortly after the elections. Not only were several of the key party organisers defeated at the polls, but tensions between extremists and moderates amongst the expatriates had broken out into open conflict—a situation made worse by the lack of any recognised leadership. In Goroka, the organisational centre of the party, the influence of two expatriate extremists (Fox[3] and Kingsford Smith, an accountant and a plantation owner respectively) had discredited the party by association with extremist racial views which ultimately saw Rhodesia as a model for PNG's future. The two men also influenced Dennis Buchanan, a businessman with a variety of interests, principally the country's major third-level airline (Territory Air Lines) and one of the UP's principal financial patrons. The irresponsible and politically ill-advised way in which these men conducted the UP's election campaign in the Eastern Highlands resulted in a decision by the central committee of the party to exclude them from its activities.

12. This particular crisis reflected a more widespread fragmentation of outlooks and policies amongst the expatriate leadership of the UP. The lack of leadership, of a common sense of purpose and an extremely amateurish approach to politics at least saved the party from drifting towards a Rhodesia Front type role in PNG affairs. Although the party paid lip-service to majority rule, most of its expatriate core saw the future of PNG in the hands of the white man. However, the party never overrode personality difficulties between its expatriate leadership,

---

3   Don Woolford has noted that 'Peter Fox, a Goroka accountant and political activist of the Right, feared
     early independence could lead to a Russian takeover'. Don Woolford, *Papua New Guinea: Initiation and
     Independence*, University of Queensland Press, Brisbane, 1976, p. 95.

let alone proved capable of spreading roots into the indigenous participants (predominantly highlanders) who were expected to acquiesce in prolonged white rule. In fact, the leadership of the party was a shambles, depending upon whoever could hold the floor or attract the attention of the press at a particular moment. This same pattern of disorganisation would have prevailed, if the UP had achieved power in the 1972 elections, but some attempt might have been able to halt the course of constitutional development and gain at least four years of false security and protection for expatriate business and political interests in PNG.

13. The melodramatic and unrealistic nature of these ambitions is a tribute to the political naivety of expatriates within the party many of whom accepted them as serious goals. The results of any attempt to follow these policies can only be guessed at, but the UP had seriously miscalculated if it believed that the highlanders could be counted on to remain conservative and docile—most had few reasons to like or admire the expatriate businessmen who so confidently discounted the intellectual capacity and political awareness of the party's indigenous members. On the national level, the UP's ambitions would probably have soon foundered but not before tempting racial animosity and political unrest on a scale not yet envisaged in this country thus sacrificing most prospects for an orderly transfer to self-government and independence.

14. Fortunately, the UP's leadership troubles were at a peak during the period of the elections, although a group of more responsible expatriates (representing both highland and coastal business interests) made some attempt to keep the party going as a viable political force. However, the UP lacked the indigenous leadership to match the energy and organisation which Somare was meanwhile injecting into the disparate array of progressive groups and members. By the time the House assembled, the UP had not only failed to pick up the mere handful of members it needed to pre-empt Somare's attempts to amass a majority, but there is no evidence that it even saw the need to try to outwit what it assumed was a hopelessly fragmented opposition. To add to the UP's humiliation, Somare's national coalition finally managed to win over a considerable bloc of highland members by building on the one-member National Party as a progressive highlands alternative to the UP.

15. Thus by the first and second sittings of the new House, the UP was a badly defeated group, seriously divided amongst itself and deprived of much of its former organisational and financial support. Although still by far, the biggest party in the House, it had not only failed to form a majority in the House, but its lack of both expatriate and indigenous leadership had proved fatal, it had been deserted by those in the Administration who had given it encouragement (the Administration was by now only too willing to offload most of its decision-making tasks on to an indigenous leadership) and it was no longer the undisputed voice of highland views in the house.

16. At the time, the UP's failure to galvanise itself appeared inexplicable but when all the factors which affected the party at the time are considered the party's lack of initiative is not surprising. Perhaps, ultimately, the most crucial factor was that the UP forces in the House were just not the right material to form a government which would be obliged to assume most of the task of governing the country on its own initiative. Ron Neville (the Regional MHA for Southern Highlands and an influential figure in the UP) admitted to me that the UP simply did not have the members capable of forming a government of the calibre of the NCG[4]—it lacked sufficient literate MHAs who are prepared to accept the responsibilities demanded by the present stage of political development. (It should be added that it also lacks the NCG's geographically comprehensive membership which can now claim support from every district in PNG.)

---

4   National Coalition Government.

(c) *Reaction to NCG*

17. Since the elections, the formation of the NCG; the failure of the UP, as the largest party, to form a government; the 'defection' of several formerly pro-UP or independent highlands members to the National Party; and the NCG's promise of early progress to self-government raised the possibility of a highlands backlash against the NCG. The NCG faced the task not only of convincing the highlanders that it should accept its proposals for early-self-government but of persuading them that a black government was now empowered to take decisions on most issues which would affect the future of the country. The transition from paternal white administration to de facto black self-rule encountered all the shibboleths so eagerly promoted in the past by the UP, of self-government bringing the flight of white capital and expertise and the collapse of effective administration. The NCG faced its first challenge in this field in the form of demonstrations in Chimbu accompanied by threats against Iambakey Okuk, the Chimbu Regional member who had joined the National Party and supported the NCG. This and other sporadic attempts to hold out the threat of a widespread popular rejection of the NCG's authority were the handiworks of Fox, the Goroka accountant mentioned above as repudiated by the UP at the time of the elections, probably assisted by Buchanan and with the indigenous front provided by Sinake Giregire (the former Minister for Posts and Telegraph and member for Asaro in the Eastern Highlands). The attempts to use demonstrations to stir up popular feeling against the NCG and its supporters were a failure. A strong undercurrent of feeling against the coalition simply did not exist to be exploited. Most highlanders were ignorant of the intricacies of national politics but, more significantly, among those who were aware, there was no inbuilt resistance to a national coalition as long as the highlanders were seen to have an adequate share in the decision-making.

18. Although Fox's attempt to lead the UP into an extremist's course of action was repudiated by the party and ignored by the highlanders, the UP has yet to adopt any other path to recovery. The UP of the post-election period is a different mixture of elements from the collection of three main interest groups which supported the party from 1970 to 1972. The administration no longer tacitly supports the party's slow and steady approach to constitutional and social development—by the forces of constitutional change it is committed to working with the NCG (as it once worked through the UP on the basis of a different calculation of where PNG's national interest lay). The highlanders themselves have been offered alternative means of political expression (through the National Party and the NCG itself), and have shown they are prepared to accept the concept of a national government, as a successor to white administration. Perhaps most surprisingly, however, many expatriate businessmen, who once saw the UP as the only responsible political force in PNG, now consider that it was a mistake to have become directly involved in national politics and recognise that the NCG under Somare offers a better and more viable political climate and thus a reasonable economic environment for their investment.

19. The effect of the NCG has therefore been to overturn the basis on which the UP was held together. The outcome of this disruption as it is likely to affect Highland politics is not yet clear, particularly as the party still lacks any real sense of direction or unanimity on its future role. As this indecision is partly a reflection of changing attitudes in the Highlands (as well as a lack of any consensus amongst the UP leadership) these attitudes will be examined in some detail at this stage before the suspects for the UP are touched on again at the conclusion of the report.

Attitudes to Constitutional Change

20. As indicated before any simplistic distinction between 'conservative' highlanders and 'radical' coastal distorts the complexities and uncertainties of the situation, [and] there was no unique ethnic or social basis for attempts to describe inherent differences in outlook between highlanders and the rest. Highlanders have shown themselves to be more ready to accept change than other groups in PNG, but they are anxious to ensure that they will be in a position to benefit from change as much as the others who have had a greater exposure to the development, which has taken place so far. In economic development, the highlands have made comparatively rapid progress and have already outstripped many coastal districts. In education, the gap has been closed over the past few years and the present rate of expansion in education could bring the highlands' rates of school attendance close to parity with most other districts in the foreseeable future. The factor which worries many highlanders, however, is that the comparatively recent advent of administration and education has resulted in few highlanders passing through higher education to senior positions in the civil service. The outlook of Anton Parao, the secretary of the UP and Western Highlands Regional MHA is dominated by a fear of a form of 'nambis' (coastal) colonialism which would replace white administration in the highlands if self-government came before the highlands had achieved a fair share of public service positions.

21. An additional factor which has fostered the illusion of conservatism is the influence of elders in most highlands societies. Respect for the old leaders has naturally lingered longer in the highlands where education is only now beginning to bring forth a new generation to challenge conventional wisdom and authority. To the old generation, many of whom spent their childhood, youth and perhaps half their manhood in a pristine traditional environment, the coming of the white man in the middle ages of their lives has brought cataclysmic changes and bewilderment. The impact of administration, cash economy and physical development over the last ten or twenty years has left them with a profound respect for Australian administration and a concern that this new phenomenon should stay and plant deeper roots. The younger generation, with a more blasé attitude to the wonders of European presence, are more willing to accept that the system can be indigenised and is not an exotic import that can only be maintained in white hands.

22. To the UP, the older generation formed a genuinely conservative indigenous element which could be exploited to represent the views of the highlanders as a whole. But the role of elders in society is steadily being eroded not merely by the younger and better educated but by a centre group—those who are now middle-aged (in terms of the short life expectancy in PNG) who have spent their adult life under administration and respect the benefits it has brought, but are aware that inevitably the highlands must prepare for self-rule in PNG. It is this middle-aged segment which is, in fact, numerically predominant in political life in the highlands and is now re-evaluating its earlier support for the UP. Many MHAs in this category have transferred their allegiance to the NCG. Meanwhile the younger generation, too, is split between those who look to the National Party as a vehicle for nationalist and progressive views and those who see the UP as a party which could be adopted [*sic*] to serve as an expression of this aggressive and xenophobic interpretation of the highlands' role in national affairs.

23. While these generalisations concerning attitudes amongst generations are of some use as a guide to one aspect of the problem, they must be considered together with other patterns which fragment attitudes in the highlands. Mention, for example, has already been made of the fragmentation of social units in pre-contact culture. This fragmentation is not total and was perhaps being corrected by a trend towards larger units at the time of Australian contact (para. 4 above). Several large linguistic groups such as the Enga (147,000) and the

Koman[5] (Chimbu, 120,000)[6] are evidence of some relatively large-scale cultural units—but the functional political divisions within traditional society were based on clans which formed the units on which rivalries or alliances were built. Administration has suddenly introduced wider loyalties, particularly to the district, but the political perspective of a highlander us still a series of horizons, the basic one being the clan, followed in receding order of importance by the language group, district, region (highlands), and the nation.

24. Although an attempt has been made above to identify a common thread running through highlanders' attitudes, cutting across geographic and linguistic divisions, there are many factors which although they do not necessarily break this pattern could increasingly disrupt it in the future. Some indication of this variety is given in the following brief survey of the four highlands districts in order to suggest the diversity of conditions found in each.

[*matter omitted*][7]

Conclusions—Implications for National Politics

38. If any consistent thread can be found in this survey of diverse attitudes and conditions, it is the fears resulting from the highlanders' lack of prolonged exposure to European presence and its trappings. He does not share the coastal Papuan or New Guinean's familiarity with (and, frequently, his indifference towards) European gadgets, concepts and methods. He has not yet gone through all the stages of bewilderment, hostility and disenchantment with Administration through which some coastal areas have graduated many decades ago. In most cases, the highlanders have adapted themselves enthusiastically and skilfully to introduce methods and attitudes. Whereas frequently the coastal Melanesian has resisted many aspects of administration (and reactions in the form of cargo cults still persist in areas first administered almost a century ago) the highlands have eagerly accepted the changes which have been offered in a relatively compressed span of time.

39. The issues in dispute between highlanders and coastals are not questions of conservative versus radical attitudes, of traditionalist versus progressive peoples, but concern problems of synchronising different stages of development and of familiarity with modern methods and attitudes. The fact that the highlanders demand so energetically that the gap be closed is a result of their realisation that the gap is on the verge of being closed under present administration policies and a breakthrough in the highlands' access to European technology and education is not far off. They fear that if they now lose their chance to close the gap, it could begin to widen again in the future and the highlands would irretrievably lose their opportunity to come to terms with the modern world on the same basis as other Papua New Guineans.

40. In political terms, then, the issue at stake is that present polices should not be halted or reversed by an indigenous government dominated by coastals. To pursue this goal, highlanders have now chosen two separate courses of action. On the one hand, many have stayed with the UP because they prefer to encourage a sense of chauvinism amongst highlanders, or because

---

5   Koman: Kuman. According to the late Bill Standish, 'Kuman ..., which means "west" (of the Chimbu River), is the most widely spoken [language in Chimbu]. It was used by some 80,000 or more people in the north and west of the province [of Chimbu] in 1975'. William Austin Standish, 'Simbu Paths to Power: Political Change and Cultural Continuity in the Papua New Guinea Highlands,' PhD Thesis, Australian National University, 1991, p. 24.

6   This number appears to refer to the total population of Chimbu, rather than to the members of the Kuman linguistic-cultural grouping.

7   The omitted matter contained a survey of the conditions found in the then four districts (later renamed provinces) in the highlands region—Western Highlands, Chimbu, Eastern Highlands and Southern Highlands.

they believe the tactic of delaying self-government will allow the gap to be closed under a benign Australian administration. On the other hand, other highlanders have recently come to believe that the gap can be closed just as quickly by highlanders joining the coalition and ensuring that they have a proportionate voice in national affairs. However, these are only tactical moves and there are few clues as yet as to how the highlanders will seek to prepare for their future in an independent PNG. Broadly, the choice lies between working through the NCG or using the UP as a basis for a truly highlands party. The NCG has made considerable gains in attracting highlands support and Somare's recent tour of three highlands districts was both an endorsement of his personal standing as a national leader and a preliminary indication that most highlanders are prepared to accept his government's authority. The pro-UP highlanders still appear too weak to reverse this trend but in the long rum they could exploit the highlands' fear for its future in an independent PNG to form a party determined to seize for the highlands a position of supremacy at the national level.

[NAA: A1838, 3036/10/6/2, PART 1]

377   CABINET SUBMISSION 897[1]

Canberra, September 1972

SECRET

Papua New Guinea Internal Security

Purpose

The purpose of this submission is to place before Cabinet the conclusions of a study in relation to internal security in Papua New Guinea and to seek Cabinet's approval to discussions between Papua New Guinea leaders and myself concerning the devolution of authority in the field of internal security along the lines recommended at the resumed constitutional talks in October.

Background

2.   Decision No. 452 of 23 June 1970 (Submission No. 327—Implications of Early Self-Government in Papua New Guinea)[2] directed that '… a special study of the situation in relation to internal security ought to be prepared by the Departments of External Territories and Defence.'

3.   This study has been completed and its conclusions are attached as Annex A to this submission.

[*matter omitted*]

5.   The Study Group noted Australia's continuing responsibilities to maintain law and order until independence and the consequences both internationally and domestically of its breakdown before that occurred. It also drew attention to the connection between the maintenance of order in emergency situations and the possible deployment of Australian defence forces if those situations should occur and deteriorate beyond a certain point. Approval of a request for assistance would require Cabinet consideration and "call-out" of the forces by the Governor-General. These considerations suggested to the Study Group the need for some continuing Australian influence over internal security. I agree with these views. It is to be noted that the retention of some residual authority along the lines proposed in the Report is compatible with self-government. In the case of the United Kingdom such an authority was frequently retained.

6.   At the same time it is necessary in my view that Papua New Guinea should be increasingly involved in the field of internal security both to enable it to gain the necessary experience and because its leaders have foreshadowed a request for further authority. In addition it is consistent with the present state of constitutional development.

7.   At the August discussions the Chief Minister informed me that the Papua New Guinea Government would wish to be more closely involved. This had been anticipated and acting with the advice of the Administrator I approved the appointment of a Police Spokesman as an interim measure. At the same time the Chief Minister has stated to the House of Assembly that Australia's ultimate authority to revoke power transferred in this area before independence is accepted. The Administrator has confirmed that in his view it is likely the proposals put forward in the Study would be acceptable.

---

1   Submitted by Peacock.

2   Document 53.

8.   In its conclusions the Study stated as a basic principle that:

'a considerable degree of responsibility for internal security should be assigned to the Papua New Guinea Government as part of its evolution to self-government but that it is essential that the Commonwealth Government should retain *until independence* at least a residual power to intervene and exercise ultimate control in internal security matters'.

9.   The Study Group, for reasons elaborated in its Report, recommended that transfer of authority, during the period to self-government, might be achieved by formally reserving to the Administrator control over internal security matters but providing that he may, by revocable transfer or revocable delegation, assign authority over the organs of internal security to Papua New Guinea Ministers.

10.   The Department of Foreign Affairs proposed as an alternative that internal security powers should be handed over rather than delegated to the Papua New Guinea Government but that the Administrator should be empowered to declare a state of emergency and, through this, resume control of the organs of internal security. The Department considered that such an arrangement would have the advantage of avoiding a situation where the prestige and authority of the Chief Minister would be undermined, or appear to be undermined, if powers delegated to him were taken away at a time of crisis or potential crisis. The Study Group accepted that the power to intervene should, in practice, only be exercised in situations of an emergency or potential emergency character. It preferred, however, that Australia's authority to intervene should be kept flexible and not circumscribed by specific legal procedures. It also noted that the Constitutional Planning Committee which has been established by the House of Assembly has, as part of its terms of reference, been deputed to consider constitutional provisions relating to emergency situations and felt it would be premature to provide by legislation for the declaration of states of emergency prior to the Report of this Committee. If provision is made for emergency situations it would be possible however for the proposal of the Department of Foreign Affairs to be implemented at the time of self-government.

11.   In accordance with wishes expressed in August by the Chief Minister, Mr Michael Somare, that the Papua New Guinea Government be given some immediate responsibility for internal security matters, including the Police, the Report favoured the transfer of authority of the Police, as well as those elements of the Department of the Administrator with an internal security character, to take place at the same time as transfer of control over District Commissioners and the Division of District Administration. This transfer is expected to take place at about the end of this year, but at least by March 1973.

RECOMMENDATION

12.   It is recommended that Ministers:

(i)   note the conclusions (at Annex A to this Submission) of the Study in relation to internal security in Papua New Guinea;

(ii) endorse the basic principle of the Report as set out in the conclusions (a) and (b);

(iii) endorse as a primary basis for discussion with the PNG leadership group at the October talks the principle of revocable delegation or revocable transfer of authority over internal security to the PNG Government. However such endorsement is not to preclude the discussion of other alternatives including that proposed by the Department of Foreign Affairs to take effect at the time of self-government;

(iv) that the Minister for External Territories be authorised to agree to a transfer of responsibility in accordance with the Conclusions (g), (h), (i), (j) and (k).

Annex A
Summary of Conclusions

The Interdepartmental Committee has concluded:

(a) There are good reasons for assigning a considerable degree of responsibility for internal security to the PNG Government in the light of the wishes of that government as part of its evolution to self-government.

(b) However, because of Australia's responsibility, the uncertain outlook, the need for experience and proven capacity to deal with difficult situations, it is essential that the Commonwealth Government should retain until independence at least a residual power to intervene and exercise ultimate control in internal security matters.

(c) The foregoing should be achieved by formally reserving to the Administrator control over internal security matters, but providing that he may by revocable transfer or delegation assign authority over the organs of internal security to PNG Ministers under suitable conditions.

(d) The recently revised Internal Security Committee structure in Papua New Guinea (including the Internal Security Committee which advises the Administrator on internal security matters) meets present requirements but its operation will need to be kept under review in the changing conditions. In particular there will be a requirement for adequate indigenous representation.

(e) Since the elections changes in the intelligence organisation in PNG, to meet both Australian and PNG requirements have acquired a new urgency. The committee notes that these changes are being implemented.

(f) The appointment of the Chief Minister as Ministerial Spokesman for the Police in the House of Assembly with effect from August is seen as an interim measure.

(g) As a result of constitutional talks with the Papua New Guinea Government it has been agreed that the Division of District Administration should be transferred to the Chief Minister following the October constitutional talks either by the end of this year or at least by March, 1973. The Committee believes that at the same time authority over the police should be delegated to a Police Minister. The Division would also be transferred to the Chief Minister in a similar way to the Division of District Administration. The Chief Minister would become Chairman of the Internal Security Committee [ISC]. However, the Administrator would retain the right to sit on the Internal Security Committee, to address it, and receive its reports. The transfer of powers in all instances would be revocable.

(h) The proposed delegation of authority over the police can be conveniently effected by the Administrator making a delegation of his statutory authority to direct the Commissioner under the Administrative Arrangements (Vesting of Powers) Ordinance 1971 which would permit him to revoke this delegation. Transfer of control over those elements of the Department of the Administrator which have an internal security character would be by approved arrangements under the Papua New Guinea Act but would be revocable.

(i) Subject to (j) below, the Police Minister should exercise full responsibility in police matters. It is important however that he should understand the need to consult with the Administrator and the AEC, and where appropriate receive the advice of the Internal Security Committee. He should also accept the need to observe the normal convention of leaving the day-to-day running of the police to the Commissioner.

(j) Particular consideration will be necessary whether, and if so at what time, certain miscellaneous powers relating to the police, e.g. terms and conditions of service, senior appointments and promotions should be delegated at the same time as the Division of District Administration is transferred to the Chief Minister.

(k) If the Minister for Police is other than the Chief Minister, he should be accorded membership of the Internal Security Committee. The Chief Minister in any case should have the right to nominate two additional members of the AEC to the ISC.

(l) Certain legislative measures are necessary before self-government. The Commonwealth Crimes Act and the Crimes (Aircraft) Act should be repealed in their extension to PNG and appropriate provisions incorporated in PNG legislation. Similarly, various powers in the Royal PNG Constabulary Ordinance vested in the Minister for External Territories should be vested in the Administrator, to enable the Administrator to delegate powers as necessary.

(m) The Commonwealth Act conferring internal self-government on PNG should preserve the Commonwealth's interest in internal security matters either by revocable delegation or, if sought by the Papua New Guinea Government, by specific provision empowering the Administrator to declare a state of emergency and so intervene.

(n) Agreement should also be reached with the PNG Government, to come into effect on self-government, to ensure the continued right of the Administrator to necessary access on internal security matters, e.g. the right to attend the AEC and ISC, and the right to continue to receive PNGIC[3] assessments.[4]

[NAA: A5908, 897]

---

3 Papua New Guinea Intelligence Committee.

4 On 17 October 1972, Cabinet: (a) noted the conclusions—at Annex A to the Submission—of the study in relation to internal security in Papua New Guinea; (b) endorsed the basic principle of the Report as set out in conclusions (a) and (b) of Annex A; (c) endorsed as a primary basis for discussion with the Papua New Guinea leadership group the principle of revocable delegation or revocable transfer of authority over internal security to the Papua New Guinea Government, with, however, the discussion of other options, including that proposed by DFA (paragraph 10 of the submission refers) not precluded; and, (d) agreed that the External Territories Minister be authorised to agree to a transfer of responsibility in accordance with conclusions (g), (h), (i), (j) and (k) of Annex A. Cabinet Decision 1432, 'Papua New Guinea Internal Security', 17 October 1972, NAA: A5908, 897.

378   JOINT STATEMENT BY PEACOCK, SINCLAIR AND SOMARE

Port Moresby, 3 October 1972

Fisheries Talks

The Chief Minister of Papua New Guinea, Mr Michael Somare, and the Australian Ministers for Primary Industry and External Territories, Messrs Sinclair and Peacock, have issued a joint communiqué concerning the talks on fisheries matters held in Port Moresby on 2–3 October.

The arrangements agreed on regarding fisheries are as follows:

• Delegation to the Papua New Guinea Government of licensing powers—subject to agreement on interim arrangements.

• Work to be commenced on the preparation of separate fisheries legislation for Papua New Guinea (to replace the Commonwealth Fisheries Act as it applies to Papua New Guinea). Review of the amendments currently proposed to the Commonwealth Fisheries Act with a view to exclusion of Papua New Guinea from the provisions of the Act. No date to be set at this stage for the implementation of these arrangements.

• Interim arrangements—to apply during the period after delegation of licensing powers and before the transfer of powers. The interim arrangements to be concluded as soon as possible and set down in an exchange of letters between the Papua New Guinea and Australian Governments.

• The Papua New Guinea Government has asked that the interim arrangements include the following provisions:

(a) Papua New Guinea to license an appropriate number of prawn catcher and carrier vessels to fish in all Commonwealth proclaimed waters outside the Declared Fisheries Zone;

(b) Agreement by all Papua New Guinea vessels licensed under (a) above to comply with Australian conservation and management measures as applied to other Australian vessels licensed under the Commonwealth Fisheries Act.

[NAA: A1838, 3080/11/2/1 PART 2]

379   TELEX FROM GALVIN TO CANBERRA

Port Moresby, 4 October 1972

668. Secret

Administrator has read through your 612[1] concerning defence and has asked me to convey his initial reaction ahead of a more considered message which will be sent tomorrow on his return to Port Moresby.

2.   Whilst he has no objections to the proposed meetings in Canberra he considers that they may not prove very productive and indeed could be counter-productive for the Commonwealth.

Neither the Chief Minister nor his Ministry (nor indeed his advisers) have any developed views on defence matters nor are they likely to have until the Defence Branch is properly established and they have had to consider some of the issues through consultation a process which envisaged AEC submissions on a whole variety of matters).

3.   The proposed November visit is unlikely to be convenient and that too would be far too early for discussion in detail if we are to avoid being seen to be thrusting subjects on to the Ministry which they are not in a position to take their own advice. The subjects you mentioned in 5(A)–(E) will properly be seen as ones of major policy importance and on which considerable consideration would be necessary to arrive at a PNG Government view.

4.   For my own part, I consider that the approach envisaged will not do much to remove the concern about the Commonwealth defence intentions that I mentioned to you in Port Moresby and is dealt with at length in my memorandum to FAS (GL) of 15 September.[2]

5.   You should also know that if the Chief Minister has stated clearly to Webb[3] and Murray[4] that if the Defence Branch is not transferred to the office of the Chief Minister he will have to establish a separated defence branch there or go elsewhere for his advice (e.g. UPNG).[5] In this regard he is not seeking power over defence but rather that his government has available to it in the most convenient way advice free from Commonwealth direction so that it can form up PNG views. I doubt if he will see that the location of the branch in his office is in any way precluded by Australia's maintaining power and responsibility for defence and of equal importance none of his key advisers, e.g. Ryan, Barnett, [and] Voutas, sees it that way. They will probably draw the analogy with other areas where the Commonwealth retains responsibility and final power but the PNG advisers are within a department for which a PNG Minister has day to day concern.

[NAA: A452, 1972/2801]

1   Not published.

2   Document 372.

3   Nick Webb.

4   Probably Commodore Brian Stewart (Chick) Murray (later Sir Brian), Director, Joint Operations and Plans, Department of Defence.

5   University of Papua New Guinea.

380   LETTER FROM WALLER TO BESLEY

Canberra, 5 October 1972

CONFIDENTIAL

PNG–Indonesian Relations: Border Regime

We have been informed that the Chief Minister of Papua New Guinea has the following general reservations concerning a border regime with Indonesia:

  i)   He has not yet considered the basic question of whether a border regime agreement is necessary (nor the financial/personnel implications);

  ii)   Until this has been done, he prefers that PNG delegates do *not* enter into substantive discussions on a border regime and he would not wish to set a date to participate in such talks (e.g. early in 1973);

  iii)   He feels it is too early to agree to a visit by HANKAM[1] (as has been suggested by the Indonesians);

  iv)   He is sceptical of the need for exchanges on border questions, as proposed by Indonesia, at chief executive level;

  v)   He has indicated interest in a visit to Indonesia early next year and believes this might be an opportunity for Indonesians to put their points although he would not be in a position to enter into commitments;

  vi)   The PNG Government is anxious to establish warm relations with Indonesia, including satisfactory border relations, but due to pre-occupation with urgent political matters it is not yet ready to enter into discussion on a regime.

2.   We are concerned that the reservations expressed by the Chief Minister may be misinterpreted by the Indonesians. This could have serious implications for future relations between Indonesia and an independent PNG. We believe that it is important that the Australian Embassy in Djakarta should be in a position to convey to the Indonesians some more forthcoming response to their proposals than that in paragraph 1 above.

3.   As previously discussed between our two Departments, we therefore suggest that the opportunity might be taken, during the Chief Minister's presence in Canberra for the Japan/Australia Ministerial consultations, for the Minister for External Territories to discuss these matters with him. We attach some suggested points on which the Minister might wish to draw if he approves the suggestion.

Attachment

PNG–Indonesian Relations: Border Regime Talking Points

We believe that it is in the best interests of both Papua New Guinea and Australia that there should be good relations and understanding between an independent Papua New Guinea and her powerful Indonesian neighbour. The Indonesians and the New Guineans do not know one another very well yet, and we need to work hard to build up a strong foundation of understanding and good will for the future.

The present Government in Indonesia, unlike the Sukarno regime, is pursuing moderate and constructive policies at home and abroad. It is not interested in external adventures, as Sukarno was. It now has close and friendly relations with Australia.

---

1   The Indonesian Ministry of Defence (*Pertahanan dan Keamanan*, or HANKAM).

History shows that border problems are a major source of dispute between countries. The Indonesians have recently been expressing increased concern over the activities of Irianese rebels operating near the common border. They say that these people are using 'bases' in Papua New Guinea. (It is true that some of these people cross and recross the border from time to time.)

The Indonesians have suggested joint patrolling of the border and discussions about a border regime. We do not favour joint patrols as such but we think it would be wise to appear responsive to the Indonesian proposal for talks. We believe it would be in PNG's interest to take advantage of Australia's present good relationship with Indonesia to secure arrangements advantageous to Papua New Guinea.

'Border regime' is the normal instrument which governments sharing a common border agree upon to regulate matters of common interest on the border.

Some form of 'border regime' will be essential, sooner or later, although there need not be any elaborate machinery or many additional personnel. (Judged on present indications the work involved could be done by officials normally otherwise engaged, and should absorb them for only two or three days a month). Some preparatory work has been done already.

On PNG's border with Indonesia, there are several matters on which it would be difficult to serve PNG's interests without some form of agreement with Indonesia. These are:

a)   Arrangements to protect land rights across the border.

b)   Arrangements to continue the border liaison procedures which have proved very useful to date in resolving problems which come up from time to time along the border.

c)   Arrangements to replace the rights which Indonesia may have as of now as to navigation on the Fly River.

d)   Administration and Commonwealth officials are examining several other matters in which they feel that PNG would benefit by agreed arrangements with Indonesia.

The Indonesians will want agreements on some of these matters. PNG can hardly refuse to talk about them. To do so might leave the Indonesians with the impression that PNG had some ulterior motive for not wishing to regulate border arrangements.

It is possible that the Indonesians could ask for much more elaborate border policing than takes place at present. This could require considerable deployment of personnel; but PNG does not have to agree if it thinks the procedures proposed by the Indonesians are unnecessary. It should, however, explain why to the Indonesians.

A visit by officials from the Indonesian Defence Ministry (HANKAM) and later on, high-level talks with West Irian provincial authorities (not necessarily involving the Chief Minister in person), would serve a useful purpose in acquainting the Indonesians with PNG's needs and wishes. If the Indonesians have only very little contact with PNG, they cannot be expected to appreciate its point of view.

If the PNG Government wishes to establish warm and friendly relations with Indonesia, an early and positive response on the subject of a border regime would establish a good basis for further friendly relations.

[NAA: A452, 1972/3190]

381   LETTER FROM BOWEN TO PEACOCK

Canberra, 6 October 1972

I would like to raise with you some thoughts arising out of our experience to date with foreign service training for Papua New Guineans.[1]

Seven officers have now completed the Foreign Service training course in Canberra. Two of these are now overseas (Djakarta and Brussels) and the other five are working in the Department of Foreign Affairs prior to posting later this year (Tokyo, Bangkok, Nairobi, New York, and Geneva). Generally speaking, they have done well and have found the course valuable. The only real problem which has emerged is that those with limited academic background have had some difficulties with the course and, later, with their work in the Department. It seems therefore that, while we do not need to insist on university graduates, officers training for foreign service work ought to have at least some tertiary education, e.g. Goroka Teachers' College. Officers with lower educational standards could however be given administrative training in the special problems with running an overseas service and my Department is very willing to arrange such training.

In view of recent estimates of the date of independence, I am a little concerned over whether we will have enough people trained to enable PNG to handle its foreign relations. It is not possible to hire qualified advisers on foreign policy in the same way as technical people like doctors and engineers can be hired. It is also certain that from the date of independence PNG will be faced with all kinds of pressure from abroad. It is in both PNG's and Australia's interest that PNG be in a position to handle these effectively.

If we assume that independence will come at the end of 1974, we have two years left to train people. If we take ten a year, that gives us 27 trained diplomatic officers to staff the Port Moresby office and whatever overseas posts are set up. Even without allowing for the inevitable drop-outs, this number would be an absolute minimum. To achieve it we must have five officers of suitable educational standard for each of the two foreign service courses to be run in 1973, and five for each of the 1974 courses. This is in addition to those officers who might be given special administrative training. (I imagine we should be thinking in terms of twenty or thirty officers in this latter category.)

It is not necessary that all the people trained in foreign service work spend all their time on it before independence, although obviously the more experience they get the more efficient they will be. But it is important that the PNG Government, the Administrator and the PNG Public Service Board be made aware of the pressing need in this field. Australia will be judged internationally to a large, and perhaps unfair, extent by the performance of independent PNG in handling its international relations.

I am fully aware of the personnel problems facing PNG. The kind of people needed for a foreign service are those who are desperately needed in so many other fields as well. Nevertheless, I feel that the PNG Government should be made aware of the kinds of problems which will face them at independence and of the ways in which their interests will suffer if PNG is not equipped to deal with those problems. Perhaps you might be able to raise these points with PNG leaders.

[NAA: A1838, 3080/10/4/7]

---

1   DFA had engaged with DET on several occasions on the establishment of an embryonic foreign affairs ministry in PNG and on training its staff. DFA had been frustrated, however, by the slow progress achieved, which appears to have resulted from DET giving these matters a lower priority than DFA. This letter from Bowen to his fellow minister is directed to getting DET to give PNG foreign affairs training greater priority and to engage with Somare's government on this matter. For background on the training question, see Documents 151 (para. 14), 153 (paras 7–11), 161, 170, 187 (paras 5–11) & 200 (paras 2–6).

382   LETTER FROM MCMAHON TO SOMARE

Canberra, 10 October 1972

Thank you for your letter of 2 August 1972,[1] expressing personal regret that I was unable to visit Papua New Guinea as planned. Your constructive understanding in this matter has been most helpful.

You mentioned the importance you attach to the concept of a cultural development programme. You may be assured that it is a matter to which we would also attach significance. I have referred your letter to my colleague, the Minister for External Territories for his attention.

I note the emphasis your Government gives to the Employment Security Scheme and to land matters, and that you will be discussing these matters with Mr Peacock.

[NAA: A452, 1972/3207]

---

1   Document 342.

383   STATEMENT BY PEACOCK[1]

Canberra, 10 October 1972

Throughout the year this House has been kept informed of developments in Papua New Guinea, most recently when on 31 August 1972 I tabled two statements[2] which resulted from Constitutional discussions held with Papua New Guinea leaders in late July and early August.

The Papua New Guinea House of Assembly has recently debated the timing of self-government. On 27 June the Chief Minister made a statement in the House of Assembly in which he said:

'The view of my Government is that self-government should not occur before 1 December 1973 but that it should come as soon as possible after that.'[3]

He moved that the House take note of the paper. The debate was adjourned until the September meeting of the House. On 5 September the Chief Minister moved an amendment to the motion, adding two clauses:

'That the House:

(1) Requests that constitutional changes necessary for internal self-government be brought into effect on 1 December 1973 or as soon as possible thereafter; and

(2) Interprets full self-government for Papua New Guinea as leaving with the Commonwealth of Australia final powers only in the matters of defence and external affairs which it will exercise with the fullest consultation with the Government of Papua New Guinea.'[4]

In speaking to the amendment the Chief Minister also cited internal security as one of the powers to remain in the hands of the Commonwealth after self-government.

After further debate, the House of Assembly on 19 September 1972 voted in favour of the Resolution as amended by a majority of 18 (52 in favour, 34 against and 13 not voting).

In doing so the Government has been obliged to consider whether a majority vote in the House of Assembly conforms to the terms of the UN Charter which requires that self-government be brought about in accordance with the freely expressed wishes of the people. The Commonwealth Government has followed the policy that it should look to the House of Assembly to represent the wishes of the majority of the people. During my visit to Port Moresby on which I reported to the House on 31 August, I discussed with the Chief Minister and his colleagues how this policy should be put into practice. We agreed that important constitutional changes required a recorded vote in favour in the House of Assembly by a substantial majority of members, the majority being broadly representative of the country as a whole.

In respect of the resolution on the timing of self-government, I point out first that there was an interval of two months between the tabling of the motion and the vote on it. I also record that in only one of the 18 administrative districts was there no vote in favour of the motion.

Honourable members will note that the Chief Minister referred to self-government as leaving with the Commonwealth such powers as Defence, Internal Security and External Affairs. This broadly accords with the approach of the Commonwealth.

Given the complicated nature of the administrative and legislative steps, some flexibility may be necessary in determining the full list of powers handed over by the chosen date for

---

1   The statement was delivered to the House of Representatives.

2   See Documents 336 & 347 (respectively).

3   Document 318.

4   See Documents 367 & 373.

self-government. Self-government will be formally signified by amendments to the Papua New Guinea Act which will vest in the Papua New Guinea Government executive authority which now legally lies in the hands of the Commonwealth. I see no reason why this formal step should not be completed by the date set for self-government in terms of the motion just approved by the House of Assembly.

The Australian Government's policy towards Papua New Guinea has been to encourage self-government but not to impose it. Australia's formal obligations to Papua New Guinea under the UN Charter are not completed until that country's independence. We have pledged aid and assistance beyond that time. Australia will not remain involved in Papua New Guinea except in accordance with the wishes of the majority of the people as represented by the House of Assembly. If we are asked to continue to assist we will. There is no question of Australia deciding unilaterally to withdraw its involvement in Papua New Guinea.

In informing the House of the Government's acceptance of the timing for self-government as endorsed by the House of Assembly, I affirm that it is our intention to put our utmost effort into preparations for effective and responsible self-government in Papua New Guinea. The Government has confidence in Papua New Guinea's leaders and their deep concern for planning the future of their country.

[*CPD*, HR, vol. 81, 10 October 1972, pp. 2292–97]

384   SUBMISSION FROM KELLOWAY TO PEACOCK

Canberra, 10 October 1972

Bougainville Copper Agreement

According to press reports, three prominent members of the National Coalition have called for renegotiation of the Bougainville Copper Agreement in the last week. They are the Minister for Mines Mr Lapun, the Deputy Chairman of the Constitutional Committee Father Momis, and finally, the Chief Minister Mr Somare.

2.   The Chief Minister is reported to have said that the Papua New Guinea Government would have to examine all agreements made for Papua New Guinea in the past by Australia. Mr Somare went on to say that his Cabinet had not *yet* considered renegotiation of the Bougainville Agreement and according to another report made it clear that he was speaking personally.

3.   Father Momis has moved in the House of Assembly a motion setting out the principles on which future mining agreements should be negotiated. In principle these do not differ radically from the existing investment guidelines except in calling for a majority holding in normal circumstances to be financed as far as possible out of future earnings.

4.   The Agreement between Bougainville Copper and the Administration was endorsed by the House of Assembly in the Mining (Bougainville Copper Agreement) Ordinance 1967 and in other debates. In spite of this it is apparent that there is a feeling in Papua New Guinea that the Agreement was basically one negotiated by Australia through Australian officials.

5.   It has always been our view that the Bougainville Agreement represented the best deal that could be negotiated at the time. Various criticisms of the return to Papua New Guinea from the project have been put forward and it is basically a matter of opinion whether this return should be greater. It cannot, however, in our view be reasonably argued that the Agreement is of an exploitive nature—it does provide substantial benefits to Papua New Guinea.[1]

6.   Mr Lapun has claimed that the Agreement is not as good as those current in Peru, Zambia and Chile, but he ignores the fact that these agreements have been renegotiated under pressure and probably were not as good as the Bougainville Agreement in the first place.

7.   We are re-examining the impact of the Bougainville Agreement in the light of up-to-date figures from the Company and at this stage we would not like to make any public comment on the benefits derived by the Government and the Company. It is clear, however, that in the initial period most of the cash flow will have to be used for the repayment of loans. In this respect the situation is not comparable with those of the countries mentioned by Mr Lapun where the mines were older and presumably most, or all, of the loans have been repaid.

8.   We are concerned that Papua New Guinea should not take any action which will result in a distraction of investment confidence and a consequent drying-up of investment. It will be of little benefit to Papua New Guinea to obtain a larger share of the Bougainville earnings if other potential projects fail to eventuate and result in a greater loss in income than the gain from Bougainville. In our opinion this result could very easily come about if the Papua New Guinea

---

1   In a separate assessment DET noted: 'In retrospect, the Agreement lacks flexilibity (but in its negotiations the company had insisted upon certainty of future mining rights). For example there is no clause requiring renegotiation in the event of changing circumstances, such as a substantial increase in the size of ore reserves. Even so, the Agreement compares favourably with other current projects. To attempt to renegotiate at this stage could well have disastrous effects on the whole economy which is very dependent on a continuing capital inflow.' See Note by DET, 'Renegotiation of Bougainville Copper Agreement', undated (c. October 1972), NAA: A452, 1972/3386.

Government used its power to force a renegotiation which was obviously unacceptable to the Company (whatever agreement might ultimately be signed) especially within a few months of the mine coming into production. The Government will need to think about the impact on the international investment community through the widespread influence of the CRA[2] Group and also through the international lenders such as the Bank of America.

9.   The Papua New Guinea Government should also realise that any forced renegotiation is bound to arouse an unfavourable reaction in the Australian financial community and this in turn could conceivably react on the attitude of the Australian public to Papua New Guinea. It is not suggested that the Australian Government would wish to use the aid relationship as a threat to the Papua New Guinea Government in this matter. It is to be remembered, however, that governments are necessarily responsive to public opinion and an unfavourable reaction to Papua New Guinea in Australia might make it difficult for the Government to maintain its present generous attitude to aid to Papua New Guinea.[3]

10. For these reasons we hope that the Papua New Guinea Government will examine the situation very carefully before it comes to a decision on this matter. It is, in our view, vital that a very thorough examination should be made of the terms of the Agreement and of the wider consequences we have mentioned above before the AEC comes to a view.

11. You might consider it advisable to mention these considerations to the Chief Minister during your forthcoming visit to Papua New Guinea.[4]

[NAA: A452, 1972/3386]

---

2   Conzinc Riotinto of Australia.

3   Here Peacock commented: 'This is an implied threat and should not be put to PNG at this stage.'

4   Here Peacock commented: 'Without being bound, I will certainly give consideration to raising the matter with the Chief Minister.'

385   RECORD OF CONVERSATION BETWEEN ANDERSON AND JOHNSON

Canberra, 12 October 1972

CONFIDENTIAL

Papua New Guinea Border Regime

At dinner last night I mentioned to the Administrator the recent evidence of growing Indonesian concern over rebel activities in the border areas and the increased interest the Indonesians were taking in discussions about a border regime.[1]

2.   The Administrator said he had no doubt that Irianese rebels moved into Papua New Guinea and back from time to time although he thought it would be wrong to speak of their having any fixed base or camp in PNG. He knew that the Indonesians would like stronger action taken against the rebels but for one thing the rebels were very hard to locate—the terrain in the area concerned being almost impossible—and for another, the New Guinea people on our side of the border would be very opposed to seeing such action taken. Somare himself came from the Sepik area where there was much sympathy for the rebels. The Administrator suggested that the problem was a relatively small one since only a small number of rebels were involved, and said he hoped it would be possible to keep the Indonesians quiet at diplomatic level and to maintain the present border liaison arrangements.

3.   I said that although there had not yet been any formal diplomatic protests, the Indonesians were not treating the problem as a small one and it was not going to go away. We were concerned not to let it get out of hand, both because of the importance of our own relations with Indonesia and because of the importance of Indonesia to an independent Papua New Guinea. Even if it was difficult to do much about the rebels, it was important—all the more important—for New Guinea leaders to appear responsive to Indonesian initiatives like the proposals for a visit by a HANKAM[2] team and for high-level meetings, and for the Australia/ New Guinea side to be ready to talk about other aspects of a border regime.

4.   Although the Administrator said that he hoped Somare's proposed visit to Indonesia and the opening of an Indonesian consulate in Port Moresby would help towards better understanding between Indonesia and Papua New Guinea, I did not get the impression that he saw the problem as urgent or even very important.

[NAA: A1838, 752/1/23/1 PART 4]

---

1   See also, among others, Documents 325, 330, 334 (paras 13 & 14), 353 & 360.

2   The Indonesian Ministry of Defence (*Pertahanan dan Keamanan*, or HANKAM).

386   RECORD OF MEETING BETWEEN TANGE AND SOMARE[1]

Canberra, 12 October 1972

CONFIDENTIAL

Sir Arthur Tange welcomed the Chief Minister to the Department of Defence. He recalled the discussions which the Minister for Defence had had with the Administrator's Executive Council in June 1972 and emphasised the value which Australia saw in the development of consultation with PNG on defence matters, in view of the pace of political and constitutional events there.[2]

The Australian side had been endeavouring to list the subjects relevant to the future of PNG defence and to identify the areas in which practical attention was required.

It was not the Australian intention at this meeting to make any proposals to the PNG side or to ask for any decisions. It hoped to hear PNG views and in particular to try and work out a practical basis for future discussions. Australia wanted to know what it should do to hand over a defence force which an independent Government would want.

Australia recognised that many of its decisions today on defence matters would have their main effect several years hence, after independence. This was an added reason for the two countries to talk.

The *Chief Minister* said that he and the Administrator were agreed on the need for the PNG Government to re-examine the present defence set-up in the light of the needs of independent PNG and to discuss its thoughts with the Australian Government. With the quickening pace of the movement towards self-government and independence, both countries needed to consider what was involved in handing over defence. The earlier these processes began the better. PNG welcomed the establishment of the Defence Branch and the appointment of Mr Webb.

The *Chief Minister* went on to say that there were a number of specific issues he wished to raise. In broaching some of these matters he—and the Constitutional Planning Committee— had considered carefully what moves were essential now and what could be considered at a later stage.

His first request was that the Defence Branch be transferred from its present location in the Administrator's Department to the Office of the Chief Minister. The PNG Ministry attached considerable importance to this proposal and would otherwise feel itself unable to place confidence in the Branch as a source of advice on post-independence defence policy. Without this confidence, the Branch Head would be severely inhibited in his tasks of training his staff for their further departmental role, and in providing policy advice. The Administrator would not be cut off from the Branch Head but the Commonwealth Government would need to make arrangements to provide its advice to the Administrator.

The second matter he wished to raise was the use of patrol boats for fisheries control. The present boats performed some duties in this regard, but as more foreign fishing boats entered PNG waters the requirement had expanded. There was also the growing need for PNG to be able to exercise control over its seabed resources generally. There were problems of distance

---

1   Along with Tange and Somare, those present included Johnson, Nick Webb, Admiral Sir Victor Smith (Chairman, Chiefs of Staff Committee), G. E. (Gordon) Blakers (Deputy Secretary B, Department of Defence), Thomas E. (Tos) Barnett (Constitutional Adviser to the Chief Minister) and J. Yocklunn (Private Secretary to the Chief Minister).

2   See Document 311.

and problems of communication. A greater effort in this field would require a greater number of patrol boats than at present.

Thirdly, the *Chief Minister* raised the question of the position of the two senior indigenous officers in the Joint Force. Both were to attend Queenscliff[3] in Australia during the next twelve months, a time when crucial constitutional developments would be taking place in PNG. He believed it to be most important that they should be able to return to PNG at intervals during their course in order to keep in touch with developments in PNG.

This matter was part of a broad problem in ensuring that in future the loyalties of the PNG Force and its officers were towards PNG rather than to an Australian Army.[4] In Australia, there was an established tradition that the Army should be isolated from politics. But the social system was very different in PNG. Experience in some other countries, for example in Africa, had shown the danger of Army coups in situations where the Army was isolated from the political life of the country. It was vital that officers should identify with PNG and feel a sense of loyalty and responsibility to the PNG government. One of the senior local officers (there were two majors now and the third was expected to be promoted shortly) could be the next Force Commander. It could be desirable to attach one of the local officers to the Defence Branch.

Sir Arthur Tange assured the Chief Minister that the Australian side would approach sympathetically the matters he had raised, and would be responsive in the advice given to Australian Ministers.

Attendance at Queenscliff and Service Loyalties

Turning to the Chief Minister's last main point, *Sir Arthur Tange* said that there would be understanding and acceptance in Australia of the need to shift the focus of loyalty of the PNG Force towards the PNG Government. He agreed with the view that the Army should be seen as part of the constitutional fabric of the country, rather than apart from it, and that officers should understand and accept PNG's national priorities.

Admiral Smith saw no difficulties in arrangements to facilitate the periodic return of the two PNG majors from Queenscliff to PNG. This was a unique situation with no parallel in regard to, for example, Asian students undertaking the course. It was suggested that there might be 3 or 4 return visits to PNG during the course, each of about a week. The *Chief Minister* indicated that he might wish them to sit in on constitutional talks.

[*matter omitted*]

Location of the Defence Branch

Sir Arthur Tange said that while the Chief Minister's proposal raised no difficulties in principle, there was a need to reach clear understandings on the complicated questions of channels of communication and lines of responsibility. Clarification was needed as the channel for conveying Australian official advice to the Spokesman, and the means of keeping the Administrator informed on developments.

[*matter omitted*]

Mr Barnett suggested that useful precedent could be seen in his own position as head of the Constitutional Branch, which had been transferred from the Department of the Administrator to the Chief Minister's Office. While he remained in contact with both the Chief Minister and the Administrator, it had been established that he was directly and chiefly responsible

---

3   The Australian Staff College at Fort Queenscliff in Victoria.

4   See Documents 354 (para. 7) & 363.

to the Chief Minister. Generally he kept the Administrator fully informed on constitutional developments, but several delicate situations had arisen where, because of his primary loyalty to the Chief Minister, he had had to tell the Administrator that he could no longer keep him fully informed on the subjects in question.

Sir Arthur Tange and *Mr Johnson* agreed that the kind of arrangement outlined by Mr Barnett would be acceptable.

[*matter omitted*]

Fisheries Control

[*matter omitted*]

It was agreed that the possibility of making greater use of existing patrol boats should be explored and that the Administration should in future be consulted by the Joint Force Commander when programmes of operations for the patrol boats were being prepared.

[*matter omitted*]

[NAA: A452, 1973/470]

387   LETTER FROM WHITELAW TO KELLOWAY

Canberra, 12 October 1972

Future Currency Arrangements for Papua New Guinea[1]

As you are aware, it is our firm opinion that, if PNG is to achieve self-government and independence in any meaningful sense, then the attainment of financial independence must be part of the process. Implicit in this is the creation of a separate PNG monetary area with its own identifiable currency. To our minds, there can be no 'half-way house' so far as currency is concerned. For the same reasons that transfer of the individual political and administrative powers to the PNG Government must be complete, so the power to issue currency and to manage the PNG monetary area must also be complete. Such expedients as the 'linked currency' arrangement outlined in the report by the Central Banking Service of the International Monetary Fund[2] could, we think, involve more difficulties and problems on both sides than they would solve.

Nevertheless, we do not think that the Commonwealth should be seen to be pressing this matter vigorously at the present time. Any specific proposals by the Commonwealth at that stage would, in our opinion, have been out of place. This is not to imply that the Commonwealth should not be ready to respond quickly and effectively to any expressed wish by the PNG Government for a separate currency—far from it. As noted above, we see the introduction of a separate PNG currency as an inevitable development. If PNG Ministers at or after the forthcoming constitutional tasks were to decide to introduce a separate PNG currency in the near future then Australia should, we believe, do all that it can to help in the implementation of that decision.

It is not for us to determine what form the future currency arrangements in PNG might take. Much of the areas of decision here will lie with the PNG Government. In our opinion, it would not be fruitful to speculate on what Australia's attitude would, or should, be to particular questions until we know in more detail precisely what course PNG Ministers wish to follow. Clearly, the views of our own Ministers would need to be sought at that time.

[NAA: A452, 1971/4971]

---

1   For background on the currency issue, see especially Documents 321, 323 & 326.
2   Not published.

388   MEMORANDUM FROM BURNS

Port Moresby, 13 October 1972

CONFIDENTIAL

Constitutional Planning Committee

At the request of the Chief Minister's Department the Constitutional Planning Committee (CPC) has presented its first progress report (copy attached)[1] to the Chief Minister this week summarising the committee's activities to date. Most of the report is spent in arguing that the committee be more closely involved in negotiations over the transfer of powers leading to self-government and brings to a head a conflict of interests between the committee and the Constitutional Development Branch of the Office of the Chief Minister.

It has been evident for some time that the committee overreached the guidelines established for it by the coalition government. The committee was deliberately established to be responsible to the NCG[2] and the Chief Minister and not as a select committee of the House of Assembly. However, the ambitions of two of the expatriate advisers, Prof. Davidson[3] and Dr Stone,[4] has obviously been to turn the CPC into a constitution-making body with status verging on that of a constituent assembly which could hold the reins controlling constitutional and political development in the period up to self-government. The advisors have tended to see if as an academic exercise in moulding a constitution divorced as much as possible from the immediate environment in which day-to-day political developments are occurring at a rapid pace. Thus the committee has developed into a paper monster which it may be difficult for the coalition to control. The extremity of the CPC's demands to be involved in government-to-government negotiations can be seen in the following extract from its progress report:

> ... [T]he transfer of power and the shaping of the system of government are closely related processes. To that degree, the Deputy Chairman of the Constitutional Planning Committee will need to watch over more than the subject-areas which are clearly recognised to lie within his province; even beyond 'the potential grey area' ... where the committee's work clearly overlaps that of the constitutional talks, there are many technical and procedural matters, even concerning avowed interim arrangements, in which the constitutional implications will have to be spelt out. It is unlikely that the Papua New Guinea Government could agree not to act or to accept additional responsibilities in such cases. The Committee should, however, resist suggestions by the Australian Government that consideration of certain matters by the committee prior to their final transfer would unnecessarily delay progress towards self-government. That suggestion is properly a matter for negotiation between the Papua New Guinea Government and the Committee alone.

The [PNG] coalition government might by now have cause to reconsider its decision to provide Papua New Guinea with a written constitution by the time of self-government. The committee has spent all of its time so far in digging in and acquiring ammunition to be used against constitutional development officials. It is devoting this week to culling all the files in the Constitutional Development Branch of the Chief Minister's Office in order to establish whether there are any other areas in the present constitutional negotiations where the committee's views should have been sought.

---

1   Not published.

2   National Coalition Government.

3   Jim Davidson, Founding Professor of Pacific History, Australian National University.

4   David Stone, New Guinea Research Unit, Australian National University.

It is difficult to see how the committee can be dislodged at this stage, or prevented from harassing, if not delaying, constitutional negotiations. In an AEC meeting on Monday at which the CPC's report was tabled, the Chief Minister did not accept the points made by the committee. Somare's role as the coordinator of the activities of his Department on the one hand and the committee on the other will be crucial. Should he decide to exert his authority over the committee and restrict its empire building the path towards self-government might be made smoother. But Somare's style of government does not encourage such attempts to provoke open confrontations and it is more likely that he will continue to play the role of mediator, seeking a broad consensus of views amongst all elements contributing to constitutional change. In this, Father Momis will probably serve as a useful intermediary. He is the best educated and one of the most astute members of the NCG and has applied himself seriously to his role as deputy chairman which should serve as a firm foundation for his political career. He faces an unenviable task in conforming to the NCG's guidelines without alienating his expatriate advisors while at the same time avoiding the temptation to use the CPC to advance his own status.

[NAA: A9334, 201/1/4 PART 1]

389   SPEECH BY SOMARE

Port Moresby, 16 October 1972

Opening Address by the Chief Minister, Mr M. Somare
to the Senior Executive Programme Seminar

I am very pleased to have the opportunity to open this seminar and to stress to you the importance my Government attaches to the localisation programme generally and to the Senior Executive Programme in particular.

Members of the SEP and overseas officers associated with it will be aware of the change in emphasis that has taken place since the formation of the National Coalition—in particular

(i)   the shift in policy-making on all important issues from Canberra to Port Moresby; and

(ii) the setting of a target date for self-government.

Many present will also be aware of changes of emphasis foreshadowed by the PNG. Government in national development planning—changes in the direction of more balanced development throughout the country as a whole and development more closely geared to the needs of the people of Papua New Guinea.

Inevitably much of what has taken place in the past has been governed by expatriate (mainly Australian) thinking about what is good for this country, and the development of the PNG Public Service has taken place equally inevitably in line with Australian Public Service concepts.

In saying this I do not wish to detract from the remarkable progress that has been made since World War 2 and the efforts of the overseas staff who have made this progress possible and have brought us to the stage we have reached today. We are grateful for all that has been done and for the dedication of those overseas officers who have taken part in bringing us to this point.

But the time has now come when we must begin to shape our own future and to shape it in accordance with our national needs as Papua New Guineans see them.

During the short time we have been operating as a PNG Ministry, we have seen a need for three things so far as our Public Service is concerned:

(a) a need to bring more and more Papua New Guinean thinking into the policy-making side of the role of the Public Service; we are looking to those PNG officers who are here today to play an increasing part in advising the Government about what should be done, as well as carrying out the policies which the Government itself decides;

(b) a need for more and more of the day to day work of government administration to be carried out by Papua New Guineans themselves, so that our people throughout the country may see and understand that our own people are able to carry out the work of government and may gain confidence in their own future through that knowledge;

(c) and thirdly, a cutting back of the cost of the Public Service to a scale that we can afford in the immediate future. If we are to be fully independent we must rely on our own efforts to the greatest extent possible both financially and in terms of staff resources.

In my Budget Speech to the House of Assembly on 26th September 1972, I informed members of my Government's plans for a reduction in the number of expatriates in the Public Service.[1]

---

1   Not published. For Somare's concerns, see Document 340.

We have set as a target a reduction from 7,500 to 3,000–4,000 overseas staff over the next 3½ years.

If we are unable to achieve this target, then we will get as close to it as we can. But we certainly have no intention of permitting a breakdown in the Public Service just to achieve the target figure.

In fact, these reductions should lead to a more streamlined, cheaper and more New Guinean type of Public Service, and that is our real aim.

Do not forget that we are proposing to continue to employ 3,000–4,000 overseas officers after independence in a population of 2½ million people. Nigeria with 40 million people only had 1,000 white officers at independence, while Kenya with 13 million people had 4,000 European officers in 1969. Therefore we will still have a very high proportion of Europeans in our Public Service compared with other developing countries.

My Budget Speech made it clear that we do not want a purge.

Once the conditions of the Employment Security Scheme has been settled, there will be a number of permanent overseas officers who will wish to accept their compensation and seek employment elsewhere.

Many of the public servants are contract officers who will be terminating contracts within the next 3 ½ years.

Others are temporary employees, who pull out at the rate of hundreds every year.

Some of the overseas public servants can be eliminated because they are now engaged purely in servicing other public servants—teaching their children, calculating their salaries and other entitlements, maintaining their homes, and so on.

Some positions will no longer be required after we have rationalised Public Service functions, eliminate duplication of work, and simplified Public Services procedures.

We do not want an Australian or European type Public Service, geared to 20th century technology, nor can we afford to maintain such [a] Public Service.

By making our Public Service one that is most suited to the need of Papua New Guinea and one that is localised wherever possible, we will substantially reduce the cost of the Public Service.

It should be remembered that the reductions we propose in the number of overseas officers will not only mean savings in salaries but also in housing, leave fares and other benefits that the expatriate public servant presently demands.

We are keen that these savings will allow us money for other purposes—for example, rural development and more houses for local officers.

For these reasons, the Public Service Board is examining ways to try and achieve our target.

I have also set up a special Cabinet Committee to ensure that the reduction is carried out in an organised manner. The Chairman of the Public Service Board will be a member of this Committee. I know it is not usual to have Public Servants on Cabinet Committees in Australia, but Papua New Guinea must make its own rules in accordance with its own needs.

Further, we have instructed our Ministers to give full support through their departmental heads, to the efforts of departmental localisation committees in bringing as many local officers in their departments as possible to the stage where they can take over competently from overseas officers. Naturally Ministers will also be looking to the problem of the extent to which over-rapid localisation may interfere with what we, as a Ministry, regard as essential departmental functions. It will not be a case of rapid localisation at any cost.[2]

---

2   See also Documents 267, 268, 327 & 371.

Before leaving the question of localisation generally and the target we have set, I would like to say that my Ministry is well aware of the state of uncertainty in which many overseas officers are at present working. I mean, of course, uncertainty about their own futures in this country and the conditions under which they may expect to leave to continue their careers elsewhere. We, too, have been concerned at the delay in bringing the provisions of the Employment Security Scheme for permanent overseas officers to clear and satisfactory finality. However, we have now received drafts of the Simpson Report, and we expect to receive the final report in about two weeks. I hope that this matter will be settled shortly after that.[3]

I want to say also that my Government realises only too well that it will have to rely heavily on the dedication of those overseas officers—and I speak especially on this point to those of you who are here today—who realise what we are trying to do and who are helping to prepare our own local officers to take over your positions. We would certainly wish to retain overseas officers who can help us to prepare local officers for senior level responsibility. We also realise that there are many specialist positions for which overseas officers will be needed for a number of years to come—in some cases well into independence; and that in the servicing areas at the lower and middle levels on which the Service relies for its effective operation, dedicated contract officers and temporary employees including married women will be needed for quite some time to carry on essential functions and assist with training until PNG staff are available in sufficient numbers.

We realise too that all those overseas staff we are looking to help us to achieve our goals have their own lives to lead, their own careers to plan and their families to look after, and our aim will be, in close cooperation with the Public Service Board, to give them the clearest possible information about how long their services will be needed. His Honour the Administrator has told me that, at a recent meeting with departmental heads, he indicated that clear plans to enable this information to be given to all concerned would be drawn up at the earliest possible date, and you may be assured that my Government will do all in its power to provide early guidelines on which such plans can be based. His Honour has also informed me of various problems connected with the localisation programme that were raised by departmental heads at that meeting. To those departmental heads who are here today I would say that the Government will be giving very close attention to these problems in consultation with His Honour and the Public Service Board.

I have also been informed of the steps being taken by the Public Service Board to strengthen localisation committees in departments and speed up localisation generally. These moves have our full backing and we are looking forward to the speedy advancement of all local officers to positions equal to their present competence, and also to their further effective development.

Local officers themselves must realise the importance of their day-to-day efforts in the building of our nation. We do not want to push them beyond their capabilities, but they must realise that if localisation is to be effective they must apply themselves whole-heartedly to their training opportunities both on-the-job and through formal training courses. It is not enough for them to take over the jobs from overseas officers. They must be efficient operators when they do so. We do not wish standards of efficiency to fall. The Government does not want mere window-dressing in its localisation programme.

I would like now to move from the localisation programme generally to the Senior Executive Programme, which is the reason we have met here today.

Firstly, I would like to emphasise that the time left before self-government is short—1st December, 1973 or as soon thereafter as possible and the need to advance as many local officers into senior executive and policy making positions is therefore urgent, the Senior

---

3   See Documents 344 & 394.

Executive Programme has been largely based on on-the-job training. A number of you may be conscious of gaps in your formal training. These can, and I hope will, be made good as your duties as senior officers permit, so that you will be able to advance still further in the Service.

Secondly the programme for your meeting provides for a full and frank discussion of your on-the-job working and training arrangements. We on the Government side see this as essential. We hope your discussions will not only bring about greater understanding between you, but will provide ideas and guidelines for the development of present members of the Programme and of those who enter it in the future. My Government and the Public Service Board are relying on you for this. We hope your other discussions, including the involvement of PNG officers' wives in the SEP, will prove equally fruitful. Your women folk have a great part to play in the building of this country. I am happy to see many of the wives here today. If their husbands are to be successful in what they are trying to achieve, they must have the understanding and support of their wives. The burdens will be heavy and the wives have their part to play in helping to bear them.

Thirdly, we, the Government, look at you as the first pool of senior local officers on whom we can draw to help us in our common task of building a Papua New Guinean nation. We know that you have your own personal problems and are placed under unusual stresses—stresses which in more developed countries few officers of your experience are called upon to undergo. We respect you for this and we look forward to a full and frank discussion with you this afternoon of our common problems and objectives.

Fourthly, I can assure members of the SEP that you will quickly attain top positions in the Public Service, if you can show that you have the potential and can handle such positions. My Government intends to localise a number of District Commissioner and permanent departmental head positions in the next six months or so. Some of you will be promoted to these positions. However, promotion will not be automatic—you must show us that you can do the job.

Fifthly, I realise that there has been some dissatisfaction with the SEP programme. I do not wish to lay the blame on anyone for not achieving all the goals that were set. But I do wish to say that both my Government and the Public Service realise the urgent need to develop our local officers for the most senior positions as rapidly as possible, and see the SEP as a very high national priority. Finally, I wish you all success in your talks during this coming week, and I now have much pleasure in declaring this seminar open.

[NAA: A452, 1972/3694]

390 SUBMISSION FROM HAY TO PEACOCK

Canberra, undated [c. 17 October 1972]

SECRET

Renegotiation Bougainville Copper Agreement[1]

On 27th September Father Momis (Bougainville Regional) moved in the House of Assembly for the adoption of a set of principles for mining projects in PNG (see Attachment No 1 extracted from PNG Gazette).[2] Father Momis spoke to the motion and indicated his dissatisfaction with the Bougainville Copper Agreement in its present form.

2.   Mr Lapun, speaking personally in the debate and in support of Father Momis's motion advocated renegotiation of the Bougainville Copper Agreement and examination of all other Agreements to be inherited by the Papua New Guinea Government from the Australian Administration (see Attachment No 2).[3]

3.   Mr Somare is reported [...] as saying that he personally considered it inevitable that the Papua New Guinea Government would review its joint venture agreements with foreign investors as it approaches self-government and independence. On the question of renegotiation of the Bougainville Copper Agreement Mr Somare stated that the matter has still to be considered by the AEC and its attitude would be guided by the vote on Father Momis's motion in the House.

Background

4.   The Bougainville Copper Agreement was ratified without dissent or opposition in 1967 after the House of Assembly had examined the Bill and pursued enquiries about the project for three months. Since 1967 the House has had regular reports on progress and in all cases endorsed the project.

5.   The Agreement has supporters and critics from the time of its ratification to the present. The present movement seems to have commenced in July 1972 with a report of a motion passed by the Kieta Local Government Council on Bougainville that the Bougainville Copper Agreement be renegotiated before self government.

6.   The recent UNDP Report[4] was also critical of the Agreement, and when the UNDP views became known publicly further impetus was given to the movement for renegotiation.

---

1   See also Document 384.

2   Not published.

3   Not published.

4   Not published. A United Nations Development Programme team led by Professor Michael Faber of the University of East Anglia visited Australia and Papua New Guinea for six weeks from March to May, 1972. After further discussions in both countries in August the mission submitted its draft report in September. Details of the report soon circulated. Downs has noted that 'the mission proposed a radical change in economic emphasis. Their proposals stressed localisation rather than increase of GNP'. The report criticised the Bougainville mining agreement and proposed that Australia be asked to bring the parties together for a renegotiation. Ian Downs, *The Australian Trusteeship: Papua New Guinea, 1945–1975*, Australian Government Publishing Service, Canberra, 1980, pp. 538, 540. See also James Griffin, 'Papua New Guinea', in W. J. Hudson (ed.), *Australia in World Affairs, 1971–75*, George Allen & Unwin, Sydney, 1980, pp. 347–383, 357; and Don Woolford, *Papua New Guinea: Initiation and Independence*, University of Queensland Press, Brisbane, 1976, pp. 219, 225.

7.   The Company has set up a study group which will prepare a case in support of the project in readiness for any possible talks with the Papua New Guinea Government that may result from moves to have the Agreement renegotiated.

8.   Arrangements have been made for Departmental and Company officials to keep in close contact on the matter to ensure that the results of the investigations under way are adequately coordinated.

9.   In the light of the statements which have been made by members of the House and the proposal that the matter be referred to the AEC the Department has obtained up to date figures from the company and is re-examining the Agreement and the benefits derived by PNG. The draft AEC submission (see attached)[5] states in Para 27 that 'The approval of the Minister is required with respect to all motions regarding special mining leases' and that 'the views of the Minister have been requested'!

10. As a result of our preliminary examination of the draft submission it is considered that:

(a) The comparisons between the Bougainville agreement and arrangements in other countries appear to over simplify the position
  −   in most cases quoted the mines have been worked for many years and company profits would have far exceeded capital expenditure
  −   returns to Government until comparatively recently would probably have been less favourable than provided for under the Bougainville Agreement
  −   at the time of renegotiation it would have been unlikely that the companies would have carried a substantial debt burden
  −   It is understood that where mining projects were nationalised or agreements renegotiated under duress there were some unfavourable consequences in terms of: −

  •   overseas investment
  •   international lending
  •   mining efficiency

(b) The comparison of other mining projects would have better balance if it included examples of new projects in developing countries such as Ertsberg in West Irian[6] where the conditions are not likely to be so favourable and probably would not measure up to those provided for under the Bougainville Agreement. Inclusion of some Australian mining projects such as Gove and Utah would probably also show the Bougainville Agreement in more favourable light.

(c) The comparison of the Company's estimates of Government receipts with Treadgold's estimates[7] is somewhat unfair. Treadgold's estimates were based on some doubtful information (although the best available at the time) and a company tax rate of $22^{1}/_{2}\%$. Both the Administration and the Department considered that Treadgold's estimates were

---

5   Not published.

6   In 1936 Dutch geologist, Jean Jacques Dozy discovered extensive copper deposits while on an expedition to climb Mount Carstenz, the highest mountain in what was then Dutch New Guinea (and part of the then Dutch East Indies). The Freeport mining group began work on the Ertsberg ('Ore Mountain') mine in 1967, at high altitudes in a remote area. Production of copper and gold began in 1972. *PNG Post Courier*, 18 January 1973, p. 15.

7   This is a reference to the research findings of M. L. (Malcolm) Treadgold. See his chapter entitled 'Projections of Economic Activity in Papua New Guinea (with special reference to the Bougainville Copper Project)' in R. T. Shand and M. L. Treadgold, (eds) *The Economy of Papua New Guinea: Projections and Policy Issues*, Department of Economics, Research School of Pacific Studies, The Australian National University, Canberra, 1971, pp. 1–53.

conservative. The Company's estimates are up-to-date and based on operating experience. They provide for dividend withholding tax and assume that the normal tax rate will be 33% by the time tax becomes payable.

11. The major objection to the AEC submission, however, is that it prejudges the outcome of the re-examination of the Agreement and leaves decisions about future action on a matter of great importance to Papua New Guinea in the hands of officials. It would be expected that the AEC would wish to come to its own conclusion after considering the work of the working group and any comments which the Commonwealth Government may wish to make rather than leave officials to decide whether a renegotiation was justified.

12. In view of the issues involved it may be preferable for your attitude to be conveyed verbally to the AEC by the Administrator. The attached reply to the Chief Minister indicates that this will be done.[8]

RECOMMENDATION

13. It is recommended that you sign the attached letter[9] to the Chief Minister and ask the Administrator to convey your attitude of the AEC as follows:

(i) you would expect the AEC to consider carefully the report of the working group before coming to a conclusion as to whether an invitation to Bougainville Copper Pty. Ltd. to renegotiate the Agreement is justified;

(ii) the Commonwealth Government may wish to comment on the position before any such invitation is issued;

(iii) if the AEC so wishes you would be willing to have officers from the Department of External Territories assist the working group;

(iv) the working group should be made aware of the preliminary departmental comments outlined in paragraph 10 above.[10]

[NAA: A1838, 846/1/6 PART 1]

---

8 Not published.

9 Not published.

10 In 1974, after Bougainville Copper Limited had announced a substantial profit, the PNG Government successfully renegotiated the Agreement. See Donald Denoon, *A Trial Separation: Australia and the Decolonisation of Papua New Guinea*, Australian National University, Pandanus Books, 2005, pp. 133–6; Don Woolford, *Papua New Guinea: Initiation and Independence*, University of Queensland Press, Brisbane, 1976, pp. 204–5; and Donald Denoon, *Getting Under the Skin: The Bougainville Copper Agreement and the Creation of the Panguna Mine*, Melbourne University Press, Carlton South, 2000.

391   LETTER FROM BORDER TO HAY

Canberra, 19 October 1972

Thank you for your letter of 13 October.[1]

It seems to us important that the international relations establishment in Papua New Guinea—on which we are generally agreed—should be formalised as soon as possible. We have noted the Chief Minister's wish that the PNG Government participate in foreign policy decisions affecting PNG and your Minister's general agreement that PNG should be closely consulted. If the PNG Government is to start being involved in international relations issues—and we agree that they should—then it is essential that they have some kind of machinery to back them up. They need their own people to identify PNG interests and problems, especially where these may differ from Australia's. Similarly, if their international relations organisation is to be functioning at independence it will need a year or so before then to settle down. Furthermore, there is the question of training. If there is to be a combined department, the kind of training to be given to its staff will be affected.

May I therefore suggest that, during your visit to Port Moresby next week, you might discuss with the Administrator and appropriate officials ways in which the new department can be speedily brought into being. This would seem to require early discussions between officers such as Messrs Conroy, Pearsall[2] and McDonald and representatives from the Trade department and the Public Service Board, to consider:

  (a) the range of activity to be undertaken by the new department;

  (b) the establishment required—both in the immediate future and in the longer term;

  (c) the formulation of an integrated training programme covering general foreign service work, trade promotion and negotiation, migration (possibly), and administrative support for overseas missions. In this latter connection it seems to us that most of the officers in the new department should be capable of handling both trade and foreign office work in view of the small size and limited resources of the PNG Public Service; and

  (d) the accommodation requirements for this establishment, and ways in which any special needs might be met, for example, the building up of a reference library and a registry system.

I appreciate that discussions on these lines might cut across discussions in the Constitutional Planning Committee. On the other hand such discussions might even be of assistance to the Committee, and in any case the arrangements and decisions which might flow from the discussions need not be regarded as an attempt to prejudge the work of the Committee and could in fact be regarded as being of a temporary nature only at this stage.

On the general question of training, I think you should know that some of the officers undertaking our foreign service training course have found it heavy going because of their lack of academic background. I do not suggest that all such trainees must be university graduates, but they should have at least some tertiary education, for example, from Goroka Teachers College. If, as seems possible, officers are selected by PNG who do not meet these academic standards, we could provide some training in administrative and consular work overseas. Some officers might also show a particular aptitude for commercial work and they should be encouraged to undertake attachments with the Department of Trade and Industry. Whatever arrangements we make in this regard, however, I feel I should re-emphasise our strong conviction that it will

---

1   Not published.

2   S. J. (Stan) Pearsall, Assistant Secretary, Secretariat Services, Department of the Administrator.

be of great importance to PNG to have at independence a group of trained advisers who can assist their Government to handle the host of international problems and pressures with which they will be faced immediately, and this demands the selection of enough officers capable of undertaking the foreign service training course. Without this backing, Papua New Guinea will quite simply be buffeted by all and sundry, and Australia will be seen to have failed in her obligations towards PNG in this respect.[3]

[NAA: A1838, 3080/10/4/7 PART 1]

---

3   On the training question, see, among others, Document 381.

392   SUBMISSION FROM WALLER TO BOWEN

Canberra, 19 October 1972

CONFIDENTIAL

Foreign Affairs Spokesman in Papua New Guinea

On 22 July you agreed (submission attached)[1] I should suggest to the Department of External Territories that they might brief their Minister, and I might advise the PNG Administrator, that:

(a) we would not object to a Foreign Affairs Spokesman being appointed;

(b) Foreign Affairs should provide back-up and head an embryo foreign office in the Chief Minister's Department;

(c) a Foreign Affairs Representative, primarily responsible to this Department, be sent to Port Moresby.

It is possible that the PNG side will ask for a Foreign Affairs Spokesman during the constitutional talks beginning on 25 October in Port Moresby. I have informed External Territories that we do not object to this being granted. I have also indicated that we see no objection to new arrangements now proposed for supporting the Spokesman. While consistent with our general approach, these arrangements differ in detail from our earlier proposal (paragraph 5(ii) in the attached submission).

The new proposal is that there be a combined Department under the present Minister for Trade,[2] who would also become Foreign Affairs Spokesman. The Department would be headed by the present Director of Agriculture, Stock and Fisheries (Mr W. L. Conroy) who has been PNG's chief international trade negotiator. He is a highly regarded permanent officer, with appropriate experience and background for the position. Under him there would be two branches—Foreign Affairs headed by one of our officers, and Trade.

This approach would be consistent with our Departmental view that PNG should have one Department dealing with all international relations, including trade. It does not seem of great importance whether such an office is located within the Chief Minister's Department (as earlier envisaged) or in some other Department. The Minister to be Spokesman seems to be a matter for the PNG Government to decide.

Regarding (c) above, I have appointed a Foreign Affairs Officer Class 3 (Burns)[3] to be Liaison Officer in the Commonwealth office, Port Moresby, and have asked the Public Service Board to create an Assistant Secretary position. I propose to appoint an officer at that level as Foreign Affairs Representative early next year.

Defence Adviser

The arrangements being made for the other reserved power—Defence—are slightly different. Briefly, [the] Defence Department has agreed to the Chief Minister's request that the Defence Adviser (Assistant Secretary level) be part of the Chief Minister's Department and advise PNG Ministers on defence. (The Chief Minister is also the Defence Spokesman). Consideration may be given later to the appointment of a Defence Representative along the lines of our Foreign Affairs Representative in the Commonwealth office, but the Defence Adviser will for the time being also communicate directly with the Commonwealth Government and the Administrator.

---

1   Not included.

2   John Poe, MHA for Rai Coast and Minister for Trade and Industry.

3   R. A. (Ross) Burns.

It was originally intended that the Defence Adviser be in the Administrator's Department, but Somare are argued—successfully it seems—that the Adviser should work to the Chief Minister, and develop PNG defence policies rather than give advice 'through the Administrator'—even though he retains a link with the Administrator. This is a sign of the times and tends to endorse the position we have taken all along that the sooner a PNG 'foreign office' is established, developing PNG policies, the better. A system involving divided loyalties does not appeal to me, and cannot be expected to work well.

[NAA: A1838, 3080/10/4/7 PART 1]

393   MEMORANDUM FROM BURNS

Port Moresby, 20 October 1972

CONFIDENTIAL

October Constitutional Talks

You will by now have probably received through DOET[1] documents relating to the two series of constitutional talks between Australian and PNG officials held this month in Port Moresby.

The talks have made little headway in advancing issues left unresolved after the first round of talks in July/August.[2] The immediate reason has been that the interval between the two rounds of talks has been too brief to allow either side to develop its position. A more basic problem is that the NCG's[3] programme of rapid constitutional change is going somewhat adrift for a variety of reasons—partly due to the differences between the Chief Minister's advisers, the bureaucracy as a whole, and the Constitutional Planning Committee (CPC).[4] It is now recognised that the arrangement for two series of constitutional talks at both official and ministerial level was too ambitious and that it would have been better to have followed up the July/August round not with another full-scale series of meetings but by maintaining contact through normal channels. Hence the two rounds of constitutional discussions between PNG ministers and the Minister for External Territories scheduled for October have not been held and even the two series of officials' talks have been unproductive.

The NCG's frustrations in meeting its timetable for constitutional development leading up to self-government at the end of 1973 are now evident. There is considerably more pressure from within the NCG that decisions on future arrangements should not be taken precipitately. The voices urging caution come not only from the PPP[5] but even from Pangu ministers who feel that the Chief Minister is relying too heavily on his expatriate advisers, particularly Voutas. Ministers, in addition, are somewhat wary of the extent to which they must rely on their expatriate departmental officials some of whom have long ago lost interest in their work and are totally inexperienced in dealing with ministers and accepting political direction. Consequently there is a tendency to question proposals put to Cabinet and decisions on constitutional change are more frequently referred back for further consideration.

The gulf between ministers and officials is matched by a lack of coordination between departments and between the NCG's expatriate advisers and the rest of the public service. All of these factors have been exacerbated by the sheer number and variety of decisions which are required by the sudden increase in the pace of constitutional development. In the face of the plethora of matters with which advisers must now deal there has been not surprisingly a tendency to leap inconclusively from subject to subject.

The role of the Constitutional Planning Committee and its concerns that no change should be implemented without the CPC deciding on its constitutional implications have been reported in earlier correspondence. In the recent talks, the CPC Deputy Chairman[6] and the advisers again followed a strong line and questioned details of transfer arrangements. This was particularly

---

1   Department of External Territories [DET].

2   See Documents 336–37, 339, 345–48, 351, 354–55 and 361.

3   National Coalition Government.

4   See Document 388.

5   People's Progress Party.

6   Father John Momis.

evident in the fields of internal security where the CPC's interests, combined with the failure of the Chief Minister's Office to arrive at an agreed position, have resulted in this issue being referred back to a PNG committee on internal security [...]

The role of the CPC and the lack of coordination at an administrative and political level on the PNG side must cast doubts on whether the NCG's plans for self-government by the end of 1973 are realistic. Even the Chief Minister's advisers now concede that it may be mid–1974 before the last details can be settled. If it wishes to observe its published timetable, the NCG may be forced to accept as an interim measure, many features of the present arrangements under the PNG Act and concentrate on the major issues which must be decided in order to achieve self-government, especially the questions of a Head of State and of central/regional relations. However, these major issues are political minefields and the NCG has so far shown few qualities of bravery in confronting contentious issues.

[NAA: A9334, 201/1/2/3 PART 2]

394   CABINET SUBMISSION 919[1]

Canberra, 24 October 1972

CONFIDENTIAL

Papua New Guinea: Future Security of Overseas Officers of the Public Service

In May this year I sought Cabinet's approval to certain proposals for the employment security of overseas officers of the Public Service of Papua New Guinea. Cabinet decided on the appointment of an independent enquiry into the total arrangements to be made (Decision No. 981/PNG of 15 May 1972).[2] Mr A. M. Simpson, CMG, Chairman of Simpson Pope Ltd. carried out the enquiry. He has now presented his report jointly to me and the Papua New Guinea Chief Minister. It is attached.[3]

2.   Mr Simpson's recommendations are set out in paragraph 102 of his report. The most important recommendations and my comment on them are:

(1). Permanent and contract overseas officers engaged by the Australian Government up to the time when responsibility for the Papua New Guinea Public Service is transferred to local executive authority to be separated from that Service and deemed to be Commonwealth employees by special provision to be made in the Papua New Guinea Act (paragraph 32 of report).

Comment

This approach is not dissimilar to that put forward in my submission No. 638 of April 1972.[4] Mr Simpson does not recommend however, as I did, the creation of a new and separate Commonwealth service as a means of the Commonwealth assuming responsibility for overseas officers.

(2). The provisions of [the] Papua New Guinea Superannuation Ordinance, the Contract Officers Retirement Benefits Ordinance and the Public Officers (Employment Security Ordinance) (amended as recommended by him) to be covered by Commonwealth legislation (paragraphs 89 and 96 of report).

Comment

This follows from (1) above and is an important consideration in removing uncertainty amongst overseas officers. This recommendation obviates the need for the existing Commonwealth guarantee of payments in the Papua New Guinea Act.

(3). The Commonwealth to meet directly the cost of all emoluments and benefits of the officers concerned rather than only those already paid or guaranteed by the Commonwealth (paragraphs 89 and 97 of report).

Comment

The Commonwealth already accepts responsibility for the emoluments of overseas officers in excess of the local salary rates. It also accepts responsibility for pensions and retirement benefits. In so far as the existing Employment Security Scheme is concerned, the maximum contingent liability if all eligible officers were to be declared redundant at say December 1973 would be in the order of $75m but could be considerably less.

---

1   Submitted by Peacock.
2   See Documents 279 & 344.
3   Not published.
4   Document 279.

The greater part of this expenditure would be incurred over a period of up to 5 years. It is not practicable to estimate the incidence of expenditure in any one year. The financial position of the Papua New Guinea Government is such that it is clearly impracticable for that Government to make even a minor contribution towards these costs from its own resources. It would be reasonable, as Mr Simpson says, for them to be taken into account when fixing future aid to PNG.

(4). The amalgamation of the existing Employment Security Scheme, the modifications proposed to it in August 1971 and the additional arrangements outside the Scheme proposed at that time, into a new composite Employment Security Scheme, the major changes being removal of the mandatory nature of the existing alternative public employment provisions (but without removal of the objective of placing officers in such employment) and the payment of compensation by instalments instead of a lump sum (these and other detailed changes are set out in paragraphs 83, 64 and 69–70 of the report).

Comment

Basically the report accepts the efficacy of the arrangements so far made and proposed for the employment security of overseas officers.

(5). The establishment of the Australian Service for Overseas Cooperation (ASOC) endorsed in principle by Cabinet in Decision No. 454 of 23 June 1970[5] not be proceeded with (paragraph 44 of report).

Comment

I agree with Mr Simpson that the total arrangements regarding provision and retention of overseas staff recommended by him obviate the need to proceed with ASOC.

3.   The Papua New Guinea Government, through the Administrator's Executive Council agrees with the recommendations in the report and recommends their acceptance. It has indicated that it is prepared to stand by these recommendations but it would need to reconsider its attitude if there is any major departure from them. This has been stated to me in firm and unequivocal terms by the Chief Minister.

4.   I urge the acceptance of Mr Simpson's report and recommendations. Although they do not meet all the representations to the Government by Papua New Guinea staff associations they are, in my view, a fair response to the very real difficulties faced by expatriate officers in this transitional period. They open the way to the retention of key officers whose services are essential to effective government in Papua New Guinea and many of whom would otherwise be lost to it. The urgency of a decision by the Commonwealth is accentuated by the desire of Papua New Guinea (accepted by the Commonwealth) for self-government by 1 December 1973 or as soon as possible thereafter. At the same time the Papua New Guinea Government has decided to hasten the process of localisation. This has added to the insecurity of overseas officers whose presence is essential to the process of orderly localisation. I consider that Mr Simpson's recommendations, if accepted, will go a long way towards remedying the present most unsatisfactory situation; at the same time the Commonwealth Government by assuring overseas officers about their future, will be helping Papua New Guinea to build up an efficient national Public Service.

5.   Acceptance of Mr Simpson's recommendations will require both Commonwealth and Papua New Guinea legislation changes. The recommendations are geared basically to the date of transfer of responsibility for control of the Papua New Guinea Public Service to local executive authority (present planning is August 1973). The legislation would therefore have to come into force not later than the date of transfer.

---

5   Not published. See Document 48, para. 22.

RECOMMENDATION

6. I recommend that:

(a) Mr Simpson's report be accepted;

(b) the report be made public;

(c) I be permitted, in conjunction with the PNG Chief Minister, to announce the results of the enquiry immediately; and

(d) the drafting of the necessary Commonwealth legislation be commenced to enable it to be dealt with during the 1973 Autumn Session of Parliament.

[NAA: A5908, 919]

395   CABINET DECISION 1453 (PNG)

Canberra, 26 October 1972

CONFIDENTIAL

Submission No. 919: Papua New Guinea:
Future Security of Overseas Officers of the Public Service[1]

The Committee accepted in principle the recommendation at paragraph 2 (1) of the Submission.

2.   It asked that, in the light of this decision, the Standing Interdepartmental Committee on Papua New Guinea meet as a matter of urgency to consider the proposals and that each Department take up with its own Minister any consequential problems of significance which, after consideration in the interdepartmental committee, it considers need to be brought to his attention.

3.   The Committee had in mind that a final decision be taken the next day by the Prime Minister in consultation with the Treasurer, the Minister for Foreign Affairs and the Minister for External Territories.

[NAA: A5908, 919]

---

1   Document 394.

396   SUBMISSION FROM BLAKERS TO FAIRBAIRN

Canberra, 26 October 1972

Secret

Functions and Roles of the PNG Security Forces—Post independence

One of the more important items being undertaken under the programme of studies on PNG Defence matters is on the functions and roles of the PNG security forces following independence. An inter-departmental working party recently completed an examination of this matter and their report has been considered by the PNG Defence Coordinating Committee (PNGDCC).[1]

2.   The report was wide-ranging and looked at many possibilities. The PNGDCC recommended that the PNG security forces should consist of the Defence Force, comprising the three elements—land, maritime and air—and the Police Force. The reasons for not proposing a single Security Force which would combine the Defence Force and the Police included:

    a.   although there is quite a degree of common training in both forces, there are certain fundamental differences in the essential character of the forces quite apart from particular differences in training, organisation and equipment;

    b.   to abolish the armed forces which currently exist and which form the foundation for PNG's own future forces could result in a gap which would, among other things, greatly prejudice the formation of armed forces if required in the future;

    c.   despite the lack of threat at present it cannot be stated that this situation will continue indefinitely; and

    d.   in certain circumstances it may be desirable for the PNG Government to have two different forces, e.g. if the police went on strike or if either force were disaffected.

3.   On this basis the PNGDCC, with whom the Department of External Territories was associated, endorsed the attached functions and roles for the Police Force and the Defence Force which in their totality will comprise the security forces of PNG. These functions and roles, very broadly, provide for increased involvement of the PNG Defence Force:

    a.   in support of the Police in internal security roles;

    b.   in undertaking, when authorised, police roles in remote and difficult areas; and

    c.   in contributing to nation building tasks within the capability of the force.

4.   Proposed functions and roles of the PNG security forces post-independence will obviously need to be fully acceptable to local PNG authorities and will ultimately be a matter for their decision. The PNGDCC accordingly observed that before any finality was reached on these matters, it was desirable as a first step that the views of the Administrator be obtained. He, by virtue of his post and continued responsibilities, could be expected to be in close touch with local needs and circumstances and local PNG opinion.

5.   At discussions between the Administrator and the Secretaries, Departments of Defence and External Territories and Chairman, Chiefs of Staff Committee at a meeting on 11th October, 1972, the Administrator supported the recommendations of the PNGDCC and thought they would be acceptable to PNG authorities. He commented that an important point was that although there were to be separate Defence and Police forces, there would be common logistic

---

1   For the PNGDCC's assessment of the report by a working group, see Document 369.

support; for example the air transport forces would operate in support of the Defence Force and the Police.

6.   The meeting discussed whether it would be better to allow the PNG authorities to develop their own views on future functions and roles of the forces before undertaking consultation on whether, as an educational exercise, the Head of Defence Branch should introduce the PNGDCC proposals. The meeting agreed that the latter course was preferable and should be undertaken quickly. Formal consultations involving perhaps a visit to PNG by the Chairman, Chiefs of Staff Committee could then take place during the first quarter of 1973. Meanwhile, we are proceeding with other studies on the shape and size of the security forces required to meet the proposed functions and roles.

Recommendation

7.   It is recommended that you endorse in principle at this stage the attached proposed functions and roles of the PNG security forces as a basis for opening discussions with the PNG authorities along the lines set out in paragraph 6 above. The Department of External Territories is seeking similar endorsement in principle from the Minister for External Territories.

[NAA: A452, 1972/1111]

397   REPORT BY BURNS

Port Moresby, undated [c. October 1972]

CONFIDENTIAL

Papua New Guinea's National Coalition—The First Six Months

Papua New Guinea's third House of Assembly opened on 20 April, 1972 amidst considerable confusion as to what combination of the various parties and groups in the House could form a viable majority. In the absence of any real challenge, the Pangu Party was able to put together a national coalition comprising the more progressive elements which gained control of the floor of the House. On 26 April, the coalition announced its ministry. It is now six months since the National Coalition Government (NCG) assumed power and for the first time provided PNG with an effective indigenous political leadership.

The coalition was composed of three parties—Pangu Party, Peoples Progress Party (PPP) and New Guinea National Party—and of several other groups including the Mataungan Association,[1] Bougainvillean supporters of Napidakoe Navitu,[2] and a group of east Papuan supporters of John Guise, as well as a handful of other independents. Pangu provides almost 50% of the coalition's strength and forms the backbone of this disparate collection of political forces which has owed most of its strength and probably its survival to the leadership of the Chief Minister, Michael Somare.

Issues

The coalition has not faced any serious opposition from the United Party (UP) which with an original strength of 42 formed the largest single party in the House. Through complacency and disorganisation the UP failed to use this advantage of strength to win a majority in the House during April.[3] The UP has since become demoralised and ineffectual in its leadership of its main support groups in the House, namely the genuinely conservative element and the highlanders. Except for a half-hearted attempt to block a decision on the date for self-government, the UP has not produced any issues on which to consistently challenge the government.

In effect, there is no ideological or other dividing line to separate the forces in the House and the Opposition is as much a combination of a variety of interests as the government. The only way to describe the difference between the two groups is in terms of political sophistication— the NCG is a coalition of the politically sophisticated forces in the House, while the UP is a grouping of all those elements who for various reasons would prefer a slower pace of political advancement. In view of this vague dividing line, it is perhaps surprising that both blocs have been able to attract consistent voting support. There has been some wavering and confusion on both sides, but generally the pattern has been consistent with an overall trend towards a slow rate of defections towards the coalition, especially amongst highlanders for whom fears of early self-government are a diminishing factor.

While the government has failed so far to produce any significant controversial issues to disturb this balance and the opposition has been too weak even to exploit the remaining uncertainty amongst members over the question of self-government, the House has continued to serve as a forum for parochial controversy and parish pump demands. In spite of the far-reaching

---

1   For background on the Mataungan Association, see Document 49, fn. 3.

2   For background on Napidakoe Navitu, see Document 350, fn. 5.

3   See Document 376.

decisions being gradually determined within the NCG, there is still little public appreciation of the issues at stake either in the House, in the press or amongst the educated and town-dwellers. The process of constitutional development thus continues to outstrip political awareness, and the country lacks a dominant theme to attract public involvement at what remains a very formative stage of its political life.

Policies

If there have been no real issues against which to measure the government's performance, likewise there has been nothing distinctive about the policies so far adopted. These have basically consisted of carrying through decisions already in the pipeline originating from administration initiatives or of changes in the emphasis with which policies are implemented. On the outstanding major policy questions (of which land, central/regional relations, and a new approach to economic development are the most significant) the coalition has made exploratory gestures and although its approach so far has been cautions this does not rule out the possibility that it might rush into precipitate decisions under the pressure of future events.

Its most consistent preoccupation has been the transfer of powers leading up to full self-government by the end of next year, although even here the mechanics of transfer are now proving more complex than the NCG had anticipated. Nevertheless, PNG already has de facto self-government, encumbered only by the formality of seeking concurrence on some questions from Canberra. The coalition has taken full advantage of the powers already transferred and has confirmed the existing undertaking that the PNG cabinet will be consulted on all questions where final power still rests with Canberra. In the process of these negotiations, some changes in the administrative and constitutional structure of the country have been foreshadowed and the NCG has clearly shown its concern to trim the cumbersome structure of government which has grown up under Australian administration. The policies which have been implemented to date are minor and even those which have been foreshadowed are not startling or radical. They are basic reforms which could be expected from any nationalist government of a moderate character taking over from a colonial system of government and economic development.

Decision-making

In the style of government and decision-making there have been many traces of inexperience and lack of confidence. Once it had recovered from the initial shock of actually gaining power, the NCG leaders found it difficult to overcome their suspicions that the predominantly expatriate public service could not be relied on to give disinterested advice or respond sympathetically to its priorities. As a result, the NCG has surrounded itself with a buffer of advisers almost all of whom are expatriates known to be sympathetic to its aims and who can be counted on to produce initiatives which could not be expected from the public service. The group of advisers around the Chief Minister forms the inner core of whom the most important figure is Tony Voutas. Most are men of moderate and thoughtful views, although they are often regarded with suspicion as dangerous radicals by public servants who have spent most of their careers in the small pond of the PNG public service. The advisers' good intentions however do not make up for their lack of experience in decision-making outside the tutorial room or the party branch.

Nevertheless the gifted amateur approach has probably served the government well to date and has pushed it headlong to explore many areas where it otherwise might have foundered through hesitation. But the stage has now been reached where many basic approaches worked out amongst the circle of advisers and the key ministers must be implemented through the cabinet, the public service and negotiations with the Australian [government.] At this point, the advisers' attempts to keep the bandwagon moving are meeting with frustrations from several quarters—from the public service which in some quarters continues to move at a lethargic pace and to react awkwardly to political direction and ministerial authority (which is often erratically wielded); from the circle of advisers themselves who are beginning to separate into distinct interest groups; and from the ministry which has tended to demand a closer scrutiny of proposals before they reach decisions.

The calibre of ministers is higher than might have been expected in a country where for many years there has been a deliberate policy of not encouraging the emergence of an elite and where few Papua New Guineans have had the demands of responsibility laid on them except in the past five to ten years. There has been a certain rashness and abrasiveness in the outlook of some ministers but so far these trends have not found their way into the actual process of decision-making. Ministers have generally accepted the [Westminster] rule that cabinet decisions are group responsibility but some have tended to make personal statements on sensitive issues which appear to bind the NCG to policies on which it has not yet made decisions.

Perhaps the most serious incident of the latter has been statements by Paul Lapun, the Minister for Mines, urging renegotiation of the Bougainville Copper agreement.[4] Inexperience and differences of opinion within the NCG as well as the Melanesian tendency not to highlight differences or to shame a colleague, has resulted in the government neither rebuking nor supporting Lapun in his views and thus creating an atmosphere of uncertainty and doubt about the NCG's good faith which could have important repercussions on the future of the economy.

Tensions

Although the achievements of the past six months are hard to describe in terms of issues raised or policies implemented, it is reasonable to conclude that in view of the initial difficulties faced by the coalition and its inexperience, the transition to a national government has been made relatively smoothly. There are, however, several disruptive issues waiting in the wings. Tensions within the coalition have been real and persistent even if they have not broken out publicly into differences over policies or struggles between personalities. The two major sources of disharmony within the leadership have been, first, the PPP's unease that decisions are often arrived at too rashly and may have an adverse effect on the country's economy and, second, rivalry between the Chief Minister and his deputy, Dr John Guise. The first has been a constant theme in cabinet discussions but so far there has been room for compromise on the subjects in dispute. The danger will come if the PPP pushes its case too far—it has so far gained a slightly disproportionate share of portfolios (including all the economic ministries) and most of the concessions made so far to arrive at an agreed coalition viewpoint appear to have been made on the Pangu side.

The second issue, is probably a more avoidable source of tension. The ambitions of Dr Guise to be Prime Minister or President are real but he has no solid basis of support in the coalition outside a few fellow East Papuan independents What he lacks in terms of ability or capacity to develop independent thought, he makes up in self-assurance and [persistence.] By excluding him as far as possible from any real influence in the coalition, Somare has hoped to isolate and neutralise him. A more effective means of reducing his potential as a threat to the stability of the coalition may have been to neutralise him with flattery and cater to his sense of self-importance by bringing him more closely into the limelight. By being more openly identified with the decisions of the present government, Guise would be even less likely to be able credibly to offer himself as an alternative to it.

---

4   See Documents 384 & 390.

The government's survival has most ably been assisted by the weak performance of the opposition which under the leadership of Mr Toliman has been unable to control its own forces, let alone drive a wedge between any of the gaps in the government ranks. But within its own ranks, in addition to Guise and Chan, the present cabinet contains several ambitious men who also realise, that there is no alternative at the moment to Somare's leadership—Olewale and perhaps Kavali could be singled out as Ministers who are prepared to give their allegiance to the coalition at present but have separate ambitions in the long term. In the immediate future their ambitions serve as irritants to the coalition's unity, although none of their chances of leadership could be rated as good and they lack the all round qualities which have marked Somare's performance as the leader of the government and of the nation.

Ultimately, the NCG exists because of the cohesion which Somare himself is able to impart to it. In this his assets are an open straightforward personality, a genuinely nationalist outlook (he is one of the few PNG politicians who put national interests above parochial or personal concerns), and an energetic devotion to his role. However, the system within which he must work imposes stress and he lacks the support to override its constraints. He has been under considerable pressure during the past six months and although he returns to Wewak to relax when engagements permit, he at times becomes over-tired by the pace of duties and social engagements in Port Moresby. He is too soft-hearted to refuse many of the social obligations of the role of Chief Minister; some of his many appearances in Port Moresby may take up an undue proportion of his time but he is very conscious of the need for PNG's first indigenous political leader to make the office a visible one and establish the authority of his government. As a good Melanesian, he is not inclined to bring issues to a head, hence his style of government is to search for the broadest possible consensus on an issue rather than to seek to impose a decision by his personal authority. As long as the consensus is not so generalised that it is meaningless, this could form a solid basis for coalition government. It can, however, bring about prolonged delays in reaching decisions and is yet another complication in the process of decision-making.

Unity

The other area of uncertainty which not only poses problems for the present coalition government but would threaten the stability of the country under any regime, is the attraction of regional chauvinism. The NCG is vulnerable to all three forms of regional separatism which are gaining political [coherence] in PNG—Bougainville, the Highlands, and the Gazelle. Bougainvillean feeling is represented in the leadership by two strong advocates of Bougainvillean self-determination; the National Party which is largely composed of highlanders who have defected from the United Party holds three ministries; and the Mataungan Association's three members support the coalition in the House and will probably be offered a ministry in the future. The National Party has yet to show any [separatist] tendencies but the nature of political alignment in the highlands is still so fluid that there is scope for the evolution of a group which would promote the interests of highlanders and demand a greater share of jobs in the civil service.

It is the pressure from the Tolai[5] and Bougainvillean groups however, which is already beginning to put strains on the coalition and hampering its attempts to develop national policies. In the transition from colonial to a nationalist government the danger is that ethnocentric and parochial attitudes which are a strong feature of Melanesian politics pass from being directed away from the centre and develop into regional chauvinism which is directed against the centre. At the parochial level the issues on the Gazelle and in Bougainville have developed a fierce intensity in the past. If, in the future, they develop into a confrontation between a

---

5   The large (by PNG standards) and self-confident Tolai community numbered around 70,000 and comprised a large majority of the population of the Gazelle Peninsula.

nationalist point of view and the forces advocating local self-determination, feeling could be further intensified.

There have been a few indications so far as to how the NCG will handle this issue. With its proposals for local self-government on the Gazelle, the NCG has sought to turn the Gazelle question over to the Tolais themselves for solution and to emphasise that it is essentially a quarrel over leadership amongst the Tolais rather than a question of confrontation between central and local interests. By seeking to appear as little as possible to be imposing a solution from afar and by exploiting the presence of the MA within the coalition the NCG has probably defused the issue for a time. Ultimately, however, a solution depends upon the good faith of the MA which it may be no more willing to extend towards the NCG than it was towards an Australian administration. In that case the NCG would simply find itself back where it started from with little choice but to regard it as a conflict between central authority and self-determination.

The Bougainville problem is potentially even more difficult.[6] The NCG has not made any pronouncements which would prejudice its future options. It presumably hopes that the question of central/regional relations may be settled by consensus through the Constitutional Planning Committee (CPC). The effective chairman of the CPC, Father John Momis, is a Bougainvillean and committed to seeking some form of autonomous status for the island. Momis will play a key role in the coalition and as one of its most astute members will press the Bougainvillean case to greatest advantage. Because of this and because the Bougainville copper mine is a critical component in the future of PNG's economy, Bougainville is a weapon which, if allowed to become a question of unchecked political controversy, could deal maximum damage to PNG's political future.

[NAA: A1838, 3080/1/1 PART 2]

---

6   See Document 350.

398   MINUTE FROM DUNN[1] TO HAY

Canberra, 3 November 1972

Visit to PNG by Officers of the Australian
Department of Trade and Industry (Sectrade)[2]

I accompanied Messrs R. Somes[3] and N. Bayley[4] of Sectrade on their familiarisation tour of Papua New Guinea from 30 October to 6 November. The areas visited were Port Moresby, Lae, Madang and Goroka.

2.   The tour was [a] great success. Both Somes and Bayley told me on the return flight that they had achieved much more than they thought possible in such a short time. They were most impressed by the quality and dedication of both the Administration officers and representatives of the private sector whom they met. Consequently they were confident that future trading relations between Australia and Papua New Guinea should be as good as those between Australia and other major trading partners. They expressed their appreciation of the itinerary arranged for them and said that seeing such diverse aspects of Papua New Guinea and talking to people in a wide variety of situations in the private and public sectors had given them a great insight into the country and its problems.

3.   At the outset Somes and Bayley explained to Administration officers that the purpose of their visit was broadly twofold, namely to discuss the question of future trading relations between Australia and Papua New Guinea as self-government and independence approached and second to assure the Administration that Sectrade would be happy to assist in any way possible, for example training local officers in Canberra or sending Sectrade officers to Papua New Guinea to train and advise.

4.   [PNG] Trade and Industry were given a large amount of briefing material specifically prepared for them to acquaint them with the functions of Sectrade and explain Australian trade relations and the operations of international agencies like GATT[5] and UNCTAD.[6] Their idea was that the documents be read at leisure after which the Administration could come back to Sectrade for whatever further information advice or assistance they might want.

5.   The talks with Bill Conroy were very fruitful as indicated by the fact that although originally he allocated an hour for discussion he gave us about two and a half hours. He ranged over the whole field of international commodity trade and gave his views on the problems likely to emerge in the future.

6.   Discussions with people in the private sector also went off well and the company representatives responded enthusiastically to the opportunity to discuss their marketing and other problems, especially as they related to Australia.

7.   I am sure that as a result of the cordial relationships and goodwill established by Somes and Bayley much closer ties between the Administration and Sectrade will ensue. I would

---

1   N. D. Dunn, Economic Division, DET.

2   See Documents 374 and 375. 'Sectrade' was the address for telegrams of the Department of Trade and Industry. It appears to be used here as an acronym for this Department.

3   F. R. Somes, Director, Food Section, Secondary Industry Operations Division, Department of Trade and Industry.

4   N. J. S. Bayley, Assistant Director and project officer on Papua New Guinea, Trade Relations Division, Department of Trade and Industry.

5   General Agreement on Tariffs and Trade.

6   United Nations Conference on Trade and Development.

strongly suggest that a follow-up visit be made in the near future, say early in the New Year. The itinerary could then cover places not visited, for example New Britain, New Ireland, Bougainville and the Western Highlands.

8.   Already [PNG] Trade & Industry have taken up the offer of assistance by asking Sectrade to enquire about GATT status pertaining to countries on the road to independence. They also said that they would like a Sectrade expert on documentation to visit and advise them. Moreover tentative agreement was reached that local officers would come to Canberra to participate in the preparation of briefs for appropriate international conferences.

[*matter omitted*]

[NAA: A452, 1972/2640]

399   PAPER BY DET[1]

Canberra, 6 November 1972

SECRET

Australian National Interests Regarding an Independent Papua New Guinea

Foreword

1.   This paper attempts to identify and assess the likely significance of factors and relations with Papua New Guinea that may be material to Australia's national interests in the short term post-independence period, following the termination of the Trusteeship Agreement. The paper does not seek to determine the policies that Australia should adopt in the light of its national interests in any particular area but attempts to set down the various factors that will be need to be used as guidelines within which particular policy issues should be determined.

[*matter omitted*][2]

Part Two: Australian PNG relationships at Independence

9.   At independence Australia's formal international responsibilities for PNG will cease. Australia will be able to reassess its national interests in response to then-current political and economic realities. It will not be possible, however, to ignore certain distinctive features of the relationship resulting from Australia's former status as the power administering the Territories[sic]. Although PNG is economically and militarily weak, and there are other countries of equal or greater importance to Australia, none is so close or has the same Australian presence, involvement, and historical links. At the same time consideration will have to be given to the extent to which Australia would be prepared to follow policies in relation to PNG which would impinge on its relations with other countries.

10.   Australia's international reputation will be affected by its relationship with Papua New Guinea and the attitudes to Australia expressed by Papua New Guinea leaders. The successful handover of a viable PNG would be to our credit. The national pride of Australians in Australian achievements in Papua New Guinea, and friendship for Papua New Guineans, will also be affected by the course of events in the newly independent country and the attitudes taken by Papua New Guineans to Australia and Australians. Australian decisions with respect to Papua New Guinea, notably in relation to the continuation of aid will be substantially influenced by these considerations. Independence, however, is likely to be marked by an increasing Papua New Guinean desire for self-assertion, and possibly by a reaction against introduced economic

---

1   On 18 May 1972 Cabinet had decided that the Department of External Territories, in conjunction with the Department of Foreign Affairs and in consultation with other departments, should undertake a study of 'Australia's national interests in relation to an independent Papua New Guinea and the arrangements between it and Australia which ought to be entered into in the light of these interests', with the conclusions and proposed guidelines with respect to the consideration of policy issues to be put before Cabinet (Document 296).

   At the same meeting Cabinet had decided to establish a standing interdepartmental committee (IDC) on Papua New Guinea. The draft paper was circulated in early November. The IDC had held its first meeting on 16 June and met every two or three weeks. Details of the IDC's activities are held on NAA: A1838, 3080/11/1/2, PART 1.

2   The omitted material, comprising part one of the paper, reviewed 'the relationship to date' and 'Present Australian involvement in PNG'.

and social forms. There will probably be attempts to adopt a 'Melanesian' way of doing things. Conscious resentment against Australia may appear.

11. Papua New Guinea will have to devote most of its energies to the problems of economic and social development and a number of potential internal problems. Foreign policy will be mainly directed towards exporting products; obtaining aid, investment and loans; and avoiding interference from outside. The countries which seem likely to be of most concern to Papua New Guinea are Australia, Indonesia and Japan. The EEC, USA, South East Asia, the South Pacific and the Solomon Islands will also be considerable importance. Practical evaluation of Papua New Guinea's interests leads to the conclusion that it will wish to maintain good relations with Australia. In particular it will look to Australia for financial and military aid while seeking to diversify its aid sources, especially from Japan. Similarly it will be concerned to develop new trade partners but also to preserve the trade advantages it already has. PNG shares a common land border with Indonesia which has a much larger population and greater military strength. It will need to take this into account, and seek good relations with Indonesia.

Part Three: Australia's broad national interests and PNG

12. The relevance of any country to Australia's pursuit of its political, strategic or economic national interests depends largely upon the potentiality of that country to assist or obstruct the attainment by Australia of its foreign policy objectives, to enhance Australia's security, or to further or hinder Australia's economic advancement and well-being. Key factors governing the importance of any country in relation to Australia's pursuit of its national interests include that country's geographical location and resource base vis-à-vis Australia, the degree of international influence it commands, its size and national wealth, its trading or investment relationships with Australia, and its military strength and consequent capability to threaten or help safeguard Australia's security.

13. PNG will be of direct importance to Australia in the pursuit of its national interests in the period under study largely because of its geographical location and its commercial, financial and other links with Australia. Its relevance to Australia's national interests can be summarised as follows:

(a) Political—As the closest foreign neighbour and because of its geographical location at the conjunction of two key areas for Australia—South East Asia and the South Pacific—Papua New Guinea will need to be taken into account in formulating and pursuing our foreign policy objectives. Australia's national interests will best be served by the development of close and friendly political relations with Papua New Guinea and by encouraging its contribution to the general peace and stability of the area.

(b) Strategic—While Papua New Guinea lacks the military capability to pose a direct threat to Australian security, its large land area and its proximity to Australia and Indonesia would render a hostile Papua New Guinea allied to a strong military power a threat to Australia. It would also obstruct Australian transport routes northwards, particularly if the Law of the Sea Conference recognises wider sovereignty over straits and archipelagos. Because of this, continuing close and friendly contact between Papua New Guinea and Australia could be valuable strategically.

(c) Economic—Australia's existing trade and investment links with Papua New Guinea and its potential future expansion of these links ensure Papua New Guinea's continuing economic importance to Australia. There is considerable scope for the complementary development of both Australian and Papua New Guinea resources to the advantage of both countries.

[matter omitted][3]

53. A clash between Papua New Guinea and Indonesia would place Australia in a very difficult position. Significant clashes seem unlikely to occur, but there are some potential sources of conflict:

(i) The feeling among some Papua New Guineans that Indonesia should never have acquired West Irian and that West Irian dissidents should be given support by Papua New Guinea.

(ii) The possibility that a change in Government in Indonesia might bring to power an expansionist, aggressive Government with designs on Papua New Guinea.

(iii) The emergence of pan-Papuanism[4] as a force to be reckoned with.

54. The greatest danger lies in a combination of any of the above, where relations gradually deteriorate without blame lying clearly on either side. If Australia had built up very close ties with Papua New Guinea, or were linked with by an inflexible defence agreement, it might be very hard to disengage sufficiently to ensure that Australia's own relations with Indonesia were not seriously damaged or that Indonesian hostility was not directed towards Australia.

55. Indonesia, largely as a result of Australia's encouragement, will shortly open a Consulate in Port Moresby which should assist in furthering relations between the two countries. Present expectations are that a border agreement between Indonesia and Papua New Guinea and border regime will be concluded before Papua New Guinea becomes independent. The early settlement of these matters will play an essential part in avoiding the emergence of serious friction between the two countries and will consequently serve Australia's own interests.

56. The general conclusion of recent studies by the Interdepartmental Committee on Japan is that the emergence of a closer Papua New Guinea relationship with Japan does not pose a serious threat to Australia. Japanese interests appear to be overwhelmingly economic and not strategic. There is no evidence that Australian investment opportunities have been reduced by Japan's participation in Papua New Guinea's economic development. On the contrary, Japan is seen as a considerable assistance in developing PNG and as a means to reduce Papua New Guinea's dependence on Australia.

[matter omitted][5]

60. The geographic proximity of PNG to Australia does not in itself make PNG of vital strategic significance to Australia from a purely military point of view. There are other points in South East Asia from which military attacks on Australia could be mounted as readily as from PNG. South West Irian[6] is, for example, little further from Sydney than PNG and Djakarta is about the same distance from Perth as Port Moresby is from Sydney. Papua New Guinea alone could not pose a military threat of any significance to Australia. The strategic significance of PNG's geographic position is related primarily to the possibility of a foreign power using PNG as a base for operations against mainland Australia, Australian forces, or Australia's lines of supply or communication. In this respect, a hostile PNG and a hostile Solomon Islands together could command 20% of Australia's sea lanes.

---

3   The omitted material, comprising a large portion of part four of the paper, considered 'Factors bearing on Australia's interests', including challenges to Papua New Guinea's viability, the Australian Aid Programme, economic development and trade and investment, and aspects of international relations.

4   This appears to be a reference to the possible development of a sense of common identity between the peoples of Papua New Guinea and those of Irian Jaya.

5   The omitted material, from part four of the paper, comprised further discussion of PNG's relationship with Japan.

6   The southern coast of West Irian.

61. It is most unlikely in the next decade that a power hostile to Australia would wish or be able to use Papua New Guinea for operations against Australia or Australian forces. China, the USSR and Indonesia are the only powers which could pose a military threat of any substance to Australia. The policy of the two super-powers is unlikely to include basing land or air forces on PNG and the possibility of them basing naval forces although greater is still slight. Present indications are that an independent PNG will not allow such bases on her soil. A change from this policy appears unlikely unless Australia negotiates to retain bases such as the naval base on Manus in an overall defence agreement with PNG.

[*matter omitted*]⁷

Part Five: Conclusions, proposed guideline implications

67. Australia's relationship with PNG in the period under study will be dictated by the proximity of the two countries and the close involvement of the Australian Government, Australian enterprises and Australian citizens in the life of PNG. Such a continuing involvement during the period will be inevitable. To a large degree it is these considerations which create then national interests which the relationship should protect—security of Australian lives, Australia's national security, economic interests, and international reputation. Although Japan and Indonesia will be of greater importance to Australia in South East Asia in some areas of interest, the foregoing considerations suggest the need for a special relationship to continue in the period under study, with the objective of keeping open the options for extending the relationship beyond that period.

[NAA: A452, 1975/78]

---

7   The omitted material reviewed external threats to Papua New Guinea, concluding that there was a 'small likelihood of external aggression'.

400   LETTER FROM WALLER TO HAY

Canberra, 7 November 1972

CONFIDENTIAL

In interdepartmental discussions on the Simpson report[1] on the employment security of oversees officers in the PNG Public Service, officers of this Department expressed their concern that decisions were being taken without sufficient study of their future implications for Australian aid programmes and which would commit the Commonwealth to expenditure in an independent Papua New Guinea for some years. In its report on the Simpson recommendations, the Inter-departmental Committee on Papua New Guinea recorded the view of this Department that it would be unfortunate if decisions entered into now without full consideration were to distort the future pattern of Australia's aid programme—both for Papua New Guinea and other countries. The Foreign Minister also raised this matter directly with the Prime Minister, recommending that:

> A study be made immediately by officials from the Departments of Foreign Affairs, External Territories and the Treasury, of the implications of Papua New Guinea's independence for Australian aid policy, and of how best to phase Australian development assistance to Papua New Guinea into an overall programme of international economic aid.

We were subsequently informed by his Department that the Prime Minister has directed that such a study be undertaken. A copy of the letter, dated 31 October 1972 conveying the Prime Minister's decision, together with the Foreign Minister's submission to him, is attached.[2]

In view of the Prime Minister's agreement that the study be undertaken immediately I should like to convene a meeting a 2 p.m. on Wednesday 15 November at this Department and should be grateful if you could arrange for your Department to be represented. I hope that at the first meeting, which I am asking Mr Border to chair, the issues likely to be involved can be identified and that we can move to the study committee's terms of reference.

You will note from the enclosures that the terms of reference of the study proposed by the Foreign Minister are as follow:

> (a) The aid policy which Australia ought to adopt towards an independent Papua New Guinea in the context of its international development assistance programme.
>
> (b) The administrative arrangements which would have to be made to implement this.
>
> (c) The mechanism which will be necessary to move from the existing arrangements for aid to Papua New Guinea to the new arrangements to be worked out in (b) above.
>
> (d) Enactment of any consequential legislation.

The meeting might like to consider employing this framework during its study.

[NAA: A1838, 3080/10/4/7 PART 1]

---

1   Not published. See Document 394.

2   Not published.

401   PAPER BY DEFENCE COMMITTEE

Canberra, 13 November 1972

Defence Aspects of PNG Constitutional Developments

The rapid progress of constitutional development in PNG necessarily has defence implications of real and immediate importance. The attached paper reviews progress on the major matters that are under consideration within the Department of Defence in consultation with other Departments where appropriate. It also discusses tentative or actual conclusions reached in respect of the more important matters which might be of interest to the Defence Committee.

[*matter omitted*]

Attachment

Defence Aspects of PNG Constitutional Developments

Introduction

The rapid progress of constitutional development in PNG has defence implications of real and immediate importance. The orderly development of the PNG Force, training of indigenous officers and technical elements, and the determination and establishment of a suitable local machinery to formulate policy and to administer and control the Force, have all had to be accelerated to meet the timings which now appear probable for self-government and independence. Australia's Defence interests in and in relation to PNG need to be reviewed, and the defence relationships which should be sought with an independent PNG Government need to be defined. Representational and consultative arrangements specifically serving our interests must be agreed and executed.

2.   The PNG Leadership is now seeking closer involvement in all aspects of evolution of the present PNG Force and the PNG defence organisation—although it is accepted that decisions on Defence matters will remain the responsibility of the Commonwealth Government until independence.

[*matter omitted*]

Lines of Action

4.   Within the Department of Defence, a number of lines of action have been pursued:

•   In consultation with the Department of External Territories, an extensive programme of defence oriented studies was agreed and initiated. These relate essentially to force roles and development up to and after independence, PNG defence organisational requirements, localisation, and internal security arrangements for PNG up to independence.

•   In February 1972 a Joint Force Headquarters was formed in PNG to replace the existing separate Service Command arrangements, to facilitate economical and effective administration and control of the forces, and to provide a basis for future assumption by an independent PNG Government of control over its own Defence Force.

•   By arrangement with the Service Ministers, the Minister for Defence has assumed full policy direction and control of the PNG Defence Force as a whole, to ensure coordinated direction and development. His directions will be legally effective through the Services Boards as necessary in the normal way.

•   A PNG Defence Coordinating Committee has been set up within the Department under the Chairman Chiefs of Staff Committee. It comprises the two Deputy Secretaries and the Director, Joint Staff of this Department, together with the 3 Deputy Chiefs of Staff. It is required to coordinate and to direct all aspects of the development of the PNG Defence Force and its support.

• Arrangements have been made with the Department of the Army for a team to prepare the draft legislation necessary for separation of the PNG Defence Force from the Australian Forces, at or before independence.

• A Defence Branch headed by a senior officer seconded from the Department has been established in PNG in the Office of the Chief Minister (who has also been appointed Ministerial Spokesman for Defence) to advise and support the Ministerial Spokesman.

[*matter omitted*]

Coordination of Development and Consultation

6.   The PNG House of Assembly has recently adopted a motion fixing the timing for self-government at 1st December, 1973 or as soon as possible thereafter.[1] The Chief Minister's view is that when self-government is achieved, powers remaining with the Commonwealth would be in respect of defence and external affairs only and the power to intervene in internal security. It seems likely that independence will be sought soon after self-government and almost certainly within the life of the present local Parliament.

[*matter omitted*]

8.   The desire for full consultation with Australia in such matters as foreign relationships and defence, which remain the final responsibility of Australia until independence, has been emphasised by the Chief Minister. Reciprocally, the Minister for Defence stated to the AEC during his visit to PNG in June that:

> Decisions taken now regarding training and accommodation facilities, equipment and so on will all have very long term effects. It is therefore desirable that there should be close consultation with and involvement of PNG Ministers' opinion on defence matters. The AEC will clearly be a focal point of this consultation. I regard these discussions today as a start point.[2]

[*matter omitted*]

Australian Interests Post-Independence and their Policy Implications

10.   In Decision 980 PNG,[3] Cabinet directed that the Departments of External Territories and Foreign Affairs should, in consultation with other Commonwealth Departments, initiate a study to define Australia's national interests in relation to an independent PNG, and the arrangements between it and Australia which ought to be entered into in the light of these interests.[4] It is understood that consultation with the Defence Department on strategic and defence interests and their implications will shortly be initiated.

11.   At this stage it can be said that, for a number of reasons outlined in the Strategic Basis of Australian Defence Policy 1971,[5] PNG is regarded as of abiding strategic interest to Australia. These reasons include its geographic position astride our military and trade lines

---

1   See Documents 367 & 383.

2   See Document 311.

3   Document 296.

4   For a DET paper prepared as part of the study, see Document 399.

5   See Stephen Frühling, *A History of Australian Strategic Policy since 1945*, Department of Defence, Canberra, 2006, pp. 413–15.

of communication to the North, and to South East Asia; its common border with Indonesia; the facilities it could provide for support of operations in the north of New Guinea or for deployment to South East Asia, or conversely, if in hostile hands, the facilities it could provide for the conduct of operations inimical to our security.

12. Threats to the integrity of PNG could arise in the future, for example from friction with Indonesia, or more probably from internal security situations. The future threat to internal security has been assessed by the National Intelligence Committee which has concluded that the state of law and order is deteriorating, with a growing possibility of significant disorders, which in certain circumstances the police may be unable to contain. Future calls for Australian support, including conceivably combat assistance, are possible. The possibility of responding to such calls is not excluded by our present policies.

13. Australia has strategic interests also in the development of defence facilities and infrastructure in PNG but in present circumstances we would need to proceed with caution on the establishment of any new facilities in PNG required for Australian forces alone.

14. Australian defence interests and their policy implications are being reviewed carefully and updated in the light of recent and prospective developments.

Functions and roles of PNG Security Forces after Independence

15. Following study of the nature of the forces which would be most suitable for an independent PNG, and subsequent discussion with the Administrator, departmental endorsement has been given to a statement of the functions and roles which would be most appropriate for those forces after independence. The broad functions proposed in consultation with the Department of External Territories for the PNG security forces as a whole, comprising the Police and the Defence Force (the latter consisting of three elements—land, maritime and air) are as follows:

- under the direction of the legally constituted Government to provide for the enforcement of national laws and processes with particular regard to preservation of internal security and the protection of national resources;

- to contribute as required to economic development and to the promotion of national administration and unity;

- to maintain a capability of external defence of the nation.

[*matter omitted*]

Development of a PNG Defence Branch and Department of the Defence Force

20. As indicated, a Defence Branch has now been established in the Office of the Chief Minister. A senior officer of the Defence Department has been seconded as its head. This action was foreshadowed by the Minister for Defence during his discussions with the AEC in June and was confirmed during the constitutional discussions in August.[6]

21. The Head of the Defence Branch provides advice in defence policy matters, and administrative support, to the PNG Spokesman on Defence, and assists in the formulation and development of PNG views on defence matters. He is to assess and recommend training requirements of local officers in appropriate Defence functions, and advise on and develop proposals for future local Defence Department organisations and arrangements in PNG. He maintains close liaison with the Commander Joint Force.

---

6   See Documents 311, 319, 352, 354 & 355.

22. The Defence Branch is seen as the first step in the development of a departmental organisation to meet PNG requirements. Study of the further development of the Defence Branch into a departmental organisation is in progress.

Australian Defence Representation in PNG

23. The establishment of the Defence Branch in the Chief Minister's Office raises the question of the need for separate defence representation in PNG explicitly of the Commonwealth Department of Defence. Having regard on the one hand to Australia's continuing responsibility for defence until independence, and on the other to increasing PNG involvement in both the development of policies affecting the PNG Force, and in the handling of a wide range of security matters, Defence Department representation at the policy level in Port Moresby will be increasingly necessary to provide advice and support to the Administrator, to ensure that Australian policies are understood and accepted, and to facilitate consultation on policy issues. Possible alternatives to be considered initially are the establishment of a full-time officer within the Commonwealth Office in Port Moresby, or for an Australian-based officer to visit. The Defence Representative would of course be advised on military matters in PNG by the Commander PNG Joint Force. The latter would continue to be responsible to the Chiefs of Staff Committee.

24. The action envisaged above would be the first step in developing Defence representation in PNG which would in due course form part of the Australian diplomatic representation there after independence. A military mission including a training group might be necessary in relation to arrangements for support of the PNG Force or of a substantial Aid Programme if approved, and this could well be located separately. Further detailed study of the tasks and personnel requirements for Australian Defence representation including military personnel post-independence will depend to a considerable extent on the further definition of Australian interests and defence support aid policies.

Australian Support for the PNG Defence Force Post-Independence

25. Although a close relationship between Australia and PNG is expected to continue, independence will also mean a broadening of PNG's relationships with other countries. Australia's contribution to the training, organisation and support of local forces, including provision of personnel to staff and technical appointments and the supply of equipment and the development of infrastructure, may well be required to continue—perhaps at significant levels.

26. It will be necessary for consideration of the level of financial support and the nature of any programme of defence aid to PNG to be undertaken in the context of proposals for Australian aid as a whole, and to have regard to possible defence relationships, and Australian interests generally, post-independence.

27. In the meantime the financial aspects and implications of proposals for PNG defence arrangements, including the development of the PNG Defence Force, are being considered within the Defence Department. This examination will enable the various proposals for defence development, together with any consequential requirements, to be costed. For their consideration of major proposals affecting Defence, for example infrastructure, or Force levels, PNG Ministers must be expected to seek an indication at least in broad terms of the extent to which the costs will be met by financial support from the Commonwealth. We shall need to be able to give this indication at the appropriate time.

[NAA: A452, 1973/470]

402   LETTER FROM WALLER TO HAY

Canberra, 14 November 1972

RESTRICTED

I refer to your letter to Mr Border of 6 November 1972[1] conveying the Administrator's views on the need to 'hasten slowly' in creating the machinery for Papua New Guinea to handle its international relations.

I am growing increasingly concerned about the delay in coming to grips with this matter. Time is rapidly running out and we face the very real risk of an independent Papua New Guinea lacking both the machinery and the experience to manage its external relations in a way which will not bring discredit both to themselves and to Australia.

An officer of this Department (Mr McDonald) was loaned to the Administration at the beginning of this year to help formulate ideas and guidelines for PNG authorities to draw up establishment proposals. I understand that some proposals have in fact been drawn up, but not yet acted on. While we stand ready and willing to offer all the advice and help we can, I feel that the next step must be for PNG to decide what suits it best. I see little to be gained by discussions among officials in Canberra until PNG itself has taken this basic decision.

It is hard to avoid the conclusion that it has not been adequately brought home to the Chief Minister and to his colleagues that the need is now urgent for PNG to decide on the arrangements for handling its foreign relations. What seems to be needed is clear and unambiguous advice to the PNG leaders that they must give this matter high priority if their country is to be able to cope at all satisfactorily with the external problems it will face at independence.

As you know, Mr Shann will be visiting Papua New Guinea next week. I hope that he will have the opportunity to impress upon PNG Ministers and the Administrator the urgency of this matter and to give them directly some awareness of the difficulties they face if quick decisions are not taken. I propose to discuss with the Minister for Foreign Affairs the possibility of his visiting Port Moresby early in the New Year for talks with PNG leaders on the handling of questions in the foreign affairs field.

I would be grateful for anything you can do, either directly or through the Administrator, to speed up a decision by PNG Ministers on this question.

[NAA: A1838, 3080/10/4/7 PART 1]

---

1   Not published.

403   MINUTE FROM GREENWELL TO PEACOCK

Canberra, 16 November 1972

Secret

Functions and Roles of the Papua New Guinea
Security Forces Post Independence

One of the major items being undertaken under the programme of studies of PNG Defence
and Internal Security matters is that of the functions and roles of the PNG security forces
(i.e. both the Police and the Defence Force) post-independence. Agreement has now been
reached between the Departments of Defence and External Territories and the Administrator
of Papua New Guinea on a statement of proposed functions and roles for the security forces.
This minute seeks your approval that this statement be discussed with the PNG Ministry and
their advisers.

2.   The proposed roles and functions for the PNG security forces upon which agreement has
been reached is set out in the attachment to this submission.[1] They were developed by the
PNG Coordinating Committee of the Department of Defence, upon which this Department
is represented after a wide-ranging study carried out by Commonwealth officers, including
officers of this Department.

[*matter omitted*]

3.   The PNG DCC[2] recommended that the PNG security forces should consist of the Defence
Force, comprising three elements—land, maritime and air—and the Police Force. Its reasons
for not proposing a single Security Force which would combine the Defence Force and the
Police included the following:

(a)   although there is quite a degree of common training in both forces, there are certain
fundamental differences in the essential character of the forces quite apart from particular
differences in training, organisation and equipment;

(b)   to abolish the armed forces which currently exist and which form the foundation for
PNG's own future forces could result in a gap which would, among other things, greatly
prejudice the formation of armed forces if required in the future;

(c)   despite the lack of an external threat at present it cannot be stated that this situation
will continue indefinitely; and

(d)   in certain circumstances it may be desirable for the PNG Government to have two
different forces, e.g. if the police went on strike or if either force were disaffected.

4.   The proposed functions and roles, very broadly, provide for increased involvement of the
PNG Defence Force:

(a)   in support of the Police in internal security roles;

(b)   in undertaking, when authorised, police roles in remote and difficult areas; and

(c)   in contributing to nation building tasks within the capability of the force.

5.   Proposed functions and roles of the PNG security forces post-independence will obviously
need to be fully acceptable to local PNG authorities and will ultimately be a matter for their
decision. The PNG DCC accordingly observed that before any finality was reached on these

---

1   Not published.

2   Defence Coordinating Committee.

matters, it was desirable as a first step that the views of the Administrator be obtained. He, by virtue of his post and continuing responsibilities, could be expected to be in close touch with local needs and circumstances and local PNG opinion.

6.   At discussions between the Administrator and the Secretaries, Departments of Defence and External Territories and Chairman, Chiefs of Staff Committee at a meeting on 11th October, 1972, the Administrator supported the recommendations of the PNG DCC and said that he thought that they would be acceptable to PNG authorities. He commented that an important point was that although there were to be separate Defence and Police forces, there would be common logistic support; for example, the air transport forces would operate in support of the Defence Force and the Police.

7.   The meeting discussed whether it would be best to allow the PNG authorities to develop their own views on future functions and roles of the forces before undertaking consultations with Australian officials. The meeting agreed that this course was preferable. However it was suggested that the PNG DCC proposals should be referred to the Administration with a view to their being considered by the Papua New Guinea authorities in the course of preparing for the formal consultations with Australian officials. Meanwhile, we are proceeding with other studies on the shape and size of the security forces required to meet the proposed functions and roles.

8.   There is no disagreement between the Administration and the Department on this matter.

Recommendation

9.   It is recommended that you endorse in principle at this stage the attached proposed functions and roles of the PNG security forces as a basis for opening discussions with the PNG authorities along the lines set out in paragraph 7 above. The Department of Defence is seeking similar endorsement in principle from the Minister for Defence.[3]

[NAA: A452, 1972/3889]

---

3   See Document 396. Peacock, for his part, annotated the DET submission: 'Approved: Andrew Peacock, 17–11–72'.

404   MINUTE FROM GUTMAN TO PEACOCK

Canberra, 20 November 1972

Report of the Committee on Banking in PNG

The final report of the Committee on Banking in Papua New Guinea was submitted to you today under cover of a separate letter.[1]

2.   On 1 November we informed you about the progress of the Committee's deliberations and indicated that the clearance of the report had been delayed because of the problems encountered by the Commonwealth Treasury regarding some aspects of the Committee's recommendations on the future of the Commonwealth Banking Corporation in Papua New Guinea. In view of this development it was decided to convene a special meeting of the Banking Committee on 8 November to endeavour to resolve this problem. At that meeting the Committee decided to modify somewhat its recommendations in relation to the Commonwealth Banking Corporation. The effect of the modification is to leave open for further examination by the appropriate authorities the question of the extent to which the Corporation should be permitted to engage in banking operations in Papua New Guinea after the establishment of a separate backing system. This modification does not alter the basic recommendation that the present business of the Corporation should be transferred to a Papua New Guinea Government owned bank. We understand that the Corporation has no objections to the recommendations as they now stand.

3.   The revised report has now been cleared by all organisations represented on the Committee, namely, the Department of External Territories, Commonwealth Treasury, the Reserve Bank of Australia and the Papua New Guinea Administration.

4.   To meet the timetable proposed in the report for the establishment of a separate Papua New Guinea banking system before self-government it is important that the views of the Papua New Guinea Government be obtained before the end of this year. We understand that the last meeting of the Administrator's Executive Council this year will be held on 14/15 December. The legislative and administrative requirements to effect the transfer of the banking function to Papua New Guinea are such that a delay in the Papua New Guinea's decision on this question until January/February next year will probably make it impossible to transfer banking controls before self-government.

5.   Your approval is therefore sought for the submission of the report to the Papua New Guinea Government for its views as soon as possible. The Commonwealth Treasury will also be seeking the Treasurer's concurrence to this course of action. It is proposed to submit the report to Cabinet early next year if the Papua New Guinea Government's views are available in December 1972.

Recommendation

6.   It is recommended that you approve the transmission of the Banking Committee's report to the Administrator with a request that he seek the view of the Papua New Guinea Government on the Committee's recommendations.[2]

[NAA: A452, 1972/3938]

---

1   Not published.

2   Peacock annotated the minute: 'Approved: Andrew Peacock, 17–11–72'.

405   PAPER FOR STANDING IDC

Canberra, 22 November 1972

CONFIDENTIAL

Programme of Movement towards Internal Self-Government

In agreeing to recommendations of the House of Assembly Select Committee on Constitutional Development in April 1971, Cabinet authorised the Department of External Territories to draw up a flexible programme of movement towards full internal self-government as a basis for negotiations with the leadership group emerging from the 1972 elections.[1] It authorised as one aspect of this the planning of legislative and administrative steps necessary to ensure that the Commonwealth is in a position to conform to such a programme.

2.   Use has been made of the programme in constitutional discussions with Papua New Guinea leaders during 1972 with the result that on most matters there has been a joint Australia/PNG assessment of the steps involved and agreement on target dates for transfer of powers and resolution of policy issues.

3.   The most recent updating of the programme (beginning of November 1972) has been charted graphically [...][2] The chart highlights major action necessary, such as Cabinet and AEC decisions, legislation in both the Commonwealth Parliament and the House of Assembly, reference to Ministers in both countries, Commonwealth/PNG official discussions, and Commonwealth inter-departmental discussions or studies.

4.   An analysis by months of the programmed action has been prepared and is attached. It indicates the volume of administrative and legislative work to be done, and the importance of adhering as closely as possible to target dates to make possible the legal attainment of self-government by Papua New Guinea by 1st December, 1973.

[NAA: A452, 1975/78]

---

1   Documents 159 & 160.

2   Not published. For an earlier version of the chart, see Document 209.

406   REPORT BY JOHNSON

Port Moresby, 27 November 1972

CONFIDENTIAL

A Review of the Development of the Papua New Guinea
National Coalition Government to November 24th 1972

The National Coalition Government (NCG) has now been in power for more than six months and it is appropriate to review its development and its problems.

House of Assembly

To date the NCG has not had any difficulty in maintaining a comfortable majority in divisions in the House, but it has done this by sometimes swimming with the tide and acceding to House of Assembly motions which look to have popular support rather than asserting a Government policy and sticking to it. Outside of Papua New Guinea, the internal politics of the House of Assembly are not well understood nor the role played by private Members' motions in the House, by informal grouping of Members, by deals made and unmade by individual Ministers irrespective of earlier AEC decisions and by the strong influence of regional groupings.

Private Members' motions in the House of Assembly, even when supported by the ruling Coalition, are sometimes treated in a rather cavalier fashion when action on them is being considered by the AEC. Motions passed by the House are transmitted by the Speaker to the Administrator who refers them to the AEC for action. The usual timing is for a motion passed in one House meeting to be considered by the AEC after the conclusion of that meeting and a reply to the Speaker prepared for delivery during the next meeting. Subsequent action would then await any House reaction, although of course, if there was full Cabinet support for the resolution, action could be initiated before the next meeting of the House. To date the House has not reacted strongly to a reasoned reply from the AEC which may, in fact, negate a House resolution which had been passed on the voices without opposition from any member of the Ministry. A number of Private Members' motions do impinge on the Government's prerogative to make policy but the NCG seems to be able to accept such motions without regarding policy implications as limiting its freedom of action.

The NCG does not act with consistent strength in the House of Assembly. There are occasions when it can and will muster its voting strength but these are usually when the United Party Opposition mounts a specific frontal attack. This means that jobs and influence are at risk and such threats rally the disparate elements within the NCG.

Much is said about consensus and, in a House in which there are no clear-cut ideological or economic divisions, perhaps broad agreement on principles without attempting to delineate specific issues is the best way to carry on parliamentary business. However, one should not be deluded into thinking that any Melanesian government will not act strongly and arbitrarily and, in so doing, override minority interests if it is confident it has the numbers and can get away with it.

Coalition Solidarity

The Coalition has a high degree of fragility in that its principal elements—Pangu, People's Progress Party [PPP], Bougainvilleans and the Mataungan Association [MA]—have very little common ground. The cement that binds is the attraction of power and of office. On the face of it one might reasonably expect the defection of the PPP on many of the economic policy issues which are now coming to the surface, but I regard this as unlikely.

The Pangu Pati appears to have a high degree of flexibility on issues which may affect its control of Government and, when it comes to the pinch, is likely to make concessions just sufficient to placate the PPP. The PPP also has only a small following, perhaps twelve or thirteen, some of whom may not be prepared to follow the party into opposition. The defection of the PPP would certainly create political chaos and quite new groupings may emerge in which a more radical Highlands group could play an important part.

The Ministry

As with all ministries everywhere, Papua New Guinea's is very uneven in capacity and understanding. It is handicapped by the fact that the best Ministers are not necessarily in charge of the more important portfolios and that some of the members of the AEC hold ministries of lesser importance. In general, Ministers arrive at Cabinet meetings poorly informed on the matters of the agenda and on very many occasions without having read the papers and without having attempted to get a briefing in any other way.

Because of political preoccupations and limited educational background, some Ministers rely very heavily on outside advice and assistance in matters relating to their portfolios and in certain cases, because of suspicion of a colonial and largely white senior public service, have been reluctant to accept departmental advice. Where extra-departmental advice is skilled and experienced, there are advantages in Ministers seeking this sort of help in addition to departmental aid, but some private advisers who have clustered around certain Ministers have neither knowledge nor experience. It will take some time for Ministers to exercise more perceptive judgment in selecting those who advise them.

A continuing problem throughout Papua New Guinea, both within and without the Government service, is the very limited number of people of high ability allied with experience and judgement.

The Opposition

The United Party Opposition has been ineffective for a number of reasons. The most obvious one is the dearth of Members with suitable education and experience and the fact that its principal strength lies in the Western and Southern Highlands Districts. Two of the more able and experienced Ministers from the previous House—Messrs Lokoloko and Giregire—have not taken an active part in politics in the present House and the remaining leaders of experience—Messrs Toliman and Abal—do not have the ruthlessness to develop strong attacks on the NCG. Two of the younger Members, Messrs Langro[1] and Parao—have taken leading roles in attacks on the Government.

In general, the concept of a government and an opposition is weakly held. Mr Abal often says that he is opposed to the Pangu Pati but supports the NCG provided it manages the country's business properly. At present the actors in the House of Assembly appear to be frozen into Westminster postures which are unsuitable to their background, needs and aspirations. This makes for a good deal of aridity in set piece debates. The committee system has never been properly developed and the experiment of the British Solomon Islands in attempting to manage the Government through this system has apparently failed.

The Chief Minister

There has been a successful effort to build up the stature of the Chief Minister and to obtain acceptance of him as the national leader. The success obtained is due first of all to the

---

1   Paul Langro, MHA for West Sepik regional.

personality and ability of Mr Somare and, secondly, to the gratifying way in which senior public servants and private citizens everywhere have cooperated to present him to the nation as a leader.

Mr Somare has had a most onerous and difficult task in first of all mastering the business of government, holding together a difficult coalition and asserting himself in Cabinet. There is no credible alternative to Mr Somare on the horizon though there are two or three members of the National Coalition Government with sufficient ambition to attempt to supplant him should an occasion arise. In my judgement, the Coalition could not hold together for any length of time with any other leader.

Policy Evolution

It might be said that the PPP supports a fairly orthodox capitalist approach to development while advocating greater equality of incomes and a wider geographic distribution of development spending. It favours a high level of foreign investment to maintain the rate of economic growth and to increase the number of jobs in towns. It advocates the maintenance of existing agreements and contracts and protection of business interests already operating here.

The Pangu Pati, insofar as it has a central policy theme, advocates a much more socialist approach, perhaps rural socialism might describe it best. The basis of life in Papua New Guinea is the rural village and the principal effort must be directed towards improving life in the village. Economic growth per se has no merit nor has foreign investment unless it can contribute to rural improvement. It is suspicious of foreign capital. There is a degree of unreality in its expectation of being able to write its own terms for foreign investors and also for international aid.

The Bougainvillean voice is principally that of Father Momis who would chase the money changers out of the temple and restore rural piety, purity and simplicity.

Out of these strands an economic policy must be woven which the Australian Government is prepared to support and which will go some way towards satisfying the demands for increased health and education services, more roads, improved agricultural extension services, improved security, more jobs in town and so on. This will entail some painful compromises but the Pangu Pati is quite determined that it should be seen to be changing direction. In the process it seems likely that small scale foreign investors will find much less attraction in Papua New Guinea but the larger projects may not be much affected if they act in conformity with existing guidelines. However, intemperate statements by individual Ministers and disinclination as a whole to deny them have created a climate of doubt and uncertainty in the board rooms of potential major investors, particularly mining and mineral exploration companies. It will be some months before there is sufficient definition of a Government investment policy to permit these companies to assess Papua New Guinea opportunities.

Localisation

Localisation is an issue on which there is little difference between any political group and it was safe enough for the Chief Minister to announce his Government's intention to reduce sharply the number of expatriates in the Public Service. It was politically necessary for him to use figures that would have some public impact and the Opposition expressed some concern that the baby might be thrown out with the bath water. The curious fact is that having made the announcement there appeared to be some reluctance to follow it through with action. Senior expatriates have been responsible for getting the project launched. The same reluctance has been evident in action to localise individual senior posts and, again, expatriate initiative has been necessary to get decisions.

The NCG has on a number of occasions asserted that it needs a simpler administrative structure and presently at least two proposals to reform departmental structure are in circulation. On the surface there is a readiness to impose radical solutions but little understanding of the difficulties facing any attempt at major reconstruction of an established and entrenched bureaucracy. There is already some evidence that senior indigenous public servants are closing ranks against the likely intrusion of politicians into managerial aspects of departmental business.

In both foreign policy and defence there has as yet been no discussion in depth and nothing more than the sporadic offering of tentative ideas. It is recognised that the major influences on Papua New Guinea will be Indonesia, Australia and Japan and Ministers appear to be groping towards a policy that will balance out the power and influence of these countries on Papua New Guinea. There is, in some quarters, a tendency to overreact against a long period of Australian paternalism but it seems that Australian ties will remain firm and enduring.

There is also a fraternal feeling for the other small Pacific nations and in particular towards those peopled by Melanesians but there is a ready appreciation that racial and cultural kinship does not do much to fill food bowls. One may confidently forecast the continuation of friendship and cultural and sporting contacts with the Pacific Island nations and perhaps some concerted action on any common political problems.

Internal security has not yet had serious consideration.

By far the greatest problem facing the National Coalition Government and one which is ever present in all policy considerations, is the secessionist threat from Bougainville. There is no doubt that at present Bougainville opinion is overwhelmingly secessionist, even though few could explain precisely what they mean by secession. The appointment of two Bougainvilleans to Cabinet rank and a third to head up the Constitutional Committee is an attempt to hold Bougainville by committing its parliamentary representatives to the Government of a united Papua New Guinea. The actions and pronouncements of Bougainville MHAs receive exaggerated attention. A good example of this is the priority attention given to Momis' successful attempt to set mining policy for the Government. The Papua New Guinea Government is playing for high stakes with a weak hand and many of its actions and statements which appear unreasonable are due to its anxiety about Bougainville.[2]

In general, the NCG has had first to overcome the problem of political survival, next to obtain some understanding of the business of government and, at the same time, to build up public acceptance of members of the Ministry as individuals and as a credible Government. It is only now beginning to evolve policies which it hopes will be distinctively Papua New Guinean.

Summary

I have not attempted to make final judgements on the effectiveness of the NCG. It will require another six months before any valid assessment can be made. In that time the weaknesses and strengths of the Ministers will become more apparent and we will have had a view of policies, even if not of their implementation, over a wide range of Government activities. It would be idle to pretend that at present the Government is working smoothly and efficiently, but the fact remains that it is working, it is making its own decisions and it is surviving.

[NAA: A452, 1971/4151]

---

2   See Documents 384 & 390.

407   MINUTES OF STANDING IDC[1]

Canberra, 29 November 1972

CONFIDENTIAL

Minutes of the Ninth Meeting held on Wednesday 29 November 1972

Programme of Movement Towards Self-Government and Role of the Constitution Planning Committee

[*matter omitted*]

5.   Note was taken of the extremely large volume of work involved and some doubts were expressed as to whether all steps could be accomplished by the time set. Against this possibility the Department of External Territories is preparing a contingency plan which would involve a fairly simple amendment of the Papua New Guinea Act to transfer the decision-making authority from Commonwealth to PNG Ministers so as to achieve self-government. To formalise such an arrangement it would be necessary to pass legislation in the PNG House of Assembly in 1974 and in these circumstances self-government would be the actual state of things which existed at the time it was declared.

6.   The Committee took note of the attitude of the PNG Constitutional Planning Committee which, if it persisted, could cause delays.[2] The Committee however had not seen the draft programme and this would be done shortly in order to ensure that members fully appreciate what it is necessary to accomplish in the time available.

7.   The validity of some of the trade assumptions and the accelerated pace of the programme in the trade area were questioned. Could for example the PNG Government legally negotiate trade agreements before independence? The view was expressed this could be done through Australia and that it was not just a question of law.

National Interests Paper

[*matter omitted*]

10.   The relationship between the National Interests Paper and the general work of the Committee was mentioned. Written comments on the draft paper[3] had been requested from members of the Committee and some other Departments and the purpose of the meeting was to give an opportunity to exchange views so as to facilitate the submission of written comments.

[*matter omitted*]

12.   Views expressed at the meeting included:

(a)   the approach of the Department of External Territories was very much in favour of a special relations concept as it saw this as important to PNG achieving a status of independence as a viable state. It might not do this without considerable support. Reference was made to public announcements by the Minister for External Territories in his speech of 8th June 1972;[4]

---

1   On 18 May 1972 Cabinet had established a standing interdepartmental committee on Papua New Guinea (Document 296). For further details on the committee, see Document 399, fn. 1.

2   See Documents 388 & 393.

3   See Document 399.

4   Document 309. See also Document 285.

(b) Treasury did not feel able to support the general approach of the Department of External Territories on the extent of support necessary since it considers PNG needs to face up to the realities of independence.[5] In particular it does not subscribe to the views on aid in the draft paper which it regards as misdirected;

(c) Foreign Affairs considers the paper is weak in the aspects of security, defence, aid, immigration and trade;

(d) the Department of Defence has set up a special working group to define Australia's defence interests and their conclusions will need to be referred to the Defence Committee before being incorporated in the paper;

(e) the Department of Trade's representative supports the special relations concept though this is not necessarily a firm departmental view. The draft paper is not seen as breaking new ground but it does forego a number of issues some of which have wider obligations than Australia's relationship with Papua New Guinea, e.g. broad GATT[6] considerations.

13. It was *agreed* that the Departments concerned should supply their comments on the paper by the end of January 1973.

[*matter omitted*]

[NAA: A1838, 3080/11/1/2 PART 1]

---

5   See Document 329.

6   General Agreement on Tariffs and Trade.

408   LETTER FROM SOMARE TO PEACOCK

Konedobu, 29 November 1972

CONFIDENTIAL

In discussions on constitutional matters in Canberra on 12th October, 1972, the Defence Department agreed in principle that the Defence support staff should be relocated in the Chief Minister's office.[1] I understand that you are also in general agreement. It was further agreed that the next step was for Papua New Guinea and Australian officials to set down the terms of this relocation so that they might be considered by yourself and myself and endorsed in an exchange of letters.

Commonwealth and PNG officials have now met in Port Moresby and submitted the following as an appropriate basis on which the Defence Support staff might be re-located in the Chief Minister's Office:

A.   It is understood that the relocation does not affect the existing constitutional position in regard to defence matters. Until Independence Australia will continue to be fully responsible for final control over the defence of PNG and for the defence forces within the country. There will continue to be a need for close consultation between Commonwealth and PNG officials regarding both day-to-day defence matters in PNG and the development of defence policy and defence organisation for PNG in this period.

B.   The Administrator should continue to be able to call on the Defence Branch for advice as well as information unless, in any particular case, the Chief Minister, the Director of the Office of the Chief Minister or the Assistant Secretary (Defence) considers that this would be inconsistent with the primary loyalty of the Defence Branch to the Chief Minister.

C.   The Defence Branch will be subject to the Director of the Office of the Chief Minister. It will use normal Administration/Department of External Territories' channels of communication when communicating with the Commonwealth Department of Defence except in urgent cases. If normal channels are bypassed in an urgent case, the Director of the Office of Chief Minister will be informed of the substance of the communication as soon afterwards as practicable.

D.   The PNG Ministry will continue to look to the Administrator as well as the Office of the Chief Minister for advice on Defence matters. In this connection, and consistent with point B above, the Office of the Chief Minister will forward to the Administrator copies of any formal advice on Defence matters given to the Defence Spokesman.

E.   The Defence Spokesman and the Defence Branch should be able to seek information regarding normal activities of the Joint Force and advice on professional military matters (but not on policy matters) from the Commander, Joint Force. When the Commander gives such advice, he would inform the Administrator accordingly.

F.   The Commonwealth Government can be expected to consider sympathetically requests for the attachment of local service officers to the Defence Branch and for the involvement of local service officers in Defence studies and also in constitutional planning in PNG. Arrangements will be made for visits to PNG by local service officers undergoing Staff College Courses in Australia for these purposes. It is realized however, that these proposals may involve problems, in view of the obligations of service officers to their

---

1   Document 386. See also Document 359.

superior officers and to the final authority of the Commonwealth Government, although with good will and trust on both sides these problems should be overcome.

G.   Except in relation to the Defence Branch and advice from the Joint Force Commander these changes are not intended to affect the arrangements for the making of public or parliamentary statements by the Defence Spokesman set out in the Administrator's letter dated 27th September,[2] appointing the Chief Minister as Defence Spokesman.

H.   PNG Ministers and officials to whom Defence documents that are confidential to the Australian Government are given will of course respect the confidentiality of these documents.

I.   The Head of the Defence Branch should be seconded to the PNG Public Service for a period of 24 months or until Independence, whichever period is the shorter. The secondment should be on terms and conditions in no way inferior to his present position as a Commonwealth Public Servant.

These proposed arrangements are acceptable to the PNG Government. I would be glad to know whether they are acceptable to the Australian Government. I suggest that we might aim to implement the changeover from 1st December, 1972.

[NAA: A452, 1972/2801]

2   Not published.

409   RECORD OF DEFENCE COMMITTEE MEETING[1]

Canberra, 30 November 1972

SECRET

Defence Aspects of PNG Constitutional Developments

The Defence Committee noted the paper prepared by the Defence Department.[2] The report described the various aspects of military organisation, future functions and roles for a PNG Defence Force, Defence organisation and Australia's future national interest in Papua New Guinea which are under study with a view to subsequent discussion or negotiation as appropriate.

2.   Having regard to the short time that is available, the Committee stressed the urgency of opening up these matters in discussions with Papua New Guinea Ministers as soon as they are ready in the New Year. Such discussions would disseminate better understanding of Defence and military concepts and would help in ensuring that Australia's own Defence interests are adequately protected in future decisions by the Papua New Guinea Government.

3.   The Committee noted the importance and necessity for consideration by the Defence Committee at the earliest possible time to define the Australian Defence interests. Definition of these interests, as part of the totality of Australian interests in Papua New Guinea, is basic to preparations for consultations and policy negotiations with PNG Ministers. The Committee was informed that a paper covering these subjects is well advanced.

4.   In the interests of both Papua and New Guinea and Australia the Committee considered that it was essential that when discussions and negotiations on matters of substance took place with PNG Ministers, the sequence and timing should be fully coordinated, with the various subjects being seen as part of a coherent programme. For example the roles and size and shape of the both Defence forces and the Police will be closely related. In addition the Australian national interest that we will be seeking to protect will have an important bearing on the way these negotiations should be handled. It was agreed that the Department of External Territories should at all times be aware of the matters under negotiation.

5.   The Committee also noted the large number of practical problems in converting the Army and Naval components of the Joint Force PNG to a locally controlled and supported force. The Committee stressed the importance of rapid development of work already in progress by relevant Australian authorities. It was important to act quickly to simplify Australian standards and methods and to shorten prevailing administrative and financial procedures in order to make it feasible for the indigenous personnel to assume responsibility for procurement, personnel management and financial control.

6.   Arising from the need for simplification of procedures and the related urgency, the Defence Committee agreed that the Secretary, Department of Defence in consultation with the Secretaries of the three Service Departments should examine the feasibility of appointing, on a full time basis, a project officer who would seek to overcome these practical problems in consultation with the Treasury.

---

1   Those present at the meeting were Tange (Chair), Bunting, Waller, Hay, Admiral Sir Victor Smith (Chair, Chiefs of Staff Committee), Vice Admiral Sir Richard Peek (Chief of Naval Staff), Lt General Sir Mervyn Brogan (Chief of the General Staff), Air Marshal C. F. Read (Chief of the Air Staff), D. R. S. Craik (Representing the Secretary to the Treasury) and Bruce White (Department of the Army Secretary).

2   Document 401.

7.   The Committee drew attention to the urgent necessity to obtain from Ministers authority for the proposed Defence discussions with PNG Ministers and [for them] to indicate Australia's willingness to provide financial support for the PNG Defence Force. The Committee noted the importance of the Defence Representatives having the requisite degree of financial authority from the Australian Government. It was considered that the PNG Ministers will seek clarification of the financial position at the outset as financial consideration must be assumed to have considerable effect on the kind and level of Defence Force support facilities which they will wish to maintain. These force levels in turn will have an impact on certain Australian decisions (for example, on works development and location of bases) which, because of the lead time, must be taken without delay to satisfy post-independence requirements. The view was expressed that it would be preferable to make a defence subvention specifically nominated by Australia for that purpose. A further view was that a time limit should be put on Australia's initial defence support programmes.

8.   A further matter raised during discussions was the need for Visiting Forces Legislation to cover the position of Australian personnel in Papua New Guinea assisting the PNG Defence Forces after independence. It was noted that there was no specific reference to this requirement in the section of the Report dealing with legislation (Attachment A paragraph 2 f).[3] The matter would be brought to the attention of the Army, who are responsible for this work.

9.   The Committee agreed that it would be timely to remind all engaged in defining the areas requiring policy decision by the PNG Government of the highly sensitive nature of the studies. It was essential that the preparatory work be done to enable formal consultations to be opened by senior personnel from Canberra. Because PNG Ministers were very sensitive about their responsibilities, preparatory work must be carried out with the utmost discretion.

[NAA: A452, 1973/470]

---

3   Not published

410   PRESS RELEASE

Port Moresby, 3 December 1972

Chief Minister Congratulates ALP

The Chief Minister, Mr Michael Somare made the following statement on the change of government in Australia.

'I offer Mr Gough Whitlam and the ALP my sincerest congratulations.

'I know that our two Governments will be able to work together, in the same spirit that has been established with Mr Peacock and the Liberals during the past nine months.

'Mr Whitlam can justifiably claim some of the credit for the recent changes of Australian policy towards Papua New Guinea, after his visits to our country in 1969 and 1971.

'Each time I visited Australia officially I made sure that I spoke to both the Liberals and the Opposition Leader.

'And when Mr Whitlam came to Papua New Guinea he made a point of meeting with some of our present Government leaders and myself.

'I believe those meetings will pay off now, as I think there is already a great deal of understanding established between us.

'Of course I regret the loss of a dynamic and proven Minister for External Territories, Mr Andrew Peacock, but I suspect that even with a Liberal Government, Mr Peacock would not have held the Territories portfolio after the elections.'

[NAA: A1838, 3080/11/6/2 PART 1]

411   CABLEGRAM TO CANBERRA

Port Moresby, 6 December 1972

049. UNCLASSIFIED

PNG Relations with Australia

Following is text of comments made yesterday (5 December) by Chief Minister on PNG/ Australia relations in response to questions submitted in advance by Post Courier and ABC:

Have you any comment on Mr Whitlam's statement that he would take Foreign Affairs himself as Prime Minister, and would probably include Papua New Guinea as part of that portfolio?

Answer:

I will be only too pleased to have Mr Whitlam attend to Papua New Guinea affairs himself as part of the Foreign Affairs portfolio. I believe that this will give us in Papua New Guinea a strong voice in Canberra and the Australian Cabinet. It will be the first time that PNG has been recognised as a really important issue in Australia, for although the past Minister, Mr Peacock, gave us every representation he could, and did that very successfully he always laboured under the disadvantage that he was not a Cabinet Minister, and must seek Cabinet approval in matters that concerned our country from outside the Cabinet room. Who is there better to represent us than the Australian Prime Minister himself? Specially a Prime Minister, who, as an Opposition Leader visited Papua New Guinea in '69 and '71, when this country was not in fashion in Australia.

Will you be seeking a confirmation on the ALP commitment when it was in Opposition for a five year development grant for PNG if it came to power?

Answer:

Yes. We have always had trouble planning our development in PNG while we are unsure of the Australian commitment to us over a period of time. It has always been difficult to produce a really meaningful five year development plan under these circumstances. I believe there are many things that we have to discuss with the new Government in Australia and I will hope to be going to Australia to meet with Mr Whitlam in the New Year.

Have you any comment on the present situation in regard to the new Government in Australia in view of ALP statements in the past that PNG would be given self-government immediately and independence within the life of the present Australian Government ... i.e. before 1975.

Answer:

I am certain that our two governments will be able to work out these issues together. These are two of the matters that I will be bringing up with Mr Whitlam at the first opportunity.

[NAA: A452, 3080/1/11]

412   CABLEGRAM TO NEW YORK

Canberra, 6 December 1972

9849. UNCLASSIFIED

Papua New Guinea

Following is an extract from the transcript of a press conference given yesterday (5 December) by the Prime Minister, Mr Whitlam, on the subject of Australia's relations with Papua New Guinea:

Reporter: Twenty six nations today moved a resolution in the Trusteeship Committee of the United Nations calling for Australia to prepare a new timetable on independence for Papua New Guinea. Australia as late as November 20 gave a timetable saying this would come in December 1973. Do you propose to update this?

Mr Whitlam: Events are moving so quickly in Papua New Guinea that it is not inconceivable that that date of December 1973 could be reached. It is altogether probable that Papua New Guinea will be fully independent and, one trusts, admitted to both the United Nations and the Commonwealth of Nations before less than two years—no more than two years from now. You know that Mr Somare has sent a message to me.[1] This is a matter where I can repeat what I said in the Parliament—what Mr Somare himself believes—that the term as Minister for External Territories of Mr Andrew Peacock made the development of, or the progress towards independence in Papua New Guinea, very much easier than any of us could have expected.

[*matter omitted*]

[NAA: A1838, 3036/10/6/2 PART 1]

---

1   Possibly a reference to Somare's statement of 3 December (Document 410).

413   TELEX TO CANBERRA

Port Moresby, 7 December 1972

976. Unclassified

At his press conference this morning the Chief Minister, Mr Somare, said that the result of the Australian elections 'would not affect us much in any way at all, whether we have to deal with a Liberal or an ALP Govt'.

Mr Somare said that he had high hopes of the new Govt. One of the matters to arise with the new Govt would be future aid to PNG. Referring to fears expressed in the past that a Labour [*sic*] Govt would try to pull out of PNG as quickly as possible, Mr Somare said 'I am quite confident that the Labour Govt would do the same as the Liberal Govt—they will consult us on any major decision.'

His impression from talking to Mr Whitlam in the past was that, if anything the Labour Govt would be more receptive to overseas aid and needs. As an Opposition Leader Mr Whitlam had said that he would consider PNG's request for aid over a five-year period so that this Govt could operate on a definite budget for its five-year development plans. Mr Somare said that this was one of the matters he would raise with the Australian Govt when he went to Australia in the New Year.

Mr Somare emphasised that it would be a good thing for this country to be elevated to Foreign Affairs portfolio. The former Minister for External Territories had done an excellent job and he got this country going at this pace. But not being a Cabinet Minister he had to push his way all the time for this country. He was pretty sure that now since the portfolio was in the hands of the Prime Minister himself PNG would be better represented in the Australian Cabinet.

Referring to Mr Whitlam's statement about independence and UN membership for PNG by 1975, Mr Somare said that it was significant that Mr Whitlam did not say at Tuesday's Press Conference in Canberra that his Govt would impose on this country independence in 1975. He was glad that Mr Whitlam did not say that—he only said that he saw it as a possibility.

Mr Somare said that the UN Trusteeship Council had called on Australia, in consultation with PNG Govt, to set a date for independence and he wanted to make it quite clear that 'any independence date should be set by the people of this country and that the date would have to be endorsed by the House of Assembly—it is not a decision that should be made by anyone else but for the moment I believe that we should cross each bridge as we come to them. We have to get over the hurdle of self-government before we can set any rigid date for independence.'

He would be seeking Mr Whitlam's 'real opinion' on this matter during his visit to Canberra. Mr Somare said he saw the main opposition to independence in this country as political and psychological and not as a matter of capability. He believed that they would continue towards self-government and eventual independence in consultation with the Australian Government and he was sure that the Opposition Leaders of Australia and PNG would be able to work together well.

Answering questions by the press Mr Somare said that he was unable to specify a date for independence for PNG and said that it would come as a normal process. Asked if Mr Whitlam's forecast was too ambitious, Mr Somare replied that this was something on which he would really like to get Mr Whitlam's opinion. Mr Whitlam had made his statement during a period of excitement after becoming the new Prime Minister. And after 23 years of Labour being in the Opposition. The press did not give him time to be able to think what was coming next.

He did not think that Mr Whitlam would thrust independence on PNG without consultations with its leaders. On the question of aid Mr Somare said his approach to Mr Whitlam, when he met him in January, would be to find out whether the Labour Govt could guarantee aid over a five or a three year period to meet PNG's planning and budgetary requirements.

Mr Somare said that it would be premature to discuss the question of [the] Queensland–PNG border with Mr Whitlam at this stage—but he was sure the question would come up when Mr Whitlam had settled down and appointed his new Ministry. It was very difficult at this stage to predict anything or say anything. He ruled out the possibility of a three-way discussion between PNG, Australia and Queensland Govts because the border was a Commonwealth responsibility.

Mr Somare said that he would like to be able to visit some South East Asian and Pacific countries next year—countries mentioned were Indonesia, Japan, Fiji, Western Samoa and Tonga.

[NAA: A452, 1973/39]

Appendixes

APPENDIX I

Biographical Guide

This guide includes brief details on the roles of most of the individuals referred to a number of times in this volume. Individuals mentioned only once or twice are generally not included. Details on these latter individuals are in most instances provided in the document in which they are mentioned, or else in a footnote. Some entries are incomplete because of gaps in the available records.

Abal, Tei
MHA for Wabag and Ministerial Member for Agriculture, Stocks and Fisheries, 1968–72; Chair of Compass Party

Anderson, H. D. (David)
First Assistant Secretary, Asia Division, Department of Foreign Affairs, 1970–71

Anthony, John Douglas (Doug)
Minister for Primary Industry, 1967–71; Deputy Prime Minister and Minister for Trade and Industry, 1971–72

Ashwin, C. R. (Robin)
Head, Trusteeship Section and then Assistant Secretary, Department of External Affairs, 1970–71; Deputy Permanent Representative and Minister to United Nations, 1971–73

Bailey, Kenneth, Sir
Special Adviser on International Law to Attorney-General's Department and Department of External Affairs/Foreign Affairs, 1970–72

Bailey, Peter
First Assistant Secretary, Department of the Cabinet Office, 1968–71; Deputy Secretary, Department of Prime Minister and Cabinet, 1971–77

Ballard, J. O. (John)
First Assistant Secretary, Government and Legal Affairs Division, Department of External Territories, 1970–71

Barnes, C. E. (Charles Edward)
Minister for Territories, 1963–68; Minister for External Territories, 1968–72

Barnett, Thomas E. (Tos)
First Assistant Secretary, PNG Administration, 1972; Legal and Constitutional Adviser to PNG Chief Minister, 1972

Beazley, Kim. E.
ALP MP for Fremantle, 1945–77

Besley, M. A (Tim)
First Assistant Secretary, Central Secretariat Division, Department of External Territories, 1968–73

Bilas, Angmai
MHA for Mabuso and Ministerial Member for Trade and Industry, 1966–72; MHA for Madang 1972–75

Blakeney, F. J. (Fred)
First Assistant Secretary, Defence Division, Department of Foreign Affairs, 1972–74

Blakers, G. E. (Gordon)   Deputy Secretary, Department of Defence, 1963–78

Border, Lewis Harold (Lew)   First Assistant Secretary, Management Services, DFA, 1970–1971; Deputy Secretary B, DFA, from July 1971

Borthwick, A. H. (Alex)   Assistant Secretary, Pacific, Department of Foreign Affairs, 1971–72

Bowen, Nigel   Minister for Education and Science, 1969–71; Attorney-General, March–August 1971; Minister for Foreign Affairs, 1971–72

Bunting, Sir John   Secretary, Department of Prime Minister, 1959–68; Secretary, Department of the Cabinet Office, 1968–71; Secretary, Department of Prime Minister and Cabinet, 1971–74

Bunting, R. (Bob)   Deputy District Commissioner, Morobe District, from June 1968; District Commissioner, West Sepik District from July 1971.

Burns, R. A. (Ross)   Trusteeship Section, Department of Foreign Affairs, 1971–72; Foreign Affairs Liaison Officer, Port Moresby, 1972–73

Bury, Leslie (Les)   Treasurer, 1969–71; Minister for Foreign Affairs, March–August 1971

Chan, Julius   MHA for Namatanai 1968–72; PNG Minister for Finance, 1972–77

Conroy, W. L. (Bill)   Director, Agriculture, Stock and Fisheries, Department of the Administrator, Port Moresby, 1970–72

Curtis, L. J. (Lindsay)   Secretary for Law in the PNG Administration, 1970.

Eldridge, Brigadier R. T. (Ralph)   Commander, PNG Command, February 1969–72; Commander Joint Task Force, January–April 1972

Ellis, T. W. (Tom)   Secretary, Department of the Administrator, 1970–73

Emanuel, Errol John (Jack)   District Commissioner, East New Britain, 1969–71

Fairbairn, David   Minister for Defence, 1971–72

Forbes, A. J. (Jim)   Minister for Immigration, 1971–72

Fraser, J. M. (Malcolm)   Minister for Defence, 1969–71; Minister for Education and Science, 1971–72

Furlonger, Robert (Bob).   Director, Joint Intelligence Organisation, 1969–72; Ambassador to Jakarta, 1972–75

Galvin, P. J. (Pat)   Assistant Secretary, Defence and International Relations, Department of External Territories, 1970–71; Assistant Secretary, office in Port Moresby, 1972–74

Giregire, Sinake   MHA for Daulo, 1968–72

Gorton, John Grey	Prime Minister, 1968–71; Minister for Defence, March–August 1971
Granger, W. (Bill)	Head, International Relations Section, Department of External Territories, 1969–72
Greenwell, J. H. (John)	First Assistant Secretary, Government and Legal Affairs Division, Department of External Territories, 1971–73
Greenwood, Ivor	Attorney-General, 1971–72
Guise, John	MHA for Alotau and Speaker of the House of Assembly, 1968–72; Deputy-Chief Minister of Papua New Guinea and Minister for the Interior (later Agriculture), 1972–75
Gutman, G. O. (Gerry)	First Assistant Secretary, Economic Affairs Division, Department of External Territories, 1965–72
Harders, C. W. (Clarrie)	Secretary, Attorney-General's Department, 1970–79
Hay, D. O. (David)	Administrator of Papua New Guinea, 1967–70; Secretary, Department of External Territories, 1970–73
Heinrich, H. G.	Assistant Secretary, International Relations, Treasury, 1969–73
Hennessy, L. F.	Assistant Secretary, Social Development Branch, Department of External Territories, 1970–73
Hewitt, C. L. (Lenox)	Secretary, Department of the Prime Minister, 1968–71
Hogue, Cavan	Director, Trusteeship Section, Department of Foreign Affairs, 1971–73
Hughes, R. L. (Ron), Major General	Director, Joint Staff, Department of Defence, 1971–72
Hughes, T. E. F. (Tom)	Attorney-General, 1961–71
Jephcott, Bruce	MHA for Madang regional and Minister for Transport, 1972–75
Jockel, G. A. (Gordon)	Ambassador to Indonesia, 1969–72; Director, Joint Intelligence Organisation, 1972–77
Johnson, Les	Assistant Administrator of Papua New Guinea (Services), 1966–70; Administrator, 1970–73
Kapena, Toua	MHA for Hiri and Ministerial Member for Labour, 1968–72
Kaputin, John	MHA for Rabaul, 1972–75; Member of the Constitutional Planning Committee
Kavali, Thomas	MHA for Jimi and Minister for Works, 1972–75
Kearney, Bill	Senior legal officer and, from circa 1971, Secretary for Law in the PNG Administration

Kelloway, Paul	Assistant Secretary, Economic Policy and Research Branch, Department of External Territories, 1970–73
Kereku, Damien	MHA for East New Britain, 1972–75; Chairman of Mataungan Association
Kerr, A. G. (Alan)	Officer in Charge, Government and Constitution Section, Department of External Territories, 1970; Assistant Secretary, Government Branch, Department of External Territories, 1971–73
Kiki, Albert Maori (Maori)	Secretary/Treasurer of Pangu Pati (Party); MHA for Moresby Inland and Minister for Lands and Environment, 1972–75
Lapun, Paul	MHA for South Bougainville, 1968–75; Minister for Mines, 1972–75
Leahy, Thomas Joseph (Tom)	MHA for Markham and Spokesman for Administrator's Executive Council, 1968–72
Lokoloko, Tore	MHA for Gulf regional, 1968–75
Lussick, Walter	MHA for Manus and New Ireland regional, 1968–72
McDonald, Colin	Foreign Affairs Adviser, International Affairs Branch, Department of the Administrator; Head of PNG's DFA Section, 1972–74
McEwen, John (Jack), Sir	Deputy Prime Minister, 1958–71; Minister for Trade and Industry, 1963–71
McIntyre, Sir Laurence	Ambassador and Permanent Representative to the United Nations, 1970–75
McMahon, William (Billy)	Minister for Foreign Affairs, 1969–71; Prime Minister, 1971–72
Mentz, Don	Assistant Secretary, Production and Trade Branch, Department of External Territories, 1970–72
Middlemiss, Barry	Secretary *Napidakoe Navitu*, 1971–72
Middleton, John Maxwell	MHA for Sumkar, 1968–72
Mola, Donatus	MHA for North Bougainville, 1968–75
Momis, John, Father	MHA for Bougainville regional, 1972–75
Moodie, Colin	First Assistant Secretary, Pacific and Western Division, Department of Foreign Affairs, 1971–72
Morgan, Leo	Assistant Executive Officer, Administrator's Executive Council, 1972
Newman, A. P. J. (Tony)	Assistant Administrator of Papua New Guinea (Economic Affairs), 1968–70; Official Member of Administrator's Executive Council, 1968–72; Deputy Administrator, 1970–73

Nicholls, N. A. M. (Norm), Brigadier	PNG Police Commissioner, 1970–73
Norrie, J. W. (Jim), Brigadier	Commander, PNG Joint Force, 1972–73
Oala-Rarua, Oala	MHA for Central regional and Assistant Ministerial Member for Treasury, 1968–72
Olewale, N. E. (Ebia)	MHA for South Fly 1968–72
Parao, Anton	MHA for Western Highlands, 1972–75
Peacock, Andrew	Minister for the Army, 1969–72; Minister for External Territories, February–December 1972
Pearsall, Stan	Assistant Secretary, Secretariat Services, Department of the Administrator.
Percival, R. J. (Ray)	Assistant Secretary, Pacific Branch, Department of Foreign Affairs, 1972–73
Pitoi, Sere	Chairman, PNG Public Service Board, 1970–73
Poyser, L. G.	Deputy Secretary, Department of Defence
Randall, Sir Richard (Dick)	Secretary, the Treasury, 1966–1971
Reiher, A. S. (Alan)	Director–General, Department of Works, 1967–1973
Ryan, Paul	Director, Office of the Chief Minister and Secretary to Cabinet, 1972–73
Scully, James (Jim)	First Assistant Secretary, Secondary Industry Operations Division, Department of Trade and Industry, 1969–72; Deputy Secretary, 1972–75
Shann, K. C. O. (Mick)	Deputy Secretary, Department of Foreign Affairs, 1970–74
Sinclair, Ian	Minister for Primary Industry, 1971–72
Smith, Vice-Admiral Sir Victor	Chair, Chiefs of Staff Committee, 1971 to 1972; Chief of Naval Staff; member Defence Committee.
Snedden, Billy Mackie	Minister Labour and National Service, 1969–71; Treasurer, 1971–72
Somare, M. T. (Michael)	MHA for East Sepik regional 1968–72; Founding Member and Parliamentary Leader of Pangu Party, 1968–88; Chief Minister of Papua New Guinea, 1972–75
Synnot, S. M. (Tony), Rear Admiral	Deputy Chief of Naval Staff, Department of Defence, 1970–74
Tammur, Oscar	MHA for Kokopo, 1968–75; Convener of Mataungan Association

Tange, Sir Arthur	Secretary, Department of Defence, 1970–79
Taureka, Reuben	MHA for Rigo-Abau and Minister for Health, 1972–75
Toliman, Matthias	MHA for Gazelle and Ministerial Member for Education and Training, 1968–72; re-elected 1972; Opposition Leader 1972–73
Unkles, Gerald	Chairman, PNG Public Service Board, 1969–70
Voutas, Anthony (Tony)	MHA for Morobe, 1966–72; Founding Member of Pangu Pati, 1968; Principal Adviser, Chief Minister's Office, 1972–74
John Wakeford	District Commissioner, West Sepik District, late 1960s to mid–1971
Waller, Sir Keith	Secretary, Department of External Affairs/Foreign Affairs, 1970–74
Warwick Smith, George	Secretary, Department of External Territories, 1968–70; Secretary, Department of the Interior, 1970–72
Webb, N. L. (Nick)	Assistant Secretary, Defence Department; Defence Branch, PNG Administration, 1972
Wheeler, Sir Frederick	Chairman, Public Service Board, 1961–71; Secretary, Department of the Treasury, 1971–79
White, Bruce	Secretary, Department of the Army, 1958–73
Whitelaw, Brigadier John	Director, Military Operations and Plans, Department of Defence, 1971–73
Whitelaw, R. J.	First Assistant Secretary, Overseas Economic Relations Division, Department of the Treasury, 1969–75
Whitlam, E. G. (Gough)	Leader of the Australian Labor Party, 1967–79; Opposition Leader, 1967–72, 1975–79; Prime Minister, 1972–75; Minister for Foreign Affairs, 1972–73
Whitrod, R. W. (Ray)	Commissioner of PNG Police Force, 1969–70
Wilton, General Sir John	Chair, Chiefs of Staff Committee, 1966–70
Yocklunn, J.	Private Secretary to Chief Minister, 1972
Yuwi, Matiabe	MHA for Tari, 1968–72

APPENDIX II

A Guide to the Records Cited in this Volume

The great majority of the documents in this volume are held on files that are available through the National Archives of Australia (NAA). An application for special access will be required with respect to some of these files because they have not been assessed and cleared for public viewing.

The following list is not exhaustive, including only files from the NAA from which documents have been sourced. The NAA contains additional valuable material on Australia's policies on Papua New Guinea in the early 1970s.

Files held by the NAA are identified by four elements. First is the series number with a letter indicating which regional office registered the series (A stands for the Australian Capital Territory), e.g. **A1838**, the main correspondence file for the Department of External Affairs/ Department of Foreign Affairs. Information on series numbers, such as the controlling government agency and a generic title, can be accessed using the record search function on the NAA website at www.naa.gov.au.

The second element is the file number (control symbol). This varies in type from single numbers, as used in Cabinet Office files (e.g. A5873, **484**) to multiple numbers, as frequently used by the Department of External Affairs/Department of Foreign Affairs (e.g. A1838, **3080/11/2/1**).

The third element is the part number. Some file numbers run to many parts, and are identified in this volume accordingly (e.g. A1838, 3034/10/1/8 **PART 2**; A1209, 1968/9698 **PART 3**)

The final element is the barcode allocated to each file held in the NAA. In the following documents these are listed in italics after the file titles (e.g. A1838, 3080/5/2 PART 2, Papua New Guinea—Judicial and Constitutional—Constitutional Development **[558255]**).

Department of External Affairs/Department of Foreign Affairs

A1838—Correspondence files, multiple number series, 1914–1989

689/1 PART 6	Papua and New Guinea—General [*1727612*]
689/2 PART 7	Papua New Guinea Defence Forces [*1755763*]
689/3/1 PART 7	Papua New Guinea Intelligence Committee Policy—General [*1728247*]
752/1/23/1 PART 4	Indonesia—Papua New Guinea–Indonesia Land Border Regime Negotiations [*558555*]
846/1/6 PART 1	Papua New Guinea—Relations with Australia—Bougainville Copper Agreements [*1553102*]
936/1/3/1 PART 1	Australian Territories—Policy Paper—PNG [Papua New Guinea] Policy Planning Group Paper—March 1971 [*546782*]

936/13/28	Prime Minister's Visit to Papua New Guinea—July 1970 [*573603*]
936/13/29	Papua New Guinea—Visits and Seminars—Visits by Departmental Representatives [*546882*]
936/3/21 PART 2	Papua New Guinea—Military Aid to the Civil Power [*546832*]
936/3/21 PART 3	Papua New Guinea—Military Aid to the Civil Power [*546833*]
936/3/21 PART 4	Papua New Guinea—Military Aid to the Civil Power [*546834*]
936/3/5 PART 2	Papua New Guinea—Ministerial Policy Statements [*574171*]
936/30/2 PART 1	Territories Papua New Guinea—Relations with ANZUS [*589277*]
936/4/13	Papua New Guinea—Political Development—Bougainville Separation Movement [*546847*]
936/4/16 PART 3	Papua New Guinea—Political Developments—Disturbances in Rabaul—1969 [*546851*]
936/4/16 PART 5	Papua New Guinea—Political Developments—Disturbances in Rabaul [*546853*]
936/4/16 PART 6	Papua New Guinea—Political Developments—Disturbances in Rabaul [*546854*]
936/4/17 PART 1	Territory of Papua New Guinea—Political—Report of Select Committee on Constitutional Development—1971 [*573522*]
936/5/5	Papua New Guinea—Scheme for Commonwealth-Backed Employment of Administration Officers [*580683*]
3034/10/1/8 PART 2	Indonesia—Relations with Australia—Official Discussions with Indonesia [*550464*]
3036/10/6/2 PART 1	West Irian—Relations with Australia in Papua New Guinea—Australian Relations with Indonesia in West Irian and Papua New Guinea [*1509586*]
3036/10/6/5 PART 1	West Irian—Relations with Australia in New Guinea—Political Consultations between DFA and Administration of Papua New Guinea [*1509593*]
3080/1/1 PART 2	Papua New Guinea—Political Situation—General—National [*551170*]
3080/1/1/1 PART 1	Papua New Guinea—Policy towards Secessionist or Autonomist Movements [*558146*]

3080/1/6 PART 1	Papua New Guinea—Political—Ministerial Statements on Independence [*558171*]
3080/1/11	Papua New Guinea—Political—Papua New Guinea Government Statements on General Policy [*558178*]
3080/1/11 PART 2	Papua New Guinea—Political—Papua New Guinea Government Statements on General Policy [*558180*]
3080/1/2/3	Papua New Guinea—Political Situation—Bougainville [*551198*]
3080/1/2/3 PART 1	Papua New Guinea—Political Situation—Papua—General [*551201*]
3080/4/4	Papua New Guinea—Defence and Security—Military Aid to Civil Power [*551296*]
3080/5/2 PART 2	Papua New Guinea—Judicial and Constitutional—Constitutional Development [*558255*]
3080/10/1 PART 1	Papua New Guinea—Relations with Australia—Transitional Arrangements up to Independence—Australian Policy on Transfer of Power [*548486*]
3080/10/1 PART 2	Papua New Guinea—Relations with Australia—Transitional Arrangements up to Independence—Australian Policy on Transfer of Power [*548487*]
3080/10/2 PART 1	Papua New Guinea—Relations with Australia—Transitional Arrangements up to Independence to Transfer of Commonwealth Assets in Papua New Guinea [*548498*]
3080/10/4/7 PART 1	Papua New Guinea—Relations with Australia—Role of Department of Foreign Affairs—Papua New Guinea Correspondence by Minister and Secretary [*558410*]
3080/11/1 PART 1	Papua New Guinea—Relations with Australia—Permanent Arrangements—Australian Policy Towards Papua New Guinea [*548533*]
3080/11/1/2 PART 1	Papua New Guinea—Australian Relations with Papua New Guinea—Permanent Arrangements—Australian Policy Towards Papua New Guinea (PNG) Australian Government Policy Coordinating Committee [*548538*]
3080/11/1/2 PART 2	Papua New Guinea—Australian Relations with Papua New Guinea—Permanent Arrangements—Australian Policy towards Papua New Guinea—Papua New Guinea—Australian Government Policy Coordinating Committee [*548539*]

3080/11/2/1	Papua New Guinea—Relations with Australia—Permanent Arrangements—Australia–Papua New Guinea Relations—General—Australia—Papua New Guinea Border [*548550*]
3080/11/2/1 PART 2	Papua New Guinea—Relations with Australia—Permanent Arrangements—Australia–Papua New Guinea Relations—General—Australia—Papua New Guinea Border [*548552*]
3080/11/6/2 PART 1	Papua New Guinea—Attitude of Australia Political Parties—Australia Labor Party [*558470*]
3080/16/2 PART 2	Papua New Guinea—Visits to Papua New Guinea by Departmental Representatives [*548620*]

A9334—Correspondence files, multiple number series (first uniform post system), Port Moresby, 1972–

| 201/1/4 PART 1 | Papua New Guinea Internal Affairs—Constitutional Planning Committee and Papua New Guinea Constitution [*11333534*] |
| 201/1/2/3 PART 2 | Constitutional Conference—General—October 1972 [*30916963*] |

Department of External Territories

A452—Correspondence files, annual single number series, 1910–76

1961/3329 PART 5	Aid to the Civil Power in the Territory of Papua New Guinea [*1111068*]
1961/3329 PART 7	Aid to the Civil Power in the Territory of Papua New Guinea [*1111072*]
1970/0240	Dossier on Visit of Mr Whitlam to Papua New Guinea—December 1969 to January 1970 [*5036833*]
1970/0637	Visit to Papua New Guinea by Mr G Whitlam and Party—December 1969 to January 1970—political effects [*12227256*]
1970/1327	Implications of Self-government for Papua New Guinea, 1972 [*3121947*]
1970/1335	Preparation and Release of Ministerial and Departmental Press Releases [*32757248*]
1970/1453	Citizenship of Residents of the Territory of Papua New Guinea [*4027667*]
1970/1645	Papua New Guinea Constitutional Development—Budget Strategy [*32757313*]
1970/1716	Notes for the Minister for Possible Questions in Parliament 1970 [*32757342*]

1970/1825	Papua New Guinea House of Assembly, 1969—Select Committee on Constitutional Development [*3122108*]
1970/1867	Policy re Political Development in Papua New Guinea [*3122112*]
1970/2031	Minister's Speech at Opening of PSA [Public Service Association] Congress 2 May 1970, Port Moresby [*32757403*]
1970/2505	Papua and New Guinea Currency [*5036830*]
1970/2570	Policy re Political Development in Papua New Guinea [*3122128*]
1970/2973	Prime Minister's Visit to Papua New Guinea July 1970—Security Arrangements [*3122132*]
1970/3045	Implications of Self-government for Papua/New Guinea—1972 [*3122142*]
1970/3046	Implications of Self-government for Papua/New Guinea—1972 [*3122147*]
1970/3199	Extension of Local Government in the Gazelle Peninsula [*3112308*]
1970/3202	Review of Immigration Policy—Papua New Guinea [*32757597*]
1970/3536	Report by Administrator, Papua New Guinea on his Visit to the Gazelle Peninsula—5–7 August 1970 [*32757666*]
1970/3718	Transfer of Responsibility to Ministerial Member for Labour, Papua New Guinea [*32757698*]
1970/3761	Size and Role of Royal Papua New Guinea Constabulary [*12166828*]
1970/3808	Defence Services Aid to the Civil Power in Papua New Guinea [*3125879*]
1970/3823	Inter-departmental Committee on the Transfer of Functions of Internal Self-government from Commonwealth Agencies to Papua New Guinea Administration—Policy [*32757720*]
1970/3961	Papua New Guinea Constitutional Changes Following from Prime Minister's Speech, 6 July 1970 [*5036851*]
1970/4193	Review of Defence Forces in Papua/New Guinea [*3125925*]
1970/4297	Defence Services Aid to the Civil Power in Papua/New Guinea [*3125963*]
1970/4523 PART 8	Papua New Guinea Act [*12103268*]

1970/460	Policy re Political Development in Papua New Guinea [*3121863*]
1970/4671	Formation of Papua New Guinea Intelligence Committee [*3122199*]
1970/4769	United Nations General Assembly—25th Session [*32757903*]
1970/4962	Papua New Guinea House of Assembly—Select Committee on Constitutional Development [*3122208*]
1970/4963	Reports on Papua New Guinea Political Parties [*3122743*]
1970/5267	Policy re political development in Papua New Guinea [*3122760*]
1970/5345	Papua New Guinea Select Committee on Constitutional Development Progress Reports on 2nd Territory Tour 1971 [*32758013*]
1970/5535	Papua and New Guinea—Status of Papua [*4027845*]
1971/0004	Dossier on Visit of Mr Whitlam to Papua New Guinea, January 1971 [*32758068*]
1971/0268	Policy Brief for the United Nations Visiting Mission to Papua New Guinea 1971 [*32758098*]
1971/0514	Policy on Selection of a Method of Expressing Majority Opinion on Constitutional Issues [*32758121*]
1971/0674	Inter-department Committee on the Transfer of Internal Self-government from Commonwealth Agencies to Papua New Guinea Administration Policy [*32758133*]
1971/0729	Establishment of a Papua New Guinea Diplomatic Service [*32758143*]
1971/1003	United Nations Visiting Mission to the Trust Territory of New Guinea, 1971 [*3122885*]
1971/1076	Outward Cablegrams to the Australian Mission to the United Nations [*3122890*]
1971/1077	Inward Cablegrams from the Australian Mission to the United Nations [*3122892*]
1971/1169	Administrative Arrangements (vesting of powers) Ordinance—Papua New Guinea [*32758192*]
1971/1463	Administrators [*sic*] Executive Council—Departmental Correspondence [*32758217*]
1971/1619	Defence Services Aid to the Civil Power in Papua New Guinea [*3125924*]

1971/1664   Future Development of the Army in Papua New
                   Guinea—Departmental Administration [*32758246*]

1971/1916   Citizenship of Residents of Papua New Guinea
                   [*11998395*]

1971/1981   Comments on the Conclusions and Recommendations of
                   the Report by the 1971 United Nations Visiting Mission
                   to Papua New Guinea [*32758276*]

1971/1995   Administrators [*sic*] Statement on National Unity—
                   Papua New Guinea [*32758278*]

1971/2098   Daily Cabled Situation Reports to New York—(38th
                   Trusteeship Council) [*32758287*]

1971/2292   38th Session of the United Nations Trusteeship Council
                   [*32758305*]

1971/2294   Papua New Guinea Law and Order Problems in the
                   Gazelle Peninsula [*3123009*]

1971/2303   Invitation for a United Nations Mission to Observe the
                   1972 Elections in Papua New Guinea [*32758306*]

1971/2323   Papua New Guinea National Unity [*11340887*]

1971/2342   Papua/New Guinea Law and Order Problems in the
                   Gazelle Peninsula [*3123027*]

1971/2441   Resolution of the Papua New Guinea House of Assembly
                   Regarding Commonwealth Parliamentary Committee to
                   Determine Wishes of Papuan People [*32758318*]

1971/2629   Confrontation between the Mataungan Association and
                   Police at Rabaul, July 1971 [*3123047*]

1971/2647   Inter-departmental Committee on Transfer of
                   International Self Government from Commonwealth
                   Agencies to Papua New Guinea—Administration
                   [*32758337*]

1971/2739   Preparation of a Plan for Internal Self-government by
                   Use of Critical Path Method—Papua New Guinea
                   (Gearing-up Plan) [*3123060*]

1971/280   Inter-departmental Committee on Internal Security
                   Arrangements after Self-government [*3122770*]

1971/2802   Establishment of a Papua New Guinea Diplomatic
                   Service [*32758353*]

1971/2828   Defence Services Aid to the Civil Power in Papua New
                   Guinea [*3125930*]

1971/297   Preparation of Briefs by the DOET (Department of
                   External Territories) on Mr Whitlam's visits to Papua
                   New Guinea, January 1971 [*3122775*]

1971/3543	Policy re Political Development in Papua New Guinea—PART 14 [*3123226*]
1971/3550	Preparation of a Plan for Internal Self-government by Use of Critical Path Method—Papua New Guinea—Gearing-up Plan [*3123231*]
1971/3895	Representation to the Minister by Mr K E Beazley regarding Social Condition in Bougainville [*32758460*]
1971/3941	Secondment of Australian Police to the Royal Papua New Guinea Constabulary [*32758466*]
1971/3947	Localisation in Public Service of Papua New Guinea Policy and Principles [*32758469*]
1971/4011	Citizenship of Residents of Papua New Guinea [*32758472*]
1971/4151	Visit to Papua New Guinea by the Minister Mr Morrison—4 to 8 January 1973 [*32758487*]
1971/4971	Working Group on Papua New Guinea Currency [*32758561*]
1971/888	Policy re Political Development in Papua New Guinea [*3122837*]
1972/0235	Britain and the EEC (European Economic Community)—Representations on Behalf of Papua New Guinea [*32758585*]
1972/0588	Papua New Guinea Increase in the Crime Rate [*11153233*]
1972/0932	Papua New Guinea Political Development 1972 [*32758652*]
1972/1079	Inter-departmental Committee on Internal Security Arrangements after Self-government—Papua New Guinea [*3123606*]
1972/1111	Future Size, Shape and Role of the Papua New Guinea Armed Forces [*3123608*]
1972/1169	6th Waigani Seminar—Port Moresby—30 April to 5 May 1972 [*32758679*]
1972/1220	Papua New Guinea Act [*32758688*]
1972/1506	Standing Committee of Cabinet on Papua New Guinea [*32758735*]
1972/1668	Meeting of Papua New Guinea House of Assembly—April 1972 [*32758749*]
1972/1993	Australia's Interest in Relation to an Independent Papua New Guinea—PART 2 [*3123658*]

1972/2015	The Question of an Act of Self-determination for Papua New Guinea [*32758788*]
1972/2263	RPNGC (Royal Papua New Guinea Constabulary)—Action Taken Subsequent to Report on Police Strength [*32758808*]
1972/2310	Application by Indonesia to Establish a Consulate in Papua New Guinea [*3123670*]
1972/2640	Constitutional Development, Papua New Guinea—Programme on Trade Matters [*32758835*]
1972/2671	Papua New Guinea Defence Coordinating Committee—Minutes of Meeting [*32758839*]
1972/2704	Constitutional Discussions Between the Minister and Papua New Guinea Leaders—Port Moresby, October 1972 [*12000652*]
1972/2801	Papua New Guinea—Appointment of Defence Spokesman and Supporting Staff [*32758849*]
1972/2841	Appointment of a Police Spokesman, Papua New Guinea [*32758855*]
1972/2883	Study Group on the Transfer of Responsibility for the Public Service, Papua New Guinea [*32758860*]
1972/3137	Indonesian Relationships With and Attitudes to Papua New Guinea [*32758875*]
1972/3190	Proposed Visit to Indonesia by Chief Minister for Papua New Guinea—Somare, Michael [*3124159*]
1972/3207	Prime Minister's Visit to Papua New Guinea—August 1972—Proposed Agreement on Cultural Development [*32758878*]
1972/3386	Re-examination and Possible Renegotiation of the Bougainville Copper Agreement [*32758893*]
1972/3607	Papua and New Guinea Currency [*12043196*]
1972/3630	Consultations on Defence Matters with the Papua New Guinea Administration, Defence Spokesman and AEC [*3124195*]
1972/3694	Localisation in the Public Service of Papua New Guinea—Policy and Principles [*12042190*]
1972/3878	Third House of Assembly—Constitutional Planning Committee [*32758953*]
1972/3889	Future Size, Shape and Role of Papua New Guinea Armed Forces [*3124217*]
1972/3938	Committee on Banking in Papua New Guinea—Final Report [*32758964*]

1972/3964	BHP—Mineral Exploration in Papua New Guinea [*32758968*]
1972/4041	Standing IDC on Papua New Guinea—Organisation [*32758976*]
1972/4109	Visit to Papua New Guinea by Minister for Defence, Mr Barnard—25 to 29 January 1973 [*3124239*]
1972/448	Measures to Increase Papua New Guinea Responsibilities in Defence Matters (Study 10) [*3123484*]
1972/763	Papua New Guinea—Gearing-up Plan for Internal Self-government [*3123575*]
1972/811	Papua New Guinea—Gearing-up plan for Internal Self-government [*3123589*]
1973/0039	Papua New Guinea Political Development, 1972 [*32759007*]
1973/470	Defence Committee Meeting—30 November 1972—Defence Aspects of Papua New Guinea Constitutional Developments [*3124298*]
1975/105	Gazelle SITREPS and Assessments, 1970 [*3124750*]
1975/108	Critchley, T K—High Commissioner of Papua New Guinea—Papers [*3124752*]
1975/78	Standing Inter-departmental Committee on Papua New Guinea—Documents [*3124723*]

Department of the Prime Minister and Cabinet/Cabinet Office

A1209—Correspondence files, annual single number series (classified), 1944–

1968/9698 PART 3	Interdepartmental Committee on the Programme for the Accelerated Development of Papua and New Guinea [*3051327*]
1970/6723	Prime Minister's Visit to Papua and New Guinea [*11970768*]
1969/9045	Review of Defence Forces in Papua New Guinea [*3054084*]
1971/9229	Preparation of Territory of Papua New Guinea for Independence as a United Country [*11971002*]

A5869—Third Gorton Ministry—Folders of Cabinet Submissions, 1969–71

| VOLUME 5 | Cabinet Submissions (and associated decisions)—Numbers 97 to 116 [*4106070*] |
| VOLUME 6 | Cabinet Submissions (and associated decisions)—Numbers 117 to 132 [*4006156*] |

VOLUME 12   Cabinet Submissions (and associated decisions)—
                                   Numbers 200 to 224 [*4037307*]

VOLUME 19   Cabinet Submissions (and associated decisions)—
                                   Numbers 321 to 331 [*4006212*]

*A5873—Third Gorton Ministry—Folders of Decisions of Cabinet and Cabinet Committees,
1969–71*

484   Cabinet Minute—Military Aid to the Civil Power in
                                   Papua and New Guinea—Call-out of the Pacific Island
                                   Regiment—Without Submission [*4102452*]

539/M   Ministry—Cabinet Minute—Aid to Papua and New
                                   Guinea Administration in 1970/1971—Submission 410
                                   [*4102345*]

A5908—McMahon Ministry—Cabinet Submissions, 1971–72

VOLUME 45   Papua and New Guinea—Constitutional Development—
                                   Decision 89 [*4290412*]

116   Papua New Guinea—Employment Security for
                                   Permanent Overseas Officers—Decision 199 [*429045*]

294   Papua New Guinea—Retention of Permanent Overseas
                                   Officers of the Public Service—Decision 361 [*4290507*]

471   Papua New Guinea—Transfer of Functions of Internal
                                   Self-government—Decision 674 [*4290628*]

655   Papua New Guinea—Creation of Ministerial Offices—
                                   Decision 979 (PNG) [*4939361*]

627   Papua New Guinea—Programme of Movement
                                   Towards Internal Self-government—Decision
                                   980(PNG) [*4939323*]

728   Aid to Papua/New Guinea 1972/1973—Treasury
                                   Analysis of Submission 728—Decision 1176(BRE)
                                   [*4939434*]

727   Banking in Papua New Guinea—Decision 1055
                                   [*4939433*]

781   Aid to Papua New Guinea 1972/1973—Treasury
                                   Analysis of Submission 728—Decision 1176(BRE)
                                   [*4962030*]

863   Papua New Guinea Programme of Movement
                                   Towards Internal Self-government—Report on Initial
                                   Discussions—Decision 1347(ad hoc) [*4252634*]

897   Papua New Guinea Internal Security—Decision 1432
                                   [*4252651*]

919   Papua New Guinea—Future Security of Overseas
                                       Officers of the Public Service—Decision 1453 (PNG)
                                       [*4939494*]

A11099—Cabinet Notebooks, 1950–96

1/111   Sir John Bunting [*31724716*]

Attorney-General's Department

A432—Correspondence files, annual single number series, 1929–96

1961/3329 Part 6   Aid to the Civil Power in the Territory of Papua New
                                       Guinea [*1111069*]

1961/3329 Part 7   Papua New Guinea—Aid to the Civil Power [*1111072*]

1971/3353   Papua New Guinea—Right of Papuans to Independent
                                       Self-determination [*9000233*]

Other

*M1767—Miscellaneous Papers Concerning the Functions of the Governor-General (Sir
Paul Hasluck)*

3   Copies of notes made by the Governor-General, the
                                       Right Honourable Sir Paul HASLUCK in his personal
                                       minute book to record conversations with successive
                                       Prime Ministers and Ministers [*11543255*]

*M3787—Subject Files of the Right Honourable John Grey Gorton as Prime Minister and
Minister for Defence*

14   Papers Relating to Visit to New Guinea, July 1970
                                       re Constitutional Development, Self-government,
                                       Mataungan Association, Land Rights etc) [*4025428*]

Books and Reference Material

There are numerous publications relevant to Australian policies with respect to Papua New
Guinea in the early 1970s. The editors have found the publications listed below particularly
useful while preparing this volume.

Commonwealth Parliamentary Debates, House of Representatives, Canberra, 1970–72

Current Notes on International Affairs, 1970–72

Denoon, Donald, *Getting Under the Skin: The Bougainville Copper Agreement and the
      Creation of the Panguna Mine*, Melbourne University Press, Melbourne, 2000

_____, *A Trial Separation: Australia and the Decolonisation of Papua New Guinea*, Pandanus
      Books, Canberra, 2005

Doran, Stuart, *Full Circle: Australia and Papua New Guinea, 1883–1970*, Department of Foreign Affairs and Trade, Canberra, 2007

_____ (ed.), *Documents on Australian Foreign Policy: Australia and Papua New Guinea, 1966–1969*, Department of Foreign Affairs and Trade, 2006

Downs, Ian, *The Australian Trusteeship: Papua New Guinea, 1945–1975*, Australian Government Publishing Service, Canberra, 1980

Frühling, Stephan (ed.), *A History of Australia Strategic Policy since 1945*, Department of Defence, Canberra, 2006

James Griffin, Hank Nelson and Stewart Firth, *Papua New Guinea: A Political History*, Heinemann Educational Australia, Richmond, Victoria, 1979.

Hunt, Bruce, *Australia's Northern Shield? Papua New Guinea and the Defence of Australia since 1880*, Monash University Publishing, Clayton, Victoria, 2017

Johnson, L. W., *Colonial Sunset: Australia and Papua New Guinea, 1970–74*, University of Queensland Press, St Lucia, 1983

Kerr, Alan, *A Federation in these Seas: An Account of the Acquisition by Australia of its External Territories*, Attorney-General's Department, Canberra, 2009

May, R. J., *State and Society in Papua New Guinea: The First Twenty-Five Years*, Crawford House Publishing, Adelaide, 2001

Moss, Tristan, *Guarding the Periphery: The Australian Army in Papua New Guinea, 1951–75*, Cambridge University Press, Cambridge, 2017.

Nelson, Hank, *Papua New Guinea: Black Unity or Black Chaos?* Penguin Australia, Ringwood, Victoria, 1972

Papua New Guinea Post–Courier, 1970–72

Papua New Guinea House of Assembly, *Debates*, 1970–72

Parker, R. S., 'Papua New Guinea', in Gordon Greenwood and Norman Harper (eds), *Australia in World Affairs, 1966–1970*, Cheshire for Australian Institute of International Affairs, Melbourne, 1974, 393–424

Ryan, Peter (ed.), *Encyclopaedia of Papua and New Guinea*, Melbourne University Press in Association with the University of Papua New Guinea, Clayton, Victoria, 1972, 2 vols.

United Nations General Assembly [UNGA] Resolutions

Woolford, Don, *Papua New Guinea: Initiation and Independence*, University of Queensland Press, St Lucia, 1976

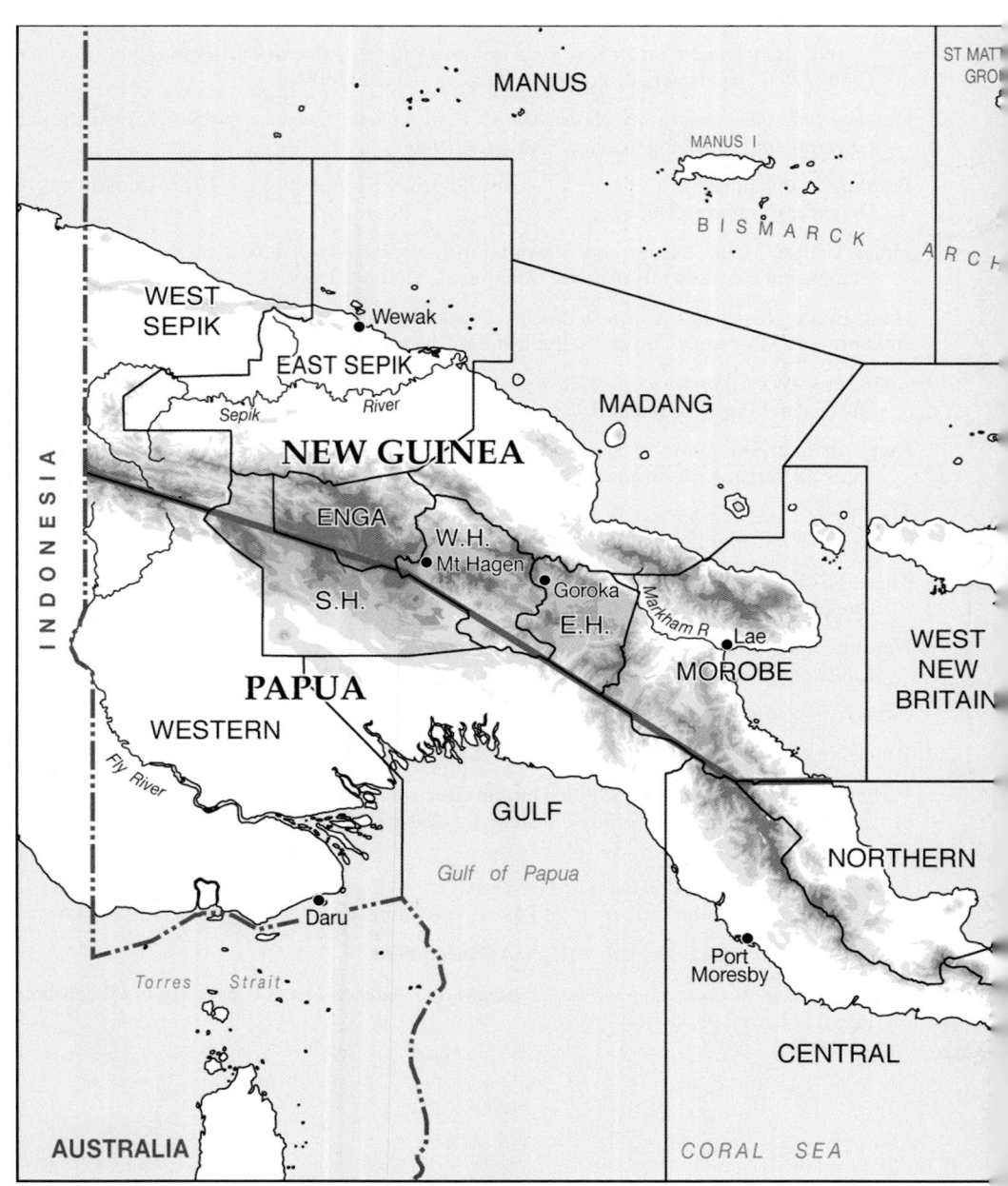

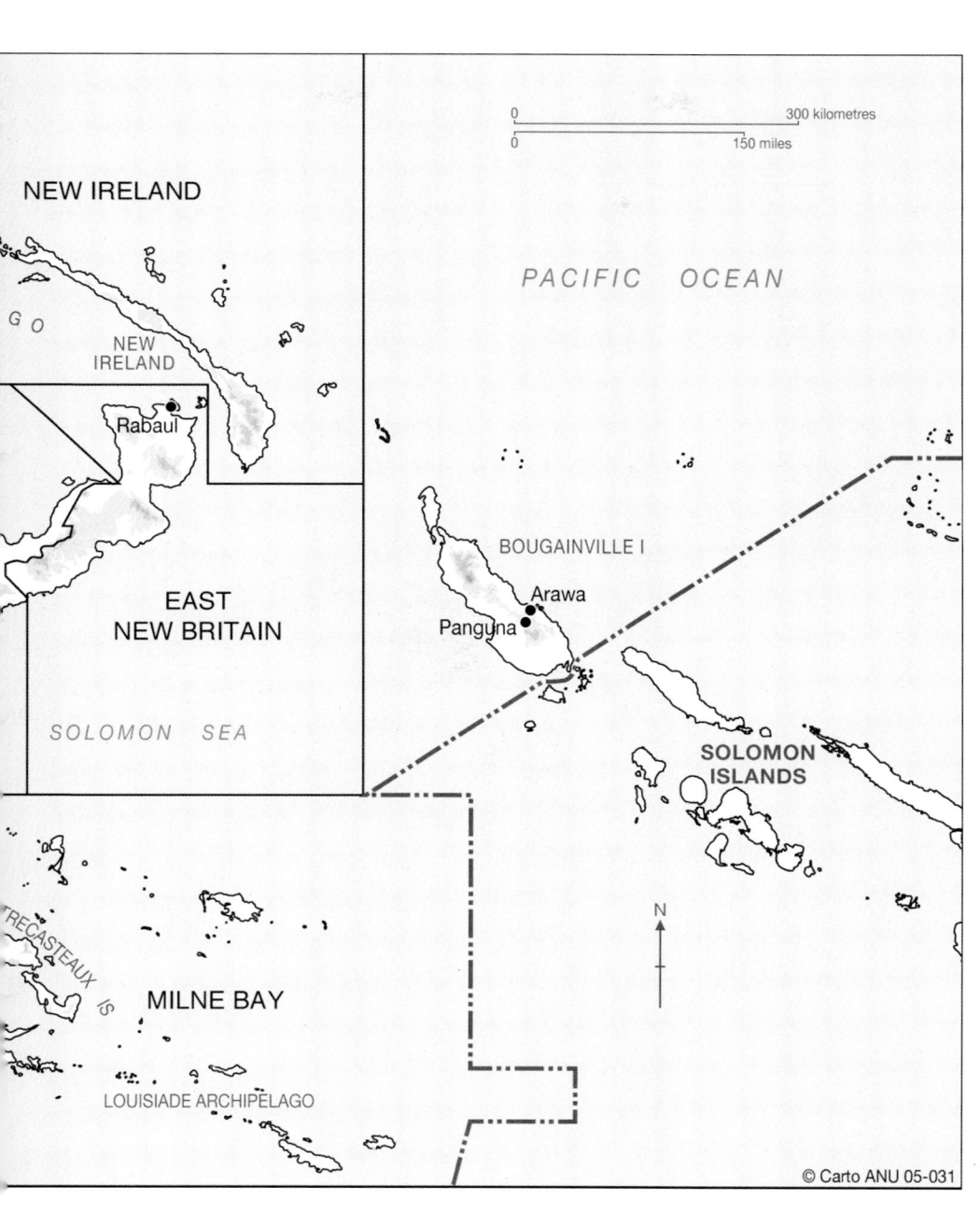

NEW IRELAND

PACIFIC OCEAN

G O

NEW
IRELAND

Rabaul

EAST
NEW BRITAIN

BOUGAINVILLE I

Arawa

Panguna

SOLOMON SEA

SOLOMON
ISLANDS

TRECASTEAUX IS

MILNE BAY

N

LOUISIADE ARCHIPELAGO

0 ——————— 300 kilometres
0 ——————— 150 miles

© Carto ANU 05-031

Indexes

Location references in arabic numerals are document numbers. They may be preceded by location references in roman numbers, which are page references to names discussed in the introduction (pp. xix–liv).

Letters placed after location references indicate the following:

n—the reference is in a footnote (or notes), the following figure indicting the note number(s)

t—the reference is to another document referred to in the main document but not identified by a footnote

tn—the reference is to a person, subject or document referred to in the main document and further identified in s footnote. In long documents they may also be used as a location device, and the note may not be directly relevant.

A span of references (158–60) indicates that the topic is discussed in each document (158, 159 and 160). It may not be a continuous reference, however.

References in brackets are used to indicate further references to the same document. They are usually to subsequent references—for example, 164 (168) indicates that document 164 is referred to in document 168, although not indicated by a footnote—but may also refer to earlier references to drafts versions etc..

Index of persons

Subject index

Documents on Australian Foreign Policy

The series *Documents on Australian Foreign Policy* (DAFP) was established by Cabinet decision in 1971 to provide an accurate, comprehensive and impartial account of Australia's foreign and trade policy based on the archival record.

DAFP is comprised of three series. The first, published between 1975 and 2001, covered Australia's approach to the world before, during and in the immediate years after the Second World War. A prequel series, which is ongoing, will document Australian policymaking in the years after Federation to the onset of the Second World War. A second series was initiated in 1997 and when completed will provide comprehensive coverage of the major events and themes in Australia's foreign relations in the post-1950 period.

Volumes published in the series to date are listed below.

Series IA: 1901–1937

W. J. Hudson and Jane North, *My Dear P.M.: Letter from R. G. Casey to S. M. Bruce, 1924–1929*

W. J. Hudson and Wendy Way, *Letters from a 'Secret Service Agent': F. L. McDougall to S. M. Bruce, 1924–1929*

James Cotton, *Documents on Australian Foreign Policy: Australia and the World, 1920–1930*

Series I: 1937–1949

R. G. Neale, *Documents on Australian Foreign Policy, 1937–38*

R. G. Neale, *Documents on Australian Foreign Policy, 1939*

H. Kenway, H. J. W. Stokes and P. G. Edwards, *Documents on Australian Foreign Policy: January–June 1940*

W. J. Hudson and H. J. W. Stokes, *Documents on Australian Foreign Policy: July 1940–June 1941*

W. J. Hudson and H. J. W. Stokes, *Documents on Australian Foreign Policy: July 1941–June 1942*

W. J. Hudson and H. J. W. Stokes, *Documents on Australian Foreign Policy: July 1942–December 1943*

W. J. Hudson, *Documents on Australian Foreign Policy: 1944*

W. J. Hudson and Wendy Way, *Documents on Australian Foreign Policy: 1945*

W. J. Hudson and Wendy Way, *Documents on Australian Foreign Policy: January–June 1946*

W. J. Hudson and Wendy Way, *Documents on Australian Foreign Policy: July–December 1946*

Philip Dorling, *Documents on Australian Foreign Policy: Indonesia 1947*

W. J. Hudson and Wendy Way, *Documents on Australian Foreign Policy: 1947*

Philip Dorling and David Lee, *Documents on Australian Foreign Policy: Indonesia, 1948*

Pamela Andre, *Documents on Australian Foreign Policy: The Commonwealth, Asia and the Pacific, 1948–1949*

David Lee, *Documents on Australian Foreign Policy: Indonesia, 1949*

Pamela Andre, *Documents on Australian Foreign Policy: Beyond the Region, 1948–1949*

Series II: 1950–1983

Wendy Way, *Australia-Japan Agreement on Commerce, 1957*

Wendy Way, *Australia and the Indonesian Incorporation of Portuguese Timor, 1974–1976*

Roger Holdich, Vivianne Johnson and Pamela Andre, *The ANZUS Treaty, 1951*

Stuart Doran and David Lee, *Australia and Recognition of the People's Republic of China, 1949–1972*

Pamela Andre, Stephen Payton and John Mills, *The Negotiation of the Australia New Zealand Closer Economic Relations Trade Agreement 1983*

David Lowe and Daniel Oakman, *Australia and the Colombo Plan, 1949–1957*

Moreen Dee, *Australia and the Formation of Malaysia, 1961–1966*

Stuart Doran, *Australia and Papua New Guinea, 1966–1969*

Carl Bridge, Steve Ashton and Stuart Ward, *Australia and the United Kingdom, 1960–1975*

Wayne Reynolds and David Lee, *Australia and the Nuclear Non-Proliferation Treaty, 1945–1974*

Matthew Jordan, *Australia and the Rhodesian Problem, 1961–1972*

Bruce Hunt and Stephen Henningham, *Australia and Papua New Guinea: The Transition to Self-Government, 1970–1972*